WEST'S ENCYCLOPEDIA
of
AMERICAN LAW

2ND EDITION

WEST'S ENCYCLOPEDIA *of* AMERICAN LAW

2ND EDITION

VOLUME 11

MILESTONES IN THE LAW

THOMSON

GALE

Detroit • San Diego • San Francisco • New Haven, Conn. • Waterville, Maine • London • Munich

West's Encyclopedia of American Law, 2nd Edition

Project Editors
Jeffrey Lehman
Shirelle Phelps

Editorial
Andrew C. Claps, Pamela A. Dear, Jason M. Everett, Lynn U. Koch, John F. McCoy, Jeffrey Wilson, Jennifer M. York, Ralph Zerbonia

Research
Barbara McNeil

Editorial Support Services
Ryan Cartmill, Mark Hefner, Sue Petrus

Data Capture
Katrina Coach, Nikita Greene, Beverly Jendrowski, Elizabeth Pilette, Beth Richardson

Indexing Services
Lynne Maday

Permissions
Margaret A. Chamberlain

Imaging and Multimedia
Dean Dauphinais, Leitha Etheridge-Sims, Mary Grimes, Lezlie Light, Dan Newell, David G. Oblender, Chris O'Bryan

Product Design
Cynthia Baldwin, Kate Scheible

Composition and Electronic Capture
Evi Seoud, Mary Beth Trimper

Manufacturing
Rhonda Williams

Library of Congress Cataloging-in-Publication Data
West's encyclopedia of American law / Jeffrey Lehman, editor, Shirelle Phelps, editor.— 2nd ed.
    p. cm.
    Includes bibliographical references and index.
    ISBN 0-7876-6367-0 (hardcover set : alk. paper)
    1. Law—United States—Encyclopedias. 2. Law—United States—Popular works. I. Lehman, Jeffrey. II. Phelps, Shirelle.
    KF154.W47 2004
    349.73'03—dc22
                                                    2004004918

ISBN 0-7876-6367-0 (set), ISBN 0-7876-6368-9 (vol. 1), ISBN 0-7876-6369-7 (vol. 2), ISBN 0-7876-6370-0 (vol. 3), ISBN 0-7876-6371-9 (vol. 4), ISBN 0-7876-6372-7 (vol. 5), ISBN 0-7876-6373-5 (vol. 6), ISBN 0-7876-6374-3 (vol. 7), ISBN 0-7876-6375-1 (vol. 8), ISBN 0-7876-6376-X (vol. 9), ISBN 0-7876-6377-8 (vol. 10), ISBN 0-7876-6378-6 (vo1. 11), ISBN 0-7876-6379-4 (vol. 12), ISBN 0-7876-9420-7 (vol. 13)

This title is also available as an e-book. ISBN 0-7876-9373-1 (set)
Contact your Gale sales representative for ordering information.

Printed in the United States of America
10 9 8 7 6 5 4 3 2

DEDICATION

West's Encyclopedia of American Law (WEAL) is dedicated to librarians and library patrons throughout the United States and beyond. Your interest in the American legal system helps to expand and fuel the framework of our Republic.

—⚏—

CONTENTS

PREFACE

The U.S. legal system is admired around the world for the freedoms it allows the individual and the fairness with which it attempts to treat all persons. On the surface, it may seem simple, yet those who have delved into it know that this system of federal and state constitutions, statutes, regulations, and common-law decisions is elaborate and complex. It derives from the English common law, but includes principles older than England, along with some principles from other lands. The U.S. legal system, like many others, has a language all its own, but too often it is an unfamiliar language: many concepts are still phrased in Latin. The second edition of *West's Encyclopedia of American Law (WEAL)* explains legal terms and concepts in everyday language, however. It covers a wide variety of persons, entities, and events that have shaped the U.S. legal system and influenced public perceptions of it.

MAIN FEATURES OF THIS SET

Entries

This encyclopedia contains nearly 5,000 entries devoted to terms, concepts, events, movements, cases, and persons significant to U.S. law. Entries on legal terms contain a definition of the term, followed by explanatory text if necessary. Entries are arranged alphabetically in standard encyclopedia format for ease of use. A wide variety of additional features, listed later in this preface, provide interesting background and supplemental information.

Definitions Every entry on a legal term is followed by a definition, which appears at the beginning of the entry and is italicized. The Dictionary and Indexes volume includes a glossary containing all the definitions from *WEAL*.

Further Readings To facilitate further research, a list of Further Readings is included at the end of a majority of the main entries.

Cross-References *WEAL* provides two types of cross-references, within and following entries. Within the entries, terms are set in small capital letters—for example, LIEN—to indicate that they have their own entry in the encyclopedia. At the end of the entries, related entries the reader may wish to explore are listed alphabetically by title.

Blind cross-reference entries are also included to direct the user to other entries throughout the set.

In Focus Essays

In Focus essays accompany related entries and provide additional facts, details, and arguments on particularly interesting, important, or controversial issues raised by those entries. The subjects covered include hotly contested issues, such as abortion, capital punishment, and gay rights; detailed processes, such as the Food and Drug Administration's approval process for new drugs; and important historical or social issues, such as debates over the formation of the U.S. Constitution.

Sidebars

Sidebars provide brief highlights of some interesting facet of accompanying entries. They complement regular entries and In Focus essays by adding informative details. Sidebar topics include the Million Man March and the branches of the U.S. armed services. Sidebars appear at the top of a text page and are set in a box.

Biographies

WEAL profiles a wide variety of interesting and influential people—including lawyers, judges, government and civic leaders, and historical and modern figures—who have played a part in creating or shaping U.S. law. Each biography includes a timeline, which shows important moments in the subject's life as well as important historical events of the period. Biographies appear alphabetically by the subject's last name.

ADDITIONAL FEATURES OF THIS SET

Enhancements Throughout *WEAL*, readers will find a broad array of photographs, charts, graphs, manuscripts, legal forms, and other visual aids enhancing the ideas presented in the text.

Indexes *WEAL* features a cases index and a cumulative general index in a separate volume.

Appendixes

Three appendix volumes are included with *WEAL*, containing hundreds of pages of documents, laws, manuscripts, and forms fundamental to and characteristic of U.S. law.

Milestone Cases in the Law

A special Appendix volume entitled Milestones in the Law, allows readers to take a close look at landmark cases in U.S. law. Readers can explore the reasoning of the judges and the arguments of the attorneys that produced major decisions on important legal and social issues. Included in each Milestone are the opinions of the lower courts; the briefs presented by the parties to the U.S. Supreme Court; and the decision of the Supreme Court, including the majority opinion and all concurring and dissenting opinions for each case.

Primary Documents

There is also an Appendix volume containing more than 60 primary documents, such as the English Bill of Rights, Martin Luther King Jr.'s Letter from Brimingham Jail, and several presidential speeches.

Citations

Wherever possible, *WEAL* entries include citations for cases and statutes mentioned in the text. These allow readers wishing to do additional research to find the opinions and statutes cited. Two sample citations, with explanations of common citation terms, can be seen below and opposite.

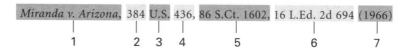

Miranda v. Arizona, 384 U.S. 436, 86 S.Ct. 1602, 16 L.Ed. 2d 694 (1966)

　　1　　　　2　3　4　　　5　　　　6　　　7

1. *Case title.* The title of the case is set in italics and indicates the names of the parties. The suit in this sample citation was between Ernesto A. Miranda and the state of Arizona.

2. *Reporter volume number.* The number preceding the reporter name indicates the reporter volume containing the case. (The volume number appears on the spine of the reporter, along with the reporter name.)

3. *Reporter name.* The reporter name is abbreviated. The suit in the sample citation is from the reporter, or series of books, called *U.S. Reports,* which contains cases from the U.S. Supreme Court. (Numerous reporters publish cases from the federal and state courts.)

4. *Reporter page.* The number following the reporter name indicates the reporter page on which the case begins.

5. *Additional reporter citation.* Many cases may be found in more than one reporter. The suit in the sample citation also appears in volume 86 of the *Supreme Court Reporter,* beginning on page 1602.

6. *Additional reporter citation.* The suit in the sample citation is also reported in volume 16 of the *Lawyer's Edition,* second series, beginning on page 694.

7. *Year of decision.* The year the court issued its decision in the case appears in parentheses at the end of the cite.

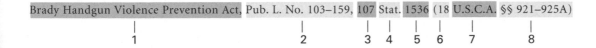

1. *Statute title.*
2. *Public law number.* In the sample citation, the number 103 indicates that this law was passed by the 103d Congress, and the number 159 indicates that it was the 159th law passed by that Congress.
3. *Reporter volume number.* The number preceding the reporter name indicates the reporter volume containing the statute.
4. *Reporter name.* The reporter name is abbreviated. The statute in the sample citation is from *Statutes at Large.*
5. *Reporter page.* The number following the reporter name indicates the reporter page on which the statute begins.

6. *Title number.* Federal laws are divided into major sections with specific titles. The number preceding a reference to the *U.S. Code Annotated* is the title number. title 18 of the U.S. Code is Crimes and Criminal Procedure.
7. *Additional reporter.* The statute in the sample citation may also be found in the *U.S. Code Annotated.*
8. *Section number.* The section numbers following a reference to the *U.S. Code Annotated* indicate where the statute appears in that reporter.

Editorial Reviewers

Matthew C. Cordon
Frederick K. Grittner
Stephanie Schmitt
Linda Tashbook
M. Uri Toch

Contributing Authors

James Cahoy
Matthew C. Cordon
Richard J. Cretan
Mark Engsberg
Frederick K. Grittner
Lauri R. Harding
David R. Johnstone
Theresa J. Lippert
Frances T. Lynch
George A. Milite
Melodie Monahan
Kelle Sisung
Scott D. Slick

Contributors to Previous Edition

Richard Abowitz
Paul Bard
Joanne Bergum
Michael Bernard
Gregory A. Borchard
Susan Buie

Terry Carter
Sally Chatelaine
Joanne Smestad Claussen
Richard Cretan
Lynne Crist
Paul D. Daggett
Susan L. Dalhed
Lisa M. DclFiacco
Suzanne Paul Dell'Oro
Dan DeVoe
Joanne Engelking
Sharon Fischlowitz
Jonathan Flanders
Lisa Florey
Robert A. Framc
John E. Gisselquist
Russell L. Gray III
Frederick K. Grittner
Victoria L. Handler
Heidi L. Headlee
James Heidberg
Clifford P. Hooker
Marianne Ashley Jerpbak
Andrew Kass
Margaret Anderson Kelliher
Christopher J. Kennedy
Anne E. Kevlin
Ann T. Laughlin
Laura Ledsworth-Wang
Linda Lincoln

Gregory Luce
David Luiken
Jennifer Marsh
Sandra M. Olson
Anne Larsen Olstad
William Ostrem
Lauren Pacelli
Randolph C. Park
Gary Peter
Michele A. Potts
Reinhard Priester
Christy Rain
Brian Roberts
Debra J. Rosenthal
Mary Lahr Schier
Mary Scarbrough
Theresa L. Schulz
John Scobey
James Slavicek
Scott D. Slick
David Strom
Wendy Tien
Douglas Tueting
Richard F. Tyson
Christine Ver Ploeg
George E. Warner
Anne Welsbacher
Eric P. Wind
Lindy T. Yokanovich

CONTENTS

APPENDIX: MILESTONES IN THE LAW

BROWN v. BOARD OF EDUCATION OF TOPEKA, KANSAS

BROWN V. BOARD OF EDUCATION OF TOPEKA, KANSAS

ISSUE

Civil Rights

MATERIALS

Opinion of U.S. District Court, D. Kansas, August, 3, 1951

Initial Briefs to the Supreme Court

Memorandum Decision to the Supreme Court, June 8, 1953

Briefs to the parties on Reargument

Opinion of the Supreme Court, May 17, 1954

Briefs to the Court of Further Reargument

Opinion of the Supreme Court, May 31, 1955

HOW TO USE MILESTONES IN THE LAW

In the materials that follow, the reader is invited to review the judicial opinions and the briefs of the parties in this milestone in U.S. law. As you read this section, you may wish to consider the following questions:

- How did the appellant's description of the issues before the Court, or questions presented, differ from the appellee's description?

- How did the parties differ in describing the history relevant to this case?

- What aspects of the conflict presented in *Brown* make it difficult for a court (as opposed to a legislature) to resolve?

- Why might *Brown* apply, or not apply, to discrimination based on a criterion other than race?

THIS CASE IN HISTORY

Brown versus Board of Education of Topeka, Kansas, or Brown as it is commonly known, is one of the most significant civil rights decisions of the twentieth century. With this decision, the Supreme Court declared that the practice of segregating children into separate schools based on race was unconstitutional under the Equal Protection Clause of the Fourteenth Amendment. *Brown* overruled the Court's prior decision in *Plessy v. Ferguson*, which had upheld segregation of the races so long as the facilities provided to each race were separate but equal. As a number of opinions* and briefs* in *Brown* demonstrate, the Court struggled with the issues presented in the case. The Court even took the extraordinary step of asking the parties for additional argument—twice—on the power and the ability of the Court to resolve the issues before it. Even today, the existence of schools with disproportionate numbers of students of one race or another continues to pose difficulties for courts and legislatures under *Brown*.

---

*The Supreme Court granted review to several similar cases from different states, which it consolidated with the *Brown* case for review. In the interest of space, the district court opinions from the other states' cases are omitted here. Also omitted are the opinion of the Supreme Court consolidating the cases and the briefs of the state of Kansas, which was asked by the Court to present its position on the issues.

Brown v. Board of Education of Topeka

CITES AS 98 F.SUPP. 707

—⚏—

BROWN ET AL. V. BOARD OF EDUCATION
OF TOPEKA, SHAWNEE COUNTY,
KANSAS ET AL.
CIV. NO. T-316.
AUG. 3, 1951.

United States District Court,
D. Kansas.
Aug. 3, 1951.

Action by Oliver Brown and others against the Board of Education of Topeka, Shawnee County, Kansas, and others for a judgment declaring unconstitutional a state statute authorizing cities of the first class to maintain separate schools for white and colored children in the grades below high school and to enjoin enforcement of the statute. The United States District Court, Huxman, Circuit Judge, held that the statute. The United States District Court, Huxman, Circuit Judge, held that the statute and the maintenance thereunder of a segregated system of schools for the first six grades do not violate constitutional guarantee of due process of law in absence of discrimination in the maintenance of the segregated schools.

Judgment for defendants.

Where physical facilities, curricula, courses of study, qualifications and quality of teachers and other educational facilities provided in separate elementary schools for colored and white children were comparable, there was no willful, intentional or substantial discrimination in such respects between colored and white schools, though absolute equality in such respects was impossible of attainment and colored children were required to travel much greater distances to school than white children, were transported to and from school free of charge. G.S.1949, 72–1724; U.S.C.A.Const. Amend. 14.

State statute authorizing cities of the first class to maintain separate schools for white and colored children in the grades below high school and the maintenance thereunder of a segregated system of elementary schools does not violate the constitutional guarantee of due process of law, in absence of discrimination between col-ored and white schools in the matter of physical facilities, curricula, courses of study, qualifications and quality of teachers, and other educational facilities. G.S.1949, 72–1724; U.S.C.A. Const. Amend. 14.

John Scott and Charles Scott, Topeka, Kan., Robert L. Carter, New York City, Jack Greenberg, New York City, and Charles Bledsoe, Topeka, Kan., for plaintiffs.

George Brewster and Lester Goodell, Topeka, Kan., for defendants.

Before HUXMAN, Circuit Judge, MELOTT, Chief Judge, and HILL, District Judge.

HUXMAN, Circuit Judge.

Chapter 72–1724 of the General Statutes of Kansas, 1949, relating to public schools in cities of the first class, so far as material, authorizes such cities to organize and maintain separate schools for the education maintain separate schools for the education of white and colored children in the grades below the high school grades. Pursuant to this authority, the City of Topeka, Kansas, a city of the first class, has established and maintains a segregated system of schools for the first six grades. It has established and maintains in the Topeka School District eighteen schools for colored students.

The adult plaintiffs instituted this action for themselves, their minor children plaintiffs, and all other persons similarly situated for an interlocutory injunction, a permanent injunction, restraining the enforcement, operation and execution of the state statute and the segregation instituted thereunder by the school authorities of the City of Topeka and for a declaratory judgment declaring unconstitutional the state statute and the segregation set up thereunder by the school authorities of the City of Topeka.

As against the school district of Topeka they contend that the opportunities provided for the infant plaintiffs in the separate all Negro schools are inferior to those provided white children in the all white schools; that the respects in which these opportunities are inferior include the physical facilities, curricula, teaching resources, student personnel services as well as all other services. As against both the state and the school district, they contend that apart from all other factors segregation in itself constitutes an inferiority in educational opportunities offered to Negroes and that all of this is in violation of due process guaranteed them by the Fourteenth

Amendment to the United States Constitution. In their answer both the state and the school district defend the constitutionality of the state law and in addition the school district defends the segregation in its schools instituted thereunder.

[1] We have found as fact that the physical, facilities, the curricula, courses of study, qualification of and quality of teachers, as well as other educational facilities in the two sets of schools are comparable. It is obvious that absolute equality of physical facilities is impossible of attainment in buildings that are erected at different times. So also absolute equality of subjects taught is impossible of maintenance when teachers are permitted to select books of their own choosing to use in teaching in addition to the prescribed courses of study. It is without dispute that the prescribed courses of study are identical in all of the Topeka schools and that there is no discrimination in this respect. It is also clear in the record that the educational qualifications of the teachers in the colored schools are equal to those in the white schools and that in all other respects the educational facilities and services are comparable. It is obvious from the fact that there are only four colored schools as against eighteen white schools as against eighteen white schools in the Topeka School District, that colored children in many instances are required to travel much greater distances than they would be required to travel could they attend a white school, and are required to travel much greater distances than white children are required to travel. The evidence, however, establishes that the school district transports colored children to and from school free of charge. No such service is furnished to white children. We conclude that in the maintenance and operation of the schools there is no willful, intentional or substantial discrimination in the matters referred to above between the colored and white schools. In fact, while plaintiffs' attorneys have not abandoned this contention, they did not give it great emphasis in their presentation before the court. They relied primarily upon the contention that segregation in and of itself without more violates their rights guaranteed by the Fourteenth Amendment.

This contention poses a question not free from difficulty. As a subordinate court in the federal judicial system, we seek the answer to this constitutional question in the decisions of the Supreme Court when it has spoken on the subject and do not substitute our own views for the declared law by the Supreme Court. The difficult question as always is to analyze the decisions and seek to ascertain the trend as revealed by the later decisions.

There are a great number of cases, both federal and state, that have dealt with the many phases of segregation. Since the question involves a construction and interpretation of the federal Constitution and the pronouncements of the Supreme Court. we will consider only those cases by the Supreme Court with respect to segregation in the schools. In the early case of *Plessy v. Ferguson*, 163 U.S. 537, 16 S.Ct. 1138. 1140, 41 L.Ed. 256, the Supreme Court said: "The object of the amendment was undoubtedly to enforce the absolute equality of the two races before the law, but, in the nature of things, it could not have been intended to abolish distinctions based upon color, or to enforce social, as distinguished from political equality, or a commingling of the two races upon terms unsatisfactory to either. Laws permitting, and even requiring, their separation, in places where they are liable to be brought into contact, do not necessarily imply the inferiority of either race to the other, and have been generally, if not universally, recognized as within the competency of the state legislatures in the exercise of their police power. The most common instance of this is connected with the establishment of separate schools for white an colored children, which has been held to be a valid exercise of the legislative power even by courts of states where the political rights of the colored race have been longest and most earnestly enforced."

It is true as contended by plaintiffs that the Plessy case involved transportation and that the above quoted statement relating to schools was not essential to the decision of the question before the court and was therefore somewhat in the nature of dicta. But that the statement is considered more than dicta is evidenced by the treatment accorded it by those seeking to strike down segregation as well as by statements in subsequent decisions of the Supreme Court. On numerous occasions the Supreme Court has been asked to overrule the Plessy case. This is the Supreme Court has refused to do, on the sole ground that a decision of the question was not necessary to a disposal of the controversy presented. In the late case of *Sweatt v. Painter*, 339 U.S. 629, 70 S.Ct. 848, 851, 94 L.Ed. 1114, the Supreme Court again refused to review the Plessy case. The Court said: "Nor need we reach petitioner's contention that *Plessy v. Ferguson* should be reexamined in the light of contemporary knowledge respecting the purposes of the Fourteenth Amendment and the effects of racial segregation."

Gong Lum v. Rice, 275 U.S. 78, 48 S.Ct. 91, 93, 72 L.Ed. 172, was a grade school segregation case. It involved the segregation law of Mississippi. Gong Lum was a Chinese child and, because of color, was required to attend the separate schools provided for colored children. The opinion of the court assumes that the educational facilities in the colored schools were adequate and equal to those of the white schools. Thus the court said: "The question here is whether a Chinese citizen of the United States is denied equal protection of the laws when he is classed among the colored races and furnished facilities for education equal to that offered to all, whether white, brown, yellow, or black." In addition to numerous state decisions on the subject, the Supreme Court in support of its conclusions cited *Plessy v. Ferguson, supra*. The Court also pointed out that the question was the same no matter what the color of the class that was required to attend separate schools. Thus the Court said: "Most of the cases cited arose, it is true, over the establishment of separate schools as between white pupils and black pupils; but we cannot think that the question is any different, or that any different result can be reached, assuming the cases above cited to be rightly decided, where the issue is as between white pupils and the pupils of the yellow races." The court held that the question of segregation was within the discretion of the state in regulating it public schools and did not conflict with the Fourteenth Amendment.

It is vigorously argued and not without some basis therefore that the later decisions of the Supreme Court in *McLaurin v. Oklahoma*, 339 U.S. 637, 70 S.Ct. 851, 84 L.Ed. 1149, and *Sweatt v. Painter*, 339 U.S. 629, 70 S.Ct. 848, 94 L.Ed. 1114, show a trend away from the Plessy and Lum cases. *McLaurin v. Oklahoma* arose under the segregation laws of Oklahoma. McLaurin, a colored student, applied for admission to the University of Oklahoma in order to pursue studies leading to a doctorate degree in education. He was denied admission solely because he was a Negro. After litigation in the courts, which need not be reviewed herein, the legislature amended the statute permitting the admissions of colored students to institutions of higher learning

attended by white students, but providing that such instruction should be given on a segregated basis; that the instruction be given in separate class rooms or at separate times. In compliance with this statute McLaurin was admitted to the university but was required to sit at a separate desk in the ante room adjoining the class room; to sit at a designated desk on the mezzanine floor of the library and to sit at a designated table and eat at a different time from the other students in the school cafeteria. These restrictions were held to violate his rights under the federal Constitution. The Supreme Court held that such treatment handicapped the student in his pursuit of effective graduate instruction.[1]

In *Sweatt v. Painter*, 339 U.S. 629, 70 S.Ct. 848, 850, 94 L.Ed. 1114, petitioner, a colored student, filed an application for admission to the University of Texas Law School. His application was rejected solely on the ground that he was a Negro. In its opinion the Supreme Court stressed the educational benefits from commingling with white students. The court concluded by stating: "we cannot conclude that the education offered petitioner [in a separate school] is substantially equal to that which he would receive if admitted to the University of Texas Law School." If segregation within a school as in the McLaurin case is a denial of due process, it is difficult to see why segregation in separate schools would not result in the same denial. Or if the denial of the right to commingle with the majority group in higher institutions of learning as in the Sweatt case and gain the educational advantages resulting therefrom, is lack of due

---

[1] The court said: "Our society grows increasingly complex, and our need for trained leaders increases correspondingly. Appellant's case represents, perhaps, the epitome of that need, for he is attempting to obtain an advanced degree in education, to become, by definition, a leader and trainer of others. Those who will come under his guidance and influence must be directly affected by the education he receives. Their own education and development will necessarily suffer to the extent that his training is unequal to that of his classmates. State-imposed restrictions which produce such inequalities cannot be sustained.

"It may be argued that appellant will be in no better position when these restrictions are removed, for he may still be set apart by his fellow students. This we think irrelevant. There is a vast difference—a Constitutional difference—between restrictions imposed by the state which prohibit the intellectual commingling of students, and the refusal of individuals to commingle where the state presents no such bar. * * * having been admitted to a state-supported graduate school, (he), must receive the same treatment at the hands of the state as students of other races." [339 U.S. 637, 70 S.Ct. 853.]

U.S. DISTRICT COURT, AUGUST 1951

process, it is difficult to see why such denial would not result in the same lack of due process if practiced in the lower grade.

It must however be remembered that in both of these cases the Supreme Court made it clear that it was confining itself to answering the one specific question, namely: "To what extent does the Equal Protection Clause * * * limit the power of a state to distinguish between students of different races in professional and graduate education in a state university?", and that the Supreme Court refused to review the Plessy case because that question was not essential to a decision of the controversy in the case.

[2] We are accordingly of the view that the Plessy and Lum cases, *supra*, have not been overruled and that they still presently are authority for the maintenance of a segregated school system in the lower grades.

The prayer for relief will be denied and judgment will be entered for defendants for costs.

In the Supreme Court of the United States October Term, 1952

NO. 8

OLIVER BROWN, MRS. RICHARD LAWTON, MRS. SADIE EMMANUEL, ET AL., APPELLANTS,

V.

BOARD OF EDUCATION OF TOPEKA, SHAWNEE COUNTY, KANSAS, ET AL.

APPEAL FROM THE UNITED STATES DISTRICT COURT FOR THE DISTRICT OF KANSAS

BRIEF FOR APPELLANTS

WILLIAM T. COLEMAN JR.,
GEORGE E. C. HAYES,
GEORGE M. JOHNSON,
WILLIAM R. MING JR.,
CONSTANCE BAKER MOTLEY,
JAMES M. NABRIT JR.,
FRANK D. REEVES,
JOHN SCOTT,
JACK B. WEINSTEIN, *of Counsel.*
ROBERT L. CARTER,
THURGOOD MARSHALL,
SPOTTSWOOD W. ROBINSON III,
CHARLES S. SCOTT,
Counsel for Appellants.

Table of Contents

OPINION BELOW

The opinion of the statutory three-judge-District Court for the District of Kansas (R. 238-244) is reported at 98 F. Supp. 797.

JURISDICTION

The judgment of the court below was entered on August 3, 1951 (R. 247). On October 1, 1951, appellants filed a petition for appeal (R. 248), and an order allowing the appeal was entered (R. 250). Probable jurisdiction was noted on June 9, 1952 (R. 254). Jurisdiction of this Court rests on Title 28, United States Code, §§ 1253 and 2201(b).

QUESTIONS PRESENTED

1. Whether the State of Kansas has power to enforce a state statute pursuant to which racially segregated public elementary schools are maintained.

2. Whether the finding of the court below— that racial segregation in public elementary schools has the detrimental effect of retarding the mental and educational development of colored children and connotes governmental acceptance of the conception of racial inferiority—compels the conclusion that appellants here are deprived of their rights to share equally in educational opportunities in violation of the equal protection clause of the Fourteenth Amendment.

THE LAW OF KANSAS AND THE STATUTE INVOLVED

All boards of education, superintendents of schools and school districts in the state are prohibited from using race as a factor in affording educational opportunities in the public schools within their respective jurisdictions unless expressly empowered to do so by statute. *Knox* v. *Board of Education*, 54 K. 152, 25 P. 616 (1891); *Cartwright* v. *Board of Education*, 73 K. 32, 84 P. 382 (1906); *Rowles* v. *Board of Education*, 76 K. 361, 91 P. 88 (1907); *Woolridge, et al.* v. *Board of Education*, 98 K. 397, 157 P. 1184 (1916); *Thurman-Watts* v. *Board of Education*, 115 K. 328, 222 P. 123 (1924); *Webb* v. *School District*, 167 K. 395, 206 P. 2d 1066 (1949).

Segregated elementary schools in cities of the first class are maintained solely pursuant to authority of Chapter 72-1724 of the General Statutes of Kansas, 1949, which reads as follows:

"Powers of board; separate schools for white and colored children; manual training. The board of education shall have power to elect their own officers, make all necessary rules for the government of the schools of such city under its charge and control and of the board, subject to the provisions of this act and the laws of this state; to organize and maintain separate schools for the education of white and colored children, including the high schools in Kansas City, Kans.; no discrimination on account of color shall be made in high schools except as provided herein; to exercise the sole control over the public schools and school property of such city; and shall have the power to establish a high school or high schools in connection with manual training and instruction or otherwise, and to maintain the same as a part of the public-school system of said city. (G. S. 1868, Ch. 18, § 75; L. 1879, Ch. 81, § 1; L. 1905, Ch. 414, § 1; Feb. 28; R. S. 1923, § 72-1724.)"

STATEMENT OF THE CASE

Appellants are of Negro origin and are citizens of the United States and of the State of Kansas (R. 3-4). Infant appellants are children eligible to attend and are now attending elementary schools in Topeka, Kansas, a city of the first class within the meaning of Chapter 72-1724, General Statutes of Kansas, 1949, hereinafter referred to as the statute. Adult appellants are parents of minor appellants and are required by law to send their respective children to public schools designated by appellees (R. 3-4). Appellees are state officers empowered by state law to maintain and operate the public schools of Topeka, Kansas.

For elementary school purposes, the City of Topeka is divided into 18 geographical divisions designated as territories (R. 24). In each of these territories one elementary school services white children exclusively (R. 24). In addition, four schools are maintained for the use of Negro children exclusively (R. 11, 12). These racial distinctions are enforced pursuant to the statute. In accordance with the terms of the statute there is no segregation of Negro and white children in junior and senior high schools (R. 12).

On March 22, 1951, appellants instituted the instant action seeking to restrain the enforcement, operation and execution of the statute on the ground that it deprived them of equal educational opportunities within the meaning of the Fourteenth Amendment (R. 2-7). In their answer, appellees admitted that they acted pursuant to the statute, and that infant appellants were not eligible to attend any of the 18 white

elementary schools solely because of their race and color (R. 12). The Attorney General of the State of Kansas filed a separate answer for the specific purpose of defending the constitutional validity of the statute in question (R. 14).

Thereupon, the court below was convened in accordance with Title 28, United States Code, § 2284. On June 25–26, a trial on the merits took place (R. 63 *et seq.*). On August 3, 1951, the court below filed its opinion (R. 238-244), its findings of fact (R. 244-246), and conclusions of law (R. 246-247), and entered a final judgment and decree in appellees' favor denying the injunctive relief sought (R. 247).

SPECIFICATIONS OF ERROR

The District Court erred:

1. In refusing to grant appellants' application for a permanent injunction to restrain appellees from acting pursuant to the statute under which they are maintaining separate public elementary schools for Negro children solely because of their race and color.

2. In refusing to hold that the State of Kansas is without authority to promulgate the statute because it enforces a classification based upon race and color which is violative of the Constitution of the United States.

3. In refusing to enter judgment in favor of appellants after finding that enforced attendance at racially segregated elementary schools was detrimental and deprived them of educational opportunities equal to those available to white children.

SUMMARY OF ARGUMENT

The Fourteenth Amendment precludes a state from imposing distinctions or classifications based upon race and color alone. The State of Kansas has no power thereunder to use race as a factor in affording educational opportunities to its citizens.

Racial segregation in public schools reduces the benefits of public education to one group solely on the basis of race and color and is a constitutionally proscribed distinction. Even assuming that the segregated schools attended by appellants are not inferior to other elementary schools in Topeka with respect to physical facilities, instruction and courses of study, unconstitutional inequality inheres in the retardation of intellectual development and distortion of personality which Negro children suffer as a result of enforced isolation in school from the general public school population. Such injury and inequality are established as facts on this appeal by the uncontested findings of the District Court.

The District Court reasoned that it could not rectify the inequality that it had found because of this Court's decisions in *Plessy* v. *Ferguson*, 163 U.S. 537 and *Gong Lum* v. *Rice*, 275 U.S. 78. This Court has already decided that the *Plessy* case is not in point. Reliance upon *Gong Lum* v. *Rice* is mistaken since the basic assumption of that case is the existence of equality while no such assumption can be made here in the face of the established facts. Moreover, more recent decisions of this Court, most notably *Sweatt* v. *Painter*, 339 U.S. 629 and *McLaurin* v. *Board of Regents*, 339 U.S. 637, clearly show that such hurtful consequences of segregated schools as appear here constitute a denial of equal educational opportunities in violation of the Fourteenth Amendment. Therefore, the court below erred in denying the relief prayed by appellants.

ARGUMENT

I. The State of Kansas in affording opportunities for elementary education to its citizens has no power under the Constitution of the United States to impose racial restrictions and distinctions While the State of Kansas has undoubted power to confer benefits or impose disabilities upon selected groups of citizens in the normal execution of governmental functions, it must conform to constitutional standards in the exercise of this authority. These standards may be generally characterized as a requirement that the state's action be reasonable. Reasonableness in a constitutional sense is determined by examining the action of the state to discover whether the distinctions or restrictions in issue are in fact based upon real differences pertinent to a lawful legislative objective. *Bain Peanut Co.* v. *Pinson*, 282 U.S. 499; *Lindsley* v. *Natural Carbonic Gas Co.*, 220 U.S. 61; *Asbury Hospital* v. *Cass County*, 326 U.S. 207; *Metropolitan Casualty Insurance Co.* v. *Brownell*, 294 U.S. 580; *Dominion Hotel* v. *Arizona*, 249 U.S. 265.

When the distinctions imposed are based upon race and color alone, the state's action is patently the epitome of that arbitrariness and capriciousness constitutionally impermissive under our system of government. *Yick Wo* v. *Hopkins*, 118 U.S. 356; *Skinner* v. *Oklahoma*, 316 U.S. 535. A racial criterion is a constitutional irrelevance, *Edwards* v. *California*, 314 U.S. 160,

184, and is not saved from condemnation even though dictated by a sincere desire to avoid the possibility of violence or race friction. *Buchanan* v. *Warley*, 245 U.S. 60; *Morgan* v. *Virginia*, 328 U.S. 373. Only because it was a war measure designed to cope with a grave national emergency was the federal government permitted to level restrictions against persons of enemy descent. *Hirabayashi* v. *United States*, 320 U.S. 81; *Oyama* v. *California*, 332 U.S. 633. This action, "odious," *Hirabayashi* v. *United States*, *supra*, at page 100, and "suspect," *Korematsu* v. *United States*, 323 U.S. 214, 216, even in times of national peril, must cease as soon as that peril is past. *Ex Parte Endo*, 323 U.S. 283.

This Court has found violation of the equal protection clause in racial distinctions and restrictions imposed by the states in selection for jury service, *Shepherd* v. *Florida*, 341 U.S. 50; ownership and occupancy of real property, *Shelley* v. *Kramer*, 334 U.S. 1; *Buchanan* v. *Warley*, *supra*; gainful employment, *Takahashi* v. *Fish and Game Commission*, 334 U.S. 410; voting, *Nixon* v. *Condon*, 286 U.S. 73; and graduate and professional education. *McLaurin* v. *Board of Regents*, *supra*; *Sweatt* v. *Painter*, *supra*. The commerce clause in proscribing the imposition of racial distinctions and restrictions in the field of interstate travel is a further limitation of state power in this regard. *Morgan* v. *Virginia*, 328 U.S. 373.

Since 1940, in an unbroken line of decisions, this Court has clearly enunciated the doctrine that the state may not validly impose distinctions and restrictions among its citizens based upon race or color alone in each field of governmental activity where question has been raised. *Smith* v. *Allwright*, 321 U.S. 649; *Sipuel* v. *Board of Education*, 332 U.S. 631; *Sweatt* v. *Painter*, *supra*; *Pierre* v. *Louisiana*, 306 U.S. 354; *Hill* v. *Texas*, 316 U.S. 400; *Morgan* v. *Virginia*, *supra*; *McLaurin* v. *Board of Regents*, *supra*; *Oyama* v. *California*, *supra*; *Takahashi* v. *Fish and Game Commission*, *supra*; *Shelley* v. *Kraemer*, *supra*; *Shepherd* v. *Florida*, *supra*; *Cassell* v. *Texas*, 339 U.S. 282. On the other hand, when the state has sought to protect its citizenry against racial discrimination and prejudice, its action has been consistently upheld, *Railway Mail Association* v. *Corsi*, 326 U.S. 88, even though taken in the field of foreign commerce. *Bob-Lo Excursion Co.* v. *Michigan*, 333 U.S. 28.

It follows, therefore, that under this doctrine, the State of Kansas which by statutory sanctions

U.S. SUPREME COURT, OCTOBER 1952

BRIEF FOR APPELLANTS

U.S. SUPREME
COURT,
OCTOBER 1952

BRIEF FOR
APPELLANTS

seeks to subject appellants, in their pursuit of elementary education, to distinctions based upon race or color alone, is here attempting to exceed the constitutional limits to its authority. For that racial distinction which has been held arbitrary in so many other areas of governmental activity is no more appropriate and can be no more reasonable in public education.

II. The court below, having found that appellants were denied equal educational opportunities by virtue of the segregated school system, erred in denying the relief prayed The court below made the following finding of fact:

> "Segregation of white and colored children in public schools has a detrimental effect upon the colored children. The impact is greater when it has the sanction of the law; for the policy of separating the races is usually interpreted as denoting the inferiority of the negro group. A sense of inferiority affects the motivation of a child to learn. Segregation with the sanction of law, therefore, has a tendency to retard the educational and mental development of negro children and to deprive them of some of the benefits they would receive in a racially integrated school system."

This finding is based upon uncontradicted testimony that conclusively demonstrates that racial segregation injures infant appellants in denying them the opportunity available to all other racial groups to learn to live, work and cooperate with children representative of approximately 90% of the population of the society in which they live (R. 216); to develop citizenship skills; and to adjust themselves personally and socially in a setting comprising a cross-section of the dominant population (R. 132). The testimony further developed the fact that the enforcement of segregation under law denies to the Negro status, power and privilege (R. 176); interferes with his motivation for learning (R. 171); and instills in him a feeling of inferiority (R. 169) resulting in a personal insecurity, confusion and frustration that condemns him to an ineffective role as a citizen and member of society (R. 165). Moreover, it was demonstrated that racial segregation is supported by the myth of the Negro's inferiority (R. 177), and where, as here, the state enforces segregation, the community at large is supported in or converted to the belief that this myth has substance in fact (R. 156, 169, 177). It was testified that because of the peculiar educational system in Kansas that requires segregation only in the lower grades, there is an additional injury in that segre-

gation occurring at an early age is greater in its impact and more permanent in its effects (R. 172) even though there is a change to integrated schools at the upper levels.

That these conclusions are the consensus of social scientists is evidenced by the appendix filed herewith. Indeed, the findings of the court that segregation constitutes discrimination are supported on the face of the statute itself where it states that: " * * * no discrimination on account of color shall be made in high schools *except as provided herein* * * * " (emphasis supplied).

Under the Fourteenth Amendment equality of educational opportunities necessitates an evaluation of all factors affecting the educational process. *Sweatt* v. *Painter, supra; McLaurin* v. *Board of Regents, supra.* Applying this yardstick, any restrictions or distinction based upon race or color that places the Negro at a disadvantage in relation to other racial groups in his pursuit of educational opportunities is violative of the equal protection clause.

In the instant case, the court found as a fact that appellants were placed at such a disadvantage and were denied educational opportunities equal to those available to white students. It necessarily follows, therefore, that the court should have concluded as a matter of law that appellants were deprived of their right to equal educational opportunities in violation of the equal protection clause of the Fourteenth Amendment.

Under the mistaken notion that *Plessy* v. *Ferguson* and *Gong Lum* v. *Rice* were controlling with respect to the validity of racial distinctions in elementary education, the trial court refused to conclude that appellants were here denied equal educational opportunities in violation of their constitutional rights. Thus, notwithstanding that it had found inequality in educational opportunity as a fact, the court concluded as a matter of law that such inequality did not constitute a denial of constitutional rights, saying:

> "*Plessy* v. *Ferguson,* 163 U.S. 537, and *Gong Lum* v. *Rice,* 275 U.S. 78, uphold the constitutionality of a legally segregated school system in the lower grades and no denial of due process results from the maintenance of such a segregated system of schools absent discrimination in the maintenance of the segregated schools. We conclude that the above-cited cases have not been overruled by the later case of *McLaurin* v. *Oklahoma,* 339 U.S. 637, and *Sweatt* v. *Painter,* 339 U.S. 629."

Plessy v. *Ferguson* is not applicable. Whatever doubts may once have existed in this respect were removed by this Court in *Sweatt* v. *Painter, supra,* at page 635, 636.

Gong Lum v. *Rice* is irrelevant to the issues in this case. There, a child of Chinese parentage was denied admission to a school maintained exclusively for white children and was ordered to attend a school for Negro children. The power of the state to make racial distinctions in its school system was not in issue. Petitioner contended that she had a constitutional right to go to school with white children, and that in being compelled to attend school with Negroes, the state had deprived her of the equal protection of the laws.

Further, there was no showing that her educational opportunities had been diminished as a result of the state's compulsion, and it was assumed by the Court that equality in fact existed. There the petitioner was not inveighing against the system, but that its application resulted in her classification as a Negro rather than as a white person, and indeed by so much conceded the propriety of the system itself. Were this not true, this Court would not have found basis for holding that the issue raised was one "which has been many times decided to be within the constitutional power of the state" and, therefore, did not "call for very full argument and consideration."

In short, she raised no issue with respect to the state's power to enforce racial classifications, as do appellants here. Rather, her objection went only to her treatment under the classification. This case, therefore, cannot be pointed to as a controlling precedent covering the instant case in which the constitutionality of the system itself is the basis for attack and in which it is shown the inequality in fact exists.

In any event the assumptions in the *Gong Lum* case have since been rejected by this Court. In the *Gong Lum* case, without "full argument and consideration," the Court assumed the state had power to make racial distinctions in its public schools without violating the equal protection clause of the Fourteenth Amendment and assumed the state and lower federal court cases cited in support of this assumed state power had been correctly decided. Language in *Plessy* v. *Ferguson* was cited in support of these assumptions. These assumptions upon full argument and consideration were rejected in the *McLaurin*

and *Sweatt* cases in relation to racial distinctions in state graduate and professional education. And, according to those cases, *Plessy* v. *Ferguson* is not controlling for the purpose of determining the state's power to enforce racial segregation in public schools.

Thus, the very basis of the decision in the *Gong Lum* case has been destroyed. We submit, therefore, that this Court has considered the basic issue involved here only in those cases dealing with racial distinctions in education at the graduate and professional levels. *Missouri ex rel. Gaines* v. *Canada,* 305 U.S. 337; *Sipuel* v. *Board of Education, supra; Fisher* v. *Hurst,* 333 U.S. 147; *Sweatt* v. *Painter, supra; McLaurin* v. *Board of Regents, supra.*

In the *McLaurin* and *Sweatt* cases, this Court measured the effect of racial restrictions upon the educational development of the individual affected, and took into account the community's actual evaluation of the schools involved. In the instant case, the court below found as a fact that racial segregation in elementary education denoted the inferiority of Negro children and retarded their educational and mental development. Thus the same factors which led to the result reached in the *McLaurin* and *Sweatt* cases are present. Their underlying principles, based upon sound analyses, control the instant case.

CONCLUSION

In light of the foregoing, we respectfully submit that appellants have been denied their rights to equal educational opportunities within the meaning of the Fourteenth Amendment and that the judgment of the court below should be reversed.

WILLIAM T. COLEMAN JR.,
JACK GREENBERG,
GEORGE E. C. HAYES,
GEORGE M. JOHNSON,
WILLIAM R. MING JR.,
CONSTANCE BAKER MOTLEY,
JAMES M. NABRIT JR.,
FRANK D. REEVES,
JOHN SCOTT,
JACK B. WEINSTEIN, *of Counsel.*

ROBERT L. CARTER,
THURGOOD MARSHALL,
SPOTTSWOOD W. ROBINSON III,
CHARLES S. SCOTT,
Counsel for Appellants.

U.S. SUPREME COURT, OCTOBER 1952

BRIEF FOR APPELLANTS

U.S. SUPREME
COURT,
OCTOBER 1952

APPENDIX TO
APPELLANTS'
BRIEFS

IN THE SUPREME COURT OF THE UNITED STATES OCTOBER TERM, 1952

NO. 8

OLIVER BROWN, MRS. RICHARD LAWTON,
MRS. SADIE EMMANUEL, ET AL., APPELLANTS,

VS.

BOARD OF EDUCATION OF TOPEKA, SHAWNEE
COUNTY, KANSAS, ET AL., APPELLEE

NO. 101

HARRY BRIGGS, JR., ET AL., APPELLANTS,

VS.

R. W. ELLIOTT, CHAIRMAN, J. D. CARSON, ET
AL., MEMBERS OF BOARD OF TRUSTEES OF
SCHOOL DISTRICT NO. 22, CLARENDON
COUNTY, S.C., ET AL., APPELLEE

NO. 191

DOROTHY E. DAVIS, BERTHA M. DAVIS AND
INEZ D. DAVIS, ETC., ET AL., APPELLANTS,

VS.

COUNTY SCHOOL BOARD OF PRINCE
EDWARD COUNTY, VIRGINIA, ET AL., APPELLEE

APPENDIX TO APPELLANTS' BRIEFS

THE EFFECTS OF SEGREGATION AND THE CONSEQUENCES OF DESEGREGATION: A SOCIAL SCIENCE STATEMENT

STATEMENT OF COUNSEL

The following statement was drafted and signed by some of the foremost authorities in sociology, anthropology, psychology and psychiatry who have worked in the area of American race relations. It represents a consensus of social scientists with respect to the issue presented in these appeals. As a summary of the best available scientific evidence relative to the effects of racial segregation on the individual, we file it herewith as an appendix to our briefs.

ROBERT L. CARTER,
THURGOOD MARSHALL,
SPOTTSWOOD W. ROBINSON III,
Counsel for Appellants.

I

The problem of the segregation of racial and ethnic groups constitutes one of the major prob-

lems facing the American people today. It seems desirable, therefore, to summarize the contributions which contemporary social science can make toward its resolution. There are, of course, moral and legal issues involved with respect to which the signers of the present statement cannot speak with any special authority and which must be taken into account in the solution of the problem. There are, however, also factual issues involved with respect to which certain conclusions seem to be justified on the basis of the available scientific evidence. It is with these issues only that this paper is concerned. Some of the issues have to do with the consequences of segregation, some with the problems of changing from segregated to unsegregated practices. These two groups of issues will be dealt with in separate sections below. It is necessary, first, however, to define and delimit the problem to be discussed.

Definitions

For purposes of the present statement, *segregation* refers to that restriction of opportunities for different types of associations between the members of one racial, religious, national or geographic origin, or linguistic group and those of other groups, which results from or is supported by the action of any official body or agency representing some branch of government. We are not here concerned with such segregation as arises from the free movements of individuals which are neither enforced nor supported by official bodies, nor with the segregation of criminals or of individuals with communicable diseases which aims at protecting society from those who might harm it.

Where the action takes place in a social milieu in which the groups involved do not enjoy equal social status, the group that is of lesser social status will be referred to as the *segregated* group.

In dealing with the question of the effects of segregation, it must be recognized that these effects do not take place in a vacuum, but in a social context. The segregation of Negroes and of other groups in the United States takes place in a social milieu in which "race" prejudice and discrimination exist. It is questionable in the view of some students of the problem whether it is possible to have segregation without substantial discrimination. Myrdal[1] states: "Segregation * * * is

---

[1] Myrdal, G., *An American Dilemma*, 1944.

financially possible and, indeed, a device of economy only as it is combined with substantial discrimination" (p. 629). The imbeddedness of segregation in such a context makes it difficult to disentangle the effects of segregation *per se* from the effects of the context. Similarly, it is difficult to disentangle the effects of segregation from the effects of a pattern of social disorganization commonly associated with it and reflected in high disease and mortality rates, crime and delinquency, poor housing, disrupted family life and general substandard living conditions. We shall, however, return to this problem after consideration of the observable effects of the total social complex in which segregation is a major component.

II

At the recent Mid-century White House Conference on Children and Youth, a fact-finding report on the effects of prejudice, discrimination and segregation on the personality development of children was prepared as a basis for some of the deliberations.[2] This report brought together the available social science and psychological studies which were related to the problem of how racial and religious prejudices influenced the development of a healthy personality. It highlighted the fact that segregation, prejudices and discriminations, and their social concomitants potentially damage the personality of all children—the children of the majority group in a somewhat different way than the more obviously damaged children of the minority group.

The report indicates that as minority group children learn the inferior status to which they are assigned—as they observe the fact that they are almost always segregated and kept apart from others who are treated with more respect by the society as a whole—they often react with feelings of inferiority and a sense of personal humiliation. Many of them become confused about their own personal worth. On the one hand, like all other human beings they require a sense of personal dignity; on the other hand, almost nowhere in the larger society do they find their own dignity as human beings respected by others. Under these conditions, the minority group child is thrown into a conflict with regard to his feelings about himself and his group. He wonders whether his group and he himself are worthy of no more respect than they receive. This conflict and confusion leads to self-hatred and rejection of his own group.

The report goes on to point out that these children must find ways with which to cope with this conflict. Not every child, of course, reacts with the same patterns of behavior. The particular pattern depends upon many interrelated factors, among which are: the stability and quality of his family relations; the social and economic class to which he belongs; the cultural and educational background of his parents; the particular minority group to which he belongs; his personal characteristics, intelligence, special talents, and personality pattern.

Some children, usually of the lower socio-economic classes, may react by overt aggressions and hostility directed toward their own group or members of the dominant group.[3] Anti-social and delinquent behavior may often be interpreted as reactions to these racial frustrations. These reactions are self-destructive in that the larger society not only punishes those who commit them, but often interprets such aggressive and anti-social behavior as justification for continuing prejudice and segregation.

Middle class and upper class minority group children are likely to react to their racial frustrations and conflicts by withdrawal and submissive behavior. Or, they may react with compensatory and rigid conformity to the prevailing middle class values and standards and an aggressive determination to succeed in these terms in spite of the handicap of their minority status.

The report indicates that minority group children of all social and economic classes often react with a generally defeatist attitude and a lowering of personal ambitions. This, for example, is reflected in a lowering of pupil morale and a depression of the educational aspiration level among minority group children in segregated schools. In producing such effects, segregated schools impair the ability of the child to profit from the educational opportunities provided him.

U.S. SUPREME
COURT,
OCTOBER 1952

APPENDIX TO
APPELLANTS'
BRIEFS

---

[2] Clark, K. B., *Effect of Prejudice and Discrimination on Personality Development*, Fact Finding Report Mid-century White House Conference on Children and Youth, Children's Bureau, Federal Security Agency, 1950 (mimeographed).

[3] Brenman, M., The Relationship Between Minority Group Identification in a Group of Urban Middle Class Negro Girls, *J. Soc. Psychol.*, 1940, 11, 171-197; Brenman, M., Minority Group Membership and Religious, Psychosexual and Social Patterns in a Group of Middle-Class Negro Girls, *J. Soc. Psychol,* 1940, 12, 179-196; Brenman, M., Urban Lower-Class Negro Girls, *Psychiatry,* 1943, 6, 307-324; Davis, A., The Socialization of the American Negro Child and Adolescent, *J. Negro Educ.*, 1939, 8, 264-275.

U.S. SUPREME
COURT,
OCTOBER 1952

APPENDIX TO
APPELLANTS'
BRIEFS

Many minority group children of all classes also tend to be hypersensitive and anxious about their relations with the larger society. They tend to see hostility and rejection even in those areas where these might not actually exist.

The report concludes that while the range of individual differences among members of a rejected minority group is as wide as among other peoples, the evidence suggests that all of these children are unnecessarily encumbered in some ways by segregation and its concomitants.

With reference to the impact of segregation and its concomitants on children of the majority group, the report indicates that the effects are somewhat more obscure. Those children who learn the prejudices of our society are also being taught to gain personal status in an unrealistic and non-adaptive way. When comparing themselves to members of the minority group, they are not required to evaluate themselves in terms of the more basic standards of actual personal ability and achievement. The culture permits and, at times, encourages them to direct their feelings of hostility and aggression against whole groups of people the members of which are perceived as weaker than themselves. They often develop patterns of guilt feelings, rationalizations and other mechanisms which they must use in an attempt to protect themselves from recognizing the essential injustice of their unrealistic fears and hatreds of minority groups.[4]

The report indicates further that confusion, conflict, moral cynicism, and disrespect for authority may arise in majority group children as a consequence of being taught the moral, religious and democratic principles of the brotherhood of man and the importance of justice and fair play by the same persons and institutions who, in their support of racial segregation and related practices, seem to be acting in a prejudiced and discriminatory manner. Some individuals may attempt to resolve this conflict by intensifying their hostility toward the minority group. Others may react by guilt feelings which are not necessarily reflected in more humane attitudes toward the minority group. Still others react by developing an unwholesome, rigid, and uncritical idealization of all authority figures—their parents, strong political and economic leaders. As described in *The Authoritarian Personality*,[5] they despise the weak, while they obsequiously and unquestioningly conform to

the demands of the strong whom they also, paradoxically, subconsciously hate.

With respect to the setting in which these difficulties develop, the report emphasized the role of the home, the school, and other social institutions. Studies[6] have shown that from the earliest school years children are not only aware of the status differences among different groups in the society but begin to react with the patterns described above.

Conclusions similar to those reached by the Mid-century White House Conference Report have been stated by other social scientists who have concerned themselves with this problem. The following are some examples of these conclusions:

Segregation imposes upon individuals a distorted sense of social reality.[7]

Segregation leads to a blockage in the communications and interaction between the two groups. Such blockages tend to increase mutual suspicion, distrust and hostility.[8]

Segregation not only perpetuates rigid stereotypes and reinforces negative attitudes toward members of the other group, but also leads to the development of a social climate within which violent outbreaks of racial tensions are likely to occur.[9]

We return now to the question, deferred earlier, of what it is about the total society complex of which segregation is one feature that produces the effects described above—or, more precisely, to the question of whether we can justifiably conclude that, as only one feature of a

---

[4] Adorno, T. W.; Frenkel-Brunswik, E.; Levinson, D. J.; Sanford, R. N., *The Authoritarian Personality*, 1951.

[5] Adorno, T. W.; Frenkel-Brunswik, E.; Levinson, D. J.; Sanford, R. N., *The Authoritarian Personality*, 1951.

[6] Clark, K. B. & Clark, M. P., Emotional Factors in Racial Identification and Preference in Negro Children, *J. Negro Educ.*, 1950, 19, 341-350; Clark, K. B. & Clark, M. P., Racial Identification and Preference in Negro Children, *Readings in Social Psychology*, Ed. by Newcomb & Hartley, 1947; Radke, M.; Trager, H.; Davis, H., Social Perceptions and Attitudes of Children, *Genetic Psychol. Monog.*, 1949, 40, 327-447; Radke, M.; Trager, H.; Children's Perceptions of the Social Role of Negroes and Whites, *J. Psychol.*, 1950, 29, 3-33.

[7] Reid, Ira, What Segregated Areas Mean; Brameld, T., Educational Cost, *Discrimination and National Welfare*, Ed. by MacIver, R. M., 1949.

[8] Frazier, E., *The Negro in the United States*, 1949; Krech, D. & Crutchfield, R. S., *Theory and Problems of Social Psychology*, 1948; Newcomb, T., *Social Psychology*, 1950.

[9] Lee, A. McClung and Humphrey, N. D., *Race Riot*, 1943.

complex social setting, segregation is in fact a significantly contributing factor to these effects.

To answer this question, it is necessary to bring to bear the general fund of psychological and sociological knowledge concerning the role of various environmental influences in producing feelings of inferiority, confusions in personal roles, various types of basic personality structures and the various forms of personal and social disorganization.

On the basis of this general fund of knowledge, it seems likely that feelings of inferiority and doubts about personal worth are attributable to living in an underprivileged environment only insofar as the latter is itself perceived as an indicator of low social status and as a symbol of inferiority. In other words, one of the important determinants in producing such feelings is the awareness of social status difference. While there are many other factors that serve as reminders of the differences in social status, there can be little doubt that the fact of enforced segregation is a major factor.[10]

This seems to be true for the following reasons among others: (1) because enforced segregation results from the decision of the majority group without the consent of the segregated and is commonly so perceived; and (2) because historically segregation patterns in the United States were developed on the assumption of the inferiority of the segregated.

In addition, enforced segregation gives official recognition and sanction to these other factors of the social complex, and thereby enhances the effects of the latter in creating the awareness of social status differences and feelings of inferiority.[11] The child who, for example, is compelled to attend a segregated school may be able to cope with ordinary expressions of prejudice by regarding the prejudiced person as evil or misguided; but he cannot readily cope with symbols of authority, the full force of the authority of the State—the school or the school board, in this instance—in the same manner. Given both the ordinary expression of prejudice and the school's policy of segregation, the former takes on greater force and seemingly becomes an official expression of the latter.

Not all of the psychological traits which are commonly observed in the social complex under discussion can be related so directly to the awareness of status differences—which in turn is, as we have already noted, materially contributed to by the practices of segregation. Thus, the low level of aspiration and defeatism so commonly observed in segregated groups is undoubtedly related to the level of self-evaluation; but it is also, in some measure, related among other things to one's expectations with regard to opportunities for achievement and, having achieved, to the opportunities for making use of these achievements. Similarly, the hypersensitivity and anxiety displayed by many minority group children about their relations with the larger society probably reflects their awareness of status differences; but it may also be influenced by the relative absence of opportunities for equal status contact which would provide correctives for prevailing unrealistic stereotypes.

The preceding view is consistent with the opinion stated by a large majority (90%) of social scientists who replied to a questionnaire concerning the probable effects of enforced segregation under conditions of equal facilities. This opinion was that, regardless of the facilities which are provided, enforced segregation is psychologically detrimental to the members of the segregated group.[12]

Similar considerations apply to the question of what features of the social complex of which segregation is a part contribute to the development of the traits which have been observed in majority group members. Some of these are probably quite closely related to the awareness of status differences, to which, as has already been pointed out, segregation makes a material contribution. Others have a more complicated relationship to the total social setting. Thus, the acquisition of an unrealistic basis for self-evaluation as a consequence of majority group membership probably reflects fairly closely the awareness of status differences. On the other hand, unrealistic fears and hatreds of minority groups, as in the case of the converse phenomenon among minority group members, are probably significantly influenced as well by the lack of opportunities for equal status contact.

---

[10] Frazier, E., *The Negro in the United States*, 1949; Myrdal, G., *An American Dilemma*, 1944.

[11] Reid, Ira, What Segregated Areas Mean, *Discrimination and National Welfare*, Ed. by MacIver, R. M., 1949.

[12] Deutscher, M. and Chein, I., The Psychological Effects of Enforced Segregation: A Survey of Social Science Opinion, *J. Psychol.*, 1948, 26, 259-287.

U.S. SUPREME
COURT,
OCTOBER 1952

APPENDIX TO
APPELLANTS'
BRIEFS

With reference to the probable effects of segregation under conditions of equal facilities on majority group members, many of the social scientists who responded to the poll in the survey cited above felt that the evidence is less convincing than with regard to the probable effects of such segregation on minority group members, and the effects are possibly less widespread. Nonetheless, more than 80% stated it as their opinion that the effects of such segregation are psychologically detrimental to the majority group members.[13]

It may be noted that many of these social scientists supported their opinions on the effects of segregation on both majority and minority groups by reference to one or another or to several of the following four lines of published and unpublished evidence.[14] First, studies of children throw light on the relative priority of the awareness of status differentials and related factors as compared to the awareness of differences in facilities. On this basis, it is possible to infer some of the consequences of segregation as distinct from the influence of inequalities of facilities. Second, clinical studies and depth interviews throw light on the genetic sources and causal sequences of various patterns of psychological reaction; and, again, certain inferences are possible with respect to the effects of segregation *per se.* Third, there actually are some relevant but relatively rare instances of segregation with equal or even superior facilities, as in the cases of certain Indian reservations. Fourth, since there are inequalities of facilities in racially and ethnically homogeneous groups, it is possible to infer the kinds of effects attributable to such inequalities in the absence of effects of segregation and, by a kind of subtraction to estimate the effects of segregation *per se* in situations where one finds both segregation and unequal facilities.

III

Segregation is at present a social reality. Questions may be raised, therefore, as to what are the likely consequences of desegregation.

One such question asks whether the inclusion of an intellectually inferior group may jeopardize the education of the more intelligent group by lowering educational standards or damage the less intelligent group by placing it in a situation where it is at a marked competitive disadvantage. Behind this question is the assumption, which is examined below, that the presently segregated groups actually are inferior intellectually.

The available scientific evidence indicates that much, perhaps all, of the observable differences among various racial and national groups may be adequately explained in terms of environmental differences.[15] It has been found, for instance, that the differences between the average intelligence test scores of Negro and white children decrease, and the overlap of the distributions increases, proportionately to the number of years that the Negro children have lived in the North.[16] Related studies have shown that this change cannot be explained by the hypothesis of selective migration.[17] It seems clear, therefore, that fears based on the assumption of innate racial differences in intelligence are not well founded.

It may also be noted in passing that the argument regarding the intellectual inferiority of one group as compared to another is, as applied to schools, essentially an argument for homogeneous groupings of children by intelligence rather than by race. Since even those who believe that there are innate differences between Negroes and whites in America in average intelligence grant that considerable overlap between the two groups exists, it would follow that it may be expedient to group together the superior whites and Negroes, the average whites and Negroes, and so on. Actually, many educators have come to doubt the wisdom of class groupings made homogeneous solely on the basis of intelligence.[18] Those who are opposed to such homogeneous grouping believe that this type of segregation, too, appears to create generalized

[13] Deutscher, M. and Chein, I., The Psychological Effects of Enforced Segregation: A Survey of Social Science Opinion, *J. Psychol.,* 1948, 26, 259-287.

[14] Chein, I., What Are the Psychological Effects of Segregation Under Conditions of Equal Facilities?, *International J. Opinion and Attitude Res.,* 1949, 2, 229-234.

[15] Klineberg, O., *Characteristics of American Negro,* 1945; Klineberg, O., *Race Differences,* 1936.

[16] Klineberg, O., *Negro Intelligence and Selective Migration,* 1935.

[17] Klineberg, O., *Negro Intelligence and Selective Migration,* 1935.

[18] Brooks, J. J., Interage Grouping on Trial-Continuous Learning, *Bulletin #87, Association for Childhood Education,* 1951; Lane, R. H., Teacher in Modern Elementary School, 1941; Educational Policies Commission of the National Education Association and the American Association of School Administration Report in *Education For All Americans,* published by the N. E. A. 1948.

feelings of inferiority in the child who attends a below average class, leads to undesirable emotional consequences in the education of the gifted child, and reduces learning opportunities which result from the interaction of individuals with varied gifts.

A second problem that comes up in an evaluation of the possible consequences of desegregation involves the question of whether segregation prevents or stimulates interracial tension and conflict and the corollary question of whether desegregation has one or the other effect.

The most direct evidence available on this problem comes from observations and systematic study of instances in which desegregation has occurred. Comprehensive reviews of such instances[19] clearly establish the fact that desegregation has been carried out successfully in a variety of situations although outbreaks of violence had been commonly predicted. Extensive desegregation has taken place without major incidents in the armed services in both Northern and Southern installations and involving officers and enlisted men from all parts of the country, including the South.[20] Similar changes have been noted in housing[21] and industry.[22] During the last war, many factories both in the North and South hired Negroes on a non-segregated, non-discriminatory basis. While a few strikes occurred, refusal by management and unions to yield quelled all strikes within a few days.[23]

Relevant to this general problem is a comprehensive study of urban race riots which found that race riots occurred in segregated neighborhoods, whereas there was no violence in sections of the city where the two races lived, worked and attended school together.[24]

Under certain circumstances desegregation not only proceeds without major difficulties, but has been observed to lead to the emergence of more favorable attitudes and friendlier relations between races. Relevant studies may be cited with respect to housing,[25] employment,[26] the armed services[27] and merchant marine,[28] recreation agency,[29] and general community life.[30]

Much depends, however, on the circumstances under which members of previously segregated groups first come in contact with others in unsegregated situations. Available evidence suggests, first, that there is less likelihood of unfriendly relations when the change is simultaneously introduced into all units of a social institution to which it is applicable—*e.g.,* all of the schools in a school system or all of the shops in a given factory.[31] When factories introduced Negroes in only some shops but not in others the prejudiced workers tended to classify the desegregated shops as inferior, "Negro work." Such objections were not raised when complete integration was introduced.

U.S. SUPREME COURT, OCTOBER 1952

APPENDIX TO APPELLANTS' BRIEFS

[19] Delano, W., Grade School Segregation: The Latest Attack on Racial Discrimination, *Yale Law Journal,* 1952, 61, 5, 730-744; Rose, A., The Influence of Legislation on Prejudice; Chapter 53 in *Race Prejudice and Discrimination,* Ed. by Rose, A., 1951; Rose, A., *Studies in Reduction of Prejudice,* Amer. Council on Race Relations, 1948.

[20] Kenworthy, E. W., The Case Against Army Segregation, *Annals of the American Academy of Political and Social Science,* 1951, 275, 27-33; Nelson, Lt. D. D., *The Integration of the Negro in the U.S. Navy,* 1951; Opinions About Negro Infantry Platoons in White Companies in Several Divisions, *Information and Education Division, U.S. War Department, Report No. B-157,* 1945.

[21] Conover, R. D., *Race Relations at Codornices Village, Berkeley-Albany, California: A Report of the Attempt to Break Down the Segregated Pattern on A Directly Managed Housing Project,* Housing and Home Finance Agency, Public Housing Administration, Region I, December 1947 (mimeographed); Deutsch, M. and Collins, M. E., *Interracial Housing, A Psychological Study of A Social Experiment,* 1951; Rutledge, E., *Integration of Racial Minorities in Public Housing Projects: A Guide for Local Housing Authorities on How to Do It,* Public Housing Administration, New York Field Office (mimeographed).

[22] Minard, R. D., The Pattern of Race Relationships in the

Pocahontas Coal Field, *J. Social Issues,* 1952, 8, 29-44; Southall, S. E., *Industry's Unfinished Business,* 1951; Weaver, G. L-P, *Negro Labor, A National Problem,* 1941.

[23] Southall, S. E., *Industry's Unfinished Business,* 1951; Weaver, G. L-P, *Negro Labor, A National Problem,* 1941.

[24] Lee, A. McClung and Humphrey, N. D., *Race Riot,* 1943; Lee, A. McClung, Race Riots Aren't Necessary, *Public Affairs Pamphlet,* 1945.

[25] Deutsch, M. and Collins, M. E., *Interracial Housing, A Psychological Study of A Social Experiment,* 1951; Merton, R. K.; West, P. S.; Jahoda, M., *Social Fictions and Social Facts: The Dynamics of Race Relations in Hilltown,* Bureau of Applied Social Research Columbia, Univ., 1949 (mimeographed); Rutledge, E., *Integration of Racial Minorities in Public Housing Projects; A Guide for Local Housing Authorities on How To Do It,* Public Housing Administration, New York Field Office (mimeographed); Wilner, D. M.; Walkley, R. P.; and Cook, S. W., Intergroup Contact and Ethnic Attitudes in Public Housing Projects, *J. Social Issues,* 1952, 8, 45-69.

[26] Harding, J., and Hogrefe, R., Attitudes of White Department Store Employees Toward Negro Co-workers, *J. Social Issues,* 1952, 8, 19-28; Southall, S. E., *Industry's Unfinished Business,* 1951; Weaver, G. L-P., *Negro Labor, A National Problem,* 1941.

[27] Kenworthy, E. W., The Case Against Army Segregation,

U.S. SUPREME
COURT,
OCTOBER 1952

APPENDIX TO
APPELLANTS'
BRIEFS

The available evidence also suggests the importance of consistent and firm enforcement of the new policy by those in authority.[32] It indicates also the importance of such factors as: the absence of competition for a limited number of facilities or benefits;[33] the possibility of contacts which permit individuals to learn about one another as individuals;[34] and the possibility of equivalence of positions and functions among all of the participants within the unsegregated situation.[35] These conditions can generally be satisfied in a number of situations, as in the armed services, public housing developments, and public schools.

IV

The problem with which we have here attempted to deal is admittedly on the frontiers of scientific knowledge. Inevitably, there must be some differences of opinion among us concerning the conclusiveness of certain items of evidence, and concerning the particular choice of words and placement of emphasis in the preceding statement. We are nonetheless in agreement that this statement is substantially correct and justified by the evidence, and the differences among us, if any, are of a relatively minor order and would not materially influence the preceding conclusions.

FLOYD H. ALLPORT
Syracuse, New York

GORDON W. ALLPORT
Cambridge, Massachusetts

CHARLOTTE BABCOCK, M.D.
Chicago, Illinois

VIOLA W. BERNARD, M.D.
New York, New York

JEROME S. BRUNER
Cambridge, Massachusetts

HADLEY CANTRIL
Princeton, New Jersey

ISIDOR CHEIN
New York, New York

KENNETH B. CLARK
New York, New York

MAMIE P. CLARK
New York, New York

STUART W. COOK
New York, New York

BINGHAM DAI
Durham, North Carolina

Annals of the American Academy of Political and Social Science, 1951, 275, 27-33; Nelson, Lt. D. D., *The Integration of the Negro in the U.S. Navy,* 1951; Stouffer, S., et al., *The American Soldier,* Vol. I, Chap. 19, A Note on Negro Troops in Combat, 1949; Watson, G., *Action for Unity,* 1947; Opinions About Negro Infantry Platoons in White Companies in Several Divisions, *Information and Education Division,* U.S. War Department, Report No. B-157, 1945.

[28] Brophy, I. N., The Luxury of Anti-Negro Prejudice, *Public Opinion Quarterly,* 1946, 9, 456-466 (Integration in Merchant Marine); Watson, G., *Action for Unity,* 1947.

[29] Williams, D. H., *The Effects of an Interracial Project Upon the Attitudes of Negro and White Girls Within the Young Women's Christian Association,* Unpublished M. A. thesis, Columbia University, 1934.

[30] Dean, J. P., *Situational Factors in Intergroup Relations: A Research Progress Report.* Paper Presented to American Sociological Society, 12/28/49 (mimeographed); Irish, D. P., Reactions of Residents of Boulder, Colorado, to the Introduction of Japanese Into the Community, *J. Social Issues,* 1952, 8, 10-17.

[31] Minard, R. D., The Pattern of Race Relationships in the Pocahontas Coal Field, *J. Social Issues,* 1952, 8, 29-44; Rutledge, E., *Integration of Racial Minorities in Public Housing Projects; A Guide for Local Housing Authorities on*

How to Do It, Public Housing Administration, New York Field Office (mimeographed).

[32] Deutsch, M. and Collins, M. E., *Interracial Housing, A Psychological Study of A Social Experiment,* 1951; Feldman, H., The Technique of Introducing Negroes Into the Plant, *Personnel,* 1942, 19, 461-466; Rutledge, E., *Integration of Racial Minorities in Public Housing Projects; A Guide for Local Housing Authorities on How to Do It,* Public Housing Administration, New York Field Office (mimeographed); Southall, S. E., *Industry's Unfinished Business,* 1951; Watson, G., *Action for Unity,* 1947.

[33] Lee, A. McClung and Humphrey, N. D., *Race Riot,* 1943; Williams, R., Jr., *The Reduction of Intergroup Tensions,* Social Science Research Council, New York, 1947; Windner, A. E., *White Attitudes Towards Negro-White Interaction In An Area of Changing Racial Composition.* Paper Delivered at the Sixtieth Annual Meeting of the American Psychological Association, Washington, September 1952.

[34] Wilner, D. M.; Walkley, R. P.; and Cook, S. W., Intergroup Contact and Ethnic Attitudes in Public Housing Projects, *J. Social Issues,* 1952, 8, 45-69.

[35] 35. Allport, G. W., and Kramer, B., Some Roots of Prejudice, *J. Psychol.,* 1946, 22, 9-39; Watson, J., Some Social and Psychological Situations Related to Change in Attitude, *Human Relations,* 1950, 3, 1.

ALLISON DAVIS
Chicago, Illinois

ELSE FRENKEL-BRUNSWIK
Berkeley, California

NOEL P. GIST
Columbia, Missouri

DANIEL KATZ
Ann Arbor, Michigan

OTTO KLINEBERG
New York, New York

DAVID KRECH
Berkeley, California

ALFRED McCLUNG LEE
Brooklyn, New York

R. M. MACIVER
New York, New York

ROBERT K. MERTON
New York, New York

GARDNER MURPHY
Topeka, Kansas

THEODORE M. NEWCOMB
Ann Arbor, Michigan

ROBERT REDFIELD
Chicago, Illinois

IRA DeA. REID
Haverford, Pennsylvania

ARNOLD M. ROSE
Minneapolis, Minnesota

GERHART SAENGER
New York, New York

R. NEVITT SANFORD
Poughkeepsie, New York

S. STANFIELD SARGENT
New York, New York

M. BREWSTER SMITH
New York, New York

SAMUEL A. STOUFFER
Cambridge, Massachusetts

WELLMAN WARNER
New York, New York

ROBIN M. WILLIAMS
Ithaca, New York

Dated: September 22, 1952.

U.S. SUPREME
COURT,
OCTOBER 1952

APPENDIX TO
APPELLANTS'
BRIEFS

U.S. SUPREME
COURT,
OCTOBER 1952

BRIEF FOR
APPELLEES

In the Supreme Court of the United States
October Term, 1952

OLIVER BROWN, MRS. RICHARD LAWTON,
MRS. SADIE EMMANUEL, ET AL., APPELLANTS,
VS.
BOARD OF EDUCATION OF TOPEKA, SHAWNEE
COUNTY, KANSAS, ET AL., APPELLEES.

APPEAL FROM THE UNITED STATES DISTRICT
COURT FOR THE DISTRICT OF KANSAS

BRIEF FOR APPELLEES

HAROLD R. FATZER, Attorney General,
PAUL E. WILSON, Asst. Attorney General, Counsel for
the State of Kansas, State House, Topeka, Kansas,
PETER F. CALDWELL, Counsel for the Board of
Education of Topeka, Kansas. 512 Capitol Federal
Bldg., Topeka, Kansas.

Table of Contents

injunctive relief and to require reversal of the
judgment below

I. PRELIMINARY STATEMENT

The issue presented by this case is whether
the Fourteenth Amendment to the Constitution
of the United States is violated by a statute which
permits boards of education in designated cities
to maintain separate elementary school facilities
for the education of white and colored children.

At the outset, counsel for the appellees desire
to state that by appearing herein they do not propose to advocate the policy of segregation of any
racial group within the public school system. We
contend only that policy determinations are
matters within the exclusive province of the legislature. We do not express an opinion as to
whether the practice of having separate schools
of equal facility for the white and colored races is
economically expedient or sociologically desirable, or whether it is consistent with sound ethical or religious theory. We do not understand
that these extra-legal questions are now before
the Court. The only proposition that we desire to
urge is that the Kansas statute which permits
racial segregation in elementary public schools
in certain cities of the state does not violate the
Fourteenth Amendment to the Constitution of
the United States as that amendment has been
interpreted and applied by this Court.

II. OPINION BELOW

The opinion of the three-judge District
Court below: (R-238-244) is reported at 98 Fed.
Supp. 797.

III. JURISDICTION

The judgment of the court below was
entered on August 3, 1951 (R. 247). On October
1, 1951, appellants filed a petition for appeal (R.
248), and an order allowing the appeal was
entered (R. 251). Probable jurisdiction was
noted on June 9, 1952 (R. 254). Jurisdiction of
this Court rests on Title 28 U. S. C. Sec. 1253 and
2201 (b).

IV. QUESTIONS PRESENTED

1. Does a statute which permits but does not
require cities of more than 15,000 population to
maintain separate school facilities for colored
and white students, violate the Fourteenth

Amendment to the Constitution of the United States in a situation where a court has specifically found that there is no discrimination or distinction in physical facilities, educational qualifications of teachers, curricula or transportation facilities?

2. Is a general finding of the trial court that segregation is detrimental to colored children and deprives them of some benefits they would receive in a racial integrated school sufficient to entitle the individual colored plaintiffs to an injunction prohibiting the maintenance of an existing system of segregated schools, and to require reversal of a judgment denying such relief?

V. THE STATUTE

The statute under attack in the present litigation is section 72-1724, General Statutes of Kansas of 1949, which is quoted hereafter:

> "*Powers of board; separate schools for white and colored children; manual training.* The board of education shall have power to elect their own officers, make all necessary rules for the government of the schools of such city under its charge and control and of the board, subject to the provisions of this act and the laws of this state; to organize and maintain separate schools for the education of white and colored children, including the high schools in Kansas City, Kansas; no discrimination on account of color shall be made in high schools, except as provided herein; to exercise the sole control over the public schools and school property of such city; and shall have the power to establish a high school or high schools in connection with manual training and instruction or otherwise, and to maintain the same as a part of the public school system of said city."

VI. STATEMENT OF THE CASE

The appellants here, who are plaintiffs below, are Negro citizens of the United States and the State of Kansas, who reside in Topeka, Shawnee County, Kansas. The infant plaintiffs are children of common school age. The defendants below and appellees herein are the duly constituted governing body and certain administrative officers of the public school system of Topeka, Kansas. The State of Kansas has intervened in the District Court to defend the constitutionality of the state statute under attack.

Acting pursuant to the authority conferred by G. S. 1949, 72-1724, *supra*, the appellee, Board of Education, many years ago created within the city of Topeka, which is one school

district, eighteen school areas, and now maintains in each of said areas a kindergarten and elementary school for white children only. (R. 24.) At the same time the present Board of Education of Topeka and prior boards of education, acting under same statutory authority, have established and operated in said city four elementary schools in the same grades for Negro children. Negro children may attend any one of said elementary schools that they or their parents may select. It was stipulated in the Court below that the Negro schools are located in neighborhoods in which the population is predominantly Negro. (R. 31.) The stipulation also indicates that at the time the action was brought, the enrollment in the eighteen white schools was 6,019, as compared to 658 students enrolled in the four Negro schools. (R. 37.)

The administration of the entire Topeka school system is under the Board of Education, and the same administrative regulations govern both the white and Negro schools. The Court found specifically that there is no material difference in the physical facilities in colored and white schools; that the educational qualifications of the teachers and the quality of instruction in the colored schools are not inferior to, but are comparable with those in the white schools; and that the courses of study followed in the two groups of schools are identical, being that prescribed by state law. (R. 245.) Also, it was found that colored students are furnished transportation to the segregated schools without cost to the children or their parents. No such transportation is furnished to the white children in the segregated schools. (R. 246.)

VII. SUMMARY OF ARGUMENT

1. The Kansas statute which permits cities of the first class to maintain separate grade school facilities for colored and white students does not *per se* violate the Fourteenth Amendment to the Constitution of the United States.

The Court below found facilities provided for Negro children in the city of Topeka to be substantially equal to those furnished to white children. The appellants, in their specifications of error and in their brief, do not object to that finding. Under those circumstances and under authority of the decisions of the Supreme Court of the United States, the inferior federal courts, and the courts of last resort in numerous state jurisdictions, and particularly the decisions of the Kansas Supreme Court, the appellants here-

U.S. SUPREME
COURT,
OCTOBER 1952

BRIEF FOR
APPELLEES

in are not denied equal protection of the laws by virtue of their being required to attend schools separate from those which white children are required to attend.

The decision of the court below should be affirmed.

2. Irrespective of the question of the constitutionality of the Kansas statute, the trial court's findings of fact are insufficient to establish appellants' right to injunctive relief and to require reversal of the judgment below. The only finding of fact relied upon by appellants is Finding of Fact No. VIII. That finding is couched in general language and in effect simply shows that segregation in the public schools has a detrimental effect upon colored children and a tendency to retain or retard their educational and mental development and to deprive them of some of the benefits they would receive in a racially integrated school system. The finding does not specifically show that any of the appellants have actually and personally suffered by reason of segregation in the public schools of Topeka nor that the mental development of any of the appellants in this case has been retarded; and the finding does not even purport to show discrimination against the appellants and in favor of any other students in the Topeka school system. It no where discusses the effect of segregation upon children of any race other than colored children. Therefore, the District Court's Finding of Fact No. VIII fails to show either that the appellants have suffered any personal harm, or that they are being deprived of benefits or subjected to detriments which do not equally apply to other students in the Topeka school system. Thus, the appellants have failed to secure findings of fact sufficient to entitle them to injunctive relief or to a reversal of the judgment below.

VIII. ARGUMENT

1. Does a statute which permits but does not require cities of more than 15,000 population to maintain separate school facilities for colored and white students violate the Fourteenth Amendment to the Constitution of the United States in a situation where a court has specifically found that there is no discrimination or distinction in physical facilities, educational qualifications of teachers, curricula or transportation facilities?

Appellees contend that only a negative answer to this question is possible.

Background of segregation in Kansas A meaningful examination of any statute must necessarily be made in the light of its context. In *Plessy v. Ferguson,* 163 U.S. 357, the Court comments:

"So far, then, as a conflict with the 14th Amendment is concerned, the case reduces itself to the question of whether the statute … is a reasonable regulation, and with respect to this, there must necessarily be a large discretion on the part of the legislature. In determining the question of reasonableness, it is at liberty to act with reference to the established usages, customs, and traditions of the people, and with a view to the promotion of their comfort, and the preservation of the public peace and good order."

Therefore, we deem it proper to pause briefly to examine the origins and attitudes of the people of the State of Kansas.

The birth of the State of Kansas was an incident of the intersectional struggle that culminated in the war between the states. Located midway between the north and the south, the territory of Kansas was coveted by both the pro-slavery and free-state elements. The Kansas-Nebraska Act which announced the principle of "squatter sovereignty" formally opened the territory for settlement and resulted in migration of large numbers of people from both the north and the south. In these early settlers were reflected the diverse attitudes and cultures of the regions from which they came. While the free-state elements from the north gained political ascendency, there remained in Kansas people who, in good faith, believed that the welfare of both the colored and the white races required that they live apart from one another. Migration following the war between the states followed the same pattern. While the greatest number came from Illinois, Ohio, Indiana and other northern states, a considerable segment of the population had its origin in Kentucky, Tennessee and Missouri. (Clark & Roberts, People of Kansas, 1936, p. 18.)

The early legislatures were faced with the task of reconciling the divergent attitudes of the settlers from such varied cultural backgrounds.

The Wyandotte Constitution, under which the State of Kansas was admitted to the Union, provided for a system of public education specifically requiring the legislature to "encourage the promotion of intellectual, moral, scientific and agricultural improvement, by establishing a uniform system of common schools and schools of a higher grade, embracing normal, preparatory, collegiate and university departments." (Const., Art. 6, Sec. 1.) It is significant that an effort was made in the Wyandotte convention to obtain a constitutional requirement for the separate education of Negro children. The proposal was defeated, not because of objection to the intrinsic policy of segregation, but because the dominant faction in the constitutional convention believed that the power to govern the public schools and to classify students therein should rest with the legislature. At no time was doubt expressed that the constitutional provision adopted at Wyandotte would preclude classification of students on the basis of color (Wyandotte Constitutional Convention, Proceedings and Debates, 1859, pp. 171 to 174).

As early as 1862 the power to classify students was exercised by the enactment of section 18, article 4, chapter 46, Compiled Laws of 1862, applying to cities of not less than 7,000 inhabitants. That statute provided:

> "The city council of any city under this act shall make provisions for the appropriation of all taxes for school purposes collected from black or mulatto persons, so that the children of such persons shall receive the benefit of all moneys collected by taxation for school purposes from such persons, in schools separate and apart from the schools hereby authorized for the children of white persons."

Chapter 18, Laws of 1868, entitled "An Act to Incorporate Cities of the First Class" authorized the organization and maintenance of separate schools for the education of white and colored children in cities of over 15,000 population. In 1876 the laws of the state pertaining to the common schools were codified and embodied in one comprehensive statute. (Chapter 122.) Article X of this chapter related to the public schools and cities of the first class, and provided that all cities of more than 15,000 inhabitants shall be governed thereby. The provision of the law of 1868 authorizing the maintenance of separate schools for white and colored children was omitted from that section and was thus deemed to have been repealed by implication. However, in 1879 a statute was passed (Laws of 1879, Chapter 81) amending the law relating to cities of the first class and specifically authorizing the boards of

education therein to organize and maintain separate elementary schools for the education of white and colored children. The section was again amended by Laws of 1905, Chapter 414, and now appears without further change in G. S. 1949, 72-1724, quoted above.

Two features of the Kansas statute should be emphasized. In the first place, we invite the court's attention to the fact that the statute is permissive only and does not, as may be inferred from appellants' brief, require any board of education to maintain separate schools for colored children.

In the second place, it is again pointed out that the statute applies only to cities of the first class. Cities of the first class in Kansas include those cities having a population of more than 15,000 persons. Presently there are 12 cities in the state so classified. The special provision affecting only these communities may be accounted for by reference to the fact that the Negro population of Kansas is largely urban. According to the 1950 census, less than four percent of the total population of Kansas belongs to the Negro race. However, more than ninety percent of this colored population lives in cities classified as urban. Sixty percent of the total colored population live in the three largest cities of Kansas City, Wichita and Topeka, and at least thirty-five percent of this total live in Kansas City alone. Thus, in enacting a school segregation statute applicable only to cities of the first class the Kansas legislature has simply recognized that there are situations where Negroes live in sufficient numbers to create special school problems and has sought to provide a law sufficiently elastic to enable Boards of Education in such communities to handle such problems as they may, in the exercise of their discretion and best judgment, deem most advantageous to their local school system under their local conditions.

The Kansas decisions The Supreme Court of Kansas has uniformly held that the governing bodies of school districts in the state may maintain separate schools for colored children only when expressly authorized by statute. *Board of Education v. Tinnon*, 26 Kan. 1 (1881); *Knox v. Board of Education*, 45 Kan. 152, 25 Pac. 616 (1891); *Cartwright v. Board of Education*, 73 Kan. 302, 84 Pac. 382 (1906); *Rowles v. Board of Education*, 76 Kan. 361, 91 Pac. 88 (1907); *Woolridge, et al., v. Board of Education*, 98 Kan. 397, 157 Pac. 1184 (1916); *Thurman-Watts v. Board of Education*, 115 Kan. 328, 22 Pac. 123

U.S. SUPREME COURT, OCTOBER 1952

BRIEF FOR APPELLEES

(1924); *Webb v. School District*, 167 Kan. 395, 206 Pac. 2d 1066 (1949).

The rationale of each of these cases is expressed in *Thurman-Watts v. Board of Education*, supra, as follows:

> "The power and duty of the school board are derived exclusively from the statutes. The school board has no greater power than is conferred on it by the statutes."

It is significant that in each of the cases cited above, the court expressly recognized or conceded that the legislature has power to classify students in the public schools on the basis of color. Illustrative of this attitude is the following statement from *Board of Education v. Tinnon*, supra, appearing on p. 16 of the reported decision:

> "For the purpose of this case we shall assume that the legislature has the power to authorize the board of education of any city or the officers of any school district to establish separate schools for the education of white and colored children, and to exclude the colored children from the white schools notwithstanding the Fourteenth Amendment to the Constitution of the United States;"

In each of the subsequent cases where the power to segregate was denied by reason of the absence of statutory authority, the court specifically recognized that the legislature had such authority to confer. (See cases above cited.)

The question of the constitutionality of a statute, antecedent to but substantially like the one here under attack, was squarely presented to the Supreme Court of Kansas in the case of *Reynolds v. Board of Education*, 66 Kan. 672, 72 Pac. 274. That was a proceeding in the nature of mandamus brought against the board of education of the city of Topeka by a colored resident. In the action he sought to compel the board of education to admit his child to a school maintained for white children only. In an exhaustive opinion the court found that the statute which permitted the policy of racial segregation to be valid and not in violation of the Fourteenth Amendment to the Constitution of the United States. The court relied specifically on the decision of the Supreme Court of the United States in the case of *Plessy v. Ferguson*, supra, and held that where facilities are equal, the mere fact of separation of races within a school system does not constitute a violation of the Fourteenth Amendment to the Constitution of the United States.

Quoting with approval from the New York case of *People, ex rel., Cisco v. School Board*, 161 N. Y. 598, 56 N. E. 81, 48 L. R. A. 115, the Court said:

> "The most that the constitution requires the legislature to do is to furnish a system of common schools where each and every child may be educated; not that all must be educated in any one school, but that it shall provide or furnish a school or schools where each and all may have the advantages guaranteed by that instrument. If the legislature determined that it was wise for one class of pupils to be educated by themselves, there is nothing in the constitution to deprive it of the right to so provide. It was the facilities for and the advantages of an education that it was required to furnish to all the children, and not that it should provide for them any particular class of associates while such education was being obtained."

And the court found merit in the quoted portion of the decision in the Massachusetts case of *Roberts v. City of Boston*, 5 Cush. 198:

> "It is urged that this maintenance of separate schools tends to deepen and perpetuate the odious distinction of caste, founded in a deep-rooted prejudice in public opinion. This prejudice, if it exists, is not created by law, and probably cannot be changed by law. Whether this distinction and prejudice, existing in the opinion and feelings of the community, would not be as effectually fostered by compelling colored and white children to associate together in the same schools, may well be doubted; at all events, it is a fair and proper question for the committee to consider and decide upon, having in view the best interests of both classes of children placed under thier superintendence, and we cannot say, that their decision upon it is not founded on just grounds of reason and experience, and in the results of a discriminating and honest judgment."

Consistent with its finding that the statute did not violate the equal protection guarantee of the Fourteenth Amendment, the Court said on page 689: "The design of the common-school system of this state is to instruct the citizen, and where for this purpose they have placed within his reach equal means of acquiring an education with other persons, they have discharged their duty to him, and he has received all that he is entitled to ask of the government with respect to such privileges."

Finally on page 292 the court holds:

> "The act of the legislature of 1879 providing for the education of white and colored children in separate schools in cities of the first

class except in the high school is, therefore, in all respects constitutional and valid."

At the same time the Kansas court has always insisted that facilities must be equal for all groups. Particularly significant is the case of *Williams v. Parsons*, 79 Kan. 202, decided in 1908. There objection was made that the school provided for colored children was located in such close proximity to the railroad tracks that such location produced an undue hazard to the children attending the school. The court stated, at page 209:

> "Having power to maintain separate schools in cities of the first class, the duty rests upon the board of education therein to give equal educational facilities to both white and colored children in such schools. This requirement must have a practical interpretation so that it may be reasonably applied to varying circumstances. . . . Where the location of a school is such as to substantially deprive some of the children of the district of any educational facilities, it is manifest that this equality is not maintained and the refusal to furnish such privileges, where it is practicable to do so, is an abuse of discretion for which the courts will afford a remedy."

A later expression of the Supreme Court of Kansas is found in *Graham v. Board of Education*, 153 Kan. 840, decided in 1941. There the court said on page 842:

> "The authorities are clear that separate schools may be maintained for the white and colored races if the educational facilities provided for each are equal, unless such separation is in contravention of a specific state law."

Again on p. 846 the court comments with reference to the rule expressed in *Reynolds v. Board of Education*, supra:

> "The defendants cite the case of *Reynolds v. Board of Education*, 66 Kan. 672, 72 Pac. 274. The rules of law set out in that case are sound and are applied in this case."

These cases demonstrate that the Supreme Court of Kansas has never doubted that G. S. 1949, 72-1724, and its antecedent statutes is without the scope of the prohibitions imposed on the legislature by the Fourteenth Amendment to the Constitution of the United States.

The controlling principles The position taken by the Supreme Court of Kansas in the cases cited, *supra*, is sustained by the weight of the decisions of this Court in *Plessy v. Ferguson*, supra, and *Gong Lum v. Rice*, 275 U.S. 78; and in numerous decisions of the inferior federal courts and the appellate courts in other states.

Appellants suggest that the Plessy case is not applicable to the situation before us. Admittedly, the question presented in the Plessy case arose out of segregation of white and colored races in railroad cars and not segregation in the public schools. However, the decision of the Court rises above the specific facts in issue and announces a doctrine applicable to any social situation wherein the two races are brought into contact. In commenting upon the purpose and the limitations of the Fourteenth Amendment the Court makes the following statement:

> "The object of the Amendment was undoubtedly to enforce the absolute equality of the two races before the law, but in the nature of things it could not have been intended to abolish distinctions based upon color, or to enforce social, as distinguished from political equality, or a commingling of the two races upon terms unsatisfactory to either. Laws permitting and even requiring their separation in places where they are liable to be brought into contact do not necessarily imply the inferiority of either race to the other, and have been generally, if not universally, recognized as within the competency of the state legislatures in the exercise of their police power. The most common instance of this is connected with the establishment of separate schools for white and colored children which has been held to be a valid exercise of the legislative power even by courts of States where the political rights of the colored race have been longest and most earnestly enforced." (p. 554.)

Certainly this language refutes appellants' contention that the Plessy case has no application to these facts.

Appellants further state that *Gong Lum v. Rice* "is irrelevant to the issues in this case." This statement appears to justify a brief examination of the facts in the Gong case. Those facts may be summarized as follows:

The Constitution and statutes of the State of Mississippi provided for two school systems in each county. One system was for "white" children and the other system for "colored" children. Plaintiff sought to have his child who was a citizen of Chinese extraction admitted to the school maintained for white students in the county where she lived. She was refused admission by the school authorities. The Supreme Court of the United States unanimously affirmed the decision

U.S. SUPREME
COURT,
OCTOBER 1952

BRIEF FOR
APPELLEES

of the Supreme Court of Mississippi, refusing to grant a Writ of Mandamus to compel the school authorities to admit the Chinese-American citizen to the white school.

The opinion by Chief Justice Taft includes the following statement (pp. 85–86): "The question here is whether a Chinese citizen of the United States is denied equal protection of the laws when he is classed among the colored races and furnished facilities for education equal to that offered to all, whether white, brown, yellow or black. Were this a new question it would call for very full argument and consideration but we think that it is the same question which has been many times decided to be within the constitutional power of the state legislature to settle without intervention of the federal courts under the Federal Constitution."

To support this proposition the Court cites sixteen cases decided by federal courts and state courts of last resort, including *Plessy v. Ferguson,* supra.

We do not believe that appellants suggest that the rights of the Negro citizens differ from the rights of the Mongolian citizen, Martha Lum. If such an idea is advanced herein, this Court should have no more difficulty in disposing of that contention than it did of that phase of the Gong case where it seemed to be contended that a yellow child had different rights than a Negro child. The Court simply held that children of all races have equal rights but that those rights are not infringed upon when the state provides that the different races shall be educated in separate schools of equal facility.

Appellants further contend that whatever force the Plessy and Gong-Lum cases may have had has been overcome by the recent decisions of *Sweatt v. Painter,* 339 U.S. 629, and *McLaurin v. Oklahoma,* 339 U.S. 637. Appellees concede that if there has been any change in the attitude of this Court as to the constitutionality of the separate but equal doctrines as it affects segregation, it must be found in these two cases. Thus, we have examined them carefully. But we find no statement therein that would cause us to believe the Court intended to reverse or modify its earlier decisions. In the Sweatt case, the Court held that a Negro prospective law student could not be denied admission to the renowned University of Texas Law School—"one of the nation's ranking law schools" (p. 663), and be compelled to accept instruction in a new school of perhaps

questionable worth, inferior as to faculty, plant and student body. The McLaurin case only found that a Negro graduate student, who had successfully compelled his admission to the University of Oklahoma to do graduate work in education, was still being denied equal rights when he was segregated inside the university as to his seat in class, in the library and in the dining hall. Unquestionably, these cases sustain the position that equal facilities must be provided. However, that point is not at issue in this case.

We think the Sweatt case has no greater significance than the following expression of the Court's attitude indicates:

"This case and *McLaurin v. Oklahoma State Regents* ... present different aspects of this general question: To what extent does the Equal Protection Clause of the Fourteenth Amendment limit the power of a state to distinguish between students of different races in professional and graduate education in a state university? Broader issues have been urged for our consideration, but we adhere to the principle of deciding constitutional questions only in the context of the particular case before the court." (p. 631.)

Squarely in point is the following statement:

"We cannot, therefore, agree with respondents that the doctrine of *Plessy v. Ferguson,* 1896, 163 U.S. 537, 16 S. Ct. 1138, 41 L. Ed. 256, requires affirmance of the judgment below. Nor need we reach the petitioner's contention that *Plessy v. Ferguson* should be re-examined in the light of contemporary knowledge respecting the purposes of the Fourteenth Amendment and the effects of racial segregation. See, *supra,* pg. 631." (pp. 635–636.)

And in the McLaurin case the significance of the special situation is noted by the Court:

"Our society grows increasingly complex, and our need for trained leaders increases correspondingly. Appellant's case represents, perhaps, the epitome of that need, for he is attempting to obtain an advanced degree in education, to become, by definition, a leader and trainer of others. Those who will come under his guidance and influence must be directly affected by the education he receives. Their own education and development will necessarily suffer to the extent that his training is unequal to that of his classmates. State-imposed restrictions which produce such inequalities cannot be sustained.

"It may be argued that appellant will be in no better position when these restrictions are removed, for he may still be set apart by his fellow students. This we think is irrelevant. There is a vast difference—a constitutional difference between restrictions imposed by the state which prohibit the intellectual commingling of students, and the refusal of individuals to commingle where the state presents no such bar ... Appellant having been admitted to a state-supported graduate school, he must receive the same treatment at the hands of the state as students of other races." (pp. 641, 642.)

In the Sweatt and McLaurin cases the Court specifically refused to consider the issue of constitutionality of racial separation in schools of equal facility in view of contemporary knowledge and held only that where the State did not furnish equal facilities for one race, the students of that race were being denied equal protection of the laws. Appellees contend that this refusal by the Court to review the Plessy and Gong-Lum doctrines in its later decisions can only be interpreted to support the view that those cases still stand as expressions of the rule established by the Supreme Court upon the question of racial segregation within the public schools.

Notable among decisions since the Sweatt and McLaurin cases are *Carr v. Corning,* 182 F. 2d 14; *Briggs v. Elliott,* 98 F. Supp. 529; and *Davis v. County School Board,* 103 F. Supp. 337, the latter two cases now pending before this Court on appeal. *Carr v. Corning* involved the public school system of the District of Columbia. There the Court noted a fact that we deem most significant with respect to the original meaning and intent of the Fourteenth Amendment. It was pointed out that in the same year that Congress proposed the amendment, federal legislation was enacted providing for segregation of the races in the public schools in the District of Columbia.

"We are not unmindful of the debates which occurred in Congress relative to the Civil Rights Act of April 9, 1866, the Fourteenth Amendment, and the Civil Rights Act of March 1, 1875. But the actions of Congress, the discussion in the Civil Rights Cases, and the fact that in 1862, 1864, 1866 and 1874 Congress, as we shall point out in a moment, enacted legislation which specifically provided for separation of the races in the schools of the District of Columbia, conclusively support our view of the Amendment and its effect." (p. 17.)

Here we note the parallel situation in the State of Kansas. There the State, through its Legislature, ratified the Fourteenth Amendment in 1867, and only one year later legislation providing for separation of the races in the public schools of first class cities was enacted. (L. 1868, ch. 18.)

An examination of all the cases in American jurisdictions supporting the appellants' position would become repetitious and tedious. Thus, we refrain from an exhaustive survey. We believe the comment of Circuit Judge Parker in *Briggs v. Elliott,* supra, aptly summarizes the law and its justification:

"One of the great virtues of our constitutional system is that, while the federal government protects the fundamental rights of the individual, it leaves to the several states the solution of local problems. In a country with a great expanse of territory with peoples of widely differing customs and ideas, local self government in local matters is essential to the peace and happiness of the people in the several communities as well as to the strength and unity of the country as a whole. It is universally held, therefore, that each state shall determine for itself, subject to the observance of the fundamental rights and liberties guaranteed by the federal Constitution, how it shall exercise the police power, *i.e.,* the power to legislate with respect to the safety, morals, health and general welfare. And in no field is this right of the several states more clearly recognized than in that of public education." (p. 532.)

Justice Holmes has expressed the following view:

"I must add one general consideration. There is nothing that I more deprecate than the use of the Fourteenth Amendment beyond the absolute compulsion of its words to prevent the making of social experiments that an important part of the community desires, in the insulated chambers afforded by the several states, even though the experiments may seem futile or even noxious to me and to those whose judgment I most respect. (Holmes, J., dissenting opinion, *Truax v. Corrigan,* 257 U.S. 312, p. 344, 42 S. Ct. 124, 66 L. Ed. 254, 27 A. L. R. 375.)"

It is undoubtedly true that the separate but equal doctrine is susceptible of abuse. In many instances it has resulted in a separate and unequal rule in practice. However, it is the impossibility of equality under such a doctrine, and not the difficulty of administering and applying the same with equality, that would make such a doctrine unconstitutional *per se.* The situation in Topeka is one where substantial equality has been reached. Such was the finding of the Court below (R. 245) and such is apparently conceded by the appellants (Appellants' Brief, p. 5). These facts, under authority of decisions heretofore reviewed, compel an inescapable conclusion: Neither the statute of Kansas nor the action of the appellee, Board of Education, offends the Fourteenth Amendment to the Federal Constitution.

The prospect At the outset we suggested that the Kansas statute is permissive and that any Board of Education included in the statute may adopt a policy consistent with local conditions and local attitudes. We believe it is significant that under this statute by a process of evolution the people in Kansas communities are arriving at their own solutions to this problem. Under the statute 12 cities are authorized to maintain separate schools for colored students. The files of the State Superintendent of Public Instruction indicate that at the present time, only nine cities exercise the power conferred by statute. Wichita, the largest city in the state, has abandoned segregation only recently. The city of Pittsburg abandoned the policy of segregation only two years ago. Lawrence, seat of the state university, is now in the process of ending the operation of segregated schools.

This account of events not in the record is related to illustrate the wisdom which underlies the Kansas statute. Only those cities where local conditions produce special problems making segregation desirable need adopt the expedient of segregation. In the orderly progress of the community, these special problems are either solved or vanish, and when the need for segregation disappears, its practice may be discontinued. This was the method provided by the legislature of the State of Kansas to achieve the goal of an integrated school system where segregation is not needed. We respectfully suggest to the court that this evolutionary process permitting an autonomous solution in the community is consistent with the purpose and intent of the Fourteenth Amendment.

2. The District Court's finding of Fact No. VIII is insufficient to establish appellants' right to injunctive relief and to require reversal of the judgment below

A. Counsel for Appellants have overstated their case. Appellant has raised and preserved this issue by its third Assignment of Error, to wit:

"The District Court erred:

"… … … …

"3. In refusing to enter judgment in favor of plaintiffs, after the court found that plaintiffs suffered serious harm and detriment in being required to attend segregated elementary schools in the City of Topeka, and were deprived thereby of benefits they would have received in a racially integrated school system." (R. 250.)

And by adopting its Assignment of Errors in its Statement of Points to Be Relied Upon (R. 253).

The District Court's Findings of Fact and Conclusions of Law appear at pp. 244 to 247 of the Transcript of the Record.

There is no Finding of Fact which literally and specifically corresponds to the finding mentioned in Appellants' third Assignment of Error.

At page 2 of the Brief for Appellants under the heading *Questions Presented,* appellants state the second issue, as follows:

"Whether the finding of the court below— that racial segregation in public elementary schools has the detrimental effect of retarding the mental and educational development of colored children and connotes governmental acceptance of the conception of racial inferiority—compels the conclusion that appellants here are deprived of their rights to share equally in educational opportunities in violation of the equal protection clause of the Fourteenth Amendment."

There is no Finding of Fact which literally and specifically corresponds to the finding mentioned in appellants' statement of the second issue.

At page 10 of the Brief for Appellant, counsel state:

"Applying this yardstick, any restrictions or distinction based upon race or color that places the Negro at a disadvantage in relation to other racial groups in his pursuit of educational opportunities is violative of the equal protection clause.

"In the instant case, the court found as a fact that appellants were placed at such a disadvantage and were denied educational opportunities equal to those available to white students.

"… … … … … …

"Thus, notwithstanding that it had found inequality in educational opportunity as a fact, the court concluded as a matter of law that such inequality did not constitute a denial of constitutional rights, saying: …"

There is no such finding of fact in the Record in this case.

With all respect due to able counsel for appellants we believe that in their zeal for their cause, they have overstated their case. The only existing Finding of Fact which is relied upon by appellants and the only one quoted in their brief is the District Court's Finding of Fact No. VIII, which we quote accurately:

> "Segregation of white and colored children in public schools has a detrimental effect upon the colored children. The impact is greater when it has the sanction of the law; for the policy of separating the races is usually interpreted as denoting the inferiority of the Negro group. A sense of inferiority affects the motivation of a child to learn. Segregation with the sanction of law, therefore, has a tendency to retain the educational and mental development of Negro children and to deprive them of some of the benefits they would receive in a racial integrated school system."

We call attention to the fact that the foregoing Finding is couched only in broad and general language; it makes no specific or particular reference to any of the appellants, nor to the grade schools in Topeka, nor to racial groups other than Negroes, nor to inequality of educational opportunities between Negroes and other racial groups. The substance of the finding can be summarized in the following statement: "Generally speaking, segregation is detrimental to colored children, and deprives them of some benefits they would receive in a racial integrated school system."

The Finding of Fact No. VIII cannot be stretched, as counsel for appellants apparently would like to stretch it, into a finding that the appellants in this case have "suffered serious harm in being required to attend segregated elementary schools in Topeka" and that "appellants were placed at such a disadvantage (in relation to other racial groups in [their] pursuit of educational opportunities) and were denied educational opportunities equal to those available to white students."

"B. Elements necessary to entitle appellants to injunctive relief and to a reversal of the judgment in this case. To establish appellants' right to injunctive relief and to reversal of the judgment in this case, the Findings of Fact No. VIII would have to show:

(1) That the appellants have actually suffered personal harm as the result of attending segregated schools in Topeka; and,

(2) Either that appellants are being deprived of benefits which other students in the Topeka school system enjoy, or that appellants are being subjected to detriments to which other students in the Topeka school system are not being subjected, by reason of maintenance of a segregated school system.

The mere showing that appellants may be members of a class which is being discriminated against by reason of a statute is not sufficient to entitle them to injunctive relief, unless appellants can also show that they personally are suffering harm. The Fourteenth Amendment protects only personal and individual rights.

The mere showing that appellants can show that they are being deprived of benefits they would receive under a different system of schools is not sufficient to show that they are being deprived of equal protection of the law, unless appellants can also show that under the existing segregate school system there are others who are not deprived of such benefits.

And finally, the mere showing that segregation is detrimental to appellants is not sufficient to show that they are being deprived of equal protection of the laws, unless they also show that segregation is not similarly detrimental to others in the Topeka school system.

McCabe v. A. T. & S. F. Ry. Co., 235 U.S. 151, 59 Law Ed. 149:

> "There is, however, an insuperable obstacle to the granting of the relief sought by this bill. It was filed, as we have seen, by five persons against five railroad corporations to restrain them from complying with the state statute. The suit had been brought before the law went into effect, and this amended bill was filed very shortly after. It contains some general allegations as to discriminations in the supply of facilities and as to the hardships which will ensue. It states that there will be 'A multiplicity of suits,' there being at least 'fifty thousand persons of the Negro race in the state of Oklahoma' who will be injured and deprived of their civil rights. But we are dealing here with the case of the complainants, and nothing is shown to entitle them to an injunction. It is an elementary principle that, in order to justify the granting of this extraordinary relief, the complainant's need of it, and the absence of an adequate remedy at law, must clearly appear. The complainant cannot succeed because someone else may be

U.S. SUPREME COURT, OCTOBER 1952

BRIEF FOR APPELLEES

U.S. SUPREME
COURT,
OCTOBER 1952

BRIEF FOR
APPELLEES

hurt. Nor does it make any difference that other persons who may be injured are persons of the same race or occupation. It is the fact, clearly established, of injury to the complainant—not to others—which justifies judicial intervention." (p. 162.)

Turpin v. Lemon, 187 U.S. 51, 47 Law Ed. 70:

"This is an effort to test the constitutionality of the law, without showing that the plaintiff had been injured by its application, and, in this particular, the case falls without ruling in *Tyler v. Registration Court Judges,* 179 U.S. 405, 45 L. ed. 252, 21 Sup. Ct. Rep. 206, wherein we held that the plaintiff was bound to show he had personally suffered an injury before he could institute a bill for relief. In short, the case made by the plaintiff is purely academic." (pp. 60, 61.)

Thomas Cusack Co. v. Chicago, 242 U.S. 526, 61 Law Ed. 472:

"He who is not injured by the operation of a law or ordinance cannot be said to be deprived by it of either constitutional right or of property." (p. 530.)

Mallinckrodt Chemical Works v. Missouri ex rel. Jones, 238 U.S. 41, 59 L. ed. 1192:

"As has been often pointed out, one who seeks to set aside a state statute as repugnant to the Federal Constitution must show that he is within the class with respect to whom the act is unconstitutional, and that the alleged unconstitutional feature injures him." (p. 54.)

C. Finding of Fact No. VIII fails to disclose that any of the appellants have been actually and personally harmed by segregation in the Topeka Schools. Finding of Fact No. VIII makes no specific reference to the individual appellants. It expresses only in broad generalities the effect of segregation in the public schools upon colored children as a class. There is no specific finding that segregation has had a personal detrimental effect upon any of the appellants. There is no specific finding that any of the appellants personally has interpreted segregation as denoting inferiority of the Negro group, or that the motivation to learn of any of the appellants has been affected by a sense of inferiority. There is no finding that the educational and mental development of any of the appellants has actually been retained or retarded by reason of segregation in the Topeka schools. In short there is no finding that any of the appellants individually and actually has been harmed by segregation in the Topeka school system.

D. Finding of Fact No. VIII fails to disclose that appellants are being deprived of equal protection of the laws, or that they are being discriminated against by segregation in the Topeka Schools. Denial of equal protection of the laws, or discrimination, logically and necessarily involves at least two persons who are being treated differently. Denial of equal protection must mean denial of protection or opportunity equal to that afforded to someone else. There can be no such thing as "unilateral discrimination."

Since the Finding of Fact No. VIII is limited solely to a statement of the effect of segregation on colored children as a group, and nowhere mentions the effect of segregation upon any other race or group, it cannot reasonably or logically show discrimination or a denial of equal protection of the laws.

Nowhere in the finding has the court disclosed any facts upon which it can be claimed to show discrimination in favor of white children over colored in segregated schools.

It is idle on this appeal to speculate upon what the trial court might have found had it been requested to make additional findings. No request for additional findings was made in the trial court. We therefore refrain from speculating as to whether the court would also have found that segregation was detrimental to white children and impaired their educational and mental development.

E. The District Court did not intend nor consider its Finding of Fact No. VIII to be a finding of discrimination against appellants. The last sentence in Finding of Fact No. VIII summarizes the entire finding. We quote:

"Segregation with the sanction of law, therefore, has a tendency to retain the educational and mental development of Negro children and to deprive them of some of the benefits they would receive in a racial integrated school system."

We believe the court intended the finding to mean simply that colored children would be better off in integrated schools than they are in segregated schools. Conceding that that is the meaning of the finding, it does not amount to a finding of actual discrimination against colored children and in favor of white children upon the facts in this case. White children are not permitted to attend integrated schools in Topeka. The mere fact, if it be a fact, that the Topeka school system could be improved so far as education of colored children is concerned, does not prove discrimination against them.

In the opinion of the District Court (R. 238 to 244), 98 F. Supp. 797, no mention is made of Finding of Fact No. VIII. It is clear the District Court did not consider or intend to attach to that finding the same significance which appellants seek to place upon it.

We do not question that if the Finding of Fact No. VIII means everything appellants claim it means, they would be entitled to an injunction and reversal of the judgment, if this court should overrule the "separate but equal doctrine." However, it is clear that the District Court did not intend or consider the finding to mean all the things appellants claim for it. As stated in the Decree of the District Court:

"The Court has heretofore filed its Findings of Fact and Conclusions of Law together with an opinion and has held as a matter of law that the plaintiffs have failed to prove they are entitled to the relief demanded."

IX. CONCLUSION

In view of the authorities heretofore cited, appellees respectfully submit that the judgment of the court below should be affirmed.

HAROLD R. FATZER,
Attorney General,

PAUL E. WILSON,
Asst. Attorney General,
Counsel for the State of Kansas,
State House, Topeka, Kansas,

PETER F. CALDWELL,
Counsel for the Board of Education of
　　Topeka, Kansas.
512 Capitol Federal Bldg., Topeka, Kansas.

U.S. Supreme Court,
October 1953
Brown v. Board of Education
of Topeka

———m———

I

**Oliver Brown, Mrs. Richard Lawton,
Mrs. Sadie Emmanuel, et al., appellants,
v. Board of Education of Topeka, Shawnee County,
Kansas, et al. No. 8, 345 U.S. 972.**

Former decision, 72 S.Ct. 1070; 344 U.S. 1, 73 S.Ct. 1; 344 U.S. 141, 73 S.Ct. 124.

Facts and opinion, 98 F.Supp. 797.

June 8, 1953. Case ordered restored to the docket and is assigned for reargument on Monday, October 12, next. In their briefs and on oral argument counsel are requested to discuss particularly the following questions insofar as they are relevant to the respective cases:

"I. What evidence is there that the Congress which submitted and the State legislatures and conventions which ratified the Fourteenth Amendment contemplated or did not contemplate, understood or did not understand, that it would abolish segregation in public schools?

"2. If neither the Congress in submitting nor the States in ratifying the Fourteenth Amendment understood that compliance with it would require the immediate abolition of segregation in public schools, was it nevertheless the understanding of the framers of the Amendment

"(a) that future Congresses might, in the exercise of their power under section 5 of the Amendment, abolish such segregation, or

"(b) that it would be within the judicial power, in light of future conditions, to construe the Amendment as abolishing such segregation of its own force?

"3. On the assumption that the answers to questions 2(a) and (b) do not dispose of the issue, is it within the judicial power, in construing the Amendment, to abolish segregation in public schools?

"4. Assuming it is decided that segregation in public schools violates the Fourteenth Amendment

"(a) would a decree necessarily follow providing that, within the limits set by normal geographic school districting, Negro children should forthwith be admitted to schools of their choice, or

"(b) may this Court, in the exercise of its equity powers, permit an effective gradual adjustment to be brought about from existing segregated systems to a system not based on color distinctions?

"5. On the assumption on which questions 4(a) and (b) are based, and assuming further that this Court will exercise its equity powers to the end described in question 4(b),

"(a) should this Court formulate detailed decrees in this case;

"(b) if so what specific issues should the decrees reach;

"(c) should this Court appoint a special master to hear evidence with a view to recommending specific terms for such decree;

"(d) should this Court remand to the courts of first instance with directions to frame decrees in this case and if so what general directions should the decrees of this Court include and what procedures should the courts of first instance follow in arriving at the specific terms of more detailed decrees?

"The Attorney General of the United States in invited to take part in the oral argument and to file an additional brief if he so desires."

The Supreme Court of the United States October Term, 1953

NO. 1

OLIVER BROWN, ET AL., APPELLANTS,

VS.

BOARD OF EDUCATION OF TOPEKA, ET AL., APPELLEES.

NO. 2

HARRY BRIGGS, JR., ET AL., APPELLANTS.

VS.

R. W. ELLIOTT, ET AL., APPELLEES.

NO. 4

DOROTHY E. DAVIS, ET AL., APPELLANTS,

VS.

COUNTY SCHOOL BOARD OF PRINCE EDWARDS COUNTY, APPELLEES.

NO. 10

FRANCIS B. GEBHART, ET AL., PETITIONERS,

VS.

ETHEL LOUISE BELTON, ET AL., RESPONDENTS.

APPEALS FROM THE UNITED STATES DISTRICT COURT FOR THE DISTRICT OF KANSAS, THE EASTERN DISTRICT OF SOUTH CAROLINA AND THE EASTERN DISTRICT OF VIRGINIA, AND ON PETITION FOR A WRIT OF CERTIORARI TO THE SUPREME COURT OF DELAWARE, RESPECTIVELY

BRIEF FOR APPELLANTS IN NOS. 1, 2 AND 4 AND FOR RESPONDENTS IN NO. 10 ON REARGUMENT

CHARLES L. BLACK JR.,
ELWOOD H. CHISOLM,
WILLIAM T. COLEMAN JR.
CHARLES T. DUNCAN,
GEORGE E. C. HAYES,
WILLIAM R. MING JR.,
CONSTANCE BAKER MOTLEY,
JAMES M. NABRIT JR.,
DAVID E. PINSKY,
FRANK E. REEVES,
JOHN SCOTT,
JACK B. WEINSTEIN, *of Counsel.*
HAROLD BOULWARE,
ROBERT L. CARTER,
JACK GREENBERG,

OLIVER W. HILL,
THURGOOD MARSHALL,
LOUIS L. REDDING,
SPOTTSWOOD W. ROBINSON, III,
CHARLES S. SCOTT, *Attorneys for Appellants in Nos. 1, 2, 4 and for Respondents in No. 10.*

—⁊⁊⁊—

U.S. SUPREME COURT, OCTOBER 1953

BRIEF FOR THE APPELLANTS AND RESPONDENTS ON REARGUMENT

Table of Contents

I. Normal exercise of the judicial function calls for a declaration that the state is without power to enforce distinctions based upon race or color in affording educational opportunities in the public schools

II. The statutory and constitutional provisions involved in these cases cannot be validated under separate but equal concept

   A. Racial segregation cannot be squared with the rationale of the early cases interpreting the reach of the Fourteenth Amendment

   B. The first time the question came before the Court, racial segregation in transportation was specifically disapproved

U.S. SUPREME
COURT,
OCTOBER 1953

BRIEF FOR THE
APPELLANTS AND
RESPONDENTS
ON REARGUMENT

C. The separate but equal doctrine marked an unwarranted departure from the main stream of constitutional development and permits the frustration of the very purposes of the Fourteenth Amendment as defined by this Court

D. The separate but equal doctrine was conceived in error

    1. The dissenting opinion of Justice Harlan in *Plessy v. Ferguson*

    2. Custom, usage and tradition rooted in the slave tradition cannot be the constitutional yardstick for measuring state action under the Fourteenth Amendment

    3. Preservation of public peace cannot justify deprivation of constitutional rights

    4. The separate but equal doctrine deprives Negroes of that protection which the Fourteenth Amendment accords under the general classification test

E. The separate but equal doctrine has not received unqualified approval in this Court

F. The necessary consequence of the Sweatt and McLaurin decisions is repudiation of the separate but equal doctrine

III. Viewed in the light of history the separate but equal doctrine has been an instrumentality of defiant nullification of the Fourteenth Amendment

A. The status of the Negro, slave and free, prior to the Civil War

B. The post war struggle

C. The Compromise of 1877 and the abandonment of Reconstruction

D. Consequences of the 1877 Compromise

E. Nullification of the rights guaranteed by the Fourteenth Amendment and the reestablishment of the Negro's pre–Civil War inferior status fully realized

Conclusion to Part I

Part Two

I. The Fourteenth Amendment was intended to destroy all caste and color legislation in the United States, including racial segregation

A. The era prior to the Civil War was marked by determined efforts to secure recognition of the principle of complete and real equality for all men within the existing constitutional framework of our government

Equality under law

B. The movement for complete equality reached its successful culmination in the Civil War and the Fourteenth Amendment

C. The principle of absolute and complete equality began to be translated into federal law as early as 1862

D. From the beginning the thirty-ninth Congress was determined to eliminate race distinctions from American law

The framers of the Fourteenth Amendment

E. The Fourteenth Amendment was intended to write into the organic law of the United States the principle of absolute and complete equality in broad constitutional language

F. The Republican majority in the 39th Congress was determined to prevent future Congresses from diminishing federal protection of these rights

G. Congress understood that while the Fourteenth Amendment would give authority to Congress to enforce its provisions, the amendment in and of itself would invalidate all class legislation by the states

Congress intended to destroy all class distinction in law

H. The treatment of public education or segregation in public schools during the 39th Congress must be considered in the light of the status of public education at that time

I. During the congressional debates on proposed legislation which culminated in the Civil Rights Act of 1875 veterans of the thirty-ninth Congress adhered to their conviction that the Fourteenth Amendment had proscribed segregation in public schools

II. There is convincing evidence that the State Legislatures and conventions which ratified the Fourteenth Amendment contemplated and understood that it prohibited State legislation which would require racial segregation in public schools

A. The eleven states seeking readmission understood that the Fourteenth Amendment stripped them of power to maintain segregated schools

Arkansas

North Carolina, South Carolina, Louisiana, Georgia, Alabama, and Florida

Texas

Virginia

Mississippi

Tennessee

B. The majority of the twenty-two Union States ratifying the 14th Amendment understood that it forbade compulsory segregation in public schools

EXPLANATORY STATEMENT

One brief is being filed in these four cases. They fundamentally involve the same questions and issues. As an aid to the Court, we are restating below a full history of each case.

NO. 1

Opinion below

The opinion of the statutory three-judge District Court for the District of Kansas (R. 238–244) is reported at 98 F. Supp. 797.

Jurisdiction

The judgment of the court below was entered on August 3, 1951 (R. 247). On October 1, 1951, appellants filed a petition for appeal (R. 248), and an order allowing the appeal was entered (R. 250). Probable jurisdiction was noted on June 9, 1952 (R. 254). Jurisdiction of this Court rests on Title 28, United States Code, §§ 1253 and 2101(b).

Statement of the case

Appellants are Negro students eligible to attend and attending elementary schools in Topeka, Kansas, and their parents (R. 3–4). Appellees are state officers empowered to maintain and operate the public schools of Topeka, Kansas (R. 4–5). On March 22, 1951, appellants commenced this class action against appellees to restrain them from enforcing and executing that part of Chapter 72–1724, General Statutes of Kansas, 1949, which permitted racial segregation in public elementary schools, on the ground that it violated the Fourteenth Amendment by depriving the infant appellants of equal educational opportunities (R. 2–7), and for a judgment declaring that the practice of appellees under said statute of maintaining and operating racially segregated elementary schools is in violation of the Fourteenth Amendment.

Appellees admitted in their answer that they acted pursuant to the statute and that, solely because of their color, the infant appellants were not eligible to attend any of the elementary schools maintained exclusively for white students (R. 12). The Attorney General of the State of Kansas filed a separate answer specifically to defend the constitutional validity of the statute (R. 14).

The court below was convened in accordance with Title 28, United States Code, § 2284, and, on June 25–26, a trial on the merits was held (R. 63 *et seq.*). On August 3, 1951, the court below filed its opinion (R. 238–244), findings of fact (R. 244–246) and conclusions of law (R. 246–247) and entered a final judgment denying the injunctive relief sought (R. 247).

Specification of errors

The court below erred:

1. In refusing to grant appellants' application for a permanent injunction to restrain appellees from acting pursuant to the statute under which they are maintaining separate

U.S. SUPREME COURT, OCTOBER 1953

BRIEF FOR THE APPELLANTS AND RESPONDENTS ON REARGUMENT

U.S. SUPREME
COURT,
OCTOBER 1953

BRIEF FOR THE
APPELLANTS AND
RESPONDENTS
ON REARGUMENT

public elementary schools for Negro children, solely because of their race and color.

2. In refusing to hold that the State of Kansas is without authority to promulgate the statute because it enforces a classification based upon race and color which is violative of the Constitution of the United States.

3. In refusing to enter judgment in favor of appellants after finding that enforced attendance at racially segregated elementary schools was detrimental and deprived them of educational opportunities equal to those available to white children.

NO. 2

Opinions below

The majority and dissenting opinions of the statutory three-judge District Court for the Eastern District of South Carolina on the first hearing (R. 176–209) are reported in 98 F. Supp. 529–548. The opinion on the second hearing (R. 301–306) is reported in 103 F. Supp. 920–923.

Jurisdiction

The judgment of the court below was entered on March 13, 1952 (R. 306). A petition for appeal was filed below and allowed on May 10, 1952 (R. 309). Probable jurisdiction was noted on June 9, 1952 (R. 316). Jurisdiction of this Court rests on Title 28, United States Code, §§ 1253 and 2101(b).

Statement of the case

Appellants are Negro children who reside in and are eligible to attend the public schools of School District No. 22, Clarendon County, South Carolina, and their respective parents and guardians (R. 4–5). Appellees are the public school officials of said district who, as officers of the state, maintain and operate the public schools of that district (R. 5–6). On December 22, 1950, appellants commenced this class action against appellees to enjoin enforcement of Article XI, Section 7, of the Constitution of South Carolina and Section 5377 of the Code of Laws of South Carolina of 1942, which require the segregation of races in public schools, on the ground that they deny to appellants the equal protection of the laws secured by the Fourteenth Amendment, and for a judgment declaring that said laws violate the Fourteenth Amendment and are invalid (R. 2–11).

Appellees in their answer admitted adherence to the said constitutional and statutory provisions requiring racial segregation in public schools and asserted that such provisions were a reasonable exercise of the police powers of the state and, therefore, were valid (R. 13–17).

A three-judge District Court was convened, pursuant to Title 28, United States Code, §§ 2284, and on July 25, 1951, a trial on the merits was held (R. 30 *et seq.*). On June 23, 1951, the court below filed its opinion (R. 176) and entered a final decree (R. 209): (1) upholding the constitutional validity of the contested state constitutional and statutory provisions; (2) denying the injunctive relief which was sought; (3) requiring appellees to furnish to appellants educational facilities equal to those furnished to white students; and (4) requiring appellees within six months to file a report of action taken toward that end.

An appeal from this judgment was allowed by this Court on July 20, 1951. The report required by the decree of the court below was filed on December 21, 1951, and subsequently forwarded to this Court. On January 28, 1952, this Court vacated the judgment of the court below and remanded the case for the purpose of obtaining the views of the court below on the additional facts in the record and to give it the opportunity to take such action as it might deem appropriate in light of the report. 342 U.S. 350. Mr. Justice Black and Mr. Justice Douglas dissented on the ground that the additional facts in the report were "wholly irrelevant to the constitutional questions presented by the appeal to this Court." 342 U.S. 350.

Pursuant to the mandate of this Court, a second trial was held in the court below on March 3, 1953 (R. 271), at which time the appellees filed an additional report showing progress made since the filing of the original report (R. 273). On March 13, 1952, the court below filed its opinion (R. 301) and entered a final decree (R. 306) again upholding the validity of the contested constitutional and statutory provisions, denying the injunctive relief requested and requiring appellees to afford to appellants educational facilities equal to those afforded to white students.

Specification of errors

The court below erred:

1. In refusing to enjoin the enforcement of the laws of South Carolina requiring racial segregation in the public schools of Clarendon County on the ground that these laws violate rights secured under the equal protection clause of the Fourteenth Amendment.

2. In refusing to grant to appellants immediate and effective relief against the unconstitutional practice of excluding appellants from an opportunity to share the public school facilities of Clarendon County on an equal basis with other students without regard to race or color.

3. In predicating its decision on the doctrine of *Plessy v. Ferguson* and in disregarding the rationale of *Sweatt v. Painter* and *McLaurin v. Board of Regents*.

NO. 4

Opinion below

The opinion of the statutory three-judge District Court for the Eastern District of Virginia (R. 617–623) is reported at 103 F. Supp. 337–341.

Jurisdiction

The judgment of the court below was entered on March 7, 1952 (R. 623). A petition for appeal was filed below and allowed on May 5, 1952 (R. 625, 630, 683). Probable jurisdiction was noted on October 8, 1952. ___U.S. ___, 97 L. ed. (Advance p. 27). Jurisdiction of this Court rests on Title 28, United States Code, §§ 1253 and 2101(b).

Statement of the case

Appellants, high school students residing in Prince Edward County, Virginia, and their parents and guardians, brought a class action against appellees, the County School Board and the Division Superintendent of Schools on May 23, 1951. The complaint (R. 5–30) alleged that said appellees maintained separate public secondary schools for Negro and white children pursuant to Article IX, Section 140 of the Constitution of Virginia, and Title 22, Chapter 12, Article 1, section 22–221, of the Code of Virginia of 1950; that the Negro school was inferior and unequal to the white schools; and that it was impossible for the infant appellants to secure educational opportunities or facilities equal to those afforded white children similarly situated as long as said appellees enforce said

laws or pursued a policy of racial segregation. It sought a judgment declaratory of the invalidity of said laws as a denial of rights secured by the due process and equal protection clauses of the Fourteenth Amendment, and an injunction restraining said appellees from enforcing said laws and from making any distinction based on race or color among children attending the secondary schools of the County.

Appellees admitted maintenance of said schools, enforcement of said laws, and inequalities as to physical plant and equipment, but denied that the segregation violated the Constitution (R. 32–36). Appellee, the Commonwealth of Virginia, intervened (R. 37) and made the same admissions and defense (R. 37–39).

On March 7, 1952, a three-judge District Court found the Negro school inferior in plant, facilities, curricula and means of transportation (R. 622–623) and ordered appellees forthwith to provide "substantially" equal curricula and transportation facilities and to "proceed with all reasonable diligence and dispatch to remove" the existing inequality "by building, furnishing and providing a high school building and facilities for Negro students" (R. 624). It refused to enjoin enforcement of the constitutional and statutory segregation provisions on the grounds: (1) that appellants' evidence as to the effects of educational segregation did not overbalance appellees', and that it accepted as "apt and able precedent" *Briggs v. Elliott*, 98 F. Supp. 529 (E. D. S. C. 1951) and *Carr v. Corning*, 182 F. 2d 14 (C. A. D. C. 1950) which "refused to decree that segregation be abolished incontinently" (R. 619); (2) that nullification of the segregation provisions was unwarranted in view of evidence that racial segregation was not based on prejudice or caprice but, rather, was "one of the ways of life in Virginia" (R. 620); (3) that segregation has begotten greater opportunities for the Negro (R. 621); (4) that elimination of segregation would lessen interest in and financial support of public schools (R. 621); and (5) that, finding "no hurt or harm to either race," it was not for the court "to adjudge the policy as right or wrong" (R. 621–622).

Specification of errors

The court below erred:

1. In refusing to enjoin the enforcement of Article IX, Section 140 of the Constitution of Virginia, and Title 22, Chapter 12, Article 1,

U.S. SUPREME COURT, OCTOBER 1953

BRIEF FOR THE APPELLANTS AND RESPONDENTS ON REARGUMENT

U.S. SUPREME
COURT,
OCTOBER 1953

BRIEF FOR THE
APPELLANTS AND
RESPONDENTS
ON REARGUMENT

Section 22–221, of the Code of Virginia of 1950, upon the grounds that these laws violate rights secured by the due process and equal protection clauses of the Fourteenth Amendment to the Constitution of the United States.

2. In refusing to forthwith restrain appellees from using race as a factor in determining the assignment of public secondary educational facilities in Prince Edward County, Virginia, after it had found that appellants are denied equality of buildings, facilities, curricula and means of transportation in violation of the due process and equal protection clauses of the Fourteenth Amendment.

3. In refusing to hold that appellants are entitled to equality in all aspects of the public secondary educational process, in addition to equality in physical facilities and curricula.

4. In issuing a decree ordering appellees to equalize secondary school facilities in the County where such decree cannot be effectively enforced without involving the court in the daily operation and supervision of schools.

NO. 10

Opinions below

The opinion of the Chancellor of the State of Delaware (A. 338) is reported at 87 A. (2d) 862. The opinion of the Supreme Court of Delaware (R. 37) is reported at 91 A. (2d) 137.*

Jurisdiction

The judgment of the court below was entered on August 28, 1952 (R. 37). On November 13, 1952 petition for writ of certiorari was filed herein. On November 20, 1952, respondents waived the filing of a brief in opposition to the petition for writ of certiorari and moved that, if certiorari were granted, the argument be advanced and heard immediately following argument in Nos. 8, 101 and 191. On November 24, 1952, the petition for writ of certiorari and motion to advance were granted. ___U.S. ___; 97 L. ed. (Advance, p. 124). Jurisdiction of this Court rests upon Title 28, United States Code, § 1257(3).

Statement of the case

No. 10 arises from two separate class actions filed in the Court of Chancery of the State of Delaware by Negro school children and their guardians seeking admittance of the children to two public schools maintained by petitioners exclusively for white children in New Castle County, Delaware. In the courts below, plaintiffs prevailed, and they and members of their class are now attending the schools to which they sought admission, an application for stay of final order having been denied. (Brief of Respondents, No. 448, October Term, 1952, pp. 25–27). Thus, in this case, unlike the other school segregation cases now under consideration, plaintiffs are respondents in this Court. Nevertheless, they file their brief at this time along with appellants in Numbers 1, 2 and 4, because, on the fundamental issues, they take the same position as do those appellants, and because they believe that by so filing they will facilitate the Court's consideration of the matters at bar.

The complaint (A 3–13) in one of the two cases from which No. 10 arises, alleged that respondents residing in the Claymont Special School District were refused admittance to the Claymont High School maintained by petitioner-members of the State Board of Education and members of the Board of Education of the Claymont Special School District solely because of respondents' color. Because of this, these respondents were compelled to attend Howard High School (RA 47), a public school for Negroes only, in Wilmington, Delaware. Howard High School is operated and controlled by the Corporate Board of Public Education in Wilmington, not a party to this case (A 314–15, 352; R 57, RA 203). The second complaint (A 14–30) out of which No. 448 arises alleged that respondent was excluded from Hockessin School No. 29, a public elementary school maintained for white children only, by petitioner-members of the State Board of Education and petitioner-members of the Board of School Trustees of Hockessin School No. 29.

---

* The record in this case consists of five separate parts: appendix to petitioners' brief in the court below, the supplement thereto, appendix to respondents' brief in the court below, the supplement thereto, and the record of proceedings in the Supreme Court of Delaware. These will be referred to in respondents' brief as follows:

Appendix to petitioners' brief below will be indicated by A; the supplement to the petitioners' appendix below will be referred to as SA; respondents' appendix below will be referred to as RA; the supplement to respondents' appendix below will be referred to as RSA; the record of proceedings in the Supreme Court of Delaware will be referred to as R.

Respondent and the class she represented at the time of the complaint, attended Hockessin School No. 107, maintained solely for Negroes by the State Board of Education. Respondents in both complaints asserted that the aforesaid state-imposed racial segregation required by Par. 2631, Revised Code of Delaware, 1935, and Article X, Section 1 of the Constitution of Delaware: (1) compelled them to attend schools substantially inferior to those for white children to which admittance was sought; and (2) injured their mental health, impeded their mental and personality development and made inferior their educational opportunity as compared with that offered by the state to white children similarly situated. Such treatment, respondents asserted, is prohibited by the equal protection clause of the Fourteenth Amendment to the Constitution of the United States.

Petitioners' answers (A 31–33, A 34–37) defended the exclusion: (1) upon mandatory constitutional and statutory provisions of the State of Delaware which require separate public schools for white and colored children; and (2) upon the fact that the educational opportunities offered respondents were equal to those offered white children similarly situated.

The two cases were consolidated and tried before the Chancellor. In an opinion (A 348–356; 87 A. (2d) 862) filed on April 1, 1952, the Chancellor found as a fact that in "our Delaware society" segregation in education practiced by petitioners "itself results in Negro children, as a class, receiving educational opportunities which are substantially inferior to those available to white children otherwise similarly situated." However, the Chancellor denied respondents' prayers for a judgment on this ground and refused to declare that the Delaware constitutional and statutory provisions violated respondents' right to equal protection. But the Chancellor did award respondents the relief which they requested because other inequalities were found to exist. These included, in the high school, teacher training, pupil-teacher ratio, extra-curricular activities, physical plant and esthetic considerations, and time and distance involved in travel. As to the elementary schools in question, the court found the Negro facilities inferior in building and site, esthetic considerations, teacher preparation and transportation facilities. A more detailed exposition of the facts upon which these findings were based is set

forth in respondents' Brief in No. 448, October Term, 1952, pp. 27–44.

The Chancellor, as stated above, ordered that respondents be granted immediate relief in the only way that it was then available, that is, by admission to the superior facilities. On August 28, 1952, the Supreme Court of Delaware affirmed. 91 A. (2d) 137. Its findings on some of the facts were somewhat different than the Chancellor's but, on the whole, it agreed with him. Upholding the Chancellor's determination that the requested relief could not be granted because of the harmful psychological effect of racial segregation, it did not otherwise review his factual findings in this regard. Denying petitioners' plea for time to equalize the facilities in question, the Supreme Court held that in the high school case: (1) a decree ordering petitioners to equalize the facilities in question could have no effect on the legal entity having control of the Wilmington public schools which was not a party to the cause; and (2) that the court did not see how it could supervise and control the expenditure of state funds in a matter committed to the administrative discretion of school authorities. Finally, the court held that it could not issue a decree which would, in effect, deny to plaintiffs what it had held they rightfully deserved. As to the elementary school, the court also noted that defendants had not assumed the burden of showing to what extent remedial legislation had improved or could improve conditions in the future. Alluding to its antecedent discussion of the question of relief for high school respondents, it affirmed the Chancellor's finding on this issue also.

Stay of the order was denied by the Chancellor and by the Supreme Court of Delaware (Brief of Respondents, No. 448, October Term, 1952, pp. 25–27) and respondents and members of their class are now enjoying their second year of equal educational opportunities under the decree.

This court's order

These four cases were argued and submitted to the Court on December 9–11, 1952. Thereafter, on June 8, 1953, this Court entered its order for reargument, as follows, ____ U.S. ____; 97 L. ed. (Advance p. 956):

> "Each of these cases is ordered restored to the docket and is assigned for reargument on Monday, October 12, next. In their briefs and on oral argument counsel are requested to

U.S. SUPREME
COURT,
OCTOBER 1953

BRIEF FOR THE
APPELLANTS AND
RESPONDENTS
ON REARGUMENT

discuss particularly the following questions insofar as they are relevant to the respective cases:

"1. What evidence is there that the Congress which submitted and the State legislatures and conventions which ratified the Fourteenth Amendment contemplated or did not contemplate, understood or did not understand, that it would abolish segregation in public schools?

"2. If neither the Congress in submitting nor the States in ratifying the Fourteenth Amendment understood that compliance with it would require the immediate abolition of segregation in public schools, was it nevertheless the understanding of the framers of the Amendment

"(a) that future Congresses might, in the exercise of their power under Sec. 5 of the Amendment, abolish such segregation, or

"(b) that it would be within the judicial power, in light of future conditions, to construe the Amendment as abolishing such segregation of its own force?

"3. On the assumption that the answers to questions 2(a) and (b) do not dispose of the issue, is it within the judicial power, in construing the Amendment, to abolish segregation in public schools?

"4. Assuming it is decided that segregation in public schools violates the Fourteenth Amendment

"(a) would a decree necessarily follow providing that, within the limits set by normal geographic school districting, Negro children should forthwith be admitted to schools of their choice, or

"(b) may this Court, in the exercise of its equity powers, permit an effective gradual adjustment to be brought about from existing segregated systems to a system not based on color distinctions?

"5. On the assumption on which questions 4(a) and (b) are based, and assuming further that this Court will exercise its equity powers to the end described in question 4(b),

"(a) should this Court formulate detailed decrees in these cases;

"(b) if so what specific issues should the decrees reach;

"(c) should this Court appoint a special master to hear evidence with a view

to recommending specific terms for such decrees;

"(d) should this Court remand to the courts of first instance with directions to frame decrees in these cases, and if so, what general directions should the decrees of this Court include and what procedures should the courts of first instance follow in arriving at the specific terms of more detailed decrees?

"The Attorney General of the United States is invited to take part in the oral argument and to file an additional brief if he so desires."

On August 4, 1953, upon motion of the Attorney General of the United States and without objection by the parties, this Court entered its order postponing the date assigned for reargument of these cases until December 7, 1953.

SUMMARY OF ARGUMENT

These cases consolidated for argument before this Court present in different factual contexts essentially the same ultimate legal questions.

The substantive question common to all is whether a state can, consistently with the Constitution, exclude children, solely on the ground that they are Negroes, from public schools which otherwise they would be qualified to attend. It is the thesis of this brief, submitted on behalf of the excluded children, that the answer to the question is in the negative: the Fourteenth Amendment prevents states from according differential treatment to American children on the basis of their color or race. Both the legal precedents and the judicial theories, discussed in Part I hereof, and the evidence concerning the intent of the framers of the Fourteenth Amendment and the understanding of the Congress and the ratifying states, developed in Part II hereof, support this proposition.

Denying this thesis, the school authorities, relying in part on language originating in this Court's opinion in *Plessy v. Ferguson*, 163 U.S. 537, urge that exclusion of Negroes, *qua* Negroes, from designated public schools is permissible when the excluded children are afforded admittance to other schools especially reserved for Negroes, *qua* Negroes, if such schools are equal.

The procedural question common to all the cases is the role to be played, and the time-table to be followed, by this Court and the lower courts in directing an end to the challenged exclusion, in the event that this Court determines, with respect to the substantive question, that exclusion of Negroes, *qua* Negroes, from public schools contravenes the Constitution.

The importance to our American democracy of the substantive question can hardly be overstated. The question is whether a nation founded on the proposition that "all men are created equal" is honoring its commitments to grant "due process of law" and "the equal protection of the laws" to all within its borders when it, or one of its constituent states, confers or denies benefits on the basis of color or race.

1. Distinctions drawn by state authorities on the basis of color or race violate the Fourteenth Amendment. *Shelley v. Kraemer,* 334 U.S. 1; *Buchanan v. Warley,* 245 U.S. 60. This has been held to be true even as to the conduct of public educational institutions. *Sweatt v. Painter,* 339 U.S. 629; *McLaurin v. Oklahoma State Regents,* 339 U.S. 637. Whatever other purposes the Fourteenth Amendment may have had, it is indisputable that its primary purpose was to complete the emancipation provided by the Thirteenth Amendment by ensuring to the Negro equality before the law. The *Slaughter-House Cases,* 16 Wall. 36; *Strauder v. West Virginia,* 100 U.S. 303.

2. Even if the Fourteenth Amendment did not *per se* invalidate racial distinctions as a matter of law, the racial segregation challenged in the instant cases would run afoul of the conventional test established for application of the equal protection clause because the racial classifications here have no reasonable relation to any valid legislative purpose. See *Quaker City Cab Co. v. Pennsylvania,* 277 U.S. 389; *Truax v. Raich,* 239 U.S. 33; *Smith v. Cahoon,* 283 U.S. 553; *Mayflower Farms v. Ten Eyck,* 297 U.S. 266; *Skinner v. Oklahoma,* 316 U.S. 535. See also *Tunstall v. Brotherhood of Locomotive Firemen,* 323 U.S. 192; *Steele v. Louisville & Nashville R. R. Co.,* 323 U.S. 192.

3. Appraisal of the facts requires rejection of the contention of the school authorities. The educational detriment involved in racially constricting a student's associations has already been recognized by this Court. *Sweatt v. Painter,* 339 U.S. 629; *McLaurin v. Oklahoma State Regents,* 339 U.S. 637.

4. The argument that the requirements of the Fourteenth Amendment are met by providing alternative schools rests, finally, on reiteration of the separate but equal doctrine enunciated in *Plessy v. Ferguson.*

Were these ordinary cases, it might be enough to say that the *Plessy* case can be distinguished—that it involved only segregation in transportation. But these are not ordinary cases, and in deference to their importance it seems more fitting to meet the *Plessy* doctrine head-on and to declare that doctrine erroneous.

Candor requires recognition that the plain purpose and effect of segregated education is to perpetuate an inferior status for Negroes which is America's sorry heritage from slavery. But the primary purpose of the Fourteenth Amendment was to deprive the states of *all* power to perpetuate such a caste system.

5. The first and second of the five questions propounded by this Court requested enlightment as to whether the Congress which submitted, and the state legislatures and conventions which ratified, the Fourteenth Amendment contemplated or understood that it would prohibit segregation in public schools, either of its own force or through subsequent legislative or judicial action. The evidence, both in Congress and in the legislatures of the ratifying states, reflects the substantial intent of the Amendment's proponents and the substantial understanding of its opponents that the Fourteenth Amendment would, of its own force, proscribe all forms of state-imposed racial distinctions, thus necessarily including all racial segregation in public education.

The Fourteenth Amendment was actually the culmination of the determined efforts of the Radical Republican majority in Congress to incorporate into our fundamental law the well-defined equalitarian principle of complete equality for all without regard to race or color. The debates in the 39th Congress and succeeding Congresses clearly reveal the intention that the Fourteenth Amendment would work a revolutionary change in our state-federal relationship by denying to the states the power to distinguish on the basis of race.

The Civil Rights Bill of 1866, as originally proposed, possessed scope sufficiently broad in the opinion of many Congressmen to entirely destroy all state legislation based on race. A great majority of the Republican Radicals—who later formulated the Fourteenth Amendment—understood and intended that the Bill would prohibit segregated schools. Opponents of the measure shared this understanding. The scope

U.S. SUPREME
COURT,
OCTOBER 1953

BRIEF FOR THE
APPELLANTS AND
RESPONDENTS
ON REARGUMENT

U.S. SUPREME
COURT,
OCTOBER 1953

BRIEF FOR THE
APPELLANTS AND
RESPONDENTS
ON REARGUMENT

of this legislation was narrowed because it was known that the Fourteenth Amendment was in process of preparation and would itself have scope exceeding that of the original draft of the Civil Rights Bill.

6. The evidence makes clear that it was the intent of the proponents of the Fourteenth Amendment, and the substantial understanding of its opponents, that it would, of its own force, prohibit all state action predicated upon race or color. The intention of the framers with respect to any specific example of caste state action—in the instant cases, segregated education—cannot be determined solely on the basis of a tabulation of contemporaneous statements mentioning the specific practice. The framers were formulating a constitutional provision setting broad standards for determination of the relationship of the state to the individual. In the nature of things they could not list all the specific categories of existing and prospective state activity which were to come within the constitutional prohibitions. The broad general purpose of the Amendment—obliteration of race and color distinctions—is clearly established by the evidence. So far as there was consideration of the Amendment's impact upon the undeveloped educational systems then existing, both proponents and opponents of the Amendment understood that it would proscribe all racial segregation in public education.

7. While the Amendment conferred upon Congress the power to enforce its prohibitions, members of the 39th Congress and those of subsequent Congresses made it clear that the framers understood and intended that the Fourteenth Amendment was self-executing and particularly pointed out that the federal judiciary had authority to enforce its prohibitions without Congressional implementation.

8. The evidence as to the understanding of the states is equally convincing. Each of the eleven states that had seceded from the Union ratified the Amendment, and concurrently eliminated racial distinctions from its laws, and adopted a constitution free of requirement or specific authorization of segregated schools. Many rejected proposals for segregated schools, and none enacted a school segregation law until after readmission. The significance of these facts is manifest from the consideration that ten of these states, which were required, as a condition of readmission, to ratify the Amendment and to

modify their constitutions and laws in conformity therewith, considered that the Amendment required them to remove all racial distinctions from their existing and prospective laws, including those pertaining to public education.

Twenty-two of the twenty-six Union states also ratified the Amendment. Although unfettered by congressional surveillance, the overwhelming majority of the Union states acted with an understanding that it prohibited racially segregated schools and necessitated conformity of their school laws to secure consistency with that understanding.

9. In short, the historical evidence fully sustains this Court's conclusion in the *Slaughter House Cases,* 16 Wall. 61, 81, that the Fourteenth Amendment was designed to take from the states all power to enforce caste or class distinctions.

10. The Court in its fourth and fifth questions assumes that segregation is declared unconstitutional and inquires as to whether relief should be granted immediately or gradually. Appellants, recognizing the possibility of delay of a purely administrative character, do not ask for the impossible. No cogent reasons justifying further exercise of equitable discretion, however, have as yet been produced.

It has been indirectly suggested in the briefs and oral argument of appellees that some such reasons exist. Two plans were suggested by the United States in its Brief as *Amicus Curiae.* We have analyzed each of these plans as well as appellees' briefs and oral argument and find nothing there of sufficient merit on which this Court, in the exercise of its equity power, could predicate a decree permitting an effective gradual adjustment from segregated to non-segregated school systems. Nor have we been able to find any other reasons or plans sufficient to warrant the exercise of such equitable discretion in these cases. Therefore, in the present posture of these cases, appellants are unable to suggest any compelling reasons for this Court to postpone relief.

ARGUMENT

PART ONE

The question of judicial power to abolish segregated schools is basic to the issues involved in these cases and for that reason we have undertaken to analyze it at the outset before dealing with the other matters raised by the Court, although formally this means that the first section of this brief comprehends Question No. 3:

> On the assumption that the answers to question 2(a) and (b) do not dispose of the issue, is it within the judicial power, in construing the Amendment, to abolish segregation in public schools?

I. NORMAL EXERCISE OF THE JUDICIAL FUNCTION CALLS FOR A DECLARATION THAT THE STATE IS WITHOUT POWER TO ENFORCE DISTINCTIONS BASED UPON RACE OR COLOR IN AFFORDING EDUCATIONAL OPPORTUNITIES IN THE PUBLIC SCHOOLS

This Court in a long line of decisions has made it plain that the Fourteenth Amendment prohibits a state from making racial distinctions in the exercise of governmental power. Time and again this Court has held that if a state's power has been exercised in such a way as to deprive a Negro of a right which he would have freely enjoyed if he had been white, then that state's action violated the Fourteenth Amendment.

In *Shelley v. Kraemer,* 334 U.S. 1, for example, an unanimous Court held that States of Missouri and Michigan had violated the 14th Amendment when their courts ruled that a Negro could not own real property whose ownership it was admitted the state law would have protected him in, had he been white. This, despite the fact that the state court was doing no more than enforcing a private agreement running with the land. The sole basis for the decision, then, was that the Fourteenth Amendment compels the states to be color blind in exercising their power and authority.

Buchanan v. Warley, 245 U.S. 60, was an earlier decision to the same effect. There, this Court invalidated a Louisville, Kentucky ordinance which required racial residential segregation. Though it applied to Negro and white alike, the Court rightly recognized that the ordinance was an exercise of the state's power based on race and race alone. This, the Court ruled, was a violation of the Fourteenth Amendment. To the same effect is *Barrows v. Jackson,* 346 U.S. 249, 97 (L. Ed. Advance p. 261). And see *Oyama v. California,* 332 U.S. 633.

This Court has applied the same rigorous requirement to the exercise of the state's power in providing public education. Beginning with *Missouri ex rel. Gaines v. Canada,* 305 U.S. 337, this Court has uniformly ruled that the Fourteenth Amendment prohibits a state from using race or color as the determinant of the quantum, quality or type of education and the place at which education is to be afforded. Most recently, this Court in *McLaurin v. Oklahoma State Regents,* 339 U.S. 637, held that rules which made distinctions among students in the same school solely on the basis of color were forbidden by the Fourteenth Amendment. Thus, this Court has made it plain that no state may use color or race as the axis upon which the state's power turns, and the conduct of the public education system has not been excepted from this ban.

This judicial recognition that race is an irrational basis for governmental action under our Constitution has been manifested in many decisions and opinions of this Court. In *Yick Wo v. Hopkins,* 118 U.S. 356, this Court struck down local administrative action which differentiated between whites and Chinese. In *Hirabayashi v. United States,* 320 U.S. 81, 100, Chief Justice Stone, in a majority opinion, characterized racial distinctions as "odious to a free people." In *Korematsu v. United States,* 323 U.S. 214, 216, the Court viewed racial restrictions as "immediately suspect." Mr. Justice Jackson, concurring in *Edwards v. California,* 314 U.S. 180, 185, referred to race and color as "constitutionally an irrelevance." Mr. Justice Douglas, dissenting in *South v. Peters,* 339 U.S. 276, 278, considered discriminations based upon race, creed, or color "beyond the pale." In an unanimous opinion in *Henderson v. United States,* 339 U.S. 816, 825, the Court, while not reaching the constitutional question raised, described signs, partitions and curtains segregating Negroes in railroad dining cars as emphasizing "the artificiality of a difference in treatment which serves only to call attention to a racial classification of passengers holding identical tickets and using the same public dining facility." Every member of the present Court has from time to time subscribed to this view of race as an irrational premise for government action.

The restrictions placed upon persons of Japanese origin on the West Coast during World War II were sustained in *Hirabayashi v. United States, supra,* and in *Korematsu v. United States, supra,* as emergency war measures taken by the national government in a dire national peril of the gravest nature. The military decision was upheld as within an implied war power, and the Court was unwilling to interfere with measures considered necessary to the safety of the nation

U.S. SUPREME COURT, OCTOBER 1953

BRIEF FOR THE APPELLANTS AND RESPONDENTS ON REARGUMENT

U.S. SUPREME
COURT,
OCTOBER 1953

BRIEF FOR THE
APPELLANTS AND
RESPONDENTS
ON REARGUMENT

by those primarily responsible for its security. Yet, in upholding these orders, the Court made some of the most sweeping condemnations of governmentally imposed racial and color distinctions ever announced by our judiciary. And while departure from accepted standards of governmental conduct was sustained in order to remove persons of Japanese origin from areas where sabotage and espionage might have worked havoc with the national war effort, once this removal was accomplished and individual loyalty determined, further restrictions based upon race or color could no longer be countenanced. *Ex Parte Endo,* 323 U.S. 283.

Tunstall v. Brotherhood of Locomotive Firemen & Enginemen, 323 U.S. 210, and *Steele v. Louisville & Nashville R. R. Co.,* 323 U.S. 192, while not deciding the constitutional question, left no doubt that the Fifth Amendment had stripped the national government of power to enforce the racial discrimination assailed.

These decisions serve to underscore the constitutional prohibition against Congressional action grounded upon color except in so far as it may have temporary justification to meet an overwhelming national emergency such as that which led to decisions in the *Hirabayashi* and *Korematsu* cases.

The power of states is even more rigidly circumscribed. For there is grave doubt that their acts can be sustained under the exception made in the *Hirabayashi* and *Korematsu* cases with respect to the national government. See *Oyama v. California,* 332 U.S. 633. The Fourteenth Amendment has been defined as a broad prohibition against state enforcement of differentiations and discrimination based upon race or color. State action restricting the right of Negroes to vote has been struck down as a violation of the Fourteenth Amendment. *Nixon v. Condon,* 286 U.S. 73. Similarly, the Court has refused to sanction the systematic exclusion of Negroes from the petit or grand jury, *Hill v. Texas,* 316 U.S. 400; *Pierre v. Louisiana,* 306 U.S. 354; their representation on juries on a token or proportional basis, *Cassell v. Texas,* 339 U.S. 282; *Shepherd v. Florida,* 341 U.S. 50; or any method in the selection of juries susceptible of racial discrimination in practice. *Avery v. Georgia,* 345 U.S. 559.

Legislation depriving persons of particular races of an opportunity to pursue a gainful occupation has been held a denial of equal protection. *Truax v. Raich,* 239 U.S. 33; *Takahashi v. Fish and Games Commission,* 334 U.S. 410. It is now well settled that a state may not make racial differences among its employees the basis for salary differentiations. *Alston v. School Board,* 112 F. 2d 992 (CA 4th 1940), *cert. denied,* 311 U.S. 693.

Indeed, abhorrence of race as a premise for governmental action pervades a wide realm of judicial opinion dealing with other constitutional provisions. Sweeping decisions have enforced the right of Negroes to make effective use of the electoral process consistent with the requirements of the Fifteenth Amendment. *Guinn v. United States,* 238 U.S. 347; *Lane v. Wilson,* 307 U.S. 268; *Smith v. Allwright,* 321 U.S. 649; *Terry v. Adams,* 345 U.S. 461.

It should be added parenthetically that these decisions are not mere *pro forma* applications of the self-evident requirements of the Fifteenth Amendment. On the contrary, the concept of state action has been utilized in a dynamic and expanding fashion as the Court has sought to reach any method or subterfuge with which the state has attempted to avoid its obligation under that constitutional amendment. *Smith v. Allwright, supra; Terry v. Adams, supra.* See *Rice v. Elmore,* 165 F. 2d 387 (CA 4th 1947), *cert. denied,* 333 U.S. 875 and *Baskin v. Brown,* 174 F. 2d 391 (CA 4th 1949), cases holding state nonaction violative of the Fifteenth Amendment the principle of which was expressly approved in *Terry v. Adams.*

State laws requiring racial segregation in interstate commerce have been declared an invalid invasion of commerce power reserved to the Congress. *Morgan v. Virginia,* 328 U.S. 373. But where a state sought to enforce against a carrier engaged in foreign commerce its local nonsegregation policy, the state law was upheld. The Court considered it inconceivable that the Congress in the exercise of its plenary power over commerce would take any action in conflict with the local nondiscriminatory regulations imposed. *Bob-Lo Excursion Co. v. Michigan,* 333 U.S. 28. These two cases considered together strikingly exemplify this Court's position that fundamental national policy is offended by a requirement of segregation, but implemented by its prohibition.

The contention by a labor union that a state civil rights law which prohibited racial discrimination in union membership offended the

Fourteenth Amendment was dismissed because such a position "would be a distortion of the policy manifested in that amendment which was adopted to prevent state legislation designed to perpetuate discrimination on the basis of race and color." *Railway Mail Association v. Corsi,* 326 U.S. 88, 94.

Thus, the Court has all but universally made short shrift of attempts to use governmental power to enforce racial distinctions. Yet, where such power has prohibited racial discrimination, it has been sustained even where it has been urged that the state is acting in derogation of other constitutional rights or protected interests.

At the graduate and professional school level, closest to the cases here, racial distinctions as applied have been struck down. *McLaurin v. Oklahoma State Regents,* 339 U.S. 637; *Sweatt v. Painter,* 339 U.S. 629. In those cases the educational process was viewed as a totality. The faculty of the school, the prestige of the institution, the fact that segregation deprived the Negro applicant of the benefits which he might secure in attending school with representatives of the state's dominant racial majority, the value judgment of the community with respect to the segregated school, and the impact of segregation on the individual were among the factors considered by the Court in determining that equal educational opportunities were not available. Those cases, we submit, control disposition of the cases here.

Since segregation was found to impair and inhibit an adult's ability to study in the *McLaurin* case, it seems clear that such segregation has even more far reaching adverse consequences on the mental development of the children involved here.

Sweatt's isolation from the dominant racial majority in a segregated law school was held to deprive him of an effective opportunity to learn the law. The basic function of the public school is to instruct each succeeding generation in the fundamental traditions of our democracy. The child can best come to believe in and respect these traditions by learning them in a setting in which they are in practical operation. But to be taught that our society is founded upon a concept of equality in a public school from which those racial groups are excluded which hold preeminence in every field in his community makes it all but impossible for such teachings to take root. Segregation here is detrimental to the

Negro child in his effort to develop into a useful and productive citizen in a democracy.

The *Sweatt* and *McLaurin* cases teach that the Court will consider the educational process in its entirety, including, apart from the measurable physical facilities, whatever factors have been shown to have educational significance. This rule cannot be peculiar to any level of public education. Public elementary and high school education is no less a governmental function than graduate and professional education in state institutions. Moreover, just as Sweatt and McLaurin were denied certain benefits characteristic of graduate and professional education, it is apparent from the records of these cases that Negroes are denied educational benefits which the state itself asserts are the fundamental objectives of public elementary and high school education.

South Carolina, like the other states in this country, has accepted the obligation of furnishing the extensive benefits of public education. Article XI, section 5, of the Constitution of South Carolina, declares: "The General Assembly shall provide for a liberal system of free public schools for all children between the ages of six and twenty-one years." Some 410 pages of the Code of Laws of South Carolina deal with "education." Title 31, Chapters 122–23, S. C. Code, pp. 387–795 (1935). Provision is made for the entire state-supported system of public schools, its administration and organization, from the kindergarten through the university. Pupils and teachers, school buildings, minimum standards of school construction, and specifications requiring certain general courses of instruction are dealt with in detail. In addition to requiring that the three "R's" must be taught, the law compels instruction in "morals and good behaviour" and in the "principles" and "essentials of the United States Constitution, including the study of and devotion to American institutions." Title 31, Chapter 122, sections 5321, 5323, 5325, S. C. Code (1935). The other states involved here are attempting to promote the same objectives.

These states thus recognize the accepted broad purposes of general public education in a democratic society. There is no question that furnishing public education is now an accepted governmental function. There are compelling reasons for a democratic government's assuming the burden of educating its children, of

U.S. SUPREME COURT, OCTOBER 1953

BRIEF FOR THE APPELLANTS AND RESPONDENTS ON REARGUMENT

U.S. SUPREME
COURT,
OCTOBER 1953

BRIEF FOR THE
APPELLANTS AND
RESPONDENTS
ON REARGUMENT

increasing its citizens' usefulness, efficiency and ability to govern.

In a democracy citizens from every group, no matter what their social or economic status or their religious or ethnic origins, are expected to participate widely in the making of important public decisions. The public school, even more than the family, the church, business institutions, political and social groups and other institutions, has become an effective agency for giving to all people that broad background of attitudes and skills required to enable them to function effectively as participants in a democracy. Thus, "education" comprehends the entire process of developing and training the mental, physical and moral powers and capabilities of human beings. See *Weyl v. Comm. of Int. Rev.*, 48 F. 2d 811, 812 (CA 2d 1931); *Jones v. Better Business Bureau*, 123 F. 2d 767, 769 (CA 10th 1941).

The records in instant cases emphasize the extent to which the state has deprived Negroes of these fundamental educational benefits by separating them from the rest of the school population. In the case of *Briggs v. Elliott* (No. 101), expert witnesses testified that compulsory racial segregation in elementary and high schools inflicts considerable personal injury on the Negro pupils which endures as long as these students remain in the segregated school. These witnesses testified that compulsory racial segregation in the public schools of South Carolina injures the Negro students by: (1) impairing their ability to learn (R. 140, 161); (2) deterring the development of their personalities (R. 86, 89); (3) depriving them of equal status in the school community (R. 89, 141, 145); (4) destroying their self-respect (R. 140, 148); (5) denying them full opportunity for democratic social development (R. 98, 99, 103); (6) subjecting them to the prejudices of others (R. 133) and stamping them with a badge of inferiority (R. 148).

Similar testimony was introduced in each of the other three cases here involved, and that testimony was undisputed in the case of *Briggs v. Elliott* (No. 101); *Brown v. Board of Education of Topeka, et al.* (No. 8); *Gebhart v. Belton* (No. 448). In *Davis v. County School Board* (No. 191), while witnesses for the appellees disputed portions of the testimony of appellants' expert witnesses, four of appellees' witnesses admitted that racial segregation has harmful effects and another recognized that such segregation could be injurious.

In the *Gebhart* case (No. 448) the Chancellor filed an opinion in which he set forth a finding of fact, based on the undisputed oral testimony of experts in education, sociology, psychology, psychiatry and anthropology (A. 340–341) that in "our Delaware society," segregation in education practiced by petitioners as agents of the state "itself results in the Negro children, as a class, receiving educational opportunities which are substantially inferior to those available to white children otherwise similarly situated."

And the court below in the *Brown* case (No. 8) made the following Finding of Fact (R. 245–246):

> "Segregation of white and colored children in public schools has a detrimental effect upon the colored children. The impact is greater when it has the sanction of the law; for the policy of separating the races is usually interpreted as denoting the inferiority of the negro group. A sense of inferiority affects the motivation of a child to learn. Segregation with the sanction of law, therefore, has a tendency to retard the educational and mental development of negro children and to deprive them of some of the benefits they would receive in a racially integrated school system."

The testimony of the expert witnesses in the cases now under consideration, the Opinion of the Chancellor in the Delaware case and the Finding of Fact by the lower court in the Kansas case are amply supported by scientific studies of recognized experts. A compilation of these materials was assembled and filed as an Appendix to the briefs in these cases on the first hearing. The observation of Mr. Justice Jackson in *West Virginia State Board of Education v. Barnette*, 319 U.S. 624, 636 that public school children, being educated for citizenship, must be scrupulously protected in their constitutional rights, "if we are not to strangle the free mind at its source and teach youth to discount important principles of our government as mere platitudes," while made in somewhat different context, appropriately describes the high public interest which these cases involve.

In sum, the statutes and constitutional provisions assailed in these cases must fall because they are contrary to this Court's basic premise that, as a matter of law, race is not an allowable basis of differentiation in governmental action; they are inconsistent with the broad prohibition of the Fifth and Fourteenth Amendments as defined by this Court; they are clearly within that category of racism in state action specifically prohibited by the *McLaurin* and *Sweatt* decisions.

II. THE STATUTORY AND CONSTITUTIONAL PROVISIONS INVOLVED IN THESE CASES CANNOT BE VALIDATED UNDER ANY SEPARATE BUT EQUAL CONCEPT

The basic principles referred to in Point I above, we submit, control these cases, and except for the mistaken belief that the doctrine of *Plessy v. Ferguson,* 163 U.S. 537, is a correct expression of the meaning of the Fourteenth Amendment, these cases would present no difficult problem.

This Court announced the separate but equal doctrine in a transportation case, and proponents of segregation have relied upon it repeatedly as a justification for racial segregation as if "separate but equal" had become *in haec verba* an amendment to the Fourteenth Amendment, itself. Under that anomalous doctrine, it is said that racial differentiations in the enjoyment of rights protected by the Fourteenth Amendment are permitted as long as the segregated facilities provided for Negroes are substantially equal to those provided for other racial groups. In each case in this Court where a state scheme of racism has been deemed susceptible of rationalization under the separate but equal formula, it has been urged as a defense.

A careful reading of the cases, however, reveals that this doctrine has received only very limited and restricted application in the actual decisions of this Court, and even that support has been eroded by more recent decisions. See particularly *McLaurin v. Oklahoma State Regents; Sweatt v. Painter.* Whatever appeal the separate but equal doctrine might have had, it stands mirrored today as the faulty conception of an era dominated by provincialism, by intense emotionalism in race relations caused by local and temporary conditions and by the preaching of a doctrine of racial superiority that contradicted the basic concept upon which our society was founded. Twentieth-century America, fighting racism at home and abroad, has rejected the race views of *Plessy v. Ferguson* because we have come to the realization that such views obviously tend to preserve not the strength but the weaknesses of our heritage.

A. Racial segregation cannot be squared with the rationale of the early cases interpreting the reach of the Fourteenth Amendment

In the *Slaughter House Cases,* 16 Wall. 36—the first case decided under the Fourteenth Amendment—the Court, drawing on its knowledge of an almost contemporaneous event, recognized that the Fourteenth Amendment secured to Negroes full citizenship rights and prohibited any state action discriminating against them as a class on account of their race. Thus, addressing itself to the intent of the Thirteenth, Fourteenth and Fifteenth Amendments, the Court said at pages 71 and 72:

"We repeat, then, in the light of this recapitulation of events, almost too recent to be called history, but which are familiar to us all; and on the most casual examination of the language of these amendments, no one can fail to be impressed with the one pervading purpose found in them all, lying at the foundation of each, and without which none of them would have been even suggested; we mean the freedom of the slave race, the security and firm establishment of that freedom, and the protection of the newly made freeman and citizen from the oppressions of those who had formerly exercised unlimited dominion over him. It is true that only the 15th Amendment, in terms, mentions the negro by speaking of his color and his slavery. But it is just as true that each of the other articles was addressed to the grievances of that race, and designed to remedy them as the fifteenth."

The real purpose of the equal protection clause was discussed in these terms at page 81:

"In the light of the history of these amendments, and the pervading purpose of them, which we have already discussed, it is not difficult to give a meaning to this clause. *The existence of laws in the states where the newly emancipated negroes resided, which discriminated with gross injustice and hardship against them as a class, was the evil to be remedied by this clause, and by it such laws are forbidden.*" (Emphasis supplied.)

So convinced was the Court that the overriding purpose of the Fourteenth Amendment was to protect the Negro against discrimination that it declared further at page 81:

"We doubt very much whether any action of a state not directed by way of discrimination against the negroes as a class, or on account of their race, will ever be held to come within the purview of this provision. It is so clearly a provision for that race and that emergency,

U.S. SUPREME COURT, OCTOBER 1953

BRIEF FOR THE APPELLANTS AND RESPONDENTS ON REARGUMENT

U.S. SUPREME
COURT,
OCTOBER 1953

BRIEF FOR THE
APPELLANTS AND
RESPONDENTS
ON REARGUMENT

that a strong case would be necessary for its application to any other."

In *Strauder v. West Virginia,* 100 U.S. 303, the Court, on page 306, viewed the Fourteenth Amendment in the same light and stated that its enactment was aimed to secure for the Negro all the civil rights enjoyed by white persons:

> "It was in view of these considerations the 14th Amendment was framed and adopted. *It was designed to assure to the colored race the enjoyment of all the civil rights that under the law are enjoyed by white persons,* and to give to that race the protection of the General Government, in that enjoyment, whenever it should be denied by the States. It not only gave citizenship and the privileges of citizenship to persons of color, but *it denied to any State the power to withhold from them the equal protection of the laws,* and authorized Congress to enforce its provisions by appropriate legislation." (Emphasis supplied).

Clearly recognizing the need to construe the Amendment liberally in order to protect the Negro, the Court noted at page 307:

> "If this is the spirit and meaning of the Amendment, whether it means more or not, it is to be construed liberally, to carry out the purposes of its framers. It ordains that no State shall make or enforce any laws which shall abridge the privileges or immunities of citizens of the United States (evidently referring to the newly made citizens, who, being citizens of the United States, are declared to be also citizens of the State in which they reside)."

It was explicitly stated at pages 307, 308 that the Amendment prevented laws from distinguishing between colored and white persons:

> "What is this but declaring *that the law in the States shall be the same for the black as for the white;* that all persons, whether colored or white, shall stand equal before the laws of the States and, in regard to the colored race, for whose protection the Amendment was primarily designed, that no discrimination shall be made against them by law because of their color? The words of the Amendment, it is true, are prohibitory, but they contain a necessary implication of a positive immunity, or right, most valuable to the colored race—the right to exemption from unfriendly legislation against them distinctly as colored; exemption from legal discriminations, implying inferiority in civil society, lessening the security of their enjoyment of the rights which others enjoy, and discriminations which are steps towards reducing them to the condition of a subject race." (Emphasis supplied).

Any distinction based upon race was understood as constituting a badge of inferiority, at page 308:

> "The very fact that colored people are singled out and expressly denied by a statute all right to participate in the administration of the law, as jurors, because of their color, though they are citizens and may be in other respects fully qualified, is practically a brand upon them, affixed by the law; an assertion of their inferiority, and a stimulant to that race prejudice which is an impediment to securing to individuals of the race that equal justice which the law aims to secure to all others."

There was no doubt that this new constitutional provision had changed the relationship between the federal government and the states so that the federal courts could and should now protect these new rights. At page 309 the Court said:

> "The framers of the constitutional Amendment must have known full well the existence of such prejudice and its likelihood to continue against the manumitted slaves and their race, and that knowledge was, doubtless, a motive that led to the Amendment. By their manumission and citizenship the colored race became entitled to the equal protection of the laws of the States in which they resided; and the apprehension that, through prejudice, they might be denied that equal protection, that is, that there might be discrimination against them, was the inducement to bestow upon the National Government the power to enforce the provision that no State shall deny to them the equal protection of the laws. Without the apprehended existence of prejudice that portion of the Amendment would have been unnecessary, and it might have been left to the States to extend equality of protection."

That law must not distinguish between colored and white persons was the thesis of all the early cases. *United States v. Cruikshank,* 92 U.S. 542, 554, 555; *Virginia v. Rives,* 100 U.S. 313; *Ex Parte Virginia,* 100 U.S. 339; *Neal v. Delaware,* 103 U.S. 370, 386; *Bush v. Kentucky,* 107 U.S. 110; *Civil Rights Cases,* 109 U.S. 3, 36, 43. As early as *Yick Wo v. Hopkins,* 118 U.S. 356, it became settled doctrine that the Fourteenth Amendment was a broad prohibition against state enforcement of racial differentiations or discrimination—a prohibition totally at war with any separate but equal notion. There can be no doubt, we submit, that, had the state regulation approved in *Plessy v. Ferguson* been before the Court that rendered the initial interpretations of the Fourteenth Amendment, the regulation would have been held a violation of the Federal Constitution.

B. The first time the question came before the Court, racial segregation in transportation was specifically disapproved

In *Railroad Co. v. Brown*, 17 Wall. 445, the first case involving the validity of segregation to reach this Court after the adoption of the Fourteenth Amendment, segregation was struck down as an unlawful discrimination. While the Fourteenth Amendment was not before the Court, the decision in the *Brown* case was in line with the spirit of the new status that the Negro had gained under the Thirteenth, Fourteenth and Fifteenth Amendments.

The problem before the Court concerned the validity of the carrier's rules and regulations that sought to segregate its passengers because of race. The pertinent facts are described by the Court as follows at page 451:

> "In the enforcement of this regulation, the defendant in error, a person of color, having entered a car appropriated to white ladies, was requested to leave it and take a seat in another car used for colored persons. This she refused to do, and this refusal resulted in her ejectment by force and with insult from the car she had first entered."

The Court characterized the railroad's defense that its practice of providing separate accommodations for Negroes was valid, as an ingenious attempt at evasion, at page 452:

> "The plaintiff in error contends that it has literally obeyed the direction, because it has never excluded this class of persons from the cars, but on the contrary, has always provided accommodations for them.

> "This is an ingenious attempt to evade a compliance with the obvious meaning of the requirement. It is true the words taken literally might bear the interpretation put upon them by the plaintiff in error, but evidently Congress did not use them in any such limited sense. There was no occasion, in legislating for a railroad corporation, to annex a condition to a grant of power, that the company should allow colored persons to ride in its cars. This right had never been refused, nor could there have been in the mind of anyone an apprehension that such a state of things would ever occur, for self-interest would clearly induce the carrier—South as well as North—to transport, if paid for it, all persons whether white or black, who should desire transportation."

The Court stressed with particularity the fact that the discrimination prohibited was discrimination in the use of the cars, at pages 452–453:

> "It was the discrimination in the use of the cars on account of color, where slavery obtained, which was the subject of discussion at the time, and not the fact that the colored race could not ride in the cars at all. Congress, in the belief that this discrimination was unjust, acted. It told this company, in substance, that it could extend its road in the District as desired, but that this discrimination must cease, and the colored and white race, in the use of the cars, be placed on an equality. This condition it had the right to impose, and in the temper of Congress at the time, it is manifest the grant could not have been made without it."

The regulation that was struck down in the *Brown* case sought to accomplish exactly what was achieved under a state statute upheld subsequently in *Plessy v. Ferguson*—the segregation of Negro and white passengers. It is clear, therefore, that in this earlier decision the Court considered segregation *per se* discrimination and a denial of equality.

C. The separate but equal doctrine marked an unwarranted departure from the main stream of constitutional development and permits the frustration of the very purposes of the Fourteenth Amendment as defined by this Court

In *Plessy v. Ferguson*, this Court for the first time gave approval to state imposed racial distinctions as consistent with the purposes and meaning of the Fourteenth Amendment. The Court described the aims and purposes of the Fourteenth Amendment in the same manner as had the earlier cases, at page 543:

> "… its main purpose was to establish the citizenship of the negro; to give definitions of citizenship of the United States and of the states, and to protect from the hostile legislation of the states the privileges and immunities of citizens of the United States, as distinguished from those of citizens of the states."

But these defined aims and purposes were now considered consistent with the imposition of legal distinctions based upon race. The Court said at 544, 551–552:

> "The object of the amendment was undoubtedly to enforce the absolute equality of the two races before the law, but in the nature of things it could not have been intended to

U.S. SUPREME COURT, OCTOBER 1953

BRIEF FOR THE APPELLANTS AND RESPONDENTS ON REARGUMENT

U.S. SUPREME
COURT,
OCTOBER 1953

BRIEF FOR THE
APPELLANTS AND
RESPONDENTS
ON REARGUMENT

abolish distinctions based upon color, or to enforce social, as distinguished from political, equality, or a commingling of the two races upon terms unsatisfactory to either.

* * *

Legislation is powerless to eradicate racial instincts or to abolish distinctions based upon physical differences, and the attempt to do so can only result in accentuating the difficulties of the present situation. If the civil and political rights of both races be equal, one cannot be inferior to the other civilly or politically. If one race be inferior to the other socially, the Constitution of the United States cannot put them upon the same plane."

And reasonableness of the regulation was found in established social usage, custom and tradition, at page 550:

"So far, then, as a conflict with the 14th Amendment is concerned, the case reduces itself to the question whether the statute of Louisiana is a reasonable regulation and with respect to this there must necessarily be a large discretion on the part of the legislature. In determining the question of reasonableness it is at liberty to act with reference to the established usages, customs, and traditions of the people, and with a view to the promotion of their comfort, and the preservation of the public peace and good order."

In *Plessy*, through distortion of the concept of "social" rights as distinguished from "civil" rights, the right to civil equality as one of the purposes of the Fourteenth Amendment was given a restricted meaning wholly at variance with that of the earlier cases and the intent of the framers as defined by this Court. Indeed, civil rights, as defined by that Court, seem merely to encompass those rights attendant upon use of the legal process and protection against complete exclusion pursuant to state mandate. Race for the first time since the adoption of the Fourteenth Amendment was sanctioned as a constitutionally valid basis for state action, and reasonableness for the racial distinctions approved was found in the social customs, usages and traditions of a people only thirty-one years removed from a slave society.

Under this rationale the Court sought to square its approval of racial segregation with the *Slaughter House Cases, Strauder v. West Virginia* and the other precedents. It is clear, however, that the early cases interpreted the Fourteenth Amendment as encompassing that same category of rights which were involved in *Plessy v. West*

Virginia—the right to be free of a racial differentiation imposed by the state in the exercise of any civil right. And the Court's attempt to distinguish *Railroad Co. v. Brown*, as a case of exclusion, was the very argument that has been specifically rejected in the *Brown* case as a sophisticated effort to avoid the obvious implications of the Congressional requirement. Thus, the separate but equal doctrine is a rejection of the precedents and constitutes a break in the development of constitutional law under which the Fourteenth Amendment has been interpreted as a fundamental interdiction against state imposed differentiations and discriminations based upon color.

D. The separate but equal doctrine was conceived in error

The separate but equal doctrine of *Plessy v. Ferguson*, we submit, has aided and supported efforts to nullify the Fourteenth Amendment's undoubted purpose—equal status for Negroes—as defined again and again by this Court. The fallacious and pernicious implications of the doctrine were evident to Justice Harlan and are set out in his dissenting opinion. It is clear today that the fact that racial segregation accords with custom and usage or is considered needful for the preservation of public peace and good order does not suffice to give constitutional validity to the state's action. What the doctrine has in fact accomplished is to deprive Negroes of the protection of the approved test of reasonable classifications which is available to everyone else who challenges legislative categories or distinctions of whatever kind.

1. The dissenting opinion of Justice Harlan in *Plessy v. Ferguson*. Justice Harlan recognized and set down for history the purpose of segregation and the implications of the separate but equal doctrine and evidenced prophetic insight concerning the inevitable consequences of the Court's approval of racial segregation. He said at page 557: "The thing to accomplish was, under the guise of giving equal accommodations for whites and blacks to compel the latter to keep to themselves while traveling in railroad passenger coaches."

He realized at page 560, moreover, that the approved regulations supported the inferior caste thesis of *Scott v. Sandford*, 19 How. 393, supposedly eradicated by the Civil War Amendments: "But it seems that we have yet, in some of the states, a dominant race, a superior class of citizens, which assumes to regulate the enjoyment of civil rights, common to all citizens, on the basis of race." And at page 562: "We boast of the freedom enjoyed by our people above all other people. But it is difficult to reconcile that boast with a state of the law which, practically, puts the brand of servitude and degradation upon a large class of our fellow citizens, our equals before the law."

While the majority opinion sought to rationalize its holding on the basis of the state's judgment that separation of races was conducive to public peace and order, Justice Harlan knew all too well that the seeds for continuing racial animosities had been planted. He said at pages 560–561:

> "The sure guaranty of peace and security of each race is the clear, distinct, unconditional recognition by our governments, national and state, of every right that inheres in civil freedom, and of equality before the law of all citizens of the United States without regard to race. State enactments, regulating the enjoyment of civil rights, upon the basis of race, and cunningly devised to defeat legitimate results of the war, under the pretense of recognizing equality of rights, can have no other result than to render permanent peace impossible and to keep alive a conflict of races, the continuance of which must do harm to all concerned."

"Our Constitution," said Justice Harlan at 559, "is color-blind, and neither knows nor tolerates classes among citizens." It is the dissenting opinion of Justice Harlan, rather than the majority opinion in *Plessy v. Ferguson*, that is in keeping with the scope and meaning of the Fourteenth Amendment as consistently defined by this Court both before and after *Plessy v. Ferguson*.

2. Custom, usage and tradition rooted in the slave tradition cannot be the constitutional yardstick for measuring state action under the Fourteenth Amendment. The analysis by Justice Harlan of the bases for the majority opinion in *Plessy v. Ferguson* was adopted by this Court in *Chiles v. Chesapeake & Ohio Railroad Company*, 218 U.S. 71, 77, 78. There this Court cited *Plessy v. Ferguson* as authority for sustaining the validity of legislative distinctions based upon race and color alone.

The importance of this case is its clear recognition and understanding that in *Plessy v. Ferguson* this Court approved the enforcement of racial distinctions as reasonable because they are in accordance with established social usage, custom and tradition. The Court said at pages 77, 78:

> "It is true the power of a legislature to recognize a racial distinction was the subject considered, but if the test of reasonableness in legislation be, as it was declared to be, 'the established usages, customs and traditions of the people,' and the 'promotion of their comfort and the preservation of the public peace and good order,' this must also be the test of reasonableness of the regulations of a carrier, made for like purposes and to secure like results."

But the very purpose of the Thirteenth, Fourteenth and Fifteenth Amendments was to effectuate a complete break with governmental action based on the established usages, customs and traditions of the slave era, to revolutionize the legal relationship between Negroes and whites, to destroy the inferior status of the Negro and to place him upon a plane of complete equality with the white man. As we will demonstrate, post Civil War reestablishment of ante-bellum custom and usage, climaxed by the decision in *Plessy v. Ferguson*, reflected a constant effort to return the Negro to his pre-Thirteenth, Fourteenth Amendment inferior status. When the Court employed the old usages, customs and traditions as the basis for determining the reasonableness of segregation statutes designed to resubjugate the Negro to an inferior status, it nullified the acknowledged intention of the framers of the Amendment, and made a travesty of the equal protection clause of the Fourteenth Amendment.

Here, again, the *Plessy v. Ferguson* decision is out of line with the modern holdings of this Court, for in a variety of cases involving the rights of Negroes it has constantly refused to regard custom and usage, however widespread, as determinative of reasonableness. This was true in *Smith v. Allwright*, of a deeply entrenched custom and usage of excluding Negroes from voting in the primaries. It was true in *Shelley v. Kraemer*, of a long standing custom excluding Negroes from the use and ownership of real property on the basis of race. In *Henderson v. United States*, a discriminatory practice of many years was held to violate the Interstate Commerce Act. In the *Sweatt* and *McLaurin* decisions, the Court broke a southern tradition of state-enforced racial distinctions in graduate and professional education—a custom almost as old as graduate and professional education, itself.

U.S. SUPREME COURT, OCTOBER 1953

BRIEF FOR THE APPELLANTS AND RESPONDENTS ON REARGUMENT

U.S. SUPREME
COURT,
OCTOBER 1953

BRIEF FOR THE
APPELLANTS AND
RESPONDENTS
ON REARGUMENT

In each instance the custom and usage had persisted for generations and its durability was cited as grounds for its validity. If this were the only test, ours indeed would become a stagnant society. Even if there be some situations in which custom, usage and tradition may be considered in testing the reasonableness of governmental action, customs, traditions and usages rooted in slavery cannot be worthy of the constitutional sanction of this Court.

3. Preservation of public peace cannot justify deprivation of constitutional rights. The fallacy underlying *Plessy v. Ferguson* of justifying racially-discriminatory statutes as essential to the public peace and good order has been completely exposed by Frederick W. Lehmann, a former Solicitor General of the United States, and Wells H. Blodgett in their Brief as *amici curiae* in *Buchanan v. Warley,* 245 U.S. 60. Their statements warrant repetition here:

> "The implication of the title of the ordinance is, that unless the white and colored people live in separate blocks, ill feeling will be engendered between them and conflicts will result and so it is assumed that a segregation of the races is necessary for the preservation of the public peace and the promotion of the general welfare. There is evidence in the record that prior to the enactment of the ordinance there were instances of colored people moving into white blocks and efforts by the white people to drive them out by violence. So to preserve the peace, the ordinance was enacted not to repress the lawless violence, but to give the sanction of the law to the motives which inspired it and to make the purpose of it lawful.

> "The population of Louisville numbers two hundred and fifty thousand, of whom about one-fifth are colored. The ordinance, almost upon its face, and clearly by the evidence submitted and the arguments offered in support of it is a discriminating enactment by the dominant majority against a minority who are held to be an inferior people. It cannot be justified by the recitals of the title, even if they are true. Many things may rouse a man's prejudice or stir him to anger, but he is not always to be humored in his wrath. The question may arise, 'Dost thou well to be angry?'" (*Brief Amici Curiae,* pp. 2 and 3).

Accepting this view, the Court in *Buchanan v. Warley* rejected the argument that a state could deny constitutional rights with impunity in its efforts to maintain the public peace:

> "It is urged that this proposed segregation will promote the public peace by preventing race conflicts. Desirable as this is, and important as is the preservation of the public peace, this aim cannot be accomplished by laws or ordinances which deny rights created or protected by the Federal Constitution" (245 U.S. 60, 81).

Accord, *Morgan v. Virginia, supra; Monk v. City of Birmingham,* 185 F. 2d 859 (CA 5th 1950), *cert. denied,* 341 U.S. 940.

Thus, the bases upon which the separate but equal doctrine was approved in the *Plessy v. Ferguson* case have all been uprooted by subsequent decisions of this Court. All that remains is the naked doctrine itself, unsupported by reason, contrary to the intent of the framers, and out of tune with present notions of constitutional rights. Repudiation of the doctrine itself, we submit, is long overdue.

4. The separate but equal doctrine deprives Negroes of that protection which the Fourteenth Amendment accords under the general classification test. One of the ironies of the separate but equal doctrine of *Plessy v. Ferguson* is that under it, the Fourteenth Amendment, the primary purpose of which was the protection of Negroes, is construed as encompassing a narrower area of protection for Negroes than for other persons under the general classification test.

Early in its history, the Fourteenth Amendment was construed as reaching not only state action based upon race and color, but also as prohibiting all unreasonable classifications and distinctions even though not racial in character. *Barbier v. Connolly,* 113 U.S. 27, seems to be the earliest case to adopt this concept of the Amendment. There the Court said on page 31:

> "The Fourteenth Amendment ... undoubtedly intended, not only that there should be no arbitrary deprivation of life or liberty or arbitrary spoliation of property but that equal protection and security should be given to all under like circumstances in the enjoyment of their personal and civil rights."

Accord: *Minneapolis & St. Louis Ry. Co. v. Beckwith,* 129 U.S. 26, 28, 29; *Bell's Gap R. R. Co. v. Pennsylvania,* 134 U.S. 232, 237; *McPherson v. Blacker,* 146 U.S. 1, 39; *Yesler v. Board of Harbor Line Commissioners,* 146 U.S. 646, 655; *Giozza v. Tiernan,* 148 U.S. 657, 662; *Marchant v. Pennsylvania R. Co.,* 153 U.S. 380, 390; *Moore v. Missouri,* 159 U.S. 673, 678.

In effectuating the protection afforded by this secondary purpose, the Court has required the classification or distinction used be based upon some real or substantial difference pertinent to a valid legislative objective. *E.g., Quaker City Cab Co. v. Pennsylvania,* 277 U.S. 389; *Truax v. Raich,* 239 U.S. 33; *Smith v. Cahoon,* 283 U.S. 553; *Mayflower Farms v. Ten Eyck,* 297 U.S. 266; *Skinner v. Oklahoma,* 316 U.S. 535. See also *Cities Service Gas Co. v. Peerless Oil & Gas Co.,* 340 U.S. 179, 186.

Justice Holmes in *Nixon v. Herndon,* 273 U.S. 536, 541, recognized and restated a long established and well settled judicial proposition when he described the Fourteenth Amendment's prohibition against unreasonable legislative classification as less rigidly proscriptive of state action than the Amendment's prohibition of color differentiation. There he concluded:

> "States may do a good deal of classifying that it is difficult to believe rational, but there are limits, and it is too clear for extended argument that color cannot be made the basis of a statutory classification affecting the right set up in this case."

But the separate but equal doctrine substitutes race for reasonableness as the constitutional test of classification. We submit, it would be a distortion of the purposes and intendment of the Fourteenth Amendment to deny to those persons for whose benefit that provision was primarily intended the same measure of protection afforded by a rule of construction evolved to reach the Amendment's subsidiary and secondary objectives. We urge this Court to examine the segregation statutes in these cases to determine whether the statutes seek to serve a permissible legislative objective; and, if any permissible objective is found, whether color differentiation has pertinence to it. So examined, the constitutional provisions and statutes involved here disclose unmistakably their constitutional infirmity.

E. The separate but equal doctrine has not received unqualified approval in this Court

Even while the separate but equal doctrine was evolving, this Court imposed limitations upon its applications. In *Buchanan v. Warley,* the Court, after reviewing the limited acceptance which the doctrine had received, concluded that its extension to approve state enforced segregation in housing was not permissible.

Ten years later in *Gong Lum v. Rice,* 275 U.S. 78, 85, 86, without any intervening development in the doctrine in this Court, sweeping language was used which gave the erroneous impression that this Court already had extended the application of the doctrine to the field of education. And in *Missouri ex rel. Gaines v. Canada,* 305 U.S. 337, the doctrine is mentioned in passing as if its application to public education were well established. But, what Justice Day was careful to point out in *Buchanan v. Warley,* was true then and is true now—the separate but equal doctrine has never been extended by this Court beyond the field of transportation in any case where such extension was contested.

While the doctrine itself has not been specifically repudiated as a valid constitutional yardstick in the field of public education, in cases in which this Court has had to determine whether the state had performed its constitutional obligation to provide equal education opportunities— the question presented here—the separate but equal doctrine has never been used by this Court to sustain the validity of the state's separate school laws. *Missouri ex rel. Gaines v. Canada; Sipuel v. Board of Regents,* 332 U.S. 631; *Sweatt v. Painter; McLaurin v. Oklahoma State Regents.*

Earlier educational cases, not concerned with equality, did not apply the doctrine. In *Cumming v. County Board of Education,* 175 U.S. 528, the question was explicitly beyond the scope of the decision rendered. In *Berea College v. Kentucky,* 211 U.S. 45, the question was reserved. In *Gong Lum v. Rice,* the separate but equal doctrine was not put in issue. Instead of challenging the validity of the Mississippi school segregation laws, the Chinese child merely objected to being classified as a Negro for public school purposes.

Even in the field of transportation, subsequent decisions have sapped the doctrine of vitality. *Henderson v. United States,* in effect overruled *Chiles v. Chesapeake & Ohio Railway Co.,* 218 U.S. 71. See *Chance v. Lambeth,* 186 F. 2d 879 (CA 4th 1951), *cert. denied,* 341 U.S. 91. *Morgan v. Virginia,* places persons traveling in interstate commerce beyond the thrust of state segregation statutes. Thus, the reach of the separate but equal doctrine approved in the *Plessy* case has now been so severely restricted and narrowed in scope that, it may be appropriately said of *Plessy v. Ferguson* as it was said of *Crowell v. Benson,* 285 U.S. 22, "one had supposed that the doctrine had earned a deserved repose." *Estep v. United States,* 327 U.S. 114, 142 (concurring opinion).

U.S. SUPREME COURT, OCTOBER 1953

BRIEF FOR THE APPELLANTS AND RESPONDENTS ON REARGUMENT

U.S. SUPREME
COURT,
OCTOBER 1953

BRIEF FOR THE
APPELLANTS AND
RESPONDENTS
ON REARGUMENT

F. The necessary consequence of the Sweatt and McLaurin decisions is repudiation of the separate but equal doctrine

While *Sweatt v. Painter* and *McLaurin v. Oklahoma State Regents* were not in terms rejections of the separate but equal doctrine, their application in effect destroyed the practice of segregation with respect to state graduate and professional schools. *Wilson v. Board of Supervisors,* 92 F. Supp. 986 (E. D. La. 1950), *aff'd,* 340 U.S. 909; *Gray v. Board of Trustees of University of Tennessee,* 342 U.S. 517; *McKissick v. Carmichael,* 187 F. 2d 949 (CA 4th 1951), *cert. denied,* 341 U.S. 951; *Swanson v. University of Virginia,* Civil Action #30 (W. D. Va. 1950) unreported; *Payne v. Board of Supervisors,* Civil Action #894 (E. D. La. 1952) unreported; *Foister v. Board of Supervisors,* Civil Action #937 (E. D. La. 1952) unreported; *Mitchell v. Board of Regents of University of Maryland,* Docket #16, Folio 126 (Baltimore City Court 1950) unreported.[1]

In the *Sweatt* case, the Court stated that, with members of the state's dominant racial groups excluded from the segregated law school which the state sought to require Sweatt to attend, "we cannot conclude that the education offered petitioner is substantially equal to that he would receive if admitted to the University of Texas." If this consideration is one of the controlling factors in determining substantial equality at the law school level, it is impossible for any segregated law school to be an equal law school. And pursuant to that decision one of the oldest and best state-supported segregated law schools in the country was found unequal and Negro applicants were ordered admitted to the University of North Carolina. *McKissick v. Carmichael.* Thus, substantial equality in professional education is "substantially equal" only if there is no racial segregation.

In the *McLaurin* case, the racial distinctions imposed in an effort to comply with the state's segregation laws were held to impair and inhibit ability to study, to exchange views with other students and, in general, to learn one's profession. The state, therefore, was required to remove all restrictions and to treat McLaurin the same way as other students are treated. Consequently these decisions are a repudiation of the separate but equal doctrine.

III. VIEWED IN THE LIGHT OF HISTORY THE SEPARATE BUT EQUAL DOCTRINE HAS BEEN AN INSTRUMENTALITY OF

DEFIANT NULLIFICATION OF THE FOURTEENTH AMENDMENT

The history of segregation laws reveals that their main purpose was to organize the community upon the basis of a superior white and an inferior Negro caste. These laws were conceived in a belief in the inherent inferiority of Negroes, a concept taken from slavery. Inevitably, segregation in its operation and effect has meant inequality consistent only with the belief that the people segregated are inferior and not worthy, or capable, of enjoying the facilities set apart for the dominant group.

Segregation originated as a part of an effort to build a social order in which the Negro would be placed in a status as close as possible to that he had held before the Civil War. The separate but equal doctrine furnished a base from which those who sought to nullify the Thirteenth, Fourteenth and Fifteenth Amendments were permitted to operate in relative security. While this must have been apparent at the end of the last century, the doctrine has become beclouded with so much fiction that it becomes important to consider the matter in historical context to restore a proper view of its meaning and import.

A. The status of the Negro, slave and free, prior to the Civil War

One of the basic assumptions of the slave system was the Negro's inherent inferiority.[2] As the invention of the cotton gin rendered slavery essential to the maintenance of the plantation economy in the South, a body of pseudo-scientific thought developed in passionate defense of slavery, premised on the Negro's

---

[1] Negroes are now attending state graduate and professional schools in West Virginia, Maryland, Arkansas, Delaware, Oklahoma, Kentucky, Texas, Missouri, North Carolina, Virginia, and Louisiana. See (Editorial Comment), THE COURTS AND RACIAL INTEGRATION IN EDUCATION, 21 J. NEG. EDUC. 3 (1952).

Negroes are also now attending private universities and colleges in Missouri, Georgia, Kentucky, Louisiana, Texas, Maryland, West Virginia, North Carolina, District of Columbia, and Virginia. See THE COURTS AND RACIAL INTEGRATION IN EDUCATION, 21 J. NEG. EDUC. 3 (1952): SOME PROGRESS IN ELIMINATION OF DISCRIMINATION IN HIGHER EDUCATION IN THE UNITED STATES, 19 J. NEG. EDUC. 4–5 (1950); LEE AND KRAMER, RACIAL INCLUSION IN CHURCH-RELATED COLLEGES IN THE SOUTH, 22 J. NEG. EDUC. 22 (1953); A NEW TREND IN PRIVATE COLLEGES, 6 NEW SOUTH 1 (1951).

[2] For an illuminating discussion of these assumptions, see JOHNSON, THE IDEOLOGY OF WHITE SUPREMACY, 1876–1910, IN ESSAYS IN SOUTHERN HISTORY PRESENTED TO JOSEPH GREGOIRE DEROULHAC HAMILTON, GREEN ED., 124–156 (1949).

unfitness for freedom and equality.[3] Thus, the Negro's inferiority with respect to brain capacity, lung activity and countless other physiological attributes was purportedly established by some of the South's most respected scientists.[4] In all relationships between the two races the Negro's place was that of an inferior, for it was claimed that any other relationship status would automatically degrade the white man.[5]

This concept of the Negro as an inferior fit only for slavery was complicated by the presence of several hundred thousand Negroes, who although not slaves, could not be described as free men.[6] In order that they would not constitute a threat to the slave regime, free Negroes were denied the full rights and privileges of citizens. They enjoyed no equality in the courts, their right to assemble was denied, their movements were proscribed, and education was withheld.[7] Their plight, in consequence of these proscriptions, invited the unfavorable comparison of them with slaves and confirmed the views of many that Negroes could not profit by freedom. They were regarded by the white society as the "very drones and pests of society," pariahs of the land, and an incubus on the body politic.[8] Even this Court, in *Scott v. Sandford*, recognized this substantial body of opinion to the effect that free Negroes had no rights that a white man was bound to respect.

The few privileges that free Negroes enjoyed were being constantly whittled away in the early nineteenth century. By 1836, free Negroes were denied the ballot in every southern state and in many states outside the South.[9] In some states, they were denied residence on penalty of enslavement; and in some, they were banned from the mechanical trades because of the economic pressure upon the white artisans.[10] Before the outbreak of the Civil War, the movement to reenslave free Negroes was under way in several states in the South.[11]

This ante-bellum view of the inferiority of the Negro persisted after the Civil War among those who already regarded the newly freed slaves as simply augmenting the group of free Negroes who had been regarded as "the most ignorant … vicious, impoverished, and degraded population of this country."[12]

B. The post war struggle

The slave system had supported and sustained a plantation economy under which 1,000 families received approximately $50,000,000 a year with the remaining 600,000 families receiving about $60,000,000 per annum. The perfection of that economy meant the ruthless destruction of the small independent white farmer who was either bought out or driven back to the poorer lands—the slaveholders controlled the destiny of both the slave and the poor whites.[13] Slaves were not only farmers and unskilled laborers but were trained by their masters as skilled artisans. Thus, slave labor was in formidable competition with white labor at every level, and the latter was the

U.S. SUPREME
COURT,
OCTOBER 1953

BRIEF FOR THE
APPELLANTS AND
RESPONDENTS
ON REARGUMENT

[3] Jenkins, Pro-Slavery Thought in the Old South 243 (1935); Johnson, The Negro in American Civilization 5–15 (1930).

[4] See Van Evrie, Negroes and Negro Slavery 120 ff, 122 ff, 214 ff (1861); Cartwright, Diseases and Peculiarities of the Negro Race, 2 DeBow, The Industrial Resources, etc., of the Southern and Western States 315–329 (1852); Nott, Two Lectures On the Natural History of the Caucasian and Negro Races (1866); Van Evrie, Negroes and Negro "Slavery"; The First An Inferior Race— The Latter Its Normal Condition (1853); Van Evrie, Subgenation: The Theory of the Normal Relation of the Races (1864); Cartwright, Diseases and Peculiarities of the Negro Races, 9 DeBow's Review 64–69 (1851); Cartwright, Essays, Being Inductions Drawn From the Baconian Philosophy Proving the Truth of the Bible and the Justice and Benevolence of the Decree Dooming Canaan to Be A Servant of Servants (1843).

[5] Jenkins, Pro-Slavery Thought In the Old South 242 ff (1935); The Pro-Slavery Argument, especially Harper's Memoir on Slavery, pp. 26–98; and Simms, The Morals of Slavery, pp. 175–275 (1835); Johnson, The Ideology of White Supremacy, *op. cit. supra*, n. 2 at 135.

[6] See Franklin, From Slavery to Freedom: A History of American Negroes 213–238 (1947).

[7] Franklin, The Free Negro in North Carolina, 1790–1860 59–120 (1943).

[8] Dew, Review of the Debates In the Virginia Legislature of 1831–1832, The Pro-Slavery Argument, 422 ff (1853); Jenkins, *op. cit. supra*, n. 5, 246.

[9] Weeks, History of Negro Suffrage in the South, 9 Pol. Sci. Q. 671–703 (1894); Porter, A History of Suffrage in the United States 87 ff (1918); Shugg, Negro Voting in the Ante-Bellum South, 21 J. Neg. Hist. 357–364 (1936).

[10] Va. House J. 84 (1831–1832); Va. Laws 1831. p. 107; Channing, History of the United States 136–137 (1921); Greene and Woodson, The Negro Wage Earner 15 ff (1930).

[11] Franklin, The Enslavement of Free-Negroes in North Carolina, 29 J. Neg. Hist. 401–428 (1944).

[12] See Jenkins, *op. cit. supra*, n. 5, 246.

[13] Weston, The Progress of Slavery (1859); Helper, The Impending Crisis of the South (1863); Johnson, The Negro in American Civilization, *op. cit. supra*, n. 2; Phillips, American Negro Slavery, Documentary History of American Industrial Society-Plantation and Frontier Documents (1910–11).

U.S. SUPREME
COURT,
OCTOBER 1953

BRIEF FOR THE
APPELLANTS AND
RESPONDENTS
ON REARGUMENT

more expendable for it did not represent property and investment. Only a few white supervisory persons were needed to insure the successful operation of the plantation system.

After the Civil War, the independent white farmer entered into cotton cultivation and took over the lands of the now impracticable large plantations. Within a few years the independent farmer was engaged in 40% of the cotton cultivation, and by 1910 this percentage had risen to 67%.[14] To the poor white Southerner the new Negro, as a skilled farmer and artisan in a free competitive economy, loomed as an even greater economic menace than he had been under the slave system. They became firm advocates of the Negro's subjugation to insure their own economic well being.[15]

The plantation aristocracy sought to regain their economic and political pre-eminence by rebuilding the prewar social structure on the philosophy of the Negro's inferiority. This group found that they could build a new economic structure based upon a depressed labor market of poor whites and Negroes. Thus, to the aristocracy, too, the Negro's subjugation was an economic advantage.

The mutual concern of these two groups of white Southerners for the subjugation of the Negro gave them a common basis for unity in irreconcilable resistance to the revolutionary change in the Negro's status which the Civil War Amendments were designed to effect. Their attitude towards the Fourteenth Amendment is best described by a Mississippi editor who said that the southern states were not prepared "to

become parties to their own degradation."[16] There were white southerners, however, as there always had been, who sought to build a society which would respect and dignify the rights of the Freedmen. But this group was in the minority and southern sentiment in bitter opposition to Negro equality prevailed. Accordingly, as a temporary expedient, even as an army of occupation has been necessary recently in Germany and Japan to prevent lawlessness by irreconcilables and the recrudescense of totalitarianism, so Union forces were needed during Reconstruction to maintain order and to make possible the development of a more democratic way of life in the states recently in rebellion.

The Thirteenth, Fourteenth and Fifteenth Amendments and the Reconstruction effort, implemented by those in the South who were coming to accept the new concept of the Negro as a free man on full terms of equality, could have led to a society free of racism. The possibility of the extensive establishment and expansion of mixed schools was real at this stage. It was discussed in every southern state, and in most states serious consideration was given to the proposal to establish them.[17]

C. The Compromise of 1877 and the abandonment of Reconstruction

The return to power of the southern irreconcilables was finally made possible by rapprochement between northern and southern economic interests culminating in the compromise of 1877. In the North, control of the Republican Party passed to those who believed that the protection and expansion of their eco-

---

[14] VANCE, HUMAN FACTORS IN COTTON CULTIVATION (1926); SIMKINS, THE TILLMAN MOVEMENT IN SOUTH CAROLINA (1926).
[15] For discussion of this whole development see JOHNSON, THE NEGRO IN AMERICAN CIVILIZATION (1930).
[16] COULTER, THE SOUTH DURING RECONSTRUCTION 434 (1947).
[17] KNIGHT, PUBLIC EDUCATION IN THE SOUTH 320 (1922). See also Part II *infra*, at pages 142–157.
There were interracial colleges, academies, and tributary grammar schools in the South established and maintained largely by philanthropic societies and individuals from the North. Although they were predominantly Negro institutions, in the Reconstruction period and later, institutions such as Fisk University in Nashville, Tennessee, and Talladega College in Alabama usually had some white students. In the last quarter of the nineteenth century most of the teachers in these institutions were white. For accounts of co-racial education at Joppa Institute and Nat School in Alabama, Piedmont College in Georgia, Saluda Institute in North Carolina and in other southern schools, see BROWNLEE, NEW DAY ASCENDING 98–110 (1946).

The effect of these institutions in keeping alive the possibility of Negroes and whites living and learning together on the basis of complete equality was pointed out by one of the South's most distinguished men of letters, George W. Cable. "In these institutions," he said:

"… there is a complete ignoring of those race distinctions so religiously enforced on every side beyond their borders; and yet none of those unnamable disasters have come to or from them which the advocates of these onerous public distinctions and separations predict and dread. On scores of Southern hilltops these schools stand out almost totally without companions or competitors in their peculiar field, so many refutations, visible and complete, of the idea that any interest requires the colored American citizen to be limited in any of the civil rights that would be his without question if the same man were white." Cable, The Negro Question 19 (1890).

nomic power could best be served by political conciliation of the southern irreconcilables, rather than by unswerving insistence upon human equality and the rights guaranteed by the post war Amendments. In the 1870's those forces that held fast to the notion of the Negro's preordained inferiority returned to power in state after state, and it is significant that one of the first measures adopted was to require segregated schools on a permanent basis in disregard of the Fourteenth Amendment.[18]

In 1877, out of the exigencies of a close and contested election, came a bargain between the Republican Party and the southern leaders of the Democratic Party which assured President Hayes' election, led to the withdrawal of federal troops from the non-redeemed states and left the South free to solve the Negro problem without apparent fear of federal intervention. This agreement preserved the pragmatic and material ends of Reconstruction at the expense of the enforcement of not only the Fourteenth Amendment but the Fifteenth Amendment as well.[19] For it brought in its wake peonage and disfranchisement as well as segregation and other denials of equal protection. Although there is grave danger in oversimplification of the complexities of history, on reflection it seems clear that more profoundly than constitutional amendments and wordy statutes, the Compromise of 1877 shaped the future of four million freedmen and their

progeny for generations to come. For the road to freedom and equality, which had seemed sure and open in 1868, was now to be securely blocked and barred by a maze of restrictions and limitations proclaimed as essential to a way of life.

D. Consequences of the 1877 Compromise

Once the South was left to its own devices, the militant irreconcilables quickly seized or consolidated power. Laws and practices de-signed to achieve rigid segregation and the disfranchisement of the Negro came on in increasing numbers and harshness.

The policy of the southern states was to destroy the political power of the Negro so that he could never seriously challenge the order that was being established. By the poll tax, the Grandfather Clause, the white primary, gerrymandering, the complicated election procedures, and by unabated intimidation and threats of violence, the Negro was stripped of effective political participation.[20]

The final blow to the political respectability of the Negro came with disfranchisement in the final decade of the Nineteenth Century and the early years of the present century when the discriminatory provisions were written into the state constitutions.[21] That problem the Court dealt with during the next forty years from *Guinn v. United States,* 238 U.S. 347 to *Terry v. Adams,* 345 U.S. 461.

U.S. SUPREME COURT, OCTOBER 1953

BRIEF FOR THE APPELLANTS AND RESPONDENTS ON REARGUMENT

---

[18] Georgia, where the reconstruction government was especially short-lived, passed a law in 1870 making it mandatory for district school officials to "make all necessary arrangements for the instruction of the white and colored youth … in separate schools. They shall provide the same facilities for each … but the children of the white and colored races shall not be taught together in any sub-district of the state." Ga. Laws 1870, p. 56. As soon as they were redeemed, the other southern states enacted similar legislation providing for segregated schools and gradually the states incorporated the provision into their constitutions. See, for example, Ark. Laws 1873, p. 423; THE JOURNAL OF THE TEXAS CONSTITUTIONAL CONVENTION 1875, pp. 608–616; Miss. Laws 1878, p. 103; STEPHENSON, RACE DISTINCTIONS IN AMERICAN LAW 170–176 (1908). When South Carolina and Louisiana conservatives secured control of their governments in 1877, they immediately repealed the laws providing for mixed schools and established separate institutions for white and colored youth.

[19] The explanation for this reversal of national policy in 1877 and the abandonment of an experiment that had enlisted national support and deeply aroused the emotions and hopes has been sought in many quarters. The most commonly accepted and often repeated story is that authorized spokesmen of Hayes met representatives of the Southern

Democrats at the Wormley House in Washington in late February, 1877, and promised the withdrawal of troops and abandonment of the Negro in return for the support of southern Congressmen for Hayes against the Democratic candidate Samuel J. Tilden in the contested Presidential election. Recent investigation has demonstrated that the so-called "Wormley House Bargain", though offered by southern participants as the explanation, is not the full relevation of the complex and elaborate maneuvering which finally led to the agreement. See WOODWARD, REUNION AND REACTION: THE COMPROMISE OF 1877 AND THE END OF RECONSTRUCTION (1951) for an elaborate and detailed explanation of the compromise agreement.

[20] In 1890, Judge J. Chrisman of Mississippi could say that there had not been a full vote and a fair count in his state since 1875, that they had preserved the ascendancy of the whites by revolutionary methods. In plain words, he continued, "We have been stuffing the ballot boxes, committing perjury and here and there in the State carrying the elections by fraud and violence until the whole machinery for election was about to rot down." Quoted in WOODWARD, ORIGINS OF THE NEW SOUTH 58 (1951).

[21] KEY, SOUTHERN POLITICS IN STATE AND NATION 539–550 (1949); WOODWARD, ORIGINS OF THE NEW SOUTH 205, 263 (1951).

U.S. SUPREME
COURT,
OCTOBER 1953

BRIEF FOR THE
APPELLANTS AND
RESPONDENTS
ON REARGUMENT

A movement to repeal the Fourteenth and Fifteenth Amendments shows the extremity to which the irreconcilables were willing to go to make certain that the Negro remained in an inferior position. At the Mississippi Constitutional Convention of 1890, a special committee studied the matter and concluded that "the white people only are capable of conducting and maintaining the government" and that the Negro race, "even if its people were educated, being wholly unequal to such responsibility," should be excluded from the franchise. It, therefore, resolved that the "true and only efficient remedy for the great and important difficulties" that would ensue from Negro participation lay in the "repeal of the Fifteenth Amendment ... whereby such restrictions and limitations may be put upon Negro suffrage as may be necessary and proper for the maintenance of good and stable government ... "[22]

A delegate to the Virginia Constitutional Convention of 1901–1902 submitted a resolution calling for a repeal of the Fifteenth Amend-ment because it is wrong, "in that it proceeds on the theory that the two races are equally competent of free government."[23] Senator Edward Carmack of Tennessee gave notice in 1903 that he would bring in a bill to repeal the Amendments.[24] The movement, though unsuccessful, clearly illustrates the temper of the white South.

Having consigned the Negro to a permanently inferior caste status, racist spokesmen, with unabashed boldness, set forth views regarding the Negro's unassimilability and uneducability even more pernicious than those held by the old South. Ben Tillman, the leader of South Carolina, declared that a Negro should not have the same treatment as a white man, "for the simple reason that God Almighty made him colored and did not make him white." He lamented the end of slavery which reversed the process of improving the Negro and "inoculated him with the virus of equality."[25] These views were expressed many times in the disfranchising conventions toward the end of the century.[26] Nor were the politicians alone in uttering such views about the Negro. Drawing on the theory of evolution as expressed by Darwin and the theory of progress developed by Spencer, persons of scholarly pretension speeded the work of justifying an inferior status for the Negro.[27] Alfred H. Stone, having the reputation of a widely respected scholar in Mississippi, declared that the "Negro was an inferior type of man with predominantly African customs and character traits whom no amount of education or improvement of environmental conditions could ever elevate to as high a scale in the human species as the white man." As late as 1910, E. H. Randle in his *Characteristics of the Southern Negro* declared that "the first important thing to remember in judging the Negro was that his mental capacity was inferior to that of the white man."[28]

[22] JOURNAL OF THE MISSISSIPPI CONSTITUTIONAL CONVENTION, 1890, 303–304. Tillman, Vardaman, and other Southern leaders frequently called for the repeal of the Amendments. Tillman believed "that such a formal declaration of surrender in the struggle to give the Negro political and civil equality would confirm the black man in his inferior position and pave the way for greater harmony between the races." SIMKINS, PITCHFORK BEN TILLMAN 395 (1944). Vardaman called for repeal as a recognition that the Negro "was physically, mentally, morally, racially, and eternally inferior to the white man." See KIRWAN, REVOLT OF THE REDNECKS (1951).

[23] JOURNAL OF THE VIRGINIA CONSTITUTIONAL CONVENTION, 1901–1902, pp. 47–48.

[24] JOHNSON, THE IDEOLOGY OF WHITE SUPREMACY, *op. cit. supra*, n. 2, 136 ff.

[25] SIMKINS, PITCHFORK BEN TILLMAN 395, 399 (1944). Tillman's Mississippi counterpart, J. K. Vardaman, was equally vigorous in denouncing the Negro. He described the Negro as an "industrial stumbling block, a political ulcer, a social scab, 'a lazy, lying, lustful animal which no conceivable amount of training can transform into a tolerable citizen.'" Quoted in KIRWAN, *op. cit. supra*, n. 22, at 146.

[26] See, for example, Alabama Constitutional Convention, 1901, Official Proceedings, Vol. I, p. 12, Vol. II, pp.

2710–2711, 2713, 2719, 2782, 2785–2786, 2793; Journal of the South Carolina Convention, 1895, pp. 443–472; Journal of the Mississippi Constitutional Convention, 1890, pp. 10, 303, 701–702; Journal of the Louisiana Constitutional Convention, 1898, pp. 9–10.

[27] See ROWLAND, A MISSISSIPPI VIEW OF RELATIONS IN THE SOUTH, A PAPER (1903); HERBERT, et al., WHY THE SOLID SOUTH? OR RECONSTRUCTION AND ITS RESULTS (1890); BRUCE, THE PLANTATION NEGRO AS A FREEMAN: OBSERVATIONS ON HIS CHARACTER, CONDITION AND PROSPECTS IN VIRGINIA (1889); STONE, STUDIES IN THE AMERICAN RACE PROBLEM (1908); CARROLL, THE NEGRO A BEAST (1908); CARROLL, THE TEMPTER OF EVE, OR THE CRIMINALITY OF MAN'S SOCIAL, POLITICAL, AND RELIGIOUS EQUALITY WITH THE NEGRO, AND THE AMALGAMATION TO WHICH THESE CRIMES INEVITABLY LEAD 286 ff (1902); PAGE, THE NEGRO: THE SOUTHERNER'S PROBLEM 126 ff (1904); RANDLE, CHARACTERISTICS OF THE SOUTHERN NEGRO 51 ff (1910).

[28] Quoted in JOHNSON, IDEOLOGY OF WHITE SUPREMACY, *op. cit., supra*, n. 2, p. 151. That the South was not alone in these views is clearly shown by Logan's study of the Northern press between 1877 and 1901. See LOGAN, THE NEGRO IN AMERICAN LIFE AND THOUGHT: THE NADIR 1877–1901, cc. 9–10 (unpub. ms., to be pub. early in 1954 by the Dial Press).

Such was the real philosophy behind the late 19th Century segregation laws—an essential part of the whole racist complex. Controlling economic and political interests in the South were convinced that the Negro's subjugation was essential to their survival, and the Court in *Plessy v. Ferguson* had ruled that such subjugation through public authority was sanctioned by the Constitution. This is the overriding vice of *Plessy v. Ferguson.* For without the sanction of *Plessy v. Ferguson,* archaic and provincial notions of racial superiority could not have injured and disfigured an entire region for so long a time. The full force and effect of the protection afforded by the Fourteenth Amendment was effectively blunted by the vigorous efforts of the proponents of the concept that the Negro was inferior. This nullification was effectuated in all aspects of Negro life in the South, particularly in the field of education, by the exercise of state power.

As the invention of the cotton gin stilled the voices of Southern Abolitionists, *Plessy v. Ferguson* chilled the development in the South of opinion conducive to the acceptance of Negroes on the basis of equality because those of the white South desiring to afford Negroes the equalitarian status which the Civil War Amendments had hoped to achieve were barred by state law from acting in accordance with their beliefs. In this connection, it is significant that the Populist movement flourished for a short period during the 1890's and threatened to take over political control of the South through a coalition of the poor Negro and poor white farmers.[29] This movement was completely smashed and since *Plessy v. Ferguson* no similar phenomenon has taken hold.

Without the "constitutional" sanction which *Plessy v. Ferguson* affords, racial segregation could not have become entrenched in the South, and individuals and local communities would have been free to maintain public school systems in conformity with the underlying purposes of the Fourteenth Amendment by providing education without racial distinctions. The doctrine of *Plessy v. Ferguson* was essential to the successful maintenance of a racial caste system in the United States. Efforts toward the elimination of race discrimination are jeopardized as long as the separate but equal doctrine endures. But for this doctrine we could more confidently assert

that ours is a democratic society based upon a belief in individual equality.

E. Nullification of the rights guaranteed by the Fourteenth Amendment and the reestablishment of the Negro's pre–Civil War inferior status fully realized

Before the end of the century, even without repeal of the Fourteenth and Fifteenth Amendments, those forces committed to a perpetuation of the slave concept of the Negro had realized their goal. They had defied the federal government, threatened the white defenders of equal rights, had used intimidation and violence against the Negro and had effectively smashed a political movement designed to unite the Negro and the poor whites. Provisions requiring segregated schools were written into state constitutions and statutes. Negroes had been driven from participation in political affairs, and a veritable maze of Jim Crow laws had been erected to "keep the Negro in his place" (of inferiority), all with impunity. There was no longer any need to pretend either that Negroes were getting an education equal to the whites or were entitled to it.

In the Constitutional Convention of Virginia, 1901–1902, Senator Carter Glass, in explaining a resolution requiring that state funds be used to maintain primary schools for four months before being used for establishment of higher grades, explained that "white people of the black sections of Virginia should be permitted to tax themselves, and after a certain point had been passed which would safeguard the poorer classes of those communities, divert that fund to the exclusive use of white children. . . ."[30]

Senator Vardaman thought it was folly to make such pretenses. In Mississippi there were too many people to educate and not enough money to go around, he felt. The state, he insisted, should not spend as much on the education of Negroes as it was doing. "There is no use multiplying words about it," he said in 1899, "the negro will not be permitted to rise above the sta-

---

[29] See CARLETON, THE CONSERVATIVE SOUTH—A POLITICAL MYTH, 22 Va. Q. Rev. 179–192 (1946); LEWINSON, RACE, CLASS AND PARTY (1932); MOON, THE BALANCE OF POWER—THE NEGRO VOTE, c. 4 (1948).

[30] REPORT OF THE PROCEEDINGS AND DEBATES OF THE CONSTITUTIONAL CONVENTION, State of Virginia, Richmond, June 12, 1901–June 26, 1902, p. 1677 (1906).

U.S. SUPREME
COURT,
OCTOBER 1953

BRIEF FOR THE
APPELLANTS AND
RESPONDENTS
ON REARGUMENT

tion he now fills." Money spent on his education was, therefore, a "positive unkindness" to him. "It simply renders him unfit for the work which the white man has prescribed and which he will be forced to perform."[31] Vardaman's scholarly compatriot, Dunbar Rowland, seconded these views in 1902, when he said that "thoughtful men in the South were beginning to lose faith in the power of education which had been heretofore given to uplift the negro," and to complain of the burden thus placed upon the people of the South in their poverty.[32]

The views of Tillman, Vardaman, Stone, Rowland, Glass and others were largely a justification for what had been done by the time they uttered them. The South had succeeded in setting up the machinery by which it was hoped to retain the Negro in an inferior status. Through separate, inferior schools, through an elaborate system of humiliating Jim Crow, and through effective disfranchisement of the Negro, the exclusive enjoyment of first-class citizenship had now become the sole possession of white persons.

And, finally, the Negro was effectively restored to an inferior position through laws and through practices, now dignified as "custom and tradition." Moreover, this relationship—of an inferior Negro and superior white status—established through laws, practice, custom and tradition, was even more rigidly enforced than in the ante-bellum era. As one historian has aptly stated:

> "Whether by state law or local law, or by the more pervasive coercion of sovereign white opinion, 'the Negro's place' was gradually defined—in the courts, schools, and libraries, in parks, theaters, hotels, and residential districts, in hospitals, insane asylums—everywhere including on sidewalks and in cemeteries. When complete, the new codes of White Supremacy were vastly more complex than the antebellum slave codes or the Black Codes of 1865–1866, and, if anything, they were stronger and more rigidly enforced."[33]

This is the historic background against which the validity of the separate but equal doctrine must be tested. History reveals it as a part of an overriding purpose to defeat the aims of the Thirteenth, Fourteenth and Fifteenth Amendments. Segregation was designed to insure inequality—to discriminate on account of race and color—and the separate but equal doctrine accommodated the Constitution to that purpose. Separate but equal is a legal fiction. There never was and never will be any separate equality. Our Constitution cannot be used to sustain ideologies and practices which we as a people abhor.

That the Constitution is color blind is our dedicated belief. We submit that this Court cannot sustain these school segregation laws under any separate but equal concept unless it is willing to accept as truths the racist notions of the perpetuators of segregation and to repeat the tragic error of the Plessy court supporting those who would nullify the Fourteenth Amendment and the basic tenet of our way of life which it incorporates. We respectfully suggest that it is the obligation of this Court to correct that error by holding that these laws and constitutional provisions which seek to condition educational opportunities on the basis of race and color are historic aberrations and are inconsistent with the federal Constitution and cannot stand. The separate but equal doctrine of *Plessy v. Ferguson* should now be overruled.

CONCLUSION TO PART ONE

In short, our answer to Question No. 3 proposed by the Court is that it is within the judicial power, whatever the evidence concerning Questions 2(a) and (b) may disclose, to hold that segregated schools violate the Fourteenth Amendment, and for the reasons herein above stated that such power should now be exercised.

WHEREFORE, it is respectfully submitted that constitutional provisions and statutes involved in these cases are invalid and should be struck down.

---

[31] KIRWAN, *op. cit. supra*, n. 22, at 145–146.

[32] JOHNSON, IDEOLOGY OF WHITE SUPREMACY, *op. cit. supra*, n. 2, at 153. That this pattern is not an antiquated doctrine but a modern view may be seen in the current expenditure per pupil in average daily attendance 1949–1950: In Alabama, $130.09 was spent for whites against $92.69 for Negroes; in Arkansas $123.60 for whites and $73.03 for Negroes; in Florida $196.42 for whites, $136.71 for Negroes; in Georgia, $145.15 for whites and $79.73 for Negroes; in Maryland, $217.41 for whites and $198.76 for Negroes; in Mississippi, $122.93 for whites and $32.55 for Negroes; in North Carolina, $148.21 for whites and $122.90 for Negroes; in South Carolina, $154.62 for whites and $79.82 for Negroes; in the District of Columbia, $289.68 for whites and $220.74 for Negroes. BLOSE AND JARACZ, BIENNIAL SURVEY OF EDUCATION IN THE UNITED STATES, 1948–50, TABLE 43, "STATISTICS OF STATE SCHOOL SYSTEMS, 1949–50" (1952).

[33] WOODWARD, ORIGINS OF THE NEW SOUTH 212 (1951).

PART TWO

This portion of the brief is directed to questions one and two propounded by the Court:

"1. What evidence is there that the Congress which submitted and the State legislatures and conventions which ratified the Fourteenth Amendment contemplated or did not contemplate, understood or did not understand, that it would abolish segregation in public schools?

2. If neither the Congress in submitting nor the States in ratifying the Fourteenth Amendment understood that compliance with it would require the immediate abolition of segregation in public schools, was it nevertheless the understanding of the framers of the Amendment

(a) that future Congresses might, in the exercise of their power under Sec. 5 of the Amendment, abolish such segregation, or

(b) that it would be within the judicial power, in light of future conditions, to construe the Amendment as abolishing such segregation of its own force?"

I. THE FOURTEENTH AMENDMENT WAS INTENDED TO DESTROY ALL CASTE AND COLOR LEGISLATION IN THE UNITED STATES, INCLUDING RACIAL SEGREGATION

Research by political scientists and historians, specialists on the period between 1820 and 1900, and other experts in the field, as well as independent research by attorneys in these cases, convinces us that: (1) there is ample evidence that the Congress which submitted and the states which ratified the Fourteenth Amendment contemplated and understood that the Amendment would deprive the states of the power to impose any racial distinctions in determining when, where, and how its citizens would enjoy the various civil rights afforded by the states; (2) in so far as views of undeveloped public education in the 1860's can be applied to universal compulsory education in the 1950's, the right to public school education was one of the civil rights with respect to which the states were deprived of the power to impose racial distinctions; (3) while the framers of the Fourteenth Amendment clearly intended that Congress should have the power to enforce the provisions of the Amendment, they also clearly intended that the Amendment would be prohibitory on the states without Congressional action.

The historic background of the Fourteenth Amendment and the legislative history of its adoption show clearly that the framers intended that the Amendment would deprive the states of power to make any racial distinction in the enjoyment of civil rights. It is also clear that the statutes involved in these cases impose racial distinctions which the framers of the Amendment and others concerned with its adoption understood to be beyond the power of a state to enforce.

The framers of the Fourteenth Amendment were men who came to the 39th Congress with a well defined background of Abolitionist doctrine dedicated to the equalitarian principles of real and complete equality for all men. Congressional debates during this period must be read with an understanding of this background along with the actual legal and political status of the Negro at the end of the Civil War. This background gives an understanding of the determination of the framers of the Fourteenth Amendment to change the inferior legal and political status of Negroes and to give them the full protection of the Federal Government in the enjoyment of complete and real equality in all civil rights.[34]

A. The era prior to the Civil War was marked by determined efforts to secure recognition of the principle of complete and real equality for all men within the existing constitutional framework of our government

The men who wrote the Fourteenth Amendment were themselves products of a gigantic antislavery crusade which, in turn, was an expression of the great humanitarian reform movement of the Age of Enlightenment. This philosophy upon which the Abolitionists had taken their stand had been adequately summed up in Jefferson's basic proposition "that all men are created equal" and "are endowed by their Creator with certain unalienable Rights." To this philosophy they adhered with an almost fanatic devotion and an unswerving determination to obliterate any obstructions which stood in the way of its fulfillment. In their drive toward this goal, it may be that they thrust aside some then accepted notions of law and, indeed, that they attempted to give to the Declaration of Independence a substance which might have sur-

U.S. SUPREME COURT, OCTOBER 1953

BRIEF FOR THE APPELLANTS AND RESPONDENTS ON REARGUMENT

---

[34] tenBroek, The Antislavery Origins of the Fourteenth Amendment 185, 186 (1951).

U.S. SUPREME
COURT,
OCTOBER 1953

BRIEF FOR THE
APPELLANTS AND
RESPONDENTS
ON REARGUMENT

prised its draftsmen. No matter, the crucial point is that their revolutionary drive was successful and that it was climaxed in the Amendment here under discussion.

The first Section of the Fourteenth Amendment is the legal capstone of the revolutionary drive of the Abolitionists to reach the goal of true equality. It was in this spirit that they wrote the Fourteenth Amendment and it is in the light of this revolutionary idealism that the questions propounded by this Court can best be answered.

In the beginning, the basic and immediate concern of the Abolitionists was necessarily slavery itself. The total question of removing all other discriminatory relationships after the abolition of slavery was at first a matter for the future. As a consequence, the philosophy of equality was in a state of continuous development from 1830 through the time of the passage of the Fourteenth Amendment. However, the ultimate objective was always clearly in mind—absolute and complete equality for all Americans.

During the pre–Civil War decades, the antislavery movement here and there began to develop special meaning and significance in the legal concept of "privileges and immunities," the concept of "due process" and the most important concept of all for these cases, "equal protection of the laws." In the immediately succeeding sections, we shall show how the development of these ideas culminated in a firm intention to obliterate all class distinction as a part of the destruction of a caste society in America.

The development of each of these conceptions was often ragged and uneven with much overlapping: what was "equal protection" to one was "due process" or "privilege and immunity" to another. However, regardless of the phrase used, the basic tenet of all was the uniform belief that Negroes were citizens and, as citizens, freedom from discrimination was their right. To them "discrimination" included all forms of racial distinctions.

Equality under law One tool developed to secure full standing for Negroes was the concept of equal protection of the laws. It was one thing, and a very important one, to declare as a political abstraction that "all men are created equal," and quite another to attach concrete rights to this state of equality. The Declaration of Independence did the former. The latter was Charles Sumner's outstanding contribution to American law.

The great abstraction of the Declaration of Independence was the central rallying point for the Abolitionists. When slavery was the evil to be attacked, no more was needed. But as some of the New England states became progressively more committed to abolition, the focus of interest shifted from slavery itself to the status and rights of the free Negro. In the Massachusetts legislature in the 1840's, Henry Wilson, manufacturer, Abolitionist, and later United States Senator and Vice President, led the fight against discrimination, with "equality" as his rallying cry.[35] One Wilson measure adopted by the Massachusetts Legislature in 1845 gave the right to recover damages to any person "unlawfully excluded" from the Massachusetts public schools.[36]

Boston thereafter established a segregated school for Negro children, the legality of which was challenged in *Roberts v. City of Boston*, 5 Cush. (Mass.) 198 (1849). Charles Sumner, who later was to play such an important role in the Congress that formulated the Fourteenth Amendment, was counsel for Roberts. His oral argument, which the Abolitionists widely circulated, is one of the landmarks in the crystallization of the equalitarian concept.

This case was technically an action for damages under the Wilson Act. However, Sumner attacked segregation in public schools on the broader ground that segregation violated the Massachusetts Constitution which provided: "All men are created free and equal," and it was from this base that he launched his attack.

"Of Equality I shall speak, not as a sentiment, but as a principle. . . .*** Thus it is with all moral and political ideas. First appearing as a sentiment, they awake a noble impulse, filling the soul with generous sympathy, and encouraging to congenial effort. Slowly recognized, they finally pass into a formula, to be acted upon, to be applied, to be defended in the concerns of life, as principles."[37]

"Equality before the law"[38] was the formula he employed. He traced the equalitarian theory from the eighteenth century French philoso-

---

[35] For an account of Wilson's struggles against anti-miscegenation laws, against jim-crow transportation and jim-crow education, see NASON, LIFE OF HENRY WILSON 48 *et seq.* (1876).

[36] Massachusetts Act 1845, § 214.

[37] 2 WORKS OF CHARLES SUMNER 330, 335–336 (1875). The entire argument is reprinted at 327 *et seq.*

[38] *Id.* at 327, 330–331.

phers through the French Revolution into the language of the French Revolutionary Constitution of 1791,[39] the Constitution of February 1793,[40] the Constitution of June 1793[41] and the Charter of Louis Phillipe.[42] Equality before the law, i.e., equality of rights, was the real meaning of the Massachusetts constitutional provision. Before it "all … distinctions disappear":

> "He may be poor, weak, humble, or black— he may be Caucasian, Jewish, Indian or Ethiopian race—he may be of French, German, English or Irish extraction; but before the Constitution of Massachusetts all these distinctions disappear. He is not poor, weak, humble, or black; nor is he French, German, English or Irish; he is a MAN, the equal of all his fellowmen."[43]

Hence, he urged, separate schools are illegal.

The Massachusetts court rejected Sumner's argument and refused to grant relief. Subsequent thereto, in 1853, the Legislature of Massachusetts, after careful consideration of the problem involving hearings and reports, amended the Wilson statute by providing, among other things, that in determining the qualifications of school children in public schools in Massachusetts "no distinction was to be made on account of the race, color or religious opinions of the appellant or scholar."[44]

The Committee on Education of the House of Representatives in its report recommending adoption of this bill carefully considered the arguments for and against the measure and concluded:

> "Your committee believe, in the words of another, that 'The only security we can have for a healthy and efficient system of public instruction rests in the deep interest and vigilant care with which the more intelligent watch over the welfare of the schools. This only will secure competent teachers, indefatigable exertion, and a high standard of excellence; and where the colored children are mingled up with the mass of their more favored fellows, they will partake of the advantages of this watchful oversight. Shut out and separated, they are sure to be neglected and to experience all the evils of an isolated and despised class. One of the great merits of our system of public instruction is the fusion of all classes which it produces. From a childhood which shares the same bench and sports there can hardly arise a manhood of aristocratic prejudice or separate castes and classes. Our common-school system suits our institutions, promotes the feeling of brotherhood, and the

habit of republican equality. To debar the colored race from these advantages, even if we still secured to them equal educational results, is a sore injustice and wrong, and is taking the surest means of perpetuating a prejudice that should be depreciated and discountenanced by all intelligent and Christian men."[45]

Thus, the argument and theories advanced by Sumner, although rejected by the Supreme Court of Massachusetts, finally became incorporated into the law of the State of Massachusetts. More important, however, is the fact that the argument of Sumner was widely distributed throughout the country during the period immediately preceding the consideration of the Fourteenth Amendment.[46] As a consequence it became a fundamental article of faith among the Radical Republicans that from a constitutional standpoint racial segregation was incompatible with constitutional guarantees of equal protection.[47]

The analysis of the available materials covering the period from 1830 to 1860, while important to this point, is too voluminous to be included in the argument at this point. We have, therefore, placed this analysis in a supplement at the end of the brief. The analysis of these materials compels the following historical conclusions:

1. To the Abolitionists, equality was an absolute—not a relative—concept which comprehended that no legal recognition be given to racial distinctions of any kind. The notion that any state could require racial segregation was totally incompatible with this doctrine.

2. The phrases—"privileges and immunities," "equal protection," and "due process"— that were to appear in the Amendment had

U.S. SUPREME COURT, OCTOBER 1953

BRIEF FOR THE APPELLANTS AND RESPONDENTS ON REARGUMENT

[39] "Men are born and continue free and *equal in their rights.*" *Id.* at 337.

[40] "The law ought to be equal for all." *Id.* at 338.

[41] "All men are equal by nature *and before the law.*" *Id.* at 339.

[42] "Frenchmen are *equal before the law… .*" *Ibid.*

[43] *Id.* at 341–342.

[44] General Laws of Mass. c. 256. § 1 (1855).

[45] Report of Committee on Education to House of Representatives, Commonwealth of Massachusetts, March 17, 1855.

[46] Among those active in distributing the argument was SALMON P. CHASE. DIARY AND CORRESPONDENCE OF SALMON P. CHASE, Chase to Sumner, Dec. 14, 1849, in 2 Ann. Rep. Am. Hist. Ass'n. 188 (1902).

[47] See, for example, Sumner resolution offered Congress on December 4, 1865 which called for "The organization of an educational system for the equal benefit of all without distinction of color or race." Cong. Globe, 39th Cong., 1st Sess. 2 (1865–1866).

U.S. SUPREME
COURT,
OCTOBER 1953

BRIEF FOR THE
APPELLANTS AND
RESPONDENTS
ON REARGUMENT

come to have a specific significance to opponents of slavery in the United States. Proponents of slavery knew and understood what that significance was, even as they disagreed with these theories. Members of the Congress that proposed the Amendment, shared this knowledge.

3. These radical Abolitionists, who had been in the minority prior to the Civil War, gained control of the Republican party in Congress during the course of the war and thus emerged in a dominant position in the Congress which was to write the Fourteenth Amendment. Ten of the members of the Joint Committee of Fifteen were men who had definite antislavery backgrounds and two others had likewise opposed slavery.

4. When the Joint Committee of Fifteen translated into constitutional provisions the equalitarian concepts held and widely bruited about in the struggle against slavery, it used the traditional phrases that had all become freighted with equalitarian meaning in its widest sense: "equal protection," "privileges and immunities" and "due process."

In these respects history buttresses and gives particular content to the recent admonition of this Court that "[w]hatever else the framers sought to achieve, it is clear that the matter of primary concern was the establishment of equality in the enjoyment of basic civil and political rights and the preservation of those rights from discriminatory action on the part of the States based on considerations of race and color." *Shelley v. Kraemer,* 334 U.S. 1, 23.

Despite the high principles and dedication of the leaders of the Abolitionist movement, their program ran into repeated roadblocks from both individual groups and state machinery. The movement was not only blocked in so far as the abolition of slavery itself was concerned, but was met by an ever increasing tendency on the part of all the southern states and some northern states to gradually cut down on the rights of free Negroes and to bring their status nearer and nearer to that of slaves. This countermovement culminated in the decision of the Supreme Court in the *Dred Scott* case (*Scott v. Sandford,* 19 How. 393) that no person of the "African race, whether free or not" could enjoy, under the Constitution of the United States, any right or protection whatsoever. All Negroes were thereby left, by the principles of that case, to the absolute, unrestrained power of the several states.

B. The movement for complete equality reached its successful culmination in the Civil War and the Fourteenth Amendment

The onset of the Civil War marked the turning point of the Abolitionists' drive to achieve absolute equality for all Americans. The first great success came on January 1, 1863, when President Lincoln's Emancipation Proclamation freed all slaves in those areas in insurrection against the United States. Obviously this was far from a complete victory. The doctrines enunciated by Chief Justice Taney in the *Dred Scott* case were still unqualified and remained as a part of the "constitutional law" of the time.

In February, 1865, the Abolitionist-dominated 38th Congress adopted and submitted to the states what was to become the Thirteenth Amendment to the Constitution. However, the Radical Republicans in Congress were intensely aware that the abolition of slavery constituted only a partial attainment of their goal of complete political and legal equality for Negroes. They had already determined as early as the spring and summer of 1862 to strike at the objective of federal statutory and constitutional guarantees for Negro equality. As yet, however, their thinking had not succeeded in distilling clearly a series of specifically defined legal and political objectives which they proposed to write into federal law and Constitution.

It should be observed in passing that their reason for this obviously was not necessarily pure Abolitionist idealism. They were in part motivated by hard practical considerations of Republican Party ascendency, and the fear that a restored South, in which Negroes were not given complete legal and political equality, would fall into the hands of a pre-war conservative white political leadership which would threaten the national political control of the Radical Republicans themselves. Thus their idealistic, social philosophy and their hard practical considerations of party interest dovetailed very nicely.[48]

It was to require the events of 1865–66, most notably the attempt to restore political rule in the South and the attempt to impose an inferior non-citizenship status upon the Negro in the restored southern states, to make clear to the Radical Republicans their new constitutional

_____

[48] tenBroek, THE ANTISLAVERY ORIGINS OF THE FOURTEENTH AMENDMENT 117–119 (1951).

objectives and the means they would seek to obtain it.

C. The principle of absolute and complete equality began to be translated into federal law as early as 1862

In 1862 Congress addressed itself to an immediate problem over which it had authority. In debating the bill which was to abolish slavery in the District of Columbia, Representative Bingham said: "The great privilege and immunity of an American citizen to be respected everywhere in this land, and especially in this District, is that they shall not be deprived of life, liberty, or property without due process of law."[49] Representative Fessenden concluded: "If I do not mistake, it is quite apparent that when this bill shall be put on its final passage it will proclaim liberty to the slaves within this District. These men—for God created them men, though man has used them as goods and chattels—slaves—these men and women and children will, when the President of the United States signs this bill, be translated ... [to a] condition in which they are invested with the rights of freemen, upon which none can trespass with impunity; since over the person of the free black as well as the free white man there is thrown the broad shield of the nation's majesty."[50] The bill was enacted into law.[51]

Simultaneously Congress discontinued the application of the Black Codes of Maryland and Virginia to the District of Columbia.[52]

Between the time of the Emancipation Proclamation in 1863 and the formulation of the Fourteenth Amendment, Congress took several forward steps to secure complete equality for the class so recently freed. These steps came in the form of particular solutions to particular problems. To this Congress (38th), the most immediate problem was one which fell under their glance daily, the problem of transportation in the District of Columbia. Congressional treatment of this problem is of significance because it reveals the early determination of the Radical Republicans to prohibit racial segregation.

In 1863, Congress amended the charter of the Alexandria and Washington Railroad to eliminate the practice of putting white and Negro passengers in separate parts of the street cars.[53] When, in 1864, the Washington and Georgetown street car company attempted to put colored passengers in cars separate from those of the white passengers, Senator Sumner denounced the practice in the Senate and set forth on his crusade to prohibit all racial distinctions by first eliminating street car segregation in the District.[54] In 1865, he carried to passage a law applicable to all District carriers that "no person shall be excluded from any car on account of color."[55]

The debate on the street car bill covered the entire issue of segregation in transportation. Those who supported prohibition of segregation did so on the ground that any such separation was a denial of equality itself. Senator Wilson denounced the "Jim Crow car," declaring it to be "in defiance of decency."[56] Senator Sumner persuaded his brethren to accept the Massachusetts view, saying that in Massachusetts, "the rights of every colored person are placed on an equality with those of white persons. They have the same right with white persons to ride in every public conveyance in the Commonwealth."[57] Thus, when Congress in 1866 framed the Fourteenth Amendment, it did so against a background of Congressional determination that segregation in transportation was unequal, unjust, and was "in defiance of decency."

D. From the beginning the thirty-ninth Congress was determined to eliminate race distinctions from American law

The 39th Congress which was to propose the Fourteenth Amendment convened in December 1865 with the realization that, although slavery had been abolished, the overall objective, the complete legal and political equality for all men had not been realized. This was dramatically emphasized by the infamous Black Codes being enacted throughout the southern states. These Black Codes had the single purpose of providing additional legislative sanction to maintain the inferior status for all Negroes which had been judicially decreed in the opinion in the case of *Scott* v. *Sandford,* 19 How. 393.

The Black Codes, while they grudgingly admitted that Negroes were no longer slaves, nonetheless used the states' power to impose and

U.S. SUPREME COURT, OCTOBER 1953

BRIEF FOR THE APPELLANTS AND RESPONDENTS ON REARGUMENT

---

[49] Cong. Globe, 37th Cong., 2d Sess. 1639 (1862).
[50] *Id.* at 1642.
[51] 12 Stat. 376 (1862).
[52] 12 Stat. 407 (1862).
[53] 12 Stat. 805 (1863).
[54] Cong. Globe, 38th Cong., 1st Sess. 553, 817 (1864).
[55] 13 Stat. 536, 537 (1865).
[56] Cong. Globe, 38th Cong., 1st Sess. 3132, 3133 (1864).
[57] *Id.* at 1158.

U.S. SUPREME
COURT,
OCTOBER 1953

BRIEF FOR THE
APPELLANTS AND
RESPONDENTS
ON REARGUMENT

maintain essentially the same inferior, servile position which Negroes had occupied prior to the abolition of slavery. These codes thus followed the legal pattern of the ante-bellum slave codes. Like their slavery forerunners, these codes compelled Negroes to work for arbitrarily limited pay; restricted their mobility; forbade them, among other things, to carry firearms; forbade their testimony in a court against any white man; and highly significant here, contained innumerable provisions for segregation on carriers and in public places. In at least three states these codes prohibited Negroes from attending the public schools provided for white children.[58]

It was this inferior caste position which the Radical Republicans in Congress were determined to destroy. They were equally determined that by federal statutory or constitutional means, or both, Congress would not only invalidate the existing Black Codes but would proscribe any and all future attempts to enforce governmentally-imposed caste distinctions.

Congress was well aware of the fact that to take this step involved a veritable revolution in federal-state relations. A number of Senators and Representatives in the 39th Congress, by speech and resolution, made it eminently clear that they aimed at nothing less than the total destruction of all hierarchy, oligarchy and class rule in the southern states. One of the more notable resolutions of this kind was that of Senator Charles Sumner, introduced on December 4, 1865, at the opening of the session. This resolution asserted that no state formerly declared to be in rebellion was to be allowed to resume its relation to the Union until "the complete reestablishment of loyalty … " and:

> "The complete suppression of all oligarchical pretensions, and the complete enfranchisement of all citizens, so that there shall be no denial of rights on account of color or race; but justice shall be impartial, and all shall be equal before the law."

Another requirement of Sumner's resolution called for:

> "The organization of an educational system for the equal benefit of all without distinction of color or race."[59]

Sumner thus recognized the close relationship between the destruction of the southern ruling class and the elimination of segregation in the educational system.

Representative Jehu Baker of Illinois introduced a similar resolution in the House of Representatives, which read in part as follows:

> "Whereas class rule and aristocratic principles of government have burdened well nigh all Europe with enormous public debts and standing armies, which press as a grievous incubus on the people, absorbing their substance, impeding their culture, and impairing their happiness; and whereas the class rule and aristocratic element of slaveholding which found a place in our Republic has proved itself, in like manner, hurtful to our people … Therefore,

> "*Resolved*, (as the sense of this House,) That once for all we should have done with class rule and aristocracy as a privileged power before the law in this nation, no matter where or in what form they may appear; and that, in restoring the normal relations of the States lately in rebellion, it is the high and sacred duty of the Representatives of the people to proceed upon the true, as distinguished from the false, democratic principle, and to realize and secure the largest attainable liberty to the whole people of the Republic, irrespective of class or race."[60]

There were numerous other resolutions and speeches expressing similar sentiments. All of the resolutions were referred to the Joint Committee on Reconstruction and are a part of the background of that committee's work in the framing of the Fourteenth Amendment.

These expressions of principle were started toward statutory fruition by Senator Trumbull's Bill to enlarge the powers of the Freedmen's Bureau. The debates which followed the introduction of his Senate Bill No. 60 are of particular interest because they make it clear that a large number of the Radical Republicans regarded the destruction of segregation in the school districts of the southern states as a highly desirable legislative objective. What followed amounted to a forthright assault on the idea that there could be racial segregation in the public schools.

---

[58] See the summary in Senator Wilson's speech before Congress, Cong. Globe, 39th Cong., 1st Sess. 39–40, 589 (1866); 1 Fleming, Documentary History of Reconstruction 273–312 (1906); McPherson, The Political History of the United States During the Period of Reconstruction 29–44 (1880).

[59] Cong. Globe, 39th Cong., 1st Sess. 2 (1865–1866).

[60] Cong. Globe, 39th Cong. 1st Sess. 69 (1865–1866).

Representative Hubbard of Connecticut expressed the broad pattern of thinking of which this bill was a part:

"The words, caste, race, color, ever unknown to the Constitution, ... are still potent for evil on the lips of men whose minds are swayed by prejudice or blinded by passion, and the freedmen need the protection of this bill.

"The era is dawning when it will be a reproach to talk in scorn about the distinctions of race or color. Our country is, and must be, cosmopolitan....

"It is in vain that we talk about race, caste, or color. . . ."[61]

Likewise, Representative Rousseau of Kentucky stated:

"... Here are four school-houses taken possession of, and unless they mix up white children with black, the white children can have no chance in these schools for instruction. And so it is wherever this Freedmen's Bureau operates."[62]

Representative Dawson of Pennsylvania recognized that the supporters of the bill:

"... hold that the white and black race are equal. . . . Their children are to attend the same schools with white children, and to sit side by side with them. . . ."[63]

Of more importance was S.61 "A Bill to Protect All Persons in the United States in Their Civil Rights and Furnish the Means of Vindication." This bill, though introduced through Senator Trumbull in his capacity as Chairman of the Judiciary Committee, was in fact a measure sponsored by the entire Radical Republican majority.

The bill forbade any "discrimination in civil rights or immunities" among "the people of the United States on account of race, color, or previous condition of slavery." It provided that all persons should have "full and equal benefits of all laws" for the security of their persons and their property.

In a lengthy speech, Senator Trumbull defended the wisdom and constitutionality of this bill in detail. The Thirteenth Amendment, he argued, made the bill both constitutional and necessary.

"Then, sir, I take it that any statute which is not equal to all, and which deprives any citizen of civil rights which are secured to other citizens, is an unjust encroachment upon his liberty; and is, in fact, a badge of servitude which, by the Constitution, is prohibited."[64]

Senator Trumbull's argument precipitated a lengthy debate on the constitutional issues. Opponents of the measure, conceding that Congress had the power under the Thirteenth Amendment to assure freedom of Negroes, denied that Congress had the power to endow Negroes with citizenship and civil rights. To sustain their position they pointed to the fact that Negroes who were freed prior to the Emancipation Proclamation were not treated as citizens and under the authority of the *Dred Scott* case could not be citizens.[65]

In reply, Trumbull advanced the additional constitutional argument that, once slavery was abolished, the naturalization clause of the Constitution provided Congress with the power to endow Negroes with the citizenship the *Dred Scott* case had held they could not otherwise enjoy. Trumbull thus adopted the position of Chief Justice Taney in the *Dred Scott* case that the power to confer citizenship was vested in the federal, not the state government.

Another major area of controversy with respect to the bill was as to its scope. Time and again the Democrats and the more conservative Republicans in the Senate asserted that the bill would invalidate every state law which provided for racial segregation, or provided a different rule for persons of different races.[66] For example, there was the charge of Senator Cowan, a Republican of Pennsylvania, who said:

"Now, as I understand the meaning ... of this bill, it is that there shall be no discrimination made between the inhabitants of the several States of this Union, none in any way. In Pennsylvania, for the greater convenience of the people, and for the greater convenience, I may say, of both classes of the people, in certain districts the Legislature has provided schools for colored children, has discriminated as between the two classes of children. We put the African children in this school-house and the white children over in that school-house, and educate them there as we best can. Is this amendment to the Constitution of the United States abolishing slavery to break up that system which Pennsylvania has adopted for the education of her white and colored

---

[61] *Id.* at 630.

[62] *Id.* at App. 71.

[63] *Id.* at 541.

[64] *Id.* at 474.

[65] See statements of Senators Van Winkle of West Virginia and Saulsbury of Delaware. *Id.* at 475 ff.

[66] *Id.* at 500 ff.

U.S. SUPREME
COURT,
OCTOBER 1953

BRIEF FOR THE
APPELLANTS AND
RESPONDENTS
ON REARGUMENT

children? Are the school directors who carry out that law and who make this distinction between these classes of children to be punished for a violation of this statute of the United States? To me it is monstrous."[67]

Senator Howard in reply gave the Conservatives no comfort:

"I do not understand the bill which is now before us to contemplate anything else but this, that in respect to all civil rights ... there is to be hereafter no distinction between the white race and the black race. It is to secure to these men whom we have made free the ordinary rights of a freeman and nothing else.... There is no invasion of the legitimate rights of the States."[68]

But, perhaps the best answer of all to these assertions of the sweeping character of the bill was given by Senator Morrill of Vermont, a member of the Joint Committee of Fifteen:

"The Senator from Kentucky tells us that the proposition [federal guarantee of civil rights] is revolutionary, ... I admit that this species of legislation is absolutely revolutionary. But are we not in the midst of revolution? Is the Senator from Kentucky utterly oblivious to the grant results of four years of war?"[69]

It is highly significant that Senator Morrill was not only a member of the Joint Committee of Fifteen, even then engaged in drafting the Fourteenth Amendment, but that he later was to insist that the Fourteenth Amendment prohibited separate but equal provisions in state school legislation.

After two full days of debate, the Senate passed the Trumbull bill by a vote of 33 to 12.

The only rational inference to be drawn from the legislative history of the Trumbull bill in the Senate is that the great majority of that body was determined to bar the states from using their power to impose or maintain racial distinctions. The same majority was of the opinion that the federal government had constitutional authority so to delimit such action by the state.

In the House, the Conservatives pointed out forcefully that the text of the bill presented would destroy all limitations on federal power over state legislation and would likewise destroy all state legislative and judicial provisions making distinctions against Negroes. Representative Rogers observed:

"In the State of Pennsylvania there is a discrimination made between the schools for white children and the schools for black. The

laws there provide that certain schools shall be set apart for black persons, and certain schools shall be set apart for white persons. Now, if this Congress has a right, by such a bill as this, to enter the sovereign domain of a State ... then, by parity of reasoning, it has a right to enter the domain of that State and inflict upon the people there, without their consent, the right of the negro to enjoy the elective franchise...."[70]

In a somewhat disingenuous attempt to deal with the argument of the Conservatives, Representative Wilson of Iowa, chairman of the House Judiciary Committee, argued vaguely that the bill would not have the effect of destroying all legislation discriminating on the basis of race.[71] Nevertheless Wilson broadly defined the term civil rights as used in the bill as being "the natural rights of man." Moreover, he observed that "immunities" secured "to citizens of the United States equality in the exemptions of the law."[72]

At this point, Representative Bingham of Ohio, who had become converted to the Conservatives' constitutional power argument, made a notable address to the House. While admitting that perhaps Congress was at that time without constitutional authority to enact so sweeping a bill, he said it was nevertheless true that the bill as it stood was as sweeping as was charged by the Conservatives.

Representative Bingham then made it preeminently clear that he entirely approved of the sweeping objectives of the bill as it came from the Senate. His willingness to accept any modification of the bill was *solely* on the grounds of an overwhelming present constitutional objection which he himself was even then in the process of curing with a proposal for a constitutional amendment. He said:

"If civil rights has this extent, what, then, is proposed by the provision of the first section? Simply to strike down by congressional enactment every State constitution which makes a discrimination on account of race or color in any of the civil rights of the citizen. I might say here, without the least fear of contradiction, that there is scarcely a State in this Union which does not, by its Constitution or by its statute laws, make some discrimination on

[67] *Id.* at 500.
[68] *Id.* at 504.
[69] *Id.* at 570.
[70] *Id.* at 1121.
[71] *Id.* at 1117.
[72] *Ibid.*

account of race or color between citizens of the United States in respect of civil rights."[73]

Bingham then insisted that he believed that all discriminatory legislation should be wiped out by amending the Constitution.

"The law in every State should be just; it should be no respecter of persons. It is otherwise now, and it has been otherwise for many years in many of the States of the Union. I should remedy that not by an arbitrary assumption of power, but by amending the Constitution of the United States, expressly prohibiting the States from any such abuse of power in the future."[74]

Bingham's prestige as a leader of the Radical Republican majority obliged Wilson to accept the Ohioan's interpretation. Consequently, the bill was returned to the Judiciary Committee and amended to eliminate the sweeping phrase "there shall be no discrimination in civil rights and immunities." Wilson no doubt comforted himself with the fact that even as amended the language of the bill was still revolutionary. At any rate, the Conservatives were still convinced that the bill invalidated state racial segregation laws. With considerable force, they argued that the phrase "the inhabitants of every state" … shall have the rights to full and equal benefits of all laws and proceedings for the "security of persons and property … " was properly to be broadly interpreted. In fact, Senator Davis of Kentucky had this to say:

"… [T]his measure proscribes all discriminations against negroes in favor of white persons that may be made anywhere in the United States by any 'ordinance, regulation, or custom,' as well as by 'law or statute.' …

But there are civil rights, immunities, and privileges 'which ordinances, regulations, and customs' confer upon white persons everywhere in the United States, and withhold from negroes. On ships and steamboats the most comfortable and handsomely furnished cabins and state-rooms, the first tables, and other privileges; in public hotels the most luxuriously appointed parlors, chambers, and saloons, the most sumptuous tables, and baths; in churches not only the most softly cushioned pews, but the most eligible sections of the edifices; on railroads, national, local, and street, not only seats, but whole cars, are assigned to white persons to the exclusion of negroes and mulattoes. All these discriminations in the entire society of the United States are established by ordinances, regulations, and customs. This bill proposes to break down and sweep them all away and to con-

summate their destruction, and bring the two races upon the same great plane of perfect equality, declares all persons who enforce those distinctions to be criminals against the United States, and subjects them to punishment by fine and imprisonment. . . ."[75]

Significantly, there was no attempt to reply to this interpretation of the amended bill.

The bill in its amended form was adopted by Congress and vetoed by President Johnson.

Representative Lawrence, who spoke in favor of overriding President Johnson's veto said:

"This section does not limit the enjoyment of privileges to such as may be accorded only to citizens of 'some class,' or 'some race,' or 'of the least favored class,' or 'of the most favored class,' or of a particular complexion, for these distinctions were never contemplated or recognized as possible in fundamental civil rights, which are alike necessary and important to all citizens, and to make inequalities in which is rank injustice."[76]

He also said:

"… distinctions created by nature of sex, age, insanity, etc., are recognized as modifying conditions and privileges, but mere race or color, as among citizens never can [be]."[77]

Numerous newspapers also thought the bill destroyed all segregation in schools, theatres, churches, public vehicles and the like.[78] Flack said of the bill:

"Many [Congressmen] believed that the negro would be entitled to sit on juries, to attend the same schools, etc., since, if the States undertook to legislate on those matters, it might be claimed that he was denied the equal rights and privileges accorded to white men. It does not appear that all of these contentions were specifically contradicted.

* * *

It would seem reasonable to suppose that if the bill should prove to be constitutional that

[73] *Id.* at 1291.

[74] *Id.* at 1294.

[75] *Id.* at App. 183.

[76] *Id.* at 1836.

[77] *Id.* at 1835.

[78] New York Herald, March 29 and April 10, 1866: Commercial March 30, 1866; National Intelligencer, April 16, 1866 and May 16, 1866. There were a number of suits against local segregation laws banning Negroes from theatres, omnibuses, etc., McPherson's Scrap Book, The Civil Rights Bill, pp. 110 ff. None of these suits appear to have involved school segregation laws.

U.S. SUPREME
COURT,
OCTOBER 1953

BRIEF FOR THE
APPELLANTS AND
RESPONDENTS
ON REARGUMENT

these rights could not be legally denied them."[79]

* * *

"… many of the leading papers of the country, including some of the principal Republican papers, regarded the Civil Rights Bill as a limitation of the powers of the States, and as a step towards centralization, in that it interfered with the regulation of local affairs which had hitherto been regulated by state and local authorities or by custom. This opinion was held in the North as well as in the South. There also seems to have been a general impression among the press that negroes would, by the provisions of the bill, be admitted, on the same terms and conditions as the white people, to schools, theaters, hotels, churches, railway cars, steamboats, etc."[80]

* * *

"What the papers gave as their opinion must necessarily have been the opinion of large numbers of people. There is much evidence to substantiate this conclusion, for almost immediately after the passage of the bill over the President's veto, efforts were made by the negroes to secure these rights."[81]

The following generalizations are pertinent to the relationship of the Civil Rights Act (S. 61 as amended) to the problem of segregation in schools and the Fourteenth Amendment:

1. As originally drafted, the Act contained a phrase "there shall be no discrimination in civil rights and immunities among the inhabitants of any state …" This was so broad in scope that most Senators and Representatives believed that it would have the effect of destroying entirely all state legislation which distinguished or classified in any manner on the basis of race. School segregation laws, statutes establishing unequal penalties in criminal codes, laws banning Negroes from juries, all alike would have become invalid as against the federal statute.

2. A great majority of the Republicans—the men who formulated the Fourteenth Amendment—had no objection to a bill which went this far. Men like Rogers, Kerr and Cowan objected to the bill on the ground that it would end all caste legislation, including segregated schools, and this was the view of the Senate. None of the bill's supporters in the House, except Wilson, denied that the bill had that effect.

3. The Bingham amendment was finally adopted in the House which struck out the "no discrimination" clause, simply because a majority of the members of the House believed that so sweeping a measure could not be justified under the Constitution as it stood. They accepted Bingham's argument that the proper remedy for removing racial distinctions and classifications in the states was a new amendment to the Constitution.

4. The logic of the Bingham constitutional objections aside, the persuasiveness of his technical objection to the Trumbull bill was immeasurably enhanced by the fact that several days before his motion to amend the Civil Rights Bill, Bingham had in fact proposed to the House, on behalf of the Joint Committee, a constitutional amendment by the terms of which his constitutional objections to the Trumbull bill were obviated. That measure, H. R. 63, with some significant changes intended to underscore the prohibition on state governmental action with the addition of the citizenship clause became the Fourteenth Amendment.[82]

5. The law as finally enacted enumerated certain rights which Trumbull and other Radicals had felt were inseparably connected with the status of freedom. However, there is no evidence that even after the modification of the bill, the enumeration in the bill was considered to exclude rights not mentioned. Kerr, Rogers, Cowan, Grimes and other conservatives still insisted that the bill, even in its final form, banned segregation laws. The phrase "the inhabitants of every race … shall have the right … to full and equal benefit of all laws and proceedings for the security of persons and property" still stood in the bill and was susceptible of broad interpretation.

6. Finally, it may be observed that a majority of both Houses of Congress were ready to go beyond the provisions of the Civil Rights

---

[79] FLACK, THE ADOPTION OF THE FOURTEENTH AMENDMENT 40 (1908).

[80] Id. at 45.

[81] Ibid.

[82] "The Congress shall have power to make all laws which shall be necessary and proper to secure to the citizens of each state all privileges and immunities of citizens in the several states (Art. 4, Sec. 2); and to all persons in the several States equal protection in the rights of life, liberty and property (5th Amendment)." THE JOURNAL OF THE JOINT COMMITTEE OF FIFTEEN ON RECONSTRUCTION, 61 (Kendrick ed. 1914).

Act. Congressmen as diverse in their views as John A. Bingham and Henry J. Raymond, a moderate Republican and editor of the *New York Times*, united in proposing a constitutional amendment which would remove doubts as to the ability of Congress to destroy all state legislation discriminating and segregating on the basis of race. The forthcoming amendment, at all odds, was to set at rest all doubts as to the power of Congress to abolish all state laws making any racial distinctions or classifications.

The framers of the Fourteenth Amendment While Congress was engaged in the passage of the Civil Rights Act, a powerful congressional committee was even then wrestling with the problem of drafting a constitutional amendment which they hoped would definitely destroy all class and caste legislation in the United States. This committee was the now famous Joint Committee of Fifteen, which the two houses of Congress had established by Joint Resolution in December, 1865, to "inquire into the conditions of the states which formed the so-called Confederate States of America and report whether any or all of them were entitled to representation in Congress." It is extremely important for the purpose of this brief to observe that the Joint Committee of Fifteen was altogether under the domination of a group of Radical Republicans who were products of the great Abolitionist tradition, the equalitarianism which has been set forth earlier in this brief.

Section 1 of the Fourteenth Amendment, and particularly the equal protection clause, is peculiarly the product of this group, plus Senators Sumner, Wilson and Trumbull.[83]

Co-chairmen of the Committee were Representative Thaddeus Stevens of Pennsylvania and Senator William P. Fessenden of Maine.

Stevens was virtually dictator of the House. It was his dedicated belief that the Negro must be immediately elevated to a position of unconditional, legal, economic, political and social equality; and to this end he was determined to destroy every legal and political barrier that stood in the way of his goal.[84] Obviously, any constitutional amendment affecting the Negro would very heavily reflect his point of view.

Stevens believed that the law could not permit any distinctions between men because of their race. It was his understanding of the first section of the Fourteenth Amendment that: "…

where any State makes a distinction in the same law between different classes of individuals, Congress shall have power to correct such discrimination and inequality …"[85] He believed that it was up to Congress to repudiate "… the whole doctrine of the legal superiority of families or races,"[85a] and that under the Amendment, "… no distinction would be tolerated in this purified Republic but what arose from merit and conduct."[86]

Senator Fessenden undoubtedly held moderate views on the Reconstruction and, these views probably accounted for his selection as Co-chairman of the Joint Committee. Although Fessenden hoped that the Republican Party would work successfully with President Johnson, he broke with Johnson on the Civil Rights Act, which he supported with conviction. He was a staunch champion of the Fourteenth Amendment. Fessenden believed that all distinctions in civil rights based upon race must be swept away, and he was in favor of excluding the southern states from any representation in Congress until this end was assured.[87]

His son reports that the essence of his views was "all civil and political distinctions on account of race or color [would] be inoperative and void. …"[88]

Senator James W. Grimes, Republican of Iowa, was a Moderate and a close friend of Fessenden.[89] While he was governor of Iowa, prior to his election to the Senate the state constitution was revised to provide schools free and

U.S. SUPREME COURT, OCTOBER 1953

BRIEF FOR THE APPELLANTS AND RESPONDENTS ON REARGUMENT

---

[83] KELLY AND HARBISON, THE AMERICAN CONSTITUTION, ITS ORIGIN AND DEVELOPMENT 460–463 (1948); BOUDIN, TRUTH AND FICTION ABOUT THE FOURTEENTH AMENDMENT, 16 N. Y. U. L. Q. REV. 19 (1938); FRANK AND MUNRO, THE ORIGINAL UNDERSTANDING OF "EQUAL PROTECTION OF THE LAWS," 50 COL. L. REV. 131, 141 (1950).

[84] See for example, Stevens' speech attacking the "doctrine of the legal superiority of families or races" and denouncing the idea that "this is a white man's government." Cong. Globe, 39th Cong., 1st Sess. 75 (1865). "Sir," he said on this occasion, "this doctrine of a white man's Government is as atrocious as the infamous sentiment that damned the late Chief Justice to everlasting fame; and, I fear, to everlasting fire." See also similar observations on Stevens in BOWERS, THE TRAGIC ERA (1929) and WOODBURN, THE LIFE OF THADDEUS STEVENS (1913).

[85] Cong. Globe, 39th Cong., 1st Sess. 1063 (1866).

[85a] *Id.* at 74.

[86] *Id.* at 3148.

[87] KENDRICK, *op. cit. supra* n. 82, at 172–177; 6 DICTIONARY OF AMERICAN BIOGRAPHY 349–350 (1931).

[88] 2 FESSENDEN, LIFE AND PUBLIC SERVICES OF WILLIAM PITT FESSENDEN 36 (1931).

[89] KENDRICK, *op. cit. supra* n. 82, at 190–191.

U.S. SUPREME
COURT,
OCTOBER 1953

BRIEF FOR THE
APPELLANTS AND
RESPONDENTS
ON REARGUMENT

open to all children.[90] He insisted upon free schools open to all,[91] and Lewellen, who analyzed Grimes' political ideas, concluded that—

> "Special legislation, whether for individual or class, was opposed by Grimes as contrary 'to the true theory of a Republican government' and as the 'source of great corruption.' Although he sympathized with the newly freed Negroes after the Civil War, he opposed any attempt to make them wards of the Federal government. They had been made citizens and had been given the right to vote; there was no reason in the world why a law should be passed 'applicable to colored people' and not to white people. While his ideas on the Negro question were colored by his radical opinions on the slavery question his opposition to race legislation would probably have been practically as firm upon any other subject."[92]

Senator Ira Harris of New York, one of the least vocal members of the Committee of Fifteen, was a close friend of Charles Sumner,[93] and "acted with the radicals in all matters pertaining to reconstruction."[94] His explicit views on segregation are unascertained.[95] He was, however, so closely allied to the insiders on the Committee who considered race and color an indefensible basis for making legal distinctions,[96] that it is safe to conclude that he espoused, or at least acquiesced in, this viewpoint.

Senator George H. Williams, an Oregon Republican and former Douglas Democrat, claimed authorship of the First Reconstruction Act of 1867, originally called the Military Reconstruction Bill, which he introduced in the Senate on February 4, 1867.[97] In commenting upon this bill he said:

> "I will say that in preparing this bill, I had no desire to oppress or injure the people of the South, but my sole purpose was to provide a system by which all classes would be protected in life, liberty, and property …"[98]

His views on segregation are also unascertained.[99] It should be noted, however, that there is no record of his ever lending his voice or his votes to any law providing segregation based upon race or color.

Senator Jacob H. Howard of Michigan was clearly in the vanguard of that group which worked to secure full equality for Negroes.[100] He was clear and definite in his interpretation of the Civil Rights Act of 1866 and the Fourteenth Amendment. He said after the passage of the former that "in respect of all civil

rights, there is to be hereafter no distinction between the white race and the black race."[101] In explaining the intention of the Joint Committee during discussion of the joint resolution to propose what was to become the Fourteenth Amendment, he said:

> "He desired to put this question of citizenship and the rights of citizens and freedmen under the civil rights bill beyond the legislative power of such gentlemen as [Senator Doolittle of Wisconsin] who would pull the whole system up by the roots and destroy it, and expose the freedmen again to the oppressions of their old masters."[102]

In another speech, while acting for Senator Fessenden as floor leader for the Amendment, Howard interpreted Section 1 as follows:

> "The last two clauses of first section … disable a state from depriving … any person … of life, liberty or property without due process of law, or from denying to him the equal protection of the laws of the state. This abolishes all class legislation and does away with the injustice of subjecting one caste of persons to a code not applicable to another … Ought not the time to be now passed when one measure of justice is to be meted out to a member of one caste while another and a different measure is meted out to the member of another caste, both castes being alike citizens of the United States …[103]

The evidence conclusively establishes that Howard's interpretation of the equal protection clause precluded any use whatever of color as a basis for legal distinctions.[104]

Senator Reverdy Johnson, Democrat of Maryland, was attorney for the defense in *Dred*

---

[90] DICTIONARY OF AMERICAN BIOGRAPHY 632 (1931).

[91] *Ibid.*; SALTER, LIFE OF JAMES W. GRIMES, c. 3 (1876).

[92] LEWELLEN, POLITICAL IDEAS OF JAMES W. GRIMES 42 IOWA HIST. & POL. 339, 347 (1944).

[93] 8 DICTIONARY OF AMERICAN BIOGRAPHY 310 (1932).

[94] KENDRICK, *op. cit. supra* n. 82, at 195.

[95] FRANK AND MUNRO, THE ORIGINAL UNDERSTANDING OF EQUAL PROTECTION OF THE LAWS, 50 COL. L. REV. 131, 142 (1950).

[96] *Ibid.*

[97] KENDRICK, *op. cit. supra* n. 82, at 191; Williams, *Six Years in the United States Senate, Daily Oregonian,* Dec. 3, 10, 1905.

[98] CHRISTENSEN, THE GRAND OLD MAN OF OREGON: THE LIFE OF GEORGE H. WILLIAMS 26 (1939).

[99] FRANK AND MUNRO, *op. cit. supra* n. 83, at 142.

[100] KENDRICK, *op. cit. supra* n. 82, at 192.

[101] FRANK AND MUNRO, *op. cit. supra* n. 83, at 140.

[102] Cong. Globe, 39th Cong., 1st Sess. 2896 (1866).

[103] *Id.* at 2766.

[104] FRANK AND MUNRO, *op. cit. supra* n. 83, at 142.

Scott v. *Sandford*.[105] George I. Curtis, one of Scott's attorneys, credited Johnson with being the major influence in shaping the decision.[106] Where segregation was concerned, Johnson was not entirely consistent or predictable.

In 1864 he supported the motion of Senator Charles Sumner that the Washington Railroad end the exclusion of persons of color.[107] During the debate upon Sumner's motion, Johnson said:

> "It may be convenient, because it meets with the public wish or with the public taste of both classes, the white and the black, that there should be cars in which the white men and ladies are to travel, designated for that purpose, and cars in which the black men and black women are to travel, designated for that purpose. But that is a matter to be decided as between these two classes. There is no more right to exclude a black man from a car designated for the transportation of white persons than there is a right to refuse to transport in a car designated for black persons white men; and I do not suppose that anybody will contend ... that there exists any power in the company to exclude white men from a car because the company have appropriated that car for the general transportation of black passengers.[108]

Two years later, Johnson said:

> "... as slavery has been abolished in the several States, those who were before slaves are now citizens of the United States, standing ... upon the same condition, therefore, with the white citizens. If there is an authority in the Constitution to provide for the black citizen, it cannot be because he is black; it must be because he is a citizen; and that reason [is] equally applicable to the white man as to the black man. ..."[109]

Thus it appears that he understood that the granting of citizenship rights to Negroes meant that racial distinctions could no longer be imposed by law.

U.S. SUPREME COURT, OCTOBER 1953

BRIEF FOR THE APPELLANTS AND RESPONDENTS ON REARGUMENT

Representative John A. Bingham of Ohio, a member of the committee who has been described as the "Madison of the first section of the Fourteenth Amendment"[110] and undoubtedly its author, was a strong and fervent Abolitionist, classified with those whose views of equal protection "precluded any use whatsoever of color as a basis of legal distinctions."[111]

While the Fourteenth Amendment was pending, Representative Bingham took the view that state constitutions which barred segregated schools were "in accordance with the spirit and letter of the Constitution of the United States ... [if] the utterance of Jefferson ever meant anything ... it meant precisely that when he declared for equal and exact justice. ..."[112]

Representative George Boutwell of Massachusetts, was a hard, practical politician rather than an idealist. He was however, no less extreme in his demands for Negro civil rights and Negro suffrage than men like Stevens and Sumner. Indicative of his views is his vote on May 22, 1874 against the Sargent amendment to the Civil Rights Act of 1875, which would have permitted separate but equal schools.[113] During Reconstruction Alabama was "flooded with the radical speeches of Morton and Boutwell in favor of mixed schools."[114] He was among those whose interpretation of "equal protection" would not admit color as a basis for legal distinctions.[115]

Representative Roscoe Conkling, a New York Republican, was thought to have taken his views on Reconstruction from Stevens.[116] He was called by some a protege of Stevens; at any rate, they worked as partners on much reconstruction legislation.[117] In 1868, when the readmission of Arkansas was being discussed, he voted against the Henderson Amendment to the bill which would have permitted the state to establish segregated schools.[118] In 1872 he favored the supplementary civil rights bill and voted against the Thurman amendment which would have struck

[105] 19 How. 393.

[106] 10 DICTIONARY OF AMERICAN BIOGRAPHY 113 (1933).

[107] WILSON, HISTORY OF THE RISE AND FALL OF THE SLAVE POWER IN AMERICA 507 (1877).

[108] Cong. Globe, 38th Cong., 1st Sess. 1156 (1864).

[109] Cong. Globe, 39th Cong., 1st Sess. 372–374 (1865–1866).

[110] Dissent of Mr. Justice Black in Adamson v. California, 332 U.S. 46, 74.

[111] "FRANK AND MUNRO, THE ORIGINAL UNDERSTANDING OF EQUAL PROTECTION OF THE LAWS, 50 COL. L. REV. at 151. See GRAHAM, THE "CONSPIRACY THEORY" OF THE FOURTEENTH AMENDMENT, 47 YALE L. J. 371, 400–401 (1938); GRAHAM,

THE EARLY ANTISLAVERY BACKGROUNDS OF THE FOURTEENTH AMENDMENT, 1950 WIS. L. REV. 479 at 492; Cong. Globe, 39th Cong., 1st Sess. 1291, 1293, 2461–2462 (1866). For other sketches of Bingham see 2 DICTIONARY OF AMERICAN BIOGRAPHY 278 (1929) and KENDRICK, op. cit. supra n. 82 at 183.

[112] Cong. Globe, 40th Cong., 1st Sess. 2462 (1868).

[113] 2 Cong. Rec. 4167 (1874).

[114] BOWERS, THE TRAGIC ERA 427 (1929).

[115] FRANK AND MUNRO, op. cit. supra n. 83, at 142.

[116] KENDRICK, op. cit. supra n. 82, at 186.

[117] CHIDSEY, THE GENTLEMAN FROM NEW YORK 34–35 (1935).

[118] Cong. Globe, 40th Cong., 2nd Sess. 2748 (1868).

U.S. SUPREME
COURT,
OCTOBER 1953

BRIEF FOR THE
APPELLANTS AND
RESPONDENTS
ON REARGUMENT

out a clause permitting colored persons to enter "any place of public amusement or entertainment."[119] He was in the Senate majority which on May 22, 1874, voted down the Sargent amendment to the Civil Rights Bill, an amendment which would have permitted separate but equal schools.[120] Conkling must be classified as one of those who agreed to no legal classifications or distinctions based upon color.[121]

Representative Henry T. Blow, a Missouri Republican, first supported the views of Thaddeus Stevens in the Joint Committee and then in the second session gave his support to Bingham.[122] In either case, he acted with those who favored a broad and sweeping denial of the right of the states to make legal classifications on the basis of race or color. Blow came to Congress with a strong antislavery background and took the position that color discrimination could not be defended, as a matter of course.[123]

Representative Justin S. Morrill of Vermont is characterized as "an extreme radical," one "regularly on the side of radicalism." It is said of him that "the only part taken by him in Reconstruction was to attend the meetings of the Committee and cast his vote."[124] However, he was among those voting against the "white" clause in the Nebraska constitution when the bill to admit that state to the union was under consideration.[125] He voted against the Henderson amendment to permit segregated schools in the bill to readmit Arkansas.[126] He voted against the Sargent Amendment to allow separate but equal schools, during the debates on the bill that became the Civil Rights Act of 1875.[127] Morrill thus belongs in the group of those who did not consider color a reasonable ground for legal distinctions.[128]

Representative Elihu Washburne of Illinois was a staunch member of the House Radical bloc, and a pronounced enemy of the more moderate Reconstruction policies of President Johnson. He supported both the Civil Rights Act and the Fourteenth Amendment and his remarks make it clear that he favored a revolution in the southern social order.[129]

The two Democratic members of the Joint Committee from the House were both enemies of the Civil Rights Act and the Fourteenth Amendment. Representative Henry Grider of Kentucky was without influence in the drafting of the Fourteenth Amendment by the Joint Committee.[130] However, remarks of Represen-

tative Andrew Jackson Rogers of New Jersey, in opposition to these measures, are significant indication of contemporary understanding of their reach and thrust. Thus, in speaking of the Civil Rights Bill, Rogers said:

"In the State of Pennsylvania there is a discrimination made between the schools for white children and the schools for black. The laws there provide that certain schools shall be set apart for black persons, and certain schools shall be set apart for white persons. Now, if this Congress has a right, by such a bill as this, to enter the sovereign domain of a State and interfere with these statutes ... , then ... it has a right to ... , inflict upon the people ... the right of the negro to [vote]... ."[131]

Similarly, in speaking of the proposed Section 1 of the Fourteenth Amendment on February 26, 1866, he said:

"... Under this amendment, Congress would have power to compel the State to provide for white children and black children to attend the same school, upon the principle that all the people ... shall have equal protection in all the rights of life, liberty, and property, and all the privileges and immunities of citizens...."[132]

Again, in denouncing the Amendment, he declared:

"This section of the joint resolution is no more nor less than an attempt to embody in the Constitution of the United States that outrageous and miserable civil rights bill...."

"... I hold [the amendment] will prevent any State from refusing to allow anything to anybody."[133]

---

[119] CONKLING, LIFE AND LETTERS OF ROSCOE CONKLING 432 (1869).

[120] 2 Cong. Rec. 4167 (1874).

[121] FRANK AND MUNRO, op. cit. supra n. 83, at 142.

[122] KENDRICK, op. cit. supra n. 82, at 194.

[123] FRANK AND MUNRO, op. cit. supra n. 83, at 142.

[124] KENDRICK, op. cit. supra n. 82, at 140, 193.

[125] CONG. Globe, 39th Cong., 1st Sess. 4275–4276 (1866).

[126] Cong. Globe, 40th Cong., 2nd Sess. 2748 (1868).

[127] 2 Cong. Rec. 4167 (1874).

[128] FRANK AND MUNRO, op. cit. supra n. 83, at 142.

[129] 19 DICTIONARY OF AMERICAN BIOGRAPHY 504 (1936);, op. cit. supra n. 82, at 194.

[130] KENDRICK, op. cit. supra n. 82, at 196. Grider is not even listed in the DICTIONARY OF AMERICAN BIOGRAPHY. He died before the second session of the 39th Congress. KENDRICK, op. cit. supra n. 82, at 197.

[131] Cong. Globe., 39th Cong., 1st Sess. 1121 (1866).

[132] Id. at App. 134 (1866).

[133] Id. at 2538.

E. The Fourteenth Amendment was intended to write into the organic law of the United States the principle of absolute and complete equality in broad constitutional language

While the Civil Rights Act of 1866 was moving through the two Houses of Congress, the Joint Committee of Fifteen was engaged in the task of drafting a constitutional amendment as a part of a program for the "readmission" of the southern states to the Union. When the Committee began its meetings in January 1866, several of its members introduced proposals for constitutional amendments guaranteeing civil rights to the freedmen. After a series of drafting experiments, Representative Bingham on February 3 proposed the following:

> "The Congress shall have power to make all laws which shall be necessary and proper to secure to the citizens of each State all privileges and immunities of citizens in the several States (Art. 4, Sec. 2); and to all persons in the several States equal protection in the rights of life, liberty and property (5th Amendment)."[134]

The Joint Committee found this proposal satisfactory and accordingly on February 13th introduced it in the House as H. R. 63.[135]

By now the dedicated purpose of the Radical Republicans based in part upon the ante-war equalitarian principles as opposed to caste and class legislation had to be crystallized in a Fourteenth Amendment. Necessarily, the drafters of this amendment and those who participated in the debates on the amendment recognized that constitutional amendments are properly worded in the broadest and most comprehensive language possible.

It must be borne in mind that Representative Bingham, and those who supported his position on the amendment to the Civil Rights Bill of 1866, had already demonstrated that the constitutional amendment under consideration would be at least as comprehensive in its scope and effect as the original sweeping language of the Trumbull Civil Rights Bill *before* it was amended in the House, and that it would be far broader than the scope of the bill as finally enacted into law. On this point, Bingham repeatedly made his

intentions clear, both in his discussion on the power limitations on the Civil Rights Bill itself and in his defense of his early drafts of the proposed constitutional amendment.

Representative Rogers immediately attacked the proposed constitutional amendment (H. R. 63) as "more dangerous to the liberties of the people and the foundations of the government" than any proposal for amending the Constitution heretofore advanced. This amendment, he said, would destroy all state legislation distinguishing Negroes on the basis of race. Laws against racial intermarriage, laws applying special punishments to Negroes for certain crimes, and laws imposing segregation, including school segregation laws, alike would become unconstitutional. He said:

> "Who gave the Senate the constitutional power to pass that bill guarantying equal rights to all, if it is necessary to amend the organic law in the manner proposed by this joint resolution? ... It provides that all persons in the several States shall have equal protection in the right of life, liberty, and property. Now, it is claimed by gentlemen upon the other side of the House that Negroes are citizens of the United States. Suppose that in the State of New Jersey Negroes are citizens, as they are claimed to be by the other side of the House, and they change their residence to the State of South Carolina, if this amendment be passed Congress can pass under it a law compelling South Carolina to grant to Negroes every right accorded to white people there; and as white men there have the right to marry white women, Negroes, under this amendment, would be entitled to the same right; and thus miscegenation and mixture of the races could be authorized in any State, as all citizens under this amendment are entitled to the same privileges and immunities, and the same protection in life, liberty, and property.

> * * *

> "In the State of Pennsylvania there are laws which make a distinction with regard to the schooling of white children and the schooling of black children. It is provided that certain schools shall be designated and set apart for white children, and certain other schools designated and set apart for black children. Under this amendment, Congress would have power to compel the State to provide for white children and black children to attend the same school, upon the principle that all the people ... shall have equal protection in all the rights of life, liberty, and property, and

U.S. SUPREME COURT, OCTOBER 1953

BRIEF FOR THE APPELLANTS AND RESPONDENTS ON REARGUMENT

---

[134] This proposal with some changes was destined to become eventually the second portion of Section 1 of the Fourteenth Amendment. KENDRICK, *op. cit. supra* n. 82, at 61.

[135] Globe, 39th Cong., 1st Sess. 813 (1865–1866).

U.S. SUPREME
COURT,
OCTOBER 1953

BRIEF FOR THE
APPELLANTS AND
RESPONDENTS
ON REARGUMENT

all the privileges and immunities of citizens in the several States."[136]

Representative Bingham, who was contemporaneously amending the original Trumbull Civil Rights Bill because its broad anti-discrimination provisions lacked constitutional foundation, naturally did not dispute Representative Rogers' appraisal of the wide scope of H. R. 63. On the contrary, Representative Bingham two days later indicated his concurrence in that appraisal in the course of a colloquy with Representative Hale.

Representative Hale inquired of Representative Bingham whether his proposed constitutional amendment did not "confer upon Congress a general power of legislation for the purpose of securing to all persons in the several states protection of life, liberty and property, subject only to the qualification that the protection shall be equal." And Representative Bingham replied, "I believe it does …"

In order to nail down the precise source of the proposed grant of power, Representative Hale then asked Representative Bingham to "point me to that clause or part … which contains the doctrine he here announces?" To which the answer was, "The words 'equal protection,' contain it, and nothing else."[137]

The House at the end of February was preoccupied with debating Reconstruction generally as well as the Civil Rights Bill, and it showed itself in no hurry to take up Bingham's proposal, especially since it was obvious that a more comprehensive measure would soon be forthcoming from the Joint Committee. Following the debate on February 28, the House postponed further consideration of the proposed amendment until mid-April.[138] In fact, "H. R. 63" was not to be heard from in that form again. Yet its protective scope presently passed into the more extensive proposal which the Joint Committee brought forward at the end of April and which became, after some changes, the amendment which Congress finally submitted to the states.

During most of March and April, the Joint Committee paid little attention to the question of civil rights. It was concerned, for a time, with the question of the admission of Tennessee; then, for a time, it appears to have been inactive. Not until late April did it resume sessions looking forward to the drafting of a comprehensive constitutional amendment on Reconstruction. On April 21, Stevens offered to the committee a draft of a proposed constitutional amendment, covering civil rights, representation, Negro suffrage and the repudiation of the "rebel" debt.

This proposal became the frame upon which the Fourteenth Amendment was constructed. Most significant from our point of view was section 1:

"No discrimination shall be made by any state, nor by the United States, as to the civil rights of persons because of race, color, or previous condition of servitude."[139]

Section 2 provided that on and after July 4, 1876, no discrimination should be made between persons in the rights of suffrage on account of race, color, or previous condition of servitude. Section 3 provided that until that time, no class of persons against whom a state imposed suffrage discrimination because of race, color or previous condition of servitude should be included in the state's basis of representation. Section 4 invalidated the "rebel" debt. Section 5, which passed substantially intact into the Fourteenth Amendment, provided that Congress was to have the power to enforce the provisions of the amendment by appropriate legislation.[140]

Section 1 was to pass through several critical changes in the next few days. Almost at once, Senator Bingham moved to have the following provision added to section 1:

"… nor shall any state deny to any person within its jurisdiction the equal protection of the laws, nor take private property for public use without just compensation."[141]

It will be noticed that Bingham's suggestion had within it the substance of the equal protection clause of the Fourteenth Amendment. After some discussion, the committee voted this suggestion down, seven to five.

Other changes followed. After some further discussion, Bingham moved that the following be added as a new section of the amendment:

"No state shall make or enforce any law which shall abridge the privileges or immunities of citizens of the United States; nor shall any state deprive any person of life, liberty or property without due process of law; nor

---

[136] Cong. Globe, 39th Cong., 1st Sess., App. 134 (1865–1866).
[137] Id. at 1094.
[138] Id. at 1095.
[139] KENDRICK, op. cit. supra n. 82, at 83.
[140] Ibid.
[141] Id. at 85.

deny to any person within its jurisdiction the equal protection of the laws."[142]

This was substantially Bingham's earlier amendment, submitted to Congress in February as H. R. 63 with the addition of the equal protection clause. One significant difference lay in the fact that Bingham's new section did not confer power upon Congress to legislate; instead, it made privileges and immunities, due process and equal protection constitutional guarantees against state interference.

F. The Republican majority in the 39th Congress was determined to prevent future Congresses from diminishing federal protection of these rights

There were two rather obvious reasons for Senator Bingham's last two amendments. First, a number of committee members had earlier expressed some concern over the phraseology of H. R. 63 because it allowed Congress to refuse to enforce the guarantees if it saw fit. The Radical Republicans were openly fearful lest later and more conservative Congresses destroy their work.[143] But direct constitutional guarantees would be beyond the power of Congress to impair or destroy. Second, Bingham was acting with the knowledge that section 5 of the proposed amendment already granted Congress full power to legislate to enforce the guarantees of the amendment. In other words, the Radical Republicans had no thought of stripping Congress of the power to enforce the amendment by adequate legislation. They put the guarantees themselves beyond the reach of a hostile Congress.[144]

The Committee at once adopted Representative Bingham's suggested addition by a vote of ten to two.[145] Four days later, however, on April 25, the Committee on Williams' motion, struck out Bingham's latest suggested revision, only Stevens, Bingham, Morrill, Rogers and Blow voting to retain it.[146] On April 28, in the final stages of committee discussion, Bingham moved to strike out section 1, reading "no discrimination shall be made …" and insert his proposal of April 21 in its place. Although the Committee had voted only three days earlier to kill Bingham's proposal entirely, it now passed his new motion.[147] Thus, Bingham's proposal ultimately became section 1 of the amendment which the Committee now submitted to Congress. As such, and with the addition of the citizenship clause adopted from the Civil Rights

Act of 1866, it was to pass into the Fourteenth Amendment as finally accepted by Congress.

On April 30, Representative Stevens introduced the text of the Committee's proposed amendment in the House of Representatives. As presented, the amendment differed in two particulars from the Fourteenth Amendment as finally adopted: the first section as yet did not contain the citizenship clause; and the third section carried a clause for the complete disfranchisement of Confederate supporters until 1870. An accompanying resolution proposed to make successful ratification of the amendment, together with ratification by the several southern states, a condition precedent to the readmission of the southern states to representation in Congress.[148]

On May 8, Stevens opened debate in the House on the proposed amendment. In a sharp speech he emphasized the legislative power of Congress under the proposed amendment:

> "I can hardly believe that any person can be found who will not admit that every one of these provisions [in the first section] is just. They are all asserted, in some form or other, in our DECLARATION or organic law. But the Constitution limits only the action of Congress, and is not a limitation on the States. This amendment supplies that defect, and allows Congress to correct the unjust legislation of the States, so far that the law which operates upon one man shall operate *equally* upon all. Whatever law punishes a white man for a crime, shall punish the black man precisely in the same way and to the same degree. Whatever law protects the white man shall afford 'equal' protection to the black man."[149]

The amendment, he added, was made necessary by the "oppressive codes" which had become law in the southern states. "Unless the Constitution should restrain them, those States will all, I fear, keep up this discrimination and crush to death the hated freedmen."[150]

---

[142] *Id.* at 87.

[143] See speeches of Representatives Garfield, Broomall, Eldridge, and Stevens and Senator Howard, Cong. Globe, 39th Cong., 1st Sess. 2459, 2462, 2498, 2506, 2896 (1865–1866).

[144] See for example Stevens's explanations on the reasons for reenforcing the Civil Rights Act by constitutional guarantees. *Id.* at 2459.

[145] KENDRICK, *op. cit. supra* n. 82, at 87.

[146] *Id.* at 98.

[147] *Id.* at 106.

[148] Cong. Globe, 39th Cong., 1st Sess. 2459 (1866).

[149] *Ibid.* (italics in original).

[150] *Ibid.*

U.S. SUPREME
COURT,
OCTOBER 1953

BRIEF FOR THE
APPELLANTS AND
RESPONDENTS
ON REARGUMENT

Finally, he stated that the purpose of section 1 was to place the Civil Rights Act beyond the reach of a hostile Congress:

"Some answer, 'Your civil rights bill secures the same things.' That is partly true, but a law is repealable by a majority. And I need hardly say that the first time that the South with their copperhead allies obtain the command of Congress it will be repealed … This amendment once adopted cannot be annulled without two-thirds of Congress. That they will hardly get."[151]

There was general agreement among subsequent speakers that one of the purposes of section 1 of the amendment was to reinforce the Civil Rights Act. Enemies of the proposed amendment charged that Radical Republicans, having forced through what was an unconstitutional statute, were now attempting to clear up the constitutional issue by writing the statute into the supreme law.[152]

The Radical Republicans refused to admit that they were attempting to cover up the passage of an unconstitutional statute. Instead, they insisted that one of the purposes of the present proposed amendment was to place the guarantees of the Civil Rights Act beyond attack by future Congresses unfriendly to the rights of the freedman. "The Civil Rights Bill is now part of the law of this land," said Representative James A. Garfield of Ohio in defending the amendment. "But every gentleman knows it will cease to be a part of the law whenever the sad moment arrives when that gentleman's party comes into power … For this reason, and not because I believe the civil rights bill to be unconstitutional, I am glad to see that first section here."[153] Representative John Broomall of Ohio, making the same point, said, "If we are already safe with the civil rights bill, it will do no harm to become the more effectually so, and to prevent a mere majority from repealing the law and thus thwarting the will of the loyal people." Broomall pointed out, also, that no less a friend of the Negro than Representative John A. Bingham, had entertained grave doubts as to the constitutionality of the measure, and thought a constitutional amendment necessary. He disagreed, Broomall said, with Bingham's doubts, but he was not so sure of himself that he felt justified "in refusing to place the power to enact the law unmistakably in the Constitution."[154]

Probably other moderate Republicans agreed with Representative Henry J. Raymond of New York who had voted against the Civil Rights bill because he "regarded it as very doubtful, to say the least, whether Congress, under the existing Constitution had any power to enact such a law. …" But he nonetheless had heartily favored the principles and objectives of the bill, and because he still favored "securing an equality of rights to all citizens" he would vote "very cheerfully" for the present amendment.[155]

There was little discussion during the debate in the House of the scope of the civil rights which would be protected by the proposed amendment, apparently because both sides realized that debate on the original Civil Rights Bill had exhausted the issue. The indefatigable Rogers, fighting to the last against any attempt to guarantee rights for the Negro, repeatedly reminded Congress that the amendment would sweep the entire range of civil rights under the protection of the Federal Government and so work a revolution in the constitutional system.[156]

Although it was not necessary to answer Rogers, Bingham reminded Congress:

"The necessity for the first section of this amendment to the Constitution, Mr. Speaker, is one of the lessons that have been taught to your committee and taught to all the people of this country by the history of the past four years of terrific conflict—that history in which God is, and in which He teaches the profoundest lessons to men and nations. There was a want hitherto, and there remains a want now, in the Constitution of our country, which the proposed amendment will supply. What is that? It is the power in the people, the whole people of the United States, by express authority of the Constitution to

---

[151] *Ibid.*
[152] Representative William Finck of Ohio asserted, for example, that "all I have to say about this section is, that if it is necessary to adopt it … then the civil rights bill, which the President vetoed, was passed without authority and was clearly unconstitutional." *Id.* at 2461. Representative Benjamin Boyer of Pennsylvania, another enemy of the amendment, after observing that "the first section embodies the principles of the civil rights bill," twitted the Republicans for seeking to rectify their own constitutional error and attacked the present amendment as "objectionable, also, in its phraseology, being open to ambiguity and admitting the conflicting constructions." *Id.* at 2467. Representative Charles Eldridge of Wisconsin asked ironically, "What necessity is there, then, for this amendment if that bill was constitutional at the time of its passage?" *Id.* at 2506.
[153] *Id.* at 2462.
[154] *Id.* at 2498.
[155] *Id.* at 2502.
[156] *Id.* at 2537.

do that by congressional enactment which hitherto they have not had the power to do, and have never even attempted to do; that is, to protect by national law the privileges and immunities of all the citizens of the Republic and the inborn rights of every person within its jurisdiction whenever the same shall be abridged or denied by the unconstitutional acts of any State.

Allow me, Mr. Speaker, in passing, to say that this amendment takes from no State any right that ever pertained to it. No State ever had the right, under the forms of law or otherwise, to deny to any freeman the equal protection of the laws or to abridge the privileges or immunities of any citizen of the Republic, although many of them have assumed and exercised the power, and that without remedy."[157]

G. Congress understood that while the Fourteenth Amendment would give authority to Congress to enforce its provisions, the amendment in and of itself would invalidate all class legislation by the states

On May 10, the House passed the amendment without modification by a vote of 128 to 37. The measure then went to the Senate.[158]

On the same day, Senator Howard opened the debate in the Senate. Speaking for the Joint Committee because of Senator Fessenden's illness, Howard gave a broad interpretation of the first section of the proposed amendment. He emphasized the scope of legislative power which Congress would possess in the enforcement of the Amendment.

"How will it be done under the present amendment? As I have remarked, they are not [at present] powers granted to Congress, and therefore it is necessary, if they are to be effectuated and enforced, as they assuredly ought to be, that additional power be given to Congress to that end. This is done by the fifth section of this amendment which declares that 'the Congress shall have power to enforce by appropriate legislation the provisions of this article.' Here is a direct affirmative delegation of power to Congress to carry out all the principles of all these guarantees, a power not found in the Constitution."[159]

Senator Howard's interpretation of the legislative power of Congress under the proposed amendment makes it obvious that the Joint Committee, in separating the guarantees of civil rights from the congressional power to legislate thereon, had not at all intended to weaken the legislative capacity of Congress to enforce the rights conferred by the amendment. The guarantees, however, no longer depended upon congressional fiat alone for their effectiveness as they had in Bingham's proposed civil rights amendment of January (H. R. 63). But in Howard's view and that of the Committee, this meant merely that future Congresses could not destroy the rights conferred.

Senator Howard then passed to an equally expansive interpretation of the due process and equal protection clauses of the amendment:

"The last two clauses of the first section of the amendment disabled a State from depriving not merely a citizen of the United States, but any person, whoever he may be, of life, liberty, or property without due process of law or from denying to him the equal protection of the laws of the State. *This abolishes all class legislation in the States and does away with the injustice of subjecting one caste of persons to a code not applicable to another.* It prohibits the hanging of a black man for a crime for which the white man is not to be hanged. It protects the black man in his fundamental rights as a citizen with the same shield which it throws over the white man."[160] (Italics added.)

The only class of rights, Howard added, which were not conferred by the first section of the amendment was "the right of suffrage." Howard concluded this analysis by asserting that the entire first section, taken in conjunction with the legislative power of Congress conferred in section five, was of epoch-making importance:

"I look upon the first section, taken in connection with the fifth, as very important. It will, if adopted by the States, forever disable everyone of them from passing laws trenching upon those fundamental rights and privileges which pertain to citizens of the United States, and to all persons who may happen to be within their jurisdiction. It establishes equality before the law, and it gives to the humblest, the poorest, the most despised of the race the same rights and the same protection before the law as it gives to the most powerful, the most wealthy, or the most haughty. That, sir, is republican government, as I understand it, and the only one which can claim the praise of a just Government."[161]

---

[157] *Id.* at 2542.

[158] *Id.* at 2545.

[159] *Id.* at 2766.

[160] *Id.* at 2766.

[161] *Id.* at 2766.

U.S. SUPREME
COURT,
OCTOBER 1953

BRIEF FOR THE
APPELLANTS AND
RESPONDENTS
ON REARGUMENT

Thus, Senator Howard understood that due process and equal protection would sweep away entirely "all class legislation" in the states. By implication, he subscribed to a "substantive interpretation" of due process of law, thus making due process a limitation upon state governments to subvert civil liberties.

No Senator thereafter challenged these sweeping claims for the efficacy of the civil rights portion of Section 1. Howard's allies subscribed enthusiastically to his interpretation. Senator Luke Poland of Vermont, a staunch Radical Republican, regarded the amendment as necessary to set to rest all questions of congressional competence in enacting the civil rights bill:

> "Congress has already shown its desire and intention to uproot and destroy all such partial State legislation in the passage of what is called the civil rights bill. The power of Congress to do this has been doubted and denied by persons entitled to high considera tion. It certainly seems desirable that no doubt should be left existing as to the power of Congress to enforce principles lying at the very foundation of all republican government if they be denied or violated by the States. . . ."[162]

Certainly the Conservatives in the Senate agreed altogether with Senator Howard and the other Senate Republicans about the sweeping impact which the prospective amendment would have upon state caste legislation. Senator Thomas Hendricks of Indiana, in condemning the legislative power to enforce the amendment which Congress would acquire from the operation of section 5, said that these words had

> "… such force and scope of meaning as that Congress might invade the jurisdiction of the States, rob them of their reserved rights, and crown the Federal Government with absolute and despotic power. As construed this provision is most dangerous."[163]

The prospective amendment moved forward rapidly in the Senate, with comparatively little debate. The Radical Republicans were confident of their objectives. The conservative Republicans and Democrats despaired of arresting the tide of events. One significant change occurred on May 30 when Howard brought forward the citizenship clause of the Civil Rights Act and successfully moved it as an amendment to section 1. Few Republicans doubted that Congress already had the power to legislate upon the question of citizenship. However, the new provision cleared up a serious hiatus in the original

Constitution by settling in unequivocal fashion the definition of national and state citizenship. Needless to say, the new provision, like its predecessor in the Civil Rights Act, specifically endowed Negroes with citizenship and reversed the dictum of the *Dred Scott* case that no Negro could be a citizen of the United States.

The Radical Republicans were well aware that by endowing the Negro with citizenship, they strengthened his claim to the entire scope of civil rights. Bingham had mentioned as much in debate in the House, while Representative Raymond of New York had added that once the Negro became a citizen, it would not be possible in a republican government to deny him any right or to impose upon him any restriction, even including that of suffrage. The force of this stratagem did not escape the Conservatives in the Senate. Senator Garrett Davis of Kentucky had this to say of the citizenship provision of the amendment:

> "The real and only object of the first provision of this section, which the Senate has added to it, is to make Negroes citizens, to prop the civil rights bill, and give them a more plausible, if not a valid, claim to its provisions, and to press them forward to a full community of civil and political rights with the white race, for which its authors are struggling and mean to continue to struggle."[164]

The Senate passed the amendment in June, 33 to 11. Congress formally proposed the amendment on June 13 and it was submitted to the states.

Congress intended to destroy all class distinctions in law What, then, may one conclude concerning the intent of Congress with regard to segregation in the framing of the amendment?

Both Senator Howard and Representative Stevens made it definitely clear that the scope of the rights guaranteed by the amendment was much greater than that embraced in the Civil Rights Act.

It is evident that the members of the Joint Committee intended to place all civil rights within the protection of the Federal Government and to deny the states any power to interfere with those rights on the basis of color. The scope of the concept of liberties entertained by the

---

[162] *Id.* at 2961.

[163] *Id.* at 2940.

[164] *Id.* at App. 240.

Committee was very broad. The breadth of this concept was recognized by this Court in all of its decisions up to *Plessy v. Ferguson*.

In adopting the Civil Rights Act of 1866, Congress had enumerated the rights protected. This was done because Bingham and others doubted that Congress had the power to take all civil liberties under federal protection. Unrestricted by this consideration in drafting a constitutional provision, Congress used broad comprehensive language to define the standards necessary to guarantee complete federal protection. This was promptly recognized by this Court in one of the earliest decisions construing the Amendment when it was held: "The 14th Amendment makes no effort to enumerate the rights it designs to protect. It speaks in general terms, and those are as comprehensive as possible." *Strauder v. West Virginia*, 100 U.S. 303, 310.

Did Congress specifically intend to ban state laws imposing segregation by race? And more specifically, did it intend to prohibit segregation in school systems, even where a state provided a separate but equal system for Negroes? To begin with it must be recognized that the "separate but equal" doctrine was yet to be born. The whole tenor of the dominant argument in Congress was at odds with any governmentally enforced racial segregation as a constitutionally permissible state practice.

Senator Howard, among others, asserted categorically that the effect of the due process and equal protection clauses of the Fourteenth Amendment would be to sweep away entirely all caste legislation in the United States. Certainly a number of Conservatives, notably Representative Rogers of New Jersey, a member of the Joint Committee and Senator Davis of Kentucky, were convinced that the effect of the amendment would be to prohibit entirely all laws classifying or segregating on the basis of race. They believed, and stated, that school laws providing separate systems for whites and Negroes of the kind which existed in Pennsylvania, Ohio and in several of the Johnson–Reconstructed southern states would be made illegal by the amendment.

It is notable that while there were some assurances extended by Radical Republicans to the Moderates and Conservatives as to the scope of the Civil Rights Act of 1866 in this regard, there were no such assurances in the debates on the Fourteenth Amendment.

The Republican majority realized full well that it could not envisage all possible future applications of the amendment to protect civil rights. By separating section 1 of the amendment, which provides an absolute federal constitutional guarantee for those rights, from section 5, which endows Congress with legislative capacity to protect such rights, the framers of the amendment assured continued protection of these rights, by making it possible to win enforcement of them in the courts and eliminated the power of Congress alone to diminish them.

H. The treatment of public education or segregation in public schools during the 39th Congress must be considered in the light of the status of public education at that time

Although today, compulsory free public education is universally regarded as a basic, appropriate governmental function, there was no such unanimity existing at the time the Fourteenth Amendment was adopted. Arrayed against those who then visualized education as vital to effective government, there were many who still regarded education as a purely private function.

While it has already been shown that the conception of equal protection of the laws and due process of law, developed by the Abolitionists before the Civil War, was so broad that it would necessarily cover such educational segregation as is now before this Court, compulsory public education at that time was the exception rather than the rule. The conception of universal compulsory free education was not established throughout the states in 1866. The struggle for such education went on through most of the 19th century and, even where accepted in principle in some of the states, it sometimes was not fully put into practice.

Prior to the first quarter of the nineteenth century childhood education was considered an individual private responsibility.[165] The period 1830–1860 was one of marked educational advancement. It has commonly been termed as the era of the Common School Revival, a movement to extend and improve facilities for general education. This movement flourished in New England under the leadership of Horace Mann, Henry Barnard and others. There was a definite tendency throughout the country to shift from

U.S. SUPREME COURT, OCTOBER 1953

BRIEF FOR THE APPELLANTS AND RESPONDENTS ON REARGUMENT

---

[165] CUBBERLY, A BRIEF HISTORY OF EDUCATION, cc. XXV–XXVI (1920).

U.S. SUPREME
COURT,
OCTOBER 1953

BRIEF FOR THE
APPELLANTS AND
RESPONDENTS
ON REARGUMENT

private to public support of education and this trend extended to normal schools and facilities for secondary and higher education. Many states, urged on by educational leaders, publicists and statesmen, began making legislative provisions for public education.

On the other hand, these gains have been commonly exaggerated and in some respects misinterpreted. The laws were by no means always carried into effect and the recommendations of the reformers were, in most instances, accepted with great hesitancy.[166] Another authority after appraising public education during the period just prior to the Civil War made the following generalizations:

> "Practically all the states were making substantial progress in the development of systems of public education. (2) At the close of the period no single state can be said to have been providing any large percentage of its children and youth with schools well-supported and well-taught. (3) The facilities for secondary education were by no means as extensive as has commonly been reported. (4) Regional differences in educational development have been exaggerated; and (5) where sectional differences in school support and attendance did exist they appear to have been due more to differentials in urban and rural development than to differences in social attitudes and philosophies."[167]

In general, it should be noted that in New England and in New York the main problem during this period was to improve the educational systems which had already been established and to secure additional support for them. In the Middle Atlantic states the major problem was to establish systems of public schools and to provide effective public education. In the West, the prevailing political and social philosophy required that at least some degree of education be provided to as large an element of the population as possible.

Public education was much slower in getting under way in the South. In most of the southern states, despite some promising beginnings, an educational system was not created until after the close of the Civil War. One historian concluded:

> "... although the 'common school awakening' which took place in the Northern States after Horace Mann began his work in Massachusetts (1837) was felt in some of the Southern States as well, and although some very commendable beginnings had been made in a few of these States before 1860, the

establishment of state educational systems in the South was in reality the work of the period following the close of the Civil War. The coming of this conflict, evident for a decade before the storm broke, tended to postpone further educational development."[168]

Public education in the South made progress only after it became acceptable as being compatible with its ideal of a white aristocracy.[169]

Among the factors responsible for this condition were the aristocratic attitude which held that it was not necessary to educate the masses, the reluctance of the people to tax themselves for educational purposes, the marked individualism of the people, born of isolation, and the imperfect state of social and political institutions. Most southerners saw little or no relation between education and life. Consequently, the view prevailed that those who could afford education could indulge themselves in securing it and those who could not afford it lost little, if anything. This southern attitude was aptly summed up fifteen years after the close of the war by the statement of Virginia's Governor F. W. M. Holliday that public schools were "a luxury ... to be paid for like any other luxury, by the people who wish their benefits."[170] Education in the South was not so much a process of individual and community improvement as it was an experience that carried with it a presumption of social equality for those who shared it, a view hardly compatible with any notion of universal education which included persons of diverse social and ethnic backgrounds.

Between 1840 and 1860, public education began to advance in the South but its benefits were denied Negroes. It is significant that racist and other types of intolerant legislation increased markedly during this period. While education could be extended to all whites who, for political purposes, belonged to one big happy family, there was nothing in such a conception that suggested that Negroes should be included.[171] The editor of the authoritative antebellum organ of southern opinion, *DeBow's*

---

[166] EDWARDS AND RICHEY, THE SCHOOL IN THE SOCIAL ORDER 421 (1947).

[167] *Id.* at 423.

[168] CUBBERLY, PUBLIC EDUCATION IN THE UNITED STATES 251 (1919).

[169] EDWARDS AND RICHEY, *op. cit. supra* n. 166, at 434.

[170] Quoted in WOODWARD, ORIGINS OF THE NEW SOUTH 61 (1951).

[171] DEBOW, THE INTEREST IN SLAVERY OF THE SOUTHERN NON-SLAVEHOLDER 3–12 (1860).

Review, summed up the matter of education for Negroes during slavery as follows: "Under the institution of slavery we used to teach them everything nearly except to read."[172]

The framers of the Fourteenth Amendment were familiar with public education, therefore, only as a developing concept. We have already demonstrated that they were determined to eliminate all governmentally imposed racial distinctions—sophisticated as well as simple minded—and expressed their views in the broadest and most conclusive terms. The intentions they expressed were definitely broad enough to proscribe state imposed racial distinctions in public education as they knew it, and the language which they used in the Fourteenth Amendment was broad enough to forever bar racial distinctions in whatever public educational system the states might later develop.

Furthermore, the framers intended that Congress would have the power under section 5 to provide additional sanctions, civil and criminal, against persons who attempted to enforce states statutes made invalid by section 1 of the Amendment. As stated above, Representative Bingham purposely revised an earlier draft of the Amendment so that the prohibitions of section 1 would be self-executing against state statutes repugnant thereto and would be beyond the threat of hostile Congressional action seeking to repeal civil rights legislation. In other words, the judicial power to enforce the prohibitory effect of section 1 was not made dependent upon Congressional action.

Thus, the exercise of this Court's judicial power does not await precise Congressional legislation. This Court has repeatedly declared invalid state statutes which conflicted with section 1 of the Fourteenth Amendment, even though Congress had not acted.[173] For example,

---

[172] REPORT OF THE JOINT COMMITTEE ON RECONSTRUCTION, 39th Cong., 1st Sess., Pt. IV, 135 (1866).

[173] Of course, Title 8 provides a remedy in law or equity against any person acting under color of State law who deprives anyone within the jurisdiction of the United States of rights secured by the Federal Constitution or laws. It provides: "Every person who, under color of any statute, ordinance, regulation, custom, or usage, of any State or Territory, subjects, or causes to be subjected, any citizen of the United States or other person within the jurisdiction thereof to the deprivation of any rights, privileges, or immunities secured by the Constitution and laws, shall be liable to the party injured in an action at law, suit in equity, or other proper proceeding for redress." 8 U.S.C. § 43.

there is no federal statute to the effect that a state which permits released time for religious instructions is acting in a way prohibited by the Fourteenth Amendment. This Court, nevertheless, held that such state action conflicted with section 1 of the Fourteenth Amendment and directed the trial court to enjoin the continuance of the proscribed state action. *Illinois ex rel. McCollum v. Board of Education,* 333 U.S. 203.

Similarly, this Court has acted to redress violations of constitutional rights, even in the absence of specific Congressional statute, in a long series of cases involving the rights of freedom of expression and freedom of worship under the Fourteenth Amendment. See *e.g., De Jonge v. Oregon,* 299 U.S. 353. And this Court has often vindicated the constitutional rights of members of minority groups in the area of public education in the absence of any Congressional statute. *Sweatt v. Painter, supra.*

Indeed, this rule has been applied in all areas in which the prohibitory effect of section 1 has been employed by the Court. *E.g., Miller v. Schoene,* 276 U.S. 272; *McCardle v. Indianapolis Water Co.,* 272 U.S. 400. To now hold Congressional action a condition precedent to judicial action would be to stultify the provisions in the Federal Constitution protecting the rights of minorities. In effect, this Court would be holding that action by a state against an unpopular minority which the Constitution prohibits cannot be judicially restrained unless the unpopular minority convinces a large majority (the whole country as represented in Congress) that a forum in which to ask relief should be provided for the precise protection they seek.

I. During the congressional debates on proposed legislation which culminated in the Civil Rights Act of 1875 veterans of the thirty-ninth Congress adhered to their conviction that the Fourteenth Amendment had proscribed segregation in public schools

At various times during the 1870's, Congress considered bills for implementing the Fourteenth Amendment as well as the Civil Rights Act of 1866. Debate on these measures was on occasion extremely significant, since it gave members of Congress an opportunity to express themselves as to the meaning and scope of the Amendment. These observations were the more significant in that perhaps two-fifths of the members of both Houses in the early seventies were veterans of the Thirty-ninth Congress

U.S. SUPREME COURT, OCTOBER 1953

BRIEF FOR THE APPELLANTS AND RESPONDENTS ON REARGUMENT

U.S. SUPREME
COURT,
OCTOBER 1953

BRIEF FOR THE
APPELLANTS AND
RESPONDENTS
ON REARGUMENT

which had formulated the Amendment. More-over, the impact of the Amendment upon segregated schools had by this time moved into the public consciousness so that Congressmen now had an opportunity to say specifically what they thought about the validity under the Amendment of state statutes imposing segregation upon public school systems.

The second session of the Forty-second Congress, which convened in December, 1871, soon found itself involved in a fairly extended discussion of the effect of the Fourteenth Amendment upon racial segregation, particularly in school systems. Early in the session the Senate took under consideration an amnesty bill to restore the political rights of ex-Confederate officials in accordance with the provisions of section 3 of the Amendment. On December 20, Senator Sumner of Massachusetts, now a veteran champion of the rights of the Negro, moved the following as an amendment to the measure under consideration:

> "Section—That all citizens of the United States, without distinction of race, color, or previous condition of servitude, are entitled to the equal and impartial enjoyment of any accommodation, advantage, facility, or privilege furnished by common carriers, whether on land or water; by inn-keepers; by licensed owners, managers, or lessees of theaters or other places of public amusement; by trustees, commissioners, superintendents, teachers, or other officers of common schools and other public institutions of learning, the same being supported or authorized by law ... and this right shall not be denied or abridged on any pretense of race, color, or previous condition of servitude."[174]

Here was a provision, which if adopted would commit Congress to the proposition that under the Fourteenth Amendment it could do away entirely with state school statutes providing for segregated school systems. Sumner attacked school segregation at length. The public school, he asserted, "must be open to all or its designation is a misnomer and a mockery. It is not a school for whites or a school for blacks, but a school for all; in other words a common school for all." Segregation he called an "odius discrimination" and an "ill-disguised violation of the principle of Equality."[175]

In the debate that followed, it was apparent that a large majority of the Republicans in the Senate were convinced that Congress quite appropriately might enact such legislation in accordance with section 5 of the Fourteenth Amendment.

Senator Carpenter of Wisconsin, one of the best constitutional lawyers in the Upper House, was doubtful of the constitutionality of Sumner's measure insofar as it applied to churches. But he had no doubt on the authority of Congress to guarantee the right of all persons, regardless of race or color, to attend public schools, to use transportation facilities, and the like, and he offered a resolution of his own to this end.[176] Even the conservative Kentuckian Garrett Davis admitted that there was no question of congressional competence under the Amendment to guarantee these rights as against state action, though he challenged the validity of any statute protecting rights against private discrimination.[177] And Senator Stevenson of Kentucky, another strong enemy of mixed schools, confined his attack to discussion of the evil involved in an attempt to "coerce social equality between the races in public schools, in hotels, in theatres. . . ."; he spoke not at all of constitutional objections.[178]

The real objection to Sumner's measure, however, was not the constitutionality of the measure itself, but the incongruity of its attachment as a rider to an amnesty bill, which required a two-thirds majority of both Houses of Congress. Nonetheless, the Senate, after extended debate, adopted Sumner's amendment, including the provision banning segregated schools, by a vote of 28–28, the ballot of the Vice President breaking the tie.[179] The amnesty measure itself later failed to obtain the necessary two-thirds majority of the Senate.

The impressive Senate support in favor of a bill which would have banned segregation in state school systems alarmed Conservatives in both Houses, who now began to advance, very deliberately, the idea that "separate but equal" facilities would be constitutional under the limitations of the equal protection clause of the Fourteenth Amendment. In the House, a few days after the defeat of the amnesty bill, Representative Frank Hereford of West Virginia

---

[174] Cong. Globe, 42nd Cong., 2nd Sess. 244 (1871).

[175] *Id.* at 383–384.

[176] *Id.* at 760.

[177] *Id.* at 764.

[178] *Id.* at 913.

[179] *Id.* at 919. The Senate vote on the amnesty bill was 33 to 19 in favor of the measure. *Id.* at 929.

offered the following resolution as an expression of conservative sentiment:

> "*Be it resolved,* That it would be contrary to the Constitution and a tyrannical usurpation of power for Congress to force mixed schools upon the States, and equally unconstitutional and tyrannical for Congress to pass any law interfering with churches, public carriers, or inn-keepers, such subjects of legislation belonging of right to the States respectively."

There was no debate on the Hereford resolution, which was put to an immediate vote and defeated, 85 to 61, 94 not voting.[180]

Later in the session, there was still further debate in the Senate concerning segregated schools. With a second amnesty bill up for consideration, Sumner on May 8 again moved an amendment providing:

> "That no citizen of the United States shall, by reason of race, color, or previous condition of servitude, be excepted or excluded from the full and equal enjoyment of any accommodation, advantage, facility, or privilege furnished by inn-keepers; by common carriers ... or ... by trustees, commissioners, superintendents, teachers, and other officers of common schools and other public institutions of learning, the same being supported by moneys derived from general taxation, or authorized by law... ."[181]

This proposal led to sharp debate and decided differences of opinion among the Republican majority. Senator Trumbull of Illinois, who was the author of the Civil Rights Act of 1866 and who had become decidedly more conservative in his political outlook since the early Reconstruction era, now insisted that the right to attend public schools was in any event not a civil right, so that Congress could not legislate on the subject under the Fourteenth Amendment. But Senator George Edmunds of Vermont, already known as a distinguished constitutional lawyer and who had entered the Senate in 1866 in time to participate in the debates on the Fourteenth Amendment, dissented sharply, insisting that the right to attend tax-supported public schools was a civil right and therefore subject to regulation by Congress.[182] Senator Morton taking the same view, insisted that "if the right to participate in these schools is to be governed by color, I say that it is a fraud upon those who pay the taxes." And he added that where there are public schools supported by common taxation upon everybody, white and black, then there is a civil right that there shall be equal participation in those schools.

Observing that the Ohio Supreme Court had but lately held constitutional a state statute providing for segregation in public schools, he argued that Congress was entirely competent under the Fourteenth Amendment to prohibit segregated schools.

Senator Arthur Boreman of West Virginia also took it as a matter of course that Congress had the power under the amendment to prohibit separate but equal facilities in school systems; he thought that Congress ought not to force the issue at present:

> "The time will come when ... these distinctions will pass away in all the States, when school laws will be passed without this question appearing upon the face of those laws; but it is not so now, and for the present I am willing to allow the laws of the State to remain as they are where they provide schools for both classes."[183]

At the close of the debate, the proponents of segregated school systems tried unsuccessfully to modify the Sumner measure to eliminate the requirement for mixed school systems. Senator Orris Ferry of Connecticut first moved to strike out entirely the provisions of the Sumner amendment which related to public school systems. This motion the Senate defeated 26 to 25.[184] Senator Francis P. Blair of Missouri then offered another amendment to allow "local option" elections within the states on the question of mixed versus segregated schools. Sumner, Edmunds and Howe all strongly condemned this proposal, which the border and southern Senators as strongly commended. The Blair amendment in turn met defeat, 23 to 30.[185] Finally, an amendment to strike out the first five sections of the Sumner measure, thereby completely destroying its effect, was defeated 29 to 29, with the Vice President casting a deciding negative vote.[186] The Senate then formally adopted the Sumner amendment to the amnesty bill, 28 to 28, with the Vice President voting in the affirmative.[187]

---

[180] *Id.* at 1582.

[181] *Id.* at 3181.

[182] *Id.* at 3190.

[183] *Id.* at 3195.

[184] *Id.* at 3256, 3258.

[185] *Id.* at 3262.

[186] *Id.* at 3264–3265.

[187] *Id.* at 3268. The amnesty bill itself subsequently received a favorable vote of 32 to 22, thereby failing to receive the necessary two-thirds majority. *Id.* at 3270.

U.S. SUPREME COURT, OCTOBER 1953

BRIEF FOR THE APPELLANTS AND RESPONDENTS ON REARGUMENT

U.S. SUPREME
COURT,
OCTOBER 1953

BRIEF FOR THE
APPELLANTS AND
RESPONDENTS
ON REARGUMENT

The conclusion seems inescapable that as of 1872 a substantial majority of the Republican Senators and perhaps half of the Senate at large believed that the prohibitions of the Fourteenth Amendment extended to segregated schools.

The authority of the judiciary to act in this field was specifically recognized and not disputed.[188] A significant number of the Senators in question, among them Edmunds, Howe, Sumner, Conkling, and Morrill, had been in Congress during the debates on the adoption of the Amendment, while Conkling and Morrill had been members of the Joint Committee. And Vice President Henry Wilson, who several times cast a deciding vote in favor of prohibiting segregated schools not only had been in Congress during the debates on the Amendment but had also authored one of the early civil rights bills of the Thirty-ninth Congress.

The first session of the Forty-third Congress, which opened in December, 1873, saw extended discussion of the issue of segregated schools in both Houses. On December 18, Representative Benjamin F. Butler of Massachusetts, chairman of the House Judiciary Committee and long one of the most outspoken leaders of the Radical faction of the Republican party, introduced the following measure from his committee:

> "... whoever, being a corporation or natural person and owner, or in charge of any public inn, or of any place of public amusement or entertainment for which a license from any legal authority is required, or of any line of stage-coaches, railroad, or other means of public carriage of passengers or freight, or of any cemetery or other benevolent institution, or any public school supported in whole or in part at public expense or by endowment for public use, shall make any distinction as to admission or accommodation therein of any citizen of the United States because of race, color, or previous condition of servitude, shall, on conviction thereof, be fined not less than $100 nor more than $5000 for each offense...."[189]

This measure inspired a somewhat bitter two-day debate early in January, 1874, during which the power of Congress to prohibit segregated schools received more attention than any other single issue involved. The most extended defense of the constitutionality of Butler's measure was made by Representative William Lawrence of Ohio, who began with the flat assertion that "Congress has the constitutional power to pass this bill." Denying that civil rights

were any longer in the exclusive care of the states, he asserted that since the passage of the Fourteenth Amendment, "if a state permits any inequality in rights to be created or meted out by citizens or corporations enjoying its protection, it denied the equal protection of laws." He then launched into an extended historical analysis of the debates in the Thirty-ninth Congress before and during the passage of the Amendment. He recalled Bingham's statement in opposition to the original extreme language of the Civil Rights bill, in which the Ohioan had said that the proper remedy for state violation of civil rights was to be achieved not by an "arbitrary assumption of power," but "by amending the Constitution of the United States expressly prohibiting the States from any such abuse of power in the future." He quoted Stevens' and Howard's speeches introducing the Amendment in Congress to show the broad purpose which they had represented to be the objectives of the Joint Committee. In some irony, he quoted various conservatives in the House, among them Finck, Boyer and Shanklin, who had asserted again and again that the Amendment would place all civil rights within the protective custody of the federal government.[190] Lawrence's speech was the more impressive in that he was a veteran of the Thirty-ninth Congress who had actively supported both the Civil Rights Act and the passage of the Fourteenth Amendment. Moreover, he was held in great respect in Congress as an able jurist and constitutional lawyer.[191]

The most extended argument in opposition to Lawrence was advanced by Representative Roger Q. Mills of Texas, who presented the contention that civil rights, in spite of the Fourteenth Amendment, were still entrusted entirely to the care of the states. Congress, he thought, had no right to touch the public school system of the several states. "The States," he said, "have ... [an] unquestioned right ... to establish universities, colleges, academies, and common schools, and govern them according to their own pleasure." He relied upon the narrow interpretation of the "privileges or immunities" clause of the Fourteenth Amendment recently

---

[188] *Id.* at 3192.

[189] 2 CONG. REC. 318 (1873–1874).

[190] *Id.* at 412 ff.

[191] 11 DICTIONARY, *op. cit. supra* n. 129, at 52. He was later the author of the statute creating the Department of Justice.

advanced by the Supreme Court in the *Slaughter House Cases* as a new argument in support of his contention. And he finished with the warning, not entirely unheard in the twentieth century, that if Congress passed any such measure as the Butler bill, "the Legislatures of every State where the white people have control will repeal the common-school laws."[192] At the end of debate, Butler's bill was recommitted on the motion of its sponsor, and was not heard of again during the session.

More significant events were occurring in the Senate. On December 2, Sumner had once more presented his now well-known civil rights measure, this time as an independent Senate bill instead of a proposed amendment to an amnesty resolution.[193] This bill finally came up for debate in late April and May, although Sumner himself had died in March. Conkling of New York, Boutwell of Massachusetts, Howe of Wisconsin, Edmunds of Vermont, and Frelinghuysen of New Jersey all gave it very effective support in debate.[194]

In a strong speech, Senator Frelinghuysen pointed out that a variety of conflicting state decisions had introduced some confusion into the question of whether or not state statutes setting up segregated school systems were constitutional under the Amendment. The present measure, he thought, would destroy "injurious agitation" on that subject. There could be no question of the constitutional power of Congress to enact the bill; the "privileges or immunities" and "the equal protection" clauses, in particular, were especially germane to congressional power. And he pointed out that if the present bill became law, it would still be possible to pursue an informal voluntary segregation by the consent of both parents and school boards, where for a time that seemed advisable. But he added that segregated school systems established by law were in complete violation of the whole spirit of the Amendment; separate schools for colored people were inevitably inferior to those for whites. "Sir," he said in conclusion, "if we did not intend to make the colored race full citizens … we should have left them slaves."[195]

Senator Edmunds used both constitutional and pragmatic arguments in support of the bill. "What the Constitution authorizes us to do is to enforce equality," he said, "and … not half-equality, for there is no such thing as half-equality. It is entire equality or none at all." And

segregated schools imposed inequality on Negroes. He quoted figures from Georgia school statistics, to demonstrate that although forty-three percent of the children in that state were colored, there were nonetheless only 356 schools for colored children as against 1379 for whites. In the light of this kind of evidence, he thought, the duty of Congress was clear.[196]

Senator Boutwell declared that "opening the public schools of this country to every class and condition of people without distinction of race and color, is security … that … the rising … generations will advance to manhood with the fixed purpose of maintaining these principles [of the Republic]." Like Edmunds, he argued that segregation made either adequate or equal facilities impossible; there was not enough money in the South to support two school systems.[197]

Senator Howe asserted that "… I am of the opinion that the authority of Congress to issue these commands, to enact this bill into law, is as clear, as indisputable as its authority to lay taxes or do any other one thing referred to in the Constitution." Like Frelinghuysen he thought that voluntary segregation might exist in some places for a time without violating the amendment. "Open two school houses wherever you please;" he said, and "furnish in them equal accommodations and equal instruction, and the whites will for a time go by themselves, and the colored children will go by themselves for the same reason, because each will feel more at home by themselves than at present either can feel with the other. . . ." But legally segregated schools, he thought would not in fact be equal, and it was the duty of Congress to prohibit them.[198]

Senator Pease of Mississippi shortly before the bill was passed speaking in favor of the bill said in unequivocal terms:

> "The main objection that has been brought forward by the opponents of this bill is the objection growing out of mixed schools. . . . There has been a great revolution in public sentiment in the South during the last three

U.S. SUPREME COURT, OCTOBER 1953

BRIEF FOR THE APPELLANTS AND RESPONDENTS ON REARGUMENT

---

[192] 2 Cong. Rec. 383 ff. (1873–1874).

[193] *Id.* at 2.

[194] Boutwell and Conkling, it will be recalled, had both served as members of the Joint Committee.

[195] *Id.* at 3451–3455.

[196] *Id.* at 4173.

[197] *Id.* at 4116.

[198] *Id.* at 4151.

U.S. SUPREME
COURT,
OCTOBER 1953

BRIEF FOR THE
APPELLANTS AND
RESPONDENTS
ON REARGUMENT

or four years, and I believe that to-day a majority of the southern people are in favor of supporting, maintaining, and fostering a system of common education ... I believe that the people of the South so fully recognize this, that if this measure shall become a law, there is not a State south of Mason and Dixon's line that will abolish its school system. . . .

"...:" I say that whenever a State shall legislate that the races shall be separated, and that legislation is based upon color or race, there is a distinction made; it is a distinction the intent of which is to foster a concomitant of slavery and to degrade him. The colored man understands and appreciates his former condition; and when laws are passed that say that 'because you are a black man you shall have a separate school,' he looks upon that, and justly, as tending to degrade him. There is no equality in that.

"... because when this question is settled I want every college and every institution of learning in this broad land to be open to every citizen, that there shall be no discrimination."[199]

The opponents of the Sumner bill meantime had become aware of the epoch-making significance of the Supreme Court's decision in the *Slaughter House Cases,* and they leaned very heavily upon Justice Miller's opinion during the debate. Thurman of Ohio analysed the *Slaughter House Cases* at length to prove his former contention that the main body of civil rights was still in the custody of the states and that the present bill was unconstitutional."[200] Senator Henry Cooper of Tennessee, after citing Justice Miller's opinion to make the same constitutional point, asked the Republican majority, "... what good are you to accomplish thus by forcing the mixture of the races in schools?"[201] And Senator Saulsbury of Delaware, who, in 1866 had insisted that if Congress enacted the Fourteenth Amendment it would work an entire revolution in state-federal relations, now argued flatly that the Sumner bill was unconstitutional under Justice Miller's interpretation of the limited scope of the "privileges or immunities" clause of the Amendment.[202]

However, the Senate majority remained firm in its intention to pass the bill with the ban on segregated schools. At the close of debate, Senator Aaron Sargent of California presented an amendment that "nothing herein contained shall be construed to prohibit any State or school district from providing separate schools

for persons of different sex or color, where such separate schools are equal in all respects to others of the same grade established by such authority, and supported by an equal *pro rata* expenditure of school funds." This amendment the Senate promptly defeated, 21 to 26.[203] Senator McCreery then moved an amendment providing that "nothing herein contained shall be so construed as to apply to schools already established." This, too, met defeat, mustering but eleven "ayes" in its support.[204] Immediately after this, the Senate, on May 22, passed the Sumner bill, by a vote of 29 to 16, and sent it to the House.[205]

Again the conclusion with respect to congressional intent as regards segregated schools seems fairly clear: a majority of the Senate in the Forty-third Congress, under control of leaders, a number of whom had supported the passage of the Fourteenth Amendment eight years earlier, thought Congress had the constitutional power to ban segregated schools and that it would be good national policy to do so.[206]

Congress adjourned before the House could take action on the Sumner bill, so that the measure carried over to the second session of the Congress, beginning in December, 1874. And now occurred a curious anticlimax with respect to the prohibition of segregated schools; Congress speedily enacted what virtually amounted to the Sumner bill of 1874 into law, but with the provision banning segregated schools eliminated from the bill.

The critical action occurred in the House of Representatives, where Butler on December 16 introduced what amounted to a somewhat modified draft of the measure passed by the Senate the previous spring. The constitutional debates produced little that was new. It was apparent that Congress by virtue of Section 5 had the constitutional power to take all civil liberties under its protection. Representative

---

[199] *Id.* at 4153–4154.

[200] *Id.* at 4089.

[201] *Id.* at 4154.

[202] *Id.* at 4159.

[203] *Id.* at 4167.

[204] *Id.* at 4171.

[205] *Id.* at 4176.

[206] Flack long ago reached a similar conclusion, that the great majority in Congress who voted for Sumner's bill "fully believed they had the power to pass it." "Of all the evidence," he said, "only a very minor part of it against this conclusion." FLACK, *op. cit. supra* n. 79, at 271.

Robert Hale of New York, a veteran of the Thirty-ninth Congress, twitted Finck of Ohio for his fallible memory in forgetting so conveniently that in 1866, he had solemnly warned that the impending amendment would place all civil rights under federal protection.[207]

Whatever may be said about the quantum or quality of Congressional debates on one side or the other no one can deny that the 39th Congress opened with a determination on the part of the Radical Republican majority to deprive the states of all power to maintain racial distinctions in governmental functions. No one can gainsay that this determination permeated the 39th Congress and continued through the passage adoption of the Fourteenth Amendment. The debates and all of the related materials show conclusively that the Fourteenth Amendment effectively gave constitutional sanction to the principle that states are thereby deprived of all power to enforce racial distinctions in governmental functions including public schools.

II. THERE IS CONVINCING EVIDENCE THAT THE STATE LEGISLATURES AND CONVENTIONS WHICH RATIFIED THE FOURTEENTH AMENDMENT CONTEMPLATED AND UNDERSTOOD THAT IT PROHIBITED STATE LEGISLATION WHICH WOULD REQUIRE RACIAL SEGREGATION IN PUBLIC SCHOOLS

The Fourteenth Amendment was submitted to the states for consideration on June 16, 1866. 14 Stat. 358. It was deliberated by thirty-seven states and ratified by thirty-three.[208] We urge that the evidence with respect to the states' understanding indicates that three-fourths of the states understood and contemplated the Amendment to forbid legislation compelling the assignment of white and Negro youth to separate schools.

---

[207] 3 Cong. Rec. 979, 980 (1875).

[208] The ratifying states included twenty free or non-slaveholding states (Connecticut, New Hampshire, New Jersey, Oregon, Vermont, New York, Ohio, Illinois, Kansas, Maine, Nevada, Indiana, Minnesota, Rhode Island, Wisconsin, Pennsylvania, Michigan, Massachusetts, Nebraska and Iowa), two former slave-holding but loyal states (West Virginia and Missouri), and the eleven former slaveholding states which had seceded (Alabama, Arkansas, Florida, Georgia, Louisiana, Mississippi, North Carolina, South Carolina, Tennessee, Texas and Virginia). Delaware, Kentucky and Maryland, three former slave-holding but non-seceding states, expressly rejected the Amendment. California, probably because the control of its legislature differed in each house, was unable to take any definitive action.

The evidence which compels this conclusion is adduced from governors' messages, reports of the legislative committees on federal relations and entries in the journals of the legislatures. At that time, the legislatures, almost without exception, kept no verbatim record of debates and speeches; and the journals merely noted motions and votes. There are, however, newspaper summaries of some speeches and proceedings. But much of the evidence from these sources is inadequate.

More significant is the modifications which the states made in their schools' laws. For if it was understood in the legislatures, which considered the proposed Amendment, that ratification would perforce forbid compulsory segregated schools, it seems certain that the legislatures would have apprehended its effect upon the state's constitutional or statutory provisions for public schools. If, for example, a state required or authorized segregated schools under existing law, presumably the legislature would not knowingly adopt the Amendment without giving some thought to its implications. After adoption, it would be expected that measures would be taken to conform the school laws to the new constitutional mandate. If, however, a state's school laws and practices already conformed to the understanding that the Fourteenth Amendment forbade segregated schools, it is probable that its legislature would not have objected to the Amendment on this question and would afterwards either retain or reinforce its school laws. On the other hand, if there was an authorization or requirement of segregation in a state's school laws, and, after ratification, the legislature took no action to end this disparity, undoubtedly it would appear that this state did not understand the Amendment to have the effect which Appellants urge. Yet, if a state under these same conditions had rejected the Amendment, it would suggest that the Amendment's impact upon the school segregation law was a controlling factor. We submit, the new constitutional and statutory provisions enacted with respect to public schools during the critical period, i.e., from 1866, the year the Amendment was submitted, until several years following adoption, constitute strong evidence on the question of the understanding of the Amendment in the state legislatures.

Then, too, we note that the Fourteenth Amendment was designed particularly as a limitation upon the late Confederate States.

U.S. SUPREME COURT, OCTOBER 1953

BRIEF FOR THE APPELLANTS AND RESPONDENTS ON REARGUMENT

U.S. SUPREME
COURT,
OCTOBER 1953

BRIEF FOR THE
APPELLANTS AND
RESPONDENTS
ON REARGUMENT

Slaughter House Cases, 16 Wall. 36. Each of them, except Tennessee, was required to endorse the Amendment and the price of readmission also required each to demonstrate that it "modified its constitution and laws in conformity therewith." 14 Stat. 428 (Act of March 2, 1867). In this connection, Representative Boutwell significantly declared:[209]

> "We are engaged in the great work of reconstructing this Government, and I suppose if we are committed to anything, it is this: that in the ten States not now represented there shall hereafter be no distinction on account of race or color."

These new constitutions, and the proposals and debates of the conventions which framed them, then are of utmost significance. Certainly, they had to measure up to the requirements of the Fourteenth Amendment and, therefore, their educational provisions apparently reflect the understanding of the draftsmen as to the Amendment's effect upon compulsory public school segregation. Similarly, since the constitutions of these states, were subject to the scrutiny of Congress, an additional insight into the understanding of Congress is provided. For it would hardly be possible to maintain that Congress contemplated the Fourteenth Amendment as a prohibition on compulsory segregated schools if it had approved a constitution having a provision inconsistent with this proposition.

We now turn to the legislative history of the Fourteenth Amendment in the states. The proceedings in the several states shall be taken up in turn. Because of the geographic origin of certain of the instant cases and the significance of the contemporary understanding and contemplation of the effect of the Amendment upon Southern institutions, we will first treat the evidence from the states whose readmission to the Union was conditioned upon their conformity with the Amendment.

A. The eleven states seeking readmission understood that the Fourteenth Amendment stripped them of power to maintain segregated schools

Subsequent to the proclamation of the Thirteenth Amendment the South sought to define the relations between the new freedmen and white men in a manner which retained most of the taint of the former master-slave relationship. The ante-bellum constitutions remained inviolate although prohibitions against slavery

were added. Laws were passed which restricted Negroes in their freedom of movement, employment, and opportunities for learning. *Slaughter House Cases,* 16 Wall. 36, 71–72; *Strauder* v. *West Virginia,* 100 U.S. 303, 306–307. In Arkansas[210] and Florida,[211] the so-called Black Codes required separate schools for the children of the two races.

After March 2, 1867, the date of the First Reconstruction Act, 14 Stat. 428, the South was obliged to redefine the status of the freedmen in conformity with their understanding of the Fourteenth Amendment. New constitutions were adopted which without exception were free of any requirement or specific authorization of segregated schools. It is also significant that in almost all of these constitutional conventions and legislatures, the issue of segregated schools was specifically raised and rejected. And no law compelling segregated schools was enacted in any state until after it had been readmitted.

Arkansas The first of these states to be readmitted was Arkansas. 15 Stat. 72 (Act of June 22, 1868). The constitution which it submitted to Congress had not one reference to race; the education article merely obligated the general assembly to "establish and maintain a system of free schools for all persons" of school age.[212] It is reported that this article was adopted to nullify the segregated school law passed by the legislature earlier in 1867.[213] Its adoption had been generally opposed in the Convention on the ground that it would "establish schools in which there would be 'indiscriminate social intercourse between whites and blacks.'"[214] The electorate was warned that this constitution would "force children into mixed schools."[215] But the new constitution was adopted and proclaimed law on April 1, 1868.[216]

The general assembly convened on April 3, and ratified the Fourteenth Amendment on April 6, 1868.[217] It then proceeded to repeal the former school statute and a new school law was proposed

---

[209] Cong. Globe, 39th Cong., 2nd Sess. 472 (1867).
[210] Ark. Acts 1866–67 p. 100.
[211] Cong. Globe, 39th Cong., 1st Sess. 217 (1866).
[212] ARK. CONST. 1868, Art. IX, § 1.
[213] STAPLES, RECONSTRUCTION IN ARKANSAS 28 (1923).
[214] *Id.* at 247.
[215] Daily Arkansas Gazette, March 19, 1868; *Id.,* March 15, 1868.
[216] *Id.,* April 2, 1868.
[217] Ark. Sen. J., 17th Sess. 19–21 (1869).

whereby taxes were to be assessed to support a system of common schools for the education of all children. This law was interpreted as establishing "a system of schools where the two races are blended together."[218] And it was attacked because it granted white parents "no option to their children … but to send them to the negro schools … unless, as is now rarely the case, they are able to give their children education in other schools."[219]

These provisions for public schools were included in the legislative record which Arkansas submitted to the scrutiny of Congress. Whereupon, Arkansas was re-admitted on June 22, 1868. 15 Stat. 72. One month later, but after readmission, the legislature amended the public school statute and directed the Board of Education to "make the necessary provisions for establishing separate schools for white and colored children and youths. . . ."[220]

North Carolina, South Carolina, Louisiana, Georgia, Alabama and Florida The North Carolina, South Carolina, Louisiana, Georgia, Alabama and Florida modifications in their constitutions and laws were approved by Congress in the Omnibus Act of June 25, 1868 and Congress authorized readmittance effective on the date each ratified the Amendment. 15 Stat. 73. The constitution which Florida offered for congressional review imposed a specific duty on the state to provide "for the education of all children residing within its borders without distinction or preference."[221] The legislature ratified the Amendment on June 9, 1868 and when it next convened passed a law to maintain "a uniform system of instruction, free to all youth of six to twenty-one years."[222] It is agreed that this law was not designed to foster segregated schools and by its operation "mixed schools" were authorized or required.[223]

Several years later the Florida Legislature passed a sweeping law which forbade any racial distinction in the full and equal enjoyment of public schools, conveyances, accommodations and amusements.[224] The first compulsory school segregation provision did not appear until over twenty years after readmission.[225]

In the North Carolina Constitution of 1868, the education article called for the general assembly to maintain "a general and uniform system of public schools, wherein tuition shall be free of charge to all the children of the State between the ages of six and sixteen."[226] Furthermore, the general assembly was "empowered to enact that every child of sufficient mental and physical ability, shall attend the public schools" unless otherwise educated.[227] It is reported that the Constitutional Convention refused by a vote of 86 to 11 to adopt a section which provided that "The General Assembly shall provide separate and distinct schools for the black children of the state, from those provided for white children."[228] The adopted article also survived amendments which would have permitted separate schools "for any class of the population" providing each class shared equally in the school fund.[229] Some proponents of the education article said that it did not force racial commingling but they frankly admitted that it did not prevent it and contended that separate schools, if established, should only develop out of the mutual agreement of parents rather than through legislation.[230] Available contemporary comment upon the education article of the 1868 constitution uniformly agreed that it either authorized or required mixed schools.[231]

The 1868 Constitution, with this education article, was submitted to Congress and treated as being in conformity with the Amendment. North Carolina's readmission was thus assured contingent upon its ratification of the Fourteenth Amendment.

The state legislature convened on July 1, 1868 and ratified the Amendment on July 4th.[232]

U.S. SUPREME COURT, OCTOBER 1953

BRIEF FOR THE APPELLANTS AND RESPONDENTS ON REARGUMENT

---

[218] *Ibid.*

[219] Daily Arkansas Gazette, April 10, 1868.

[220] Act of July 23, 1868 as amended by Ark. Acts 1873, p. 42. See Ark. Dig. Stats., c. 120 § 5513 (1874).

[221] FLA. CONST. 1868, Art. VIII § 1.

[222] Fla. Laws 1869, Act of Jan. 30, 1869.

[223] KNIGHT, PUBLIC EDUCATION IN THE SOUTH 306 (1922) EATON, "SPECIAL REPORT TO THE UNITED STATES COMMISSION OF EDUCATION", REP. U.S. COMMR. EDUC. TO SECY. INT. (1871).

[224] Fla. Laws 1873, c. 1947.

[225] FLA. CONST. 1885, Art. XII § 2.

[226] N. C. CONST. 1868, Art. IX § 2.

[227] *Id.,* § 17.

[228] Motion of Mr. Durham reported in KNIGHT, INFLUENCE OF RECONSTRUCTION ON EDUCATION 22 (1913).

[229] Motions of Messrs. Graham and Tourgee reported in *Id.* at 22.

[230] NOBLE, A HISTORY OF PUBLIC SCHOOLS IN NORTH CAROLINA 340–41 (1930).

[231] Wilmington Morning Star, March 27, 1868; >*id.,* March 28, 1868, p. 2; Charlotte Western Democrat, March 24, 1868; *id.,* April 17, 1868, p. 2; Greensboro Times, April 2, 1868, p. 3; *id.,* April 16, 1868, p. 1; Fayetteville News, April 14, 1868, p. 2; *id.,* June 2, 1868, p. 1.

[232] N. C. Laws 1867, ch. CLXXXIV, Sec. 50.

U.S. SUPREME
COURT,
OCTOBER 1953

BRIEF FOR THE
APPELLANTS AND
RESPONDENTS
ON REARGUMENT

Three days later the lower house adopted a resolution providing for the establishment of separate schools, but it failed to win support in the upper house which successfully carried a resolution instructing the Board of Education to prepare a code for the maintenance of the system of free public schools contemplated in the constitution.[233] Significantly, this measure made no reference to race. It was enrolled on July 28, 1868.[234]

At the next regular session after readmission, the legislature passed a school law which required separate schools.[235] However doubtful the validity of this law was to some as late as 1870,[236] the state constitution as amended in 1872, settled the issue by specifically requiring racial separation in education.[237]

South Carolina and Louisiana both ratified the Amendment on July 9, 1868 and were readmitted as of that date pursuant to the Omnibus Act. 15 Stat. 73. The educational articles in their 1868 constitutions were of the same cloth. The Louisiana article flatly said: "There shall be no separate schools or institutions of learning established exclusively for any race by the State of Louisiana."[238] South Carolina's constitution provided that: "All the public schools, colleges and universities of this State, supported in whole or in part by the public school fund, shall be free and open to all the children and youths of the State, without regard to race or color."[239] In addition to this, the South Carolina Constitution required the legislature to pass a compulsory school law after it organized facilities for the education of all children.[240] The 1868 constitutions of both states also declared that all citizens, without regard to race or color, were entitled to equal civil and political rights.[241]

The proponents of the education articles in the Louisiana and South Carolina conventions defended the provisions prohibiting segregation by force of law in public schools as an incident of equal justice or equal benefits in return for equal

burdens; and they overwhelmingly considered compulsory segregation to be a hostile distinction based on race and previous condition.[242] The chairman of the Education Committee of the South Carolina Convention, defending the proposed education article, explained:[243]

"The whole measure of Reconstruction is antagonistic to the wishes of the people of the State, and this section is a legitimate portion of that scheme. It secures to every man in this State full political and civil equality, and I hope members will not commit so suicidal an act as to oppose the adoption of this section."

Continuing, he explained:[244]

We only compel parents to send their children to some school, not that they shall send them with the colored children; we simply give those colored children who desire to go to white schools, the privilege to do so." (Emphasis supplied.)

After the Louisiana and South Carolina constitutions were approved by Congress, the South Carolina Legislature, in a special session, ratified the Amendment and temporarily organized the school system in conformity with the education article, despite Governor Scott's plea for a law which would require racial separation in schools as a preventive against "educational miscegenation."[245] At the next regular session, the school system was permanently organized, and a law was passed forbidding officials of the state university to "make any distinction in the admission of students or management of the university on account of race, color or creed."[246]

The Louisiana legislature acted with similar celerity and consistency. It assembled on June 29, 1868, ratified the Amendment on July 9, 1868 and enacted laws conforming to the constitutional mandate against segregated schools.[247] At its next session, it supplemented the school laws by imposing penal and civil sanctions against any teacher refusing to accept a pupil of either race.[248] Subsequent laws forbade racial

---

[233] NOBLE, *op. cit. supra* n. 230, at 297, 299.

[234] See List of Public Acts and Resolutions Passed by the General Assembly of North Carolina, Spec. Sess. of July, 1868.

[235] N. C. Laws 1868–69, c. CLXXXIV, § 50.

[236] NOBLE, *op. cit. supra* n. 230, at 325.

[237] Art. IX, § 2.

[238] LA. CONST. 1868, Title VII, Art. 135.

[239] S. C. CONST. 1868, Art. XX § 10.

[240] *Id.,* § 4.

[241] *Id.,* Art. I, § 7; LA. CONST. 1868, Title I, Art 2.

[242] Proceedings of the South Carolina Constitutional

Convention of 1868, Held at Charleston, S. C., Beginning January 14th and Ending March 17th, 1868, pp. 654–900 (1868); Official Journal of the Proceedings for Framing a Constitution for Louisiana, 1867–1868, *passim* (1868).

[243] Proceedings, *op. cit. supra* n. 242, at 899.

[244] *Id.* at 690.

[245] S. C. House J., Spec. Sess., p. 51 *et seq.* (1868). See Charleston Daily News, July 10, 1868.

[246] S. C. Acts 1868–69, pp. 203–204.

[247] DABNEY, UNIVERSAL EDUCATION IN THE SOUTH 370 (1936).

[248] FAY, "THE HISTORY OF EDUCATION IN LOUISIANA", 1 U.S. Bu. Educ. Cir. No. 1, p. 101 (1898).

---

distinctions at a state institution for the instruction of the blind, prohibited racial separation on common carriers, and provided that there should be no racial discrimination in admission, management and discipline at an agricultural and mechanical college.[249]

More than a quarter-century elapsed before South Carolina and Louisiana in 1895 and 1898, respectively, changed these laws to require racial segregation in public education.[250]

The Alabama Constitutional Convention assembled on November 4, 1867, but the education article was not adopted until December 5th, the final day of the session. What emerged was borrowed directly from the Iowa Constitution of 1857, in most particulars, plus the language of a statute passed by the 1865–66 Iowa legislature to specifically bar segregation in schools.[251] This anti-segregation article survived two attempts to introduce provisos specifically requiring the establishment of separate schools.[252]

Congress found that Alabama had conformed its constitution with the Amendment and considered the state qualified for readmission as soon as it ratified the Fourteenth Amendment. On July 13th, 1868, the General Assembly fulfilled the final requirement. Thereafter, on August 11th, the State Board of Education, acting under the legislative powers conferred upon it in the constitution, passed a regulation which made it unlawful "to unite in one school both colored and white children, unless it be by the unanimous consent of the parents and guardians of such children ... "[253] But the significant point again is that this was done only after readmission.

Georgia, like most of the South, had no public school system prior to Reconstruction. In fact, no reference to public schools appears in either the ante-bellum Georgia Constitution or

the Constitution of 1865 which was substantially a reenactment of the former.[254]

The Constitutional Convention of 1867–68, however, rewrote the basic state document and the committee on education reported a proposal to establish a thorough system of public education "without partiality or distinction."[255] During the drafting and consideration of the proposed education article, several efforts to include provisions requiring segregated schools were defeated.[256] The Convention adopted an article which directed the General Assembly to "provide a thorough system of general education to be forever free to all children of the State. . . ."[257]

After this constitution was approved by Congress, the legislature ratified the Fourteenth Amendment on July 21, 1868 and Georgia apparently qualified for readmission. But the General Assembly forcibly expelled its Negro complement at this session on the ground that their color made them ineligible to hold office. This action prompted Congress to refuse to seat the Georgia congressional delegation.[258] The General Assembly then reconvened on January 10, 1870, re-seated its Negro members, ratified the Fourteenth Amendment again, and expunged the word "white" from all state laws.[259] The conduct of this legislature satisfied Congress and Georgia was readmitted to the Union on July 15, 1870. 16 Stat. 363.

Three months later, on October 13, 1870, the state legislature passed a public school act which in section 32 established a system of segregated schools.[260] The state constitution was amended in 1877 and validated this legislation by an express requirement for racial separation in public schools.[261]

Texas In Texas a Constitutional Convention met in June 1868 to frame the constitution under which it was subsequently readmitted. Drafted to secure the approval of Congress,[262] it required

---

[249] La. Acts 1869, p. 37; La. Laws 1871, pp. 208–10; La. Laws 1875, pp. 50–52.

[250] S. C. Const. 1895, Art. XI § 7; La. Const. 1898, Art. 248.

[251] Compare Ala. Const. 1867, Art. XI with Iowa Const. 1857, Art. IX and Iowa Laws 1865–66, p. 158.

[252] Official Journal of the Constitutional Convention of the State of Alabama 1867–68, pp. 237, 242 (1869).

[253] Ala. Laws 1868, App., Acts Ala. Bd. of Educ. It would appear that had this law been tested, application of the rule applicable to borrowed statutes would have invalidated it inasmuch as a similar statute in Iowa had been struck down on the basis of a less stringent constitutional provision. Clark v. Board of School Directors, 24 Iowa 266 (1868).

[254] 2 Thorpe, Federal and State Constitutions 765 et seq. (1909).

[255] Journal of the Constitutional Convention of Georgia, 1867–68, p. 151 (1868).

[256] Id., at 69, 151, 479, 558. See Orr, History of Education in Georgia 187 (1950).

[257] Ga. Const. 1868, Art. VI.

[258] Orr, op. cit. supra n. 256, at 195–196.

[259] Ga. Sen. J. Pt. II, p. 289 (1870); Ga. House J. pp. 307, 1065 (1870).

[260] Ga. Laws 1870, p. 57.

[261] Ga. Const. 1877, Art. VIII § 1.

[262] Tex. Const. 1871, Art. I § 1.

U.S. SUPREME
COURT,
OCTOBER 1953

BRIEF FOR THE
APPELLANTS AND
RESPONDENTS
ON REARGUMENT

the legislature to maintain "a system of public free schools, for the gratuitous instruction of all the inhabitants of this State of school age."[263] This constitution was accepted at the elections in 1869, and the legislature, without discussion, ratified the three Civil War Amendments on February 18, 1870.[264] Texas was readmitted on March 30, 1870, 16 Stat. 80, and the legislature drafted a public school law which provided that local boards of education, "when in their opinion the harmony and success of the schools require it, ... *may* make any separation of the students or schools necessary to secure success in operation . . . ."[265] Contemporary opinion was that this grant of discretion to school boards was a restrained effort to achieve racial separation without offending Congress and that the Fourteenth Amendment forbade the requirement of separate schools although it did not compel mixed schools.[266] It was not until 1876, when Texas adopted a new constitution, that racial separation in schools was expressly required by law.[267]

Virginia Virginia submitted to Congress a constitution which contained no reference to race or racial separation in public schools.[268] In the Constitutional Convention, the issue of segregation was introduced when the report of the committee on education was being considered. First, an amendment was proposed to provide "that in no case shall white and colored children be taught in the same school."[269] This amendment was defeated.[270] Subsequently, a proposal to add an independent section providing for the establishment of segregated schools met a like fate.[271] A provision was also submitted to require that public schools be open to all classes without distinction and that the legislature be denied the power to make any law which would admit of any invidious distinctions.[272] This proposal and a substitute to the same effect were also defeated.[273] Opponents of the proposals to prohibit segregat-

ed schools explained the failure of passage, not on the grounds of fundamental objection, but because it was feared that the adoption of such an article in the constitution would doom its chance of ratification.[274] Thus, an article merely directing the general assembly to provide for a uniform system of public free schools was adopted "rather than risk having the Congress or Union Leagues force an obnoxious law on them."[275]

After the election of 1869, at which the constitution was adopted, the General Assembly convened and ratified the Fourteenth Amendment on October 8, 1869. This session passed no school laws and the establishment of the public school system was deferred until after readmission. Full statehood status was regained on January 26, 1870. 16 Stat. 62. Six months later, on June 11th, the General Assembly established a "uniform system of schools" in which separate schools were required.[276] A specific constitutional mandate for segregated[277] schools, however, did not appear until 1902.

Mississippi Mississippi followed the general pattern of the former seceded states. The Constitutional Convention of 1868, adopted an education article which made no mention of race or racial separation.[278] At least two unsuccessful attempts were also made in the Convention to require segregated schools.[279]

While the convention journal does not specifically indicate that the Fourteenth Amendment was raised as an objection to segregated schools, the convention had passed a resolution which declared that:

"... the paramount political object ... is the restoration or reconstruction of our government upon a truly loyal and national basis, or a basis which will secure liberty and equality before the law, to all men, regardless of race, color or previous conditions."[280]

The convention also framed a Bill of Rights which required all public conveyances to accord

---

[263] *Id.* Art. IX §§ 1–4.

[264] Daily State Journal, February 20, 1870.

[265] 6 Tex. Laws 1866–71, p. 288. (Emphasis added.)

[266] Flake's Daily Bulletin, March 3, 1870; *Id.* March 13, 1870.

[267] TEX. CONST. 1876, Art. VII § 7; 8 TEX. Laws 1873–79 CXX § 54.

[268] VA. CONST. 1868, Art. VIII § 3.

[269] JOURNAL OF THE VIRGINIA CONSTITUTIONAL CON-VENTION, 1867–68, p. 299 (1868).

[270] *Id.* at 300: Richmond Enquirer, March 31, 1868.

[271] Journal, *op cit. supra* n. 269, at 301.

[272] *Id.,* at 333.

[273] *Id.,* at 335–40.

[274] ADDRESS OF THE CONSERVATIVE MEMBERS OF THE LATE STATE CONVENTION TO THE VOTERS OF VIRGINIA (1868).

[275] DABNEY, UNIVERSAL EDUCATION IN THE SOUTH 143–44 (1936).

[276] Va. Acts 1869–70, c. 259 § 47, p. 402.

[277] VA. CONST. 1902, Art. IX § 140.

[278] MISS. CONST. 1868, Art. VIII.

[279] JOURNAL OF THE MISSISSIPPI CONSTITUTIONAL CONVENTION OF 1868, pp. 316–18, 479–80 (1868).

[280] *Id.* at 123.

all persons the same rights,[281] and it refused to adopt an article forbidding intermarriage.[282]

The next legislature convened in January, 1870, ratified the Fourteenth and Fifteenth Amendments, repealed all laws relative to Negroes in the Code of 1857, as amended by the Black Code of 1865, and indicated that it intended to remove all laws "which in any manner recognize any natural difference or distinction between citizens and inhabitants of the state."[283]

The Constitution and actions of the legislature proved acceptable to Congress, and Mississippi was restored to the Union on February 23, 1870. 16 Stat. 77. It was not until 1878 that Mississippi passed a law requiring segregated schools;[284] and it was still later when the Constitution was altered to reiterate this requirement.[285]

Tennessee Tennessee, although a member state in the late Confederacy, was not subjected to the requirements of the First Reconstruction Act, inasmuch as it had promptly ratified the Fourteenth Amendment and had been readmitted prior to the passage of that Act. Nevertheless, this state likewise reentered the Union with compulsory racial segregation absent from its constitution and statutory provisions on public schools. Readmission was under the Constitution of 1834, inasmuch as the Constitutional Convention of 1865 merely amended it to abrogate slavery and authorize the general assembly to determine the qualifications of the exercise of the elective franchise.[286] The education article in this constitution merely required the legislature to encourage and support common schools "for the benefit of all the people" in the state.[287] The first law providing for tax supported schools, on its face, also made no racial distinction.[288] The next law, however,

prohibited compulsory integrated schools.[289] Contemporary federal authorities noted that ante-bellum practice apparently had restricted the benefits of the school system to white children; but approved these provisions because, in sum, they provided a sufficient guarantee for the support and enjoyment of common schools for the equal benefit of all the people without distinction on the basis of race or color.[290]

The Governor convened the legislature in special session on July 4, 1866 to consider the Fourteenth Amendment. In urging its adoption, he summarized Section 1, and said that its practical effect was to protect the civil rights of Negroes and to "prevent unjust and oppressive discrimination" in the exercise of these citizenship rights.[291] A joint resolution to ratify was introduced in the upper house; and a resolution to amend it with a proviso that the proposed Amendment should not be construed to confer upon a person of color rights to vote, to hold office, to sit on juries or to intermarry with whites or to "prevent any state from enacting and enforcing such laws" was voted down.[292] Then the Senate approved the joint resolution and the House concurred.[293]

After ratification, a group in the lower house formally protested its confirmation of the Amendment on the ground that it invaded state rights "and obliterates all distinctions in regard to races, except Indians not taxed."[294] A similar protest was filed in the upper house.[295] Such of the debates as were reported in the press indicate that the legislators understood the Amendment to force absolute equality[296] and that under the inhibitions of Section 1 "distinctions in schools cannot be made, and the same privileges the one has cannot be denied the other...."[297]

U.S. SUPREME COURT, OCTOBER 1953

BRIEF FOR THE APPELLANTS AND RESPONDENTS ON REARGUMENT

---

[281] *Id.* at 47; MISS. CONST. 1868, Art. I, § 24.

[282] JOURNAL OF THE MISSISSIPPI CONSTITUTIONAL CONVENTION OF 1868, pp. 199, 212 (1868).

[283] GARNER, RECONSTRUCTION IN MISSISSIPPI 285 (1901).

[284] Miss. Laws 1878, p. 103.

[285] MISS. CONST. 1890, Art. IX, § 2.

[286] TENN. CONST. 1834 as amended by §§ 1 and 9 of "Schedule" ratified February 22, 1865. In conformity with the Schedule's directive the legislature enacted that Negroes could exercise and pursue all types of employment and business under the laws applicable to white persons, Tenn. Acts. 1865–66, c. 15; that Negroes were competent witnesses, *Id.*, c. 18; and that persons of color henceforth had the same rights in courts, contracts and property as white persons except that Negroes could not serve on juries and that this act "shall not

be construed as to require the education of white and colored children in the same school." *Id.*, c. 40, § 4.

[287] TENN. CONST. 1834, Art. XI § 10.

[288] Tenn. Acts. 1853–54, c. 81.

[289] Tenn. Acts. 1865–66, c. 40, § 4.

[290] Rep. U.S. Commr. Educ. 1867–68, 101 (18).

[291] Tenn. House J., Called Sess. 3, 26–27 (1866); Tenn. Sen. Called Sess. 8 (1866).

[292] Tenn. Sen. J., Called Sess. 26 (1866).

[293] *Id.* at p. 24; Tenn. House J., Called Sess. 24 (1866).

[294] Tenn. House J., Called Sess. 38 (1866).

[295] Tenn. Sen. J., Called Sess. 41–42 (1866).

[296] Nashville Dispatch, July 12, 1866.

[297] *Id.*, July 25, 1866.

U.S. SUPREME
COURT,
OCTOBER 1953

BRIEF FOR THE
APPELLANTS AND
RESPONDENTS
ON REARGUMENT

Tennessee was readmitted July 24, 1866. 15 Stat. 708–711. After readmission, a school law was passed on March 5, 1867 whereby boards of education were "authorized and required to establish … special schools for colored children, when the whole number by enumeration exceeds twenty-five."[298] It also provided for the discontinuance of these separate schools when the enrollment fell below fifteen. The law, however, did not forbid non-segregated schools. But it was repealed in 1869 and replaced with a requirement that racial separation in schools be observed without exception.[299] Finally, the constitution was amended in 1870 to secure the same result.[300]

In summary, therefore, as to these eleven states the evidence clearly reveals that the Fourteenth Amendment was understood as prohibiting color distinctions in public schools.

B. The majority of the twenty-two union states ratifying the 14th Amendment understood that it forbade compulsory segregation in public schools.

Other than the states already treated, twenty-six Union States considered the Amendment. Twenty-two of them ratified it. The evidence adduced here is of a somewhat less uniform character than that from the states which formed the late Confederacy for the simple reason that the legislatures in the North were unfettered by any congressional surveillance, and they did not experience the imperative necessity of re-examining their constitutions and laws at the time the proposed Fourteenth Amendment was considered by them. Thus, it is to be expected that some of these legislatures deferred attuning their school laws with the keynote of the Amendment until several years after it had become the law of the land. In other states, the legislatures adjusted their school laws almost simultaneously with their ratification of the Amendment. Still others, because existing laws and practices conformed with their basic understanding with respect to the impact of the Amendment, were not required to act. In the end, nevertheless, we submit that the overwhelming majority of the Union States ratified or did not ratify the Fourteenth Amendment with an understanding or contemplation that it commanded them to refrain from compelling segregated schools and obliged them to conform their school laws to assure consistency with such an understanding.

West Virginia and Missouri West Virginia, a state created during the Civil War when forty western counties refused to follow Virginia down the road to secession, and Missouri, a former slaveholding state comprised the small minority of states which ratified the Fourteenth Amendment and perpetuated laws requiring segregated schools without any subsequent enactment consistent with a discernment that such laws and the Amendment were incompatible.

Both states required separate schools for the two races prior to the submission of the Amendment.[301] These laws were continued after the Amendment was proclaimed as ratified;[302] and both states subsequently strengthened the requirement of separate schools in the 1870's by amending their constitutions to specifically proscribe racial integration in public schools.[303]

The New England States Segregated schools also existed in some of the strongly abolitionist New England states prior to their consideration and ratification of the Amendment. But their reaction to the prohibitions of Section 1 was directly contrary to the course taken in West Virginia and Missouri.

In Connecticut, prior to the adoption of the Amendment, racial segregation was not required by state law but segregated schools were required in some cities and communities, e.g., in Hartford pursuant to an ordinance enacted in 1867 and in New Haven by administrative regulation.[304] On August 1, 1868, four days after the Amendment was proclaimed, however, the legislature expressly forbade separate schools.[305] Interestingly, during the course of debate on this bill, amendments which would have required segregation or permitted separate "equal" schools were introduced and rejected.[306]

---

[298] Tenn. Laws 1867, c. 27, § 17.

[299] Tenn. Laws 1870, c. 33, § 4.

[300] TENN. CONST. 1870, Art. XI, § 12.

[301] W. Va. Laws 1865, p. 54; Mo. Laws 1864, p. 126.

[302] W. Va. Laws 1867, c. 98; W. Va. Laws 1871, p. 206; Mo. Laws 1868, p. 170; Mo. Laws 1869, p. 86.

[303] W. VA. CONST. 1872, Art. XII, § 8; MO. CONST. 1875, Art. IX.

[304] MORSE, THE DEVELOPMENT OF FREE SCHOOLS IN THE UNITED STATES AS ILLUSTRATED BY CONNECTICUT AND MICHIGAN 127, 144, 192 (1918); WARNER, NEW HAVEN NEGROES 34, 71–72 (1940).

[305] Conn. Acts 1866–68, p. 206. See Conn. House J. 410 (1866); Conn. Sen. J. 374 (1866).

[306] Conn. Sen. J. 247–48 (1868); Conn. House J. 595 (1868). See New Haven Evening Register, June 17, 1868.

Similarly, racial separation in schools was never required by the constitution or laws of Rhode Island, but segregated schools existed at least in Providence, Newport and Bristol.[307] Here, too, the same legislature which ratified the Amendment enacted a law prohibiting racial segregation in public schools.[308]

In Maine, there was no racial separation in public schools prior to the adoption of the Amendment.[309] However, the leading supporter of ratification extolled in the broadest terms its equality provisions and indicated that the proponents expected it to compel in the other states the same equality in civil and political rights as existed in Maine, itself.[310]

Massachusetts too, had already made unlawful any racial segregation in schools prior to the submission of the Amendment.[311] Thus, since Massachusetts had already considered state required racial segregation completely inconsistent with a system of laws and government which treats all persons alike irrespective of color,[312] there was no subsequent legislative action interpretative of the impact of the Amendment on segregation.

The deliberations of the legislature on the proposed Amendment opened with its reference to the body by the governor. He recommended ratification and his speech indicates that he understood Section 1 of the Amendment to be a reinforcement of the Civil Rights Act of 1866 and observed: "Whatever reasons existed at the time for the enactment of that bill, apply to the incorporation of its provisions into the state law."[313] Surprisingly, strong opposition to ratification developed. A majority of the joint committee recommended rejection on the ground

that the proposed Amendment neither specifically guaranteed Negro suffrage nor added anything to what was already in the constitution "possibly excepting the last clause" of Section 1. Of this, is concluded:[314]

"The denial by any state to any person within its jurisdiction, of the equal protection of the laws, would be a flagrant perversion of the guarantees of personal rights. . . . [But] such denial would be equally possible and probable hereafter, in spite of an indefinite reiteration of these guarantees by new amendments."

The minority reported that:[315]

"Without entering into any argument upon the merits of the amendment, they would express the opinion that its ratification is extremely important in the present condition of national affairs."

When these reports were presented in the lower house of the legislature, a motion was passed to substitute the minority report.[316] Suffrage had claimed much of the strident debate on the motion. But a speech of one of the last members to speak for the motion was reported as follows:[317]

"To the first article of this amendment, there had been no objection brought by those who favored rejection. . . . The speaker felt that this was a most important article; by it the question of equal rights was taken from the supreme courts of the States and given to the Supreme Court of the United States for decision; the adoption of the article was the greatest movement that the country had made toward centralization, and was a serious and most important step. This was taken solely for the reason of obtaining protection for the colored people of the South; the white men who do not need this article and do not

U.S. SUPREME
COURT,
OCTOBER 1953

BRIEF FOR THE
APPELLANTS AND
RESPONDENTS
ON REARGUMENT

---

[307] BARTLETT, FROM SLAVE TO CITIZEN, c. 6 *passim.* (unpub. ms., pub. expected in Dec. 1953). See Ammons v. School Dist. No. 5, 7 R. I. 596 (1864).

[308] R. I. LAWS 1866, C. 609. The Committee on Education recommended passage of this act, saying: "The great events of the time are, also, all in favor of the elevation of the colored man. They are all tending to merge the distinctions of race and of class in the common brotherhood of humanity. They have already declared the Negro and the white man to be equal before the law; and the privileges here asked for by these petitioners, are simply a necessary result of this recognized equality." It went on to say, "We have no right to withhold it from him in any case," and asked, "With what consistency can we demand that these colored people shall be equal before the law in other states or the territories, while we, ourselves, deprive them of one of their most important civil rights?" Report of Committee on Education, Pub. Doc. No. 4 (1896).

[309] See CHADBOURNE, A HISTORY OF EDUCATION IN MAINE (1936).

[310] Speech of Senator Crosby in the Maine Senate, January 16, 1867, reported in Kennebec Journal, January 22, 1867, p. 1.

[311] Mass. Acts & Res. 1854–1855, p. 650; Mass. Acts & Res. 1864–1865, pp. 674–75.

[312] This was precisely the fundamental proposition underlying the enactment of the Act of 1855 prohibiting racial segregation in public schools. Report of the Committee on Education, Mass. House Doc. No. 167, March 17, 1855.

[313] Mass. Acts and Res. 1867, pp. 789, 820; Boston Daily Advertiser, January 5, 1867, Sat. Supp.

[314] Mass. House Doc. 149, pp. 23–24 (1867).

[315] *Id.,* at 25.

[316] Boston Daily Advertiser, March 13, 1867, p. 2; *Ibid.,* March 14, 1867, p. 1.

[317] *Id.,* March 14, 1867, p. 1 (Speech of Richard Henry Dana, Jr.).

U.S. SUPREME
COURT,
OCTOBER 1953

BRIEF FOR THE
APPELLANTS AND
RESPONDENTS
ON REARGUMENT

like it, sacrifice some of their rights for the purpose of aiding the blacks."

The upper house considered the motion several days later, re-echoed the theme of the speeches previously made in the lower house, and voted for ratification.[318]

The New Hampshire legislature took up the proposed Amendment in June of 1866. The governor's message urged ratification but its brief comment was not revealing.[319] The majority report of the house committee with respect to the Amendment merely offered a resolution to modify.[320] But the minority reported a number of reasons for rejection which, *inter alia,* criticized section 1 on the grounds of ambiguity and furthermore:[321]

> "Because said amendment is a dangerous infringement upon the rights and independence of all the states, north as well as south, assuming as it does, control their legislation in matters purely local in their character, and impose disabilities upon them for regulating, in their own way [such matters]."

The same set of objections was presented by a minority of the special committee of the upper house.[322] Both chambers voted for ratification, however, within a month after the Amendment was offered to the state.[323]

Laws governing public schools in New Hampshire appear to have never been qualified on the basis of race or color at any time after its organic law obligated the legislature to stimulate public education.[324] Similarly, Vermont seems to have no history of segregated schools. Neither did its laws sanction such a policy.[325] When the legislature convened in 1866, the Governor's opening message discussed the proposed Fourteenth Amendment at some length. He urged that it be ratified to secure "equal rights and impartial liberty," otherwise a small number of whites in the South and the entire colored race would be left unprotected. In concluding, he said Vermont welcomed "such a reorganization of the rebellious communities, as would have given the people, white and black, the equal civil and political rights secured to the people of the State, by our Bill of Rights and Constitution, and under which peace, order, civilization, *education,* contentment, Christianity and liberty have shed their benign and blessed influence alike upon every home and household in our beloved Commonwealth."[326] Thereupon, both houses routinely voted for ratification.[327]

The Middle Atlantic States Three Mid-Atlantic States, New York, New Jersey and Pennsylvania ratified the Amendment. The Pennsylvania evidence is in some detail because it was one of the few states to preserve the full discussions and debates of its legislature. Furthermore, its statutes, previous to the adoption of the Amendment, authorized segregation in schools;[328] and public carriers had regulations which excluded or segregated Negroes. See *West Chester & Phila. R. Co. v. Miles,* 5 Smith (55 Pa.) 209 (1867).

On January 2, 1867, the Governor transmitted the Fourteenth Amendment to the Legislature. He called for its adoption primarily upon political grounds but strenuously urged that every citizen of the United States had certain rights that no state had a right to abridge and the proposed Amendment asserted "these vital principles in an authoritative manner, and this is done in the first clause of the proposed amendments [sic]."[329]

The resolution recommending ratification was introduced in the Pennsylvania Senate by its floor leader. He urged that one of the reasons why it had to be adopted was because Mississippi had enacted a law requiring segregation on railroads and the Amendment was necessary to overcome all state legislation of this character.[330] In summary of his concept of the purpose of section 1, he said:

> "The South must be fenced in by a system of positive, strong, just legislation. The lack of this has wrought her present ruin; her future renovation can come only through pure and equitable law; law restraining the vicious and protecting the innocent, making all castes

---

[318] Mass. Acts and Res. 1867, p. 787; Mass. Leg. Doc. Sen. Doc. No. 25 (1867); Boston Daily Advertiser, March 21, 1867, p. 1.

[319] N. H. House J. 137 (1866).

[320] *Ibid.,* p. 174.

[321] *Id.* at 176.

[322] N. H. Sen. J. 70 (1866).

[323] *Id.* at 94, N. H. House J. 231–33 (1866).

[324] N. H. CONST. 1792, § LXXXIII.

[325] VT. CONST. 1777, c. II, § XXXIX; VT. CONST. 1786, c. II, § XXXVIII; VT. CONST. 1793, c. II, § 41. See Report of the Indiana Department of Public Instruction 23–28 (1867–68).

[326] Vt. Sen. J. 28 (1866); Vt. House J. 33 (1866). (Emphasis added.)

[327] Vt. House J. 139 (1866); Vt. Sen. J. 75 (1866).

[328] Act of May 8, 1854, Pa. L. 617 § 24.

[329] Pa. Sen. J. 16 (1867).

[330] 2 Pa. Leg. Rec., app., p. III (1867).

and colors equal before its solemn bar, that, sir, is the *sine qua non*. . . ."

The pith of the speeches of both the proponents and opponents of ratification are as follows:

Senator Bingham, a leading supporter of the resolution, noted that "it has been only a question of time how soon all legal distinctions will be wiped out."[331]

Another announced, "I shall vote for it with satisfaction for my own conscience and gratitude to Congress for squarely meeting the universal demand of the loyal states to destroy all legal caste within our borders."[332]

The leading opponent of ratification interpreted the Amendment as follows:[333]

"By the first section it is intended to destroy every distinction founded upon a difference in the caste, nationality, race or color of persons … which has found its way into the laws of the Federal or State Governments which regulate the civil relations or rights of the people. No law shall be made or executed which does not secure equal rights to all. *In all matters of civil legislation and administration there shall be perfect equality in the advantages and securities guaranteed by each state to everyone here declared a citizen, without distinction of race or color,* every one being equally entitled to demand from the state and state authorities full security in the enjoyment of such advantages and securities." (Emphasis supplied).

The legislature ratified the Amendment on January 17, 1867.[334]

About two weeks later, on February 5th, a bill was introduced making it unlawful for public conveyances to exclude or segregate Negroes.[335] In introducing this bill, its sponsor announced that the doctrine of equality before the law required the passage of this bill. Both he and another supporter of the bill pointed out that these practices were pursuant to carrier regulations and policies and had to be eradicated by legislative action. It was also pointed out that the bill did not effect social equality because that is regulated solely by the personal tastes of each individual.[336] The bill was overwhelmingly enacted into law the following month.[337]

The school law authorizing separate schools was not specifically repealed until 1881 when the legislature made it unlawful for any school official to make any distinction on account of race or color in students attending or seeking to attend any public school.[338]

It appears, however, that when the state constitution was amended in 1873, the 1854 school law was viewed as having been brought into conformity with the adoption of a provision for a school system "wherein all children of this Commonwealth above the age of six years shall be educated. . . ."[339] The Secretary of State, official reporter of the Convention, states particular attention was paid to "that part which confers authority on the subject of education." And he noted that the new article was formulated to conform with the policy of protest against all racial discrimination and, specifically, to remove the "equivocal and invidious provision."[340] These purposes are further borne out when the sponsor of the 1881 bill stated:[341]

"In proposing the repeal of the act of 1854, which in terms would be prohibited by the present State and Federal Constitutions, it seems a matter of surprise that an act so directly in conflict with the Fourteenth and Fifteenth Amendments of the Constitution of the United States should have been permitted to have remained in the statute book until this time."

New Jersey, as early as 1844, enacted general legislation for the establishment and support of a public school system "for the equal benefit of all persons. . . ."[342] In 1850, special legislation was enacted which enabled Morris Township to establish a separate colored school district if the local town meeting voted to do so.[343] The state superintendent of schools construed this act and concluded that it in combination with the earlier law of 1844 permitted any local school system to maintain separate schools provided both schools offered the same advantages and no child was excluded.[344]

U.S. SUPREME
COURT,
OCTOBER 1953

BRIEF FOR THE
APPELLANTS AND
RESPONDENTS
ON REARGUMENT

---

[331] *Id.* at XVI.

[332] *Id.* at XXII (speech of Senator Taylor).

[333] *Id.* at XLI (speech of Mr. Jenks).

[334] Pa. Laws 1867, 1334.

[335] 2 Pa. Leg. Rec., app. p. LXXXIV (1867).

[336] Id. at pp. LXXXIV *et seq.* (Remarks of Senators Lowery and Brown.)

[337] Act of March 22, 1867, Pa. Laws 1867, pp. 38–39.

[338] Act of June 8, 1881, Pa. L. 76, § 1, Pa. Laws 1881, p. 76.

[339] Pa. Const. 1873, Art. X, § 1.

[340] Jordan, Official Convention Manual 44 (1874).

[341] Pa. Sen. J. (entry dated May 26, 1881).

[342] N. J. Const. 1844, Art. IV § 7(6); N. J. Rev. Stats., c. 3 (1847).

[343] N. J. Laws 1850, pp. 63–64.

[344] Annual Report of the State Superintendent of Schools 41–42, (1868).

U.S. SUPREME
COURT,
OCTOBER 1953

BRIEF FOR THE
APPELLANTS AND
RESPONDENTS
ON REARGUMENT

The New Jersey Legislature convened in a special session and hastily ratified the Amendment on September 11, 1866.[345] The dispatch with which this was done was made a focal issue in the following elections. The Republicans broadly defended the Amendment as "forbidding class legislation, or the subjecting of one class of people to burdens that are not equally laid upon all."[346] The Democrats more specifically contended that their candidates opposed the Amendment because they were "against Negro suffrage and the attempt to mix negroes with workingmen's children in public schools."[347] When the Republicans captured the governorship and elected a radical congressional delegation, the Democrats captured the state legislature and immediately proceeded to rescind New Jersey's ratification.[348]

When the Republicans recaptured control of the legislature in 1870 the school law was amended to require "a thorough and effective system of public schools for the instruction of all children. . . ."[349] And this was later reinforced by an enactment which made it unlawful to exclude any child from any public school on account of color.[350] As a result of this law, separate schools soon disappeared except in a few counties where Negro citizens generally accepted them. When Negroes chose not to accept these segregated schools the school authorities were required to admit them to the white schools pursuant to the prohibition of the 1881 school law.[351]

New York, like the other Middle-Atlantic states, had ante-bellum constitutions which merely authorized the legislature to establish a common school fund.[352] There was never any general legislation on the subject of racial separation in schools sharing in the common school fund. The legislature, however, granted charters to Brooklyn, Canandaigua, Buffalo and Albany which permitted these cities to maintain segregated schools as early as 1850.[353] The Common School Act of 1864 was in the same vein. It only permitted school boards in certain political subdivisions to establish and maintain segregated schools "when the inhabitants of any school district shall so determine, by resolution at any annual meeting called for that purpose, establish a separate school or separate schools for the instruction of such colored children. . . ."[354] Communities exercising the option under this law comprised the exception rather than the rule.[355]

Shortly after New York ratified the Amendment,[356] a constitutional convention was held and it adopted a new constitution which provided for free instruction of all persons of school age.[357] The convention approved a committee report which contained a ringing declaration that Negroes should have full equality in the enjoyment of all civil and political rights and privileges.[358]

Subsequently, in 1873, the legislature passed an "Act to Provide for the Protection of Citizens in Their Civil and Public Rights."[359] The Act

---

[345] N. J. Sen. J., Extra Sess., 1866, p. 14; MINUTES OF THE ASSEMBLY, Extra Sess., 1866, p. 8.

[346] Newark Daily Advertiser, October 25, 1866; Trenton State Gazette, November 3, 1866.

[347] Trenton Daily True American, November 3, 1866.

[348] N. J. Sen. J. 198, 249, 356 (1868); Minutes of the Assembly; 309, 743 (1868). See KNAPP, NEW JERSEY POLITICS DURING THE PERIOD OF CIVIL WAR AND RECONSTRUCTION 167 (1924).

[349] N. J. Laws 1874, p. 135.

[350] N. J. Laws 1881, p. 186.

[351] See Pierce v. Union Dist. School Trustees, 17 Vroom (46 N. J. L.) 76 (1884).

[352] N. Y. CONST. 1821, Art. VII; N. Y. CONST. 1846, Art. IX.

[353] N. Y. Laws 1850, c. 143; N. Y. Laws 1852, c. 291. See Dallas v. Fosdick, 50 How. Prac. 249 (1869); People v. Easton, 13 Abb. Prac. N. S. 159 (1872).

[354] N. Y. Laws 1864, c. 555.

[355] ANNUAL REPORT OF THE STATE SUPERINTENDENT OF PUBLIC INSTRUCTION 131, 159, 163, 166, 170, 233, 323 (1866).

[356] N. Y. Sen. J. 33 (1867); N. Y. Ass. J. 77 (1867). The Governor's message upon transmission of the Amendment leaves little doubt that he considered it as a "moderate

proposition" containing "just the conditions for safety and justice indispensable to a permanent settlement." N. Y. Sen. J. 6 (1867); N. Y. Ass. J. 13 (1867).

[357] N. Y. CONST. 1868, Art. IX. See PROCEEDINGS AND DEBATES OF THE CONSTITUTIONAL CONVENTION OF THE STATE OF NEW YORK 1867-68 (1868).

[358] "First. Strike out all discriminations based on color. Slavery, the vital source and only plausible ground of such invidious discrimination, being dead, not only in this State, but throughout the Union, as it is soon to be, we trust, throughout this hemisphere, we can imagine no tolerable excuse for perpetuating the existing proscription. Whites and blacks are required to render like obedience to our laws, and are punished in like measure for their violation. Whites and blacks are indiscriminately drafted and held to service to fill our State's quotas in a war whereby the Republic was saved from disruption. We trust that we are henceforth to deal with men according to their conduct, without regard to their color. If so, the fact should be embodied in the Const." DOCUMENTS OF THE CONVENTION OF THE STATE OF NEW YORK, 1867–68, Doc. No. 15 (1868).

[359] N. Y. Laws 1873, c. 186 § 1.

made it unlawful for any person to exclude any other person on the ground of race or color from the equal enjoyment of any place of public accommodation, place of public amusement, public conveyance, "*common schools and public instruction* [sic] *of learning. . . .*" (emphasis supplied). It also annulled the use of the word "white" or any other discriminatory term in all existing laws, statutes, ordinances and regulations.[360] The New York Court of Appeals did not give vitality to this act in the case of *People ex rel. King v. Gallagher*, 92 N.Y. 438 (1883). But cf. *Railway Mail Association v. Corsi*, 326 U.S. 88.

The Western Reserve States The five states in the Western Reserve all ratified the Fourteenth Amendment. Each of them had rather well established public school systems prior to the Civil War. In Ohio, the first public school legislation expressly denied Negroes the benefit of free schools.[361] Twenty years later, in 1847, this act was amended to permit the maintenance of separate schools for colored children if the residents of a school district objected to their admission into the white schools.[362] At its next session, the legislature repealed the provision in an earlier law that had prohibited the application of taxes paid by white residents toward the support of colored schools.[363] And in 1853 the school law was revised to require the allocation of public school funds in proportion to the number of children of school age regardless of color.[364]

Separate schools, however, were still maintained except in Cleveland, Oberlin and other northern cities despite the general feeling that this act had relaxed the stringent restrictions of the antecedent laws. Furthermore, the State Supreme Court held this law not to entitle colored children, as of right, to admission into white schools. *Van Camp v. Board of Education*, 9 Ohio St. 406 (1859).

After ratification of the Amendment,[365] the legislature did not immediately modify the schools laws. In fact, it did nothing until after the Ohio Supreme Court upheld compulsory segregated schools in *State ex rel. Garnes v. McCann*, 21 Ohio St. 198 (1872). Then the legislature enacted a statute which permitted rather than required segregated schools.[366] Later, it denied local school authorities the power to exercise their discretion in the premises.[367] By this act, all public schools were opened to all children without distinction on account of race

or color. *State v. Board of Education*, 2 Ohio Cir. Ct. Rep. 557 (1887).

Indiana's pre-Fourteenth Amendment school law provided for the support of public schools but exempted "all Negroes and mulattoes" from the assessment.[368] This law was interpreted as excluding colored children from public schools wherever the parents of white children objected. *Lewis v. Henley*, 2 Ind. 332 (1850).

On January 11, 1867, Governor Morton submitted the Fourteenth Amendment to the legislature. His message urged ratification but suggested that schools should be provided for Negroes and that they be educated in separate schools to relieve any friction which could arise if they were required to be admitted to white schools.[369] A resolution to ratify the Amendment was introduced on the same day and referred to a joint committee. Five days later the resolution was reported out favorably with a recommendation of prompt ratification.[370] A minority report was made which objected to the Amendment primarily because it conferred civil and political equality upon Negroes, including the same rights that were then enjoyed by the white race.[371]

The resolution was adopted on the same day in the Senate.[372] No speeches were made in support of the resolution in this chamber but two senators spoke at length against it.[373] In the House, the main contention of the opponents was that the Amendment would impose Negro equality,[374] seat Negroes on juries, grant them suffrage and admit them into the white

U.S. SUPREME COURT, OCTOBER 1953

BRIEF FOR THE APPELLANTS AND RESPONDENTS ON REARGUMENT

---

[360] *Id.*, § 3.

[361] Ohio Laws 1828–29, p. 73.

[362] Ohio Laws 1847–48, pp. 81–83.

[363] Ohio Laws 1848–49, pp. 17–18.

[364] Ohio Laws 1852, p. 441.

[365] Ohio Sen. J. 9 (1867); Ohio House J. 13 (1867). The Amendment was ratified within two days of its submission to the legislature by the Governor. He observed that the Amendment had four provisions; the first of which was "the grant of power to the National Government to protect the citizens of the whole country ... should any state attempt to oppress classes or individuals, or deprive them of equal protection of the laws ..." Ohio Exec. Doc., Part I, 282 (1867).

[366] Ohio Laws 1878, p. 513.

[367] Ohio Laws 1887, p. 34.

[368] Ind. Rev. Stats. 314 (1843).

[369] Ind. Doc. J., Part I, p. 21 (1867).

[370] Ind. House J. 101 (1867).

[371] *Id.* at 102.

[372] Ind. Sen. J. 79 (1867).

[373] Brevier, Legislative Reports 44–45 (1867).

[374] *Id.* at 79.

U.S. SUPREME
COURT,
OCTOBER 1953

BRIEF FOR THE
APPELLANTS AND
RESPONDENTS
ON REARGUMENT

schools.[375] The proponents only denied that the Amendment conferred suffrage.[376] And the lower chamber adopted the resolution on January 23, 1867.[377]

Two years after ratification of the Fourteenth Amendment, the legislature revised its law to require the organization of separate schools.[378] The act also authorized the maintenance of non-segregated schools in areas where there were insufficient Negro children residing within a reasonable distance to justify a separate school. In 1874, the compulsory segregation section of this law was declared valid in the case of *Cory v. Carter,* 48 Ind. 327 (1874).

The legislature, however, revised the school laws at its next session to permit (*not require*) segregated schools.[379] The revised law, furthermore, required that colored children be admitted to the regular schools if a separate school was not maintained. This provision was applied in sustaining mixed schools in *State v. Grubbs,* 85 Ind. 213 (1883).

Illinois statutes never specifically required separate schools. But the ante-bellum school statute provided that school districts with Negro populations should allow these residents a portion of the school fund equal to the amount of taxes collected from them.[380] As construed by the state superintendent of schools, this law was applied to require segregated schools.[381]

The Illinois legislature received the governor's message endorsing ratification of the Fourteenth Amendment on January 7, 1867. Both chambers then ratified it on the same day with virtually no discussion or debate.[382] About one year later, in December 1869, Illinois called a constitutional convention. It adopted the present organic law which provides for a free public school system for the education of "all children."[383] This provision

stems from a resolution in which the convention directed the Education Committee to submit an article which would call for the establishment of a public school system for the education of every "susceptible child—without regard to color or previous condition."[384] Furthermore, the convention rejected two resolutions which would have directed the establishment of a compulsory segregated school system.[385]

Of all the states of the Western Reserve, Michigan was most deeply affected by the tide of abolitionism which swept this section during the pre-war years. By its Constitution of 1850 the word "white" was eliminated from the section establishing voting qualifications[386] and slavery was declared intolerable.[387] Neither this constitution nor the general law of the state recognized any racial distinctions in the enjoyment of public education. But as early as 1842 and as late as 1866, special statutes were passed granting school boards in certain of the larger cities discretionary power to regulate the apportionment of school funds and distribution of pupils among the several schools under their jurisdiction. Pursuant to this authority some school boards, e.g., in Detroit and Jackson, established separate schools.[388]

The Amendment was submitted to the legislature on January 6, 1867. On January 12th, a resolution was adopted in the Senate instructing the Committee on Public Instruction to report out a bill "to prevent the exclusion of children from the primary or graded or other public schools of this state on account of race or color." And four days later the general school law was amended to provide that "all residents of any district shall have an equal right to attend any school therein. . . ."[389] The Fourteenth Amendment was subsequently ratified on February 16, 1867.[390]

---

[375] *Id.* at 80, 88–89, 90.

[376] *Id.* at 90.

[377] Ind. House J. 184 (1867).

[378] Ind. Laws 1869, p. 41.

[379] Ind. Laws 1877, p. 124.

[380] Ill. Stats. 1858, p. 460.

[381] Sixth Biennial Report of the Superintendent of Public Instruction of the State of Illinois, 1865–66, pp. 27–29; 2 Reports Made to the General Assembly at its Twenty-Fifth Session, pp. 35–37.

[382] Ill. House J. 40, 154 (1867); Ill. Sen. J. 40, 76 (1867).

[383] Ill. Const. 1870, Art. VIII, § 1.

[384] Journal of the Constitutional Convention of the State of Illinois, Convened at Springfield, December 13, 1869, p. 234.

[385] *Id.* at 429–431, 860–861.

[386] Compare Mich. Const. 1850, Art. VII, § 1 with Mich. Const. 1835, Art. II, § 1.

[387] Art. XVIII, § 11.

[388] See People ex rel. Workman v. Board of Education of Detroit, 18 Mich. 400 (1869) for reference to these special statutes and notice of separate schools in these two cities. Since the decision in this case, there have been no segregated schools maintained by state authorities.

[389] 1 Mich. Laws 42 (1867); Mich. Acts 1867, Act 34 § 28.

[390] The journals of the Michigan legislature indicate that both houses promptly ratified the Amendment without reference to a committee. Mich. Sen. J. 125, 162 (1867); Mich. House J. 181 (1867).

The legislative record of Michigan during the next several years is replete with more blows against segregation and other distinctions based on race or color. In 1869, insurance companies were prohibited from making any distinction between white and Negro insureds.[391] The ban against interracial marriages was removed in 1883.[392] Then in 1885, the civil rights law was enacted prohibiting racial separation on public conveyances, in places of public accommodation, recreation, and amusement.[393]

Wisconsin, since 1848, provided for a public school system free to all children.[394] Moreover, during the crucial years, its Negro population was insignificant—less than two-tenths of one percent.[395] Thus, it seems obvious why segregation in schools or elsewhere never merited the attention of the legislature at the time of its ratification of the Amendment or thereafter.[396]

The Wisconsin legislature met on January 3, 1867 and was addressed by the Governor. His speech suggests that in his thinking the Fourteenth Amendment which he asked them to ratify was designed to apply solely to the South and required that "they must assent to the proposed amendment with all of its guarantees, securing to all men equality before the law. . . ."[397] A joint resolution was introduced to ratify the Amendment and referred to a committee of three, two of whom reported a recommendation to adopt. The report filed by the minority member condemned the Amendment at some length. "The apparent object," to him, was to allow Congress to enfranchise Negroes, legislate generally on civil rights, "give to the federal government the supervision of all the social and domestic relations of the citizen of the state and to subordinate state governments to federal power."[398]

It appears that this understanding of the Amendment was not disputed. Rather, one supporter of the Amendment is reported as stating: "If the states refuse to legislate as to give all men equal civil rights and equal protection before the laws, then, sir, there should be supervisory power to make them do that, and a consolidation of that kind will be a benefit instead of an injury."[399] And, another answered:[400]

> "We therefore need such a provision in the Constitution so that if the South discriminates against the blacks the United States courts can protect them. I know it is objected that this is an enlargement of the power of the United States Supreme Court. But it is a power given on the side of liberty—power to protect and not power to oppress. For the appeal will come up to this court from the aggrieved individual against the aggressing state. . . ."

The Western States Of the states west of the Mississippi which ratified the Amendment, Nebraska is quite significant because it was admitted to the Union during the life of the 39th Congress and conditions were imposed upon its admission which demonstrate that the Congress which prepared the Amendment intended to eradicate all distinctions based upon race. Nebraska won statehood without having ratified the Amendment. But the enabling Act provided that "this act shall take effect with the fundamental and perpetual condition that there shall be no abridgement or denial of the exercise of the elective franchise, *or any other right,* to any person by reason of race or color. . . ." Act of February 9, 1867, ch. 9, sec. 3, 14 Stat. 377 (emphasis supplied). The Act, furthermore, required Nebraska to publicly proclaim this fundamental condition "as a part of the organization of this state."

While the enabling Act was still being considered by Congress, the territorial legislature forthwith passed a "Bill to remove all distinctions on account of race or color in our public schools"[401] since the existing school law restricting the enumeration of pupils to white

U.S. SUPREME
COURT,
OCTOBER 1953

BRIEF FOR THE
APPELLANTS AND
RESPONDENTS
ON REARGUMENT

---

[391] Mich. Acts 1869, Act 77 § 32. See Mich. Comp. Laws § 7220 (1897).

[392] Mich. Acts 1883, Act 23, p. 16.

[393] Mich. Acts 1885, Act 130 § 1. See Mich. Comp. Laws § 11759 (1897).

[394] Wis. Const. 1848, Art. X, § 3; Wis. Rev. Stats. Title VII (1849).

[395] Legal Status of the Colored Population in Respect to Schools and Education, Special Report of the Commissioner of Education, 400 (1871).

[396] Wis. Sen. J. 119, 149 (1867); Wis. Ass. J. 224–226, 393 (1867). The entire series of Journals covering the War and Reconstruction years shows but a single reference to color in

connection with education. This was a proposal to amend an 1863 bill so as to limit certain educational privileges to children of "white parentage." The amendment failed and the matter was never revived. Wis. Ass. J. 618 (1863).

[397] Wis. Sen. J. 32 (1867); Wis. House J. 33 (1867).

[398] Id. at 96, 98 et seq. (Report filed by Sen. Garrett T. Thorne).

[399] Wisconsin State Journal, Feb. 7, 1867 (Reporting speech of Assemblyman C. B. Thomas).

[400] Daily Wisconsin Union, Feb. 7, 1867 (Reporting speech of Assemblyman H. C. Hobart).

[401] Neb. House J., 12th Terr. Sess. 99, 105 (1867). See Omaha Weekly Republican, January 25, 1867, p. 2; Id., February 8, 1867.

U.S. SUPREME
COURT,
OCTOBER 1953

BRIEF FOR THE
APPELLANTS AND
RESPONDENTS
ON REARGUMENT

youths[402] had heretofore been administratively construed to exclude colored children from the public schools. This bill failed to enter the statute books for lack of gubernatorial endorsement.[403]

The same session of the legislature by an appropriate resolution recognized the enabling Act's "fundamental condition" on February 20, 1867 and on March 1st Nebraska was proclaimed the 37th state. Two months later, a special session of the legislature was called to ratify the Amendment and to enact legislation to "render Nebraska second to no other state in the facilities offered to all her children, irrespective of sex or condition. . . ."[404] The Amendment was ratified in June 1867,[405] and the school law was amended to require the enumeration of "all the children" in the school census.[406] The new school law did not in specific language prohibit segregation, but colored children entered the public schools on a non-segregated basis at the next school term in September, 1867.[407]

Another school law was enacted in 1869 which provided an increase in the taxes for the support of public schools "affording the advantages of a free education to all youth;"[408] and thereafter no school law has contained any language describing the system of public schools operated by the state.

Prior to its ratification of the Amendment, Kansas, a loyal border state, had adopted a policy of permissive segregation whereby boards of education were authorized, but not required, to establish separate schools.[409] The legislature ratified the Amendment on January 16, 1867,[410] and changed the school law on February 26th by an act which made it illegal for "any" school board

to refuse to admit "any" child.[411] In 1868, it reenacted the earlier permissive school segregation law.[412] Subsequently, an 1876 revision of the school laws omitted any authorization for segregation in cities of the first class and specifically forbade segregated schools in cities of the second class.[413] The same session also passed a civil rights act which is still the law and proscribes any distinction on account of race or color in "any state university, college, or other school of public instruction" or in any licensed place of public accommodation or amusement, or on any means of public carriage.[414] In 1879, the legislature reenacted the law permitting racial separation in schools but limited it to cities of the first class.[415]

Minnesota ratified the Fourteenth Amendment on January 16, 1867.[416] Its legislature was not obliged to contemplate whether the Amendment nullified segregated schools because such practices had been made a penal offense in 1864.[417] However, in submitting the Amendment to the legislature, the governor urged that its adoption was necessary because of the failure of the former seceding states "to reorganize their civil government on the basis of equal ... rights, without distinction of color. . . ."[418] In 1873, the legislature rephrased the school law so as to specifically prohibit segregated schools.[419]

In Nevada, the school law in existence prior to its consideration of the Amendment excluded Negroes from public schools and prescribed a penalty against any school which opened its doors to such persons.[420] However, the statute provided that school authorities might, if they deemed it advisable, establish a separate school for colored children and maintain it out of the

---

[402] Neb. Comp. Laws 1855–65, pp. 92, 234, 560, 642 (1886).

[403] Messages and Proclamations of the Governors of Nebraska. Collected in Publications of the Nebraska State Historical Society, 249 (1942).

[404] Id. at 274.

[405] Neb. House J. 148 (1867); Neb. Sen. J. 174 (1867).

[406] 2 Neb. Comp. Laws 1866–77, p. 351 (1887).

[407] See Nebraska City News, August 26, 1867, p. 3; Id., September 4, 1867, p. 3.

[408] 2 Neb. Comp. Laws 1866–77, pp. 451, 453 (1887).

[409] Kan. Laws 1862, c. 46, Art. 4 §§ 3, 18; Kan. Laws 1864, c. 67, § 4; Kan. Laws 1865, c. 46, § 1.

[410] The Amendment was ratified without reference to a committee within three days after it was submitted to the legislature. Kan. Sen. J. 43, 76, 128 (1867); Kan. House J. 62, 79 (1867).

[411] Kan. Laws 1867, c. 125, § 1; Kan. Gen. Stats., c. 92, § 1 (1868). The punitive feature of this statute directed county

superintendents to withhold school funds from any offending schools.

[412] Kan. Gen. Stats., c. 18, Art. V § 75, c. 19, Art. V § 57 (1868).

[413] Kan. Laws 1876, 238.

[414] Kan. Laws 1874, c. 49, § 1. See Kan. Rev. Stats. § 21–2424 (1935).

[415] Kan. Laws 1879, c. 81, § 1. This is the current law in Kansas. Kan. Rev. Stats. § 27–1724 (1935).

[416] The governor laid the proposed Amendment before the legislature with the observation that it would secure equal civil rights to all citizens and both houses voted at once to ratify the Amendment without further reference. Minn. Exec. Doc. 26 (1866); Minn. House J. 26 (1866); Minn. Sen. J. 22, 23 (1866).

[417] Minn. Laws 1864, c. 4, § 1, amending Minn. Laws 1862, c. 1, § 33.

[418] Minn. Exec. Docs. 25 (1866).

[419] Minn. Stats., ch. 15 § 74 (1873).

[420] Nev. Laws 1864–65, p. 426.

general school fund. While the legislature took no affirmative action after it ratified the Amendment on January 22, 1867,[421] it similarly remained inactive after the decision in *State* v. *Duffy,* 7 Nev. 342 (1872), which vitiated the first section of the school law. There is no subsequent reference to the subject of separate schools in the statute books and the segregatory statute itself was dropped from subsequent compilations of laws.[422]

The Oregon evidence is singularly meager. There were no laws requiring or permitting racial separation in schools either prior or subsequent to ratification of the Amendment on September 9, 1866. What the ratifying legislature understood as to the force of the Amendment and the significance of the abortive attempt to withdraw its ratification in 1868 on this subject is unavailable from the bare notations contained in the legislative journals.[423] The contemporary newspapers are also barren of information on this point.[424] What evidence there is, indicates that separate schools did exist at least in Portland as late as 1867 and that they were discontinued in 1871.[425]

Almost two years after the Amendment was submitted to the states, Iowa ratified on April 3, 1868.[426] Neither the state constitution nor laws required or in any manner authorized racial separation in schools at that time.[427] Instances of exclusion and segregation were being quickly remedied without recourse to the courts.[428] Where the courts were called upon, local practices of segregation in schools were never sustained as lawful. *Clark v. School Directors,* 24 Iowa 266 (1868); *Smith v. Directors of Independent Schools Dist.,* 40 Iowa 518 (1875); *Dove v. Independent School Dist.,* 41

Iowa 689 (1875). The state supreme court also forbade segregation by a common carrier in its dining facilities, predicating its decision squarely upon the Fourteenth Amendment. *Coger v. N. W. Union Packet Co.,* 37 Iowa 145 (1873).

In sum, the legislatures in all of the Union States which ratified the Fourteenth Amendment, except three, understood and contemplated that the Amendment proscribed State laws compelling segregation in public schools.

C. The non-ratifying states understood that the Fourteenth Amendment forbade enforced segregation in public schools

Four states did not ratify the Amendment, three specifically withholding endorsement and the other being unable to arrive at any definitive position. Delaware, in the anomalous position of a former slave state which sided with the Union, rejected it on February 7, 1867 with a resolution which declared that "this General Assembly believes the adoption of the said proposed amendment to the Constitution would have a tendency to destroy the rights of the States in their Sovereign capacity as states, would be an attempt to establish an equality not sanctioned by the laws of nature or God. . . ."[429] Again, in 1873, the state legislators denounced

> "... all other measures intended or calculated to equalize or amalgamate the Negro race with the white race, politically or socially, and especially do they proclaim unceasing opposition to making Negroes eligible to public office, to sit on juries, and to their admission into public schools where white children attend, and to the admission on terms of equality with white people in the churches, public conveyances, places of amusement or hotels, and to any measure designed or hav-

U.S. SUPREME COURT, OCTOBER 1953

BRIEF FOR THE APPELLANTS AND RESPONDENTS ON REARGUMENT

---

[421] The governor presented the Amendment to the legislature with an admonition that they were expected to ratify it and the ratification was accomplished three days later. The journals indicate virtually no opposition or advocacy of the Amendment. Nev. Sen. J. 9, 47 (1867); Nev. Ass. J. 25 (1867).

[422] See Nev. Comp. Laws (1929).

[423] Ore. Sen. J. 25, 34–36 (1866); *Id.,* at 271–272 (1868); Ore. House J. 273 (1868); Ore. Laws 1868, 114; *Id.,* "Joint Resolutions and Memorials" 13.

[424] The Oregonian, the state's leading newspaper, purportedly carried all the legislative happenings in full. See The Oregonian, September 14, 1866. None of its 1866 issues indicate more than that the legislature considered the Amendment dealt with "equality" and that the primary controversy was with respect to suffrage. *Ibid.,* September 21, 1866.

[425] See Reynolds, Portland Public Schools, 1875, 33 Ore.

Hist. Q. 344 (1932); W. P. A. Adult Education Project, History of Education in Portland 34 (1937).

[426] Ratification was almost perfunctorily effected. Iowa Sen. J. 265 (1868) Iowa House J. 132 (1868).

[427] ;s427 Iowa Const. 1857, Art. IX. § 12; Iowa Laws 1866, p. 158, reinforcing the Acts of 1860 and 1862 which required the instruction of all children without regard to race. Schaffter, The Iowa Civil Rights Act, 14 Iowa L. Rev. 63, 64–65 (1928).

[428] Dubuque Weekly Herald, January 30, 1867, p. 2; Des Moines Iowa State Register, January 29, 1868, p. 1; *Id.,* February 19, 1868, p. 1.

[429] 13 Del. Laws 256. See Del. Sen. J. 76 (1867); Del. House J. 88 (1867) for speech of Governor Saulsbury recommending rejection on the ground that it was a flagrant invasion of state rights.

U.S. SUPREME
COURT,
OCTOBER 1953

BRIEF FOR THE
APPELLANTS AND
RESPONDENTS
ON REARGUMENT

ing the effect to promote the equality of the Negro with the white man in any of the relations of life, or which may possibly conduce to such result."[430]

Then, shortly thereafter, the General Assembly in a series of discriminatory statutes demonstrated that it fully understood that equality before the law demanded non-segregation. It passed laws permitting segregation in schools,[431] places of public accommodation, places of public amusement and on public carriers.[432] Delaware, however, deferred sanctioning compulsory racial separation in public schools until after this Court handed down the *Plessy* decision.[433]

Maryland Maryland was also a loyal former slave-holding state. It rejected the Amendment on March 23, 1867.[434] The establishment of universal free public education here coincided with the Reconstruction Period. Although Maryland has always maintained a dual school system, it has never enacted a law specifically forbidding racial integration in its public schools. Rather, separate and parallel provisions were made for the education of white and colored children.[435]

Kentucky The third of the states which rejected the Amendment was Kentucky, a state with a slaveholding background and generally sympathetic with the South with regard to the status of Negroes although it did not secede. It was the first to refuse ratification: its rejection was enrolled on January 10, 1867.[436] While Negroes were denied or severely limited in the enjoyment of many citizenship rights at that time, including exclusion from juries,[437] the legislature was silent on the specific question of compulsory segregated schools.[438] Like its Maryland brothers, it passed two discrete series of laws, one for the benefit of

white children and the other for colored children. But no definite compulsory education statute was enacted until 1904[439] although the constitution had been previously amended so as to support such legislation.[440]

California California was the only state whose legislature considered the Amendment and yet did not reach an official stand on the matter.[441] Before the Fourteenth Amendment was proclaimed the law of the land, the legislature in 1866, relaxed the pattern of compulsory segregation when the school law was revised to permit Negro children to enter "white" schools, provided a majority of the white parents did not object.[442] This provision survived changes made in the school laws in 1870 and 1872; and, in 1874, a bill to eliminate segregated schools led to the adoption of a law which required the admission of colored children "into schools for white children" if separate schools were not provided.[443] Later in this same year the state supreme court upheld segregated schools despite the petitioner's claim that this practice violated the Amendment. *Ward v. Flood*, 48 Cal. 36 (1874). The legislature then revised the school laws and eliminated the provisions which had been held to require separate schools for Negro children.[444]

The evidence from the non-ratifying states also indicates that their legislatures understood or contemplated that the Fourteenth Amendment forbade legislation which enforced the separation of white and colored children in public schools.

CONCLUSIONS OF PART II

There is, therefore, considerable evidence and, we submit, conclusive evidence that the Congress which submitted and the state legisla-

---

[430] Del. Laws 1871–73, pp. 686–87.

[431] DEL. REV. STATS. c. 42 § 12 (1874); Del. Laws 1875, pp. 82–83; Del. Laws 1881, c. 362.

[432] Del. Laws 1875–77, c. 194.

[433] DEL. CONST. 1897, Art. X, § 2.

[434] Md. Sen. J. 808 (1867); Md. House J. 1141 (1867).

[435] Md. Laws 1865, c. 160, tit. i–iv; Md. Rev. Code §§ 47, 60, 119 (1861–67 Supp.); Md. Laws 1868, c. 407; Md. Laws 1870, c. 311; Md. Laws 1872, c. 377; Md. Rev. Code, tit. xvii §§ 95, 98 (1878).

[436] Ky. House J. 60 (1867); Ky. Sen. J. 63 (1867).

[437] Ky. Laws 1865–66, pp. 38–39, 49–50, 68–69.

[438] Ky. Laws 1869, c. 1634; 1 Ky. Laws 1869–70, pp. 113–127; Ky. Laws 1871–72, ch. 112; KY. STATS., c. 18 (1873); KY. GEN. STATS., c. 18, pp. 371 *et seq.* (1881).

[439] Ky. Laws 1904, pp. 181–82.

[440] KY. CONST. 1891, § 187.

[441] The Committee on Federal Relations in the Assembly and Senate, respectively, recommended rejection and ratification of the Amendment and no further action was taken. Cal. Ass. J., 17th Sess., p. 611 (1867–68); Cal. Sen. J., 17th Sess., p. 676 (1867–68), p. 676. See FLACK, THE ADOPTION OF THE FOURTEENTH AMENDMENT 207 (1908).

[442] Cal. Stats. 1866, p. 363. Pursuant to this statute a number of "white" schools admitted colored children without untoward incident. CLOUD, EDUCATION IN CALIFORNIA 44 (1952).

[443] Cal. Stats. 1873–74, p. 97.

[444] Cal. Stats. 1880, p. 48. See Wysinger v. Crookshank, 82 Cal. 588 (1890). The laws segregating Chinese children remained on the books probably because it was the general impression that only discriminatory laws aimed at Negroes were forbidden by the Fourteenth Amendment. Debates of the California Constitutional Convention of 1873, pp. 631, 642, 649 (1880).

tures and conventions which considered the Fourteenth Amendment contemplated and understood that it would proscribe all racial distinctions in law including segregation in public schools. A part of this evidence consists of the political, social and legal theories which formed the background of the men who framed the Fourteenth Amendment and the Radical Republican majority in Congress at that time.

Congressional debates following the Civil War must be read and understood in the light of the equalitarian principles of absolute and complete equality for all Americans as exemplified throughout the Abolitionist movement prior to the Civil War.

Many of the members of Congress, in debating the bill which became the Civil Rights Act of 1875, made it clear in no uncertain terms that it was generally understood in the 39th Congress that the Fourteenth Amendment was intended to prohibit all racial distinctions, including segregation in public school systems.

Running throughout the 39th Congress was a determination of the Radical Republican majority to transform these equalitarian principles into federal statutory and constitutional law. They realized that these high principles could not be achieved without effective federal legislation. The infamous Black Codes were demonstrative proof that the southern states were determined to prevent the newly freed Negroes from escaping from an inferior status even after the Thirteenth Amendment. The Radical Republican majority realized that in the status of American law at that time, the only way to achieve fulfillment of their determination to remove caste and racial distinctions from our law would be for them to effect a revolutionary change in the federal-state relationship.

After many drafting experiments, the Committee of Fifteen introduced in Congress the proposed amendment to the Constitution which was to become the Fourteenth Amendment. The broad and comprehensive scope of the bill was clearly set forth by Senator Howard, Chairman of the Judiciary Committee. An appraisal of the Congressional debates during the period the Fourteenth Amendment was being considered show conclusively that in so far as section 1 was concerned, there could be no doubt that it was intended to not only destroy the validity of the existing Black Codes, but also to deprive the states of power to enact any future legislation which

would be based upon *class* or *caste* distinctions. It is likewise clear that the Fourteenth Amendment was intended to be even more comprehensive than the scope of the original bill which, subsequently weakened by amendment, became the Civil Rights Act of 1866.

Throughout the debates in the 39th Congress and subsequent Congresses, the framers of the Amendment, the Radical Republican majority in Congress, over and over again, made it clear that: (1) future Congresses might in the exercise of their power under section 5 take whatever action they might deem necessary to enforce the Amendment; (2) that one of the purposes of the Amendment was to take away from future Congresses the power to diminish the rights intended to be protected by the Amendment; and (3) they at all times made it clear that the Amendment was meant to be self-executing and that the judiciary would have the authority to enforce the provisions of the Amendment without further implementation by Congress. All of the decisions of this Court, without exception, have recognized this principle.

Other Congressional debates, including those on the readmission of certain states, the amnesty bills and other legislation give further evidence of the intent of Congress in regard to the broad scope of the Fourteenth Amendment. The debates in Congress on legislation which was later to become the Civil Rights Act of 1875 made it clear that efforts of states to set up segregated school systems violated the Fourteenth Amendment. These debates were more specific on the question of segregation in public education because some states were already beginning to violate the Fourteenth Amendment by setting up segregated systems.

A study of the statements and actions of those responsible for state ratification of the Amendment remove any doubt as to their understanding that the Fourteenth Amendment was intended to prohibit state imposed racial segregation in public schools.

After addressing ourselves to questions 1 and 2 propounded by this Court, we find that the evidence not only supports but also compels the conclusions reached in Part One hereof. Wherefore, we respectfully submit, this Court should decide that the constitutional provisions and statutes involved in these cases are in violation of the Fourteenth Amendment and therefore unconstitutional.

U.S. SUPREME COURT, OCTOBER 1953

BRIEF FOR THE APPELLANTS AND RESPONDENTS ON REARGUMENT

U.S. SUPREME
COURT,
OCTOBER 1953

BRIEF FOR THE
APPELLANTS AND
RESPONDENTS
ON REARGUMENT

PART THREE

This portion is directed to questions four and five of the Court's Order:

4. Assuming it is decided that segregation in public schools violates the Fourteenth Amendment,

    (a) would a decree necessarily follow providing that, within the limits set by normal geographic school districting, Negro children should forthwith be admitted to schools of their choice, or

    (b) may this Court, in the exercise of its equity powers, permit an effective gradual adjustment to be brought about from existing segregated systems to a system not based on color distinctions?

5. On the assumption on which questions 4(a) and (b) are based, and assuming further that this Court will exercise its equity powers to the end described in question 4(b),

    (a) should this Court formulate detailed decrees in these cases;

    (b) if so what specific issues should the decrees reach;

    (c) should this Court appoint a special master to hear evidence with a view to recommending specific terms for such decrees;

    (d) should this Court remand to the courts of first instance with directions to frame decrees in these cases, and if so, what general directions should the decrees of this Court include and what procedures should the courts of first instance follow in arriving at the specific terms of more detailed decrees?

I. THIS COURT SHOULD DECLARE INVALID THE CONSTITUTIONAL AND STATUTORY PROVISIONS HERE INVOLVED REQUIRING SEGREGATION IN PUBLIC SCHOOLS. AFTER CAREFUL CONSIDERATION OF ALL OF THE FACTORS INVOLVED IN TRANSITION FROM SEGREGATED SCHOOL SYSTEMS TO UNSEGREGATED SCHOOL SYSTEMS, APPELLANTS KNOW OF NO REASONS OR CONSIDERATIONS WHICH WOULD WARRANT POSTPONEMENT OF THE ENFORCEMENT OF APPELLANTS' RIGHTS BY THIS COURT IN THE EXERCISE OF ITS EQUITY POWERS.

The questions raised involve consideration of the propriety of postponing relief in these cases, should the Court declare segregation in public schools impermissible under the Constitution. The basic difficulty presented is in the correlation between a grant of effective relief and temporary postponement. After carefully addressing ourselves to the problem, we find that difficulty insurmountable.

A. The Fourteenth Amendment requires that a decree be entered directing that appellants be admitted forthwith to public schools without distinction as to race or color

"It is fundamental that these cases concern rights which are personal and present." *Sweatt v. Painter,* 339 U.S. 629, 635; see also *Sipuel v. Board of Regents,* 332 U.S. 631, 633. These rights are personal because each appellant[445] is asserting his individual constitutional right to grow up in our democratic society without the impress of state-imposed racial segregation in the public schools. They are present because they will be irretrievably lost if their enjoyment is put off. The rights of the adult students in the *Sipuel, Sweatt,* and *McLaurin* cases required, this Court held, vindication forthwith. *A fortiori,* this is true of the rights of children to a public education that they must obtain, if at all while they are children. It follows that appellants are entitled to be admitted forthwith to public schools without distinction as to race and color.

B. There is no equitable justification for postponement of appellants' enjoyment of their rights

Even if the Court should decide that enforcement of individual and personal constitutional rights may be postponed, consideration of the relevant factors discloses no equitable basis for delaying enforcement of appellants' rights.

Appellants have no desire to set precise bounds to the reserve discretion of equity. They concede that, as a court of chancery, this Court has power in a proper case to mold its relief to individual circumstances in ways and to an extent which it is now unnecessary to define with entire precision. But the rights established by these appellants are far outside the classes as to which, whether for denial or delay, a "balance of convenience" has been or ought to be struck.

These infant appellants are asserting the most important secular claims that can be put

---

[445] As used herein "appellant" includes the respondents in No. 10.

forward by children, the claim to their full measure of the chance to learn and grow, and the inseparably connected but even more important claim to be treated as entire citizens of the society into which they have been born. We have discovered no case in which such rights, once established, have been postponed by a cautious calculation of conveniences. The nuisance cases, the sewage cases, the cases of the overhanging cornices, need not be distinguished. They distinguish themselves.

The Fourteenth Amendment can hardly have been intended for enforcement at a pace geared down to the mores of the very states whose action it was designed to limit. The balance between the customs of the states and the personal rights of these appellants has been struck by that Amendment. "[A] court of equity is not justified in ignoring that pronouncement under the guise of exercising equitable jurisdiction." *Youngstown Co. v. Sawyer,* 343 U.S. 579, 610 (concurring opinion).

Affirming the decree of one of the few judges still carrying the traditional title and power of Chancellor, the highest Court of Delaware epitomized equity in one of the cases now before this bar when it declared in *Gebhart v. Belton,* 91 A. 2d 137, 149 that

> "To require the plaintiffs to wait another year under present conditions would be in effect partially to deny them that to which we have held they are entitled."

Appellants, in the main, are obliged to speculate as to factors which might be urged to justify postponement of the enforcement of their rights. Hitherto, appellees have offered no justification for any such postponement. Instead they have sought to maintain a position which is, essentially, that a state may continue governmentally enforced racism so long as the state government wills it.

In deciding whether sufficient reason exists for postponing the enjoyment of appellants' rights, this Court is not resolving an issue which depends upon a mere preponderance of the evidence. It needs no citation of authority to establish that the defendant in equity who asks the chancellor to go slow in upholding the vital rights of children accruing to them under the Constitution, must make out an affirmative case of crushing conviction to sustain his plea for delay.

The problem of effective gradual adjustment cannot fairly arise in three of the five cases consolidated for argument. In the Kansas case, there was a frank concession on oral argument that elimination of segregation would not have serious consequences. In Delaware, court-compelled desegregation in this very case has already been accomplished. The case from the District of Columbia is here on a dismissal of the complaint on motion. In the oral argument the counsel for respondents implied that he foresaw no difficulties in enforcing a decree which would abolish segregation. Surely it would be curious as well as a gratuitous assumption that such a change cannot be expeditiously handled in this nation's capital. Cf. *District of Columbia v. John R. Thompson Co.,* 346 U.S. 100.

We can, however, put out of the case what is not in dispute. We concede that there may well be delays of a purely administrative nature involved in bringing about desegregation. Any injunction requires time for compliance and we do not ask the impossible. We strongly urge, however, that no reason has been suggested and none has been discovered by us that would warrant denying appellants their full rights beyond the beginning of the next school year.

But we do not understand that the "effective gradual adjustment" mentioned in this Court's fourth and fifth questions referred to such conceded necessities. We proceed then, to consider possible grounds that might be put forth as reasons for added delay, or for the postponement of relief to appellants.

It has been suggested that desegregation may bring about unemployment for Negro teachers. (Appellees' Brief in *Davis v. County School Board,* p. 31; *Transcript of Argument* in the same case, p. 71) If this is more than a remote possibility, it undoubtedly can be offset by good faith efforts on the part of the responsible school boards.[446] On the other hand, if appellees' suggestion is based upon an unexpressed intention of discriminating against Negro teachers by wholesale firings, it is not even worthy of notice in a court of equity.

---

[446] In view of the nationwide shortage of teachers, it is doubtful that any unemployment would be more than transitory. See *e.g.,* New York Times, August 19, 1953, 31:8 (S. M. Bouthardt puts elementary teachers shortage at 116,000); August 24, 1953, 21:1 (Comm. Thurston and NEA on shortage); 22 J. Neg. Ed. 95 (1953).

U.S. SUPREME
COURT,
OCTOBER 1953

BRIEF FOR THE
APPELLANTS AND
RESPONDENTS
ON REARGUMENT

U.S. SUPREME
COURT,
OCTOBER 1953

BRIEF FOR THE
APPELLANTS AND
RESPONDENTS
ON REARGUMENT

It has been bruited about that certain of the states involved in this litigation will cease to support and perhaps even abolish their public school systems, if segregation is outlawed. (*Davis v. County School Board, Transcript of Argument*, pp. 69–70; *Gebhart v. Belton, Transcript of Argument*, p. 17; *Briggs v. Eliott, Record on Appeal*, p. 113.) We submit that such action is not permissible. *Cf. Rice v. Elmore*, 165 F. 2d 387 (CA 4th 1947), *cert. denied*, 333 U.S. 875. Any such reckless threats cannot be relevant to a consideration of effective "gradual adjustment"; they are based upon opposition to desegregation in any way, at any time.

Finally, there are hints and forebodings of trouble to come, ranging from hostility and deteriorated relations to actual violence. (Appellees' brief in *Briggs v. Eliott*, p. 267; Appellees' brief in *Davis v. County School Board*, p. 17.) Obviously this Court will not be deterred by threats of unlawful action. *Buchanan v. Warley*, 245 U.S. 60, 81.

Moreover, there are powerful reasons to confirm the belief that immediate desegregation will not have the untoward consequences anticipated. The states in question are inhabited in the main by law-abiding people who up to now have relied upon what they believe—erroneously, as we have demonstrated—to be the law. It cannot be presumed that they will not obey the law as expounded by this Court. Such evidence as there is lends no support to defendants' forebodings. Note, *Grade School Segregation: The Latest Attack on Racial Discrimination*, 61 Yale L. J. 730, 739, 743 (1952).

A higher public interest than any yet urged by appellees is the need for the enforcement of constitutional rights fought for and won about a century ago. Public interest requires that racial distinctions proscribed by our Constitution be given the fullest protection. Survival of our country in the present international situation is inevitably tied to resolution of this domestic issue.

The greatest strength of our democracy grows out of its people working together as equals. Our public schools are "[d]esigned to serve as perhaps the most powerful agency for promoting cohesion among a heterogeneous democratic people. . . ." Mr. Justice Frankfurter, concurring in *Illinois ex rel. McCollum v. Board of Education*, 333 U.S. 206, 216–217.

C. Appellants are unable, in good faith, to suggest terms for a decree which will secure effective gradual adjustment because no such decree will protect appellants' rights

Question 5 assumes that the Court, having decided that segregation in public schools violates the Fourteenth Amendment, will, nevertheless, in the exercise of its equity powers, permit an effective gradual adjustment from segregated schools to systems not operated on the basis of color distinctions. This necessarily assumes further that reasons might be produced to justify consideration of postponement of the enforcement of the present and personal rights here involved. As we have pointed out immediately hereinbefore we are unable to identify any such reason.

Appellants obviously are aware of the existence of segregated school systems throughout the South similar to those presently before this Court. Similarly, appellants realize that the thrust of decisions in these cases may appear to present complex problems of adjustment because segregated schools have existed for nearly a century in many areas of this country. Generalizations, however, as to the scope and character of the complexities which might arise from immediate enforcement of appellants' rights would be unwarranted. This is demonstrated in part by the fact that even in the five cases joined for hearing, there appears to be no uniformity in the extent of the task of adjustment from segregated to non-segregated schools.

Necessarily, consideration of the specific issues which decrees should reach on the basis of the assumptions of Question 5 likewise requires the assumption that reasons will be adduced to warrant consideration of postponement of enforcement of appellants' rights.[447]

---

[447] It follows that there is no need for this Court to appoint a Master. Since repeal in 1948 of the 1805 statute, 28 U.S.C., § 863 (1946), forbidding the introduction of new evidence at an appellate level, there would appear to be no reason why such master could not be appointed. Certainly respected authorities have recommended the practice of appellate courts' taking evidence. See 1 WIGMORE, EVIDENCE 41 (3d ed., 1940); POUND, APPELLATE PROCEDURE IN CIVIL CASES pp. 303, 387 (1941); Note, 56 HARV. L. REV. 1313 (1943), and in other times and jurisdictions it has been respected practice. See SMITH, APPEALS OF THE PRIVY COUNCIL FROM AMERICAN PLANTATIONS 310 (1950); Rules of the Supreme Court of Judicature, Order 58, Rules 1, 2; cf. New Mexico, Stat. 1949, c. 168, § 19. However, taking of evidence by a Master is undoubtedly a departure from normal practice on appeal and it may result in loss of time to the prejudice of plaintiffs' rights.

Though no cogent reasons were offered to support them, two suggestions of methods of postponement of relief to appellants were made to this Court in the original brief for the United States. The first of these was "integration on a grade basis," i.e., to integrate the first grades immediately, and to continue such integration until completed as to all grades in the elementary schools (Brief, pp. 30–31). The second was integration "on a school-by school" basis (Brief, p. 31).

The first suggestion is intolerable. It would mean the flat denial of the right of every appellant in these cases. The second plan is likewise impossible to defend because it would mean the deliberate denial of the rights of many of the plaintiffs. If desegregation is possible in some schools in a district, why not in all? Must some appellants' rights be denied altogether so that others may be more conveniently protected?

Whether any given plan for gradual adjustment would be effective would depend on the showing of reasons valid in equity for postponement of enforcement of appellants' rights. In accordance with instructions of this Court we have addressed ourselves to all of the plans for gradual adjustment which we have been able to find. None would be effective. We recognize that the appellees, as school officials and state officers, might offer reasons for seeking postponement of the effect of decrees in these cases. Therefore, we submit, affirmative answers to questions 4(b) and 5 can come only from appellees since they alone can adduce reasons for postponement of enforcement of appellants' rights.

In the absence of any such reasons the only specific issue which appellants can recommend to the Court that the decrees should reach is the substantive one presented here, namely, that appellees should be required in the future to discharge their obligations as state officers without drawing distinctions based on race and color. Once this is done not only the local communities involved in these several cases, but communities throughout the South, would be left free to work out individual plans for conforming to the then established precedent free from the statutory requirement of rigid racial segregation.

In the very nature of the judicial process once a right is judicially declared proposals for postponement of the remedy must originate with the party desiring that postponement.

We submit that it would be customary procedure for the appellees to first produce whatever reasons they might urge to justify postponement of relief. Appellants then would be in a position to advise the Court of their views with respect to the matter.

CONCLUSION

Under the applicable decisions of this Court the state constitutional and statutory provisions herein involved are clearly unconstitutional. Moreover, the historical evidence surrounding the adoption, submission and ratification of the Fourteenth Amendment compels the conclusion that it was the intent, understanding and contemplation that the Amendment proscribed all state imposed racial restrictions. The Negro children in these cases are arbitrarily excluded from state public schools set apart for the dominant white groups. Such a practice can only be continued on a theory that Negroes, *qua* Negroes, are inferior to all other Americans. The constitutional and statutory provisions herein challenged cannot be upheld without a clear determination that Negroes are inferior and, therefore, must be segregated from other human beings. Certainly, such a ruling would destroy the intent and purpose of the Fourteenth Amendment and the very equalitarian basis of our Government.

WHEREFORE, it is respectfully submitted that the judgments in cases No. 1, 2 and 4 should be reversed and the judgment in No. 10 should be affirmed on the grounds that the constitutional and statutory provisions involved in each of the cases violate the Fourteenth Amendment.

CHARLES L. BLACK JR.,

ELWOOD H. CHISOLM,

WILLIAM T. COLEMAN JR.,

CHARLES T. DUNCAN,

GEORGE E. C. HAYES,

WILLIAM R. MING JR.,

CONSTANCE BAKER MOTLEY,

JAMES M. NABRIT JR.,

DAVID E. PINSKY,

FRANK D. REEVES,

JOHN SCOTT,

JACK B. WEINSTEIN, *of Counsel.*

HAROLD BOULWARE,

ROBERT L. CARTER,

JACK GREENBERG,

U.S. SUPREME COURT, OCTOBER 1953

BRIEF FOR THE APPELLANTS AND RESPONDENTS ON REARGUMENT

U.S. SUPREME
COURT,
OCTOBER 1953

BRIEF FOR THE
APPELLANTS AND
RESPONDENTS
ON REARGUMENT

OLIVER W. HILL,

THURGOOD MARSHALL,

LOUIS L. REDDING,

SPOTTSWOOD W. ROBINSON, III,

CHARLES S. SCOTT, *Attorneys for Appellants in Nos. 1, 2, 4 and for Respondents in No. 10.*

SUPPLEMENT

AN ANALYSIS OF THE POLITICAL, SOCIAL, AND LEGAL THEORIES UNDERLYING THE FOURTEENTH AMENDMENT

The first Section of the Fourteenth Amendment did not spring full blown from the brow of any individual proponent. Primitive natural rights theories and earlier constitutional forms were the origins of its equal protection-due process-privileges and immunities trilogy. The occasion for the metamorphosis of moral premises to full-fledged constitutional status was the attack on the American system of slavery. During the long antislavery crusade, the trilogy became a form of shorthand for, and the spearhead of, the whole of the argument against distinctions and caste based on race.

Section One of the Fourteenth Amendment thus marks the "constitutionalization" of an ethico-moral argument. The really decisive shifts occurred before the Civil War, and the synthesis was made, not by lawyers or judges, but by laymen. Doctrines originally worked out and propagated by a dissident minority became, by 1866, the dominant constitutional theory of the country.

In both language and form, Section One was the distillation of basic constitutional and legal theories long understood and voiced by leaders in a Congress upon which history had cast both the opportunity and the obligation to amend the Constitution to regulate relationships profoundly altered by the abolition of slavery.[448] None can doubt that the thrust of the Amendment was equalitarian and that it was adopted to wipe out the racial inequalities that were the legacies of that system. But beyond this, the majestic generalities of the Section can be seen to have evolved naturally and logically in the minds of the antislavery generation.[449]

At the outset we point out that we do not set forth the arguments of pamphleteers, or even of lawyers or congressmen, to justify the validity of their constitutional theories. We do not say that these theories were universally held, or deny that they were vigorously challenged. Nor do we urge

that the pre–Civil War Constitution contained the sweeping guarantees that the Abolitionists claimed for Negroes. These are beside our present point. What we do undertake in this section is illumination of the constitutional language— the moral and ethical opinions that were the matrix of the Amendment, the development under terrific counter-pressures of the principal texts and forms, the meaning of "equal protection" and "due process" as understood and contemplated by those who wrote those phrases into the Amendment.

1. The declaration of the "Self-Evident Truths"

The roots of our American equalitarian ideal extend deep into the history of the western world. Philosophers of the seventeenth and eighteenth centuries produced an intellectual climate in which the equality of man was a central concept. Their beliefs rested upon the basic proposition that all men were endowed with certain natural rights, some of which were surrendered under the so-called "social contract." The state, in return, guaranteed individual rights, and owed protection equally to all men. Thus, governments existed, not to give, but to protect rights; and allegiance and protection were reciprocal. For his allegiance, the citizen was guaranteed his rights and the equal protection of the law.[450]

---

[448] Graham, *The Early Antislavery Backgrounds of the Fourteenth Amendment,* 1950 WIS. L. REV. 479–507, 610–661, hereinafter cited *Early Antislavery Backgrounds.*

[449] Basic monographs and articles on the Fourteenth Amendment and its major clauses are: 2 CROSSKEY, POLITICS AND THE CONSTITUTION IN THE HISTORY OF THE UNITED STATES cc. 31–32 (1953); FLACK, THE ADOPTION OF THE FOURTEENTH AMENDMENT (1908); THE JOURNALS OF THE JOINT COMMITTEE OF FIFTEEN ON RECONSTRUCTION (Kendrick ed. 1914); TENBROEK, THE ANTISLAVERY ORIGINS OF THE FOURTEENTH AMENDMENT (1951) hereinafter cited ANTISLAVERY ORIGINS; WARSOFF, EQUALITY AND THE LAW (1938); Boudin, *Truth and Fiction About the Fourteenth Amendment,* 16 N. Y. U. L. Q. REV. 19 (1938); Fairman, *Does the Fourteenth Amendment Incorporate the Bill of Rights? The Original Understanding,* 2 STAN. L. REV. 5 (1949); Frank and Munro, *The Original Understanding of "Equal Protection of the Laws,"* 50 COL. L. REV. 131 (1950); Graham, *The "Conspiracy Theory" of the Fourteenth Amendment,* 47 YALE L. J. 371, 48 YALE L. J. 171 (1938); McLaughlin, *The Court, The Corporation, and Conkling,* 46 AM. HIST. REV. 45 (1940).

[450] LOCKE, SECOND TREATISE ON GOVERNMENT c. 2 (1698). (1926); SMITH, AMERICAN PHILOSOPHY OF EQUALITY (1927); WRIGHT, AMERICAN INTERPRETATIONS OF NATURAL LAW (1931); Corwin, *The "Higher Law" Background of American*

This doctrine was the core of the first great statement of American principles. To Jefferson and the other draftsmen of the Declaration of Independence, it was "self-evident" that "all men are created equal," and "are endowed by their Creator with certain unalienable Rights," among which are "Life, Liberty and the pursuit of Happiness," and that "to secure these rights, Governments are instituted among Men, deriving their just powers from the consent of the governed."[451]

Abhorrence of arbitrariness—the central element of due process—and the ideal of a general and equal law—the core of equal protection—both were implicit in the Lockean-Jeffersonian premises. Slavery—with its theories of racial damnation, racial inferiority, and racial discrimination—was inherently repugnant to the American creed and the Christian ethic. This fact was being rapidly and increasingly sensed. As men sensed it, they had to fit it into the only political theory they knew: Governments existed, not to give, but to *protect* human rights; allegiance and protection were reciprocal—i.e., *ought to be reciprocal;* rights and duties were correlative—i.e., *had to be correlative* if Americans ever were to live with their consciences and to justify their declared political faith.

Long before the Revolution, Quakers and Puritans attacked slavery as a violation of the social compact and Christian ethic.[452] After 1776, Jefferson's "self-evident truths" put a cutting edge on all such pleas—made them the broadswords in every attack. Idealists demanded that America live up to her Declaration. "All men" must mean all men. "Unalienable Rights ... of Life, Liberty and the pursuit of Happiness" must be given its full human, not merely a restricted racial, application. Race and color were arbitrary, insubstantial bases for accord or denial of natural, human rights. Sensitive leaders soon found themselves confronted with what Gunnar Myrdal treated recently as *An American Dilemma.*[453] Having pledged their "Lives ... Fortunes, and sacred Honor" to the causes of liberty and freedom, either Americans endeavored to live up to their creed or stultified themselves before the world.

After the Revolution, the "self-evident truths" and the provisions of the state Bills of Rights were employed as weapons against slavery and against racial distinctions.[454] Down through the Civil War, moreover, the "self-evident truths" constituted precisely what Jefferson declared them to be—political axioms—except in the South after the invention of the cotton gin.[455] They were on every tongue as rhetorical shorthand, and were popularly regarded as the marrow of the Constitution itself. In justifying one revolution, Jefferson no less than Locke had laid the groundwork for another. The dominating premise that governments were instituted for protection and

U.S. SUPREME
COURT,
OCTOBER 1953

BRIEF FOR THE
APPELLANTS AND
RESPONDENTS
ON REARGUMENT

Constitutional Law, 42 HARV. L. REV. 149, 365 (1928); Graham, *Early Antislavery Backgrounds, supra* note 1, at 610–611; Hamilton. *Property According to Locke,* 41 YALE L. J. 864 (1932).

[451] It is interesting to note in this context that Jefferson's original draft of the Declaration, accepted by Franklin and Adams, the other members of the sub-committee responsible for the drafting, contained severe strictures on the King because of the slave trade. See BECKER, *op. cit. supra* note 3, at 212–213.

[452] German Quakers of Pennsylvania had argued as early as 1688, "Though they are black, we cannot conceive there is more liberty to have them slaves [than] ... to have other white ones... . We should do to all men like as we will be done ourselves, making no difference of what descent or colour they are... . Here is liberty of conscience, which is right and reasonable; here ought to be likewise liberty of body... ." MOORE, NOTES ON THE HISTORY OF SLAVERY IN MASSACHUSETTS 75 (1866). In 1700, in his antislavery tract, THE SELLING OF JOSEPH, the great Puritan elder, Judge Samuel Sewall, declared, "All men, as they are ... Sons of Adam, are co-heirs, and have equal Right unto Liberty." *Id.* at 83–87. See also Graham, *Early Antislavery Backgrounds, supra* note 1, at 614–615.

[453] 2 vols. (1944).

[454] In 1783, Chief Justice Cushing, pointing to the "All men

are born free and equal" clause of the Massachusetts Bill of Rights, declared that "... slavery is inconsistent with our conduct and Constitution, and there can be no such thing as perpetual servitude of a rational creature." MOORE, *op. cit. supra* note 5, at 209–221. Four years later, Congress passed the Northwest Ordinance outlawing slavery in the territories. 2 THORPE, THE FEDERAL AND STATE CONSTITUTIONS, COLONIAL CHARTERS, AND OTHER ORGANIC LAWS 957–962 (1909). Vermont effected abolition by constitutional clause; other northern states by prospective legislative action. Graham, *Early Antislavery Backgrounds, supra* note 1, at 617. [455] While early southern leaders in Virginia accepted Jeffersonian concepts of natural rights, contract, and equality, later leaders and theorists defended the slave society on the basis of Greek concepts. Man had no rights save those created by the state. Men were inherently unequal, and the end of the state was not equality but justice. Each man would have status in accordance with his ability. Such theorists posited the inherent inferiority of the Negro. Their theory was broad enough to justify slavery for any man, irrespective of race or color. See THE PRO-SLAVERY ARGUMENT, AS MAINTAINED BY THE MOST DISTINGUISHED WRITERS OF THE SOUTHERN STATES (1853). See also 1 THE WORKS OF JOHN C. CALHOUN 393–394, 6 *id.* at 182–183 (Crallé ed. 1854–1855);

U.S. SUPREME
COURT,
OCTOBER 1953

BRIEF FOR THE
APPELLANTS AND
RESPONDENTS
ON REARGUMENT

that they derived their just powers from the consent of the governed had begun to make slavery, and with it race distinctions, untenable. What slowly took shape was an ethical interpretation of American origins and destiny.

2. The moral suasion campaign and its rejection

The Age of Enlightenment of the seventeenth and eighteenth centuries gave birth to a world-wide antislavery movement. A wave of humanitarianism, embracing quests for abolition of slavery, suffrage for women, and penal, land, and other reforms, swept across the United States of the early nineteenth century. Because of its dramatic qualities, the American anti-slavery movement assumed even larger proportions and eventually overshadowed the other phases.[456] Like them, it was based fundamentally on Judeo-Christian ethic and was formulated in terms of equalitarianism and natural rights.

The early antislavery movement was a campaign of moral suasion. Rational men appealed to other rational men to square precept with practice. Proponents of equality, who were by that definition opponents of slavery, sought to persuade slaveholders of the error of enslaving other men, i.e., of denying equality to those held as slaves. That campaign bore early fruit in Virginia, in the uplands of the Carolinas, and even in the deeper South. The appeal to the South ultimately broke on the hard rock of economic self-interest after invention of the cotton gin. Geography and migrations tended further to sectionalize the institution. Quakers and Scotch-Irish yeomen from Virginia and the Carolinas, unable to arrest spread of a labor system they detested, and others from the deeper South, fled *en masse,* settling generally in Ohio and Indiana. There they were joined by staunch Puritan and Calvinist stocks from New York and New England. Thus, the antislavery movement became sectionalized with important centers in Ohio, western New York, and Pennsylvania.

Spearheading the movement was the American Anti-Slavery Society, founded in 1833 and headed by the wealthy Tappan brothers. Recruited and led by Theodore Weld,[457] a brilliant orator and organizer, and by his co-leader, James G. Birney,[458] a converted Alabama slaveholder and lawyer, whole communities were abolitionized in the years 1835–1837. Appeals were aimed at influential leaders; lawyers in particular were sought out and recruited by the score.

This appeal was an ethico-moral-religious-natural rights argument. It was addressed by the revivalists to their countrymen as patriots, Christians, and "free moral agents." "The law of nature *clearly teaches the natural* republican equality of all mankind. *Nature* revolts at human slavery. . . . The Law of God renders all Natural Rights inalienable. . . . Governments and laws are established, not to give, but to protect ... rights."[459] Negroes, they continued, were "not naturally inferior." They simply had been degraded by slavery. They were persons, endowed by God with all the attributes of personality. Their enslavement could no more be justified than could chattelization of men with red hair. Slavery rested on a capricious, discredited classification.[460] It simply was institutionalized false imprisonment. White men were protected against enslavement and against false imprisonment.

Spain, The Political Theory of John C. Calhoun c. 8 (1951).

[456] Nye, Fettered Freedom 2, 10–11, 217–218, and *passim* (1949).

[457] See Thomas, Theodore Weld (1950); Letters of Theodore Dwight Weld, Angelina Grimke Weld and Sarah Grimke, 1822–1844, 2 vols. (Barnes and Dumond ed. 1934) cited hereinafter as Weld-Grimke Letters.1830–1844 (1933). Weld was a tireless speaker and pamphleteer who turned out documents that became guide posts in the antislavery movement: Slavery As It Is (1839); The Power of Congress Over the District of Columbia (1838); The Bible Against Slavery (1837). Such persons as William Jay, John Quincy Adams and Senator Robert C. Winthrop relied on Weld for legal research. See 2 Weld-Grimke Letters 748, 956–958. The evangelical character of the antislavery movement helps account for the flood of arguments that poured from it. It was even organized on an analogy drawn from early Christian evangelists with its Seventy and its Council of Twelve.

[458] See Birney, James G. Birney and His Times (1890); Letters of James G. Birney, 1831–1857, 2 vols. (Dumond ed. 1938), referred to hereinafter as Birney Letters.

[459] Olcott, Two Lectures on the Subject of Slavery and Abolition 24–29 (1838).

[460] The idea that race and color were arbitrary, capricious standards on which to base denial of human rights was implicit in all antislavery attacks on discrimination and prejudice. Yet it was when the constitutional-legal attack began to reinforce the religious one that such arguments became explicit, and the concept of an arbitrary classification developed. Lawyers like Ellsworth, Goddard, Birney (Philanthropist, Dec. 9, 1836, p. 3, cols. 4–5), Gerrit Smith (see American Anti-Slavery Society, 3 Annual Reports 16–17 (1836)) and Salmon P. Chase (Speech ... in the Case of the Colored Woman, Matilda ... 32 (1837)) helped to formulate the concept and linked it with the principles of equality, affirmative protection, and national citizenship.

"What abolitionists demand as naked justice is that the benefit and protection of these just laws be extended to all human beings alike ... without regard to color or any other physical peculiarities."[461]

Racial discrimination, in short, was repugnant both as a breach of equality and as a breach of protection. Because it was a breach of protection, it also was a breach of equality; and because it was a breach of equality, it was thereby an even greater breach of protection. This was the outcome of Americans' triple-barreled major premise which posited the purpose of *all* government to be the protection of inalienable rights bestowed upon *all* men by their Creator. Once that compound premise was granted—and in the generations since 1776 virtually all Americans outside the South had *spoken* as if they granted it—the abolitionists' conclusions were unassailable. The heart of it was that these basic ideals of liberty, equality, and protection were deemed to be paramount by reason of their place in the Declaration and determinative by reason of the place of the Declaration in American life and history.

The issue had to be resolved within the framework of the constitutional system. Appeals to ethico-moral concepts and to natural rights were good enough to argue as to what ought to be. Reality was something else again. Constitutional reality was that the status of inhabitants of the United States, white or Negro, was fixed by the Constitution. Social reality was that the great mass of Negroes were slaves.

Inevitably, then, the first skirmishes as to the rights claimed for Negroes had to be fought out in the case of free Negroes.[462] The targets here were northern black laws—the laws in Ohio and Connecticut; the techniques were persuasion, conversion, and demonstration. It was in the course of this campaign that what presently became the constitutional trinity of the antislavery movement received its decisive synthesis.

The first comprehensive crystallization of antislavery constitutional theory occurred in 1834 in the arguments of W. W. Ellsworth and Calvin Goddard, two of the outstanding lawyers and statesmen of Connecticut, on the appeal[463] of the conviction of Prudence Crandall for violation of an ordinance forbidding the education of non-resident colored persons without the consent of the civil authorities.[464] They reveal this theory as based on broad natural rights premises and on an ethical interpretation of

American origins and history. Four ideals were central and interrelated: the ideal of human equality, the ideal of a general and equal law, the ideal of reciprocal protection and allegiance, and the ideal of reason and substantiality as the true bases for the necessary discriminations and classifications by government. Race as a standard breached every one of these ideals, as did color. What was attacked was denial of human equality and denial of protection of the laws—denials inherent in any racial discrimination backed by public authority. Slavery was the arch evil in this respect, and the primary one, both because of the magnitude of its denials and deprivations and abridgments, and because these necessarily established a whole pattern of discrimination based upon race and color alone. It was this pattern of public discrimination that was combatted no less than slavery. It had to be combatted because it was deemed a part of slavery.

Although neither slavery nor segregated schools was the issue in the case, the Ellsworth-Goddard argument is one of the classic statements of the social and ethical case for equality of opportunity irrespective of race. It gave immense impetus to the emerging concept of American nationality and citizenship. Fully reported and widely circulated as a tract, it soon became one of the fountainheads of antislavery constitutional theory. It figured prominently in Abolitionist writings throughout the 'thirties. In the spring of 1835, Judge William Jay, Abolitionist son of the first Chief Justice and one of the founders and vice-presidents of the American Anti-Slavery

U.S. SUPREME COURT, OCTOBER 1953

BRIEF FOR THE APPELLANTS AND RESPONDENTS ON REARGUMENT

---

[461] OLCOTT, *op. cit. supra* note 12, at 44.

[462] For characteristic references to plans for bettering the lot of the free Negro, see 1 WELD-GRIMKE LETTERS, *op. cit. supra* note 10, at 132–135, 262; AMERICAN ANTI-SLAVERY SOCIETY, 4 ANNUAL REPORTS 32–35, 105–111 (1837). 5 ANNUAL REPORTS 127 (1838). For evidence of how large the condition of the free Negroes, and plans for their betterment, figured in the early A. A. S. S. strategy, see *The Condition of Free People of Color in the United States,* The Anti-slavery Examiner #13a (1839), apparently written by Judge William Jay, reprinted in his MISCELLANEOUS WORKS 371–395 (1853).

[463] Crandall v. State, 10 Conn. 339 (1834).

[464] REPORT OF THE ARGUMENTS OF COUNSEL IN THE CASE OF PRUDENCE CRANDALL, PLFF. IN ERROR, VS. STATE OF CONNECTICUT, BEFORE THE SUPREME COURT OF ERRORS, AT THEIR SESSION AT BROOKLYN, JULY TERM, 1834. The arguments are printed in condensed form in the official report, Crandall v. State, *supra* note 16, at 349–353 (1834).34–51 (1853); STIENER, HISTORY OF SLAVERY IN CONN. 45–52 (1893); VON HOLST, CONSTITUTIONAL HISTORY 1828–1846 98, 99 (1881); McCarron, *Trial of Prudence Crandall,* 12 CONN. MAG. 225–232 (1908); NYE, *op. cit. supra* note 9, at 83.

U.S. SUPREME
COURT,
OCTOBER 1953

BRIEF FOR THE
APPELLANTS AND
RESPONDENTS
ON REARGUMENT

Society, devoted fifteen pages of his *Inquiry into the Character and Tendency of the Colonization and Anti-Slavery Societies*[465] to a slashing attack on the trial court's decision.

The due process element of our modern trilogy was introduced in the course of a determined attack made in 1835 by the Weld-Birney group upon Ohio's black laws. Enacted in 1807, these laws embodied prohibitions against Negro immigration, employment, education, and testimony. A report[466] prepared at Weld's direction by a committee of the newly formed Ohio Anti-Slavery Society appealed to the American and Christian conscience. Notwithstanding the affirmative duty of all government to "promote the happiness and secure the rights and liberties of man," and despite the fact that American government was predicated on the "broad and universal principle of equal and unalienable rights," these statutes had singled out a "weak and defenseless class of citizens—a class convicted of no crime— no natural inferiority," and had invidiously demanded their exclusion from "the rights and privileges of citizenship." This, it was argued, the Constitution forbade. "Our Constitution does not say, *All men* of a *certain color* are entitled to certain rights, and are born free and independent. . . . The expression is unlimited. . . . *All* men are so born, and have the *unalienable* rights of life and liberty—the pursuit of happiness, and the acquisition and possession of wealth."

These were the doctrinal cornerstones.[467] They were the heart of the ethico-moral-historical-natural rights argument which the American Anti-Slavery Society broadcast in the mid- and late-'thirties. They were broadcast particularly throughout Ohio, western New York and Pennsylvania, Rhode Island, and Massachusetts.[468] Weld was the director and master strategist; Birney, the forensic quartermaster and attorney general. The "Twelve" and the "Seventy" were the chosen instruments. These were the two dedicated hand-picked groups of trained teachers, ministers, divinity students, self-named after the early Christian Apostles. Their revivals converted thousands before funds ran out and southern antagonism crippled the movement. Numerous anti-slavery newspapers and coordinated pamphlet and petition campaigns were reinforcing media.

The trouble, of course, was that northerners were still largely indifferent to or unreached by this program, while the South rejected it almost without a hearing. Coincidence played a great part here. Alarmed lest educated Negroes foment slave insurrections, the South further tightened its controls.[469] Fortuitously, the Vesey and Turner uprisings had seemed to offer frightening confirmation of fears in this regard. Meanwhile, cotton profits and politics had begun to rationalize slavery as "a positive good." The insidious belief spread that the South must insulate herself, safeguard her "peculiar institu-

[465] Reprinted in JAY, MISCELLANEOUS WRITINGS ON SLAVERY 36 (1853).
[466] PROCEEDINGS OF THE OHIO ANTI-SLAVERY CONVENTION HELD AT PUTNAM 17–36 (April 22–24, 1835).
[467] It is not implied that these arguments were without ante-cedents. Earlier (1819–21) in the controversy over Missouri's admission, the provision in its Constitution prohibiting immigration of free Negroes prompted anti-slavery arguments based on the republican form of government and comity clauses. See BURGESS, THE MIDDLE PERIOD, 1817–58 c. 4 (1897); McLAUGHLIN, CONSTITUTIONAL HISTORY OF THE UNITED STATES c. 29 (1935); WILSON, RISE AND FALL OF THE SLAVE POWER cc. 11–12 (1872), especially at 154. Later, the Horton episode, and the protracted controversy over southern seamen's laws whereunder northern and British free Negro seamen were confined to quarters or jailed while in southern ports, gave further impetus to theories of *national* or *American* citizenship. The former was a *cause cél;agebre* of 1826–1827 involving a statute of the District of Columbia which authorized sale for jail fees of *suspected* fugitive slaves. Horton, a free Negro of New York, who had been arrested and threatened with sale, was saved by timely aid of Abolitionist friends who capitalized the incident. See JAY, MISCELLANEOUS WRITINGS ON SLAVERY 48,

238–242 (1853); TUCKERMAN, WILLIAM JAY AND THE CONSTITUTIONAL MOVEMENT FOR ABOLITION OF SLAVERY 31–33 (1893); 3 CONG. DEB. 555 (1826). Regarding the seamen's controversy, see Hamer, *Great Britain, the United States and the Negro Seamen Acts, 1822–1848*, 1 J. OF SO. HIST. 1–28 (1935); H. R. REP. NO. 80, 27th Cong., 3rd Sess. (1843). Later, in 1844, the Hoar incident occurred, in which Judge Samuel Hoar of Massachusetts, proceeding to Charleston to defend imprisoned Negro seamen, was expelled from South Carolina by legislative resolution. See Hamer, *supra,* and the elaborate documentation in STATE DOCUMENTS ON FEDERAL RELATIONS: THE STATES AND THE UNITED STATES 237–238 (Ames ed. 1904). The Hoar expulsion and the numerous laws, both North and South, excluding free Negroes and mulattoes, were cited repeatedly in the debates of the 'fifties and in 1866. See, for example, CONG. GLOBE, 39th Cong., 1st Sess. 475 (1866) (Remarks of Sen. Trumbull).
[468] See especially BARNES, *op. cit. supra* note 10, cc. 2, 3, 4, and WELD-GRIMKE LETTERS and BIRNEY LETTERS, *op. cit. supra* notes 10, 11.
[469] See EATON, FREEDOM OF THOUGHT IN THE OLD SOUTH c. 5 (1940) and statutes there cited; SYDNOR, DEVELOPMENT OF SOUTHERN SECTIONALISM 1819–1848 (1948).

U.S. SUPREME
COURT,
OCTOBER 1953

BRIEF FOR THE
APPELLANTS AND
RESPONDENTS
ON REARGUMENT

tions," and remove them even from discussion and criticism.[470] In the Pinckney Report of 1836,[471] pro-slave theorists sought to implement these convictions. To reinforce Calhoun's defensive doctrines of concurrent majority and state interposition, and in a determined attempt to protect slavery in the Federal District from possible interference or abolition by Congress under its sweeping powers over the District and territories, Pinckney and his colleagues in the House employed the due process clause of the Fifth Amendment and "the principles of natural justice and of the social compact."[472]

3. The political action campaign

A. Systemization Thus, the antislavery campaign was set back, its piecemeal conversion and demonstration program was frustrated at the outset by barriers that held slavery to be a positive good—untouchable even where Congress had full powers over it. Antislavery men were denied the use of the mails. Their anti-slavery petitions were throttled by Congressional "gags." They were forced to defend even their own rights to speak and write and proselytize. In consequence, the antislavery leaders had to reorient their whole movement and strategy.[473]

This reorientation, greatly accelerated by the Pinckney Report, was marked by rapid "constitutionalization" of the higher law argument. There was a shift from an overwhelming faith in moral suasion to a reluctant resort to political action, from efforts to convince Americans of the expediency and justice of freeing their slaves, to a search for constitutional power to free them.[474]

These tendencies may be traced today in the pages of the *Weld-Grimke* and *Birney Letters,* in a vast pamphlet literature, in annual reports of the state and national societies,[475] but most satisfactorily in the columns of Birney's *Philanthropist.*[476] Calhoun and "positive good" theorists had fashioned a constitutional system that promised absolute protection for slavery and ignored the constitutional reference to slaves as "persons," referring to them whenever possible as "property." These theorists also employed the "compact" and "compromises" of 1787 as a device that removed slavery from the reach not merely of state and federal legislatures but from adverse discussion and criticism.

Birney and his colleagues now formulated a countersystem, one which exalted liberty and exploited the founding fathers' use of "persons." Denying all limiting force to the "compact" or "compromises," this group hailed the spirit of the Declaration, of the Constitution, and American institutions generally. They seized on the leading provisions of the state and federal bills of rights as affirmative guarantees of the freedom of the slaves.[477]

In his earlier writings,[478] Birney's ethical interpretation of American origins and history was essentially that of the *Crandall* argument and the Ohio Anti-Slavery Society reports. The natural rights creed of the Declaration, the universality of guarantees of the state bills of rights, the Signers' and the Fathers' known aversion to slavery, the "color blindness" of the Articles of Confederation, the outright prohibition of slavery in the territories by the Northwest Ordinance,

---

[470] See JENKINS, PROSLAVERY THOUGHT IN THE OLD SOUTH (1935); and the histories of Eaton and Sydnor, *op. cit. supra* note 22; and WILTSIE, JOHN C. CALHOUN, NULLIFIER, 1828–1839 c. 20, esp. 283–286 (1949); *cf.* Corwin, *National Power and State Interposition, 1787–1861,* 10 MICH. L. REV. 535 (1912).

[471] H. R. REP. NO. 691, 24th Cong., 1st Sess. (1836).

[472] *Id.* at 14.

[473] DUMOND, THE ANTISLAVERY ORIGINS OF THE CIVIL WAR (1938); NYE, *op. cit. supra* note 9.

[474] DUMOND, *op. cit. supra* note 26, especially cc. 5–6; T. C. SMITH, THE LIBERTY AND FREE SOIL PARTIES IN THE NORTHWEST (1897); NYE, *op. cit. supra* note 9. *Cf.* CRAVEN, THE COMING OF THE CIVIL WAR (1943); NEVINS, ORDEAL OF THE UNION (1947).

[475] Read straight through, the six ANNUAL PROC. AND REP. OF AMERICAN ANTISLAVERY SOCIETY (1833–1839) and the five ANNIVERSARY PROC. OF THE OHIO ANTISLAVERY SOCIETY (1836–1840) reveal the shift from confident evangelism to determined self-defense and political action. Not until after the Pinckney Report (*supra* note 24), the "Gags" denying

antislavery petitions, and the refusal of the South to countenance discussion of the issue, does one find serious interest in political movements and tactics. The THIRD ANNUAL REPORT OF THE A. A. S. S. (May 10, 1836) signed by Elizur Wright is thus the turning point and a catalog of the factors that had reoriented opinion. By the SIXTH ANNUAL REPORT OF THE A. A. S. S. (1839), the "imperative necessity of political action" caused Wright to devote much of his space to convincing the still hesitant and divided membership.

[476] Birney's career as an editor can be followed in the BIRNEY LETTERS, *op. cit. supra* note 11 (see index entries "Philanthropist"), and in his pamphlet NARRATIVE OF THE LATE RIOTOUS PROCEEDINGS AGAINST THE LIBERTY OF THE PRESS IN CINCINNATI (1836).

[477] Sometimes Abolitionists, in desperation, appealed to a higher law beyond the Constitution, but this was not a consistent argument or one possible within the legal framework.

[478] BIRNEY LETTERS, *op. cit. supra* note 11. For a fuller and documented summary, see Graham, *Early Antislavery Backgrounds, supra* note 1, at 638–650.

U.S. SUPREME
COURT,
OCTOBER 1953

BRIEF FOR THE
APPELLANTS AND
RESPONDENTS
ON REARGUMENT

and above all, the silence, the euphemisms, the circumlocutions of the Constitution—these were the recurrent and expanding points. Not merely slavery, but *all public race discrimination* was ethically and morally wrong. It was so because it was a denial of the rights and protections that governments were established to secure.

After the Pinckney Report, however, and especially after the growing mob action against Abolitionists began to make it clear that state bills of rights were not self-executing but rested on local enforcement, Birney reexamined his position. Everywhere there was this anomaly: the great natural and fundamental rights of conscience, inquiry and communication, secured *on paper* in every constitution, nevertheless were denied and abridged daily for want of sanctions. All men by nature "possessed" these indispensable rights; all constitutions "declared" and "secured" them. It was the bounden duty of all governments "created for the purposes of protection" to safeguard and enforce them. Yet the hard fact was that state and local governments were flagrantly, increasingly derelict. Nothing, southerners argued, could be done about it.

Challenged in this manner, Birney and his aides shifted their ground. They advanced from the old position that the Federal Constitution was neutral—"or at least not pro-slavery"—to the stand that the document was antislavery. Constitutionalization of the natural rights argument proceeded at a much more rapid pace. No longer was the fight waged merely defensively in behalf of the right to proselytize, or counter-defensively to support sweeping Federal powers over the District and territories; more and more the antislavery forces took the offensive against slavery itself.[479]

Thus, by December 1836, the Abolitionists' argument was recrystallizing around three major propositions:

First, the great natural and fundamental rights of life, liberty, and property, long deemed inherent and inalienable, were now held to be secured by *both* state and national constitutions.

Second, notwithstanding this double security, and in disregard of the obligation of governments to extend protection in return for allegiance, these rights were being violated with impunity both on national soil and in the states, (a) by the fact of slavery itself, (b) by mob action directed against those working for abolition, (c)

by flagrant discriminations against free Negroes and mulattoes.

Third, race and color—"grades and shades" —whenever and wherever employed as criteria and determinants of fundamental rights, violated both the letter and spirit of American institutions; race *per se* was not only an ignoble standard; it was an irrational and unsubstantial one.

The problems of implementing this theory, Birney worked out in several series of articles during 1837. Rescrutinizing the document, he began to make the same rigorous use of the Federal Bill of Rights that previously he and others had made of Ohio's. Ultimately, he focused on the due process clause employed in Pinckney's Report:[480] "The Constitution contains provisions which, if literally carried out, would extinguish the entire system of slavery. It guarantees to every state in the union a republican form of government, Art. IV, Sec. 4th. A majority of the people of South Carolina are slaves; can she be said properly to have a republican form of government? It says, that 'the right of the people to be secure in their *persons,* houses, papers and effects … against unreasonable searches and *seizures,* shall not be violated.' Slaves, Sir, are men, constitute a portion of the people: Is that no 'unreasonable seizure,' by which the man is deprived of all his earnings [effects?]—by which in fact he is robbed of his own person? Is the perpetual privation of liberty 'no unreasonable seizure'? Suppose this provision of the Constitution were literally and universally enforced; how long would it be before there would not be a single *slave* to mar the prospect of American liberty? Again, '*no* person shall be held to answer for a capital or otherwise infamous crime unless on the presentment or indictment of a grand jury, except in cases arising in the land or naval forces, [sic] nor shall any person be compelled in any case to witness against himself; nor be deprived of life, liberty or property without due process of law.' Art. V Amendments.

"Are slaves ever honored with indictment by a grand jury? Are they never compelled 'to wit-

---

[479] See Graham, *Early Antislavery Backgrounds, supra* note 1, at 650–653.

[480] Philanthropist, Jan. 13, 1837, p. 2. Birney continued his "Reply to Judge L" in the Jan. 20 and 27, 1837 numbers, and in the former demonstrated his forensic powers by brilliant caricature of the South's efforts to suppress discussion of slavery.

U.S. SUPREME
COURT,
OCTOBER 1953

BRIEF FOR THE
APPELLANTS AND
RESPONDENTS
ON REARGUMENT

ness against themselves'? never tortured until they lie against their own lives? never deprived of life without 'due process of law'? By what 'due process of law' is it, that two millions of 'persons' are deprived every year of the millions of dollars produced by their labor? By what due process of law is it that 56,000 'persons,' the annual increase of the slave population, are annually deprived of their 'liberty'? Such questions may seem impertinent, to Mr. L., but when he shall feel that the slave is a 'person,' in very deed, and has rights, as inalienable as his own, he will acknowledge their propriety. Again 'In all criminal prosecutions, the accused shall enjoy the right to a speedy and public trial, by an impartial jury … and to be informed of the nature and cause of the accusation; to be confronted with the witnesses against him; to have compulsory process for obtaining witnesses in his favor; and to have the assistance of Counsel for his defense.' Art. VI of the Amendments. Take all the above provisions in connection with that clause under Art. VI, which declares that 'This Constitution and the laws of the United States which shall be made in pursuance thereof' etc., 'shall be the supreme law of the land, and the judges in every state shall be bound thereby, anything in the Constitution or laws of any state to the contrary notwithstanding'—and then carry them out to their full extent, and how long would it be ere slavery would be utterly prostrated? I do not say they were inserted with a specific view toward this end, but I do say, that so long as they shall stand, the Constitution of these U[nited] States will be a perpetual rebuke to the selfishness and injustice of the whole policy of the slaveholder. The provisions embody principles which are at entire enmity with the spirit and practice of slavery. How an instrument, containing such principles, can be tortured to express a *sanction* to slavery, I am yet to learn."[481]

Reassimilation of the old theory into the Bill of Rights now proceeded rapidly.[482] The various clauses restraining the powers of Congress began to be popularly regarded as *sources* of Congressional power. The initial premise in this regard was that the provisions of the Bill of Rights were not *rights,* they were *guarantees,* and guarantees customarily presumed the intent and capacity, as well as the duty, to make them good.[483] An open letter[484] to his Congressman from an unnamed Abolitionist in Batavia[485] reveals the hold and spread and reach of these ideas:

"The very Constitution of the United States is attempted to be distorted and made an ally of domestic slavery. That Constitution was established, not by the *citizens* or *voters,* but

by '*the people*' of the United States to secure the blessings of *liberty* and establish *justice.* The Union … was formed for the same great purposes, … yet we have been told that petitioning for *liberty* endangers this Union, that the partnership will be dissolved by extending to all the very right it was intended to secure.

"Slavery in the District of Columbia violates the most important and sacred principles of the Constitution.… . I speak not of the mere *letter,* but of the *principles* …—of the *rights* it guarantees, of the *form,* in which the guarantee is expressed. The 5th Amendment declares 'no person shall be deprived of life, *liberty* or property without due process of law.' This petition informs you free men in the District … have been first imprisoned, and then sold for their jail fees. [Suppose, he continued, this had happened to American seamen in a foreign port.] Would not Congress upon petition enquire into the fact and redress the wrong if it existed? Would not you, Sir, be one of the foremost in repelling the insult to our seamen and punishing the aggressor? Would you not consider it your *duty*—your *official* duty to do so? And yet you have no power to discriminate in the object of your protection—a colored sailor is entitled to the *protection* of his country's laws, and Constitution, and flag, and honor, as well as a white one,—he is as much entitled to that protection in Washington city beneath the flag of his country and while he reposes under the tower of the Capitol as he is at *Qualla Balloo* or Halifax, or anywhere on the face of the earth. And all should be protected with equal and exact justice, whether sailors or laborers—citizens or soldiers: if so, you are bound to enquire into the alleged abuses, and if they exist to redress them."

Thus, by October, 1837, the date of Birney's retirement as editor of the Philanthropist, the motivating premise of Abolitionism already was

---

481 *Ibid.*

482 Resolutions and petitions still were the chief media in evolving this system of constitutional shorthand. Similarity of the revivalists' lectures from place to place, their widespread circulation of the Philanthropist and printed tracts, Birney's own speaking tours, all contributed to resulting stereotypes.

483 For a striking statement of this theory in 1866 see CONG. GLOBE, 39th Cong., 1st Sess. 1270 (Rep. Thayer, later a distinguished Philadelphia judge).

484 Graham, *Early Antislavery Backgrounds, supra* note 1, at 655.

485 Perhaps John Joliffe, a local antislavery lawyer, who was a close friend of Birney. See Graham, *Early Antislavery Backgrounds, supra* note 1, at 655, n. 256.

U.S. SUPREME
COURT,
OCTOBER 1953

BRIEF FOR THE
APPELLANTS AND
RESPONDENTS
ON REARGUMENT

coming to be this: Americans' basic civil rights were truly national, but in practice their basic civil liberty was not. By acts in support and in toleration of slavery and by failure to protect the friends of the enslaved race, the states and the federal government all abridged, and all allowed to be abridged, the dearest privileges and immunities of citizenship. Humanitarianism had attempted to soften race prejudice and meet this challenge squarely but had been frustrated. Failure left no alternative but political action and the instinctive answer that government had the power to do what the governed had the job to do. The answer to denied power and to defective power was the concept of an inherent power derived from the standing duty to protect. The gist of it was that because allegiance and protection were reciprocal—i.e., ought to be reciprocal—because the government protected its citizens abroad without discrimination, and because the text of the Federal Bill of Rights gave no warrant for discrimination, Congress was duty bound *not* to discriminate. It must do "equal and exact justice" irrespective of race. It had no other choice. It lacked power to discriminate between those persons who were equally entitled to protection. It was duty bound also to remove such discrimination as existed. Implicitly, and morally, these same obligations rested on the states; yet respect for the constitutional division of power here introduced conflict. Few were yet ready for the extreme proposition that Congress might *constitutionally* abolish slavery *in the states*. The original form, as shown by the Batavian communication, was more often that Congress was duty bound to hear petitions to abolish slavery, or that slavery had been abolished in federal territory by the force of the Preamble and Declaration. Because the great natural rights were now also national constitutional rights, they began to generate and carry with them—*even into the states*—the power for their enforcement.

B. Popularization

Four routes and media of political action "constitutionalizing" the anti-slavery argument are to be noted.

First were the countless petitions, resolutions, declarations, letters, editorials, speeches, and sermons broadcast by the original anti-slavery proponents and converts—uniformly men and women of influence and position whose idealism was extraordinary and un-

doubted. One has to read only the *Weld-Grimke* and the *Birney*[486] *Letters,* or the monographs of Barnes,[487] Dumond[488] and Nye[489]—and Nevins's great history[490]—to realize the appeal of these peoples' character and of their example and argument. Moreover, many of them were southerners, and of the proudest type who practiced what they preached—Birney alone freeing slaves to the value of thousands of dollars,[491] and the Grimke sisters doing likewise with those they inherited. Every antislavery society was a band of disciples, workers, petitioners, writers, and "free moral agents" committed to the spread of doctrine that had immense intrinsic appeal.

In consequence, simply as an incident of the intense revival campaigns, the equal protection–due process–privileges and immunities theory became the core of thousands of abolitionist petitions, resolutions, and lectures. Now one, now another of the elements was accented, depending on the need and circumstances, but in an astonishing number of cases two or three parts of the trilogy were used. The whole thus became, even before 1840, a form of popular constitutional shorthand.

After that date even stronger forces enter the picture. First, were the compilers and synthesizers—pamphleteers and journalists like Tiffany[492] and Goodell[493] and Mellen[494] who wrote the articles and treatises on the "Unconstitutionality of Slavery" which Dr.

---

[486] The legal and constitutional argument in the Birney Letters is remarkable both in range and interest. Note especially the due process arguments at 293, 647, 805–806, 835; the declaration that colored people are "citizens" at 815, and "persons" at 658 and 835; the exceptionally strong references to "natural equality of men" at 272; the composite synthesis of all these elements in the Declaration of 1848 drafted by William Goodell at 1048–1057; the various references to major law cases at 386–387 (Nancy Jackson v. Bulloch, 12 Conn. 38 (1837)), at page 658, 667–670 (Birney's arguments in The Creole, 2 Moore, Digest of International Law 358–361 (1906), for which Weld did much of the research), at 758 (Jones v. Van Zandt, 46 U.S. 215 (1846) in which Salmon P. Chase was of counsel). By contrast, the legal argument in the Weld-Grimke Letters is more limited, but see page 798 for the letter of Ebenezer Chaplin, an Athol, Massachusetts physician, to Weld, dated October 1, 1839, urging greater emphasis on the unconstitutionality of slavery and less on its cruelties, and specifically mentioning the Declaration of Independence, the common law, the Ordinance of 1787, the Preamble, and the due process clause of the Fifth Amendment.

[487] *Op. cit. supra* note 10.

[488] *Op. cit. supra* note 26.

[489] *Op. cit. supra* note 9.

[490] The Ordeal of the Union, 2 vols. (1947).

tenBroek analyzes so well.[495] Others annotated copies of *Our National Charters*[496] setting down after each clause or phrase of the Constitution and the Declaration (much as Birney had done in his early articles) antislavery arguments and doctrines gleaned "both from reason and authority." Such materials, broadcast by the thousand, reprinted, condensed and paraphrased, were themselves powerful disseminators.

It was the minority party platform that gave antislavery theory its most concise, effective statement. Drafted generally by Salmon P. Chase or Joshua R. Giddings, these documents, first of the Liberty and Free Soil parties in the 'forties, then of the Free Democracy and Republican parties in the 'fifties, and in 1860, all made use, in slightly varying combination, of the cardinal articles of faith: human equality, protection, and equal protection from the Declaration, and due process both as a restraint and a source of congressional power. Such consistent repetition testifies both to the nature and extent of previous distillations and to the power and significance of current ones:

1. Liberty Party Platform (adopted in 1843 for the 1844 campaign):

"*Resolved,* That the fundamental truth of the Declaration of Independence, that all men are endowed by their Creator with certain unalienable rights, among which are life, liberty, and the pursuit of happiness, was made the fundamental law of our national government by that amendment of the Constitution which declares that no person shall be deprived of life, liberty, or property without due process of law."[497]

2. Free Soil Party Platform, 1848:

"*Resolved,* That our fathers ordained the Constitution of the United States in order, among other great national objects, to establish justice, promote the general welfare, and secure the blessings of liberty, but expressly denied to the federal government, which they created, all constitutional power to deprive

any person of life, liberty, or property without due legal process.

"*Resolved,* that, in the judgment of this convention, Congress has no more power to make a slave than to make a king; no more power to institute or establish slavery than to institute or establish a monarchy. No such power can be found among those specifically conferred by the Constitution, or derived by any just implication from them."[498]

3. Free Democracy Platform, 1852:

"1. That governments deriving their just powers from the consent of the governed are instituted among men to secure to all those unalienable rights of life, liberty, and the pursuit of happiness with which they are endowed by their Creator, and of which none can be deprived by valid legislation, except for crime.

"4. That the Constitution of the United States, ordained to form a more perfect Union, to establish justice, and secure the blessings of liberty, expressly denies to the general government all power to deprive any person of life, liberty, or property without due process of law; and, therefore, the government, having no more power to make a slave than to make a king, and no more power to establish slavery than to establish a monarchy, should at once proceed to relieve itself from all responsibility for the existence of slavery wherever it possesses constitutional power to legislate for its extinction."[499]

4. Republican Party Platform, 1856:

"*Resolved,* That with our republican fathers we hold it be a self-evident truth, that all men are endowed with the unalienable rights to life, liberty, and the pursuit of happiness, and that the primary object and ulterior designs of our federal government were to secure these rights to all persons within its exclusive jurisdiction; that, as our republican fathers, when they had abolished slavery in all our national territory, ordained that no person should be deprived of life, liberty, or property without due process of law, it becomes our duty to maintain this

U.S. SUPREME COURT, OCTOBER 1953

BRIEF FOR THE APPELLANTS AND RESPONDENTS ON REARGUMENT

---

491 1 Birney Letters, *op. cit. supra* note 11, at 52, 494, 498, 500–501.

492 Tiffany, A Treatise on the Unconstitutionality of American Slavery (1849).

493 Goodell, Views of American Constitutional Law in its Bearing Upon American Slavery (1844).

494 Mellen, An Argument on the Unconstitutionality of Slavery ... (1841).

495 tenBroek, Antislavery Origins, *op. cit. supra* note 2, c. 3 and pp. 86–91.

496 (Goodell ed. 1863).

497 The full platform is in Stanwood, History of the Presi-

dency 216–220 (1904). In addition to the plank quoted, it contains numerous references to "equality of the rights among men," "the principle of equal rights with all its practical consequences and applications," the "higher law" and "moral law," and the sacredness of rights of speech, press and petition.

498 *Id.* at 240. This platform was drafted by Salmon P. Chase. See Smith, The Liberty and Free Soil Parties in the Northwest 140 (1897).

499 Stanwood, *op. cit. supra* note 50, 253–254. This platform was drafted by Salmon P. Chase (see Warden, Life of Chase 338 (1874)) and Joshua R. Giddings (see Smith, *op. cit. supra* note 51, 247–248).

U.S. SUPREME
COURT,
OCTOBER 1953

BRIEF FOR THE
APPELLANTS AND
RESPONDENTS
ON REARGUMENT

provision of the Constitution against all attempts to violate it for the purpose of establishing slavery in any Territory of the United States, by positive legislation prohibiting its existence or extension therein; that we deny the authority of Congress, of a territorial legislature, of any individual or association of individuals, to give legal existence to slavery in any Territory of the United States, while the present Constitution shall be maintained."[500]

5. Republican Party Platform, 1860:

"8. That the normal condition of all the territory of the United States is that of freedom; that as our republican fathers, when they had abolished slavery in all our national territory, ordained that no person should be deprived of life, liberty, or property without due process of law, it becomes our duty, by legislation whenever such legislation is necessary, to maintain this provision of the Constitution against all attempts to violate it; and we deny the authority of Congress, of a territorial legislature, or of any individual, to give legal existence to slavery in any Territory of the United States.

"14. That the Republican party is opposed to any change in our naturalization laws, or any state legislation by which the rights of citizenship hitherto accorded to immigrants from foreign lands shall be abridged or impaired; and in favor of giving a full and efficient protection to the rights of all classes of citizens, whether native or naturalized, both at home and abroad."[501]

True, these were party platforms, but these were the platforms of parties to which leaders in the Congress that would frame the Fourteenth Amendment had given their allegiance.[502]

Many Congressmen whose names later loomed large in the formulation of and debates on the Thirteenth and Fourteenth Amendments and the Civil Rights Acts were men of antislavery backgrounds[503] which, it will be recalled, had sought out community leaders, particularly lawyers.[504] Even in the 'forties, antislavery Whigs, Liberty Party-Free Soilers, and later, members of the Free Democracy, converted by the Weld-Birney group, began to enter Congressmen like Joshua R. Giddings,[505] E. S. Hamlin,[506] the Wade brothers,[507] Horace Mann,[508] Philomen Bliss,[509] A. P. Granger,[510] Thaddeus Stevens,[511] Gerrit Smith,[512] William Lawrence,[513] James M. Ashley[514] (who introduced the Thirteenth Amendment in the House), Samuel Galloway[515] (a former member of the "Seventy") and John A. Bingham.[516] All were either associates, converts, or disciples of the Weld-Birney group; and after 1854, all were Republicans.

In addition to the western group of antislavery leaders, there was an equally strong and determined group with its focus in New England. From this group emerged Charles Sumner, Wendell Phillips, and Henry Wilson. Sumner later became one of the most intransigent leaders of the Republican party during and

[500] STANWOOD, op. cit. supra note 50, at 271. This platform was drafted by Joshua R. Giddings. JULIAN, THE LIFE OF JOSHUA R. GIDDINGS 335–336 (1892).

[501] STANWOOD, op. cit. supra note 50, at 293.

[502] See infra pp. 27–36, and notes 56–69.

[503] Among them the following members of the Joint Committee on Reconstruction: George H. Williams, Oregon; Henry W. Grimes, Iowa; William Pitt Fessenden, Maine; Henry T. Blow, Missouri; John A. Bingham, Ohio; George S. Boutwell, Massachusetts; Justin S. Morrill, Vermont; Roscoe Conkling, New York; Elihu B. Washburne, Illinois; and Thaddeus Stevens, Pennsylvania. Two others, Jacob M. Howard of Michigan and Ira Harris of New York, invariably voted with the so-called Radicals. See KENDRICK op. cit. supra note 2, at 155 195.

[504] Among Weld's converts were Reps. Edward Wade, and Philemon Bliss, and John H. Paine, Liberty Party leader. See 1 WELD-GRIMKE LETTERS, op. cit. supra note 10, at 236–240.

[505] 1795–1864; represented Ohio's Ashtabula and Jefferson Counties (Western Reserve) in House, 25th–34th Congresses, 1838–1859; with John Quincy Adams one of the original antislavery leaders in the House. 7 DICT. AM. BIOG. 260 (1931).

[506] 1808–1894; represented Lorain County district in 28th Cong. 1844–45; one of the political lieutenants of Salmon P.

Chase in the 'fifties. See 2 BIRNEY LETTERS, op. cit. supra note 11, at 1025.

[507] Edward Wade, 1803–1862, elected as a Free Soiler from Cleveland, 1853–55, and as a Republican, 1855–61 Ben Wade, 1800–1878, law partner of Giddings, and Radical Senator, 1851–1869. See 2 BIRNEY LETTERS, op. cit. supra note 11, at 710. 19 DICT. AM. BIOG. 303 (1936).

[508] 1796–1859; one of the organizers of the American public school system; elected as a Whig to succeed J. Q. Adams, Mass. district; reelected as Free Soiler, served 1848–53; President, Antioch College, 1852–59. 12 DICT. AM. BIOG. 240 (1933).

[509] 1813–1889; Ohio Circuit Judge, 1848–51; elected as a Republican from Elyria-Oberlin district, Ohio, served 1855–59; Chief Justice of Dakota Territory, 1861; Assoc. Justice Missouri Supreme Court, 1868–72; Dean of Univ. of Missouri Law School, 1872–1889. 2 DICT. AM. BIOG. 374 (1929).

[510] 1789–1866; antislavery Whig from Syracuse, N.Y.; served 1855–59. BIOG. DIR. AM. CONG., H. R. DOC. NO. 607, 81st Cong. 2d Sess. 1229 (1950).

[511] 1792–1868; elected as a Whig from Lancaster, Pa. district, 1849–53; as a Republican, 1859–68; Radical Republican leader in the House. 17 DICT. AM. BIOG. 620 (1935).

[512] 1797–1874; elected from Peterboro, N.Y. district, one of

after the Civil War.[517] Wilson was also in Congress during the Reconstruction period; and became Vice-President and voted with the Radicals on important tie votes.[518] Other New Englanders who served in Congress, and were members of the Joint Committee on Reconstruction, include William Pitt Fessenden of Maine, Justin Morrill of Vermont, and George S. Boutwell of Massachusetts.[519]

Because Bingham is known to have drafted Sections One and Five of the Fourteenth Amendment, his speeches are of special interest. From 1855–63 and from 1865–73, he represented the Twenty-first Ohio District, which included the Cadiz-Mt. Pleasant Quaker settlements, antislavery strongholds. Furthermore, as a youth he had attended Franklin College at New Athens in 1837–38. At that date Franklin was second only to Oberlin as an antislavery stronghold;[520] the Weld-Birney crusade was at its height. Indeed, in Birney's Philanthropist, 1836–37, we find various anti-slavery petitions and resolutions from the Cadiz and Mt. Pleasant societies.[521] These are couched in the very phraseology for which Bingham in 1856–66 manifested his decisive preference.

Four of Bingham's speeches are of particular significance:

I. In his maiden speech in the House, March 6, 1856, attacking laws recently passed by the Kansas pro-slavery legislature which declared it a felony even to agitate against slavery, Bingham argued:

> "These infamous statutes ... [contravene] the Constitution of the United States. . . . [A]ny territorial enactment which makes it a felony for a citizen of the United States, within the

territory of the United States 'to know, to argue and to utter freely,' according to conscience is absolutely void. . . . [A] felony to utter there, in the hearing of a slave, upon American soil, beneath the American flag ... the words of the Declaration 'All men are born free and equal, and endowed by their Creator with the inalienable rights of life and liberty;' ... [A] felony to utter ... those other words. . . . 'We, the people of the United States, in order to establish justice,' the attribute of God, and 'to secure liberty,' the imperishable right of man, do 'ordain this Constitution'. . . . It is *too late* to make it a felony to utter the self-evident truth that life and liberty belong of right to every man. . . . This pretended legislation ... violates the Constitution in this—that it abridges the freedom of speech and of the press, and deprives persons of liberty without due process of law, or any process but that of brute force, while the Constitution provides that Congress shall make no law abridging the freedom of speech or of the press; and it expressly prescribes that 'no person shall be deprived of life, liberty, or property without due process of law."[522]

II. On January 13, 1857, Bingham spoke in support of Congress' power over slavery in the territory and attacked President Buchanan's recent defense of the Kansas-Nebraska Act of 1854 repealing the Missouri Compromise. After a long analysis of the provisions of the Federal Bill of Rights, of the Northwest Ordinance, the enabling acts and constitutions of the states carved from the Ohio Territory—emphasizing especially the Federal due process clause and the "all men are born equally free and independent" clauses of the state constitution, he said:

U.S. SUPREME COURT, OCTOBER 1953

BRIEF FOR THE APPELLANTS AND RESPONDENTS ON REARGUMENT

the regions converted by Weld; served 1853–1854, resigned. 17 DICT. AM. BIOG. 270 (1935).

[513] 1819–1899; grad. Franklin College, New Athens, Ohio, 1838; Cincinnati Law School, 1840; Supreme Court Reporter, 1851; Judge, 1857–64; elected as a Republican, served 1865–71, 1873–77. 11 >DICT. AM. BIOG. 52 (1933).

[514] 1824–1896; elected as a Republican from Scioto County, 1859–69. See 1 WELD-GRIMKE LETTERS, *op. cit. supra* note 10, at 333. 1 DICT. AM. BIOG. 389 (1928).

[515] 1811–1872, elected as a Republican from Columbus, 1855–57. See WELD-GRIMKE LETTERS, *op. cit. supra* note 10, at 228.

[516] For eight terms (1855–63, 1865–73) Bingham represented the 21st Ohio District, composed of Harrison, Jefferson, Carroll and Columbiana Counties, including the Quaker settlements along Short Creek and the Ohio. See 3 BRENNAN, BIOGRAPHICAL ENCYCLOPEDIA ... OF OHIO 691 (1884).

[517] 18 DICT. AM. BIOG. 208 (1936).

[518] 20 DICT. AM. BIOG. 322 (1936).

[519] Fessenden was the son of General Samuel Fessenden, the leading Abolitionist of Maine, who was one of the national vice-presidents of the American Anti-Slavery Society, 6 DICT. AM. BIOG. 348 (1931); on Morrill, see 13 DICT. AM. BIOG. 198 (1934); on Boutwell, see 2 DICT. AM. BIOG. 489 (1929).

[520] See Graham, *Early Antislavery Backgrounds, op. cit. supra* note 1, at 624, n. 150.

[521] For an example see Philanthropist, Mar. 10, 1837, p. 3, col. 4.

[522] CONG. GLOBE, 34th Cong., 1st Sess. app. 124 (1856). Three other antislavery Republicans representing constituencies converted in the Weld-Birney crusade also used all the old rhetoric and theory including due process: Rep. Granger (N.Y.) *id.* at 295–296; Reps. Edward Wade (*id.* at 1076–1081) and Philemon Bliss (*id.* at 553–557), both Ohioans and among Weld's early converts. See also the speech of Rep. Schuyler Colfax (Ind.), *id.* at 644.

U.S. SUPREME
COURT,
OCTOBER 1953

BRIEF FOR THE
APPELLANTS AND
RESPONDENTS
ON REARGUMENT

"The Constitution is based upon EQUALITY of the human race.... A State formed under the Constitution and pursuant to its spirit, must rest upon this great principle of EQUALITY. Its primal object must be to protect each human being within its jurisdiction in the free and full enjoyment of his natural rights...."

"It must be apparent that the absolute equality of all, and the equal protection of each, are principles of our Constitution, which ought to be observed and enforced in the organization and admission of new States. The Constitution provides ... that *no person* shall be deprived of life, liberty, or property, without due process of law. It makes no distinction either on account of complexion or birth—it secures these rights to all persons within its exclusive jurisdiction. This is equality. It protects not only life and liberty, but also property, the product of labor. It contemplates that no man shall be wrongfully deprived of the fruit of his toil any more than of his life."[523]

III. On January 25, 1858, attacking "The Lecompton Conspiracy"—the proposed proslave constitution of Kansas declaring that only "All *freemen,* when they form a compact, are equal in rights,"—and absolutely barring free Negroes from the state, Bingham declared:

"The [Federal] Constitution ... declares upon its face that no person, whether white or black, shall be deprived of life, liberty, or property, but by due process of law; and that it was ordained by the people to establish justice! ... [By sanctioning these provisions] we are asked to say, that the self-evident truth of the Declaration, 'that ALL MEN ARE CREATED EQUAL' is a self-evident lie. . . . We are to say ... to certain human beings in the Territory of Kansas, though you were born in this Territory, and born of free parents, though you are human beings, and no chattel, yet you are not free to live here ...; you must be disseized of your freehold liberties and privileges, without the judgment of your peers and without the protection of law. Though born here, you shall not, under any circumstances, be permitted to live here."[524]

IV. On February 11, 1859, Bingham attacked the admission of Oregon because its constitution forbade immigration of free Negroes and contained other discriminations against them:

"[T]his constitution ... is repugnant to the Federal Constitution, and violative of the *rights of citizens of the United States.* . . .

"Who *are citizens of the United States?* They are those, and those only, who owe allegiance to the Government of the United States; not the base allegiance imposed upon the Saxon by the Conqueror ...; but the allegiance which requires the citizen not only to obey, but to support and defend, if need be with his life, the Constitution of his country. All free persons born and domiciled within the jurisdiction of the United States; all aliens by act of naturalization, under the laws of the United States."

"The people of the several States," who according to the Constitution are to choose the representatives in Congress, and to whom political powers were reserved by the Tenth Amendment, were to Bingham "the same community, or body politic, called by the Preamble ... 'the people of the United States.'" Morcover, certain "distinctive political rights"—for example the right to choose representatives and officers of the United States, to hold such offices, etc.—were conferred only on "citizens of the United States."

"... I invite attention to the significant fact that natural or inherent rights, which belong to all men irrespective of all conventional regulations, are by this Constitution guaranteed by the broad and comprehensive word 'person,' as contradistinguished from the limited term citizen—as in the fifth article of amendments, guarding those *sacred rights* which *are* as *universal and indestructible* as the human race, that 'no person shall be deprived of life, liberty, or property, but by due process of law, nor shall private property be taken without just compensation.' And this guarantee *applies* to all citizens within the United States."

Against infringement of "these wise and beneficent guarantees of political rights to the citizens of the United States as such, and of natural rights to all persons, whether citizens or strangers," stood the supremacy clause.

"There, sir, is the limitation upon State sovereignty—simple, clear, and strong. No State may *rightfully,* by Constitution or statute law, impair any of these guarantied rights, either political or natural. They may not *rightfully or lawfully* declare that the strong citizens may deprive the weak citizens of their rights, natural or political. . . .

"... This provision [excluding free Negroes and mulattoes] seems to me ... injustice and

---

[523] CONG. GLOBE, 34th Cong., 3rd Sess. app. 135–140 (1857).
[524] CONG. GLOBE, 35th Cong., 1st Sess. 402 (1858).

oppression incarnate. This provision, sir, excludes from the State of Oregon eight hundred thousand of the native-born citizens of the other States, who are, therefore, *citizens of the United States.* I grant you that a State may restrict the exercise of the elective franchise to certain classes of citizens of the United States, to the exclusion of others; but I deny that any State may exclude a law abiding citizen of the United States from coming within its territory, or abiding therein, or acquiring and enjoying property therein, or from the enjoyment therein of the 'privileges and immunities' of *a citizen of the United States.* What says the Constitution:

" 'The citizens of each State shall be entitled to all privileges and immunities of citizens in the several States. Art. 4, Section 2.'

"Here is no qualification. . . . The citizens of each State, all the citizens of each State, *being citizens of the United States,* shall be entitled to 'all privileges and immunities of citizens of the several States.' Not to the rights and immunities of the several States; not to those constitutional rights and immunities which result exclusively from State authority or State legislation; but to 'all privileges and immunities' of citizens of the United States in the several States. *There is an ellipsis in the language employed in the Constitution, but its meaning is self-evident that it is 'the privileges and immunities of citizens of the* United States ...' that it guaranties. . . .

"...[S]ir, I maintain that the persons thus excluded from the State by this section of the Oregon Constitution, are citizens by birth of the several States, and therefore *are citizens of the United States,* and as such are entitled to all the privileges and immunities of citizens of the United States, amongst which *are* the rights of life and liberty and property, and their due protection in the enjoyment thereof by law; . . . .

"Who, sir, are citizens of the United States? First, all free persons born and domiciled within the United States—not all free white persons, but all free persons. You will search in vain, in the Constitution of the United States, for that word *white;* it is not there. You will look in vain for it in that first form of national Government—the Articles of Confederation; it is not there. The omission of this word—this phrase of caste—from our national charter, was not accidental, but intentional. . . .

"... This Government rests upon the absolute equality of natural rights amongst men. . . .

"... Who ... will be bold enough to deny that all persons are equally entitled to the enjoy-

ment of the rights of life and liberty and property; and that no one should be deprived of life or liberty, but as punishment for crime; nor of his property, against his consent and without due compensation? ...

"*The equality of all* to the right to live; *to the right to know;* to argue and to utter, according to conscience; to work and enjoy the product of their toil, is the rock on which that Constitution rests—. . . . The charm of that Constitution lies in the great democratic idea which it embodies, that *all men, before the law, are equal in respect of those rights of person which God gives* and *no man or State may rightfully take away,* except as a forfeiture for crime. Before your Constitution, sir, *as it is,* as I trust it ever will be, all men are sacred, whether white or black. . . ."[525]

Several points must here be emphasized. It will be noted that Bingham disavows the color line as a basis for citizenship of the United States; that he regards Milton's rights of communication and conscience, including the *right to know,* to *education,* as one of the great fundamental natural "rights of person which God gives and no man or *state* may *rightfully* take away," and which hence are "embodied" also within, and secured by, "the great democratic idea that all men before the law are equal." In short, the concept and guarantee of the equal protection of the laws is already "embodied" in the Federal Constitution as of 1859; this same concept, moreover, embraces "*the equality of all ... to the right to know*"; and above all, there is no color line in the Constitution, even of 1859.

Conclusions

From this consideration of the historical background against which the Fourteenth Amendment was written, submitted by Congress, and ratified by the requisite number of states, these important facts develop:

1. To the opponents of slavery, equality was an absolute, not a relative, concept which comprehended that no legal recognition be given to racial distinctions of any kind. Their theories were formulated with reference to the free Negro as well as to slavery—that great reservoir of prejudice and evil that fed the whole system of racial distinctions and caste. The notion that any state could impose such distinctions was totally incompatible with antislavery doctrine.

---

[525] CONG. GLOBE, 35th Cong., 2nd Sess. 981–985 (1859) (emphasis added throughout).

U.S. SUPREME COURT, OCTOBER 1953

BRIEF FOR THE APPELLANTS AND RESPONDENTS ON REARGUMENT

U.S. SUPREME
COURT,
OCTOBER 1954

BRIEF FOR THE
APPELLANTS AND
RESPONDENTS
ON REARGUMENT

2 These proponents of absolute equalitarianism emerged victorious in the Civil War and controlled the Congress that wrote the Fourteenth Amendment. Ten of the fifteen members of the Joint Committee on Reconstruction were men who had antislavery backgrounds.

3 The phrases—"privileges and immunities," "equal protection," and "due process"— that were to appear in the Amendment had come to have specific significance to opponents of slavery. Proponents of slavery, even as they disagreed, knew and understood what that significance was. Members of the Congress that formulated and submitted the Amendment shared that knowledge and understanding. When they translated the antislavery concepts into constitutional provisions, they employed these by now traditional phrases that had become freighted with equalitarian meaning in its widest sense.

In the Supreme Court of the United States October Term, 1953

No. 1

OLIVER BROWN, ET AL., APPELLANTS

VS.

BOARD OF EDUCATION OF TOPEKA, SHAWNEE COUNTY, KANSAS, ET AL., APPELLEES

APPEAL FROM THE UNITED STATES DISTRICT COURT FOR THE DISTRICT OF KANSAS

BRIEF FOR THE BOARD OF EDUCATION, TOPEKA, KANSAS, ON QUESTIONS PROPOUNDED BY THE COURT

PETER F. CALDWELL, Counsel for the Board of Education of Topeka, Kansas, 512 Capitol Federal Building, Topeka, Kansas.

INDEX

I. STATEMENT

This brief is filed in response to the order of the Court, entered June 8, 1953, propounding five questions on which briefs were requested. Since the date of that order the Topeka Board of Education on September 3, 1953, duly adopted the following resolution:

"Be it resolved that it is the policy of the Topeka Board of Education to terminate maintenance of segregation in the elementary schools as rapidly as is practicable.";

and on September 8, 1953, it passed a motion, "... that segregation be terminate in the Southwest and Randolph Schools this year ...". Prior to the adoption of said resolution the Board of Education maintained twenty separate elementary schools for white children, each of which schools was attended by white children residing within a limited geographic area or boundaries near the school, and it also maintained four separate schools for negro children with large area or district boundaries. Negro students living some distance from school were furnished transportation to and from school if they requested it.

Since September 8, 1953, negro children living within the area boundaries of the Southwest School and the Randolph School are assigned to and are attending those schools along with and equally with white children. The Board is still maintaining the four separate negro schools and eighteen separate white schools.

By reason of its having resolved to terminate segregation in the elementary schools of Topeka "as rapidly as is practicable," the Topeka Board of Education no longer has an actual interest in the controversy over the constitutionality of segregation in such schools, and it therefore prefers to refrain from arguing and briefing Questions 1, 2, and 3 as propounded by the Court, which are directed to the constitutional questions involved.

The Board of Education of Topeka is, however, actually and directly interested in Questions 4 and 5 as propounded by the Court. Briefly summarized, we contend;

First, That termination of segregation in the elementary schools of Topeka will involve difficult and far reaching administrative decisions, affecting nearly all school children, nearly all teachers, and nearly all school buildings, so that to attempt to accomplish it in a hurried or summary manner will be both impossible and impractical.

Second, The public interest, including the interest of negro children in Topeka, equity, and practical considerations require that termination of segregation in the elementary schools of Topeka shall be permitted to be accomplished in a gradual and orderly manner.

II. QUESTION 4(A) SHOULD BE ANSWERED IN THE NEGATIVE: AND QUESTION 4(B) IN THE AFFIRMATIVE

Both Questions 4(a) and 4(b) contemplate the possibility that this Court might issue a broad, general order requiring abolition of segregation in the elementary schools of Topeka, rather than a limited order relating to the rights of the few particular negro children who are parties to this suit.

U.S. SUPREME COURT, OCTOBER 1953

BRIEF FOR THE BD. OF EDUC., TOPEKA, KS. ON QUESTIONS PROPOUNDED BY THE COURT

U.S. SUPREME
COURT,
OCTOBER 1953

BRIEF FOR THE
BD. OF EDUC.,
TOPEKA, KS,
ON QUESTIONS
PROPOUNDED
BY THE COURT

Such a general order would necessitate almost a complete readjustment of the elementary school system as now maintained in Topeka, so far as fixing attendance areas and boundaries for all the elementary school buildings in Topeka; it would require the transfer of many white and negro children from the schools they now attend to other buildings, as well as the transfer and assignment of many teachers to serve the resulting new classes in the various buildings.

Many of the grade schools now used for white children in the city are already full, and some are badly overcrowded. A school building program has been carried on and is being carried on now. The Southwest School was completed and opened in 1952; two other new schools are under construction now, and the Board is deciding on new sites for still two more schools to be constructed as quickly as possible. All five of these new buildings are, or will be, in areas where there have been new housing projects, and where the school population is now and probably will remain predominantly white children. These schools will probably not serve many negro children even when segregation is finally abolished.

The majority of the negro school population resides in a few scattered areas throughout the older parts of the city, and is not evenly distributed throughout the entire city. Many negro children live nearest to white schools which are already overcrowded. To transfer and admit these negro children to the schools nearest their residences will require either that many white children now attending such schools will have to be transferred to other schools, or that annexes will have to be provided. In short we have little doubt that the area boundaries of the existing white and negro schools will have to be redefined. This will necessarily require reassigning students, both white and negro, to schools which they do not now attend, and this in turn will require changing the classes to fit the new children in, and may involve transferring teachers from building to building as well.

It is the plan of the Board of Education of Topeka to make the transition from segregated to integrated elementary schools gradually and in an orderly manner on a school by school basis, but as rapidly as is practically possible. Such changes will be made at convenient times between semesters, and in such a manner that the administrative decisions and changes can be conveniently and efficiently handled without interrupting the continuity of the regular school program. The Board has discussed its policy and plans in open, public meetings attended by members of both white and negro races. It has invited and secured cooperation and suggestions, and the public generally in the community is assisting the Board in achieving its objective of terminating segregation "as rapidly as is practicable."

If this Court should enter an order to abolish segregation in the public schools of Topeka "forthwith," as suggested in Question 4(a), the Topeka Board would, of course, do its best to comply with the order. We believe, however, that it would probably require that the regular classes be suspended, while the many administrative changes and adjustments are being made, and while the necessary transfers of and reassignment of students and teachers are being made. Important decisions would have to be hurriedly made, without time for careful investigation of the facts nor for careful thought and reflection. Most decisions would have to be made on a temporary or an emergency basis. We believe the attendant confusion and interruption of the regular school program would be against the public interest, and would be damaging to the children, both negro and white alike.

We respectfully urge that in making and issuing its decree this Court has equitable power and discretion to shape the decree and to control its execution in such a manner as to protect the public interest:

United States v. Morgan, 307 U.S. 183, 81 L. Ed. 1211, 59 S. Ct. 795:

"It is familiar doctrine that the extent to which a court of equity may grant or withhold its aid, and the manner of moulding its remedies, may be affected by the public interest involved." (p. 1219, L. Ed.)

Virginia Ry. Co. v. System Federation No. 40, 300 U.S. 515, 81 L. Ed. 789, 52 S. Ct. 512:

"6. The extent to which equity will go to give relief where there is no adequate remedy at law is not a matter of fixed rule, but rests rather in the sound discretion of the court.

"7. Courts of equity may, and frequently do, go much further to give and withhold relief in furtherance of the public interest than they are accustomed to go when only private interests are involved." (Syll. 6. and 7.)

Securities Exch. Comm. v. U. S. R. and Imp. Co., 310 U.S. 434, 84 L. Ed. 1293, 60 S. Ct. 1044:

"7. A court of equity has discretion, in the exercise of jurisdiction committed to it, to grant or deny relief upon performance of conditions which will safeguard the public interest." (Syll. 7.)

Because the Board of Education believes that a "forthwith" order to abolish segregation in the Topeka school system would seriously damage and interrupt the operation and administration of the schools and would be plainly against public interest, and because it believes that an order to abolish segregation, in the public interest, should permit "an effective gradual adjustment"; we respectfully submit that Question 4(a) propounded by the Court should be answered in the negative, and that Question 4(b) should be answered in the affirmative.

III. QUESTIONS 5(A), (B) AND (C) SHOULD BE ANSWERED IN THE NEGATIVE

If segregation in the public schools of Topeka is to be abolished by decree of the Court permitting an "effective gradual adjustment" as suggested in Question 4(b), then the Board of Education should be permitted to manage the readjustment, subject only to the usual and normal jurisdiction always retained by a court of equity for the enforcement of its decree or judgment.

We have heretofore pointed out the many intricate administrative decisions which will be involved in the transition to an integrated system of grade schools in Topeka. These are the problems and decisions which the Board of Education is organized to handle. Clearly there will be considerable administrative expense involved in making the adjustment. In Kansas the Board of Education is required to comply with cash basis and budget laws in connection with such expenditures, and taxes must be levied for such expenses within the levy limitation laws. Thus the necessary adjustments for a transition from segregated to integrated schools will affect nearly all the other administrative actions of the Board of Education. For this Court or a special master to undertake to control the necessary readjustments or to draw detailed orders and decrees will involve them in the control and direction of the administration of the entire school program either directly or indirectly.

We believe such detailed control by this Court or a special master is unnecessary and undesirable. We therefore submit that Questions 5(a), (b) and (c) should be answered in the negative.

IV. QUESTION 5(D) SHOULD ALSO BE ANSWERED IN THE NEGATIVE

If this Court should enter an order or decree as suggested in Question 4(b), there is no need for a more specific or detailed decree in this case.

The Board of Education of Topeka has already on its own initiative resolved to terminate segregation in the elementary schools "as rapidly as is practicable" and has already taken its first step toward that end by providing for an integrated system in two schools which were formerly used only for white children. Certainly at this time there is no need for a more detailed decree than the decree suggested in Question 4(b). The District Court will always have jurisdiction to enforce the decree. If the need for a more specific decree should arise in the future, the District Court will have ample power to make such a decree under its general power to enforce the judgment and decree of the court.

We respectfully submit that Question 5(d) should be answered in the negative.

Peter F. Caldwell,
    Counsel for the Board of Education of
       Topeka, Kansas,
    512 Capitol Federal Building,
    Topeka, Kansas.

U.S. SUPREME COURT, OCTOBER 1953

BRIEF FOR THE BD. OF EDUC., TOPEKA, KS, ON QUESTIONS PROPOUNDED BY THE COURT

U.S. SUPREME
COURT, MAY
1954

Brown v. Board of Education of Topeka

BROWN ET AL.

V.

BOARD OF EDUCATION OF TOPEKA,
SHAWNEE COUNTY, KAN., ET AL.

BRIGGS ET AL. V. ELLIOTT ET AL.

DAVIS ET AL. V. COUNTY SCHOOL BOARD OF
PRINCE EDWARD COUNTY, VA., ET AL.

GEBHART ET AL. V. BELTON ET AL.

Nos. 1, 2, 4, 10.

Reargued Dec. 7, 8, 9, 1953.
Decided May 17, 1954.

347 U.S. 483

Class action originating in the four states of Kansas, South Carolina, Virginia, and Delaware, by which minor Negro plaintiffs sought to obtain admission to public schools on a nonsegregated basis. On direct appeals by plaintiffs form adverse decisions in the United States District Courts, District of Kansas, 98 F.Supp. 797, Eastern District of South Carolina, 103 F.Supp. 337, and on grant of certiorari after decision favorable to plaintiffs in the Supreme Court of Delaware, 91 A.2d 137, the United States Supreme Court, Mr. Chief Justice Warren, held that segregation of children in public schools solely on the basis race, even though the physical facilities and other tangible factors may be equal, deprives the children of the minority group of equal educational opportunities, in contravention of the Equal Protection Clause of the Fourteenth Amendment.

Cases ordered restored to docket for further argument regarding formulation of decrees.

In resolving question whether segregation of races in public schools constituted a denial of equal protection of the laws, even though the tangible facilities provided might be equal, court would consider public education in light of its full development and present status throughout the nation, and not in light of conditions prevailing at time of adoption of the amendment. U.S.C.A.Const. Amend. 14.

The opportunity of an education, where the state has undertaken to provide it, is a right which must be made available to all on equal terms. U.S.C.A.Const. Amend. 14.

The segregation of children in public schools solely on the basis of race, even though the physical facilities and other tangible factors may be equal, deprives the children of minority group of equal educational opportunities, and amounts to a deprivation of the equal protection of the laws guaranteed by the Fourteenth Amendment to the Federal Constitution. U.S.C.A.Const. Amend. 14.

The doctrine of "separate but equal" has no place in the field of public education, since separate educational facilities are inherently unequal. U.S.C.A.Const. Amend. 14.

In view of fact that actions raising question of constitutional validity of segregation of races in public schools were class actions, and because of the wide applicability of decisions holding that segregation was denial of equal protection of laws, and the great variety of local conditions, the formation of decrees presented problems of considerable complexity, requiring that cases be restored to the docket so that court might have full assistance of parties in formulating appropriate decrees. U.S.C.A.Const. Amend. 14.

No. 1:

Mr. Robert L. Carter, New York City, for appellants Brown and others.

Mr. Paul E. Wilson, Topeka, Kan., for appellees Board of Education of Topeka and others.

Nos. 2, 4:

Messrs. Spottswood Robinson III, Thurgood Marshall, New York City for appellants Briggs and Davis and others.

Messrs. John W. Davis, T. Justin Moore, J. Lindsay Almond Jr., Richmond, Va., for appellees Elliott and County School Board of Prince Edward County and others.

Asst. Atty. Gen. J. Lee Rankin for United States amicus curiae by special leave of Court.

No. 10:

Mr. H. Albert Young, Wilmington, Del., for petitioners Gerbhart et al.

Mr. Jack Greenberg, Thurgood Marshall, New York City, for respondents Belton et al.

Mr. Chief Justice Warren delivered the opinion of the Court.

These cases come to us from the States of Kansas, South Carolina, Virginia, and Delaware. They are premised on different facts and different local conditions, but a common legal question justifies their consideration together in this consolidated opinion.[1]

In each of the cases, minors of the Negro race, through their legal representatives, seek the aid of the courts in obtaining admission to the public schools of their community on a nonsegregated basis. In each instance, they have been denied admission to schools attended by white children under laws requiring or permitting segregation according to race. This segregation was alleged to deprive the plaintiffs of the equal protection of the laws under the Fourteenth Amendment. In each of the cases other than the Delaware case, a three-judge federal district court denied relief to the plaintiffs on the so-called "separate but equal" doctrine announced by this Court in *Plessy v. Ferguson*, 163 U.S. 537, 16 S.Ct. 1138, 41 L.Ed. 256. Under that doctrine, equality of treatment is accorded when the races are provided substantially equal facilities, even though these facilities be separate. In the Delaware case, the Supreme Court of Delaware adhered to that doctrine, but ordered that the plaintiffs be admitted to the white schools

because of their superiority to the Negro schools.

The plaintiffs contend that segregated public schools are not "equal" and cannot be made "equal," and that hence they are deprived of the equal protection of the laws. Because of the obvious importance of the question presented, the Court took jurisdiction.[2] Argument was heard in the 1952 Term, and reargument was heard this Term on certain questions propounded by the Court.[3]

Reargument was largely devoted to the circumstances surrounding the adoption of the Fourteenth Amendment in 1868. It covered exhaustively consideration of the Amendment in Congress, ratification by the states, then existing practices in racial segregation, and the views of proponents and opponents of the Amendment. This discussion and our own investigation convince us that, although these sources cast some light, it is not enough to resolve the problem with which we are faced. At best, they are inconclusive. The most avid proponents of the post-War Amendments undoubtedly intended them to remove all legal distinctions among "all persons born or naturalized in the United States." Their opponents, just as certainly, were antagonistic to both the letter and the spirit of the Amendments and wished them to have the most limited effect.

U.S. SUPREME COURT, MAY 1954

---

[1] In the Kansas case, *Brown v. Board of Education*, the plaintiffs are Negro children of elementary school age residing in Topeka. They brought this action in the United States District Court for the District of Kansas to enjoin enforcement of a Kansas statute which permits, but does not require, cities of more than 15,000 population to maintain separate school facilities for Negro and white students. Kan.Gen.Stat1949, § 72–1724. Pursuant to the authority, the Topeka Board of Education elected to establish segregated elementary schools. Other public schools in the community, however, are operated on a nonsegregated basis. The three-judge District Court, convened under 28 U.S.C. §§ 2281 and 2284, 28 U.S.C.A. §§ 2281, 2284, found that segregation in public education has a detrimental effect upon Negro children, but denied relief on the ground that the Negro and white schools were substantially equal with respect to buildings, transportation, curricula, and educational qualifications of teachers. 98 F.Supp. 797. The case is here on direct appeal under 28 U.S.C.A. § 1253.

In the South Carolina case, *Briggs v. Elliott*, the plaintiffs are Negro children of both elementary and high school age residing in Clarendon County. They brought this action in the United States District Court for the Eastern District of South Carolina to enjoin enforcement of provisions in the state constitution and statutory code which require the segregation of Negroes and whites in public schools. S.C.Const. Art. XI, § 7; S.C. Code 1942 § 5377. The three-judge District

Court, convened under 28 U.S.C. §§ 2281 and 2284, 28 U.S.C.A.§§ 2281, 2284, denied the requested relief. The court found that the Negro schools were inferior to the white schools and ordered the defendants to begin immediately to equalize the facilities. But the court sustained the validity of the contested provisions and denied the plaintiffs admission to the white schools during the equalization program. 98 F.Supp. 529. This Court vacated the District Court's judgment and remanded the case for the purpose of obtaining the court's reviews on a report filed by the defendants concerning the progress made in the equalization program. 342 U.S. 350, 72 S.Ct. 327, 96 L.Ed. 392. On remand, the District Court found that substantial equality had been achieved except for buildings and that the defendants were proceeding to rectify this inequality as well. 103 F.Supp. 920. The case is again here in direct appeal under 28 U.S.C. § 1253, 28 U.S.C.A. § 1253.

In the Virginia case, *Davis v. County School Board*, the plaintiffs are Negro children of high school age residing in Prince Edward County. They brought this action in the United States District Court for the Eastern District of Virginia to enjoin enforcement of provisions in the state constitution and statutory code which require the segregation of Negroes and whites in public schools. Va.Const. § 140; Va.Code 1950, § 22–221, The three-judge District Court, convened under 28 U.S.C. §§ 2281 and 2284, 28 U.S.C.A. §§ 2281, 2284, denied the requested relief. The court found the

U.S. SUPREME
COURT, MAY
1954

What others in Congress and the state legislatures had in mind cannot be determined with any degree of certainty.

An additional reason for the inconclusive nature of the Amendment's history, with respect to segregated schools, is the status of public education at that time.[4] In the South, the movement toward free common schools, supported by general taxation, had not yet taken hold. Education of white children was largely in the hands of private groups. Education of Negroes was almost nonexistent, and practically all of the race were illiterate. In fact, any education of Negroes was forbidden by the law in some states. Today, in contrast, many Negroes have achieved outstanding success in the arts and sciences as well as in the business and professional world. It is true that public school education at the time of the Amendment had advanced further in the North, but the effect of the Amendment on Northern States was generally ignored in the congressional debates. Even in the North, the conditions of public education did not approximate those existing today. The curriculum was usually rudimentary; ungraded schools were common in rural areas; the school term was but three months a year in many states; and compulsory school attendance was virtually unknown. As a consequence, it is not surprising that there should be so little in the history of the Four-teenth Amendment relating to its intended effect on public education.

In the first cases in this Court construing the Fourteenth Amendment, decided shortly after its adoption, the Court interpreted it as proscribing all state-imposed discriminations against the Negro race.[5] The doctrine of "separate but equal" did not make its appearance in this Court until 1896 in the case of *Plessy v. Ferguson, supra*, involving not education but transportation.[6] American courts have since labored with the doctrine for over half a century. In this Court, there have been six cases involving the "separate but equal" doctrine in the field of public education.[7] In *Cumming v. Board of Education of Richmond County*, 175 U.S. 528, 20 S.Ct. 197, 44 L.Ed. 262, and *Gong Lum v. Rice*, 275 U.S. 78, 48 S.Ct. 91, 72 L.Ed. 172, the validity of the doctrine itself was not challenged.[8] In more recent cases, all on the graduate school level, inequality was found in that specific benefits enjoyed by white students were denied to Negro students were denied to Negro Students of the same educational qualifications. *State of Missouri ex rel. Gaines v. Canada*, 305 U.S. 337, 59 S.Ct. 232, 83 L.Ed. 208; *Sipuel v. Board of Regents of University of Oklahoma*, 332 U.S. 631, 68 S.Ct. 299, 92 L.Ed. 247; *Sweatt v. Painter*, 339 U.S. 629, 70 S.Ct. 848,

---

Negro school inferior in physical plant, curricula, and transportation, and ordered the defendants forthwith to provide substantially equal curricula and transportation and to "proceed with all reasonable diligence and dispatch to remove" the inequality in physical plant. But, as in the South Carolina case, the court sustained the validity of the contested provisions and denied the plaintiffs admission to the white schools during the equalization program. 103 F.Supp. 337. The case is here on direct appeal under 28 U.S.C. § 1253.

In the Delaware case, *Gebhart v. Belton*, the plaintiffs are Negro children of both elementary and high school age residing in New Castle County. They brought this action in the Delaware Court of Chancery to enjoin enforcement of provisions in the state constitution and statutory code which require the segregation of Negroes and whites in public schools. Del.Const. Art. X, § 2; Del.Rev.Code, 1935, § 2631, 14 Del.C. § 141. The Chancellor gave judgment for the plaintiffs and ordered their immediate admission to schools previously attended only by white children, on the ground that the Negro schools were inferior with respect to teacher training, pupil-teacher ratio, extracurricular activities, physical plant, and time and distance involved in travel. Del.Ch., 87 A.2d 862. The Chancellor also found that segregation itself results in an inferior education for Negro children (see note 10, *infra*), but did not rest his decision on that ground. 87 A.2d at page 865. The Chancellor's decree was affirmed by the Supreme Court of

Delaware, which intimated, however, that the defendants might be able to obtain a modification of the decree after equalization of the Negro and white schools had been accomplished. 91 A.2d 137, 152. The defendants, contending only that the Delaware courts had erred in ordering the immediate admission of the Negro plaintiffs to the white schools, applied to this Court for certiorari. The writ was granted, 344 U.S, 891, 73 S.Ct. 213, 97 L.Ed. 689. The plaintiffs, who were successful below, did not submit a cross-petition.

[2] 344 U.S. 1, 73 S.Ct. 1, 97 L.Ed. 3, Id., 344 U.S. 141, 73 S.Ct. 124, 97 L.Ed. 152, *Gebhart v. Belton*, 344 U.S. 891, 73 S.Ct. 213, 97 L.Ed. 689.

[3] 345 U.S. 972, 73 S.Ct. 1118, 97 L.Ed. 1388. The Attorney General of the United States participated both Terms as *amicus curiae*. 3. 345 U.S. 972, 73 S.Ct. 1118, 97 L.Ed. 1388. The Attorney General of the United States participated both Terms as *amicus curiae*.

[4] For a general study of the development of public education prior to the Amendment, see Butts and Cremin, *A History of Education in American Culture* (1953), Pts. I, II; Cubberley, *Public Education in the United States* (1934 ed.), cc. II-XII. School practices current at the time of the adoption of the Fourteenth Amendment are described in Butts and Crimin, *supra*, at 269–275; Cubberley, *supra*, at 288–339, 408–431; Knight, *Public Education in the South* (1922), ecc. VIII, IX. See also H. Ex. Doc. No. 315, 41st Cong., 2d Sees. (1871).

94 L.Ed. 1114; *McLaurin v. Oklahoma State Regents*, 339 U.S. 637, 70 S.Ct. 851, 94 L.Ed. 1149. In none of these cases was it necessary to re-examine the doctrine to grant relief to the Negro plaintiff. And in *Sweatt v, Painter*, supra, the Court expressly reserved decision on the question whether *Plessy v. Ferguson* should be held inapplicable to public education.

In the instant cases, that question is directly presented. Here, unlike *Sweatt v. Painter*, there are findings below that the Negro and white schools involved have been equalized, or are being equalized, with respect to buildings, curricula, qualifications and salaries of teachers, and other "tangible" factors.[9] Our decision, therefore, cannot turn on merely a comparison of these tangible factors in the Negro and white schools involved in each of the cases. We must look instead to the effect of segregation itself on public education.

[1] In approaching this problem, we cannot turn the clock back to 1868 when the Amendment was adopted, or even to 1896 when *Plessy v. Ferguson* was written. We must consider public education in the light of its full development and its present place in American life throughout the Nation. Only in this way can it be determined if segregation in public schools deprives these plaintiffs of the equal protection of the laws.

[2] Today, education is perhaps the most important function of state and local governments. Compulsory school attendance laws and the great expenditures for education both demonstrate our recognition of the importance of education to our democratic society. It is required in the performance of our most basic public responsibilities, even service in the armed forces. It is the very foundation of good citizenship. Today it is a principal instrument in awakening the child to cultural values, in preparing him for later professional training, and in helping him to adjust normally to his environment. In these days, it is doubtful that any child may reasonably be expected to succeed in life if he is denied the opportunity, where the state has undertaken to provide it, is a right which must be made available to all on equal terms.

[3] We come then to the question presented: Does segregation of children in public schools solely on the basis of race, even though the physical facilities and other "tangible" factors may be equal, deprive the children of the minority group of equal educational opportunities? We believe that it does.

In *Sweatt v. Painter*, supra [339 U.S. 629, 70 S.Ct. 850], in finding that a segregated law school for Negroes could not provide them equal educational opportunities, this Court

U.S. SUPREME
COURT, MAY
1954

Although the demand for free public schools followed substantially the same pattern in both the North and the South, the development in the South and did not begin to gain momentum until about 1850, some twenty years after that in the North. The reasons for the somewhat slower development in the South (e.g., the rural character of the South and the different regional attitudes toward state assistance) are well explained in Cubberley, *supra*, at 408–424. In the country as a whole, but particularly in the South, the War virtually stopped all progress in public education. Id., at 427–428. The low status of Negro education in all sections of the country, both before and immediately after the War, is described in Beale, *A History of Freedom of Teaching in American Schools* (1941), 112–132, 175–195. Compulsory school attendance laws were not generally adopted until after the ratification of the fourteenth Amendment, and it was not until 1918 that such laws were in force in all the states. Cubberley, *supra*, at 563–565.

[5] *In re Slaughter-House Cases*, 1873, 16 Wall. 36, 67–72, 21 L.Ed. 394; *Strauder v. West Virginia*, 1880, 100 U.S. 303, 307–308, 25 L.Ed. 664.

"It ordains that no State shall deprive any person of life, liberty, or property. without due process of deny, to any person within its jurisdiction the equal protection of the laws. What is this but declaring that the law in the States shall be the same for the black as for the white; that all persons, whether colored or white,

shall stand equal before the laws of the States, and, in regard to the colored race, for whose protection the amendment was primarily designed, that no discrimination shall be made against them by law because of their color? The words of the amendment, it is true, are prohibitory, but they contain a necessary implication of a positive immunity, or right, most valuable to the colored race,—the right to exemption from un-friendly legislation against them distinctively as colored,—exemption from legal discrimination, implying inferiority in civil society, lessening the security of their enjoyment of the rights which others enjoy, and discriminations which are steps towards reducing them to the condition of a subject race." See also *State of Virginia v. Rives*, 1879, 100 U.S. 313, 318, 25 L.Ed. 667; *Ex parte Virginia*, 1879, 100 U.S. 339, 344–345, 25 L.Ed. 676.

The doctrine apparently originated in *Roberts v. City of Boston*, 1850, 5 Cush. 198, 59 Mass. 198, 206, upholding school segregation against attack as being violative of a state constitutional guarantee of equality. Segregation in Boston public schools was eliminated in 1855. Mass. Acts 1855, c. 256. But elsewhere in the North segregation in public education has persisted in some communities until recent years. It is apparent that such segregation has long been a nationwide problem, not merely one of sectional concern.

relied in large part on "those qualities which are incapable of objective measurement but which make for greatness in a law school." In *McLaurin v. Oklahoma State Regents*, supra [339 U.S. 67, 70 S.Ct. 853], the Court, in requiring that a Negro admitted to a white graduate school be treated like all other students, again resorted to intangible considerations: "* * * his ability to study, to engage in discussions and exchange views with other students, and, in general, to learn his profession." Such considerations apply with added force to children in grade and high schools. To separate them from others of similar age and qualifications solely because of their race generates a feeling of inferiority as to their hearts and minds in a way unlikely ever to be undone. The effect of this separation on their educational opportunities was well stated by a finding in the Kansas case by a court which nevertheless felt compelled to rule against the Negro plaintiffs.

> "Segregation of white and colored children in public schools has a detrimental effect upon the colored children. The impact is greater when it has the sanction of the law; for the policy of separating the races is usually interpreted as denoting the inferiority of the Negro group. A sense of inferiority affects the motivation of a child to learn. Segregation with the sanction of law, therefore, has a tendency to [retard] the educational and mental development of Negro children and to

deprive them of some of the benefits they would receive in a racial[ly] integrated school system."[10]

Whatever may have been the extent of psychological knowledge at the time of *Plessy v. Ferguson*, this finding is amply supported by modern authority.[11] Any language in *Plessy v. Ferguson* contrary to this finding is rejected.

[4] We conclude that in the field of public education the doctrine of "separate but equal" has no place. Separate educational facilities are inherently unequal. Therefore, we hold that the plaintiffs and others similarly situated for whom the actions have been brought are, by reason of the segregation complained of, deprived of the equal protection of the laws guaranteed by the Fourteenth Amendment. This disposition makes unnecessary any discussion whether such segregation also violates the Due Process Clause of the Fourteenth Amendment.[12]

[5] Because these are class actions, because of the wide applicability of third decision, and because of the great variety of local conditions, the formulation of decrees in these cases presents problems of considerable complexity. On reargument, the consideration of appropriate relief was necessarily subordinated to the primary question—the constitutionality of segregation in public education. We have now announced that such segregation is a denial of

---

7 See also *Berea College v. Kentucky*, 1908, 211 U.S 45, 29 S.Ct. 33, 53 L.Ed. 81.

8 In the Cumming case, Negro taxpayers sought an injunction requiring the defendant school board to discontinue the operation of a high school for white children until the board resumed operation of a high school for Negro children. Similarly, in the Gong Lum case, the plaintiff, a child of Chinese descent, contended only that state authorities had misapplied the doctrine by classifying him with Negro children and requiring him to attend a Negro school.

9 In the Kansas case, the court below found substantial equality as to all such factors. 98 F.Supp. 797, 798. In the South Carolina case, the court below found that the defendants were proceeding "promptly and in good faith to comply with the court's decree." 103 F.Supp. 920, 921. In the Virginia case, the court below noted that the equalization program was already "afoot and progressing," 103 F.Supp. 337, 341; since then, we have been advised, in the Virginia Attorney General's brief on reargument, that the program has now been completed. In the Delaware case, the court below similarly noted that the state's equalization program was well under way. 91 A.2d 137, 139.

10 A similar finding was made in the Delaware case: "I conclude from the testimony that in our Delaware society, State-imposed segregation in education itself results in the Negro children, as a class, receiving educational opportunities

which are substantially inferior to those available to white children otherwise similarly situated." 87 A.2d 862, 865.

11 K. B. Clark, "Effect of Prejudice and Discrimination on Personality Development" (Midcentury White House Conference on Children and Youth, 1950); Witmer and Kotinsky, *Personality in the Making* (1952), c. VI; Deutscher and Chein, "The Psychological Effects of Enforced Segregation: A Survey of Social Science Opinion," 26 J.Psychol. 259 (1948); Chein, "What are the Psychological Effects of Segregation Under Conditions of Equal Facilities?," 3 Int. J. Opinion and Attitude Res. 229 (1949); Brameld, "Educational Costs," in *Discrimination and National Welfare* (MacIver, ed., 1949), 674–681. And see generally Myrdal, *An American Dilemma* (1944).

12 See *Bolling v. Sharpe*, 347 U.S. 497, 74 S.Ct. 693, concerning the Due Process Clause of the Fifth Amendment.

13 "4. Assuming it is decided that segregation in public schools violates the Fourteenth Amendment

"(*a*) would a decree necessarily follow providing that, within the limits set by normal geographic school districting, Negro children should forthwith be admitted to schools of their choice, or

"(*b*) may this Court, in the exercise of its equity powers, permit an effective gradual adjustment to be brought about from existing segregated systems to a system not based on color distinctions?

---

the equal protection of the laws. In order that we may have the full assistance of the parties in formulating decrees, the cases will be restored to the docket, and the parties are requested to present further argument on Questions 4 and 5 previously propounded by the Court for the reargument this Term.[13] The Attorney General of the United States is again invited to participate. The Attorneys General of the states requiring or permitting segregation in public education will also be permitted to appear as *amici curiae* upon request to do so by September 15, 1954, and submission of briefs by October 1, 1954.[14]

It is so ordered.

"5. On the assumption on which questions 4(a) and (b) are based, and assuming further that this Court will exercise its equity powers to the end described in question 4(b),

"(*a*) should this Court formulate detailed decrees in these cases;

"(*b*) if so, what specific issues should the decrees reach;

"(*c*) should this Court appoint a special master to hear evidence with a view to recommending specific terms for such decrees;

"(*d*) should this Court remand to the courts of first instance with directions to frame decrees in these cases, and if so what general directions should the decrees of this Court include and what procedures should the courts of first instance follow in arriving at the specific terms of more, detailed decrees?"

[14] See Rule 42, Revised Rules of this Court, effective July 1, 1954, 28 U.S.C.A.

U.S. SUPREME
COURT,
OCTOBER 1954

BRIEF FOR
APPELLANTS AND
RESPONDENTS
ON FURTHER
REARGUMENT

In The Supreme Court of the United States
October Term, 1954

NO. 1

OLIVER BROWN, ET AL., APPELLANTS,

VS.

BOARD OF EDUCATION OF TOPEKA, ET AL.,

APPELLEES.

NO. 2

HARRY BRIGGS, JR. ET AL., APPELLANTS,

VS.

R. W. ELLIOTT, ET AL., APPELLEES.

NO. 3

DOROTHY E. DAVIS, ET AL., APPELLANTS,

VS.

COUNTY SCHOOL BOARD OF PRINCE
EDWARD COUNTY, VIRGINIA, ET AL., APPELLEES.

NO. 5

FRANCIS B. GEBHART, ET AL., PETITIONERS,

VS.

ETHEL LOUISE BELTON, ET AL., RESPONDENTS.

**APPEALS FROM THE UNITED STATES
DISTRICT COURTS FOR THE DISTRICT OF
KANSAS, THE EASTERN DISTRICT OF
SOUTH CAROLINA AND THE EASTERN
DISTRICT OF VIRGINIA, AND ON
PETITION FOR A WRIT OF CERTIORARI TO
THE SUPREME COURT OF DELAWARE,
RESPECTIVELY**

**BRIEF FOR APPELLANTS IN NOS. 1, 2
AND 3 AND FOR RESPONDENTS IN NO. 5
ON FURTHER REARGUMENT**

CHARLES L. BLACK JR.,
ELWOOD H. CHISOLM,
WILLIAM T. COLEMAN JR.,
CHARLES T. DUNCAN,
GEORGE E. C. HAYES,
LOREN MILLER,
WILLIAM R. MING JR.,
CONSTANCE BAKER MOTLEY,
JAMES M. NABRIT JR.,
DAVID E. PINSKY,
FRANK D. REEVES,
JOHN SCOTT,

JACK B. WEINSTEIN, *of Counsel.*
HAROLD BOULWAR,
ROBERT L. CARTER,
JACK GREENBERG,
OLIVER W. HILL,
THURGOOD MARSHALL,
LOUIS L. REDDING,,
SPOTTSWOOD W. ROBINSON III,
CHARLES S. SCOTT,
*Attorneys for Appellants in Nos. 1, 2, 3 and for
Respondents in No. 5.*

—m—

Table of Contents

—m—

PRELIMINARY STATEMENT

On May 17, 1954, this Court disposed of the basic constitutional question presented in these cases by deciding that racial segregation in public education is unconstitutional. The Court said, however, that the formulation of decrees was made difficult "because these are class actions, because of the wide applicability of this decision and because of the great variety of local conditions. . . ." The cases were restored to the docket, and the parties were requested to present further argument on Questions 4 and 5 previously propounded by the Court for the reargument last Term.

QUESTIONS INVOLVED

Questions 4 and 5, left undecided and now the subject of discussion in this brief, follow:

4. Assuming it is decided that segregation in public schools violates the Fourteenth Amendment

   (a) would a decree necessarily follow providing that, within the limits set by normal geographic school districting, Negro children should forthwith be admitted to schools of their choice, or

   (b) may this Court, in the exercise of its equity powers, permit an effective gradual adjustment to be brought about from existing segregated systems to a system not based on color distinctions?

5. On the assumption on which question 4(a) and (b) are based, and assuming further that this Court will exercise its equity powers to the end described in question 4 (b)

   (a) should this Court formulate detailed decrees in these cases;

   (b) if so, what specific issues should the decrees reach;

   (c) should this Court appoint a special master to hear evidence with a view to recommending specific terms for such decrees;

   (d) should this Court remand to the courts of first instance with directions to frame decrees in these cases, and if so, what general directions should the decrees of this Court include and what procedures should the courts of first instance follow in arriving at the specific terms of more detailed decrees?

DEVELOPMENTS IN THESE CASES SINCE THE LAST ARGUMENT

The Kansas case

On September 3, 1953, the Topeka School Board adopted the following resolution:

> Be it resolved that it is the policy of the Topeka Board of Education to terminate the maintenance of segregation in the elementary schools as rapidly as is practicable.

On September 8, 1953, appellees ordered segregation terminated in two of the nineteen school districts in Topeka. In September, 1954, segregation was completely terminated in ten other school districts and partially in two.

There is now a total school enrollment of approximately 8,500 children of elementary school age attending 23 elementary schools. Of the 8,500 children enrolled, approximately 700 Negro children are in four elementary schools for Negroes. There are 123 Negro children now attending schools on a non-segregated basis pursuant to appellees' implementation of its policy of removing segregation from the public school system. The blunt truth is that 85% of the Negro children in Topeka's elementary schools are still being denied the constitutional rights for which appellants sought redress in their original action.

While Topeka has been effectuating its plan, several other cities of the first class have undertaken the abolition of segregated schools. Lawrence and Pittsburg have completely desegregated. Kansas City, Abilene, Leavenworth and Parsons have ordered partial desegregation. Wichita and Salina have revised their school regulations to permit Negro children to attend schools nearest their homes. Only Coffeeville and Fort Scott have not taken any affirmative action whatsoever.

The Delaware case

By order of the Court of Chancery, affirmed by the Supreme Court of Delaware, the named plaintiffs were immediately admitted to the schools to which they applied. These plaintiffs and other members of the class are in their third year of uninterrupted attendance in the two Delaware schools named in the order. That attendance has been marked by no untoward incident. The order, however, did not result in elimination of separate schools for Negroes in the two school districts involved, in each of

U.S. SUPREME COURT, OCTOBER 1954

BRIEF FOR APPELLANTS AND RESPONDENTS ON FURTHER REARGUMENT

U.S. SUPREME
COURT,
OCTOBER 1954

BRIEF FOR
APPELLANTS AND
RESPONDENTS
ON FURTHER
REARGUMENT

which one segregated elementary school is yet maintained by petitioners.

The State Board of Education has statutory authority to "exercise general control and supervision over the public schools of the State, including … the determination of the educational policies of the State and the seeking in every way to direct and develop public sentiment in support of public education." DELAWARE CODE, Title 14, Section 121 (1953). Accordingly, the State Board of Education, on June 11, 1954, adopted a statement of "Policies Regarding Desegregation of Schools of the State" and announced "a general policy" that it "intends to carry out the mandates of the United States Supreme Court decision as expeditiously as possible." It further requested that "the school authorities together with interested citizen groups throughout the State should take immediate steps to hold discussions for the purpose of (1) formulating plans for desegregation in their respective districts and (2) presenting said plans to the State Board of Education for review."

On August 19, 1954, the State Board of Education requested "that *all schools,* maintaining four or more teachers, present a *tentative plan* for desegregation in their area on or before *October 1, 1954.*"

The desegregation plans of the Claymont Board of Education, whose members are petitioners here, providing for the complete termination of segregation, were approved by the State Board of Education on August 26, 1954. These plans have been partially put into operation.

No plan ending segregation in the Hockessin schools, the other Delaware area in the litigation here, has yet been formulated.

Delaware statutes provide for two types of public school districts, exclusive of the public school system in Wilmington which is practically autonomous. One type is commonly known as the State Board District. As to it, the statute provides that the "Board of School Trustees shall be the representative in the District of the State Board of Education." DELAWARE CODE, Title 14, Section 702 (1953). There are 98 such units. The other type is the Special School District, concerning which the statute provides that "There shall be a Board of Education which shall be responsible for the general administration and supervision of the free public schools and educational interests of the District." DELAWARE

CODE, Title 14, Section 902 (1953). There are fifteen Special School Districts.

Desegregation in the school districts of Delaware is illustrated by the table below:

State Board Districts

	Partial Desegregation	Complete Desegregation	No Desegregation	Total
New Castle County	4	1	26	31
Kent County	0	0	24	24
Sussex County	0	0	43	43
				98

Special School Districts

	Partial Desegregation	Complete Desegregation	No Desegregation	Total
New Castle County	3	1	1	5
Kent County	1	0	3	4
Sussex County *	0	0	6	6
				15

Wilmington, which is in New Castle County and contains 34% of the population of the State, in June desegregated all elementary and secondary schools for the 1954 summer session. It has also completely desegregated its night school sessions. Beginning in September, 1954, desegregation of all elementary schools was effectuated, with some integration of teachers.

The school districts involved in this litigation also are in New Castle County, which has 68% of the State's population. Desegregation in varying degrees has started in every major school district in this county, except one.

The State Board of Education has made specific requests to 58 of the 113 school districts in the State to submit such plans. Another six districts have stated that any kind of plan they may have would be more or less nullified by overcrowded classroom conditions. Fourteen others have indicated that they desire to await the mandate of this Court. The remaining districts have not responded to the State Board.

In summary, school districts in areas comprising more than 50% of the population of Delaware have undertaken some desegregation of the public schools. Many school districts in semi-urban and rural areas have undertaken no step. The ultimate responsibility for effectuating desegregation throughout Delaware rests with petitioners here, members of the State Board of Education.

The South Carolina case

Since May 17, 1954, South Carolina's fifteen-man legislative "Segregation Study Committee" was reorganized and has conferred with the Governor, State education officials, other legislators and spokesmen from various civic and teacher organizations. All of their meetings have been closed to the public. The Committee also visited Louisiana and Mississippi "to observe what was being done in those states to preserve segregated schools."

On July 28, the committee issued an interim report which recommended that public schools be operated during the coming year "in keeping with previously established policy." The committee construed its assignment as being the formulation of courses of action whereby the State could continue public education "without unfortunate disruption by outside forces and influences which have no knowledge of recent progress and no understanding of the problems of the present and future. . . ." Moreover, the report stated that the committee also recognized "the need for a system in keeping with public opinion and established traditions and living patterns."

The State Attorney General insisted that this Court should not undertake to direct further action even by the school district involved and announced that he considered the Clarendon County case "purely a local matter as far as the parties to the suit are concerned."

In Rock Hill (population 25,000 with 20% Negroes) a Catholic grade school voluntarily desegregated. Opening day enrollment was 29 white students and five Negroes. There has been no report of overt action against this development; but the parents of some of the children have been remonstrated with by neighbors and workers.[1]

A newspaper report[1a] of a public speech of E. B. McCord, one of the appellees herein, superintendent of education for Clarendon County, states in part:

> There will be no mixed schools in Clarendon County as long as there is any possible way for present leadership to prevent them.

So declared L. B. McCord of Manning, Clarendon County superintendent of educa-

tion, in an address before the Lions Club here Monday night.

Decrying the fact that "Our churches seem to be letting their zeal run away in leading the way," he denounced de-segregation as contrary to the Scriptures and to good sense.

The Virginia case

On May 27, 1954, the State Board of Education advised city and county school boards to continue segregation during the present school year.

On August 28, the Governor named a thirty-two-man, all-white legislative commission to study the problems raised by the Court's ruling and to prepare a report and recommendations to the legislature and to him. The Governor then announced:

> … I am inviting the commission to ascertain, through public hearings and such other means as appear appropriate, the wishes of the people of Virginia; to give careful study to plans or legislation or both, that should be considered for adoption in Virginia after the final decree of the Court is entered, and to offer such other recommendations as it may deem proper as a result of the decision of the Supreme Court affecting the public schools.[2]

At its first meeting the commission adopted a rule that:

> All meetings of the commission shall be executive and its deliberations confidential, except when the meeting consists of a public hearing or it is otherwise expressly decided by the commission.[3]

By October, the local school boards or boards of supervisors of approximately 25 of the state's 98 counties had adopted and forwarded

---

* Partial desegregation, that is, on the high school level, was instituted by the Milford Board of Education, in Sussex County. This action was later revoked and a test of the revocation is now pending in the Delaware courts. See Simmons v. Steiner, 108 A. 2d 173 (Del. Ct. Chanc. 1954). In that case the Vice-Chancellor found the Negro plaintiffs' rights to remain as students in Milford High School "clear and convincing" and restrained the Board of Education from excluding them. However, the Supreme Court of Delaware temporarily stayed the injunction to give that court sufficient time to examine "serious questions of law." Argument has been scheduled for December 13, 1954. Steiner v. Simmons (Del Sup. Ct. No. 27, 1954).

[1] Southern School News, Sept. 3, 1954, p. 12, col. 3–4.
[1a] Charleston News and Courier, August 4, 1954.
[2] Southern School News, Sept. 3, 1954, p. 13, col. 5.
[3] Southern School News, Oct. 1, 1954, p. 14, col. 2–3.

U.S. SUPREME COURT, OCTOBER 1954

BRIEF FOR APPELLANTS AND RESPONDENTS ON FURTHER REARGUMENT

U.S. SUPREME
COURT,
OCTOBER 1954

BRIEF FOR
APPELLANTS AND
RESPONDENTS
ON FURTHER
REARGUMENT

to the Governor resolutions urging the continuation of segregated schools.

In May, 1954, the Richmond Diocese of the Roman Catholic Church, which includes all but 6 of Virginia's counties, announced that during the Fall of 1954, Negroes would for the first time be admitted to previously all-white Catholic parochial schools where there was no separate parochial school for Negroes. Approximately 40 Negro pupils of a total of 3,527 are enrolled in four high and six elementary parochial schools formerly attended only by white pupils. The Superintendent of the Richmond Diocese states that integration in these schools "has worked out magnificently, without a ripple of discontent, ..."[4]

ARGUMENT

I. Answering Question 4: Only a decree requiring desegregation as quickly as prerequisite administrative and mechanical procedures can be completed will discharge judicial responsibility for the vindication of the constitutional rights of which appellants are being deprived In the normal course of judicial procedure, this Court's decision that racial segregation in public education is unconstitutional would be effectuated by decrees forthwith enjoining the continuation of that segregation. Indeed, in *Sipuel* v. *Board of Regents,* 332 U.S. 631, when effort was made to secure postponement of the enforcement of similar rights, this Court not only refused to delay action but accelerated the granting of relief by ordering its mandate to issue forthwith.

In practical effect, such disposition of this litigation would require immediate initiation of the administrative procedures prerequisite to desegregation, to be followed by the admission of the complaining children and others similarly situated to unsegregated schools at the beginning of the next academic term. This means that appellees will have had from May 17, 1954, to September, 1955, to complete whatever adjustments may be necessary.

If appellees desire any postponement of relief beyond that date, the affirmative burden must be on them to state explicitly what they propose and to establish that the requested postponement has judicially cognizable advantages greater than those inherent in the prompt vindication of appellants' adjudicated constitutional rights. Moreover, when appellees seek to post-

pone the enjoyment of rights which are personal and present, *Sweatt* v. *Painter,* 339 U.S. 629; *Sipuel* v. *Board of Regents,* 332 U.S. 631, that burden is particularly heavy. When the rights of school children are involved the burden is even greater. Each day relief is postponed is to the appellants* a day of serious and irreparable injury; for this Court has announced that segregation of Negroes in the public schools "generates a feeling of inferiority as to their status in the community that may affect their hearts and minds in a way unlikely ever to be undone. . . ." And, time is of the essence because the period of public school attendance is short.

A. Aggrieved parties showing denial of constitutional rights in analogous situations have received immediate relief despite arguments for delay more persuasive than any available here. Where a substantial constitutional right would be impaired by delay, this Court has refused to postpone injunctive relief even in the face of the gravest of public considerations suggested as justification therefor. In *Youngstown Sheet & Tube Co.* v. *Sawyer,* 343 U.S. 579, this Court upheld the issuance of preliminary injunctions restraining the Government's continued possession of steel mills seized under Presidential order intended to avoid a work stoppage that would imperil the national de-fense during the Korean conflict. The Govern-ment argued that even though the seizure might be unconstitutional, the public interest in uninterrupted production of essential war materials was superior to the owners' rights to the immediate return of their properties. It is significant that in the seven opinions filed no Justice saw any merit in this position. If equity could not appropriately exercise its broad discretion to withhold the immediate grant of relief in the *Youngstown* case, such a postponement must certainly be inappropriate in these cases where no comparable overriding consideration can be suggested.

Similarly in Ex parte *Endo,* 323 U.S. 283, this Court rejected the Government's argument that hardship and disorder resulting from racial prejudice could justify delay in releasing the petitioner. There, the argument made by the Government to justify other than immediate

---

[4] *Id.* at p. 14, col. 5.

24 *As used in this Brief, "appellants" include the respondents in No. 5.

relief was summarized in the Court's opinion as follows (pp. 296–297):

It is argued that such a planned and orderly relocation was essential to the success of the evacuation program; that but for such supervision there might have been a dangerously disorderly migration of unwanted people to unprepared communities; that unsupervised evacuation might have resulted in hardship and disorder; that the success of the evacuation program was thought to require the knowledge that the Federal government was maintaining control over the evacuated population except as the release of individuals could be effected consistently with their own peace and well-being and that of the nation; that although community hostility towards the evacuees has diminished, it has not disappeared and the continuing control of the Authority over the relocation process is essential to the success of the evacuation program. It is argued that supervised relocation, as the chosen method of terminating the evacuation, is the final step in the entire process and is a consequence of the first step taken. It is conceded that appellant's detention pending compliance with the leave regulations is not directly connected with the prevention of espionage and sabotage at the present time. But it is argued that Executive Order No. 9102 confers power to make regulations necessary and proper for controlling situations created by the exercise of the powers expressly conferred for protection against espionage and sabotage. The leave regulations are said to fall within that category.

In a unanimous decision, with the Court's opinion by Mr. Justice Douglas and two concurring opinions, the Court held that the petitioner must be given her unconditional liberty because the detention was not permissible by either statutory or administrative authorization. Viewing the petitioner's right as being in that "sensitive area of rights specifically guaranteed by the Constitution" (p. 299), the Court rejected the Government's contention that a continuation of its unlawful course of conduct was necessary to avoid the harmful consequences which otherwise would follow.

It is true that in the *Endo* case the contention rejected was that an executive order (which on its face did not authorize the petitioner's detention) ought to be extended by "construction" so as to entitle the Relocation Authority to delay the release of the petitioner until it felt that social conditions made it convenient and prudent to do so. In this case, the suggestion is that this Court,

in the exercise of its equity powers, ought to withhold appellants' constitutional rights on closely similar grounds. But this is not a decisive distinction. If, as the *Endo* case held, the enjoyment of a constitutional right may not be deferred by a process of forced construction on the basis of factors closely similar to the ones at work in the instant case, then certainly this Court ought not to find in its equitable discretion a mandate or empowerment to obtain the same result.

In the *Endo* case, the national interest in time of war was present. In these cases, no such interest exists. Thus, there is even less basis for delaying the immediate enjoyment of appellants' rights.

Counsel have discovered no case wherein this Court has found a violation of a present constitutional right but has postponed relief on the representation by governmental officials that local mores and customs justify delay which might produce a more orderly transition.

It would be paradoxical indeed if, in the instant cases, it were decided for the first time that constitutional rights may be postponed because of anticipation of difficulties arising out of local feelings. These cases are brought to vindicate rights which, as a matter of common knowledge and legal experience, need, above all others, protection against local attitudes and patterns of behavior.[5] They are brought, specifically, to uphold rights under the Fourteenth Amendment which are not to be qualified, substantively or remedially, by reference to local mores. On the contrary, the Fourteenth Amendment, on its face and as a matter of history, was designed for the very purpose of affording protection against local mores and customs, and Congress has implemented that design by providing redress against aggression under color of state laws, customs and usages. 28 U.S.C. § 1343; 42 U.S.C. § 1983.

Surely, appellants' rights are not to be enforced at a pace geared down to the very customs which the Fourteenth Amendment and implementing federal laws were designed to combat.

Cases in which delays in enforcement of rights have been granted involve totally dissimilar considerations. Such cases generally deal

---

[5] In the instant cases, dark and uncertain prophecies as to anticipated community reactions to school desegregation are speculative at best.

U.S. SUPREME COURT, OCTOBER 1954

BRIEF FOR APPELLANTS AND RESPONDENTS ON FURTHER REARGUMENT

U.S. SUPREME
COURT,
OCTOBER 1954

BRIEF FOR
APPELLANTS AND
RESPONDENTS
ON FURTHER
REARGUMENT

with the abatement of nuisances, e.g., *New Jersey v. New York,* 283 U.S. 473; *Wisconsin v. Illinois,* 278 U.S. 367; *Arizona Copper Co. v. Gillespie,* 230 U.S. 46; *Georgia v. Tennessee Copper Co.,* 206 U.S. 230; or with violations of the anti-trust laws, e.g., *Schine Chain Theaters v. United States,* 334 U.S. 110; *United States v. National Lead Co.,* 332 U.S. 319; *United States v. Crescent Amusement Co.,* 323 U.S. 173; *Hartford-Empire Co. v. United States,* 323 U.S. 386; *United States v. American Tobacco Co.,* 221 U.S. 106; *Standard Oil Co. of New Jersey v. United States,* 221 U.S. 1.

These cases are readily distinguishable, and are not precedents for the postponement of relief here. In the nuisance cases, the Court allowed the offending parties time to comply because the granting of immediate relief would have caused great injury to the public or to the defendants with comparatively slight benefit to the plaintiffs. In the instant cases, a continuation of the unconstitutional practice is as injurious to the welfare of our government as it is to the individual appellants.

In the anti-trust cases, delay could be granted without violence to individual rights simply because there were no individual rights on the plaintiff's side. The suits were brought by the Government and the only interest which could have been prejudiced by the delays granted is the diffuse public interest in free competition. The delays granted in anti-trust cases rarely, if ever, permit the continuance of active wrongful conduct, but merely give time for dissolution and dissipation of the effects of past misconduct. Obviously, these cases have nothing to do with ours.

It should be remembered that the rights involved in these cases are not only of importance to appellants and the class they represent, but are among the most important in our society. As this Court said on May 17th:

> Today, education is perhaps the most important function of state and local governments. Compulsory school attendance laws and the great expenditures for education both demonstrate our recognition of the importance of education to our democratic society. It is required in the performance of our most basic public responsibilities, even service in the armed forces. It is the very foundation of good citizenship. Today it is a principal instrument in awakening the child to cultural values, in preparing him for later professional training, and in helping him to adjust normally to his environment. In these days, it is doubtful that any child may reasonably be

expected to succeed in life if he is denied the opportunity of an education. Such an opportunity, where the state has undertaken to provide it, is a right which must be made available to all on equal terms.

Neither the nuisance cases nor the anti-trust cases afford any support for delay in these cases. On the contrary, in cases more nearly analogous to the instant cases, this Court has held that the executive branch of the government could not justify the detention of wrongfully seized private property on the basis of a national economic crisis in the midst of the Korean conflict. Nor could the War Relocation Authority wrongfully detain a loyal American because of racial tension or threats of disorder. It follows that in these cases this Court should apply similar limitations to the judiciary in the exercise of its equity power when a request is made that it delay enjoyment of personal rights on grounds of alleged expediency.

B. Empirical data negate unsupported speculations that a gradual decree would bring about a more effective adjustment. Obviously, we are not aware of what appellees will advance on further argument as reasons for postponing the enforcement of the rights here involved. Therefore, the only way we can discuss Question 4(b) is by conjecture in so far as reasons for postponement are concerned.

There is no basis for the assumption that gradual as opposed to immediate desegregation is the better, smoother or more "effective" mode of transition. On the contrary, there is an impressive body of evidence which supports the position that gradualism, far from facilitating the process, may actually make it more difficult; that, in fact, the problems of transition will be a good deal less complicated than might be forecast by appellees. Our submission is that this, like many wrongs, can be easiest and best undone, not by "tapering off" but by forthright action.

There is now substantial documented experience with desegregation in this country, in schools and elsewhere.[6] On the basis of this experience, it is possible to estimate with some accuracy the chances of various types of "gradual" plans for success in minimizing trouble during the period of transition.

---

[6] See ASHMORE, THE NEGRO AND THE SCHOOLS (1954); CLARK, DESEGREGATION: AN APPRAISAL OF THE EVIDENCE, 9 J. SOCIAL ISSUES 1–77 (1953); NEXT STEPS IN RACIAL DESEGREGATION IN EDUCATION, 23 J. NEGRO ED. 201–399 (1954).(1950).

Some plans have been tried involving a set "deadline" without the specification of intervening steps to be taken. Where such plans have been tried, the tendency seems to have been to regard the deadline as the time when action is to be initiated rather than the time at which desegregation is to be accomplished. Since there exists no body of knowledge that is even helpful in selecting an optimum time at the end of which the situation may be expected to be better, the deadline date is necessarily arbitrary and hence may be needlessly remote.[7]

A species of the "deadline" type of plan attempts to prepare the public, through churches, radio and other agencies, for the impending change. It is altogether conjectural how successful such attempts might be in actually effecting change in attitude. The underlying assumption—that change in attitude must precede change in action—is itself at best a highly questionable one. There is a considerable body of evidence to indicate that attitudemay itself be influenced by situation[8] and that, where the situation demands that an individual act as if he were not prejudiced, he will so act, despite the continuance, at least temporarily, of the prejudice.[9] We submit that this Court can itself contribute to an effective and decisive change in attitude by insistence that the present unlawful situation be changed forthwith.

As to any sort of "deadline" plan, even assuming that community leaders make every effort to build community support for desegregation, experience shows that other forces in the community will use the time allowed to firm up and build opposition.[10] At least in South Carolina and Virginia, as well as in some other states affected by this decision, statements and action of governmental officials since May 17th demonstrate that they will not use the time allowed to build up community support for desegregation.[11] Church groups and others in the South who are seeking to win community acceptance for the Court's May 17th decision cannot be effective without the support of a forthwith decree from this Court.

Besides the "deadline" plans, various "piecemeal" schemes have been suggested and tried. These seem to be inspired by the assumption that it is always easier and better to do something slowly and a little at a time than to do it all at once. As might be expected, it has appeared that the resistance of some people affected by such schemes is increased since they feel arbitrarily selected as experimental animals. Other members in the community observe this reaction and in turn their anxieties are sharpened.[12]

Piecemeal desegregation of schools, on a class-by-class basis, tends to arouse feelings of the same kind[13] and these feelings are heightened by the intra-familial and intra-school dif-

U.S. SUPREME
COURT,
OCTOBER 1954

BRIEF FOR
APPELLANTS AND
RESPONDENTS
ON FURTHER
REARGUMENT

---

[7] ASHMORE, *op. cit. supra* note 6, at 70, 71, 79, 80; CLARK, *op. cit. supra* note 6, at 36, 45.

[8] CLARK, *op. cit. supra* note 6, at 69–76.

[9] KUTNER, WILKINS and YARROW, VERBAL ATTITUDES AND OVERT BEHAVIOR INVOLVING RACIAL PREJUDICE, 47 J. ABNORMAL AND SOCIAL PSYCH. 649–652 (1952); LA PIERE, ATTITUDES VS. ACTION, 13 SOCIAL FORCES 230–237 (1934); SAENGER and GILBERT, CUSTOMER REACTIONS TO THE INTEGRATION OF NEGRO SALES PERSONNEL, 4 INT. J. OPINION AND ATTITUDES RESEARCH 57–76 (1950); DEUTSCH and COLLINS, INTERRACIAL HOUSING, A PSYCHOLOGICAL STUDY OF A SOCIAL EXPERIMENT (1951); CHEIN, DEUTSCH, HYMAN and JAHODA, CONSISTENCY AND INCONSISTENCY IN INTERGROUP RELATIONS, 5 J. SOCIAL ISSUES 1–63 (1949). ASHMORE, *op. cit. supra* note 6, at 42; New York Times, "Mixed Schools Set in 'Border' States", August 29, 1954, p. 88, col. 1–4; New York Times, "New Mexico Town Quietly Ends Pupil Segregation Despite a Cleric", August 31, 1954, p. 1, col. 3–4; ROSE, YOU CAN'T LEGISLATE AGAINST PREJUDICE—OR CAN YOU?, 9 COMMON GROUND 61–67 (1949), reprinted in RACE PREJUDICE AND DISCRIMINATION, (Rose ed. 1951); NICHOLS, BREAKTHROUGH ON THE COLOR FRONT (1954); MERTON, WEST and JAHODA, SOCIAL FICTIONS AND SOCIAL FACTS: THE DYNAMICS OF RACE RELATIONS IN HILLTOWN, COLUMBIA UNIVERSITY BUREAU OF APPLIED SOCIAL RESEARCH (mimeographed); MERTON, WEST, JAHODA and SELDEN,

SOCIAL POLICY AND SOCIAL RESEARCH IN HOUSING, 7 J. SOCIAL ISSUES, 132–140 (1951); MERTON, THE SOCIAL PSYCHOLOGY OF HOUSING (1948). South as well as North, people's actions and attitudes were changed not in advance of but after the admission of Negroes into organized baseball. See CLEMENT, RACIAL INTEGRATION IN THE FIELD OF SPORTS, 23 J. NEGRO ED. 226–228 (1954). Objections to desegregation have generally been found to be greater before than after its accomplishment. CLARK, *op. cit. supra* note 6, *passim*; CONFERENCE REPORT, ARIZONA COUNCIL FOR CIVIC UNITY CONFERENCE ON SCHOOL SEGREGATION (Phoenix, Arizona, June 2, 1951).

[10] CLARK, *op. cit. supra* note 6, at 43, 44; BROGAN, THE EMERSON SCHOOL—COMMUNITY PROBLEM, GARY, INDIANA, BUREAU OF INTERCULTURAL EDUCATION REPORT (October 1947, mimeographed); TIPTON, COMMUNITY IN CRISIS 15–76 (1953).

[11] For the latest example of this, see New York Times, "7 of South's Governors Warn of 'Dissensions' in Curb on Bias—Avow Right of States to Control Public School Procedures—Six at Meeting Refrain from Signing Statement", November 14, 1954, p. 58, col. 4–5.

[12] TIPTON, *op. cit. supra* note 11, at 42, 47, 57, 71; CLARK, SOME PRINCIPLES RELATED TO THE PROBLEM OF DESEGREGATION, 23 J. NEGRO ED. 343 (1954); CULVER, RACIAL DESEGREGATION IN EDUCATION IN INDIANA, 23 J. NEGRO ED. 300 (1954).

[13] ASHMORE, *op. cit. supra* note 6, at 79, 80; CLARK,

U.S. SUPREME
COURT,
OCTOBER 1954

BRIEF FOR
APPELLANTS AND
RESPONDENTS
ON FURTHER
REARGUMENT

ferences thus created.[14] It would be hard to imagine any means better calculated to increase tension in regard to desegregation than to so arrange matters so that some children in a family were attending segregated and others unsegregated classes. Hardly more promising of harmony is the prospect of a school which is segregated in the upper parts and mixed in the lower.

When one looks at various "gradual" processes, the fact is that there is no convincing evidence which supports the theory that "gradual" desegregation is more "effective."[15] On the contrary, there is considerable evidence that the forthright way is a most effective way.[16]

The progress of desegregation in the Topeka schools is an example of gradualism based upon conjecture, fears and speculation regarding community opposition which might delay completion of desegregation forever. The desegregation plan adopted by the Topeka school authorities called for school desegregation first in the better residential areas of the city and desegregation followed in those areas where the smallest number of Negro children lived. There is little excuse for the school board's not having already completed desegregation. Apparently either the fact that the school board, in order to complete the transition, may have to utilize one or more of the former schools for Negroes and assign white children to them or the fact that it must now reassign some 700 Negro children to approximately seven former all-white schools, seems to present difficulties to appellees. One must remember that in Topeka there has been complete integration above the sixth grade for many years. The schools already desegregated have reported no difficulties. There can hardly be any basic resistance to nonsegregated schools

in the habits or customs of the city's populace. The elimination of the remnants of segregation throughout the city's school system should be a simple matter.

No special public preparations involving teachers, parents, students or the general public were made, nor were they necessary in advance of either the first or second step in the implementation of the Board's decision to desegregate the school system. Indeed, the Board of Education adopted the second step in January, 1954, and the only reports of what was involved were those published in the newspapers. Negro parents living in these territories were not notified by appellees regarding the change, but transferred their children to the schools in question on the basis of information provided in the newspapers. As far as the teachers in those schools were concerned, they were merely informed in the Spring of 1954 that their particular schools would be integrated in September. Thus, delay here cannot be based upon need for public orientation.

It should be pointed out that of the 23 public elementary schools, there exists potential space for some additional 83 classrooms of which 16 such potential classrooms are in the four schools to which the majority of the Negroes are now assigned. No claim can be made that the school system is overcrowded and unable to absorb the Negro and white children under a reorganization plan. There is no discernable reason why all of the elementary schools of Topeka have not been desegregated.

As is pointed out in the Brief for Petitioners on Further Reargument in *Bolling* v. *Sharpe* (No. 4, October Term, 1954) the gradualist approach adopted by the Board of Education in Washington, D.C., produced confusion, hard-

DESEGREGATION: AN APPRAISAL OF THE EVIDENCE, *op. cit. supra* note 6, at 36, 45.

[14] CLARK, EFFECTS OF PREJUDICE AND DISCRIMINATION ON PERSONALITY DEVELOPMENTS, MID-CENTURY WHITE HOUSE CONFERENCE ON CHILDREN AND YOUTH (mimeographed, 1950).

[15] ASHMORE, *op. cit. supra* note 6, at 80:
> Proponents of the gradual approach argue that it minimizes public resistance to integration. But some school officials who have experienced it believe the reverse is true. A markedly gradual program, they contend, particularly one which involves the continued maintenance of some separate schools, invites opposition and allows time for it to be organized. Whatever the merit of this argument, the case histo-

ries clearly indicate a tendency for local political pressure to be applied by both sides when the question of integration is raised, and when policies remain unsettled for a protracted period the pressures mount. One school board member in Arizona privately expressed the wish that the state had gone all the way and made integration mandatory instead of optional— thus giving the board something to point to as justification for its action.

[16] CLARK, *op. cit. supra* note 6, at 46, 47; WRIGHT, RACIAL INTEGRATION IN THE PUBLIC SCHOOLS OF NEW JERSEY, 23 J. NEGRO ED. 283 (1954); KNOX, RACIAL INTEGRATION IN THE SCHOOLS OF ARIZONA, NEW MEXICO, AND KANSAS, 23 J. NEGRO ED. 291, 293 (1954); CULVER, RACIAL DESEGREGATION IN EDUCATION IN INDIANA, 23 J. NEGRO ED. 296, 300–302 (1954).

ship and unnecessary delay. Indeed, the operation of the "Corning Plan" has produced manifold problems in school administration which could have been avoided if the transition had been immediate. The argument that delay is more sound educationally has been shown to be without basis in fact in the operation of the District of Columbia plan—so conclusively, in fact, that the time schedule has been accelerated. The experience in the District argues for immediate action.

To suggest that this Court may properly mold its relief so as to serve whatever theories as to educational policy may be in vogue is to confuse its function with that of a school board, and to confuse the clear-cut constitutional issue in these cases with the situation in which a school board might find itself if it were unbound by constitutional requirements and were addressing itself to the policy problem of effecting desegregation in what seems to it the most desirable way. But even if a judgment as to the abstract desirability of gradualism could be supported by evidence, it is outside the province of this Court to balance the merely desirable against the adjudicated constitutional rights of appellants. The Constitution has prescribed the educational policy applicable to the issue tendered in this case, and this Court has no power, under the guise of a "gradual" decree, to select another.

We submit that there are various necessary administrative factors which would make "immediate" relief as of tomorrow physically impossible. These include such factors as need for redistricting and the redistribution of teachers and pupils. Under the circumstances of this case, the Court's mandate will probably come down in the middle or near the close of the 1954 school term, and the decrees of the courts of first instance could not be put into effect until September, 1955. Appellees would, therefore, have had from May 17, 1954, to September, 1955, to make necessary administrative changes.

II. Answering Question 5: If this court should decide to permit an "effective gradual adjustment" from segregated school systems to systems not based on color distinctions, it should not formulate detailed decrees but should remand these cases to the courts of first instance with specific directions to complete desegregation by a day certain In answering Question 5, we are required to assume that this

Court "will exercise its equity powers to permit an effective gradual adjustment to be brought about from existing segregated systems to a system not based on color distinctions" thereby refusing to hold that appellants were entitled to decrees providing that, "within the limits set by normal geographic school districting, Negro children should forthwith be admitted to schools of their choice." While we feel most strongly that this Court will not subordinate appellants' constitutional rights to immediate relief to any plan for an "effective gradual adjustment," we must nevertheless assume the contrary for the purpose of answering Question 5.[17]

Question 5 assumes that there should be an "effective gradual adjustment" to a system of desegregated education. We have certain difficulties with this formulation. We have already demonstrated that there is no reason to believe that any form of gradualism will be more effective than forthwith compliance. If, however, this Court determines upon a gradual decree, we then urge that, as a minimum, certain safeguards must be embodied in that "gradual" decree in order to render it as nearly "effective" as any decree can be which continues the injury being suffered by these appellants as a consequence of the unconstitutional practice here complained of.

Appellants assume that "the great variety of local conditions," to which the Court referred in its May 17th opinion, embraces only such educationally relevant factors as variations in administrative organization, physical facilities, school population and pupil redistribution, and does not include such judicially non-cognizable factors as need for community preparation, Ex Parte *Endo*, 323 U.S. 283, and threats of racial hostility and violence, *Buchanan* v. *Warley*, 245

U.S. SUPREME
COURT,
OCTOBER 1954

BRIEF FOR
APPELLANTS AND
RESPONDENTS
ON FURTHER
REARGUMENT

---

[17] "5. On the assumption on which question 4(*a*) and (*b*) are based, and assuming further that this Court will exercise its equity powers to the end described in question 4(*b*).

"(*a*) should this Court formulate detailed decrees in these cases;

"(*b*) if so, what specific issues should the decrees reach;

"(*c*) should this Court appoint a special master to hear evidence with a view to recommending specific terms for such decrees;

"(*d*) should this Court remand to the courts of first instance with directions to frame decrees in these cases, and if so, what general directions should the decrees of this Court include and what procedures should the courts of first instance follow in arriving at the specific terms of more detailed decrees?"

U.S. SUPREME
COURT,
OCTOBER 1954

BRIEF FOR
APPELLANTS AND
RESPONDENTS
ON FURTHER
REARGUMENT

U.S. 60; *Monk* v. *City of Birmingham,* 185 F. 2d 859 (C. A. 5th 1950), *cert. denied,* 341 U.S. 940.

Further we assume that the word "effective" might be so construed that a plan contemplating desegregation after the lapse of many years could be called an "effective gradual adjustment." For, whenever the change is in fact made, it results in a desegregated system. We do not understand that this type of adjustment would be "effective" within the meaning of Question 5 nor do we undertake to answer it in this framework. Rather, we assume that under any circumstances, the question encompasses due consideration for the constitutional rights of each of these appellants and those presently in the class they represent to be free from enforced racial segregation in public education.

Ordinarily, the problem—the elimination of race as the criterion of admission to public schools—by its very nature would require only general dispositive directions by this Court. Even if the Court decides that the adjustment to non-segregated systems is to be gradual, no elaborate decree structure is essential at this stage of the proceedings. In neither event would appellants now ask this Court, or any other court, to direct or supervise the details of operation of the local school systems. In either event, we would seek effective provisions assuring their operation—forthwith in the one instance and eventually in the other—in conformity with the Constitution.

These considerations suggest appellants' answers to Question 5. Briefly stated, this Court should not formulate detailed decrees in these cases. It should not appoint a special master to hear evidence with a view to recommending specific terms for such decrees. It should remand these cases to the courts of first instance with directions to frame decrees incorporating certain provisions, hereinafter discussed, that appellants believe are calculated to make them as nearly effective as any gradual desegregation

decree can be. The courts of first instance need only follow normal procedures in arriving at such additional provisions for such decrees as circumstances may warrant.

Declaratory provisions This Court should reiterate in the clearest possible language that segregation in public education is a denial of the equal protection of the laws. It should order that the decrees include a recital that constitutional and statutory provisions, and administrative and judicial pronouncements, requiring or sanctioning segregated education afford no basis for the continued maintenance of segregation in public schools.

The important legal consequence of such declaratory provisions would be to obviate the real or imagined dilemma of some school officials who contend that, pending the issuance of injunctions against the continuation of segregated education in their own systems, they are entitled or even obliged to carry out state policies the invalidity of which this Court has already declared. The dilemma is well illustrated by the case of *Steiner* v. *Simmons* (Del. Sup. Ct. No. 27, 1954), pending in the Delaware Supreme Court, wherein plaintiffs are suing for readmission to Milford's high school from which, on September 30, 1954, they were expelled because they are Negroes. The Vice Chancellor granted the requested mandatory injunction, finding that plaintiffs had a constitutional right to readmission to school. The Delaware Supreme Court, however, granted a stay pending determination of the appeal on the basis of its preliminary conclusion that "there are serious questions of law touching the existence of that legal right."[18]

This Court's decision of May 17th put state authorities on notice that thereafter they could not with impunity abrogate the constitutional rights of American children not to be segregated in public schools on the basis of race. This type of recital in the decree should foreclose further

---

[18] Cf. Burr v. Bd. of School Commrs. of Baltimore, Superior Court of Baltimore City, Oct. 5, 1954 (unreported), in which case Judge James K. Cullen stated in part: In the instant case this Court is asked to issue a writ of mandamus requiring these defendants, the School Board, to continue with its policy of segregation. This Court finds the Board of School Commissioners have exercised their discretion legally and in accordance with a final and enforceable holding and decision of the Supreme Court. Those cases were undoubtedly argued before the Supreme Court fully, and the views of every division of thought of our citizenry was undoubtedly presented to the Court; but the Court has spoken. Whether

the individual agrees or disagrees with the finding, he is bound thereby so long as it remains the law of the land. The Court realizes the change and the difficulty some may have accepting the reality or the inevitable from the standpoint of enforcement. We live in a country where our rights and liberties have been protected under a system of laws which has withstood the test of time. We must allow ourselves to be governed by those laws, realizing there are many differences among our people. Respect for the law is of paramount importance. The law must be accepted. We must all be forced to abide by it. We can gain nothing by demonstrations of violence except sorrow and possible destructions.

misunderstanding, real or pretended, of the principle of law that continuation of racial segregation in public education is in direct violation of the Constitution—state constitutions, statutes, custom or usage requiring such segregation to the contrary notwithstanding.

Time provisions We do not know what considerations may be presented by appellees to warrant gradualism. But whatever these considerations may be, appellants submit that any school plan embracing gradualism must safeguard against the gradual adjustment becoming an interminable one. Therefore, appellants respectfully urge that this Court's opinion and mandate also contain specific directions that any decree to be entered by a district court shall specify (1) that the process of desegregation be commenced immediately, (2) that appellees be required to file periodic reports to the courts of first instance, and (3) an outer time limit by which desegregation must be completed.

Even cases involving gradual decrees have required some amount of immediate compliance by the party under an obligation to remedy his wrongs to the extent physically possible.[19] In *Wisconsin* v. *Illinois,* 281 U.S. 179, the Court said:

> It already has been decided that the defendants are doing a wrong to the complainants, and that they must stop it. They must find out a way at their peril. We have only to consider what is possible if the state of Illinois devotes all its powers to dealing with an exigency to the magnitude of which it seems not yet to have fully awaked. It can base no defenses upon difficulties that it has itself created. If its Constitution stands in the way of prompt action, it must amend it or yield to an authority that is paramount to the state (p. 197).

* * *

> 1. On and after July 1, 1930,[20] the defendants, the state of Illinois and the sanitary district of Chicago are enjoined from diverting any of the waters of the Great Lakes–St. Lawrence system or watershed through the Chicago drainage canal and its auxiliary channels or otherwise in excess of an annual average of 6,500 c.f.s. in addition to domestic pumpage (p. 201).

Considering the normal time consumed before the issuance of the mandate of this Court and the time for submission and preparation of decrees by the courts of first instance, decrees in these cases will not issue until after February, 1955—after the normal mid-term in most school

systems. Thus, the school boards would have until September, 1955—sixteen months after the May 17th opinions—to change to a system not based on color distinctions. This time could very well be considered as necessarily incidental to any decision by this Court requiring "forthwith" decrees by the courts of first instance.

Whatever the reasons for gradualism, there is no reason to believe that the process of transition would be more effective if further extended. Certainly, to indulge school authorities until September 1, 1956, to achieve desegregation would be generous in the extreme. Therefore, we submit that if the Court decides to grant further time, then the Court should direct that all decrees specify September, 1956, as the outside date by which desegregation must be accomplished. This would afford more than a year, in excess of the time necessary for administrative changes, to review and modify decisions in the light of lessons learned as these decisions are put into effect.

We submit that the decrees should contain no provision for extension of the fixed limit, whatever date may be fixed. Such a provision would be merely an invitation to procrastinate.[21]

We further urge this Court to make it plain that the time for completion of the desegregation program will not depend upon the success or failure of interim activities. The decrees in the instant cases should accordingly provide that in the event the school authorities should for any reason fail to comply with the time limitation of the decree, Negro children should then be immediately admitted to the schools to which they apply.[22]

All states requiring segregated public education were by the May 17th decision of this Court

U.S. SUPREME
COURT,
OCTOBER 1954

BRIEF FOR APPEL-
LANTS AND
RESPONDENTS
ON FURTHER
REARGUMENT

---

[19] See Wisconsin v. Illinois, 281 U.S. 179; Arizona Copper Co. v. Gillespie, 230 U.S. 46; Georgia v. Tennessee Copper Co., 206 U.S. 230; Westinghouse Air Brake Co. v. Great Northern Ry. Co., 86 Fed. 132 (C. C. S. D. N. Y. 1898).

[20] This opinion was rendered April 30, 1930.

[21] ASHMORE, THE NEGRO AND THE SCHOOLS 70–71 (1954); CULVER, RACIAL DESEGREGATION IN EDUCATION IN INDIANA, 23 J. NEGRO ED. 296–302 (1954).

[22] See United States v. American Tobacco Co., 221 U.S. 106, where this Court directed the allowance of a period of six months, with leave to grant an additional sixty days if necessary, for activities dissolving an illegal monopoly and recreating out of its components a new situation in harmony with the law, but further directed that if within this period a legally harmonious condition was not brought about, the lower court should give effect to the requirements of the Sherman Act.

U.S. SUPREME
COURT,
OCTOBER 1954

BRIEF FOR
APPELLANTS AND
RESPONDENTS
ON FURTHER
REARGUMENT

put upon notice that segregated systems of public education are unconstitutional. A decision granting appellees time for gradual adjustment should be so framed that no other state maintaining such a system is lulled into a period of inaction and induced to merely await suit on the assumption that it will then be granted the same period of time after such suit is instituted.

CONCLUSION

Much of the opposition to forthwith desegregation does not truly rest on any theory that it is better to accomplish it gradually. In considerable part, if indeed not in the main, such opposition stems from a desire that desegregation not be undertaken at all. In consideration of the type of relief to be granted in any case, due consideration must be given to the character of the right to be protected. Appellants here seek effective protection for adjudicated constitutional rights which are personal and present. Consideration of a plea for delay in enforcement of such rights must be preceded by a showing of clear legal precedent therefor and some public necessity of a gravity never as yet demonstrated.

There are no applicable legal precedents justifying a plea for delay. As a matter of fact, relevant legal precedents preclude a valid plea for delay. And, an analysis of the non-legal materials relevant to the issue whether or not relief should be delayed in these cases shows that the process of gradual desegregation is at best no more effective than immediate desegregation.

WHEREFORE, we respectfully submit that this Court should direct the issuance of decrees in each of these cases requiring desegregation by no later than September of 1955.

CHARLES L. BLACK JR.,

ELWOOD H. CHISOLM,

WILLIAM T. COLEMAN JR.,

CHARLES T. DUNCAN,

GEORGE E. C. HAYES,

LOREN MILLER,

WILLIAM R. MING JR.,

CONSTANCE BAKER MOTLEY,

JAMES M. NABRIT JR.,

DAVID E. PINSKY,

FRANK D. REEVES,

JOHN SCOTT,

JACK B. WEINSTEIN, *of Counsel.*

HAROLD BOULWARE,

ROBERT L. CARTER,

JACK GREENBERG,

OLIVER W. HILL,

THURGOOD MARSHALL,

LOUIS L. REDDING,

SPOTTSWOOD W. ROBINSON III,

CHARLES S. SCOTT, *Attorneys for Appellants in Nos. 1, 2, 3 and for Respondents in No. 5.*

In the Supreme Court of the United States

No. 1, October Term, 1954

OLIVER BROWN, ET AL., APPELLANTS

VS.

BOARD OF EDUCATION OF TOPEKA, SHAWNEE COUNTY, KANSAS ET AL., APPELLEES

APPEAL FROM THE UNITED STATES DISTRICT COURT FOR THE DISTRICT OF KANSAS

SUPPLEMENTAL BRIEF FOR THE BOARD OF EDUCATION, TOPEKA, KANSAS, ON QUESTIONS 4 AND 5 PROPOUNDED BY THE COURT

PETER F. CALDWELL,
Counsel for the Board of Education of Topeka,
Kansas,
512 Capitol Federal Building,
Topeka, Kansas.

———ᵐ———

This supplemental brief is filed in response to the order of this Court directing and requesting further briefs and argument on questions 4 and 5 heretofore propounded by the Court.

In its brief, heretofore filed herein in December, 1953, The Board of Education of Topeka urged that in the event segregation in its elementary schools were held to be unconstitutional, this case should simply be remanded to the lower court with instructions to reverse its judgment and to enter a decree requiring that segregation be terminated "as rapidly as is practicable" by the defendant Board of Education. It was suggested that by such a decree the lower court could retain jurisdiction for enforcement of the decree, and that if a need for a more specific decree should arise in the future, the lower court would have power to amplify its decree under the general power of an equity court to enforce its decree.

As was pointed out in its brief filed in December, 1953, The Board of Education of Topeka in September, 1953, adopted a resolution to terminate segregation in its elementary schools "as rapidly as is practicable"; and on September 8, 1953, terminated segregation at two of its elementary schools, to wit: Southwest and Randolph Schools.

Since that time, the Board of Education of Topeka has already taken its second far-reaching step or stride toward termination of segregation by adopting the recommendations of its superintendent of schools as set out in the following report which was made on January 20, 1954, and was approved and adopted by the Board of Education on the same date:

SECOND STEP IN TERMINATION OF SEGREGATION IN TOPEKA ELEMENTARY SCHOOLS

I. In implementation of the Board's policy to terminate segregation in elementary schools as soon as practicable, I propose that the second step be taken at the opening of school in September, 1954. The step should be acted upon by the Board at this time in order to enable everybody concerned to make necessary plans for next year.

II. In the second step, I propose that segregation be terminated in the following school districts and that transportation not be provided for Negro children who are affected, but that such child be given the privilege of attending the nearest Negro School if his parents want him to do so. (All pupil accounting is based on the number belonging on October 16, 1953.)

	Negro Children to Integrated Schools	Negro Children to Come from Following Schools			
		McKinley	Buchanan	Monroe	Washington
1. Central Park	21		16	5	
2. Clay	13		12	1	
3. Crestview	0				
4. Gage	1				
5. Grant (Limited)*	3	3	1		
6. Oakland	0				
7. Polk (Limited)**	3			3	
8. Potwin	0				
9. Quincy	34	34			
10. Quinton Heights	10		5	5	

*The limitation suggested at Grant is that three Negro children isolated in the extreme northern part of Grant School district be permitted to attend Grant, while the remainder of the Negro children continue at McKinley.

**The limitation suggested at Polk School is as follows: Several Negro children in this district live very close to Buchanan School. They should continue at this school. There would not be room for them at Polk and there is plenty of room at Buchanan. However, there are three Negro children now attending Monroe School but residing in the Polk district. I suggest that they be allowed to attend Polk School.

U.S. SUPREME COURT, OCTOBER 1954

SUPPLEMENTAL BRIEF FOR THE BD. OF EDUC., TOPEKA, KS, ON QUESTIONS PROPOUNDED BY THE COURT

U.S. SUPREME
COURT,
OCTOBER 1954

SUPPLEMENTAL
BRIEF FOR THE
BD. OF EDUC..
TOPEKA, KS,
ON QUESTIONS
PROPOUNDED
BY THE COURT

	Negro Children to Integrated Schools	Negro Children to Come from Following Schools			
		McKinley	Buchanan	Monroe	Washington
11. State Street	21			9	12
12. Sumner	7	1	5	1	
	113	38	39	24	12
Randolph	2				
Southwest	8				
	123				

III. The effects of taking this step would be as follows:

1. It would reduce the enrollments of Negro Schools as indicated.

	From	To
McKinley	127	89
Buchanan	160	121
Monroe	245	221
Washington	292	280
	824	711

2. It would place 123 Negro children in integrated schools.

3. It would leave, in addition to the four schools for Negro children, 12 schools integrated, 2 schools (Grant and Polk) on a basis of partial integration, and 5 schools continuing on a segregated basis (Lafayette, Lincoln, Lowman Hill, Parkdale and Van Buren.)

Thus, by announcing the changes in the spring of 1954, all parties affected had ample opportunity to adjust themselves to the changes before they became effective the following September.

Segregation has been completely terminated in 12 elementary school districts, and partially terminated in two others; and, as of September, 1954, there will remain only four Negro schools and five white schools in which segregation is being continued.

The Board of Education has requested the superintendent, and he plans, to make recommendations for the third step toward termination of segregation early in 1955 to become effective in September, 1955. In the meantime, of course, he will have had an opportunity to observe the results and the operation of the second step which became effective in September, 1954. Thus before taking the third step, the board of education will have the benefit of its experiences with the first and second steps.

It is gratifying to be able to report to the Court that The Board of Education has been carrying out its policy of termination of segregation "as rapidly as is practicable" with full public cooperation and acceptance by both white and Negro pupils, teachers and parents.

The administrative problems, which were discussed in the brief filed in December, 1953, are the chief problems with which The Board of Education is confronted; but with practical experience, they are being satisfactorily solved. Their solution, however, cannot be effected "forthwith," but require time for a gradual adjustment.

It is respectfully submitted that The Board of Education of Topeka is in good faith carrying out its adopted policy to terminate segregation "as rapidly as is practicable," and that there is no need at this time for the appointment of a special master or for the Court to undertake to formulate specific decrees directing the particular steps to be taken to terminate segregation in the schools of Topeka.

Respectfully submitted,
PETER F. CALDWELL,
Counsel for the Board of Education of Topeka, Kansas,
512 Capitol Federal Building,
Topeka, Kansas.

In the Supreme Court of the United States October Term, 1954

NO. 1

OLIVER BROWN, ET AL., APPELLANTS,
VS.
BOARD OF EDUCATION OF TOPEKA, ET AL.,
APPELLEES.

NO. 2

HARRY BRIGGS, JR., ET AL., APPELLANTS,
VS.
R. W. ELLIOTT, ET AL., APPELLEES.

NO. 3

DOROTHY E. DAVIS, ET AL., APPELLANTS,
VS.
COUNTY SCHOOL BOARD OF PRINCE
EDWARD COUNTY, VIRGINIA, ET AL., APPELLEES.

NO. 5

FRANCIS B. GEBHART, ET AL., PETITIONERS,
VS.
ETHEL LOUISE BELTON, ET AL., RESPONDENTS.

APPEALS FROM THE UNITED STATES DISTRICT COURTS FOR THE DISTRICT OF KANSAS, THE EASTERN DISTRICT OF SOUTH CAROLINA AND THE EASTERN DISTRICT OF VIRGINIA, AND ON PETITION FOR A WRIT OF CERTIORARI TO THE SUPREME COURT OF DELAWARE, RESPECTIVELY

REPLY BRIEF FOR APPELLANTS IN NOS. 1, 2 AND 3 AND FOR RESPONDENTS IN NO. 5 ON FURTHER REARGUMENT

CHARLES L. BLACK JR.,
ELWOOD H. CHISOLM,
WILLIAM T. COLEMAN JR.,
CHARLES T. DUNCAN,
GEORGE E. C. HAYES,
LOREN MILLER,
WILLIAM R. MING JR.,
CONSTANCE BAKER MOTLEY,
JAMES M. NABRIT JR.,
LOUIS H. POLLAK,
FRANK D. REEVES,
JOHN SCOTT,
JACK B. WEINSTEIN, *of Counsel.*
HAROLD BOULWARE,

ROBERT L. CARTER,
JACK GREENBERG,
OLIVER W. HILL,
THURGOOD MARSHALL,
LOUIS L. REDDING,
SPOTTSWOOD W. ROBINSON III,
CHARLES S. SCOTT, *Attorneys for Appellants in Nos. 1, 2, 3 and for Respondents in No. 5.*

—⟫⟫⟫—

TABLE OF CONTENTS

—⟫⟫⟫—

The briefs filed on this reargument by appellees and *amici curiae* (with the exception of those in Nos. 1 and 5, and the brief filed on behalf of the Attorney General of The United States) are similar in substance despite some differences in details. Our reply to them can, therefore, be made in one joint brief.

ARGUMENT

Briefs filed by appellees and state Attorneys General do not offer any affirmative plan for desegregation but are merely restatements of arguments in favor of interminable continuation of racial segregation In our Brief on Further Reargument, we stated:[1]

---

[1] Brief for Appellants in Nos. 1, 2 and 3 and for Respondents in No. 5 on Further Reargument, 1954 Term, p. 31.

U.S. SUPREME
COURT,
OCTOBER 1954

REPLY BRIEF FOR
APPELLANTS AND
RESPONDENTS
ON FURTHER
REARGUMENT

Much of the opposition to forthwith desegregation does not truly rest on any theory that it is better to accomplish it gradually. In considerable part, if indeed not in the main, such opposition stems from a desire that desegregation not be undertaken at all.

Similarly, the briefs filed at this time, both by appellees and state attorneys general seem to be directed against ending racial segregation in our time, rather than toward desegregation within a reasonable time. First, these briefs do not in fact offer any affirmative plan or elements of such a plan for accomplishing the task of desegregation. Secondly, and equally significant, the main reasons now proffered in support of indefinite delay are identical with arguments previously advanced for denying relief on the merits.

This Court has decided that racial segregation is unconstitutional—that it is a practice, moreover, which has such effects on its victims that it can only be described as abhorrent. Yet, in answering questions 4 and 5, propounded by the Court, the States do not even get around to what must, in the light of that decision, be the main problem underlying those questions: How can this practice be most expeditiously done away with? Reasons for delay, which would seem to occupy at best a subsidiary position, are the sole preoccupation of state counsel, and the affirmative problem gets virtually no attention.[2]

The brief of the Attorney General of Florida does contain a Point entitled "Specific Suggestions to the Court in Formulating a Decree."[3] But, the effect of the suggested plan[4] would be to subject the constitutional rights of Negro children to denial on the basis of such a variety of intangible factors that the plan itself cannot be seriously regarded as one for implementing the May 17th decision.

Each individual Negro child must, under the Florida plan, petition a court of the first instance for admission to an unsegregated school, after exhausting his administrative remedies. It is up to him to establish to that court's satisfaction that there exists no "reasonable grounds" for delay in his admission. "Reasonable grounds" include lack of a reasonable time to amend the state school laws, good faith efforts of the school board in promoting citizens' educational committees, administrative problems, and "evidence of … a strong degree of *sincere* opposition and sustained hostility" [emphasis supplied] giving the school board ground to believe that admission of the applicant would "… create emotion-

al responses among the children which would seriously interfere with their education." In other words, the applicant's right is to be postponed until everything seems entirely propitious for granting it. It is submitted that this is not a plan for granting rights, but a plan for denying them just as long as can possibly be done without a direct overruling of the May 17th decision.

Lest there be any doubt about this, the final criterion for admission to unsegregated schooling should be quoted:[5]

(6) Evidence that the petitioner's application was made in good faith and not for *capricious* reasons. Such evidence should demonstrate:

(a) That the petitioner personally feels that he would be handicapped in his education, either because of lack of school plant facilities or psychological or sociological reasons if his application for admission is denied.

(b) That the petitioner is not motivated in his application solely by a desire for the advancement of a racial group on economic, social or political grounds, as distinguished from his personal legal right to equality in public school education as guaranteed by the 14th Amendment. This distinction should be carefully drawn [emphasis supplied].

Where the devisers of a plan are disposed to characterize opposition to desegregation as "sincere" and reasons for desiring admission as "capricious," we cannot be surprised at a rather peculiar procedural consequence of the dispensation they set up. The "petitioner," if he is to make timely application, exhaust his administrative remedies, and allow time for appeal, will have to draw this fine distinction at about four years of age, if he is to start the first grade in a desegregated school. Out of the mouths of babes and sucklings will have to come a wisdom in self-analysis which surely has never in the history of this country been required of any applicant for relief from the denial of a personal constitu-

---

[2] It is true that Delaware and Kansas catalogue the progress they have made thus far in accomplishing integration. But both states plead for delay without offering any valid reasons therefor.

[3] Brief of the Attorney General of the State of Florida as *amicus curiae*, pp. 57–65. Hereinafter, citations to briefs of appellees and *amici curiae* will be abbreviated. See, e.g., fn. 5, *infra*.

[4] Set out commencing at p. 61 of the Florida Brief.

[5] Florida Brief, p. 63.

U.S. SUPREME
COURT,
OCTOBER 1954

REPLY BRIEF FOR
APPELLANTS AND
RESPONDENTS
ON FURTHER
REARGUMENT

tional right. The Florida Brief is no real exception to the statement that none of the States has offered any plan for actually implementing the decision of this Court.

The quality and thrust of the reasons now advanced for delay may best be evaluated by noting that (except for those that deal with purely administrative matters obviously requiring little time for solution) they are arguments which were advanced at an earlier stage in this litigation as grounds for denying relief on the merits, and now, under slightly altered guise, they walk again after their supposed laying to rest on May 17. Thus, the impossibility of procuring community acceptance of desegregation, urged earlier as a ground for decision on the merits,[6] now turns up as an argument for indefinite postponement[7] with no convincing reasons given for supposing that community attitudes will change within the segregated pattern.

The prediction that white parents will withdraw their children from public schools is repeated,[8] with the implied hope, no doubt, that at some remote date they will have attained a state of mind that will result in their leaving their children in school. "Racial tensions" are again predicted.[9] Negro teachers may lose their jobs.[10] Violence is warned of.[11] The people and the legislature will abolish the school system or decline to appropriate money for its support.[12]

All these are serious matters, but we have elsewhere shown solid reason for believing that those dire predictions, one and all, are unreliable. There is no reason for supposing that delay can minimize whatever unpleasant consequences might follow from the eradication of this great evil. Here, however, the point is that, where these arguments are resuscitated as grounds for delay, the inference is that their sponsors favor delay as long as present conditions prevail—that, in other words, they now want to delay desegregation just as long as the

conditions exist which they formerly regarded as sufficient grounds for imposing segregation as a matter of legal right. The distinction is too fine to make such practical difference, either to the Negro child who is growing up or to this Court.

That it is opposition to the principle of the May 17th decision that animates these briefs is made clear by noting that the equality of schools, *Plessy* style, is now being urged as a ground for delay.[13] Nothing could make it clearer, moreover, that many responsible officials, taking a realistic view, will not regard the "separate but equal" doctrine as abolished until this Court orders its abandonment in practice. Most significant here is the *amicus curiae* brief of the Attorney General of Texas which, after making a straight-out *Plessy* argument, continues with the statement: "However, if the occasion arises whereby we are compelled to abolish segregation in Texas, it should be a gradual adjustment in view of the complexities of the problem" (p. 4).

Opinion polls are immaterial to the issues herein and do not afford any basis to support an argument that a gradual adjustment would be more effective Several of the briefs filed herein refer to polls of public opinion in their respective States in support of arguments to postpone desegregation indefinitely.[14] These polls appear to have been made for the purpose of sampling opinions of various groups within the State as to whether they approved of the May 17th decision and whether they thought it could be enforced immediately without friction.

The information as to racial hostility obtained from these polls is indecisive of the issues before this Court. In *Buchanan* v. *Warley*, 245 U.S. 60, 80, this Court stated:

> That there exists a serious and difficult problem arising from a feeling of race hostility which the law is powerless to control, and to which it must give a measure of consideration, may be freely admitted. But its solution

---

[6] South Carolina Brief (1952) p. 27. Cf. *Id.* at p. 35; Virginia Brief (1952) pp. 24–25.

[7] Virginia Brief (1954) p. 13; Delaware Brief (1954) pp. 16, 25; Florida Brief (1954) p. 201 ff.; Texas Brief (1954) pp. 16–17; North Carolina Brief (1954) pp. 7–8.

[8] *Compare* Florida Brief (1954) pp. 26–27 and North Carolina Brief (1954) pp. 36–37 *with* Virginia Brief (1952) p. 30.

[9] *Compare* Florida Brief (1954) p. 95 *with* Virginia Brief (1952) p. 27.

[10] *Compare* Florida Brief (1954) pp. 31–32; North Carolina Brief (1954) pp. 24–25; and Texas Brief (1954) pp. 10–11, *with* Virginia Brief (1952) p. 31.

[11] *Compare* North Carolina Brief (1954) p. 37 and Florida Brief (1954) p. 25 *with* South Carolina Brief (1952) p. 27.

[12] *Compare* North Carolina Brief (1954) p. 36; Virginia Brief (1954) p. 15; and Arkansas Brief (1954) pp. 7–8 *with* South Carolina Brief (1952) p. 27.

[13] *Compare* North Carolina Brief (1954) pp. 25–35, 43; Texas Brief (1954) pp. 2–4; and Maryland Brief (1954) p. 10 *with* Virginia Brief (1952) pp. 18–19 and South Carolina Brief (1952) pp. 8–9.

[14] Texas Brief, pp. 16–17; Virginia Brief pp. 13–14; North Carolina Brief pp. 7–9; Florida Brief pp. 23–24, 105 ff; Delaware Brief p. 12.

U.S. SUPREME
COURT,
OCTOBER 1954

REPLY BRIEF FOR
APPELLANTS AND
RESPONDENTS
ON FURTHER
REARGUMENT

cannot be promoted by depriving citizens of their constitutional rights and privileges.

We believe the same answer should be given to any suggestion that the enforcement of constitutional rights be deferred to a time when it will have uniform public acceptance.

Even if relevant, results of polls are often not conclusive. For example, the Florida survey polled eleven "leadership" groups. These groups give evidence of a very high degree of "willingness" to comply. Although peace officers are greatly opposed to desegregation (Table 3, p. 138), only two of the eleven groups would not positively comply, and in those cases there is a very even division (Table 4, p. 139). Overall, six of the eleven groups are not opposed to the decision (Table 3, p. 138); 84.5% of white principals and supervisors who, would be charged with the duty of implementation, would comply (Table 4, p. 139). A majority of all groups expect neither mob violence nor "serious violence" (Table 5, p. 140).

Moreover, such polls are not a valid index of how the individuals questioned will in fact act in the event of desegregation. Modern psychological research shows that, especially in the case of broad public issues, many persons simply "do not follow through even on actions which they say they personally will take in support of an opinion."[15]

The Attorney General of Texas sets out in his brief in these cases a survey by the "Texas Poll" showing 71% disapproval of the May 17th decision and 65% approval of continued segregation notwithstanding this Court's decision. It is interesting to note that in *Sweatt* v. *Painter,* 339 U.S. 629, respondents included in their brief a survey made by the same "Texas Poll" showing that 76% of all Texans were "against Negroes and whites going to the same universities." However, this Court ordered Sweatt admitted to the University of Texas. He and other Negroes attended the University.[16] Since then Negroes have been admitted to and are attending this and other public universities in twelve southern States.[16a]

Finally, there is nothing to indicate that an extended delay in ordering the elimination of all segregation will improve public attitudes or eliminate the objections presently interposed. Clearly the polls are irrelevant and should be so treated by this Court.

The wide applicability of the decision in these cases should not affect the relief to which appellants are entitled Effort is made throughout the briefs for appellees and the several attorneys general to balance the personal and present rights here involved against the large number of children of both races now attending public school on a segregated basis. This argument is made for a twofold purpose: to escape the uniformity of decisions of this Court on the personal character of the rights involved and, secondly, to destroy the present character of the right involved.

---

[15] BUCHANAN, KRUGMAN AND VAN WAGENEN, AN INTERNATIONAL POLICE FORCE AND PUBLIC OPINION 13 (1954). For other studies dealing with the discrepancy between verbal statements and actions, see Link and Freiberg, "THE PROBLEM OF VALIDITY VS. RELIABILITY IN PUBLIC OPINION POLLS," 6 PUBLIC OPINION QUARTERLY 87–98, esp. 91–92 (1942); JENKINS AND CORBIN, "DEPENDABILITY OF PSYCHOLOGICAL BRAND BAROMETERS II, THE PROBLEM OF VALIDITY," 22 JOURNAL OF APPLIED PSYCHOLOGY, 252–260 (1938); HYMAN, "DO THEY TELL THE TRUTH?," 8 PUBLIC OPINION QUARTERLY 557–559 (1944); SOCIAL SCIENCE RESEARCH COUNCIL, COMMITTEE ON ANALYSIS OF PRE–ELECTION POLLS AND FORECASTS 302–303 (1949); LA PIERE, "ATTITUDES VS. ACTIONS," 13 SOCIAL FORCES 230–237 (1934); DOOB, PUBLIC OPINION AND PROPAGANDA 151 (1948); HARTLEY AND HARTLEY, FUNDAMENTALS OF SOCIAL PSYCHOLOGY 657 (1952). See also *Irvin* v. *State,* 66 So. 2d 288, 290–292, *cert. denied* 346 U.S. 927, *reh. denied* 347 U.S. 914.

[16] It is also significant that many municipal junior colleges in Texas have also desegregated their student bodies. See SOUTHERN SCHOOL NEWS, October 1, 1954, p. 13, c. 5.

[16a] JOHNSON, "PUBLIC HIGHER EDUCATION IN THE SOUTH," 23 JOURNAL OF NEGRO EDUCATION 317 (1954), especially at 328

where Dr. Johnson, University of North Carolina Sociologist, concludes:

> The transition from complete segregation to some degree of integration of Negroes into the publicly-supported institutions of higher learning in the South has already been accomplished in all except five of the Southern states, and most of this change has occurred in the brief period, 1948–1953. Despite numerous predictions of violence, this transition has been accomplished without a single serious incident of interracial friction. We put to one side as obviously immaterial the mere technical character of these suits as class actions under Rule 23(a)(3). Obviously, the mere joinder of plaintiffs in a spurious class suit for reasons of convenience cannot have any effect on the nature of the rights asserted or on the availability of normal relief remedy. Whether a suit is or is not a class action tells us little, in this field of law, as to the magnitude of the interests involved; *Sweatt* v. *Painter* was an individual mandamus suit, but the effect of that decision spread throughout the segregating states.

Of course, the decision of this Court in the instant cases will have wide effect involving public school systems of many states and many public school children. The mere fact of numbers involved is not sufficient to delay enforcement of rights of the type here involved.[17]

On the face of it, their position is both ill-taken and self-defeating. That it is ill-taken becomes clear when the suggestion itself is clearly stated; obviously, there is nothing in mere numerousness as such which has any tendency whatever to create or destroy rights to efficacious legal relief. Behind every numeral is a Negro child, suffering the effects spoken of by the Court on May 17. It is a manifest inconsequence to say that the rights or remedial needs of each child are diminished merely because others are in the same position. That this argument is self-defeating emerges when it is considered that its tendency is simply to establish that we have to do with an evil affecting a great many people; presumably, the abolition of a widespread evil is even more urgent than dealing with isolated cases of wrongdoing.

This Court has consistently treated the personal rights of litigants on a personal basis. Every leading case involving discrimination against Negroes has necessarily and demonstrably involved large numbers of people; yet this Court has given present relief on a personal basis to those who showed themselves entitled to it, without any hint of the possibility that the rights of citizenship are diminished because many people are being denied them. The *Sweatt, Sipuel* and *McLaurin* cases and *Smith* v. *Allwright,* all, as was well known to this Court and to the country, involved not merely the individuals or class-plaintiffs or geographical subdivision actually before the Court, but also the whole framework of law school, graduate school or primary election segregation. All major constitutional cases involve large numbers of people. Yet there is not a hint, in words or in action, in any past case, to the effect that the wide applicability of a decision was considered material to the right to relief. It is unthinkable that this Court would apply any such doctrine to limit the enjoyment of constitutional rights in general; there is no reason for its making a special and anomalous exception of the case at bar.

Actually, to point to the vast numbers of people whose lives will be affected by the relief granted here is only a diffuse way of raising all the questions as to the consequences of immediate desegregation. We have dealt with these questions elsewhere. The suggestion that mere numerousness makes a difference adds nothing new, but merely serves to confuse the issues by diverting attention from the extremely personal plight of each child, and from his need for present relief.

Average differences in student groups have no relevance to the individual rights of pupils: individual differences can be handled administratively without reference to race Having attempted to subordinate appellants' personal and present constitutional rights to an alleged overriding consideration of the large numbers of people involved, these briefs for appellees then seek to further limit the individual rights of Negro students by broad characterizations of group intelligence, group morality and health.[18] Specifically, it is pointed out that statistics show that *on the average* Negro children in segregated schools score lower on achievement tests and are *in general* more retarded culturally than white children. This data, contrary to the conclusions advanced thereupon, merely underscores and further documents the finding quoted in this Court's opinion:

> "Segregation of white and colored children in public schools has a detrimental effect upon the colored children. The impact is greater when it has the sanction of the law; for the policy of separating the races is usually interpreted as denoting the inferiority of the Negro group. A sense of inferiority affects the motivation of a child to learn. Segregation with the sanction of law, therefore, has a tendency to [retard] the educational and mental development of Negro children and to deprive them of some of the benefits they would receive in a racial[ly] integrated school system."

We have come too far not to realize that educability and absorption and adoption of cultural values has nothing to do with race. What is achieved educationally and culturally, we now

---

[18] North Carolina Brief, pp. 39–41; Florida Brief, pp. 19–21, 189.

[19] KLINEBERG, RACE DIFFERENCES: THE PRESENT POSITION OF THE PROBLEM, 2 INTERNATIONAL SOCIAL SCIENCE BULLETIN 460 (1950); MONTAGUE, STATEMENT ON RACE, THE UNESCO STATEMENT BY EXPERTS ON RACE PROBLEMS 14–15 (1951); MONTAGUE, MAN'S MOST DANGEROUS MYTH: THE FALLACY OF RACE 286 (1952); KIRKPATRICK, PHILOSOPHY OF EDUCATION 399–433 (1951). See KLINEBERG, RACE AND PSYCHOLOGY, UNESCO (1951); ALLPORT, THE NATURE OF PREJUDICE (1954); COMAS, RACIAL MYTHS, UNESCO (1951).

U.S. SUPREME COURT, OCTOBER 1954

REPLY BRIEF FOR APPELLANTS AND RESPONDENTS ON FURTHER REARGUMENT

U.S. SUPREME
COURT,
OCTOBER 1954

REPLY BRIEF FOR
APPELLANTS AND
RESPONDENTS
ON FURTHER
REARGUMENT

know to be largely the result of opportunity and environment.[19] That the Negro is so disadvantaged educationally and culturally in the states where segregation is required is the strongest argument against its continuation for any period of time. Yet those who use this argument as a basis for interminable delay in the elimination of segregation in reality are seeking to utilize the product of their own wrongdoing as a justification for continued malfeasance.

Our public school systems have grown and improved as an American institution. And in every community it is obvious that children of all levels of culture, educability, and achievement must be accounted for within the same system. In some school systems the exceptional children are separated from the rest of the children. In others there are special classes for retarded children, for slow readers and for the physically handicapped. But these factors have no relation to race. These are administrative problems with respect to conduct of the public school.

In the past, large city school systems, North and South, have had the problem of absorbing children from rural areas where the public schools and cultural backgrounds were below the city standards. On many occasions these migrations have been very sudden and in proportionately very large numbers. This problem has always been solved as an administrative detail. It has never been either insurmountable nor has it been used as an excuse to force the rural children to attend sub-standard schools. Similarly, large cities have met without difficulty the influx of immigrants from foreign countries.

Cultural and health standards have always been maintained in public schools and there could be no objection to the continuation of such standards without regard to race. All social scientists seem to be in agreement that race and color have no connection whatsoever with a student's ability to be educated. Achievement and cultural deficiencies are nonracial in character, also. Hence these factors in no wise relate to questions posed as to whether desegregation should take place immediately or over an extended period.

Perhaps the main reasons for rejecting appellees' argument are that the conditions they complain of can never be remedied as long as segregation in public schools is continued and these so-called problems, *i.e.,* average on achievement tests, health, etc., are administrative problems which can be solved by recognized administrative

regulations made to fit the problems without regard to pigmentation of the skin. It is significant that appellees and the Attorneys-General who advance these arguments do not give any hope to anyone that the continuation of segregated public education will ever remove these problems which are the product of this segregation.

On the other hand, appellants have shown in their Brief on Further Reargument that on the basis of substantial documented experience: "There is no basis for the assumption that gradual as opposed to immediate desegregation is the better, smoother or more 'effective' mode of transition. On the contrary, there is an impressive body of evidence which supports the position that gradualism, far from facilitating the process, may actually make it more difficult; that, in fact, the problems of transition will be a good deal less complicated than might be forecast by appellees. Our submission is that this, like many wrongs, can be easiest and best undone, not by 'tapering off' but by forthright action" (p. 31).

Official reactions in states affected by the May 17th decision make it plain that delay will detract from rather than contribute to the "effectiveness" of the transition to desegregated schools Events occurring in the states affected by the decision of May 17, 1954, do not support the suggestions of appellees and *amici curiae* that further (and limitless) postponement of relief to Negro children will assure an "effective" adjustment from segregated to non-segregated school systems. In terms of legislative, executive or administrative reaction, the southern and border states may now be grouped in three loose categories:

(1) Those which have not waited for further directions from the Court, but have undertaken desegregation in varied measure during the current school year. Typical of the states falling in this category are Delaware,[20] Kansas,[21] Missouri,[22]

---

[20] Brief for Appellants in Nos. 1, 2 and 3 and for Respondents in No. 5 on Further Reargument, pp. 4–7; Brief for Petitioners on the Mandate in No. 5, pp. 10–12.

[21] Brief for Appellants in Nos. 1, 2 and 3 and for Respondents in No. 5 on Further Reargument, pp. 3–4; Supplemental Brief for the State of Kansas on Questions 4 and 5 Propounded by the Court, pp. 13–22; Supplemental Brief for the Board of Education, Topeka, Kansas on Questions 4 and 5 Propounded by the Court, pp. 2–4.

[22] SOUTHERN SCHOOL NEWS, September 3, 1954, p. 9, c. 2–5; *Id.,* October 1, 1954, p. 10, c. 1–5; *Id.,* November 4, 1954, p. 12, c. 1–5; *Id.,* December 1, 1954, p. 10, c. 1–5; *Id.,* January 6, 1955, p. 11, c. 1; *Id.,* February 3, 1955, p. 15, c. 1–5.

and West Virginia.[23] Although not a state, the District of Columbia would fall within this group.

(2) Those which have decided to await a decision on the question of relief but have indicated an intention to obey the Court's directions. Kentucky,[24] Oklahoma,[25] and Tennessee[26] are among the states in this category.

(3) Those which have indicated an intention to circumvent the decision of this Court or interminably delay the enjoyment by Negro children of their constitutionally protected rights not to be segregated in public schools. Included in this category are states like South Carolina[27] and Mississippi,[28] which have enacted legislation designed to nullify any decision of this Court in these cases, and states like Virginia[29] and Florida,[30] where either the governors or special legislative committees studying the problem have recommended that "every legal means" be used to preserve segregated school systems.[31]

Against this background of state reaction to the decision of May 17, 1954, it is clear that postponement of relief will serve no purpose. The states in the first category have already begun to implement this Court's decision and any delay as to them may imperil the progress already made.[32] The states in the second category have indicated a willingness to do whatever this Court directs and there is certainly no reason for delay as to them. The probable effect of delay, as to states in the third category, must be evaluated in the light of their declared intentions; we are justified in assuming that it would have no affirmative effect, but would merely provide additional time to devise and put into practice schemes expressly designed to thwart this Court's decision.

CONCLUSION

Appellants recognize that the problems confronting this Court, as it turns to the implementation of its decision in these cases, are of primary magnitude. Their high seriousness is enhanced by the fact that sovereign states are in effect, though not formally, at the bar and that the evil to which the Court's decree must be directed is no transitory wrong but is of the essence of the social structure of a great section of our nation.

Yet, it should be borne in mind that the very magnitude of these problems exists because of the assumption, tacitly indulged up to now, that the Constitution is not to be applied in its full force and scope to all sections of this country alike, but rather that its guarantees are to be enjoyed, in one part of our nation, only as molded and modified by the desire and customs of the dominant component of the sectional population. Such a view, however expressed, ignores the minimum requirement for a truly national constitution. It ignores also a vast part of the reality of the sectional interest involved, for that interest must be composed of the legitimate aspirations of Negroes as well as whites. It certainly ignores the repercussions which any reluctance to forthrightly enforce appellants' rights would have on this nation's international relations. Every day of delay means that this country is failing to develop its full strength.

The time has come to end the division of one nation into those sections where the Constitution is and those where it is not fully respected. Only by forthright action can the country set on the road to a uniform amenability to its Constitution. Finally, the right asserted by these appellants is not the only one at stake. The fate of other great constitutional freedoms,

U.S. SUPREME COURT, OCTOBER 1954

REPLY BRIEF FOR APPELLANTS AND RESPONDENTS ON FURTHER REARGUMENT

[23] SOUTHERN SCHOOL NEWS, October 1, p. 14, c. 1, 5; *Id.,* January 6, 1955, p. 2, c. 4–5.

[24] SOUTHERN SCHOOL NEWS, September 3, 1954, p. 7, c. 3; *Id.,* November 4, 1954, p. 16, c. 1; *Id.,* December 1, 1954, p. 9, c. 1, 3.

[25] SOUTHERN SCHOOL NEWS, February 3, 1955, p. 10, c. 1–2; *Id.,* March 3, 1955, p. 16, c. 1; THE NEW YORK TIMES, April 6, 1955, p. 20, c. 5.

[26] SOUTHERN SCHOOL NEWS, October 1, 1954, p. 11, c. 1; *Id.,* December 1, 1954, p. 12, c. 4; NEW YORK POST, March 16, 1955, p. 58, c. 4.

[27] SOUTHERN SCHOOL NEWS, September 3, 1954, p. 12, c. 1–2; *Id.,* February 3, 1955, p. 3, c. 2–4, *Id.,* March 3, 1955, p. 14, c. 1 3.

[28] SOUTHERN SCHOOL NEWS, September 3, 1954, p. 8, c. 3; *Id.,* October 1, 1954, p. 9, c. 4–5; *Id.,* November 4, 1954, p. 11, c.

4–5; *Id.,* January 6, 1955, p. 10, c. 1–2; THE NEW YORK TIMES, April 6, 1955, p. 20, c. 5.

[29] SOUTHERN SCHOOL NEWS, February 3, 1955, p. 10, c. 4.

[30] SOUTHERN SCHOOL NEWS, January 6, 1955, p. 6, c. 2.

[31] Indeed, Governor Marvin B. Griffin of Georgia has asserted: "However, if this court is so unrealistic as to attempt to enforce this unthinkable evil upon us, I serve notice now that we shall resist it with all the resources at our disposal and we shall never submit to the proposition of mixing the races in the classrooms of our schools."

[32] See, *e.g., Steiner v. Simmons,* 111 A. 2d 574 (Del. 1955), rev'g 108 A. 2d 173 (Del. 1954). There the Supreme Court reversed a chancery court determination that forthwith desegregation was proper under the decision of this Court of May 17, 1954.

U.S. SUPREME
COURT,
OCTOBER 1954

REPLY BRIEF FOR
APPELLANTS AND
RESPONDENTS
ON FURTHER
REARGUMENT

whether secured by the Fourteenth Amendment or by other provisions, is inevitably bound up in the resolution to be made in these cases. For delay in enforcement of these rights invites the insidious prospect that a moratorium may equally be placed on the enjoyment of other constitutional rights.

In disposing of the great issues before it, this Court should do no less than order the abolition of racial segregation in public education by a day certain, as heretofore set forth in Appellants' Brief on Further Reargument.

Respectively submitted,

CHARLES L. BLACK JR.,

ELWOOD H. CHISOLM,

WILLIAM T. COLEMAN JR.,

CHARLES T. DUNCAN,

GEORGE E. C. HAYES,

LOREN MILLER,

WILLIAM R. MING JR.,

CONSTANCE BAKER MOTLEY,

JAMES M. NABRIT JR.,

LOUIS H. POLLAK,

FRANK D. REEVES,

JOHN SCOTT,

JACK B. WEINSTEIN, *of Counsel.*

HAROLD BOULWARE,

ROBERT L. CARTER,

JACK GREENBERG,

OLIVER W. HILL,

THURGOOD MARSHALL,

LOUIS L. REDDING,

SPOTTSWOOD W. ROBINSON III,

CHARLES S. SCOTT, *Attorneys for Appellants in Nos. 1, 2, 3 and for Respondents in No. 5.*

In the Supreme Court of the United States

CITE AS 75 S.CT. 753

— ᘉ —

OLIVER BROWN, ET AL., APPELLANTS,
V.
BOARD OF EDUCATION OF TOPEKA,
SHAWNEE COUNTY, KANSAS, ET AL.

HARRY BRIGGS, JR., ET AL., APPELLANTS,
V.
R. W. ELLIOTT, ET AL.

DOROTHY E. DAVIS, ET AL., APPELLANTS,
V.
COUNTY SCHOOL BOARD OF PRINCE
EDWARD COUNTY, VIRGINIA,
ET. AL.

SPOTTSWOOD THOMAS BOLLING, ET AL.,
PETITIONERS,
V.
C. MELVIN SHARPE, ET AL.

FRANCIS B. GEBHART, ET AL., PETITIONERS,
V.
ETHEL LOUISE BELTON, ET AL.

NOS. 1–5.

Argued April 11, 12, 13, and 14, 1955.
Decided May 31. 1955.

349 U.S. 294

Class actions by which minor plaintiffs sought to obtain admission to public schools on a nonsegregated basis. On direct appeals by plaintiffs from adverse decisions in United States District Courts, District of Kansas, 98 F.Supp. 797, Eastern District of South Carolina, 103 F.Supp. 920, and Eastern District of Virginia, 103 F.Supp. 337, on certiorari before judgment on appeal to the United States Court of Appeals for the District of Columbia from adverse decision in the United States District Court for the District of Columbia, and on certiorari from decision favorable to plaintiffs in the Supreme Court of Delaware, 91 A.2d 137, the Supreme Court, 347 U.S. 483, 74 S.Ct. 686, 98 L.Ed. 873, and 347 U.S.

497, 74 S.Ct. 693, 98 L.Ed. 884, held that racial discrimination in public education was unconstitutional and restored cases to docket for further argument regarding formulation of decrees. On further argument, the Supreme Court, Mr. Chief Justice Warren, held that in proceedings to implement Supreme Court's determination, inferior courts might consider problems related to administration, arising from physical condition of school plant, school transportation system, personnel, revision of school districts and attendance areas into compact units to achieve system of determining admission to public schools on a nonracial basis, and revision of local laws and regulations, and might consider adequacy of any plan school authorities might propose to meet these problems and to effectuate a transition to racially nondiscriminatory school systems.

Judgments, except that in case No. 5, reversed and cases remanded with directions; judgment in case No. 5 affirmed and case remanded with directions.

All provisions of federal, state, or local law requiring or permitting racial discrimination in public education must yield to principle that such discrimination is unconstitutional. U.S.C.A. Const. Amend.

School authorities have primary responsibility for elucidating, assessing, and solving problems arising from fact that racial discrimination in public education is unconstitutional.

Question whether school authorities' actions constitute good faith implementation of principle that racial discrimination in public education is unconstitutional could best be appraised by courts which originally heard cases raising questions of constitutionality of such discrimination, and it was appropriate to remand cases to such courts. 28 U.S.C.A.§§ 2281, 2284.

Traditionally, equity has been characterized by a practical flexibility in shaping its remedies and by a facility for adjusting and reconciling public and private needs.

Courts of equity, in implementing Supreme Court's determination that racial discrimination in public education is unconstitutional, may properly take into account the public interest in elimination, in a systematic and effective manner, of obstacles to transition to school systems operated in accordance with constitutional principles, but constitutional principles cannot be allowed to yield because of disagreement with them.

U.S. SUPREME
COURT, 1955

On remand from Supreme Court after determination in several cases that racial discrimination in public education is unconstitutional. inferior courts should, while giving weight to public considerations and private interest of litigants, require that school authorities make prompt and reasonable start toward full compliance with ruling.

In proceedings to implement Supreme Court's decision that racial discrimination in public education is unconstitutional, public school authorities have burden of establishing that grant of additional time for transition is necessary in public interest and is consistent with good faith compliance at earliest practicable date.

Inferior courts, in implementing Supreme Court's determination that racial discrimination in public education is unconstitutional, may consider problems related to administration, arising from physical condition of school plant, school transportation system, personnel, revision of school districts and attendance areas into compact units to achieve system of determining admission to public schools on a nonracial basis, and revision of local laws and regulations, and many consider adequacy of any plans school authorities may propose to meet these problems and to effectuate a transition to racially nondiscriminatory school system.

Inferior courts, on remand from Supreme Court's determination that discrimination in public education is unconstitutional, were directed to retain jurisdiction of cases during period of transition to nondiscriminatory school systems.

Mr. Robert L. Carter, New York City, for appellants in No. 1.

Mr. Harold R. Fatzer, Topeka, Kan., for appellees in No. 1.

Messrs. Thurgood Marshall, New York City, and Spottswood W. Robinson, III, Richmond, VA., for appellants in Nos. 2 and 3.

Messrs. S. E. Rogers, Summerton, S. C., and Robert McC. Figg, Jr., Charleston, S.C., for appellees in No. 2.

Messrs. Archibald G. Robertson, Richmond, Va., and J. Lindsay Almond, Jr., Atty. Gen., for appellees in No. 3.

Messrs. George E. C. Hayes and James M. Nabrit, Jr., Washington, D.C., for petitioners in No. 4.

Mr. Milton D. Korman, Washington, D.C., for respondents in No. 4.

Mr. Joseph Donald Craven, Wilmington, Del., for petitioners in No. 5.

Mr. Louis L. Redding, Wilmington. Del., for respondents in No. 5.

Messrs. Richard W. Ervin and Ralph E. Odum, Tallahassee, Fla., for State of Florida, I. Beverly Lake, Raleigh, N.C., for State of North Carolina, Thomas J. Gentry, Little Rock, Ark., for State of Arkansas, Mac Q. Williamson Oklahoma, City, Okla., for State of Oklahoma, C. Ferdinand Sybert, Ellicott City, Md., for State of Maryland, John Ben Shepperd and Burnell Waldrep, Austin, Tex., for State of Texas, Sol. Gen. Simon E. Sobeloff, Washington, D.C., for United States, amici curiae.

Mr. Chief Justice Warren delivered the opinion of the Court.

[1] These cases were decided on May 17, 1954. The opinions of that date,[1] declaring the fundamental principle that racial discrimination in public education is unconstitutional, are incorporated herein by reference. All provisions of federal, state, or local law requiring or permitting such discrimination must yield to this principle. There remains for consideration the manner in which relief is to be accorded.

Because these cases arose under different local conditions and their disposition will involve a variety of local problems, we requested further argument on the question of relief.[2] In view of the nationwide importance of the deci-

---

[1] 347 U.S. 43, 74 S.Ct. 686, 98 L.Ed. 873, 347 U.S. 497, 74 S.Ct. 693, 98 L.Ed. 884.

[2] Further argument was requested on the following questions, 347 U.S. 483, 495–496, note 13, 74 S.Ct. 686, 692, 98 L.Ed. 873, previously propounded by the Court:

"4. Assuming it is decided that segregation in public schools violates the Fourteenth Amendment

"(a) would a decree necessarily follow providing that, within the limits set by normal geographic school districting, Negro children should forthwith be admitted to schools of their choice, or

"(b) may this Court, in the exercise of its equity powers, permit an effective gradual adjustment to be brought about from existing segregated systems to a system not based color distinctions?

"5. On the assumption on which questions 4 (a) and (b) are based, and assuming further that this Court will exercise its equity powers to the end described in question 4 (b),

"(a) should this Court formulate detailed decrees in these cases;

"(b) if so, what specific issues should the decrees;

"(c) should this Court appoint a special master to hear evidence with a view to recommending specific terms for such decrees;

U.S. SUPREME
COURT, 1955

sion. we invited the Attorney General of the United States and the Attorneys General of all states requiring or permitting racial discrimination in public education to present their views on that question. The parties, the United States, and the States of Florida, North Carolina, Arkansas, Oklahoma, Maryland, and Texas filed briefs and participated in the oral argument.

These presentations were informative and helpful to the Court in its consideration of the complexities arising from the transition to a system of public education freed of racial discrimination. The presentations also demonstrated that substantial steps to eliminate racial discrimination in public schools have already been taken, not only in some of the communities in which these cases arose, but in some of the states appearing as *amici curiae*, and in other states as well. Substantial progress has been made in the District of Columbia and in the communities in Kansas and Delaware involved in this litigation. The defendants in the cases coming to us from South Carolina and Virginia are awaiting the decisions of this Court concerning relief.

[2,3] Full implementation of these constitutional principles may require solution of varied local school problems. School authorities have the primary responsibility of elucidating, assessing, and solving these problems; courts will have to consider whether the action of school authorities constitutes good faith implementation of the governing constitutional principles. Because of their proximity to local conditions and the possible need for further hearings, the courts which originally heard these cases can best perform this judicial appraisal. Accordingly, we believe it appropriate to remand the cases to those courts.[3]

"(*d*) should this Court remand to the courts of first instance with directions to frame decrees in these cases, and if so what general directions should the decrees of this Court include and what procedures should the courts of first instance follow in arriving at the specific terms of more detailed decrees?"

[3] The cases coming to us from Kansas, South Carolina, and Virginia were originally heard by three-judge District Courts convened under 28 U.S.C. §§ 2281 and 2284, 28 U.S.C.A. §§ 2281, 2284. These cases will accordingly be remanded to those three-judge courts. See *Briggs v. Elliott*, 342 U.S. 350, 72 S.Ct. 327, 96 L.Ed. 392.

[4] See *Alexander v. Hillman*, 296 U.S. 222, 239, 56 S.Ct. 204, 209, 80 L.Ed. 192.

[5] See *Hecht Co, v. Bowles*, 321 U.S. 321, 329–330, 64 S.Ct. 587, 591, 592, 88 L.Ed. 754.

[4,5] In fashioning and effectuating the decrees, the courts will be guided by equitable principles. Traditionally, equity has been characterized by a practical flexibility in shaping its remedies[4] and by a facility for adjusting and reconciling public and private needs.[5] These cases call for the exercise of these traditional attributes of equity power. At stake is the personal interest of the plaintiffs in admission to public schools as soon as practicable on a nondiscriminatory basis. To effectuate this interest may call for elimination of a variety of obstacles in marking the transition to school systems operated in accordance with the constitutional principles set forth in our May 17, 1954, decision. Courts of equity may properly take into account the public interest in the elimination of such obstacles in a systematic and effective manner. But it should go without saying that the vitality of these constitutional principles cannot be allowed to yield simply because of disagreement with them.

[6–9] While giving weight to these public and private considerations, the courts will require that the defendants make a prompt and reasonable start toward full compliance with our May 17, 1954, ruling. Once such a start has been made, the courts may find that additional time is necessary to carry out the ruling in an effective manner. The burden rests upon the defendants to establish that such time is necessary in the public interest and is consistent with good faith compliance at the earliest practicable date. To that end, the courts may consider problems related to administration, arising from the physical condition of the school plant, the school transportation system, personnel, revision of school districts and attendance areas into compact units to achieve a system of determining admission to the public schools on a nonracial basis, and revision of local laws and regulations which may be necessary in solving the foregoing problems. They will also consider the adequacy of any plans the defendants may propose to meet these problems and to effectuate a transition to a racially nondiscriminatory school system. During this period of transition, the courts will retain jurisdiction of these cases.

The judgments below, except that in the Delaware case, are accordingly reversed and the cases are remanded to the District Courts to take such proceedings and enter such orders and decrees consistent with this opinion as are necessary and proper to admit to public schools on a racially nondiscriminatory basis with all deliberate speed the parties to these cases. The judgment in the Delaware case—ordering the immediate admission of the plaintiffs to schools previously attended only by white children—is affirmed on the basis of the principles stated in our May 17, 1954, opinion, but the case is remanded to the Supreme Court of Delaware for such further proceedings as that Court may deem necessary in light of this opinion.

It is so ordered.

Judgments, except that in case No. 5, reversed and cases remanded with directions; judgment in case No. 5 affirmed and case remanded with directions.

LAWRENCE v. TEXAS

LAWRENCE V. TEXAS

ISSUE

Gay and Lesbian Rights

HOW TO USE MILESTONES IN THE LAW

This section allows readers to investigate the facts, the arguments, and the legal reasoning that produced the *Lawrence v. Texas* decision. It also sheds light on the roles and required skills of attorneys and judges in resolving disputes.

As you read this section you may wish to consider the following issues:

- How did the appellant's description of the issues before the Court, or questions presented, differ from the appellee's description?

- How did the courts and the two parties differ in describing the meaning of particular prior cases to the present case?

- How did the holdings (conclusions of law) of the appeals court differ from those of the Supreme Court?

- On what points in the Supreme Court's majority opinion do the concurring and dissenting justices agree and disagree?

THIS CASE IN HISTORY

Lawrence v. Texas was a significant gain for the cause of gay and lesbian civil rights. In this decision, the Supreme Court held that state laws prohibiting sodomy were unconstitutional, arguing that any government interest in consensual sex between adults, either homosexual or heterosexual, infringed upon the right to liberty protected by the Due Process clause of the Fourteenth Amendment. This argument follows the analysis made in rulings such as *Roe v. Wade* and *Griswold v. Connecticut,* which struck down bans on abortion and birth control (respectively) on the basis that such bans infringed on a person's right to liberty, which has been determined to include the rights to privacy and autonomy. *Lawrence* essentially overturned the 1986 precedent of *Bowers v. Hardwick,* in which the Court upheld a Georgia law prohibiting sodomy similar to the one struck down in *Lawrence.* A central argument for the decision in *Bowers* was that a long history of laws existed in Western civilization that have sought to repress homosexual conduct. The majority in *Lawrence* noted, however, that many sodomy laws have been overturned since *Bowers,* reflecting a new trend. Only 13 states in 2003, as compared to all 50 in 1961, still had laws prohibiting sodomy.

The *Lawrence* ruling caused considerable controversy. Opponents to the ruling contended that the majority manipulated the due process clause to push the cause of gay rights. They also disagreed with the overturning of *Bowers v. Hardwick,* because it took away from the states the power to determine their own moral laws.

IN COURT OF APPEALS OF TEXAS, FOURTEENTH DISTRICT, HOUSTON

NO. 14–99–00109–CR & NO. 14–99–00111–CR

JOHN GEDDES LAWRENCE AND TYRON GARNER, APPELLANTS

V.

THE STATE OF TEXAS, APPELLEE

March 15, 2001, Substituted Majority, Concurring, and Dissenting Opinions Filed

PRIOR HISTORY: On Appeal from County Criminal Court at Law No. 10. Trial Court Cause Nos. 98–48530 and 98–48531. Harris County, Texas. Sherman A. Ross, Judge.

This Opinion Substituted on Grant of Rehearing for Withdrawn Opinion of June 8, 2000.

DISPOSITION: Judgment of trial court affirmed.

Mitchell Katine of Houston, TX, Susanne B. Goldberg of New York, NY, Ruth E. Harlow of New York, NY, *for appellants.*

William Delmore, III of Houston, TX, *for appellee.*
J. Harvey Hudson, Justice. Justices Yates, Fowler, Edelman, Wittig, Frost, and Amidei join this opinion; Justice Yates also filed a concurring opinion in which Justices Hudson, Fowler, Edelman, and Frost join; Justice Fowler also filed a concurring opinion in which Justices Yates, Edelman, Frost, and Amidei join. Justice Anderson filed a dissenting opinion in which Senior Chief Justice Murphy joins.
Senior Chief Justice Paul C. Murphy and Former Justice Maurice Amidei sitting by assignment.

STATEMENT OF THE CASE

Appellants, John Geddes Lawrence and Tyron Garner, were convicted of engaging in homosexual conduct. They were each assessed a fine of two hundred dollars. On appeal, appellants challenge the constitutionality of Section 21.06 of the Texas Penal Code, contending it offends the equal protection and privacy guarantees assured by both the state and federal constitutions. For the reasons set forth below, we find no constitutional infringement.

While investigating a reported "weapons disturbance," police entered a residence where they observed appellants engaged in deviate sexual intercourse.[1] It is a Class C misdemeanor in the State of Texas for a person to engage "in deviate sexual intercourse with another individual of the same sex." TEX. PEN. CODE ANN. § 21.06 (Vernon 1994). However, because appellants subsequently entered pleas of nolo contendere, the facts and circumstances of the offense are not in the record. Accordingly, appellants did not challenge at trial, and do not contest on appeal, the propriety of the police conduct leading to their discovery and arrest. Thus, the narrow issue presented here is whether Section 21.06 is facially unconstitutional.

ARGUMENT

EQUAL PROTECTION

In their first point of error, appellants contend Section 21.06 violates federal and state equal protection guarantees by discriminating both in regard to sexual orientation and gender.[2]

The universal application of law to all citizens has been a tenet of English common law since at least the Magna Carta, and our whole system of law is predicated on this fundamental principle. *Truax v. Corrigan,* 257 U.S. 312, 332, 66 L. Ed. 254, 42 S. Ct. 124 (1921). Nevertheless, our federal constitution did not originally contain an express guarantee of equal protection. While an assurance of equal protection could be implied from the Due Process Clause of the Fifth Amendment, this rudimentary guarantee was

---

[1] "Deviate sexual intercourse" is defined in Texas as "any contact between any part of the genitals of one person and the mouth or anus of another person; or . . . the penetration of the genitals or the anus of another person with an object." TEX. PEN. CODE ANN. § 21.01 (Vernon 1994).

[2] Appellants rely upon the Fourteenth Amendment of the United States Constitution and two provisions of the Texas Constitution, namely, Article I, sections 3 and 3a:

No State shall make or enforce any law which shall . . . deny to any person within its jurisdiction the equal protection of the laws.

U.S. CONST. amend. XIV, § 1.

All free men, when they form a social compact, have equal rights, and no man, or set of men, is entitled to exclusive separate public emoluments, or privileges, but in consideration of public service.

TEX. CONST. art. I, § 3.

Equality under the law shall not be denied or abridged because of sex, race, color, creed, or national origin. This amendment is self-operative.

TEX. CONST. art. I, § 3a.

COURT OF
APPEALS OF
TEXAS,
MARCH 2001

complicated by constitutional distinctions between "free" persons and persons "held to service or labour." U.S. CONST. arts. I, § 2 & IV, § 2.[3]

Although the constitution did not establish or legalize slavery, it certainly recognized its existence within the states which tolerated it. See *The Amistad,* 40 U.S. 518, 551, 10 L. Ed. 826 (1841). This constitutional recognition of slavery undoubtedly facilitated a union of the original colonies, but it postponed until a later day a resolution of the tension between involuntary servitude and the concept of equal protection of laws implied by the Fifth Amendment.[4] Reconciling the institution of slavery with the notion of equal protection ultimately proved to be impossible. In the end, a constitutional "clarification" was obtained by the force of arms, six hundred thousand lives, and two constitutional amendments.

In 1863, while the outcome of the civil war remained very much in doubt, President Lincoln issued his Emancipation Proclamation purporting to free slaves found within the confederate states. In 1865, just months after general hostilities had ended, the Thirteenth Amendment was adopted. It declared that "neither slavery nor involuntary servitude . . . shall exist within the United States, or any place subject to their jurisdiction." U.S. CONST. amend. XIII, § 1. The abolition of slavery, however, was not immediately effective in bestowing the equal protection of law upon all persons. Several centuries of slavery had instilled a deep cultural bias against people of color. Individual southern states began enacting the so-called Black Codes which were designed to repress their black citizens and very nearly resurrect the institution of slavery. *City of Memphis v. Greene,* 451 U.S. 100, 132, 67 L. Ed. 2d 769, 101 S. Ct. 1584 (1981) (White, J., concurring). In response to these events, the Republican Congress passed the Civil Rights Act of 1866 in an attempt to ensure equal rights for former slaves. *General Bldgs. Contrs. Assn., Inc. v. Pennsylvania,* 458 U.S. 375, 389, 73 L. Ed. 2d 835, 102 S. Ct. 3141 (1982). In 1868, the Fourteenth

Amendment was adopted and its Equal Protection Clause enjoined the states from denying to any person the equal protection of the laws.

Thus, the central purpose of the Equal Protection Clause "is to prevent the States from purposefully discriminating between individuals on the basis of race." *Shaw v. Reno,* 509 U.S. 630, 642, 125 L. Ed. 2d 511, 113 S. Ct. 2816 (1993). While the guarantees of "equal protection" and "due process of law" may overlap, the spheres of protection they offer are not coterminous. *Truax,* 257 U.S. at 332, 42 S. Ct. at 129. Rather, the right to "'equal protection of the laws' is a more explicit safeguard of prohibited unfairness than 'due process of law.'" Bolling, 347 U.S. 497, 499, 98 L. Ed. 884, 74 S. Ct. 693 (1954). It is aimed at undue favor and individual or class privilege, on the one hand, and at hostile discrimination or the oppression of inequality, on the other. See *Truax,* 257 U.S. at 332–33, 42 S. Ct. at 129. It was not intended, however, "to interfere with the power of the state . . . to prescribe regulations to promote the health, peace, morals, education, and good order of the people." *Barbier v. Connolly,* 113 U.S. 27, 31, 28 L. Ed. 923, 5 S. Ct. 357 (1884).

Similarly, Article I, § 3 of the Texas Constitution also guarantees equality of rights to all persons. *Burroughs v. Lyles,* 142 Tex. 704, 181 S.W.2d 570, 574 (Tex. 1944). It was designed to prevent any person, or class of persons, from being singled out as a special subject for discriminating or hostile legislation. *Id.* Because the state and federal equal protection guarantees share a common aim and are similar in scope, Texas cases have frequently followed federal precedent when analyzing the scope and effect of Article I, § 3. *Hogan v. Hallman,* 889 S.W.2d 332, 338 (Tex. App.—Houston [14th Dist.] 1994, writ denied).

The Texas Equal Rights Amendment, however, has no federal equivalent. See TEX. CONST. art. I, § 3a. When Texas voters adopted it in 1972 by a four to one margin, both the United States and Texas constitutions already provided due process and equal protection guarantees. In the Interest of *McLean,* 725 S.W.2d 696, 698 (Tex. 1987). Thus, unless the amendment was an exercise in futility, it must have been intended to be more extensive and provide greater specific protection than either the

---

[3] These articles were subsequently amended by the Thirteenth and Fourteenth Amendments.

[4] The Due Process Clause of the Fifth Amendment "requires that every man shall have the protection of his day in court, and the benefit of the general law . . . so that every citizen shall hold his life, liberty, property and immunities under the protection of the general rules which govern society." U.S. CONST. amend. V.

United States or Texas due process and equal protection guarantees. *Id.*

All of the aforementioned state and federal guarantees of equal protection are tempered somewhat by the practical reality that the mere act of governing often requires discrimination between groups and classes of individuals. *Casarez v. State*, 913 S.W.2d 468, 493 (Tex. Crim. App. 1994). A state simply cannot function without classifying its citizens for various purposes and treating some differently than others. See *Sullivan v. U.I.L.*, 616 S.W.2d 170, 172 (Tex. 1981). For example, able-bodied citizens may be required to serve in the armed forces, while the infirm are not. *Casarez,* 913 S.W.2d at 493.

The conflict between the hypothetical ideal of equal protection and the practical necessity of governmental classifications has spawned a series of judicial tests for determining when classifications are and are not permissible. The general rule is that legislation is presumed to be valid and will be sustained if the classification drawn by the statute is rationally related to a legitimate state interest. *City of Cleburne v. Cleburne Living Center*, 473 U.S. 432, 440, 87 L. Ed. 2d 313, 105 S. Ct. 3249 (1985). The general rule gives way, however, when a statute classifies persons by race, alienage, or national origin. *Id.* These factors are so seldom relevant to the achievement of any legitimate state interest that laws separating persons according to these "suspect classifications" are subject to strict scrutiny. *Id.* Accordingly, laws directed against a "suspect class," or which infringe upon a "fundamental right," will be sustained only if they are suitably tailored to serve a compelling state interest. *Id.*; *Kadrmas v. Dickinson Public Schools*, 487 U.S. 450, 457–58, 101 L. Ed. 2d 399, 108 S. Ct. 2481 (1988).

Sexual Orientation

Relying on the Fourteenth Amendment of the United States Constitution, Article I, § 3 of the Texas Constitution, and the Texas Equal Rights Amendment, appellants contend that Section 21.06 of the Texas Penal Code unconstitutionally discriminates against homosexuals.[5] In other words, the statute improperly punishes persons on the basis of their sexual orientation.

The threshold issue we must decide is whether Section 21.06 distinguishes persons by sexual orientation. On its face, the statute makes no classification on the basis of sexual orientation; rather, the statute is expressly directed at conduct. While homosexuals may be disproportionately affected by the statute, we cannot assume homosexual conduct is limited only to those possessing a homosexual "orientation." Persons having a predominately heterosexual inclination may sometimes engage in homosexual conduct.[6] Thus, the statute's proscription applies, facially at least, without respect to a defendant's sexual orientation.

However, a facially neutral statute may support an equal protection claim where it is motivated by discriminatory animus and its application results in a discriminatory effect. *Village of Arlington Heights v. Metropolitan Housing Dev. Corp.*, 429 U.S. 252, 264–65, 50 L. Ed. 2d 450, 97 S. Ct. 555 (1977). Appellants contend this discriminatory intent is evident in the evolution of Section 21.06. For most of its history, Texas has deemed deviate sexual intercourse, i.e., sodomy, to be unlawful whether performed by persons of the same or different sex.[7] In 1973, however, the Legislature repealed its prohibition of sodomy generally, except when performed by persons of the same sex. Because "homosexual sodomy" is unlawful, while "heterosexual

W E S T ' S   E N C Y C L O P E D I A   O F   A M E R I C A N   L A W ,   2 N D   E D I T I O N

---

[5] There is some authority recognizing a distinction between homosexual orientation and homosexual conduct. *Meinhold v. United States Dept. of Defense*, 34 F.3d 1469, 1477 (9th Cir. 1994); *Pruitt v. Cheney*, 963 F.2d 1160, 1164 (9th Cir. 1991); see also *Watkins v. United States Army*, 875 F.2d 699, 725 (9th Cir. 1989) (Norris, J., concurring) (stating that "any attempt to criminalize the status of an individual's sexual orientation would present grave constitutional problems").

[6] In his study of human sexuality, Dr. Alfred C. Kinsey classified the "sexual orientation" of his subjects on a seven point continuum: (1) exclusively heterosexual; (2) predominantly heterosexual, only incidentally homosexual; (3) heterosexual, but more than incidentally homosexual; (4) equally heterosexual and homosexual; (5) predominantly homosexual, but more than incidentally heterosexual; (6) predominantly

homosexual, but incidentally heterosexual; and (7) exclusively homosexual. Jeffrey S. Davis, Military Policy Toward Homosexuals: Scientific, Historical, and Legal Perspectives, 131 MIL. L. REV. 55, 58 (1991). Kinsey estimated that approximately 50 per cent of the population is exclusively heterosexual; 4 per cent is exclusively homosexual. Id. at 64. See also Sharon Elizabeth Rush, Equal Protection Analogies—Identity and "Passing": Race and Sexual Orientation, 13 HARV. BLACKLETTER J. 65, 83–84 (1997); Odeana R. Neal, The Limits of Legal Discourse: Learning From the Civil Rights Movement in the Quest for Gay and Lesbian Civil Rights, 40 N.Y.L. SCH. L. REV. 679, 705 (1996).

[7] See Acts 1943, 48th Leg., p. 194, ch.112, § 1; Vernon's Ann. P.C. (1925) art. 524; Rev. P.C. 1911, art. 507; Rev. P.C. 1895, art. 364; and Rev.P.C.1879, art. 342.

sodomy" is not, appellants contend the statute evidences a hostility toward homosexuals, not shared by heterosexuals.

While we find this distinction may be sufficient to support an equal protection claim, neither the United States Supreme Court, the Texas Supreme Court, nor the Texas Court of Criminal Appeals has found sexual orientation to be a "suspect class."[8] Thus, the prohibition of homosexual sodomy is permissible if it is rationally related to a legitimate state interest.

The State contends the statute advances a legitimate state interest, namely, preserving public morals. One fundamental purpose of government is "to conserve the moral forces of society." *Grigsby v. Reib,* 105 Tex. 597, 607, 153 S.W. 1124, 1129 (Tex. 1913). In fact, the Legislature has outlawed behavior ranging from murder to prostitution precisely because it has deemed these activities to be immoral. Even our civil law rests on concepts of fairness derived from a moral understanding of right and wrong. The State's power to preserve and protect morality has been the basis for upholding such diverse statutes as requiring parents to provide medical care to their children,[9] prohibiting the sale of obscene devices,[10] forbidding nude dancing where liquor is sold,[11] criminalizing child endangerment,[12] regulating the sale of liquor,[13] and punishing incest.[14] Most, if not all, of our law is "based on notions of morality." *Bowers v. Hardwick,* 478 U.S. 186, 196, 92 L. Ed. 2d 140, 106 S. Ct. 2841 (1986).

Appellants claim the concept of "morality" is simply "the singling out [of] groups of people based on popular dislike or disapproval." Contending this practice was specifically condemned in *Romer v. Evans,* appellants argue that classifications based on sexual orientation can no longer be rationally justified by the State's interest in protecting morality. 517 U.S. 620, 116 S. Ct. 1620, 134 L. Ed. 2d 855 (1996). We find, however, that appellant's broad interpretation of *Romer* is not supported by the text or rationale of the Court's opinion.

In *Romer,* the Supreme Court considered the constitutionality of Colorado's universal prohibition of any statute, regulation, ordinance, or policy making homosexual orientation the basis of any claim of minority status, quota preferences, protected status, or claim of discrimination. Justice Kennedy, writing for the majority, first observed that the Fourteenth Amendment does not give Congress a general power to prohibit discrimination in public accommodations. *Romer,* 517 U.S. at 627–28. Thus, discrimination in employment, accommodations, and other commercial activities has historically been rectified by the enactment of detailed statutory schemes. *Id.* at 628. The Court cited, for illustration, several municipal codes in Colorado that prohibited discrimination on the basis of age, military status, pregnancy, parenthood, custody of a minor child, political affiliation, physical or mental disability, or sexual orientation. *Id.* at 629. To the extent these codes protected homosexuals, however, they were rendered invalid by Colorado's constitutional amendment.

In striking down the amendment, the Supreme Court declared that all citizens have the right to petition and seek legislative protection from their government. "A law declaring that in general it shall be more difficult for one group of citizens than for all others to seek aid from the government is itself a denial of equal protection of the laws in the most literal sense."

---

[8] The Ninth Circuit Court of Appeals briefly held that homosexuals constitute a "suspect class," but that opinion was later withdrawn. *Watkins v. United States Army,* 847 F.2d 1329, 1349 (9th Cir. 1988), withdrawn, 875 F.2d 699, 711 (9th Cir. 1989), cert. denied, 498 U.S. 957, 111 S. Ct. 384, 112 L. Ed. 2d 395 (1990). No other federal court of appeals has ever applied heightened scrutiny when considering equal protection claims in the context of sexual orientation. See *High Tech Gays v. Defense Indus.* Sec. Clearance Office, 895 F.2d 563, 571 (9th Cir. 1990); *Ben-Shalom v. Marsh,* 881 F.2d 454, 464 (7th Cir. 1989); *Woodward v. United States,* 871 F.2d 1068, 1076 (Fed. Cir. 1989); *Padula v. Webster,* 261 U.S. App. D.C. 365, 822 F.2d 97, 103 (D.C. Cir. 1987) (all holding that homosexuals do not constitute a suspect or quasi-suspect class entitled to greater than rational basis scrutiny for equal protection purposes). See also *Romer v. Evans,* 517 U.S. 620, 631–32, 134 L. Ed. 2d 855, 116 S. Ct.

[continued] 1620 (1996) (relying on the "rational relationship" test rather than "strict scrutiny" when assessing the constitutionality of Colorado's Second Amendment barring legislation favorable to homosexuals).

[9] *Commonwealth v. Nixon,* 563 Pa. 425, 761 A.2d 1151, 2000 WL 1741296, *5 (Pa. 2000).

[10] *Yorko v. State,* 690 S.W.2d 260, 265–66 (Tex. Crim. App. 1985).

[11] *El Marocco Club, Inc. v. Richardson,* 746 A.2d 1228, 1237–38 (R.I. 2000).

[12] *State v. Wilson,* 267 Kan. 550, 987 P.2d 1060, 1067 (Kan. 1999).

[13] *Altshuler v. Pennsylvania Liquor Control Bd.,* 729 A.2d 1272, 1277 (Pa. Commw. Ct. 1999).

[14] *Smith v. State,* 6 S.W.3d 512, 519–20 (Tenn. Crim. App. 1999).

COURT OF
APPEALS OF
TEXAS,
MARCH 2001

Id. at 633. "A State cannot . . . deem a class of persons a stranger to its laws." *Id.* at 635. Thus, while no individual, class, or group is guaranteed success, all persons have the right to seek legislation favoring their interests.

Here, appellants do not suggest that Section 21.06 unconstitutionally encumbers their right to seek legislative protection from discriminatory practices. Hence, *Romer* provides no support for appellants' position. *Romer,* for example, does not disavow the Court's previous holding in *Bowers*; it does not elevate homosexuals to a suspect class; it does not suggest that statutes prohibiting homosexual conduct violate the Equal Protection Clause; and it does not challenge the concept that the preservation and protection of morality is a legitimate state interest.[15]

Moreover, while appellants may deem the statute to be based on prejudice, rather than moral insight, our power to review the moral justification for a legislative act is extremely limited. The constitution has vested the legislature, not the judiciary, with the authority to make law. In so doing, the people have granted the legislature the exclusive right to determine issues of public morality.[16] If a court could overturn a statute because it perceived nothing wrong with the prohibited conduct, the judiciary would at once become the rule making authority for society—this the people have strictly forbidden. Accordingly, we must assume for the purposes of our analysis that the Legislature has found homosexual sodomy to be immoral.

The State also contends the legislature could have rationally concluded that "homosexual sodomy" is a different, and more reprehensible, offense than "heterosexual sodomy." This proposition is difficult to confirm because in American jurisprudence courts and legislatures have historically discussed the topic only in terms of vague euphemisms. In fact, statutes often made sodomy a criminal offense without ever defining the conduct. See *Commonwealth v. Poindexter,* 133 Ky. 720, 118 S.W. 943, 944 (Ky. 1909).

In its broadest common law form, the offense "consists in a carnal knowledge committed against the order of nature by man with man, or in the same unnatural manner with woman; or by man or woman, in any manner, with beast." *Prindle v. State,* 31 Tex. Crim. 551, 21 S.W. 360 (Tex. Crim. App. 1893). More restrictive definitions of sodomy, however, were commonly recognized. In many instances, for example, sodomy was restricted to carnal copulation between two human beings—sometimes further restricted to males (perhaps because it was difficult to "imagine that such an offense would ever be committed between a man and a woman"). *Wise v. Commonwealth,* 135 Va. 757, 115 S.E. 508, 509 (Va. 1923). In any event, only homosexual conduct between two men was included among the early capital crimes of the Massachusetts Bay Colony.[17] Moreover, in some jurisdictions, including Texas, sodomy did not include oral sex. *Prindle,* 21 S.W. at 360; *Poindexter,* 118 S.W. at 944. Again, it is difficult to know whether this more narrow definition arose deliberately or was simply the product of legislative ignorance and/or judicial innocence. Conceivably, oral sex was "so unusual and unthinkable as perhaps not to have been even contemplated in the earlier stages of the law." *Wise,* 115 S.E. at 509.

Regardless of how these differing definitions of sodomy arose, we agree with the State's general contention that it has always been the legislature's prerogative to deem some acts more egregious

---

[15] In fact, the State of Colorado did not cite the preservation of morality as one of its legitimate interests in attempting to uphold the amendment. Rather, the state argued that it had a legitimate interest in: (1) protecting the freedom of association of its citizens, particularly those who might have personal or religious objections to homosexuality, and (2) conserving its resources to combat discrimination against other groups. Id. at 635.

[16] Where a statute does not run afoul of explicit constitutional protections, its moral justification is virtually unreviewable by the judiciary. When the rational basis for an Alabama statute outlawing certain sexual devices was challenged, the United States Eleventh Circuit Court of Appeals wrote:

> However misguided the legislature of Alabama may have been in enacting the statute challenged in this case, the statute is not constitutionally irrational under rational basis

scrutiny because it is rationally related to the State's legitimate power to protect its view of public morality. "The Constitution presumes that ... improvident decisions will eventually be rectified by the democratic process and that judicial intervention is generally unwarranted no matter how unwisely we may think a political branch has acted." *Vance v. Bradley,* 440 U.S. 93, 97, 99 S. Ct. 939, 942–943, 59 L. Ed. 2d 171 (1979). This Court does not invalidate bad or foolish policies, only unconstitutional ones; we may not "sit as a superlegislature to judge the wisdom or desirability of legislative policy determinations made in areas that neither affect fundamental rights nor proceed along suspect lines." *New Orleans v. Dukes,* 427 U.S. 297, 303, 96 S. Ct. 2513, 2517, 49 L. Ed. 2d 511 (1976).

For the foregoing reasons, we hold the Alabama statute challenged in this case has a rational basis. *Williams v. Pryor,* 229 F.3d 1331, 1339 (11th Cir. 2000).

than others. For example, the legislature has not chosen to make every homicide a capital offense; depending upon the circumstances, some homicides are first degree felonies,[18] some are second degree felonies,[19] some are state jail felonies,[20] and others are lawful.[21] Moreover, it is the duty of this Court to construe every statute in a manner that renders it constitutional if it is possible to do so consistent with a reasonable interpretation of its language. *Trinity River Authority v. UR Consultants, Inc.* Texas, 869 S.W.2d 367, 370 (Tex. App.—Dallas 1993), aff'd, 889 S.W.2d 259 (Tex. 1994). Accordingly, we find the legislature could have concluded that deviant sexual intercourse, when performed by members of the same sex, is an act different from or more offensive than any such conduct performed by members of the opposite sex.

Because (1) there is no fundamental right to engage in sodomy, (2) homosexuals do not constitute a "suspect class," and (3) the prohibition of homosexual conduct advances a legitimate state interest and is rationally related thereto, namely, preserving public morals, appellant's first contention is overruled.

Gender

Appellants also contend Section 21.06 unconstitutionally discriminates on the basis of gender. In Texas, gender is recognized as a "suspect class." *Barber v. Colorado Independent School Dist.*, 901 S.W.2d 447, 452 (Tex. 1995). In light of the Texas Equal Rights Amendment, classifications by gender are subject to "strict scrutiny" and will be upheld only if the State can show such classifications have been suitably tailored to serve a compelling state interest.[22]

---

[17] Bestiality, however, was a capital offense whether committed by a man or a woman. THE LAWS AND LIBERTIES OF MASSACHUSETTS, at 5 (Cambridge 1648).

[18] TEX. PEN. CODE ANN. § 19.02 (Vernon 1994).

[19] TEX. PEN. CODE ANN. § 19.04 (Vernon 1994).

[20] TEX. PEN. CODE ANN. § 19.05 (Vernon 1994).

[21] TEX. PEN. CODE ANN. §§ 9.32, 9.33, 9.42, & 9.43 (Vernon 1994).

[22] Under the Fourteenth Amendment, gender classifications are analyzed according to an intermediate "heightened scrutiny" falling somewhere between the rational relationship test and strict scrutiny. *Mississippi University for Women v. Hogan*, 458 U.S. 718, 724, 73 L. Ed. 2d 1090, 102 S. Ct. 3331 (1982); see also *Craig v. Boren*, 429 U.S. 190, 197, 50 L. Ed. 2d 397, 97 S. Ct. 451 (1976) (holding that under the Fourteenth Amendment, classifications by gender must serve important governmental objectives and must be substantially related to the achievement of those objectives.

Appellants claim Section 21.06 discriminates on the basis of sex because criminal conduct is determined to some degree by the gender of the actors. For example, deviate sexual intercourse is not unlawful per se in Texas. While the physical act is not unlawful as between a man and woman, it is unlawful when performed between two men or two women. Appellants contend that because criminality under the statute is, in some respects, gender-dependent, Section 21.06 runs afoul of state and federal equal protection guarantees.

The State asserts the statute applies equally to men and women, i.e., two men engaged in homosexual conduct face the same sanctions as two women. Thus, the State maintains the statute does not discriminate on the basis of gender. Appellants respond by observing that a similar rationale was expressly rejected in the context of racial discrimination. *Loving v. Virginia*, 388 U.S. 1, 9, 18 L. Ed. 2d 1010, 87 S. Ct. 1817 (1967).

In *Loving*, the State of Virginia attempted to uphold its miscegenation statute in the face of an equal protection challenge by arguing that the statute did not discriminate on the basis of race because it applied equally to whites and blacks. The Supreme Court traced the origins of Virginia's miscegenation statute and concluded that "penalties for miscegenation arose as an incident to slavery." *Loving*, 388 U.S. at 6. Because the clear and central purpose of the Fourteenth Amendment was "to eliminate all official state sources of invidious racial discrimination," the court determined the statute was unconstitutional. *Id.*, at 10.

Here, the State of Texas employs a comparable argument, namely, Section 21.06 does not discriminate on the basis of gender because it applies equally to men and women. Appellants' contend the argument was discredited by *Loving* and should not be followed here. But while the purpose of Virginia's miscegenation statute was to segregate the races and perpetuate the notion that blacks are inferior to whites, no such sinister motive can be ascribed to the criminalization of homosexual conduct. In other words, we find nothing in the history of Section 21.06 to suggest it was intended to promote any hostility between the sexes, preserve any unequal treatment as between men and women, or perpetuate any societal or cultural bias with regard to gender. Thus, we find appellants' reliance on *Loving* unpersuasive.[23]

While Section 21.06 alludes to sex, not every statutory reference to gender constitutes an unlawful "gender-classification." Texas law provides, for example, that counties are authorized to increase participation by "women-owned businesses" in public contract awards by establishing a contract percentage goal for those businesses;[24] when jurors are sequestered overnight, separate facilities must be provided for male and female jurors;[25] employers are prohibited from permitting, requesting, or requiring female children to work topless;[26] the Director of the Texas Department of Transportation must report to each house of the legislature regarding the department's progress in recruiting and hiring women;[27] where a child is adopted by two parents, one must be female and the other male;[28] female patients being transported from a jail to a mental health facility must be accompanied by a female attendant;[29] circumcision of a female under the age of 18 is unlawful;[30] etc. Whether these and many other gender-specific statutes, violate the Texas Equal Rights Amendment is not before us. We must assume, however, that the legislature enacted these provisions with full knowledge of Article I, section 3a of the Texas Constitution and perceived no conflict. The legislature, for example, has specifically admonished the governor and supreme court to ensure the full and fair representation of women when making their appointments to the Board of Directors of the State Bar of Texas, but to also make no "regard to race, creed, sex, religion, or national origin." TEX. GOV'T CODE ANN. § 81.020 (Vernon 1998).

The mere allusion to gender is not a talisman of constitutional invalidity. If a statute does not impose burdens or benefits upon a particular gender, it does not subject individuals to unequal treatment. See *Coalition for Economic Equity v. Wilson,* 122 F.3d 692, 702 (9th Cir. 1997) (holding that while California's Proposition 209 mentions race and gender, it does not logically classify persons by race and gender); see also *Hayden v. County of Nassau,* 180 F.3d 42, 48–49 (2nd Cir. 1999) (entrance exam designed to diminish cultural bias on black applicants did not constitute a "racial classification" because it did not promote one race over another). While Section 21.06 includes the word "sex," it does not elevate one gender over the other. Neither does it impose burdens on one gender not shared by the other.

Where, as here, a statute is gender-neutral on its face, appellants bear the burden of showing the statute has had an adverse effect upon one gender and that such disproportionate impact can be traced to a discriminatory purpose. *Sylvia Development Corp. v. Calvert County, Md.,* 48 F.3d 810, 819 (4th Cir. 1995); *Keevan v. Smith,* 100 F.3d 644, 650 (8th Cir. 1996). Appellants have made no attempt to establish, nor do they even contend, that Section 21.06 has had any disparate impact between men and women. Rather,

COURT OF
APPEALS OF
TEXAS,
MARCH 2001

---

[23] See also *Boutwell v. State,* 719 S.W.2d 164 (Tex. Crim. App. 1985). There the Court of Criminal Appeals considered the applicability of the Texas Equal Rights Amendment to Section 21.10 of the Penal Code which, until its repeal in 1983, provided legal defenses to certain heterosexual acts that were specifically denied in the context of homosexual acts. Act of May 24, 1973, 63rd Leg., R.S., ch. 399, § 21.10, 1973 Tex. Gen. Laws 918. When Boutwell was charged with sexual abuse of several boys, he argued the statute was unconstitutional under the Texas Equal Rights Amendment because it discriminated against him on the basis of sex. *Boutwell,* 719 S.W.2d at 167. The Court of Criminal Appeals rejected the contention, stating:

But clearly, a female defendant situated similarly to appellant—that is, a female who had engaged in deviate sexual intercourse with a child 14 years or older who was of the same sex—would likewise be denied the "promiscuity" defense under § 21.10. Thus, appellant's reasoning proceeds upon a fallacy of amphiboly: his complaint is not that he is discriminated against on the basis of "sex" in the sense of "gender;" but rather, that his "sex" act is entitled to protection equal to that given heterosexual conduct under the law as stated in § 21.10(b). Id. at 169; see also *Boulding v. State,*

719 S.W.2d 333 (Tex. Crim. App. 1986). *Boutwell* has been severely criticized, but on grounds different than those at issue here. *McGlothlin v. State,* 848 S.W.2d 139, 139 (Tex. Crim. App. 1992); *Vernon v. State,* 841 S.W.2d 407, 410 (Tex. Crim. App. 1992).

[24] TEX. LOC. GOV'T. CODE ANN. § 381.004 (Vernon 1999).

[25] TEX. CODE CRIM. PROC. ANN. art. 35.23 (Vernon Supp. 2000).

[26] TEX. PEN. CODE ANN. § 43.251 (Vernon 1994).

[27] TEX. TRANS. CODE ANN. § 201.403 (Vernon 1999).

[28] TEX. HEALTH & SAFETY CODE ANN. § 192.008 (Vernon Supp. 2000).

[29] TEX. CODE CRIM. PROC. ANN. art. 46.04 (Vernon Pamph. 2000).

[30] TEX. HEALTH & SAFETY CODE ANN. § 166.001 (Vernon Supp. 2000).

The legislature has mistakenly designated two different statutes as Section 166.001 of the Health and Safety Code. Act of May 18, 1999, 76th Leg., R.S., ch. 450, § 1.02, 1999 Tex. Gen. Laws 2835 (Advance Directives Act) and Act of May 26, 1999, 76th Leg., R.S., ch. 642, § 1, 1999 Tex. Gen. Laws 3213 (Female Genital Mutilation Prohibited).

appellants complain only that the statute has had a disparate impact between homosexuals and heterosexuals. While we recognize the statute may adversely affect the conduct of male and female homosexuals, this simply does not raise the specter of gender-based discrimination.

As we already have determined, the police power of a state may be legitimately exerted in the form of legislation where such statute bears a real and substantial relation to the public health, safety, morals, or some other phase of the general welfare. *Louis K. Liggett Co. v. Baldridge,* 278 U.S. 105, 111–12, 73 L. Ed. 204, 49 S. Ct. 57 (1928). To the extent the statute has a disproportionate impact upon homosexual conduct, the statute is supported by a legitimate state interest. The first point of error is overruled.

PRIVACY

In their second point of error, appellants contend Section 21.06 violates the right to privacy guaranteed by both the state and federal constitutions. Appellants claim the intimate nature of the conduct at issue, when engaged in by consenting adults in private, is beyond the scope of governmental interference.

Neither the state nor federal constitutions contain an explicit guarantee of privacy. Thus, there is no general constitutional right to privacy. However, both constitutions contain express limitations on governmental power from which "zones of privacy" may be inferred. The United States Supreme Court has found five such zones in the Bill of Rights:

Various guarantees create zones of privacy. The right of association contained in the penumbra of the First Amendment. . . . The Third Amendment in its prohibition against the quartering of soldiers "in any house" in time of peace without the consent of the owner is another facet of that privacy. The Fourth Amendment explicitly affirms the "right of the people to be secure in their persons, houses, papers, and effects, against unreasonable searches and seizures." The Fifth Amendment in its Self-Incrimination Clause enables the citizen to create a zone of privacy which government may not force him to surrender to his detriment. The Ninth Amendment provides: "The enumeration in the Constitution, of certain rights, shall not be construed to deny or disparage others retained by the people." *Griswold v. Connecticut,* 381 U.S. 479, 484, 14 L. Ed. 2d 510, 85 S. Ct. 1678 (1965).

Similarly, the Texas Supreme Court has found "constitutionally protected zones of privacy emanating from several sections of article I of the Texas Constitution." *City of Sherman v. Henry,* 928 S.W.2d 464, 472 (Tex. 1996). These include: section 6, concerning freedom of worship; section 8, concerning freedom of speech and press; section 9, concerning searches and seizures; section 10, concerning the rights of an accused in criminal prosecutions; section 19, concerning deprivation of life, liberty and property, and due course of law; and section 25, concerning quartering soldiers in houses. Id.

Appellants do not specifically identify the constitutional provision which they claim creates a zone of privacy protecting consensual sexual behavior from state interference. However, we find there are but two provisions of the federal constitution which could arguably be construed to apply here—the Fourth and Ninth Amendments.

The Fourth Amendment is not applicable because appellants do not contest, and have never contested, the entry by police into the residence where they were discovered. Thus, we must assume the police conduct was both reasonable and lawful under the Fourth Amendment.

The Ninth Amendment also offers no support. In *Bowers v. Hardwick,* the defendants were convicted of violating the Georgia sodomy statute. 478 U.S. at 190–91. Relying upon *Griswold v. Connecticut*[31] and other decisions recognizing "reproductive rights," the defendants argued that the Ninth Amendment creates a zone of privacy regarding consensual sexual activity that encompasses homosexual sodomy. The court rejected the argument and said "the position that any kind of private sexual conduct between consenting adults is constitutionally insulated from state proscription is unsupportable." *Bowers,* 478 U.S. at 191.

Likewise, under the Texas Constitution, we perceive that there are but two provisions that would arguably support appellants' position— sections 9 and 19 of Article I. Again, because appellants have not challenged the search leading to their arrest, we must conclude the police did not violate section 9 of the Texas Constitution.

---

[31] 381 U.S. 479, 85 S. Ct. 1678, 14 L. Ed. 2d 510 (1965).

Although neither the Texas Supreme Court nor Texas Court of Criminal Appeals has considered whether section 19 creates a zone of privacy that would protect private homosexual behavior, the Supreme Court has held it does not protect private heterosexual behavior. In *City of Sherman v. Henry,* the court was confronted with a case where the city had denied a promotion to a police officer because he was having an adulterous affair with the wife of another officer. See *Henry* 928 S.W.2d at 465. The court held that Article I, section 19 does not create a right of privacy protecting adulterous conduct without state interference.

Sexual relations with the spouse of another is not a right that is "implicit in the concept of ordered liberty" or "deeply rooted in this Nation's history and tradition." Prohibitions against adultery have ancient roots. In the latter half of the 17th century in England, adultery was a capital offense. 4 WILLIAM BLACKSTONE, COMMENTARIES *64. The common law brought to this country by the American colonists included the crime of adultery as previously defined by the canon law of England. *United States v. Clapox,* 13 Sawy. 349, 35 F. 575, 578 (D.Or.1888); FRANCIS WHARTON, A TREATISE ON CRIMINAL LAW vol. 11, §§ 1719–20, p. 524 (9th ed. 1885). Adultery was still considered a crime by courts and commentators in the latter half of the 19th century when the Fourteenth Amendment was ratified. See *Clapox,* 35 F. at 578; WHARTON, supra. In fact, adultery is a crime today in half of the states and the District of Columbia.

* * *

While other states, including Texas, have recently repealed laws criminalizing adultery, the mere fact that such conduct is no longer illegal in some states does not cloak it with constitutional protection. *Henry,* 928 S.W.2d at 470.

Similarly, we find homosexual conduct is not a right that is "implicit in the concept of ordered liberty" or "deeply rooted in this Nation's history and tradition." In America, homosexual conduct was classified as a felony offense from the time of early colonization.[32] In fact, there was such unanimity of condemnation that sodomy was, before 1961, a criminal offense in all fifty states and the District of Columbia. *Bowers v. Hardwick,* 478 U.S. at 193. In Texas, homosexual conduct has been a criminal offense for well over a century.[33]

In addition to an American tradition of statutory proscription, homosexual conduct has historically been repudiated by many religious faiths.[34] Moreover, Western civilization has a long history of repressing homosexual behavior by state action. Under Roman law, Justinian states that a lex Iulia imposed severe criminal penalties against "those who indulge in criminal intercourse with those of their own sex."[35] Blackstone states that the "infamous crime against nature, committed either with man or beast" was a grave offense among the ancient Goths and that it continued to be so under English common law at the time of his writing.[36] In his survey of the law, Montesquieu was prompted to conclude that "the crime against nature" is a "crime, which religion, morality, and civil government equally condemn."[37]

Nevertheless, appellants contend that Texas should join several of our sister states who have legalized homosexual conduct. Certainly, the modern national trend has been to decriminalize many forms of consensual sexual conduct even when such behavior is widely perceived to be destructive and immoral, e.g., seduction, fornication, adultery, bestiality, etc.[38] Our concern, however, cannot be with cultural trends and political movements because these can have no place in our decision without usurping the role of the Legislature. While the Legislature is not infallible in its moral and ethical judgments, it

[32] See LAWS AND LIBERTIES 5 (Cambridge 1648) (collection of the general laws of the Massachusetts Bay Colony).

[33] See Tex. Penal Code art. 342 (1879); Tex. Penal Code art. 364 (1895); Tex. Penal Code art. 507 (1911); and Tex. Penal Code art. 524 (1925).

[34] "Our society's three major religions—Judaism, Christianity, and Islam—historically have viewed homosexuality as immoral." Richard F. Duncan, Who Wants to Stop the Church: Homosexual Rights Legislation, Public Policy, and Religious Freedom, 69 NOTRE DAME L. REV. 393, 404 n.40 (1994) [citing The Jewish Torah (Leviticus 18:22, 20:13), the New Testament (Romans 1:26–28, I Timothy 1:9–10, I Corinthians 6:9–10) and the Koran (The Heights 7:80)].

[35] FLAVIUS JUSTINIAN, THE INSTITUTES OF JUSTINIAN 205 (J. B. Moyle trans., 5th ed., Oxford 1913).

[36] 4 WILLIAM BLACKSTONE, COMMENTARIES * 215–16.

[37] 1 Bankr.N DE MONTESQUIEU, THE SPIRIT OF LAWS 231 (Dublin 1751).

[38] Despite this trend, there are still today many types of "private" conduct which courts have recognized are not protected from state interference. See generally *Washington v. Glucksberg,* 521 U.S. 702, 138 L. Ed. 2d 772, 117 S. Ct. 2258 (1997) (holding there is no protected right to commit suicide); *Osborne v. Ohio,* 495 U.S. 103, 109 L. Ed. 2d 98, 110 S.

alone is constitutionally empowered to decide which evils it will restrain when enacting laws for the public good.[39]

Our role was aptly defined over a hundred years ago by Justice Noggle who, while writing for the Idaho Supreme Court, observed: "The court is not expected to make or change the law, but to construe it, and determine the power of the law and the power the legislature had to pass such a law; whether that power was wisely or unwisely exercised, can be of no consequence." *People v. Griffin*, 1 Idaho 476, 479 (1873). Because we find no constitutional "zone of privacy" shielding homosexual conduct from state interference, appellants' second point of error is overruled.

The judgment of the trial court is affirmed.

/s/ J. Harvey Hudson

Justice

Judgment rendered and Majority, Consenting, and Dissenting Opinions filed March 15, 2001. (Justices Yates, Fowler, Edelman, Wittig, Frost, and Amidei join this opinion; Justice Yates also filed a concurring opinion in which Justices Hudson, Fowler, Edelman, and Frost join; Justice Fowler also filed a concurring opinion in which Justices Yates, Edelman, Frost, and Amidei join. Justice Anderson filed a dissenting opinion in which Senior Chief Justice Murphy joins.)*

En banc.

Affirmed on Rehearing En Banc; Majority and Dissenting Opinions of June 8, 2000, are

Withdrawn and Substituted with Majority, Concurring, and Dissenting Opinions filed March 15, 2001.

CONCURRING OPINION ON MOTION FOR REHEARING EN BANC

I agree with the result reached by, and reasoning utilized by, the majority opinion. However, I write separately only to address one of the arguments raised by *amicus curiae*. *Amicus curiae* alleges that by overruling the prior panel's decision, this Court will have succumbed to improper political pressure and asserts "the best way for this Court to rebuke those who attempted to exercise improper political influence in the present case is to affirm the well-reasoned panel opinion."

The Texas Code of Judicial Conduct provides the guiding principals for every judge of this State in the performance of his or her judicial duties. TEX. CODE JUD. CONDUCT, reprinted in TEX. GOV'T CODE ANN., tit. 2, subtit. G app. B (Vernon 1998 & Supp. 2000). Each judge in Texas is instructed to "not be swayed by partisan interests, public clamor, or fear of criticism." *Id.* at Canon 3(B)(2). What *amicus curiae* requests this Court to do is, in effect, no different from what those who leveled political attacks against the majority in the panel opinion hoped to achieve, i.e., a certain desired result.[1] In other words, *amicus curiae* asks this Court to shirk its bound duty in order to decide a difficult question of law differently from what

---

Ct. 1691 (1990) (possession of child pornography not a protectable privacy interest even when possessed inside the home); *Bowers*, 478 U.S. at 195 (suggesting that adultery, even when committed in the home, is not a constitutionally protected behavior); *United States v. Miller*, 776 F.2d 978 (11th Cir. 1985) (holding that constitutional right of privacy does not shield a person from personal possession of pornography outside the home); *Potter v. Murray City*, 760 F.2d 1065 (10th Cir. 1985) (holding that because monogamy is inextricably woven into the fabric of our society, ban on plural marriage did not violate right of privacy); *United States v. Fogarty*, 692 F.2d 542 (8th Cir. 1982) (holding there is no fundamental right to possess marijuana); *J.B.K., Inc. v. Caron*, 600 F.2d 710 (8th Cir. 1979) (holding right of privacy does not extend to commercialized sexual activities); *Kuromiya v. United States*, 37 F. Supp. 2d 717 (E.D. Penn. 1999) (holding there is no fundamental right to smoke marijuana).

[39] The fact that unlawful behavior is conducted in private between consenting adults may complicate detection and prosecution, but it does not, ipso facto, render its statutory prohibition unconstitutional. In upholding its sodomy statute, the Supreme Court of Louisiana wrote:

The question of whether or not a third party is harmed by a consensual and private act of oral or anal sex is a debate which has been ongoing for many years and is nothing which this court needs to address. The legislature is within constitutional authority to proscribe its commission. Any claim that private sexual conduct between consenting adults is constitutionally insulated from state proscription is unsupportable.

* * *

There has never been any doubt that the legislature, in the exercise of its police power, has authority to criminalize the commission of acts which, without regard to the infliction of any other injury, are considered immoral.

Simply put, commission of what the legislature determines as an immoral act, even if consensual and private, is an injury against society itself. See *State v. Smith*, 766 So. 2d 501, 509 (La. 2000).

* Senior Chief Justice Paul C. Murphy and Former Justice Maurice Amidei sitting by assignment.

[1] In its brief to this Court, *amicus curiae* describes the political attacks as including a "letter circulated by local [Republican party] officials in an attempt to influence the outcome of the case."

it believes to be the correct resolution. *Amicus curiae's* request is grounded on the mistaken notion that any different result must surely be on the basis of political pressure, without crediting the members of this Court with the integrity to carry out their duties in strict accordance with the Texas Code of Judicial Conduct and with careful consideration of the legal issues presented in this appeal. As *amicus curiae* suggests, attacks on the judiciary, like the one following the panel opinion, may have the effect of increasing the potential that the public's confidence in our courts will diminish because of a perception, however erroneous, that we have made a political decision, not a legal one. But the response to such a reckless and irresponsible act cannot be that we ignore our duty to decide the law we have been entrusted to interpret. Attempts to politicize this opinion—regardless of their origin—have no place in our decision-making process, nor are attacks from opposing interests immune from creating the very same perception in the mind of the public that may now exist as a result of earlier inappropriate attempts to influence this decision.

"Judges are called upon to make hundreds of decisions each year. These decisions are made after consideration of opposing contentions, both of which are often based on reasonable interpretations of the laws of the United States and the Constitution." Second Circuit Chief Judges Criticize Attacks on Judge Baer, 215 N.Y.L.J. 4 (March 29, 1996). Unless there is a basis for disqualification or recusal, all judges must decide the matter brought before them. TEX. CODE JUD. CONDUCT, Canon 3(B)(1); *Rogers v. Bradley,* 909 S.W.2d 872, 879 (Tex. 1995) (Enoch, J., responding to Justice Gammage's declaration of recusal) (citing *Sun Oil Co. v. Whitaker,* 483 S.W.2d 808, 823–24 (Tex. 1972)). As one jurist has commented with regard to our duty to decide difficult matters presented to us:

All judges face the likelihood of being publicly criticized . . . for decisions that they render. It goes with the territory. A judge's oath is to decide cases based on the law and the facts . . . . Carl E. Stewart, Contemporary Challenges to Judicial Independence, 43 LOY. L. REV. 293, 306 (1997). There is simply no place for suggesting that the members of this Court are pandering to certain political groups or deciding a case as a means to achieve a politically desired end.[2] And

to do so only adds unnecessarily to the already politically charged climate created by the people *amicus curiae* purports to condemn.

Today we have been called upon to decide whether section 21.06 of the Texas Penal Code lacks a rational basis or otherwise violates the constitutional right to privacy found in the constitutions of either Texas or the United States. We have done so—not because of political pressures, as *amicus curiae* has suggested, but despite them.

/s/ Leslie Brock Yates

Justice

Judgment rendered and Concurring Opinion filed March 15, 2001.

En banc.

CONCURRING OPINION ON MOTION FOR REHEARING EN BANC

Today the Court holds that section 21.06 of the Texas Penal Code is not unconstitutional. I join in the court's opinion, however I write separately to make the following comments.

First, once the decision is made that the classifications in section 21.06 are not gender based, the analysis is relatively straightforward. A gender-based classification would require a heightened scrutiny of section 21.06 because gender is a protected class. However, sexual preference has not been designated a protected class by the United States Supreme Court, the Texas Supreme Court, or the Texas Court of Criminal Appeals. See Majority Op. n. 8 supra. Consequently, in deciding whether 21.06 is constitutionally sound, we look only for a rational relationship between section 21.06 and the State's reasons for enacting it.[1]

The State argues that 21.06 is directly related to the legislature's right to legislate morality. The United States Supreme Court has held that it is within a State's legitimate police power to legis-

---

[2] See, e.g., Stephen B. Bright, Policital Attacks on the Judiciary: Can Justice Be Done Amid Efforts to Intimidate and Remove Judges from Office for Unpopular Decisions?, 72 N.Y.U. L. Rev. 308, 313 (1997) (observing that "it is irresponsible for critics of the courts to argue that only results matter, without regard to the legal principles that govern judicial decisionmaking.").

[1] The dissent argues that the rational relationship test we are to use here is a higher standard than the rational relationship test normally is; however, that distinction is not apparent in the case law, and the dissent does not point to any particular language that supports this argument.

late on grounds of morality. *Bowers v. Hardwick,* 478 U.S. 186, 196, 92 L. Ed. 2d 140, 106 S. Ct. 2841 (1986); *Berman v. Parker,* 348 U.S. 26, 32, 99 L. Ed. 27, 75 S. Ct. 98 (1954). Thus, we need only determine if section 21.06 is related "to the pursuit" of implementing morality.

The United States Circuit Court for the Fifth Circuit has already held that 21.06 concerns issues of morality. *Baker v. Wade,* 769 F.2d 289, 292 (5th Cir. 1985). In reviewing section 21.06, that court held, "in view of the strong objection to homosexual conduct, which has prevailed in Western culture for the past seven centuries, we cannot say that section 21.06 is 'totally unrelated to the pursuit of,' implementing morality, a permissible state goal." (internal citations omitted). That is the same justification upon which the majority relies to reach the conclusion that the Texas Legislature was exercising valid legislative powers in enacting section 21.06. I agree that the justification is legally sound. It is not our duty to assess the wisdom or desirability of the law, see *New Orleans v. Dukes,* 427 U.S. 297, 303, 49 L. Ed. 2d 511, 96 S. Ct. 2513 (1976), nor does "this court ... invalidate bad or foolish policies, only unconstitutional ones; we may not 'sit as a super-legislature to judge the wisdom or desirability of legislative policy determinations made in areas that neither affect fundamental rights nor proceed along suspect lines.'" *Id.* As the majority states, "our power to review the moral justification for a legislative act is extremely limited."

Secondly, I concur with the majority in its rationale and holdings as to both the Equal Protection and Privacy sections of the opinion. I would only add that, as to whether section 21.06 unconstitutionally discriminates on the basis of gender, it clearly does not. This is not merely because of the equal application of the statute to men and women, but because this statute does not contain a discriminatory classification based on gender.

The dissent contends that, like the statute struck down in *Loving v. Virginia,* this statute "equally punishes," in this case, based on gender classification, which makes the statute gender based. 388 U.S. 1, 87 S. Ct. 1817, 18 L. Ed. 2d 1010 (1967). That argument is creative, but misguided. In *Loving,* the Court struck down a statute because the statute furthered a loathsome discrimination—racism that implied a "superior" white person marrying an "inferior" black person does so at the risk of both being

punished. The *Loving* court correctly recognized that this was the kind of discriminatory law sought to be vanquished by the Fourteenth Amendment; one that advanced the fallacy of racial superiority. However, *Loving* is not on point in this case because section 21.06 does not advance the fallacy of gender superiority. It prohibits a same-sex sexual relationship. The fact that sexual orientation necessarily depends upon the sex of the parties does not mean that section 21.06 is the kind of statute that discriminates on the basis of gender. Gender is treated as an elevated class under the Fourteenth Amendment because this country saw a need to rid itself of outdated notions of a woman's inferiority to a man.[2] *Reed v. Reed,* 404 U.S. 71, 30 L. Ed. 2d 225, 92 S. Ct. 251 (1971); *Phillips v. Marietta Corp.,* 400 U.S. 542, 27 L. Ed. 2d 613, 91 S. Ct. 496 (1971); *Seidenberg v. McSorleys' Old Ale House, Inc.,* 317 F. Supp. 593 (S.D.N.Y. 1970); *Sail'er Inn, Inc. v. Kirby,* 5 Cal. 3d 1, 485 P.2d 529, 95 Cal. Rptr. 329 (Cal. 1971). There is nothing in section 21.06 that furthers any unequal treatment between the sexes. The dissent's argument to the contrary is not a legally sustainable one.

Finally, I also take issue with the dissent's treatment of the majority's reliance on *Bowers v. Hardwick.* The dissent correctly points out that *Bowers v. Hardwick* deals with the Due Process Clause, while the majority's analysis depends upon the Equal Protection Clause of the Fourteenth Amendment. The dissent remarks that "this blending of quite distinct elements of the Federal Constitution blunts the force of the majority's equal protection arguments." I disagree.

First, the dissent overlooks the fact that the ultimate analysis in both *Bowers* and this case turns on the application of the rational basis test. This test does not differ depending on whether it is applied in a "due process" or an "equal protection" context. The test remains the same: does the statute further some legitimate, articulated state purpose? *Kadrmas v. Dickinson Pub. Sch.,* 487 U.S. 450, 461–62, 101 L. Ed. 2d 399, 108 S. Ct. 2481 (1988) (analyzing a Fourteenth Amendment Equal Protection claim based on whether the statute at issue had a

---

[2] As the majority stated, "neither the United States Supreme Court, the Texas Supreme Court, nor the Texas Court of Criminal Appeals has found sexual orientation to be a 'suspect class.'"

"rational relation to a legitimate government objective . . ."); *Williamson v. Lee Optical of Okla.,* 348 U.S. 483, 488, 99 L. Ed. 563, 75 S. Ct. 461, (1955) (analyzing a Fourteenth Amendment Due Process claim under the rational basis test by stating, ". . . to be constitutional, it is enough that there is an [issue] at hand for correction, and that it might be thought that the particular legislative measure was a rational way to correct it."); see *Richardson v. Belcher,* 404 U.S. 78, 81, 30 L. Ed. 2d 231, 92 S. Ct. 254 (1971) (analyzing a Fifth Amendment Due Process claim using a rational basis test drawn from Equal Protection cases that stated the statute must be "rationally based and free from invidious discrimination . . ."). *Bowers* holds that states are within the scope of legislative authority— and further a legitimate state purpose—when their legislatures base laws on concepts of morality. Therefore, the application of *Bowers* does not "blunt[] the force of the majority's equal protection arguments." Secondly, the dissent charges that the majority merges *Bowers*' due process analysis with the equal protection issue in this case. That statement is incorrect. The majority cites *Bowers* only three times: (1) in reference to legislating on notions of morality; (2) in reference to the privacy issue; and (3) for the contention that sodomy was an offense in all fifty states and in the District of Columbia prior to 1961. The majority's analysis of whether section 21.06 should be subject to some level of heightened scrutiny in an equal protection analysis does not depend on the *Bowers* decision. The dissent's implication to the contrary is inaccurate.

/s/ Wanda McKee Fowler

Justice

Judgment rendered and Concurring Opinion filed March 15, 2001.

En banc.

DISSENTING OPINION

I respectfully dissent to the majority's Herculean effort to justify the discriminatory classification of section 21.06 of the Penal Code despite the clear prohibitions on such discrimination contained in the Equal Protection Clause of the United States Constitution and the Texas Equal Rights Amendment in the Bill of Rights of the Texas Constitution.

Appellants are before this court challenging the constitutionality of Texas Penal Code section

21.06. They bring four issues: (1) whether the statute violates the right to federal constitutional equal protection as applied and on its face; (2) whether the statute violates the right to state constitutional equal protection as applied and on its face; (3) whether the statute violates the appellants' right to privacy under the Texas Constitution; and (4) whether the statute violates the appellants' right to privacy under the United States Constitution.

I believe appellants' federal right to privacy challenge is controlled by the Supreme Court's determination in *Bowers v. Hardwick.* The Due Process Clause of the Federal Constitution does not confer a fundamental right upon homosexuals to engage in sodomy. 478 U.S. 186, 106 S. Ct. 2841, 92 L. Ed. 2d 140 (1986). I would reach the same conclusion on appellants' privacy claim under the Texas Constitution. The Texas Supreme Court, borrowing heavily from *Bowers,* denied the existence of an asserted privacy right by insisting that adultery is "not a right implicit in the concept of liberty in Texas or deeply rooted in this state's history and tradition." *Henry v. City of Sherman,* 928 S.W.2d 464, 470 (Tex. 1996). "Because homosexual conduct is not a fundamental right under the United States Constitution, adultery, likewise, cannot be a fundamental right." *Id.* Accordingly, I concur in the result reached by the majority on appellants' third and fourth issues, but for the reasons set forth below, strongly disagree with the majority's treatment of appellants' state and federal equal protection arguments.

I.

Application of Equal Protection to Section 21.06: An Overview

Appellants contend section 21.06 violates their rights of equal protection under the United States and Texas Constitutions. Under the Fourteenth Amendment, the statute must fail because even applying the most deferential standard, the rational basis standard, the statute cannot be justified on the majority's sole asserted basis of preserving public morality, where the same conduct, defined as "deviate sexual intercourse" is criminalized for same sex participants but not for heterosexuals. The contention that the same conduct is moral for some but not for others merely repeats, rather than legitimizes, the Legislatures' unconstitutional edict. The statute must also fail because statutory classifications that are not gender neutral are analyzed under the heightened scrutiny standard of review, and there is no showing by the State either that there is an exceedingly persuasive justification for the classification, or that there is a direct, substantial relationship between the classification and the important government objectives it purports to serve.

Similarly, section 21.06 cannot withstand scrutiny under the Texas ERA, Article I, § 3a of the Texas Constitution. The ERA is part of the Texas Bill of Rights. Under Article I, § 29 of the Bill of Rights, the Inviolability Clause, statutes that contravene anything in the Bill of Rights are per se void. Because section 21.06 discriminates on the basis of gender, thus violating Article I, § 3a, it is void. Moreover, applying the less rigorous standard of strict scrutiny, mandated by *McLean*, produces the same result. *In re McLean*, 725 S.W.2d 696 (Tex. 1987). Under strict scrutiny as applied in Texas, the proponent of gender discrimination must demonstrate a compelling interest and that there is no other manner to protect the state's compelling interest. *Id.* This requirement places the burden to support the statute squarely upon the State and not on the challenger, and the State, as discussed here and in this Court's original opinion, has failed to make the required showing to defeat a challenge under the Texas ERA.

II.

Section 21.06 and the Fourteenth Amendment: Equal Protection, Gender, and Heightened Scrutiny Review

The Equal Protection Clause of the Fourteenth Amendment commands that no State shall "deny to any person within its jurisdiction the equal protection of the laws," which is essentially a direction that all persons similarly situated should be treated alike. *City of Cleburne, Tex. v. Cleburne Living Center*, 473 U.S. 432, 439, 87 L. Ed. 2d 313, 105 S. Ct. 3249 (1985). The general rule is that legislation is presumed valid and will be sustained if the classification drawn by the statute is rationally related to a legitimate state interest. *Id.* However, within the three-tiered federal equal protection scheme, legislative classifications based on gender call for a heightened standard of review, one step below the most rigorous strict scrutiny review applied to statutory classifications based on race, alienage, or national origin. *Id.* Under the heightened standard, a gender classification fails unless it is

substantially related to a sufficiently important governmental interest. *Mississippi Univ. for Women v. Hogan*, 458 U.S. 718, 73 L. Ed. 2d 1090, 102 S. Ct. 3331 (1982).[1]

A. Section 21.06 Is Not Gender Neutral

In its analysis of appellants' gender discrimination contention, the majority attempts to transfer the burden of proof to appellants to show the statute has had an adverse effect upon one gender, and that such disproportionate impact can be traced to a discriminatory purpose. This transfer is based on the naked assertion that section 21.06 is gender-neutral because it does not impose burdens on one gender not shared by the other. That 21.06 is not gender neutral is manifest based on application of the statute to the following events:

There are three people in a room: Alice, Bob, and Cathy. Bob approaches Alice, and with her consent, engages with her in several varieties of "deviate sexual intercourse," the conduct at issue here. Bob then leaves the room. Cathy approaches Alice, and with her consent, engages with her in several kinds of "deviate sexual intercourse." Cathy is promptly arrested for violating section 21.06.

I have indulged in this tableau to demonstrate one important point: one person simply committed a sex act while another committed a crime. While the acts were exactly the same, the gender of the actors was different, and it was this difference alone that determined the criminal nature of the conduct. In other words, because he is a man, Bob committed no crime and may freely indulge his predilection for "deviate sexual intercourse," but because she is a woman, Cathy is a criminal. Thus, women are treated differently in this scenario, and therefore, are discriminated against by the explicit gender-based prohibition of section 21.06, and to suggest oth-

---

[1] The best short analysis of the three tests for considering whether legislation violates the Equal Protection Clause of the Fourteenth Amendment is set out in *Clark v. Jeter*, 486 U.S. 456, 461, 100 L. Ed. 2d 465, 108 S. Ct. 1910 (1988):

At a minimum, a statutory classification must be rationally related to a legitimate governmental purpose. Classifications based on race or national origin, and classifications affecting fundamental rights, are given the most exacting [or strict] scrutiny. Between these extremes of rational basis review and strict scrutiny lies a level of intermediate scrutiny, which generally has been applied to discriminatory classifications based on sex or illegitimacy.

erwise is disingenuous at best.[2] It is also no answer to insist that because the statute also subjects men to similar discrimination in different scenarios, somehow the discrimination here is rendered constitutionally acceptable. Discrimination in one instance is not cured by additional discrimination in another. Moreover, section 21.06 grew out of the revision of the penal code in 1973.[3] In the new statute, two standards were created, demarcated by the sex of the actors: deviate sexual intercourse when performed by a man and a woman would henceforth be legal, but deviate sexual intercourse performed by two men or two women would remain illegal. Thus, after 1974, the distinction between legal and illegal conduct was clearly not the act, but rather the sex of one of the participants.

B. Equal Discrimination Argument Not A Cure

While not precisely a model of clarity, the majority appears to accept the State's contention that because section 21.06 applies equally to men and women, the statute does not discriminate on the basis of gender. I draw this conclusion based on the majority's rejection of appellants' argument that *Loving v. Virginia*, 388 U.S. 1, 18 L. Ed. 2d 1010, 87 S. Ct. 1817 (1967) discredited the "equal application" defense of 21.06, and conclusion that 21.06 does not impose burdens on one gender not shared by the other. However, the United States Supreme Court has rejected the majority's position in a variety of cases.

One example of the Court's rejection of the "equal discrimination" argument is found in *United Bldg. and Const. Trades Council of Camden County and Vicinity v. Mayor and Council of City of Camden*, 465 U.S. 208, 217–18, 79 L. Ed. 2d 249, 104 S. Ct. 1020 (1984). In that case, the Supreme Court invalidated a municipal ordinance in Camden, New Jersey, requiring that at least forty percent of employees working on city construction projects be city residents. Camden's Mayor and City Council argued the ordinance did not violate the strictures of the Privileges and Immunities Clause of the Four-

teenth Amendment, which requires that out-of-state residents be afforded the same job opportunities as in-state residents, because not only out-of-state residents were burdened by the ordinance. In fact, the respondents argued, many in-state residents, who did not live within the city of Camden, were as burdened by the ordinance as the out-of-state workers who brought the suit. Rejecting the "equal discrimination" argument, the Supreme Court stated "the Camden ordinance is not immune from constitutional review at the behest of out-of-state residents merely because some in-state residents are similarly disadvantaged." *Id.* (citing *Zobel v. Williams*, 457 U.S. 55, 75, 72 L. Ed. 2d 672, 102 S. Ct. 2309 [1982] [O'Connor, J., concurring]).

A second example of the Court's rejection of additional "curative" discrimination is noted in *Hunter v. Underwood*, 471 U.S. 222, 85 L. Ed. 2d 222, 105 S. Ct. 1916 (1985). In *Hunter*, the Court struck down a provision of the Alabama Constitution that mandated disenfranchisement for people who committed "crimes of moral turpitude." Although facially neutral, the Court determined the provision was enacted with the intent of discriminating against blacks and disparately impacted blacks as well because it had disenfranchised ten times as many blacks as whites. *Id.* at 227. Appellant, the State of Alabama, argued that although the constitutional provision was intended to discriminate against blacks, it did not violate the Equal Protection Clause because it was also intended to discriminate against poor whites. The Court held that the intention to additionally discriminate against whites "hardly saves [the Alabama provision] from invalidity." *Id.* at 231. An additional purpose to discriminate against poor whites would not render nugatory the purpose to discriminate against blacks. *Id.* at 232. Thus, again, the Court declined to accept additional discrimination as a purported cure for a clearly discriminatory law.

Finally, the Supreme Court discussed the logic of an argument analogous to the State's argument here in *Loving v. Virginia*, 388 U.S. 1, 18 L. Ed. 2d 1010, 87 S. Ct. 1817 (1967). There, the State of Virginia argued that Virginia's miscegenation statutes do not constitute invidious racial discrimination because the statutes apply equally to whites and blacks. *Id.* at 8. The miscegenation statutes, the State contended, equally penalized both whites who intermarried and blacks who intermarried; therefore, the "equal

COURT OF APPEALS OF TEXAS, MARCH 2001

---

[2] The characteristic injury of gender discrimination lies not in the failure to be treated on a gender-blind basis, but rather in being deprived of opportunity because one is a woman, or because one is a man. LAURENCE H. TRIBE, AMERICAN CONSTITUTIONAL LAW § 16–29 (2d. ed. 1988).

[3] Convening in 1973, the 63rd Legislature, passed the revised Penal Code, which was enacted in 1974. See Acts 1973, 63rd Leg., ch. 399, § 1, 1973 Tex. Gen. Laws 917.

application" of the statutes rendered them acceptable under the Fourteenth Amendment using a rational basis standard. *Id.* Rejecting this sophistry, the Court responded that the mere equal application of a statute containing racial classifications does not remove the classifications from the Fourteenth Amendment's proscription of all invidious racial discrimination. *Id.* By using the race of an individual as the sole determinant of the criminality of his conduct, the State created and perpetuated an invidious racial classification in violation of the Fourteenth Amendment. *Loving,* 388 U.S. at 11. Accordingly, the Court reaffirmed the propriety of strict scrutiny and struck down the Virginia statutes as unconstitutional. *Id.* at 12.

I would also reject the equal application argument offered here. Merely punishing men who engage in sodomy with other men and women who engage in sodomy with other women equally, neither salvages nor cures the discriminatory classification contained in this statute. The simple fact is, the same behavior is criminal for some but not for others, based solely on the sex of the individuals who engage in the behavior. In other words, the sex of the individual, not the conduct, is the sole determinant of the criminality of the conduct.

Indeed, the State's and the majority's utilization of the equal application justification for 21.06 detrimentally impacts their unified position. If in *Loving* the equal application of the anti-miscegenation statutes to both blacks and whites did not negate the existence of a racial classification, then here, equal application of the anti-homosexual-sodomy statute to both men and women does not negate the existence of a sex classification. Alternatively, if 21.06 does not contain a sex-based classification because it applies equally to men and women, then the anti-miscegenation statutes in *Loving* did not contain a race-based classification, with the logical corollary that *Loving* was wrongly decided. Here, the State and the majority go to great lengths to manufacture a conclusion that 21.06 is gender neutral. They must, because acknowledging the facial and as applied gender discrimination within 21.06 vitiates any defense of that statute inasmuch as the State has failed to establish either that the classification created by the statute is substantially related to important and legitimate government objectives, the test applied under heightened

scrutiny, or identify a compelling state interest for purposes of strict scrutiny.

The issue regarding whether 21.06 is gender neutral lies at the core of this case. The majority, in a somewhat cursory fashion, dispenses with *Loving* and moves quickly to the conclusion of gender neutrality without addressing, among other things, the tableau set forth above in this part II. This conclusion of neutrality is essential for the majority to access the rational basis review, avoid heightened scrutiny mandated for gender discrimination, and most importantly, avoid any analysis of appellants' claims under the Texas ERA. However, limiting analysis of 21.06 to rational basis review is incomplete.

In an equal protection analysis of a legislative classification such as that drawn in 21.06, the appropriate framework for reviewing the scheme is to first ask whether the law survives rational basis analysis, and, if it does, the second inquiry is whether the distinction will pass heightened scrutiny. *Hooper v. Bernalillo County Assessor,* 472 U.S. 612, 618, 86 L. Ed. 2d 487, 105 S. Ct. 2862 (1985). Both *Hooper* and *Zobel v. Williams,* 457 U.S. 55, 72 L. Ed. 2d 672, 102 S. Ct. 2309 (1982) analyzed statutory classifications violating the Equal Protection Clause by deferring heightened scrutiny analysis until a determination is made that it survived a rational basis analysis. *Attorney Gen. of New York v. Soto-Lopez,* 476 U.S. 898, 904, 90 L. Ed. 2d 899, 106 S. Ct. 2317 (1986). Thus, here, because the majority has determined that 21.06 survives rational basis scrutiny, and fails to then apply heightened scrutiny review, its analysis under the Equal Protection Clause is incomplete. *Romer v. Evans,* 517 U.S. 620, 134 L. Ed. 2d 855, 116 S. Ct. 1620 (1996) is consistent with this approach. There, because Amendment 2 was in violation of the Equal Protection Clause applying rational basis review, there was no need to examine the statute under heightened scrutiny. Thus, the majority's conclusion that 21.01 is gender neutral will not allow omission of heightened scrutiny review.

C. Standard of Review For Gender Discrimination

Inasmuch as section 21.06 is not gender-neutral, the next inquiry is determining the appropriate burden of proof and assigning that burden. In 1982, in Mississippi University for Women, the Court held that the party seeking to uphold a statute that classifies individuals on the basis of their gender must carry the burden of showing an "exceedingly persuasive justification" for the classification. 458 U.S. at 724. The burden is met only by showing, at a minimum, that the classification serves important governmental objectives. *Id.* There is, however, a further inquiry if the State's objective is legitimate and important. The reviewing court must then determine whether the requisite direct, substantial relationship between the objective sought and means used is present. *Id.* This is heightened scrutiny.

The Supreme Court again addressed the issue of whether the Equal Protection Clause forbids gender based discrimination in *J.E.B. v. Alabama* ex rel. T.B., 511 U.S. 127, 128 L. Ed. 2d 89, 114 S. Ct. 1419 (1994). Specifically, the Court examined the use of peremptory challenges on the basis of gender under the dictates of the Equal Protection Clause and the court's holding in *Batson v. Kentucky,* which prohibits peremptory strikes solely on the basis of race. 476 U.S. 79, 106 S. Ct. 1712, 90 L. Ed. 2d 69 (1986). The court held the Equal Protection Clause prohibits discrimination in jury selection on the basis of gender. *J.E.B.,* 511 U.S. at 146. In reaching that conclusion, the *J.E.B.* Court acknowledged that "our Nation has had a long and unfortunate history of sex discrimination," a history which warrants the heightened scrutiny afforded all gender-based classifications. *Id.*

In *United States v Virginia,* 518 U.S. 515, 533, 135 L. Ed. 2d 735, 116 S. Ct. 2264 (1996), the Supreme Court reiterated the burden of proof for cases of official classification based on gender as requiring the reviewing court to determine whether the proffered justification is exceedingly persuasive, and declared "the burden of justification is demanding and it rests entirely on the State." Further, the Court held that the justification must be genuine, not hypothesized or invented post hoc in response to litigation. *Id.* And, it must not rely on overbroad generalizations about different talents, capacities, or preferences of males and females. *Id.* This is the heightened review standard applied to classifications based on sex. *Id.*

D. Failure to Satisfy the Heightened Scrutiny Standard

In its original brief filed with this court, the State contends that section 21.06 must be upheld if there is any rational relationship between the disparity of treatment reflected in that statute and a legitimate state interest. The State seeks to apply the general rule that legislation is presumed to be valid and will be sustained if the classification drawn by the statute is rationally related to a legitimate state interest. *City of Cleburne,* 473 U.S. at 440. To satisfy the rational relationship burden, the State asserts the statute is rationally related to permissible governmental purposes, the discouragement of behavior historically perceived to be immoral, and the promotion of family values. This assertion was reiterated in the State's brief in support of its motion for rehearing en banc. The majority also adopts this rational relationship standard.[4] The State's and the majority's arguments that 21.06 survives a challenge under federal equal protection are untenable.[5]

First, the State and the majority have applied the wrong standard. As set out in *City of Cleburne,* the three standards of equal protection review, from highest to lowest, are strict scrutiny, heightened review, and rational relationship. 473 U.S. at 440–441. Under *Heitman v. State,* the court held that decisions of the Supreme Court represent the minimum protections that a state must afford its citizens. 815 S.W.2d 681, 690 (Tex. Crim. App. 1991). The federal constitution sets the floor for individual rights, and state constitutions cannot subtract from the rights guaranteed by the United States Constitution; however, they can provide additional rights to their citizens. *Id.* It appears, therefore, that the State and the majority have

---

[4] The majority's entire analysis of appellants' equal protection issues is premised on the belief that 21.06 is gender neutral on its face. The comparison of 21.06 and the definition of "deviate sexual intercourse" in 21.01 set out in note 9 below, I believe, adequately dismantles facial neutrality contentions. This misinterpretation of 21.06 has led the majority into error. Moreover, for unexplained reasons, the majority has merged a due process analysis with an equal protection analysis by stating there is no fundamental right to engage in sodomy. Whatever the merits of that contention, it is sourced from the Court's analysis of the Due Process Clause in *Bowers v. Hardwick* where the Court was unwilling to extend the Due Process Clause to confer "a fundamental right to engage in acts of consensual sodomy." 478 U.S. 186, 192, 106 S. Ct. 2841, 92 L. Ed. 2d 140 (1986). This blending of quite distinct elements of the Federal Constitution blunts the force of the majority's equal protection arguments. Indeed, that the majority is in fact attempting to analyze 21.06 under the Due Process Clause is manifest from (a) its failure to address how a ban of homosexual sodomy preserves public morals while permitting heterosexual sodomy, but (b) justifying the statute based on historical analysis and the common law, and references to seventeenth century laws banning homosexual conduct in the Massachusetts Bay Colony. See discussion of Cass

COURT OF APPEALS OF TEXAS, MARCH 2001

COURT OF
APPEALS OF
TEXAS,
MARCH 2001

attempted to apply a lower threshold standard of review to gender-based discrimination than the heightened standard mandated by the United States Supreme Court. It is not within the discretion of an intermediate court to ignore United States Supreme Court precedent regarding the appropriate standard of review for gender based classifications challenged, as appellants have done here, under the Equal Protection Clause of the Fourteenth Amendment. The court in *Heitman* stated the rule more succinctly: this court is not at liberty to reduce the protections afforded its citizens to a level less than that established under the federal constitution. 815 S.W.2d at 690. A fortiori, by applying the improper standard of review, the majority has accomplished the following: it has afforded appellants a level of protection less than that prescribed by courts whose opinions we are required to follow.

Second, the majority apparently has accepted the State's obfuscation of the issue of gender discrimination in 21.06, thus lowering the State's burden of proof. It is well established that a gender classification fails unless the party seeking to uphold the statute satisfies the dual burden of showing a persuasive justification or objective for the classification and that the discriminatory means employed are substantially related to the objective. *Mississippi Univ. for Women,* 458 U.S. at 724–725. Where, as here, there is not even a whisper or hint in the majority opinion purporting to demonstrate how the State satisfied the minimum rational relationship showing required to sustain 21.06 in the face of an equal protection challenge, it is difficult to understand how the majority can con-

clude 21.06 does not violate appellants' federal equal protection rights.[6]

E. Proper Application of Heightened Scrutiny Review

Turning now to the case sub judice, a rather succinct two part test exists for evaluating the validity of the gender-based classification in 21.06 against a federal equal protection challenge, and it is couched in terms of dual burdens on the proponent of the statute: (1) has the proponent demonstrated a legitimate and exceedingly persuasive justification for the gender based classification contained in 21.06; and (2) has the proponent demonstrated the requisite direct, substantial relationship between the classification and the important government objectives it purports to serve. *Heckler v. Mathews,* 465 U.S. 728, 745, 79 L. Ed. 2d 646, 104 S. Ct. 1387 (1984).

(1). The justification asserted here for 21.06 is promotion of family values and discouragement of immoral behavior. At the outset, it should be noted that "promotion of family values" has not been defined by the State, but it is not illogical to assume that it has some relationship to the institution of marriage and procreation. Thus, the State's contention must be that permitting deviate sexual intercourse between heterosexual couples promotes family values while such conduct by same sex couples promotes something less than that. What is interesting to note is the fact that deviate sexual intercourse, as defined in section 21.01 of the Penal Code, regardless of the gender of one's sex partner, will not permit a female's ovum to be fertilized, thus creating a pregnancy. It must, therefore, be concluded that the State's acquies-

---

Sunstein's analysis of the distinctions between the Due Process and Equal Protection Clauses at note 12 below.

Nevertheless, even assuming the statute is gender neutral on its face, it is not gender neutral as applied, an argument also advanced by appellants. I have, in part II A above, demonstrated the application of section 21.06 is not gender neutral when applied to appellants. The majority recognizes that a facially neutral statute may support an equal protection claim where it is motivated by discriminatory intent and its application results in a discriminatory effect, citing *Village of Arlington Heights v. Metropolitan Housing Dev. Corp.,* 429 U.S. 252, 50 L. Ed. 2d 450, 97 S. Ct. 555 (1977). Despite this acknowledgment of the rule, the majority prefers here, as elsewhere in the opinion, to impose a burden of proof not required in an inquiry based on gender discrimination. The Supreme Court has consistently subjected gender-based classifications to heightened scrutiny in recog-

nition of the real danger that government policies that professedly are based on reasonable considerations in fact may be reflective of archaic and overbroad generalizations. *J.E.B.,* 511 U.S. 127, 135, 128 L. Ed. 2d 89, 114 S. Ct. 1419 (1994).

[5] The majority's statement that the State can, in many instances, pass laws the purpose of which is to preserve morals is correct. However, that license is subject to the Equal Protection Clause, and if the statute is not rationally related to the asserted State interest, or classifies on the basis of gender without a compelling state interest, the license is revoked.

[6] As noted above, the majority's equal protection analysis is incomplete because it fails to engage in intermediate scrutiny required for review of a challenged classification under the Equal Protection Clause where, as here, the majority has concluded 21.06 satisfies rational basis review. *Hooper,* 472 U.S. at 618.

COURT OF
APPEALS OF
TEXAS,
MARCH 2001

cence in heterosexual deviate sexual intercourse permits heterosexuals, whether married or not, to engage in a variety of historically repugnant "recreational sex" acts. To contend, as the State must, that a man somehow promotes family values by engaging in deviate sexual intercourse with a woman, but undermines those values by performing the same deviate sex act with a man, does not, in my view, constitute a showing of an exceedingly persuasive justification for the gender based classification in 21.06.[7]

Nor does the asserted justification of discouraging immoral behavior constitute such a showing. The behavior to be discouraged is deviate sexual intercourse between same sex couples. That same behavior between heterosexual couples is, by implication, moral and something to be encouraged. Sodomy is either immoral or it is not. It appears that the State's vigorous defense of 21.06 has been advanced without due consideration of the inconsistency of, on the one hand, condemning sodomy as immoral, but on the other implicitly embracing sodomy as perfectly moral. Again, such incongruity is not exceedingly persuasive.

(2). Because the test articulated in *Heckler* is described in the conjunctive, it follows that if the State has failed to articulate a legitimate and exceedingly persuasive justification, we need not reach the second part of the test. Nevertheless, even if family values and prevention of immoral behavior were legitimate and persuasive justifications for the gender classification, the discussion above demonstrates there is no connection between penalizing homosexual sodomy and the achievement of those objectives. Neither heterosexual sodomy nor homosexual sodomy can create a new life. Further, encouraging heterosexual sodomy and punishing homosexual sodomy, as a Class C misdemeanor with a fine only, scuttles the State's asserted purpose of preventing immoral behavior inasmuch as 21.06 permits deviate sexual intercourse by any man with any woman. Thus, the State has failed to make a showing of how the gender-based classification is substantially and directly related to the proffered objective of discouraging immoral behavior. Perhaps this failure rests, in part, on the apparent impossibility of logically explaining how the classification in 21.06 is even remotely related to that objective where such behavior is simultaneously sanctioned and is presumably engaged in routinely. Where, as here, the proponent of a gender-based statutory classification fails to establish the requisite relationship between the objective and the means used to achieve it, the statute is invalid. See *Mississippi Univ. for Women*, 458 U.S. at 730.

The mere recitation of a benign purpose is not an automatic shield that protects against any inquiry into the actual purposes underlying a statutory scheme. *Mississippi Univ. for Women*, 458 U.S. at 728. Having performed the analysis dictated by intermediate scrutiny, it must be concluded the State failed both to articulate a persuasive justification and to demonstrate a direct relationship between the tendered objectives and the means utilized to achieve those objectives in 21.06. In the absence of legitimate objectives, the inevitable inference is raised that the disadvantage to homosexuals contained in 21.06 is born of animosity toward the persons affected. See *Romer*, 517 U.S. at 634. The Legislature's removal of the prohibition on heterosexual sodomy while retaining it for homosexual sodomy cannot, in my view, be explained by anything but animus toward the persons it affects.[8]

Indeed, the State's purported justification for the classification in 21.06 in terms of upholding public morality founders on the distinction between public and private morality. The private morality of an individual is not synonymous with nor necessarily has an effect on what is known as public morality. The majority believes 21.06 preserves public morals. That conclusion is apparently reached *sua sponte* without the slightest showing by the State that such consequence flows from enforcement of 21.06. As set forth above, the State's general contention is that the statute discourages immoral

---

[7] Because the Court in *Romer v. Evans*, 517 U.S. 620, 134 L. Ed. 2d 855, 116 S. Ct. 1620 (1996), implicitly rejected the justification of promoting family values in a rational basis analysis of a statute that discriminated against homosexuals based on sexual orientation, it follows that those same justifications, advanced here, could not satisfy heightened scrutiny. See part III below.

[8] My conclusion that 21.06 was born out of animus towards the persons affected thereunder is buttressed by the statute's evolution. Until 1974, the penal code prohibited oral and anal copulation "with another human being." Thus, the statute prohibited all acts of sodomy, whether performed by members of the opposite or the same sex. *Pruett v. State*, 463 S.W.2d 191, 193 (Tex. Crim. App. 1970). In 1974, a new penal code was enacted wherein sodomy performed by members of the same sex continued to be proscribed, but the same act performed by members of the opposite sex became, for the first time in 114 years, legal.

COURT OF
APPEALS OF
TEXAS,
MARCH 2001

behavior, without regard to the public or private nature thereof. Nevertheless, addressing the majority's contention, we are not told how government interference with the practice of adult only, consensual personal choice in matters of intimate sexual behavior out of view of the public and with no commercial component will serve to advance the cause of "public morality" or do anything other than restrict individual conduct and impose a concept of private morality chosen by the State. Here again, when one applies the clear test, articulated in Heckler and elsewhere, that a gender-based classification must fail an equal protection challenge absent a showing that the classification is substantially and directly related to the preservation of public morality, the conclusion is obvious. Perhaps this is the reason the majority labors so hard to conclude 21.06 is gender neutral.[9]

III.

Equal Protection, Improper Classifications and Rational Basis Review

A. Romer v. Evans I firmly believe 21.06 establishes a gender-based classification, on its face and as applied, in the Penal Code of the State of Texas that will not withstand middle tier scrutiny mandated for the analysis of such classifications under the Equal Protection Clause of the Fourteenth Amendment. Appellants, however, also challenge the statute because it unconstitutionally discriminates against homosexuals, thus imposing an unequal burden on them based on their sexual orientation because heterosexuals are not targeted by 21.06 when engaging in the same conduct. Here, the rational basis test, much preferred by the State, is applicable, but the result of a correct analysis applying federal precedent is contrary to the outcome sought by the State. The case that controls the disposition of appellants' contention that section 21.06 discriminates against a class based on sexual orientation is *Romer v. Evans,* 517 U.S. 620, 134 L. Ed. 2d 855, 116 S. Ct. 1620 (1996).[10] In *Romer,* the United States Supreme Court held that a Colorado constitutional amendment (Amendment 2) prohibiting official protection from discrimination on the basis of sexual orientation violated the Fourteenth Amendment's Equal Protection Clause. Using a rational basis standard of review, the most deferential test, the Court invalidated Amendment 2 which (1) contained a classification of "homo-

sexuals," and (2) withdrew from homosexuals, but no others, legal protection from discrimination and prohibited reinstatement of these laws and policies. *See id.* at 627.

The primary rationale advanced by the State for Amendment 2, adverted to in the opinion, was respect for other citizens' freedom of association, and, in particular, the liberties of landlords or employers who have personal or religious objections to homosexuality. *Id.* at 635. In striking down Amendment 2, the Court stated, that "equal protection of the laws is not achieved through indiscriminate imposition of inequalities." *Id.* at 633. The inequality the Court detected was that homosexuals were singled out by Amendment 2 and accorded less protection of the law solely by virtue of their membership in the class. *Id.* at 635. Although the Court utilized a rational basis standard for its analysis, Amendment 2 still failed this most deferential standard because the Court found the amendment advanced no legitimate government interest. *Id.* Thus, the *Romer* Court concluded Amendment 2 classified homosexuals not to further a proper legislative end, but to make them unequal to everyone else. *Id.*

Interestingly, Petitioner, the State of Colorado, offered other justifications for Amendment 2 similar to those offered by the State here.[11] In *Romer,* the State argued the "legitimate governmental interests" of Amendment 2 were the promotion of traditional moral norms

---

[9] That 21.06 is not gender neutral on its face is demonstrated by the language in the statute. "A person commits an offense if he engages in deviate sexual intercourse with another individual of the same sex." TEX. PEN. CODE ANN. § 21.06 (Vernon 1994) (emphasis added). The statute clearly specifies what the gender of the actors must be to constitute a criminal offense. Curiously, the definition of "deviate sexual intercourse" contained in section 21.01 is gender neutral. Such conduct is defined as "any contact between any part of the genitals of one person and the mouth or anus of another person; or ...the penetration of the genitals or the anus of another person with an object." TEX. PEN. CODE ANN. § 21.01 (Vernon 1994) (emphasis added).

[10] Section B of this part III examines the application of the rational basis review to a city ordinance where the justifications for the classification it contained did not justify singling out one group for different treatment, thus rendering the classification irrational and unconstitutional as applied.

[11] In note 15, the majority refused to accept the fact that the State of Colorado did in fact make those arguments in its brief. Even though the arguments are not set out in the opinion, a reader may access them by going through the WestLaw reference in the *Romer* opinion, which brings up the briefs containing the rejected arguments. 517 U.S. at 621.

and family values. See Petitioner's Brief at 45–47, *Romer* (1995 WL 310026). Specifically, the State posited the amendment fostered "family privacy and the ability to convey values to their children," by disallowing the "implicit endorsement of homosexuality fostered by laws granting special protections [that] could undermine the efforts of some parents to teach traditional moral values," and deterred factionalism within the state by "maximizing individual liberty, including the preservation of traditional norms." *Id.*

Far from accepting these justifications as legitimate, the Court apparently did not find they even merited review in the opinion. Thus, the Court, *sub silentio*, rejected the "implementation of traditional notions of morality" justification deemed sufficient in *Bowers v. Hardwick*, 478 U.S. at 196, and *Baker v. Wade*, 769 F.2d 289, 292 (5th Cir. 1985), both of which are relied upon by the State here.[12] In *Romer*, the Supreme Court focused, instead, upon the animus apparent from a provision that drew a classification "for the purpose of disadvantaging the group burdened by the law." 517 U.S. at 633. Because Amendment 2 drew such a classification, and then proceeded to disadvantage homosexuals because of their membership in the class, the amendment violated the equal protection of the law guaranteed by the Fourteenth Amendment.

The statute at issue here, much like Amendment 2, draws a classification for the purpose of disadvantaging the group burdened by the law. In fact, Justice Scalia, in his dissent to *Romer* readily agreed that, "here can hardly be more palpable discrimination against a class than making the conduct that defines the class criminal." *Id.* at 641. I agree with Justice Scalia that the statute at issue here, by proscribing "deviate sexual intercourse" only when engaged in with members of one's own sex, does discriminate against homosexuals. However, following *Romer*, I view the justifications proffered by the State, enforcement of traditional norms of morality and family values, as nothing more than politically-charged, thinly-veiled, animus-driven cliches.[13] Section 21.06 is, like Amendment 2, a status-based enactment divorced from any factual context from which one can discern a relationship to legitimate state interests; it is a classification of persons undertaken for its own sake, something the Equal Protection Clause does not permit. *Id.* at 635. Although a state's police powers are broad and comprehensive, the constitution, both state and federal, "forbids its exercise when the result would be the destruction of the rights, guarantees, privileges, and restraints excepted from the powers of government by the Bill of Rights." *Fazekas v. University of Houston*, 565 S.W.2d 299, 305 (Tex. Civ. App.—Houston [1st Dist.] 1978, writ ref'd

---

[12] Justice Scalia's dissent in *Romer* concedes as much. He notes, that in "placing the prestige of [the Supreme Court] behind the proposition that opposition to homosexuality is as reprehensible as racial or religious bias," the Court has essentially sub silentio overruled *Bowers*. *Romer*, 517 U.S. at 636–37. I agree with this characterization of *Romer*, and further note the rational basis analysis employed by the *Romer* Court may be more exacting than that employed by the Court in *Bowers*. The concurring opinion by Justice Fowler fails to appreciate the difference in the rational basis test as applied in a *Bowers* due process analysis versus a *Romer* equal protection analysis.

Although both *Bowers* and *Romer* applied the rational basis analysis to the state action in question, there is, nevertheless, a difference in the analysis of rational basis review under the Due Process Clause and under the Equal Protection Clause. These two clauses perform quite different functions. In its substantive dimension, the Due Process Clause protects a range of basic rights; it does not speak to the constitutionality of classifications. The Equal Protection Clause operates as a functional complement to the Due Process Clause, addressing a different set of questions. The Due Process Clause has frequently been understood as an effort to restrict short-term or shortsighted deviations from widely held social norms; it has an important backward

looking dimension. For purposes of due process, the baseline for inquiry has tended to be the common law, Anglo American practice, or the status quo. The Due Process Clause is, therefore, closely associated with the view that the role of the Supreme Court is to limit dramatic and insufficiently reasoned change, to protect tradition and to bring a more balanced and disinterested perspective to legislation. See Cass R. Sunstein, Sexual Orientation and the Constitution: A Note on the Relationship Between Due Process and Equal Protection, 55 U. CHI. L. REV. 1161, 1171 (1988). Thus, in *Bowers*, the Court declined to find, as respondent requested, a fundamental right to engage in homosexual sodomy because sodomy was not a fundamental liberty that was deeply rooted in this Nation's history and tradition. *Bowers*, 478 U.S. at 192.

The Equal Protection Clause, on the other hand, has served an entirely different set of purposes from the Due Process Clause. That clause is emphatically not an effort to protect traditionally held values against novel or short-term deviations. The clause is not backward looking at all; it was consciously designed to eliminate practices that existed at the time of ratification and that were expected to endure. The function of the Equal Protection Clause is to protect disadvantaged groups against the effects of past and present discrimination by political majorities. It is not rooted in

n.r.e.) (citing *Travelers' Ins. Co. v. Marshall*, 124 Tex. 45, 76 S.W.2d 1007 [1934]). Thus, stripped of its asserted justifications, the classification drawn in 21.06 is arbitrary and irrational, and fails the rational basis test.

Regarding appellants' issue on sexual orientation discrimination aspect of 21.06, the majority, *inter alia*, concludes there is no fundamental right to engage in sodomy, and homosexuals do not constitute a suspect class. These two conclusions are irrelevant here because appellants do not raise these arguments, and the first conclusion implicates *Bowers v. Hardwick* where equal protection was not argued or addressed.

B. *City of Cleburne* Legislation containing a classification challenged under the Equal Protection Clause must, in order to withstand rational basis review, be rationally related to a legitimate governmental purpose. *City of Cleburne*, 473 U.S. at 446. The State may not rely, however, on a classification whose relationship to an asserted goal is so attenuated as to render the distinction arbitrary or irrational. *Zobel*, 457 U.S. at 61–63. Objectives such as a bare desire to harm a politically unpopular group are not legitimate State interests. *City of Cleburne*, 473 U.S. at 447.

In *City of Cleburne*, the Court struck down a city zoning ordinance requiring a special use permit for a home for the mentally retarded, but exempting from such a permit apartment houses, fraternity houses, apartment hotels, hospitals, private clubs and other specified uses. *Id.* Plainly stated, the equal protection issue there presented was: "May the city require the permit for this facility when other care and multiple dwelling facilities are freely permitted?" *City of*

Cleburne, 473 U.S. at 448. The Federal District Court had found, and the Court of Appeals and Supreme Court repeated the obvious fact that if the potential residents of the home for the mentally retarded were not in fact so afflicted, and the home was the same in all other respects, its use would be authorized under the zoning ordinance. *City of Cleburne*, 473 U.S. at 449.

The city presented several bases supporting the ordinance: fear and negative attitudes by residents living near the facility; location of the home in a five hundred year flood plain; the size of the home and the number of people who would occupy it. The *City of Cleburne* Court demonstrated how each factor presented by the city made no sense in light of how the city treated other groups similarly situated in relevant respects. *City of Cleburne*, 473 U.S. at 448–450. Because none of the asserted bases rationally justified singling out a home for the retarded for the special use permit, while imposing no such restrictions on other uses freely permitted in the neighborhood, the Supreme Court concluded:

Requiring the permit in this case appears to us to rest on an irrational prejudice against the mentally retarded, including those who would occupy the [home] and who would live under the closely supervised and highly regulated conditions expressly provided for by state and federal law. *City of Cleburne*, 473 U.S. at 450.

Applying the *City of Cleburne* rational basis review here, because the State's grounds purporting to justify 21.06 do not rationally justify criminalizing same sex sodomy while imposing no such burden on others engaging in acts defined as deviate sexual intercourse, the classification is arbitrary and irrational and driven by

---

common law or status quo baselines or in Anglo-American conventions. The baseline is instead a principle of equality that operates as a criticism of existing practice. The clause does not safeguard traditions; it protects against traditions, however long standing and deeply rooted. Sunstein, 55 U. CHI. L. REV. at 1174. Thus, Justice Fowler's conclusion, that rational basis review under the Due Process Clause is the same as rational basis review under the Equal Protection Clause ignores the important distinction between the functions of the two clauses and how that distinction shapes review under each clause using the rational basis standard.

[13] I am not unmindful of the sensibilities of many persons who are deeply persuaded that homosexual sodomy is evil and should be prohibited. That is not the issue here. Rather, the federal equal protection issue before this court, which I believe should be answered in the negative, is whether the Federal Constitution permits discriminatory recourse to the sanctions of the criminal law for the achievement of that

objective. The community and its members remain entirely free to employ theological teaching, moral persuasion, parental advice, psychological and psychiatric counseling, and other noncoercive means to condemn the practice of homosexual sodomy. *People v. Onofre*, 51 N.Y.2d 476, 415 N.E.2d 936, 941 n.3, 434 N.Y.S.2d 947 (N.Y. 1980). Alternatively, if the legislature wishes to abolish what it views as immoral behavior, it is free to do so, provided that it does not single out a class of people for the prohibition, while freely permitting other classes to engage in the same behavior, thereby, again, running afoul of the federal Equal Protection Clause. But the law regarding the use of the criminal law to implement biases is clear: "private biases may be outside the reach of the law, but the law cannot, directly or indirectly, give them effect." *City of Cleburne*, 473 U.S. at 448 (using rational relationship test to invalidate zoning ordinance requiring a special use permit for home for the mentally retarded where no special permit required for other similar multiple dwelling facilities).

prejudice. It makes no sense for the State to contend that morals are preserved by criminalizing homosexual sodomy while supporting sodomy by heterosexual couples, including unmarried persons. The State simply may not rely on a classification whose relationship to an asserted goal is so attenuated as to render the distinction arbitrary or irrational. *Zobel,* 457 U.S. at 61–63. Where, as here, the State interest of preserving morality is irrational in light of authorization of the same immoral acts by others, the statute fails rational basis review under the Equal Protection Clause and should be held in violation of the United States Constitution. *Heller v. Doe by Doe,* 509 U.S. 312, 324, 125 L. Ed. 2d 257, 113 S. Ct. 2637 (1993) (stating a statutory classification fails rational basis review when it rests on grounds wholly irrelevant to achievement of the state's objective).

The majority's discussion of the historical definitions of sodomy, which includes a reference to a seventeenth century law of the Massachusetts Bay Colony, suggests that homosexuals have been subjected to a tradition of disfavor. In his concurring opinion in *City of Cleburne,* Justice Stevens, joined by Chief Justice Burger, distanced himself from the tiered analysis of equal protection claims because, he believed, the rational basis test is suitable for all such inquiries. 473 U.S. at 452. In every equal protection case, he wrote, we have to ask certain basic questions: What class is harmed by the legislation, and has it been subjected to a "tradition of disfavor" by our laws? *City of Cleburne,* 473 U.S. at 453. In a footnote to this question, Justice Stevens stated the following:

> The Court must be especially vigilant in evaluating the rationality of any classification involving a group that has been subjected to a tradition of disfavor [for] a traditional classification is more likely to be used without pausing to consider its justification than is a newly created classification. Habit, rather than analysis, makes it seem acceptable and natural to distinguish between male and female, alien and citizen, legitimate and illegitimate; for too much of our history there was the same inertia in distinguishing between black and white. But that sort of stereotyped reaction may have no rational relationship—other than pure prejudicial discrimination—to the stated purpose for which the classification is made. *Id.* at n.6.

Because the State has not shown a valid state interest for 21.06 that is rationally served by proscribing sodomy only when performed by homosexuals, the unavoidable conclusion is that the statute was merely a continuation of the stereotyped reaction to a traditionally disfavored group. By its unquestioning acceptance of the State's justification for the statute, the majority has overlooked the illegitimate stereotyping lying at the core of 21.06.

C. Judge Norris, concurring in *Watkins v. U.S. Army,* 875 F.2d 699, 720 (9th Cir. 1989), captured, in my view, the core rationale underlying the Equal Protection Clause of the Fourteenth Amendment. He wrote that the equal protection doctrine does not prevent the majority from enacting laws based on its substantive value choices. Equal protection simply requires that the majority apply its values evenhandedly. *Id.* Indeed, the equal protection doctrine plays an important role in perfecting, rather than frustrating, the democratic process. The constitutional requirement of evenhandedness advances the political legitimacy of majority rule by safeguarding minorities from majoritarian oppression. *Id.*

Therefore, I would hold section 21.06 violates the Equal Protection Clause based on appellants' contentions that it discriminates based on both gender and sexual orientation. Accordingly, I would sustain appellants' first point of error challenging 21.06 on federal equal protection grounds, as applied and on its face.

IV.

Section 21.06 and The Texas Equal Rights Amendment Appellants also challenge 21.06 contending it violates Article I, § 3a of the Texas Constitution in that it proscribes otherwise lawful behavior solely on the basis of the sex of the participants. That provision of the Texas Bill of Rights provides as follows:

> Equality under the law shall not be denied or abridged because of sex, race, color, creed, or national origin. This amendment is self-operative.

In my opinion, there are two standards by which review of section 21.06 may be made in the face of a challenge under the Texas ERA. The first is a per se rule based on the mandate of Article I, § 29 of the Texas Bill of Rights, and the second is strict scrutiny under the guidance of *In re McLean,* 725 S.W.2d 696 (Tex. 1987).

A. Per Se Rule   Article I, § 29 of the Texas Bill of Rights states the following rule regarding the power of the state government to usurp any of the rights contained in Article I of the Texas Constitution:

To guard against transgressions of the high powers herein delegated, we declare that everything in this 'Bill of Rights' is excepted out of the general powers of government, and shall forever remain inviolate, and all laws contrary thereto, or to the following provisions, shall be void.

Section 29 has been interpreted as follows: any provision of the Bill of Rights is self-executing to the extent that anything done in violation of it is void. *City of Beaumont v. Bouillion*, 896 S.W.2d 143, 148–149 (Tex. 1995). When a law conflicts with rights guaranteed by Article I, the constitution declares that such acts are void because the Bill of Rights is a limit on State power. *Id.* at 149. Indeed, the Bill of Rights consists of express limitations of power on the legislature, executive officers, and the judiciary. *Republican Party of Texas v. Dietz*, 940 S.W.2d 86, 90 (Tex. 1997) (citing *Travelers' Ins. Co. v. Marshall*, 124 Tex. 45, 76 S.W.2d 1007 (Tex. 1934)). The framers of the Texas Constitution articulated what they intended to be the means of remedying a constitutional violation: a law contrary to a constitutional provision is void. *Bouillion*, 896 S.W.2d at 149.

Thus, while the State, in the exercise of its police powers, may enact legislation reasonably tending to promote the health, comfort or welfare of the public, the extent of this power is limited and must be exercised in conformance with the limitations prescribed by the constitution. *Faulk v. Buena Vista Burial Park Ass'n*, 152 S.W.2d 891, 891–95 (Tex. Civ. App.—El Paso 1941, no writ); see also *Villarreal v. State*, 935 S.W.2d 134, 139 (Tex. Crim. App. 1996) (McCormick, P.J., concurring) (characterizing dissent's approach to "privacy expectation" analysis as coming "perilously close to subjecting our constitutional rights too closely to majoritarian political processes and temporary passions of the moment, which is inconsistent with the idea underlying the Bill of Rights.").

Therefore, when the equality guaranteed by the Texas ERA is viewed through the prism of the Texas "Inviolability Clause,"[14] it becomes clear that section 21.06, as a non-gender neutral classification created by the legislature in violation of Article I, § 3a, is void.[15]

B. Strict Scrutiny Under *In re McLean*   Before examining the precise manner in which the *McLean* court analyzed a statute that discriminated on the basis of sex, it is informative to review what that court had to say about the meaning of the Texas ERA.

The *McLean* court declined to give the Texas ERA an interpretation identical to that given state and federal due process and equal guarantees. 725 S.W.2d at 697. Both the United States Constitution and the Texas Constitution had due process and equal protection guarantees before the ERA was adopted in Texas in 1972. Id. If the due process and equal protection provisions and the ERA are given identical interpretations, then the 1972 amendment, adopted by a four to one margin by Texas voters, was an exercise in futility. *Id.* Thus, the *McLean* court concluded the Equal Rights Amendment is more extensive and provides more specific protection than both the United States and Texas due process and equal protection guarantees. *McLean*, 725 S.W.2d at 698. The *McLean* court did not, however, adopt a per se standard,[16] but instead concluded the Texas ERA elevated sex to a suspect class, thus subjecting any gender discrimination to strict scrutiny, placing the burden on the proponent of the discriminatory provision to demonstrate a compelling interest, and that there is no other manner to protect the state's compelling interest. *Id.* (citing *Mercer v. Board of Trust.*, North Forest Indep. Sch. Dist., 538 S.W.2d 201, 206 [Tex. Civ. App.—Houston

---

[14] Article I, § 29 excepts everything in the bill of rights out of the general powers of government and states such rights included therein are to remain inviolate, thus placing these rights beyond the power of the state government to usurp. TEX. CONST. Art. I, § 29 interp. commentary (Vernon 1997).

[15] The majority never really addresses the Texas ERA, or the companion Inviolability Clause, in its analysis of appellants' challenge to 21.06 on the basis of gender discrimination under the Texas Constitution, even though Rule 47.1 requires that opinions from this Court "address[] every issue raised and necessary to final disposition of the appeal." TEX. R. APP. P. 47.1. Nevertheless, by its decision today the majority renders meaningless the action of the people of Texas in placing the ERA in the state constitution, engaging in nothing less than the gratuitous nullification of an act of the people of Texas and totally disregarding their expressed constitutional will. See *Barber v. Colorado Indep.Sch.Dist.*, 901 S.W.2d 447, 455 (Tex. 1995) (Gammage, J., dissenting to majority's refusal to intervene and apply Texas ERA to a class action challenging high school's hair length and earring restrictions under the ERA based on gender discrimination).

[16] There is no reference in *McLean* to Article I, § 29.

(14th Dist.) 1976, writ ref'd n.r.e.] [holding any classification based on sex is suspect classification; thus any law or regulation classifying persons for different treatment on basis of their sex is subject to strictest judicial scrutiny]). The Austin Court of Appeals has also concluded the Equal Rights Amendment elevates sex to a suspect class, thereby invoking strict scrutiny review when a law differentiates on the basis of gender. *Lens Express, Inc. v. Ewald,* 907 S.W.2d 64, 69 (Tex. App.—Austin 1995, no writ).

Neither the State nor the majority have applied the strict scrutiny mandated by *McLean* and Mercer. Nevertheless, that standard must be applied. *McLean* established a two step process for examining a statute challenged as a violation of the ERA. The first step is to determine whether equality under the law has been denied. 725 S.W.2d at 697. That first inquiry is relatively simple. The denial of equality here was under the law because appellants were prosecuted under 21.06 of the Texas Penal Code. In *McLean,* the court held that because disparate treatment of an illegitimate child's father and mother was required by a statute in the Texas Family Code, the denial of equality was under the law. *Id.*

The second inquiry is whether equality was denied because of a person's membership in a protected class of sex, race, color, creed, or national origin. *Id.* As I have discussed above in connection with the analysis of appellants' federal equal protection challenge to 21.06, it is manifest on the face of that statute it is the gender of the particular actors that serves as the trigger for 21.06's prohibitions, so that discussion need not be repeated here. Thus, addressing the second part of the *McLean* test, the focus is on whether the discrimination in 21.06 is prohibited by the ERA. *Id.* Sex-based discrimination is allowed to co-exist with the ERA only when the proponent of the discrimination can prove there is no other manner to protect the state's compelling interest. *Id.* Surprisingly, counsel for the State conceded at oral argument that he could not "even see how he could begin to frame an argument that there was a compelling State interest," much less demonstrate that interest for this Court. The State did offer, however, what it characterized as legitimate purposes for the statute: enforcement of principles of morality and promotion of family values.

It is simply not enough for the State to say it has an important interest furthered by the discriminatory law. *McLean,* 725 S.W.2d at 698. Even the loftiest goal does not justify sex-based discrimination in light of the clear constitutional prohibition contained in the Texas ERA. *Id.* Strict scrutiny is not satisfied until the State has met a two part test: articulation of a compelling state interest, and a showing that there is no other manner to protect the state's compelling interest. *Id.* Thus, even accepting the morality and family values bases supporting the discrimination as compelling state interests, there is no showing here that there is no other manner of protecting morality and family values other than prosecuting same sex sodomy. It would appear that the state's goal of protecting these interests was originally achieved on a non-discriminatory basis when the prohibition of sodomy applied to all persons. See n.8, supra. There are other avenues for achieving the State's objectives without resorting to 21.06 as pointed out by the court in Onofre. See n.13, supra. It is manifestly illogical to suggest that sodomy, when performed by heterosexuals promotes morality and family values, and that the same acts when performed by same sex couples, denigrates morality and family values.

As noted above, implicitly rejecting "morality" and "family values" as justifications for Colorado's discriminatory constitutional amendment, the United States Supreme Court struck down the amendment under a rational basis standard. See n.12, supra. Logic dictates that if the promotion of morality norms and family values as rationalizations for state sponsored discrimination will not pass a rational basis standard of review, such contentions would wilt in the face of strict scrutiny mandated by *McLean.* I conclude, therefore, that because the State has not shown there are no alternate means to protect the State's asserted interests of family values and morality other than through the gender-based discrimination in 21.06, the statute violates Article I, § 3a of the Texas Constitution and is, therefore, void. See TEX. CONST. Art. I, § 29.

Accordingly, I would sustain appellant's point of error two challenging 21.06 under the Texas ERA.

V.

Conclusion Analyzed correctly under binding Supreme Court precedent, Texas Penal Code section 21.06 is in violation of the Equal Protection Clause of the Federal Constitution because it is neither rationally related to the legitimate State objective presented for its support, nor viable under heightened scrutiny because the State failed to articulate a compelling interest served by the gender discrimination exhibited by 21.06 on its face and as applied. Further, under the Texas Bill of Rights, because the gender discrimination in 21.06 contravenes the Equal Rights Amendment, it is automatically void without regard to any justification.

The holding here that 21.06 is unconstitutional is not tantamount to a conclusion that there is nothing wrong with the prohibited conduct. The majority correctly states that mere disagreement with the Legislature over whether the conduct proscribed by 21.06 is or is not a bad deed is not a basis for overturning a statute. This statement, however, is incomplete because it ignores the duty a judge has when confronted by a statute in conflict with the constitution.

The courts may declare legislative enactments unconstitutional and void in some cases, but not because the judicial power is superior in degree or dignity to the legislative. Being required to declare what the law is in the cases which come before them, they must enforce the constitution as the paramount law, whenever a legislative enactment comes in conflict with it.

In exercising this high authority, the judges claim no judicial supremacy; they are only the administrators of the public will [expressed in the constitution]. If an act of the legislature is held void, it is not because the judges have any control over the legislative power, but because the act is forbidden by the constitution, and because the will of the people, which is therein declared, is paramount to that of their representatives expressed in any law. *Ex parte Rodriguez,* 39 Tex. 705, 751 (1873).

The Texas Constitution does not protect morality; it does, however, guarantee equality to all persons under the law. TEX. CONST. art. I, § 3a. My personal views on the conduct involved here are irrelevant to the outcome that I believe is required. The foregoing is my duty in the preparation of opinions because Cannon 3B(5) of the Texas Code of Judicial Conduct requires a judge to "perform judicial duties without bias or prejudice." Thus, the result reached in this dissent is purely a function of the application of the Texas and Federal Constitutions to section 21.06, and nothing more. Accordingly, I respectfully dissent.

/s/ John S. Anderson

Justice

Dissenting Opinion filed March 15, 2001.

En Banc.

In the Supreme Court of the United States

JOHN GEDDES LAWRENCE AND TYRON
GARNER, PETITIONERS
V.
STATE OF TEXAS, RESPONDENT.

ON WRIT OF CERTIORARI TO THE COURT OF
APPEALS OF TEXAS FOURTEENTH DISTRICT

BRIEF OF PETITIONERS

Paul M. Smith
William M. Hohengarten
Daniel Mach
Sharon M. McGowan
JENNER & BLOCK, LLC
601 13th Street, N.W.
Washington, DC 20005
(202) 639-6000

Mitchell Katine
WILLIAMS, BIRNBERG & ANDERSEN, L. L.P.
6671 Southwest Freeway, Suite 303
Houston, Texas 77074
(713) 981-9595

Ruth E. Harlow
Counsel of Record
LAMBDA LEGAL DEFENSE AND EDUCATION
FUND, INC.
120 Wall Street, Suite 1500
New York, NY 10005
(212) 809-8585
Counsel for Petitioners

TABLE OF CONTENTS

QUESTIONS PRESENTED

1. Whether Petitioners' criminal convictions under the Texas "Homosexual Conduct" law—which criminalizes adult, consensual same-sex intimate behavior, but not identical behavior by different-sex couples—violate the Fourteenth Amendment right to equal protection of the laws?

2. Whether Petitioners' criminal convictions for adult consensual sexual intimacy in the home violate their vital interests in liberty and

privacy protected by the Due Process Clause of the Fourteenth Amendment?

3. Whether *Bowers v. Hardwick*, 478 U.S. 186 (1986), should be overruled?

BRIEF OF PETITIONERS

The State of Texas arrested Petitioners Lawrence and Garner, charged them with a crime, and convicted them under the State's "Homosexual Conduct" law for engaging in consensual same-sex intimacy in the privacy of Lawrence's home. The Texas law and Petitioners' convictions are constitutionally indefensible for two reasons. First, the law discriminates without a legitimate and rational State purpose, in violation of the Equal Protection Clause. In 1973, Texas broke with both the evenhanded laws of the past and the decisive modern trend toward decriminalization. Instead, the State chose to criminalize consensual, adult sexual behaviors *only* for those whose partners are of the same sex—gay men and lesbians. Texas's decision to classify along that line brands gay men and lesbians as lawbreakers and fuels a whole range of further discrimination, effectively relegating them to a form of second-class citizenship. Second, this criminal law directly implicates fundamental interests in intimate relationships, bodily integrity, and the home. Texas's law and the few other remaining consensual sodomy statutes—both those that discriminate and those that do not—trample on the substantive liberty protections that the Constitution erects in order to preserve a private sphere shielded from government intrusion. Here, where the State authorizes such intrusion into the homes and lives only of same sex couples, the constitutional injury is especially clear and disturbing.

OPINIONS AND ORDERS BELOW

The Texas Court of Criminal Appeals' orders refusing discretionary review are unreported. Pet. App. 1a, 2a. The decision of the *en banc* Court of Appeals for the Fourteenth District of Texas is reported at 41 S.W.3d 349. Pet. App. 4a. The court's prior panel opinion is unreported. Pet. App. 80a. The judgments of the Harris County Criminal Court are unreported. Pet. App. 107a, 109a.

JURISDICTION

The judgment of the Court of Appeals was entered on March 15, 2001. Pet. App. 3a. On April 17, 2002, the Texas Court of Criminal Appeals denied a timely consolidated petition for discretionary review. Pet. App. 1a, 2a. Petitioners filed their timely petition for a writ of certiorari in this Court on July 16, 2002. This Court's jurisdiction rests on 28 U.S.C. § 1257(a).

STATUTORY AND CONSTITUTIONAL PROVISIONS

Texas Penal Code § 21.06 ("Homosexual Conduct") provides: "(a) A person commits an offense if he engages in deviate sexual intercourse with another individual of the same sex. (b) An offense under this section is a Class C misdemeanor."

Texas Penal Code § 21.01(1) provides: "'Deviate sexual intercourse' means: (A) any contact between any part of the genitals of one person and the mouth or anus of another person; or (B) the penetration of the genitals or the anus of another person with an object."

The Fourteenth Amendment to the United States Constitution provides, in relevant part: "No State shall ... deprive any person of life, liberty, or property, without due process of law; nor deny to any person within its jurisdiction the equal protection of the laws." U.S. Const. amend. XIV, § 1.

STATEMENT OF THE CASE

A. Petitioners' Arrests, Convictions, And Appeals.

Late in the Evening of September 17, 1998, Harris County, Texas, sheriff's officers entered John Lawrence's home and there intruded on Lawrence and Tyron Garner having sex. The officers were responding to a false report of a "weapons disturbance." Pet. App. 129a, 141a.[1] They arrested petitioners, jailed them, and did not release them from custody until the next day. Clerk's Record in *State v. Lawrence*, at 3 ("C.R.L."); Clerk's Record in *State v. Garner*, at 3 ("C.R.G.").

The State charged Petitioners with violating the Texas "Homosexual Conduct" statute, Tex. Pen. Code § 21.06 (the "Homosexual Conduct

---

[1] The person who called in the report later admitted his allegations were false and was convicted of filing a false report. *See* R. A. Dyer, *Two Men Charged Under State's Sodomy Law*, Hous. Chron., Nov. 6, 1998, at A1.

Law" or "Section 21.06"), which criminalizes so-called "deviate sexual intercourse" with another person of the same sex, but not identical conduct by different-sex couples. *Id.* The sole facts alleged by the State to make out a violation were that each Petitioner "engage[d] in deviate sexual intercourse, namely anal sex, with a member of the same sex (man)." Pet. App. 127a, 139a. The State did not allege that the conduct was public, non-consensual, with a minor, or in exchange for money. *Id.* The charges rested solely on consensual, adult sexual relations with a partner of the same sex in the privacy of Lawrence's home. *Id.*

After proceedings and initial convictions in the Justice of the Peace Court, Petitioners appealed for a trial *de novo* to the Harris County Criminal Court. C.R.L. 15; C.R.G. 12. They filed motions to quash the charges on the ground that the law violates the Fourteenth Amendment's guarantees of equal protection and privacy, both on its face and as applied to their "consensual, adult, private sexual relations with another person of the same sex." Pet. App. 117a–118a, 121a–122a, 130a–131a, 134a–135a. On December 22, 1998, the court denied the motions to quash. Pet. App. 113a. Lawrence and Garner then pled *nolo contendere,* Pet. App. 114a, preserving, under Texas procedural rules, their right to pursue previously asserted defenses. Tex. Code Crim. P. § 44.02. The court imposed on each a fine of $200 and court costs of $141.25. Pet. App. 107a–108a, 109a–110a, 116a.

In consolidated appeals to the Texas Court of Appeals, Lawrence and Garner argued that Section 21.06 impermissibly discriminates between citizens "[u]nder any characterization of the classification." Amended Brief of Appellants at 4, 5, 6–17 (Tex. App. filed Apr. 30, 1999) ("Am. Br."); Additional Brief of Appellants 1 n.1, 14–22 (Tex. App. filed Aug. 11, 2000) ("Add'l Br."); Petition for Discretionary Review at 7–13 (Tex. Crim. App. filed Apr. 13, 2001) ("Pet. Disc. Rev."). Petitioners also argued that the statute invades their right of privacy and preserved their contention that *Bowers v. Hardwick,* 478 U.S. 186 (1986), was wrongly decided. Am. Br. 5, 23–26; Add'l Br. 23 n.20; Pet. Disc. Rev. 16–19.

At oral argument in the Court of Appeals, counsel for the State conceded that "he could not 'even see how he could begin to frame an argument that there was a compelling State interest'"

served by Section 21.06. Pet. App. 76a (quoting counsel for Texas). Texas has repeatedly identified its only aim as "enforcement of principles of morality and the promotion of family values." *See, e.g.,* State's Brief in Support of Rehearing En Banc 16 (Tex. App. filed Aug. 23, 2000) ("States' Br. in Supp. of Reh'g En Banc").

On June 8, 2000, a panel of the Court of Appeals reversed Petitioners' convictions under the Texas Equal Rights Amendment, holding that Section 21.06 impermissibly discriminates on the basis of sex. Pet. App. 86a–92a. After rehearing *en banc,* the Court of Appeals reinstated Petitioners' convictions on March 15, 2001. Pet. App. 3a, 4a. Citing *Bowers,* the court rejected Petitioners' substantive due process claim. Pet. App. 24a–31a. As to the federal equal protection claim, the court held that the statute was subject to and survived rational basis review, because it "advances a legitimate state interest, namely, preserving public morals." Pet. App. 13a. The court distinguished *Romer v. Evans,* 517 U.S. 620 (1996), as limited to discrimination in the right to seek legislation. Pet. App. 14a–15a.

Two Justices of the appellate court "strongly" dissented from the rejection of Petitioners' federal equal protection arguments. Pet. App. 42a. The dissent reasoned that:

> where the same conduct, defined as "deviate sexual intercourse[,]" is criminalized for same sex participants but not for heterosexuals[,] [t]he contention that the same conduct is moral for some but not for others merely repeats, rather than legitimizes, the Legislature's unconstitutional edict.

Pet. App. 44a. Petitioners timely sought discretionary review from the Texas Court of Criminal Appeals, which was refused. Pet. App. 1a, 2a.

B. THE HOMOSEXUAL CONDUCT LAW

The Homosexual Conduct Law is of comparatively recent vintage. It was enacted in 1973 when Texas repealed all of its then-existing laws that criminalized private sexual conduct between consenting adults. *See* 1973 Tex. Gen. Laws ch. 399, §§ 1, 3. Prior to that time, the criminality of consensual sexual conduct in Texas did not depend on whether a couple was same sex or different-sex. In particular, oral as well as anal sex was a crime for all. 1943 Tex. Gen. Laws ch. 112, § 1. *See generally Baker v. Wade,* 553 F. Supp. 1121, 1148–53 (N.D. Tex. 1982) (reviewing history of Texas sodomy laws),

U.S. SUPREME
COURT

BRIEF OF
PETITIONERS

rev'd, 769 F.2d 289 (5th Cir. 1985) (en banc).[2] Until 1973 Texas also criminalized fornication and adultery. *See* Tex. Pen. Code arts. 499–504 (1952) (repealed by 1973 Tex. Gen. Laws, ch. 399, § 3).

The 1973 repeals abolished all those crimes, 1973 Tex. Gen. Laws ch. 399, § 3, freeing heterosexual adult couples, married or unmarried, to engage in all forms of consensual, private, noncommercial sexual intimacy without state intrusion. In the same enactment, however, the Legislature adopted Section 21.06, *see id.* § 1, which for the first time singled out same-sex couples for criminal sanctions. Section 21.06 applies to "deviate sexual intercourse," which is defined as oral, anal, and certain other sexual conduct without regard to whether the actors are of the same or different sexes. *See* Tex. Pen. Code § 21.01(1).[3] But "deviate sexual intercourse" is *not* a crime when engaged in privately by two consenting adults of different sexes. Rather, Section 21.06 criminalizes only "Homosexual Conduct," making it a punishable offense to engage in "deviate sexual intercourse with another individual of the same sex," but not identical conduct by heterosexual couples. Tex. Pen. Code § 21.06.[4]

Texas, of course, also has and enforces other laws that criminalize sexual conduct that takes place in public, Tex. Pen. Code §§ 21.07(a)(2), 21.08, that is violent or without consent, *id.* § 22.011(a)(1), that is in exchange for money, *id.* § 43.02, or that is committed with a minor, *id.* §§ 22.011(a)(2), 21.11. All of these prohibitions apply without regard to whether the actors are of the same or different sexes. Section 21.06, in contrast, applies to non-commercial, consensu-

al, private sexual conduct between two adults— but only if they are of the same sex.

Because it singles out same-sex couples, this Texas law is unlike older legal prohibitions of "sodomy," *see infra* Point I.A.3, and differs fundamentally from the facially evenhanded Georgia law considered by the Court in *Bowers,* *see* 478 U.S. at 188 n.1. The Homosexual Conduct Law was substituted for a facially nondiscriminatory law at a time when many States, prompted by changing views about the proper limits of government power that were reflected in the American Law Institute's *Model Penal Code,* were revising their criminal codes and completely abandoning offenses like fornication and sodomy. *See Model Penal Code and Commentaries* §§ 213.2 cmt. 2, 213.6 note (1980). By 1986, 26 States had invalidated their sodomy laws. *Bowers,* 478 U.S. at 193–94. Today, only nine States retain criminal laws that bar consensual sodomy for all.[5] Between 1969 and 1989, Texas and seven other States legislatively replaced general laws with laws targeting homosexual couples. *See infra* at 21–22 & note 15. Four of those discriminatory laws have already been judicially invalidated, and one has been repealed. *See id.* Now only Texas and two other States criminalize same-sex conduct but not identical different-sex conduct by statute, while one other State has reached the same result through judicial construction of a facially evenhanded law.[6] Similarly, all but a few States have repealed criminal laws prohibiting fornication. *Infra* note 18.

Since its enactment, Section 21.06 has narrowly survived several federal and state constitutional challenges. In *Baker v. Wade,* a federal district court held that Section 21.06 violates the

---

[2] Before 1943, an 1860 statute criminalized "the abominable and detestable crime against nature," Tex. Pen. Code art. 342 (1860); *see Baker,* 553 F. Supp. at 1148, which was held *not* to apply to oral sex. *See, e.g., Munoz v. State,* 281 S.W. 857 (Tex. Crim. App. 1926); *Prindle v. State,* 21 S.W. 360, 361 (Tex. Crim. App. 1893). Like the 1943 law, however, the 1860 statute applied to heterosexual as well as homosexual conduct. *See Adams v. State,* 86 S.W. 334 (Tex. Crim. App. 1905); *Lewis v. State,* 35 S.W. 372 (Tex. Crim. App. 1896).

[3] The present definition of "deviate sexual intercourse" reflects a 1981 amendment adding § 21.01(1)(B) to encompass penetration with "objects," which has been construed to include any part of the body. *See C.M. v. State,* 680 S.W.2d 53, 55–56 (Tex. App. 1984). In 1993, facing a sunset provision, Texas reenacted most of the Penal Code, including Section 21.06. *See* 1993 Tex. Sess. Law Serv. ch. 900 (Vernon). Several attempts to repeal the law have failed, *see, e.g.,* H.B.

687, 2001 Leg. 77th (R) Sess. (Tex.); *see also Baker,* 553 F. Supp. at 1126 & n.4, 1151.

[4] "Homosexual conduct" is a Class C misdemeanor punishable by a fine of up to $500. Tex. Pen. Code §§ 21.06(b), 12.23.

[5] Ala. Code §§ 13A-6-60(2), 13A-6-65(a)(3); Fla. Stat. Ann. § 800.02; Idaho Code § 18-6605; La. Rev. Stat. Ann. § 14:89; Miss. Code Ann. § 97-29- 59; N.C. Gen. Stat. § 14-177; S.C. Code Ann. § 16-15-120; Utah Code Ann. § 76-5-403(1); Va. Code Ann. § 18.2-361(A).

[6] Kansas and Missouri have same-sex-only statutes, Kan. Stat. Ann. § 21-3505(a)(1); Mo. Rev. Stat. § 566.090, although one intermediate court of appeals in Missouri has held that State's statute applicable only to nonconsensual conduct, *State v. Cogshell,* 997 S.W.2d 534 (Mo. Ct. App. 1999). Oklahoma's general statute has been construed to exclude different-sex couples. Okla. Stat. tit. 21, § 886; *Post v. State,* 715 P.2d 1105 (Okla. Crim. App. 1986).

constitutional rights of privacy and equal protection. 553 F. Supp. at 1125. The court rejected the State's claimed justifications for Section 21.06 and found that, even when not enforced, the law results in serious harms to gay persons, including employment discrimination. *Id.* at 1130, 1146–47. Although the Texas Attorney General withdrew the State's appeal, a divided *en banc* Fifth Circuit allowed an appeal by an intervenor and reversed, citing the summary affirmance in *Doe v. Commonwealth's Attorney,* 425 U.S. 901 (1976). *Baker v. Wade,* 769 F.2d 289, 292 (5th Cir. 1985) (en banc).

In the early 1990s, Texas Courts of Appeals declared Section 21.06 unconstitutional in two cases exercising state equity jurisdiction. *City of Dallas v. England,* 846 S.W.2d 957 (Tex. App. 1993); *State v. Morales,* 826 S.W.2d 201 (Tex. App. 1992), *rev'd on jurisdictional grounds,* 869 S.W.2d 941 (Tex. 1994). In both cases, the intermediate appellate court struck down the Homosexual Conduct Law under the Texas Constitution and found that the statute inflicted severe harms beyond the direct threat of criminal convictions. *See England,* 846 S.W.2d at 959; *Morales,* 826 S.W.2d at 202. As the State itself stipulated in *Morales,* Section 21.06 "brands lesbians and gay men as criminals and thereby legally sanctions discrimination against them in a variety of ways unrelated to the criminal law." *Id.* at 202–03.

In 1994, *Morales* was set aside by the Texas Supreme Court as reaching beyond the power of the State's equity courts. 869 S.W.2d at 943–47. The court ruled that constitutional review should occur in the context of a criminal prosecution, with final review in the Texas Court of Criminal Appeals. *Id.*[7] In the present criminal case, however, the Court of Criminal Appeals refused to exercise its jurisdiction to review the validity of the law, Pet. App. 1a, 2a, leaving its burdens in effect throughout Texas.

SUMMARY OF ARGUMENT

As the experience of Lawrence and Garner vividly illustrates, Section 21.06 puts the State of Texas inside its citizens' homes, policing the details of their most intimate and private physi-

cal behavior and dictating with whom they may share a profound part of adulthood. Texas has enacted and enforced a criminal law that takes away—from same-sex couples only—the freedom to make their own decisions, based upon their own values and relationships, about the forms of private, consensual sexual intimacy they will engage in or refrain from. The State defends this law only by saying the majority wants it so. Texas asserts a power of the majority to free itself from state dictates about private, consensual sexual choices, while using the criminal law to condemn and limit the choices of a minority.

This law and its application to Petitioners violate both the guarantee of equal protection *and* fundamental liberties safeguarded by the Fourteenth Amendment. Petitioners explain below why the equality claim and the liberty claim are each well rooted in the Constitution. The Court, however, need not rule on both constitutional violations if it chooses to focus on one infirmity rather than the other. Petitioners discuss the fundamental liberty claim under the Due Process Clause first, because even if the Court were not to reach that issue, a full appreciation of the personal interests affected by Section 21.06 also illuminates and informs the equal protection analysis that follows.

Fundamental liberty and privacy interests in adults' private, consensual sexual choices are essential to the ordered liberty our Constitution protects. The State may not, without overriding need, regiment and limit this personal and important part of its citizens' lives. More so than in 1986, when *Bowers v. Hardwick* was decided, it is clear today that such a fundamental right is supported by our basic constitutional structure, by multiple lines of precedent, and by a decisive historical turn in the vast majority of the States to repudiate this type of government invasion into private life. The well-established fundamental interests in intimate relationships, bodily integrity, and the sanctity of the home all converge in the right asserted here. *See Griswold v. Connecticut,* 381 U.S. 479 (1965); *Eisenstadt v. Baird,* 405 U.S. 438 (1972); *Planned Parenthood of S.E. Pa. v. Casey,* 505 U.S. 833 (1992). That right belongs to all Americans, including gay men and lesbians, and should be shielded from Section 21.06's unjustified invasion. Much more is needed to outweigh fundamental individual interests than the majority's preferences. Indeed,

U.S. SUPREME
COURT

BRIEF OF
PETITIONERS

---

[7] Although the Texas Supreme Court did not review *England,* due to a jurisdictional defect in that court, *see Morales,* 869 S.W.2d at 942 n.5 (noting dismissal of writ of error in *England* without reaching merits), the state supreme court's ruling in *Morales* removed the underpinnings of *England.*

the Fourteenth Amendment's protection of liberty exists to guard against the very impulse Texas acted on here. Principles of *stare decisis* do not, in these circumstances, justify adherence to *Bowers*.

Texas also has violated the Fourteenth Amendment's guarantee of equal protection of the laws. The Homosexual Conduct Law creates classes of persons, treating the same acts of consensual sexual behavior differently depending on who the participants are. By this law, Texas imposes a discriminatory prohibition on all gay and lesbian couples, requiring them to limit their expressions of affection in ways that heterosexual couples, whether married or unmarried, need not. The law's discriminatory focus sends the message that gay people are second-class citizens and lawbreakers, leading to ripples of discrimination throughout society. Such a discriminatory law cannot satisfy even the minimal requirement that a legislative classification must be rationally related to a legitimate State purpose. *See Romer*, 517 U.S. 620. The bare negative attitudes of the majority, whether viewed as an expression of morality, discomfort, or blatant bias, cannot take away the equality of a smaller group. *See id.*; *United States Dep't of Agric. v. Moreno*, 413 U.S. 528, 534 (1973); *City of Cleburne v. Cleburne Living Ctr., Inc.*, 473 U.S. 432, 448 (1985).

ARGUMENT

I. Section 21.06 Violates Constitutional Rights to Liberty and Privacy Possessed by All Americans.

"It is a promise of the Constitution that there is a realm of personal liberty which the government may not enter." *Casey*, 505 U.S. at 847. It is well settled that the Due Process Clause of the Fourteenth Amendment guarantees the personal liberty of Americans against encroachment by the States, and that this protection of liberty encompasses substantive fundamental rights and interests that are unenumerated. *See, e.g., Troxel v. Granville*, 530 U.S. 57, 65–66 (2000); *Casey*, 505 U.S. at 846–51; *Cruzan v. Director, Mo. Dep't of Health*, 497 U.S. 261, 278–79 (1990); *Carey v. Population Servs. Int'l*, 431 U.S. 678, 684–85 (1977); *Moore v. City of E. Cleveland*, 431 U.S. 494, 501–03 (1977); *Roe v. Wade*, 410 U.S. 113, 152–53 (1973); *Griswold*, 381 U.S. at 482–85; *Pierce v. Society of the Sisters of the Holy Names of Jesus & Mary*, 268 U.S. 510, 534–35 (1925); *Meyer v. Nebraska*, 262 U.S. 390,

399–400 (1923). Giving substance to "liberty" is necessary to maintain the individual freedoms that are the essence of American democracy, while also allowing government action that is justified by the collective good. *See Casey*, 505 U.S. at 849–51.

Among the liberties protected by the Constitution is the right of an adult to make choices about whether and in what manner to engage in private consensual sexual intimacy with another adult, including one of the same sex. This extremely personal sphere implicates three aspects of liberty that have long been recognized as fundamental: the interests in intimate associations, in bodily integrity, and in the privacy of the home. For the State to limit and dictate the intimate choices of American couples in this realm without any substantial justification is repugnant to ordered liberty. *Stare decisis* does not require continued adherence to the Court's contrary decision in *Bowers*.

A. American Adults Have Fundamental Liberty and Privacy Interests in Making Their Own Choices About Private, Consensual Sexual Relations.

1. Well-Established Protections for Intimate Relationships, Bodily Integrity, and the Privacy of the Home Converge in This Vital Freedom.

Being forced into a life without sexual intimacy would represent an intolerable and fundamental deprivation for the overwhelming majority of individuals. Equally repugnant is any form of external compulsion to engage in sexual relations. There should be no doubt, then, that the Constitution imposes substantive limits on the power of government to compel, forbid, or regulate the intimate details of private sexual relations between two consenting adults.

All adults have the same fundamental liberty interests in their private consensual sexual choices. This fundamental protection is rooted in three well-recognized aspects of personal liberty—in intimate relationships, in bodily integrity, and in the privacy of the home. These aspects of liberty should not be viewed as "a series of isolated points," but are part of a "rational continuum" that constitutes the full scope of liberty of a free people. *Casey*, 505 U.S. at 848 (quotation marks omitted); *see also Board of Regents v. Roth*, 408 U.S. 564, 572 (1972) ("In a Constitution for a free people, there can be no doubt that the meaning of 'liberty' must be broad indeed"). Sexual intimacy marks an intensely personal and vital part of that continuum.

The Court has recognized that "choices to enter into and maintain certain intimate human relationships must be secured against undue intrusion by the State because of the role of such relationships in safeguarding the individual freedom that is central to our constitutional scheme." *Roberts v. United States Jaycees,* 468 U.S. 609, 617–18 (1984). "[T]he constitutional shelter afforded such relationships reflects the realization that individuals draw much of their emotional enrichment from close ties with others. Protecting these relationships from unwarranted state interference therefore safeguards the ability independently to define one's identity that is central to any concept of liberty." *Id.* at 619; *see also Board of Directors of Rotary Int'l v. Rotary Club of Duarte,* 481U.S. 537, 545–46 (1987).

The adult couple whose shared life includes sexual intimacy is undoubtedly one of the most important and profound forms of intimate association. The Court has rightly recognized that regulation of the private details of sexual relations between two adults sharing an intimate relationship has "a maximum destructive impact upon that relationship." *Griswold,* 381 U.S. at 485. *Griswold* struck down a law that intruded directly into a married couple's private sexual intimacy—and thus their intimate relationship—by criminalizing the use of contraceptives and allowing intercourse only if accompanied by the risk of pregnancy. *Id.* at 485–86. Since *Griswold,* the Court has recognized that all adults, regardless of marital status or other facets of their relationship, have the same interest in making their own intimate choices in this area. *See Eisenstadt,* 405 U.S. at 453 ("If the right of privacy means anything, it is the right of the *individual,* married or single, to be free from unwarranted governmental intrusion into matters so fundamentally affecting a person") (emphasis in original); *Casey,* 505 U.S. at 898 ("The Constitution protects all individuals, male or female, married or unmarried, from the abuse of governmental power"); *id.* at 852 (reaffirming *Eisenstadt* and *Griswold*).

Sexual intimacy is "a sensitive, key relationship of human existence, central to family life, community welfare, and the development of human personality." *Paris Adult Theatre I v.*

Slaton, 413 U.S. 49, 63 (1973). One's sexual orientation, the choice of one's partner, and whether and how to connect sexually are profound attributes of personhood where compulsion by the State is anathema to liberty. *Cf. Casey,* 505 U.S. at 851.[8] Thus, the essential associational freedom here is the freedom to structure one's own private sexual intimacy with another adult. Section 21.06 utterly destroys that freedom by forbidding most sexual behavior for all same-sex couples, whether they are in a committed, long-standing relationship, a growing one, or a new one.

State regulation of sexual intimacy also implicates the liberty interest in bodily integrity. "It is settled now ... that the Constitution places limits on a State's right to interfere with a person's most basic decisions about ... bodily integrity." *Casey,* 505 U.S. at 849 (citations omitted); *see also id.* at 896 ("state regulation ... is doubly deserving of scrutiny ... [where] the State has touched not only upon the private sphere of the family but upon the very bodily integrity of the pregnant woman"). Stated generally, "[e]very human being of adult years and sound mind has a right to determine what shall be done with his own body." *Glucksberg,* 521 U.S. at 777 (Souter, J., concurring) (quotation marks omitted); *see also id.* at 720; *Rochin v. California,* 342 U.S. 165, 166, 173–74 (1952); *Cruzan,* 497 U.S. at 278.

Control over one's own body is fundamentally at stake in sexual relations, involving as they do the most intimate physical interactions conceivable. Like the decision whether to continue or terminate a pregnancy, or the decision whether to permit or decline medical procedures, the physical, bodily dimensions of how two persons express their sexuality in intimate relations are profoundly personal. Indeed, consent is a critically important dividing line in legal and societal views about sexuality for the very reason that individual control over sexual activity is of fundamental importance to every person's autonomy. Texas invades the liberty

[8] For many adults in modern society, sexual intimacy is an important aspect of forming or building a committed relationship where one does not already exist. *See Roberts,* 468 U.S. at 618 (Constitution protects "the *formation* and preservation" of "highly personal relationships") (emphasis added); Richard A. Posner, *Sex and Reason* 349 (1992) ("Consensual sex in whatever form is as we know a method of cementing a relationship").

interest in bodily integrity by dictating that citizens may not share sexual intimacy unless they perform acts approved by the legislature, and by attempting to coerce them to select a sexual partner of the other sex.

The liberty interest at issue here also involves the deeply entrenched interest in the privacy of the home. "In the home, [the Court's] cases show, *all* details are intimate details, because the entire area is held safe from prying government eyes." *Kyllo v. United States*, 533 U.S. 27, 37 (2001) (emphasis in original); *Minnesota v. Olson*, 495 U.S. 91, 98 (1990) (overnight guest receives protection under "everyday expectations of privacy that we all share"). The importance of shielding the home from intrusion goes beyond the Fourth Amendment. In *Frisby v. Schultz*, 487 U.S. 474 (1988), for example, the Court relied on the constitutional status of the home in rejecting a First Amendment challenge to an ordinance against picketing targeted at a home. *Id.* at 484 ("The State's interest in protecting the well-being, tranquility, and privacy of the home is certainly of the highest order in a free and civilized society") (quotation marks omitted). And constitutional protection for the home was an important consideration in *Griswold* itself. *See* 381 U.S. at 485 (rejecting intrusion into "sacred precincts of marital bedrooms"). "[I]f the physical curtilage of the home is protected, it is surely as a result of the solicitude to protect the privacies of the life within." *Poe v. Ullman*, 367 U.S. 497, 551 (1961) (Harlan, J., dissenting); *see also Stanley v. Georgia*, 394 U.S. 557 (1969).

Even without actual physical entry by the police, Section 21.06 directly invades the privacy of the home by criminalizing the private intimate conduct taking place there. *Poe*, 367 U.S. at 549, 551–52 (Harlan, J., dissenting). But this case also graphically illustrates how laws criminalizing consensual adult sexual intimacy permit invasion of the privacy of the home in the starkest sense. Although Petitioners do not challenge the lawfulness of the police entry into Lawrence's home in response to a report of an armed gunman, the officers did not withdraw after discovering the report was false. Instead, under license of Section 21.06, they multiplied their intrusion exponentially by scrutinizing the specific intimate acts in which Petitioners were involved, arresting them, hauling them off to

jail, and charging them with a crime for which they were later convicted.

Denying the existence of a liberty interest in private consensual adult sexual activity would give constitutional legitimacy to the grossest forms of intrusion into the homes of individuals and couples. To investigate this "criminal" conduct, the police could use every investigative method appropriate when ordinary criminal activity, such as drug use or distribution, occurs in the home: obtaining warrants to search for physical evidence of sexual activity; interrogating each member of the couple about the intimate details of the relationship; and surveillance, wiretaps, confidential informants, and questioning of neighbors. That these routine police methods are so repugnant and unthinkable in the context of adult consensual sexual relations is a strong indication that the conduct at issue differs in a fundamental way from ordinary criminal conduct that happens to occur in the home. *Cf. Romer*, 517 U.S. at 645 (Scalia, J., dissenting) ("'To obtain evidence [in sodomy cases], police are obliged to resort to behavior which tends to degrade and demean both themselves personally and law enforcement as an institution'") (quoting Kadish, *The Crisis of Overcriminalization*, 374 Annals of Am. Acad. of Pol. & Soc. Sci. 157, 161 [1967]).[9]

The core liberty interests at stake in this case are a bulwark against an overly controlling and intrusive government. The "fundamental theory of liberty upon which all governments in this Union repose excludes any general power of the state to standardize," *Pierce*, 268 U.S. at 535, or "to coerce uniformity," *West Va. State Bd. of Educ. v. Barnette*, 319 U.S. 624, 640 (1943).

> The right of privacy exists because democracy must impose limits on the extent of control and direction that the state exercises over the day-to-day conduct of individual lives.... People do not meaningfully govern themselves if their lives are ... molded into standard, rigid, normalized roles.

---

[9] The argument here in no way implies that ordinary criminal conduct may find refuge in the home. In the present context, "the privacy of the home is constitutionally protected not only because the home is seen as a sanctuary, privileged against prying eyes, but also because it is the place where most intimate associations are centered." Kenneth L. Karst, *The Freedom of Intimate Association*, 89 Yale L.J. 624, 634 (1980) (footnote omitted); *see also Poe*, 367 U.S. at 551 (Harlan, J., dissenting) ("[t]he home derives its pre-eminence as the seat of family life").

Jed Rubenfeld, *The Right of Privacy*, 102 Harv. L. Rev. 783, 804–05 (1989).

2. There Is No Constitutional Exception to Liberty for Gay and Lesbian Citizens.

Gay and lesbian Americans have the same liberty interests as heterosexuals in private consensual sexual intimacy free from unwarranted intrusion by the State. Gay adults, like their heterosexual counterparts, have vital interests in their intimate relationships, their bodily integrity, and the sanctity of their homes. Today, family lives centered on same-sex relationships are apparent in households and communities throughout the country. Likewise, the special interplay between the privacy of the home and individual decisions about sexual expression applies to lesbians and gay men as it does to others.

A gay or lesbian sexual orientation is a normal and natural manifestation of human sexuality. A difference in sexual orientation means a difference only in that one personal characteristic. Mental health professionals have universally rejected the erroneous belief that homosexuality is a disease. For example, in 1973 the American Psychiatric Association concluded that "homosexuality *per se* implies no impairment in judgment, stability, reliability, or general social or vocational capabilities."[10] For gay adults, as for heterosexual ones, sexual expression is integrally linked to forming and nurturing the close personal bonds that give humans the love, attachment, and intimacy they need to thrive. *See, e.g.,* Lawrence A. Kurdeck, *Sexuality in Homosexual and Heterosexual Couples, in Sexuality in Close Relationships* 177–91 (K. McKinney & S. Sprecher eds., 1991); Christopher R. Leslie, *Creating Criminals: The Injuries Inflicted by "Unenforced" Sodomy Laws*, 35 Harv. C.R.-C.L. L. Rev. 103, 119–20 (2000). "[M]ost lesbians and gay men want intimate relationships and are successful in creating them. Homosexual partnerships appear no more vulnerable to problems and dissatisfactions than their heterosexual counterparts." Letitia A. Peplau, *Lesbian and Gay Relationships,*

in Homosexuality 177, 195 (J. Gonsiorek & J. Weinrich eds., 1991). Same-sex relationships often last a lifetime, and provide deep sustenance to each member of the couple. *See, e.g., A. Steven Bryant & Demian, Relationship Characteristics of American Gay and Lesbian Couples*, 1 J. Gay & Lesbian Soc. Servs. 101 (1994).

That gay Americans have exactly the same vital interests as all others in their bodily integrity and the privacy of their homes is so plain that it appears never to have been disputed in the law. In contrast, the vital liberty interest that gay adults have in their intimate relationships has not always been recognized. Even a few decades ago, intense societal pressure, including many anti-gay government measures, ensured that the vast majority of gay people hid their sexual orientation—even from their own parents—and thus hid the important intimate relationships that gave meaning to their lives. *See infra* Point II.B.2. Lesbians and gay men, moreover, were falsely seen as sick and dangerous. *See infra* at 46. As recently as 1986, it was still possible not to perceive the existence and dignity of the families formed by gay adults. *See, e.g., Bowers*, 478 U.S. at 191, 195.

Today, the reality of these families is undeniable. The 2000 United States Census identified more than 600,000 households of same-sex partners nationally, including almost 43,000 in Texas. These families live in 99.3% of American counties.[11] Many state and local governments and thousands of private employers have adopted domestic partner benefits or more extensive protections for same-sex couples.[12] Virtually every State permits gay men and lesbians to adopt children individually, jointly and/or through "second-parent adoptions" that are analogous to stepparent adoptions. *See, e.g., Lofton v. Kearney*, 157 F. Supp. 2d 1372, 1374 n.1 (S.D. Fla. 2001) (observing that Florida is currently "the only state" "to statutorily ban adoption by gay or lesbian adults"); American Law Inst., *Principles of the Law of Family Dissolution: Analysis and Recommendations* § 2.12 cmt. f, at

---

[10] *Resolution of the American Psychiatric Ass'n* (Dec. 15, 1973), 131 Am. J. Psychiatry 497 (1974); *accord* American Psychological Ass'n, *Minutes of the Annual Meeting of the Council of Representatives*, 30 Am. Psychologist 620, 633 (1975); National Ass'n of Social Workers, *Policy Statement on Lesbian and Gay Issues, reprinted in* Nat'l Ass'n of Social Workers, *Social World Speaks: NASW Policy Statements* 162, 162–65 (3d ed. 1994).

[11] *See* William B. Rubenstein, et al., *Some Demographic Characteristics of the Gay Community in the United States* 3 (Table 1), 5 (Williams Project, UCLA School of Law 2003), available at http://www1.law.ucla.edu/~erg/pubs/GD/Gay Demographics.pdf (accessed Jan. 15, 2003).

[12] *See Employers That Offer Domestic Partner Health Benefits, available at* http://www.hrc.org/worknet/dp/index.asp (accessed Jan. 15, 2003).

312 (2002). These and other legal doctrines have secured parental bonds for many of the estimated millions of children in the United States with gay parents. Ellen C. Perrin, *Technical Report: Coparent or Second-Parent Adoption by Same-Sex Parents*, 109 Pediatrics 341, 341 & n.1 (Feb. 2002) (estimating one to nine million children with at least one lesbian or gay parent); *see also, e.g., T.B. v. L.R.M.*, 786 A.2d 913 (Pa. 2001) (allowing claim for partial custody by lesbian second parent under *in loco parentis* doctrine).

The reality of these families cannot be disregarded just because they do not match the "nuclear" model of a married couple with their biological children. *See, e.g., Troxel*, 530 U.S. at 63 ("The demographic changes of the past century make it difficult to speak of an average American family. The composition of families varies greatly from household to household"); *id.* at 85 (Stevens, J., dissenting); *id.* at 98–101 (Kennedy, J., dissenting); *Michael H. v. Gerald D.*, 491 U.S. 110, 124 n.3 (1989) (plurality opinion) ("The family unit accorded traditional respect in our society ... includes the household of unmarried parents and their children"). For gay men and lesbians, their family life—their intimate associations and the homes in which they nurture those relationships—is every bit as meaningful and important as family life is to heterosexuals.

Thus, the liberty interest at issue here should not be defined in terms of sexual orientation as the "right of homosexuals to engage in acts of sodomy," *Bowers*, 478 U.S. at 191, or reduced in value on that account. If heterosexual adults have a fundamental interest in consensual sexual intimacy, including the choice to engage in oral or anal sex, then so too must homosexual adults. The Due Process Clause itself does not distinguish among classes of citizens, extending the Constitution's shield to the highly personal associations and choices of some, but not protecting the very same associations and choices for others. These liberties are important to and protected for all Americans.

3. Objective Considerations Support Recognition of Fundamental Interests Here.

To ensure that its decisions in this area are firmly grounded, the Court has sought objective guideposts for the recognition of fundamental liberties. *See County of Sacramento v. Lewis*, 523 U.S. 833, 857–58 (1998) (Kennedy, J., concur-

ring, joined by O'Connor, J.) (emphasizing that "objective considerations," including but not limited to "history and precedent," determine substantive due process interests). As just discussed, this Court's precedents and our constitutional structure indicate that the personal liberty protected by the Constitution must include adults' private choices about sexual intimacy. Foremost among other guideposts has been the history of legislation concerning the matter at hand, from prior centuries through the present. *See, e.g., Glucksberg*, 521 U.S. at 710–19.

In reviewing relevant legal traditions, the Court has made clear that protected liberty interests are not limited to those explicitly recognized when the Fourteenth Amendment was ratified. *Casey*, 505 U.S. at 847, 850 ("such a view would be inconsistent with our law"); *Rochin*, 342 U.S. at 171–72 ("To believe that ... judicial exercise of judgment could be avoided by freezing 'due process of law' at some fixed stage of time or thought is to suggest that the most important aspect of constitutional adjudication is a function for inanimate machines and not for judges"). Abundant examples exist of the Court giving meaning to contemporary truths about freedom, where earlier generations had failed to acknowledge and specify an essential aspect of liberty. *See, e.g., Turner v. Safley*, 482 U.S. 78, 94–99 (1987); *Roe*, 410 U.S. at 152–53; *Loving v. Virginia*, 388 U.S. 1, 12 (1967); *Griswold*, 381 U.S. at 482–85; *Pierce*, 268 U.S. at 534–35; *Meyer*, 262 U.S. at 399–400. *See generally Casey*, 505 U.S. at 847–48.

Similarly, in cases *rejecting* asserted liberty interests, the Court's decisions have never rested on past legal history alone. Because constitutional "tradition is a living thing," *Casey*, 505 U.S. at 850 (quotation marks omitted), the Court has always deemed it essential that the relevant legal tradition have continuing vitality today. In *Glucksberg*, for example, the Court rejected the claimed liberty interest in doctor-assisted suicide based not only on the common law's criminalization of assisted suicide, but also on the fact that "the States' assisted-suicide bans have in recent years been reexamined and, generally"—with a single exception—"reaffirmed." 521 U.S. at 716; *see also Michael H.*, 491 U.S. at 127. Even in *Bowers*, the Court looked not only to criminal laws concerning sodomy in 1787 and 1868, but also to the fact that half the States continued to outlaw such conduct in 1986. 478 U.S. at 192–94.[13]

Over the last half century, the Nation has firmly broken from its prior legal tradition of criminalizing many adult choices about private sexual intimacy. Even before 1960, however, the relevant legal tradition is more complicated than an initial examination might reveal. *Bowers* observed that when the Fourteenth Amendment was ratified, 32 of 37 States had criminal laws against sodomy. 478 U.S. at 192–93. But a critical feature of those 19th century and earlier laws was not discussed by the *Bowers* majority: Almost without exception, such laws historically have applied to certain specified sex acts without regard to whether same-sex or different-sex couples were involved. *See, e.g.,* Anne B. Goldstein, *History, Homosexuality, and Political Values*, 97 Yale L.J. 1073, 1082–86 (1988).[14] In addition, actual prosecutions for *private* intimacy have been exceedingly rare since the Nation's founding. *See* John D'Emilio & Estelle B. Freedman, *Intimate Matters: A History of Sexuality in America* 66–67 (1988). And the scope of the specific sexual conduct covered has varied over time. *See, e.g.,* Goldstein, 97 Yale L.J. at 1085–86.

Texas law is a case in point. A Texas statute adopted in 1860 penalized "the abominable and detestable crime against nature" for all persons, Tex. Pen. Code art. 342 (1860); *supra* note 2, and an amendment in 1943 extended that ban to oral sex for all persons, 1943 Tex. Gen. Laws ch. 112, § 1. *See supra* at 5. Only in 1973 did Texas—like a handful of other States in the same period—replace its general ban with one that singled out the sexual intimacy of same-sex couples for criminal prohibition. 1973 Tex. Gen. Laws ch. 399, §§ 1, 3.[15] Thus, our Nation has no longstanding legal tradition of defining permissible or prohibited sexual conduct in terms of sexual orientation. Rather, the tradition exemplified by actual legislation is one of facial neutrality. The few discriminatory laws singling out lesbians and gay men show the divide that existed in the 1970s and 1980s between the majority's view of its own liberties and its lingering anti-gay attitudes.

Most importantly, however, both evenhanded and discriminatory bans on private sexual conduct between consenting adults have been rejected in contemporary times. Since the 1960s, there has been a steady stream of repeals and state judicial invalidations of laws criminalizing consensual sodomy and fornication.[16] "The unmistakable trend … nationally … is to curb government intrusions at the threshold of one's door and most definitely at the threshold of one's bedroom." *Jegley v. Picado,* 80 S.W.3d 332, 356 (Ark. 2002) (Brown, J., concurring). By 1986, when *Bowers* was decided, 26 States had already removed consensual sodomy laws from their criminal codes. *See* 478 U.S. at 193–94. Today,

---

[13] The Court has repeatedly rejected the notion that fundamental rights encompass only those recognized at "the most specific level" at the time the Fourteenth Amendment was adopted. *Casey,* 505 U.S. at 847–59; *Michael H.,* 491 U.S. at 132 (O'Connor, J., joined by Kennedy, J., concurring in part) (the Court's cases have discussed "asserted rights at levels of generality that might not be 'the most specific level' available"). While the Court has sought carefully to describe fundamental liberty interests, as Petitioners do in this case, careful description means neither restriction to the most specific level nor limitation to historically recognized rights. Moreover, to the extent the Court prefers to characterize the asserted right parallel to the historical legal treatment, laws regulating consensual sex between adults, and state decisions to abolish such regulation, have almost always been written generally—*not* specifically to apply only to same-sex relationships.

[14] In 1868, at most three of the 32 States with sodomy prohibitions limited them to sexual conduct between two men; even in those three States, however, there is some uncertainty whether heterosexual couples were also covered. *See* Goldstein, 97 Yale L.J. at 1084 nn.60 & 66. Statutes using the word "mankind" frequently included sexual relations between men and women, as was the case in Texas. *See Lewis,* 35 S.W. at 372 ("Woman is included under the term 'mankind'"). In any event, three of 37 States is no legal tradition.

[15] *See also* 1977 Ark. Acts 828 (struck down by *Jegley v. Picado,* 80 S.W.3d 332 (Ark. 2002)); 1969 Kan. Sess. Laws ch. 180, *codified at* Kan. Stat. Ann. § 21-3505; 1974 Ky. Laws ch. 406 (struck down by *Commonwealth v. Wasson,* 842 S.W.2d 487 (Ky. 1992)); 1977 Mo. Laws sec. 1, § 566.090, *codified at* Mo. Rev. Stat. § 566.090; 1973 Mont. Laws ch. 513 (struck down by *Gryczan v. State,* 942 P.2d 112 (Mont. 1997)); 1977 Nev. Stat. ch. 598 (repealed by 1993 Nev. Stat. ch. 236); 1989 Tenn. Pub. Acts ch. 591 (struck down by *Campbell v. Sundquist,* 926 S.W.2d 250 (Tenn. Ct. App. 1996)).

[16] "With nonmarital sex so utterly commonplace, the word *fornication,* with its strong pejorative connotation, has virtually passed out of the language." Posner, *Sex and Reason* 55 (emphasis in original). Likewise, "sodomy" is a term now used rarely outside legal contexts, while oral sex and anal sex are openly discussed in the media and society.

Consensual sodomy and fornication have been the *only* criminal laws in American history where the State has acted solely to limit forms of intimacy by consenting adults. Other crimes relating to sexuality have included additional elements reflecting other state concerns. Adultery and bigamy laws, for example, aim to enforce the legal marriage contract. Incest and under-age sex laws, *inter alia,* seek to protect vulnerable individuals who may not be capable of true consent. Prostitution and public-sex laws address commercial or pub-

U.S. SUPREME
COURT

BRIEF OF
PETITIONERS

only 13 States still have such prohibitions.[17] Moreover, of those 13 States, Texas and the three others that have discriminatory rules have eliminated criminal prohibitions in this area for the vast majority of adult couples. Similarly, only six States and the District of Columbia still criminalize fornication.[18] In contrast, when *Loving* was decided in 1967, 16 States still had criminal laws against interracial marriage. *Loving,* 388 U.S. at 6 n.5; *see also id.* at 12 (holding that such laws violate fundamental liberty).

The "consistency of the direction of change" among the States, *Atkins v. Virginia,* 122 S. Ct. 2242, 2249 (2002), is indicative of a strong national consensus reflecting profound judgments about the limits of government's intrusive powers in a civilized society. The principles and sentiments that have led the States to eliminate these laws are yet another objective indicator of the fundamental interests at stake. For example, when the Georgia Supreme Court struck down, under the state constitution, the very law upheld by this Court in *Bowers,* it stated: "We cannot think of any other activity that reasonable persons would rank as more private and more deserving of protection from governmental interference than unforced, private, adult sexual activity." *Powell v. State,* 510 S.E.2d 18, 24 (Ga. 1998); *accord, e.g., Gryczan v. State,* 942 P.2d 112, 122 (Mont. 1997) ("all adults regardless of gender, fully and properly expect that their consen-

sual sexual activities will not be subject to the prying eyes of others or to governmental snooping or regulation"); *Campbell v. Sundquist,* 926 S.W.2d 250, 261 n.9 (Tenn. App. 1996) ("Infringement of such individual rights cannot be tolerated until we tire of democracy and are ready for communism or a despotism"); *Commonwealth v. Bonadio,* 415 A.2d 47, 50 (Pa. 1980) ("regulat[ing] the private [sexual] conduct of consenting adults ... exceeds the valid bounds of the police power"); *State v. Ciuffini,* 395 A.2d 904, 908 (N.J. Super. Ct. App. Div. 1978) (because consensual sodomy law only "serves as an official sanction of certain conceptions of desirable lifestyles, social mores, or individualized beliefs, it is not an appropriate exercise of the police power"). Legislative repeals reflect the same deepseated values. As Governor Jane Hull said when signing the bill repealing Arizona's sodomy law, "At the end of the day, I returned to one of my most basic beliefs about government—It does not belong in our private lives." Howard Fischer, *Hull OKs Repeal of 'Archaic' Sex Laws,* Ariz. Daily Star, May 9, 2001, at A1.

A final confirmation underscoring that America has repudiated a role for government as enforcer of permitted forms of intimacy is the virtually non-existent enforcement today of the laws that still are on the books. In the 13 States that still proscribe sodomy, the laws are almost never enforced in criminal proceedings against

---

lic interactions that have a negative impact on the larger community. This case concerns the narrow but important freedom to choose the expressions of sexual intimacy one shares with another adult partner in private, and does not challenge these other types of State regulation.

[17] Repeal or invalidation of same-sex-only sodomy laws since *Bowers:* 1993 Nev. Stat. ch. 236 (repealing Nev. Rev. Stat. § 201.193); *Jegley,* 80 S.W.3d 332 (Ark.); *Wasson,* 842 S.W.2d 487 (Ky.); *Gryczan,* 942 P.2d 112 (Mont.); *Campbell,* 926 S.W.2d 250 (Tenn.).

Repeal or invalidation of facially evenhanded sodomy laws since *Bowers:* 2001 Ariz. Legis. Serv. 382 (West) (repealing Ariz. Rev. Stat. §§ 13-1411, 13-1412); 1993 D.C. Laws 10–14 (amending D.C. Stat. § 22-3502 to exclude private consensual adult conduct); 1998 R.I. Pub. Laws 24 (amending R.I. Gen. Laws § 11-10-1 to exclude conduct with other persons); *Powell v. State,* 510 S.E.2d 18 (Ga. 1998); *Williams v. State,* No. 98036031/CL-1059, 1998 Extra LEXIS 260 (Md. Cir. Ct. Balt. City Oct. 15, 1998); *Michigan Org. for Human Rights v. Kelley,* No. 88-815820 CZ (Mich. Cir. Ct. Wayne County July 9, 1990); *Doe v. Ventura,* No. MC 01-489, 2001 WL 543734 (Minn. Dist. Ct. May 15, 2001). In Maryland, Michigan, and Minnesota, the States did not appeal the lower court decisions striking down the laws.

One state high court upheld a sodomy law against a constitutional challenge in recent years. *See State v. Smith,* 766 So. 2d 501 (La. 2000).

[18] As with sodomy laws, fornication laws have been struck down as contrary to the right of privacy protected by state constitutions. *See, e.g., In re J.M.,* No. SO2A1432, 2003 WL 79330 (Ga. Jan. 13, 2003) (invalidating Ga. Code Ann. § 16-6-18). The fornication laws remaining in seven jurisdictions criminalize any act of sexual intercourse between unmarried persons. *See* D.C. Stat. Ann. § 22-1602; Idaho Code § 18-6603; Mass. Gen. Laws ch. 272, § 18; *id.* ch. 277 § 39; Minn. Stat. § 609.34; Utah Code Ann. § 76-7-104; Va. Code Ann. § 18.2-344; W. Va. Code § 61-8-3. Seven other States, although purporting in some cases to proscribe "fornication," prohibit a narrower category of sexual intercourse between unmarried persons, such as where it is "open and notorious," 720 Ill. Comp. Stat. 5/11-8; N.D. Cent. Code § 12.1-20-10, or where the parties cohabit or engage in habitual intercourse, Fla. Stat. Ann. § 798.02; Mich. Comp. Laws Ann. § 750.335; Miss. Code Ann. § 97-29-1; N.C. Gen. Stat. § 14-184; S.C. Code Ann. §§ 16-15-60, 16-15-80. *See generally* Richard A. Posner & Katharine B. Silbaugh, *A Guide to America's Sex Laws* 99-102 (1996) (summarizing criminal fornication and cohabitation laws; Arizona's and New Mexico's laws cited

private consensual intimacy. *See Bowers,* 478 U.S. at 198 n.2 (Powell, J., concurring) ("prior to the complaint against respondent Hardwick, there had been no reported decision involving prosecution for private homosexual sodomy under this statute for several decades"); *Morales,* 826 S.W.2d at 203 ("The State concedes that it rarely, if ever, enforces § 21.06"). But as this rare case of prosecution vividly demonstrates, the laws remaining on the books still sometimes strike like lightning, causing the grossest of governmental invasions of privacy through criminal enforcement. The Court should recognize the liberty interests that Petitioners and all Americans have in being free from such invasions.

B. Texas Cannot Justify Section 21.06's Criminal Prohibition of Petitioners' and Other Adults' Private Sexual Intimacy.

Recognition of the fundamental liberty interest at stake here does not end the inquiry, for due regard must also be given to any countervailing interests the State may have and the means used to achieve them. The Court has rejected rigid or mechanical tests in this area. Rather, it has given careful consideration to any weighty governmental interests that stand opposed to a fundamental liberty interest, and has looked closely at the degree and nature of the burden on the liberty interest, before ruling on the ultimate question of constitutionality. *See, e.g., Casey,* 505 U.S. at 849–51 (opinion of Court); *id.* at 871–79 (plurality opinion of O'Connor, Kennedy, and Souter, JJ.); *Troxel,* 530 U.S. at 73 (plurality opinion); *id.* at 101–02 (Kennedy, J., dissenting); *Cruzan,* 497 U.S. at 280–81.

Here, however, there is no countervailing State interest remotely comparable to those weighed by this Court in other recent cases involving fundamental liberties, such as the State's interests in protecting the potentiality of human life, *Casey,* 505 U.S. at 871–79 (opinion of O'Connor, Kennedy, and Souter, JJ.), in protecting the welfare of children, *see Troxel,* 530 U.S. at 73 (plurality opinion), or in protecting and preserving existing human life, *Cruzan,* 497 U.S. at 280–81. *See also Glucksberg,* 521 U.S. at 728–35 (reviewing numerous "important and legitimate" interests furthered by ban on assisted suicide).

In stark contrast to those cases, counsel for Texas has conceded that Section 21.06 furthers

therein were since repealed, *see* 2001 Ariz. Legis. Serv. ch. 382, § 1 (West); 2001 N.M. Laws ch. 32).

no compelling state interest. Pet. App. 76a. The sole justification urged throughout this litigation by the State is the majority's desire to espouse prevailing moral principles and values. *See, e.g.,* State's Br. in Supp. of Reh'g En Banc 16. The State claims no distinct harm or public interest other than a pure statement of moral condemnation. This Court, however, has never allowed fundamental freedoms to be circumscribed simply to enforce majority preferences or moral views concerning deeply personal matters. *See, e.g., Casey,* 505 U.S. at 850–51. Indeed, the discriminatory moral standard employed in the Homosexual Conduct Law is illegitimate under the Equal Protection Clause. *See infra* Point II.

In arriving at the constitutional balance, the Court must also consider that Texas is using "the full power of the criminal law." *Poe,* 367 U.S. at 548 (Harlan, J., dissenting). Section 21.06 empowered the police to inspect closely Lawrence and Garner's intimate behavior in Lawrence's home and haul them off to jail. Although prosecutions may be rare and wholly arbitrary, this case shows that the criminal penalties of such laws are on occasion enforced. Criminal sanctions always impose an extreme burden.

Lawrence and Garner were arrested and held in custody for more than a day—a humiliating invasion of personal dignity. "A custodial arrest exacts an obvious toll on an individual's liberty and privacy, even when the period of custody is relatively brief. . . . And once the period of custody is over, the fact of the arrest is a permanent part of the public record." *Atwater v. City of Lago Vista,* 532 U.S. 318, 364–65 (2001) (O'Connor, J., dissenting). Petitioners now each have a criminal conviction for private consensual sexuality. This "finding of illegality is a burden by itself. In addition to a declaration of illegality and whatever legal consequences flow from that, the finding also poses the threat of reputational harm that is different and additional to any burden posed by other penalties." *BE &K Constr. Co. v. NLRB,* 122 S. Ct. 2390, 2398 (2002).

Moreover, "[t]he Texas courts have held that the crime of homosexual conduct ... is a crime involving moral turpitude." *In re Longstaff,* 538 F. Supp. 589, 592 (N.D. Tex. 1982) (citation omitted), *aff'd,* 716 F.2d 1439 (5th Cir. 1983). Petitioners' convictions therefore disqualify or restrict Lawrence and Garner from practicing

U.S. SUPREME
COURT

BRIEF OF
PETITIONERS

dozens of professions in Texas, from physician to athletic trainer to bus driver.[19] In four states, Lawrence and Garner are considered sex offenders and would have to register as such with law enforcement.[20] And while Section 21.06 does not authorize imprisonment as a penalty, prison terms can be imposed in the 12 other States with sodomy prohibitions, in some cases up to ten years.[21]

Even where there is no direct enforcement, Section 21.06 intrudes into the privacy of innumerable homes by regulating the actual physical details of how consenting adults must conduct their most intimate relationships. As discussed above, *see supra* Point I.A., such an invasion starkly offends the fundamental freedom of adulthood that is at stake. The Homosexual Conduct Law's absolute criminal ban is a harsh burden for all covered by the law.

The balance in this case thus heavily favors individual liberty. Texas's justification—amounting to a mere declaration that the State disapproves of same-sex couples engaging in the conduct at issue, in the absence of any asserted public need or harm—cannot be sufficient. *See Casey*, 505 U.S. at 850–53; *Roe*, 410 U.S. at 162; *Poe*, 367 U.S. at 548 (Harlan, J., dissenting). If it were, the power of the government to restrict liberty interests would be unlimited. The very meaning of fundamental liberty interests is that this kind of decision—affecting the most personal and central aspects of one's life—should be made by the individual, not the State.

While Texas may advocate a majority view about sexual morality, it may not excessively burden the liberty interests of those citizens who

profoundly disagree. *See, e.g., Maher v. Roe*, 432 U.S. 464, 475–76 (1977) ("There is a basic difference between direct state interference with a protected activity and state encouragement of an alternative activity . . . . Constitutional concerns are greatest when the State attempts to impose its will by force of law"). Texas may not impose its particular view through the intrusive force of a criminal law regulating the very forms of physical intimacy that consenting adults may choose in the privacy of their own homes. By claiming the power to impose its own moral code where constitutional guarantees of personal liberty are at stake, Texas is reversing the proper relationship between the government and a free people.

The Court long ago made clear that the Constitution "excludes any general power of the state to standardize its children" because "[t]he child is not the mere creature of the state." *Pierce*, 268 U.S. at 535; *accord Troxel*, 530 U.S. at 68 (plurality opinion). Yet, what Texas claims here is the power to standardize its adult citizens and render them mere creatures of the State by compelling conformity in the most private and intimate personal matters. By vote of the majority, one particular view of how to conduct one's most private relationships is imposed on all. But "fundamental rights may not be submitted to vote; they depend on the outcome of no election." *Barnette*, 319 U.S. at 638. The precepts advocated by Texas, aimed at "submerg[ing] the individual," are "wholly different from those upon which our institutions rest." *Meyer*, 262 U.S. at 402. Section 21.06 unjustifiably infringes the personal liberty and privacy guaranteed by the Constitution and should be struck down.

C. *Bowers* Should Not Block Recognition and Enforcement of These Fundamental Interests.

Vindication of Petitioners' constitutionally protected liberty interests should not be blocked by continued adherence to *Bowers*. In light of the fundamental interests at stake and the consistent and profound legal, political, and social developments since *Bowers*, principles of *stare decisis* do not bar the Court's reconsideration of that decision.

Stare decisis is a "principle of policy," not an "inexorable command." *Seminole Tribe of Fla. v. Florida*, 517 U.S. 44, 63 (1996) (quotation marks omitted); *see also, e.g., Agostini v. Felton*, 521 U.S. 203, 235–36 (1997) (same). That is "particularly

---

19 Tex. Occ. Code § 164.051(a)(2)(B) (physician); *id.* § 301.409(a)(1)(B) (registered nurse); *id.* § 401.453(a) (speech-language pathologist); *id.* § 451.251(a)(1) (athletic trainer); *id.* § 1053.252(2) (interior designer); *id.* § 2001.102 (bingo licensee); Tex. Transp. Code § 512.022(f) (school bus driver); Tex. Alco. Bev. Code § 11.46(a)(3) (liquor sales).

20 *See* Idaho Code § 18-8304; La. Rev. Stat. Ann. § 15:541; Miss. Code Ann. § 45-33-23; S.C. Code Ann. § 23-3-430.

21 *See* Ala. Code §§ 13A-6-60(2), 13A-5-7(a)(1) (one year); Fla. Stat. Ann. §§ 800.02, 775.082(4)(b) (60 days); Idaho Code § 18-6605 (five years); Kan. Stat. Ann. §§ 21-3505, 21-4502(1)(b) (six months); La. Rev. Stat. Ann. 14:89 (five years); Miss. Code Ann. 97-29-59 (ten years); Mo. Rev. Stat. §§ 566.090, 558.011 (one year); N.C. Gen. Stat. §§ 14-177, 15A-1340.17 (one year); Okla. Stat. tit. 21, § 886, *amended by* 2002 Okla. Sess. Law Serv. ch. 460, § 8 (West) (ten years); S.C. Code Ann. § 16-15-120 (five years); Utah Code Ann. §§ 76-5-403(1), 76-3-204(2) (6 months); Va. Code Ann. §§ 18.2-361, 18.2-10 (five years).

true in constitutional cases, because in such cases correction through legislative action is practically impossible." *Seminole Tribe,* 517 U.S. at 63 (quotation marks omitted). For these reasons, the Court has not hesitated to overrule earlier constitutional decisions that have been recognized as erroneous. *See, e.g., Payne v. Tennessee,* 501 U.S. 808, 828 & n.1 (1991) (surveying cases); Lewis F. Powell, Jr., *Stare Decisis and Judicial Restraint,* 1991 J. S. Ct. Hist. 13 (same).

Where, as here, a prior decision has erroneously *denied* a fundamental constitutional right of citizens over and against the State and no countervailing rights of other individuals are at stake, there is a compelling need to correct the error. *See, e.g., Barnette,* 319 U.S. at 630–42 (overruling *Minersville Sch. Dist. v. Gobitis,* 310 U.S. 586 [1940]); *see also, e.g., Brown v. Board of Educ.,* 347 U.S. 483, 494–95 (1954) (overruling *Plessy v. Ferguson,* 163 U.S. 537 [1896]). That is especially true here, because laws of the kind upheld by *Bowers*—whether facially evenhanded or discriminatory—are used to legitimize widespread discrimination against gay and lesbian Americans. *See infra* Point II.B.1. Indeed, the holding of *Bowers* itself has been cited as justifying state-sponsored discrimination. *See, e.g., Padula v. Webster,* 822 F.2d 97, 103 (D.C. Cir. 1987) ("If the Court [in *Bowers*] was unwilling to object to state laws that criminalize the behavior that defines the class, it is hardly open ... to conclude that state sponsored discrimination against the class is invidious"); *Romer,* 517 U.S. at 641 (Scalia, J., dissenting) (same).

In this respect *Bowers* is fundamentally different from decisions like *Roe* or *Miranda v. Arizona,* 384 U.S. 436 (1966), which recognized individual rights that then became incorporated into the very fabric of our society. *See Casey,* 505 U.S. at 854; *Dickerson v. United States,* 530 U.S. 428, 443 (2000). Indeed, there are no considerations like those identified in *Casey* or other *stare decisis* cases that might favor continued adherence to *Bowers.*

Unlike the right recognized in *Roe* and its progeny, there is no pattern of individuals who "have relied reasonably on the [*Bowers*] rule's continued application" to their advantage, *Casey,* 505 U.S. at 855; *see also, e.g., Adarand Constructors, Inc. v. Pena,* 515 U.S. 200, 233 (1995). Individuals have only been harmed by the *Bowers* decision. Nor has *Bowers* become

"part of our national culture," *Dickerson,* 530 U.S. at 443. Just the opposite is true. Developments in the law and in the facts—or in society's perception of the facts, *see Casey,* 505 U.S. at 863—have steadily eroded any support for *Bowers.* Since *Bowers,* the Nation has continued to reject the extreme intrusion into the realm of personal privacy approved in that case, so that now three-fourths of the States have repealed or invalidated such laws—including the very law upheld by *Bowers. See supra* Point I.A.3.

Also since *Bowers,* the Nation has steadily moved toward rejecting second-class-citizen status for gay and lesbian Americans. In *Romer,* this Court held that venerable equal protection principles protect gay and lesbian Americans against invidious discrimination. Thirteen States and the District of Columbia, plus countless municipalities—including at least four in Texas—have now added sexual orientation to laws barring discrimination in housing, employment, public accommodations, and other areas.[22] More than half the States now have enhanced penalties for hate crimes motivated by the victim's sexual orientation.[23] And the reality of gay and lesbian couples and families with children has been increasingly recognized by the law and by society at large. *See supra* at 17–19. This is thus a case in which the Court must respond to basic facts and constitutional principles that the country has "come to understand already, but which the Court of an earlier day ... had not been able to perceive." *Casey,* 505 U.S. at 863; *see also, e.g., Vasquez v. Hillery,* 474 U.S. 254, 266 (1986) (*stare decisis* must give way when necessary "to bring [the Court's] opinions into agreement with experience and with facts newly ascertained") (quotation marks omitted).

Bowers is an isolated decision that, like the cases overturned in *Payne,* was "decided by the

[22] 1999 Cal. Legis. Serv. ch. 592 (West); 1991 Conn. Legis. Serv. 91-58 (West); Human Rights Act of 1977, D.C. Laws 2-38; 1991 Haw. Sess. Laws Act 2; 2001 Md. Laws ch. 340; 1989 Mass. Legis. Serv. ch. 516 (West); 1993 Minn. Sess. Law Serv. ch. 22 (West); 1999 Nev. Stat. ch. 410; 1997 N.H. Laws ch. 108; 1991 N.J. Sess. Law Serv. ch. 519 (West); 2002 N.Y. Laws ch. 2; 1995 R.I. Pub. Laws ch. 95-32; 1992 Vt. Acts & Resolves 135; 1981 Wis. Laws ch. 112; Austin, Tex., City Code, vol. I, tit. VII; Dallas, Tex., Mun. Ordinance 24927 (May 8, 2002); Fort Worth, Tex., Code of Ordinances ch. 17, art. III; Houston, Tex., City Code ch. 2, tit. XIV.

[23] *See* Nat'l Gay and Lesbian Task Force, *Hate Crime Laws in the U.S., available at* http://www.ngltf.org/downloads/hate-crimeslawsmap.pdf (accessed Jan. 14, 2003).

narrowest of margins, over spirited dissents challenging [its] basic underpinnings." *Payne*, 501 U.S. at 828–29. Far from being "an essential feature of our legal tradition," *Mitchell v. United States*, 526 U.S. 314, 330 (1999), *Bowers* stands today as "a doctrinal anachronism discounted by society," *Casey*, 505 U.S. at 855. Many of the bedrock principles of contemporary constitutional law were announced in cases overruling contrary precedent—whether after only a few intervening years, or following decades of legal, political, and social development. *See, e.g., Barnette*, 319 U.S. at 630; *Brown*, 347 U.S. at 494–95; *Gitlow v. New York*, 268 U.S. 652, 666 (1925); *Malloy v. Hogan*, 378 U.S. 1, 4–6 (1964). As in those cases, the Court "cannot turn the clock back." *Brown*, 347 U.S. at 492–93. It accordingly should overturn *Bowers* and protect the fundamental liberty interests of Petitioners.

II. Section 21.06 Discriminates Without Any Legitimate and Rational Basis, Contrary to the Guarantee of Equal Protection.

Texas's Homosexual Conduct Law violates the Fourteenth Amendment for the additional reason that it "singl[es] out a certain class of citizens for disfavored legal status," *Romer*, 517 U.S. at 633, in violation of the most basic requirements of the Equal Protection Clause. The statute directly conflicts with the Constitution's "commitment to the law's neutrality." *Id.* at 623. It fails equal protection scrutiny even under the deferential "rational basis" standard.[24] And this discriminatory classification is "embodied in a criminal statute … where the power of the State weighs most heavily," a context in which the Court "must be especially sensitive to the policies of the Equal Protection Clause." *McLaughlin v. Florida*, 379 U.S. 184, 192 (1964).

By its terms, Section 21.06 treats the *same* consensual sexual behavior differently depending on *who* the participants are. The behaviors labeled "deviate sexual intercourse" by Texas are widely practiced by heterosexual as well as gay adults.[25] But the statute makes this common conduct illegal only for same-sex couples and not for different-sex ones. Tex. Pen. Code § 21.06. And the State offers only a tautological, illegitimate, and irrational purported justification for such discrimination.

The group targeted and harmed by the Homosexual Conduct Law is, of course, gay people. Gay people have a same-sex sexual orientation and heterosexuals have a different-sex

one. *See, e.g.,* John C. Gonsiorek & James D. Weinrich, *The Definition and Scope of Sexual Orientation, in Homosexuality: Research Implications for Public Policy* 1 (J. Gonsiorek & J. Weinrich eds., 1991) ("sexual orientation is erotic and/or affectional disposition to the same and/or opposite sex"); *cf. Romer*, 517 U.S. at 624, 626–31 (in civil rights laws, "sexual orientation" is defined by an individual's "choice of sexual partners" or "heterosexuality, homosexuality or bisexuality"). The Homosexual Conduct Law overtly uses that defining characteristic to set up its disparate treatment. Section 21.06 "prohibit[s] lesbians and gay men from engaging in the same conduct in which heterosexuals may legally engage." *Morales*, 826 S.W.2d at 204; *see also Wasson*, 842 S.W.2d at 502 (where same-sex but not different-sex sodomy is criminalized, "[s]exual preference, and not the act committed, determines criminality, and is being punished").

A straightforward application of the rational basis test shows that this law and Texas's attempted justification for it cannot satisfy the requirement that every classification must at least "bear a rational relationship to an independent and legitimate legislative end." *Romer*, 517 U.S. at 633. When broader realities and history are considered, as this Court appropriately does in any equal protection case, the constitutional violation is only magnified. The Homosexual Conduct Law and its badge of criminality function to make gay people unequal in myriad spheres of everyday life and continue an ignominious history of discrimination based on sexual orientation. Ultimately, the equal protection and liberty concerns in this case reinforce one

---

[24] Heightened equal protection scrutiny is appropriate for laws like Section 21.06 that use a sexual-orientation-based classification. It is also appropriate where, as here, the law employs a gender-based classification to discriminate against gay people. The classification in this law, however, does not even have a legitimate and rational basis.

Of course, if the Court agrees with Petitioners that the challenged law invades a fundamental liberty, analysis of the law's discriminatory classification would be as stringent as the analysis outlined in Point I. *See, e.g., Dunn v. Blumstein*, 405 U.S. 330, 337 (1972). In this Point II, Petitioners urge a distinct constitutional violation that does not depend on the Court finding that a fundamental liberty is at stake.

[25] *See, e.g.,* Edward O. Laumann *et al., The Social Organization of Sexuality* 98–99 (1994) (comprehensive study by University of Chicago researchers of sexual practices of American adults, finding that approximately 79% of all men and 73% of all women had engaged in oral sex, and 26% of all men and 20% of all women had engaged in anal sex).

another, and further underscore that this unequal law and its broad harms are intolerable in this country.

A. Section 21.06's Classification Is Not Rationally Related to Any Legitimate Purpose and Serves Only the Illegitimate Purpose of Disadvantaging One Group.

"[C]onventional and venerable" principles require that legislative discrimination must, at a minimum, "bear a rational relationship to an independent and legitimate legislative end." *Romer*, 517 U.S. at 633, 635; *see also, e.g., Cleburne*, 473 U.S. at 446; *Western & S. Life Ins. Co. v. State Bd. of Equalization*, 451 U.S. 648, 668 (1981). This test is deferential, but meaningful.

> [E]ven in the ordinary equal protection case ... , [the Court] insist[s] on knowing the relation between the classification adopted and the object to be attained. The search for the link between classification and objective gives substance to the Equal Protection Clause; it provides guidance and discipline for the legislature, which is entitled to know what sort of laws it can pass; and it marks the outer limits of [the judiciary's] own authority.

Romer, 517 U.S. at 632.

Under the Equal Protection Clause, the *classification*—the different treatment of different people—is what must be justified. *See Board of Trustees of the Univ. of Ala. v. Garrett*, 531 U.S. 356, 366–67 (2001) (rational basis review searches for "distinguishing characteristics" between the two groups that are "relevant to interests the State has the authority to implement") (quotation marks omitted); *Rinaldi v. Yeager*, 384 U.S. 305, 308–09 (1966) (equal protection "imposes a requirement of some rationality in the nature of the class singled out"); *McLaughlin*, 379 U.S. at 191 ("courts must reach and determine the question whether the classifications drawn in a statute are reasonable in light of its purpose—… whether there is an arbitrary or invidious discrimination between those classes covered … and those excluded"). The classification must be rationally connected to an independent and permissible government objective to "ensure that classifications are not drawn for the purpose of disadvantaging the group burdened by the law." *Romer*, 517 U.S. at 633.

Section 21.06 fails that essential test. As the Supreme Court of Kentucky observed in striking down that State's discriminatory consensual sodomy law on state equal protection grounds:

> In the final analysis we can attribute no legislative purpose to this statute except to single out homosexuals for different treatment for indulging their sexual preference by engaging in the same activity heterosexuals are now at liberty to perform . . . . The question is whether a society that no longer criminalizes adultery, fornication, or deviate sexual intercourse between heterosexuals, has a rational basis to single out homosexual acts for different treatment.

Wasson, 842 S.W.2d at 501. That court found no "rational basis for different treatment," and emphasized that "[w]e need not sympathize, agree with, or even understand the sexual preference of homosexuals in order to recognize their right to equal treatment before the bar of criminal justice." *Id.; accord Jegley*, 80 S.W.3d at 353 ("[w]e echo Kentucky in concluding that 'we can attribute no legislative purpose to this statute except to single out homosexuals'"). That conclusion applies with equal force to the identical classification employed by Texas's law.

When Texas enacted Section 21.06 in the early 1970s, there was no "practical necessity" to draw a classification among its residents with regard to the subject matter of consensual, adult oral and anal sex. *Cf. Romer*, 517 U.S. at 631. For decades, the State had included an evenhanded prohibition on those acts within its criminal code. When the legislature determined that its old law was unduly intrusive, it had the obvious choice of repealing it for *all* its citizens—as three-fourths of the States have done. *See supra* at 23 & note 17. Instead, it decided to single out same-sex couples for intrusive regulation and condemnation, and to free all heterosexual couples to make their own choices about particular forms of intimacy.

Throughout this litigation, the only justification that Texas has offered for this discriminatory classification is the moral judgment of the majority of its electorate. The State asserts that its "electorate evidently continues to believe" that the discriminatory line drawn by the Homosexual Conduct Law is desirable because it expresses the majority's moral views. Pet. Opp. 18.

The Homosexual Conduct Law's classification fails rational basis analysis, for several reasons. *First*, the State's position amounts to no "independent … legislative end" at all. *Cf. Romer*, 517 U.S. at 633. This "justification" merely restates that Texas believes in and wants to have this criminal law. The Equal Protection

Clause requires that the State's classification serve a distinct legislative end—an objective or purpose—independent of the classification itself. There must be a "link between classification and objective," *id.* at 632, or "some relation between the classification and the purpose it serve[s]," *id.* at 633. The test would be meaningless—a mere rubberstamp for discrimination—unless the purpose is independent of the classification. But the "justification" offered by Texas is circular and not an independent objective served. In the words of the dissenters below, "[t]he contention that the same conduct is moral for some but not for others merely repeats, rather than legitimizes, the Legislature's unconstitutional edict." Pet. App. 44a.

The State's approach gives *carte blanche* to presumed majority sentiment, and leaves those targeted by a discriminatory law without recourse. If majority moral or value judgments were enough to answer an equal protection challenge, the amendment struck down in *Romer* would have survived, because the votes of a majority of Coloradans clearly signaled that including gay people within civil rights protections was antithetical to their values. Instead, this Court recognized that Amendment 2—like Section 21.06 here—was a "classification of persons undertaken for its own sake, something the Equal Protection Clause does not permit." 517 U.S. at 635. Government "may not avoid the strictures of that Clause by deferring to the wishes or objections ... of the body politic." *Cleburne*, 473 U.S. at 448.

Second, even if Texas's objective could somehow be characterized as independent of the classification, mere negative views about the disfavored group—"moral" or otherwise—are not a legitimate basis for legal discrimination. *Cleburne*, 473 U.S. at 448 ("mere negative attitudes ... unsubstantiated by factors which are properly cognizable [by government] are not permissible bases" for discriminatory legal rules). This Court has many times repeated the core principle of rejecting bias, however characterized, in law: Legal distinctions may not give effect to the majority's desire to condemn an unpopular group, *see Moreno*, 413 U.S. at 534, the negative reactions of neighbors, *see Cleburne*, 473 U.S. at 448, the fears of people who are different, *see id.*, a reaction of discomfort toward a minority, *see O'Connor v. Donaldson*, 422 U.S. 563, 575 (1975); *Cleburne*,

473 U.S. at 448–49, private prejudice, *Palmore v. Sidoti*, 466 U.S. 429, 433 (1984), or any other manifestation of unfounded animosity toward one group, *Romer*, 517 U.S. at 633–35. History unquestionably teaches that the moral views of a given time, just like fears, dislikes, and blatant prejudices, often reflect prevailing negative attitudes about different groups of people in society. *Cf. Whitney v. California*, 274 U.S. 357, 376 (1927) (Brandeis, J., concurring) ("Men feared witches and burnt women"). Indeed, negative attitudes toward a group can always be recast in terms of a discriminatory moral code. Using a moral lens to describe negative attitudes about a group that are not tied to any distinct, objective and permissible factors cannot cleanse those bare negative attitudes of their illegitimacy in government decisionmaking.

Texas's approach of dictating that same-sex couples are "more 'immoral and unacceptable,'" Pet. Opp. 18, than heterosexual couples under the very same circumstances—if they choose any of the behaviors defined as "deviate sexual intercourse"—must be rejected as impermissible. *Neutral, evenhanded* laws that truly restrict all persons in the same way could, if there were no fundamental interests at stake, be justified by a moral position. Here, however, Texas impermissibly attempts to impose a *discriminatory* moral code.[26] The State's law and its proffered justification embody a bald preference for those with the most common sexual orientation and dislike of a smaller group who are different. Texas simply wants to judge those with a same-sex sexual orientation more harshly for the same behavior.[27]

The Constitution and this Court's precedents forbid that. In *Palmore*, a mother lost custody of her child because her interracial "'life-style'" was

---

[26] *See* Pet. App. 70a–71a (Anderson, J., dissenting) ("[E]qual protection doctrine does not prevent the majority from enacting laws based on its substantive value choices. Equal protection simply requires that the majority apply its values evenhandedly. . . . The constitutional requirement of evenhandedness advances the political legitimacy of majority rule by safeguarding minorities from majoritarian oppression").

[27] This conclusion is reinforced by the fact that Texas's 1973 enactment discriminates against gay people whereas traditional morality did not. "[T]he practice of deviate sexual intercourse violates traditional morality. But so does the same act between heterosexuals, which activity is decriminalized. . . . The issue here is ... whether [sexual activity traditionally viewed as immoral] can be punished solely on the basis of sexual preference." *Jegley*, 80 S.W.3d at 352 (quotation marks omitted).

"'unacceptable … to society.'" 466 U.S. at 431 (quoting investigator's report). But this Court emphatically held that such negative views have no place in the law. Id. at 433 ("Private biases may be outside the reach of the law, but the law cannot, directly or indirectly, give them effect"). Likewise, unequal treatment may not be based on archaic and unfounded negative attitudes toward a group, whether grounded in morality, religious conviction, or "nature." In *Mississippi University for Women v. Hogan*, 458 U.S. 718 (1982), for example, the Court stressed the need to set aside archaic ideas about gender, such as that women are "innately inferior" or that unique "'moral and social problems'" would arise if women tended bar or otherwise enjoyed equal opportunities. *Id.* at 725 & n.10.

Similarly, negative attitudes toward those with a particular personal characteristic—even where advanced with the toned down patina of morality—are also not a legitimate justification for discrimination under rational basis scrutiny. In *Romer*, the Court refused to endorse the dissent's position that Amendment 2's anti-gay classification could be sustained as an attempt "to preserve traditional sexual mores," *Romer*, 517 U.S. at 636 (Scalia, J., dissenting). In *Moreno*, faced with a regulation that targeted the morally disfavored group of "hippies," the Court emphasized that "if the constitutional conception of 'equal protection of the laws' means anything, it must at the very least mean that a bare … desire to harm a politically unpopular group cannot constitute a *legitimate* governmental interest." *Moreno*, 413 U.S. at 534. Instead, different treatment must be supported by "reference to [some independent] considerations in the public interest." *Id.* (alteration in original). Whether termed a moral judgment, fear, discomfort, or bias, "mere negative attitudes" about one subset of the diverse American population cannot justify distinctions in legal treatment. *See Cleburne*, 473 U.S. at 448.

Third, there is no other legitimate justification that can save this law. The distinction drawn by the Homosexual Conduct Law does not rationally further any permissible goal of the State. There are no valid concerns of the government here that correlate with sexual orientation, which is a deeply rooted personal characteristic that we all have. Variation among heterosexuals, homosexuals, and bisexuals has no "relevan[cy]" to interests the State has the authority to imple-

ment," *Garrett*, 531 U.S. at 366, or to "factors which are properly cognizable," *Cleburne*, 473 U.S. at 448, in writing the criminal law. Thus, Section 21.06's linedrawing does not turn on or respond to any differences in maturity or age, in intent, or in the specifics of the actors' relationship, other than its same-sex or different-sex nature. It does not incorporate the use of force, a public location, or a commercial context in its elements, to address those types of important concerns. Indeed, Texas has other laws that criminalize sexual conduct that is non-consensual, or public, or commercial, or with a minor. *See supra* at 6. Likewise, the law's discriminatory regulation of "deviate sexual intercourse" is unrelated to any interest in reproduction, for oral and anal sex are obviously not methods of reproduction for any couple.

Where government itself offers a reason that is illegitimate, as Texas has done here, or other factors indicate that the law rests on negative attitudes, the Court has carefully assessed any additional, purportedly rational and legitimate basis for challenged differential treatment. *See Cleburne*, 473 U.S. at 449 (careful assessment, and ultimate rejection, of other proffered reasons, where negative attitudes were clearly one basis for legal discrimination); *Moreno*, 413 U.S. at 535–38 (same). In such rational basis cases, the Court has not tried to supply new, "conceivable" reasons to support the classification. *See also Romer*, 517 U.S. at 635. It is, after all, only "*absent some reason to infer antipathy*" that the "Constitution presumes that … even improvident decisions will eventually be rectified by the democratic process and that judicial intervention is generally unwarranted." *Vance v. Bradley* 440 U.S. 93, 97 (1979) (emphasis added). Here, Texas offers nothing more than the majority's negative moral judgment to support its discrimination, and that should end the matter with a ruling of unconstitutionality.

This 1970s classification is "divorced from any factual context from which [the Court] could discern a relationship to legitimate state interests." *Romer*, 517 U.S. at 635. It is solely an effort to mark a difference in status, to send a message in the criminal law that one group is condemned by the majority. This impermissible and irrational double standard must be removed from Texas's criminal code.

U.S. SUPREME
COURT

BRIEF OF
PETITIONERS

B. The Broader Realities Reinforce This Law's Affront to Core Principles of Equal Protection.

Additional considerations confirm the violation of equal protection here. First, the Homosexual Conduct Law does not just discriminate against gay and lesbian Texans in their private intimate relations, but brands gay persons as second-class citizens and legitimizes discrimination against them in all aspects of life. Second, the discrimination worked by this law reflects and reinforces a century-long history of discrimination against gay Americans. The real-world context and history of discrimination further expose the law's illegitimacy. *See Romer,* 517 U.S. at 623–31 (considering in detail the functioning and historical background of challenged enactment); *Moreno,* 413 U.S. at 537 (considering "practical effect" of classification); *Eisenstadt,* 405 U.S. at 447–52 (considering social and legal backdrop in finding equal protection violation under rational basis standard). Where a law "circumscribe[s] a class of persons characterized by some unpopular trait or affiliation," there is a "special likelihood of bias on the part of the ruling majority." *N.Y. Trans. Auth. v. Beazer,* 440 U.S. 568, 593 (1979).

1. The Homosexual Conduct Law Brands Gay Persons as Second-Class Citizens and Licenses Wide-Ranging Discrimination Against Them.

On the surface, the Homosexual Conduct Law may appear to discriminate against gay men and lesbians in only one sphere of life—albeit a vitally important one, *see supra* Point I—by criminalizing the sexual intimacy of same-sex adult couples but not the very same conduct engaged in by different-sex couples. In reality, the scope of the discrimination is much broader. Today, sodomy laws—even facially even-handed sodomy laws—are widely understood to brand gay citizens as criminals by virtue of their sexual orientation, and are thus used to legitimate across-the-board discrimination. Texas's enactment of a facially discriminatory law formalizes that pejorative classification of lesbians and gay men as second-class citizens.

Historically, the vast majority of consensual sodomy laws have not differentiated between same-sex and different-sex couples, and nine of the 13 sodomy laws still on the books today retain that traditional characteristic of being facially evenhanded. *See supra* at 6 & note 5, 21–22. In recent eventimes, however, facially non-discriminatory laws have been understood as targeting gay men and lesbians rather than heterosexual couples who engage in identical forms of private sexual intimacy covered by the laws. This contemporary understanding of these laws was reflected in—and reinforced by—the Court's reasoning in *Bowers,* which read Georgia's facially *neutral* law as reflecting "the presumed belief of a majority of the electorate in Georgia that *homosexual* sodomy is immoral and unacceptable." 478 U.S. at 196 (emphasis added). *See generally* Nan D. Hunter, *Life After Hardwick,* 27 Harv. C.R.-C.L. L. Rev. 531, 542 (1992).

Thus, in recent decades, the existence of facially nondiscriminatory sodomy laws—indeed, the mere power of state legislatures to pass such laws, whether or not that power is exercised—has been used to justify myriad forms of discrimination against gay and lesbian Americans as presumptive criminals. For example, sodomy laws are often invoked to deny or restrict gay parents' custody of or visitation with their own children,[28] to deny public employment to gay people,[29] and to block protection of gay citizens under hate-crime legislation.[30]

---

[28] *See, e.g., Ex Parte D.W.W.,* 717 So. 2d 793, 796 (Ala. 1998) (affirming imposition of severe visitation restrictions on lesbian mother, reasoning, "the conduct inherent in lesbianism is illegal in Alabama"); *Bottoms v. Bottoms,* 457 S.E.2d 102, 108 (Va. 1995) (removing child from lesbian mother and giving custody to child's grandmother, concluding, "[c]onduct inherent in lesbianism is punishable as a Class 6 felony in the Commonwealth, Code § 18.2-361; thus, that conduct is another important consideration in determining custody"); *see also Ex parte H.H.,* 830 So. 2d 21, 35 (Ala. 2002) (Moore, C.J., specially concurring) ("disfavoring practicing homosexuals in custody matters promotes the general welfare of the people of our State in accordance with our law").

[29] *See, e.g., Shahar v. Bowers,* 114 F.3d 1097, 1105 & n.17 (11th Cir. 1997); *see also Walls v. City of Petersburg,* 895 F.2d 188, 193 (4th Cir. 1990) (upholding public employment application question about homosexual relations "because the *Bowers* decision is controlling").

[30] An amendment to include "sexual orientation" in the Utah hate crime bill was defeated after a representative referred to Utah's sodomy law, stating that the "effect of granting special protection under [the hate crime act] to homosexuals would be contradictory under Utah law." *See* Terry S. Kogan, *Legislative Violence Against Lesbians and Gay Men,* 1994 Utah L. Rev. 209, 222 (quotation marks omitted). Similarly, a hate crime bill in North Carolina covering sexual orientation was rejected in 2000 after the House heard testimony about the illegality of sodomy. People for the Am. Way Found., *Hostile Climate: Report on Anti-Gay Activity* 257 (2000).

Indeed, the dissent in *Romer* argued that the Court's holding in *Bowers* alone was sufficient justification for the sweeping discrimination against gay citizens worked by Colorado Amendment 2, *Romer*, 517 U.S. at 640–43 (Scalia, J., dissenting)—even though Colorado's former sodomy law had applied to all and had been repealed years before, *see* 1971 Colo. Sess. Laws ch. 121.

Texas has gone further, abandoning any pretense of nondiscriminatory legislation in this area by enacting a law that facially discriminates against gay and lesbian couples. By introducing that express classification into the criminal law, Texas has placed its imprimatur on discrimination based on sexual orientation. That has had far-reaching implications for gay citizens in virtually every area of their lives. As the State stipulated in an earlier challenge to Section 21.06, the law "brands lesbians and gay men as criminals and thereby legally sanctions discrimination against them in a variety of ways unrelated to the criminal law," including "in the context of employment, family issues, and housing." *Morales*, 826 S.W.2d at 202–03; *see also Jegley*, 80 S.W.3d at 343 (under same-sex-only sodomy laws, gay people "suffer the brand of criminal impressed upon them by a[n] ... unconstitutional law").

The Homosexual Conduct Law and similar statutes in other States have been routinely invoked to limit the custody or visitation that fit, gay parents would otherwise have with their own children.[31] Likewise, this law is cited as a basis for preventing lesbians and gay men from serving as foster parents, simply because of their presumed "criminal status" and wholly apart from any inquiry into the best interests of children awaiting a home. *See, e.g.,* Polly Hughes, *Bill Would Ban Gay Texans From Adopting Children*, Hous.

Chron., Dec. 11, 1998, at A38 (reporting on adoption and foster-care policies). Section 21.06 and other discriminatory consensual sodomy offenses have been used to interfere with equal employment opportunities for lesbians and gay men. *England*, 846 S.W.2d at 958; *Childers v. Dallas Police Dep't*, 513 F. Supp. 134, 144, 147–48 (N.D. Tex. 1981) (upholding denial of employment to gay man), *aff'd*, 669 F.2d 732 (5th Cir. 1982); *Baker*, 553 F. Supp. at 1130, 1147. These laws are also used to block the adoption of civil rights ordinances that would prohibit sexual orientation discrimination in employment and other core aspects of civil society.[32] The Homosexual Conduct Law has even been cited in arguments for imposing the death penalty on a gay defendant, *Burdine v. Johnson*, 66 F. Supp. 2d 854, 857 (S.D. Tex. 1999), *aff'd*, 262 F.3d 336 (5th Cir. 2001) (*en banc*), *cert. denied*, 122 S. Ct. 2347 (2002). In these many ways and others, the Homosexual Conduct Law is functioning as a legal reference point that endorses gay inequality.

Thus, even in the absence of actual arrest and prosecution, the Homosexual Conduct Law labels gay men and lesbians as criminals and legitimates discrimination against them on that basis.[33] Classification of gay Texans as second-class citizens is indeed the primary function of this law in society, as evidenced by the rarity of direct criminal enforcement. Texas makes no pretense of vigorously enforcing this law or of actually preventing any private, consensual adult sexual behavior. *Morales*, 826 S.W.2d at 203 ("The State concedes that it rarely, if ever, enforces § 21.06"). Only rare couples who are caught through some extremely unlucky series of events, like Lawrence and Garner in this case, ever directly suffer criminal prosecution and punishment for their discreet intimacy. *Model Penal Code* § 213.2 cmt. 2 ("To the extent ... that laws against deviate sexual behavior are enforced

---

[31] *See, e.g., Jegley*, 80 S.W.3d at 343 (observing that Arkansas sodomy statute had been used in harmful ways "outside the criminal context," including in prior case denying lesbian custody of her children); *see also* Jo Ann Zuniga, *Gay Parents Are Fighting Back Against Blackmail, Court Bias*, Hous. Chron., June 27, 1994, at A11 (reporting that common tactic of vilifying gay parents in custody battle is "give[n] ... teeth [by] Section 21.06"); *J.P. v. P.W.*, 772 S.W.2d 786, 792 (Mo. Ct. App. 1989) (restricting gay father's visitation rights, in part because a "statute of this state declares that deviate sexual intercourse with another person of the same sex is illegal. § 566.090.1"). *See generally* Diana Hassel, *The Use of Criminal Sodomy Laws in Civil Litigation*, 79 Tex. L. Rev. 813 (2001).

[32] *See, e.g.,* Dianna Hunt, *Plan to Ban Anti-Gay Bias in Fort*

Worth Dies, Dallas Morning News, Jan. 20, 1999, at 32A (local anti-discrimination measure in Texas abandoned after several members of town council expressed desire to wait until status of state's sodomy law was resolved); see also Arthur S. Leonard, *Legislative Notes*, 1998 Lesbian/Gay L. Notes 101, 115 (Kansas sodomy law cited in support of halting Topeka Human Rights Commission from investigating anti-gay discrimination).

[33] In Texas, calling someone a "homosexual" or using epithets that mean the same is slanderous *per se* because of the implication that he or she has violated the Homosexual Conduct Law. *Thomas v. Bynum*, No. 04-02-00036-CV, 2002 WL 31829509, at *2 (Tex. App. Dec. 18, 2002); *Head v. Newton*, 596 S.W.2d 209, 210 (Tex. App. 1980).

against private conduct between consenting adults, the result is episodic and capricious selection of an infinitesimal fraction of offenders for severe punishment"). The branding function of the Homosexual Conduct Law and the civil harms that follow from it forcefully underscore that the law violates equal protection. It "has the peculiar property of imposing a broad and undifferentiated disability on a single named group," *Romer,* 517 U.S. at 632, without rational and legitimate justification.

2. The Homosexual Conduct Law Reflects and Helps Fuel a Continuing History of Discrimination Against Gay Americans.

The Homosexual Conduct Law is only one manifestation of a history of irrational anti-gay discrimination.[34] Although our Nation has no legal tradition making the criminality of private sexuality turn on whether a couple is homosexual or heterosexual, *see supra* at 21–22, the laws of this Nation have reflected and played a role in virulent anti-gay discrimination over the last century. In enforcing the Equal Protection Clause today, this history informs the Court's assessment of whether a legal classification that discriminates against those with a same-sex sexual orientation rests on irrational bias. *See Vance,* 440 U.S. at 97 (Court is attuned to "some reason to infer antipathy"); *see also, e.g., Romer,* 517 U.S. at 624–31.

Anti-gay discrimination was long justified by the false view that gay individuals were "sick." Until 1973, the year Section 21.06 was passed, homosexuality was incorrectly classified as a mental disease. *See supra* note 10; *see also Boutilier v. INS,* 387 U.S. 118 (1967) (holding that "psychopathic personality" exclusion in immigration law applied to homosexual persons). Deeming them to be "sex deviants," States involuntarily committed gay men and lesbians to mental institutions under extremely inhumane conditions. *See, e.g.,* James A. Garland, *The Low Road to Violence: Governmental Discrimination as a Catalyst for Pandemic Hate Crime,* 10 L. & Sexuality 1, 75–76 (2001). "Treatments" to "cure" homosexuality were often sadistically cruel. *See, e.g.,* Jonathan N. Katz, *Gay/Lesbian Almanac* 156 (1983) (describing "treatment" involving "repeated searing with a hot iron or chemical of [the] 'pervert' patient's loins"); Jonathan N. Katz, *Gay American History: Lesbians and Gay Men in the U.S.A.* 129–208 (rev. ed. 1992). Even today, discredited "therapies" to "change" the very sexual

orientation of gay adults continue this destructive pathologizing of gay citizens.[35]

The Homosexual Conduct Law is a remnant of a historical pattern of repressive law enforcement measures that have reinforced an outcast status for gay citizens. In the past, state laws authorized the arrest of individuals simply for "appearing" to be gay or lesbian, and the closure of businesses simply for serving gay patrons. *See, e.g., One Eleven Wines & Liquors, Inc. v. Division of Alcohol Beverage Control,* 235 A.2d 12, 14 (N.J. 1967) (reviewing and rejecting agency policy of suspending businesses' licenses simply for "permitting the congregation of apparent homosexuals"). McCarthy-era and later witch hunts led to the firing from federal and federal-contractor employment of thousands of persons suspected of being homosexuals. Katz, *Gay American History,* at 91–109; *Norton v. Macy,* 417 F.2d 1161, 1162 (D.C. Cir. 1969).[36]

Official repression has often been directed at preventing gay Americans from organizing politically to advocate for and protect their rights. The earliest gay political organization in America, formed in Chicago in the mid-1920s, was silenced by police raids, arrests, and firings from employment. *See, e.g,* William N. Eskridge, Jr., *Channeling: Identity-Based Social Movements and Public Law,* 150 U. Pa. L. Rev. 419, 438 & n.77 (2001). Similar groups that emerged after World War II also suffered severe harassment. *See, e.g., id.* at 443–48. Educational publications about homosexuality were censored as "obscene." *See, e.g., One, Inc. v. Olesen,* 241 F.2d 772 (9th Cir. 1957), *rev'd,* 355 U.S. 371 (1958) (per curiam).

Since the late 1960s and early 1970s, gay Americans have made substantial strides toward securing equal rights. *See supra* at 17–19, 30–31.

---

[34] *See generally* Jonathan N. Katz, *Gay American History: Lesbians and Gay Men in the U.S.A.* (rev. ed. 1992); John D'Emilio & Estelle B. Freedman, *Intimate Matters: A History of Sexuality in America* (2d ed. 1997); *Hidden From History: Reclaiming the Gay and Lesbian Past* (Martin Duberman, Martha Vicinus & George Chauncey, Jr. eds., 1990); *Lesbians, Gay Men and the Law* (William B. Rubenstein ed., 1993).

[35] *See, e.g.,* American Psychiatric Ass'n, *Position Statement: Psychiatric Treatment and Sexual Orientation* (1998), *available at* http://www.psych.org/archives/980020.pdf.

[36] Private institutions like Harvard University also mounted secret but systematic efforts to root out gay people. Amit R. Paley, *The Secret Court of 1920,* Harv. Crimson, Nov. 21, 2002, *available at* http://www.thecrimson.com/article.aspx?ref=255428 (accessed Jan. 14, 2003).

But there is still substantial inequality and back-lash. In passing a statute last year that protects against sexual-orientation discrimination, the New York state legislature found that anti-gay prejudice "has severely limited or actually prevented access to employment, housing and other basic necessities of life, leading to deprivation and suffering." N.Y. Sexual Orientation Non-Discrimination Act, 2002 N.Y. Laws ch. 2. Cruel anti-gay harassment in schools remains common. *See, e.g., Nabozny v. Podlesny*, 92 F.3d 446 (7th Cir. 1996). And violence motivated by irrational hatred of gay people can result in crimes of unimaginable brutality, as occurred with the murder of college student Matthew Shepard. *See, e.g., A Vicious Attack on Gay Student, Beaten, Burned and Left for Dead*, N.Y. Newsday, Oct. 10, 1998, at A4. Such killings, together with lesser forms of violence, intimidation, and discrimination, remain extremely effective in deterring gay Americans from revealing their sexual orientation, and thus from working openly to end anti-gay discrimination. By marking gay men and lesbians as criminals, discriminatory sodomy laws reinforce and intensify the irrational prejudice that leads to such violence. *See* Leslie, *Creating Criminals*, 35 Harv. C.R.-C.L. L. Rev. at 124.

The Constitution "neither knows nor tolerates classes among citizens." *Romer*, 517 U.S. at 623 (quotation marks omitted). In distinguishing laws based on hostility from ordinary legislative linedrawing, the Court should not ignore the persistent and destructive American history of anti-gay discrimination. The Homosexual Conduct Law is the State's own endorsement of discrimination against gay men and lesbians.

C. Equal Protection Concerns Are Particularly Strong Here Because of the Personal Burdens Imposed by This Criminal Law.

The Constitution's equal protection and due process protections are articulated together. U.S. Const. amend. XIV, § 1. Those dual safeguards reinforce one another, including in cases where liberty concerns may not rise to the level of a fundamental right or may be indirectly implicated. In this case, regardless of the Court's ultimate ruling on Point I, the personal burdens and restrictions on freedom imposed by Section 21.06 strengthen the need to reject its discriminatory classification.

On numerous occasions, the Court has held that where an extremely important personal interest is at stake, the State may *not* grant some citizens the ability to vindicate that interest but altogether deny other citizens that ability, even if the State *could* employ an evenhanded denial to all citizens. For example, there is no due process right to appellate review of decrees severing the parent-child bond. *M.L.B. v. S.L.J.*, 519 U.S. 102, 120 (1996). Where, however, the State grants review of such decrees to its citizens generally, it may not deny review to the few who cannot pay costs. *Id.* at 107; *see also, e.g., Boddie v. Connecticut*, 401 U.S. 371, 374 (1971) (although there is no right to obtain divorce, where State makes divorce available to most couples, it may not bar indigent persons from divorce due to inability to pay). That is so, even though wealth classifications are not inherently suspect, *see San Antonio Indep. Sch. Dist. v. Rodriguez*, 411 U.S. 1, 28 (1973), and the imposition of costs on litigants is otherwise rationally related to a legitimate state interest, *M.L.B.*, 519 U.S. at 123. Because the imposition of costs in *M.L.B.* at least indirectly implicated "state controls or intrusions on family relationships," *id.* at 116, the Court closely examined the unique burden the State had placed on the poor and rejected it as offensive to the combined guarantees of equal protection and due process. *See id.* at 120. The constitutional challenge in this case is also of an especially serious order, because it "endeavor[s] to defend against the States's destruction of family bonds, and to resist the brand associated with" criminality that is now imposed only on the deeply personal and intimate sexual relations of gay adults. *Cf. id.* at 125. As in *M.L.B.*, the outcome here should "reflect both equal protection and due process concerns." *Id.* at 120.

Similarly, there is no fundamental right to an education, and undocumented aliens are not a suspect class, but in light of the importance of the interest in education in our society, a law barring undocumented aliens from receiving a state-funded education will be rigorously scrutinized. *Plyler v. Doe*, 457 U.S. 202, 216–24 (1982). The nature of the deprivation, though not a fundamental right, informs and strengthens the equal protection claim. As the Court reasoned in *Plyler*, exclusion of one isolated group from such an important sphere "poses an affront to one of the goals of the Equal Protection Clause: the abolition of governmental barriers presenting unreasonable obstacles to advancement on the basis of individual merit." *Id.* at 221–22. It imposes a "stigma" that "will mark them for the rest of their lives." *Id.* at 223. Here, too, the Court must not ignore the stigma and the obstacle to equal advancement in society that accompanies the discriminatory law that Texas seeks to defend in assessing its validity under the Equal Protection Clause. This classification likewise "involve[s] the State in the creation of permanent class distinctions" and relegates gay men and lesbians to "second-class social status." *Cf. id.* at 234 (Blackmun, J., concurring).

The Equal Protection Clause is a critical guardian of liberty as well as equality. It defends against unreasonable exactions by the State because it "requires the democratic majority to accept for themselves and their loved ones what they impose on you and me." *Cruzan,* 497 U.S. at 300 (Scalia, J., concurring); *accord Railway Express Agency v. New York,* 336 U.S. 106, 112–13 (1949) (Jackson, J., concurring). The Texas Homosexual Conduct Law makes a mockery of that principle. Just as the majority may not decide that the availability of divorce or education is critical for the majority itself but then deny those benefits to a few, so Texas may not determine that freedom from state intrusion into the private sexual intimacy of two consenting adults is an important aspect of liberty for most of its citizens, but then deny that liberty to a minority—particularly a minority historically subject to discrimination. Consensual sexual decisions are too clearly matters for individual decisionmaking, not for imposition by the State. The discriminatory criminal law at issue here seriously diminishes the personal relationships and legal standing of a distinct class, and under the Fourteenth Amendment cannot stand.

CONCLUSION

For the foregoing reasons, the judgment of the Texas Court of Appeals upholding Section 21.06 and affirming Petitioners' criminal convictions thereunder should be reversed.

Respectfully submitted,

Paul M. Smith
William M. Hohengarten
Daniel Mach
Sharon M. McGowan
JENNER & BLOCK, LLC
601 13th Street, N.W.
Washington, DC 20005
(202) 639-6000

Mitchell Katine
WILLIAMS, BIRNBERG & ANDERSEN, L. L.P.
6671 Southwest Freeway, Suite 303
Houston, Texas 77074
(713) 981-9595

Ruth E. Harlow
Counsel of Record
Patricia M. Logue
Susan L. Sommer
LAMBDA LEGAL DEFENCSE AND EDUCATION FUND, INC.
120 Wall Street, Suite 1500
New York, NY 10005
(212)809–8585

Counsel for Petitioners
Dated: January 16, 2003

In The Supreme Court of the United States

JOHN GEDDES LAWRENCE AND
TYRON GARNER, PETITIONERS,
V.
STATE OF TEXAS, RESPONDENT.

ON WRIT OF CERTIORARI TO THE TEXAS
COURT OF APPEALS FOR THE FOURTEENTH
DISTRICT

RESPONDENT'S BRIEF

Charles A. Rosenthal Jr.
Harris County District Attorney

William J. Delmore III*
Scott A. Durfee
Assistant District Attorneys
Harris County, Texas
1201 Franklin, Suite 600
Houston, Texas 77002
(713) 755-5826
*Counsel of Record

Counsel for Respondent

TABLE OF CONTENTS

QUESTIONS PRESENTED

1. Whether the petitioners' criminal prosecutions for the offense of engaging in homosexual conduct, as defined by section 21.06 of the Texas Penal Code, violated the Fourteenth Amendment guarantee of equal protection of the law.

2. Whether the petitioners' criminal prosecutions under section 21.06 of the Texas Penal Code violated their constitutional rights to liberty and privacy, as protected by the Due Process Clause of the Fourteenth Amendment.

3. Whether *Bowers v. Hardwick,* 478 U.S. 186 (1986), should be overruled.

STATEMENT

A citizen informed Harris County sheriff's deputies that an armed man was "going crazy" in the apartment of petitioner Lawrence. Pet. App. 129a. The investigating officers entered the apartment and observed the petitioners engaged in anal sexual intercourse. *Id.* They were then charged by complaint in a Harris County justice court with the commission of the Class C misdemeanor offense of engaging in homosexual conduct, an offense defined by TEX. PENAL CODE § 21.06(a) (Vernon 1994), as follows: "A person commits an offense if he engages in deviate sexual intercourse with another individual of the same sex."[1] A Class C misdemeanor is punishable only by a fine not to exceed five hundred dollars. TEX. PENAL CODE § 12.23 (Vernon 1994).

After the petitioners were convicted and fined in the justice court,[2] they gave notice of appeal and the proceedings were transferred to Harris County Criminal Court at Law No. 10.[3] The petitioners moved to quash the complaints on various constitutional grounds. Pet. App. 117a, 130a. In support of those motions, the petitioners offered into evidence only the complaints themselves and the supporting "probable cause affidavits" filed by a sheriff's deputy in the justice court. See Pet. App. 129a, 141a. The two affidavits contained identical descriptions of the events leading to the filing of the complaints:

Officers dispatched to 794 Normandy # 833 reference to a weapons disturbance. The reportee advised dispatch a black male was going crazy in the apartment and he was armed with a gun. Officers met with the reportee who directed officers to the upstairs apartment. Upon entering the apartment and conducting a search for the armed suspect, officers observed the defendant engaged in deviate sexual conduct namely, anal sex, with another man.

After the county court denied the petitioners' motions to quash the complaints, they entered pleas of *nolo contendere*, and the court found them guilty of engaging in homosexual conduct. The court sentenced each petitioner, pursuant to a plea bargain, to payment of a fine in the amount of two hundred dollars, and the petitioners again gave notice of appeal from their convictions.[4]

A three-judge panel of the Court of Appeals for the Fourteenth District of Texas initially held that the State's prosecution of the petitioners under section 21.06 violated the Equal Rights Amendment of the Texas Constitution,[5] with one justice dissenting. The State's motion for rehearing *en banc* was granted, however, and on March 15, 2001, the *en banc* court of appeals rejected all of the petitioners' constitutional challenges to the enforcement of section 21.06. See *Lawrence v. State,* 41 S.W.3d 349 (Tex. App.—Houston [14th Dist.] 2001, pet. ref 'd) (Pet. App. 4a, et seq.). The *en banc* opinion of the court of appeals may be briefly summarized as follows:

1. Enforcement of the statute prohibiting homosexual conduct does not violate the Equal Protection Clauses of the Fourteenth Amendment to the United States Constitution and Article I, § 3, of the Texas Constitution, because the statute does not implicate fundamental rights or a suspect class, and it has a rational basis in the Texas Legislature's determination that homosexual sodomy is immoral. The fact that heterosexual sodomy is no longer a criminal offense under Texas law is not constitutionally significant, because the Legislature could rationally distinguish between an act performed with a person of the same sex and a similar act performed with a person of different sex. Pet. App. 13a-18a.

2. Enforcement of section 21.06 does not violate the Equal Rights Amendment of the Texas Constitution, because the statute applies equally to both men and women who engage in the prohibited conduct, and it is not the product of prejudice towards persons of either gender. Pet. App. 20a-24a.

3. The State's prosecution of the petitioners for the offense of engaging in homosexual conduct did not violate any constitutional right to privacy under the State or Federal Constitutions, in light of the long history of the imposition of criminal sanctions for such conduct, because it could not be said that the State of Texas or the United States recognized any "fundamental right" to engage in homosexual activity. Pet. App. 25a-31a.

A petition for discretionary review was denied, without written opinion, by the Texas Court of Criminal Appeals. Pet. App. 1a.

---

[1] The term "deviate sexual intercourse" is defined in the Texas Penal Code as "any contact between any part of the genitals of one person and the mouth of or anus of another person," or "the penetration of the genitals or the anus of another person with an object." TEX. PENAL CODE § 21.01(1) (Vernon 1994).

[2] The record contains no information concerning the course of proceedings which occurred in the justice court.

[3] An appeal from a judgment of conviction in a Texas justice court results in a trial de novo in a county court. TEX. CODE CRIM. PROC. art. 45.042 (Vernon Supp. 2003).

[4] A case which has been appealed from a Texas justice court to a county court may be further appealed to a court of appeals if the fine exceeds $100 or the sole issue is the constitutionality of the statute on which the conviction is based. TEX. CODE CRIM. PROC. art. 4.03 (Vernon Supp. 2003).

[5] TEX. CONST. art. I, § 3a.

SUMMARY OF ARGUMENT

1. The record is inadequate to serve as a basis for recognition of a limited constitutional right to engage in extramarital sexual conduct, because the absence of information concerning the petitioners and the circumstances of their offense precludes a determination of whether they would actually benefit from the Court's recognition of the limited right which they assert. The record is also inadequate to establish that the petitioners belong to the class for which they seek equal protection relief.

2. The States of the Union have historically prohibited a wide variety of extramarital sexual conduct, a legal tradition which is utterly inconsistent with any recognition, at this point in time, of a constitutionally protected liberty interest in engaging in any form of sexual conduct with whomever one chooses. Nothing in this Court's "substantive due process" jurisprudence supports recognition of a constitutional right to engage in sexual misconduct outside the venerable institution of marriage. This Court should adhere to its previous holding on this issue in *Bowers v. Hardwick*, 478 U.S. 186 (1986), and it should reaffirm that the personal liberties protected by the Due Process Clause of the Fourteenth Amendment from State regulation are limited to those "so rooted in the traditions and conscience of our people as to be ranked as fundamental." *Palko v. Connecticut*, 302 U.S. 319, 325 (1937).

3. Since enforcement of the homosexual conduct statute does not interfere with the exercise of a fundamental right, and the statute is not based upon a suspect classification, it must only be rationally related to a permissible state goal in order to withstand equal protection challenge. This legislative proscription of one form of extramarital sexual misconduct is in keeping with longstanding national tradition, and bears a rational relationship to the worthy governmental goals of implementation of public morality and promotion of family values.

4. The petitioners cannot meet their burden of establishing a discriminatory purpose to the original enactment of a statute which is facially applicable to both persons of exclusively homosexual orientation and persons who regard themselves as bisexual or hetero-

sexual. When the statute is viewed in historical perspective, it can reasonably be inferred that the Texas Legislature acted with nondiscriminatory intent in limiting the scope of the predecessor sodomy statute to fit within the commonly understood parameters of this Court's then-emerging privacy jurisprudence.

ARGUMENT

I. Substantive Due Process Under the Fourteenth Amendment.

A. The appellate record is inadequate to support the recognition of the limited constitutional right asserted by the petitioners. The appellate record does not establish that the petitioners would actually benefit from recognition of the particular liberty interest which they assert; therefore, it does not provide this Court with a factual basis for recognizing that interest.

Precise identification of an asserted liberty interest is critical to the determination of whether it falls within the scope of the Due Process Clause of the Fourteenth Amendment. An appellate court's substantive due process analysis "must begin with a careful description of the asserted right," because the "doctrine of judicial self-restraint" requires a court "to exercise the utmost care whenever [it] is asked to break new ground in this field." *Reno v. Flores*, 507 U.S. 292, 302 (1993) (quoting *Collins v. Harker Heights*, 503 U.S. 115, 125 [1992]). The petitioners initially advocate the recognition of a broadly drawn constitutional right to choose to engage in any "private consensual sexual intimacy with another adult, including one of the same sex." Brief of Petitioners 10. However, the petitioners later clarify that their challenge does not extend to the validity of statutes prohibiting prostitution, incest or adultery, which they describe as implicating additional "state concerns" not present in this case. *Id.* at 22 n.16. In short, the petitioners are asking the Court to recognize a fundamental right of an adult to engage in private, non-commercial, consensual sex with an unrelated, unmarried adult.

The slim record reveals only that the petitioners are adult males and that they engaged in anal intercourse in an apartment that petitioner Lawrence identified as his residence. It does not answer any of the following questions concerning the factual basis of their constitutional claims:

U.S. SUPREME
COURT

BRIEF FOR
RESPONDENTS

■ Whether the petitioners' sexual conduct was noncommercial.[6]

■ Whether the petitioners' sexual conduct was mutually consensual.[7]

■ Whether the petitioners' conduct was "private."[8]

■ Whether the petitioners are related to one another.

■ Whether either of the petitioners is married.

■ Whether either (or both) of the petitioners is exclusively homosexual.[9]

While the petitioners possess standing to challenge the constitutionality of a statute under which they have actually been prosecuted and convicted, see *Eisenstadt v. Baird,* 405 U.S. 438, 443-444 (1972), they should not be permitted to argue that a protected liberty interest exists under some specified set of circumstances without showing that those circumstances actually exist. This Court will not issue an opinion "advising what the law would be upon a hypothetical state of facts," and it will not "decide questions that cannot affect the rights of litigants in the case before [it]." *North Carolina v. Rice,* 404 U.S. 244, 246 (1971) (citations omitted). For example, in cases not involving expressive activity protected by the First Amendment, litigants have no standing to argue that a statute "would be unconstitutional if applied to third parties in hypothetical situations." *County Court of Ulster County v. Allen,* 442 U.S. 140, 155 (1979).[10]

In recognizing constitutional liberty interests under the Fourteenth Amendment, appellate courts "must use considerable restraint, including careful adherence to the incremental instruction given by the precise facts of particular cases, as they seek to give further and more precise definition to the right." *Troxel v. Granville,* 530 U.S. 57, 95-96 (2000) (Kennedy, J., dissenting).

Simply put, the record in this case provides an insufficient foundation for the meaningful review of the important and complex question of whether there is a constitutional right to engage in private, non-commercial, consensual sex with an unrelated, unmarried adult. At best, the record would support only the recognition of an extremely broad right to engage in sexual conduct with any other adult, regardless of any other circumstance which might attend that conduct—a right so broad that the petitioners themselves disavow any claim to it.

Because the record is inadequate to permit this Court to scrutinize and identify the contours and limitations of any protected liberty interest that might be recognized in this case, the State respectfully suggests that this Court dismiss the petition for writ of certiorari as improvidently granted. In the alternative, the respondent asks that the Court affirm the judgment of the Texas court of appeals on ground that the record is inadequate to support an effort to identify a limited constitutional right to engage in sexual conduct.

B. The Court has adopted an historical approach to the recognition of liberty interests protected under the Due Process Clause. In addressing claims that a state has interfered with an individual's exercise of a previously unrecognized liberty interest protected by the

[6] The lack of profit motivation cannot be inferred from the lack of prosecution for the more serious offense of prostitution, see TEX. PENAL CODE § 43.02 (Vernon Supp. 2003), because the police could not possibly determine whether prostitution was occurring if both participants in the sexual conduct declined to discuss that issue.

[7] While neither of the petitioners was charged with any variant of sexual assault, prosecution for such an offense would require an acknowledgment from at least one of the parties that the sexual activity was non-consensual. Because there are any number of reasons why a person might choose not to cooperate with authorities in the investigation and prosecution of a sexual offense, mutual consent cannot necessarily be inferred from the parties' silence.

[8] While the record reflects that the sexual conduct occurred in Lawrence's apartment, the record does not indicate whether anyone else was present in that apartment at the time. Lower courts have held that any right of privacy that protects marital sex from governmental interference is

waived when an onlooker is welcomed into the marital bedchamber. See *Lovisi v. Slayton,* 539 F.2d 349, 351-352 (4th Cir. 1976), *cert. denied,* 429 U.S. 977 (1977).

[9] The sexual orientation of the petitioners appears to be irrelevant to the disposition of their substantive due process argument, because they assert a constitutional right to engage in sodomy with persons of either gender, but it may be significant in determining whether the petitioners are members of any specific class in addressing their arguments premised upon the Equal Protection Clause, *infra.*

[10] Thus, in *United States v. Lemons,* 697 F.2d 832, 834-835 (9th Cir. 1983), in which the defendant was convicted of engaging in homosexual sodomy in violation of an Arkansas statute, the court of appeals held that the defendant would not be heard to argue that the statute would be unconstitutional if applied to persons who committed sodomy in a private place, in light of the fact that the defendant was arrested while engaging in an act of oral sex in a public place, i.e., the restroom of a national park.

Fourteenth Amendment, this Court has looked to the nation's history and legal traditions to determine whether the asserted interest is actually so fundamental to our system of ordered liberty as to merit constitutional protection from state regulation. For instance, in *Moore v. City of East Cleveland*, 431 U.S. 494 (1976) (plurality opinion), the Court observed that, "Appropriate limits on substantive due process come not from drawing arbitrary lines but rather from careful 'respect for the teaching of history [and], solid recognition of the basic values that underlie our society'." *Id.* at 503 (quoting *Griswold v. Connecticut*, 381 U.S. 479, 501 [1965] [Harlan, J., concurring]). Thus the "Constitution protects the sanctity of the family precisely because the institution of the family is deeply rooted in this Nation's history and tradition." *Id.*

In *Bowers*, 478 U.S. at 192–194, the Court rejected an asserted fundamental right to engage in homosexual conduct because, in light of pervasive State criminalization of such conduct throughout the nation's history, it could not seriously be asserted that a right to engage in homosexual sodomy was "deeply rooted in this Nation's history and tradition." Three years later, in *Michael H. v. Gerald D.*, 491 U.S. 110 (1989) (plurality opinion), the Court noted that in its attempts to "limit and guide interpretation of the [Due Process] Clause," it has "insisted not merely that the interest denominated as a 'liberty' be 'fundamental' (a concept that in isolation is hard to objectify), but also that it be an interest traditionally protected by our society." *Id.* at 122–123.

Two of the opinions issued in *Planned Parenthood of Southeastern Pa. v. Casey*, 505 U.S. 833 (1992), expressed doubt or disagreement that the Due Process Clause protects only those practices, "defined at the most specific level," which were protected by law at the time of ratification of the Fourteenth Amendment.[11] Emphasis upon the nation's legal traditions appeared only in the dissenting opinions.[12] However, less than a year later, the Court's opinion in *Reno v. Flores*, 507 U.S. 292 (1993), unambiguously stated that the "mere novelty" of a

claimed constitutional liberty interest was "reason enough to doubt that 'substantive due process' sustains it," because it could not be considered "so rooted in the traditions and conscience of our people as to be ranked as fundamental." *Id.* at 303 (quoting *United States v. Salerno*, 481 U.S. 739, 751 [1987], and *Snyder v. Massachusetts*, 291 U.S. 97, 105 [1934]).

This issue of the importance of national legal tradition in substantive due process jurisprudence was resolved in *Washington v. Glucksberg*, 521 U.S. 702 (1997), in which the Court emphasized the necessity of "examining our Nation's history, legal traditions, and practices" in order to determine whether a claimed liberty interest was, "objectively, 'deeply rooted in this Nation's history and tradition'" and "implicit in the concept of ordered liberty," and, therefore, merited protection under the Fourteenth Amendment:

Our established method of substantive due process analysis has two primary features: First, we have regularly observed that the Due Process Clause specially protects those fundamental rights and liberties which are, objectively, "deeply rooted in this Nation's history and tradition," [*Moore v. City of East Cleveland*], at 503 (plurality opinion); *Snyder v. Massachusetts*, 291 U.S. 97, 105 (1934) ("so rooted in the traditions and conscience of our people as to be ranked as fundamental"), and "implicit in the concept of ordered liberty," such that "neither liberty nor justice would exist if they were sacrificed," *Palko v. Connecticut*, 302 U.S. 319, 325, 326 (1937). Second, we have required in substantive due process cases a "careful description" of the asserted fundamental liberty interest. Flores, supra, at 302; *Collins* [*v. Harker Heights*, 503 U.S. 115 (1992)] at 125; *Cruzan* [*v. Director, Missouri Department of Health*, 497 U.S. 261 (1990)] at 277–278. Our Nation's history, legal traditions, and practices thus provide the crucial "guideposts for responsible decisionmaking," *Collins, supra*, at 125, that direct and restrain our exposition of the Due Process Clause. 521 U.S. at 720–721.

The Court declined to recognize the constitutional liberty interest proposed in Glucksberg—a right to assisted suicide—because its recognition would have required the Court to "reverse centuries of legal doctrine and practice" and to elevate to the status of a protected liberty interest a practice that was traditionally prohib-

---

[11] *See Casey*, 505 U.S. at 847 (joint opinion of O'Connor, J., Kennedy, J., and Souter, J.); id. at 923 (Blackmun, J., concurring).

[12] *See Casey*, 505 U.S. at 952-953 (Rehnquist, C.J., dissenting); id. at 980 (Scalia, J., dissenting).

ited by state law. *Id.* at 723, 728. In addition to the opinion of the Court, Justice Stevens in a concurring opinion agreed that "[h]istory and tradition provide ample support for refusing to recognize an open-ended constitutional right to commit suicide." *Id.* at 740 (Stevens, J., concurring).[13]

Since Glucksberg was decided, the Court has had little opportunity to consider the recognition of previously unacknowledged liberty interests under the Due Process Clause.[14] In *County of Sacramento v. Lewis,* 523 U.S. 833 (1998), the Court held that a determination of whether executive action violated an individual's right to substantive due process did not require the same historical and traditional analysis utilized in reviewing legislative action. A concurring justice suggested that "history and tradition are the starting point, but not in all cases the ending point of the substantive due process inquiry," leaving room for an "objective assessment of the necessities of law enforcement"; but that opinion did not suggest that *Glucksberg* was incorrect in its emphasis upon American legal tradition in determining the existence of a substantive due process right in the context of review of a legislative enactment. *Id.* at 857–858 (Kennedy, J., concurring). A subsequent statement in the same concurring opinion that "objective considerations, including history and precedent, are the controlling principle, regardless of whether the State's action is legislative or executive in character," *id.* at 858 (Kennedy, J., concurring), indicated no disagreement with the basic principle expressed in *Glucksberg:* that recognition of protected liberty interests under the Fourteenth Amendment must be based upon objective historical evidence that a particular practice is a cherished American tradition, "lest the liberty protected by the Due Process Clause be subtly transformed into the policy preferences of the Members of [the] Court." *Glucksberg,* 521 U.S. at 720.

C. This nation has no deep-rooted tradition of protecting a right to engage in sodomy. Turning to the question of whether a right to engage in sodomy is "so rooted in the traditions and conscience of our people as to be ranked as fundamental," the Court's previous resolution of that issue in *Bowers v. Hardwick* is unassailable. As noted in *Bowers,* sodomy was a serious criminal offense at common law;[15] it was forbidden by the laws of the original thirteen states at the

time of the ratification of the Bill of Rights; and it was punishable as a crime in all but five of the thirty-seven states in existence at the time of the ratification of the Fourteenth Amendment. *Bowers,* 478 U.S. at 192–193.

As further noted in *Bowers,* sodomy remained punishable as a crime in every state of the Union prior to the year 1961, *id.* at 193, when Illinois became the first state to adopt the American Law Institute's Model Penal Code approach to decriminalization of some sexual offenses. *Id.* at 193 n.7.

Our nation's history has not been rewritten in the seventeen years since *Bowers* was decided, and that history contradicts any assertion that a right to engage in homosexual anal intercourse has been a valued and protected right of American citizens. The fact that the states have traditionally prohibited the act as a crime is utterly inconsistent with any claim that our legal tradition has treated the choice to engage in that act as a "fundamental" right.

It is true that some change has occurred since *Bowers* was decided: three more states and the District of Columbia, in appropriate exercise of the democratic process, have repealed or limited the scope of their statutes prohibiting sodomy in general or homosexual sodomy in particular; and a small number of state appellate courts have found that such statutes violate a state constitutional right to privacy. See Brief of Petitioners 23 n.17. The State of Texas is now one of thirteen states in which consensual

---

[13] The "traditionalistic approach" adopted by the Court in *Glucksberg* has been described as "wise, workable, and firmly grounded in principles of American constitutionalism," in that it "provides a check against particular states or local jurisdictions whose practices contradict what most Americans would deem to be fundamental rights, but does so without licensing courts to second-guess democratic judgments on the basis of their own ideological or philosophical preferences." Michael W. McConnell, The Right to Die and the Jurisprudence of Tradition, 1997 Utah L. Rev. 665, 681 (1997).

[14] The Court's opinions in *City of Chicago v. Morales,* 527 U.S. 41 (1999), and *Troxel v. Granville,* 530 U.S. 57 (2000), both included acknowledgement of the existence of substantive rights under the Due Process Clause, but in each of those cases the particular liberty interest in question had long been recognized by the Court: the freedom to loiter in a public place, see *Morales,* 527 U.S. at 53-54; and parents' liberty interest in the care, custody and control of their own children, see *Troxel,* 530 U.S. at 65-66.

[15] *See also* William N. Eskridge Jr., *Gaylaw: Challenging the Apartheid of the Closet* 157 (1999).

U.S. SUPREME
COURT

BRIEF FOR
RESPONDENTS

homosexual sodomy remains a criminal offense. *Id.* at 27 n.21. The fact that several states have ceased treating sodomy as a criminal offense, however, is no evidence of a national tradition of espousing, honoring or safeguarding a right to engage in deviate sexual intercourse.

The petitioners concede that this Court requires "objective guideposts," such as "history and precedent," in the process of identification of liberty interests protected by the Fourteenth Amendment. They point to the gradual trend towards decriminalization of consensual sexual behavior among adults as the necessary objective evidence of a fundamental right firmly rooted in the traditions and conscience of American citizens. See Brief of Petitioners 19–25. Four decades of gradual but incomplete decriminalization does not erase a history of one hundred and fifty years of universal reprobation. A recent trend towards uneasy toleration—even a trend involving a majority of the fifty states—cannot establish a tradition "deeply rooted" in our national history and tradition. The petitioners mistake new growth for deep roots.

The petitioners argue that the "consistency of the direction of change" indicates a national consensus sufficient to satisfy the need for objective indicia in identifying a constitutionally protected liberty interest, utilizing a key phrase from the Court's recent decision in *Atkins v. Virginia,* 122 S.Ct. 2242, 2249 (2002), in which the Court found that the execution of mentally retarded criminal defendants violated the Eighth Amendment. The petitioners' argument suffers from a logical flaw in that, prior to 1961, every State treated sodomy as a criminal offense, so only one direction of change is possible. Compare *Atkins,* 122 S.Ct. at 2263 (Scalia, J., dissenting). A State's affirmative choice to maintain the status quo demonstrates the absence of consensus. Several states have made such a choice, in that their appellate courts have upheld the constitutionality of statutes prohibiting the commission of sodomy or homosexual conduct. For instance, the Louisiana Supreme Court held in *State v. Smith,* 766 So.2d 501, 508-510 (La. 2000), that the constitutional right to privacy expressly recognized by that state's constitution did not extend to the commission of oral or anal sex in private, observing that there "has never been any doubt that the legislature, in the exercise of its police power, has the authority to criminalize the commission of acts which, with-

out regard to the infliction of any other injury, are considered immoral."[16] Accord *Missouri v. Walsh,* 713 S.W.2d 508 (Mo. 1986) (holding that a prosecution under the Missouri homosexual conduct statute did not violate any constitutional right to privacy under the state or federal constitution). Should just a few more states join Texas, Louisiana and Missouri in upholding the state's power to punish acts of sodomy, one could argue that the prevailing trend was actually the rejection of a constitutional privacy right extending to consensual sodomy.

In any event, currently evolving standards are an unstable basis for recognition of fundamental rights protected by the Fourteenth Amendment. The Eighth Amendment has long been construed to require consideration of "evolving standards of decency that mark the progress of a maturing society," *Trop v. Dulles,* 356 U.S. 86, 101 (1958), permitting reliance upon "contemporary values" as evidenced by recent legislative enactments. See *Penry v. Lynaugh,* 492 U.S. 302, 331 (1989). In contrast, none of this Court's precedents so much as suggests that recent legislative activity should be accepted as proof of "deeply rooted" fundamental rights, and the Court's decisions exploring the possible existence of unrecognized liberty interests under the Fourteenth Amendment have never taken into account rapidly "evolving standards." The approach advocated by the petitioners would require this Court to serve as a micro-managing super-legislature, continually assessing current legislative trends to determine the current extent of protection under the Fourteenth Amendment—an approach which is entirely inconsistent with the Court's reliance in *Glucksberg* upon history and legal tradition.

The petitioners also argue that previously recognized "fundamental interests . . . converge in the right asserted here," Brief of Petitioners 11–16, but considered separately, the recognized

---

[16] The Louisiana court also held that the separation of powers provision of its state constitution precluded the Court from usurping the legislative function of determining "the public policy of Louisiana on the practice of oral and anal sex"; and it pungently observed that the "only perceptible unconstitutionality in this case is that which would be evident if this court would . . . elevate [its] own personal notions of individual liberty over the collective wisdom of the voters' elected representatives' belief " that the proscription of "oral and anal sex, consensual or otherwise, is in furtherance of the moral welfare of the public mind." *Smith,* 766 So.2d at 510.

liberty interests upon which the petitioners rely do not implicate the conduct in question, and no logical process extends their reach when they are lumped together.

The petitioners first assert a constitutionally protected right to choose to enter into "intimate relationships," citing *Roberts v. United States Jaycees,* 468 U.S. 609, 617-618 (1984), but no court has held that this nebulously defined right extended to the protection of sexual misconduct prohibited by State law. For example, in *Marcum v. McWhorter,* 308 F.3d 635, 641-643 (6th Cir. 2002), the court held that the freedom to choose to enter into personal relationships could not extend to an adulterous relationship, since adultery has been punishable as a crime for centuries. In this case, while the petitioners may have a constitutional right to associate with one another, the right to form an "intimate relationship" does not protect any and all sexual conduct in which they might engage in the context of that relationship.[17]

The petitioners also rely upon the recognized constitutional right to "bodily integrity," but the Court's decisions regarding bodily integrity generally pertain to unwarranted government invasion of an individual's body, and the individual's right to control his own medical treatment, see *Glucksberg,* 521 U.S. at 777-778 (Souter, J., concurring), and those decisions have nothing to do with the manner in which an individual interacts with third parties or invades another person's body.

The right to privacy in the home has long been recognized under both the First Amendment, see *Stanley v. Georgia,* 394 U.S. 557, 564-565 (1969), and the Fourth Amendment, see *Kyllo v. United States,* 533 U.S. 27, 31 (2001). However, the decision in *Stanley* involved the individual's freedom of thought, rather than conduct, *Stanley* 394 U.S. at 565-566, and that decision has never been extended to prohibit state regulation of conduct that does not involve expression protected by the First Amendment. The Fourth Amendment protects against unreasonable police entry and search of the home, but it has never been found to protect one from prosecution for otherwise criminal conduct that occurs within that home.[18] See *Osborne v. Ohio,* 495 U.S. 103, 108-110 (1990); *Bowers,* 478 U.S. at 195-196; Stanley, 394 U.S. at 568 n.11.

By arguing that their asserted liberty interest under the Fourteenth Amendment may be located at the "convergence" of these previously recognized rights, the petitioners implicitly admit that none of them, standing alone, has ever been construed in a fashion that would protect an individual from state prosecution for sexual misconduct occurring in a private residence. The petitioners' assertion of a patchwork of constitutional rights which do not implicate their conduct does not logically prove that the conduct is in fact protected by a previously unrecognized liberty interest.

D. No tradition of protection exists at any level of specificity of designation of an asserted liberty interest. The petitioners' other quarrel with *Bowers* involves the level of specificity at which the nation's traditions are to be analyzed in assessing the existence of a protected liberty interest under the Fourteenth Amendment, an issue that does not seem to have been definitively resolved at this time. See Michael H., 491 U.S. 110, 127 n.6 (plurality opinion), 132 (O'Connor, J., concurring); *County of Sacramento v. Lewis,* 523 U.S. 833, 847 n.8 (1998).[19] Assuming that issue does remain open at this time, it should not be necessary to resolve it in this case, since the petitioners cannot establish a historical tradition of exalting and protecting the conduct for which they were prosecuted at any level of specificity.

At the most specific level, the nation has a longstanding tradition, only recently waning, of criminalizing anal sodomy—the offense once known as "buggery"—as a serious criminal offense. See *Bowers,* 478 U.S. 192-194; William N. Eskridge Jr., *Gaylaw: Challenging the Apartheid of the Closet* 157-158, 328-337 (App.

---

[17] Parents might well have a constitutionally protected right to maintain an intimate relationship with their children, but no one would argue that their protected liberty interest would extend to having sexual relations with the children.

[18] The petitioners understandably disavow any complaint regarding the manner in which the police entered Lawrence's apartment, Brief of Petitioners 14-15, since few citizens would want to impede an officer's ability to enter their residence to search for an armed man said to be "going crazy" on the premises. Pet. App. 129a.

[19] The opinion in Lewis noted: "*Glucksberg* presented a disagreement about the significance of historical examples of protected liberty in determining whether a given statute could be judged to contravene the Fourteenth Amendment. The differences of opinion turned on the issues of how much history indicating recognition of the asserted right, viewed at what level of specificity, is necessary to support the finding of a substantive due process right entitled to prevail over state legislation." *Id.*

A) (1999).[20] But even if the topic is broadened to include other acts of extramarital sexual intercourse, such as fornication, adultery, incest, prostitution, etc., the nation's tradition is still one characterized by prohibition and criminalization. Most of the states have maintained, through most of their history, statutes which made it a criminal offense to engage in fornication and adultery as well as sodomy, and there is no long-standing tradition of protecting the right to engage in any sort of extramarital sexual conduct. Fornication was a punishable offense in colonial times, and it remained illegal in forty states until the early 1970s. See Tracy Shallbettor Stratton, *No More Messing Around: Substantive Due Process Challenges to State Laws Prohibiting Fornication*, 73 Wash. L. Rev. 767, 780 (1998). As of 1998, it was still a crime in thirteen states and the District of Columbia. *See id.* at 767 n.2; accord, Richard Green, *Griswold's Legacy: Fornication and Adultery as Crimes*, 16 Ohio N.U.L. Rev. 545, 546 n.8 (1989).

Adultery was once a capital offense, under some circumstances, in colonial Massachusetts, and it was punished as a crime during the colonial period in almost every jurisdiction. See *Oliverson v. West Valley City*, 875 F. Supp. 1465, 1474 (D. Utah 1995). Adultery was still punishable as a crime "in most states . . . in 1900," *see id.* (quoting Lawrence M. Friedman, *Crime and Punishment in American History* 13 (1993)), and as of 1996, it remained a crime in twenty-five states and the District of Columbia. *City of*

Sherman v. Henry, 928 S.W.2d 464, 470 n.3 (Tex. 1996); Green, *supra* at n.7.

Thus, the legislatures of the various states have shown significant concern for the sexual morality of the citizenry, and statutes criminalizing extramarital sexual conduct have been pervasive throughout our national history. The constitutionality of those statutes previously has been thought to be "beyond doubt," *Griswold v. Connecticut*, 381 U.S. 479, 498 (Goldberg, J. concurring), and recent decisions from the lower courts have held that the statutes are, in fact, constitutional. See, e.g., *Henry*, 928 S.W.2d at 471-472; *Marcum*, 308 F.3d at 642-643. Furthermore, criminal prosecutions aside, the United States had no history whatsoever of protecting the right to engage in extramarital sex, at least until a few state appellate courts began in the 1990s to invalidate their sodomy statutes as violative of a state constitutional right to privacy.[21] This Court, in particular, has never recognized any right to engage in extramarital sexual conduct, and it is telling that most of the fundamental liberty interests the Court has recognized under the Fourteenth Amendment are rooted in marriage, procreation and childrearing. An asserted right to engage in homosexual sodomy is actually inimical to the fundamental rights that this Court has endeavored to protect.

The Court catalogued the liberty interests to which it has accorded Fourteenth Amendment protection in *Glucksberg*, 521 U.S. at 720, as follows: In a long line of cases, we have held that, in

U.S. SUPREME
COURT

BRIEF FOR
RESPONDENTS

---

[20] While acknowledging the widespread and longstanding existence of sodomy statutes, Professor Eskridge is critical of the historical basis for the Court's decision in *Bowers*, on grounds that early sodomy statutes were aimed primarily at the prohibition of buggery and similar forms of unnatural coitus, rather than the oral sex act for which the defendant in *Bowers* was prosecuted. See Eskridge at 156-157. That concern is absent in this case, since it is undisputed that the act of anal sodomy was a serious crime—originally a capital offense—from the earliest days of the colonization period.

[21] The handful of state appellate courts that have invalidated sodomy or homosexual conduct statutes have all predicated their holdings upon objective indications that their state constitutions provided more privacy protection than the Federal Constitution. See *Commonwealth v. Wasson*, 842 S.W.2d 487, 492 (Ky. 1992) (basing its ruling upon the "textual and structural differences between the United States Bill of Rights and our own, which suggest a different conclusion from that reached by the United States Supreme Court is more appropriate"); *Campbell v. Sundquist*, 926 S.W.2d 250, 261 (Tenn. Ct. App. 1996) (noting that both the "Tennessee

Constitution and this State's constitutional jurisprudence establish that the right to privacy provided to Tennesseans under our Constitution is in fact more extensive than the corresponding right to privacy provided by the Federal Constitution"); *Gryczan v. State*, 942 P.2d 112, 121-22 (Mont. 1997) (invalidating a statute prohibiting "deviate sexual conduct" and noting that "Montana's Constitution affords citizens broader protection of their right to privacy than does the federal constitution"); *Powell v. State*, 510 S.E.2d 18, 22 (Ga. 1998) (in which a general sodomy statute was invalidated upon a finding that the " 'right to be let alone' guaranteed by the Georgia Constitution is far more extensive than the right of privacy protected by the U.S. Constitution"); *Jegley v. Picado*, 80 S.W.3d 332, 344 (Ark. 2002) (stating that "Arkansas's Constitution can be held to provide greater privacy rights than the United States Constitution"). The fact that five state courts have invalidated sodomy statutes in the last eleven years, on state constitutional grounds, is meager evidence of a deeply rooted national tradition of protecting the privacy of the conduct in issue. Too few states have taken such a step, over too brief a period of time, to support any such inference.

addition to the specific freedoms protected by the Bill of Rights, the "liberty" specially protected by the Due Process Clause includes the rights to marry, *Loving v. Virginia,* 388 U.S. 1 (1967); to have children, *Skinner v. Oklahoma ex rel. Williamson,* 316 U.S. 535 (1942); to direct the education and upbringing of one's children, *Meyer v. Nebraska,* 262 U.S. 390 (1923); *Pierce v. Society of Sisters,* 268 U.S. 510 (1925); to marital privacy, *Griswold v. Connecticut,* 381 U.S. 479 (1965); to use contraception, ibid.; *Eisenstadt v. Baird,* 405 U.S. 438 (1972); to bodily integrity, *Rochin v. California,* 342 U.S. 165 (1952), and to abortion, *Casey, supra.* We have also assumed, and strongly suggested, that the Due Process Clause protects the traditional right to refuse unwanted lifesaving medical treatment. *Cruzan,* 497 U.S., at 278-279.

The conduct at issue in this case has nothing to do with marriage or conception or parenthood and it is not on a par with those sacred choices. Homosexual sodomy cannot occur within or lead to a marital relationship. It has nothing to do with families or children. The decision to engage in homosexual acts is not like the acts and decisions that this Court previously has found worthy of constitutional protection, and it should not be added to the list of fundamental rights protected by the Fourteenth Amendment.

The difference between protected conduct within the marriage relationship and unprotected sexual conduct outside marriage has been recognized on a number of occasions, most famously in Justice Harlan's dissenting opinion in *Poe v. Ullman,* 367 U.S. 497, 545-546, 552-553 (1961), in which he expressed the view that "any Constitutional doctrine in this area" must be built upon the division between acts occurring within and without the marital relationship:

Yet the very inclusion of the category of morality among state concerns indicates that society is not limited in its objects only to the physical well-being of the community, but has traditionally concerned itself with the moral soundness of its people as well. Indeed to attempt a line between public behavior and that which is purely consensual or solitary would be to withdraw from community concern a range of subjects with which every society in civilized times has found it necessary to deal. The laws regarding marriage which provide both when the sexual powers may be used and the legal and

societal context in which children are born and brought up, as well as laws forbidding adultery, fornication and homosexual practices which express the negative of the proposition, confining sexuality to lawful marriage, form a pattern so deeply pressed into the substance of our social life that any Constitutional doctrine in this area must build upon that basis. . . .

The right of privacy most manifestly is not an absolute. Thus, I would not suggest that adultery, homosexuality, fornication and incest are immune from criminal enquiry, however privately practiced. So much has been explicitly recognized in acknowledging the State's rightful concern for its people's moral welfare. See 367 U.S. at pages 545-548, *supra.* But not to discriminate between what is involved in this case and either the traditional offenses against good morals or crimes which, though they may be committed anywhere, happen to have been committed or concealed in the home, would entirely misconceive the argument that is being made. Adultery, homosexuality and the like are sexual intimacies which the State forbids altogether, but the intimacy of husband and wife is necessarily an essential and accepted feature of the institution of marriage, an institution which the State not only must allow, but which always and in every age it has fostered and protected. It is one thing when the State exerts its power either to forbid extra-marital sexuality altogether, or to say who may marry, but it is quite another when, having acknowledged a marriage and the intimacies inherent in it, it undertakes to regulate by means of the criminal law the details of that intimacy.

As noted in a concurring opinion in *Glucksberg,* Justice Harlan's proposed dichotomy "provides a lesson for today," in that his identification of the traditionally protected liberty interest in *Poe v. Ullman* served to distinguish "between areas in which government traditionally had regulated (sexual relations outside of marriage) and those in which it had not (private marital intimacies) and thus was broad enough to cover the claim at hand without being so broad as to be shot-through by exceptions." 521 U.S. at 770-772 (Souter, J., concurring).

Therefore, should the Court consider expanding the level of specificity with which it identifies the proposed liberty interest at issue in this case, the State urges the Court to draw the line at the threshold of the marital bedroom, in keeping with its past decisions emphasizing the American tradition of marital privacy. Outside that threshold, nothing in our nation's "history, legal traditions, and practices" offer the "crucial 'guideposts for responsible decisionmaking' . . . that direct and restrain [the Court's] exposition of the Due Process Clause." *Glucksberg,* 521 U.S. at 721 (quoting *Collins v. Harker Heights,* 503 U.S. 115, 125 (1992)).

E. Principles of stare decisis counsel against recognition of a new protected liberty interest. Stare decisis mandates that the Court adhere to its holdings in *Bowers.* Seventeen years should be considered a very brief period indeed, in the context of the development of fundamental rights under the Fourteenth Amendment, and the principle of stare decisis counsels against rapid change in this area. If a right is truly fundamental, its public acceptance and societal value should not be the subject of vehement and widespread disagreement. Fundamental rights should be rock solid, and vacillation is inconsistent with the level of durability of rights which should be deemed "fundamental" to our society. "Although adherence to precedent is not rigidly required in constitutional cases, any departure from the doctrine of stare decisis demands special justification." *Arizona v. Rumsey,* 467 U.S. 203, 212 (1984). The petitioners argue that such special justification exists in the steady "erosion" of support for *Bowers* and the concomitant advancement of the gay rights movement, Brief of Petitioners 30-31, but the Court reaffirmed in *Glucksberg* that *Bowers* utilized the correct mode of analysis in the determination of the existence of a new liberty interest under the Fourteenth Amendment. The fact that a few more states have eased criminal sanctions on sodomy or homosexual conduct since 1986 does not logically affect the validity of the conclusion in *Bowers* that no right to engage in homosexual conduct can be found "deeply rooted in this Nation's history and tradition." *Bowers,* 478 U.S. at 192.

"It is one of the happy incidents of the federal system that a single courageous State may, if its citizens choose, serve as a laboratory; and try novel social and economic experiments without risk to the rest of the country." *New State Ice Co. v. Liebmann,* 285 U.S. 262, 311 (1932) (Brandeis, J., dissenting). The principle of federalism that encourages the state to undertake such experiments also operates to permit states to decline to participate in them. All change is not for the better, and the right to be first should be accompanied by a right to be among the last to accept a change of debatable social value.

In *Atkins,* the State of Texas found itself in a minority of states which had not legislatively limited its capital punishment statutes in a particular fashion, and it was obligated to join the herd because of the Eighth Amendment requirement that it comply with "evolving standards" of "contemporary values." 122 S.Ct. at 2247. This is not an Eighth Amendment case, and any indicia of recent "evolving standards" is irrelevant to the identification of those truly fundamental rights which form the core of our democratic society. Courts cannot concern themselves "with cultural trends and political movements" without "usurping the role of the Legislature," and while the Legislature "may not be infallible in its moral and ethical judgments, it alone is constitutionally empowered to decide which evils it will restrain when enacting laws for the public good." *Lawrence,* 41 S.W.2d at 362. For these reasons, this Court should reject the petitioners' due process challenge and affirm the judgment of the court below.

II. Equal Protection Under the Fourteenth Amendment.

The petitioners also argue that their prosecution for engaging in homosexual conduct violates the Equal Protection Clause of the Fourteenth Amendment. They argue that section 21.06 improperly criminalizes sexual conduct with a person of the same sex that is otherwise legal when done with a person of the opposite sex, and they claim that the State cannot articulate any rational basis for this classification.

This challenge fails on two grounds. First, given the evolution of the Texas sodomy statute towards more liberality with respect to sexual activity, petitioners cannot establish that the Texas Legislature purposefully discriminated against persons engaging in homosexual conduct. Instead, this Court reasonably can infer that the legislature, in good faith, incrementally narrowed the State's neutral proscriptions against sodomy in accordance with contemporaneous developments in due process jurisprudence. As such, instead of being the product of a legislative choice to discriminate against homosexuals, section 21.06 is the vestigial remainder of a predecessor sodomy statute, reduced to its present form as a result of the legislature's 1973 reform of the Texas Penal Code.

Second, this Court can infer a rational basis for the legislature's enactment of section 21.06. The State of Texas has a legitimate state interest in legislatively expressing the long-standing moral traditions of the State against homosexual conduct, and in discouraging its citizens—whether they be homosexual, bisexual or heterosexual—from choosing to engage in what is still perceived to be immoral conduct. Section 21.06 rationally furthers that goal by publishing the State's moral disapproval in a penal code of conduct for its citizens and by creating a disincentive against the conduct. The Legislature reasonably could have concluded that lesser, unenforceable expressions of disapproval would be ineffective to deter that conduct. Moreover, the narrowing of the predecessor sodomy statute to avoid constitutional challenge is in itself a rational basis for the legislative action: viewed in historical context, the Texas Legislature's decision was a reasonable response to the evolving due process jurisprudence of the late 1960s and early 1970s.

This rational-basis analysis is consistent with this Court's analysis in *Bowers v. Hardwick*, 478 U.S. 186 (1986), which addressed the rationality of basing legislation on moral tradition. Although *Bowers* was decided on substantive due process grounds, it stands alone as the only modern case in which this Court has approved moral tradition as a submitted rational basis for legislation. Nothing has changed in the sixteen years since *Bowers* to justify abandonment of its conclusion.[22]

A. The Equal Protection Clause—standard of review.   The Equal Protection Clause of the Fourteenth Amendment creates no substantive rights. *Vacco v. Quill*, 521 U.S. 793, 799 (1997). Instead, it "embodies a general rule that States must treat like cases alike but may treat unlike cases accordingly." *Id*.; see also *City of Cleburne, Texas v. Cleburne Living Center*, 473 U.S. 432, 439 (1985) (construing Equal Protection Clause as "essentially a direction that all persons similarly situated should be treated alike").

Unless a classification warrants some form of heightened review because it jeopardizes the exercise of a fundamental right or categorizes on the basis of an inherently suspect characteristic, the Equal Protection Clause requires only that the classification rationally further a legitimate state interest. *Nordlinger v. Hahn,* 505 U.S. 1, 10 (1992).

1. *Rational-basis review.*   Rational-basis review is "the most relaxed and tolerant form of judicial scrutiny under the Equal Protection Clause." *City of Dallas v. Stanglin,* 490 U.S. 19, 26 (1989). "In general, the Equal Protection Clause is satisfied so long as there is a plausible policy reason for the classification, the legislative facts on which the classification is apparently based rationally may have been considered to be true by the governmental decisionmaker, and the relationship of the classification is not so attenuated as to render the distinction arbitrary or irrational." *Nordlinger,* 505 U.S. at 11 (citations omitted); see also *Romer,* 517 U.S. at 632 (1996) ("In the ordinary case, a law will be sustained if it can be said to advance a legitimate government interest, even if the law seems unwise or works to the disadvantage of a particular group, or if the rationale for it seems tenuous.")

The rational-basis standard of review is a paradigm of judicial restraint. *F.C.C. v. Beach Communications, Inc.,* 508 U.S. 307, 314 (1993). Rational-basis review in equal protection analysis is not a license for courts to judge the wisdom, fairness, or logic of legislative choices, nor does it authorize the judiciary to sit as a superlegislature to judge the wisdom or desirability of legislative policy determinations made in areas that neither affect fundamental rights nor proceed along suspect lines. *Heller v. Doe* by Doe, 509 U.S. 312, 319 (1993). The Court summarized the evidentiary presumptions in rational-basis review in *Heller* as follows:

[A] legislature that creates these categories need not "actually articulate at any time the purpose or rationale supporting its classification." Instead, a classification "must be upheld against equal protection challenge if there is any reasonably conceivable state of facts that could provide a rational basis for the classification." A State, moreover, has no obligation to produce evidence to sustain the rationality of a statutory classification. "[A] legislative choice is not subject to courtroom factfinding and may be based on rational speculation unsupported by evi-

---

[22] As discussed in more detail *infra, Romer v. Evans,* 517 U.S. 620 (1996), does not dictate otherwise. Instead, *Romer* is notable for what it does not do: in striking down a constitutional amendment remarkably overbroad for the purposes it purported to further, the majority's opinion pointedly neither revisited the rationality of moral classifications in legislation nor distinguished *Bowers*.

dence or empirical data." A statute is presumed constitutional, and "[t]he burden is on the one attacking the legislative arrangement to negative every conceivable basis which might support it," whether or not the basis has a foundation in the record. *Id.* at 320-21 (citations omitted).

When social legislation is at issue, the Equal Protection Clause allows the states wide latitude, and the Constitution presumes that even improvident decisions will eventually be rectified by the democratic processes. *Cleburne,* 473 U.S. at 440; see also *Dandridge v. Williams,* 397 U.S. 471, 486 (1970) (holding that the rational basis standard "is true to the principle that the Fourteenth Amendment gives the federal courts no power to impose upon the States their views of what constitutes wise economic or social policy").

2. Heightened review is neither sought nor required. The petitioners suggest only in a footnote that laws which incorporate a sexual-orientation-based classification, or a gender-based classification to discriminate against homosexuals, should be reviewed pursuant to a heightened scrutiny standard. Brief of Petitioners 32 n.24. This assertion is not implicated by the litigation, briefed by the petitioners, or mandated by law.

The petitioners do not brief their request for heightened review and continue to rely solely on the rational-basis standard of review in their equal protection challenge to the constitutionality of section 21.06. See *Lawrence,* 41 S.W.2d at 378 (Anderson, J., dissenting) (in response to majority's conclusions that there is no fundamental right to engage in sodomy, and homosexuals do not constitute a suspect class, dissent characterizes these conclusions as "irrelevant here because appellants do not raise these arguments") (emphasis added). Accordingly, this Court's jurisprudence would be ill-served by consideration of a new standard not actually in controversy between the parties. See *Heller,* 509 U.S. at 319 ("Even if respondents were correct that heightened scrutiny applies, it would be inappropriate for us to apply that standard here. Both parties have been litigating this case for years on the theory of rational-basis review, which . . . does not require the State to place any evidence in the record, let alone the extensive evidentiary showing that would be required for these statutes to survive heightened scrutiny. It would be imprudent and unfair to inject a new standard at this stage in the litigation.").

The appropriateness of applying a rational-basis analysis to classifications based upon sexual orientation is not a matter of controversy in this Court or the federal courts of appeals. In *Romer v. Evans,* 517 U.S. 620 (1996), a case in which the amendment in question specifically classified the affected individuals in terms of sexual orientation, this Court nonetheless utilized the rational-basis test. Id. at 631-636. Likewise, in the federal courts of appeals, the profusion of litigation involving the exclusion of homosexuals from military service has provided ample opportunity for consideration of the appropriate standard of review, and it appears that those courts are unanimous in finding that homosexuals do not constitute a suspect class and that there is no fundamental right to engage in homosexual conduct.[23]

Heightened review of section 21.06 as a statute discriminating on the basis of gender is likewise unnecessary. This Court's heightened scrutiny in gender cases has been directed at legislative classifications that "create or perpetuate

---

[23] *See, e.g., Thomasson v. Perry,* 80 F.3d 915, 928 (4th Cir.), *cert. denied,* 519 U.S. 948 (1996) ("rational basis is . . . the suitable standard for review" of the military "don't ask/don't tell" policy); *Baker v. Wade,* 769 F.2d 289, 292 (5th Cir. 1985), *cert. denied,* 478 U.S. 1022 (1986) ("the standard for review is whether § 21.06 [of the Texas Penal Code] is rationally related to a legitimate state end"); *Equality Foundation of Greater Cincinnati, Inc. v. City of Cincinnati,* 128 F.3d 289, 292-293 (6th Cir. 1997), *cert. denied,* 525 U.S. 943 (1998) (holding that city charter amendment pertaining to sexual orientation was subject to review "under the most common and least rigorous equal protection norm . . . the 'rational relationship' test"); *Ben-Shalom v. Marsh,* 881 F.2d 454, 464 (7th Cir. 1989), *cert. denied,* 494 U.S. 1004 (1990) ("deferential standard of review" held applicable to military regulation targeting homosexuals).

See also Richenberg v. Perry, 97 F.3d 256, 260 (8th Cir. 1996), *cert. denied,* sub nom. *Richenberg v. Cohen,* 522 U.S. 807 (1997) (rejecting contention that homosexuality is "suspect classification" requiring heightened scrutiny); *Holmes v. California Army National Guard,* 124 F.3d 1126, 1132 (9th Cir. 1997), *cert. denied,* 525 U.S. 1067 (1998) ("because homosexuals do not constitute a suspect or quasi-suspect class," the military "don't ask/don't tell" policy is subject only "to rational basis review"); *Rich v. Secretary of the Army,* 735 F.2d 1220, 1229 (10th Cir. 1984) ("classification based on one's choice of sexual partners is not suspect"); *Steffan v. Perry,* 41 F.3d 677, 684, n.3 (D.C. Cir. 1994) (holding that a group "defined by reference" to homosexual conduct "cannot constitute a suspect class"); *Woodward v. United States,* 871 F.2d 1068, 1076 (Fed. Cir. 1989), *cert. denied,* 494 U.S. 1003 (1990) (holding that a homosexual "is not a member of a class to which heightened scrutiny must be afforded").

the legal, social, and economic inferiority of women." *United States v. Virginia*, 518 U.S. 515, 534 (1996). Such heightened scrutiny has been mandated in recognition of the real danger that government policies that professedly are based on reasonable considerations in fact may be reflective of "archaic and overbroad" generalizations about gender, see *Schlesinger v. Ballard*, 419 U.S. 498, 506- 507 (1975), or based on "outdated misconceptions concerning the role of females in the home rather than in the 'marketplace and world of ideas.'" *Craig v. Boren*, 429 U.S. 190, 198-199 (1976). See also *Cleburne v. Cleburne Living Center, Inc.*, 473 U.S. 432, 441 (1985) (differential treatment of the sexes "very likely reflect[s] outmoded notions of the relative capabilities of men and women"). *J.E.B. v. Alabama ex rel. T.B.*, 511 U.S. 127, 135 (1994); see also *United States v. Virginia*, 518 U.S. at 532 (stating that the Court will "carefully inspect[ ] official action that closes a door or denies opportunity to women [or to men]"). Enforcement of section 21.06 does not involve gender stereotyping or exclusion. The homosexual conduct statute indulges in no stereotypes about the respective capabilities of men and women, and it does not penalize one gender at the expense of the other. See *Miller v. Albright*, 523 U.S. 420, 444-45 (1998) (rejecting claim of improper genderbased classification in Fifth Amendment equal protection analysis of statute because "[n]one of the premises on which the statutory classification is grounded can be fairly characterized as an accidental byproduct of a traditional way of thinking about the members of either sex"); *Coalition for Economic Equity v. Wilson*, 122 F.3d 692, 702 (9th Cir. 1997) (holding that, while California's Proposition 209 mentions race and gender, it does not logically classify persons by race and gender).

Given these circumstances, heightened review for statutes that classify on the basis of sexual orientation or gender is neither raised nor required in this case.

B. The petitioners have not established their membership in the class for which equal protection relief is sought Before rationalbasis review is necessary, the petitioners must establish that Texas impermissibly discriminated against them. From the record and the briefs, however, it is unclear what class the petitioners purport to represent in this challenge.

The classifications challenged in the petitioners' respective motions to quash the complaints against them in the trial court were the criminalization of "consensual sexual acts, including those in private, according to the sex and sexual orientation of those who engage in them," and the "discriminatory classification against gay people." See Pet. App. 119a-120a, 131a-132a. However, the record is silent as to the sexual orientation of the petitioners and whether the charged conduct was occurring consensually. See id., Appendices E, F & G, pp. 107a-141a (entirety of trial court record).

In *United States v. Hays*, 515 U.S. 737 (1995), the Court summarized the elements necessary to establish standing:

First, the plaintiff must have suffered an 'injury in fact'—an invasion of a legally protected interest that is (a) concrete and particularized, and (b) actual or imminent, not conjectural or hypothetical. Second, there must be a causal connection between the injury and the conduct complained of . . . Third, it must be likely, as opposed to merely speculative, that the injury will be redressed by a favorable decision. *Id.* at 742-743 (1995). The Court emphasized that, to avoid dismissal on standing grounds, the party who seeks the exercise of jurisdiction in his favor must clearly allege facts demonstrating that he is a proper party to invoke judicial resolution of the dispute, and thereafter support this allegation by evidence adduced at trial. *Id.* at 743.

In this instance, if the petitioners contend that they were denied equal protection because they belong to the class of individuals who are foreclosed from having deviate sexual intercourse with another person of the same sex, they do not state an equal protection violation. Under the facially neutral conduct prohibitions of section 21.06, everyone in Texas is foreclosed from having deviate sexual intercourse with another person of the same sex. If the petitioners contend, however, that they were denied equal protection because they belong to a class of individuals who have been disproportionately impacted by section 21.06, the record is silent as to whether they in fact belong to such a class.

This Court accords equal protection standing only to "those persons who are personally denied equal treatment." *See id.* at 743-744 (quoting *Allen v. Wright*, 468 U.S. 737, 755 (1984). While the petitioners clearly have been prosecuted under section 21.06, it is not established in this record that they possess the same-sex orientation that they contend is singled out for discrimination by the statute. As such, the writ of certiorari should be dismissed as improvidently granted, or standing should be denied to these petitioners for lack of an adequate record to establish an equal protection violation against them personally.

C. The Texas Legislature did not purposefully discriminate in the passage of section 21.06. Although the petitioners assert that the "group targeted and harmed by the Homosexual Conduct Law is, of course, gay people," see Brief of Petitioners 33, and much of their briefing is related to the unequal protection of the laws with respect to homosexuals, *see id.* at 40-50, section 21.06 does not expressly classify its offenders on the basis of their sexual orientation. Rather, it criminalizes homosexual conduct without reference to a defendant's sexual orientation. *Lawrence,* 41 S.W.2d at 353; see also Editors of the Harvard Law Review, *Sexual Orientation and the Law,* at 16 (Harvard University Press 1990) ("Although litigants and courts have assumed that [samesex] sodomy statutes classify based on sexual preference, the statutes actually prevent all persons from engaging in same-sex sodomy, regardless of sexual orientation.").[24]

The focus of section 21.06 on conduct, rather than sexual orientation, does not foreclose equal protection review. A statute, though facially neutral, may still be challenged as constitutionally infirm under the Equal Protection Clause if the challenger can prove that the statute was enacted because of a discriminatory purpose. *Personnel Administrator of Massachusetts v. Feeney,* 442 U.S. 256, 279 (1979). This intent component is significant: equal protection jurisprudence focuses on the purposeful marginalization of disfavored groups. *See id.* at 274, 279 (holding that "discriminatory purpose" implies more than intent as volition or intent as awareness of the consequences; it implies that

the decisionmaker [in that case a state legislature] selected or reaffirmed a particular course of action at least partly "because of," and not merely "in spite of," its adverse effects upon an identifiable group); *Hernandez v. New York,* 500 U.S. 352, 372-73 (1991) (O'Connor, J., concurring) ("An unwavering line of cases from this Court holds that a violation of the Equal Protection Clause requires state action motivated by discriminatory intent; the disproportionate effects of state action are not sufficient to establish such a violation.").

As such, assuming that petitioners appear as representatives of the class of individuals who are disproportionately affected by section 21.06, it is incumbent upon them to prove the purposeful intent of the Texas Legislature in order to perfect their equal protection claim. Cf. *State v. Baxley,* 656 So.2d 973, 978 (La. 1995) ("Given the presumption of the constitutionality of legislation which does not classify on its face, it is incumbent upon the challenger of the legislation to prove the discriminatory purpose. In the present case, the record is devoid of any evidence that the crime against nature statute was enacted for the purpose of discriminating against gay men and lesbians. Therefore, the statute is not constitutionally infirm on these grounds.").

The record on appeal—which essentially consists of complaints, "probable cause affidavits," motions to quash, and pleas of guilty—provides no such evidence. Likewise, the petitioners have submitted no evidence of the Legislature's intent to invidiously discriminate.

Although commentators have speculated that section 21.06 was enacted in its present form because of political concerns about the impact of decriminalizing homosexual conduct, an alternative interpretation of the Legislature's intent can be inferred from the historical context within which section 21.06 was passed.

In 1854, the State's Fifth Legislature determined that the conduct engaged in by the petitioners in this case—homosexual anal intercourse—should be punishable by hard labor in the penitentiary for up to five years: Sec. 40. If any person shall commit the abominable and detestable crime against nature, either with mankind or with any beast, he shall be punished by confinement to hard labor in the Penitentiary not exceeding five years. Act of February 9, 1854,

---

[24] The authors of the Harvard Law Review treatise go on to assert, however, that an invidious classification can be inferred from the disparate impact of the statute. Id. As will be discussed herein, disparate impact is insufficient in itself to establish an equal protection classification. There must be purposeful invidious discrimination against the affected class, and a review of the historical context in which the Texas statute was enacted does not suggest the presence of such discrimination.

5th Leg., R.S., ch. XLIX, § 40, 1854 Tex. Gen. Laws 58, 66.

Six years later, the Eighth Legislature increased both the minimum and maximum periods of confinement to be assessed upon conviction of that offense: Art. 399c. If any person shall commit with mankind or beast the abominable and detestable crime against nature, he shall be deemed guilty of sodomy, and on conviction thereof, he shall be punished by confinement in the penitentiary for not less than five nor more than fifteen years. Act of February 11, 1860, 8th Leg., R.S., ch. 74, 1860 Tex. Gen. Laws 95, 97.

A Reconstruction-era Texas Supreme Court found the prohibition of the "abominable and detestable crime against nature" to be too vague to be enforced, *Fennell v. State*, 32 Tex. 378 (1869), but by 1893, the Court of Criminal Appeals was willing to look to the common law for guidance in determining what constituted a "crime against nature," and it found that the conduct prohibited by the statute was anal sexual intercourse. See *Prindle v. State*, 21 S.W. 360 (Tex. Crim. App. 1893). In 1943, the statute was amended to the following form:

> Article 524. Sodomy.
>
> Whoever has carnal copulation with a beast, or in an opening of the body, except sexual parts, with another human being, or whoever shall use his mouth on the sexual parts of another human being for the purpose of having carnal copulation, or who shall voluntarily permit the use of his own sexual parts in a lewd and lascivious manner by any minor, shall be guilty of sodomy, and upon conviction thereof shall be deemed guilty of a felony, and shall be confined in the penitentiary not less than two (2) nor more than fifteen (15) years.

Act of April 5, 1943, 48th Leg., R.S., ch. 112, § 1, 1943 Tex. Gen. Laws 194 (hereinafter "article 524").

In 1965, this Court recognized in *Griswold v. Connecticut*, 381 U.S. 479 (1965), a constitutional right of privacy forbidding government regulation of a married couple's access to the use of contraceptives. Decisions followed that further delineated similar rights of privacy, including *Loving v. Virginia*, 388 U.S. 1 (1967), *Eisenstadt v. Baird*, 405 U.S. 438 (1972), and *Roe v. Wade*, 410 U.S. 113 (1973).[25]

As a result of those decisions, article 524 came under attack in federal district court, see

Buchanan v. Batchelor, 308 F. Supp. 729 (N.D. Tex. 1970), rev'd on other grounds, 401 U.S. 989 (1971), and in the Texas Court of Criminal Appeals. See *Pruett v. State*, 463 S.W.2d 191 (Tex. Crim. App. 1971). The *Buchanan* court, a three-judge panel, declared article 524 unconstitutional because it violated the liberty of married couples in their private conduct by subjecting them to felony prosecution for private acts of sodomy, "an intimate relation of husband and wife." *Id.* at 732-33. The court declined to extend its holding to homosexual conduct, specifically noting the limited applicability of *Griswold* to the marital context. *Id.* at 733. The Court thus held article 524 unconstitutional "insofar as it reaches the private, consensual acts of married couples." *Id.* at 735.

Although *Buchanan* was later reversed by this Court and remanded for consideration as to whether abstention was necessary in light of the Court's decision in *Younger v. Harris*, 401 U.S. 37 (1971), and the Texas Court of Criminal Appeals ultimately declined to find article 524 unconstitutional in *Pruett*,[26] these cases were certainly within the constructive knowledge of the 1973 Texas Legislature as it considered what to do with the sodomy statute.

As such, it is a reasonable inference from this context that the Texas Legislature's enactment of section 21.06 in 1973 was not purposefully discriminatory against homosexuals, but was instead a reform of article 524 in accordance with what then appeared to be the direction in which constitutional privacy law was heading. The reformatory nature of the amendments is indicated as well by the Legislature's reduction of the offense from a felony punishable by confinement in the penitentiary for a minimum two years to a misdemeanor punishable only by a fine of up to two hundred dollars, and the

---

[25] In fact, *Roe* was announced on January 23, 1973, just two weeks after the 63rd Texas Legislature convened on January 9, 1973, to enact the legislation that would ultimately include the 1974 Texas Penal Code. See 1973 Tex. Gen. Laws vi (noting date of convening as January 9, 1973).

[26] The reluctance of the Texas Court of Criminal Appeals to invalidate the sodomy statute in *Pruett* may have been related to the facts of the case. *Pruett* was essentially a homosexual rape case, in which the adult defendant "confessed that he committed the offense, after the victim had refused to consent, by striking him in the face with his fist and making him submit." *Pruett*, 463 S.W.2d at 192. The Court expressly noted that it had not been called upon to consider the "question of whether the sodomy statute may be invoked against married couples for private consenual [sic] acts." Id. at 194.

Legislature's formulation of the statute to forbid only certain kinds of homosexual conduct.[27]

The residual differences left over from this kind of benign incremental reform do not amount to purposeful discrimination.[28] See, e.g., *McDonald v. Board of Election Commissioners of Chicago*, 394 U.S. 802, 809 (1969) ("[A] legislature traditionally has been allowed to take reform 'one step at a time, addressing itself to the phase of the problem which seems most acute to the legislative mind,' and a legislature need not run the risk of losing an entire remedial scheme simply because it failed, through inadvertence or otherwise, to cover every evil that might conceivably have been attacked.") (citations omitted); *F.C.C. v. Beach Communications, Inc.*, 508 U.S. 307, 316 (1993) ("[S]cope-of-coverage provisions are unavoidable components of most economic or social legislation. [The necessity of drawing a line of demarcation] renders the precise coordinates of the resulting legislative judgment virtually unreviewable, since the legislature must be allowed leeway to approach a perceived problem incrementally."). Because there is no evidence establishing that the Texas Legislature acted with discriminatory intent in 1973, the presumption of constitutionality persists. The petitioners have not demonstrated purposeful discrimination against the class they purport to represent.

D. Section 21.06 is rationally related to a legitimate state interest.

If a rational-basis analysis is necessary with regard to the promulgation of section 21.06, the State's legitimate interest in protecting its statute from constitutional challenge was in itself a rational basis for legislative action. In addition, section 21.06 rationally furthers other legitimate state interests, namely, the continued expression of the State's long-standing moral disapproval of homosexual conduct, and the deterrence of such immoral sexual activity, particularly with regard to the contemplated conduct of heterosexuals and bisexuals.

1. *Section 21.06 was enacted for the purpose of avoiding litigation and possible invalidation of the predecessor statute.* As noted above, section 21.06 was enacted by a 1973 Texas Legislature which was cognizant of changing judicial attitudes towards the constitutionality of legislation restricting private decisions of married couples. Accordingly, the decision to narrow article 524 was not the irrational product of invidious discrimination against homosexuals, but rather a reasonable retrenchment of the statute to address what may have been perceived to be a constitutional limitation of state authority to regulate marital behavior. No similar concerns existed at that time with respect to the possible constitutional protection of homosexual conduct, thus vitiating the need for immediate legislative reform in that direction.

For the reasons more fully expressed *supra*, this neutral motivation for the amendment of article 524 into the present-day statute—i.e., to avoid a potentially successful challenge to the State's sodomy law by individuals engaging in consensual heterosexual conduct—represents a rational basis for the classification of conduct upon which section 21.06 is based.

2. *Section 21.06 furthers the legitimate governmental interest of promotion of morality.* The promotion of morality has long been recognized as a lawful function of government. See, e.g., *Barbier v. Connolly*, 113 U.S. 27, 31 (1884) (holding that the Equal Protection Clause was not intended "to interfere with the power of the state . . . to prescribe regulations to promote the health, peace, morals, education, and good order of the people"); *Louis K. Liggett Co. v. Baldridge*, 278 U.S. 105, 111-12 (1928) ("The police power may be exerted in the form of state legislation . . . only when such legislation bears a real and substantial relation to the public health, safety, morals, or some other phase of the general welfare."); *Berman v. Parker*, 348 U.S. 26, 32 (1954) (identifying "[p]ublic safety, public health, morality, peace and quiet [and] law and order" as appropriate "application[s] of the police power to municipal affairs"); *Barnes v. Glen Theatre, Inc.*, 501 U.S. 560, 569 (1991) (plurality opinion) (holding that police powers of the State extend to "public health, safety and morals").

Similarly, protection of family and morality has motivated many valid governmental actions.

---

[27] For example, the homosexual conduct statute does not forbid kissing or sexual stimulation of another person of the same sex with hands or fingers. See *Baker v. Wade*, 553 F. Supp. 1121, 1134 (N.D. Tex. 1982), rev'd, 769 F.2d 289 (5th Cir. 1985), *cert. denied*, 478 U.S. 1022 (1986).

[28] The Texas Legislature reenacted the Texas Penal Code in 1993, leaving section 21.06 intact. Act of May 29, 1993, 73rd Leg., R.S., ch. 900, § 1.01, 1993 Tex. Gen. Laws 3589. As was the case in 1973, this reenactment of the status quo was also consistent with the thenprevailing law with respect to recognition of privacy for homosexuals. See *Bowers v. Hardwick*, 478 U.S. 186 (1986). An invidious intent cannot be inferred from the Legislature's passive maintenance of the status quo.

See, e.g., *Barnes,* 501 U.S. at 569 (recognizing legislature's right to "protect 'the social interest in order and morality'" in enacting public indecency statutes); *Michael H. v. Gerald D.,* 491 U.S. 110, 131 (1989) (protection of "integrity of the marital union" as legitimate state interest for denying third-party standing to challenge legitimacy of birth); *City of Dallas v. Stanglin,* 490 U.S. 19, 27 (1989) (protection of teenagers from "corrupting influences" as legitimate state interest for limiting access to dancehall); *Ginsberg v. United States,* 390 U.S. 629, 639 (1968) (approving legislature's legislation against distribution of "girlie magazines" to minors because "legislature could properly conclude that parents and others . . . who have this primary responsibility for children's well-being are entitled to the support of laws designed to aid discharge of that responsibility").

This moral component was at the core of the Fifth Circuit's decision affirming the constitutionality of section 21.06 in 1985. Sitting *en banc,* that court found that "in view of the strong objection to homosexual conduct, which has prevailed in Western culture for the past seven centuries," section 21.06 was rationally related to the implementation of "morality, a permissible state goal," and, therefore, did not violate the Equal Protection Clause. *Baker v. Wade,* 769 F.2d 289, 292 (5th Cir. 1985), *cert. denied,* 478 U.S. 1022 (1986). Other courts at that time reached similar conclusions. See *Dronenburg v. Zech,* 741 F.2d 1388, 1397 (D.C. Cir. 1984) (upholding naval regulations excluding homosexuals from service as a permissible implementation of public morality, and noting the unlikelihood that "very many laws exist whose ultimate justification does not rest upon the society's morality"); *State v. Walsh,* 713 S.W.2d 508, 511-12 (Mo. 1986) (holding that "punishing homosexual acts as a Class A misdemeanor . . . is rationally related to the State's constitutionally permissible objective of implementing and promoting the public morality").

Shortly before the courts in *Baker and Dronenburg* upheld legislation related to homosexual conduct, the Eleventh Circuit reached an opposite conclusion with respect to Georgia's sodomy statute. See *Hardwick v. Bowers,* 760 F.2d 1202, 1212 (11th Cir. 1985) (holding that the Georgia statute implicated *Hardwick's* fundamental rights because his homosexual activity was a private and intimate association placed beyond the reach of state regulation by the

Ninth Amendment and the "notion of fundamental fairness embodied in the due process clause of the Fourteenth Amendment").

This Court granted the Georgia Attorney General's petition for *certiorari,* and declined to invalidate Georgia's sodomy statute, finding that there was no fundamental right to engage in homosexual sodomy. *Bowers,* 478 U.S. at 191. In reaching this conclusion, the Court noted the long history of moral disapproval of homosexual conduct, noting that "[p]roscriptions against that conduct have ancient roots," and that, until 1961, sodomy had been illegal in all fifty states. *Id.* at 192; *see also id.* at 196-97 (Burger, C.J., concurring) (detailing historical genesis of sodomy statutes).

This Court dismissed *Hardwick's* assertion that there was no rational basis for the Georgia sodomy statute, explicitly rejecting the notion that laws may not be based upon perceptions of morality:

Even if the conduct at issue here is not a fundamental right, respondent asserts that there must be a rational basis for the law and that there is none in this case other than the presumed belief of a majority of the electorate in Georgia that homosexual sodomy is immoral and unacceptable. This is said to be an inadequate rationale to support the law. The law, however, is constantly based on notions of morality, and if all laws representing essentially moral choices are to be invalidated under the Due Process Clause, the courts will be very busy indeed. Even respondent makes no such claim, but insists that majority sentiments about the morality of homosexuality should be declared inadequate. We do not agree, and are unpersuaded that the sodomy laws of some 25 States should be invalidated on this basis. *Id.* at 196. This Court shortly thereafter declined to review the constitutionality of section 21.06 of the Texas Penal Code. See *Baker v. Wade,* 478 U.S. 1022 (1986) (denying petition for writ of certiorari).

Nothing in this Court's jurisprudence since *Bowers* justifies revisiting its conclusion that morality constitutes an appropriate basis for legislative action. Petitioners cite *Romer v. Evans,* 517 U.S. 620 (1996) as antithetical to *Bowers,* but a careful review of *Romer* indicates that its application of equal protection principles to an overbroad state constitutional amendment does not implicate the legislature's authority to prohibit what has traditionally been perceived as immoral conduct.

In *Romer,* the citizens of the State of Colorado approved a constitutional amendment that invalidated municipal ordinances banning discrimination on the basis of sexual orientation, and prohibited all legislative, executive or judicial action at any level of state or local government designed to protect homosexuals, lesbians, or bisexuals. *See id.* at 627. The Court summarized the impact of the amendment:

Homosexuals, by state decree, are put in a solitary class with respect to transactions and relations in both the private and governmental spheres. The amendment withdraws from homosexuals, but no others, specific legal protection from the injuries caused by discrimination, and it forbids reinstatement of these laws and policies. *Id.*

In overturning the amendment on equal protection grounds, the Court found that the statute "has the peculiar property of imposing a broad and undifferentiated disability on a single named group" that is "at once too narrow and too broad," identifying "persons by a single trait and then den[ying] them protection across the board." *Id.* at 632-33. In other words, the Colorado initiative was held unconstitutional because it went beyond punishment of the act of engaging in homosexual conduct and sought to disenfranchise individuals because of the mere tendency or predilection to engage in such conduct.

Section 21.06 does not suffer from that flaw. It is the homosexual conduct that is viewed as immoral, and a statute rendering that conduct illegal is obviously related to the goal of discouraging the conduct and thereby implementing morality. A statute that, say, prohibited all individuals with a homosexual orientation from attending public schools would not be rationally related to that goal and would violate the Equal Protection Clause, but a statute imposing criminal liability only upon persons who actually engage in homosexual conduct is perfectly tailored to implement the communal belief that the conduct is wrong and should be discouraged.

Notably, the issue of morality as a rational basis for the amendment was not implicated in *Romer.*[29] The lawyers challenging Amendment 2 did not ask this Court to overrule *Bowers,* and the lawyers for the State of Colorado avoided relying on it in their arguments. *Romer,* 517 U.S. at 635 (identifying primary rationale for

Amendment 2 as "respect for other citizens' freedom of association" and Colorado's "interest in conserving resources to fight discrimination against other groups"); 517 U.S. at 641 (Scalia, J., dissenting) ("Respondents' briefs did not urge overruling *Bowers,* and at oral argument respondents' counsel expressly disavowed any intent to seek such overruling."); see generally Thomas C. Grey, *Bowers v. Hardwick Diminished,* 68 U. Colo. L. Rev. 373, 375 & notes 13-14 (1997) (discussing general absence of advocacy related to *Bowers* in the *Romer* litigation).

In the absence of any party raising morality as a justification, the *Romer* court prudentially declined to raise the issue itself. As the court below observed: *Romer . . .* does not disavow the Court's previous holding in *Bowers;* it does not elevate homosexuals to a suspect class; it does not suggest that statutes prohibiting homosexual conduct violate the Equal Protection Clause; and it does not challenge the concept that the preservation and protection of morality is a legitimate state interest.

Lawrence, 41 S.W.3d at 355. As such, *Romer* does not contradict the ultimate conclusion in *Bowers*—that majoritarian moral standards can be a rational basis for prohibitions against certain homosexual conduct. The State does not dispute that invidious intent can be inferred from classifications based on race, gender, economic status, or mental retardation. See, e.g., *Palmore v. Sidoti,* 466 U.S. 429 (1984) (reversing order denying custody based on racial considerations); *Frontiero v. Richardson,* 411 U.S. 677 (1973) (reversing gender-based classification in distribution of military benefits); *United States Department of Agriculture v. Moreno,* 413 U.S. 528 (1973) (striking down grossly overbroad classification discriminating against "individuals who live in households containing one or more members who are unrelated to the rest"); *Cleburne,* 473 U.S. 432 (1985) (striking down zoning restriction against group home for men-

---

[29] The Colorado constitutional amendment, which one commentator characterized as a "squirrelly antigay initiative adopted by narrow margins in an outlier state," see William N. Eskridge Jr., *Gaylaw: Challenging the Apartheid of the Closet* 229 (1999), lent itself to a holding that bypassed the role of morality in legislation. See also Lynn A. Baker, *The Missing Pages of the Majority Opinion in Romer v. Evans,* 68 U. Colo. L. Rev. 387, 408 (1997) (arguing that *Romer* is generally limited to its facts because "it is Amendment 2's unjustifiable and unprecedented scope, [its] 'sheer breadth,' that distinguishes it" from other legislation).

tally retarded based on negative reactions of neighbors to proximity). In those cases, the Court fairly reduced the asserted bases for discriminatory classifications to unsubstantiated negative views about the affected individuals. See *Romer*, 517 U.S. at 635 (prohibiting "status-based" legislation that is "a classification of persons undertaken for its own sake"). Those classifications do not implicate a moral component, though, as does a classification identifying types of homosexual conduct. As previously noted, the history of prohibitions against homosexual sodomy—in the common law, American law, and Texas law—is ancient, and the legislature's deference to these moral traditions is appropriate and rational.[30]

The prohibition of homosexual conduct in section 21.06 represents the reasoned judgment of the Texas Legislature that such conduct is immoral and should be deterred.[31] Although the application of sodomy statutes is not common because of the nature and circumstances of the offense, the statutes, like many others, express a baseline standard expressing the core moral beliefs of the people of the State. Whether this Court perceives this position to be wise or unwise, long-established principles of federalism dictate that the Court defer to the Texas Legislature's judgment and to the collective good sense of the people of the State of Texas, in their effort to enforce public morality and promote family values through the promulgation of penal statutes such as section 21.06.

---

[30] *See* Michael McConnell, *The Role of Democratic Politics in Transforming Moral Convictions into Law*, 98 Yale L. Rev. 1501 (1989), arguing that deference to traditions of morality is "natural and inevitable . . . but it is also sensible":

An individual has only his own, necessarily limited, intelligence and experience (personal and vicarious) to draw upon. Tradition, by contrast, is composed of the cumulative thoughts and experiences of thousands of individuals over an expanse of time, each of them making incremental and experimental alterations (often unconsciously), which are then adopted or rejected (again, often unconsciously) on the basis of experience—the experience, that is, of whether they advance the good life.

[31] In fact, although the statute is unlikely to deter many individuals with an exclusively homosexual orientation, the Legislature rationally could have concluded that section 21.06 would be effective to some degree in deterring the remaining population (i.e., persons with a heterosexual or bisexual orientation) from detrimentally experimenting in homosexual conduct.

III. Summary.

Public opinion regarding moral issues may change over time, but what has not changed is the understanding that government may require adherence to certain widely accepted moral standards and sanction deviation from those standards, so long as it does not interfere with constitutionally protected liberties. The legislature exists so that laws can be repealed or modified to match prevailing views regarding what is right and wrong, and so that the citizens' elected representatives can fine-tune the severity of the penalties to be attached to wrongful conduct. Perhaps homosexual conduct is not now universally regarded with the same abhorrence it inspired at the time of the adoption of our Federal Constitution, but any lag in legislative response to a mere change of public opinion—if such a lag actually exists—cannot and must not constitute the basis for a finding that the legislature's original enactment exceeded its constitutional authority.

As stated in *Glucksberg*, 521 U.S. at 735-36, there is "an earnest and profound debate about the morality, legality and practicality" of the statute in question; and the affirmance of the decision of the court of appeals in this case will "permit this debate to continue, as it should in a democratic society."

CONCLUSION

It is respectfully submitted that the petition for writ of certiorari should be dismissed as improvidently granted, or, in the alternative, that the judgment of the Texas Court of Appeals for the Fourteenth District should be in all things affirmed.

Charles A. Rosenthal Jr.
Harris County District Attorney

William J. Delmore III*
Scott A. Durfee
Assistant District Attorneys
Harris County, Texas
1201 Franklin, Suite 600
Houston, Texas 77002
(713) 755-5826
**Counsel of Record*

Counsel for Respondent

IN THE SUPREME COURT OF THE UNITED STATES

JOHN GEDDES LAWRENCE AND TYRON GAR-
NER, APPELLANTS

V.

THE STATE OF TEXAS, APPELLEE

In Writ of Certiorari to the Court of Appeals of
Texas, Fourteenth District

No. 02-102. Argued March 26, 2003–Decided
June 26, 2003

—m—

SUMMARY OF ARGUMENT

Responding to a reported weapons disturbance in a private residence, Houston police
entered petitioner Lawrence's apartment and saw
him and another adult man, petitioner Garner,
engaging in a private, consensual sexual act.
Petitioners were arrested and convicted of deviate
sexual intercourse in violation of a Texas statute
forbidding two persons of the same sex to engage
in certain intimate sexual conduct. In affirming,
the State Court of Appeals held, *inter alia,* that the
statute was not unconstitutional under the Due
Process Clause of the Fourteenth Amendment.
The court considered *Bowers v. Hardwick,* 478 U.
S. 186, controlling on that point.

Held: The Texas statute making it a crime for
two persons of the same sex to engage in certain
intimate sexual conduct violates the Due Process
Clause. pp. 3–18.

(a) Resolution of this case depends on
whether petitioners were free as adults to engage
in private conduct in the exercise of their liberty
under the Due Process Clause. For this inquiry
the Court deems it necessary to reconsider its
Bowers holding. The *Bowers* Court's initial substantive statement—"The issue presented is
whether the Federal Constitution confers a fundamental right upon homosexuals to engage in
sodomy ... ," 478 U. S., at 190—discloses the
Court's failure to appreciate the extent of the
liberty at stake. To say that the issue in *Bowers*
was simply the right to engage in certain sexual
conduct demeans the claim the individual put
forward, just as it would demean a married couple were it said that marriage is just about the
right to have sexual intercourse. Although the
laws involved in *Bowers* and here purport to do

not more than prohibit a particular sexual act,
their penalties and purposes have more far-
reaching consequences, touching upon the most
private human conduct, sexual behavior, and in
the most private of places, the home. They seek
to control a personal relationship that, whether
or not entitled to formal recognition in the law,
is within the liberty of persons to choose without being punished as criminals. The liberty
protected by the Constitution allows homosexual persons the right to choose to enter upon relationships in the confines of their homes and
their own private lives and still retain their dignity as free persons. pp. 3–6.

(b) Having misapprehended the liberty claim
presented to it, the *Bowers* Court stated that proscriptions against sodomy have ancient roots. 478
U. S., at 192. It should be noted, however, that
there is no longstanding history in this country of
laws directed at homosexual conduct as a distinct
matter. Early American sodomy laws were not
directed at homosexuals as such but instead
sought to prohibit nonprocreative sexual activity
more generally, whether between men and
women or men and men. Moreover, early
sodomy laws seem not to have been enforced
against consenting adults acting in private.
Instead, sodomy prosecutions often involved
predatory acts against those who could not or did
not consent: relations between men and minor
girls or boys, between adults involving force,
between adults implicating disparity in status, or
between men and animals. The longstanding
criminal prohibition of homosexual sodomy
upon which *Bowers* placed such reliance is as consistent with a general condemnation of nonprocreative sex as it is with an established tradition of
prosecuting acts because of their homosexual
character. Far from possessing "ancient roots,"
ibid., American laws targeting same-sex couples
did not develop until the last third of the 20th
century. Even now, only nine States have singled
out same-sex relations for criminal prosecution.
Thus, the historical grounds relied upon in
Bowers are more complex than the majority opinion and the concurring opinion by Chief Justice
Burger there indicated. They are not without
doubt and, at the very least, are overstated. The
Bowers Court was, of course, making the broader
point that for centuries there have been powerful
voices to condemn homosexual conduct as
immoral, but this Court's obligation is to define
the liberty of all, not to mandate its own moral
code, *Planned Parenthood of Southeastern Pa. v.*

Casey, 505 U. S. 833, 850. The Nation's laws and traditions in the past half century are most relevant here. They show an emerging awareness that liberty gives substantial protection to adult persons in deciding how to conduct their private lives in matters pertaining to sex. See *County of Sacramento v. Lewis,* 523 U. S. 833, 857. pp. 6–12.

(c) *Bowers'* deficiencies became even more apparent in the years following its announcement. The 25 States with laws prohibiting the conduct referenced in *Bowers* are reduced now to 13, of which 4 enforce their laws only against homosexual conduct. In those States, including Texas, that still proscribe sodomy (whether for same-sex or heterosexual conduct), there is a pattern of nonenforcement with respect to consenting adults acting in private. *Casey, supra,* at 851—which confirmed that the Due Process Clause protects personal decisions relating to marriage, procreation, contraception, family relationships, child rearing, and education—and *Romer v. Evans,* 517 U. S. 620, 624—which struck down class-based legislation directed at homosexuals—cast *Bowers'* holding into even more doubt. The stigma the Texas criminal statute imposes, moreover, is not trivial. Although the offense is but a minor misdemeanor, it remains a criminal offense with all that imports for the dignity of the persons charged, including notation of convictions on their records and on job application forms, and registration as sex offenders under state law. Where a case's foundations have sustained serious erosion, criticism from other sources is of greater significance. In the United States, criticism of *Bowers* has been substantial and continuing, disapproving of its reasoning in all respects, not just as to its historical assumptions. And, to the extent *Bowers* relied on values shared with a wider civilization, the case's reasoning and holding have been rejected by the European Court of Human Rights, and that other nations have taken action consistent with an affirmation of the protected right of homosexual adults to engage in intimate, consensual conduct. There has been no showing that in this country the governmental interest in circumscribing personal choice is somehow more legitimate or urgent. Stare decisis is not an inexorable command. *Payne v. Tennessee,* 501 U. S. 808, 828. *Bowers'* holding has not induced detrimental reliance of the sort that could counsel against overturning it once there are compelling reasons to do so. *Casey, supra,* at 855–856. *Bowers* causes uncertainty, for the precedents before and after it contradict its central holding. pp. 12–17.

(d) *Bowers'* rationale does not withstand careful analysis. In his dissenting opinion in *Bowers* Justice Stevens concluded that (1) the fact a State's governing majority has traditionally viewed a particular practice as immoral is not a sufficient reason for upholding a law prohibiting the practice, and (2) individual decisions concerning the intimacies of physical relationships, even when not intended to produce offspring, are a form of "liberty" protected by due process. That analysis should have controlled *Bowers,* and it controls here. *Bowers* was not correct when it was decided, is not correct today, and is hereby overruled. This case does not involve minors, persons who might be injured or coerced, those who might not easily refuse consent, or public conduct or prostitution. It does involve two adults who, with full and mutual consent, engaged in sexual practices common to a homosexual lifestyle. Petitioners' right to liberty under the Due Process Clause gives them the full right to engage in private conduct without government intervention. *Casey, supra,* at 847. The Texas statute furthers no legitimate state interest which can justify its intrusion into the individual's personal and private life. pp. 17–18.

41 S. W. 3d 349, reversed and remanded.

Kennedy, J., delivered the opinion of the Court, in which Stevens, Souter, Ginsburg, and Breyer, JJ., joined. O'Connor, J., filed an opinion concurring in the judgment. Scalia, J., filed a dissenting opinion, in which Rehnquist, C. J., and Thomas, J., joined. Thomas, J., filed a dissenting opinion.

Justice Kennedy delivered the opinion of the Court.

ARGUMENT

Liberty protects the person from unwarranted government intrusions into a dwelling or other private places. In our tradition the State is not omnipresent in the home. And there are other spheres of our lives and existence, outside the home, where the State should not be a dominant presence. Freedom extends beyond spatial bounds. Liberty presumes an autonomy of self that includes freedom of thought, belief, expression, and certain intimate conduct. The instant case involves liberty of the person both in its spatial and more transcendent dimensions.

I

The question before the Court is the validity of a Texas statute making it a crime for two persons of the same sex to engage in certain intimate sexual conduct.

In Houston, Texas, officers of the Harris County Police Department were dispatched to a private residence in response to a reported weapons disturbance. They entered an apartment where one of the petitioners, John Geddes Lawrence, resided. The right of the police to enter does not seem to have been questioned. The officers observed Lawrence and another man, Tyron Garner, engaging in a sexual act. The two petitioners were arrested, held in custody over night, and charged and convicted before a Justice of the Peace.

The complaints described their crime as "deviate sexual intercourse, namely anal sex, with a member of the same sex (man)." App. to Pet. for Cert. 127a, 139a. The applicable state law is Tex. Penal Code Ann. §21.06(a) (2003). It provides: "A person commits an offense if he engages in deviate sexual intercourse with another individual of the same sex." The statute defines "[d]eviate sexual intercourse" as follows:

"(A) any contact between any part of the genitals of one person and the mouth or anus of another person; or

"(B) the penetration of the genitals or the anus of another person with an object." §21.01(1).

The petitioners exercised their right to a trial *de novo* in Harris County Criminal Court. They challenged the statute as a violation of the Equal Protection Clause of the Fourteenth Amendment and of a like provision of the Texas Constitution. Tex. Const., Art. 1, §3a. Those contentions were rejected. The petitioners, having entered a plea of *nolo contendere,* were each fined $200 and assessed court costs of $141.25. App. to Pet. for Cert. 107a–110a.

The Court of Appeals for the Texas Fourteenth District considered the petitioners' federal constitutional arguments under both the Equal Protection and Due Process Clauses of the Fourteenth Amendment. After hearing the case en banc the court, in a divided opinion, rejected the constitutional arguments and affirmed the convictions. 41 S. W. 3d 349 (Tex. App. 2001). The majority opinion indicates that the Court of Appeals considered our decision in *Bowers v.*

Hardwick, 478 U. S. 186 (1986), to be controlling on the federal due process aspect of the case. *Bowers* then being authoritative, this was proper.

We granted certiorari, 537 U. S. 1044 (2002), to consider three questions:

1. "Whether Petitioners' criminal convictions under the Texas 'Homosexual Conduct' law—which criminalizes sexual intimacy by same-sex couples, but not identical behavior by different-sex couples—violate the Fourteenth Amendment guarantee of equal protection of laws?

2. "Whether Petitioners' criminal convictions for adult consensual sexual intimacy in the home violate their vital interests in liberty and privacy protected by the Due Process Clause of the Fourteenth Amendment?

3. "Whether *Bowers v. Hardwick,* 478 U. S. 186 (1986), should be overruled?" Pet. for Cert. i.

The petitioners were adults at the time of the alleged offense. Their conduct was in private and consensual.

II

We conclude the case should be resolved by determining whether the petitioners were free as adults to engage in the private conduct in the exercise of their liberty under the Due Process Clause of the Fourteenth Amendment to the Constitution. For this inquiry we deem it necessary to reconsider the Court's holding in *Bowers.*

There are broad statements of the substantive reach of liberty under the Due Process Clause in earlier cases, including *Pierce v. Society of Sisters,* 268 U. S. 510 (1925), and *Meyer v. Nebraska,* 262 U. S. 390 (1923); but the most pertinent beginning point is our decision in *Griswold v. Connecticut,* 381 U. S. 479 (1965).

In *Griswold* the Court invalidated a state law prohibiting the use of drugs or devices of contraception and counseling or aiding and abetting the use of contraceptives. The Court described the protected interest as a right to privacy and placed emphasis on the marriage relation and the protected space of the marital bedroom. *Id.,* at 485.

After *Griswold* it was established that the right to make certain decisions regarding sexual conduct extends beyond the marital relationship. In *Eisenstadt v. Baird,* 405 U. S. 438 (1972), the Court invalidated a law prohibiting the distribution of contraceptives to unmarried per-

U.S. SUPREME COURT, JUNE 2003

U.S. SUPREME
COURT,
JUNE 2003

sons. The case was decided under the Equal Protection Clause, *id.,* at 454; but with respect to unmarried persons, the Court went on to state the fundamental proposition that the law impaired the exercise of their personal rights, *ibid.* It quoted from the statement of the Court of Appeals finding the law to be in conflict with fundamental human rights, and it followed with this statement of its own:

> "It is true that in *Griswold* the right of privacy in question inhered in the marital relationship. . . . If the right of privacy means anything, it is the right of the individual, married or single, to be free from unwarranted governmental intrusion into matters so fundamentally affecting a person as the decision whether to bear or beget a child." *Id.,* at 453.

The opinions in *Griswold* and Eisenstadt were part of the background for the decision in *Roe v. Wade,* 410 U. S. 113 (1973). As is well known, the case involved a challenge to the Texas law prohibiting abortions, but the laws of other States were affected as well. Although the Court held the woman's rights were not absolute, her right to elect an abortion did have real and substantial protection as an exercise of her liberty under the Due Process Clause. The Court cited cases that protect spatial freedom and cases that go well beyond it. *Roe* recognized the right of a woman to make certain fundamental decisions affecting her destiny and confirmed once more that the protection of liberty under the Due Process Clause has a substantive dimension of fundamental significance in defining the rights of the person.

In *Carey v. Population Services Int'l,* 431 U. S. 678 (1977), the Court confronted a New York law forbidding sale or distribution of contraceptive devices to persons under 16 years of age. Although there was no single opinion for the Court, the law was invalidated. Both *Eisenstadt* and *Carey,* as well as the holding and rationale in *Roe,* confirmed that the reasoning of *Griswold* could not be confined to the protection of rights of married adults. This was the state of the law with respect to some of the most relevant cases when the Court considered *Bowers v. Hardwick.*

The facts in *Bowers* had some similarities to the instant case. A police officer, whose right to enter seems not to have been in question, observed Hardwick, in his own bedroom, engaging in intimate sexual conduct with another adult male. The conduct was in violation of a Georgia statute making it a criminal offense to engage in sodomy. One difference between the two cases is that the Georgia statute prohibited the conduct whether or not the participants were of the same sex, while the Texas statute, as we have seen, applies only to participants of the same sex. *Hardwick* was not prosecuted, but he brought an action in federal court to declare the state statute invalid. He alleged he was a practicing homosexual and that the criminal prohibition violated rights guaranteed to him by the Constitution. The Court, in an opinion by Justice White, sustained the Georgia law. Chief Justice Burger and Justice Powell joined the opinion of the Court and filed separate, concurring opinions. Four Justices dissented. 478 U. S., at 199 (opinion of Blackmun, J., joined by Brennan, Marshall, and Stevens, JJ.); *id.,* at 214 (opinion of Stevens, J., joined by Brennan and Marshall, JJ.).

The Court began its substantive discussion in *Bowers* as follows: "The issue presented is whether the Federal Constitution confers a fundamental right upon homosexuals to engage in sodomy and hence invalidates the laws of the many States that still make such conduct illegal and have done so for a very long time." *Id.,* at 190. That statement, we now conclude, discloses the Court's own failure to appreciate the extent of the liberty at stake. To say that the issue in *Bowers* was simply the right to engage in certain sexual conduct demeans the claim the individual put forward, just as it would demean a married couple were it to be said marriage is simply about the right to have sexual intercourse. The laws involved in *Bowers* and here are, to be sure, statutes that purport to do no more than prohibit a particular sexual act. Their penalties and purposes, though, have more far-reaching consequences, touching upon the most private human conduct, sexual behavior, and in the most private of places, the home. The statutes do seek to control a personal relationship that, whether or not entitled to formal recognition in the law, is within the liberty of persons to choose without being punished as criminals.

This, as a general rule, should counsel against attempts by the State, or a court, to define the meaning of the relationship or to set its boundaries absent injury to a person or abuse of an institution the law protects. It suffices for us to acknowledge that adults may choose to enter upon this relationship in the confines of their homes and their own private lives and still retain their dignity as free persons. When sexuality finds overt expression in intimate conduct with another person, the conduct can be but one element in a personal bond that is more enduring. The liberty protected by the Constitution allows homosexual persons the right to make this choice.

Having misapprehended the claim of liberty there presented to it, and thus stating the claim to be whether there is a fundamental right to engage in consensual sodomy, the *Bowers* Court said: "Proscriptions against that conduct have ancient roots." *Id.,* at 192. In academic writings, and in many of the scholarly amicus briefs filed to assist the Court in this case, there are fundamental criticisms of the historical premises relied upon by the majority and concurring opinions in *Bowers.* Brief for Cato Institute as *Amicus Curiae* 16–17; Brief for American Civil Liberties Union et al. as *Amici Curiae* 15–21; Brief for Professors of History et al. as *Amici Curiae* 3–10. We need not enter this debate in the attempt to reach a definitive historical judgment, but the following considerations counsel against adopting the definitive conclusions upon which *Bowers* placed such reliance.

At the outset it should be noted that there is no longstanding history in this country of laws directed at homosexual conduct as a distinct matter. Beginning in colonial times there were prohibitions of sodomy derived from the English criminal laws passed in the first instance by the Reformation Parliament of 1533. The English prohibition was understood to include relations between men and women as well as relations between men and men. See, e.g., *King v. Wiseman,* 92 Eng. Rep. 774, 775 (K. B. 1718) (interpreting "mankind" in Act of 1533 as including women and girls). Nineteenth-century commentators similarly read American sodomy, buggery, and crime-against-nature statutes as criminalizing certain relations between men and women and between men and men. See, e.g., 2 J. Bishop, Criminal Law §1028 (1858); 2 J. Chitty, Criminal Law 47–50 (5th Am. ed. 1847); R. Desty, A Compendium of American Criminal Law 143 (1882); J. May, The Law of Crimes §203 (2d ed. 1893). The absence of legal prohibitions focusing on homosexual conduct may be explained in part by noting that according to some scholars the concept of the homosexual as a distinct category of person did not emerge until the late 19th century. See, e.g., J. Katz, *The*

Invention of Heterosexuality 10 (1995); J. D'Emilio & E. Freedman, *Intimate Matters: A History of Sexuality in America* 121 (2d ed. 1997) ("The modern terms *homosexuality* and *heterosexuality* do not apply to an era that had not yet articulated these distinctions"). Thus early American sodomy laws were not directed at homosexuals as such but instead sought to prohibit nonprocreative sexual activity more generally. This does not suggest approval of homosexual conduct. It does tend to show that this particular form of conduct was not thought of as a separate category from like conduct between heterosexual persons.

Laws prohibiting sodomy do not seem to have been enforced against consenting adults acting in private. A substantial number of sodomy prosecutions and convictions for which there are surviving records were for predatory acts against those who could not or did not consent, as in the case of a minor or the victim of an assault. As to these, one purpose for the prohibitions was to ensure there would be no lack of coverage if a predator committed a sexual assault that did not constitute rape as defined by the criminal law. Thus the model sodomy indictments presented in a 19th-century treatise, see 2 Chitty, *supra,* at 49, addressed the predatory acts of an adult man against a minor girl or minor boy. Instead of targeting relations between consenting adults in private, 19th-century sodomy prosecutions typically involved relations between men and minor girls or minor boys, relations between adults involving force, relations between adults implicating disparity in status, or relations between men and animals.

To the extent that there were any prosecutions for the acts in question, 19th-century evidence rules imposed a burden that would make a conviction more difficult to obtain even taking into account the problems always inherent in prosecuting consensual acts committed in private. Under then-prevailing standards, a man could not be convicted of sodomy based upon testimony of a consenting partner, because the partner was considered an accomplice. A partner's testimony, however, was admissible if he or she had not consented to the act or was a minor, and therefore incapable of consent. See, e.g., F. Wharton, Criminal Law 443 (2d ed. 1852); 1 F. Wharton, Criminal Law 512 (8th ed. 1880). The rule may explain in part the infrequency of these prosecutions. In all events that infrequency

U.S. SUPREME
COURT,
JUNE 2003

makes it difficult to say that society approved of a rigorous and systematic punishment of the consensual acts committed in private and by adults. The longstanding criminal prohibition of homosexual sodomy upon which the *Bowers* decision placed such reliance is as consistent with a general condemnation of nonprocreative sex as it is with an established tradition of prosecuting acts because of their homosexual character.

The policy of punishing consenting adults for private acts was not much discussed in the early legal literature. We can infer that one reason for this was the very private nature of the conduct. Despite the absence of prosecutions, there may have been periods in which there was public criticism of homosexuals as such and an insistence that the criminal laws be enforced to discourage their practices. But far from possessing "ancient roots," *Bowers*, 478 U. S., at 192, American laws targeting same-sex couples did not develop until the last third of the 20th century. The reported decisions concerning the prosecution of consensual, homosexual sodomy between adults for the years 1880–1995 are not always clear in the details, but a significant number involved conduct in a public place. See Brief for American Civil Liberties Union et al. as *Amici Curiae* 14–15, and n. 18.

It was not until the 1970's that any State singled out same-sex relations for criminal prosecution, and only nine States have done so. See 1977 Ark. Gen. Acts no. 828; 1983 Kan. Sess. Laws p. 652; 1974 Ky. Acts p. 847; 1977 Mo. Laws p. 687; 1973 Mont. Laws p. 1339; 1977 Nev. Stats. p. 1632; 1989 Tenn. Pub. Acts ch. 591; 1973 Tex. Gen. Laws ch. 399; see also *Post v. State,* 715 P. 2d 1105 (Okla. Crim. App. 1986) (sodomy law invalidated as applied to different-sex couples). Post-*Bowers* even some of these States did not adhere to the policy of suppressing homosexual conduct. Over the course of the last decades, States with same-sex prohibitions have moved toward abolishing them. See, e.g., *Jegley v. Picado,* 349 Ark. 600, 80 S. W. 3d 332 (2002); *Gryczan v. State,* 283 Mont. 433, 942 P. 2d 112 (1997); *Campbell v. Sundquist,* 926 S. W. 2d 250 (Tenn. App. 1996); *Commonwealth v. Wasson,* 842 S. W. 2d 487 (Ky. 1992); see also 1993 Nev. Stats. p. 518 (repealing Nev. Rev. Stat. §201.193).

In summary, the historical grounds relied upon in *Bowers* are more complex than the majority opinion and the concurring opinion by Chief Justice Burger indicate. Their historical premises are not without doubt and, at the very least, are overstated.

It must be acknowledged, of course, that the Court in *Bowers* was making the broader point that for centuries there have been powerful voices to condemn homosexual conduct as immoral. The condemnation has been shaped by religious beliefs, conceptions of right and acceptable behavior, and respect for the traditional family. For many persons these are not trivial concerns but profound and deep convictions accepted as ethical and moral principles to which they aspire and which thus determine the course of their lives. These considerations do not answer the question before us, however. The issue is whether the majority may use the power of the State to enforce these views on the whole society through operation of the criminal law. "Our obligation is to define the liberty of all, not to mandate our own moral code." *Planned Parenthood of Southeastern Pa. v. Casey,* 505 U. S. 833, 850 (1992).

Chief Justice Burger joined the opinion for the Court in *Bowers* and further explained his views as follows: "Decisions of individuals relating to homosexual conduct have been subject to state intervention throughout the history of Western civilization. Condemnation of those practices is firmly rooted in Judeao-Christian moral and ethical standards." 478 U. S., at 196. As with Justice White's assumptions about history, scholarship casts some doubt on the sweeping nature of the statement by Chief Justice Burger as it pertains to private homosexual conduct between consenting adults. See, e.g., Eskridge, Hardwick and Historiography, 1999 U. Ill. L. Rev. 631, 656. In all events we think that our laws and traditions in the past half century are of most relevance here. These references show an emerging awareness that liberty gives substantial protection to adult persons in deciding how to conduct their private lives in matters pertaining to sex. "[H]istory and tradition are the starting point but not in all cases the ending point of the substantive due process inquiry." *County of Sacramento v. Lewis,* 523 U. S. 833, 857 (1998) (Kennedy, J., concurring).

This emerging recognition should have been apparent when *Bowers* was decided. In 1955 the American Law Institute promulgated the Model Penal Code and made clear that it did not recommend or provide for "criminal penalties for consensual sexual relations conducted in private."

ALI, Model Penal Code §213.2, Comment 2, p. 372 (1980). It justified its decision on three grounds: (1) The prohibitions undermined respect for the law by penalizing conduct many people engaged in; (2) the statutes regulated private conduct not harmful to others; and (3) the laws were arbitrarily enforced and thus invited the danger of blackmail. ALI, Model Penal Code, Commentary 277-280 (Tent. Draft No. 4, 1955). In 1961 Illinois changed its laws to conform to the Model Penal Code. Other States soon followed. Brief for Cato Institute as *Amicus Curiae* 15–16.

In *Bowers* the Court referred to the fact that before 1961 all 50 States had outlawed sodomy, and that at the time of the Court's decision 24 States and the District of Columbia had sodomy laws. 478 U. S., at 192–193. Justice Powell pointed out that these prohibitions often were being ignored, however. Georgia, for instance, had not sought to enforce its law for decades. *Id.,* at 197–198, n. 2 ("The history of nonenforcement suggests the moribund character today of laws criminalizing this type of private, consensual conduct")

The sweeping references by Chief Justice Burger to the history of Western civilization and to Judeo-Christian moral and ethical standards did not take account of other authorities pointing in an opposite direction. A committee advising the British Parliament recommended in 1957 repeal of laws punishing homosexual conduct. The Wolfenden Report: Report of the Committee on Homosexual Offenses and Prostitution (1963). Parliament enacted the substance of those recommendations 10 years later. Sexual Offences Act 1967, §1.

Of even more importance, almost five years before *Bowers* was decided the European Court of Human Rights considered a case with parallels to *Bowers* and to today's case. An adult male resident in Northern Ireland alleged he was a practicing homosexual who desired to engage in consensual homosexual conduct. The laws of Northern Ireland forbade him that right. He alleged that he had been questioned, his home had been searched, and he feared criminal prosecution. The court held that the laws proscribing the conduct were invalid under the European Convention on Human Rights. *Dudgeon v. United Kingdom,* 45 Eur. Ct. H. R. (1981) ¶ ;52. Authoritative in all countries that are members of the Council of Europe (21 nations then, 45 nations now), the decision is at odds with the premise in *Bowers* that the claim put forward was insubstantial in our Western civilization.

In our own constitutional system the deficiencies in *Bowers* became even more apparent in the years following its announcement. The 25 States with laws prohibiting the relevant conduct referenced in the *Bowers* decision are reduced now to 13, of which 4 enforce their laws only against homosexual conduct. In those States where sodomy is still proscribed, whether for same-sex or heterosexual conduct, there is a pattern of nonenforcement with respect to consenting adults acting in private. The State of Texas admitted in 1994 that as of that date it had not prosecuted anyone under those circumstances. *State v. Morales,* 869 S. W. 2d 941, 943.

Two principal cases decided after *Bowers* cast its holding into even more doubt. In *Planned Parenthood of Southeastern Pa. v. Casey,* 505 U. S. 833 (1992), the Court reaffirmed the substantive force of the liberty protected by the Due Process Clause. The *Casey* decision again confirmed that our laws and tradition afford constitutional protection to personal decisions relating to marriage, procreation, contraception, family relationships, child rearing, and education. *Id.,* at 851. In explaining the respect the Constitution demands for the autonomy of the person in making these choices, we stated as follows:

> "These matters, involving the most intimate and personal choices a person may make in a lifetime, choices central to personal dignity and autonomy, are central to the liberty protected by the Fourteenth Amendment. At the heart of liberty is the right to define one's own concept of existence, of meaning, of the universe, and of the mystery of human life. Beliefs about these matters could not define the attributes of personhood were they formed under compulsion of the State." *Ibid.*

Persons in a homosexual relationship may seek autonomy for these purposes, just as heterosexual persons do. The decision in *Bowers* would deny them this right.

The second post-*Bowers* case of principal relevance is *Romer v. Evans,* 517 U. S. 620 (1996). There the Court struck down class-based legislation directed at homosexuals as a violation of the Equal Protection Clause. *Romer* invalidated an amendment to Colorado's constitution which named as a solitary class persons who were homosexuals, lesbians, or bisexual either by "orientation, conduct, practices or relationships," *id.,* at 624 (internal quotation marks omitted), and deprived them of protection under state antidiscrimination laws. We concluded that the provision was "born of animosity toward the class of persons affected" and further that it had no rational relation to a legitimate governmental purpose. *Id.,* at 634.

As an alternative argument in this case, counsel for the petitioners and some *amici* contend that *Romer* provides the basis for declaring the Texas statute invalid under the Equal Protection Clause. That is a tenable argument, but we conclude the instant case requires us to address whether *Bowers* itself has continuing validity. Were we to hold the statute invalid under the Equal Protection Clause some might question whether a prohibition would be valid if drawn differently, say, to prohibit the conduct both between same-sex and different-sex participants.

Equality of treatment and the due process right to demand respect for conduct protected by the substantive guarantee of liberty are linked in important respects, and a decision on the latter point advances both interests. If protected conduct is made criminal and the law which does so remains unexamined for its substantive validity, its stigma might remain even if it were not enforceable as drawn for equal protection reasons. When homosexual conduct is made criminal by the law of the State, that declaration in and of itself is an invitation to subject homosexual persons to discrimination both in the public and in the private spheres. The central holding of *Bowers* has been brought in question by this case, and it should be addressed. Its continuance as precedent demeans the lives of homosexual persons.

The stigma this criminal statute imposes, moreover, is not trivial. The offense, to be sure, is but a class C misdemeanor, a minor offense in the Texas legal system. Still, it remains a criminal offense with all that imports for the dignity of the persons charged. The petitioners will bear on their record the history of their criminal convictions. Just this Term we rejected various challenges to state laws requiring the registration of sex offenders. *Smith v. Doe,* 538 U. S. ___ (2003); *Connecticut Dept. of Public Safety v. Doe,* 538 U. S. 1 (2003). We are advised that if Texas convicted an adult for private, consensual homosexual conduct under the statute here in question the convicted person would come within the registration laws of a least four States were he or she to be subject to their jurisdiction. Pet. for Cert.

13, and n. 12 (citing Idaho Code §§18–8301 to 18–8326 (Cum. Supp. 2002); La. Code Crim. Proc. Ann., §§15:540–15:549 (West 2003); Miss. Code Ann. §§45–33–21 to 45–33–57 (Lexis 2003); S. C. Code Ann. §§23–3–400 to 23–3–490 (West 2002)). This underscores the consequential nature of the punishment and the state-sponsored condemnation attendant to the criminal prohibition. Furthermore, the Texas criminal conviction carries with it the other collateral consequences always following a conviction, such as notations on job application forms, to mention but one example.

The foundations of *Bowers* have sustained serious erosion from our recent decisions in *Casey* and *Romer.* When our precedent has been thus weakened, criticism from other sources is of greater significance. In the United States criticism of *Bowers* has been substantial and continuing, disapproving of its reasoning in all respects, not just as to its historical assumptions. See, e.g., C. Fried, Order and Law: Arguing the Reagan Revolution—A Firsthand Account 81–84 (1991); R. Posner, Sex and Reason 341–350 (1992). The courts of five different States have declined to follow it in interpreting provisions in their own state constitutions parallel to the Due Process Clause of the Fourteenth Amendment, see *Jegley v. Picado,* 349 Ark. 600, 80 S. W. 3d 332 (2002); *Powell v. State,* 270 Ga. 327, 510 S. E. 2d 18, 24 (1998); *Gryczan v. State,* 283 Mont. 433, 942 P. 2d 112 (1997); *Campbell v. Sundquist,* 926 S. W. 2d 250 (Tenn. App. 1996); *Commonwealth v. Wasson,* 842 S. W. 2d 487 (Ky. 1992).

To the extent *Bowers* relied on values we share with a wider civilization, it should be noted that the reasoning and holding in *Bowers* have been rejected elsewhere. The European Court of Human Rights has followed not *Bowers* but its own decision in *Dudgeon v. United Kingdom.* See *P. G. & J. H. v. United Kingdom,* App. No. 00044787/98, ¶ ;56 (Eur. Ct. H. R., Sept. 25, 2001); *Modinos v. Cyprus,* 259 Eur. Ct. H. R. (1993); *Norris v. Ireland,* 142 Eur. Ct. H. R. (1988). Other nations, too, have taken action consistent with an affirmation of the protected right of homosexual adults to engage in intimate, consensual conduct. See Brief for Mary Robinson et al. as *Amici Curiae* 11–12. The right the petitioners seek in this case has been accepted as an integral part of human freedom in many other countries. There has been no showing that in this country the governmental interest in circumscribing personal choice is somehow more legitimate or urgent.

The doctrine of *stare decisis* is essential to the respect accorded to the judgments of the Court and to the stability of the law. It is not, however, an inexorable command. *Payne v. Tennessee,* 501 U. S. 808, 828 (1991) ("*Stare decisis* is not an inexorable command; rather, it 'is a principle of policy and not a mechanical formula of adherence to the latest decision'") (quoting *Helvering v. Hallock,* 309 U. S. 106, 119 [1940]). In *Casey* we noted that when a Court is asked to overrule a precedent recognizing a constitutional liberty interest, individual or societal reliance on the existence of that liberty cautions with particular strength against reversing course. 505 U. S., at 855–856; see also *id.,* at 844 ("Liberty finds no refuge in a jurisprudence of doubt"). The holding in *Bowers* however, has not induced detrimental reliance comparable to some instances where recognized individual rights are involved. Indeed, there has been no individual or societal reliance on *Bowers* of the sort that could counsel against overturning its holding once there are compelling reasons to do so. *Bowers* itself causes uncertainty, for the precedents before and after its issuance contradict its central holding.

The rationale of *Bowers* does not withstand careful analysis. In his dissenting opinion in *Bowers* Justice Stevens came to these conclusions:

> "Our prior cases make two propositions abundantly clear. First, the fact that the governing majority in a State has traditionally viewed a particular practice as immoral is not a sufficient reason for upholding a law prohibiting the practice; neither history nor tradition could save a law prohibiting miscegenation from constitutional attack. Second, individual decisions by married persons, concerning the intimacies of their physical relationship, even when not intended to produce offspring, are a form of 'liberty' protected by the Due Process Clause of the Fourteenth Amendment. Moreover, this protection extends to intimate choices by unmarried as well as married persons." 478 U. S., at 216 (footnotes and citations omitted).

Justice Stevens' analysis, in our view, should have been controlling in *Bowers* and should control here.

Bowers was not correct when it was decided, and it is not correct today. It ought not to remain binding precedent. *Bowers v. Hardwick* should be and now is overruled.

The present case does not involve minors. It does not involve persons who might be injured or coerced or who are situated in relationships where consent might not easily be refused. It does not involve public conduct or prostitution. It does not involve whether the government must give formal recognition to any relationship that homosexual persons seek to enter. The case does involve two adults who, with full and mutual consent from each other, engaged in sexual practices common to a homosexual lifestyle. The petitioners are entitled to respect for their private lives. The State cannot demean their existence or control their destiny by making their private sexual conduct a crime. Their right to liberty under the Due Process Clause gives them the full right to engage in their conduct without intervention of the government. "It is a promise of the Constitution that there is a realm of personal liberty which the government may not enter." *Casey, supra,* at 847. The Texas statute furthers no legitimate state interest which can justify its intrusion into the personal and private life of the individual.

Had those who drew and ratified the Due Process Clauses of the Fifth Amendment or the Fourteenth Amendment known the components of liberty in its manifold possibilities, they might have been more specific. They did not presume to have this insight. They knew times can blind us to certain truths and later generations can see that laws once thought necessary and proper in fact serve only to oppress. As the Constitution endures, persons in every generation can invoke its principles in their own search for greater freedom.

The judgment of the Court of Appeals for the Texas Fourteenth District is reversed, and the case is remanded for further proceedings not inconsistent with this opinion.

It is so ordered.

Justice O'Connor, concurring in the judgment.

The Court today overrules *Bowers v. Hardwick,* 478 U. S. 186 (1986). I joined *Bowers,* and do not join the Court in overruling it. Nevertheless, I agree with the Court that Texas' statute banning same-sex sodomy is unconstitutional. See Tex. Penal Code Ann. §21.06 (2003). Rather than relying on the substantive component of the Fourteenth Amendment's Due Process Clause, as the Court does, I base my conclusion on the Fourteenth Amendment's Equal Protection Clause.

U.S. SUPREME
COURT,
JUNE 2003

The Equal Protection Clause of the Fourteenth Amendment "is essentially a direction that all persons similarly situated should be treated alike." *Cleburne v. Cleburne Living Center, Inc.*, 473 U. S. 432, 439 (1985); see also *Plyler v. Doe*, 457 U. S. 202, 216 (1982). Under our rational basis standard of review, "legislation is presumed to be valid and will be sustained if the classification drawn by the statute is rationally related to a legitimate state interest." *Cleburne v. Cleburne Living Center, supra*, at 440; see also *Department of Agriculture v. Moreno*, 413 U. S. 528, 534 (1973); *Romer v. Evans*, 517 U. S. 620, 632-633 (1996); *Nordlinger v. Hahn*, 505 U. S. 1, 11-12 (1992).

Laws such as economic or tax legislation that are scrutinized under rational basis review normally pass constitutional muster, since "the Constitution presumes that even improvident decisions will eventually be rectified by the democratic processes." *Cleburne v. Cleburne Living Center, supra*, at 440; see also *Fitzgerald v. Racing Assn. of Central Iowa, ante*, p. ___; *Williamson v. Lee Optical of Okla., Inc.*, 348 U. S. 483 (1955). We have consistently held, however, that some objectives, such as "a bare ... desire to harm a politically unpopular group," are not legitimate state interests. *Department of Agriculture v. Moreno, supra*, at 534. See also *Cleburne v. Cleburne Living Center, supra*, at 446–447; *Romer v. Evans, supra*, at 632. When a law exhibits such a desire to harm a politically unpopular group, we have applied a more searching form of rational basis review to strike down such laws under the Equal Protection Clause.

We have been most likely to apply rational basis review to hold a law unconstitutional under the Equal Protection Clause where, as here, the challenged legislation inhibits personal relationships. In *Department of Agriculture v. Moreno*, for example, we held that a law preventing those households containing an individual unrelated to any other member of the household from receiving food stamps violated equal protection because the purpose of the law was to "'discriminate against hippies.'"413 U. S., at 534. The asserted governmental interest in preventing food stamp fraud was not deemed sufficient to satisfy rational basis review. *Id.*, at 535–538. In *Eisenstadt v. Baird*, 405 U. S. 438, 447–455 (1972), we refused to sanction a law that discriminated between married and unmarried persons by prohibiting the distribution of contraceptives to single persons. Likewise, in *Cleburne v. Cleburne Living Center, supra,* we held that it was irrational for a State to require a home for the mentally disabled to obtain a special use permit when other residences—like fraternity houses and apartment buildings—did not have to obtain such a permit. And in *Romer v. Evans*, we disallowed a state statute that "impos[ed] a broad and undifferentiated disability on a single named group"—specifically, homosexuals. 517 U. S., at 632. The dissent apparently agrees that if these cases have stare decisis effect, Texas' sodomy law would not pass scrutiny under the Equal Protection Clause, regardless of the type of rational basis review that we apply. See post, at 17–18 (opinion of Scalia, J.).

The statute at issue here makes sodomy a crime only if a person "engages in deviate sexual intercourse with another individual of the same sex." Tex. Penal Code Ann. §21.06(a) (2003). Sodomy between opposite-sex partners, however, is not a crime in Texas. That is, Texas treats the same conduct differently based solely on the participants. Those harmed by this law are people who have a same-sex sexual orientation and thus are more likely to engage in behavior prohibited by §21.06.

The Texas statute makes homosexuals unequal in the eyes of the law by making particular conduct—and only that conduct—subject to criminal sanction. It appears that prosecutions under Texas' sodomy law are rare. See *State v. Morales*, 869 S. W. 2d 941, 943 (Tex. 1994) (noting in 1994 that §21.06 "has not been, and in all probability will not be, enforced against private consensual conduct between adults"). This case shows, however, that prosecutions under §21.06 do occur. And while the penalty imposed on petitioners in this case was relatively minor, the consequences of conviction are not. As the Court notes, see *ante*, at 15, petitioners' convictions, if upheld, would disqualify them from or restrict their ability to engage in a variety of professions, including medicine, athletic training, and interior design. See, e.g., Tex. Occ. Code Ann. §164.051(a)(2)(B) (2003 Pamphlet) (physician); §451.251 (a)(1) (athletic trainer); §1053.252(2) (interior designer). Indeed, were petitioners to move to one of four States, their convictions would require them to register as sex offenders to local law enforcement. See, e.g., Idaho Code §18–8304 (Cum.

U.S. SUPREME
COURT,
JUNE 2003

Supp. 2002); La. Stat. Ann. §15:542 (West Cum. Supp. 2003); Miss. Code Ann. §45–33–25 (West 2003); S. C. Code Ann. §23–3–430 (West Cum. Supp. 2002); cf. *ante*, at 15.

And the effect of Texas' sodomy law is not just limited to the threat of prosecution or consequence of conviction. Texas' sodomy law brands all homosexuals as criminals, thereby making it more difficult for homosexuals to be treated in the same manner as everyone else. Indeed, Texas itself has previously acknowledged the collateral effects of the law, stipulating in a prior challenge to this action that the law "legally sanctions discrimination against [homosexuals] in a variety of ways unrelated to the criminal law," including in the areas of "employment, family issues, and housing." *State v. Morales*, 826 S. W. 2d 201, 203 (Tex. App. 1992).

Texas attempts to justify its law, and the effects of the law, by arguing that the statute satisfies rational basis review because it furthers the legitimate governmental interest of the promotion of morality. In *Bowers*, we held that a state law criminalizing sodomy as applied to homosexual couples did not violate substantive due process. We rejected the argument that no rational basis existed to justify the law, pointing to the government's interest in promoting morality. 478 U. S., at 196. The only question in front of the Court in *Bowers* was whether the substantive component of the Due Process Clause protected a right to engage in homosexual sodomy. *Id.*, at 188, n. 2. *Bowers* did not hold that moral disapproval of a group is a rational basis under the Equal Protection Clause to criminalize homosexual sodomy when heterosexual sodomy is not punished.

This case raises a different issue than *Bowers*: whether, under the Equal Protection Clause, moral disapproval is a legitimate state interest to justify by itself a statute that bans homosexual sodomy, but not heterosexual sodomy. It is not. Moral disapproval of this group, like a bare desire to harm the group, is an interest that is insufficient to satisfy rational basis review under the Equal Protection Clause. See, e.g., *Department of Agriculture v. Moreno, supra,* at 534; *Romer v. Evans*, 517 U. S., at 634–635. Indeed, we have never held that moral disapproval, without any other asserted state interest, is a sufficient rationale under the Equal Protection Clause to justify a law that discriminates among groups of persons.

Moral disapproval of a group cannot be a legitimate governmental interest under the Equal Protection Clause because legal classifications must not be "drawn for the purpose of disadvantaging the group burdened by the law." *Id.*, at 633. Texas' invocation of moral disapproval as a legitimate state interest proves nothing more than Texas' desire to criminalize homosexual sodomy. But the Equal Protection Clause prevents a State from creating "a classification of persons undertaken for its own sake." *Id.*, at 635. And because Texas so rarely enforces its sodomy law as applied to private, consensual acts, the law serves more as a statement of dislike and disapproval against homosexuals than as a tool to stop criminal behavior. The Texas sodomy law "raise[s] the inevitable inference that the disadvantage imposed is born of animosity toward the class of persons affected." *Id.*, at 634.

Texas argues, however, that the sodomy law does not discriminate against homosexual persons. Instead, the State maintains that the law discriminates only against homosexual conduct. While it is true that the law applies only to conduct, the conduct targeted by this law is conduct that is closely correlated with being homosexual. Under such circumstances, Texas' sodomy law is targeted at more than conduct. It is instead directed toward gay persons as a class. "After all, there can hardly be more palpable discrimination against a class than making the conduct that defines the class criminal." *Id.*, at 641 (Scalia, J., dissenting) (internal quotation marks omitted). When a State makes homosexual conduct criminal, and not "deviate sexual intercourse" committed by persons of different sexes, "that declaration in and of itself is an invitation to subject homosexual persons to discrimination both in the public and in the private spheres." *Ante*, at 14.

Indeed, Texas law confirms that the sodomy statute is directed toward homosexuals as a class. In Texas, calling a person a homosexual is slander per se because the word "homosexual" "impute[s] the commission of a crime." *Plumley v. Landmark Chevrolet, Inc.*, 122 F. 3d 308, 310 (CA5 1997) (applying Texas law); see also *Head v. Newton*, 596 S. W. 2d 209, 210 (Tex. App. 1980). The State has admitted that because of the sodomy law, being homosexual carries the presumption of being a criminal. See *State v. Morales*, 826 S. W. 2d, at 202–203 ("[T]he statute brands lesbians and gay men as criminals and

U.S. SUPREME
COURT,
JUNE 2003

thereby legally sanctions discrimination against them in a variety of ways unrelated to the criminal law"). Texas' sodomy law therefore results in discrimination against homosexuals as a class in an array of areas outside the criminal law. See *ibid.* In *Romer v. Evans,* we refused to sanction a law that singled out homosexuals "for disfavored legal status." 517 U. S., at 633. The same is true here. The Equal Protection Clause "'neither knows nor tolerates classes among citizens.'" *Id.,* at 623 (quoting *Plessy v. Ferguson,* 163 U. S. 537, 559 [1896] [Harlan, J. dissenting]).

A State can of course assign certain consequences to a violation of its criminal law. But the State cannot single out one identifiable class of citizens for punishment that does not apply to everyone else, with moral disapproval as the only asserted state interest for the law. The Texas sodomy statute subjects homosexuals to "a lifelong penalty and stigma. A legislative classification that threatens the creation of an underclass ... cannot be reconciled with" the Equal Protection Clause. *Plyler v. Doe,* 457 U. S., at 239 (Powell, J., concurring).

Whether a sodomy law that is neutral both in effect and application, see *Yick Wo v. Hopkins,* 118 U. S. 356 (1886), would violate the substantive component of the Due Process Clause is an issue that need not be decided today. I am confident, however, that so long as the Equal Protection Clause requires a sodomy law to apply equally to the private consensual conduct of homosexuals and heterosexuals alike, such a law would not long stand in our democratic society. In the words of Justice Jackson:

> "The framers of the Constitution knew, and we should not forget today, that there is no more effective practical guaranty against arbitrary and unreasonable government than to require that the principles of law which officials would impose upon a minority be imposed generally. Conversely, nothing opens the door to arbitrary action so effectively as to allow those officials to pick and choose only a few to whom they will apply legislation and thus to escape the political retribution that might be visited upon them if larger numbers were affected." *Railway Express Agency, Inc. v. New York,* 336 U. S. 106, 112–113 (1949) (concurring opinion).

That this law as applied to private, consensual conduct is unconstitutional under the Equal Protection Clause does not mean that other laws distinguishing between heterosexuals and homosexuals would similarly fail under rational-basis review. Texas cannot assert any legitimate state interest here, such as national security or preserving the traditional institution of marriage. Unlike the moral disapproval of same-sex relations—the asserted state interest in this case—other reasons exist to promote the institution of marriage beyond mere moral disapproval of an excluded group.

A law branding one class of persons as criminal solely based on the State's moral disapproval of that class and the conduct associated with that class runs contrary to the values of the Constitution and the Equal Protection Clause, under any standard of review. I therefore concur in the Court's judgment that Texas' sodomy law banning "deviate sexual intercourse" between consenting adults of the same sex, but not between consenting adults of different sexes, is unconstitutional.

Justice Scalia, with whom The Chief Justice and Justice Thomas join, dissenting.

"Liberty finds no refuge in a jurisprudence of doubt." *Planned Parenthood of Southeastern Pa. v. Casey,* 505 U. S. 833, 844 (1992). That was the Court's sententious response, barely more than a decade ago, to those seeking to overrule *Roe v. Wade,* 410 U. S. 113 (1973). The Court's response today, to those who have engaged in a 17-year crusade to overrule *Bowers v. Hardwick,* 478 U. S. 186 (1986), is very different. The need for stability and certainty presents no barrier.

Most of the rest of today's opinion has no relevance to its actual holding—that the Texas statute "furthers no legitimate state interest which can justify" its application to petitioners under rational-basis review. *Ante,* at 18 (overruling *Bowers* to the extent it sustained Georgia's anti-sodomy statute under the rational-basis test). Though there is discussion of "fundamental proposition[s]," *ante,* at 4, and "fundamental decisions," *ibid.* nowhere does the Court's opinion declare that homosexual sodomy is a "fundamental right" under the Due Process Clause; nor does it subject the Texas law to the standard of review that would be appropriate (strict scrutiny) if homosexual sodomy were a "fundamental right." Thus, while overruling the outcome of *Bowers,* the Court leaves strangely untouched its central legal conclusion: "[R]espondent would have us announce ... a fundamental right to engage in homosexual sodomy. This we are quite unwilling to do." 478 U. S., at 191. Instead the Court simply describes petitioners' conduct as "an exercise of their liberty"—which it undoubtedly is—and proceeds to apply an unheard-of form of rational-basis review that will have far-reaching implications beyond this case. *Ante,* at 3.

I

I begin with the Court's surprising readiness to reconsider a decision rendered a mere 17 years ago in *Bowers v. Hardwick.* I do not myself believe in rigid adherence to *stare decisis* in constitutional cases; but I do believe that we should be consistent rather than manipulative in invoking the doctrine. Today's opinions in support of reversal do not bother to distinguish—or indeed, even bother to mention—the paean to *stare decisis* coauthored by three Members of today's majority in *Planned Parenthood v. Casey.* There, when *stare decisis* meant preservation of judicially invented abortion rights, the widespread criticism of was strong reason to *reaffirm* it:

> "Where, in the performance of its judicial duties, the Court decides a case in such a way as to resolve the sort of intensely divisive controversy reflected in *Roe*[,] ... its decision has a dimension that the resolution of the normal case does not carry. . . . [T]o overrule under fire in the absence of the most compelling reason ... would subvert the Court's legitimacy beyond any serious question." 505 U. S., at 866–867.b

Today, however, the widespread opposition to *Bowers,* a decision resolving an issue as "intensely divisive" as the issue in *Roe,* is offered as a reason in favor of overruling it. See *ante,* at 15–16. Gone, too, is any "enquiry" (of the sort conducted in *Casey*) into whether the decision sought to be overruled has "proven 'unworkable,'" *Casey, supra,* at 855.

Today's approach to *stare decisis* invites us to overrule an erroneously decided precedent (including an "intensely divisive" decision) if: (1) its foundations have been "eroded" by subsequent decisions, *ante,* at 15; (2) it has been subject to "substantial and continuing" criticism, *ibid.*; and (3) it has not induced "individual or societal reliance" that counsels against overturning, *ante,* at 16. The problem is that *Roe* itself—which today's majority surely has no disposition to overrule—satisfies these conditions to at least the same degree as *Bowers.*

(1) A preliminary digressive observation with regard to the first factor: The Court's claim that *Planned Parenthood v. Casey, supra,* "casts some doubt" upon the holding in *Bowers* (or any other case, for that matter) does not withstand analysis. *Ante,* at 10. As far as its holding is concerned, *Casey* provided a less expansive right to abortion than did *Roe,* which was already on the books when *Bowers* was decided. And if the Court is referring not to the holding of *Casey,* but to the dictum of its famed sweet-mystery-of-life passage, *ante,* at 13 ("'At the heart of liberty is the right to define one's own concept of existence, of meaning, of the universe, and of the mystery of human life'"): That "casts some doubt" upon either the totality of our jurisprudence or else (presumably the right answer) nothing at all. I have never heard of a law that attempted to restrict one's "right to define" certain concepts; and if the passage calls into question the government's power to regulate actions based on one's self-defined "concept of existence, etc.," it is the passage that ate the rule of law.

I do not quarrel with the Court's claim that *Romer v. Evans,* 517 U. S. 620 (1996), "eroded" the "foundations" of *Bowers'* rational-basis holding. See *Romer, supra,* at 640-643 (Scalia, J., dissenting).) But *Roe* and *Casey* have been equally "eroded" by *Washington v. Glucksberg,* 521 U. S. 702, 721 (1997), which held that only fundamental rights which are "'deeply rooted in this Nation's history and tradition'" qualify for anything other than rational basis scrutiny under the doctrine of "substantive due process." *Roe* and *Casey,* of course, subjected the restriction of abortion to heightened scrutiny without even attempting to establish that the freedom to abort was rooted in this Nation's tradition.

(2) *Bowers,* the Court says, has been subject to "substantial and continuing [criticism], disapproving of its reasoning in all respects, not just as to its historical assumptions." *Ante,* at 15. Exactly what those nonhistorical criticisms are, and whether the Court even agrees with them, are left unsaid, although the Court does cite two books. See *ibid.* (citing C. Fried, Order and Law: Arguing the Reagan Revolution—A Firsthand Account 81–84 (1991); R. Posner, Sex and Reason 341–350 (1992)).[1] Of course, *Roe* too (and by extension *Casey*) had been (and still is) subject to unrelenting criticism, including criticism from the two commentators cited by the

---

[1] This last-cited critic of *Bowers* actually writes: "[*Bowers*] is correct nevertheless that the right to engage in homosexual acts is not deeply rooted in America's history and tradition." Posner, Sex and Reason, at 343.

Court today. See Fried, *supra,* at 75 ("*Roe* was a prime example of twisted judging"); Posner, *supra,* at 337 ("[The Court's] opinion in *Roe* ... fails to measure up to professional expectations regarding judicial opinions"); Posner, Judicial Opinion Writing, 62 U. Chi. L. Rev. 1421, 1434 (1995) (describing the opinion in *Roe* as an "embarrassing performanc[e]").

(3) That leaves, to distinguish the rock-solid, unamendable disposition of *Roe* from the readily overrulable *Bowers,* only the third factor. "[T]here has been," the Court says, "no individual or societal reliance on *Bowers* of the sort that could counsel against overturning its holding . . . ." *Ante,* at 16. It seems to me that the "societal reliance" on the principles confirmed in *Bowers* and discarded today has been overwhelming. Countless judicial decisions and legislative enactments have relied on the ancient proposition that a governing majority's belief that certain sexual behavior is "immoral and unacceptable" constitutes a rational basis for regulation. See, e.g., *Williams v. Pryor,* 240 F. 3d 944, 949 (CA11 2001) (citing *Bowers* in upholding Alabama's prohibition on the sale of sex toys on the ground that "[t]he crafting and safeguarding of public morality ... indisputably is a legitimate government interest under rational basis scrutiny"); *Milner v. Apfel,* 148 F. 3d 812, 814 (CA7 1998) (citing *Bowers* for the proposition that "[l]egislatures are permitted to legislate with regard to morality ... rather than confined to preventing demonstrable harms"); *Holmes v. California Army National Guard* 124 F. 3d 1126, 1136 (CA9 1997) (relying on *Bowers* in upholding the federal statute and regulations banning from military service those who engage in homosexual conduct); *Owens v. State,* 352 Md.

663, 683, 724 A. 2d 43, 53 (1999) (relying on *Bowers* in holding that "a person has no constitutional right to engage in sexual intercourse, at least outside of marriage"); *Sherman v. Henry,* 928 S. W. 2d 464, 469–473 (Tex. 1996) (relying on *Bowers* in rejecting a claimed constitutional right to commit adultery). We ourselves relied extensively on *Bowers* when we concluded, in *Barnes v. Glen Theatre, Inc.,* 501 U. S. 560, 569 (1991), that Indiana's public indecency statute furthered "a substantial government interest in protecting order and morality," *ibid.,* (plurality opinion); see also *id.,* at 575 (Scalia, J., concurring in judgment). State laws against bigamy, same-sex marriage, adult incest, prostitution, masturbation, adultery, fornication, bestiality, and obscenity are likewise sustainable only in light of *Bowers'* validation of laws based on moral choices. Every single one of these laws is called into question by today's decision; the Court makes no effort to cabin the scope of its decision to exclude them from its holding. See *ante,* at 11 (noting "an emerging awareness that liberty gives substantial protection to adult persons in deciding how to conduct their private lives in matters pertaining to sex" [emphasis added]). The impossibility of distinguishing homosexuality from other traditional "morals" offenses is precisely why *Bowers* rejected the rational-basis challenge. "The law," it said, "is constantly based on notions of morality, and if all laws representing essentially moral choices are to be invalidated under the Due Process Clause, the courts will be very busy indeed." 478 U. S., at 196.[2]

What a massive disruption of the current social order, therefore, the overruling of *Bowers* entails. Not so the overruling of *Roe,* which

---

[2] While the Court does not overrule *Bowers'* holding that homosexual sodomy is not a "fundamental right," it is worth noting that the "societal reliance" upon that aspect of the decision has been substantial as well. See 10 U. S. C. §654(b)(1) ("A member of the armed forces shall be separated from the armed forces ... if ... the member has engaged in ... a homosexual act or acts"); *Marcum v. McWhorter,* 308 F. 3d 635, 640–642 (CA6 2002) (relying on *Bowers* in rejecting a claimed fundamental right to commit adultery); *Mullins v. Oregon,* 57 F. 3d 789, 793–794 (CA9 1995) (relying on *Bowers* in rejecting a grandparent's claimed "fundamental liberty interes[t]" in the adoption of her grandchildren); *Doe v. Wigginton,* 21 F. 3d 733, 739–740 (CA6 1994) (relying on *Bowers* in rejecting a prisoner's claimed "fundamental right" to on-demand HIV testing); *Schowengerdt v. United States,* 944 F. 2d 483, 490 (CA9 1991) (relying on *Bowers* in upholding a bisexual's discharge from the armed services); *Charles v.*

Baesler, 910 F. 2d 1349, 1353 (CA6 1990) (relying on *Bowers* in rejecting fire department captain's claimed "fundamental" interest in a promotion); *Henne v. Wright,* 904 F. 2d 1208, 1214–1215 (CA8 1990) (relying on *Bowers* in rejecting a claim that state law restricting surnames that could be given to children at birth implicates a "fundamental right"); *Walls v. Petersburg,* 895 F. 2d 188, 193 (CA4 1990) (relying on *Bowers* in rejecting substantive-due-process challenge to a police department questionnaire that asked prospective employees about homosexual activity); *High Tech Gays v. Defense Industrial Security Clearance Office,* 895 F. 2d 563, 570–571 (CA9 1988) (relying on *Bowers'* holding that homosexual activity is not a fundamental right in rejecting—on the basis of the rational-basis standard—an equal-protection challenge to the Defense Department's policy of conducting expanded investigations into backgrounds of gay and lesbian applicants for secret and top-secret security clearance).

would simply have restored the regime that existed for centuries before 1973, in which the permissibility of and restrictions upon abortion were determined legislatively State-by-State. *Casey*, however, chose to base its *stare decisis* determination on a different "sort" of reliance. "[P]eople," it said, "have organized intimate relationships and made choices that define their views of themselves and their places in society, in reliance on the availability of abortion in the event that contraception should fail." 505 U. S., at 856. This falsely assumes that the consequence of overruling *Roe* would have been to make abortion unlawful. It would not; it would merely have permitted the States to do so. Many States would unquestionably have declined to prohibit abortion, and others would not have prohibited it within six months (after which the most significant reliance interests would have expired). Even for persons in States other than these, the choice would not have been between abortion and childbirth, but between abortion nearby and abortion in a neighboring State.

To tell the truth, it does not surprise me, and should surprise no one, that the Court has chosen today to revise the standards of *stare decisis* set forth in *Casey*. It has thereby exposed *Casey*'s extraordinary deference to precedent for the result-oriented expedient that it is.

II

Having decided that it need not adhere to *stare decisis*, the Court still must establish that *Bowers* was wrongly decided and that the Texas statute, as applied to petitioners, is unconstitutional.

Texas Penal Code Ann. §21.06(a) (2003) undoubtedly imposes constraints on liberty. So do laws prohibiting prostitution, recreational use of heroin, and, for that matter, working more than 60 hours per week in a bakery. But there is no right to "liberty" under the Due Process Clause, though today's opinion repeatedly makes that claim. *Ante,* at 6 ("The liberty protected by the Constitution allows homosexual persons the right to make this choice"); *ante,* at 13 ("'These matters ... are central to the liberty protected by the Fourteenth Amendment'"); *ante,* at 17 ("Their right to liberty under the Due Process Clause gives them the full right to engage in their conduct without intervention of the government"). The Fourteenth Amendment expressly allows States to deprive their citizens of "liberty," so long as "due process of law" is provided:

> "No state shall ... deprive any person of life, liberty, or property, without due process of law." Amdt. 14 (emphasis added).

Our opinions applying the doctrine known as "substantive due process" hold that the Due Process Clause prohibits States from infringing fundamental liberty interests, unless the infringement is narrowly tailored to serve a compelling state interest. *Washington v. Glucksberg,* 521 U. S., at 721. We have held repeatedly, in cases the Court today does not overrule, that only fundamental rights qualify for this so-called "heightened scrutiny" protection—that is, rights which are "'deeply rooted in this Nation's history and tradition,'" *ibid.* See *Reno v. Flores,* 507 U. S. 292, 303 (1993) (fundamental liberty interests must be "so rooted in the traditions and conscience of our people as to be ranked as fundamental" (internal quotation marks and citations omitted)); *United States v. Salerno,* 481 U. S. 739, 751 (1987) (same). See also *Michael H. v. Gerald D.,* 491 U. S. 110, 122 (1989) ("[W]e have insisted not merely that the interest denominated as a 'liberty' be 'fundamental' ... but also that it be an interest traditionally protected by our society"); *Moore v. East Cleveland,* 431 U. S. 494, 503 (1977) (plurality opinion); *Meyer v. Nebraska,* 262 U. S. 390, 399 (1923) (Fourteenth Amendment protects "those privileges long recognized at common law as essential to the orderly pursuit of happiness by free men" [emphasis added]).[3] All other liberty interests may be abridged or abrogated pursuant to a validly enacted state law if that law is rationally related to a legitimate state interest.

Bowers held, first, that criminal prohibitions of homosexual sodomy are not subject to heightened scrutiny because they do not impli-

---

[3] The Court is quite right that "history and tradition are the starting point but not in all cases the ending point of the substantive due process inquiry," *ante,* at 11. An asserted "fundamental liberty interest" must not only be "deeply rooted in this Nation's history and tradition," *Washington v. Glucksberg,* 521 U. S. 702, 721 (1997), but it must also be "implicit in the concept of ordered liberty," so that "neither liberty nor justice would exist if [it] were sacrificed," *ibid.* Moreover, liberty interests unsupported by history and tradition, though not deserving of "heightened scrutiny," are still protected from state laws that are not rationally related to any legitimate state interest. *Id.,* at 722. As I proceed to discuss, it is this latter principle that the Court applies in the present case.

U.S. SUPREME
COURT,
JUNE 2003

cate a "fundamental right" under the Due Process Clause, 478 U. S., at 191-194. Noting that "[p]roscriptions against that conduct have ancient roots," *id.,* at 192, that "[s]odomy was a criminal offense at common law and was forbidden by the laws of the original 13 States when they ratified the Bill of Rights," *ibid.,* and that many States had retained their bans on sodomy, *id.,* at 193, *Bowers* concluded that a right to engage in homosexual sodomy was not "'deeply rooted in this Nation's history and tradition,'" *id.,* at 192.

The Court today does not overrule this holding. Not once does it describe homosexual sodomy as a "fundamental right" or a "fundamental liberty interest," nor does it subject the Texas statute to strict scrutiny. Instead, having failed to establish that the right to homosexual sodomy is "'deeply rooted in this Nation's history and tradition,'" the Court concludes that the application of Texas's statute to petitioners' conduct fails the rational-basis test, and overrules *Bowers'* holding to the contrary, see *id.,* at 196. "The Texas statute furthers no legitimate state interest which can justify its intrusion into the personal and private life of the individual." *Ante,* at 18.

I shall address that rational-basis holding presently. First, however, I address some aspersions that the Court casts upon *Bowers'* conclusion that homosexual sodomy is not a "fundamental right"—even though, as I have said, the Court does not have the boldness to reverse that conclusion.

III

The Court's description of "the state of the law" at the time of *Bowers* only confirms that *Bowers* was right. *Ante,* at 5. The Court points to *Griswold v. Connecticut,* 381 U. S. 479, 481–482 (1965). But that case expressly disclaimed any reliance on the doctrine of "substantive due process," and grounded the so-called "right to privacy" in penumbras of constitutional provisions other than the Due Process Clause. *Eisenstadt v. Baird,* 405 U. S. 438 (1972), likewise had nothing to do with "substantive due process"; it invalidated a Massachusetts law prohibiting the distribution of contraceptives to unmarried persons solely on the basis of the Equal Protection Clause. Of course *Eisenstadt* contains well known dictum relating to the "right to privacy," but this referred to the right recognized in *Griswold*—a right penumbral to

the specific guarantees in the Bill of Rights, and not a "substantive due process" right.

Roe v. Wade recognized that the right to abort an unborn child was a "fundamental right" protected by the Due Process Clause. 410 U. S., at 155. The *Roe* Court, however, made no attempt to establish that this right was "'deeply rooted in this Nation's history and tradition'"; instead, it based its conclusion that "the Fourteenth Amendment's concept of personal liberty ... is broad enough to encompass a woman's decision whether or not to terminate her pregnancy" on its own normative judgment that anti-abortion laws were undesirable. See *id.,* at 153. We have since rejected *Roe's* holding that regulations of abortion must be narrowly tailored to serve a compelling state interest, see *Planned Parenthood v. Casey,* 505 U. S., at 876 (joint opinion of O'Connor, Kennedy, and Souter, JJ.); *id.,* at 951–953 (Rehnquist, C. J., concurring in judgment in part and dissenting in part)—and thus, by logical implication, *Roe's* holding that the right to abort an unborn child is a "fundamental right." See 505 U. S., at 843–912 (joint opinion of O'Connor, Kennedy, and Souter, JJ.) (not once describing abortion as a "fundamental right" or a "fundamental liberty interest").

After discussing the history of antisodomy laws, *ante,* at 7–10, the Court proclaims that, "it should be noted that there is no longstanding history in this country of laws directed at homosexual conduct as a distinct matter," *ante,* at 7. This observation in no way casts into doubt the "definitive [historical] conclusion," *id.,* on which *Bowers* relied: that our Nation has a longstanding history of laws prohibiting sodomy in general—regardless of whether it was performed by same-sex or opposite-sex couples:

> "It is obvious to us that neither of these formulations would extend a fundamental right to homosexuals to engage in acts of consensual sodomy. Proscriptions against that conduct have ancient roots. *Sodomy* was a criminal offense at common law and was forbidden by the laws of the original 13 States when they ratified the Bill of Rights. In 1868, when the Fourteenth Amendment was ratified, all but 5 of the 37 States in the Union had *criminal sodomy laws.* In fact, until 1961, all 50 States outlawed *sodomy,* and today, 24 States and the District of Columbia continue to provide criminal penalties for *sodomy* performed in private and between consenting adults. Against this background, to claim that

a right to engage in such conduct is 'deeply rooted in this Nation's history and tradition' or 'implicit in the concept of ordered liberty' is, at best, facetious." 478 U. S., at 192–194 (citations and footnotes omitted; emphasis added).

It is (as *Bowers* recognized) entirely irrelevant whether the laws in our long national tradition criminalizing homosexual sodomy were "directed at homosexual conduct as a distinct matter." *Ante,* at 7. Whether homosexual sodomy was prohibited by a law targeted at same-sex sexual relations or by a more general law prohibiting both homosexual and heterosexual sodomy, the only relevant point is that it was criminalized—which suffices to establish that homosexual sodomy is not a right "deeply rooted in our Nation's history and tradition." The Court today agrees that homosexual sodomy was criminalized and thus does not dispute the facts on which *Bowers actually* relied.

Next the Court makes the claim, again unsupported by any citations, that "[l]aws prohibiting sodomy do not seem to have been enforced against consenting adults acting in private." *Ante,* at 8. The key qualifier here is "acting in private"—since the Court admits that sodomy laws were enforced against consenting adults (although the Court contends that prosecutions were "infrequent," *ante,* at 9). I do not know what "acting in private" means; surely consensual sodomy, like heterosexual intercourse, is rarely performed on stage. If all the Court means by "acting in private" is "on private premises, with the doors closed and windows covered," it is entirely unsurprising that evidence of enforcement would be hard to come by. (Imagine the circumstances that would enable a search warrant to be obtained for a residence on the ground that there was probable cause to believe that consensual sodomy was then and there occurring.) Surely that lack of evidence would not sustain the proposition that consensual sodomy on private premises with the doors closed and windows covered was regarded as a "fundamental right," even though all other consensual sodomy was criminalized. There are 203 prosecutions for consensual, adult homosexual sodomy reported in the West Reporting system and official state reporters from the years 1880–1995. See W. Eskridge, Gaylaw: Challenging the Apartheid of the Closet 375 (1999) (hereinafter Gaylaw). There are also records of 20 sodomy prosecutions and 4 executions during the colonial peri-

od. J. Katz, Gay/Lesbian Almanac 29, 58, 663 (1983). *Bowers'* conclusion that homosexual sodomy is not a fundamental right "deeply rooted in this Nation's history and tradition" is utterly unassailable.

Realizing that fact, the Court instead says: "[W]e think that our laws and traditions in the past half century are of most relevance here. These references show an emerging awareness that liberty gives substantial protection to adult persons in deciding how to conduct their private lives in matters pertaining to sex." *Ante,* at 11 (emphasis added). Apart from the fact that such an "emerging awareness" does not establish a "fundamental right," the statement is factually false. States continue to prosecute all sorts of crimes by adults "in matters pertaining to sex": prostitution, adult incest, adultery, obscenity, and child pornography. Sodomy laws, too, have been enforced "in the past half century," in which there have been 134 reported cases involving prosecutions for consensual, adult, homosexual sodomy. Gaylaw 375. In relying, for evidence of an "emerging recognition," upon the American Law Institute's 1955 recommendation not to criminalize "'consensual sexual relations conducted in private,'" *ante,* at 11, the Court ignores the fact that this recommendation was "a point of resistance in most of the states that considered adopting the Model Penal Code." Gaylaw 159.

In any event, an "emerging awareness" is by definition not "deeply rooted in this Nation's history and tradition[s]," as we have said "fundamental right" status requires. Constitutional entitlements do not spring into existence because some States choose to lessen or eliminate criminal sanctions on certain behavior. Much less do they spring into existence, as the Court seems to believe, because *foreign nations* decriminalize conduct. The *Bowers* majority opinion *never* relied on "values we share with a wider civilization," *ante,* at 16, but rather rejected the claimed right to sodomy on the ground that such a right was not "'deeply rooted in *this Nation's* history and tradition,'" 478 U. S., at 193-194 (emphasis added). *Bowers'* rational-basis holding is likewise devoid of any reliance on the views of a "wider civilization," see *id.,* at 196. The Court's discussion of these foreign views (ignoring, of course, the many countries that have retained criminal prohibitions on sodomy) is therefore meaningless dicta. Dangerous dicta,

U.S. SUPREME
COURT,
JUNE 2003

however, since "this Court ... should not impose foreign moods, fads, or fashions on Americans." *Foster v. Florida,* 537 U. S. 990, n. (2002) (Thomas, J., concurring in denial of certiorari).

IV

I turn now to the ground on which the Court squarely rests its holding: the contention that there is no rational basis for the law here under attack. This proposition is so out of accord with our jurisprudence—indeed, with the jurisprudence of any society we know—that it requires little discussion.

The Texas statute undeniably seeks to further the belief of its citizens that certain forms of sexual behavior are "immoral and unacceptable," *Bowers, supra,* at 196—the same interest furthered by criminal laws against fornication, bigamy, adultery, adult incest, bestiality, and obscenity. *Bowers* held that this was a legitimate state interest. The Court today reaches the opposite conclusion. The Texas statute, it says, "furthers no legitimate state interest which can justify its intrusion into the personal and private life of the individual," *ante,* at 18 (emphasis addded). The Court embraces instead Justice Stevens' declaration in his *Bowers* dissent, that "the fact that the governing majority in a State has traditionally viewed a particular practice as immoral is not a sufficient reason for upholding a law prohibiting the practice," *ante,* at 17. This effectively decrees the end of all morals legislation. If, as the Court asserts, the promotion of majoritarian sexual morality is not even a legitimate state interest, none of the above-mentioned laws can survive rational-basis review.

V

Finally, I turn to petitioners' equal-protection challenge, which no Member of the Court save Justice O'Connor, *ante,* at 1 (opinion concurring in judgment), embraces: On its face §21.06(a) applies equally to all persons. Men and women, heterosexuals and homosexuals, are all subject to its prohibition of deviate sexual intercourse with someone of the same sex. To be sure, §21.06 does distinguish between the sexes insofar as concerns the partner with whom the sexual acts are performed: men can violate the law only with other men, and women only with other women. But this cannot itself be a denial of equal protection, since it is precisely the same distinction regarding partner that is drawn in

state laws prohibiting marriage with someone of the same sex while permitting marriage with someone of the opposite sex.

The objection is made, however, that the antimiscegenation laws invalidated in *Loving v. Virginia,* 388 U. S. 1, 8 (1967), similarly were applicable to whites and blacks alike, and only distinguished between the races insofar as the partner was concerned. In *Loving,* however, we correctly applied heightened scrutiny, rather than the usual rational-basis review, because the Virginia statute was "designed to maintain White Supremacy." *Id.,* at 6, 11. A racially discriminatory purpose is always sufficient to subject a law to strict scrutiny, even a facially neutral law that makes no mention of race. See *Washington v. Davis,* 426 U. S. 229, 241–242 (1976). No purpose to discriminate against men or women as a class can be gleaned from the Texas law, so rational-basis review applies. That review is readily satisfied here by the same rational basis that satisfied it in *Bowers*—society's belief that certain forms of sexual behavior are "immoral and unacceptable," 478 U. S., at 196. This is the same justification that supports many other laws regulating sexual behavior that make a distinction based upon the identity of the partner—for example, laws against adultery, fornication, and adult incest, and laws refusing to recognize homosexual marriage.

Justice O'Connor argues that the discrimination in this law which must be justified is not its discrimination with regard to the sex of the partner but its discrimination with regard to the sexual proclivity of the principal actor.

> "While it is true that the law applies only to conduct, the conduct targeted by this law is conduct that is closely correlated with being homosexual. Under such circumstances, Texas' sodomy law is targeted at more than conduct. It is instead directed toward gay persons as a class." *Ante,* at 5.

Of course the same could be said of any law. A law against public nudity targets "the conduct that is closely correlated with being a nudist," and hence "is targeted at more than conduct"; it is "directed toward nudists as a class." But be that as it may. Even if the Texas law does deny equal protection to "homosexuals as a class," that denial still does not need to be justified by anything more than a rational basis, which our cases show is satisfied by the enforcement of traditional notions of sexual morality.

U.S. SUPREME
COURT,
JUNE 2003

Justice O'Connor simply decrees application of "a more searching form of rational basis review" to the Texas statute. *Ante,* at 2. The cases she cites do not recognize such a standard, and reach their conclusions only after finding, as required by conventional rational-basis analysis, that no conceivable legitimate state interest supports the classification at issue. See *Romer v. Evans,* 517 U. S., at 635; *Cleburne v. Cleburne Living Center, Inc.,* 473 U. S. 432, 448–450 (1985); *Department of Agriculture v. Moreno,* 413 U. S. 528, 534–538 (1973). Nor does Justice O'Connor explain precisely what her "more searching form" of rational-basis review consists of. It must at least mean, however, that laws exhibiting "'a ... desire to harm a politically unpopular group,'" *ante,* at 2, are invalid even though there may be a conceivable rational basis to support them.

This reasoning leaves on pretty shaky grounds state laws limiting marriage to opposite-sex couples. Justice O'Connor seeks to preserve them by the conclusory statement that "preserving the traditional institution of marriage" is a legitimate state interest. *Ante,* at 7. But "preserving the traditional institution of marriage" is just a kinder way of describing the State's moral disapproval of same-sex couples. Texas's interest in §21.06 could be recast in similarly euphemistic terms: "preserving the traditional sexual mores of our society." In the jurisprudence Justice O'Connor has seemingly created, judges can validate laws by characterizing them as "preserving the traditions of society" (good); or invalidate them by characterizing them as "expressing moral disapproval" (bad).

* * *

Today's opinion is the product of a Court, which is the product of a law-profession culture, that has largely signed on to the so-called homosexual agenda, by which I mean the agenda promoted by some homosexual activists directed at eliminating the moral opprobrium that has traditionally attached to homosexual conduct. I noted in an earlier opinion the fact that the American Association of Law Schools (to which any reputable law school must seek to belong) excludes from membership any school that refuses to ban from its job-interview facilities a law firm (no matter how small) that does not wish to hire as a prospective partner a person who openly engages in homosexual conduct. See *Romer, supra,* at 653.

One of the most revealing statements in today's opinion is the Court's grim warning that the criminalization of homosexual conduct is "an invitation to subject homosexual persons to discrimination both in the public and in the private spheres." *Ante,* at 14. It is clear from this that the Court has taken sides in the culture war, departing from its role of assuring, as neutral observer, that the democratic rules of engagement are observed. Many Americans do not want persons who openly engage in homosexual conduct as partners in their business, as scoutmasters for their children, as teachers in their children's schools, or as boarders in their home. They view this as protecting themselves and their families from a lifestyle that they believe to be immoral and destructive. The Court views it as "discrimination" which it is the function of our judgments to deter. So imbued is the Court with the law profession's anti-anti-homosexual culture, that it is seemingly unaware that the attitudes of that culture are not obviously "mainstream"; that in most States what the Court calls "discrimination" against those who engage in homosexual acts is perfectly legal; that proposals to ban such "discrimination" under Title VII have repeatedly been rejected by Congress, see Employment Non-Discrimination Act of 1994, S. 2238, 103d Cong., 2d Sess. (1994); Civil Rights Amendments, H. R. 5452, 94th Cong., 1st Sess. (1975); that in some cases such "discrimination" is mandated by federal statute, see 10 U. S. C. §654(b)(1) (mandating discharge from the armed forces of any service member who engages in or intends to engage in homosexual acts); and that in some cases such "discrimination" is a constitutional right, see *Boy Scouts of America v. Dale,* 530 U. S. 640 (2000).

Let me be clear that I have nothing against homosexuals, or any other group, promoting their agenda through normal democratic means. Social perceptions of sexual and other morality change over time, and every group has the right to persuade its fellow citizens that its view of such matters is the best. That homosexuals have achieved some success in that enterprise is attested to by the fact that Texas is one of the few remaining States that criminalize private, consensual homosexual acts. But persuading one's fellow citizens is one thing, and imposing one's views in absence of democratic majority will is something else. I would no more require a State to criminalize homosexual acts— or, for that matter, display any moral disappro-

U.S. SUPREME
COURT,
JUNE 2003

bation of them—than I would forbid it to do so. What Texas has chosen to do is well within the range of traditional democratic action, and its hand should not be stayed through the invention of a brand-new "constitutional right" by a Court that is impatient of democratic change. It is indeed true that "later generations can see that laws once thought necessary and proper in fact serve only to oppress," *ante,* at 18; and when that happens, later generations can repeal those laws. But it is the premise of our system that those judgments are to be made by the people, and not imposed by a governing caste that knows best.

One of the benefits of leaving regulation of this matter to the people rather than to the courts is that the people, unlike judges, need not carry things to their logical conclusion. The people may feel that their disapprobation of homosexual conduct is strong enough to disallow homosexual marriage, but not strong enough to criminalize private homosexual acts—and may legislate accordingly. The Court today pretends that it possesses a similar freedom of action, so that that we need not fear judicial imposition of homosexual marriage, as has recently occurred in Canada (in a decision that the Canadian Government has chosen not to appeal). See *Halpern v. Toronto,* 2003 WL 34950 (Ontario Ct. App.); Cohen, Dozens in Canada Follow Gay Couple's Lead, Washington Post, June 12, 2003, p. A25. At the end of its opinion—after having laid waste the foundations of our rational-basis jurisprudence—the Court says that the present case "does not involve whether the government must give formal recognition to any relationship that homosexual persons seek to enter." *Ante,* at 17. Do not believe it. More illuminating than this bald, unreasoned disclaimer is the progression of thought displayed by an earlier passage in the Court's opinion, which notes the constitutional protections afforded to "personal decisions relating to marriage, procreation, contraception, family relationships, child rearing, and education," and then declares that "[p]ersons in a homosexual relationship may seek autonomy for these purposes, just as heterosexual persons do." *Ante,* at 13 (emphasis added). Today's opinion dismantles the structure of constitutional law that has permitted a distinction to be made between heterosexual and homosexual unions, insofar as formal

recognition in marriage is concerned. If moral disapprobation of homosexual conduct is "no legitimate state interest" for purposes of proscribing that conduct, *ante,* at 18; and if, as the Court coos (casting aside all pretense of neutrality), "[w]hen sexuality finds overt expression in intimate conduct with another person, the conduct can be but one element in a personal bond that is more enduring," *ante,* at 6; what justification could there possibly be for denying the benefits of marriage to homosexual couples exercising "[t]he liberty protected by the Constitution," *ibid.*? Surely not the encouragement of procreation, since the sterile and the elderly are allowed to marry. This case "does not involve" the issue of homosexual marriage only if one entertains the belief that principle and logic have nothing to do with the decisions of this Court. Many will hope that, as the Court comfortingly assures us, this is so.

The matters appropriate for this Court's resolution are only three: Texas's prohibition of sodomy neither infringes a "fundamental right" (which the Court does not dispute), nor is unsupported by a rational relation to what the Constitution considers a legitimate state interest, nor denies the equal protection of the laws. I dissent.

Justice Thomas, dissenting.

I join Justice Scalia's dissenting opinion. I write separately to note that the law before the Court today "is ... uncommonly silly." *Griswold v. Connecticut,* 381 U. S. 479, 527 (1965) (Stewart, J., dissenting). If I were a member of the Texas Legislature, I would vote to repeal it. Punishing someone for expressing his sexual preference through noncommercial consensual conduct with another adult does not appear to be a worthy way to expend valuable law enforcement resources.

Notwithstanding this, I recognize that as a member of this Court I am not empowered to help petitioners and others similarly situated. My duty, rather, is to "decide cases 'agreeably to the Constitution and laws of the United States.'" *Id.,* at 530. And, just like Justice Stewart, I "can find [neither in the Bill of Rights nor any other part of the Constitution a] general right of privacy," *ibid.,* or as the Court terms it today, the "liberty of the person both in its spatial and more transcendent dimensions," *ante,* at 1.

MIRANDA v. ARIZONA

MIRANDA V. ARIZONA

ISSUE

Criminal Procedure

HOW TO USE MILESTONES IN THE LAW

In the opinions* and briefs* that follow, the reader is invited to explore the issue of interrogation of criminal suspects and the question of when a suspect's confession to a crime should be admitted at trial. As you read this section, you may wish to consider the following questions:

■ Why does the Constitution protect a criminal suspect from being a witness against himself or herself?

■ Under what circumstances could a police officer ask an individual questions about a crime without having to give the person the Miranda warnings?

■ What is the purpose of the right to counsel?

THIS CASE IN HISTORY

You have the right to remain silent. Anything you say may be used for or against you in a court of law. You have the right to an attorney now or at any time during questioning. If you cannot afford an attorney, one will be appointed to represent you, without cost, by the courts. [sample Miranda warning]

Law enforcement officers in movies, TV shows, and real life all utter some version of the *Miranda* warnings prior to interrogating a criminal suspect. In *Miranda versus Arizona*, the Supreme Court attempted to clarify a criminal suspect's privilege against self-incrimination under the Fifth Amendment, and right to counsel under the Sixth Amendment, during interrogation. *Miranda*, which was actually a review of four similar cases at once, was the Court's attempt to balance the rights of a person accused of a crime with the rights of society to prosecute those who commit criminal acts. Since it was handed down in 1966, the *Miranda* case has been the subject of continuing analysis and debate, yet its requirements, for the most part, have withstood the test of time.

In the interest of space, only the opinions of the supreme courts of Arizona and California, which reached different results, and only the briefs in *Miranda v. Arizona*, are presented.

State v. Miranda

CITE AS 401 P.2D 721

—∿—

STATE OF ARIZONA, APPELLEE,

V.

ERNEST ARTHUR MIRANDA, APPELLANT.

NO. 1394.

Supreme Court of Arizona.
En Banc.
April 22, 1965.
98 Ariz. 18

Prosecution on count of kidnapping and rape. The Superior Court, Maricopa County, Yale McFate, J., entered judgment on guilty verdict, and defendant appealed. The Supreme Court, McFarland, J., held that confession of defendant, who from previous arrests was familiar with legal proceedings and personal rights in court and who was picked from police lineup by complaining witness as person who allegedly kidnapped and raped her, made after police had informed him of his rights but had not specifically informed him of right to assistance of council and he himself had not requested and been denied assistance of counsel, was not inadmissible by reason of defendant's lacking attorney at time it was made.

Affirmed.

Reference to "rape" in kidnapping count of information against defendant was proper where rape was alleged to be purpose of kidnapping. A.R.S. § 13–492, subsecs. A-C.

Where allegation in kidnapping information against defendant that defendant had allegedly perpetrated kidnapping for purpose of raping complaining witness was necessary and proper element of information, subsequent reiterated reference to alleged rape by use of words "and did rape" were not objectionable as being inflammatory inasmuch as those words stated no more than the original necessary reference to matter. A.R.S. § 13–492, subsecs. A-C.

Use of word "rape" in first or kidnapping count of information against defendant, to define necessary element of defendant's alleged purpose for alleged kidnapping, was not, by itself, prejudicial to defendant where use of word was necessary in second or "rape" count of information. A.R.S. § 13–492, subsecs. A-C.

Descriptive phrase "not being related in any way to the defendant" in first or kidnapping count of information against defendant, which had mere object of indicating that defendant's alleged taking of 18-year-old girl did not fall within exception in statute providing for taking of minor by parent, could not have had any inflammatory contents which prejudiced defendant. A.R.S. § 13–492, subsecs. A-C.

Where word "fear" originally alleged in second or "rape" count of indictment against defendant had been stricken from information prior to trial and, therefore, was not included in information read to jury, original inclusion could not have prejudiced defendant. A.R.S. §§ 13–492, subsecs. B, C, 13–611, subsec. A, par. 2.

Allowing defendant charged with rape and kidnapping, on his own motion, to have sanity hearing that caused delay of trial, through late filing of medical report, past 60-day period that rule required trial to be brought in, except in case of appropriate showing of good cause by affidavit or defendant's consent or action, was "good cause," within section, for continuing trial for additional five days beyond 60-day period. 17 A.R.S. Rules of Criminal Procedure, rules 236, 250.

Where prosecuting attorney, who had wide latitude in his argument to jury, stated conclusion in argument, justified by evidence, that 18-year-old complaining witness had acquiesced in alleged act of rape due to her fear of defendant, and trial court's immediate instruction to jury to disregard statement and instruction at close of trial limiting jury's consideration to rape offense charged had effect of precluding prejudice from inflammatory aspect of statement, prejudicial error did not appear. A.R.S. § 13–611, subsec. A, par. 2.

Whether defendant charged with rape of complaining witness had actually penetrated 18–year-old complaining witness, as witness affirmatively testified and as defendant's confession indicated, and whether thereby rape was actually perpetrated were questions for jury. A.R.S. § 13–611, subsec. A, par. 2.

All inferences must be construed in light most favorable to sustaining verdict in criminal case.

Where there is evidence to support criminal verdict, Supreme Court will not disturb finding of jury.

SUPREME COURT
OF ARIZONA,
APRIL 1965

SUPREME COURT
OF ARIZONA,
APRIL 1965

A chief duty of both sheriff's office and county attorney's office is to make sure that people are not unjustly charged with crime; both have duty to protect innocent as well as to detect the guilty.

Confession may be admissible when made without an attorney if it is voluntary and does not violate constitutional rights of defendant. U.S.C.A. Const. Amends. 6, 14.

Confession of defendant, who from previous arrests was familiar with legal proceedings and personal rights in court, made after police had informed him of his rights but had not specifically informed him of right to assistance of counsel and he himself had not requested and been denied assistance of counsel, was not inadmissible by reason of defendant's lacking attorney at time it was made.

Darrell F. Smith, Atty. Gen., Robert W. Pickrell, former Atty. Gen., Stirley Newell, former Asst. Atty. Gen., Allen L. Feinstein, Phoenix, of counsel, for appellee.

Alvin Moore, Phoenix, for appellant.

McFarland, Justice:

Appellant was convicted of the crime of kidnapping, Count I; and Rape, Count II; and sentenced to serve from twenty to thirty years on each count, to run concurrently. From the judgement and sentence of the court he appeals. Appellant, hereinafter called defendant, was in another information charged with the crime of robbery. After arraignment in the instant case, on motion of the county attorney, the trial on the robbery case was consolidated with the instant case, but thereafter—one day prior to the trial of this case—separate trials were granted. Defendant was tried and convicted on the robbery charge, from which he is also appealing in the companion case of State v. Miranda, No. 1397, 98 Ariz. 11, 401 P.2d 716.

The facts, as they relate to the defense as charged under Counts I and II in the instant case are as follows: On March 3, 1963, the complaining witness—a girl eighteen years of age— had been working in the concession stand at the Paramount Theatre in downtown Phoenix, and had taken the bus to 7th Street and Marlette. After getting off the bus, she had started to walk toward her home. She observed a car, which afterwords proved to be defendant's, which had been parked behind the ballet school on Marlette. The car pulled out of the lot, and came so close to her that she had to jump back to prevent being hit. It then parked across from some apartments in the same block. Defendant then left his car, walked toward her, and grabbed her. He told her not to scream, that he would not hurt her. He held her hands behind her back, put a hand over her mouth, and pulled her toward the car. He put her in the back seat, tied her hands and feet, and put a sharp thing to her neck and said to her "Feel this." She stated it all happened so suddenly that she did not have time to do anything. Defendant was unknown to the complaining witness. She had not seen him before and he was not related to her in any way.

He then drove the car for about twenty minutes, during which time complaining witness was lying in the back seat crying. When defendant stopped the car, he came to the back seat, and untied her hands and feet. He told her to pull off her clothes. She said "no," whereupon he started to remove them. She tried to push away from him, but he proceeded to remove her clothing. And, then, after one unsuccessful attempt, made a successful sexual penetration, while she pushed with her hands and was screaming. She testified:

> "I was pushing against him with my hands. I kept screaming, I was trying to get away but he was a lot stronger than I was, and I couldn't do anything."

He then drove her to 12th Street and Rose Lane, during which time she dressed. She ran home, and told her family who called the police. Her sister testified that the complaining witness came home that morning crying and looking as if she had been in a fight. On March 13, 1963, defendant was apprehended by the police. The officers who picked him up both testified that he was put into the "line-up" and was identified by complaining witness. Thereafter he confessed that he had forced complaining witness into his car, drove away with her, and raped her. After these statements he signed a statement, partly typed and partly in his own handwriting, which was substantially to the same effect as the testimony of the officers. Defendant offered no evidence in his defense at the trial of his case.

Defendant assigns as error the following: denial of the motion to quash the information; denial of his motion to dismiss the action on the ground that the case was not brought to trial within sixty days, under Rule 236, Rules of Criminal Procedure, 17 A.R.S. (1956); the county attorney's arguing the proposition of fear to the jury; the admission of the confession of defendant; that the verdict was not sustained by the evidence; and denial of defendant's motion for an instructed verdict.

We shall consider first the denial of the motion to quash the information. A.R.S. § 13–492 reads as follows:

> "A. A person, except in the case of a minor by the parent, who seizes, confines, inveigles, entices, decoys, abducts, conceals, kidnaps or carries away any individual by any means whatsoever with intent to hold or detain, or who holds or detains such individual for ransom, reward or otherwise, or to commit extortion or robbery, or to exact from relatives of such person or from any other person any money or valuable thing, or a person who aids or abets any such conduct, is guilty of a felony.

> "B. A person, except in the case of a minor by the parent, who seizes, confines, inveigles, entices, decoys, abducts, conceals, kidnaps or carries away any child under the age of fourteen years by any means whatsoever with intent to hold or detain, or who holds or detains such child for the purpose of raping or committing sodomy, or lewd or lascivious acts upon the person of such child, or a person who aids or abets any such conduct, is guilty of a felony.

> "C. A person convicted under subsections A or B of this section shall be punished as follows:

> "1. If the person subjected to the acts mentioned in subsections A or B suffers serious bodily harm inflicted by the person found guilty, the person found guilty shall be punished by death or by life imprisonment without possibility of parole, whichever the jury recommends.

> "2. If the person subjected to any acts mentioned in subsection A or B does not suffer serious bodily harm the person found guilty shall be punished by imprisonment in the state prison from twenty to fifty years without possibility of parole until the minimum sentence has been served. As amended Laws 1956, Ch. 92, § 1."

Defendant contents that there were objectionable, prejudicial and redundant, and unnecessary words in the following portion of the information:

> "[D]id then and there wilfully, unlawfully and feloniously, seize, confine, abduct, conceal, kidnap or carry away one [complaining witness] for the purpose of raping *and did*

not rape said [complaining witness], *said [complaining witness] not being related in any way to said defendant, * * *.*"(Italics added.)

The words which he complains of were the words italicized. We have held the word "otherwise," in A.R.S. § 13–492 Subsec. A, includes other crimes such as rape. *State v. Jacobs*, 93 Ariz. 336, 380 P.2d 998; and *State v. Taylor*, 82 Ariz. 289, 312 P.2d 162.

[1–4] In *State v. Jacobs*, supra, we stated:

> "We therefore now hold that the crime of kidnapping with intent to commit rape may be charged under A.R.S. § 13–492, subd. A." 93 Ariz. at 341, 380 P.2d at 1002.

The history and reason for the broadening of the kidnapping statute was well set forth in the *Jacobs* case. The information properly referred to "rape" because that was the purpose of the kidnapping. The use of the words "and did rape" was no more inflammatory than the allegation "for the purpose of raping," which was necessary and proper, as held in *Jacobs* supra. The commission of rape was charged in Count II, and so defendant could not have been prejudiced by the use of the word on Count I. The objection to the other language—namely, "not being related in any way to the defendant"—certainly is without foundation. The only object of the allegation was to show that the case did not fall within the exception, i.e., the taking of a minor by a parent. Under no stretch of the imagination could these words be construed as inflammatory, as contended by defendant.

[5] As to the second part of the information charging the crime of rape, defendant contends that because originally the word "fear" was in the information it was prejudicial. However, defendant made a motion to quash the information, and, on May 2d, before the trial, the court entered an order denying defendant's motion to quash but ordered the word "fear" to be stricken from the information. Hence the information upon which defendant was tried and which was read to the jury did not contain the word "fear." So the word "fear" originally in the information could not have had any prejudicial effect. The case was submitted under proper instructions defining rape under A.R.S. § 13–611, Subsec. A. Par. 2 namely:

> "2. Where the female resists, but her resistance is overcome by force or violence."

[6] Defendant contends that it was error to deny his motion to dismiss the action on the

ground that the case was not brought to trial within the sixty days provided for under Rule of Criminal Procedure, No. 236, which reads:

> "When a person has been held to answer for an offense, if an information is not filed against him for the offense within thirty days thereafter, or when a person has been indicted or informed against for an offense, if he is not brought to trial for the offense within sixty days after the indictment has been found or the information filed, the prosecution shall be dismissed upon the application of such person, or of the county attorney, or on the motion of the court itself, unless good cause to the contrary is shown by affidavit, or unless the action has not proceeded to trial because of the defendant's consent or by his action. When good cause is shown, the action may be continued, in which event the defendant if bailable shall be released on bail either on his own recognizance or on the undertaking of sureties." 17 A.R.S. (1956).

This contention is without merit, as defendant made application for a sanity hearing under Rules of Criminal Procedure, No. 250, 17 A.R.S. (1956), just one week prior to the time of the original trial setting. The trial setting was well within the 60–day period. It was defendant's application for the sanity hearing which caused the delay. At the hearing on this application, and without objection of defendant's counsel, a new date for trial was set—June 10, 1963—which was also within the 60–day period. One of the medical reports was not filed until June 7, 1963. Defendant was thereafter promptly tried—just two days after the ruling was made on the motion for the sanity hearing. Thus, it is evident that the delay of the trial was due to defendant's waiting until just one week before trial date to make his motion for the sanity hearing. This was good cause for continuance. Even with the delay occasioned by defendant's own action, trial was held June 20, 1963, only five days beyond the 60–day period. Where good cause is shown, under Rules of Criminal Procedure, No. 236, an action may be continued. *Westover v. State*, 66 Ariz. 145, 185 P.2d 315; *Power v. State*, 43 Ariz. 329, 30 P.2d 1059.

[7] Defendant contends that there was prejudicial error committed by the deputy county attorney when he argued before the jury that the victim acquiesced in the act due to fear. Defendant contends that this argument, notwithstanding the court's instruction to disregard it, was so prejudicial and inflammatory as to deny defendant a fair and impartial trial. We cannot agree with defendant's interpretation. Certainly the testimony justified the county attorney's conclusion of fear. There was such testimony by the complaining witness as: "He had my hands behind my back, and one hand over my mouth, and started pulling me toward the car"; "He tied my hands and my ankles, after he got out, he put this sharp thing to my neck and said 'Feel this' * * * I kept screaming 'Please let me go,'"; and when he was undressing her, she stated she was crying again and said "Please don't." This court has repeatedly held that attorneys are given a wide latitude in their arguments to the jury. *State v. Dowthard*, 92 Ariz. 44, 373 P.2d 357; *State v. Thomas*, 78 Ariz. 52, 275 P.2d 408; *State v. McLain*, 74 Ariz. 132, 245 P.2d 278. In addition, any possible prejudice was corrected by the court's prompt instruction to disregard, coupled with the instructions given at the close of a trial, viz., limiting the jury's consideration to the offense charged—Rape, A.R.S. § 13–611, Subsec. A, Par 2.

[8–10] Defendant contends that the verdict is unsupported by the evidence, viz., there is no showing that the victim resisted the perpetration of the rape. This court cannot find merit in this contention. The victim testified that she pushed against defendant with her hands, and kept screaming; that she was trying to get away, and she testified that he was a lot stronger than she was, and she could not do anything. She also testified to penetration and defendant's confession showed penetration. These were questions for the jury, and the jury decided against defendant. We have repeatedly held that all inferences must be construed in the light most favorable to sustaining the verdict, and that where there is evidence to support a verdict we will not disturb a finding of a jury. *State v. Hernandez*, 96 Ariz. 28, 391 P.2d 586; *State v. Maxwell*, 95 Ariz. 396, 391 P.2d 560.

Defendant contends that admission into evidence of his written confession was error for the reason that he did not have an attorney at the time the statement was made and signed. The police officers Young and Cooley testified to oral statements made to them before the signing of the written confession. Their testimony was substantially the same. They first saw defendant at his home at 2525 West Maricopa on March 13, 1963, when they went there for the purpose of investigating a rape. They took defendant to the police station and placed him in a "line-up" with "four other Mexican males, all approximately the same age and height, build," and brought in the complaining witness who identified him as the one who had perpetrated the acts against her. Then they immediately interrogated him. They advised him of his rights. They testified that he made the statement of his own free will; and that there were no threats, or use of force and coercion, or promises of immunity; that they had informed him of his legal rights and that any statement he made might be used against him.

The oral statement by defendant, as related to police officers, is set forth in the testimony of Detective Carroll Cooley:

> "A He saw this girl walking on the street, he said, so he decided he would pull up ahead of her and stop. He stopped and got out of his car and opened the back door of his automobile. He said when the girl approached him he told her, he said, 'Don't make any noise, and get into the car,' and he said she got into the car, he said, in the back seat.

> "After getting into the car, he said he took a small rope he had inside the car and he tied her hands and her ankles, then he got into the front seat behind the driver's wheel and he drive to a location several miles from there in the northeast direction to the area of a desert.

> "Q Did he tell you what street this took place on?

> "A He didn't know the street. I asked him the street, and he didn't know the name of the street, he didn't know exactly where he was located when he stopped. It was just in the desert area, couple of miles from where he picked the girl up.

> "He said then when he got there he noticed that the girl was untied, and he got into the back seat and he asked her if she would, or he told her to take her clothes off and she said, 'No, would you please take me home?'

> "He said then he took her clothes off for her. After he had undressed her, she began to cry, and started begging him not to do this. She said she had never had any relations with a man before.

> "He said he went ahead and performed the act of intercourse, and in so doing was only able to get about a half inch of his penis in and at which time he said he did reach a climax, but he didn't believe that he had reached a climax inside of her.

> "He said after the act of intercourse, he then told her to get dressed and asked her where

she lived and she told him in the area, she told him 10th or 12th Street. He couldn't remember where, so he said he drove her back to the area where he picked her up and dropped her off in that general area.

> "When he started to let her out, why she told him, 'Well this is not where I live.'

> "He said, 'This is as far as I am taking you,' and then he asked her if she would pray for him. She got out of the car and he left and he said then he went home.

> "Q Was that the essence of the conversation you had with him at that time?

> "A That was the essence of the conversation.

> "Q Officer, was this conversation reduced, or was the defendant's conversation with you reduced to writing?

> "A Yes, Sir it was.

> "Q Who wrote it down, Officer?

> "A He wrote his own statement down.

> "Q He wrote it down?

> "A Yes, Sir.

> "Q Were you present, Officer, when he wrote this?

> "A Yes, Sir, I was."

This oral statement was corroborated by the testimony of Officer Young. At the conclusion of Officer Cooley's testimony the statement of defendant was offered in evidence. Officer Cooley was examined on voir dire, as follows:

> "Q Is this the statement that you said the defendant reduced to writing?

> "A Yes, Sir, it is.

> "[Prosecuting Attorney]: At this time, State will move to introduce the exhibit in evidence.

> "[Defense Attorney]: May I ask some questions on voir dire?

> "THE COURT: Yes, you may.

> "[Defense Attorney]: Q Officer Cooley, in the taking of this statement, what did you say to the defendant to get him to make this statement?

> "A I asked the defendant if he would tell us, write the same story that he had just told me, and he said that he would.

> "Q Did you warn him of his rights?

> "A Yes, Sir, at the heading of the statement is a paragraph typed out, and I read this paragraph to him out loud.

> "Q Did you read that to him outloud?

"A Yes, Sir.

"Q But did you ever, before or during your conversation or before taking this statement, did you ever advise the defendant he was entitled to the services of an attorney?

"A When I read —

"Q Before he made any statement?

"A When I read the statement right there.

"Q I don't see in the statement that it says where he is entitled to the advise of an attorney before he made it.

"A No, Sir.

"Q It is not in the statement?

"A It doesn't say anything about an attorney. Would you like for me to read it?

"Q No, it will be an exhibit if it is admitted and the jury can read it, but you didn't tell him he could have an attorney?"

The signed statement admitted in evidence is as follows:

I, Ernest A. Miranda, do hereby swear that I make this statement voluntarily and out of my own free will, with no threats, coercion, or promises of immunity, and with full knowledge of my legal rights, understanding any statement I make may be used against me.

"I, Ernest A. Miranda, am 23 year of age and have completed the 8th grade in school.

"Seen a girl walking up street stopped a little ahead of her got out of car walked towards her grabbed her by the arm and asked to get in the car. Got in car without force tied hands & ankles. Drove away for a few miles. Stopped asked to take clothes off. Did not, asked me to take her back home. I started to take clothes off her without any force, and with cooperation. Asked her to lay down and she did. Could not get penis into vagina got about 1/2 (half) inch in. Told her to get clothes back on. Drove her home. I couldn't say I was sorry for what I had done. But asked her to say a prayer for me.

"I have read and understand the foregoing statement and hereby swear to its truthfulness.

"/s/ Ernest A. Miranda

"WITNESS: /s/ Carroll Cooley

/s/ Wilfred M. Young, #182

It will be noted that the only objection made to the testimony was in regard to the narrative form of the answers. The record shows the trial court did not err in the exercise of its discretion in the admission of this evidence.

The only objection made to the introduction of the signed statement was:

"We are objecting because the Supreme Court of the United States says the man is entitled to an attorney at the time of his arrest."

No objection was made on the ground that the statement was not shown to be voluntary, and no request was made for a determination of the voluntariness of the confession outside of the presence of the jury.

In *State v. Owen*, 96 Ariz. 274, 394 P.2d 206, after the Supreme Court of the United States (378 U.S. 574, 84 S.Ct. 1932, 12 L.Ed.2d 1041) granted a petition for a writ of certiorari, judgement was vacated, and the case remanded for further proceedings not inconsistent with the opinion in *Jackson v. Denno*, 378 U.S. 368, 84 S.Ct. 1774, 12 L.Ed. 2d 908, and, in accordance with the mandate of the U.S. Supreme Court, we held:

"However, since the Supreme Court vacated the judgement of this Court [*Jackson v. Denno*, 378 U.S. 368, 84 S.Ct. 1774, 12 L.Ed2d 908] we are of the opinion that it was intended that we follow the rule that statements or admissions, which have been induced by a method in violation of a defendant's constitutional rights, are subject to the same exclusionary rule as a confession. (Cases cited.)" 96 Ariz. at 276, 394 P.2d at 207.

In the instant case request was not made for a determination of the voluntariness of the testimony out of the presence of the jury, nor was its voluntariness questioned or evidence offered to prove it involuntary. No question was presented to the court—either from the evidence or by the attorney—suggesting that there should be a determination as to the voluntariness of the evidence, and no request was made therefor. Officers Cooley and Young had testified to substantially the same facts as were contained in the written statement without objection except to the form of the questions. In his appeal, defendant's only contention is that he did not have an attorney. The evidence clearly shows that the statement was voluntary. The officers testified that there were no threats or use of any force or coercion, and no promise of immunity; that defendant was advised of his rights, and that any statement he made might be used against him. The record in this case, and the companion robbery case, No. 1397, shows that defendant was identified, interrogated, and signed confessions in both cases in approximately two hours.

The procedure to be followed in regard to confessions is clearly set forth in State v. Owen, supra, where we held, in line with *Jackson v. Denno*, supra, that:

"* * * when a question is raised as to voluntariness of a statement constituting either admissions against interest, exculpatory or otherwise, or a confession, it must be resolved by the judge outside the presence of the jury. If he determines it was involuntary, it will not be admitted. If he determines it was voluntary, it may be admitted." 96 Ariz. at 277, 394 P.2d at 208.

Counsel for defendant evidently determined that the statement was voluntary, or he would have made a request for a hearing out of the presence of the jury. There not having been an issue presented in regard to voluntariness—either from evidence or by request made for a hearing on its voluntariness—and a proper foundation having been laid for its introduction, there was no question to be determined by the court. The failure of the court to give such a hearing is not assigned as error in this case. The only question presented is whether it is proper to admit a statement voluntarily made where defendant did not have an attorney at the time he signed the statement.

The facts of *Jackson v. Denno*, supra, were different from those of the instant case. In that case there was a serious question in regard to whether the confession was voluntary, so the court laid down the rule which was followed by this court in the Owen case. We held that when requested there must first be a determination by the court in the absence of the jury as to whether a statement was voluntary. If it were involuntary, that ended the matter. If the court determined it to be voluntary, following the Massachusetts rule, we held it was still the duty of the court to submit the question again to the jury, and the jury might reject it on the grounds that it was involuntary.

The voluntariness and the truth of the confession were not denied. However, the defendant did not have an attorney at the time he made the confession. The sole question before the court, then, is whether there was a violation of the rights of defendant under the Sixth and Fourteenth Amendments to the Constitution by admission of the voluntary statement made without an attorney.

We recognize that in passing upon constitutional provisions applicable to the instant case it is our duty to follow the interpretations of the Supreme Court of the United States. There is a long list of these cases, the most recent of which are *Escobedo v. State of Illinois* (1964), 378 U.S. 478, 84 S.Ct. 1758, 121 L.Ed.2d 977; and *Massiah v. United States* (1964) 377 U.S. 201, 84 S.Ct. 1199, 12 L.Ed.2d 246.

In *Massiah*, supra, the court held invalid a conviction on statements which were secured by placing a hidden radio microphone in a co-defendant's car so that government agents could pick up a conversation between defendants. Indictment already had been returned, and counsel retained by defendant.

The *Massiah* case is not in point. The defendant in that case was not aware that his conversation was being picked up by the government agents, and he had not been put on notice that what he was saying might be used against him, nor did he know that the federal agents were eavesdropping on his conversation. Under these circumstances it was evident that he did not know his statement might be used against him, and the court held that such an incriminating statement was inadmissible.

In the *Escobedo* case, supra, defendant's brother-in-law had been fatally shot on January 19, 1960. Defendant had been arrested at 2:30 a. m. the next morning without a warrant and interrogated. He was released at 5:00 p. m. pursuant to a state court writ of habeas corpus. On January 30th, one DiGerlando, who was then in custody and later indicted along with defendant, told police that Escobedo had fired the fatal shot. That evening between 8:00 and 9:00 o'clock, Escobedo and his sister, the widow of deceased, were arrested and taken to headquarters. Escobedo had been handcuffed. Escobedo was told by the detective, in his words, that "they had us pretty well, up pretty tight, and we might as well admit to this crime." Escobedo then told them he wanted a lawyer. The police officer testified that although defendant was not formally charged he was in custody and could not walk out of the door.

The facts of the case also show that shortly after defendant reached police headquarters his lawyer arrived, and that he requested to see defendant, which request was denied. This was between 9:30 and 10:00 in the evening. Also, that all during questioning defendant asked to speak

SUPREME COURT OF ARIZONA, APRIL 1965

to his lawyer, and the police said his lawyer didn't want to see him. Notwithstanding both the request of the defendant and his retained lawyer, he was denied the opportunity to consult with his lawyer during the course of the entire interrogation. The court, in discussing the testimony, stated:

> "The critical question in this case is whether, under the circumstances, the refusal by the police to honor petitioner's request to consult with his lawyer during the course of an interrogation constitutes a denial of 'the Assistance of Counsel' in violation of the Sixth Amendment to the Constitution as 'made obligatory upon the States by the Fourteenth Amendment,' *Gideon v. Wainwright*, 372 U.S. 335, 342, 83 S.Ct. 792, 795, 9 L.Ed.2d 799, and thereby renders inadmissible in a state criminal trial any incriminating statement elicited by the police during the interrogation." 378 U.S. at 479, 84 S.Ct. at 1759.

Under these circumstances, after review of the facts and the decisions on the question, the court stated:

> "We hold, therefore, that where, as the, the investigation is no longer a general inquiry into an unsolved crime but has begun to focus, on a particular suspect, the suspect has been taken into police custody, the police carry out a process of interrogations that lends itself to eliciting incriminating statements, the suspect has requested and been denied an opportunity to consult with his lawyer, and the police have not effectively warned him of his absolute constitutional right to remain silent, the accused has been denied 'the Assistance of Counsel' in violation of the Sixth Amendment to the Constitution as 'made obligatory upon the States by the Fourteenth Amendment,' *Gideon v. Wainwright*, 372 U.S., at 342, 83 S.Ct., at 795, and that no statement elicited by the police during the interrogation may be used against him at a criminal trial. [378 U.S. at 490, 84 S.Ct. at 1765]

* * * * * *

> "Nothing we have said today affects the powers of the police to investigate 'an unsolved crime,' *Spano v. [People of the State of] New York*, 360 U.S. 315, 327, 79 S.Ct. 1202, 1209 [3 L.Ed.2d 1265] (Stewart J., concurring), by gathering information from witnesses and by other 'proper investigative efforts.' *Haynes v. [State of] Washington*, 373 U.S. 503, 519, 83 S.Ct. 1336, 1346 [10 L.Ed.2d 513]. We hold only that when the process shifts from investigatory to accusatory—when its focus is on

the accused and its purpose is to elicit a confession—our adversary system beings to operate, and, under the circumstances here, the accused must be permitted to consult with his lawyer." 378 U.S. at 492, 84 S.Ct. at 1766.

It will be noted that the court in the Escobedo case set forth the circumstances under which a statement would be held inadmissible, namely: (1) The general inquiry into an unsolved crime must have begun to focus on a particular suspect. (2) The suspect must have been taken into police custody. (3) The police in its interrogation must have elicited an incriminating statement. (4) The suspect must have requested and been denied an opportunity to consult with his lawyer. (5) The police must not have effectively warned the suspect of his constitutional rights to remain silent.

[11] When all of these five factors occur, then the *Escobedo* case is a controlling precedent. As to whether identification of a defendant in a "line-up" is sufficient to focus the investigation upon a defendant depends upon all of the facts and circumstances surrounding the case. We call attention to the fact that the crime committed in the instant case occurred in the night time, and that there is always a chance of a mistake in identity under such circumstances on account of the excitement of the complaining witness, and difficulty of identity at night. Even where a complaining witness identifies a defendant in a line-up, as in the instant case, officers may well feel that a defendant should have the right and privilege of explaining his whereabouts at the particular time which could be checked by the officers. One of the chief duties of both the sheriff's office and the county attorney's office is to make sure that people are not unjustly charged with crime. It is their duty to protect the innocent as well as detect the guilty. In *United States v. Konigsberg*, 2 Cir., 336 F.2d 844 (1964), the court stated:

> "In this appeal at the time the F.B.I. agents talked with Konigsberg the process was definitely investigative and never shifted to accusatory. Its purpose was not to elicit a confession: there were no threats or attempt to extract admissions from Konigsberg, damaging or otherwise. The uncontradicted purpose of the discussion was to give Konigsberg a chance to explain his presence in the garage if he could; to hear Konigberg's side of the story." 336 F.2d at 853.

The question of whether the investigation had focused on the accused at the time of the making of the statement and thereby shifted "from investigatory to accusatory" is not the deciding factor in regard to the admissibility of the confession in the instant case. There are other factors under the ruling of the *Escobedo* case. Defendant in the instant case was advised of his rights. He had not requested counsel, and had not been denied assistance of counsel. We further call attention to the fact that, as pointed out in the companion case here on appeal, *State v. Miranda*, No. 1397, defendant had a record which indicated that he was not without courtroom experience. *State v. Cuzick*, 97 Ariz. 130, 397 P.2d 269, 631. It included being arrested in California on suspicion of armed robbery, and a conviction and sentence in Tennessee on violations of the Dyer Act. Under these circumstances he was certainly not unfamiliar with legal proceedings and his rights in court. The police testified they had informed defendant of his rights, and he stated in his written confession that he understood his rights (which would certainly include the right to counsel), and it is not for this court to dispute his statement that he did. His experience under previous cases indicate that his statement that he understood his rights was true.

In the case of *Commonwealth (Pa.) v. Coyle*, 415 Pa. 379, 203 A.2d 782, the court said:

"During the course of Lt. Cullinane's questioning, the record is convincing that the appellant did not ask for the assistance of counsel. We note that this, in itself, is not controlling since if such assistance were constitutionally required, the right thereto would not depend on a request: *Carnley v. Cochran*, 369 U.S. 506, 82 S.Ct. 884, 8 L.Ed.2d 70 (1962). However, this factor substantially distinguishes the present case from the situation presented in *Escobedo v. State of Illinois*, 378 U.S. 478, 84 S.Ct. 1758, 12 L.Ed.2d 977 (1964). Further, we do not interpret *Escobedo* mean that, counsel must immediately be afforded one taken into custody, under all circumstances, particularly where none is requested. The mere fact that appellant was unrepresented by counsel during the questioning does not invalidate admissions made against interest. See, *Commonwealth v. Graham*, 408 Pa. 155, 182 A.2d 727 (1962); *Crooker v. State of California*, 357 U.S. 433, 78 S.Ct. 1287, 2 L.Ed.2d 1488 (1958); *Cicenia v. LaGay*, 357 U.S. 504, 78 S.Ct. 1297, 2 L.Ed.2d 1523 (1958)." 203 A.2d at 794.

In *Anderson v. State of Maryland*, 237 Md. 45, 205 A.2d 281 (1964) the court stated:

"The appellant urges that the confession was inadmissible because he did not have counsel when he made it, citing *Escobedo v. [State of] Illinois*, 378 U.S. 478, 84 S.Ct. 1758, 12 L.Ed.2d 977 (1964). This contention is without merit since there is no evidence that he ever requested counsel. See *Green v. State*, supra [236 Md. 334, 203 A.2d 870], and *Mefford and Blackburn v. State*, 253 Md. 497, 201 A.2d 824 (1964).

"Careful inspection of the record concerning the circumstances surrounding the giving of the confession reveals no evidence that it was not freely and voluntarily made. There is no evidence that the appellant ever asked to contact his family or requested food. He was not questioned by relays of officers. According to the police testimony and the written confession itself, the appellant was advised that his statement must voluntary, that there would be no threats or promises, and that it could be used in a court of law against him. There was no contradictory evidence. The trial court's finding that the confession was voluntary was supported by the evidence." 205 A.2d at 285.

We also note the interpretation of the federal court of the effect of the *Escobedo* case, at set forth in *Jackson v. United States*, D.C.Cir., 337 F.2d 136 (1964).

"Defense counsel moved to suppress 'any and all confessions and admissions written or oral obtained by the United States since the date of his arrest and presentation to a committing magistrate.' As grounds for the motion, appellant claimed that the confessions and admissions were elicited from him 'involuntarily' in violation of the Fifth Amendment and of the appellant's right to counsel under the Sixth Amendment. [337 F.2d at 138].

"Obviously neither *Escobedo* nor *Massiah* can be read as barring use of this appellant's confession. Many, learned in the law, deeply believe that no accused should be convicted out of his own mouth. But the Supreme Court never announced any such proposition—not even where the accused had no attorney and had received no Rule 5 'judicial caution.' *United States v. Mitchell*, 322 U.S. 65, 70, 64 S.Ct. 896, 88 L.Ed. 1140 (1944). We said as much ourselves only a month ago in *Ramey v. United States*, 118 U.S.App.D.C. 355, 336 F.2d 743 (1964), cert. denied [379 U.S. 840], 85 S.Ct. 79 [13 L.Ed.2d 47] (1964) and see *United States v. Carignan*, 342 U.S. 36, 72 S.Ct. 97, 96 L.Ed. 48 (1951) where Rule 5

SUPREME COURT OF ARIZONA, APRIL 1965

advice had been imparted. If there were a rule that a confession may not be received *if made by an accused without counsel*, that would be the end of this case—and of scores like it.

"We conclude that no rule of law required the exclusion of this appellant's confession, voluntarily made, after he had been warned by the F.B.I., the police and the United States Commissioner acting pursuant to Rule 40(b). He had not requested that counsel be appointed; he had retained no lawyer; that one was not then appointed for him denied him no right; and as the law now stands, there is no automatic rule of exclusion which will bar use of such a confession by an accused who has no lawyer, under circumstances such as appear on the record before us." 337 F.2d at 140.

Other cases, in interpreting the effect of *Massiah* and *Escobedo*, have held that the test of admissibility of a statement was not whether defendant had counsel but whether the statement was in effect voluntary, some even holding that it was not necessary that he be warned that it might be used against him. *People v. Hartgraves*, 31 Ill.2d 375, 202 N.E.2d 33; *People v. Agar*, 44 Misc.2d 396, 253 N.Y.S.2d 761; *Commonwealth (Pa.) v. Patrick*, 416 Pa. 437, 206 A.2d 295; *United States v. Konigsberg*, supra; *State v. Fox*, 131 N.W.2d 684 (Iowa); *State v. Worley*, 178 Neb. 232, 132 N.W.2d 764.

What is the purpose of the right to counsel? What is the purpose of the Sixth and Fourteenth Amendments? Without question it is to protect individual rights which we cherish, but there must be a balance between the competing interests of society and the rights of the individual. Society has the right of protection against those who roam the streets for the purpose of violating the law, but that protection must not be at the expense of the rights of the individual guaranteed under the Sixth and Fourteenth Amendments to our Constitution.

In *Bean v. State* (Nev.), 398 P.2d 251 (1965), the court, after discussing the *Escobedo* case, stated:

"Here it is true that the investigation had begun to focus upon *Bean*; that he had been taken into police custody; that the police were about to commence a process of interrogation to elicit incriminating statements,

and did so; that *Bean* was not warned of his absolute constitutional right to remain silent. However, *Bean* did not request counsel, nor was he denied the assistance counsel. Absent such a request, and denial of counsel, rule of Escobedo does not apply.

* * * * * *

"In *Morford v. State*, 80 Nev.—, 395 P.2d 861, we discussed the Dorado case, pointing out that it is an extension of the rule announced in *Escobedo*, and chose not to follow it." 398 P.2d at 254.

We are familiar with the case of *State of California v. Dorado*, Cal., 40 Cal.Rptr. 264, 394 P.2d 952, and, like the Supreme Court of Nevada, do not choose to follow Dorado in the extension of the rule announced in Escobedo, supra.

[12] It will be noted in the discussion of these cases—particularly the *Escobedo* case—the ruling of the court is based upon the circumstances of the particular case. The court, in making its holding in the *Escobedo* case, stated "under the circumstances here, the accused must be permitted to consult with his lawyer." Most of the cases distinguish the *Escobedo* case on the grounds that the defendant.

Each case must largely turn upon its own facts, and the court must examine all the circumstances surrounding the taking of the statement in determining whether it is voluntary, and whether defendant's constitutional rights have been violated.

[13] The facts and circumstances in the instant case show that the statement was voluntary, made by defendant of his own free will, that no threats or use of force or coercion or promise, of immunity were made; and that he understood his legal right and the statement might be used against him. Under such facts and circumstances we hold that, notwithstanding the fact that he did not have an attorney at the time he made the statement, and the investigation was beginning to focus upon him, defendant's constitutional rights were not violated, and it was proper to admit the statement in evidence.

Judgment affirmed.

Lockwood, C.J., Struckmeyer, V.C.J., and Bernstein and Udall, JJ., concurring.

SUPREME COURT OF CALIFORNIA, MARCH 1965

People v. Stewart

CITE AS 400 P.2D 97

THE PEOPLE, PLAINTIFF AND RESPONDENT,
V.
ROY ALLEN STEWART, DEFENDANT
AND APPELLANT.
CR. 7662

Supreme Court of California,
In Bank.
March 25, 1965
As Modified on Denial of Rehearing
April 21, 1965.
43 Cal.Rptr. 201

Prosecution for robbery and murder. The Superior Court, Los Angeles County, Benjamin Landis, J., rendered judgment, and defendant appealed. The Supreme Court, Tobriner, J., held that accusatory stage had been reached and defendant was entitled to counsel with respect to taking of confession where defendant had been in custody for five day and had been interrogated daily, although incriminating evidence in defendant's house was found not among his possessions of another and four other suspects were in custody, and that it would not be presumed that warning had been given.

Reversed.

Schauer and McComb, J.J., dissented.

Accusatory or critical stage has been reached and suspect is entitled to counsel when officers have arrested suspect and have undertaken process of interrogation that lends itself to elicting incriminating statements.

Accusatory or critical stage at which suspect is entitled to counsel does not begin with arrest alone.

Process of interrogation following arrest is not necessarily interrogation lending itself to eliciting incriminating statements so as to entitle suspect to counsel.

To determine if police are carrying out process of interrogation that lends itself to elicting incriminating statements, so as to entitle suspect to counsel, court must analyze total situation which envelopes questioning by considering such factors as length of interrogation, place and time of interrogation, nature of questions, conduct of police and all other relevant circumstances; test is objective.

Accusatory stage had been reached and defendant was entitled to counsel with respect to taking of confession where defendant had been in custody for five days and had been interrogated daily, although incriminating evidence in defendant's house was found not among his possessions but in bureau drawer containing possessions of another and four other suspects were in custody.

Court cannot presume that police acted in accordance with unannounced constitutional principle.

It would not be presumed that suspect had been advised of his right to counsel and right to remain silent at police interrogation where, at time of interrogation, state law did not give him right to counsel during prearraignment interrogation and did not require that warning be given. West's Ann.Penn.Code. § 825.

Use of defendant's confession obtained in violation of his constitutional right to counsel required reversal of his conviction for the robbery and murder which he confessed and also reversal of his conviction for other robberies which he did not confess, where there was such an inter-relationship among these crimes that his confession composed strong evidence of his guilt of the robberies which he did not confess.

Edwin Malmuth, Los Angeles, under appointment by Supreme Court, for defendant and appellant.

Stanley Mosk and Thomas C. Lynch, Attys. Gen., William E. James, Asst. Atty. Gen., and Gordon Ringer, Deputy Atty. Gen., for plaintiff and respondent.

Tobriner, Justice.

The jury found defendant guilty of robbery and murder of the first degree and fixed the penalty at death. The trial court denied his motion for a new trial and for a reduction of the penalty. This appeal is automatic (Pen.Code, § 1239, subd. (b).

Defendant contends that his confession was improperly admitted at the trial because he was not informed of his right to counsel and of his right to remain silent prior to the time he confessed and because he gave his confession involuntarily. He also contends that during the penalty trial the trial judge gave an instruction condemned in *People v. Morse* (1964) 60 Cal. 2d 631, 36 Cal.Rptr. 201, 388 P.2d 33.

Since we conclude that the admission of defendant's confession constituted reversible error in view of our recent holding in *People v. Dorado* (1965) 62 A.C. 350, 42 Cal.Rptr. 169 398 P.2d 361, we need not reach the issues raised by defendant's other contentions.

During December 1962 and January 1963 a series of robberies accompanied by beatings took place in a neighborhood of Los Angeles. On December 21, 1962, an assailant struck Mrs. Meriwether Wells while she was walking down the street and took from her a handbag containing $5 to $10, a wallet bearing her maiden name, charge-a-plates in the names of Mr. and Mrs. Robert K. Wells, a salary check payable to Mrs. Wells, a salary check payable to Mr. Wells, and three dividend checks. Mrs. Wells, who suffered a fractured jaw, said the culprit was a "colored man," but she was unable to identify him.

On January 10, 1963, someone robbed Mrs. Tsuru Miyuchi of her leather lunch bag, containing a red change purse with her daughter's name on it, pictures, keys, and $8 to $10 in cash. As she was walking down the street, the assailant hit her on the head with a blunt instrument, causing her to suffer a fractured skull and a broken nose. She could not identify the robber.

On January 19, 1963, Miss Lucile O. Mitchell was beaten and robbed of a silver cufflink, a transistor earplug, a watch, and a charge-a-plate. Miss Mitchell, who was found on a house porch, subsequently, without having identified the attacker, died from a head wound.

On January 25, 1963, Mrs. Beatrice Dixon, while walking down a street, was hit on the head and robbed of her large leather bag containing a billfold, $23, a black coin purse, cash, and a door key on a chain bearing her initial, "B" Mrs. Dixon could not identify the person who hit and robbed her.

When, on January 30, 1963, Miss Maria Louisa Ramirez was walking down a street, someone hit her on the side of her head. When she regained consciousness, her purse containing a wallet, a coin purse, and a pair of glasses in a case were gone. The police officer investigating the robbery found the charge-a-plate taken from Miss Mitchell on the ground about 18 inches from the place where Miss Ramirez had been lying. A witness to the crime testified at the trial

that defendant looked like the assailant, but she did not make a positive identification.

Mr. Wells, husband of the first of the above victims, reported to the police that the dividend checks stolen from his wife bore the endorsement, "Robert K. Wells." He said that he had never endorsed the checks. The police then interviewed a Mr. Sam Newman, who operated the market where the checks had been cashed. Mr. Newman related that because the person who cashed the checks lacked identification, a Mrs. Lena Franklin, who was then in the store and was apparently acquainted with the defendant, cosigned them. On January 31, Mrs. Franklin pointed out to a police officer the defendant as the one who cashed the checks.

The police officer went to defendant's residence and there informed him that he was under arrest for a series of "purse snatch robberies." When the officer asked if he could search the house, the defendant replied, "Go ahead." During the search, the officer found Mrs. Wells' purse and wallet, Mrs. Miyauchi's coin purse attached to a key that operated the door to defendant's house, Miss Mitchell's watch, Mrs. Dixon's coin purse and initialed key, and Miss Ramirez' wallet. On February 3, during a further search of the house the police found Miss Ramirez' glasses and Miss Mitchell's cufflink, transistor earplug and case.

Likewise on January 31, the police arrested four other people who were in the house at the time of defendant's arrest. The police later determined that besides defendant the only other people who actually lived in the house were a woman referred to as Lillian Lara[1] and her daughter. The police interrogated all five persons.

The police officers testified at the trial that during the interrogations of the defendants on January 31 and on February 1 he denied any knowledge of the checks, even though confronted by Mrs. Franklin, the cosigner of the checks. A tape of the January 31 interrogation was introduced at the trial for impeachment purposes. According to one of the officers, on February 3 defendant said that if he could see Lillian Lara

---

[1] Some question arose as the whether defendant and Lillian Lara were married. During the January 31 interrogation, which was recorded, defendant referred to a "Lillian Davis" as a "girl friend" at whose house he spent two or three nights a week. Defendant testified that he and Lillian Lara had been married in Mexico.

he might have "something to say." After a meeting with her, defendant admitted signing Wells' name to the checks and cashing them, but he claimed that he found the checks; he also denied having seen any of Mrs. Wells' other belongings prior to the date of the interrogation.

On February 4 the police showed defendant the objects found in his residence, bur according to the police officers, he denied having seen them before. One of the officers testified that defendant then said that he had brought the purse, subsequently identified as belonging to Mrs. Wells, to his house when he had moved there two months earlier. He also told the police that other people had brought some of the other stolen objects into house. A police officer testified that defendant denied having seen Miss Ramirez' wallet; but the defendant said he found Mrs. Miysuchi's coin pates on the street. Another officer testified that when the defendant was shown Miss Mitchell's watch he at first denied having previously seen it, but then said someone brought it to his house. He later said he had bought the watch on the street and had given it to Lillian Lara.[2]

On February 5 defendant admitted that he robbed Miss Mitchell. An officer testified that defendant expressed sorrow at having killed Miss Mitchell and said, "I didn't mean to kill her." The police then recorded an interrogation during which defendant gain admitted robbing Miss Mitchell. He denied hitting Mrs. Mitchell on the head; he did say, however, that he could have kicked her in the head after she fell and while he was escaping. He continued to insist that he had not participated in the other robberies.

The police brought defendant before a magistrate for the first time shortly after his confession. They then released the other persons arrested in connection with the crimes. An officer testified that an investigation of these people revealed "no evidence to connect them with any crime."

The transcriptions of the January 31 interrogation and of the February 5 confession of the robbery and other incriminating statements were admitted into evidence without objection, although during the trial defendant contended that he gave his confession involuntarily.[3] Nothing in the record indicates whether or not defendant was informed prior to his confession of his rights to counsel and to remain silent or whether he otherwise knowingly and intelligently waived those rights.[4]

Following the decision of the United States Supreme Court in *Escobedo v. State of Illinois* (1964) 378 U.S. 478, 84 S.Ct. 1758, 12 L.Ed.2d 977, we held in *People v. Dorado* (1965) 62 A.C. 350, 365, 42 Cal. Rptr. 169, 179, 398 P.2d 361, 371, "that defendant's confession could not properly be introduced into evidence because (1) the investigation was no longer a general inquiry into an unsolved crime but had begun to focus on a particular suspect, (2) the suspect was in custody, (3) the authorities had carried out a process of interrogations that lent itself to eliciting incriminating statements, (4) the authorities had not effectively informed defendant of his right to counsel or of his absolute right to remain silent, and no evidence establishes that he had waived these rights."

The instant case presents the following principal questions: (1) whether, at the time defendant uttered the confession, the investigation had reached the accusatory or critical stage so that he was entitled to counsel, and hence to be advised of his rights to counsel and to remain silent if he did not otherwise waive those rights; (2) whether the lack of any indication in the record that defendant was advised of his rights to counsel and to remain silent preludes a finding that he was so advised. We set forth our reasons for answering each of these questions in the affirmative.

The United States Supreme Court in *Esobedo* fixed the point at which a suspect is entitled to

SUPREME COURT
OF CALIFORNIA,
MARCH 1965

---

[2] At the trial defendant denied having said at any time that he had never seen the dividend checks or that had found the checks. He asserted that a Jackie Jackson gave him the checks to cash. He also denied having said that he never saw Miss Mitchell's watch or having said that he had purchased it. He testified that Jackie Jackson and a Louis Bookman brought the stolen goods to his house. Jackie Jackson also testified that Louis Bookman brought the stolen goods to the house. Linda Lara, Lillian Lara's daughter, testified that Bookman and Jackie Jackson were in the house and that Jackie Jackson used Miss Mitchell's charge-a-plate.

[3] Although the record does not indicate that the trial judge made an independent determination of whether the confession was voluntary, we do not probe the problem raised by *Jackson v. Denno* (1964) 378 U.S. 368, 84 S.Ct. 1774, 12 L.Ed.2d 980, since we reverse on other grounds.

[4] The Attorney General admits that there is nothing "specifically showing whether appellant was or was not advised of his 'right to counsel and right to remain silent at the interrogation.'" In a number of instances, the police officers conducting the interrogations were asked to relate everything that was said during specific interrogations. They at no time indicated that they had advised defendant of his rights to counsel and to remain silent.

SUPREME COURT
OF CALIFORNIA,
MARCH 1965

counsel as that at which "the process shifts from investigators to accusatory—when its focus is on the accused and its purpose is to elicit a confession * * *." (378 U.S. at p. 492, 84 S.Ct. at p. 1766). The court also characterized the time when a person needs the "guiding hand counsel" as the when the "investigation had ceased to be a general investigation of 'an unsolved crime'"; at that time the defendant "had become the accused, and the purpose of the interrogation was to 'get him' to confess his guilt despite his constitutional right not to do so." (Id. at pp. 485, 486, 84 S.Ct. at p. 1762).

[1] Normally "the investigation is no longer a general inquiry into an unsolved crime but has begun to focus on a particular suspect:" (Id. at p. 490, 84 S.Ct. at p. 1765) at that point when the police officers place that suspect under arrest. But *Escobedo* indicates that the accusatory or critical stage is not reached unless another event occurs: the police must "carry out a process interrogations that lends itself to eliciting incriminating statements." (Id. at pp. 490–491, 84 S.Ct.at p. 1765; see also Id. at pp. 485, 492, 84 S.Ct. at pp. 1762, 1766.) That process may be undertaken either before or after arrest. Whenever the two conditions are met, that is, when the officers have arrested the suspects and the officers have undertaken a process of interrogations that lends itself to eliciting incriminating statements, the accusatory or critical stage has been reached and the suspect is entitled to counsel.

We believe that the arrest encompasses two of the circumstances which produced the accusatory stages in the *Esobedo* and *Dorado* cases: (1) the investigation is no linger a general inquiry into an unsolved crime but has begun to focus on a particular suspect, and (2) the suspect is in custody.

An arrest fulfills the first requirement that the investigation has begun to focus on a particular suspect. The Penal Code itself conditions the arrest upon the presence of reasonable ground for the belief that the individual committed the offense; section 813 predicates the issuance of a warrant upon "reasonable ground to believe that the defendant has committed" the offense; section 836 requires that the arrest must rest upon the officer's reasonable cause for believing the person committed the offense.

"Probable cause for an arrest," we have said, "is shown if a man of ordinary caution or prudence would be led to believe and conscien-

tiously entertain a strong suspicion of the guilt of the accused. * * * there may some room for doubt. * * The test in such case is not whether the evidence upon which the officer made the arrest is sufficient to convict but only whether the prisoner should stand trial." *(People v. Fischer* (1957) 49 Cal.2d 442, 446, 317 P.2d 967, 970; see generally. Witkin, Cal. Criminal Procedure (1963) pp. 102–104; Fricke, Cal. Criminal Procedure (6th ed. 1962) pp. 19–20.)

The arrest includes "custody," the second condition present in *Esobedo* and *Dorado*. By definition in this state, an element of an arrest is custody. Thus, section 834 of the Penal Code states "Am arrest is taking a person into custody * * *."

Since, once a person has been properly placed under arrest, probate cause must support it, we conclude that the investigation has at least "*begun* to focus on a particular suspect." (378 U.S. at p. 490, 84 S.Ct. at p. 1765; emphasis added.) Indeed, as the court said in a case which, although based upon the McNabb-Mallory rule, cites *Esobedo*, "Ordinarily, arrest is the culmination, not the beginning, of police investigation." *(Greenwell v. United States* (D.C.Cir.1964) 336 F.2d 962, 966.)

[2,3] We turn to the further requirement of *Esobedo* that, beyond the "focus" and custody, the accusatory stage matures upon, the undertaking by the police of a "process of interrogation that lends itself to eliciting incriminating statements." (378 U.S. at p. 491, 84 S.Ct. at p. 1765; see id. at pp. 485, 492, 84 S.Ct. at pp. 1762, 1766; *United States v. Konigsberg* (3d Cir.1964) 336 F.2d 844, 853.)[5] Although in most cases the process of interrogations following an arrest will so lend itself, it does not necessarily do so.

In the *Konigsberg* case, supra, Federal Bureau of Investigation agents apprehended the defendants in a garage containing stolen goods, arrest-

---

[5] We do not agree with the suggestion of some writers that, for purposes of Escobedo, the accusatory or critical stage begins with the arrest alone. See Anderson, Representation of Defendants, Panel Discussion (1965) 36 F.R.D. 129, 141; Enker and Elsen, Counsel for the Suspect: *Massiah v, United States* and *Esobedo v. Illinois* (1964) 49 Minn.L.Rev. 47, 70–73; Note, The Supreme Court, 1963 Term (1964) 78 Harv.L.Rev. 143, 220.

[6] Section 825 of the Penal Code, guaranteeing a person arrested the right to see an attorney, does not signify that counsel must be allowed to be present during interrogations. *(People v. Garner* (1961) 57 Cal.2d 135, 165, 18 Cal.Rptr. 40, 367 P.2d 680 (Traynor, J., concurring).)

ed them and took them to the bureau's office. At that office, prior to an arraignment, the agents asked Konigsberg "'why he was in this garage and just what had taken place * * * and * * * if he wished to cleanse himself or explain * * * what his reasons for being there, were, why at the other individuals were there.'" (Id. at p. 852.) Konigsberg then male some incriminating statements. Among other reasons for not applying *Escobedo*, the court said that the purpose of the interrogation, even though it took place after the arrest, was not to elicit a confession. The court stated, "The uncontradicted purpose of the discussion was to give Konigsberg a chance to explain his presence in the garage if he could; to hear Konigsberg's side of the story. * * If Konigsberg or any of the other people caught in the garage could account for their presence this was their opportunity," (Id. at p. 853; see *People v. Ghimenti* (1965) 232 A.C.A. 111, 119, 43 Cal.Rptr. 504.)

[4] The test which we have described does not propose a determination of the actual intent or subjective purpose of the police in undertaking the interrogations but a determination based upon the objective intent of the interrogators, we must, in order to determine if the police are carrying out "a process of interrogations that lends itself to eliciting incriminating statements" (*Escobedo v. State of Illinois*, supra, 378 U.S, ar p. 491, 84 S.Ct. at p. 1765), analyze the total situation which envelops the questioning by considering such factors as the length of the interrogation, the place and time of the interrogation, the nature of the questions, the conduct of the police and all other relevant circumstances.

As some writers have suggested, "An objective test is * * * likely for the new American rule. for it is noteworthy that the question of 'purpose to elicit a confession' may be more readily determined from the objective evidence—such as the nature of the questions and accusations put to defendant and the length of the interrogation—than the question whether the police had decision to charge the defendant." (Enker and Elsen, Counsel for the Suspect: *Massiah v. United States* and *Esobedo v. Illinois* (1964) 49 Minn.L.Rev. 47, 71.)

[5] In the instant case all of the above conditions had been fulfilled. Defendant was not only under arrest at the time he confessed but had been in custody for five days and had been interrogated daily. In his summation, the prosecutor referred to the interrogation of the defendant on January 31 concerning the robber of Mrs. Wells as an "accusatory circumstances." A police officer testified that on February 5 police office testified that on February 5 he entered the interrogation room and said to the defendant, "Roy, you killed that old woman. * * * " Such extensive interrogations during the period of defendant's incarceration could serve no other purpose than to elicit incriminating statements. Thus, prior to his confession, the defendant was entitled to counsel under the *Esobedo* case. for the "accusatory" stage had been reached.

We do not think the contrary contention of the Attorney General that defendant's confession was procured at the investigatory stage can prevail in the light of the above facts. The Attorney General argues that the fact that the Mitchell watch had not been found among defendant's possessions but in a bureau drawer containing the possessions of Lillian Lara, as well as the fact of the continued custody of four other suspects of the crime, establishes that the police were still conducting a "general inquiry" and had not "begun to focus" on the defendant demonstrates that the police believed that they had reasonable ground for attributing to him the commission of the crimes. The continued custody of other suspects does not automatically negate the advent of the accusatory stage as to defendant; the above conduct of the police destroys the contention.

Concluding, therefore, that prior to his confession defendant was entitled to counsel under *Esobedo*, we probe the second major premise of the Attorney General that, despite the absence of a showing advice to defendant of his rights to counsel and to remain silent, we can presume that such warning was given. The Attorney General bases his contention upon *People v. Farrara* (1956) 46 Cal.2d 265, 294 P.2d 21, which, in the absence of evidence to the contrary, expressed a presumption that the officers in that case lawfully performed their duties.

Farrara, we believe, can readily be distinguished from the instant case. There, appellants contended that the police obtained certain of the adduced evidence during and illegal search and seizure. Since the trial occurred prior to our decision in *People v. Cahan* (1955) 44, Cal.2d 434, 282 P.2d 905, 50 A.L.R.2d 513, declaring such evidence inadmissible, the record was barren of any showing as to the legality of the

SUPREME COURT OF CALIFORNIA, MARCH 1965

search. This court said, "It is settled * * * that error will not be presumed on appeal, * * * and in the absence of evidence to the contrary it must also presumed that the officers regularly and lawfully performed their duties. Code Civ. Proc. § 1963 (1, 15, 33) * * *." (46 Cal.2d ar p. 268, 294 P.2d ar p. 23).

[6,7] Whereas, long before *Cahan*, searches and seizures illegal under federal law had been illegal California (Cal. Const., art. I, § 19), no such antecedent illegality had been present in the *Esobedo* situation. Indeed, *Cahan* merely provided a remedy in the form of exclusion for evidence illegally seized. Until *Escobedo* and *Dorado*, however, the law of this state did not give an accused a right to counsel during prearraignment interrogations and therefore did not require that an accused be advised of his rights to counsel and to remain silent if he had not otherwise waived those rights.[6] We cannot presume that the police acted in accordance with an unannounced constitutional principle. We therefore cannot presume in the face of a silent record that the police informed defendant of his right to remain silent and of his right to counsel. (See *Carnley v. Cochran* (1962) 369 U.S. 506, 82 S.Ct. 884, 8 L.Ed.2d 70.)

In *Carnley v. Cochran* (1962) 369 U.S. 506, 82 S.Ct. 884, the United States Supreme Court, said, "The record must show, or there must be an allegation and evidence which show, that an accused was offered counsel but intelligently and understanding rejected the offer. Anything less is not waiver." (Id. at p. 516, 82 S.Ct. at p. 890.) It follows that in order to establish a waiver of the right to the assistance of counsel the record must indicate that the defendant was advised of his right to counsel and to remain silent or that he knew of these rights and intelligently and knowingly waived them.

To presume in the instant case that absent the warnings defendant knew of his right to counsel at the prearraignment stage prior to the time that the United States Supreme Court established this right in *Esobedo* would be to ascribe to him an utterly fictitious clairvoyance.

[8] Since we have said that the use of a confession obtained in violation of the defendant's constitutional right to counsel compels a reversal, we must reverse the judgment on the counts involving the robbery and murder of Miss Mitchell. (*People v. Dorado* (1965) 62 A.C. 350, 368–369, 42 Cal.Rptr. 169, 398 P.2d 361.)

Because defendant, however, confessed only to the robbery and murder of Miss Mitchell, we must determine if the erroneous admission of his confession constituted prejudicial error as to those other robberies for which he was convicted but as to which he did not confess. (See *People v. Dorado*, supra, 62 A.C. 350, 368, 42 Cal.Rptr. 169, 398 P.2d 361.) A full examination of the record indicates that the error requires the reversal of the judgment on these counts since "it is reasonably probable that a result more favorable to the appealing party would have been reached in the absence of the error." (*People v. Watson* (1956) 46 Cal.2d 818, 837, 299 P.2d 243, 255.)

Thus the evidence adduced at the trial indicated that the same person participated in all of the charge robberies. All of the robberies took place in the same neighborhood; they were all committed in the same fashion; the police found at defendant's residence items stolen during each of the robberies. Because of the inter-relationship among these crimes, defendant's confession to the robbery and murder of Miss Mitchell composed strong evidence of his guilt on each of the robberies to which he did not confess.

The judgment is reversed.

Traynor, C. J., and Peters and Peek, JJ., concur.

Burke, Justice (concurring).

The majority bases its reversal upon the admission into evidence of a voluntary confession in violation of the defendant's constitutional right to counsel, based upon this court's decision in *People v. Dorado*, 62 A.C. 350, 42 Cal.Rptr. 169, 398 P.2d 361. As noted in my dissent in *Dorado*, concurred in by Mr. Justice Schauer, assuming that there was error in the admission of such voluntary confession the mandate of section 4½ of article VI of the California Constitution requires this court to review the entire record to determine the probability that a result more favorable to the defendant would have been reached had the error not been committed (*People v. Watson* (1956) 46 Cal.2d 818, 299 P.2d 243) and that therefore there was a miscarriage of justice. The majority opinion in the case at hand does not indicate that there was a review of "the entire cause, including the evidence" and that the majority is of "the opinion that the error complained of has resulted in a miscarriage of justice." (Const., art VI, § 4½.)

Under the mandate of article VI, section 4½, and of the supplemental rule of this court as to the test to be applied in determining whether such an error in the admission of evidence compels reversal (*People v. Watson,* supra (1956) 46 Cal.2d 818, 836, 299 P.2d 243), I have reviewed the entire cause, including the evidence, and have concluded that it is reasonably probable that a result more favorable to the defendant would have been reached if the subject evidence had not been erroneously admitted against him. Under these circumstances the error compels reversal and I, therefore, concur in the reversal of the judgment of conviction.

Schauer, Justice* (dissenting).

I concur generally in the law as stated by Mr. Justice Burk in his concurring opinion, but after

_____
* Retired Associate Justice of the Supreme Court sitting under assignment by the Chairman of the Judicial Council.

review of the entire cause, including the evidence, am not affirmatively persuaded that a result more favorable to the defendant would have been reached in the absence of the declared error.

The encompassing net of interwoven circumstances established by the prosecution is to me inherently more convincing than the direct uncorroborated statement of any single witness could ordinarily be. The confession here is significant principally because it is consistent with the only conclusion reasonably supported by the proof independently made. Assuming that such additional—in effect, cumulative—proof was erroneously received does not persuade me to the conclusion that in the absence of the error a result more favorable to the defendant would have been probable.

I would affirm the judgment in its entirety.

McComb, J., concurs.

SUPREME COURT OF CALIFORNIA, MARCH 1965

U.S. SUPREME
COURT,
OCTOBER 1965

BRIEF FOR
PETITIONER

In the Supreme Court of the United States

October Term, 1965

No. 759

ERNESTO A. MIRANDA, PETITIONER,

V.

THE STATE OF ARIZONA, RESPONDENT

On Writ of Certiorari to the Supreme Court of the State of Arizona

Brief for Petitioner

LEWIS ROCA SCOVILLE BEAUCHAMP & LINTON
John J. Flynn
900 Title & Trust Building
Phoenix, Arizona 85003
Attorneys for Petitioner

Index

OPINION

This is a certiorari to the Supreme Court of Arizona, to review a decision reported at 98 Ariz. 18, 401 P. 2d 721, and reprinted R. 72.

JURISDICTION

Certiorari has been granted to review a judgment of the Supreme Court of Arizona in a criminal case, entered on April 22, 1965, which became final on May 7, 1965. The petition for writ of certiorari, filed in July of 1965, was granted on November 22, 1965, and the case, in forma pauperis, was placed on the appellate docket and summary calendar. The issue is whether the conviction of petitioner violates his constitutional rights under the Sixth and Fourteenth Amendments to the Federal Constitution. This Court has jurisdiction under 28 U.S.C. Sec. 1257(3).

CONSTITUTIONAL PROVISIONS INVOLVED

"In all criminal prosecutions, the accused shall enjoy the right to a speedy and public trial, by an impartial jury of the State and district wherein the crime shall have been committed, which district shall have been previously ascertained by law, and to be informed of the nature and cause of the accusation; to be confronted with the witnesses against him; to have compulsory process for obtaining Witnesses in his favor, and to have the Assistance of Counsel for his defence." (U.S.C. Const. Amend. VI.)

"All persons born or naturalized in the United States, and subject to the jurisdiction thereof, are citizens of the United States and of the State wherein they reside. No state shall make or enforce any law which shall abridge the privileges or immunities of citizens of the United States; nor shall any State deprive any person of life, liberty, or property, without due process of law; nor deny to any person within its jurisdiction the equal protection of the laws." (U.S.C. Const. Amend. XIV, Sec. 1.)

QUESTION PRESENTED

Whether the confession of a poorly educated, mentally abnormal, indigent defendant, not told of his right to counsel, taken while he is in police custody and without the assistance of counsel, which was not requested, can be admitted into evidence over specific objection based on the absence of counsel?

STATEMENT

A. Proceedings on interrogation and trial

Petitioner was charged with having kidnapped and raped an eighteen year old girl in the vicinity of Phoenix, Arizona, on March 3, 1963.

A psychiatric report, made by a court-appointed psychiatrist (R. 6-9), gives the background of petitioner. Miranda, an indigent, was 23 years old at the time of the interrogation, and working as a truck driver and warehouseman. He had completed eighth grade and started on ninth grade before dropping out of school. Petitioner has a considerable sexual preoccupation, as illustrated in his interpretation of certain proverbs;[1] he has been involved in a series of sex offenses. The doctor concluded that petitioner "has an emotional illness. I would classify him as a schizophrenic reaction, chronic, undifferentiated type" (R. 9).

Petitioner was, at the time of his apprehension, suspected of another, wholly unrelated crime. That incident, the robbery of a woman, may also have involved a threat of rape. The robbery occurred several months before the instant episode (R. 6-7). On March 13, 1963, defendant was arrested at his home and taken in custody to the police station where he was put in a lineup consisting of four persons.[2] He was there confronted and identified by the two complaining witnesses, the one for robbery and the other for rape. Miranda was then taken to Interrogation Room 2 at the local police headquarters (R. 37) and there interrogated on both matters.

The two matters were at first consolidated in the trial court, with one sanity examination covering both, but were later separated for trial. (See report in 401 P. 2d at 718.) The petitioner was convicted of both offenses in separate trials. The two cases were treated by the Supreme Court of Arizona as companions; *State* v. *Miranda*, 98 Ariz. 11, 401 P. 2d 716 (not this

case) and 98 Ariz. 18, 401 P. 2d 721 (this case), both decided on April 22, 1965.

Only the kidnapping-rape case has been brought here. However, since the interrogation was joint, some reference needs to be made to the other record, and, with the consent of opposing counsel, an extract has been tendered to this Court. It is reprinted as an appendix to this brief and is the basis of this paragraph. After the lineup, it was Officer Cooley, who had arrested Miranda, who took petitioner to Interrogation Room 2. There he and Officer Young conducted the questioning. Officer Young did not tell Miranda that anything he said would be held against him, nor did he tell Miranda of his right to consult an attorney (Appendix, reproduction of Transcript, p. 48). Officer Young believes that Miranda was told that he need not answer their questions (Appendix, reproduction of Transcript, p. 60) but no mention was made of the right to counsel.

The absence of advice to petitioner regarding his right to counsel is amplified by the record in the instant case. Here, Officer Cooley also testified as to interrogation in Room 2 of the Detective Bureau (R. 37), and narrated extensively a confession he attributed to the petitioner (R. 38-40). A written statement,[3] obtained from Miranda while he was under the interrogation in Room 2, was then put into evidence (R. 40, R. 69). Officer Young confirmed that defendant was not told of any right to advice of counsel (R. 45). When the confession was offered into evidence, defense counsel expressly objected "because the Supreme Court of the United States says a man is entitled to an

---

[1] "A rolling stone gathers no moss" is interpreted by Miranda to mean "if you don't have sex with a woman, she can't get pregnant." The proverb "people in glass houses shouldn't throw stones" is interpreted by Miranda to mean, "a person with one woman shouldn't go to another woman." Apart from this preoccupation, petitioner also believes that "a stitch in time saves nine" means "if you try to shut something in, you keep it from going out" (R. 8-9).

[2] See R. 37, 38 where police officers refer variously to custody and arrest. Under Arizona law, custody is arrest; see Rule 14, Arizona Rules of Criminal Procedure, Vol. 17, Ariz. Rev. Stat. p. 175; and Ariz. Rev. Stat. Sec. 13-1401.

[3] The written confession says, "I started to take clothes off her without any force and with cooperation. Asked her to lay down and she did. Could not get penis into vagina got about ½(half) inch in." It strains credulity to the breaking point to believe that this sentence was the product of a man of petitioner's mentality and comprehension as indicated by his answers to the questions set forth in footnote 1.

U.S. SUPREME
COURT,
OCTOBER 1965

BRIEF FOR
PETITIONER

attorney at the time of his arrest." The confession was admitted over this objection (R. 41). In summation, the prosecutor emphasized to the jury the officer's testimony as to the interrogation, and the written confession (R. 50-51).

The two cases, the robbery and the rape-kidnapping, were tried by this same judge. In the instant case Miranda was given a sentence of twenty to thirty years, and in the robbery case he was given a sentence of twenty to twenty-five years. He thus faces imprisonment of forty to fifty-five years.

B. Proceedings in the Arizona Supreme Court

The Arizona Supreme Court, setting forth the language of both the oral and the written confessions at length (R. 79-82), considered the admissibility of the confessions under the decisions of this Court. It held that *Escobedo* v. *Illinois,* 378 U.S. 478, 84 Sup. Ct. 1758, 12 L. Ed. 2d 977 (1964) was "a controlling precedent" only where five elements occur, one of which is that "The suspect must have requested and been denied the opportunity to consult with his lawyer" (R. 87). This element being absent, the court held that:

> "[N]otwithstanding the fact that he did not have an attorney at the time he made the statement, and the investigation was beginning to focus upon him, defendant's constitutional rights were not violated, and it was proper to admit the statement in evidence" (R. 93).

Accordingly, Miranda's conviction was affirmed.

SUMMARY OF ARGUMENT

There is a right to counsel for arrested persons when interrogated by the police. The law has been growing in this direction for more than thirty years. The federal experience from *Johnson* v. *Zerbst,* 304 U.S. 458, 58 Sup. Ct. 1019, 82 L. Ed. 1461 (1938) through the series of cases culminating in *Mallory* v. *United States,* 354 U.S. 449, 77 Sup. Ct. 1356, 1 L. Ed. 2d 1479 (1957), and the Public Defender Act of 1964 (78 Stat. 552, 18 U.S.C. Sec. 3006A), and applying Federal Criminal Rules 5 and 44, amount to a requirement that all defendants be informed of their right to counsel and be given counsel swiftly upon their arrest. In the states, *Powell* v. *Alabama,* 287 U.S. 45, 53 Sup. Ct. 55, 77 L. Ed. 158 (1932) asserted as a constitutional require-

ment of state procedure that a person charged with a capital crime have "the guiding hand of counsel at every step in the proceedings against him." 287 U.S. at 69. This requirement was buttressed by repeated decisions of this Court that it would accept no forced confessions, *Brown* v. *Mississippi,* 297 U.S. 278, 56 Sup. Ct. 461, 80 L. Ed. 682 (1936), or those obtained in such circumstances that the exclusion of "friends, advisers, or counselors" made it highly likely that force was used, *Chambers* v. *Florida,* 309 U.S. 227, 238, 60 Sup. Ct. 472, 84 L. Ed. 716 (1940).

The right to counsel remained in some suspense during the period governed by *Betts* v. *Brady,* 316 U.S. 455, 62 Sup. Ct. 1252, 86 L. Ed. 1595 (1942), but during the years following *Betts,* the views were rapidly developed by just short of a majority of this Court that secret confessions obtained without counsel between arrest and arraignment were invalid; *Haley* v. *Ohio,* 332 U.S. 596, 68 Sup. Ct. 302, 92 L. Ed. 224 (1948); *In re Groban's Petition,* 352 U.S. 330, 77 Sup. Ct. 510, 1 L. Ed. 2d 376 (1957). This view had the support of four Justices of the present Court in *Crooker* v. *California,* 357 U.S. 433, 78 Sup. Ct. 1287, 2 L. Ed. 2d 1448 (1958); *Cicenia* v. *La Gay,* 357 U.S. 504, 78 Sup. Ct. 1297, 2 L. Ed. 2d 1523 (1958).

When the right to counsel was recognized at the arraignment period, *Hamilton* v. *Alabama,* 368 U.S. 52, 82 Sup. Ct. 157, 7 L. Ed. 2d 114 (1961), and for all crimes at trial, *Gideon* v. *Wainwright,* 372 U.S. 335, 83 Sup. Ct. 792, 9 L. Ed. 2d 799 (1963), and when it was recognized that the privilege against self-incrimination applied to the states as well as the federal government, *Malloy* v. *Hogan,* 378 U.S. 1, 84 Sup. Ct. 1489, 12 L. Ed. 2d 653 (1964), any view that counsel was not required for interrogation became untenable. Hence counsel was required for interrogation at least where requested in *Escobedo* v. *Illinois,* 378 U.S. 478, 84 Sup. Ct. 1758, 12 L. Ed. 2d 977 (1964); and the fact that a request happens to have been made at that particular case cannot be controlling for *Carnley* v. *Cochran,* 369 U.S. 506, 82 Sup. Ct. 884, 8 L. Ed. 2d 70 (1962) held that the right to be furnished counsel does not depend upon a request.

We therefore urge upon the Court that line of cases interpreting *Escobedo* which holds that there is a right to counsel during the interrogation period for any person under arrest; *People* v. *Dorado,* 42 Cal. Rptr. 169, 398 P.2d 361 (1965);

U.S. SUPREME
COURT,
OCTOBER 1965

BRIEF FOR
PETITIONER

Wright v. *Dickson,* 336 F. 2d 878 (9th Cir. 1964); *United States ex rel. Russo* v. *New Jersey,* 351 F. 2d 429 (3d Cir. 1965); *Collins* v. *Beto,* 348 F. 2d 823 (5th Cir. 1965); *Commonwealth* v. *Negri,* 213 A. 2d 670 (Pa. 1965).

We deal with the basic principle, the principle expressed by Justice Douglas in his concurring opinion in *Culombe* v. *Connecticut,* 367 U.S. 568, 637, 81 Sup. Ct. 1860, 6 L. Ed. 2d 1037 (1961), that "any accused—whether rich or poor—has the right to consult a lawyer before talking with the police."

This constitutional principle is not incompatible with proper law enforcement. It will have no effect on organized crime, whose members know the method of combat with society all too well; the principle here advocated as a practical matter of solid experience applies primarily to the poor, the ignorant, and frequently, those of limited mental ability. The right to counsel under public defender systems may well be costly, but the dollar cost of preservation of a constitutional right is no reason for ignoring that right.

The larger problem is whether extending the right to counsel into the interrogation period will unduly handicap the police in their work. Numerous reports of actual experience are analyzed in the brief to show that this hazard need not be heavily weighed. Concrete experiences for various cities are reported including the observation of Judge George Edwards of the United States Court of Appeals for the Sixth Circuit who had been Detroit's police commissioner in 1962 and 1963. Judge Edwards attempted to apply "Supreme Court standards." He found no ill effects and much benefit. A review of actual experience shows that third degree abuses are not some remote fantasy; they happen now, and so does wrongful detention without charge and without counsel. These things occur in great numbers in today's United States. They are practices which, as the scrupulously meticulous Horsky Report for the District of Columbia concludes, "arrest for investigation should cease immediately."

At best, as a practical matter, confessions obtained from ignorant persons without counsel are the product of skilled leading by trained prosecutors or investigators. See the opinion of Judge Smith in *United States* v. *Richmond,* 197 F. Supp. 125 (D. Conn. 1960). Even without physical abuse, confessions are obtained by means wholly unworthy of free people. The evil of the "led con-fession" is particularly apparent in the instant case in which the defendant was clearly led into assertions which only dubiously originated with him, and without which would have led to his conviction for a grave but lesser offense.

When this defendant went into Interrogation Room 2, instead of having "the guiding hand of counsel" to which we believe the principles of *Powell* v. *Alabama* entitled him, he had the guiding hand of two policemen. When he came out of Interrogation Room 2, there was no longer any point in giving him counsel—his case was over. We believe that such practices are barred by the Sixth and Fourteenth Amendments to the Constitution of the United States.

ARGUMENT

When Miranda walked out of Interrogation Room 2 on March 13, 1963, his life for all practical purposes was over. Whatever happened later was inevitable; the die had been cast in that room at that time. There was no duress, no brutality. Yet when Miranda finished his conversation with Officers Cooley and Young, only the ceremonies of the law remained; in any realistic sense, his case was done. We have here the clearest possible example of Justice Douglas' observation, "what takes place in the secret confines of the police station may be more critical than what takes place at the trial." *Crooker* v. *California,* 357 U.S. 433, 444-45, 78 Sup. Ct. 1287, 2 L. Ed. 2d 1448 (1958) (dissenting opinion).

The question presented is whether a defendant in such circumstances is entitled to be told of his right to counsel and to have a meaningful opportunity to consult counsel before the law disposes of him. For "what use is a defendant's right to effective counsel at every stage of a criminal case if, while he is held awaiting trial, he can be questioned in the absence of counsel until he confesses?" Justices Douglas, Black, and Brennan in *Spano* v. *New York,* 360 U.S. 315, 326, 79 Sup. Ct. 1202, 3 L. Ed. 2d 1265 (1959).

I. THERE IS A RIGHT TO COUNSEL FOR ARRESTED PERSONS WHEN INTERROGATED BY THE POLICE

We deal here with growing law, and look to where we are going by considering where we have been. The existence of a right to counsel of any sort at any time did not exist in medieval England; Plucknett tells us that not until the 15th Century was counsel allowed to argue points of law; that in 1695 counsel was allowed

U.S. SUPREME
COURT,
OCTOBER 1965

BRIEF FOR
PETITIONER

in treason trials; and that not until 1836 was counsel allowed in felony cases.[4]

While English statutes did not provide for counsel in felony cases before 1836, in practice counsel did participate in English criminal trials before the American Revolution.[5] This is of consequence in understanding early American constitutional and statutory provisions of substantially the same vintage as the Bill of Rights. Many of these expressly or in practice asserted a right to counsel (New Hampshire, Vermont, Massachusetts, Rhode Island, New York, Maryland, North Carolina, Georgia), and some of them even at that early time required that appointed counsel be made available (Connecticut, New York (*dubitante*), Pennsylvania, New Jersey, Delaware, and South Carolina).[6] Speaking broadly, therefore, the Sixth Amendment was in general accord with the English and American practice of its time: "In all criminal prosecutions, the accused shall enjoy the right ... to have the assistance of counsel for his defence."

Sixth Amendment problems came to the Court surprisingly late, both as to federal and state procedure.

A. Federal experience

The leading case is *Johnson* v. *Zerbst,* 304 U.S. 458, 58 Sup. Ct. 1019, 82 L. Ed. 1461 (1938). In that case, petitioner, without counsel, had been convicted of counterfeiting. There was a conflict as to whether or not he had asked for counsel. The decision decisively establishes as an "obvious truth that the average defendant does not have the professional legal skill to protect himself when brought before a tribunal with power to take his life or liberty... ." 304 U.S. at 462-63. The opinion, quoting from *Powell* v. *Alabama,* 287 U.S. 45, 68, 69, 53 Sup. Ct. 55, 77 L. Ed. 158 (1932), repeats that a defendant "'requires the guiding hand of counsel at every step in the proceedings against him.'" 304 U.S. at 463. Hence in *Johnson* v. *Zerbst,* the Court declared that "the Sixth Amendment withholds from Federal Court, in all criminal proceedings, the power and authority to deprive an accused of his life and liberty unless he has or waives the assistance of counsel." *Ibid.*[7]

The Court further declared that "since the Sixth Amendment constitutionally entitled one charged with crime to the assistance of counsel, compliance with this constitutional mandate is an essential judicial prerequisite to a federal court's authority to deprive an accused of his life or liberty." *Id.* at 467.

The requirements of *Johnson* v. *Zerbst* were carried into effect by Rules 5 and 44 of the Rules of Criminal Procedure. Rule 5 expressly provides that any arrested person should be taken "without unnecessary delay before the nearest available commissioner" who is to tell the accused both of his right to stand silent and of his right to counsel. Rule 44 confirmed this provision by providing for appointment of counsel if need be. But it should always be remembered that these rules were simply manifestations of the Sixth Amendment as declared in *Johnson* v. *Zerbst.*

Rule 5 with its provision for arraignment "without unnecessary delay" became the battleground for the immediate issue now before the Court. If the defendant is brought before the commissioner instantly, he cannot be interrogated before being informed of his right to counsel. On the other hand, if the period pending presentment is protracted, the right to counsel can, as in the instant case, be made meaningless because the defendant may be in such a position before the arraignment that a combination of Clarence Darrow and John W. Davis reincarnated could do him no good. In *McNabb* v. *United States,* 318 U.S. 332, 63 Sup. Ct. 608, 87 L. Ed. 219 (1943), the issue was whether a confession should be excluded which was obtained in the course of an extended interrogation. The defendants "had no lawyer. There is no evidence that they requested the assistance of counsel, or that they were told that they were entitled to such assistance." 318 U.S. at 335. This Court, taking up the matter from the standpoint of "civilized standards" of justice, *id.* at 340, found that the procedure followed "tends to undermine the integrity of the criminal proceeding." *Id.* at 342. The Court, analyzing the proper division of functions in criminal law enforcement, declared that prop-

---

[4] Plucknett, *A Concise History of the Common Law,* 385-86 (2d ed. 1936), citing for the 1837 development to 6 & 7 Will. IV, c. 114.

[5] Comment, *An Historical Argument [etc.],* 73 Yale L.J. 1000, 1027-28 (1964); and see historical analysis in *Powell* v. *Alabama,* 287 U.S. 45, 53 Sup. Ct. 55, 77 L. Ed. 158 (1932).

[6] *Id.,* appendix, 73 Yale L.J. at 1055-57.

[7] The case also considered the subject of waiver, a matter we do not develop here because there is no waiver question in the *Miranda* case, there being no suggestion that the defendant had the faintest notion of any right to counsel.

cr procedure "aims to avoid all the evil implications of secret interrogation of persons accused of crimes." *Id.* at 344.

McNabb scrupulously avoids constitutional interpretation, restricting itself to a matter of proper federal practice. The *McNabb* rule was not applied in *United States* v. *Mitchell,* 322 U.S. 65, 64 Sup. Ct. 896, 88 L. Ed. 1140 (1944) where the confession was held to be so immediate that it was construed to be spontaneous. However, the rule was applied again in *Upshaw* v. *United States,* 335 U.S. 410, 69 Sup. Ct. 170, 93 L. Ed. 100 (1948), a case in which the defendant confessed during a thirty-hour detention. The Court in *Upshaw* stressed that the object of the *McNabb* rule and of Rule 5 was to "check resort by officers to 'secret interrogation of persons accused of crime.'" 335 U.S. at 412. The matter of obtaining counsel was considered by the dissent, which observed that the practical effect of speedy application of the rule was that "prompt hearing gives an accused an opportunity to obtain a lawyer," with all of the consequences of giving legal advice to "the illiterate and inexperienced." 335 U.S. at 424.

The matter was again reviewed in *Mallory* v. *United States,* 354 U.S. 449, 77 Sup. Ct. 1356, 1 L. Ed. 2d 1479 (1957). In *Mallory,* the defendant, like the defendant here, was charged with rape. He was interrogated for about ten hours after his arrest, the inquiry going deep into the night, at the end of which he made a confession. The next morning he was brought before a commissioner. The Court noted that the Criminal Rules were adopted "since such unwarranted detention led to tempting utilization of intensive interrogation, easily gliding into the evils of 'the third degree;'" and that therefore the police could detain a person only until "a committing magistrate was readily accessible." 354 U.S. at 453.

The Court held that the time interval permitted between arrest and presentation to a magistrate was intended to give "little more leeway than the interval between arrest and the ordinary administrative steps required to bring a suspect before the nearest available magistrate." It added that a person was to be arraigned "as quickly as possible so that he may be advised of his rights ... But he is not to be taken to police headquarters in order to carry out a process of inquiry that lends itself, even if not so designed, to eliciting damaging statements to support the arrest and ultimately his guilt." *Id.* at 453-54. The

Court noted that the defendant had not been "told of his rights to counsel or to a preliminary examination before a magistrate, nor was he warned that he might keep silent ... " *Id.* at 455. The opinion concluded "it is not the function of the police to arrest, as it were, at large and to use an interrogating process at police headquarters in order to determine whom they should charge before a committing magistrate on 'probable cause.'" *Id.* at 456.

Mallory was the unanimous expression of this Court. Once again the case did not formally involve a constitutional issue, but rather the interpretation of the rules of criminal procedure. Unlike its predecessor, the opinion did not refer to constitutional standards. Nonetheless, *Mallory,* by its express recognition of the legitimate need for counsel during the interrogation, went far to establish for the federal system the principle here advocated.

B. The constitutional principles applied to state criminal proceedings; the development to Escobedo

The development of constitutional doctrine as applied to state proceedings can be grouped around three key decisions, *Powell* v. *Alabama,* 287 U.S. 45, 53 Sup. Ct. 55, 77 L. Ed. 158 (1932); *Betts* v. *Brady,* 316 U.S. 455, 62 Sup. Ct. 1252, 86 L. Ed. 1595 (1942); and *Gideon* v. *Wainwright,* 372 U.S. 335, 83 Sup. Ct. 792, 9 L. Ed. 2d 799 (1963).

(a) The Powell period (1932–1942) *Powell* is too familiar to warrant restatement. In this famous rape case, counsel was appointed but exercised only a nominal function, permitting defendants to be hustled to trial. The function of counsel was described as "pro forma." The Court held that:

> "defendants were not accorded the right of counsel in any substantial sense. To decide otherwise would simply be to ignore actualities... . The prompt disposition of criminal cases is to be commended and encouraged. But in reaching that result the defendant, charged with a serious crime, must not be stripped of his right to have sufficient time to advise with counsel and prepare his defense." 287 U.S. at 58-59.

This Court in *Powell* recognized that the right to counsel was a growing, not a static, constitutional right. It refused to be guided by the standards of England at the time the Constitution was adopted, following instead the more liberal practice of the various colonies. The right to counsel was held to be one of those " 'fundamental principles of liberty and justice which lie at the base of all our civil and political institutions,'" *id.* U.S. at 67, quoting *Hebert* v. *Louisiana,* 272 U.S. 312, 316, 47 Sup. Ct. 103, 71 L. Ed. 270 (1926); it was expressly held to be an integral part of the right to a fair hearing. This led Justice Sutherland to the classic passage: the person charged with the crime "requires the guiding hand of counsel at every step in the proceedings against him." This said the Court, was true for men of intelligence and even more true for "the ignorant and illiterate, or those of feeble intellect." 287 U.S. at 69. The trial court therefore must first give the defendant the right to employ counsel, and second, if need be, must appoint counsel. The Court made no decision as to non-capital cases, but as to capital cases it held that:

> "where the defendant was unable to employ counsel, and is incapable adequately of making his own defense because of ignorance, feeble-mindedness, illiteracy, or the like, it is the duty of the court, whether requested or not, to assign counsel for him as a necessary requisite of due process of law; and that duty is not discharged by an assignment at such a time or under such circumstances as to preclude the giving of effective aid in the preparation and trial of the case."

Miranda strikingly parallels the *Scottsboro* case; here, as there, the defendant did not have counsel "at such times or under such circumstances as to preclude the giving of effective aid in the preparation and trial of the case."

Immediately after *Powell*, the right to counsel cases began to relate directly to the forced confession cases; as this Court said in *Mallory, supra,* secret interrogation, which is interrogation without counsel, tends to slide into the third degree. Thus in *Brown* v. *Mississippi,* 297 U.S. 278, 56 Sup. Ct. 461, 80 L. Ed. 682 (1936), the leading confession by torture case, the Court mentioned *Powell* as illustrative of the principles of basic justice, observing that "the state may not deny to the accused the aid of counsel." In *Brown,* trial counsel failed to make proper objections to confessions obtained by violent beating. In *Chambers* v. *Florida,* 309 U.S. 227, 60 Sup. Ct. 472, 84 L. Ed. 716 (1940), a long additional step was taken. In *Brown,* it was indisputable that physical violence had been applied to the defendants. In *Chambers* there was a fac-

tual dispute as to whether or not there had been physical compulsion. This Court nonetheless held that the protracted questioning, in all of the circumstances, banned the confession under the Fourteenth Amendment, noting that the defendants had been held and interrogated "without friends, advisers, or counselors." 309 U.S. at 238.

The state of the law as it stood in relation to right to counsel and confessions in 1940 may fairly be summarized as follows:

In the federal courts there was an absolute right to counsel in criminal cases. In the state courts there was an absolute right to counsel, and appointed counsel at that, at least in capital cases, the matter being reserved as to non-capital cases. A confession obtained by force could not be used, and a confession obtained by protracted interrogation where there was an unresolved dispute as to force, and where the defendant had been interrogated, among other things, "without counselors" denied due process. There was, however, an ambiguity left open by the *Powell* case. The Court had declared in *Powell* that a person charged with a crime "requires the guiding hand of counsel at every step in the proceedings against him;" but there had not yet been resolved the question of whether "every step in the proceedings" really meant "every step in the proceedings," which would include interrogation, or whether, despite the broad sweep in the language, something less was intended.[8]

(b) The Betts period (1942–1963) *Betts,* like *Powell,* is too familiar to need restatement. The case held, in its chief conclusions, that while counsel was required in capital cases and in some undefined other cases, it was not required

---

[8] This summary does not take account of *Lisenba* v. *California,* 314 U.S. 219, 62 Sup. Ct. 280, 86 L. Ed. 166 (1941). *Lisenba* involved a confession obtained upon protracted interrogation. The majority noted expressly that "counsel had been afforded [the petitioner] and had advised him." Apparently petitioner saw his attorney as much as he wished up to the critical day of his interrogation and confession. 314 U.S. at 230-31, 240. Hence the majority, in upholding the use of the confession, expressly noted that this was not a case in which he had been interrogated "without the advice of friends or of counsel;" (*id.* at 240) and the Court further observed that if a person held were incommunicado, subject to questioning for a long period, "and deprived of the advice of counsel," (*ibid.*) it would inspect the matter with great care. On the other hand, the dissent shows that the defendant was without counsel on the critical confession day, 314 U.S. at 242. In view of these specialized facts, we put the case aside in considering the immediate problem.

in all cases. But on the way to reaching that decision, *Betts* also decided one other point of great importance in the instant case. It expressly recognized that under the Sixth Amendment as interpreted in *Johnson* v. *Zerbst, supra,* appointed counsel was required "in all cases where a defendant is unable to procure the services of an attorney." 316 U.S. at 464. It thereupon examined the question of whether Sixth Amendment principles should in fact be imported into the interpretation of the Fourteenth Amendment. This vital question is answered in the negative, thus laying the foundation for the particular conclusion *Betts* reached. Justices Black, Douglas and Murphy dissenting did so expressly on the ground that the Sixth Amendment is applicable to state criminal proceedings, the view adopted twenty years later in *Gideon.*

During the reign of *Betts,* the confession cases turned on "special circumstances," as is illustrated in the citations in the concurring opinion of Justice Clark in *Gideon* v. *Wainwright,* 372 U.S. at 347-49. This same specialized notion of the circumstances applied also to the right to counsel as it related to the interrogation. An example is *Haley* v. *Ohio,* 332 U.S. 596, 68 Sup. Ct. 302, 92 L. Ed. 224 (1948). In this case a fifteen year old boy was interrogated for five hours before he confessed to murder. The judgment of the Court reversing the conviction was announced by Justice Douglas, and joining with him in an opinion were Justices Black, Murphy and Rutledge. This opinion particularly stressed that "at no time was this boy advised of his right to counsel." Noting the youth of the defendant, the opinion said:

> "He needs counsel and support if he is not to become the victim first of fear, then of panic. He needs someone on whom to lean lest the overpowering presence of the law, as he knows it, may not crush him. No friend stood at the side of this 15-year old boy as the police, working in relays, questioned him hour after hour, from midnight until dawn. No lawyer stood guard to make sure that the police went so far and no farther, to see to it that they stopped short of the point where he became the victim of coercion. No counsel or friend was called during the critical hours of questioning. A photographer was admitted once this lad broke and confessed. But not even a gesture towards getting a lawyer for him was ever made."

> "This disregard of the standards of decency is underlined by the fact that he was kept incommunicado for over three days during which the lawyer retained to represent him twice tried to see him and twice was refused admission." 332 U.S. at 600.

It was asserted that the petitioner had signed a confession, and that the signed confession asserted that he knew fully of his rights. Said these four Justices: "That assumes, however, that a boy of fifteen, without aid of counsel, would have a full appreciation of that advice and that on the facts of this record he had a freedom of choice. We cannot indulge those assumptions." *Id.* at 601. The four Justices made clear that they were not announcing a principle simply for boys in custody, but one which applied equally to any defendant: "The Fourteenth Amendment prohibits the police from using the private, secret custody of either man or child as a device for wringing confessions from them." *Ibid.*

We assume that the opinion in *Haley,* had it been of five Justices, would totally control in the instant situation. The interrogation, though at an odd hour, was relatively brief, and the opinion, emphasizing the necessity of counsel, tells us that the same principles apply to adults. But there were not five. Justice Frankfurter concurred specially, also noting the interrogation without counsel carries temptations for abuse. *Id.* at 605. He concluded that the confession should be barred because of specialized circumstances in the particular case, without reaching the broader question. The dissenting Justices were apparently content that the boy had not asked for counsel before his arraignment.

In 1957, two new voices were added in this Court on the right to counsel at the interrogation state. The case was *In re Groban's Petition,* 352 U.S. 330, 77 Sup. Ct. 510, 1 L. Ed. 2d 376 (1957), in which the issue was the validity of an inquiry by the Ohio State Fire Marshal into the cause of a fire, the inquiry involving compulsory testimony without presence of counsel. The majority opinion, by Justice Reed on his last day on the Court, found distinctions because this was an administrative hearing and therefore did not reach the principal question. Justice Black, for Chief Justice Warren and Justices Douglas and Brennan, did. What was said by those four Justices there synthesizes everything we have to say in the instant case (352 U.S. at 340-44). At any secret hearing,

1. "The witness has no effective way to challenge his interrogator's testimony as to what

U.S. SUPREME COURT, OCTOBER 1965

BRIEF FOR PETITIONER

was said and done at the secret inquisition. The officer's version frequently may reflect an inaccurate understanding of an accused's statements or, on occasion, may be deliberately distorted or falsified. While the accused may protest against these misrepresentations, his protestations will normally be in vain… ."

2.   "Behind closed doors he [the defendant] can be coerced, tricked or confused by officers into making statements which may be untrue or may hide the truth by creating misleading impressions. While the witness is in the custody of the interrogators, as a practical matter, he is subject to their uncontrolled will." *Id.* at 341-42.

3.   "Nothing would be better calculated to prevent misuse of official power in dealing with a witness or suspect than the scrutiny of his lawyer or friends or even of disinterested bystanders."

4.   "I also firmly believe that the Due Process Clause requires that a person interrogated be allowed to use legal counsel whenever he is compelled to give testimony to law-enforcement officers which may be instrumental in his prosecution and conviction for a criminal offense. This Court has repeatedly held that an accused in a state criminal prosecution has an unqualified right to make use of counsel at every stage of the proceedings against him."

5.   "The right to use counsel at the formal trial is a very hollow thing when, for all practical purposes, the conviction is already assured by pretrial examination."

These same dissenting Justices expressed their views again in *Crooker* v. *California,* 357 U.S. 433, 78 Sup. Ct. 1287, 2 L. Ed. 2d 1448 (1958) and *Cicenia* v. *LaGay,* 357 U.S. 504, 78 Sup. Ct. 1297, 2 L. Ed. 2d 1523 (1958). Crooker confessed during interrogation after he had asked for counsel and it was refused him. The Court, in passing upon the admissibility of the confession, concluded that the sole real issue was whether he had been coerced by the denial of his request for counsel. Citing various cases to the effect that confessions made prior to State appointment of counsel are not thereby rendered involuntary, the Court upheld the conviction. Applying the special circumstances test, it concluded that the particular petitioner was able to take care of himself without counsel at that

stage. The Court held that State refusal of a request to engage counsel was a denial of constitutional rights "if he is deprived of counsel for any part of the pretrial proceedings, provided that he is so prejudiced thereby as to infect his subsequent trial with an absence" of fundamental fairness. 357 U.S. at 439. This, it was held, depended on the circumstances of the case. The Court rejected the view, as having a "devastating effect on enforcement of criminal law," that police questioning, fair as well as unfair, should be precluded until the accused is given an opportunity to call his attorney. *Id.* at 440.

Justice Douglas, for Chief Justice Warren and Justices Black and Brennan, gave an emphatic and detailed analysis of the absolute need for counsel at the pretrial stage, first to avoid the third degree, second because of the impossibility of determining disputes over what actually happened in the secret chamber, and finally, because of the importance of pretrial period. These Justices adopted the view that "'the pre-trial period is so full of hazards for the accused that, if unaided by competent legal advice, he may lose any legitimate defense he may have long before he is arraigned and put on trial.' " *Id.* at 445-46. They also adopted the statement of Professor Chafee, "A person accused of crime needs a lawyer right after his arrest probably more than at any other time." *Id.* at 446. Adopting the views of *Powell* v. *Alabama* and the views of the dissent of *In re Groban's Petition,* both *supra,* this opinion concluded that "The demands of our civilization expressed in the Due Process Clause require that the accused who wants a counsel should have one at any time after the moment of arrest." *Id.* at 448.

Cicenia involved similar issues. The defendant, before his indictment, was interrogated at the police station. He wanted counsel then and his family wanted to provide it, but the police did not permit the petitioner to meet with his lawyer or his family until after they had the confession. A majority rejected the view "that any state denial of a defendant's request to confer with counsel during police questioning violates due process, irrespective of the particular circumstances involved." 357 U.S. at 509. The same dissenters as in *Crooker* (except Justice Brennan, not participating) disagreed; they believed that *Cicenia* was "the occasion to bring our decision into tune with the constitutional requirement for fair criminal proceedings against the citizen." *Id.* at 512.[9]

Soon after *Crooker* and *Cicenia,* the tide which was to overrule *Betts* began to flow with new vigor. In *McNeal* v. *Culver,* 365 U.S. 109, 81 Sup. Ct. 413, 5 L. Ed. 2d 445 (1961), Justices Douglas and Brennan called outright for the overruling of *Betts.* In *Culombe* v. *Connecticut,* 367 U.S. 568, 81 Sup. Ct. 1860, 6 L. Ed. 2d 1037 (1961), Justices Frankfurter and Stewart, applying the particular circumstances approach, held that a confession should not be admitted. Those Justices pointedly rejected the view that all persons under interrogation should be entitled to counsel. Observing that "Legal counsel for the suspect will generally prove a thorough obstruction to the investigation," 367 U.S. at 580, their opinion reviewed the practice of other countries and again observed that the *McNabb* principles had not been applied to state cases. Justices Douglas and Black wished to rest frankly on the principle "that any accused—whether rich or poor—has the right to consult a lawyer before talking with the police; and if he makes the request for a lawyer and it is refused," his constitutional rights are violated. *Id.* at 637. While an attorney may tell a defendant of his constitutional right not to testify, these Justices felt that all defendants are entitled to know their constitutional rights.

At the end of the *Betts* period, the condition of the constitutional law on the right to counsel at trial or during interrogation and the meaning of that right was this: a majority of this Court, so far as decisions were concerned, either had participated in *Betts* or had not yet disapproved it. The state of the law therefore was while a person was entitled to counsel of his choice in every case, *Chandler* v. *Fretag,* 348 U.S. 3, 75 Sup. Ct. 1, 99 L. Ed. 4 (1954), he was not yet entitled to appointed counsel at actual trial in every case. He was entitled to counsel in all federal cases; he was entitled to counsel at trial in all state capital cases; and he was entitled to counsel at trial in all other cases dependent upon special circumstances. This right in capital cases extended also to the arraignment, at least where the arraignment was "a critical stage in a criminal proceeding," because "What happens there may affect the whole trial." *Hamilton* v. *Alabama,* 368 U.S. 52, 54, 82 Sup. Ct. 157, 7 L. Ed. 2d 114 (1961). Four Justices of this Court (Chief Justice Warren and Justices Black, Douglas and Brennan) had expressed views indicating a belief that there was a right to counsel at interrogation, but a majority was not ready to go so far.

(c) **The Gideon period (1963–)** In overruling *Betts,* Justice Black for the Court closed the circle by applying the principle of his own 1938 opinion of *Johnson* v. *Zerbst, supra,* to state proceedings. This Court in *Gideon* thus erased the fundamental distinction between the state and federal cases by holding that the Sixth Amendment guarantee of counsel was of such character that it applied to the states in full. The Court, readopting the conclusive authority of *Powell* v. *Alabama,* declared that "The right of one charged with crime to counsel may not be deemed fundamental and essential to fair trials in some countries, but it is in ours." 372 U.S. at 344. Justice Douglas, concurring, noted that this did not mean that some kind of a watered-down version of the Sixth Amendment was made applicable to the states—its totality applied to both.

It follows that so far as the Sixth Amendment is concerned, after March 18, 1963, there is no difference between the right to counsel as provided in that Amendment in the two court systems. *Gideon* was followed shortly by *Haynes* v. *Washington,* 373 U.S. 503, 83 Sup. Ct. 1336, 10 L. Ed. 2d 513 (1963), holding that the failure to tell a defendant under interrogation that he is entitled to be represented by counsel is one of the factors relevant to determining whether his confession was voluntary, 373 U.S. at 516-17;

---

[9] Another case of this special circumstances type is *Reck* v. *Pate,* 367 U.S. 433, 81 Sup. Ct. 1541, 6 L. Ed. 2d 948 (1961). Justice Douglas concurring said, "I would hold that any confession obtained by the police while the defendant is under detention is inadmissible unless there is prompt arraignment and unless the accused is informed of his right to silence and accorded an opportunity to consult counsel." 367 U.S. at 448. See also *Spano* v. *New York,* 360 U.S. 315, 79 Sup. Ct. 1202, 3 L. Ed. 2d 1265 (1959), in which the defendant had been indicted and thereafter confessed without counsel. Chief Justice Warren for the Court said that the "abhorrence of society to the use of involuntary confessions" among other things "turns on the deep rooted feeling that the police must obey the law while enforcing the law; that in the end life and liberty can be as much endangered from illegal methods used to convict those thought to be criminals as from the actual criminals themselves." 360 U.S. at 320-21, footnote 2 on 321 summarizing the confession cases from *Brown* to this point. Justices Douglas, Black and Brennan, concurring, held that after indictment certainly the Government can never interrogate the accused in secret when he has asked for his lawyer. Justice Stewart, concurring, rested heavily on the fact that this defendant was under indictment.

and by *White* v. *Maryland, 373* U.S. 59, 83 Sup. Ct. 1050, 10 L. Ed. 2d 193 (1963), which further extended the rule of *Hamilton* v. *Alabama*. In *White,* at a preliminary hearing, defendant pled guilty without counsel. Thereafter he was always afforded counsel. This Court held in effect that any stage at which a person can plead guilty is "critical" and he is entitled to counsel then.

C. Escobedo and the present day

The welter of cases obscures the simple lines of the situation. As of the spring of 1963, this law applied to these situations:

1. Defendants were entitled to counsel at all trials in the federal courts under *Johnson* v. *Zerbst, supra*.

2. Defendants in state courts were entitled to counsel in all trials, *Gideon* v. *Wainwright, supra*.

3. Persons were entitled to counsel in all federal arraignments (Rule 5 of the Rules of Criminal Procedure, as repeatedly interpreted), and in all arraignments or analogous proceedings under state law at which anything of consequence can happen; *Hamilton* v. *Alabama, supra;* and *White* v. *Maryland, supra*.

4. Several Justices believed that in all cases, a person who requested counsel at pre-arraignment investigation was entitled to it, at least in cases in which he wanted to consult his own lawyer; but this was not yet a majority view, *Crooker* v. *California, supra,* and *Cicenia* v. *La Gay, supra*.

5. Several Justices believed that, requested or not, a person has a right to counsel upon interrogation unless he intelligently waived that right. See for the views of Chief Justice Warren and Justices Black, Douglas, and Brennan, variously the *Groban, Crooker,* and *Cicenia* cases, *supra*.

Situation 5 is that presented in the instant case. *Escobedo* v. *Illinois, 378* U.S. 478, 84 Sup. Ct. 1758, 12 L. Ed. 2d 977 (1964) settled point 4. In *Escobedo,* the defendant, after arrest but before indictment, repeatedly asked to see his counsel and was effectively barred from doing so by the police. The Court held that it was immaterial whether the defendant had yet been indicted— "It would exalt form over substance to make the right to counsel, under these circumstances, depend on whether at the time of the interrogation, the authorities had secured a formal indict-

ment." *Id.* at 486. The Court, following the New York rule in *People* v. *Donovan,* 13 N.Y. 2d 148, 243 N.Y.S. 2d 841, 193 N.E. 2d 628 (1963) held that a confession even prior to indictment after an attorney had been requested and denied access to see the person, could not be used in a criminal trial.[10]Following the dissenting opinion of *In re Groban, supra,* the Court held that it would make a mockery of the right to counsel if a person were entitled to counsel at trial but not at an earlier stage which in truth disposed of the case. *Cicenia* and *Crooker,* after some attempt to distinguish them, were put aside with the observation that insofar as they might "be inconsistent with the principles announced today, they are not to be regarded as controlling." *Id.* at 492. In summary, *Escobedo* held: "We hold only that when the process shifts from investigatory to accusatory—when its focus is on the accused and its purpose is to elicit a confession—our adversary system begins to operate, and, under the circumstances here, the accused must be permitted to consult with his lawyer." *Ibid.*[11]

We cannot in candor assert that *Escobedo* unequivocally establishes a right to counsel at the interrogation stage in all situations. Certainly, the three dissenting Justices so construed it, *Id.* at 496-97. On the other hand, any case may depend on its facts. In *Escobedo,* without doubt, the defendant did ask for counsel at the interrogation stage, this was denied him, and

---

[10] This had special importance because of *Malloy* v. *Hogan,* 378 U.S. 1, 84 Sup. Ct. 1489, 12 L. Ed. 2d 653 (1964), holding that the states cannot, any more than the federal government, abridge the privilege against self-incrimination. Since a principal function of counsel is to advise a defendant of his constitutional rights, including specifically the right against self-incrimination, and since the most significant point of this abridgment is at the interrogation stage, *Malloy* buttressed the necessity of the right to counsel at this point.

[11] *Escobedo* further developed *Massiah* v. *United States,* 377 U.S. 201, 84 Sup. Ct. 1199, 12 L. Ed. 2d 246 (1964) an opinion by Justice Stewart in which the defendant was induced to make statements, without counsel present, after his indictment. The Court adopted the rule that any "secret interrogation" after the indictment without the protection of counsel vitiated any confession so obtained. Three dissenting judges in *Massiah* thought that the reasoning of the case should apply equally to "statements obtained at any time after the right to counsel attaches, whether there has been an indictment or not," 377 U.S. at 208; and in *Escobedo,* the majority took the view that no meaningful distinction can be drawn between interrogation of an accused before indictment or after. However, in *Escobedo* Justice Stewart expressed his own view that the fact of indictment "makes all the difference." 378 U.S. at 493.

U.S. SUPREME
COURT,
OCTOBER 1965

BRIEF FOR
PETITIONER

the Court did mention this as one of the factual elements in its decision. For an expression of honest puzzlement as to the scope of *Escobedo,* see *Miller* v. *Warden, Maryland Penitentiary,* 338 F. 2d 201, 204 (4th Cir. 1964).

Shortly before *Escobedo,* Justice Douglas, in discussing the need for counsel at the interrogation stage, said that "the federal law here is still halting or yet unborn." Douglas, *The Right to Counsel,* 45 Minn. L. Rev. 693-94 (1961). The new birth which Justice Douglas anticipated in 1961 has led to a nationwide series of conflicting decisions of which the instant case and *People* v. *Dorado,* 42 Cal. Rptr. 169, 398 P. 2d 361 (1965), are typical. The Arizona Supreme Court in the instant case focused upon the fact that in *Escobedo,* the defendant asked for counsel whereas in the instant case, he did not, and therefore reached opposite results dependent upon that request. Chief Justice Traynor had already, before *Escobedo,* led the way toward a right to counsel at the interrogation stage in *People* v. *Garner,* 57 Cal. 2d 135, 18 Cal. Rptr. 40, 367 P. 2d 680, 693 (1961) (concurring). This landmark analysis put aside any distinction between a right to counsel after as distinguished from before indictment.[12]

The only difference between *Escobedo* and *Dorado* was that Dorado had neither retained nor requested counsel. The California court concluded that whether or not the accused had requested counsel was "a formalistic distinction." It read *Escobedo* to mean that defendant's right to counsel did mature at the accusatory stage; "the stage when legal aid and advice were most critical" to defendant; therefore California held that his vocalization of that right cannot be the determinative factor. 42 Cal. Rptr. At 175, with comprehensive citations following. Hence, California concluded that "the right to counsel matures at this critical accusatory stage; the right does not originate in the accused's assertion of it." *Id.* at 176.

Indeed, there are numerous decisions of this Court holding that the right to counsel, where it indisputably exists, does not depend upon a request for it; see for example, *Carnley* v. *Cochran,* 369 U.S. 506, 82 Sup. Ct. 884, 8 L. Ed. 2d 70 (1962), holding with numerous citations that "it is settled that where the assistance of counsel is a constitutional requisite, the right to be furnished counsel does not depend on a request." 369 U.S. at 513; and see, for post-*Gideon* application of this rule, *Doughty* v. *Maxwell,* 376 U.S. 202, 84 Sup. Ct. 702, 11 L. Ed. 2d 650 (1964). Relying on the *Carnley* opinion, the California court concluded that the presence or absence of the request was immaterial, a conclusion reached also because "we must recognize that the imposition of the requirement for the request would discriminate against the defendant who does not know his rights. The defendant who does not ask for counsel is the very defendant who most needs counsel. We cannot penalize the defendant who, not understanding his constitutional rights, does not make the formal request and by such failure demonstrates his helplessness. To require the request would be to favor the defendant whose sophistication or status had fortuitously prompted him to make it." 42 Cal. Rptr. At 177-78. Hence, it held that at the interrogation stage a defendant must be informed of his rights so that he can intelligently waive them.

As noted, the cases have divided. *Wright* v. *Dickson,* 336 F. 2d 878, 882 (9th Cir. 1964) expressly holds that under *Escobedo,* the test is whether "the investigation was then no longer a general inquiry but had focused on appellant," and it is immaterial whether or not "appellant asked to consult retained counsel or to be provided with the assistance of appointed counsel, nor, indeed, whether he requested counsel at all, except as the latter fact might bear upon waiver." See to the same effect, *United States ex rel. Russo* v. *New Jersey,* 351 F. 2d 429, 438 (3d Cir. 1965);[13] and see the opinion of Tuttle, J., in *Collins* v. *Beto,* 348 F. 2d 823, 830-31 (5th Cir. 1965), with abundant citations. See also, as an example of a state reversing itself to accord with this position, *Commonwealth* v. *Negri,* 213 A. 2d 670 (Pa. 1965).

---

[12] "It is a formalistic assumption that indictment is the point when a defendant particularly needs the advice and protection of counsel. Often a defendant is arrested under highly suspicious circumstances and from the time he is apprehended his guilt is a foregone conclusion in the minds of the police. Frequently too, suspicion falls upon him at some intermediate point before indictment. In some cases the evidence against the accused may be stronger at the moment of arrest than it may be in other cases when the indictment is returned. It is hardly realistic to assume that a defendant is less in need of counsel an hour before indictment than he is an hour after." 367 P. 2d at 695.

[13] "No sound reasoning that we can discover will support the conclusion that although at other stages in the proceedings in which the right attaches there must be an intelligent waiver, at the interrogation level a failure to request counsel may be deemed to be a waiver."

Yet not only the instant case, but numerous others go the other way. See for example, *People v. Gunner*, 15 N.Y. 2d 226, 205 N.E. 2d 852 (1965), although Chief Judge Desmond and Judge Fuld disagree with that conclusion; see 205 N.E. 2d at 855-56. See also as illustrations of cases limiting *Escobedo* to its facts, *Latham v. Crouse*, 338 F. 2d 658 (10th Cir. 1964); *Jackson v. United States*, 337 F. 2d 136 (D. C. Cir. 1964); *United States v. Ogilvie*, 334 F. 2d 837 (7th Cir. 1964); *Mefford v. States*, 235 Md. 497, 201 A. 2d 824 (1964).[14]

D. The right to counsel at interrogation: 1966

The issue is whether, under the Sixth Amendment to the Federal Constitution as made applicable to the states by the Fourteenth, there is the same right to counsel at interrogation of an arrested suspect as there is at arraignment (*Hamilton v. Alabama, supra; People v. White, supra*) or at trial (*Johnson v. Zerbst, supra; Gideon v. Wainwright, supra*).

The right does exist. It is the same. This is not the result of a single case, *Escobedo* or any other. Rather, there is a tide in the affairs of men, and it is this engulfing tide which is washing away the secret interrogation of the unprotected accused. The *McNabb-Mallory* line of cases may in terms be restricted to the rules, but the rules themselves are a reflection of the Sixth Amendment as interpreted in *Johnson v. Zerbst, supra*. Once the Sixth Amendment is clearly applicable to the states (*Gideon v. Wainwright*), then the constitutional standards are the same. *Escobedo*, although all that was involved there was a fact situation in which a request had been made and denied, necessarily transcends its facts because it recognizes the interrogation as one of the sequence of proceedings covered by the Sixth Amendment. Since *Carnley v. Cochran, supra*, bars unwitting waiver under the Sixth Amendment, it necessarily applies to the totality of that to which the Sixth Amendment applies, and this must necessarily run, as it does, from the interrogation after arrest through the appeal.[15]

We have in this galaxy of cases not a series of isolated phenomena, but reflections of basic belief, beliefs which were expressed in the dissents in *In re Groban; Crooker;* and *Cicenia;* in *Gideon;* in *Malloy v. Hogan, supra*, extending the freedom from self-incrimination to the states; and in *Escobedo*. These are all different manifes-

tations of the view expressed by Justice Douglas in *Culombe v. Connecticut, supra*, concurring, where he said, the "principle is that any accused—whether rich or poor—has the right to consult a lawyer before talking with the police."

This case is not to be decided by the color-matching technique of determining whether one case looks just like another case. We deal with fundamentals of liberty, and so, in consequence, with basic belief. The suggestion that the defendant must ask for counsel is to make a great matter depend upon a formal distinction. We warmly commend to this Court *Oregon v. Neely*, 239 Ore. 487, 398 P. 2d 482, 486 (1965):

> "Adoption of the distinction advanced by the state would lead to results contrary to the basic beliefs of the United States Supreme Court and of this court.... If the state's distinction were accepted, we would grant the assistance of counsel to those educated enough to demand it and deny it to those too ignorant to ask for it. The United States Constitution demands equal treatment during the criminal process for the inexperienced and the uneducated."

II. PRACTICAL CONSIDERATIONS OF LAW ENFORCEMENT ACCORD WITH GIVING THE SIXTH AMENDMENT ITS FULL MEANING

Whenever rights are recognized for those charged with crime, sincere people will inescapably be concerned as to the effect of those rights on law enforcement. In *Powell v. Alabama, supra*, the defendants were tried within a few days of the crime, and in holding that this matter had been hustled too much, this Court found it necessary to discuss also the problem of the "great and inexcusable delay in the enforcement of our criminal law" as "one of the grave evils of our time." 287 U.S. at 59. In

---

[14] For other cases to the same effect, see Note, *The Right to Counsel During Police Interrogation*, 25 Md. L. Rev. 165, 172, n. 58 (1965); and see Dowling, *Escobedo and Beyond*, 56 J. Crim. Law 143, 155, notes 81 and 82 (1965). Outstandingly useful articles relating to the problems of this case are Comments at 53 Calif. L. Rev. 337 (1965); 52 Geo. L.J. 825 (1964); 25 Md. L. Rev. 165 (1965); and 32 U. Chi. L. Rev. 560 (1965).

[15] For able development of a similar approach and view, see the dissenting opinion of Chief Judge Brune in *Prescoe v. State*, 231 Md. 486, 191 A. 2d 226, 232 (1963). We have not considered any of the problems of waiver or any of the problems of pre-arrest interrogation in this case since they are not here.

Chambers v. *Florida, supra,* the Court observed that "we are not impressed by the argument that law enforcement methods such as those under review are necessary to uphold our laws," 309 U.S. at 240, with a note analyzing the literature in relation to the use of the third degree to obtain confessions. Justice Jackson, in *Watts* v. *Indiana,* 338 U.S. 49, 57, 69 Sup. Ct. 1347, 93 L. Ed. 1801 (1949) made the classic statement of the conflict:

> "To subject one without counsel to questioning which may and is intended to convict him, is a real peril to individual freedom. To bring in a lawyer means a real peril to solution of crime … [A]ny lawyer worth his salt will tell the suspect in no uncertain terms to make no such statement to police under any circumstances."[16]

Justice White, dissenting for himself and Justices Clark and Stewart in *Escobedo,* expressed concern for the crippling effect of the decision on law enforcement, 378 U.S. at 499. Justice White, joined by Justices Clark and Harlan, in their dissent in *Massiah, supra,* also developed the matter largely in terms of the effect of the rule on law enforcement, moving from the premise that "a civilized society must maintain its capacity to discover transgressions of the law and to identify those who flout it." 377 U.S. at 207.

With so many members of this Court concerned with the constitutional rule from the practical standpoint of law enforcement, that matter requires independent consideration. The principal practical concerns are two: first, that the system established will be expensive; and second, that it will prevent the detection and punishment of the guilty. At a time when American society is deeply and justly concerned both with rising crime rates and with the menacing existence of organized crime, these are genuinely serious problems.

We begin by observing that the principles here advocated will have exactly zero effect on organized crime. This case involves an important constitutional principle, but it must not be made more important than it is. This case is not a grand caucus on whether sin or virtue should be the order of the day; we are dealing with the precise problem of whether a person charged with crime is to be made effectively aware of his right to counsel at the interrogation stage, and whether he is to be supplied counsel if he needs it at that point. None of this has any application

to organized crime at all. The criminal gangs know perfectly well what tools, both physical and legal, they may use in their battle with society. The confession and right to counsel cases which have been before this Court so constantly since *Powell* v. *Alabama* have almost never involved gang-type criminals. The crimes from *Powell* (rape) to *Miranda* (rape) have almost always been rapes and murders, involving defendants poor, poorly educated, and very frequently, as here, of very limited mental abilities. The rich, the wellborn, and the able are adequately protected under existing constitutional standards, and the sophisticates of crime do not need this protection. We are talking here about precisely what was involved in *Chambers* v. *Florida* twenty-five years ago, the "helpless, weak, outnumbered." 309 U.S. at 241.

A. Cost factors

Public defender systems cost money. Many defendants are indigents, and extending the right to counsel into the interrogation stage will increase personnel, paperwork, costs of all kinds. It will make some kind of public defender system virtually obligatory.[17] But the cost increase will by no means be limited to defense costs. As Mr. J. Edgar Hoover observed in 1952, full use of proper scientific methods should make it unnecessary for officers to use dishonorable methods of detection;[18] this inescapably means increased prosecution costs. A laboratory costs more than a strap, and so does the training of those who wield a microscope rather than a whip.

---

[16] Justice Jackson continued: "If the State may rest on suspicion and interrogate without counsel, there is no denying the fact that it largely negates the benefits of the constitutional guarantee of the right to assistance of counsel. Any lawyer who has ever been called into a case after his client has 'told all' and turned any evidence he has over to the Government knows how helpless he is to protect his client against the facts thus disclosed." 338 U.S. at 59.

[17] Pollock, *Equal Justice in Practice,* 45 Minn. L. Rev. 737, 738-39 (1961) estimates 2,000,000 arrests for major offenses in a year, with 1,000,000 needing free legal representation and only 100,000 getting it. Birzon, Kasanof and Forma, in *The Right to Counsel,* 14 Buff. L. Rev. 428, 433 (1965) estimate 65% to 90% indigency among felony defendants in New York. For brief references, see Note, 1962 U. Ill. L.F. 645, n. 37, and for more extensive citations on the burdens involved, Comment, *Escobedo v. Illinois,* 32 U. Chi. L. Rev. 560, 580, n. 92 (1965); and see for anticipated cost analysis under federal legislation, Rep. Emanuel Celler, *Federal Legis. Proposals,* 45 Minn. L. Rev. 697 (1961).

[18] FBI Law Enforcement Bull., Sept., 1952.

U.S. SUPREME COURT, OCTOBER 1965

BRIEF FOR PETITIONER

There are undoubtedly cheaper methods of law enforcement than those contemplated by the American Constitution. While some critics have contested the right to counsel in cost terms, no member of this Court has ever attempted to put a price tag on constitutional rights. Pepper in the eyes is cheaper than a fair trial and respect for constitutional rights in law enforcement will inescapably cost money.

Let it.

B. The effect on law enforcement

Some members of this Court have had severe doubts about the effect of the application of these principles in the operation of the criminal law, and some outside criticisms have been uninhibited. Professor Inbau regards *Escobedo* as "the hardest body blow the Court has struck yet against enforcement of law in this nation."[19] More temperate criticism of *Escobedo* develops the view that it "creates unnecessary and undesirable impediments to police investigation."[20]

While figures vary as to the number of crimes which are solved by confessions, that number is clearly extremely large. As Justice Jackson observed in the passage quoted above from *Watts* v. *Indiana,* a lawyer at the interrogation stage may well tell his client to stand mute, and the practical effect will be to eliminate large numbers of confessions.[21]

There have been several congressional inquiries into the problems of police interrogation.[22] Professor Louis B. Schwartz of the

University of Pennsylvania has testified that in his experience, very few proper convictions had been lost because of the *Mallory* rule.[23] Senator Dominick noted the contradictory attitudes of the police and prosecutors as to the effect of the *Mallory* rule on the crime rate, with the police uniformly taking the position that the increase in crime in the District is directly related to the *Mallory* rule, while the United States Attorney and the Department of Justice indicate that the rule has very little effect on the releasing of guilty persons.[24]

Deputy Attorney General Ramsay Clark for the Department of Justice testified that the *Mallory* rule had not been shown to be a direct causative factor in crime or its increase; and the report of the United States Attorney attributes only two "lost" cases a year to the operation of the *Mallory* rule.[25] On the other hand, a report from the House Committee of the District of Columbia, H. Rep. 176, 89th Cong., 1st Sess. (1965) accompanying House Bill 5688, providing for amendment to the *Mallory* rule, does report an apparent relationship of the increase of the District of Columbia crime rate with *Mallory.*[26] A strong minority report shows that while there is a rise in crime in the District, nothing connects it to the *Mallory* rule or makes the rise attributable to *Mallory* in any way.[27]

There are other conflicting views. The New York City Police Commissioner in September of 1965 estimated that confessions were essential to conviction in 50 per cent of the homicides com-

---

[19] As quoted in Dowling, *Escobedo and Beyond,* 56 J. Crim. L. 143, 145 (1965). Professor Inbau expresses himself also in *Restrictions in the Law of Interrogations and Confessions,* 52 Nw. U. L. Rev. 77 (1957).

[20] Enker and Elsen, *Counsel for the Suspect,* 49 Minn. L. Rev. 47, 48 (1965). See in particular, *Id.* at 62-63, n. 52, on the current developments under the English Judges' Rules.

[21] See Weisberg, "Police Interrogation of Arrested Persons," in *Police Power and Individual Freedom.* 153, 179 (Sowle Ed. 1962).

[22] See *Hearings on the Constitutional Aspects of Police Detention Before the Subcommittee on Constitutional Rights of the Senate Committee on the Judiciary,* 85th Cong., 2d Sess. (1958) (hereafter, *1958 Hearings*). See also the various Hearings on bills to alter the rule of *Mallory* v. *United States, supra.* E.g., *Hearings on H.R. 5688 and 5.1526 Before the Senate Committee on the District of Columbia,* 89th Cong., 1st Sess., pts. 1-2 (1965) (hereafter *1965 Hearings*). Prior to these Senate Hearings, the House Committee on the District of Columbia had submitted H.R. Rep. No. 176, 89th Cong., 1st Sess. (1965) (hereafter, *1965 Report*) to accompany H.R. 5688.

[23] *1965 Hearings,* pt. 1, at 107.

[24] *Id.* at 299. In earlier hearings, the Deputy Chief of Police for Washington, D.C., had contended that the *Mallory* rule results in freeing guilty persons and unduly hampers law enforcement, *1958 Hearings* 124-35. See also the testimony of Chief Layton, *1965 Hearings,* pt. 1, at 299.

The District Attorney of the District of Columbia, Mr. David Acheson, in 1964 said:

" ... Prosecution procedure has, at most, only the most remote causal connection with crime. Changes in court decisions and prosecution procedure would have about the same effect on the crime rate as an aspirin would have on a tumor of the brain... ."

Quoted in the address of Judge J. Skelly Wright before the Annual Convention of the International Academy of Trial Lawyers, p. 10 (unpub., 1965), from which many of the conceptions of this brief are drawn.

[25] For Mr. Clark's statement, see *id.,* pt. 2, at 495; for that of Mr. Acheson, see note 36, *infra.*

[26] *1965 Report* 5. There is some testimony to the effect that it is very difficult to obtain convictions of criminals where neither scientific evidence nor eye witness identification is available. *Id.* at 65.

[27] *Id.* at 119.

mitted in New York in 1964 and, on the other hand, State Supreme Court Justice Nathan R. Sobel describes the view that confessions are the backbone of law enforcement as "carelessly nurtured nonsense."[28] New York District Attorney Frank S. Hogan says that the police are heavily dependent on confessions to get convictions in many cases and that "the whole purpose of a police investigation is frustrated if a suspect is entitled to have a lawyer during preliminary questioning, for any lawyer worth his fee will tell him to keep his mouth shut."[29] On the other hand, Brooklyn District Attorney Aaron E. Koota believes that a person should have a lawyer "at the moment he comes into contact with the law." While some law enforcement officials claim that 75 to 85 per cent of all convictions are based on confessions, Judge Sobel's study, based on 1,000 Brooklyn indictments from February to April, 1965, showed that fewer than 10 per cent involved confessions.[30]

An extremely experienced point of view is that of Judge George Edwards of the United States Court of Appeals for the Sixth Circuit, who resigned from the Michigan Supreme Court to be Detroit Police Commissioner in 1962 and 1963. Judge Edwards said, "We did take prisoners promptly before a judge. And the town did not fall apart. Murder and pillage did not run rampant." He added that he had attempted to run the Detroit Police Department by United States Supreme Court standards, and that it made law enforcement more effective, convincing more people that "we were moving toward making it more nearly equal in its application to all people, regardless of race or color."[31]

The Criminal Justice Act of 1964, 78 Stat. 552, 18 U.S.C. Sec. 3006A, reflects the belief that early advice of right to counsel is compatible with good law enforcement. The Congressional Committee considered a report of the special committee of the Association of the Bar of the City of New York and of the National Legal Aid Association, which concluded that the public defender "system should come into operation at a sufficiently early stage of the proceedings so that it can fully advise and protect and should continue through appeal."[32] The Congress was also advised of the report of the Attorney General's Committee on Poverty and Administration of Federal Justice, February 25, 1963. This report in turn referred to the 1958 report of the New York City Bar and National Legal Aid

Association Committee, asserting that "if the rights of the defendant are to be fully protected, the defense of his criminal case should begin as soon after the arrest as possible." A majority of the Attorney General's Committee endorsed this view, and recognized "strong argument that the time the defendant needs counsel most is immediately after his arrest and until trial."[33]

The Attorney General's Committee "after careful consideration" did not adopt that view for legislative purposes at that time but the actual bill which passed provides that the United States Commissioner for the Court should advise the defendant of his right to be represented by counsel and in appropriate circumstances should appoint counsel for him. 18 U.S.C. Sec. 3006A(b). Coupled with the *Mallory* rule, this for all practical purposes means forthwith advice of the right to counsel almost at once upon arrest.

The District of Columbia is the best testing ground for the effect of the Court's standards since it has been most affected by the *McNabb-Mallory* line of cases and at the same time is most analogous to the states of any part of the federal system. The leading study is *Report and Recommendations of the Commissioner's Committee on Police Arrests for Investigation* (1962), commonly known as the Horsky Report, for its chairman, Mr. Charles A. Horsky. The Horsky study shows that a very large number of arrests for investigation have been made in the District of Columbia, the number of persons being arrested on suspicion running about a third of those arrested for felonies.[34] An analysis of hundreds of cases of arrest for investigation, in which persons were interrogated privately,

---

[28] *New York Times*, Nov. 20, 1965, p. 1. Judge Sobel's views are published in N.Y.L.J., Nov. 22, 1965, p. 1, 4-5, and have very comprehensive statistics on various crimes and their relation to confessions.

[29] *New York Times*, Dec. 2, 1965, p. 1.

[30] *New York Times*, Nov. 22, 1965, p. 1, pt. 2.

[31] *New York Times*, Dec. 7, 1965, p. 33.

[32] Hearing Before Senate Committee on the Judiciary on S. 1057, p. 24 (1963).

[33] *Id.* 197-205.

[34] Horsky Report, p. 9. For comparable Chicago experience, with statistical detail on the numbers of persons detained for investigation, see American Civil Liberties Union "Secret Detention by the Chicago Police" (Free Press, Glencoe, Ill., 1959). Based on a study of police records, the report concludes that in 1956 approximately 20,000 persons were held incommunicado for at least 17 hours, and 2,000 for 48 hours or more.

showed that this was not in fact a fruitful source of criminal convictions; only about five per cent were ever charged, and even this exaggerates the practical importance of the procedure.[35] As noted, the former United States Attorney, Mr. David Acheson, reported that only an average of about two cases a year were lost because of the *Mallory* decision.[36]

The Horsky Report is the richest single source on the practical aspects of secret interrogations. On both principle and practical considerations "the committee recommends that arrest for 'investigation' should cease immediately."[37] They invoked directly the principle of Blackstone's Commentaries:

> "To bereave a man of life, or by violence to confiscate his estate, without accusation or trial, would be so gross and notorious an act of despotism, as must at once convey the alarm of tyranny throughout the whole kingdom; but confinement of the person, by secretly hurrying him to a gaol, where his sufferings are unknown or forgotten, is a less public, a less striking, and therefore a more dangerous engine of arbitrary government."[38]

As a practical matter, we cannot know with assurance whether the amplification of the right to counsel in the interrogation period will severely handicap the police; we end by trading opinions.[39] The best of interrogation, as expounded for example by the principal publicist for secret inquiries, Professor Inbau, makes a poor case for itself as is illustrated in the note attached.[40] But assuming that there may be some unpredictable decline in the efficiency of the conviction machinery, there are some distinctly practical plusses to be balanced against this. As Justice Douglas said in *United States* v. *Carignan,* 342 U.S. 36, 46, 72 Sup. Ct. 97, 96 L. Ed. 48 (1951), when a person is detained without arraignment,

> "the accused is under the exclusive control of the police, subject to their mercy, and beyond the reach of counsel or of friends. What happens behind doors that are opened and closed at the sole discretion of the police is a black chapter in every country—the free as well as the despotic, the modern as well as the ancient."

We are not talking with some learned historicity about the *lettre de cachet* of pre-Revolutionary France or the secret prisons of a distant Russia. We are talking about conditions in the United States, in the Twentieth Century, and now.[41]

Moreover, some of the cost and efficiency comes from giving American citizens exactly what they are entitled to under the Constitution. It is, after all, the man's privilege to be silent, *Mallory* v. *Hogan, supra,* and it does smack of denial of equal protection to say that this is a right only for those well educated enough to know about it. But one need not reach to constitutional principle; there are, practically, equally impor-

---

[35] Horsky Report, pp. 33-34.

[36] Horsky Report, p. 17.

[37] Horsky Report, pp. 41-71.

[38] Quoted at Report, p. 43.

[39] See for example the conflict between Inbau, *Police Interrogation—a Practical Necessity, in Police Power and Individual Freedom,* 147 (Sowle ed. 1962) with Weisberg, *Police Interrogation of Arrested Persons: A Skeptical View, id.,* 153.

[40] The following note is taken bodily from Comment, *The Right to Counsel During Police Interrogation,* 53 Cal. L. Rev. 337, 351-52, note 75 (1965):

> "75. See Inbau & Reid, *Criminal Interrogation and Confessions* (1962); Kidd, *Police Interrogation* (1954); Gerber & Schroeder, *Criminal Investigation and Interrogation* (1962). The Inbau and Reid book is a very specific and highly illuminating study of recommended techniques of interrogation. A paraphrase of the author's advice to the would-be interrogator might read: Impress the accused with your certainty of his guilt, and comment upon his psychological symptoms of guilt, such as the pulsation of a carotid artery, nail biting, dryness of the mouth, etc.; smoking should be discouraged because this is a tension-reliever for the guilty subject trying desperately not to confess; the sympa-

thetic approach—anyone else under such circumstances would have acted the same way, suggests a less repulsive reason for the crime, and, once he confesses, extract the real reason, condemn the victim, the accomplice or anyone else upon whom some degree of moral responsibility might be placed; understanding approach—a gentle pat on the shoulder, a confession is the only decent thing to do, I would tell my own brother to confess; forceful approach—exaggerate the charges against the accused, sweet and sour technique (one policeman is hostile to him while other acts as his friend); interrogation of the recalcitrant witness—at first be gentle and promise him police protection, then, if he still refuses to talk, attempt to break the bond of loyalty between him and the accused or even accuse him of the offense and interrogate him as if he were the offender.

> "The book written by Lt. Kidd provides fascinating reading for the novice. The following paraphrased extracts offer examples: The officer should not interrogate in a business office where there might be a recording device because he may make some statements which would be embarrassing if played back in court to rebut his testimony; feed

tant workaday considerations. As is well developed by Judge Smith in *United States* v. *Richmond*, 197 F. Supp. 125, 129 (D. Conn. 1960):

> "Statements elicited during questioning are bound to be colored to some extent by the purpose of the questioner who inevitably leads the witness in the absence of court control. This coloring is compounded where the statement is not taken down stenographically, but written out as a narrative in language supplied by the questioner. Where the state of mind of the defendant is an issue in the case, as in determining the degree of a homicide, this wording of his account of the crime is of vital importance... . Had counsel been available to Reid he might have advised Reid of the danger to one on trial for his life on charges such as were faced by Reid of adopting the language of another in a statement signed by him.

> "Reid appears to have been suggestible, as might be expected in view of his age, mentality and education."[42]

Judge Smith's highly practical observations are of special application in the instant case. We deal here with rape and with what is, on the facts, an actual issue of penetration.[43] This defendant was obviously led in his alleged talk about vagina and penis, and had he not made or acquiesced in this very clearly led statement, might have been convicted for a lesser offense.

CONCLUSION

The day is here to recognize the full meaning of the Sixth Amendment. As a matter of constitutional theory and of criminal procedure, if a defendant cannot waive counsel unwittingly in one part of the conviction procedure, he should not be able to waive it at another. As a matter of practicality in law enforcement, we cannot know the precise effects of giving counsel at the beginning as the law does at the end; but we can know that there is not the faintest sense in deliberately establishing an elaborate and costly system of counsel—to take effect just after it is too late to matter. Yet that is precisely the *Miranda* case.

We invoke the basic principles of *Powell* v. *Alabama*: "He requires the guiding hand of counsel at every step in the proceedings against him." When Miranda stepped into Interrogation Room 2, he had only the guiding hand of Officers Cooley and Young.

We respectfully submit that the decision of the court below should be reversed.

Respectfully submitted,

LEWIS ROCA SCOVILLE BEAUCHAMP & LINTON

By John P. Frank[44]

John J. Flynn

January, 1966.

U.S. SUPREME COURT, OCTOBER 1965

BRIEF FOR PETITIONER

---

upon suspect's likes and dislikes—love of mother, hatred of father, concern for children; never release pressure even when tears begin to flow; don't allow the accused any form of tension release at a critical moment in the questioning, such as a cigarette, a drink of water, or a trip to the washroom; play two co-conspirators against each other (often termed bluffing on a split pair)—claim that one talked and blamed the other, possibly using a false recording to substantiate this claim, continually take one out separately but never question him—the other will believe it necessary to tell his side of the story; aggressive approach—blame accused for crimes he didn't commit, play on the fact that many defendants fear the mental asylum more than jail. "An interesting article in the Gerber and Schroeder book noted the similarity between the methods of interrogation used today and the practices of the German Inquisition. See Gerber & Schroeder, *op. cit. supra* at 361-62." .

See also, for illustration of interrogation methods, Sutherland, *Crime and Confession*, 79 Harv. L. Rev. 21, 31-32 (1965).

[41] "The 'war on crime' is not a sporadic crisis, here today and gone tomorrow, justifying during its brief combat stage a

shelving of long-standing immunities of the citizen." Sutherland, *supra*, n. 40, 79 Harv. L. Rev. at 40-41, supported by contemporary illustrations; and see citations collected in the Horsky Report, pp. 46-47.

[42] We are not unaware that this case was reversed on other grounds, three to two by the Second Circuit, Judges Clark and Waterman dissenting on the issue of rehearing, 295 F. 2d 83 (2d Cir. 1961) and that certiorari was denied, 368 U.S. 948, 82 Sup. Ct. 390, 7 L. Ed. 2d 344 (1962). We respectfully commend it as a good case all the same.

[43] Without the "half-inch" statement in the confession (R. 69), there might have been no rape in this case at all. There was no medical testimony of any rape. In response to the prosecution's questions, the prosecutrix testified that at first the defendant was unable to make penetration; that later he did, but whether with his finger or his penis, she "was not sure" (R. 19). A few lines later, she said he made penetration with his penis (R. 20); but on cross, in response to the question of whether entry had been made "with his finger or his penis," she replied, "I don't know" (R. 32), and later she said, "I guess it was with his penis" (R. 33).

[44] Counsel notes with appreciation the research assistance of Mr. Robert Jensen of the Minnesota bar and Mr. Paul Ulrich of the California bar, both clerks in the office of counsel.

U.S. SUPREME
COURT,
OCTOBER 1965

BRIEF FOR
PETITIONER

APPENDIX

Extracts from record in the companion case of *State* v. *Miranda,* 98 Ariz. 11, 401 P. 2d 716 (1965).

Mr. Turoff: What was your answer to this? Let me repeat the question. Did you make any threats to the defendant? Did you answer that?

A. Yes, I answered that. I didn't make any threats.

Q. Did you use any force on the defendant?

A. No, Sir.

Q. Did you offer the defendant any promises of immunity?

A. No, Sir, I did not.

Q. Officer, were you the arresting officer?

A. Yes, Sir.

Q. Did you arrest the defendant?

A. Yes, Sir.

Q. Are you the officer who brought him into the Interrogation Room?

A. Yes, Sir.

Q. Officer Young, was he also in the Interrogation Room?

A. Yes, Sir, he was with me during the time.

Q. And in your presence, did Officer Young make any threats?

A. No, Sir, he did not.

Q. Did Officer Young use any force on the defendant?

A. No, Sir, he did not.

Q. Did Officer Young make any promises of immunity to the defendant?

A. No, Sir, he did not.

Q. Officer, I ask you again, what was your question to the defendant and what was his answer to that question?

Mr. Moore: Comes now the defendant and objects for the reason—I would like to ask a question on voir dire before I make the objection.

The Court: All right, Mr. Moore.

By Mr. Moore:

Q. Did you say to the defendant at any time before he made the statement you are about to answer to, that anything he said would be held against him?

A. No, Sir.

Q. You didn't warn him of that?

A. No, Sir.

Q. Did you warn him of his rights to an attorney?

A. No, Sir.

Mr. Moore: We object, not voluntarily given.

Mr. Turoff: I don't believe that is necessary.

The Court: Overruled.

By Mr. Turoff:

Q. Would you tell us, Officer, now, what you said to the defendant after Miss McDaniels made her statement and what the defendant said to you regarding this charge.

A. I asked him, I said, "Is this the woman that you took money from?" and he said, "Yes, this is her."

Q. Did you ask him anything else? Was there any further conversation regarding the taking of this money?

A. Yes, Sir, we then—I believe he just volunteered the information and was saying—part of the conversation was with the woman at the time that the occurrence had happened.

Q. I didn't get that, Officer. He told you what conversation he had with her?

A. Yes, he did.

Q. I see; did he tell you also where this took place and when?

A. He wasn't exactly sure of the exact location. It was at approximately 2nd Street just north of Van Buren up around Taylor, somewhere in that vicinity. He wasn't sure of the exact location of the occurrence, but just the approximate location.

Mr. Turoff: I have no further question of this witness.

A. No, not right away.

Q. Later on when Miss McDaniels was present, did you have a discussion with the defendant concerning that charge?

A. Yes, Sir.

Q. Who was present at that conversation, Officer?

A. Myself, Detective Cooley, Mr. Miranda and Barbara McDaniels.

Q. I see; prior to that, had you made any threats or used any force on the defendant?

A. No, Sir.

Q. Had you offered the defendant any immunity?

A. No, Sir.

Q. In your presence, had Officer Cooley done any of these acts?

A. No, Sir.

Q. About what time did this conversation take place, Officer?

A. Approximately 1:30.

Q. Shortly after Miss McDaniels made her first statement, is that correct?

A. Yes, Sir.

Q. Can you tell us now, Officer, regarding the charge of robbery, what was said to the defendant and what the defendant answered in your presence?

A. I asked Mr. Miranda if he recognized * * *

A. When Mrs. McDaniels was in there, we were not armed—I was not.

Q. You were not?

A. No, Sir.

Q. But the defendant did know you were policemen?

A. Yes, Sir.

Q. And you did question him?

A. Yes, Sir.

Q. And you didn't warn him of his rights?

A. What is that?

Q. You never warned him he was entitled to an attorney nor anything he said would be held against him, did you?

A. We told him anything he said would be used against him, he wasn't required by law to tell us anything.

Q. Did you tell him that or did Mr. Cooley tell him that?

A. We both had told him.

Q. That is all you know about this? You don't know a thing about this except the conversation you heard, this robbery trial, isn't that right?

A. Yes.

Q. The conversation you heard in the interrogation room?

U.S. SUPREME
COURT,
OCTOBER 1965

BRIEF FOR
RESPONDENT

In the Supreme Court of the United States

October Term, 1965

No. 759

ERNESTO A. MIRANDA, PETITIONER,

V.

THE STATE OF ARIZONA, RESPONDENT

ON WRIT OF CERTIORARI TO THE SUPREME COURT OF THE STATE OF ARIZONA

BRIEF FOR RESPONDENT

DARRELL F. SMITH,
The Attorney General of Arizona
GARY K. NELSON,
Assistant Attorney General
Rm. 159, State Capitol Bldg.,
Phoenix, Arizona 85007
Attorneys for Respondent
GARY K. NELSON,
Assistant Attorney General,
Of Counsel

Index

OPINION BELOW, JURISDICTION, CONSTITUTIONAL PROVISIONS INVOLVED

Pursuant to Rule 40, Subd. 3, Rules of the Supreme Court, 28 U.S.C. Rules, as amended, the respondent accepts petitioner's presentation of the above referenced portions of the brief.

QUESTION PRESENTED

While your respondent accepts the legal substance of the Question Presented as posed by the petitioner, serious issue is taken with the descriptive phrases, "poorly educated, mentally abnormal".[1] The propriety of this description of the petitioner, insofar as it may enhance the question presented for review, is no doubt one of the key issues to be decided by the Court and respondent reserves the right to present argument, *infra,* concerning the description's accuracy and impact.

STATEMENT OF THE CASE

Pursuant to Rule 40 of this Court, *supra,* respondent deems it necessary to set forth additional facts from the record of this case which are considered essential to the complete resolution of the issues presented for review.

A psychiatric report is part of the record (R. 6) and has been referred to by petitioner in his Statement of the Case.[2] The totality of this report is essential for an adequate determination of critical factual and background matters, and the report is therefore fully incorporated by reference into this Statement of the Case and reprinted verbatim in Appendix A, *infra.*

The psychiatrist quoted the petitioner as making the following statements:[3]

> "Don't worry. If I had wanted to rape you, I would have done it before. [R. 7]

---

[1] Brief of Petitioner, at 2.

[2] *Id.* at 3.

[3] These are in addition to those quoted responses to proverbs cited in petitioner's brief, *Id.* n. 1.

"You don't have to scream. I am not going to hurt you. [R. 7]

"I didn't know how to ask her for forgiveness. [R. 7]

"I never could get adjusted to her. [R. 8]"

The psychiatrist sets forth in detail Miranda's experience with law enforcement agencies.[4](R. 8)

Petitioner made a written statement concerning the events in question (State's Exhibit 1; R. 41, 69). Petitioner makes selected references to the statement.[5] Respondent incorporates the whole of this written instrument into this brief; it is reprinted herein as Appendix B, *infra*.

A portion of the statement was typewritten and part of it was written in long-hand by the petitioner himself (R. 40, 41). The following portion of the statement was actually written by the petitioner in his own hand:

"E.A.M. Seen a girl walking up street stopped a little ahead of her got out of car walked towards her grabbed her by the arm and asked to get in the car. Got in car without force tied hands & ankles. Drove away for a few miles. Stopped asked to take clothes off. Did not, asked me to take her back home. I started to take clothes off her without any force and with cooperation. Asked her to lay down and she did could not get penis into vagina got about ½(half) inch in. Told her to get clothes back on. Drove her home. I couldn't say I was sorry for what I had done. But asked her to say a prayer for me. E.A.M." (R. 69)

Finally, petitioner cites the Court to the opinion of the Arizona Supreme Court (R. 72-93), but once again is selective in the portions set forth in the Statement of the Case.[6] Acting on the assumption that petitioner considered the selected portions of the opinion "all that is material to the consideration of the Questions Presented,"[7] the respondent must expand this Statement of the Case to include the whole of the opinion below of the Arizona Supreme Court (98 Ariz. 18, 401 P. 2d 721) and hereby incorporates the whole of the opinion herein by reference.

The following specific excerpts, at a minimum, are vital for a determination of the factual and legal predicate of the Arizona Court in its resolution of the Federal Constitutional Question:

"The question of whether the investigation had focused on the accused at the time of the making of the statement and thereby shifted

'from investigatory to accusatory' is not the deciding factor in regard to the admissibility of the confession in the instant case. There are other factors under the ruling of the *Escobedo* case. Defendant in the instant case was advised of his rights. He had not requested counsel, and had not been denied assistance of counsel. We further call attention to the fact that, as pointed out in the companion case here on appeal, *State v. Miranda*, No. 1397 [98 Ariz. 11, 401 P. 2d 716] defendant had a record which indicated he was not without courtroom experience. [Citation omitted] It included being arrested in California on suspicion of armed robbery, and a conviction and sentence in Tennessee on violations of the Dwyer [sic] Act. Under the circumstances he was certainly not unfamiliar with legal proceedings and his rights in court. The police testified they had informed defendant of his rights, and he stated in his written confession that he understood his rights (which would certainly include his right to counsel), and it is not for this court to dispute his statement that he did. His experience under previous cases would indicate that his statement that he understood his rights was true. (R. 88-89)

* * *

"What is the purpose of the right to counsel? What is the purpose of the Sixth and Fourteenth Amendments? Without question it is to protect individual rights which we cherish, but there must be a balance between the competing interests of society and the rights of the individual. Society has the right of protection against those who roam the streets for the purpose of violating the law, but that protection must not be at the expense of the rights of the individual guaranteed under the Sixth and Fourteenth Amendments to our Constitution. (R. 91-92)

* * *

U.S. SUPREME
COURT,
OCTOBER 1965

BRIEF FOR
RESPONDENT

---

[4] 1) Aged 14, Stolen Car, Probation.

2) Three weeks later, Fort Grant (Arizona Industrial School for Boys), 6 months.

3) Assault and Attempted Rape, 1 year sentence.

4) Aged 17, Peeping Tom charge, Los Angeles, Probation.

5) Arrested twice, Los Angeles, Suspicion of Armed Robbery.

6) Military service, Peeping Tom charge, confinement and Undesirable Discharge.

7) December 1959, Dwyer Act Violation, Federal Penitentiary.

[5] Brief of Petitioner, n. 3.

[6] *Id.* at 5-6.

[7] Rule 40, Subd. 1 (e), Supreme Court Rules, 28 U.S.C., Rules, as amended.

U.S. SUPREME
COURT,
OCTOBER 1965

BRIEF FOR
RESPONDENT

"It will be noted in the discussion of these cases—particularly the *Escobedo* case—the ruling of the court is based upon the circumstances of the particular case. The court, in making its holding in the *Escobedo* case, stated 'under the circumstances here the accused must be permitted to consult with his lawyer.'"

"Most of the cases distinguished the Escobedo case on the grounds that the defendant requested and was denied the right to counsel during interrogation. The *Escobedo* case merely points out factors under which—if all exist—it would not be admissible. We hold that a confession may be admissible when made without an attorney if it is voluntary and does not violate the constitutional rights of the defendant."

"Each case must largely turn upon its own facts, and the court must examine all the circumstances surrounding the taking of the statement in determining whether it is voluntary and whether defendant's constitutional rights have been violated."

"The facts and circumstances in the instant case show that the statement was voluntary, made by defendant of his own free will, that no threats or use of force or coercion or promise of immunity were made; and that he understood his legal rights and the statement might be used against him. Under such facts and circumstances we hold that, notwithstanding the fact that he did not have an attorney at the time he made the statement, and the investigation was beginning to focus upon him, defendant's constitutional rights were not violated, and it was proper to admit the statement in evidence." (R. 92-93)

SUMMARY OF ARGUMENT

Petitioner was in no way denied his constitutional right to counsel in this case. He neither merits, nor is he reason for, the pronouncement of the broad constitutional principle which is sought.

Petitioner received a full elementary education and, although he had an emotional illness, he had sufficient mentality and emotional stability to understand what he was doing when he was doing it, and to fully appreciate all the potential consequences of his act.

Clearly there was no police brutality or any possible official overreaching in the acquisition of the statements here in question. Yet petitioner, nonetheless, portrays the police generally in the worst possible light, in attempting to justify the need for the rule he seeks. The examples of bad police activity represent the exceptions to the general rule as regards police conduct and attitude, and do not merit or require an overly broad constitutional rule which would strike down the good with the bad.

Petitioner infers that since he stood no chance of victory in the trial of the case after the statements were given, he was therefore deprived of some right. Nothing could be further from the truth. He has no such right to "win." The Constitution insures that he must not be convicted as a result of any violations of those rights which we all cherish; it doesn't insure that he won't be convicted.

The decision of the Arizona Supreme Court below rested on many factors, of which the lack of a request for counsel was but one. It determined that the totality of these factors did not result in affirmative conduct which denied petitioner his right to counsel. There was no element of waiver involved in the Arizona Court's decision.

The decision of this Court in *Escobedo v. Illinois,* 378 U.S. 478 (1964) does not require the reversal of this case. The facts are significantly different. The legal principles therein announced, considered within the context of that decision as it discusses not only the particular facts of the case but also the significance of the prior decisions of this Court on the same subject matter, implement an exclusionary rule directed to deter the police from affirmative conduct calculated, under the facts of any given case, to deny an accused from consulting with counsel. Such a rule, in proper perspective and balance, will protect the accused from any infringement of his right to counsel, while not unduly or unnecessarily curtailing the oft times essential investigative questioning of a suspect.

ARGUMENT

I. Introduction

Petitioner states that his life for all practical purposes was over when he walked out of Interrogation Room #2 on March 13, 1963.[8] The real fact is that Miranda's life was unalterably destined ten days earlier during the late evening hours of March 2 and the early morning hours of March 3, when he kidnapped and raped his victim, Patricia Weir. What followed must not be described in cynical terms as "the ceremonies of the law";[9] they

---

[8] Brief of Petitioner, at 10.
[9] *Ibid.*

were, and are, the carefully ordained processes of our judicial system, designed, at the optimum, to discover the truth, mete out justice to all, insure the guilty their just and proper recompense and vindicate the innocent. To be sure, thoroughly interwoven into these processes at all stages and levels is the implementation and zealous protection of those cherished rights and privileges guaranteed to all by the Constitutions of the United States and the several states; no police officer, prosecutor or judge dedicated to the basic precepts of our system of government advocates that it should be any different.

Unfortunately, or perhaps fortunately, so long as human beings rather than computers administer the processes of justice, mistakes and error will occur and injustices will be done. The courts of our land, including this Court with its highest and most final jurisdiction, are daily exposing and correcting these mistakes to the best of their ability. The question here before the Court is whether there was such a mistake or error in this case of a dimension to result in the denial of petitioner's right to counsel as set down in the Constitution of the United States, and as proclaimed by this Court in its decisions thereunder.

II. There are no inherent defects either in this defendant, the operation of law enforcement agencies, or in our system of criminal justice, which require a rule of the constitutional impact and proportions here sought by petitioner

A. The defendant The very description of the petitioner in his Question Presented[10] subtly introduces a factual issue into this case which is of the gravest importance in resolving the ultimate legal question.

The words so carefully used were "poorly educated, mentally abnormal." No doubt other descriptive words and phrases could have been added—poor, motherless, unloved, downtrodden, culturally deprived, misguided, unguided, harassed, *ad infinitum.*

It is practically impossible to pick up a national magazine, professional journal, or listen to an address without some dramatic usage of these descriptive adjectives to characterize some greater or lesser portion of the American population.[11] And in the proper perspective, such attention, whether it be by this Court,[12] the Congress,[13] the executive,[14] or state and local governments,[15] is long overdue and, hopefully, will do something about the root-source of our

most perplexing problems—not the least of which is the rising crime rate.[16]

However, to use these heart-rending descriptions in an attempt to justify or excuse the knowing and deliberate violation of our criminal statutes and the imposition of violence and suffering and depravation upon some individuals of our society by others, is misleading to say the least. Of this ilk, Miranda is a clear example.

Perhaps an eighth grade education, under a literal definition of the term and in the context of our affluent society, is a "poor education." Under no stretch of the imagination, however, can Miranda be deemed to be uneducated or illiterate. In addition to his formal schooling, petitioner had considerable and varied experiences which broadened his knowledge, particularly in the area which is of primary importance to us now.[17]

Counsel would have us believe that petitioner was incapable of producing the statement which was admitted against him (Appendix B. *infra*).[18] A simple reading and viewing of the statement refutes such a contention. The portion of the statement describing the actual events of the incident is in petitioner's hand and was written by him. Certainly the officers, if they were interested in putting words into Miranda's mouth, could have typed in these words also, in a favorable context, and simply obtained Miranda's signature to the whole. And although petitioner's grammar, sentence structure and punctuation leave much to be desired, the conclusion is inescapable that his knowledge and

---

[10] *Id.* at 2.

[11] E.g. *Nine "Unadoptable" Children Joined by Love,* Look Magazine, Oct. 19, 1965, at 54; *Winters, Counsel for the Indigent Accused in Wisconsin,* 49 Marq. L. J. 1 (1965); Inaugural Address of President John F. Kennedy, January 20, 1961, 107 Congressional Record, 1013.

[12] E.g. *Brown v. Board of Education,* 347 U.S. 483 (1954).

[13] E.g. Public Works and Economic Development Act of 1965, 42 U.S.C. §§ 3121-3226.

[14] E.g. State of the Union Address, President Lyndon B. Johnson, January 12, 1966, 112 Congressional Record 129.

[15] E.g. Operation LEAP (Leadership and Education for the Advancement of Phoenix), Ordinance No. S-3205, Dec. 15, 1964, City Council of Phoenix, Arizona, Implementing Resolution No. 11887, November 4, 1964.

[16] E.g. Hoover, *Annual Report of the Federal Bureau of Investigation, Fiscal Year 1965,* U.S. Department of Justice.

[17] See n. 4, *supra.*

[18] Brief of Petitioner, n. 3.

U.S. SUPREME COURT, OCTOBER 1965

BRIEF FOR RESPONDENT

understanding of the difference between simple promiscuity and the crime of rape is more highly sophisticated than most of the Ph.Ds in our country.[19]

Miranda is also labeled as "mentally abnormal." The basis for this is the psychiatric report (Appendix A, *infra*). While Miranda had an "emotional illness," it is questionable that this even made him "abnormal."[20] Clearly the diagnosis of the psychiatrist was to the effect that the illness was not disabling and that Miranda was able to understand the predicament he was in and knew the conduct society demanded of him at the time he chose to ignore those demands.[21]

B. The police Admittedly there is no possible element of police brutality or coercion in this case, whether direct or subtle.[22] Yet petitioner, nevertheless, paints a picture of police disregard for rights guaranteed by our Constitution. The picture is inaccurate—but proving it so is almost a practical impossibility.

The articles, the studies, and the cases,[23] dealing, as they almost unanimously do, with the negative aspect of the problem, make it difficult to see the rule because of the emphasis on the exception. It is true that all police officers are not interested in protecting the rights of the accused; it is true that there are convictions obtained by use of trumped-up evidence and wrongfully elicited incriminating statements and confessions; but these are the very few

exceptions to the general rule. For every case of police insensitivity to individual rights, there are literally thousands of unreported incidents of the unstinting efforts of police and prosecutors which result in the extrication of an otherwise helpless and innocent victim, hopelessly intertwined in a web of circumstantial evidence of guilt.[24] The prime reason the vast majority of such instances go unreported and unstatisticized, is that the police and the prosecutor alike consider this just another important, but routine part of their work, which they do with the same dedication as they do the more spectacular phases.[25]

This Court, together with all the courts of our land, should and will continue to firmly and courageously deal with the exceptions to this rule. We must be careful, however, not to foreclose, limit or unduly hamper investigative techniques which, in their legitimate use, are not barred by any Constitutional mandate, solely because a few use the techniques to effect an unconstitutional result. The promulgation of such a rule of constitutional dimension in any given case would be as necessary as "Dr." Jerry Colona's recently suggested solution to Bob Hope's medical problem of a sore and infected big toe—to cut off Hope's head to relieve the excess weight on the toe.[26] While it goes without saying that the problem of the big toe would most certainly be forever solved, it is question-

---

[19] Note petitioner's careful use of the words "without force," "without force and with cooperation," "asked her to lay down, and she did." Appendix B, *infra*. See also petitioner's quoted sentence responses, statement of the case, *supra*, at 2.

[20] It has been estimated that at least 10% of our entire population have emotional illnesses of one type or another which should be treated professionally. Milt, *How to Deal With Mental Problems*, (National Association for Mental Health, Booklet, 1962).

[21] "It is my opinion that Mr. Mirande [sic] is aware of the charges that have been brought against him and is able to cooperate with his attorney in his own defense. Although Mr. Mirande [sic] has an emotional illness, I feel that at the time the acts were committed that he was aware of the nature and quality of the acts and that he was further aware that what he did was wrong." Appendix A, *infra*.

[22] Brief of Petitioner, at 10.

[23] E.g. LaFave, *Detention for Investigation by the Police: An Analysis of Current Practices*, 1962 Wash. U.L.Q. 331; Smith, *Police Systems in the United States*, (2d rev. ed. 1960); *Ashcraft v. Tennessee*, 322 U.S. 143 (1944).

[24] A person cannot talk to a police officer or prosecutor of many years tenure without hearing of numerous such incidents, many made possible by not only investigating extrinsic physical facts, but also by investigative questioning.

[25] The Law Enforcement Code of Ethics, as set forth in The Detroit Police Manual, and cited in Norris, *Constitutional Law Enforcement is effective Law Enforcement*: [Etc.], 43 U. Det. L. J. 203 (1965), n. 30, clearly reflects the importance of this particular responsibility, and represents the rule and not the exception:

"Law Enforcement Code of Ethics"

As a Law Enforcement Officer, my fundamental duty is to serve mankind; to safeguard lives and property; to protect the innocent against deception, the weak against oppression or intimidation, and the peaceful against violence or disorder; and to respect the Constitutional rights of all men to liberty, equality and justice.

I will keep my private life unsullied as an example to all, maintain courageous calm in the face of danger, scorn or ridicule; develop self-restraint; and be constantly mindful of the welfare of others. Honest in thought and deed in both my personal and official life, I will be exemplary in obeying the laws of the land and the regulations of my department. Whatever I see or hear of a confidential nature or that is confided to me in my official capacity will be kept ever secret unless revelation is necessary in the performance of my duty.

I will never act officiously or permit personal feelings, prejudices, animosities, or friendships to influence my deci-

able whether the patient would be at all happy with the ancillary side effects of the treatment. As to whether a similarly undesirable side effect would be forthcoming from an unnecessarily broad constitutional rule in this case, we must look ahead.

C. The nature of the contest Petitioner, it seems, would have us interpret our adversary system of criminal justice as giving the accused a right to "win" the contest.[27] While it may be inherent in the very nature of our system, with its vital and essential safeguards to individual freedom, that a person who actually commits a criminal act may have extra opportunities to escape punishment for his crime, it must be clear without comment or citation that the intent of the Constitutional safeguards were to insure, as much as humanly possible, that the innocent and unpopular would not be wrongfully harassed, intimidated or convicted—not that the guilty should have any special chances for acquittal or other favorable result.

If the prosecuting authorities have gained an overwhelming advantage over a particular defendant, assuming they have done so by proper methods, and not by violating any of his constitutional rights, this is to be highly commended, not condemned. It is a vital attribute of our society that the law enforcement machinery apprehend, convict and punish and/or rehabilitate those who would break the laws and endanger, if not destroy, our domestic tranquility. Law enforcement is not a game of chance, *Massiah v. United States,* 377 U.S. 201, 213 (1964) (Dissenting Opinion); *McGuire v. United States,* 273 U.S. 95 (1927). There is no "gamesmanship"

or "sportsmanship" involved here, at least insofar as the criminal is concerned. He follows no code of conduct or canons of ethics. The death, suffering, and depravation caused by crime is as real to those who are touched by its sting as is that of any war ever fought. Certainly the criminal gives no quarter; and none should be given in return except as is required to insure the integrity and continuation of the system which we all cherish.

Criminals, like the rest of us, are inherently unequal. Some are skilled, some not; some intelligent, some not; some trained, some not; some blabbermouths, some not; some strong, some not; some cruel, some not, etc. It certainly would not be urged that if a criminal is foolish enough to leave physical clues, the police should not be allowed to use them because X, who committed the same crime, was more careful. Or if Y was callous enough, or "intelligent" enough, to kill his rape victim to prevent identification, certainly Z, who also raped, should not be given the same opportunity to kill so as to have an equal chance at the trial to "win." So, too, are there differences between what happened to Ernesto A. Miranda as contrasted with what happened to Danny Escobedo[28] which militate in favor of a different resolution of their problem by this Court.

III. Miranda was not denied his right to counsel as guaranteed to him by the Sixth and Fourteenth Amendments to the Constitution of the United States

The decision in this case must rest upon the scope and effect to be attributed to this Court's decision concerning right to counsel at the interrogation stage, in *Escobedo v. Illinois,* 378 U.S. 478 (1964). While petitioner's historical analysis is to be highly commended for the care and effort which it reflects, his almost cursory treatment of *Escobedo,* coupled as it is with an inaccurate treatment of the Arizona Court's decision in the instant case, belies some doubt as to the absolute accuracy of the conclusion forecast as unassailable. Rather than obscuring the "simple lines of the situation,"[29] the welter of the cases, the majority of which disagree with petitioner's conclusion,[30] coupled with the rather sharp divergence of opinion on this Court, not only in the recent decisions on this point, e.g., *Massiah v. United States,* 377 U.S. 201 (1964) and *Escobedo v. Illinois, supra,* but in the earlier decisions as well, e.g., *Crooker v. California,* 357 U.S.

U.S. SUPREME COURT, OCTOBER 1965

BRIEF FOR RESPONDENT

sions. With no compromise for crime and with relentless prosecution of criminals, I will enforce the law courteously and appropriately without fear or favor, malice or ill will, never employing unnecessary force or violence and never accepting gratuities.

I recognize the badge of my office as a symbol of public faith, and I accept it as a public trust to hold so long as I am true to the ethics of police service. I will constantly strive to achieve these objectives and ideals, dedicating myself before God to my chosen profession—Law Enforcement."

[26] Bob Hope Christmas Special, N.B.C. Television Network, January 26, 1966, 8:30 P.M., M.S.T.

[27] Brief of Petitioner, at 9.

[28] *Escobedo v. Illinois,* 378 U.S. 478 (1964).

[29] Brief of Petitioner, at 28.

[30] For an exhaustive citation of the cases construing *Escobedo,* both on a State and Federal level, see: Sokol, *Brief of Amicus Curiae in The Escobedo Cases* (The Michie Company, 1966).

U.S. SUPREME
COURT,
OCTOBER 1965

BRIEF FOR
RESPONDENT

433 (1958) and *Cicenia v. LaGay*, 357 U.S. 504 (1958), indicate the problem posed here to be anything but simple.

A. The Arizona court's decision Petitioner, at least twice,[31] states that the Arizona Supreme Court rested its opinion on petitioner's refusal to request counsel. A reading of the opinion clearly reveals that this was only one factor in many which resulted in a determination that Miranda was not denied his right to counsel (Statement of the Case, *supra*, at 4). The nature and length of the questioning, the warning advice given, and the background of the petitioner were equally important factors. Petitioner is correct in stating that the Arizona Court's decision did not in any way purport to rest on a waiver doctrine.[32] This is made amply clear in the Arizona Supreme Court's decision in *State v. Goff*, ___Ariz. ___, 407 P. 2d 55 (1965), where the court referred to this aspect of its decision in *Miranda*:

> "We did not conclude from Escobedo that the Supreme Court of the United States held that arbitrarily and in every instance admissions made to police officers after an investigation has become accusatory are inadmissible in evidence unless a suspect has knowingly waived his right to counsel." *Id*, 407 P. 2d at 57.

The Supreme Court of California, in *People v. Dorado*, 42 Cal. Rptr. 169, 398 P. 2d 361 (1965), and indeed the dissenting Justices of this Court in *Escobedo v. Illinois, supra*, 378 U.S. at 495, have forecast, as a minimum, a contrary conclusion. If this latter view is proved to be correct, that is the end of this case, and untold thousands like it throughout the length and breadth of this land. We choose, however, in turning our attention to *Escobedo*, to approach the import of that decision with the "hope" expressed by Justice Stewart in concluding his separate dissenting opinion in *Escobedo v. Illinois, Ibid.*

B. Escobedo v. Miranda Petitioner prefers to dwell on the implicit in *Escobedo*.[33] The explicit facts of the case are considered by respondent to be highly relevant and very crucial to the indicated result in Miranda.

Danny Escobedo had retained counsel and repeatedly requested to consult with him. The requests were all denied. Escobedo was even told at one time that his lawyer didn't want to see him. On the contrary, Escobedo's lawyer was trying desperately to see his client, and was thwarted at every turn by the police, in spite of a specific Illinois statute requiring the police to admit the lawyer. *Escobedo v. Illinois, supra*, 378 U.S. at 480. Escobedo had no record of previous experience with the police. He was interrogated not only by police officers, but by a skilled and experienced lawyer. Escobedo was told that another suspect had pointed the finger at him as the guilty one. At no time was he ever advised of his constitutional rights by either the police or the prosecutor.

Ernesto A. Miranda was not represented by counsel at the time of the questioning here involved. He had not requested that counsel be provided, or that he be given an opportunity to consult with counsel prior to talking to the police. The officers did not deny him an opportunity to consult with counsel, nor did they in any way use chicanery in their questioning of Miranda. Petitioner had had considerable and varied experience with the police on previous occasions. Petitioner was advised of his constitutional rights, specifically including his right to remain silent, the fact that his statement had to be voluntary, and that anything he did say could be used against him.[34]

In setting forth the holding of the case, this Court very carefully enumerated the factors which resulted in the denial of counsel to *Escobedo*:

> "We hold, therefore, that where, as here, the investigation is no longer a general inquiry into an unsolved crime but has begun to focus on a particular suspect, the suspect has been taken into police custody, the police carry out a process of interrogations that lends itself to eliciting incriminating statements, the suspect has requested and been denied counsel, and the police have not effectively warned him of his absolute constitutional right to remain silent, the accused has been denied 'the assistance of counsel' in violation of the Sixth Amendment to the Constitution as 'made obligatory upon the states by the Fourteenth Amendment,' *Gideon v. Wainright*, 372 U.S. at 342, and that no statement elicited by the police during the

---

[31] Brief of Petitioner, at 6, 30.

[32] *Id*, nn. 7 and 15.

[33] *Id*, at 30—in fact, it would appear, on the following page of his brief, that he relies perhaps more upon the guiding light of the California Supreme Court than the pronouncements of this Court.

[34] It is not here disputed that petitioner was not specifically advised of his right to counsel.

interrogation may be used against him at a criminal trial." *Escobedo v. Illinois, supra,* 378 U.S. at 490 and 491.

Of the five specific elements, which might be set forth as: (1) Accusatory Stage; (2) Police Custody; (3) Interrogation to elicit incriminating statements; (4) Request and Denial of an opportunity to consult counsel; and (5) Effective Warning of his absolute right to remain silent, petitioner contends that only (4) is absent here and that its absence is not crucial. Both premises are incorrect.

The Arizona Court clearly considered that Miranda had been warned of his absolute right to remain silent. The facts cited in that opinion, together with the Appendix to Petitioner's Brief, provided an ample basis for such a conclusion. And to discount item (4) concerning the request, is to completely ignore not only the plain wording of the opinion in *Escobedo,* but to completely disregard the factual and legal bases for the opinions cited in petitioner's historical analysis as demanding the ultimate ruling sought herein. E.g., *Crooker v. California, supra,* (Douglas, J., dissenting):[35] *Spano v. New York,* 360 U.S. 315, 325 (1959), (Douglas, J., concurring).[36] The court lays a great stress on this factor, together with the failure of the police to warn the accused of his absolute right to remain silent. *Escobedo v. Illinois, supra,* 378 U.S. at 479, 480, 481, 482, 485, 486, 491, 492.

There are two other matters in the opinion itself which militate against petitioner's sought-for rule being all but announced. They are: (1) The treatment accorded the prior decisions of this Court in *Crooker v. California, supra,* 357 U.S. 433 and *Cicenia v. LaGay, supra* 357 U.S. 504, and (2) The Court's special and clear emphasis of the request for and denial of counsel in spite of its recent restatement that the right to counsel did not depend upon a formal request, *Carnley v. Cochran,* 369 U.S. 506 (1962).

Instead of completely overruling *Crooker* and *Cicenia,* the Court noted that the holding itself in *Crooker,* on the distinguishable facts in that case, which were set forth in some detail (*Escobedo v. Illinois, supra,* 378 U.S. at 491, 492), would possibly have been the same under the principles announced in *Escobedo.* In implicitly accepting the result in *Crooker,* while discarding the language inconsistent with the principles of *Escobedo,* the Court specifically approves the rejection of the absolute rule sought by *Crooker:*

"That 'every state denial of a request to contact counsel [is] an infringement of the constitutional right *without regard to the circumstances of the case.*" *Id,* at 491. (Emphasis in *Crooker.*)

The continued rejection of the absolute rule sought by *Crooker,* implying as it does that in some cases a state could even deny a request without denying an accused his constitutional right to counsel, clearly rejects, *a fortiori,* the absolute rule sought by petitioner.

This result is also pointed to by the inclusion and emphasis of the request for counsel as a vital factor in *Escobedo* while not even including a reference to this Court's recent reemphasis of the unimportance of a request for counsel in the implementation of the absolute right to be provided counsel in *Carnley v. Cochran, supra,* 369 U.S. 506. The omission of reference to *Carnley* must be considered to have been by design and not accident. Thus the scope of the rule, and the force of its emphasis, must be and is different.

The decision in *Escobedo* announces an exclusionary rule directed against the affirmative conduct of police and prosecutors calculated to deny to an accused his right to counsel. Any incriminating statements received thereafter, regardless of the fact that they are clearly the product of the free and uncoerced will of the accused, are inadmissible, *Escobedo v. Illinois, supra,* 378 U.S. at 491. The decision in *Massiah v. United States, supra,* 377 U.S. 201, although involving a federal prosecution, certainly reinforces this view of the *Escobedo* doctrine, particularly the last two paragraphs thereof.[37]

U.S. SUPREME COURT, OCTOBER 1965

BRIEF FOR RESPONDENT

---

[35] "This demand for an attorney was made over and again prior to the time a confession was extracted from the accused. Its denial was in my view a denial of that due process of law guaranteed the citizen by the Fourteenth Amendment." 357 U.S. at 442.

[36] "The question is whether after the indictment and before the trial the Government can interrogate the accused **in secret** when he asked for his lawyer and when his request was denied." 360 U.S. at 325. (Emphasis in original.)

[37] "The Solicitor General, in his brief and oral argument, has strenuously contended that the federal law enforcement agents had the right, if not indeed the duty, to continue their investigation of the petitioner and his alleged criminal associates even though the petitioner had been indicted. He points out that the Government was continuing its investigation in order to uncover not only the source of narcotics found on the S.S. Santa Maria, but also their intended buyer. He says that the quantity of narcotics involved was such as to suggest that the petitioner was part of a large and well-organized ring, and indeed that the continuing investigation confirmed this suspicion, since it resulted in criminal

The rule announced is a parallel to that announced in *Mapp v. Ohio,* 367 U.S. 643 (1961), designed as a specific deterrent to police activity calculated to render meaningless the citizen's rights under the search and seizure provision of the Fourth Amendment to the Federal Constitution. It must also be applied with the same practical, non-technical, common sense approach as is the *Mapp* exclusionary rule. *United States v. Ventresca,* 380 U.S. 102 (1965).

A contrary application would result in attempting to make police officers part-time defense counsel and part-time magistrates, or deprive them completely of an investigative technique which, in its proper use and application, is as invaluable as any modern, scientific tool for the detection and prevention of crime.

The legal scholars and commentators have produced volumes of material on *Escobedo.*[38] It ranges the complete spectrum, from law professors and lawyers[39] to second and third year law students.[40] Both poles of the controversy are forcefully presented, including extensive citations to both primary and secondary authority, in the very recent publication of the University Press of Virginia: Kamisar, Inbau, and Arnold, *Criminal Justice in Our Time,* (Magna Carta Essays, Howard ed. 1965).

Ultimately, however, neither the overwhelming weight of the writings of the commentators, nor the weight of the decisions of the Judges and Justices of the other appellate tribunals of our land, whether state or federal, can dictate or necessarily foreshadow this Court's determination of the scope and effect of the principles announced in *Escobedo.*

If the rule sought by petitioner is forthcoming, we can only re-echo the ominous warnings and misgivings of the dissenters in *Massiah* and *Escobedo, supra.* Miranda and Escobedo are not

equal and there is no Constitutional reason for this Court to equate them in the manner sought by petitioner, any more than there would be for this Court to balance their skill in committing and concealing their crime. No amount of scientific advancements in crime detection will produce evidence which a clever criminal has not been foolish enough to provide for discovery. If a criminal has been clever in the commission of his crime, but is foolish or careless in his handling of the police interrogation of him concerning that crime, the evidence obtained as a result of the only honest investigative avenue left open to the law enforcement agency, should not be suppressed unless that evidence is determined not to be the product of the free and uncoerced will of the accused, or if it is obtained after the police have undertaken a course of conduct calculated to deny the accused his right to counsel. Certainly nothing less will be tolerated, but the United States Constitution requires no more.

CONCLUSION

Quite appropriately, Justice Goldberg, who authored *Escobedo v. Illinois, supra,* provides the words most appropriate to conclude this brief. Speaking for the Court in *United States v. Ventresca, supra,* 380 U.S. 102, he said:

"This court is alert to invalidate unconstitutional searches and seizures whether with or without a warrant. [Presumably, for purposes of this case, confessions and admissions may be substituted for the final phrase concerning searches and seizures.] [Citations omitted.] By doing so, it vindicates individual liberties and strengthens the administration of justice by promoting respect for law and order. This court is equally concerned to uphold the actions of law enforcement officers consistently following the proper constitutional course. This is no less important to the administration of justice than the invali-

---

charges against many defendants. Under these circumstances the Solicitor General concludes that the government agents were completely 'justified in making use of Colson's cooperation by having Colson continue his normal associations and by surveilling them.'

"We may accept and, at least for present purposes, completely approve all that this argument implies, Fourth Amendment problems to one side. We do not question that in this case, as in many cases, it was entirely proper to continue an investigation of the suspected criminal activities of the defendant and his alleged confederates, even though the defendant had already been indicted. All that we hold is that the defendant's own incriminating statements, obtained by federal agents under the circumstances here disclosed, could

not constitutionally be used by the prosecution as evidence against **him** at his trial." *Massiah v. United States,* 377 U.S. at pages 206 and 207. (Emphasis in original.)

[38] For an exhaustive collection of citations see: Sokol, *Brief of Amicus Curiae in the Escobedo Cases, supra,* n. 29.

[39] E.g. Sutherland, *Crime and Confession,* 79 Harv. L. Rev. 21 (1965); Dowling, *Escobedo and Beyond,* 56 J. Crim. L., C.&P.S., 143 (1965); Herman, *The Supreme Court and Restrictions on Police Interrogation,* 25 Ohio St. L.J. 449 (1964).

[40] E.g. Comment, *Escobedo v. Illinois,* 25 Md. L. Rev. 165 (1965); Comment, *Right to Counsel During Police Interrogation, The Aftermath of Escobedo,* 53 Calif. L. Rev. 337 (1965); Note, *Escobedo in the courts, May Anything You Say Be Held Against You,* 19 Rutgers L. Rev. 111 (1964).

dation of convictions because of disregard of individual rights or official overreaching. In our view the officers in this case did what the Constitution requires.

* * *

"It is vital that having done so their actions should be sustained under a system of justice responsive both to the needs of individual liberty and to the rights of the community." Id, at 111 and 112. (Emphasis added).

The officers in this case also acted within the constitutional standards, and it is equally vital that their actions be sustained.

The judgment and decision of the Arizona Supreme Court in this case below should be affirmed.

Respectfully submitted,

DARREL F. SMITH,
The Attorney General of Arizona.

GARY K. NELSON,
Assistant Attorney General,
Rm. 159, State Capitol Bldg.,
Phoenix, Arizona 85007,
Attorneys for Respondent.

GARY K. NELSON,
Assistant Attorney General,
of Counsel
February, 1966

APPENDIX A

JAMES M. KILGORE JR., M.D.
Suite 209
461 West Catalina Drive
Phoenix 13, Arizona
PSYCHIATRY
May 28, 1963

Honorable Warren L. McCarthy
Judge of the Superior Court
Maricopa County
Court House
Phoenix, Arizona

MIRANDA, Ernest Arthur Criminal Cause #41947, #41948

Ernest Arthur Miranda is a 23-year-old Mexican male who was examined by me in the County Jail on May 26, 1963.

Mr. Miranda is charged with the offense of robbery in relation to one Barbara Sue McDaniel

on November 27, 1962. Mr. Miranda states that on that evening approximately 9:30 p.m. he saw a lady go to her car in the parking lot alone. He approached the car and got in the front seat. He stated at the time that he didn't know whether he would rob or rape the lady. She asked him if he didn't want to go to her apartment. Mr. Miranda stated that this frightened him in that she was so eager for sex and decided at that point to ask for money which she readily gave to him. He then said, "Don't worry. If I had wanted to rape you, I would have done it before."

The second offense for which Mr. Miranda is charged occurred on March 3, 1963, at which time he is supposed to have kidnapped and raped Patricia Ann Weir. Mr. Miranda stated that he knew Patricia Ann Weir, an 18-year-old single girl who worked in the theater. He had occasionally seen her there and on the evening of March 3 at approximately 11:00 p.m. he saw her walking toward the bus stop. He drove ahead of the bus and when she got off close to her home he was waiting for her. As she came close to the car he said to her, "You don't have to scream. I am not going to hurt you." He then told her to get into the car, which she did, and they drove out into the desert. He asked her to remove her clothing, which she did without resistance. He removed his clothes and performed the act of sexual intercourse. Miss Weir, according to the patient, did not resist, but during the process of sexual relations was tearful. Mr. Miranda was somewhat upset when he learned that the girl had not previously had sexual relations. He stated that if at any time the girl had refused or resisted, that he would not have proceeded. He then took her within a block or two of her house where he let her out. He asked if she would "tell on me." The girl did not respond. He stated "I didn't know how to ask her for forgiveness."

Mr. Miranda is age 23 and he has a common-law wife, age 30. They have been living together since August, 1961. His wife has two children by her first husband, a son, 11, and a daughter, 10. Mr. Miranda and his wife have a daughter, 9½ months of age. He has worked as a truck driver and also as a worker in a warehouse. Mr. Miranda's father is age 55 and works as a painter in Mesa. He stated that he did not get along with his father during his adolescent years and was frequently beaten up by his father when he got into trouble. Mr. Miranda's mother died in 1946 at the age of 34 when Mr. Miranda was

U.S. SUPREME COURT, OCTOBER 1965

BRIEF FOR RESPONDENT

six years of age. He was reared by his step-mother, age unknown. He stated with reference to her, "I never could get adjusted to her." Mr. Miranda completed half of the ninth grade at the age of 15. Mr. Miranda was first placed on probation at the age of 14 after having stolen a car. Three months later he was sent to Fort Grant for a period of six months. Shortly after returning he was sentenced for a year on an attempted rape and assault charge. According to Mr. Miranda's description of this incident, he was walking by a home in which he saw a lady lying in bed with no clothes on. He went up to the front door and it was open; he entered the home and crawled in bed with the woman. Her husband returned home shortly and the police were called. In 1957 at the age of 17 Mr. Miranda was picked up in Los Angeles for being a peeping tom and charged with lack of supervision and was placed on probation. He was also arrested twice in L.A. on suspicion of armed robbery. He was in the Army from April, 1958, to July, 1959. He was placed in the brig for being a peeping tom and given an undesirable discharge. In December, 1959, he was sentenced to the Federal Penitentiary for transporting a stolen automobile across state lines.

Mr. Miranda is a 23-year-old Mexican man who is alert and oriented as to time, place, and person. His general knowledge and information is estimated to be within normal limits as is his intelligence. He is emotionally bland, showing little if any effect. He is shy, somewhat withdrawn. He tends to be somewhat hypoactive. The patient's responses to proverbs are autistic and somewhat bizarre; for example, to the proverb "a rolling stone gathers no moss," the patient interpreted this to mean "If you don't have sex with a woman, she can't get pregnant." To the proverb "a stitch in time saves nine," Mr. Miranda's response is "If you try to shut something in, you keep it from going out." To the proverb "people in glass houses shouldn't throw stones," Mr. Miranda states "A person with one woman shouldn't go to another women." Mr. Miranda states that he is not particularly concerned about himself at this point or the trouble that he is in except in that it might interfere with his looking after his wife and child.

It is my diagnostic impression that Mr. Miranda has an emotional illness. I would classify him as a schizophrenic reaction, chronic, undifferentiated type.

It is my opinion that Mr. Miranda is aware of the charges that have been brought against him and is able to cooperate with his attorney in his own defense. Although Mr. Miranda has an emotional illness, I feel that at the time the acts were committed that he was aware of the nature and quality of the acts and that he was further aware that what he did was wrong.

/s/ JAMES M. KILGORE JR.

JAMES M. KILGORE JR., M.D.

JMK/db

APPENDIX B

STATE'S EXHIBIT 1

CITY OF PHOENIX, ARIZONA

POLICE DEPARTMENT

| Form 2000-66-D | Witness/Suspect |
| Rev. Nov. 59 | Statement |

SUBJECT: Rape D.R. 63-08380

STATEMENT OF: Ernest Arthur Miranda

TAKEN BY: C. Cooley #413—W. Young #182

| DATE: 3-13-63 | Time: 1.30 P.M. |

PLACE TAKEN: Interr Rm #2

I, Ernest A. Miranda, do hereby swear that I make this statement voluntarily and of my own free will, with no threats, coercion, or promises of immunity, and with full knowledge of my legal rights, understanding any statement I make may be used against me.

I, Ernest A. Miranda, am 23 years of age and have completed the 8th grade in school.

E.A.M. Seen a girl walking up street stopped a little ahead of her got out of car walked towards her grabbed her by the arm and asked to get in the car. Got in car without force tied hands & ankles. Drove away for a few miles. Stopped asked to take clothes off. Did not, asked me to take her back home. I started to take clothes off her without any force and with cooperation. Asked her to lay down and she did could not get penis into vagina got about ½(half) inch in. Told her to get clothes back on. Drove her home. I couldn't say I was sorry for what I had done. But asked her to say a prayer for me. E.A.M.

I have read and understand the foregoing statement and hereby swear to its truthfulness.

/s/ ERNEST A. MIRANDA

WITNESS /s/ Carroll Cooley

Wilfred M. Young #182

Miranda v. State of Arizona

—⁓—

ERNESTO A. MIRANDA, PETITIONER,
V.
STATE OF ARIZONA.

MICHAEL VIGNERA, PETITIONER,
V.
STATE OF NEW YORK.

CARL CALVIN WESTOVER, PETITIONER,
V.
UNITED STATES.

STATE OF CALIFORNIA, PETITIONER,
V.
ROY ALLEN STEWART.

NOS. 759–761, 584.

Argued Feb. 28, March 1 and 2, 1966.
Decided June 13, 1966.
Rehearing Denied No. 584
Oct. 10, 1966.
See 87 S.Ct. 11.

384 U.S. 436

Criminal prosecutions. The Superior Court, Maricopa County, Arizona, rendered judgment, and the Supreme Court of Arizona, 98 Ariz. 18, 401 P.2d 721, affirmed. The Supreme Court, Kings County, New York, rendered judgment, and the Supreme Court, Appellate Division, Second Department, 21 A.D.2d 752, 252 N.Y.S.2d 19, affirmed, as did the Court of Appeals of the State of New York at 15 N.Y.2d 970, 259 N.Y.S.2d 857, 207 N.E.2d 527. The United States District Court for the Northern District of California, Northern Division, rendered judgment, and the United States Court of Appeals for the Ninth Circuit, 342 F.2d 684, affirmed. The Superior Court, Los Angeles County, California, rendered judgment and the Supreme Court of California, 62 Cal.2d 571, 43 Cal. Rptr. 201, 400 P.2d 97, reversed. In the first three cases, defendants obtained certiorari, and the State of California obtained certiorari in the fourth case. The Supreme Court, Mr. Chief Justice Warren, held that statements obtained from defendants during incommunicado interrogation in police-dominated atmosphere, without full warning of constitutional rights, were inadmissible as having been obtained in violation of Fifth Amendment privilege against self-incrimination.

Judgments in first three cases reversed and judgment in fourth case affirmed.

Mr. Justice Harlan, Mr. Justice Stewart, and Mr. Justice White dissented; Mr. Justice Clark dissented in part.

Certiorari was granted in cases involving admissibility of defendants' statements to police to explore some facets of problems of applying privilege against self-incrimination to in-custody interrogation and to give concrete constitutional guidelines for law enforcement agencies and courts to follow.

Constitutional rights to assistance of counsel and protection against self-incrimination were secured for ages to come and designed to approach immortality as nearly as human institutions can approach it. U.S.C.A.Const. Amends. 5, 6.

Prosecution may not use statements, whether exculpatory or inculpatory, stemming from custodial interrogation of defendant unless it demonstrates use of procedural safeguards effective to secure privilege against self-incrimination. U.S.C.A.Const. Amend. 5.

"Custodial interrogation," within rule limiting admissibility of statements stemming from such interrogation, means questioning initiated by law enforcement officers after person has been taken into custody or otherwise deprived of his freedom of action in any significant way. U.S.C.A.Const. Amend. 5.

Unless other fully effective means are devised to inform accused person of the right to silence and to assure continuous opportunity to exercise it, person must, before any questioning, be warned that he has the right to remain silent, that any statement he does make may be used as evidence against him, and that he has right to presence of attorney, retained or appointed. U.S.C.A.Const. Amend. 5.

Defendant may waive effectuation of right to counsel and to remain silent, provided that waiver is made voluntarily, knowingly and intelligently. U.S.C.A.Const. Amends. 5, 6.

There can be no questioning if defendant indicates in any manner and at any stage of interrogation process that he wishes to consult with attorney before speaking. U.S.C.A.Const. Amend. 6.

Police may not question individual if he is alone and indicates in any manner that he does not wish to be interrogated.

Mere fact that accused may have answered some questions or volunteered some statements on his own does not deprive him of right to refrain from answering any further inquiries until he has consulted with attorney and thereafter consents to be questioned. U.S.C.A.Const. Amends. 5, 6.

Coercion can be mental as well as physical and blood of accused is not the only hallmark of unconstitutional inquisition. U.S.C.A.Const. Amend. 5.

Incommunicado interrogation of individuals in police-dominated atmosphere, while not physical intimidation, is equally destructive of human dignity, and current practice is at odds with principle that individual may not be compelled to incriminate himself. U.S.C.A.Const. Amend. 5.

Privilege against self-incrimination is in part individual's substantive right to private enclave where he may lead private life. U.S.C.A.Const. Amend. 5.

Constitutional foundation underlying privilege against self-incrimination is the respect a government, state or federal, must accord to dignity and integrity of its citizens.

Government seeking to punish individual must produce evidence against him by its own independent labors, rather than by cruel, simple expedient of compelling it from his own mouth. U.S.C.A.Const. Amend. 5.

Privilege against self-incrimination is fulfilled only when person is guaranteed right to remain silent unless he chooses to speak in unfettered exercise of his own will. U.S.C.A.Const. Amend. 5.

Individual swept from familiar surroundings into police custody, surrounded by antagonistic forces and subjected to techniques of persuasion employed by police, cannot be otherwise than under compulsion to speak. U.S.C.A.Const. Amend. 5.

When federal officials arrest individuals they must always comply with dictates of congressional legislation and cases thereunder. Fed.Rules Crim.Proc.rule 5(a), 18 U.S.C.A.

Defendant's constitutional rights have been violated if his conviction is based, in while or in part, on involuntary confession, regardless of its truth or falsity, even if there is ample evidence aside from confession to support conviction.

Whether conviction was in federal or state court, defendant may secure post-conviction hearing based on alleged involuntary character of his confession, provided that he meets procedural requirements.

Voluntariness doctrine in state cases encompasses all interrogation practices which are likely to exert such pressure upon individual as to disable him from making free and rational choice. U.S.C.A.Const. Amend. 5.

Independent of any other constitutional proscription, preventing attorney from consulting with client is violation of Sixth Amendment right to assistance of counsel and excludes any statement obtained in its wake. U.S.C.A.Const. Amend. 6.

Presence of counsel in cases presented would have been adequate protective device necessary to make process of police interrogation conform to dictates of privilege; his presence would have insured that statements made in government-established atmosphere were not product of compulsion. U.S.C.A.Const. Amends. 5, 6.

Fifth Amendment privilege is available outside of criminal court proceedings and serves to protect persons in all settings in which their freedom of action is curtailed from being compelled to incriminate themselves. U.S.C.A.Const. Amend. 5.

To combat pressures in in-custody interrogation and to permit full opportunity to exercise privilege against self-incrimination, accused must be adequately and effectively apprised of his rights and exercise of these rights must be fully honored. U.S.C.A.Const. Amend. 5.

If person in custody is to be subjected to interrogation, he must first be informed in clear and unequivocal terms that he has right to remain silent, as threshold requirement for intelligent decision as to its exercise, as absolute prerequisite in overcoming inherent pressures of interrogation atmosphere, and to show that interrogators are prepared to recognize privilege should accused choose to exercise it. U.S.C.A.Const. Amend. 5.

Awareness of right to remain silent is threshold requirement for intelligent decision as to its exercise. U.S.C.A.Const. Amend. 5.

It is impermissible to penalize individual for exercising his Fifth Amendment privilege when he is under police custodial interrogation. U.S.C.A.Const. Amend. 5.

Prosecution may not use at trial fact that defendant stood mute or claimed his privilege in face of accusation.

Whatever background of person interrogated, warning at time of interrogation as to availability of right to remain silent is indispensable to overcome pressures of in-custody interrogation and to insure that individual knows that he is free to exercise privilege at that point and time. U.S.C.A.Const. Amend. 5.

Warning of right to remain silent, as prerequisite to in-custody interrogation, must be accompanied by explanation that anything said can and will be used against individual; warning is needed to make accused aware not only of privilege but of consequences of foregoing it and also serves to make him more acutely aware that he is faced with phase of adversary system. U.S.C.A.Const. Amend. 5.

Right to have counsel present at interrogation is indispensable to protection of Fifth Amendment privilege. U.S.C.A.Const. Amend. 5.

Need for counsel to protect Fifth Amendment privilege comprehends not merely right to consult with counsel prior to questioning but also to have counsel present during any questioning if defendant so desires. U.S.C.A.Const. Amends. 5, 6.

Preinterrogation request for lawyer affirmatively secures accused's right to have one, but his failure to ask for lawyer does not constitute waiver. U.S.C.A.Const. Amend. 5.

No effective waiver of right to counsel during interrogation can be recognized unless specifically made after warnings as to rights have been given. U.S.C.A.Const. Amend. 5.

Proposition that right to be furnished counsel does not depend upon request applies with equal force in context of providing counsel to protect accused's Fifth Amendment privilege in face of interrogation. U.S.C.A.Const. Amend. 5.

Individual held for interrogation must be clearly informed that he has right to consult with lawyer and to have lawyer with him during interrogation, to protect Fifth Amendment privilege. U.S.C.A.Const. Amend. 5.

Warning as to right to consult lawyer and have lawyer present during interrogation is absolute prerequisite to interrogation, and no amount of circumstantial evidence that person may have been aware of this right will suffice to stand in its stead. U.S.C.A.Const. Amend. 5.

If individual indicates that he wishes assistance of counsel before interrogation occurs, authorities cannot rationally ignore or deny request on basis that individual does not have or cannot afford retained attorney.

Privilege against self-incrimination applies to all individuals U.S.C.A.Const. Amend. 5.

With respect to affording assistance of counsel, while authorities are not required to relieve accused of his poverty, they have obligation not to take advantage of indigence in administration of justice. U.S.C.A.Const. Amend. 6.

In order fully to apprise person interrogated of extent of his rights, it is necessary to warn him not only that he has right to consult with attorney, but also that if he is indigent lawyer will be appointed to represent him. U.S.C.A.Const. Amend. 6.

Expedient of giving warning as to right to appointed counsel is too simple and rights involved too important to engage in ex post facto inquiries into financial ability when there is any doubt at all on that score, but warning that indigent may have counsel appointed need not be given to person who is known to have attorney or is known to have ample funds to secure one. U.S.C.A.Const. Amend. 6.

Once warnings have been given, if individual indicates in any manner, at any time prior to or during questioning, that he wishes to remain silent, interrogation must cease. U.S.C.A.Const. Amend. 5.

If individual indicates desire to remain silent, but has attorney present, there may be some circumstances in which further questioning would be permissible; in absence of evidence of overbearing, statements then made in presence of counsel might be free of compelling influence of interrogation process and might fairly be construed as waiver of privilege for purposes of these statements. U.S.C.A.Const. Amend. 5.

Any statement taken after person invokes Fifth Amendment privilege cannot be other than product of compulsion. U.S.C.A.Const. Amend. 5.

If individual states that he wants attorney, interrogation must cease until attorney is pres-

U.S. SUPREME COURT, OCTOBER 1966

ent; at that time, individual must have opportunity to confer with attorney and to have him present during any subsequent questioning. U.S.C.A.Const. Amends. 5, 6.

While each police station need not have "station house lawyer" present at all times to advise prisoners, if police propose to interrogate person they must make known to him that he is entitled to lawyer and that if he cannot afford one, lawyer will be provided for him prior to any interrogation. U.S.C.A.Const. Amend. 5.

If authorities conclude that they will not provide counsel during reasonable period of time in which investigation in field is carried out, they may refrain from doing so without violating person's Fifth Amendment privilege so long as they do not question him during that time. U.S.C.A.Const. Amend. 5.

If interrogation continues without presence of attorney and statement is taken, government has heavy burden to demonstrate that defendant knowingly and intelligently waived his privilege against self-incrimination and his right to retained or appointed counsel. U.S.C.A.Const. Amend. 5.

High standards of proof for waiver of constitutional rights apply to in-custody interrogation.

State properly has burden to demonstrate knowing and intelligent waiver of privilege against self-incrimination and right to counsel, with respect to incommunicado interrogation, since state is responsible for establishing isolated circumstances under which interrogation takes place and has only means of making available corroborated evidence of warnings given.

Express statement that defendant is willing to make statement and does not want attorney, followed closely by statement, could constitute waiver, but valid waiver will not be presumed simply from silence of accused after warnings are given or simply from fact that confession was in fact eventually obtained.

Presuming waiver from silent record is impermissible, and record must show, or there must be allegations and evidence, that accused was offered counsel but intelligently and understandingly rejected offer.

Where in-custody interrogation is involved, there is no room for contention that privilege is waived if individual answers some questions or gives some information on his own before

invoking right to remain silent when interrogated. U.S.C.A.Const. Amend. 5.

Fact of lengthy interrogation or incommunicado incarceration before statement is made is strong evidence that accused did not validly waive rights. U.S.C.A.Const. Amend. 5.

Any evidence that accused was threatened, tricked, or cajoled into waiver will show that he did not voluntarily waive privilege to remain silent. U.S.C.A.Const. Amend. 5.

Requirement of warnings and waiver of right is fundamental with respect to Fifth Amendment privilege and not simply preliminary ritual to existing methods of interrogation.

Warnings or waiver with respect to Fifth Amendment rights are, in absence of wholly effective equivalent, prerequisites to admissibility of any statement made by a defendant, regardless of whether statements are direct confessions, admissions of part or all of offense, or merely "exculpatory." U.S.C.A.Const. Amend. 5.

Privilege against self-incrimination protects individual from being compelled to incriminate himself in any manner; it does not distinguish degrees of incrimination.

Statements merely intended to be exculpatory by defendant, but used to impeach trial testimony or to demonstrate untruth in statements given under interrogation, are incriminating and may not be used without full warnings and effective waiver required for any order statement. U.S.C.A.Const. Amend. 5.

When individual is in custody on probable cause, police may seek out evidence in field to be used at trial against him, and may make inquiry of persons not under restraint.

Rules relating to warnings and waiver in connection with statements taken in police interrogation do not govern general on-the-scene questioning as to facts surrounding crime or other general questioning of citizens in fact-finding process. U.S.C.A.Const. Amend. 5.

Confessions remain a proper element in law enforcement.

Any statement given freely and voluntarily without compelling influences is admissible.

Volunteered statements of any kind are not barred by Fifth Amendment; there is no requirement that police stop person who enters police station and states that he wishes to confess a crime or a person who calls police to offer confession or any other statements he desires to make. U.S.C.A.Const. Amend. 5.

When individual is taken into custody or otherwise deprived of his freedom by authorities in any significant way and is subjected to questioning, privilege against self-incrimination is jeopardized, and procedural safeguards must be employed to protect privilege. U.S.C.A.Const. Amend. 5.

Unless other fully effective means are adopted to notify accused in custody or otherwise deprived of freedom of his right of silence and to assure that exercise of right will be scrupulously honored, he must be warned before questioning that he has right to remain silent, that anything he says can be used against him in court, and that he has right to presence of attorney and to have attorney appointed before questioning if he cannot afford one; opportunity to exercise these rights must be afforded to him throughout interrogation; after such warnings have been given and opportunity afforded, accused may knowingly and intelligently waive rights and agree to answer questions or make statements, but unless and until such warnings and waiver are demonstrated by prosecution at trial, no evidence obtained as a result of interrogation can be used against them. U.S.C.A.Const. Amends. 5, 6.

Fifth Amendment provision that individual cannot be compelled to be witness against himself cannot be abridged. U.S.C.A.Const. Amend. 5.

In fulfilling responsibility to protect rights of client, attorney plays vital role in administration of criminal justice. U.S.C.A.Const. Amend. 6.

Interviewing agent must exercise his judgment in determining whether individual waives right to counsel, but standard for waiver is high and ultimate responsibility for resolving constitutional question lies with courts.

Constitution does not require any specific code of procedures for protecting privilege against self-incrimination during custodial interrogation, and Congress and states are free to develop their own safeguards for privilege, so long as those required by court. U.S.C.A.Const. Amend. 5.

Issues of admissibility of statements taken during custodial interrogation were of constitutional dimension and must be determined by courts.

Where rights secured by Constitution are involved, there can be no rule making or legislation which would abrogate them.

Statements taken by police in incommunicado interrogation were inadmissible in state prosecution, where defendant had not been in any way apprised of his right to consult with attorney or to have one present during interrogation, and his Fifth Amendment right not to be compelled to incriminate himself was not effectively protected in any other manner, even though he signed statement which contained typed in clause that he had full knowledge of his legal rights. U.S.C.A.Const. Amends. 5, 6.

Mere fact that interrogated defendant signed statement which contained typed in clause stating that he had full knowledge of his legal rights did not approach knowing and intelligent waiver required to relinquish constitutional rights to counsel and privilege against self-incrimination.

State defendant's oral confession obtained during incommunicado interrogation was inadmissible where he had not been warned or any of his rights before questioning, and thus was not effectively apprised of Fifth Amendment privilege or right to have counsel present. U.S.C.A.Const. Amends. 5, 6.

Confessions obtained by federal agents in incommunicado interrogation were not admissible in federal prosecution, although federal agents gave warning of defendant's right to counsel and to remain silent, where defendant had been arrested by state authorities who detained and interrogated him for lengthy period, both at night and the following morning, without giving warning, and confessions were obtained after some two hours of questioning by federal agents in same police station. U.S.C.A.Const. Amends. 5, 6.

Defendant's failure to object to introduction of his confession at trial was not a waiver of claim of constitutional inadmissibility, and did not preclude Supreme Court's consideration of issue, where trial was held prior to decision in *Escobedo v. Illinois.*

Federal agents' giving of warning alone was not sufficient to protect defendant's Fifth Amendment privilege where federal interrogation was conducted immediately following state interrogation in same police station and in same compelling circumstances, after state interrogation in which no warnings were given, so that federal agents were beneficiaries of pressure applied by local in-custody interrogation; however, law enforcement authorities are not necessarily precluded from questioning any individual who has been held for period of time by other authorities and interrogated by them without appropriate warning.

California Supreme Court decision directing that state defendant be retired was final judgment, from which state could appeal to federal Supreme Court, since in event defendant were successful in obtaining acquittal on retrial state would have no appeal. 28 U.S.C.A. § 1257(3).

In dealing with custodial interrogation, court will not presume that defendant has been effectively apprised of rights and that has privilege against self-incrimination has been adequately safeguarded on record that does not show that any warnings have been given or that any effective alternative has been employed, nor can knowing and intelligent waiver of those rights be assumed on silent record. U.S.C.A.Const. Amend. 5.

State defendant's inculpatory statement obtained in incommunicado interrogation was inadmissible as obtained in violation of Fifth Amendment privilege where record did not specifically disclose whether defendant had been advised of his rights, he was interrogated on nine separate occasions over five days' detention, and record was silent as to waiver. U.S.C.A.Const. Amend. 5.

No. 759:

John J. Flynn, Phoenix, Ariz., for petitioner.

Gary K. Nelson, Phoenix, Ariz., for respondent.

Telford Taylor, New York City, for State of New York, as amicus curiae, by special leave of Court. (Also in Nos. 584, 760, 761 and 762)

Duane R. Nedrud, for National District Attorneys Ass'n, as amicus curiae, by special leave of Court. (Also in Nos. 760, 762 and 584)

No. 760:

Victor M. Earle, III, New York City, for petitioner.

William I. Siegel, Brooklyn, for respondent.

No. 761:

F. Conger Fawcett, San Francisco, Cal., for petitioner.

Sol. Gen. Thurgood Marshall, for respondent.

No. 584:

Gordon Ringer, Los Angeles, Cal., for petitioner.

William A. Norris, Los Angeles, Cal., for respondent.

Mr. Chief Justice Warren delivered the opinion of the Court.

The cases before us raise questions which go to the roots of our concepts of American criminal jurisprudence: the restraints society must observe consistent with the Federal Constitution in prosecuting individuals for crime. More specifically, we deal with the admissibility of statements obtained from an individual who is subjected to custodial police interrogation and the necessity for procedures which assure that the individual is accorded his privilege under the Fifth Amendment to the Constitution not to be compelled to incriminate himself.

We dealt with certain phases of this problem recently in *Escobedo v. State of Illinois*, 378 U.S. 478, 84 S.Ct. 1758, 12 L.Ed.2d 977 (1964). There, as in the four cases before us, law enforcement officials took the defendant into custody and interrogated him in a police station for the purpose of obtaining a confession. The police did not effectively advise him of his right to remain silent or of his right to consult with his attorney. Rather, they confronted him with an alleged accomplice who accused him of having perpetrated a murder. When the defendant denied the accusation and said "I didn't shoot Manuel, you did it," they handcuffed him and took him to an interrogation room. There, while handcuffed and standing, he was questioned for four hours until he confessed. During this interrogation, the police denied his request to speak to his attorney, and they prevented his retained attorney, who had come to the police station, from consulting with him. At his trial, the State, over his objection, introduced the confession against him. We held that the statements thus made were constitutionally inadmissible.

[1] This case has been the subject of judicial interpretation and spirited legal debate since it was decided two years ago. Both state and federal courts, in accessing its implications, have arrived at varying conclusions.[1] A wealth of

---

[1] Compare *United States v. Childress*, 347 F.2d 448 (C.A. 7th Cir. 1965), with *Collins v. Beto*, 348 F.2d 823 (C.A. 5th Cir. 1965). Compare *People v. Dorado*, 62 Cal.2d 338, 42 Cal.Rptr. 169, 398 P.2d 361 (1964) with *People v. Hartgraves*, 31 Ill.2d 375, 202 N.E.2d 33 (1964).

scholarly material has been written tracing its ramifications and underpinnings.[2] Police and prosecutor have speculated on its range and desirability.[3] We granted certiorari in these cases, 382 U.S. 924, 925, 937, 86 S.Ct. 318, 320, 395, 15 L.Ed. 2d 338, 339, 348, in order further to explore some facets of the problems, thus exposed, of applying the privilege against self-incrimination to in-custody interrogation, and to give concrete constitutional guidelines for law enforcement agencies and courts to follow.

[2] We start here, as we did in *Escobedo* decision and the principles it announced, and we reaffirm it. That case was but an explication of basic rights that are enshrined in our Constitution—that "No person * * * shall be compelled in any criminal case to be a witness against himself," and that "the accused shall * * * have the Assistance of Counsel"—rights which were put in jeopardy in that case through official overbearing. These precious rights were fixed in our Constitution only after centuries of persecution and struggle. And in the words of Chief Justice Marshall, they were secured "for ages to come, and * * * designed to approach immortality as nearly as human institutions can approach it," *Cohens v. Commonwealth of Virginia,* 6 Wheat. 264, 387, 5 L.Ed. 257 (1821).

Over 70 years ago, our predecessors on this Court eloquently stated:

"The maxim *'Nemo tenetur seipsum accusare,'* had its origin in a protest against the inquisitorial and manifestly unjust methods of interrogating accused persons, which [have] long obtained in the continental system, and, until the expulsion of the Stuarts from the British throne in 1688, and the erection of additional barriers for the protection of the people against the exercise of arbitrary power, [were] not uncommon even in England. While the admissions or confessions of the prisoner, when voluntarily and freely made, have always ranked high in the scale of incriminating evidence, if an accused person be asked to explain his apparent connection with a crime under investigation, the ease with which the questions put to him my assume an inquisitorial character, the temptation to press the witness unduly, to browbeat him if he be timid or reluctant, to push him into a corner, and entrap him into fatal contradictions, which is so painfully evident in many of the earlier state trials, notably in those of Sir Nicholas Throckmorton, and Udal, the Puritan minister, made the system so odious as to give rise to a demand for its total abolition. The change in the English criminal procedure in that particular seems to be founded upon no statute and no judicial opinion, but upon a general and silent acquiescence of the courts in a popular demand. But, however adopted, it has become firmly embedded in English, as well as in American jurisprudence. So deeply did the iniquities of the ancient system impress themselves upon the minds of the American colonists that the states, with one accord, made a denial of the right to question an accused person a part of their fundamental law, so that a maxim, which in England was a

---

[2] See, e. g., Enker & Elsen, Counsel for the Suspect: *Messiah v. United States,* 377 U.S. 201, 84 S.Ct. 1199, 12 L.Ed.2d 246 and *Escobedo v. State of Illinois,* 49 Minn.L.Rev. 47 (1964); Herman, The Supreme Court and Restrictions on Police Interrogation, 25 Ohio St.L.J. 449 (1964); Kamisar, Equal Justice in the Gatehouses and Mansions of American Criminal Procedure, in Criminal Justice in Our Time 1 (1965); Dowling, Escobedo and Beyond: The Need for a Fourteenth Amendment Code of Criminal Procedure, 56 J.Crim.L., C. & P.S. 143, 156 (1965).

The complex problems also prompted discussions by jurists. Compare Bazelon, Law, Morality, and Civil Liberties, 12 U.C.L.A.L.Rev. 13 (1964), with Friendly, The Bill of Rights as a Code of Criminal Procedure, 53 Calif.L.Rev. 929 (1965).

[3] For example, the Los Angeles Police Chief stated that "If the police are required * * * to * * * establish that the defendant was apprised of his constitutional guarantees of silence and legal counsel prior to the uttering of any admission or confession, and that he intelligently waived these guarantees * * * a whole Pandora's box is opened as to under what circumstances * * * can a defendant intelligently waive these rights. * * * Allegations that modern criminal investigations can compensate for the lack of a confession or admission in

every criminal case it totally absurd!" Parker, 40 L.A.Bar Bull. 603, 607, 642 (1965). His prosecutorial counterpart, District Attorney Younger, stated that "[I]t begins to appear that many of these seemingly restrictive decisions are going to contribute directly to a more effective, efficient and professional level of law enforcement." *L. A. Times,* Oct. 2, 1965, p. 1. The former Police Commissioner of New York, Michael J. Murphy, stated of *Escobedo:* "What the Court is doing is akin to requiring one boxer to fight by Marquis of Queensbury rules while permitting the other to butt, gouge and bite." *N. Y. Times,* May 14, 1965, p. 39. The former United States Attorney for the District of Columbia, David C. Acheson, who is presently Special Assistant to the Secretary of the Treasury (for Enforcement), and directly in charge of the Secret Service and the Bureau of Narcotics, observed that "Prosecution procedure has, at most, only the most remote casual connection with crime. Changes in court decisions and prosecution procedure would have about the same effect on the crime rate as an aspirin would have on a tumor of the brain." Quoted in Herman, supra, n. 2, at 500, n. 270. Other views on the subject in general are collected in Weisberg, Police Interrogation of Arrested Persons; A Skeptical View, 52 J.Crim.L., C. & P.S. 21 (1961).

U.S. SUPREME
COURT,
OCTOBER 1966

mere rule of evidence, became clothed in this country with the impregnability of a constitutional enactment." *Brown v. Walker,* 161 U.S. 591, 596–597, 16 S.Ct. 644, 646, 40 L.Ed. 819 (1896).

In stating the obligation of the judiciary to apply these constitutional rights, this Court declared in *Weems v. United States,* 217 U.S. 349, 373, 30 S.Ct. 544, 551, 54 L.Ed. 793 (1910):

"* * * our contemplation cannot be only of what has been, but of what may be. Under any other rule a constitution would indeed be as easy of application as it would be deficient in efficacy and power. Its general principles would have little value, and be converted by precedent into impotent and lifeless formulas. Rights declared in words might be lost in reality. And this has been recognized. The meaning and vitality of the Constitution have developed against narrow and restrictive construction."

This was the spirit in which we delineated, in meaningful language, the manner in which the constitutional rights of the individual could be enforced against overzealous police practices. It was necessary in *Escobedo,* as here, to insure that what was proclaimed in the Constitution had not become but a "form of words," *Silverthorne Lumber Co. v. United States,* 251 U.S. 385, 392, 40 S.Ct. 182, 64 L.Ed. 319 (1920), in the hands of government officials. And it is in this spirit, consistent with our role as judges, that we adhere to the principles of *Escobedo* today.

[3–9] Our holding will be spelled out with some specificity in the pages which follow but briefly stated it is this: the prosecution may not use statements, whether exculpatory or inculpatory, stemming from custodial interrogation of the defendant unless it demonstrates the use of procedural safeguards effective to secure the privilege against self-incrimination. By custodial interrogation, we mean questioning initiated by law enforcement officers after a person has been taken into custody or otherwise deprived of his freedom of action in any significant way.[4] As for the procedural safeguards to be employed, unless other fully effective means are devised to inform accused persons of their right of silence and to assure a continuous opportunity to exercise it, the following measures are required. Prior to any questioning, the person must be warned that he has a right to remain silent, that any statement he does make may be used as evidence against him, and that he has a right to the presence of an attorney, either

retained or appointed. The defendant may waive effectuation of these rights, provided the waiver is made voluntarily, knowingly and intelligently. If, however, he indicates in any manner and at any stage of the process that he wishes to consult with an attorney before speaking there can be no questioning. Likewise, if the individual is alone and indicates in any manner that he does not wish to be interrogated, the police may not question him. The mere fact that he may have answered some questions or volunteered some statements on his own does not deprive him of the right to refrain from answering any further inquiries until he has consulted with an attorney and thereafter consents to be questioned.

I.

The constitutional issue we decide in each of these cases is the admissibility of statements obtained from a defendant questioned while in custody or otherwise deprived of his freedom of action in any significant way. In each, the defendant was questioned by police officers, detectives, or a prosecuting attorney in a room in which he was cut off from the outside world. In none of these cases was the defendant given a full and effective warning of his rights at the outset of the interrogation process. In all the cases, the questioning elicited oral admissions, and in three of them, signed statements as well which were admitted at their trials. They all thus share salient features—incommunicado interrogation of individuals in a police-dominated atmosphere, resulting in self-incriminating statements without full warnings of constitutional rights.

An understanding of the nature and setting of this in-custody interrogation is essential to our decisions today. The difficulty in depicting what transpires at such interrogation stems from the fact that in this country they have largely taken place incommunicado. From extensive factual studies undertaken in the early 1930's, including the famous Wickersham Report to Congress by a Presidential Commission, it is clear that police violence and the "third degree" flourished at that time.[5] In a series of cases decid-

---

[4] This is what we meant in *Escobedo* when we spoke of an investigation which had focused on an accused.

[5] See, for example, IV National Commission on Law Observance and Enforcement, Report on Lawlessness in Law Enforcement (1931) [Wickersham Report]; Booth, Confessions and Methods Employed in Procuring Them, 4 So.Calif.L. Rev. 83 (1930); Kauper, Judicial Examination of the Accused — A Remedy for the Third Degree, 30 Mich.L.Rev.

U.S. SUPREME
COURT,
OCTOBER 1966

ed by this Court long after these studies, the police resorted to physical brutality — beatings, hanging, whipping—and to sustained and protracted questioning incommunicado in order to extort confessions.[6] The Commission on Civil Rights in 1961 found much evidence to indicate that "some policemen still resort to physical force to obtain confessions," 1961 Comm'n on Civil Rights Rep., Justice, pt. 5, 17. The use of physical brutality and violence is not, unfortunately, relegated to the past of to any part of the country. Only recently in Kings County, New York, the police brutally beat, kicked and placed lighted cigarette butts on the back of a potential witness under interrogation for the purpose of securing a statement incriminating a third party. *People v. Portelli,* 15 N.Y.2d 235, 257 N.Y.S.2d 931, 205 N.E.2d 857 (1965).[7]

The examples given above are undoubtedly the exception now, but they are sufficiently widespread to be the object of concern. Unless a proper limitation upon custodial interrogation is achieved—such as these decisions will advance—there can be no assurance that practices of this nature will be eradicated in the foreseeable future. The conclusion of the Wickersham Commission Report, made over 30 years ago, is still pertinent:

> "To the contention that the third degree is necessary to get the facts, the reporters aptly reply in the language of the present Lord Chancellor of England (Lord Sankey): 'It is not admissible to do a great right by doing a little wrong. * * * It is not sufficient to do justice by obtaining a proper result by irregular

or improper means.' Not only does the use of the third degree involve a flagrant violation of law by the officers of the law, but it involves also the dangers of false confessions, and it tends to make police and prosecutors less zealous in the search for objective evidence. As the New York prosecutor quoted in the report said, 'It is a short cut and makes the police lazy and unenterprising.' Or, as another official quoted remarked: 'If you use your fists, you are not so likely to use your wits.' We agree with the conclusion expressed in the report, that 'The third degree brutalizes the police, hardens the prisoner against society, and lowers the esteem in which the administration of justice is held by the public.'" IV National Commission on Law Observance and Enforcement, Report on Lawlessness in Law Enforcement 5 (1931).

[10] Again we stress that the modern practice of in-custody interrogation is psychologically rather than physically oriented. As we have stated before, "Since *Chambers v. State of Florida,* 309 U.S. 227, 60 S. Ct. 472, 84 L.Ed. 716, this Court has recognized that coercion can be mental as well as physical, and that the blood of the accused is not the only hallmark of an unconstitutional inquisition." *Blackburn v. State of Alabama,* 361 U.S. 199, 206, 80 S.Ct. 274, 279 4 L.Ed.2d 242 (1960). Interrogation still takes place in privacy. Privacy results in a gap in our knowledge as to what in fact goes on in the interrogation rooms. A valuable source of information about present police practices, however, may be found in various police manuals and texts which document procedures employed with success in the past, and which recommend

---

1224 (1932). It is significant that instances of third-degree treatment of prisoners almost invariably took place during the period between arrest and preliminary examination. Wickersham Report, at 169; Hall, the Law of Arrest in Relation to Contemporary Social Problems, 3 U.Chi.L. Rev. 345, 357 (1936). See also Foote, Law and Police Practice: Safeguards in the Law of Arrest, 52 Nw.U.L.Rev. 16 (1957).

[6] *Brown v. State of Mississippi,* 297 U.S. 278, 56 S.Ct. 461, 80 L.Ed. 682 (1936); *Chambers v. State of Florida,* 309 U.S. 227, 60 S.Ct. 472, 84 L.Ed. 716 (1940); *Canty v. State of Alabama,* 309 U.S. 629, 60 S.Ct. 612, 84 L.Ed. 988 (1940); *White v. State of Texas,* 310 U.S. 530, 60 S.Ct. 1032, 84 L.ED. 1342 (1940); *Vernon v. State of Alabama,* 313 U.S. 547, 61 S.Ct. 1092, 85 L.Ed. 1513 (1941); *Ward v. State of Texas,* 316 U.S. 547, 62 S.Ct. 1139, 86 L.Ed. 1663 (1942); *Ashcraft v. State of Tennessee,* 322 U.S. 143, 64 S.Ct. 921, 88 L.Ed. 1192 (1944); *Malinski v. People of State of New York,* 324 U.S. 401, 65 S.Ct. 781, 89 L.Ed. 1029 (1945); *Leyra v. Denno,* 347 U.S. 556, 74 S.Ct. 716, 98 L.Ed. 948 (1954). See also *Williams v. United States,* 341 U.S. 97, 71 S.Ct. 576, 95 L.Ed. 774 (1951).

[7] In addition, see *People v. Wakat,* 415 Ill. 610, 114 N.E.2d 706

(1953); *Wakat v. Harlib,* 253 F.2d 59 (C.A. 7th Cir.1958) (defendant suffering from broken bones, multiple bruises and injuries sufficiently serious to require eight months' medical treatment after being manhandled by five policeman); *Kier v. State,* 213 Md. 556, 132 A.2d 494 (1957) (police doctor told accused, who was strapped to a chair completely nude, that he proposed to take hair and skin scrapings from anything that looked like blood or sperm from various parts of his body); *Bruner v. People,* 113 Colo. 194, 156 P.2d 111 (1945) (defendant held in custody over two months, deprived of food for 15 hours, forced to submit to a lie detector test when he wanted to go to the toilet); *People v. Matlock,* 51 Cal.2d 682, 336 P.2d 505, 71 A.L.R.2d 605 (1959) (defendant questioned incessantly over an evening's time, made to lie on cold board and to answer questions whenever it appeared he was getting sleepy). Other cases are documented in American Civil Liberties Union, Illinois Division, Secret Detention by the Chicago Police (1959); Potts, The Preliminary Examination and "The Third Degree," 2 Baylor L.Rev. 131 (1950); Sterling, Police Interrogation and the Psychology of Confession, 14 J.Pub.L. 25 (1965).

various other effective tactics.[8] These texts are used by law enforcement agencies themselves as guides.[9] It should be noted that these texts professedly present the most enlightened and effective means presently used to obtain statements through custodial interrogation. By considering these texts and other data, it is possible to describe procedures observed and noted around the country.

The officers are told by the manuals that the "principal psychological factor contributing to a successful interrogation is privacy—being alone with the person under interrogation."[10] The efficacy of this tactic has been explained as follows:

> "If at all practicable, the interrogation should take place in the investigator's office or at least in a room of his own choice. The subject should be deprived of every psychological advantage. In his own home he may be confident, indigent, or recalcitrant. He is more keenly aware of his rights and more reluctant to tell of his indiscretions or criminal behavior within the walls of his home. Moreover his family and other friends are nearby, their presence lending moral support. In his office, the investigator possesses all the advantages. The atmosphere suggests the invincibility of the forces of the law."[11]

To highlight the isolation and unfamiliar surroundings, the manuals instruct the police to display an air of confidence in the suspect's guilt and from outward appearance to maintain only an interest in confirming certain details. The guilt of the subject is to be posited as a fact. The interrogator should direct his comments toward the reasons why the subject committed the act,

rather than court failure by asking the subject whether he did it. Like other men, perhaps the subject has had a bad family life, had an unhappy childhood, had too much to drink, had an unrequited desire for women. The officers are instructed to minimize the moral seriousness of the offense,[12] to cast blame on the victim or on society.[13] These tactics are designed to put the subject in a psychological state where his story is but an elaboration of what the police purport to know already—that he is guilty. Explanations to the contrary are dismissed and discouraged.

The texts thus stress that the major qualities an interrogator should possess are patience and perseverance. One writer describes the efficacy of these characteristics in this manner:

> "In the preceding paragraphs emphasis has been placed on kindness and stratagems. The investigator will, however, encounter many situations where the sheer weight of his personality will be the deciding factor. Where emotional appeals and tricks are employed to no avail, he must rely on an oppressive atmosphere of dogged persistence. He must interrogate steadily and without relent, leaving the subject no prospect of surcease. He must dominate his subject and overwhelm him with his inexorable will to obtain the truth. He should interrogate for a spell of several hours pausing only for the subject's necessities in acknowledgement of the need to avoid a charge of duress that can be technically substantiated. In a serious case, the interrogation may continue for days, with the required intervals for food and sleep, but with no respite from the atmosphere of domination. It is possible in this way to induce the

---

[8] The manuals quoted in the text following are the most recent and representative of the texts currently available. Material of the same nature appears in Kidd, Police Interrogation (1940); Mulbar, Interrogation (1951); Dienstein, Technics for the Crime Investigator 97–115 (1952). Studies concerning the observed practices of the police appear in LaFave, Arrest: The Decision To Take a Suspect Into Custody 244–437, 490–521 (1965); LaFave, Detention for Investigation by the Police: An Analysis of Current Practices, 1962 Wash.U.L.Q. 331; Barrett, Police Practices and the Law—From Arrest to Release or Charge, 50 Calif.L.Rev. 11 (1962); Sterling, supra, n. 7, at 47–65.

[9] The methods described in Inbau & Reid Criminal Interrogation and Confessions (1962), are a revision and enlargement of material presented in three prior editions of a predecessor text, Lie Detection and Criminal Interrogation (3d ed. 1953). The authors and their associates are officers of the Chicago Police Scientific Crime Detection Laboratory and have had extensive experience in writing, lecturing and speaking to law enforcement authorities over a 20–year period. They say that the techniques portrayed in their manuals

reflect their experiences and are the most effective psychological stratagems to employ during interrogation. Similarly, the techniques described in O'Hara, Fundamentals of Criminal Investigation (1956), were gleaned from long service as observer, lecturer in police science, and work as a federal criminal investigator. All these texts have had rather extensive use among law enforcement agencies and among students of police science, with total sales and circulation of over 44,000.

[10] Inbau & Reid, Criminal Interrogation and Confessions (1962), at 1.

[11] O'Hara, supra, at 99.

[12] Inbau & Redi, supra, at 34–43, 87. For example, in *Leyra v. Denno*, 347 U.S. 556, 74 S.Ct. 716, 98 L.Ed. 948 (1954), the interrogator-psychiatrist told the accused, "We do sometimes things that are not right, but in a fit of temper or anger we sometimes do things we aren't really responsible for," id., at 562, 74 S.Ct. at 719, and again, "We know that morally you were just in anger. Morally, you are not to be condemned," id., at 582, 74 S.Ct. at 729.

[13] Inbau & Reid, supra, at 43–55.

subject to talk without resorting to duress or coercion. The method should be used only when the guilt of the subject appears highly probable."[14]

The manuals suggest that the suspect be offered legal excuses for his actions in order to obtain an initial admission of guilt. Where there is a suspected revenge-killing, for example, the interrogator may say:

"Joe, you probably didn't got out looking for this fellow with the purpose of shooting him. My guess is, however, that you expected something from him and that's why you carried a gun—for your own protection. You knew him for what he was, no good. Then when you met him he probably started using foul, abusive language and he gave some indication that he was about to pull a gun on you, and that's when you had to act to save your own life. That's about it, isn't it, Joe?"[15]

Having then obtained the admission of shooting, the interrogator is advised to refer to circumstantial evidence which negates the self-defense explanation. This should enable him to secure the entire story. One text notes that "Even if he fails to do so, the inconsistency between the subject's original denial of the shooting and his present admission of at least doing the shooting will serve to deprive him of a self-defense 'out' at the time of trial."[16]

When the techniques described above prove unavailing, the texts recommend they be alternated with a show of some hostility. One ploy often used has been termed with the "friendly-unfriendly" or the "Mutt and Jeff" act:

"* * * In this technique, two agents are employed. Mutt, the relentless investigator, who knows the subject is guilty and is not going to waste any time. He's sent a dozen men away for this crime and he's going to send the subject away for the full term. Jeff, on the other hand, is obviously a kindhearted man. He has a family himself. He has a brother who was involved in a little scrape like this. He disapproves of Mutt and his tactics and will arrange to get him off the case if the subject will cooperate. He can't hold Mutt off for very long. The subject would be wise to make a quick decision. The technique is applied by having both investigators present while Mutt acts out his role. Jeff may stand by quietly and demur at some of Mutt's tactics. When Jeff makes his plea for cooperation, Mutt is not present in the room."[17]

The interrogators sometimes are instructed to induce a confession out of trickery. The technique here is quite effective in crimes which require identification or which run in series. In the identification situation, the interrogator may take a break in his questioning to place the subject among a group of men in a line-up. "The witness or compliant (previously coached, if necessary) studies the line-up and confidently points out the subject as the guilty party."[18] Then the questioning resumes "as though there were no doubt about the guilt of the subject." A variation on this technique is called the "reverse line-up:"

"The accused is placed in a line-up, but this time he is identified by several fictitious witnesses or victims who associated him with different offenses. It is expected that the subject will become desperate and confess to the offense under investigation in order to escape from the false accusations."[19]

The manuals also contain instructions for police on how to handle the individual who refuses to discuss the matter entirely, or who asks for an attorney or relatives. The examiner is to concede him the right to remain silent. "This usually has a very undermining effect. First of all, he is disappointed in his expectation of an unfavorable reaction on the part of the interrogator. Secondly, a concession of this right to remain silent impresses the subject with the apparent fairness of his interrogator."[20] After this psychological conditioning, however, the officer is told to point out the incriminating significance of the suspect's refusal to talk:

"Joe, you have a right to remain silent. That's your privilege and I'm the last person in the world who'll try to take it away from you. If that's the way you want to leave this, O.K. But

---

[14] O'Hara, supra, at 112.

[15] Inbau & Reid, supra, at 40.

[16] Ibid.

[17] O'Hara, supra, at 104, Inbau & Reid, supra, at 58–59. See *Spano v. People of State of New York*, 360 U.S. 315, 79 S.Ct. 1202, 3 L.Ed.2d 1265 (1959). A variant on the technique of creating hostility is one of engendering fear. This is perhaps best described by the prosecuting attorney in *Malinski v. People of State of New York*, 324 U.S. 401, 407, 65 S.Ct. 781, 784, 89 L.Ed. 1029 (1945): "Why this talk about being undressed? Of course, they had a right to undress him to look for bullet scars, and keep the clothes off him. That was quite proper police procedure. That is some more psychology—let him sit around with a blanket on him, humiliate him there for a while; let him sit in the corner, let him think he is going to get a shellacking."

[18] O'Hara, supra, at 105–106.

[19] Id., at 106.

[20] Inbau & Reid, supra, at 111.

U.S. SUPREME
COURT,
OCTOBER 1966

let me ask you this. Suppose you were in my shoes and I were in yours and you called me in to ask me about this and I told you, 'I don't want to answer any of your questions.' You'd think I had something to hide, and you'd probably be right in thinking that. That's exactly what I'll have to think about you, and so will everybody else. So let's sit here and talk this whole thing over."[21]

Few will persist in their initial refusal to talk, it is said, if this monologue is employed correctly.

In the event that the subject wishes to speak to a relative or an attorney, the following advice is tendered:

"[T]he interrogator should respond by suggesting that the subject first tell the truth to the interrogator himself rather than get anyone else involved in the matter. If the request is for an attorney, the interrogator may suggest that the subject save himself or his family the expense of any such professional service, particularly if he is innocent of the offense under investigation. The interrogator may also add, 'Joe, I'm only looking for the truth, and if you're telling the truth, that's it. You can handle this by yourself.'"[22]

From these representative samples of interrogation techniques, the setting prescribed by the manuals and observed in practice becomes clear. In essence, it is this: To be alone with the subject is essential to prevent distraction and to deprive him of any outside support. The aura of confidence in his guilt undermines his will to resist. He merely confirms the preconceived story the police seek to have him describe. Patience and persistence, at times relentless questioning, are employed. To obtain a confession, the interrogator must "patiently maneuver himself or his quarry into a position from which the desired objective may be attained."[23] When normal procedures fail to produce the needed result, the police may resort to deceptive strata-

gems such as giving false legal advice. It is important to keep the subject off balance, for example, by trading on his insecurity about himself or his surroundings. The police then persuade, trick, or cajole him out of exercising his constitutional rights.

Even without employing brutality, the "third degree" or the specific stratagems described above, the very fact of custodial interrogation exacts a heavy toll on individual liberty and trades on the weakness of individuals.[24] This fact may be illustrated simply by referring to three confession cases decided by this Court in the Term immediately preceding our *Escobedo* decision. In *Townsend v. Sain,* 372 U.S. 293, 83 S.Ct. 745, 9 L.Ed.2d 770 (1963), the defendant was a 19–year-old heroin addict, described as a "near mental defective," id., at 307–310, 83 S.Ct. at 754–755. The defendant in *Lynumn v. State of Illinois,* 372 U.S. 528, 83 S.Ct. 917, 9 L.Ed.2d 922 (1963), was a woman who confessed to the arresting officer after bring importuned to "cooperate" in order to prevent her children from being taken by relief authorities. This Court as in those cases reversed the conviction of a defendant in *Haynes v. State of Washington,* 373 U.S. 503, 83 S.Ct. 1336, 10 L.Ed.2d 513 (1963), whose persistent request during his interrogation was to phone his wife or attorney.[25] In other settings, these individuals might have exercised their constitutional rights. In the incommunicado police-dominated atmosphere, they succumbed.

In the cases before us today, given this background, we concern ourselves primarily with this interrogation atmosphere and the evils it can bring. In No. 759, *Miranda v. Arizona,* the police arrested the defendant and took him to a special interrogation room where they secured a confession. In No. 760, *Vignera v. New York,* the

---

[21] Ibid.

[22] Inbau & Reid, supra, at 112.

[23] Inbau & Reid, Lie Detection and Criminal Interrogation 185 (3d ed. 1953).

[24] Interrogation procedures may even give rise to a false confession. The most recent conspicuous example occurred in New York, in 1964, when a Negro of limited intelligence confessed to two brutal murders and a rape which he had not committed. When this was discovered, the prosecutor was reported as saying: "Call if what you want—brain-washing, hypnosis, fright. They made him give an untrue confession. The only thing I don't believe is that Whitmore was beaten." *N. Y. Times,* Jan. 28, 1965, p. 1, col. 5. In two other instances, similar events had occurred. *N. Y. Times,* Oct. 20, 1964, p. 22,

col. 1; *N. Y. Times,* Aug. 25, 1965, p. 1, col. 1. In general, see Borchard, Convicting the Innocent (1932); Frank & Frank, Not Guilty (1957).

[25] In the fourth confession case decided by the Court in the 1962 Term, *Fay v. Noia,* 372 U.S. 391, 83 S.Ct. 822, 9 L.Ed.2d 837 (1963), our disposition made it unnecessary to delve at length into the facts. The facts of the defendant's case there, however, paralleled those of his co-defendants, whose confessions were found to have resulted from continuous and coercive interrogation for 27 hours, with denial of requests for friends or attorney. See United States ex rel. *Caminito v. Murphy,* 222 F.2d 698 (C.A.2d Cir. 1955) (Frank, J.); *People v. Bonino,* 1 N.Y.2d 752, 152 N.Y.S.2d 298, 135 N.E. 2d 51 (1956).

defendant made oral admissions to the police after interrogation in the afternoon, and then signed an inculpatory statement upon being questioned by an assistant district attorney later the same evening. In No. 761, *Westover v. United States,* the defendant was handed over to the Federal Bureau of Investigation by local authorities after they had detained and interrogate him for a lengthy period, both at night and the following morning. After some two hours of questioning, the federal officers had obtained signed statements from the defendant. Lastly, in No. 584, *California v. Stewart,* the local police held the defendant five days in the station and interrogated him on nine separate occasions before they secured his inculpatory statement.

In these cases, we might not find the defendant's statements to have been involuntary in traditional terms. Our concern for adequate safeguards to protect precious Fifth Amendment rights is, of course, not lessened in the slightest. In each of the cases, the defendant was thrust into an unfamiliar atmosphere and run through menacing police interrogation procedures. The potentiality for compulsion is forcefully apparent, for example, in *Miranda,* where the indigent Mexican defendant was a seriously disturbed individual with pronounced sexual fantasies, and in *Stewart,* in which the defendant was an indigent Los Angeles Negro who had dropped out of school in the sixth grade. To be sure, the records do not evince overt physical coercion or patent psychological ploys. The fact remains that in none of these cases did the officers undertake to afford appropriate safeguards at the outset of the interrogation to insure that the statements were truly the product of free choice.

[11] It is obvious that such an interrogation environment is created for no purpose other than to subjugate the individual to the will of his examiner. This atmosphere carries its own badge of intimidation. To be sure, this is not physical intimidation, but it is equally destructive of human dignity.[26] The current practice of incommunicado interrogation is at odds with one of our Nation's most cherished principles—that the individual may not be compelled to incriminate himself. Unless adequate protective devices are employed to dispel the compulsion inherent in custodial surroundings, no statement obtained from the defendant can truly be the product of his free choice.

From the foregoing, we can readily perceive an intimate connection between the privilege against self-incrimination and police custodial questioning. It is fitting to turn to history and precedent underlying the Self-Incrimination Clause to determine its applicability in this situation.

II.

We sometimes forget how long it has taken to establish the privilege against self-incrimination, the sources from which it came and the fervor with which it was defended. Its roots go back into ancient times.[27] Perhaps the critical historical event shedding light on its origins and evolution was the trial of one John Lilburn, a vocal anti-Stuart Leveller, who was made to take the Star Chamber Oath in 1637. The oath would have bound him to answer all questions posed to him on any subject. The Trial of John Liburn and John Wharton, 3 How.St.Tr. 1315 (1637). He resisted the oath and declaimed the proceedings, stating:

> "Another fundamental right I then contended for, was, that no man's conscience ought to be racked by oaths imposed, to answer to questions concerning himself in matters criminal, or pretended to be so." Haller & Davies, The Leveller Tracts 1647–1653, p. 454 (1944).

On account of the Liburn Trial, Parliament abolished the inquisitorial Court of Star

_____

[26] The absurdity of denying that a confession obtained under these circumstances is compelled is aptly portrayed by an example in Professor Sutherland's recent article, Crime and Confession, 79 Harv.L. Rev. 21, 37 (1965):

> "Suppose a well-to-do testatrix says she intends to will her property to Elizabeth. John and James want her to bequeath it to them instead. They capture the testatrix, put her in a carefully designed room, out of touch with everyone but themselves and their convenient 'witnesses,' keep her secluded there for hours while they make insistent demands, weary her with contradictions of her assertions that she wants to leave her money to Elizabeth, and finally induce her to execute the will in their favor. Assume that John and James are deeply and correctly convinced that Elizabeth is unworthy and will make base use of the property if she gets her hands on it, whereas John and James have the noblest and most righteous intentions. Would any judge of probate accept the will so procured as the 'voluntary' act of the testatrix?"

[27] Thirteenth century commentators found an analogue to the privilege grounded in the Bible. "To sum up the matter, the principle that no man is to be declared guilty on his own admission is a divine decree." Maimonides, Mishneh Torah

Chamber and went further in giving him generous reparation. The lofty principles to which Liburn had appealed during his trial gained popular acceptance in England.[28] These sentiments worked their way over to the Colonies and were implanted after great struggle into the Bill of Rights.[29] Those who framed our Constitution and the Bill of Rights were ever aware of subtle encroachments on individual liberty. They knew that "illegitimate and unconstitutional practices get their first footing * * * by silent approaches and slight deviations from legal modes of procedure." *Boyd v. United States,* 116 U.S. 616, 635, 6 S.Ct. 524, 535, 29 L.Ed. 746 (1886). The privilege was elevated to constitutional status and has always been "as broad as the mischief against which it seeks to guard." *Counselman v. Hitchcock,* 142 U.S. 547, 562, 12 S.Ct. 195, 198, 35 L.Ed. 1110 (1892). We cannot depart from this noble heritage.

[12–15] Thus we may have view the historical development of the privilege as one which groped for the proper scope of governmental power over the citizen. As a "noble principle often transcends its origins," the privilege has come rightfully to be recognized in part as an individual's substantive right, a "right to a private enclave where he may lead a private life. That right is the hallmark of our democracy." *United States v. Grunewald,* 233 F.2d 556, 579, 581–582 (Frank, J., dissenting), rev'd, 353 U.S. 391, 77 S.Ct. 963, 1 L.Ed.2d 931 (1957). We have recently noted that the privilege against self-incrimination—the essential mainstay of our adversary system—is founded on a complex of values, *Murphy v. Waterfront Comm. of New York Harbor,* 378 U.S. 52, 55–57, n. 5, 84 S.Ct. 1594, 1596–1597, 12 L.Ed.2d 678 (1964); *Tehan v. United States ex rel. Shott,* 382 U.S. 406, 414–415, n. 12, 86 S.Ct. 459, 464, 15 L.Ed.2d 453 (1966). All these policies point to one overriding thought: the constitutional foundation underlying the privilege is the respect a government— state or federal—must accord to the dignity and integrity of its citizens. To maintain a "fair state-individual balance," to require the government "to shoulder the entire load," 8 Wigmore, Evidence 317 (McNaughton rev. 1961), to respect the inviolability of the human personality, our accusatory system of criminal justice demands that the government seeking to punish an individual produce the evidence against him by its own independent labors, rather than by the cruel, simple expedient against him by its

own independent labors, rather than by the cruel, simple expedient of compelling it from his own mouth. *Chambers v. State of Florida,* 309 U.S. 227, 235–238, 60 S.Ct. 472, 476–477, 84 L.Ed. 716 (1940). In sum, the privilege is fulfilled only when the person is guaranteed the right "to remain silent unless he chooses to speak in the unfettered exercise of his own will." *Malloy v. Hogan,* 378 U.S. 1, 8, 84 S.Ct. 1489, 1493, 12 L.Ed.2d 653 (1964).

[16] The question in these cases is whether the privilege is fully applicable during a period of custodial interrogation. In this Court, the privilege has consistently been accorded a liberal construction. *Albertson v. Subversive Activities Control Board,* 382 U.S. 70, 81, 86 S.Ct. 194, 200, 15 L.Ed.2d 165 (1965); *Hoffman v. United States,* 341 U.S. 479, 486, 71 S.Ct. 814, 818, 95 L.Ed.2d 1118 (1951); *Arnstein v. McCarthy,* 254 U.S. 71, 72–73, 41 S.Ct. 26, 65 L.Ed. 138 (1920); *Counselman v. Hitchcock,* 142 U.S. 547, 562, 12 S.Ct. 195, 197, 35 L.Ed. 1110 (1892). We are satisfied that all the principles embodied in the privilege apply to informal compulsion exerted by law-enforcement officers during in-custody questioning. An individual swept from familiar surroundings into police custody, surrounded by antagonistic forces, and subjected to the techniques of persuasion described above cannot be otherwise than under compulsion to speak. As a practical matter, the compulsion to speak in the isolated setting of the police station may well be greater than in courts or other official investigations, where there are often impartial observers to guard against intimidation or trickery."[30]

This question, in fact, could have been taken as settled in federal courts almost 70 years ago, when, in *Bram v. United States,* 168 U.S. 532,

---

(Code of Jewish Law), Book of Judges, Laws of the Sanhedrin, c. 18, ¶ 6, III Yale Judaica Series 52–53. See also Lamm, The Fifth Amendment and Its Equivalent in the Halakhah, 5 Judaism 53 (Winter 1956).

[28] See Morgan, The Privilege Against Self-Incrimination, 34 Minn.L.Rev. 1, 9–11 (1949); 8 Wigmore, Evidence 285–295 (McNaughton rev. 1961). See also Lowell, The Judicial Use of Torture, Parts I and II, 11 Harv.L.Rev. 220, 290 (1897).

[29] See Pittman, The Colonial and Constitutional History of the Privilege Against Self-Incrimination in America, 21 Va.L. Rev. 763 (1935); *Ullmann v. United States,* 350 U.S. 422, 445–449, 76 S.Ct. 497, 510–512, 100 L.Ed. 511 (1956) (Douglas, J., dissenting).

[30] Compare *Brown v. Walker,* 161 U.S. 591, 16 S.Ct. 644, 40 L.Ed. 819 (1896); *Quinn v. United States,* 349 U.S. 155, 75 S.Ct. 668, 99 L.Ed. 964 (1955).

542, 18 S.Ct. 183, 187, 42 L.Ed. 568 (1897), this Court held:

> "In criminal trials, in the courts of the United States, wherever a question arises whether a confession is incompetent because not voluntary, the issue is controlled by that portion of the fifth amendment * * * commanding that no person 'shall be compelled in any criminal case to be a witness against himself.'"

In *Bram,* the Court reviewed the British and American history and case law and set down the Fifth Amendment standard for compulsion which we implement today:

> "Much of the confusion which has resulted from the effort to deduce from the adjudged cases what would be a sufficient quantum of proof to show that a confession was or was not voluntary has arisen from a misconception of the subject to which the proof must address itself. The rule is not that, in order to render a statement admissible, the proof must be adequate to establish that the particular communications contained in a statement were voluntarily made, but it must be sufficient to establish that the making of the statement was voluntary; that is to say, that, from the causes which the law treats as legally sufficient to engender in the mind of the accused hope or fear in respect to the crime charged, the accused was not involuntarily impelled to make a statement when but for the improper influences he would have remained silent. * * *" 168 U.S., at 549, 18 S.Ct. at 189. And see, id., at 542, 18 S.Ct. at 186.

The Court has adhered to this reasoning. In 1924, Mr. Justice Brandeis wrote for a unanimous Court in reversing a conviction resting on a compelled confession, *Ziang Sung Wan v. United States,* 266 U.S. 1, 45 S.Ct. 1, 69 L.Ed. 131. He stated:

> "In the federal courts, the requisite of voluntariness is not satisfied by establishing merely that the confession was not induced by a promise or a threat. A confession is voluntary in law if, and only if, it was, in fact, voluntarily made. A confession may have been given voluntarily, although it was made to police officers, while in custody, and in answer to an examination conducted by them. But a confession obtained by compulsion must be excluded whatever may have been the character of the compulsion, and whether the compulsion was applied in a judicial proceeding or otherwise. *Bram v. United States,* 168 U.S. 532, 18 S.Ct. 183, 42 L.Ed. 568." 266 U.S., at 14–15, 45 S.Ct. at 3.

In addition to the expansive historical development of the privilege and the sound policies which have nurtured its evolution, judicial precedent thus clearly establishes its application to incommunicado interrogation. In fact, the Government concedes this point as well established in No. 761, *Westover v. United States,* stating: "We have no doubt * * * that it is possible for a suspect's Fifth Amendment right to be violated during in-custody questioning by a law-enforcement officer."[31]

[17] Because of the adoption by Congress of Rule 5(a) of the Federal Rules of Criminal Procedure, and the Court's effectuation of that Rule in *McNabb v. United States,* 318 U.S. 332, 63 S.Ct. 608, 87 L.Ed. 819 (1943), and *Mallory v. United States,* 354 U.S. 449, 77 S.Ct. 1356, 1 L.Ed.2d 1479 (1957), we have had little occasion in the past quarter century to reach the constitutional issues in dealing with federal interrogations. These supervisory rules, requiring production of an arrested person before a commissioner "without unnecessary delay" and excluding evidence obtained in default of that statutory obligation, were nonetheless responsive to the same considerations of Fifth Amendment policy that unavoidably face us now as to the States. In *McNabb,* 318 U.S., at 343–344, 63 S.Ct. at 614, and in *Mallory,* 354 U.S., at 455–456, 77 S.Ct. at 1359–1360, we recognized both the dangers of interrogation and the appropriateness of prophylaxis stemming from the very fact of interrogation itself.[32]

[18–20] Our decision in *Malloy v. Hogan,* 378 U.S. 1, 84 S.Ct. 1489, 12 L.Ed.2d 653 (1964), necessitates an examination of the scope of the privilege in state cases as well. In *Malloy,* we squarely held the privilege applicable to the States, and held that the substantive standards underlying the privilege applied with full force to state court proceedings. There, as in *Murphy v. Waterfront Comm. of New York Harbor,* 378 U.S. 52, 84 S.Ct. 1594, 12 L.Ed.2d 678 (1964), and *Griffin v. State of California,* 380 U.S. 609, 85 S.Ct. 1229, 14 L.Ed.2d 106

---

[31] Brief for the United States, p. 28. To the same effect, see Brief for the United States, pp. 40–49, n. 44, *Anderson v. United States,* 318 U.S. 350, 63 S.Ct. 599, 87 L.Ed. 829 (1943); Brief for the United States, pp. 17–18, *McNabb v. United States,* 318 U.S. 332, 63 S.Ct. 608 (1943).

[32] Our decision today does not indicate in any manner, of course, that these rules can be disregarded. When federal officials arrest an individual, they must as always comply with the dictates of the congressional legislation and cases thereunder. See generally, Hogan & Snee, The McNabb-Mallory Rule: Its Rise, Rationale and Rescue, 47 Geo.L.J.1 (1958).

(1965), we applied the existing Fifth Amendment standards to the case before us. Aside from holding itself, the reasoning in *Malloy* made clear what had already become apparent—that the substantive and procedural safeguards surrounding admissibility of confessions exacting, reflecting all the policies embedded in the privilege, 378 U.S., at 7–8, 84 S.Ct. at 1493.[33] The voluntariness doctrine in the state cases, as *Malloy* indicates, encompasses all interrogation practices which are likely to exert such pressure upon an individual as to disable him from making a free and rational choice.[34] The implications of this proposition were elaborated in our decision in *Escobedo v. State of Illinois*, 378 U.S. 478, 84 S.Ct. 1758, 12 L.Ed.2d 977, decided one week after *Malloy* applied the privilege to the States.

Our holding there stressed the fact that the police had not advised the defendant of his constitutional privilege to remain silent at the outset of the interrogation, and we drew attention to that fact at several points in the decision, 378 U.S., at 483, 485, 491, 84 S.Ct. at 1761, 1762, 1765. This was no isolated factor, but an essential ingredient in our decision. The entire thrust of police interrogation there, as in all the cases today, was to put the defendant in such an emotional state as to impair his capacity for rational judgment. The abdication of the constitutional privilege—the choice on his part to speak to the police—was not made knowingly or competently because of the failure to apprise him of his

rights; the compelling atmosphere of the in-custody interrogation, and not an independent decision on his part, cause the defendant to speak.

[21, 22] A different phase of the *Escobedo* decision was significant in its attention to the absence of counsel during the questioning. There, as in the cases today, we sought a protective device to dispel the compelling atmosphere of the interrogation. In *Escobedo*, however, the police did not relieve the defendant of the anxieties which they had created in the interrogation rooms. Rather, they denied his request for the assistance of counsel, 378 U.S., at 481, 488, 491, 84 S.Ct. at 1760, 1763, 1765.[35] This heightened his dilemma, and made his later statements the product of this compulsion. Cf. *Haynes v. State of Washington*, 373 U.S. 503, 514, 83 S.Ct. 1336, 1343 (1963). The denial of the defendant's request for his attorney thus undermined his ability to exercise the privilege—to remain silent if he chose or to speak without any intimidation, blatant or subtle. The presence of counsel, in all the cases before us today, would be the adequate protective device necessary to make the process of police interrogation conform to the dictates of the privilege. His presence would insure that statements made in the government-established atmosphere are not the product of compulsion.

It was in this manner that *Escobedo* explicated another facet of the pre-trial privilege, noted in many of the Court's prior decisions: the protection of rights at trial.[36] That counsel is

---

[33] The decision of this Court have guaranteed the same procedural protection for the defendant whether his confession was used in a federal or state court. It is now axiomatic that the defendant's constitutional rights have been violated if his conviction is based, in whole or in part, on an involuntary confession, regardless of its truth or falsity. *Rogers v. Richmond*, 365 U.S. 534, 544, 81 S.Ct. 735, 741, 5 L.Ed.2d 760 (1961); *Siang Sung Wan v. United States*, 266 U.S. 1, 45 S.Ct. 1, 69 L.Ed. 131 (1924). This is so even if there is ample evidence aside from the confession to support the conviction, e. g., *Malinski v. People of State of New York*, 324 U.S. 401, 404, 65 S.Ct. 781, 783, 89 L.Ed. 1029 (1945); *Bram v. United States*, 168 U.S. 532, 540–542, 18 S.Ct. 183, 185–186 (1897). Both state and federal courts now adhere to trial procedures which seek to assure a reliable and clear-cut determination of the voluntariness of the confession offered at trial, *Jackson v. Denno*, 378 U.S. 368, 84 S.Ct. 1774, 12 L.Ed.2d 904 (1964); *United States v. Carignan*, 342 U.S. 36, 38, 72 S.Ct. 97, 98, 96 L.Ed. 48 (1951); see also *Wilson v. United States*, 162 U.S. 613, 624, 16 S.Ct. 895, 900, 40 L.Ed. 1090 (1896). Appellate review is exacting, see *Haynes v. State of Washington*, 373 U.S. 503, 83 S.Ct. 1336, 10 L.Ed.2d 513 (1963); *Blackburn v. State of Alabama*, 361 U.S. 199, 80 S.Ct. 274, 4 L.Ed.2d 242 (1960). Whether his convic-

tion was in a federal or state court, the defendant may secure a post-conviction hearing based on the alleged involuntary character of his confession, provided he meets the procedural requirements, *Fay v. Noia*, 372 U.S. 391, 83 S.Ct. 822, 9 L.Ed.2d 837 (1963); *Townsend v. Sain*, 372 U.S. 293, 83 S.Ct. 745, 9 L.Ed.2d 770 (1963). In addition, see *Murphy v. Waterfront Comm. of New York Harbor*, 378 U.S. 52, 84 S.Ct. 1594 (1964).

[34] See *Lisenba v. People of State of California*, 314 U.S. 219, 241, 62 S.Ct. 280, 292, 86 L.Ed. 166 (1941); *Ashcraft v. State of Tennessee*, 322 U.S. 143, 64 S.Ct. 921, 88 L.Ed. 1192 (1944); *Malinski v. People of State of New York*, 324 U.S. 401, 65 S.Ct. 781 (1945); *Spano v. People of State of New York*, 360 U.S. 315, 79 S.Ct. 1202, 3 L.Ed.2d 1265 (1959); *Lynumn v. State of Illinois*, 372 U.S. 528, 83 S.Ct. 917, 9 L.Ed.2d 922 (1963); *Haynes v. State of Washington*, 373 U.S. 503, 83 S.Ct. 1336, 10 L.Ed.2d 513 (1963).

[35] The police also prevented the attorney from consulting with his client. Independent of any other constitutional proscription, this action constitutes a violation of the Sixth Amendment right to the assistance of counsel and excludes any statement obtained in its wake. See *People v. Donovan*, 13 N.Y.2d 148, 243 N.Y.S. 2d 841, 193 N.E.2d 628 (1963) (Fuld, J.).

present when statements are taken from an individual during interrogation obviously enhances the integrity of the fact-finding processes in court. The presence of an attorney, and the warnings delivered to the individual, enable the defendant under otherwise compelling circumstances to tell his story without fear, effectively, and in a way that eliminates the evils in the interrogation process. Without the protections flowing from adequate warning and the rights of the counsel, "all the careful safeguards erected around the giving of testimony, whether by an accused or any other witness, would become empty formalities in a procedure where the most compelling possible evidence of guilt, a confession, would have already been obtained at the unsupervised pleasure of the police." Mapp v. Ohio, 367 U.S. 643, 685, 81 S.Ct. 1684, 1707, 6 L.Ed.2d 1081 (1961) (Harlan, J., dissenting). Cf. *Pointer v. State of Texas*, 380 U.S. 400, 85 S.Ct. 1065, 13 L.Ed.2d 923 (1965).

III.

[23, 24] Today, then, there can be no doubt that the Fifth Amendment privilege is available outside of criminal court proceedings and serves to protect persons in all settings in which their freedom of action is curtailed in any significant way from being compelled to incriminate themselves. We have concluded that without proper safeguards the process of in-custody interrogation of persons suspected or accused of crime contains inherently compelling pressures which work to undermine the individual's will to resist and to compel him to speak where he would not otherwise do so freely. In order to combat these pressures and to permit a full opportunity to exercise the privilege against self-incrimination, the accused must be adequately and effectively apprised of his rights and the exercise of those rights must be fully honored.

It is impossible for us to foresee the potential alternatives for protecting the privilege which might be devised by Congress or the States in the exercise of their creative rule-making capacities. Therefore we cannot say that the Constitu-tion necessarily requires adherence to any particular solution for the inherent compulsions of the interrogation process as it is presently conducted. Our decision in no way creates a constitutional strait-jacket which will handicap sound efforts at reform, nor is it intended to have this effect. We encourage Congress and the States to continue their laudable search for increasingly effective ways of protecting the rights of the individual while promoting efficient enforcement of our criminal laws. However, unless we are shown other procedures which are at least as effective in apprising accused persons of their right of silence and in assuring a continuous opportunity to exercise it, the following safeguards must be observed.

[25–28] At the outset, if a person in custody is to be subjected to interrogation, he must first be informed in clear and unequivocal terms that he has the right to remain silent. For those unaware of the privilege, the warning is needed simply to make them aware of it—the threshold requirement for an intelligent decision as to its exercise. More important, such a warning is an absolute prerequisite in overcoming the inherent pressures of the interrogation atmosphere. It is not just the subnormal or woefully ignorant who succumb to an interrogator's imprecations, whether implied or expressly stated, that the interrogation will continue until a confession is obtained or that silence in the face of accusation is itself damning and will bode ill when presented to a jury.[37] Further, the warning will show the individual that his interrogators are prepared to recognize his privilege should he choose to exercise it.

[29] The Fifth Amendment privilege is so fundamental to our system of constitutional

---

[36] *In re Groban*, 352 U.S. 330, 340–352, 77 S.Ct. 510, 517–523, 1 L.Ed.2d 376 (1957) (Black, J., dissenting); Note, 73 Yale L.J. 1000, 1048–1051 (1964); Comment, 31 U.Chi.L.Rev. 313, 320 (1964) and authorities cited.

[37] See p. 1617, supra. Lord Devlin has commented:

"It is probable that even today, when there is much less ignorance about these matters than formerly, there is still a general belief that you must answer all questions put to you by a policeman, or at least that it will be the worse for you if you do not." Devlin, The Criminal Prosecution in England 32 (1958).

In accord with our decision today, it is impermissible to penalize an individual for exercising his Fifth Amendment privilege when he is under police custodial interrogation. The prosecution may not, therefore, use at trial the fact that he stood mute or claimed his privilege in the face of accusation. Cf. *Griffin v. State of California*, 380 U.S. 609, 85 S.Ct. 1229, 14 L.Ed.2d 106 (1965); *Malloy v. Hogan*, 378 U.S. 1, 8, 84 S.Ct. 1489, 1493, 12 L.Ed.2d 653 (1964); Comment, 31 U.Chi.L.Rev. 556 (1964); Developments in the Law—Confessions, 79 Harv.L.Rev. 935, 1041–1044 (1966). See also *Bram v. United States*, 168 U.S. 532, 562, 18 S.Ct. 183, 194, 42 L.Ed. 568 (1897).

U.S. SUPREME
COURT,
OCTOBER 1966

rule and the expedient of giving an adequate warning as to the availability of the privilege so simple, we will not pause to inquire in individual cases whether the defendant was aware of his rights without a warning being given. Assessments of the knowledge the defendant possessed, based on information as to his age, education, intelligence, or prior contact with authorities, can never be more than speculation;[38] a warning is a clearcut fact. More important, whatever the background of the person interrogated is indispensable to overcome its pressures and to insure that the individual knows he is free to exercise the privilege at that point in time.

[30] The warning of the right to remain silent must be accompanied by the explanation that anything said can and will be used against the individual in court. This warning is needed in order to make him aware not only of the privilege, but also of the consequences of forgoing it. It is only through an awareness of these consequences that there can be any assurance of real understanding and intelligent exercise of the privilege. Moreover, this warning may serve to make the individual more acutely aware that he is faced with a phase of the adversary system— that he is not in the presence of persons acting solely in his interest.

[31, 32] The circumstances surrounding incustody interrogation can operate very quickly to overbear the will of one merely made aware of his privilege by his interrogators. Therefore, the right to have counsel present at the interrogation is indispensable to the protection of the Fifth Amendment privilege under the system we delineate today. Our aim is to assure that the individual's right to choose between silence and speech remains unfettered throughout the interrogation process. A once-stated warning, delivered by those who will conduct the interrogation, delivered by those who will conduct the interrogation, cannot itself suffice to that end among those who most require knowledge of their rights. A mere warning given by the interrogators is not alone sufficient to accomplish that end. Prosecutors themselves claim that the admonishment of the right to remain silent

without more "will benefit only the recidivist and the professional." Brief for the National District Attorneys Association as *amicus curiae*, p. 14. Even preliminary advice given to the accused by his own attorney can be swiftly overcome by the secret interrogation process. Cf. *Escobedo v. State of Illinois*, 378 U.S. 478, 485, n. 5, 84 S.Ct. 1758, 1762. Thus, the need for counsel to protect the Fifth Amendment privilege comprehends not merely a right to consult with counsel prior to questioning, but also to have counsel present during any questioning if the defendant so desires.

The presence of counsel at the interrogation may serve several significant subsidiary functions as well. If the accused decides to talk to his interrogators, the assistance of counsel can mitigate the dangers of untrustworthiness. With a lawyer present the likelihood that the police will practice coercion is reduced, and if coercion is nevertheless exercised the lawyer can testify to it in court. The presence of a lawyer can also help to guarantee that the accused gives a fully accurate statement to the police and that statement is rightly reported by the prosecution at trial. See *Crooker v. State of California*, 357 U.S. 433, 443–448, 78 S.Ct. 1287, 1293–1296, 2 L.Ed.2d 1448 (1958) (Douglas, J., dissenting).

[33–35] An individual need not make a preinterrogation request for a lawyer. While such request affirmatively secures his right to have one, his failure to ask for a lawyer does not constitute a waiver. No effective waiver of the right to counsel during interrogation can be recognized unless specifically made after the warnings we here delineate have been given. The accused who does not know his rights and therefore does not make a request may be the person who most needs counsel. As the California Supreme Court has aptly put it:

> "Finally, we must recognize that the imposition of the requirement for the request would discriminate against the defendant who does not know his rights. The defendant who does not ask for counsel is the very defendant who most needs counsel. We cannot penalize a defendant who, not understanding his constitutional rights, does not make the formal request and by such failure demonstrates his helplessness. To require the request would be to favor the defendant whose sophistication or status had fortuitously prompted him to make it." *People v. Dorado*, 62 Cal.2d 338, 351, 42 Cal. Rptr. 169, 177–178, 398 P.2d 361, 369–370, (1965) (Tobriner, J.).

---

[38] Cf. *Betts v. Brady*, 316 U.S. 455, 62 S.Ct. 1252, 86 L.Ed. 1595 (1942), and the recurrent inquiry into special circumstances it necessitated. See generally, Kamisar, Betts v. Brady Twenty Years Later: The Right to Counsel and Due Process Values, 61 Mich.L.Rev. 219 (1962).

In *Carnley v. Cochran,* 369 U.S. 506, 513, 82 S.Ct. 884, 889, 8 L.Ed.2d 70 (1962), we stated: "[I]t is settled that where the assistance of counsel is a constitutional requisite, the right to be furnished counsel does not depend on a request." This proposition applies with equal force in the context of providing counsel to protect an accused's Fifth Amendment privilege in the face of interrogation.[39] Although the role of the counsel at trial differs from the role during interrogation, the differences are not relevant to the question whether a request is a prerequisite.

[36, 37] Accordingly we hold that an individual held for interrogation must be clearly informed that he has the right to consult with a lawyer and to have the lawyer with him during interrogation under the system for protecting the privilege we delineate today. As with the warnings of the right to remain silent and that anything stated can be used in evidence against him, this warning is an absolute prerequisite to interrogation. No amount of circumstantial evidence that the person may have been aware of this right will suffice to stand in its stead. Only through such a warning is there ascertainable assurance that the accused was aware of this right.

[38–40] If an individual indicates that he wishes the assistance of counsel before any interrogation occurs, the authorities cannot rationally ignore or deny his request on the basis that the individual does not have or cannot afford a retired attorney. The financial ability of the individual has no relationship to the scope of the rights involved here. The privilege against self-incrimination secured by the Constitution applies to all individuals. The need for counsel in order to protect the privilege exists for the indigent as well as the affluent. In fact, were we to limit these constitutional rights to those who can retain an attorney, our decisions today would be of little significance. The cases before us as well as the vast majority of confession cases with which we have dealt in the past involve those unable to retain counsel.[40] While authorities are not required to relieve the accused of his poverty, they have the obligation not to take advantage of indigence in the administration of justice.[41] Denial of counsel to the indigent at the time of interrogation while allowing an attorney to those who can afford one would be no more supportable by reason or logic than the similar situation at trial and on appeal struck down in *Gideon v. Wainwright,* 372 U.S. 335, 83 S.Ct. 792, 9 L.Ed.2d 799 (1963), and *Douglas v. People of State of California,* 372 U.S. 353, 83 S.Ct. 814, 9 L.Ed.2d 811 (1963).

[41, 42] In order fully to apprise a person interrogated of the extent of his rights under this system then, it is necessary to warn him not only that he has the right to consult with an attorney, but also that if he is indigent a lawyer will be appointed to represent him. Without this additional warning, the admonition of the right to consult with counsel would often be understood as meaning only that he can consult with a lawyer if he has one or has the funds to obtain one. The warning of a right to counsel would be hollow if not couched in terms that would convey to be indigent—the person most often subjected to interrogation—the knowledge that he too has a right to have counsel present.[42] As with the warnings of the right to remain silent and of the general right to counsel, only by effective and express explanation to the indigent of this right can there be assurance that he was truly in a position to exercise it.[43]

---

[39] See Herman, The Supreme Court and Restrictions on Police Interrogation, 25 Ohio St.L.J. 449, 480 (1964).

[40] Estimates of 50–90% indigency among felony defendants have been reported. Pollock, Equal Justice in Practice, 45 Minn.L.Rev. 737, 738–739 (1961); Birzon, Kasanof & Forma, The Right to Counsel and the Indigent Accused in Courts of Criminal Jurisdiction in New York State, 14 Buffalo L.Rev. 428, 433 (1965).

[41] See Kamisar, Equal Justice in the Gatehouses and Mansions of American Criminal Procedure, in Criminal Justice in Our Time 1, 64–81 (1965). As was stated in the Report of the Attorney General's Committee on Poverty and the Administration of Federal Criminal Justice 9 (1963):

"When government chooses to exert its powers in the criminal area, its obligation is surely no less than that of taking reasonable measures to eliminate those factors that are irrelevant to just

administration of the law but which, nevertheless, may occasionally affect determinations of the accused's liability or penalty. While government may not be required to relieve the accused of his poverty, it may properly be required to minimize the influence of poverty on its administration of justice."

[42] Cf. *United States ex rel. Brown v. Fay,* 242 F.Supp. 273, 277 (D.C.S.D.N.Y. 1965); *People v. Witenski,* 15 N.Y.2d 392, 259 N.Y.S.2d 413, 207 N.E.2d 358 (1965).

[43] While a warning that the indigent may have counsel appointed need not be given to the person who is known to have an attorney or is known to have ample funds to secure one, the expedient of giving a warning is too simple and the rights involved too important to engage in *ex post facto* inquiries into financial ability when there is any doubt at all on that score.

U.S. SUPREME
COURT,
OCTOBER 1966

[43–46] Once warnings have been given, the subsequent procedure is clear. If the individual indicates in any manner, at any time prior to or during questioning, that he wishes to remain silent, the interrogation must cease.[44] At this point he has shown that he intends to exercise his Fifth Amendment privilege; any statement taken after the person invokes his privilege cannot be other than the product of compulsion, subtle or otherwise. Without the right to cut off questioning, the setting of in-custody interrogation operates on the individual to overcome free choice in producing a statement after the privilege has been once invoked. If the individual states that he wants an attorney, the interrogation must cease until an attorney is present. At that time, the individual must have an opportunity to confer with the attorney and to have him present during any subsequent questioning. If the individual cannot obtain an attorney and he indicates that he wants one before speaking to police, they must respect his decision to remain silent.

[47, 48] This does not mean, as some have suggested, that each police station must have a "station house lawyer" present at all times to advise prisoners. It does mean, however, that if police propose to interrogate a person they must make known to him that he is entitled to a lawyer and that if he cannot afford one, a lawyer will be provided for him prior to any interrogation. If authorities conclude that they will not provide counsel during a reasonable period of time in which investigation in the field is carried out, they may refrain from doing so without violating the person's Fifth Amendment privilege so long as they do not question him during that time.

[49–51] If the interrogation continues without the presence of an attorney and a statement is taken, a heavy burden rests on the government to demonstrate that the defendant knowingly and intelligently waived his privilege against self-incrimination and his right to retained or appointed counsel. *Escobedo v. State of Illinois,* 378 U.S. 478, 490, n. 14, 84 S.Ct. 1758, 1764, 12 L.Ed.2d 977. This Court has always set high standards of proof for the waiver of constitutional rights, *Johnson v. Zerbst,* 304 U.S. 458, 58 S.Ct. 1019, 82 L.Ed. 1461 (1938), and we reassert these standards as applied to in-custody interrogation. Since the State is responsible for establishing the isolated circumstances under which the interrogation takes place and has the only means of making available corroborated evidence of warnings given during incommunicado interrogation, the burden is rightly on its shoulders.

[52–54] An express statement that the individual is willing to make a statement and does not want an attorney followed closely by a statement could constitute a waiver. But a valid waiver will not be presumed simply from the silence of the accused after warnings are given or simply from the fact that a confession was in fact eventually obtained. A statement we made in *Carnley v. Cochran,* 369 U.S. 506, 516, 82 S.Ct. 884, 890, 8 L.Ed.2d 70 (1962), is applicable here:

> "Presuming waiver from a silent record is impermissible. The record must show, or there must be an allegation and evidence which show, that an accused was offered counsel but intelligently and understandingly rejected the offer. Anything less is not waiver."

See also *Glasser v. United States,* 315 U.S. 60, 62 S.Ct. 457, 86 L.Ed. 680 (1942). Moreover, where in-custody interrogation is involved, there is no room for the contention that the privilege is waived if the individual answers some questions or gives some information on his own prior to invoking his right to remain silent when interrogated.[45]

[55–57] Whatever the testimony of the authorities as to waiver of rights by an accused, the fact of lengthy interrogation or incommunicado incarceration before a statement is made is strong evidence that the accused did not validly waive his rights. In these circumstances the fact that the individual eventually made a statement is consistent with the conclusion that the compelling influence of the interrogation finally forced him to do so. It is inconsistent with any

[44] If an individual indicates his desire to remain silent, but has an attorney present, there may be some circumstances in which further questioning would be permissible. In the absence of evidence of overbearing, statements then made in the presence of counsel might be free of the compelling influence of the interrogation process and might fairly be construed as a waiver of the privilege for purposes of these statements.

[45] Although this Court held in *Rogers v. United States,* 340 U.S. 367, 71 S.Ct. 438, 95 L.Ed. 344 (1951), over strong dissent, that a witness before a grand jury may not in certain circumstances decide to answer some questions and then refuse to answer others, that decision has no application to the interrogation situation we deal with today. No legislative or judicial fact-finding authority is involved here, nor is there a possibility that the individual might make self-serving statements of which he could make use at trial while refusing to answer incriminating statements.

U.S. SUPREME
COURT,
OCTOBER 1966

notion of a voluntary relinquishment of the privilege. Moreover, any evidence that the accused was threatened, tricked, or cajoled into a waiver will, of course, show that the defendant did not voluntarily waive his privilege. The requirement of warnings and waiver of rights is a fundamental with respect to the Fifth Amendment privilege and not simply a preliminary ritual to existing methods of interrogation.

[58–60] The warnings required and the waiver necessary in accordance with our opinion today are, in the absence of a fully effective equivalent, prerequisites to the admissibility of any statement made by a defendant. No distinction can be drawn between statements which are direct confessions and statements which amount to "admissions" of part or all of an offense. The privilege against self-incrimination protects the individual from being compelled to incriminate himself in any manner; it does not distinguish degrees of incrimination. Similarly, for precisely the same reason, no distinction may be drawn between inculpatory statements and statements alleged to be merely "exculpatory." If a statement made were in fact truly exculpatory it would, of course, never be used by the prosecution. In fact, statements merely intended to be exculpatory by the defendant are often used to impeach his testimony at trial or to demonstrate untruths in the statement given under interrogation and thus to prove guilty by implication. These statements are incriminating in any meaningful sense of the word and may not be used without the full warnings and effective waiver required for any other statement. In *Escobedo* itself, the defendant fully intended his accusation of another as the slayer to be exculpatory as to himself.

The principles announced today deal with the protection which must be given to the privilege against self-incrimination when the individual is first subjected to police interrogation while in custody at the station or otherwise deprived of his freedom of action in any significant way. It is at this point that our adversary system of criminal proceedings commences, distinguishing itself at the outset from the inquisitorial system recognized in some countries. Under the system of warnings we delineate today or under any other system which may be devised and found effective, the safeguards to be erected about the privilege must come into play at this point.

[61, 62] Our decision is not intended to hamper the traditional function of police officers in investigating crime. See *Escobedo v. State of Illinois,* 378 U.S. 478, 492, 84 S.Ct. 1758, 1765. When an individual is in custody on probable cause, the police may, of course, seek out evidence in the field to be used at trial against him. Such investigation may include inquiry of persons not under restraint. General on-the-scene questioning as to facts surrounding a crime or other general questioning of citizens in the fact-finding process is not affected by our holding. It is an act of responsible citizenship for individuals to give whatever information they may have to aid in law enforcement. In such situations the compelling atmosphere inherent in the process of in-custody interrogation is not necessarily present.[46]

[63–65] In dealing with statements obtained through interrogation, we do not purport to find all confessions inadmissible. Confessions remain a proper element in law enforcement. Any statement given freely and voluntarily without any compelling influences is, of course, admissible in evidence. The fundamental import of the privilege while an individual is in custody is not whether he is allowed to talk to the police without the benefit of warnings and counsel, but whether he can be interrogated. There is no requirement that police stop a person who enters a police station and states that he wishes to confess to a crime,[47] or a person who calls the police to offer a confession or any other statement he desires to make. Volunteered statements of any kind are not barred by the Fifth Amendment and their admissibility is not affected by our holding today.

[66, 67] To summarize, we hold that when an individual is taken into custody or otherwise deprived of his freedom by the authorities in any significant way and is subjected to questioning, the privilege against self-incrimination is jeop-

---

46 The distinction and its significance has been aptly described in the opinion of a Scottish court:

"In former times such questioning, if undertaken, would be conducted by police officers visiting the house or place of business of the suspect and there questioning him, probably in the presence of a relation or friend. However convenient the modern practice may be, it must normally create a situation very unfavorable to the suspect." *Chalmers v. H. M. Advocate,* [1954] Sess.Cas. 66, 78 (J.C.).

47 See *People v. Dorado,* 62 Cal.2d 338, 354, 42 Cal.Rptr. 169, 179, 398 P.2d 361, 371 (1965).

ardized. Procedural safeguards must be employed to protect the privilege and unless other fully effective means are adopted to notify the person of his right of silence and to assure that the exercise of the right will be scrupulously honored, the following measures are required. He must be warned prior to any questioning that he has the right to remain silent, that anything he says can be used against him in the court of law, that he has the right to the presence of an attorney, and that if he cannot afford an attorney one will be appointed for him prior to any questioning if he so desires. Opportunity to exercise these rights must be afforded to him throughout the interrogation. After such warnings have been given, and such opportunity afforded him, the individual may knowingly and intelligently waive these rights and agree to answer questions or make a statement. But unless and until such warnings and waiver are demonstrated by the prosecution at trial, no evidence obtained as a result of interrogation can be used against him.[48]

IV.

[68] A recurrent argument made in these cases is that society's need for interrogation outweighs the privilege. This argument is not unfamiliar to this Court. See, e. g., *Chambers v. State of Florida*, 309 U.S. 227, 240–241, 60 S.Ct. 472, 478–479, 84 L.Ed. 716 (1940). The whole thrust of our foregoing discussion demonstrates that the Constitution has prescribed the rights of the individual when confronted with the power of government when it provided in the Fifth Amendment that an individual cannot be compelled to be a witness against himself. That right cannot be abridged. As Mr. Justice Brandeis once observed:

"Decency, security, and liberty alike demand that government officials shall be subjected to the same rules of conduct that are commands to the citizen. In a government of laws, existence of the government will be imperilled if it fails to observe the law scrupulously. Our government is the potent, the omnipresent teacher. For good or for ill, it teaches the whole people by its example. Crime is contagious. If the government becomes a lawbreaker, it breeds contempt for law; it invites every man to become a law unto himself; it invites anarchy. To declare that in the administration of the criminal law the end justifies the means * * * would bring terrible retribution. Against that pernicious doctrine this court should resolutely set its

face." *Olmstead v. United States,* 227 U.S. 438, 485, 48 S.Ct. 564, 575, 72 L.Ed. 944 (1928) (dissenting opinion).[49]

In this connection, one of our country's distinguished jurists has pointed out: "The quality of a nation's civilization can be largely measured by the methods it uses in the enforcement of its criminal law."[50]

[69] If the individual desires to exercise his privilege, he has the right to do so. This is not for the authorities to decide. An attorney may advise his client not to talk to police until he has had an opportunity to investigate the case, or he may wish to be present with his client during any police questioning. In doing so an attorney is merely exercising the good professional judgment he has been taught. This is not cause for considering the attorney a menace to law enforcement. He is merely carrying out what he is sworn to do under his oath—to protect to the extent of his ability the rights of his client. In fulfilling this responsibility the attorney plays a vital role in the administration of criminal justice under our Constitution.

In announcing these principles, we are not unmindful of the burdens which law enforcement officials must bear, often under trying circumstances. We also fully recognize the obligation of all citizens to aid in enforcing the criminal laws. This Court, while protecting individual rights, has always given ample latitude to law enforcement agencies in the legitimate exercise of their duties. The limits we have placed on the interrogation process should not constitute an undue interference with a proper system of law enforcement. As we have noted, our decision does not in a way preclude police from carrying out their traditional investigatory functions. Although confessions may play an important role in some convictions, the cases before us present graphic examples of the overstatement of the "need" for confessions. In each case authorities conducted interrogations ranging up to five days in duration despite the presence,

---

[48] In accordance with our holdings today and in *Escobedo v. State of Illinois*, 378 U.S. 478, 492, 84 S.Ct. 1758, 1765; *Crooker v. State of California*, 357 U.S. 433, 78 S.Ct. 1287, 2 L.Ed.2d 1448 (1958) and *Cicenia v. La Gay*, 357 U.S. 504, 78 S.Ct. 1297, 2 L.Ed.2d 1523 (1958) are not to be followed.

[49] In quoting the above from the dissenting opinion of Mr. Justice Brandeis we, of course, do not intend to pass on the constitutional questions involved in the *Olmstead* case.

[50] Schaefer, Federalism and State Criminal Procedure, 70 Harv.L.Rev. 1, 26 (1956).

through standard investigating practices, of considerable evidence against each defendant.[51] Further examples are chronicled in our prior cases. See, e. g., *Haynes v. State of Washington*, 373 U.S. 503, 518–519, 83 S.Ct. 1336, 1345, 1346, 10 L.Ed.2d 513 (1963); *Rogers v. Richmond*, 365 U.S. 534, 541, 81 S.Ct. 735, 739, 5 L.Ed.2d 760 (1961); *Malinski v. People of State of New York*, 324 U.S. 401, 402, 65 S.Ct. 781, 782 (1945).[52]

It is also urged that an unfettered right to detention for interrogation should be allowed because it will often redound to the benefit of the person questioned. When police inquiry determines that there is no reason to believe that the person has committed any crime, it is said, he will be released without need for further formal procedures. The person who has committed no offense, however, will be better able to clear himself after warnings with counsel present than without. It can be assumed that in such circumstances a lawyer would advise his client to talk freely to police in order to clear himself.

Custodial interrogation, by contrast, does not necessarily afford the innocent an opportunity to clear themselves. A serious consequence of the present practice of interrogation alleged to be beneficial for the innocent is that many arrests "for investigation" subject large numbers of innocent persons to detention and interrogation. In one of the cases before us, No. 584, *California v. Stewart*, police held four persons,

who were in the defendant's house at the time of the arrest, in jail for five days until defendant confessed. At that time they were finally released. Police stated that there was "no evidence to connect them with any crime." Available statistics on the extent of this practice where it is condoned indicate that these four are far from alone in being subjected to arrest, prolonged detention, and interrogation without the requisite probable cause.[53]

Over the years the Federal Bureau of Investigation has compiled an exemplary record of effective law enforcement while advising any suspect or arrested person, at the outset of an interview, that he is not required to make a statement, that any statement may be used against him in court, that the individual may obtain the services of an attorney of his own choice and, more recently, that he has a right to free counsel if he is unable to pay.[54] A letter received from the Solicitor General is response to a question from the Bench makes it clear that the present pattern of warnings and respect for the rights of the individual followed as a practice by the FBI is consistent with the procedure which we delineate today. It states:

"At the oral argument of the above cause, Mr. Justice Fortas asked whether I could provide certain information as to the practices followed by the Federal Bureau of Investigation. I have directed these questions to the attention of the Director of the Federal Bureau of

---

[51] Miranda, Vignera, and Westover were identified by eyewitnesses. Marked bills from the bank robbed were found in Westover's car. Articles stolen from the victim as well as from several other robbery victims were found in Stewart's home at the outset of the investigation.

[52] Dealing as we do here with constitutional standards in relation to statements made, the existence of independent corroborating evidence produced at trial is, of course, irrelevant to our decisions. *Haynes v. State of Washington*, 373 U.S. 503, 518–519, 83 S.Ct. 1336, 1345–1346 (1963); *Lynumn v. State of Illinois*, 372 U.S. 528, 537–538, 83 S.Ct. 917, 922, 9 L.Ed.2d 922 (1963); *Rogers v. Richmond*, 365 U.S. 534, 541, 81 S.Ct. 735, 739 (1961); *Blackburn v. State of Alabama*, 361 U.S. 199, 206, 80 S.Ct. 274, 279, 4 L.Ed.2d 242 (1960).

[53] See, e. g., Report and Recommendations of the [District of Columbia] Commissioners' Committee on Police Arrests for Investigation (1962); American Civil Liberties Union, Secret Detention by the Chicago Police (1959). An extreme example of this practice occurred in the District of Columbia in 1958 . Seeking three "stocky" young Negroes who had robbed a restaurant, police rounded up 90 persons of that general description. Sixty-three were held overnight before being released for lack of evidence. A man not among the 90 arrested was ultimately charged with the crime. *Washington Daily News*, January 21, 1958, p. 5, col. 1; Hearings before a

Subcommittee of the Senate Judiciary Committee on H.R. 11477, S. 2970, S. 3325, and S. 3355, 85th Cong., 2d Sess. (July 1958), pp. 40, 78.

[54] In 1952, J. Edgar Hoover, Director of the Federal Bureau of Investigation, stated:

"Law enforcement, however, in defeating the criminal, must maintain inviolate the historic liberties of the individual. To turn back the criminal, yet, by so doing, destroy the dignity of the individual, would be a hollow victory.

* * * * *

"We can have the Constitution, the best laws in the land, and the most honest reviews by courts — but unless the law enforcement profession is stepped in the democratic tradition, maintains the highest in ethics, and makes its work a career of honor, civil liberties will continually — and without end — be violated. * * * The best protection of civil liberties is an alert, intelligent and honest law enforcement agency. There can be no alternative."

* * * * *

"* * * Special Agents are taught that any suspect or arrested person, at the outset of an interview, must be advised that he is not required to make a

Investigation and am submitting herewith a statement of the questions and of the answers which we have received."

"'(1) When an individual is interviewed by against of the Bureau, what warning is given to him?"

"'The standard warning long given by Special Agents of the FBI to both suspects and persons under arrest is that the person has a right to say nothing and a right to counsel, and that any statement he does make may be used against him in court. Examples of this warning are to be found in the *Westover* case at 342 F.2d 684 (1965), and *Jackson v. U.S.*, [119 U.S.App.D.C. 100] 337 F.2d 136 (1964), cert. den. 380 U.S. 935, 85 S.Ct. 1353,

"'After passage of the Criminal Justice Act of 1964, which provides free counsel for Federal defendants unable to pay, we added to our instructions to Special Agents the requirement that any person who is under arrest for an offense under FBI jurisdiction, or whose arrest is contemplated following the interview, must also be advised of his right to free counsel if he is unable to pay, and the fact that such counsel will be assigned by the Judge. At the same time, we broadened the right to counsel warning to read counsel of his own choice, or anyone else with whom he might wish to speak."

"'(2) When is the warning given?"

"The FBI warning is given to a suspect at the very outset of the interview, as shown in the *Westover* case, cited above. The warning may be given to a person arrested as soon as practicable after the arrest, as shown in the *Jackson* case, also cited above, and in *U.S. v. Konigsberg*, 336 F.2d 844 (1964), cert. den. [*Celso v. United States*] 379 U.S. 933 [85 S.Ct. 327, 13 L.Ed.2d 342] but in any event it must precede the interview with the person for a confession or admission of his own guilt."

"'(3) What is the Bureau's practice in the event that (a) the individual requests counsel and (b) counsel appears?"

"'When the person who has been warned of his right to counsel decides that he wishes to consult with counsel before making a statement, the interview is terminated at that point, *Schultz v. U.S.*, 351 F.2d 287 ([10 Cir.] 1965). It may be continued, however, as to all matters *other* than the person's own guilt or innocence. If he is indecisive in his request for counsel, there may be some question on whether he did or did not waive counsel. Situations of this kind must necessarily be left to the judgment of the interviewing Agent. For example, in *Hiram v. U.S.*, 354 F.2d 4 ([9 Cir.] 1965), the Agent's conclusion that the person arrested had waived his right to counsel was upheld by the courts.

"'A person being interviewed and desiring to consult counsel by telephone must be permitted to do so, as shown in *Caldwell v. U.S.*, 351 F.2d 459 ([1 Cir.] 1965). When counsel appears in person, he is permitted to confer with his client in private.'"

"'(4) What is the Bureau's practice if the individual requests counsel, but cannot afford to retain an attorney?'"

"'If any person being interviewed after warning of counsel decides that he wishes to consult with counsel before proceeding further the interview is terminated, as shown above. FBI Agents do not pass judgment on the ability of the person to pay for counsel. They do, however, advise those who have been arrested for an offense under FBI jurisdiction, or whose arrest is contemplated following the interview, of a right to free counsel *if* they are unable to pay, and the availability of such counsel from the Judge.'"[55]

[70] The practice of the FBI can readily be emulated by state and local enforcement agencies. The argument that the FBI deals with different crimes than are dealt with by state authorities does not mitigate the significance of the FBI experience.[56]

The experience in some other countries also suggests that the danger to law enforcement in curbs on interrogation is overplayed. The

---

statement and that any statement given can be used against him in court. Moreover, the individual must be informed that, if he desires, he may obtain the services of an attorney of his own choice."
Hoover, Civil Liberties and Law Enforcement: The Role of the FBI, 37 Iowa L. Rev. 175, 177–182 (1952).

[55] We agree that the interviewing agent must exercise his judgment in determining whether the individual waives his right to counsel. Because of the constitutional basis of the right, however, the standard for waiver is necessarily high.

And, of course, the ultimate responsibility for resolving this constitutional question lies with the courts.
[56] Among the crimes within the enforcement jurisdictions of the FBI are kidnapping, 18 U.S.C. § 1201 (1964 ed.), white slavery, 18 U.S.C. §§ 2421–2423 (1964 ed.), bank robbery, 18 U.S.C. § 2113 (1964 ed.), interstate transportation and sale of stolen property, 18 U.S.C. §§ 2311–2317 (1964 ed.), all manner of conspiracies, 18 U.S.C. § 371 (1964 ed.), and violation of civil rights, 18 U.S.C. §§ 241–242 (1964 ed.). See also 18 U.S.C. § 1114 (1964 ed.) (murder of officer or employee of the United States).

U.S. SUPREME
COURT,
OCTOBER 1966

English procedure since 1912 under the Judge's Rule is significant. As recently strengthened, the Rules require that a cautionary warning be given an accused by a police officer as soon as he has evidence that affords reasonable grounds for suspicion; they also require that any statement made be given by the accused without questioning by police.[57] The right of the individual to consult with an attorney during this period is expressly recognized.[58]

The safeguards present under Scottish law may be even greater than in England. Scottish judicial decisions bar use in evidence of most confessions obtained through police interrogation.[59] In India, confessions made to police not in the presence of a magistrate have been excluded by rule of evidence since 1872, at a time when it operated under British law.[60] Identical provisions appear in the Evidence Ordinance of Ceylon, enacted in 1895.[61] Similarly, in our country the Uniform Code of Military Justice has long provided that no suspect may be interrogated without first being warned of his right not to make a statement and that any statement he makes may be used against him.[62] Denial of the right to consult counsel during interrogation has also been proscribed by military tribunals.[63] There appears to have been no marked detrimental effect on criminal law enforcement in these jurisdictions as a result of these rules. Conditions of law enforcement in our country are sufficiently similar to permit reference to this experience as assurance that lawlessness will not result from warning an individual of his rights or allowing him to exercise them. Moreover, it is consistent with our legal system that we give at least as much protection to these rights as is given in the jurisdiction described. We deal in our country with rights grounded in a specific requirement of the Fifth Amendment of the Constitution, whereas other jurisdictions arrived at their conclusions on the basis of principles of justice not so specifically defined.[64]

[71–73] It is also urged upon us that we withhold decision on this issue until state legislative bodies and advisory groups have had an opportunity to deal with these problems by rule making.[65] We have already pointed out that the Constitution does not require any specific code of procedures for protecting the privilege against self-incrimination during custodial interrogation. Congress and the States are free to develop their own safeguards for the privilege, so long as they are fully as effective as those described above in informing accused persons of their right of silence and in affording a continuous opportunity to exercise it. In any event, however, the issues presented are of constitutional dimensions and must be determined by the courts. The admissibility of a statement in the face of a claim that it was obtained in viola-

---

[57] [1964] Crim.L.Rev., at 166–170. These Rules provide in part:

> "II. As soon as a police officer has evidence which would afford reasonable grounds for suspecting that a person has committed an offense, he shall caution that person or cause him to be cautioned before putting to him any questions, or further questions, relating to that offence."
>
> "The caution shall be in the following terms:
> 'You are not obliged to say anything unless you wish to do so but what you say may be put into writing and given in evidence.'"
>
> "When after being cautioned a person is being questioned, or elects to make a statement, a record shall be kept of the time and place at which any such questioning or statement began and ended and of the persons present."

* * * * *

> "III. * * *

* * * * *

> "(b) It is only in exceptional cases that questions relating to the offence should be put to the accused person after he has been charged or informed that he may be prosecuted.

* * * * *

> "IV. All written statements made after caution shall be taken in the following manner:"
>
> "(a) If a person says that he wants to make a statement he shall be told that it is intended to make a written record of what he says."
>
> "He shall always be asked whether he wishes to write down himself what he wants to say; if he says that he cannot write or that he would like someone to write it for him, a police officer may offer to write the statement for him." * * *
>
> "(b) Any person writing his own statement shall be allowed to do so without any prompting as distinct from indicating to him what matters are material."

* * * * *

> "(d) Whenever a police officer writes the statement, he shall take down the exact words spoken by the person making the statement, without putting any questions other than such as may be needed to make the statement coherent, intelligible and relevant to the material matters: he shall not prompt him."

The prior Rules appear in Devlin, The Criminal Prosecution in England 137–141 (1958).

tion of the defendant's constitutional rights is an issue the resolution of which has long since been undertaken by this Court. See *Hopt v. People of Territory of Utah,* 110 U.S. 574, 4 S.Ct. 202, 28 L.Ed. 262 (1884). Judicial solutions to problems of constitutional dimension have evolved decade by decade. As courts have been presented with the need to enforce constitutional rights, they have found means of doing so. That was our responsibility when *Escobedo* was before us and it is our responsibility today. Where rights secured by the Constitution are involved, there can be no rule making or legislation which would abrogate them.

V.

Because of the nature of the problem and because of its recurrent significance in numerous cases, we have to this point discussed the relationship of the Fifth Amendment privilege to police interrogation without specific concentration on the facts of the case before us. We turn now to these facts to consider the application to these cases of the constitutional principles discussed above. In each instance, we have concluded that statements were obtained from the defendant under circumstances that did not meet constitutional standards for protection of the privilege.

No. 759. *Miranda v. Arizona*

On March 13, 1963, petitioner, Ernesto Miranda, was arrested at his home and taken into custody to a Phoenix police station. He was there identified by the complaining witness. The police then took him to "Interrogation Room No. 2" of the detective bureau. There he was questioned by two police officers. The officers admitted at trial that Miranda was not advised that he had a right to have an attorney present.[66] Two hours later, the officers emerged from the interrogation room with a written confession signed by Miranda. At the top of the statement was a typed paragraph stating that the confession was made voluntarily, without threats or promises of immunity and "with full knowledge of my legal rights, understanding any statement I make may be used against me."[67]

At his trial before a jury, the written confession was admitted into evidence over the objection of defense counsel, and the officers testified to the prior oral confession made by Miranda during the interrogation. Miranda was found guilty of kidnapping and rape. He was sentenced to 20 to 30 years' imprisonment on each count, the sentences to run concurrently. On appeal, the Supreme Court of Arizona held that Miranda's constitutional rights were not violated in obtaining the confession and affirmed the conviction. 98 Ariz. 18, 401 P.2d 721. In reaching its decision, the court emphasized heavily the fact that Miranda did not specifically request counsel.

Despite suggestions of some laxity in enforcement of the Rules and despite the fact some discretion as to admissibility is invested in the trial judge, the Rules are a significant influence in the English criminal law enforcement system. See, *e. g.,* [1964] Crim.L.Rev., at 182; and articles collected in [1960] Crim.L.Rev., at 298–356.

[58] The introduction to the Judge's Rules states in part:
These Rules do not affect the principles

* * * * *

"(c) That every person at any stage of an investigation should be able to communicate and to consult privately with a solicitor. This is so even if he is in custody provided that in such a case no unreasonable delay or hindrance is caused to the processes of investigation or the administration of justice by his doing so. * * *" [1964] Crim.L.Rev., at 166–167.

[59] As stated by the Lord Justice General in *Chalmers v. H. M. Advocate,* [1954] Sess.Cas. 66, 78 (J.C.):
"The theory of our law is that at the stage of initial investigation the police may question anyone with a view to acquiring information which may lead to the detection of the criminal; but that, when the stage has been reached at which suspicion, or more than suspicion, has in their view centred upon

some person as the likely perpetrator of the crime, further interrogation of that person becomes very dangerous, and, if carried too far, *e. g.,* to the point of extracting a confession by what amounts to cross-examination, the evidence of that confession will almost certainly be excluded. Once the accused has been apprehended and charged he has the statutory right to a private interview with a solicitor and to be brought before a magistrate with all convenient speed so that he may, if so advised, emit a declaration in presence of his solicitor under conditions which safeguard him against prejudice."

[60] "No confession made to a police officer shall be proved as against a person accused of any offense." Indian Evidence Act § 25.
"No confession made by any person whilst he is in the custody of a police officer unless it be made in the immediate presence of a Magistrate, shall be proved as against such person." Indian Evidence Act § 26. See 1 Ramaswami & Rajagopalan, Law of Evidence in India 553–569 (1962). To avoid any continuing effect of police pressure or inducement, the Indian Supreme Court has invalidated a confession made shortly after police brought a suspect before a magistrate, suggesting: [I]t would, we think, be reasonable to insist upon giving an accused person at least 24 hours to

[74, 75] We reverse. From the testimony of the officers and by the admission of respondent, it is clear that Miranda was not in any way apprised of his right to consult with an attorney and to have one present during the interrogation, nor was his right not to be compelled to incriminate himself effectively protected in any other manner. Without these warnings the statements were inadmissible. The mere fact that he signed a statement which contained a typed-in clause stating that he had "full knowledge" of his "legal rights" does not approach the knowing and intelligent waiver required to relinquish constitutional rights. Cf. *Haynes v. State of Washington*, 373 U.S. 503, 512–513, 83 S.Ct. 1336, 1342, 10 L.Ed.2d 513 (1963); *Haley v. State of Ohio*, 332 U.S. 596, 601, 68 S.Ct. 302, 304, 92 L.Ed.224 (1948) (opinion of Mr. Justice Douglas).

No. 760 *Vignera v. New York*.

Petitioner, Michael Vignera, was picked up by New York police on October 14, 1960, in connection with the robbery three days earlier of a Brooklyn dress shop. They took him to the 17th Detective Squad headquarters in Manhattan. Sometime thereafter he was taken to the 66th Detective Squad. There a detective questioned Vignera with respect to the robbery. Vignera orally admitted the robbery to the detective. The detective was asked on cross-examination at trial by defense counsel whether Vignera was warned of his right to counsel before being interrogated. The prosecution objected to the question and the trial judge sustained the objection. Thus, the defendant was precluded from making any showing that warnings had not been given. While at the 66th Detective Squad, Vignera was identified by the store owner and a saleslady as the man who robbed the dress shop. At about 3 p.m. he was formally arrested. The police then transported him to still another station, the 70th Precinct in Brooklyn, "for detention." At 11 p.m. Vignera was questioned by an assistant district attorney in the presence of a hearing reporter who transcribed the questions and Vignera's answers. This verbatim account of these proceedings contains no statement of any warnings given by the assistant district attorney. At Vignera's trial on charge of first degree robbery, the detective testified as to the oral confession. The transcription of the statement taken was also introduced in evidence. At the conclusion of the testimony, the trial judge charged the jury in part as follows:

> "The law doesn't say that the confession is void or invalidated because the police officer didn't advise the defendant as to his rights. Did you hear what I said? I am telling you what the law of the State of New York is."

Vignera was found guilty of first degree robbery. He was subsequently adjudged a third-felony offender and sentenced to 30 to 60 years' imprisonment.[68] The conviction was affirmed without opinion by the Appellate Division, Second Department, 21 A.D.2d 752, 252 N.Y.S.2d 19, and by the Court of Appeals, also without opinion, 15 N.Y.2d 970, 259 N.Y.S.2d 857, 207 N.E.2d 527, remittitur amended, 16 N.Y.2d 614, 261 N.Y.S.2d 65, 209 N.E.2d 110. In argument to the Court of Appeals, the State contended that Vignera had no constitutional right to be advised of his right to counsel or his privilege against self-incrimination.

[76] We reverse. The foregoing indicates that Vignera was not warned of any of his rights

---

decide whether or not he should make a confession." *Sarwan Singh v. State of Punjab*, 44 All India Rep. 1957, Sup.Ct. 637, 644.

[61] I Legislative Enactments of Ceylon 211 (1958).

[62] 10 U.S.C. § 831(b) (1964 ed.).

[63] *United States v. Rose*, 24 CMR 251 (1957); *United States v. Gunnels*, 23 CMR 354 (1957).

[64] Although no constitution existed at the time confessions were excluded by rule of evidence in 1872, India now has a written constitution which includes the provision that "No person accused of any offence shall be compelled to be a witness against himself." Constitution of India, Article 20(3). See Tope, The Constitution of India 63–67 (1960).

[65] Brief for United States in No. 761, *Westover v. United States*, pp. 44–47; Brief for the State of New York as *amicus curiae*, pp. 35–39. See also Brief for the National District Attorneys Association as *amicus curiae*, pp. 23–26.

[66] Miranda was also convicted in a separate trial on an unrelated robbery charge not presented here for review. A statement introduced at that trial was obtained from Miranda during the same interrogation which resulted in the confession involved here. At the robbery trial, one officer testified that during the interrogation he did not tell Miranda that anything he said would be held against him or that he could consult with an attorney. The other officer stated that they had both told Miranda that anything he said would be used against him and that he was not required by law to tell them anything.

[67] One of the officers testified that he read this paragraph to Miranda. Apparently, however, he did not do so until after Miranda had confessed orally.

[68] Vignera thereafter successfully attacked the validity of one of the prior convictions, *Vignera v. Wilkins*, Civ. 9901 (D.C.W.D. N.Y. Dec. 31, 1961) (unreported), but was then resentenced as a second-felony offender to the same term of imprisonment as the original sentence. R. 31–33.

before the questioning by the detective and by the assistant district attorney. No other steps were taken to protect these rights. Thus he was not effectively apprised of his Fifth Amendment privilege or of his right to have counsel present and his statements are inadmissible.

No. 761. *Westover v. United States.*

At approximately 9:45 p.m. on March 20, 1963, petitioner, Carl Calvin Westover, was arrested by local police in Kansas City as a suspect in to Kansas City robberies. A report was also received from the FBI that he was wanted on a felony charge in California. The local authorities took him to a police station and placed him in a line-up on the local charges, and at about 11:45 p.m. he was booked. Kansas City police interrogated Westover on the night of his arrest. He denied any knowledge of criminal activities. The next day local officers interrogated him again throughout the morning. Shortly before noon they informed the FBI that they were through interrogating Westover and that the FBI could proceed to interrogate him. There is nothing in the record to indicate that Westover was ever given any warning as to his rights by local police. At noon, three special agents of the FBI continued the interrogation in a private interview room of the Kansas City Police Department, this time with respect to the robbery of a savings and loan association and bank in Sacramento, California. After two or two and one-half hours, Westover signed separate confessions to each of these two robberies which had been prepared by one of the agents during the interrogation. At trial one of the agents testified, and a paragraph on each of the statements states, that the agents advised Westover that he did not have to make a statement, that any statement he made could be used against him, and that he had the right to see an attorney.

[77, 78] Westover was tried by a jury in federal court and convicted of the California robberies. His statements were introduced at trial. He was sentenced to 15 years' imprisonment on each count, the sentences to run consecutively. On appeal, the conviction was affirmed by the Court of Appeals for the Ninth Circuit. 342 F.2d 684.

We reverse. On the facts of this case we cannot find that Westover knowingly and intelligently waived his right to remain silent and his right to consult with counsel prior to the time he made the statement.[69] At the time the FBI agents began questioning Westover, he had been in custody for over 14 hours and had been interrogated at length during that period. The FBI interrogation began immediately upon the conclusion of the interrogation by Kansas City police and was conducted in local police headquarters. Although the two law enforcement authorities are legally distinct and the crimes for which they interrogated Westover were different, the impact on him was that of a continuous period of questioning. There is no evidence of an articulated waiver of rights after the FBI commenced its interrogation. The record simply shows that the defendant did in fact confess a short time after being turned over to the FBI following interrogation by local police. Despite the fact that the FBI agents gave warnings at the outset of their interview, from Westover's point of view the warnings came at the end of the interrogation process. In these circumstances an intelligent waiver of constitutional rights cannot be assumed.

[79] We do not suggest that law enforcement authorities precluded from questioning any individual who has been held for a period of time by other authorities and interrogated by them without appropriate warnings. A different case would be presented if an accused were taken into custody by the second authority, removed both in time and place from his original surroundings, and then adequately advised of his rights and given an opportunity to exercise them. But here the FBI interrogation was conducted immediately following the state interrogation in the same police station—in the same compelling surroundings. Thus, in obtaining a confession from Westover the federal authorities were the beneficiaries of the pressure applied by the local in-custody interrogation. In these circumstances the giving of warnings alone was not sufficient to protect the privilege.

No. 584. *California v. Stewart.*

---

[69] The failure of defense counsel to object to the introduction of the confession at trial, noted by the Court of Appeals and emphasized by the Solicitor General, does not preclude our consideration of the issue. Since the trial was held prior to our decision in *Escobedo* and, of course, prior to our decision today making the objection available, the failure to object at trial does not constitute a waiver of the claim. See, e. g., *United States ex rel. Angelet v. Fay*, 333 F.2d 12, 16 (C.A.2d Cir. 1964), aff'd, 381 U.S. 654, 85 S.Ct. 1750, 14 L.Ed.2d 625 (1965). Cf. *Ziffrin, Inc. v. United States*, 318 U.S. 73, 78, 63 S.Ct. 465, 87 L.Ed. 621 (1943).

In the course of investigating a series of purse-snatch robberies in which one of the victims had died of injuries inflicted by her assailant, respondent, Roy Allen Stewart, was pointed out to Los Angeles police as the endorser of dividend checks taken in one of the robberies. At about 7:15 p.m., January 31, 1963, police officers went to Stewart's house and arrested him. One of the officers asked Stewart if they could search the house, to which he replied, "Go ahead." The search turned up various items taken from the robbery victims. At the time of Stewart's arrest, police also arrested Stewart's wife and three other persons who were visiting him. These four were jailed along with Stewart and were interrogated. Stewart was taken to the University Station of the Los Angeles Police Department where he was placed in a cell. During the next five days, police interrogated Stewart on nine different occasions. Except during the first interrogation session, when he was confronted with an accusing witness, Stewart was isolated with his interrogators.

During the ninth interrogation session, Stewart admitted that he had robbed the deceased and stated that he had not meant to hurt her. Police then brought Stewart before a magistrate for the first time. Since there was no evidence to connect them with any crime, the police then released the other four persons arrested with him.

Nothing in the record specifically indicates whether Stewart was or was not advised of his right to remain silent or his right to counsel. In a number of instances, however, the interrogating officers were asked to recount everything that was said during the interrogations. None indicated that Stewart was ever advised of his rights.

[80] Stewart was charged with kidnapping to commit robbery, rape, and murder. At his trial, transcripts of the first interrogation and the confession at the last interrogation were introduced in evidence. The jury found Stewart guilty of robbery and first degree murder and fixed the penalty as death. On appeal, the Supreme Court of California reversed. 62 Cal.2d 571, 43 Cal.Rptr. 201, 400 P.2d 97. It held that under this Court's decision in *Escobedo*, Stewart should have been advised of his right to remain silent and of his right to counsel and that it would not presume in the face of a silent record that the police advised Stewart of his rights.[70]

[81, 82] We affirm.[71] In dealing with custodial interrogation, we will not presume that a defendant has been effectively apprised of his rights and that his privilege against self-incrimination has been adequately safeguarded on a record that does not show that any warnings have been given or that any effective alternative has been employed. Nor can a knowing and intelligent waiver of these rights be assumed on a silent record. Furthermore, Stewart's steadfast denial of the alleged offenses through eight of the nine interrogations over a period of five days is subject to no other construction than that he was compelled by persistent interrogation to forgo his Fifth Amendment privilege.

Therefore, in accordance with this foregoing, the judgments of the Supreme Court of Arizona in No. 759, of the New York Court of Appeals in No. 760, and of the Court of Appeals for the Ninth Circuit in No. 761 are reversed. The judgment of the Supreme Court of California in No. 584 is affirmed. It is so ordered.

Judgments of Supreme Court of Arizona in No. 759, of New York Court of Appeals in No. 760, and of the Court of Appeals for the Ninth Circuit in No. 761 reversed.

Judgment of Supreme Court of California in No. 584 affirmed.

Mr. Justice Clark, dissenting in Nos. 759, 760, and 761, and concurring in the result in No. 584.

It is with regret that I find it necessary to write in these cases. However, I am unable to join the majority because its opinion goes too far on too little, while my dissenting brethren do not go quite far enough. Nor can I join in the

---

[70] Because of this disposition of the case, the California Supreme Court did not reach the claims that the confession was coerced by police threats to hold his ailing wife in custody until he confessed, that there was no hearing as required by *Jackson v. Denno,* 378 U.S. 368, 84 S.Ct. 1774, 12 L.Ed.2d 908 (1964), and that the trial judge gave an instruction condemned by the California Supreme Court's decision in *People v. Morse,* 60 Cal.2d 631, 36 Cal. Rptr. 201, 388 P.2d 33 (1964).

[71] After certiorari granted in this case, respondent moved to dismiss on the ground that there was no final judgment from which the State could appeal since the judgment below directed that he be retried. In the event respondent was successful in obtaining an acquittal on retrial, however, under California law the State would have no appeal. Satisfied that in these circumstances the decision below constituted a final judgment under 28 U.S.C. § 1257(3) (1964 ed.), we denied the motion. 383 U.S. 903, 86 S.Ct. 885.

U.S. SUPREME
COURT,
OCTOBER 1966

Court's criticism of the present practices of police and investigatory agencies as to custodial interrogation. The materials it refers to as "police manuals"[1] are, as I read them, merely writings in this field by professors and some police officers. Not one is shown by the record here to be the official manual of any police department, much less in universal use in crime detection. Moreover the examples of police brutality mentioned by Court[2] are rare exceptions to the thousands of cases that appear every year in the law reports. The police agencies—all the way from municipal and state forces to the federal bureaus—are responsible for law enforcement and public safety in this country. I am proud of their efforts, which in my view are not fairly characterized by the Court's opinion.

I.

The *ipse dixit* of the majority has no support in our cases. Indeed, the Court admits that "we might not find the defendant's statements [here] to have been involuntary in traditional terms." Ante, p. 1618. In short, the Court has added more to the requirements that the accused is entitled to consult with his lawyer and that he must be given the traditional warning that he may remain silent and that anything he says may be used against him. *Escobedo v. State of Illinois,* 378 U.S. 478, 490–491, 84 S.Ct. 1758, 1764–1765, 12 L.Ed.2d 977 (1964). Now, the Court fashions a constitutional rule that the police may engage in no custodial interrogation without additionally advising the accused that he has a right under the Fifth Amendment to the presence of counsel during interrogation and that, if he is without funds, counsel will be furnished him. When at any point during an interrogation the accused seeks affirmatively or impliedly to invoke his rights to silence or counsel, interrogation must be forgone or postponed. The Court further holds that failure to follow the new procedures requires inexorably the exclusion of any statement by the accused, as well as the fruits thereof. Such a strict constitutional specific inserted at the nerve center of crime detection may well kill the patient.[3] Since there is at this time a paucity of information and an almost total lack of empirical knowledge on the practical operation of requirements truly comparable to those announced by the majority, I would be more restrained lest we go too far too fast.

II.

Custodial interrogation has long been recognized as "undoubtedly an essential tool in effective law enforcement." *Haynes v. State of Washington,* 373 U.S. 503, 515, 83 S.Ct. 1336, 1344, 10 L.Ed.2d 513 (1963). Recognition of this fact should put us on guard against the promulgation of doctrinaire rules. Especially is this true where the Court finds that "the Constitution has prescribed" its holding and where the light of our past cases, from *Hopt v. People of Territory of Utah,* 110 U.S. 574, 4 S.Ct. 202, 28 L.Ed. 262 (1884), down to *Haynes v. State of Washington,* supra, is to the contrary. Indeed, even in *Escobedo* the Court never hinted that an affirmative "waiver" was a prerequisite to questioning; that the burden of proof as to waiver was on

---

[1] *E.g.,* Inbau & Reid, Criminal Interrogation and Confessions (1962); O'Hara, Fundamentals of Criminal Investigation (1956); Dienstein, Technics for the Crime Investigator (1952); Mulbar, Interrogation (1951); Kidd, Police Interrogation (1940).

[2] As developed by my Brother Harlan, post, pp. 1644–1649, such cases, with the exception of the long-discredited decision in *Bram v. United States,* 168 U.S. 532, 18 S.Ct. 183, 42 L.Ed. 568 (1897), were adequately treated in terms of due process.

[3] The Court points to England, Scotland, Ceylon and India as having equally rigid rules. As my Brother Harlan points out, post, pp. 1652–1653, the Court is mistaken in this regard, for it overlooks counterbalancing prosecutorial advantages. Moreover, the requirements of the Federal Bureau of Investigation do not appear from the Solicitor General's letter, ante, pp. 1633–1634, to be as strict as those imposed today in at least two respects: (1) The offer of counsel is articulated only as "a right to counsel," nothing is said about a right to have counsel present at the custodial interrogation. (See also the examples cited by the Solicitor General,

Westover v. United States, 342 F.2d 684, 685 (9 Cir., 1965) ("right to consult counsel"); *Jackson v. United States,* 119 U.S.App.D.C. 100, 337 F.2d 136, 138 (1964) (accused "entitled to an attorney").) Indeed, the practice is that whenever the suspect "decides that he wishes to consult with counsel before making a statement, the interview is terminated at that point. * * * When counsel appears in person, he is permitted to confer with his client in private." This clearly indicates that the FBI does not warn that counsel may be present during custodial interrogation. (2) The Solicitor General's letter states: "[T]hose who have been arrested for an offense under FBI jurisdiction, or whose arrest is contemplated following the interview, [are advised] of a right to free counsel *if* they are unable to pay, and the availability of such counsel from the Judge." So phrased, this warning does not indicate that the agent will secure counsel. Rather, the statement may well be interpreted by the suspect to mean that the burden is placed upon himself and that he may have counsel appointed only when brought before the judge or at trial — but not at custodial interrogation. As I view the FBI practice, it is not as broad as the one laid down today by the Court.

the prosecution; that the presence of counsel—absent a waiver—during interrogation was required; that a waiver can be withdrawn at the will of the accused; that counsel must be furnished during an accusatory stage to those unable to pay; nor that admissions and exculpatory statements are "confessions." To require all those things at one gulp should cause the Court to choke over more cases than *Crooker v. State of California,* 357 U.S. 433, 78 S.Ct. 1287, 2 L.Ed.2d 1448 (1958), and *Cicenia v. La Gay,* 357 U.S. 504, 78 S.Ct. 1297, 2 L.Ed.2d 1523 (1958), which it expressly overrules today.

The rule prior to today—as Mr. Justice Goldberg, the author of the Court's opinion in *Escobedo,* stated it in *Haynes v. Washington*—depended upon "a totality of circumstances evidencing an involuntary * * * admission of guilt." 373 U.S., at 514, 83 S.Ct. at 1343. And he concluded:

> "Of course, detection and solution of crime is, at best, a difficult and arduous task requiring determination and persistence on the part of all responsible officers charged with the duty of law enforcement. And, certainly, we do not mean to suggest that all interrogation of witnesses and suspects is impermissible. Such questioning is undoubtedly an essential tool in effective law enforcement. The line between proper and permissible police conduct and techniques and methods offensive to due process is, at best, a difficult one to draw, particularly in cases such as this where it is necessary to make fine judgments as to the effect of psychologically coercive pressures and inducements on the mind and will of an accused. * * * We are here impelled to the conclusion, from all of the facts presented, that the bounds of due process have been exceeded." Id., at 514–515, 83 S.Ct. at 1344.

III.

I would continue to follow that rule. Under the "totality of circumstances" rule of which my Brother Goldberg spoke in *Haynes,* I would consider in each case whether the police officer prior to custodial interrogation added the warning that the suspect might have counsel present at the interrogation and, further, that a court would appoint one at his request if he was too poor to employ counsel. In the absence of warnings, the burden would be on the State to prove that counsel was knowingly and intelligently waived or that in the totality of the circumstances, includ-

ing the failure to give the necessary warnings, the confession was clearly voluntary.

Rather than employing the arbitrary Fifth Amendment rule[4] which the Court lays down I would follow the more pliable dictates of the Due Process Clauses of the Fifth and Fourteenth Amendments which we are accustomed to administrating and which we know from our cases are effective instruments in protecting persons in police custody. In this way we would not be acting in the dark nor in one full sweep changing the traditional rules of custodial interrogation which this Court has for so long recognized as a justifiable and proper tool in balancing individual rights against the rights of society. It will be soon enough to go further when we are able to appraise with somewhat better accuracy the effect of such a holding.

I would affirm the conviction in *Miranda v. Arizona,* No. 759; *Vignera v. New York,* No. 760; and *Westover v. United States,* No. 761. In each of those cases I find from the circumstances no warrant of reversal. In *California v. Stewart,* No. 584, I would dismiss the writ of certiorari for want of a final judgment, 28 U.S.C. § 1257(3) (1964 ed.); but if the merits are to be reached I would affirm on the ground that the State failed to fulfill its burden, in the absence of a showing that appropriate warnings were given, of proving a waiver or a totality of circumstances showing voluntariness. Should there be a retrial, I would leave the State free to attempt to prove these elements.

Mr. Justice Harlan, whom Mr. Justice Stewart and Mr. Justice White join, dissenting.

I believe the decision of the Court represents poor constitutional law and entails harmful consequences for the country at large. How serious these consequences may prove to be only time can tell. But the basic flaws in the Court's justification seem to me readily apparent now once all sides of the problem are considered.

I. INTRODUCTION

At the outset, it is well to note exactly what is required by the Court's new constitutional code of rules for confessions. The foremost require-

---

[4] In my view there is "no significant support" in our cases for the holding of the Court today that the Fifth Amendment privilege, in effect, forbids custodial interrogation. For a discussion of this point see the dissenting opinion of my Brother White, post, pp. 1655–1657.

ment, upon which later admissibility of a confession depends, is that a fourfold warning be given to a person in custody before he is questioned, namely, that he has a right to remain silent, that anything he says may be used against him, that he has a right to have present an attorney during the questioning, and that if indigent he has a right to a lawyer without charge. To forgo these rights, some affirmative statement of rejection is seemingly required, and threats, tricks, or cajolings to obtain this waiver are forbidden. If before or during questioning the suspect seeks to invoke his right to remain silent, interrogation must be forgone or cease; a request for counsel brings about the same result until a lawyer is produced. Finally, there are a miscellany of minor directives, for example, the burden of proof of waiver is on the State, admissions and exculpatory statements are treated just like confessions, withdrawal of a waiver is always permitted, and so forth.[1]

While the fine points of this scheme are far less clear than the Court admits, the tenor is quite apparent. The new rules are not designed to guard against police brutality or other unmistakably banned forms or coercion. Those who use third-degree tactics and deny them in court are equally able and destined to lie as skillfully about warnings and waivers. Rather, the thrust of the new rules is to negate all pressures, to reinforce the nervous or ignorant suspect, and ultimately to discourage any confession at all. The aim in short is toward "voluntariness" in a utopian sense, or to view it from a different angle, voluntariness with a vengeance.

To incorporate this notion into the Constitution requires a strained reading of history and precedent and a disregard of the very pragmatic concerns that alone may on occasion justify such strains. I believe that reasoned examination will show that the Due Process Clauses provide an adequate tool for coping with confessions and that, even if the Fifth Amendment privilege against self-incrimination be invoked, its precedents taken as a whole do not sustain the present rules. Viewed as a choice based on pure policy, these new rules prove to be a highly debatable, if not one-sided, appraisal of the competing interests, imposed over widespread objection, at the very time when judicial restraint is most called for by the circumstances.

II. CONSTITUTIONAL PREMISES

It is most fitting to begin in inquiry into the constitutional precedents by surveying the limits on confessions the Court has evolved under the Due Process Clause of the Fourteenth Amendment. This is so because these cases show that there exists a workable and effective means of dealing with confessions in a judicial manner; because the cases are the baseline from which the Court now departs and so serve to measure the actual as opposed to the professed distance it travels; and because examination of them helps reveal how the Court has coasted into its present position.

The earliest confession cases in this Court emerged from federal prosecutions and were settled on a nonconstitutional basis, the Court adopting the common-law rule that the absence of inducements, promises, and threats made a confession voluntary and admissible. *Hopt v. People of Territory of Utah,* 110 U.S. 574, 4 S.Ct. 202, 28 L.Ed. 262; *Pierce v. United States,* 160 U.S. 355, 16 S.Ct. 321, 40 L.Ed. 454. While a later case said the Fifth Amendment privilege controlled admissibility, this proposition was not itself developed in subsequent decisions.[2] The Court did, however, heighten the test of admissibility in federal trials to one of voluntariness "in fact," *Ziang Sung Wan v. United States,* 266 U.S. 1, 14, 45 S.Ct. 1, 3, 69 L.Ed. 131 (quoted, ante, p. 1621), and then by and large left federal judges to apply the same standards the Court began to drive in a string of state court cases.

---

[1] My discussion in this opinion is directed to the main questions decided by the Court and necessary to its decision; in ignoring some of the collateral points, I do not mean to imply agreement.

[2] The case was *Bram v. United States,* 168 U.S. 532, 18 S.Ct. 183, 42 L.Ed. 568 (quoted, ante, p. 1621). Its historical premises were afterwards disproved by Wigmore, who concluded "that no assertions could be more unfounded." 3 Wigmore, Evidence § 823, at 250, n. 5 (3d ed. 1940). The Court in *United States v. Carignan,* 342 U.S. 36, 41, 72 S.Ct. 97, 100, 96 L.Ed. 48, declined to choose between *Bram* and Wigmore, and *Stein v. People of State of New York,* 346 U.S. 156, 191, n. 35, 73 S.Ct. 1077, 1095, 97 L.Ed. 1522, cast further doubt on *Bram.* There are, however, several Court opinions which assume in dicta the relevance of the Fifth Amendment privilege to confessions. *Burdeau v. McDowell,* 256 U.S. 465, 475, 41 S.Ct. 574, 576, 65 L.Ed. 1048; see *Shotwell Mfg. Co. v. United States,* 371 U.S. 341, 347, 83 S.Ct. 448, 453, 9 L.Ed.2d 357. On *Bram* and the federal confession cases generally, see Developments in the Law—Confessions, 79 Harv.L.Rev. 935, 959–961 (1966).

This new line of decisions, testing admissibility by the Due Process Clause, began in 1936 with *Brown v. State of Mississippi,* 297 U.S. 278, 56 S.Ct. 461, 80 L.Ed. 682, and must now embrace somewhat more than 30 full opinions of the Court.[3] While the voluntariness rubric was repeated in many instances, e. g., *Lyons v. State of Oklahoma,* 322 U.S. 596, 64 S.Ct. 1208, 88 L.Ed. 1481, the Court never pinned it down to a single meaning but on the contrary infused it with a number of different values. To travel quickly over the main themes, there was an initial emphasis on reliability, e. g., *Ward v. State of Texas,* 316 U.S. 547, 62 S.Ct. 1139, 86 L.Ed. 1663, supplemented by concern over the legality and fairness of the police practices, e. g., *Ashcraft v. State of Tennessee,* 322 U.S. 143, 64 S.Ct. 921, 88 L.Ed. 1192, in an "accusatorial" system of law enforcement, *Watts v. State of Indiana,* 338 U.S. 49, 54, 69 S.Ct. 1347, 1350, 93 L.Ed. 1801, and eventually by close attention to the individual's state of mind and capacity for effective choice, e.g., *Gallegos v. State of Colorado,* 370 U.S. 49, 82 S.Ct. 1209, 8 L.Ed.2d 325. The outcome was a continuing re-evaluation on the facts of each case of *how much* pressure on the suspect was permissible.[4]

Among the criteria often taken into account were threats or imminent danger, e.g., *Payne v. State of Arkansas,* 356 U.S. 560, 78 S.Ct. 844, 2 L.Ed.2d 975, physical deprivations such as lack of sleep or food, e. g., *Reck v. Pate,* 367 U.S. 433, 81 S.Ct. 1541, 6 L.Ed.2d 948, repeated or extended interrogation, e.g., *Chambers v. State of Florida,* 309 U.S. 227, 60 S.Ct. 472, 84 L.Ed. 716, limits on access to counsel or friends, *Crooker v. State of California,* 357 U.S. 433, 78 S.Ct. 1287, 2 L.Ed.2d 1448; *Cicenia v. La Gay,* 357 U.S. 504, 78 S.Ct. 1297, 2 L.Ed.2d 1523, length and illegality of detention under state law, e.g., *Haynes v. State of Washington,* 373 U.S. 503, 83 S.Ct. 1336, 10 L.Ed.2d 513, and individual weakness or incapacities, *Lynumn v. State of Illinois,* 372 U.S. 528, 83 S.Ct. 917, 9 L.Ed.2d 922. Apart from direct physical coercion, however, no single default or fixed combination of defaults guaranteed exclusion, and synopses of the cases would serve little use because the overall gauge has been steadily changing, usually in the direction of restricting admissibility. But to mark just what point had been reached before the Court jumped the rails in *Escobedo v. State of Illinois,* 378 U.S. 478, 84 S.Ct. 1758, 12 L.Ed.2d 977, it is worth capsulizing the then-recent case of *Haynes v. State of Washington,* 373 U.S. 503, 83 S.Ct. 1366. There, Haynes had been held some 16 or more hours in violation of state law before signing the disputed confession, had received no warnings of any kind, and despite requests had been refused access to his wife or to counsel, the police indicating that access would be allowed after a confession. Emphasizing especially this last inducement and rejecting some contrary indicia of voluntariness, the Court in a 5-to-4 decision held the confession inadmissible.

There are several relevant lessons to be drawn from this constitutional history. The first is that with over 25 years of precedent the Court has developed an elaborate, sophisticated, and sensitive approach to admissibility of confessions. It is "judicial" in its treatment of one case at a time, see *Culombe v. Connecticut,* 367 U.S. 568, 635, 81 S.Ct. 1860, 1896, 6 L.Ed.2d 1037 (concurring opinion of The Chief Justice), flexible in its ability to respond to the endless mutations of fact presented, and ever more familiar to the lower courts. Of course, strict certainty is not obtained in this developing process, but this is often so with constitutional principles, and disagreement is usually confined to that borderland of close cases where it matters least.

The second point is that in practice and from time to time in principle, the Court has given ample recognition to society's interest in suspect questioning as an instrument of law enforcement. Cases countenancing quite significant pressures can be cited without difficulty,[5] and the lower courts may often have been yet

---

[3] Comment, 31 U.Chi.L.Rev. 313 & n. 1 (1964), states that by the 1963 Term 33 state coerced-confession cases had been decided by this Court, apart from *per curians. Spano v. People of State of New York,* 360 U.S. 315, 321, n. 2, 79 S.Ct. 1202, 1206, 3 L.Ed.2d 1265, collects 28 cases.

[4] Bator & Vorenberg, Arrest, Detention, Interrogation and the Right to Counsel, 66 Col.L.Rev. 62, 73 (1966); "In fact, the concept of involuntariness seems to be used by the courts as a shorthand to refer to practices which are repellent to civilized standards of decency or which, under the circumstances, are thought to apply a degree of pressure to an individual which unfairly impairs his capacity to make a rational choice." See Herman, The Supreme Court and Restrictions on Police Interrogation, 25 Ohio St.L.J. 449, 452–458 (1964); Developments, supra, n. 2, at 964–984.

[5] See the cases synopsized in Herman, supra, n. 4, at 456, nn. 36–39. One not too distant example is *Stroble v. State of California,* 343 U.S. 181, 72 S.Ct. 599, 96 L.Ed. 872, in which the suspect was kicked and threatened after his arrest, questioned a little later for two hours, and isolated from a lawyer trying to see him; the resulting confession was held admissible.

U.S. SUPREME
COURT,
OCTOBER 1966

more tolerant. Of course the limitations imposed today were rejected by necessary implication in case after case, the right to warnings having been explicitly rebuffed in this Court many years ago. *Powers v. United States,* 223 U.S. 303, 32 S.Ct. 281, 56 L.Ed. 448; *Wilson v. United States,* 162 U.S. 613, 16 S.Ct. 895, 40 L.Ed. 1090. As recently as *Haynes v. State of Washington,* 373 U.S. 503, 515, 83 S.Ct. 1336, 1344, the Court openly acknowledged that questioning of witnesses and suspects "is undoubtedly an essential tool in effective law enforcement." Accord, *Crooker v. State of California,* 357 U.S. 433, 441, 78 S.Ct. 1287, 1292.

Finally, the cases disclose that the language in many of the opinions overstates the actual course of decision. It has been said, for example, that an admissible confession must be made by the suspect "in the unfettered exercise of his own will," *Malloy v. Hogan,* 378 U.S. 1, 8, 84 S.Ct. 1489, 1493, 12 L.Ed.2d 653, and that "a prisoner is not 'to be made the deluded instrument of his own conviction,'" *Culombe v. Connecticut,* 367 U.S. 568, 581, 81 S.Ct. 1860, 1867, 6 L.Ed.2d 1037 (Frankfurter, J., announcing the Court's judgment and an opinion). Though often repeated, such principles are rarely observed in full measure. Even the word "voluntary" may be deemed somewhat misleading, especially when one considers many of the confessions that have been brought under its umbrella. See, e. g., supra, n. 5. The tendency to overstate may be laid in part to the flagrant facts often before the Court; but in any event one must recognize how it has tempered attitudes and lent some color of authority to the approach now taken by the Court.

I turn now to the Court's asserted reliance on the Fifth Amendment, an approach which I frankly regard as a *trompe l'oeil.* The Court's opinion in my view reveals no adequate basis for extending the Fifth Amendment's privilege against self-incrimination to the police station. Far more important, it fails to show that the Court's new rules are well supported, let alone compelled, by Fifth Amendment precedents. Instead, the new rules actually derive from quotation and analogy drawn from precedents under the Sixth Amendment, which should properly have no bearing on police interrogation.

The Court's opening contention, that the Fifth Amendment governs police station confessions, is perhaps not an impermissible extension of the law but it has little to comment itself in the present circumstances. Historically, the privilege against self-incrimination did not bear at all on the use of extra-legal confessions, for which distinct standards evolved; indeed, "the *history* of the two principles is wide apart, differing by one hundred years in origin, and derived through separate lines of precedents. * * *" 8 Wigmore, Evidence § 2266, at 401 (McNaughton rev. 1961). Practice under the two doctrines has also differed in a number of important respects.[6] Even those who would readily enlarge the privilege must concede some linguistic difficulties since the Fifth Amendment in terms proscribes only compelling any person "in any criminal case to be a witness against himself." Cf. Kamisar, Equal Justice in the Gatehouses and Mansions of American Criminal Procedure, in Criminal Justice in Our Time 1, 25–26 (1965).

Though weighty, I do not say these points and similar ones are conclusive, for, as the Court reiterates, the privilege embodies basic principles always capable of expansion.[7] Certainly the perspective does represent a protective concern for the accused and an emphasis upon accusatorial rather than inquisitorial values in law enforcement, although this is similarly true of other limitations such as the grand jury requirement and the reasonable doubt standard. Accusatorial values, however, have openly been absorbed into the due process standard governing confessions; this indeed is why at present "the kinship of the two rules [governing confessions and self-incrimination] is too apparent for denial." McCormick, Evidence 155 (1954). Since extension of the general principle has already occurred, to insist that the privilege applies as such serves only to carry over inapposite historical details and engaging rhetoric and to obscure the policy choices to be made in regulating confessions.

---

[6] Among the examples given in 8 Wigmore, Evidence § 2266, at 401 (McNaughton rev. 1961), are these: the privilege applies to any witness, civil or criminal, but the confession rule protects only criminal defendants; the privilege deals only with compulsion, while the confession rule may exclude statements obtained by trick or promise; and where the privilege has been nullified — as by the English Bankruptcy Act — the confession rule may still operate.

[7] Additionally, there are precedents and even historical arguments that can be arrayed in favor of bringing extra-legal questioning within the privilege. See generally Maguire. Evidence of Guilt § 2.03, at 15–16 (1959).

U.S. SUPREME
COURT,
OCTOBER 1966

Having decided that the Fifth Amendment privilege does apply in the police station, the Court reveals that the privilege imposes more exacting restrictions than does the Fourteenth Amendment's voluntariness test.[8] It then emerges from a discussion of *Escobedo* that the Fifth Amendment requires for an admissible confession that it be given by one distinctly aware of his right not to speak and shielded from "the compelling atmosphere" of interrogation. See ante, pp. 1623–1624. From these key premises, the Court finally develops the safeguards of warning, counsel, and so forth. I do not believe these premises are sustained by precedents under the Fifth Amendment.[9]

The more important premise is that pressure on the suspect must be eliminated though it be only the subtle influence of the atmosphere and surroundings. The Fifth Amendment, however, has never been thought to forbid *all* pressure to incriminate one's self in the situations covered by it. On the contrary, it has been held that failure to incriminate one's self can result in denial of removal of one's case from state to federal court, *State of Maryland v. Soper,* 270 U.S. 9, 46 S.Ct. 185, 70 L.Ed. 449; in refusal of a military commission, *Orloff v. Willoughby,* 345 U.S. 83, 73 S.Ct. 534, 97 L.Ed. 842; in denial of a discharge in bankruptcy, *Kaufman v. Hurwitz,* 4 Cir., 176 F.2d 210; and in numerous other adverse consequences. See 8 Wigmore, Evidence § 2272, at 441–444, n. 18 (McNaughton rev. 1961); Maguire, Evidence of Guilt § 2.062 (1959). This is not to say that short of jail or torture any sanction is permissible in any case; policy and history alike may impose sharp limits. See, e. g., *Griffin v. State of California,* 380 U.S. 609, 85 S.Ct. 1229, 14 L.Ed.2d 106. However, the Court's unspoken assumption that *any* pressure violates the privilege is not supported by the precedents and it has failed to show why the Fifth Amendment prohibits that relatively mild pressure the Due Process Clause permits.

The Court appears similarly wrong in thinking that precise knowledge of one's rights is a settled prerequisite under the Fifth Amendment to the loss of its protections. A number of lower federal court cases have held that grand jury witnesses need not always be warned of their privilege, e. g., *United States v. Scully,* 2 Cir., 225 F.2d 113, 116, and Wigmore states this to be the better rule for trial witnesses. See 8 Wigmore, Evidence § 2269 (McNaughton rev. 1961). Cf. *Henry v. State of Mississippi,* 379 U.S. 443, 451–452, 85 S.Ct. 564, 569, 13 L.Ed.2d 408 (waiver of constitutional rights by counsel despite defendant's ignorance held allowable). No Fifth Amendment precedent is cited for the Court's contrary view. There might of course be reasons apart from Fifth Amendment precedent for requiring warning or any other safeguard on questioning but that is a different matter entirely. See infra, pp. 1649–1650.

A closing word must be said about the Assistance of Counsel Clause of the Sixth Amendment, which is never expressly relied on by the Court but whose judicial precedents turn out to be linchpins of the confession rules announced today. To support its requirement of a knowing and intelligent waiver, the Court cites *Johnson v. Zerbst,* 304 U.S. 458, 58 S.Ct. 1019, 82 L.Ed. 1461, ante, p. 1628; appointment of counsel for the indigent suspect is tied to *Gideon v. Wainwright,* 372 U.S. 335, 83 S.Ct. 792, 9 L.Ed.2d 799, and *Douglas v. People of State of California,* 372 U.S. 353, 83 S.Ct. 884, 8 L.Ed.2d 70, ante, p. 1628, as is the right to an express offer of counsel, ante, p. 1626. All these cases imparting glosses to the Sixth Amendment concerned counsel at trial or on appeal. While the Court finds no pertinent difference between judicial proceedings and police interrogation, I believe the differences are so vast as to disqualify wholly the Sixth Amendment precedents as suitable analogies in the present cases.[10]

The only attempt in this Court to carry the right to counsel into the station house occurred in *Escobedo,* the Court repeating several times that the stage was no less "critical" than trial itself. See 378 U.S. 485–488, 84 S.Ct. 1762–1763. This is hardly persuasive when we consider that a grand jury inquiry, the filing of a certiorari petition, and certainly the purchase of narcotics by an undercover agent from a prospective

---

[8] This, of course, is implicit in the Court's introductory announcement that "[o]ur decision in *Malloy v. Hogan,* 378 U.S. 1, 84 S.Ct. 1489, 12 L.Ed.2d 653 (1964) [extending the Fifth Amendment privilege to the States] necessitates an examination of the scope of the privilege in state cases as well." Ante, p. 1622. It is also inconsistent with *Malloy* itself, in which extension of the Fifth Amendment to the States rested in part on the view that the Due Process Clause restriction on state confessions has in recent years been "the same standard" as the imposed in federal prosecutions assertively by the Fifth Amendment. 378 U.S., at 7, 84 S.Ct., at 1493.

U.S. SUPREME
COURT,
OCTOBER 1966

defendant may all be equally "critical" yet provision of counsel and advice on the score have never been thought compelled by the Constitution in such cases. The sound reason why this right is so freely extended for a criminal trial is the severe injustice risked by confronting an untrained defendant with a range of technical points of law, evidence, and tactics familiar to the prosecutor but not to himself. This danger shrinks markedly in the police station where indeed the lawyer in fulfilling his professional responsibilities of necessity may become an obstacle of truthfinding. See infra, n. 12. The Court's summary citation of the Sixth Amendment cases here seems to me best described as "the domino method of constitutional adjudication * * * wherein every explanatory statement in a previous opinion is made the basis for extension to a wholly different situation." Friendly, supra, n. 10, at 950.

III. POLICY CONSIDERATIONS

Examined as an expression of public policy, the Court's new regime proves so dubious that there can be no due compensation for its weakness in constitutional law. The foregoing discussion has shown, I think, how mistaken is the Court in implying that the Constitution has struck the balance in favor of the approach the Court takes. Ante, p. 1630. Rather, precedent reveals that the Fourteenth Amendment in practice has been construed to strike a different balance, that the Fifth Amendment gives the Court little solid support in this context, and that the Sixth Amendment should have no bearing at all. Legal history has been stretched before to satisfy deep needs of society. In this instance, however, the Court has not and cannot make the powerful showing that its new rules are plainly desirable in the context of our society, something which is surely demanded before those rules are engrafted onto the Constitution and imposed on every State and county in the land.

Without at all subscribing to the generally black picture of police conduct painted by the Court, I think it must be frankly recognized at the outset that police questioning allowable under due process precedents may inherently entail some pressure on the suspect and may seek advantage in his ignorance or weaknesses. The atmosphere and questioning techniques, proper and fair though they be, can in themselves exert a tug on the suspect to confess, and in this light "[t]o speak of any confession of

crime made after arrest as being 'voluntary' or 'uncoerced' is somewhat inaccurate, although traditional. A confession is wholly and incontestably voluntary only if a guilty person gives himself up to the law and becomes his own accuser." *Ashcraft v. State of Tennessee,* 322 U.S. 143, 161, 64 S.Ct. 921, 929, 88 L.Ed. 1192 (Jackson, J., dissenting). Until today, the role of the Constitution has been only to sift out *undue* pressure, not to assure spontaneous confessions.[11]

The Court's new rules aim to offset these minor pressures and disadvantages intrinsic to any kind of police interrogation. The rules do not serve due process interests in preventing blatant coercion since, as I noted earlier, they do nothing to contain the policeman who is prepared to lie from the start. The rules work for reliability in confessions almost only in the Pickwickian sense that they can prevent some from being given at all.[12] In short, the benefit of this new regime is simply to lessen or wipe out the inherent compulsion and inequalities to which the Court devotes some nine pages of description. Ante, pp. 1614–1618.

What the Court largely ignores is that its rules impair, if they will not eventually serve wholly to frustrate, an instrument of law enforcement that has long and quite reasonably been thought worth the price paid for it.[13] There can be little doubt that the Court's new code would markedly decrease the number of confessions. To warn the suspect that he may remain silent and remind him that his confession may

---

[11] See supra, n. 4, and text. Of course, the use of terms like voluntariness involves questions of law and terminology quite as much as questions of fact. See *Collins v. Beto,* 5 Cir., 348 F.2d 823, 832 (concurring opinion); Bator & Vorenberg, supra, n. 4, at 72–73.

[12] The Court's vision of a lawyer "mitigat[ing] the dangers of untrustworthiness" ante, p. 1626, by witnessing coercion and assisting accuracy in the confession is largely a fancy; for if counsel arrives, there is rarely going to be a police station confession. *Watts v. State of Indiana,* 338 U.S. 49, 59, 69 S.Ct. 1347, 1358, 93 L.Ed. 1801 (separate opinion of Jackson, J.): "[A]ny lawyer worth his salt will tell the suspect in no uncertain terms to make no statement to police under any circumstances." See Enker & Elsen, Counsel for the Suspect, 49 Minn.L.Rev. 47, 66–68 (1964).

[13] This need is, of course, what makes so misleading the Court's comparison of a probate judge readily setting aside as involuntary the will of an old lady badgered and beleaguered by the new heirs. Ante, p. 1619, n. 26. With wills, there is no public interest save in a totally free choice; with confessions, the solution of crime is a countervailing gain, however the balance is resolved.

U.S. SUPREME
COURT,
OCTOBER 1966

be used in court are minor obstructions. To require also an express waiver by the suspect and an end to questioning whenever he demurs must heavily handicap questioning. And to suggest or provide counsel for the suspect simply invites the end of interrogation. See, supra, n. 12.

How much harm this decision will inflict on law enforcement cannot fairly be predicted with accuracy. Evidence on the role of confessions is notoriously incomplete, see Developments, supra, n. 2, at 941–944, and little is added by the Court's reference to the FBI experience and the resources believed wasted in interrogation. See infra, n. 19, and text. We do know that some crimes cannot be solved without confessions, that ample expert testimony attests to their importance in crime control,[14] and that the Court is taking a real risk with society's welfare in imposing its new regime on the country. The social costs of crime are too great to call the new rules anything but a hazardous experimentation.

While passing over the costs and risks of its experiment, the Court portrays the evils of normal police questioning in terms which I think are exaggerated. Albeit stringently confined by the due process standards interrogation is no doubt often inconvenient and unpleasant for the suspect. However, it is no less so for a man to be arrested and jailed, to have his house searched, or to stand trial in court, yet all this may properly happen to the most innocent given probable cause, a warrant, or an indictment. Society has always paid a stiff price for law and order, and peaceful interrogation is not one of the dark moments of the law.

This brief statement of the competing considerations seem to me ample proof that the Court's preference is highly debatable at best and therefore not to be read into the Constitution. However, it may make the analysis more graphic to consider the actual facts of one of the four cases reversed by the Court. *Miranda v. Arizona* serves best, being neither the hardest nor easiest of the four under the Court's standards.[15]

On March 3, 1963, an 18-year-old girl was kidnapped and forcibly raped near Phoenix, Arizona. Ten days later, on the morning of March 13, petitioner Miranda was arrested and taken to the police station. At this time Miranda was 23 years old, indigent, and educated to the extent of completing half the ninth grade. He had "an emotional illness" of the schizophrenic type, according to the doctor who eventually examined him; the doctor's report also stated that Miranda was "alert and oriented as to time, place, and person," intelligent within normal limits, competent to stand trial, and sane within legal definition. At the police station, the victim picked Miranda out of a line-up, and two officers then took him into a separate room to interrogate him, starting about 11:30 a.m. Though at first denying his guilt, within a short time Miranda gave a detailed oral confession and then wrote out in his own hand and signed a brief statement admitting and describing the crime. All this was accomplished in two hours or less without any force, threats or promises and —I will assume this though the record is uncertain, ante, 1636–1637 and nn. 66–67—without any effective warnings at all.

Miranda's oral and written confessions are now held inadmissible under the Court's new rules. One is entitled to feel astonished that the Constitution can be read to produce this result. These confessions were obtained during brief, daytime questioning conducted by two officers and unmarked by any of the traditional indicia of coercion. They assured a conviction for a brutal and unsettling crime, for which the police had and quite possibly could obtain little evidence other than the victim's identifications, evidence which is frequently unreliable. There was, in sum, a legitimate purpose, no perceptible unfairness, and certainly little risk of injustice in the interrogation. Yet the resulting confession, and the responsible course of police practice they represent, are to be sacrificed to the Court's own finespun conception of fairness which I seriously doubt is share by many thinking citizens in this country.[16] The tenor of judicial opinion also falls well short of supporting the Court's new approach. Although *Escobedo* has widely been interpreted as an open invitation to lower courts to rewrite the law of confessions, a

---

[15] In *Westover*, a seasoned criminal was practically given the Court's full complement of warnings and did not heed them. The *Stewart* case, on the other hand, involves long detention and successive questioning. In *Vignera*, the facts are complicated and the record somewhat incomplete.

[16] "[J]ustice, though due to the accused, is due to the accuser also. The concept of fairness must not be strained till it is narrowed to a filament. We are to keep the balance true." *Snyder v. Commonwealth of Massachusetts*, 291 U.S. 97, 122, 54 S.Ct. 330, 338, 78 L.Ed. 674 (Cardozo, J.).

U.S. SUPREME
COURT,
OCTOBER 1966

significant heavy majority of the state and federal decisions in point have sought narrow interpretations.[17] Of the courts that have accepted the invitation, it is hard to know how many have felt compelled by their best guess as to this Court's likely construction; but none of the state decisions saw fit to rely on the state privilege against self-incrimination, and no decision at all has gone as far as this Court goes today.[18]

It is also instructive to compare the attitude in this case of those responsible for law enforcement with the official views that existed when the Court undertook three major revisions of prosecutorial practice prior to this case, *Johnson v. Zerbst,* 304 U.S. 458, 58 S.Ct. 1019, 82 L.Ed. 1461; *Mapp v. Ohio,* 367 U.S. 643, 81 S.Ct. 1684, 6 L.Ed.2d 1081, and *Gideon v. Wainwright,* 372 U.S. 335, 83 S.Ct. 792, 0 L.Ed.2d 799. In *Johnson,* which established that appointed counsel must be offered the indigent in federal criminal trials, the Federal Government all but conceded the basic issue, which had in fact been recently fixed as Department of Justice policy. See Beaney, Right to Counsel 29–30, 36–42 (1955). In *Mapp,* which imposed the exclusionary rule on the States for Fourth Amendment violations, more than half of the States had themselves already adopted some such rule. See 367 U.S., at 651, 81 S.Ct., at 1689. In *Gideon,* which extended *Johnson v. Zerbst* to the States, an *amicus* brief was filed by 22 States and Commonwealths urging that course; only two States besides that of the respondent came forward to protest. See 372 U.S., at 345, 83 S.Ct., at 797. By contrast, in this case new restrictions on police questioning have been opposed by the United States and in an *amicus* brief signed by 27 States and Commonwealths, not including the three other States which are parties. No State in the country

has urged this court to impose the newly announced rules, nor has any State chosen to go nearly so far on its own.

The Court in closing its general discussion invokes the practice in federal and foreign jurisdictions as lending weight to its new curbs on confessions for all the States. A brief résumé will suffice to show that none of these jurisdictions has struck so one-sided a balance as the Court does today. Heaviest reliance is placed on the FBI practice. Differing circumstances may make this comparison quite untrustworthy,[19] but in any event the FBI falls sensibly short of the Court's formalistic rules. For example, there is no indication the FBI agents must obtain an affirmative "waiver" before they pursue their questioning. nor is it clear that one invoking his right to silence may not be prevailed upon to change his mind. And the warning as to appointed counsel apparently indicates only that one will be assigned by the judge when the suspect appears before him; the trust of the Court's rules is to induce the suspect to obtain appointed counsel before continuing the interview. See ante, pp. 1633–1634. Apparently American military practice, briefly mentioned by the Court, has these same limits and is still less favorable to the suspect than the FBI warning, making no mention of appointed counsel. Developments, supra, n. 2, at 1084–1089.

The law of the foreign countries described by the Court also reflects a more moderate conception of the rights of the accused as against those of society when other data are considered. Concededly, the English experience is most relevant. In that country, a caution as to silence but not counsel has long been mandated by the "Judge's Rules," which also place other somewhat imprecise limits on police cross-

---

[17] A narrow reading is given in: *United States v. Robinson,* 354 F.2d 109 (C.A.2d Cir.): *Davis v. State of North Carolina,* 339 F.2d 770 (C.A.4th Cir.); *Edwards v. Holman,* 342 F.2d 679 (C.A.5th Cir.); *United States ex rel. Townsend v. Ogilvie,* 334 F.2d 837 (C.A.7th Cir.); *People v. Hartgraves,* 31 Ill.2d 375, 202 N.E.2d 33; *State v. Fox,* 131 N.W.2d 684 (Iowa); *Rowe v. Commonwealth,* 394 S.W.2d 751 (Ky.); *Parker v. Warden,* 236 Md. 236, 203 A.2d 418; *State v. Howard,* 383 S.W.2d 701 (Mo.); *Bean v. State,* 398 P.2d 251 (Nev.); *State of New Jersey v. Hodgson,* 44 N.J. 151, 207 A.2d 542; *People v. Gunner,* 15 N.Y.2d 226, 257 N.Y.S.2d 924, 205 N.E.2d 852; *Commonwealth ex rel. Linde v. Maroney,* 416 Pa. 331, 206 A.2d 288; *Browne v. State,* 24 Wis.2d 491, 129 N.W.2d 175, 131 N.W.2d 169.

An ample reading is given in: *United States ex rel. Russo v. State of New Jersey,* 351 F.2d 429 (C.A.3d Cir.); *Wright v.*

Dickson, 336 F.2d 878 (C.A. 9th Cir.); *People v. Dorado,* 62 Cal.2d 338, 42 Cal.Rptr. 169, 398 P.2d 361; *State v. Dufour,* 206 A.2d 82 (R.I.); *State v. Neely,* 239 Or. 487, 395 P.2d 557, modified 398 P.2d 482.

The cases in both categories are those readily available; there are certainly many others.

[18] For instance, compare the requirements of the catalytic case of *People v. Dorado,* 62 Cal.2d 338, 42 Cal.Rptr. 169, 398 P.2d 361, with those laid down today. See also Traynor, The Devils of Due Process in Criminal Detection, Detention, and Trial, 33 U.Chi.L.Rev. 657, 670.

[19] The Court's *obiter dictum* notwithstanding ante, p. 1634, there is some basis for believing that the staple of FBI criminal work differs importantly from much crime within the ken of local police. The skill and resources of the FBI may also be unusual.

examination of suspects. However, in the court's discretion confessions can be and apparently quite frequently are admitted in evidence despite disregard of the Judge's Rule, so long as they are found voluntary under the common-law test. Moreover, the check that exists on the use of pretrial statements is counterbalanced by the evident admissibility of fruits of an illegal confession and by the judge's often-used authority to comment adversely on the defendant's failure to testify.[20]

India, Ceylon and Scotland are the other examples chosen by the Court. In India and Ceylon the general ban on police-adduced confessions cited by the Court is subject to a major exception: if evidence is uncovered by police questioning, it is fully admissible at trial along with the confession itself, so far as it relates to the evidence and is not blatantly coerced. See Developments, supra, n. 2, at 1106–1110; *Reg v. Ramasamy* [1965] A.C. 1 (P.C.). Scotland's limits on interrogation do measure up to the Court's; however, restrained comment at trial on the defendant's failure to take the stand is allowed the judge, and in many other respects Scotch law redresses the prosecutor's disadvantage in ways not permitted in this country.[21] The Court ends its survey by imputing added strength to our privilege against self-incrimination since, by contrast to other countries, it is embodied in a written Constitution. Considering the liberties the Court has today taken with constitutional history and precedent, few will find this emphasis persuasive.

In closing this necessarily truncated discussion of policy considerations attending the new confession rules, some reference must be made to their ironic untimeliness. There is now in progress in this country a massive re-examination of criminal law enforcement procedures on a scale never before witnessed. Parcipitants in this undertaking include a Special Committee of the American Bar Association, under the chairmanship of Chief Judge Lumbard of the Court of Appeals for the Second Circuit; a distinguished study group of the American Law Institute, headed by Professors Vorenberg and Bator of the Harvard Law School; and the President's Commission on Law Enforcement and Administration of Justice, under the leadership of the Attorney General of the United States.[22] Studies are also being conducted by the District of Columbia Crime Commission, the Gerogetown Law Center, and by others equipped to do practical research.[23] There are also signs that legislatures in some of the States may be preparing to re-examine the problem before us.[24]

It is no secret that concern has been expressed lest long-range and lasting reforms be frustrated by this Court's too rapid departure from existing constitutional standards. Despite the Court's disclaimer, the practical effect of the decision made today must inevitably be to handicap seriously sound efforts at reform, not least by removing options necessary to a just compromise of competing interests. Of course legislative reform is rarely speedy or unanimous, though this Court has been more patient in the past.[25] But the legislative reforms when they come would have the vast advantage of empirical data and comprehensive study, they would allow experimentation and use of solutions not open to the courts, and they would restore the initiative in criminal law reform to those forums where it truly belongs.

U.S. SUPREME
COURT,
OCTOBER 1966

---

[20] For citations and discussion covering each of these points, see Developments, supra, n. 2, at 1091–1097, and Enker & Elsen, supra, n. 12, at 80 & n. 94.

[21] On Comment, see Hardin, Other Answers: Search and Seizure, Coerced Confession, and Criminal Trial in Scotland, 113 U.Pa.L.Rev. 165, 181 and nn. 96–97 (1964). Other examples are less stringent search and seizure rules and no automatic exclusion for violation of them, id., at 167–169; guilt based on majority jury verdicts, id., at 185; and pre-trial discovery of evidence on both sides, id., at 175.

[22] Of particular relevance is the ALI's drafting of a Model Code of Pre-Arraignment Procedure, now in its first tentative draft. While the ABA and National Commission studies have wider scope, the former is lending its advice to the ALI project and the executive director of the latter is one of the reporters for the Model Code.

[23] See Brief for the United States in *Westover,* p. 45. The *N. Y. Times,* June 3, 1966, p. 41 (late city ed.) reported that the Food Foundation has awarded $1,100,000 for a five-year study of arrests and confessions in New York.

[24] The New York Assembly recently passed a bill to require certain warnings before an admissible confession is taken, though the rules are less strict than are the Court's. *N. Y. Times,* May 24, 1966, p. 35 (late city ed.).

[25] The Court waited 12 years after *Wolf v. People of State of Colorado,* 338 U.S. 25, 69 S.Ct. 1359, 93 L.Ed. 1782, declared privacy against improper state intrusions to be constitutionally safeguarded before it concluded in *Mapp v. Ohio,* 367 U.S. 643, 81 S.Ct. 1684, 6 L.Ed.2d 1081, that adequate state remedies had not been provided to protect this interest so the exclusionary rule was necessary.

IV. CONCLUSIONS

All four of the cases involved here present express claims that confessions were inadmissible, not because of coercion in the traditional due process sense, but solely because of lack of counsel or lack of warnings concerning counsel and silence. For the reasons stated in this opinion, I would adhere to the due process test and reject the new requirements inaugurated by the Court. On this premise my disposition of each of these cases can be stated briefly.

In two of the three cases coming from state courts, *Miranda v. Arizona* (No. 759) and *Vignera v. New York* (No. 760), the confessions were held admissible and no other errors worth comment are alleged by petitioners. I would affirm in these two cases. The other state case is *California v. Stewart* (No. 584), where the state supreme court held the confession inadmissible and reversed the conviction. In that case I would dismiss the writ of certiorari on the ground that no final judgment is before us, 28 U.S.C. § 1257 (1964 ed.); putting aside the new trial open to the State in any event, the confession itself has not even been finally excluded since the California Supreme Court left the State free to show proof of a waiver. If the merits of the decision in *Stewart* be reached, then I believe it should be reversed and the case remanded so the state supreme court may pass on the other claims available to respondent.

In the federal case, *Westover v. United States* (No. 761), a number of issues are raised by petitioner apart from the one already dealt with in this dissent. None of these other claims appears to me tenable, nor in this context to warrant extended discussion. It is urged that the confession was also inadmissible because not voluntary even measured by due process standards and because federal-state cooperation brought the McNabb-Mallory rule into play under *Anderson v. United States,* 318 U.S. 350, 63 S.Ct. 599, 87 L.Ed. 829. However, the facts alleged fall well short of coercion in my view, and I believe the involvement of federal agents in petitioner's arrest and detention by the State too slight to invoke *Anderson.* I agree with the Government that the admission of the evidence now protested by petitioner was at most harmless error, and two final contentions—one involving weight of the evidence and another improper prosecutor comment—seem to me without merit. I would therefore affirm Westover's conviction.

In conclusion: Nothing in the letter or the spirit of the Constitution or in the precedents squares with the heavy-handed and one-sided action that is so precipitously taken by the Court in the name of fulfilling its constitutional responsibilities. The foray which the Court makes today brings to mind the wise and far-sighted words of Mr. Justice Jackson in *Douglas v. City of Jeannette,* 319 U.S. 157, 181, 63 S.Ct. 877, 889, 87 L.Ed. 1324 (separate opinion): "This Court is forever adding new stories to the temples of constitutional law, and the temples have a way of collapsing when one story too many is added."

Mr. Justice White, with whom Mr. Justice Harlan and Mr. Justice Stewart join, dissenting.

I.

The proposition that the privilege against self-incrimination forbids in-custody interrogation without the warnings specified in the majority opinion and without a clear waiver of counsel has no significant support in the history of the privilege or in the language of the Fifth Amendment. As for the English authorities and the common-law history, the privilege, firmly established in the second half of the seventeenth century, was never applied except to prohibit compelled judicial interrogations. The rule excluded coerced confessions matured about 100 years later, "[b]ut there is nothing in the reports to suggest that the theory has its roots in the privilege against self-incrimination. And so far as the cases reveal, the privilege, as such, seems to have been given effect only in judicial proceedings, including the preliminary examinations by authorized magistrates." Morgan, the Privilege Against Self-Incrimination, 34 Minn.L.Rev. 1, 18 (1949).

Our own constitutional provision provides that no person "shall be compelled in any criminal case to be a witness against himself." These words, when "[c]onsidered in the light to be shed by grammar and the dictionary * * * appear to signify simply that nobody will be compelled to give oral testimony against himself in a criminal proceeding under way in which he is defendant." Corwin, The Supreme Court's Construction of the Self-Incrimination Clause, 29 Mich.L.Rev. 1, 2. And there is very little in the surrounding circumstances of the adoption of the Fifth Amendment or in the provisions of the then existing state constitutions or in state practice which would give the constitutional provision any broader meaning. Mayers, The Federal Witness' Privilege Against Self-Incrimination: Constitutional or Common-Law? 4 American Journal of Legal History 107 (1960). Such a construction, however, was considerably narrower than the privilege at common law, and when eventually faced with the issues, the Court extended the constitutional privilege to the compulsory production of books and papers, to the ordinary witness before the grand jury and to witnesses generally. *Boyd v. United States,* 116 U.S. 616, 6 S.Ct. 524, 29 L.Ed. 746, and *Counselman v. Hitchcock,* 142 U.S. 547, 12 S.Ct. 195, 35 L.Ed. 1110. Both rules had solid support in common-law history, if not in the history of our own constitutional provision.

A few years later the Fifth Amendment privilege was similarly extended to encompass the then well-established rule against coerced confessions: "In criminal trials, in the courts of the United States, wherever a question arises whether a confession is incompetent because not voluntary, the issue is controlled by that portion of the fifth amendment to the constitution of the United States, commanding that no person shall be compelled in any criminal case to be a witness against himself." *Bram v. United States,* 168 U.S. 532, 542, 18 S.Ct. 183, 187, 42 L.Ed. 568. Although this view has found approval in other cases, *Burdeau v. McDowell,* 256 U.S. 465, 475, 41 S.Ct. 574, 576, 65 L.Ed. 1048; *Powers v. United States,* 223 U.S. 303, 313, 32 S.Ct. 281, 283, 56 L.Ed. 448; *Shotwell Mfg. Co. v. United States,* 371 U.S. 341, 347, 83 S.Ct. 448, 453, 9 L.Ed.2d 357, it has also been questioned, see *Brown v. State of Mississippi,* 297 U.S. 278, 285, 56 S.Ct. 461, 464, 80 L.Ed. 682; *United States v. Carignan,* 342 U.S. 36, 41, 72 S.Ct. 97, 100, 96 L.Ed. 48; *Stein v. People of State of New York,* 346 U.S. 156, 191, n. 35, 73 S.Ct. 1077, 1095, 97 L.Ed. 1522, and finds scant support in either the English or American authorities, see generally *Regina v. Scott, Dears. & Bell* 47; 3 Wigmore, Evidence § 823 (3d ed. 1940), at 249 ("a confession is not rejected because of any connection with the *privilege against self-incrimination*"), and 250, n. 5 (particularly criticizing *Bram*); 8 Wigmore, Evidence § 2266, at 400–401 (McNaughton rev. 1961). Whatever the source of the rule excluding coerced confessions, it is clear that prior to the application of the privilege itself to state courts, *Malloy v. Hogan,* 378 U.S. 1, 84 S.Ct. 1489, 12 L.Ed.2d 653, the admissibility of a confession in a state criminal prosecution was tested by the same standards as were applied in federal prosecutions. Id., at 6–7, 10, 84 S.Ct., at 1492–1493, 1494.

Bram, however, itself rejected the proposition which the Court now espouses. The question in *Bram* was whether a confession, obtained during custodial interrogation, had been compelled, and if such interrogation was to be deemed inherently vulnerable the Court's inquiry could have ended there. After examining the English and American authorities, however, the Court declared that:

> "In this court also it has been settled that the mere fact that the confession is made to a police officer, while the accused was under arrest in or out of prison, or was drawn out by his questions, does not necessarily render the question involuntary; but, as one of the circumstances, such imprisonment or interrogation may be taken into account in determining whether or not the statements of the prisoner were voluntary." 168 U.S., at 558, 18 S.Ct., at 192.

In this respect the Court was wholly consistent with prior and subsequent pronouncements in this Court.

Thus prior to *Bram* the Court, in *Hopt v. People of Territory of Utah,* 110 U.S. 574, 583–587, 4 S.Ct. 202, 206, 28 L.Ed. 262, had upheld the admissibility of a confession made to police officers following arrest, the record being silent concerning what conversation had occurred between the officers and the defendant in the short period preceding the confession. Relying on *Hopt,* the Court ruled squarely on the issue in *Sparf and Hansen v. United States,* 156 U.S. 51, 55, 15 S.Ct. 273, 275, 39 L.Ed. 343:

> "Counsel for the accused insist that there cannot be a voluntary statement, a free, open confession, while a defendant is confined and in irons, under an accusation of having committed a capital offence. We have not been referred to any authority in support of that position. It is true that the fact of a prisoner being in custody at the time he makes a confession is a circumstance not to be overlooked, because it bears upon the inquiry whether the confession was voluntarily made, or was extorted by threats or violence or made under the influence of fear. But confinement or imprisonment is not in itself sufficient to justify the exclusion of a confession, if it appears to have been voluntary and was not obtained by putting the prisoner in fear or by promises. Whart[on's] Cr.Ev. (9th Ed.) §§ 661, 663, and authorities cited."

Accord, *Pierce v. United States,* 160 U.S. 355, 357, 16 S.Ct. 321, 322, 40 L.Ed. 454.

And in *Wilson v. United States,* 162 U.S. 613, 623, 16 S.Ct. 895, 899, 40 L.Ed. 1090, the Court had considered the significance of custodial interrogation without any antecedent warnings regarding the right to remain silent or the right to counsel. There the defendant had answered questions posed by a Commissioner, who had failed to advise him of his rights, and his answers were held admissible over his claim of involuntariness. "The fact that [a defendant] is in custody and manacled does not necessarily render his statement involuntary, nor is that necessarily the effect of popular excitement shortly proceeding. * * * And it is laid down that it is not essential to the admissibility of a confession that it should appear that the person was warned that what he said would be used against him; but, on the contrary, if the confession was voluntary, it is sufficient, though it appear that he was not so warned."

Since *Bram,* the admissibility of statements made during custodial interrogation has been frequently reiterated. *Powers v. United States,* 223 U.S. 303, 32 S.Ct. 281, cited *Wilson* approvingly and held admissible as voluntary statements the accused's testimony at a preliminary hearing even though he was not warned that what he said might be used against him. Without any discussion of the presence or absence of warnings, presumably because such discussion was deemed unnecessary, numerous other cases have declared that "[t]he mere fact that a confession was made while in the custody of the police does not render it admissible," *McNabb v. United States,* 318 U.S. 332, 346, 63 S.Ct. 608, 615, 87 L.Ed. 819; accord, *United States v. Mitchell,* 322 U.S. 65, 64 S.Ct. 896, 88 L.Ed. 1140, despite its having been elicited by police examination. *Ziang Sung Wan v. United States,* 266 U.S. 1, 14, 45 S.Ct. 3; *United States v. Carignan,* 342 U.S. 36, 39, 72 S.Ct. 97, 99. Likewise, in *Crooker v. State of California,* 357 U.S. 433, 437, 78 S.Ct. 1287, 1290, 2 L.Ed.2d 1448, the Court said that "[t]he bare fact of police 'detention and police examination in private of one in official state custody' does not render involuntary a confession by the one so detained." And finally, in *Canada v. La Gay,* 357 U.S. 504, 78 S.Ct. 1297, 2 L.Ed.2d 1523, a confession obtained by police interrogation after arrest was held voluntary even through the authorities refused to permit the defendant to

consult with his attorney. See generally *Culombe v. Connecticut,* 367 U.S. 568, 587–602, 81 S.Ct. 1860, 1870, 6 L.Ed.2d 1037 (opinion of Frankfurter, J.); 3 Wigmore, Evidence § 851, at 313 (3d ed. 1940); see also Jay, Admissibility of Confessions 38, 46 (1842).

Only a tiny minority of our judges who have dealt with the question, including today's majority, have considered in-custody interrogation, without more, to be a violation of the Fifth Amendment. And this Court, as every member knows, has left standing literally thousands of criminal convictions that rested at least in part on confessions taken in the course of interrogation by the police after arrest.

II.

That the Court's holding today is neither compelled nor even strongly suggested by the language of the Fifth Amendment, is at odds with American and English legal history, and involves a departure from a long line of precedent does not prove either that the Court is wrong or unwise in its present reinterpretation of the Fifth Amendment. It does, however, underscore the obvious—that the Court has not discovered or found the law in making today's decision, nor has it derived it from some irrefutable sources; what it has done is to make new law and new public policy in much the same way that it has in the course of interpreting other great clauses of the Constitution.[1] This is what the Court historically has done. Indeed, it is what it must do and will continue to do until and unless there is some fundamental change in the constitutional distribution of governmental powers.

But if the Court is here and now to announce new and fundamental policy to govern certain aspects of our affairs, it is wholly legitimate to examine the mode of this or any other constitutional decision in this Court and to inquire into the advisability of its end product in terms of the long-range interest of the country. At the very least, the Court's text and reasoning should withstand analysis and be a fair exposition of the constitutional provision which its opinion interprets. Decisions like these can-

---

[1] Of course the Court does not deny that it is departing from prior precedent; it expressly overrules *Crooker* and *Cicenia,* ante, at 1630, n. 48, and it acknowledges that in the instant "cases we might not find the defendants' statements to have been involuntary in traditional terms," ante, at 1618.

not rest alone on syllogism, metaphysics or some ill-defined notions of natural justice, although each will perhaps play its part. In proceeding to such constructions as it now announces, the Court should also duly consider all the factors and interests bearing upon the cases, at least insofar as the relevant materials are available; and if the necessary considerations are not treated in the record or obtainable from some other reliable source, the Court should not proceed to formulate fundamental policies based on speculation alone.

III.

First, we may inquire what are the textual and factual bases of this new fundamental rule. To reach the result announced on the grounds it does, the Court must stay within the confines of the Fifth Amendment, which forbids self-incrimination only if *compelled*. Hence the core of the Court's opinion is that because of the "compulsion inherent in custodial surroundings, no statement obtained from [a] defendant [in custody] can truly be the product of his free choice," ante, at 1619, absent the use of adequate protective devices as described by the Court. However, the Court does not point to any sudden inrush of new knowledge requiring the rejection of 70 years' experience. Nor does it assert that its novel conclusion reflects a changing consensus among state courts, see *Mapp v. Ohio,* 367 U.S. 643, 81 S.Ct. 1684, 6 L.Ed.2d 1081, or that a succession of cases had steadily eroded the old rule and proved it unworkable, see *Gideon v. Wainwright,* 372 U.S. 355, 83 S.Ct. 792, 9 L.Ed.2d 799. Rather than asserting new knowledge, the Court concedes that it cannot truly know what occurs during custodial questioning, because of the innate secrecy of such proceedings. It extrapolates a picture of what it conceives to be the norm from police investigatorial manuals, published in 1959 and 1962 or earlier, without any attempt to allow for adjustments in police practices that may have occurred in the wake of more recent decisions of state appellate tribunals or this Court. But even if the relentless application of the described procedures could lead to involuntary confessions, it most assuredly does not follow that each and every case will disclose this kind of interrogation or this kind of consequence.[2] Insofar as appears from the Court's opinion, it has not examined a single transcript of any police interrogation, let alone the interrogation that took place in any one of these cases which it decides today. Judged by any of the standards for empirical investigation utilized in the social sciences the factual basis for the Court's premise is patently inadequate.

Although in the Court's view in-custody interrogation is inherently coercive, the Court says that the spontaneous product of the coercion of arrest and detention is still to be deemed voluntary. An accused, arrested on probable cause, may blurt out a confession which will be admissible despite the fact that he is alone and in custody, without any showing that he had any notion of his right to remain silent or of the consequences of his admission. Yet, under the Court's rule, if the police ask him a single question such as "Do you have anything to say?" or "Did you kill your wife?" his response, if there is one, has somehow been compelled, even if the accused has been clearly warned of his right to remain silent. Common sense informs us to the contrary. While one may say that the response was "involuntary" in the sense the question provoked or was the occasion for the response and thus the defendant was induced to speak out when he might have remained silent if not arrested and not questioned, it is patently unsound to say the response is compelled.

Today's result would not follow even if it were agreed that to some extent custodial interrogation is inherently coercive. See *Ashcraft v. State of Tennessee,* 322 U.S. 143, 161, 64 S.Ct. 921, 929, 88 L.Ed. 1192 (Jackson, J., dissenting). The test has been whether the totality of circumstances deprived the defendant of a "free choice to admit, to deny, or to refuse to answer," *Lisenba v. People of State of California,* 314 U.S. 219, 241, 62 S.Ct. 280, 292, 86 L.Ed. 166, and whether physical or psychological coercion was of such a degree that "the defendant's will was overborne at the time he confessed," *Haynes v. State of Washington,* 373 U.S. 503, 513, 83 S.Ct. 1336, 1343, 10 L.Ed.2d 513; *Lynumn v. State of*

U.S. SUPREME
COURT,
OCTOBER 1966

---

[2] In fact, the type of sustained interrogation described by the Court appears to be the exception rather than the rule. A survey of 399 cases in one city found that in almost half of the cases the interrogation lasted less than 30 minutes. Barrett, Police Practices and the Law—From Arrest to Release or Charge, 50 Calif.L.Rev. 11, 41–45 (1962). Questioning tends to be confused and sporadic and is usually concentrated on confrontations with witnesses or new items of evidence, as these are obtained by officers conducting the investigation. See generally LaFave, Arrest: The Decision to Take a Suspect into Custody 386 (1965); ALI, A Model Code of Pre-Arraignment Procedure, Commentary § 5.01, at 170, n. 4 (Tent.Draft No. 1, 1966).

U.S. SUPREME
COURT,
OCTOBER 1966

Illinois, 372 U.S. 528, 534, 83 S.Ct. 917, 920, 9 L.Ed.2d 922. The duration and nature of incommunicado custody, the presence or absence of advice concerning the defendant's constitutional rights, and the granting or refusal of requests to communicate with lawyers, relatives or friends have all been rightly regarded as important data bearing on the basic inquiry. See, e. g., *Ashcraft v. State of Tennessee,* 322 U.S. 143, 64 S.Ct. 921; *Haynes v. State of Washington,* 373 U.S. 503, 83 S.Ct. 1336.[3] But it has never been suggested, until today, that such questioning was so coercive and accused persons so lacking in hardihood that the very first response to the very first question following the commencement of custody must be conclusively presumed to be the product of an overborne will.

If the rule announced today were truly based on a conclusion that all confessions resulting from custodial interrogation are coerced, then it would simply have no rational foundation. Compare *Tot v. United States,* 319 U.S. 463, 466, 63 S.Ct. 1241, 1244, 87 L.Ed. 1519; *United States v. Romano,* 382 U.S. 136, 86 S.Ct. 279, 15 L.Ed.2d 210. A *fortiori* that would be true of the extension of the rule to exculpatory statements, which the Court effects after a brief discussion of why, in the Court's view, they must be deemed incriminatory but without any discussion of why they must be deemed coerced. See *Wilson v. United States,* 162 U.S. 613, 624, 16 S.Ct. 895, 900, 40 L.Ed. 1090. Even if one were to postulate that the Court's concern is not that all confessions included by police interrogation are coerced but rather that some such confessions are coerced and present judicial procedures are believed to be inadequate to identify the confessions that are coerced and those that are not, it

would still not be essential to impose the rule that the Court has now fashioned. Transcripts or observers could be required, specific time limits, tailored to fit the cause, could be imposed, or other devices could be utilized to reduce the chances that otherwise indiscernible coercion will produce inadmissible confession.

On the other hand, even if one assumed that there was an adequate factual basis for the conclusion that all confessions obtained during in-custody interrogation and the product of compulsion, the rule propounded by the Court will still be irrational, for, apparently, it is only if the accused is also warned of his right to counsel and waives both that right and the right against self-incrimination that the inherent compulsiveness of interrogation disappears. But if the defendant may not answer without a warning a question such as "Where were you last night?" without having his answer be a compelled one, how can the Court ever accept his negative answer to the question of whether he wants to consult his retained counsel or counsel whom the court will appoint? And why if counsel is present and the accused nevertheless confesses, or counsel tells the accused to tell the truth, and that is what the accused does, is the situation any less coercive insofar as the accused is concerned? The Court apparently realizes its dilemma of foreclosing questioning without the necessary warnings but at the same time permitting the accused, sitting in the same chair in front of the same policeman, to waive his right to consult an attorney. It expects, however, that the accused will not often waive the right; and if it is claimed that he has, the State faces a severe, if not impossible burden of proof.

All of this makes very little sense in terms of the compulsion which the Fifth Amendment proscribes. That amendment deals with compelling the accused himself. It is his free will that is involved. Confessions and incriminating admissions, as such, as not forbidden evidence; only those which are compelled are banned. I doubt that the Court observes these distinctions today. By considering any answers to any interrogation to be compelled regardless of the content and course of examination and by escalating the requirements to prove waiver, the Court not only prevents the use of compelled confessions but for all practical purposes forbids interrogation except in the presence of counsel. That is, instead of confining itself to protection of the right

---

[3] By contrast, the Court indicates that in applying this new rule it "will not pause to inquire in individual cases whether the defendant was aware of his rights without a warning being given." Ante, at 1625. The reason given is that assessment of the knowledge of the defendant based on information as to age, education, intelligence, or prior contact with authorities can never be more than speculation, while a warning is a clear-cut fact. But the officers' claim that they gave the requisite warnings may be disputed, and facts respecting the defendant's prior experience may be undisputed and be of such a nature as to virtually preclude any doubt that the defendant knew of his rights. See *United States v. Bolden,* 355 F.2d 453 (C.A.7th Cir.1965), petition for cert. pending No. 1146, O.T. 1965 (Secret Service agent); *People v. Du Bont,* 235 Cal.App.2d 844, 45 Cal.Rptr. 717, pet. for cert. pending No. 1053, Misc., O. T. 1965 (former police officer).

against compelled self-incrimination the Court has created a limited Fifth Amendment right to counsel—or, as the Court expresses it, a "need for counsel to protect the Fifth Amendment privilege * * *." Ante, at 1625. The focus then is not on the will of the accused but on the will of the counsel and how much influence he can have on the accused. Obviously there is no warrant in the Fifth Amendment for thus installing counsel as the arbiter of the privilege.

In sum, for all the Court's expounding on the menacing atmosphere of police interrogation procedures, it has failed to supply any foundation for the conclusions it draws or the measures it adopts.

IV.

Criticism of the Court's opinion, however, cannot stop with a demonstration that the factual and textual bases for the rule it propounds are, at best, less than compelling. Equally relevant is an assessment of the rule's of the rule's consequences measured against community values. The Court's duty to assess the consequences of its action is not satisfied by the utterance of the truth that a value of our system of criminal justice is "to respect the inviolability of the human personality" and to require government to produce the evidence against the accused by its own independent labors. Ante, at 1620. More than the human dignity of the accused is involved; the human personality of others in the society must also be preserved. Thus the values reflected by the privilege are not the sole desideratum; society's interest in the general security is of equal weight.

The obvious underpinning of the Court's decision is a deep-seated distrust of all confessions. As the Court declares that the accused may not be interrogated without counsel present, absent a waiver of the right to counsel, and as the Court all but admonishes the lawyer to advise the accused to remain silent, the result adds up to a judicial judgment that evidence from the accused should not be used against him in any way, whether compelled or not. This is the not so subtle overtone of the opinion—that it is inherently wrong for the police to gather evidence from the accused himself. And this is precisely the nub of this dissent. I see nothing wrong or immoral, and certainly nothing unconstitutional, in the police's asking a suspect whom they have reasonable cause to arrest whether or not he killed his wife or in confronting him with the evidence on which the arrest was based, at least where he has been plainly advised that he may remain completely silent, see *Escobedo v. State of Illinois,* 378 U.S. 478, 499, 84 S.Ct. 1758, 1769, 12 L.Ed.2d 977 (dissenting opinion). Until today, "the admissions or confessions of the prisoner, when voluntarily and freely made, have always ranked high in the scale of incriminating evidence." *Brown v. Walker,* 161 U.S. 591, 596, 16 S.Ct. 644, 646, 40 L.Ed. 819, see also *Hopt v. People of Territory of Utah,* 110 U.S. 574, 584–585, 4 S.Ct. 202, 207. Particularly when corroborated, as where the police have confirmed the accused's disclosure of the hiding place of implements or fruits of the crime, such confessions have the highest reliability and significantly contribute to the certitude with which we may believe the accused is guilty. Moreover, it is by no means certain that the process of confessing is injurious to the accused. To the contrary it may provide psychological relief and enhance the prospects for rehabilitation.

This is not to say that the value of respect for the inviolability of the accused's individual personality should be accorded no weight or that all confessions should be indiscriminately admitted. This Court has long read the Constitution to proscribe compelled confessions, a salutary rule from which there should be no retreat. But I see no sound basis, factual or otherwise, and the Court gives none, for concluding that the present rule against the receipt of coerced confessions is inadequate for the task of sorting out inadmissible evidence and must be replaced by the *per se* rule which is now imposed. Even if the new concept can be said to have advantages of some sort over the present law, they are far outweighed but its likely undesirable impact on other very relevant and important interests.

The most basic function of any government is to provide for the security of the individual and for his property. *Lanzetta v. State of New Jersey,* 306 U.S. 451, 455, 59 S.Ct., 618, 619, 83 L.Ed. 888. These ends of society are served by the criminal laws which for the most part are aimed at the prevention of crime. Without the reasonably effective performance of the task of preventing private violence and retaliation, it is idle to talk about human dignity and civilized values.

The modes by which the criminal laws serve the interest in general security are many. First

U.S. SUPREME COURT, OCTOBER 1966

the murderer who has taken the life of another is removed from the streets, deprived of his liberty and thereby prevented from repeating his offense. In view of the statistics on recidivism in this country[4] and of the number of instances in which apprehension occurs only after repeated offenses, no one can sensibly claim that this aspect of the criminal law does not prevent crime or contribute significantly to the personal security of the ordinary citizen.

Secondly, the swift and sure apprehension of those who refuse to respect the personal security and dignity of their neighbor unquestionably has its impact on others who might be similarly tempted. That the criminal law is wholly or partly ineffective with a segment of the population or with many of those who have been apprehended and convicted is a very faulty basis for concluding that it is not effective with respect to the great bulk of our citizens or for thinking that without the criminal laws, or in the absence of their enforcement, there would be no increase in crime. Arguments of this nature are not borne out by any kind of reliable evidence that I have seen to this date.

Thirdly, the law concerns itself with those whom it has confined. The hope and aim of modern penology, fortunately, is as soon as possible to return the convict to society a better and more law-abiding man than when he left. Sometimes there is success, sometimes failure.

But at least the effort is made, and it should be made to the very maximum extent of our present and future capabilities.

The rule announced today will measurably waken the ability of the criminal law to perform these tasks. It is a deliberate calculus to prevent interrogations, to reduce the incidence of confessions and pleas of guilty and to increase the number of trials.[5] Criminal trials, no matter how efficient the police are, are not sure bets for the prosecution, nor should they be if the evidence is not forthcoming. Under the present law, the prosecution fails to prove its case in about 30% of the criminal cases actually tried in the federal courts. See Federal Offenders: 1964, supra, note 4, at 6 (Table 4), 59 (Table 1); Federal Offenders; 1963, supra, note 4, at 5 (Table 3); District of Columbia Offenders; 1963, supra, note 4, at 2 (Table 1). But it is something else again to remove from the ordinary criminal case all those confessions which heretofore have been held to be free and voluntary acts of the accused and to thus establish a new constitutional barrier to the ascertainment of truth by the judicial process. There is, in my view, every reason to believe that a good many criminal defendants who otherwise would have been convicted on what this Court has previously thought to be the most satisfactory kind of evidence will now under this new version of the Fifth Amendment, either not be tried at all or will be acquitted if

---

[4] Precise statistics on the extent of recidivism are unavailable, in part because not all crimes are solved and in part because criminal records of convictions in different jurisdictions are not brought together by a central data collection agency. Beginning in 1963, however, the Federal Bureau of Investigation began collating data on "Careers in Crime," which it publishes in its Uniform Crime Reports. Of 92,869 offenders processed in 1963 and 1964, 76% had a prior arrest record on some charge. Over a period of 10 years the group had accumulated 434,000 charges. FBI, Uniform Crime Reports — 1964, 27–28. In 1963 and 1964 between 23% and 25% of all offenders sentenced in 88 federal district courts (excluding the District Court for the District of Columbia) whose criminal records were reported had previously been sentenced to at term of imprisonment of 13 months or more. Approximately an additional 40% had a prior record less than prison (juvenile record, probation record, etc.). Administrative Office of the United States Courts, Federal Offenders in the United States District Courts: 1964, x, 36 (hereinafter cited as Federal Offenders: 1964); Administrative Office of the United States Courts, Federal Offenders in the United States District Courts: 1963, 25–27 (hereinafter cited as Federal Offenders: 1963). During the same two years in the District Court for the District of Columbia between 28% and 35% of those sentenced had prior prison records

and from 37% to 40% had a prior record less than prison. Federal Offenders: 1964, xii, 64, 66; Administrative Office of the United States Courts, Federal Offenders in the United States District Court for the District of Columbia; 1963, 8, 10 (hereinafter cited as District of Columbia Offenders: 1963).

A similar picture is obtained if one looks at the subsequent records of those released from confinement. In 1964, 12.3% of persons on federal probation had their probation revoked because of the commission of major violations (defined as one in which the probationer has been committed to imprisonment for a period of 90 days or more, been placed on probation for over one year on a new offense, or has absconded with felony charges outstanding). Twenty-three and two-tenths percent of paroles and 16.9% of those who had been mandatorily released after service of a portion of their sentence likewise committed major violations. Reports of the Proceedings of the Judicial Conference of the United States and Annual Report of the Director of the Administrative Office of the United States Courts: 1965, 138. See also Mandel et al., Recidivism Studied and Defined, 56 J. Crim.L., C. & P.S. 59 (1965) (within five years of release 62.33% of sample had committed offenses placing them in recidivist category).

[5] Eighty-eight federal district courts (excluding the District Court for the District of Columbia) disposed of the cases of

U.S. SUPREME
COURT,
OCTOBER 1966

the State's evidence, minus the confessions, is put to the test of litigation.

I have no desire whatsoever to share the responsibility for any such impact on the present criminal process.

In some unknown number of cases the Court's rule will return a killer, a rapist or other criminal to the streets and to the environment which produced him, to repeat his crime whenever it pleases him. As a consequence, there will not be a gain, but a loss, in human dignity. The real concern is not the unfortunate consequences of this new decision on the criminal law as an abstract, disembodied series of authoritative proscriptions, but the impact on those who rely on the public authority for protection and who without it can only engage in violent self-help with guns, knives and the help of their neighbors similarly inclined. There is, of course, a saving factor: the next victims are uncertain, unnamed and unrepresented in this case.

Nor can this decision do other than have a corrosive effect on the criminal laws as an effective device to prevent crime. A major component in its effectiveness in this regard is its swift and sure enforcement. The easier it is to get away with rape and murder, the less the deterrent effect on those who are inclined to attempt it. This is still good common sense. If it were not, we should posthaste liquidate the whole law enforcement establishment as a useless, misguided effort to control human conduct.

33,381 criminal defendants in 1964. Only 12.5% of those cases were actually tried. Of the remaining cases, 89.9% were terminated by convictions upon pleas of guilty and 10.1% were dismissed. Stated differently, approximately 90% of all convictions resulted from guilty pleas. Federal Offenders: 1964, supra, note 4, 3–6. In the District Court for the District of Columbia a higher percentage, 27%, went to trial, and the defendant pleaded guilty in approximately 78% of the cases terminated prior to trial. *Id.*, at 58–59. No reliable statistics are available concerning the percentage of cases in which guilty pleas are induced because of the existence of a confession or of physical evidence unearthed as a result of a confession. Undoubtedly the number of such cases is substantial.

Perhaps of equal significance is the number of instances of known crimes which are not solved. In 1964, only 388, 946, or 23.9% of 1,626,574 serious known offenses were cleared. The clearance rate ranged from 89.8% for homicides to 18.7% for larceny. FBI, Uniform Crime Reports — 1964, 20–22, 101. Those who would replace interrogation as an investigatorial tool by modern scientific investigation techniques significantly overestimate the effectiveness of present procedures, even when interrogation is included.

And what about the accused who has confessed or would confess in response to simple, noncoercive questioning and whose guilt could not otherwise be proved? Is it so clear that release is the best thing for him in every case? Has it so unquestionably been resolved that in each and every case it would be better for him not to confess and to return to his environment with no attempt whatsoever to help him? I think not. It may well be that in many cases it will be no less than a callous disregard for his own welfare as well as for the interests of his next victim.

There is another aspect to the effect of the Court's rule on the person whom the police have arrested on probable cause. The fact is that he may not be guilty at all and may be able to extricate himself quickly and simply if he were told the circumstances of his arrest and were asked to explain. This effort, and his release, must now await the hiring of a lawyer or his appointment by the court, consultation with counsel and then a session with the police or the prosecutor. Similarly, where probable cause exists to arrest several suspects, as where the body of the victim is discovered in a house having several residents, compare *Johnson v. State*, 238 Md. 140, 207 A.2d 643 (1965), cert. denied, 382 U.S. 1013, 86 S.Ct. 623, 15 L.Ed.2d 528, it will often be true that a suspect may be cleared only through the results of interrogation of other suspects. Here too the release of the innocent may be delayed by the Court's rule.

Much of the trouble with the Court's new rule is that it will operate indiscriminately in all criminal cases, regardless of the severity of the crime or the circumstances involved. It applies to every defendant, whether the professional criminal or one committing a crime of momentary passion who is not part and parcel of organized crime. It will slow down the investigation and the apprehension of confederates in those cases where time is of the essence, such as kidnapping, see *Brinegar v. United States*, 338 U.S. 160, 183, 69 S.Ct. 1302, 1314, 93 L.Ed 1879 (Jackson, J., dissenting); *People v. Modesto*, 62 Cal.2d 436, 446, 42 Cal.Rptr. 417, 423, 398 P.2d 753, 759 (1965), those involving the national security, see *United States v. Drummond*, 354 F.2d 132, 147 (C.A.2d Cir. 1965) (*en banc*) (espionage case), pet. for cert. pending, No. 1203, Misc., O.T. 1965; cf. *Gessner v. United States*, 354 F.2d 726, 730, n. 10 (C.A.10th Cir. 1965) (upholding, in espionage case, trial ruling that

U.S. SUPREME
COURT,
OCTOBER 1966

Government need not submit classified portions of interrogation transcript), and some of those involving organized crime. In the later context the lawyer who arrives may also be the lawyer for the defendant's colleagues and can be relied upon to insure that no breach of the organization's security takes place even though the accused may feel that the best thing he can do is to cooperate.

At the same time, the Court's *per se* approach may not be justified on the ground that it provides a "bright line" permitting the authorities to judge in advance whether interrogation may safely be pursued without jeopardizing the admissibility of any information obtained as a consequence. Nor can it be claimed that judicial time and effort, assuming that is a relevant consideration, will be conserved because of the ease of application of the new rule. Today's decision leaves open such questions as whether the accused was in custody, whether his statements were spontaneous or the product of interrogation, whether the accused has effectively waived his rights, and whether nontestimonial evidence introduced at trial is the fruit of statements made during a prohibited interrogation, all of which are certain to prove productive of uncertainty during investigation and litigation during prosecution. For all these reasons, if further restrictions on police interrogation are desirable at this time, a more flexible approach makes much more sense than the Court's constitutional straightjacket which forecloses more discriminating treatment by legislative or rule-making pronouncements.

Applying the traditional standards to the cases before the Court, I would hold these confessions voluntary. I would therefore affirm in Nos. 759, 760, and 761, and reverse in No. 584.

NEW YORK TIMES v. SULLIVAN

NEW YORK TIMES V. SULLIVAN

ISSUE

Freedoms of Speech and Press

HOW TO USE MILESTONES IN THE LAW

In this section, the reader is invited to study the court opinions and briefs* that shaped a major facet of First Amendment law. As you read the following pages, you may wish to consider these issues:

- What were the inaccuracies upon which Sullivan's claims of libel were based?

- What about the advertisement made Sullivan believe it was directed at him?

- How did the descriptions of the issues before the Court, and of their significance, differ as presented by the different parties?

- What facts and legal principles did the Alabama Supreme Court rely on for its decision, and how was the U.S. Supreme Court's approach different?

- What sorts of misstatements about a government official do you think would be permissible, and impermissible, under this case?

------

*The Court heard the cases between Sullivan and the *Times*, and Sullivan and the four clergymen, together. Both sets of briefs are included.

THIS CASE IN HISTORY

New York Times v. Sullivan, handed down in the midst of the civil rights movement, changed the inquiry for libel actions, strengthening the freedoms of speech and press when directed at government behavior. L. B. Sullivan, a city commissioner in Montgomery, Alabama, sued the *Times* and four black clergymen over an advertisement placed by the Committee to Defend Martin Luther King and the Struggle for Freedom in the South. The full page ad, which described abuses that students and civil rights activists had suffered at the hands of police and state authorities in various southern cities, contained several inaccuracies. Though the inaccuracies were minor, the Supreme Court of Alabama upheld a judgment of $500,000 against the defendants. In a unanimous 9–0 decision, the U.S. Supreme Court reversed, holding that public officials cannot recover damages for false statements regarding their official conduct unless they can prove actual malice—that is, that the defendant or defendants knew the statements were false or made them with reckless disregard as to whether they were true or false. The decision freed the press and others to comment on government conduct by reducing fears of enormous damage awards based on minor inaccuracies.

New York Times Company v. Sullivan

CITE AS 144 SO.2D 25

—⟋⟍⟋—

THE NEW YORK TIMES COMPANY ET AL.
V.
L. B. SULLIVAN.
3 DIV. 961.

Supreme Court of Alabama.
Aug. 30, 1962.

Suit for libel against nonresident, corporate, newspaper publisher and others. The Circuit Court, Montgomery County, Walter B. Jones, J., entered a judgment for the plaintiff and the defendants appealed. The Supreme Court, Harwood, J., held that the publication of libelous matter in another state and the distribution of such matter within Alabama gave rise to a cause of action for libel in Alabama, and the evidence justified an award of $500,000 damages.

Affirmed.

Activities of foreign corporation, which published newspaper and sent representatives into Alabama to solicit advertisements and gather news stories, were amply sufficient to meet minimal standards required for service of process in libel suit on corporation's resident "stringer" correspondent who was paid only for such articles as were accepted by corporation. Laws 1953, p. 347.

Statute providing for substituted service on nonresident corporations fully meets requirements of due process. Laws 1953, p. 347.

Affidavit filed by plaintiff, suing foreign newspaper corporation for libel, stated, sufficient facts to invoke statute providing substituted service on nonresident corporation. Laws 1953, p. 347.

Legislature's purpose in calling for affidavit to invoke substituted service statute was not to require detailed quo modo of business done but to furnish Secretary of Stare with sufficient information so that he could perform duties imposed on him. Laws 1953, p. 347.

Ultimate determination of whether nonresident corporation has done business in state or performed work or services in state, and whether cause of action accrues from such acts, thereby coming within substituted service statute, is judicial and not ministerial. Laws 1953, p. 347.

When nonresident prints libel beyond boundaries of state and distributes published libel in Alabama, cause of action for libel arises in Alabama as well as in state of printing or publishing of libel.

Where foreign newspaper corporation published libelous advertisement in New York and sent its papers into Alabama with carrier as its agent, freight prepaid, and with title passing on delivery to consignee, cause of action for libel arose from acts of newspaper in Alabama. Code 1940, Tit. 57, § 25; Laws 1953, p. 347.

Scope of substituted service is as broad as permissible limits of due process. Laws 1953, p. 347.

Nonresident corporation, by including in motion to quash service of process, prayer that court dismiss action as to corporation for lack of jurisdiction of subject matter of action, went beyond question of jurisdiction over corporate person and made a general appearance which waived any defects in service of process and submitted its corporate person to jurisdiction of court.

Pleading based on lack of jurisdiction of person are in their nature pleas in abatement which find no special favor in law, are purely dilatory and amount to no more than declaration that defendant is in court in proper action, after actual notice, but because of defect in service he is not legally before court.

Where words published tend to injure person libeled by them in his reputation, profession, trade or business, or charge him with indictable offense, or tend to bring individual into public contempt words are libelous per se.

Publication is not to be measured by its effect when subjected to critical analysis of trained legal mind, but must be construed and determined by its natural and probable effect upon mind of average lay reader.

Impersonal reproach of indeterminate class is not actionable but if words may by any reasonable application import charge against several defendants, under some general description of general name, it is for jury to decide whether charge has personal application averred by plaintiff.

Court would judicially know that City of Montgomery operates under commission form

SUPREME COURT
OF ALABAMA,
AUGUST 1962

SUPREME COURT
OF ALABAMA,
AUGUST 1962

of government and that by provision of statute executive and administrative powers are distributed into departments of public health and public safety; streets, parks and public property and improvements; accounts, finances, and public affairs; and that assignments of commissioners may be changed at any time by majority of board. Laws 1931, p. 30; Code 1940, Tit. 37, § 51.

It is common knowledge that average person knows that municipal agents such as police and firemen are under control and direction of city governing body, and more particularly under direction and control of a single commissioner. Code 1940, Tit. 37, § 51.

Advertisement which falsely recounted activities of city police on college campus and elsewhere was libelous per se, and libelous matter was of and connected with plaintiff police commissioner.

Where advertisement was libelous per se it was not necessary to allege special damages and complaint could be very simple and brief and there was no need to set forth innuendo.

Complaint referring to false advertisement concerning police activities was sufficient to state a cause of action for libel in favor of plaintiff police commissioner.

Broad right of parties to interrogate jurors as to interest or bias is limited by propriety and pertinence and is exercised within sound discretion of trial court. Code 1940, Tit. 30, § 52.

Refusal to allow newspaper sued for libel to ask certain questions of jury venire as to bias against newspaper was not an abuse of discretion where prospective jurors had already indicated that there was no reason which would cause them to hesitate to return a verdict for newspaper. Code 1940, Tit. 30, § 52.

Refusal to allow defendant newspaper, being sued for libel, to ask of jury venire if any of them had been plaintiffs in litigation in court was not an abuse of discretion, considering completeness of qualification of prospective jurors and remoteness of question. Code 1940, Tit. 30, § 52.

First Amendment of United States Constitution does not protect libelous publications. U.S.C.A.Const. Amend. 1.

Fourteenth Amendment of United States Constitution is directed against state and not private action. U.S.C.A.Const. Amend. 14.

Where words are actionable per se complaint need not specify damages and proof of pecuniary injury is not required since such injury is implied.

Testimony of witness that they associated libelous statements in advertisement with plaintiff who was suing defendant newspaper was admissible. Code 1940, Tit. 7, § 910.

Admission of testimony by witness, who had already testified that they had associated plaintiff with libelous advertisement, that if they had believed matter contained in advertisement they would have thought less of plaintiff was not error on ground that answers were hypothetical and implied that witness thought ad was published of an concerning plaintiff.

Proof of common knowledge is harmless though it is unnecessary to offer such proof. Supreme Court Rules, rule 45.

It is matter of common knowledge that publication of matter that is libelous per se would, of believed, lessen person in eyes of any recipient of libel.

Court's reference to witness for defendant newspaper in libel action as a very high official of newspaper was not, in view of witness' background and state of record, reversible error. Supreme Court Rules, rule 45.

Where no objections were interposed to argument of counsel nothing was presented for review by claim of prejudicial statements of counsel in argument.

Defendant newspaper could not predicate error in libel trial because of hostile newspaper articles where at no time did defendant suggest continuance or charge of venue.

Defendant newspaper could not predicate error in libel trial due to presence of photographers in courtroom where at no time did was an objection interposed to their presence.

Where newly discovered evidence was not basis of motion for new trial court was confined, upon hearing motion, to matters contained in record of trial.

Court's oral charge must be considered as whole and if instruction as a whole states law correctly there is no reversible error even though part of instruction, when considered alone, might be erroneous.

Charge of court, when considered as whole, was a fair, accurate, and clear expression of governing principles and that portion of charge which referred to libelous advertisement aimed at plaintiff did not remove from jury question of whether advertisement was of an concerning plaintiff.

Statement that counsel excepted to described portions of court's charge was descriptive of subject matter only and was too indefinite to invite review.

Charges instructing jury that if the jury "find" or "find from the evidence" were refused without error in that predicate for jury's determination in civil suit is "reasonably satisfied from the evidence."

Court cannot be reversed for refusal of charges which are not expressed in exact and appropriate terms of law.

Judgment will not be reversed or affirmed because of refusal, or giving, of "belief" charges.

Refusal to sustain individual defendant's objection in libel action to way one of plaintiff's counsel pronounced word "Negro" presented nothing for review where no further objections were interposed after colloquy between court and counsel and no exceptions were reserved.

Claims that error infected record in libel action because courtroom was segregated during trial and because judge was not legally elected due to alleged deprivation of Negro voting rights could not be presented for review where such matters were not presented in trial below.

Claim that parties were deprived of fair trial in that judge was, by virtue of statute, member of jury commission must be considered waived where it was not raised in trial below. Loc.Laws 1939, p. 66.

Where there are no judgments on motion for new trial and such motions had become discontinued, assignments attempting to raise questions as to weight of evidence and excessiveness of damages were ineffective and presented nothing for review on appeal.

Questions as to weight of evidence and excessiveness of damages can be presented only by motion for new trial.

Evidence authorized award of $500,000 damages against defendant newspaper for publication of libelous advertisement and against individual defendants who subscribed their names to such advertisement.

There is presumption of correctness of verdict where trial judge has refused to grant new trial.

T. Eric Embry, Beddow, Embry & Beddow and Fred Blanton, Birmingham, and Lord, Day & Lord and Herbert Wechsler, New York City, for appellant New York Times.

Chas. S. Conley and Vernon Z. Crawford, Montgomery. for individual appellants.

R. E. Steiner, III, Sam Rice Baker, M. R. Nachman, Jr., Steiner, Crum & Baker and Calvin M. Whitesell, Montgomery, for appellee.

Harwood, Justice.

This is an appeal from a judgment in the amount of $500,000.00 awarded as damages in a libel suit. The plaintiff below was L. B. Sullivan, a member of the Board of Commissioners of the City of Montgomery, where he served as Police Commissioner. The defendants below were *The New York Times*, a corporation, and four individuals, Ralph D. Abernathy, Fred L. Shuttlesworth, S. S. Seay, Sr., and J. E. Lowery.

Service of the complaint upon *The New York Times* was by personal service upon Dan McKee as an agent of the defendant, and also by publication pursuant to the provisions of Sec. 199(1) of Tit. 7, Code of Alabama 1940.

The Times moved to quash service upon it upon the grounds that McKee was not its agent, and *The Times*, a foreign corporation, was not doing business in Alabama, and that service under Sec. 199(1) was improper, and to sustain either of the services upon it would be unconstitutional.

After hearing upon the motion to quash, the lower court denied such motion.

In this connection the plaintiff presented evidence tending to show *The Times* gathers new from national press services, from its staff correspondents, and from string correspondents, sometimes called "stringers."

The Times maintained a staff correspondent in Atlanta, Claude Sitton, who covered eleven southern states, including Alabama.

During the period from 1956 through April 1960, regular staff correspondents of *The Times* spent 153 days in Alabama to gather new articles for submission to *The Times*. Forty-nine staff news articles so gathered were introduced in evidence.

SUPREME COURT OF ALABAMA, AUGUST 1962

Sitton himself was assigned to cover in Alabama, at various times, the so-called "demonstrations," the hearings of the Civil Rights Commission in Montgomery, and proceedings in the United States District Court in Montgomery. During his work in Alabama, he also conducted investigations and interviews in such places as Clayton and Union Springs. On some of his visits to Alabama, Sitton would stat as long as a week or ten days.

In May of 1960, he came to Alabama for the purpose of covering the Martin Luther King trial. After his arrival in Montgomery, he "understood" an attempt would be made to serve him. He contacted Mr. Roderick McLeod Jr., an attorney representing The Times, and was advised to leave Alabama. Shortly after this he call McKee, the "stringer" in Montgomery, and talked generally about the King trial with him.

In addition, The Times made an active effort to keep a resident "stringer" in Montgomery at all times, and as a matter of policy wanted to have three "stringers" in Alabama at all times.

The work of "stringers" was outlined by Sitton as follows: "When The Times feels there is a news story of note going on in an area where a particular stringer lives * * * The Times calls on a stringer for a story."

"Stringers" fill out blank cards required by The Times, which refer to them as "our correspondents." Detailed instructions are also given to "stringers" by The Times.

"Stringers" also on occasions initiate stories to The Times by telephone recordation. If these stories were not accepted, The Times pays the telephone tolls.

A "stringer" is usually employed by another newspaper, or news agency and is called upon for stories occasionally, or offers upon for stories his own. A "stringer" is paid at about the rate of a penny a word. No deductions are made from these payments for such things as income tax, social security, insurance contributions, etc., and "stringers" are not carried on the payroll of The Times. Up to July 25 for the year 1960, The Times he paid Chadwick, the "stringer" in Birmingham, $135.00 for stories accepted, and paid McKee $90.00.

It further appears that upon receipt of a letter from the plaintiff Sullivan demanding a retraction and apology for the statements appearing in the advertisement, which is the basis of this suit, the general counsel of The Times in New York requested the Assistant Managing Editor of The Times to have an investigation made of the correctness of the facts set forth in the advertisement in question. The Times thereupon communicated with McKee and asked for a report. After his investigation, McKee sent a lengthy wire to The Times setting forth facts which demonstrated with clarity the utter falsity of the allegations contained in the advertisement. McKee was also paid $25.00 by The Times for help given Harrison Salisbury, a staff correspondent of The Times when he was in Alabama on an assignment in the spring of 1960.

The Times also has a news service and sells to other papers stories sent it by its staff correspondents, "stringers," and local reporters. In this connection the lower court observed:

"Obviously, The Times considered the news gathering activities of these staff correspondents and 'stringers' a valuable and unique complement to the news gathering facilities of the Associated Press and other wire services of which The Times is a member. The stories of the 'stringers' appear under the 'slug' 'Special to The New York Times,' and there were 59 such 'specials' in the period from January 1, 1956, through April of 1960."

ADVERTISING

About three quarters of the revenue of The Times comes from advertisements. In 1956, The New York Times Sales, Inc., was set up. This a wholly owned subsidiary of The Times and its sole function is to solicit advertising for The Times only.

All of the officials of "Sales" are also officials of The Times.

Two solicitors for "Sales," as well as two employees of The Times have at various times come into Alabama seeking advertising for the The Times. Between July 1959 and June 3, 1960, one representative spent over a week in this State, another spent a week and a third spent three days. Advertising business was solicited in Birmingham, Montgomery, Mobile, and Selma. Between January 1, 1960 and May 1960, inclusive, approximately seventeen to eighteen thousand dollars worth of advertising was thus sold in Alabama, while in the period of 1956 through April 1960, revenues of $26, 801.64 were realized by The Times from Alabama advertisers.

CIRCULATION

The Times sends about 390 daily, and 2,500 Sunday editions into Alabama.

Shipments are made by mail, rail, and air, with transportation charges being prepaid by *The Times*. Dealers are charged for the papers.

Credit is given for unsold papers and any loss in transit is paid by *The Times*.

Claims for losses are handled by baggagemen in Alabama, and *The Times* furnished claim cards to dealers who bring them to the baggagemen, *The Times* paying for losses or incomplete copies upon substantiation by the local Alabama baggagemen.

Account cards of various Alabama *Times* dealers show that credit was thus given for unsold merchandise.

We are here confronted with the question of in personal jurisdiction acquired by service upon an alleged representative of a foreign corporation.

The severe limitations of the doctrine of *Bank of Augusta v. Earle* (1839) 13 Pet. 519, 13 U.S. 519, 10 L.Ed.2d 274, that a corporation "must dwell in the place of its creation, and cannot migrate to another sovereignty," proving unsatisfactory, the courts, by resort to fictions of "presence," "consent," and "doing business," attempted to find answers compatible with social and economic needs. Until comparatively recent years these bases of jurisdictions have tended only to confuse rather than clarify, leading the late Judge Learned Hand to remark that it was impossible to determine any established rule, but that "we must step from tuft to tuft across the morass." *Htuchinson v. Chase and Gilbert*, (2 Cir.) 45 F.2d 139.

In *Pennoyer v. Neff*, 95 U.S. 714, 24 L.Ed. 565, the court held that the Fourteenth Amendment to the Federal Constitution required a relationship between the State and the person jurisdiction, and there must be a reasonable notification to the person upon whom the state seeks to exercise its jurisdiction. The required relationship between the State and the person was held to be presence within the State, and as a corollary, no state could "extend its process beyond that territory so as to subject either persons or property to its decisions."

In *Hess v. Pawloski*, 274 U.S. 352, 47 S.Ct. 632, 71, L.Ed. 1091 (1927), the United States Supreme Court sustained the validity of a non-

resident motorist statute which provided that the mere act of driving an automobile in a state should be deemed an appointment of a named state official as agent to receive service in a suit arising out of the operation of the motor vehicle on the highway of such state. The dangerous nature of motor vehicle was deemed to justify the statute as a reasonable exercise of police power to preserve the safety of the citizens of the state, and the consent for service exacted by the State for use of its highways was reasonable.

In 1935 the same reasoning was applied in upholding a state statute permitting service on an agent of a non-resident individual engaged in the sale of corporate securities in the state in claims arising out of such business.*Henry L. Doherty and Co. v. Goodman*,

Corporations being mere legal entities and incapable of having physical presence as such in a foreign state, and its agents being limited by the scope of their employment, neither the "presence" theory nor the "consent" theory could satisfactorily be applied as a basis for personal jurisdiction.

As to personal jurisdiction over non-resident corporation, the rule therefore evolved that such jurisdiction could be based upon the act of such corporations "doing business" in a state, though echoes of the "presence" and "consent" doctrines may be found in some decisions purportedly applying the "doing business" doctrine in suits against foreign corporations. See *Green v. Chicago Burlington and Quincy Ry.*, 205 U.S. 530, 27 S.Ct. 595, 51 L.Ed. 916, when "presence" of a corporation was found to exist from business done in a state, and *Old Wayne Mutual Life Ass'n. of Indianapolis v. McDonough*, 204 U.S. 8, 27 S.Ct. 236, 51 L.Ed. 345, where implied consent to jurisdiction was said to arise from business done in the state of the forum.

The term "doing business" carries no inherent criteria. It is a concept dependent upon each court's reaction to facts. These reactions were varied, and the conflicting decisions evoked the observation of Judge Learned Hand, then fully justified, but no longer apt since the "morass" has been considerably firmed up by subsequent decisions of the United States Supreme Court.

In *International Shoe v. State of Washington et al.*, 326 U.S. 310, 66 S.Ct. 154, 90 L.Ed. 95, the old bases of personal jurisdiction were re-cast, the court saying:

SUPREME COURT
OF ALABAMA,
AUGUST 1962

SUPREME COURT
OF ALABAMA,
AUGUST 1962

"To say that the corporation is so far 'present' there as to satisfy due process requirements * * * is to beg the question to be decided. For the terms 'present' or 'presence' are used merely to symbolize those activities of the corporation's agent within the state which courts will deem to be sufficient to satisfy the demands of due process. * * * Those demands may be met by such contacts of the corporation with the state of the forum as make it reasonable, in the context of our federal system of government, to require the corporation to defend the particular suit which is brought there. An 'estimate of the inconveniences' which would result to the corporation from a trial away from its 'home' or principal place a business is relevant in this connection.

That the new test enunciated is dependent upon the degree of contacts and activities exercised in the forum state is made clear, the court saying:

"* * * due process requires only that in order to subject a defendant to a judgment in personal, if he be not present within the territory of the forum, we have certain minimum contacts with it such that the maintenance of the suit does not offend 'traditional notions of fair play and substantial justice.'"

In accord with the above doctrine is our case of Boyd v. Warren Paint and Color Co., 254 Ala. 687, 49 So.2d 559.

In 1957 the United States Supreme Court handed down its opinion in McCoy v. International Life Insurance Co., 355 U.S. 220, 78 S.Ct. 199, 2 L.Ed.2d 223.This case involved the validity of a California judgment rendered in a processing where service was had upon the defendant company by registered mail addressed to the respondent at its principal place of business in Texas. A California statute subjecting foreign corporations to suit in California on insurance contracts with California residents even though such corporations could not be served with process within its borders.

The facts show that petitioner's son, a resident of California, bought a life insurance policy from an Arizona corporation, naming petitioner as beneficiary. Later, respondent, a Texas corporation, agreed to assume the insurance obligations of the Arizona company, and mailed a re-insurance certificate to the son in California, offering to insure him in accordance with his policy. He accepted the offer and paid premiums by mail from California to the company's office in Texas. Neither corporation ever had any office

in California, nor any agent therein, nor had solicited or done any other business in the state. Petitioner sent proofs of her son's death to respondent, but it refused to pay the claim.

The Texas court refused to enforce the California judgment holding it void under the Fourteenth Amendment because of lack of valid service. McGee v. International Life Insurance Company, Tex.Civ.App., 288 S.W.2d 579.

In reversing the Texas Court, the United States Supreme Court wrote:

"Since Pennoyer v. Neff, 95 U.S. 714, 24 L.Ed. 565, this Court has held that Due Process Clause of the Fourteenth Amendment places some limit on the power of state courts to enter binding judgments against persons not served with process within their boundaries. But just where this line of limitation falls has been the subject of prolific controversy, particularly with respect to foreign corporations. In a continuing process of evolution this Court accepted and then abandoned 'consent,' 'doing business,' and 'presence' as the standard for measuring the extent of state judicial power over such corporations. See Henderson, The Position of Foreign Corporations in American Constitutional Law, c. V. Mores recently in International Shoe Co. v. State of Washington, 326 U.S. 310, 66 S.Ct. 154, 90 L.Ed. 95, the Court decided that 'due process requires only that order to subject a defendant to a judgment in personam, if he be not present within the territory of the forum. he have certain minimum contacts with it such that the maintenance of the suit does not offend 'traditional notions of fair play and substantial justice.'" 326 U.S. at 316, 66 S.Ct. at 158.

"Looking back over this long history of litigation a trend is clearly discernible toward expanding the permissible scope of state jurisdiction over foreign corporations and other nonresidents. In part this attributable to the fundamental transformation of our national economy over the years. Today many commercial transactions touch two or more States and may involve parties separated by the full continent. With this increasing nationalization of commerce has come a great increase in the amount of business conducted by mail across state lines. At the same time modern transportation and communication have made it much less burdensome for a party sued to defend himself in a State where he engages in economic activity.

[1] Under the above and more recent doctrines, we are clear to the conclusion that the activities of The New York Times as heretofore set

out, are amply sufficient to more than meet the minimal standards required for service upon its representative McKee.

The adjective "string" in McKee's designation is redundant, and in no wise lessens his status as a correspondent and agent of *The New York Times* in Alabama. Justice demands that Alabama be permitted to protect its citizens from tortious libels, the effects of such libels certainly occurring to a substantial degree in this State.

SUBSTITUTED SERVICE

By Act No. 282, approved 5 August 1953 (Acts of Alabama, Reg.Sess.19s3, page 347) amending a prior Act of 1949, it was provided that any non-resident person, firm, partnership or corporation, not qualified to do business in this State, who shall do any business or perform any character of work or service in this State shall by so doing, be deemed to have appointed the Secretary of State to be his lawful attorney or agent of such non-resident, upon whom process may be served in any action accruing from the acts in this State, or incident thereto, by any non-resident, or his or its agent, servant or employee.

The act further provides that service of process may be made by service of three copies of the process on the Secretary of State, upon the non-resident, provided that notice of such service and a copy of the process are forthwith sent by registered mail by the Secretary of State to the defendant, at his last known address, which shall be stated in the affidavit of the plaintiff, said matter so mailed shall be marked "Deliver to Addressee Only" and "Return Receipt Requested," and provided further that such return receipt shall be received by the Secretary of State purporting to have been signed by the said non-resident.

It is further provided in the Act that any party desiring to obtain service under that Act shall make and file in the cause an affidavit stating facts showing that this Act is applicable.

[2] A mere reading of the above Act demonstrates the sufficiency of the provisions for notice to the non-resident defendant, and that service under the provisions of the Act fully meet the requirements of due process.

Counsel for appellant argues however that the service attempted under Act 282, supra, is defective in two aspects. First, that the affidavit in accompanying the complaint is conclusionary and does not show facts bringing the Act into operation, and second, that the Act complained of did not accrue from acts done in Alabama.

The affidavit filed by the plaintiff avers that the defendant " * * * has actually done and is doing business or performing work or services in the State of Alabama; that this cause of action has arisen out of the doing of such business or as an incident thereof by said defendant in the State of Alabama."

[3–5] The affidavit does state facts essential to the invocation of Act 282, supra. We do not think the legislative purpose in requiring the affidavit was to require a detailed quo modo of the business done, but rather was to furnish the Secretary of State with information sufficient upon which to perform the duties imposed upon that official. The ultimate determination of whether the non-resident has done business or performed work or services in this State, and whether the cause of action accrues from such acts, is judicial, and not ministerial, as demonstrated by appellant's motion to quash.

As to appellant's second contention that the cause did not accrue from any acts of *The Times* in Alabama, it is our conclusion that this contention is without merit.

Equally applicable to newspaper publishing are the observations made in *Consolidated Cosmetics v. D-A Pub. Co., Inc., et al.*, 7 Cir. 186 F.2d 906 at 908, relative to the functions of a magazine publishing company:

> "The functions of a magazine publishing company, obviously, include gathering material to be printed, obtaining advertisers and subscribers, printing, selling and delivering the magazines for sale. Each of these, we think, constitutes as essential factor of the magazine publication business. Consequently if a non-resident corporation sees fit to perform any one of those essential functions in a given jurisdiction, it necessarily follows that it is conducting its activities in such a manner as to be subject to jurisdiction."

[6,7] It is clear under our decisions that when a non-resident prints a libel beyond the boundaries of the State, and distributes and publishes the libel in Alabama, a cause of action arises in Alabama, as well as in the State of the printing or publishing of the libel. *Johnson Publishing Co. v. Davis*, 271 Ala. 474, 124 So.2d 441; *Weir v. Brotherhood of Railroad Trainmen*, 221 Ala. 494, 129 So. 267; *Bridwell v. Brotherhood of Railroad Trainmen*, 227 Ala. 443, 150 So. 338;

SUPREME COURT OF ALABAMA, AUGUST 1962

Collins v. Brotherhood of Railroad Trainmen, 226 Ala. 659, 148 So. 133

[8] The scope of substituted service is as broad as the process. *Boyd v. Warren Paint & Color Co.,* 254 Ala. 687, 49 So.2d 559; *Ex parte Emerson,* 270 Ala. 697, 121 So.2d 914.

The evidence shows that *The Times* sent its papers into Alabama, with its carrier as its agent, freight prepaid, with title passing on delivery to the consignee. See Tit. 57, Sec.25, Code of Alabama 1940; 2 Williston on Sales, Sec. 279(b), p. 90. Thence the issue went to newsstands for sale to the public in Alabama, in accordance with a long standing business practice.

The Times or its wholly owned advertising subsidiary, on several occasions, had agents in Alabama for substantial periods of time soliciting, and procuring in substantial amounts advertising to appear in *The Times.*

Furthermore, upon the receipt of the letter from the plaintiff demanding a retraction of the matter appearing in the advertisement, *The Times* had its string correspondent in Montgomery, Mr. McKee, investigate the truthfulness of the assertions in the advertisement. The fact that McKee was not devoting his full time to the service of *The Times* is "without constitutional significance." *Scripto Inc, v. Carson, Sheriff, et al.,* 362 U.S. 207, 80 S.Ct 619, 4 L.Ed.2d 660.

In *WSAZ, Inc. v. Lyons,* 254 F.2d 242 (6 Cir.), the defendant television corporation was located in West Virginia. Its broadcasts covered several counties in Kentucky, and the defendant contracted for advertising in the Kentucky counties, all contracts for such advertising being sent to the corporation West Virginia for acceptance.

The alleged libel sued upon occurred during a news broadcast.

Service was obtained by serving the Kentucky Secretary of State under the provisions of a Kentucky statute providing for such service upon a foreign corporation doing business in Kentucky where the action arose out of or was "connected" with the business done by such corporation in Kentucky.

In sustaining the judgment awarded the plaintiff, the court wrote in connection with the validity of the service to support the judgment:

> "All that is necessary here is that the cause of action asserted shall be 'connected' with the business done. Defendant asserts that the alleged libel has no connection with its busi-

ness done in Kentucky. But in view of its admission that its usual business was the business of telecasting and that this included new programs, and in view of the undisputed fact that the alleged libel was part of new programs regularly broadcast by defendant, this contention has no merit.

> "The question due process would seem to be settled by the case of *McGee v. International Life Insurance Co.* (citation), as well as by *International Shoe Co. v. State of Washington,* supra. While defendant was not present in the territory of the forum, it certainly had substantial contacts with it . It sought and executed contracts with it. It sought and executed contracts for the sale of advertising service to be performed and actually performed by its own act within the territory of the forum. We conclude that the maintenance of the suit does not offend 'traditional notions of fair play and substantial notions of fair play and substantial justice.'"

In the present case the evidence shows that the publishing of advertisements was a substantial part of the business of *The Times,* and its newspapers were regularly sent into Alabama. Advertising was solicited in Alabama. Its correspondent McKee was called upon by *The Times* to investigate the truthfulness or falsity of the matters contained in the advertisement after the letter from the plaintiff. The acts therefore disclose not only certain general conditions with reference to newspaper publishing, but also specific acts directly connected with, and directly incident to the business of *The Times* done in Alabama.

The service acquired under the provisions of Act No. 282, supra, was valid.

GENERAL APPEARANCE BY THE TIMES

[9] The trial court also found that *The Times,* by including as a ground of the prayer in its motion to quash, the following, "* * * that this court dismiss this action as to The New York Times Company, A Corporation, for lack of jurisdiction of the subject matter of said action * * *" did thereby go beyond the question of jurisdiction over the corporate person of *The Times,* and made a general appearance, thereby waiving any defects in service of process, and thus submitted its corporate person to the jurisdiction of the court.

The conclusions of the trial court in this aspect are in accord with the doctrines of a majority of our sister states, and the doctrines of our own decisions.

[10] Pleadings based upon lack of jurisdiction of the person are in their nature pleas in abatement, and find no special favor in the law. They are purely dilatory and amount to no more than a declaration by a defendant that he is in court in a proper action, after actual notice, but because of a defect in service, he is not legally before the court. See *Olcese v. Justice's Court*, 156 Cal. 82, 103 P. 317.

In *Roberts v. Superior Court*, 30 Cal.App. 714, 159 P. 465, the court observed:

> "The motion to dismiss the complaint on the ground that the court was without jurisdiction of the subject-matter of the action amounted, substantially or in legal effect, to a demurrer to the complaint on that ground. At all events, a motion to dismiss on the ground of want of jurisdiction of the subject-matter of the action necessarily calls for relief which may be demanded only by a party to the record. It has been uniformly so held, as logically it could not otherwise be held, and, furthermore, that where a party appears and asks for such relief, although expressly characterizing his appearance as special and for the special purpose of objecting to the jurisdiction of the court over his person, he as effectually submits himself to the jurisdiction of the court as though he had legally been served with process."

The reason dictating such conclusion is stated by the Supreme Court of North Carolina in *Dailey Motor Co. v. Reaves*, 184 N.C. 260 114 S.E. 175, to be:

> "Any course that, in substance, is the equivalent of an effort by the defendants to try the matter and obtain a judgment on the merits, in any material aspect of the case, while standing just outside the threshold of the court, cannot be permitted to avail them. A party will not be allowed to occupy so ambiguous a position. He cannot deny the authority of the court to take cognizance of his action for want of jurisdiction of the person or proceeding, and at the same time seek a judgment in his favor on the ground that there is no jurisdiction of the cause of action.

>   * * * * * *

> "We might cite cases and authorities indefinitely to the same purpose and effect, but those to which we have briefly referred will suffice to show how firmly and unquestionable it is established, that it is not only dangerous, but fatal, to couple with a demurrer, or other form of objection based upon the ground that the court does not have jurisdiction of the person, an objection in the form of a demurrer, answer, or otherwise, which substantially pleads to the merits, and, as we have seen, such an objection is presented when the defendant unites with his demurrer for lack of jurisdiction of the person, a cause of demurrer for want of jurisdiction of the cause or subject of the action, and that is exactly what was done in this case."

We will excerpt further from the decisions from other jurisdictions in accord with the doctrine of the above cases, but point out that innumerable authorities from a large number of states may be founds set forth in an annotation to be found in 25 A.L.R.2d, pages 838 through 842.

In *Thompson v. Wilson*, 224 Ala., 299, 140 So. 439, this court stated:

> "If there was a general appearance made in this case, the lower court had jurisdiction of the person of the appellant. (Authorities cited).

> "The filing of a demurrer, unless based solely on the ground of lack of jurisdiction of the person, constitutes a general appearance."

Again, in *Blankenship v. Blankenship*, 263 Ala. 297, 82 So.2d 335, the court reiterated the above doctrine.

Thus the doctrine of our cases is in accord with that of a majority of our sister states that despite an allegation in a special appearance that it is for the sole purpose of questioning the jurisdiction of the court, if matters going beyond the question of jurisdiction of the person are set forth, then the appearance is deemed general, and defects in the service are to be deemed waived.

We deem the lower court's conclusions correct, that *The Times*, by questioning the jurisdiction of the lower court over the subject matter of this suit, made a general appearance, and thereby submitted itself to the jurisdiction of the lower court.

Appellant's assignment No. 9 is to the effect the lower court erred in overruling defendant's demurrers as last amended to plaintiff's complaint.

The defendant's demurrers contain a large number of grounds, and the argument of the appellant is directed toward the propositions that:

> "1. As a matter of law, the advertisement was not published of an concerning the plaintiff, as appears in the face of the complaint.

> 2. The publication was not libelous per se.

3. The complaint was defective in failing to allege special damages

4. The complaint was defective in failing to allege facts or innuendo showing how plaintiff claimed the article had defamed him.

5. The complaint was bad because it stated two causes of action."

Both counts of the complaint aver among other things that " * * * defendants falsely and maliciously published in the City of New York, State of New York, and in the City of Montgomery, Alabama. and throughout the State of Alabama, of and concerning the plaintiff, in a paper entitled *The New York Times*, in the issue of March 29, 1960, on page 25, in an advertisement entitled 'Heed Their Rising Voices' (a copy of said advertisement being attached hereto and made a part hereof as Exhibit 'A'), false and defamatory matter or charges reflecting upon the conduct of the plaintiff as a member of the Board of Commissioners of the City of Montgomery, Alabama, and imputing improper conduct to him, and subjecting him to public contempt, ridicule and shame, and prejudicing the plaintiff in his office, profession, trade or business, with an intent to defame the plaintiff, and particularly the following false and defamatory matter contained therein:

" 'In Montgomery, Alabama, after students sang "My Country 'Tis of Thee" on the State Capitol steps, their leaders were expelled from school, and truckloads of police armed with shotguns and tear-gas ringed the Alabama State College Campus. When the entire student body protested to state authorities by refusing to re-register, their dining hall was padlocked in an attempt to starve them into submission.

* * * * * *

" 'Again and again the Southern violators have answered Dr. King's peaceful protests with intimidation and violence. They have bombed his home almost killing his wife and child. They have assaulted his person. They have arrested him seven times—for "speeding," "loitering," and similar "offenses." And now they have charged him with "perjury"—a *felony* under which they could imprison him for *ten years*."

[11] Where the words published tend to injure a person libeled by them in his reputation, profession, trade or business, or charge him with an indictable offense, or tends to bring the individual into public contempt are libelous

per se. *White v. Birmingham Post Co.*, 233 Ala. 547, 172 So. 649; Iron Age Pub. Co. v. Crudup, 85 Ala. 519, 5 So. 332.

[12] Further, "the publication is not to be measured by its effects when subjected to the critical analysis of a trained legal mind, but must be construed and determined by its natural and probable effect upon the mind of the average lay reader." *White v. Birmingham Post Co.*, supra.

We hold that the matter complained of is, under the above doctrine. libelous per se, if it was published of and concerning the plaintiff.

In "Dangerous Words—A Guide to the Law of Libel," by Philip Wittenberg, we find the following observations, at pages 227 and 228:

"There are groupings which may be finite enough so that a description of the body is a description of the members. Here the problem is merely one of evaluation. Is the description of the member implicit in the description of the body, or is there a possibility that a description of the body may consist of a variety of persons, those included within the charge, and those excluded from it?

* * * * * *

"The groupings in society today are innumerable and varied. Chances of recovery for libel of the members of such groups diminish with increasing size, and increase as the class or group decreases. Whenever a class or group decreases. Whenever a class decreases so that the individuals become obvious, they may recover for a libel descriptive of the group. In cases where the group is such that it is definite in number; where its composition is easily recognizable and the forms of its organization are apparent, then recognition of individuals libeled by group defamation becomes clear."

[13] The same principle is aptly stated in *Gross v. Cantor*, 270 N.Y. 93, 200 N.E. 592, as follows:

"An action for defamation lies only in case the defendant has published the matter 'of and concerning the plaintiff.' * * * Consequently an impersonal reproach of an indeterminate class is not actionable. * * * 'But if the words may by any reasonable application, import a charge against several individuals, under some general description or general name, the plaintiff has the right to go on to trial, and it is for the jury to decide, whether the charge has the personal application averred by the plaintiff.'

"We cannot go beyond the face of this complaint. It does not there appear that the publication was so scattered a generality or described so large a class as such that no one could have been personally injured by it. Perhaps the plaintiff will be able to satisfy a jury of the reality of his position that the article was directed at him as an individual and did not miss the mark."

And in *Wofford v. Meeks*, 129 Ala.; 349, 30 So. 625, we find this court saying:

"Mr. Freeman, in his note to case of *Jones v. Stare*, (Tex.Cr.App.) 43 S.W. 78,70 Am.St.Rep. 756, after reviewing the cases, says: 'We apprehend the true rule is that, although the libelous publication is directed against a particular class of persons or a group, yet any one of the class or group may maintain an action, upon showing that the words apply especially to him.' And further, he cites the cases approvingly which hold that each of the persons composing the class may maintain the action. We think this the correct doctrine, and it is certainly supported by the great weight of authority. 13 Am. & Eng.Enc.Law, 392, and note 1; *Hardy v. Williamson*, 86 Ga.551, 12 S.E. 874, 22 Am.St.Rep. 479."

[14] We judicially know that the City of Montgomery operates under a commission form of government. (See Act 20, Gen.Acts of Alabama 1931, page 30.) We further judicially know that under the provisions of Sec. 51, tit. 37, Code of Alabama 1940, that under this form of municipal government the executive and administrative powers are distributed into departments of (1) public health and public safety, (2) streets, parks and public property and improvements, and , (3) accounts, finances, and public affairs; and that the assignments of the commissioners may be changed at any time by a majority of the board.

The appellant contends that the word "police" encompasses too broad a group to permit the conclusion that the statement in the advertisement was of and concerning the plaintiff since he was not mentioned by name.

[15] We think it common knowledge that the average person knows that municipal agents, such as police and firemen, and others, are under the control and direction of the city governing body and more particularly under the direction and control of a single commissioner. In measuring the performance or deficiencies of such groups, praise or criticism is usually attached to the official in complete control of the body. Such common knowledge and belief has its origin in established legal patterns as illustrated by Sec. 51, supra.

In *De Hoyos v. Thornton*, 259 App.Div. 1, 18 N.Y.S.2d 121, a resident of Monticello, New York, a town of 4000 population, had published in a local newspaper an article in which she stated that a proposed acquisition of certain property by the municipality was "another scheme to bleed the taxpayers and force more families to lose their homes. * * * It seems to me it might be better to relieve the tension on the taxpayers right now and get ready for the golden age * * * and not be dictated to by gangsters and Chambers of Commerce."

The mayor and the three trustees of Monticello brought libel actions. The court originally considering the complaint dismissed the actions on the grounds that the plaintiffs were not mentioned in the article, and their connection with the municipality was not stated in the complaint. In reversing this decision the Appellate Division of the Supreme Court wrote: "There is no room for doubt as to who were the objects of her attack. Their identity is as clear to local readers from the article itself as if they were mentioned by name."

[16] The court did not err in overruling the demurrer in the aspect that the libelous matter was not of and concerning the plaintiffs.

[17] The advertisement being libelous per se, it was not necessary to allege special damages in the complaint. *Iron Age Pub. Co. v. Crudup*, 85 Ala. 519, 5 So. 332.

[18] Where, as in this case, the matter published is libelous per se, then the complaint may be very simple and brief (*Penry v. Dozier*, 161 Ala. 292, 49 So. 909), and there is no need to set forth innuendo. *White v. Birmingham Post Co.*, 233 Ala. 547, 172 So. 649. Further, a complaint in all respects similar to the present was considered sufficient in our recent case of *Johnson Publishing Co. v. Davis*, 271 Ala. 474, 124 So.2d 441.

The *Johnson* case, supra, is also to the effect that where a newspaper publishes a libel in New York, and by distribution of the paper further publishes the libel in Alabama, a cause of action arises in Alabama, as well as in New York, and that the doctrine of *Age-Herald Pub. Co, v. Huddleston*, 207 Ala. 40, 92 So. 193, 37 S.L.R. 898, concerned venue, and venue statutes do not apply to a foreign corporation not qualified to do business in Alabama.

SUPREME COURT OF ALABAMA, AUGUST 1962

In view of the principles above set forth, we hold that the lower court did not err in overruling the demurrer to the complaint in the aspects contended for and argued in appellant's brief.

Assignments of error Nos. 14, 15, 16 and 17, related to the court's refusal to permit certain questions to be put to the venire in qualifying the jurors.

The appellant contends that *The Times* was unlawfully deprived of its right to question the jury venire to ascertain the existence of bias or prejudice. The trial court refused to allow four questions which were in effect, (1) Do you have any conviction, opinion or pre-disposition which would compel you to render a verdict against *The Times*? (2) Have any of you been plaintiffs in litigation in this court? (3) If there is no evidence of malice, would you refuse to punish *The Times*? (4) Is there any reason which would cause you to hesitate to return a verdict in favor of the *The Times*?

The prospective jurors had already indicated that the were unacquainted with any of the facts in the case, that they had not discussed the case with anyone nor had it been discussed in their presence nor were they familiar in any manner with the contentions of the parties. Appellant was permitted to propound at some length other questions designed to determine whether there was any opinion or pre-disposition which would influence the juror's judgment. The jurors indicated that there was no reason whatsoever which would cause them to hesitate to return a verdict for *The Times*.

[19, 20] Sec. 52, Tit. 30 Code of Alabama 1940, gives the parties a broad tight to interrogate jurors as to interest or bias. This right is limited by propriety and pertinence. It is exercised within the sound discretion of the trial court. has been abused where similar questions have already been answered by the prospective jurors. *Dyer v. State*, 241 Ala. 679, 4 So.2d 311.

[21] Only the second question could have conceivably revealed anything which was not already brought out by appellant's interrogation of the prospective jurors. Considering the completeness of the qualification and the remoteness of the second question, the exclusion of that inquiry by the trial court will not be regarded as an abuse of discretion. *Noah v. State*, 38 Ala. App. 531, 89 So.2d 231.

Appellant contends that without the right to adequately question the prospective jurors, a defendant cannot adequately ensure that his case is being tried before a jury which meets the federal constitutional standards laid downing such decisions as *Irvin v. Dowd*, 366 U.S. 717, 81 S.Ct. 1639, 6 L.Ed. 751. It is sufficient to say that the jurors who tried this case were asked repeatedly, and in various forms, by counsel for *The Times* about their impartiality in every reasonable manner.

Appellant's assignment of error 306 pertains to the refusal of requested charge T. 22, which was affirmative in nature.

It is appellant's contention that refusal of said charge contravenes Amendment One of the United States Constitution and results in an improper restraint of freedom of the press, further, that refusal of said charge is violative of the Fourteenth Amendment of the federal constitution.

In argument in support of this assignment, counsel for appellant asserts that the advertisement was only an appeal for support of King and "thousands of Southern Negro students" said to be "engaged in widespread non-violent demonstrations in positive affirmation of the right to live in human dignity as guaranteed by the U.S. Constitution and the Bill of Rights."

The fallacy of such argument is that is overlooks the libelous portions of the advertisement which are the very crux of this suit.

[22] The First Amendment of the U.S. Constitution does not protect libelous publications. *Near v. Minnesota*, 283 U.S. 697, 51 S.Ct. 625, 75 L.Ed. 1357; *Konigsberg v. State Bar of California*, 366 U.S. 36, 81 S.Ct. 997, 6 L.Ed.2d 105; *Times Film Corporation v. City of Chicago*, 365 U.S. 43, 81 S.Ct. 391, 5 L.Ed.2d 403; *Chaplinsky v. Ne Hampshire*, 315 U.S. 568, 62 S.Ct. 766, 86 L.Ed. 1031; *Beauharnais v. Illinois*, 343 U.S. 250, 72 S.Ct. 725, 96 L.Ed. 919.

[23] The Fourteenth Amendment is directed against State action and not private action. *Collins v. Hardyman*, 341 U.S. 651, 71 S.Ct. 937, 95 L.Ed. 1253.

Assignment of error No, 306 is without merit.

Appellant's assignment of error No. 94 also pertains to the court's refusal of its requested charge T. 22.

SUPREME COURT
OF ALABAMA,
AUGUST 1962

Appellant's argument under this assignment asserts it was entitled to have charge T. 22 given because of the plaintiff's failure to plead or prove special damages.

[24] In libel action, where the words are actionable per se, the complaint need not specify damages (*Johnson v. Robertson*, 8 Port. 486), nor is proof of pecuniary injury required, such injury being implied. *Johnson Publishing Co. v. Davis*. supra.

[25] Assignments 18, 19, 21, 23, 25, 27, 30 and 32, relate to the action of the court in overruling defendant's objections to questions propounded to six witnesses presented by the plaintiff as to whether they associated the statements in the advertisement with the plaintiff. All of the witnesses answered such questions in such manner as to indicate that they did so associate the advertisement.

Without such evidence the plaintiff's cause would of necessity fall, for that the libel was of or concerning the plaintiff is the essence of plaintiff's claim.

Section 910 of Title 7, Code of Alabama 1940, pertaining to libel, among other things, provides that " * * * and if the allegation be denied, the plaintiff must prove, on the trial, the facts showing that the defamatory matter was published or spoken of him." This statute would seem to require the proof here admitted. And in *Wofford v. Meeks*, 129 Ala. 349, 30 So. 625, 55 L.R.A. 214, the court stated that where the libel is against a group, any one of that group may maintain an action "upon showing that the words apply specially to him," and in *Chandler v. Birmingham New Co.*, 209 Ala. 208 95 So. 886, this court said, "Any evidence which tended to show it was not intended 'of and concerning him' was material and relevant to the issue."

In *Hope v. Hearst Consolidated Publications*, (2 Cir.1961), 294 F.2d 681, the court said as to the admissibility of testimony that a witness believed the defamatory matter referred to the plaintiff:

> "In this regard it appears that the New York exclusionary rule represents a distinct, if not a lone, minority voice. The vast majority of reported cases, from both American state and British courts, espouse the admission of such evidence; the text writers similarly advocate its admissibility."

* * * * * *

"The plaintiff, as a necessary element in obtaining relief, would have to prove that the coercive lies were understood, by customers, to be aimed in his direction. In a case where the plaintiff was not specifically named, the exact issue now before us would be presented."

In accord with the doctrine that the instant evidence was admissible may be cited, among authorities *Marr v. Putnam Oil Co.*, 196 Or. 1, 246 P.2d 509; *Red River Valley Pub. Co., Inc. v. Bridges*, (Tex.Civ.App.) 254 S.W.2d 854; *Colbert v. Journal Pub. Co.*, 19 N.M. 156, 142 P. 146; *Prosser v. Callis et al.*, 117 Ind. 105, 19 N.E. 735; *Martin County Bank v. Day*, 73 Minn. 195, 75 N.W. 1115; *Ball v. Evening American Pub. Co.*, 237 Ill. 592, 86 N.E. 1097; *Children v. Shinn*, 168 Iowa 531, 150 N.W. 864.

Counsel for appellant argues that the questions " * * * inescapably carried the implication that the witness thought the ad was published of and concerning the plaintiff." Each and every one of the above named witnesses had testified previous to the instant questions, that they had associated the City Commissioners, or the plaintiff, with the advertisement upon reading it. The questions where therefore based upon the witnesses' testimony that they associated the advertisement with the plaintiff, and not merely an implication that might be read into the question.

Counsel further argues that the question is hypothetical in that none of the witnesses testified they believed the advertisement, or that they thought less of the plaintiff.

While we think such evidence of small probative value, yet it would have relevancy not only as to its effect upon the recipient, but also as to the effect such publication may reasonably have had upon other recipients. See "Defamation," 69 Harv.L.R., 877, at 884.

[27] This aside, we cannot see that the answers elicited were probably injurious to the substantial rights of the appellant. Sup.Court Rule 45. Proof of common knowledge is without injury, though it be unnecessary to offer such proof.

[28] Clearly we think it common knowledge that publication of matter libelous per se would, if believed, lessen the person concerned in the eyes of any recipient of the libel. See *Tidmore v. Mills*, 33 Ala. App. 243, 32 So.2d 769, and cases cited therein.

[29] Assignment of error No. 63 asserts error arising out of the following instance during the cross-examination of Gershon Aronson, a witness for *The Times*, which matter, as shown by the record, had been preceded by numerous objections, and considerable colloquy between counsel and court:

"Q Would you state now sir, what that word means to you; whether it has only a time meaning or whether it also to your eye and mind has a cause and effect meaning?

"Mr. Embry: Now, we object to that, Your Honor. That's a question for the jury to determine—

"The Court: Well, of course, it probably will be a question for the jury, but this gentleman here is a very high official of *The Times and I should think he can testify*—

Mr. Daly: I object to that, Your Honor. He isn't a high official of *The Times* at all—

Mr. Embry: He is just a man that has a routine job there, Your Honor. He is not—

"The Court: Let me give you an exception to the Court's ruling.

"Mr. Embry: We except."

We do not think it can be fairly said that the record discloses a ruling by the trial court on counsel's objection to the use of the term "very high official." The ruling made by the court is palpably to the question to which the objection was interposed. Counsel interrupted the court to object to the term "very high official," and second counsel added, "He is just man that has a routine job there, Your Honor." Apparently this explanation satisfied counsel, as the court's use of the term was not pursued to the extent of obtaining a ruling upon this aspect, and the court's ruling was upon the first, and main objection.

Mr. Aronson testified that he had been with *The Times* for twenty-five years, and Assistant Manager of the Advertising Acceptability Department of *The Times*, and was familiar with the company's policies regarding advertising in all it aspects, that is, sales, acceptability, etc., and that advertisements of organizations and committees that express a point of view comes within the witness's particular duties.

In view of the above background of Mr. Aronson, and the state of the record immediately above referred to, we are unwilling to cast error upon the lower court in the instance brought forth under assignment No. 63.

Assignment of error No. 81 is to the effect that the lower court erred in denying appellant's motion for a new trial. Such an assignment is an indirect assignment of all of the grounds of the motion for a new trial which appellant sees fit to bring forward and specify as error in his brief.

The appellant under this assignment has sought to argue several grounds of its motion for a new trial.

Counsel, in this connection, seeks to cast error on the lower court because of an alleged prejudicial statement made by counsel for the appellee in his argument to the jury.

[30] The record fails to show any objections were interposed to any argument by counsel for any of the litigants during the trial. There is therefore nothing presented to us for review in this regard. *Woodward Iron Co. v. Earley*, 247 Ala. 556, 25 So.2d 267, and cases therein cited.

Counsel also argues two additional grounds contained in the motion for a new trial, (1) that the appellant was deprived of due process in the trial below because of hostile articles in Montgomery newspapers, and (2) because of the presence of photographers in the courtroom and the publication of the names and pictures of the jury prior to the rendition of the verdict.

[31] As to the first point, the appellant sought to introduce in the hearing on the motion for a new trial newspaper articles dated prior to, and during, the trial. The court refused to admit these articles.

At no time during the course of the trial below did the appellant suggest a continuance, or a change of venue, or that it did not have knowledge of said articles.

[32] Likewise, at no time was any objection interposed to the presence of photographers in the courtroom.

[33] Newly discovered evidence was not the basis of the motion for a new trial. This being so, the court was confined upon the hearing on the motion to matters contained in the record of the trial. *Thomason v. Silvey*, 123 Ala. 694, 26 So. 644; *Alabama Gas Co, v. Jones*, 244 Ala. 413, 13 So.2d 873.

Assignment of error 78 pertains to an alleged error occurring in the court's oral charge.

In this connection the record shows the following:

"Mr. Embry: We except, your Honor. We except, your Honor. We except the oral portions of Your's Charge wherein Your Honor charged on libel per se. We object to that portion of Your Honor's Charge wherein Your Honor charged as follows: 'So, as I said, if you are reasonably satisfied from the evidence before you, considered in connection with the rules of the law the Court has stated to you, you would come to consider the question of damages and, where as here, the Court has ruled the matter complained of proved to your reasonable satisfaction and aimed at the plaintiff in this case, is libelous per se then punitive damages may be awarded by the jury even though the amount of actual damages is neither found nor shown.'

"The Court: Overruled and you have an exception."

Preceding the above exception the court had instructed the jury as follows:

"Now, as stated, the defendants say that the ad complained of does not name the plaintiff, Sullivan, by name and that the ad is not published of an concerning him. * * * The plaintiff, Sullivan, as a member of the group referred to must show by the evidence to your reasonable satisfaction that the words objected to were spoken of an concerning him. The reason for this being that while any one of a class or group may maintain an action because of alleged libelous words, he must show to the reasonable satisfaction of the jury that the words he complained of apply especially to him or are published of and concerning him.

* * * * * *

"So, at the very outset of our deliberations you come to this question: Were the words complained of in counts 1 and 2 of this complaint spoken of and concerning the plaintiff, Sullivan? That's the burden he has. He must show that to your reasonable satisfaction and if the evidence in this case does not reasonably satisfy you that the words published were spoken of or concerning Sullivan or that they related to him, why then of course he would not be entitled to any damages and you would not go any further."

In addition the court gave some eleven written charges at defendant's request, instructing the jury in substance that the burden was upon the plaintiff to establish to the reasonable satisfaction of the jury that the advertisement in question was of an concerning the plaintiff, and that without such proof the plaintiff could not recover.

It is to be noted that in the portion of the complained of instructions excerpted above, the court first cautioned the jury they were to consider the evidence in connection with the rules of law stated to them. The court had previously made it crystal clear that he jury were to determine to their reasonable satisfaction from the evidence that the words were spoken of and concerning the plaintiff.

Counsel for appellant contend that because of the words "and aimed at the plaintiff in this case," the instruction would be taken by the jury as charge that the advertisement was of an concerning the plaintiff, and hence the instruction was invasive of the province of the jury.

Removed from the full context of the court's instructions the charge complained of, because of its inept mode of expression, might be criticized as confused and misleading.

[34] However, it is basic that a court's oral charge must be considered as a whole and the part excepted to should be considered in the light of the entire instruction. If as a whole the instructions state the law correctly, there is no reversible error even though a part of the instructions, if considered alone, might even erroneous.

Innumerable authorities enunciating the above doctrines may be found in 18 Ala.Dig. Trial 295(1) through (11).

Specially, in reference to portions of oral instructions that might be criticized because tending to be invasive of the province of the jury, we find the following stated in 89 C.J.S. Trial § 438, the text being amply supported by citations:

"A charge which, taken as a whole, correctly submits the issues to the jury will not be held objectionable because certain instructions, taken in their severalty, may be subject to criticism on the ground they invade the province of the jury, * * * *."

To this same effect, see *Abercombie v. Martin and Hoyt Co.*, 227 Ala. 510, 150 So. 497; *Choctaw Coal and Mining Co., v. Dodd*, 201 Ala. 622, 79 So. 54.

[35] We have carefully read the court's entire oral instruction to the jury. It is a fair, accurate, and clear expression of the governing legal principles. In light of the entire charge we consider that the portion of the charge complained of to be inconsequential, and unlikely to have affected the jury's conclusion. We do not consider it

SUPREME COURT
OF ALABAMA,
AUGUST 1962

probable that this appellant was injured in any substantial right by this alleged misleading instruction in view of the court's repeated and clear exposition of the principles involved, and the numerous written charges given at the defendant's request further correctly instructing the jury in the premises.

The individual appellants, Ralph D. Abernathy, Fred L. Shuttlesworth, S. S. Seay, Sr., and J. E. Lowery have also filed briefs and arguments in their respective appeals. Many of the assignments of error in these individual appeals are governed by our discussion of the principles relating to the appeal of *The Times*. We therefore will now confine our review in the individual appeals to those assignments that may present questions not already covered.

[36] In their assignment of error No. 41, the individual appellants assert that the lower court erred in it oral instructions as to ratification of the use of their names in the publication of the advertisement. The instructions of the court in this regard run for a half a page or better. The record shows that an exception was attempted in the following language:

> "Lawyer Gray: Your Honor, we except to the Court's charge dealing with ratification as well as the Court's charge in connection with the advertisement being libelous per se in behalf of each of individual defendants."

The above attempted exception was descriptive of the subject matter only, and is too indefinite to invite our review. *Birmingham Ry. Light and Power Co. v. Friedman*, 187 Ala. 562, 65 So. 939; *Conway v, Robinson*, 216 Ala. 495, 113 So. 531; *Birmingham Ry, Light and Power Co. v. Jackson*, 198 Ala. 378, 73 So. 627.

[37, 38] Several of the charges instruct the jury that if the jury "find" etc., while others use the term "find from the evidence." These charges were refused without error in that the predicate for the jury's determination in a civil suit is "reasonably satisfied from the evidence." A court cannot be reversed for its refusal of charges which are not expressed in the exact and appropriate terms of the law. *W. P. Brown and Sons Lumber Co, v. Rattray*, 238 Ala. 406, 192 So. 851, 129 A.L.R. 526.

[39] Others of the refused charges, not affirmative in nature, are posited on "belief," or "belief from the evidence." A judgment will not be reversed or affirmed because of the refusal, or giving, of "belief" charges. *Sovereign Camp, W.*

O. W. v. Sirten, 234 Ala. 421, 175 So. 539; *Pan American Petroleum Co. v. Byars*, 228 Ala. 372, 153 So. 616; *Casino Restaurant v. McWhorter*, 35 Ala.App. 332, 46 So.2d 582.

[40] Specification of error number 6 asserts error in the court's action in refusing to sustain the individual defendants' objection to the way one of the plaintiff's counsel pronounced the word "negro." When this objection was interposed, the court instructed plaintiff's counsel to "read it jut like it is," and counsel replied, "I have pronouncing it that way all my life." The court then instructed counsel to proceed. No further objections were interposed, nor exceptions reserved.

We consider this assignment mere quibbling, and certainly nothing is presented for our review in the state of the record.

[41] Counsel have also argued assignments to the effect that error infects this record because, (1) the courtroom was segregated during the trial below, and (2) the trial judge was not duly and legally elected because of alleged deprivation of voting rights to negroes.

Neither of the above matters were presented in trial below, and cannot now be presented for review.

[42] Counsel further argues that the appellants were deprived of a fair trial in that the trial judge was, by virtue of Local Act No. 118, 1939 Local Act of Alabama, p. 66, a member of the jury commission of Montgomery County. This act is constitutional. *Reeves v. State*, 260 Ala. 66, 68 So.2d 14.

Without intimating that any merit attaches to this correction it is sufficient to point out that this point was not raised in the trial below, and must be considered as having been waived. *De Moville v. Merchants & Farmers Bank of Greene County*, 237 Ala. 347, 186 So. 704.

Assignments 42, 121, 122, assert error in the court's refusal to hear the individual appellant's motions for new trials, and reference in brief is made to pages 2058–2105 of the record in this connection.

These pages of the record merely show that the individual appellants filed and presented to the court their respective motions for a new trial on 2 December 1960, the respective motions were continued to 14 January 1961. No further orders in reference to the motions of the individual appellants appear in the record, no judgment of any of the motions of the individual appellants appears in the record.

The motions of the individual appellants therefore became discontinued after 14 January 1961.

[43, 44] There being no judgments on the motion for a new trial of the individual appellants, and they having become discontinued, those assignments by the individual appellants attempting to raise questions as to the weight of the evidence, and the excessiveness of the damages are ineffective and present nothing for review. Such matters can be presented only by a motion for a new trial. See 2 Ala.Dig. Appeal and Error 294(1) and 295, for innumerable authorities.

Other matters are argued in the briefs of the individual appellants. We conclude they are without merit and do not invite discussion, though we observe that some of the matters attempted to be brought forward are insufficiently presented to warrant review.

EVIDENCE ON THE MERITS

The plaintiff first introduced the depositional testimony of Harding Bancroft, secretary of *The Times*.

Mr. Bancroft thus testified that one John Murray brought the original of the advertisement to *The Times* where it was delivered to Gershon Aronson, an employee of *The Times* a Thermo-fax copy of the advertisement was turned over to Vincent Redding, manager of the advertising department, and Redding approved it for insertion in *The Times*. The actual insertion order issued by the Union Advertising Service of New York City.

Redding determined that the advertisement was endorsed by a large number of people who reputation for truth he considered good.

Numerous new stories from its correspondents, published in *The Times*, relating to certain events which formed the basis of the advertisement and which had been published from time to time in *The Times* were identified. These new stories were later introduced in evidence as exhibits.

Also introduced through this witness was a letter from A. Philip Randolph certifying that the four individual defendants had all given permission to use their names in furthering the work of the "Committee to Defend Martin Luther King and the Struggle for Freedom in the South."

Mr. Bancroft further testified that *The Times* received a letter from the plaintiff date 7 April 1960, demanding a retraction of the advertisement. They replied by letter dared 15 April 1960, which they asked Mr. Sullivan what statements in the advertisement reflected on him.

After the receipt of the letter from the plaintiff, *The Times* had McKee its "string" correspondent in Montgomery, and Sitton, its staff correspondent in Atlanta, investigate the truthfulness of the allegations in the advertisement. Their lengthy telegraphic reports, introduced in evidence showed that the Alabama College officials had informed them that the statement that the dining room at the College had been padlocked to starve the students into submission was absolutely false; that all but 28 of the 1900 students had re-registered and meal service was furnished all students on the campus and was available even to those who had not registered, upon payment for the meals; that the Montgomery police entered the campus upon request of the College officials, and then only after a mob of rowdy students had threatened the negro college custodian, and after a college policeman had fired his pistol in the air several times in an effort to control the mob. The city police had merely tried to see that the orders of the Alabama College officials were not violated.

Sitton's report contained the following pertinent statements:

 " * * * Paragraph 3 of the advertisement, which begins, 'In Montgomery, Alabama, after students sang' and so forth, appears t be virtually without any foundation. The students sand the National Anthem. Never at any time did police 'ring' the campus although on three occasions they were deployed near the campus in large numbers. Probably a majority of the student body was at one time or another involved in the protest but not 'entire student body.' I have been unable to find any one who has heard that the campus dining room was padlocked. * * * In reference to the 6th paragraph, beginning: 'Again and again the Southern violators' and so forth, Dr. King's home was bombed during the bus boycott some four years ago. his wife and child were there but were not (repeat not) injured in any way. King says that the only assault against his person took place when he was arrested some four years ago for loitering outside a courtroom. The arresting

SUPREME COURT
OF ALABAMA,
AUGUST 1962

SUPREME COURT
OF ALABAMA,
AUGUST 1962

officer twisted King's arm behind the minister's back in taking him to be booked.

The reports further show that King had been arrested only twice by the Montgomery police. Once for spending on which charge he was convicted and paid a $10.00 fine, and once for "loitering"on which charge he was convicted and fined $14.00, this fine being paid by the then police commissioner whom the plaintiff succeeded in office.

Mr. Bancroft further testified that upon receipt of a letter from John Patterson, Governor of Alabama, *The Times'* judgment no statement in the advertisement in the advertisement referred to John Patterson either personally or as Governor of Alabama. However, *The Times* felt that since Patterson held the high office of Governor of Alabama and believed that he had been libeled, they should apologize.

Grover C. Hall, Jr., Arnold D. Blackwell, William H. MacDonald, Harry W. Kaminsky, H. M. Price, Sr., William M. Parker, Jr., and Horace W. White, all residents of the city of Montgomery, as well as the plaintiff, testified over the defendant's objections that upon reading the advertisement they associated it with the plaintiff, who was Police Commissioner.

E. Y. Lacy, Lieutenant of detectives for the City of Montgomery, testified that he had investigated the bombings, "The Police Department did extensive research work with overtime and extra personnel and we did everything that we knew including inviting and working with other departments throughout the country."

O. M. Strickland, a police officer of the City of Montgomery, testified that he had arrested King on the loitering charge after King had attempted to force his way into an already overcrowded courtroom, Strickland having been instructed not to admit any additional persons to the courtroom unless they had been subpoenaed as a witness. At no time did he nor anyone else assault King in any manner, and King was permitted to make his own bond and was released.

In his own behalf the plaintiff, Sullivan, testified that he first read the advertisement in the Mayor's office in Montgomery. He testified that he took office as a Commissioner of the City of Montgomery in October 1959, and had occupied that position since. Mr. Sullivan testified that upon reading the advertisement he associated it with himself, and in response to a question on cross-examination, stated that he felt that he had been greatly injured by it.

Mr. Sullivan gave further testimony as to the falsity of the assertions contained in the advertisement.

For the defense, Gershon Aronson, testified that the advertisement was brought to him by John Murray and he only scanned it hurriedly before the advertisement was sent to the Advertising Acceptability Department of *The New York Times*. As to whether the word "they" as used in the paragraph of the advertisement charging that "Southern violators" had bombed King's home, assaulted his person, arrested him seven times, etc., referred to the same people as "they" in the paragraph wherein it was alleged that the Alabama College students were padlocked out of their dining room in an attempt to starve them into submission and that the campus was ringed with police, armed with shotguns, tear gas, etc. Aronson first stated, "Well, it may have referred to the same people. It is rather difficult to tell"and a short while later Aronson stated, "Well, I think now it probably refers to the same people."

The Times was paid in the vicinity of $4,800 for publishing the advertisement.

D. Vincent Redding, assistant to the manager of the Advertising Acceptability Department of *The Times*, testified that he examined the advertisement and approved it, seeing nothing in it to cause him to believe it was false, and further he placed reliance upon the endorsers "whose reputations I had no reason to question." On cross-examination Mr. Redding testified he had not checked with any of the endorsers as their familiarity with the events in Montgomery to determine the accuracy of their statements, nor could he say whether he had read any news accounts concerning such events which had been published in *The Times*. The following is an excerpt from Mr. Redding's cross-examination:

"Q Now, Mr. Redding, wouldn't't it be a fair statement to say that you really didn't check this ad at all for accuracy?"

"A That's a fair statement, yes."

Mr. Harding Bancroft, Secretary of *The Times*, whose testimony taken by deposition had been introduced by the plaintiff, testified in the trial below as a witness for the defendants. His testimony is substantially in accord with that given in his deposition and we see no purpose in an additional delineation of it.

As a witness for the defense, John Murray testified that he was a writer living in New York City. He was a volunteer worker for the "Committee to Defend Martin Luther King," etc., and as such was called upon, together with two other writers, to draft the advertisement in question.

These three were given material by Bayard Rustin, the Executive Director Committee, a basis for composing the advertisement. Murray stated that Rustin is a professional organizer, he guessed along the line of raising funds. Murray knew that Rustin had been affiliated with the War Resisters League, among others.

After the first proof of the advertisement was ready, Rustin called Jim to his office and stated he was dissatisfied with it as it did not have the kind of appeal it should have if it was to get the response in funds the Committee needed.

Rustin then stated they could add the names of the individual defendants since by virtue of their membership in the Southern Christian Leadership Conference, which supported the work of the Committee, he felt they need not consult them.

The individual defendants' names were them placed on the advertisement under the legend "We in the South who are struggling daily for dignity and freedom warmly endorse this appeal."

Murray further testified that he and Rustin rewrote the advertisement "to get money" and "project the ad in the most appealing form from the material we were getting."

As to the accuracy of the advertisement, Murray testified:

> "Well, that did not enter the—it did not enter into consideration at all except we took it for granted that it was accurate—we took it for granted that it was accurate—they were accurate—and if they hadn't been—I mean we would have stopped to question it—I mean we would have stopped to question it. We had every reason to believe it."

The individual defendants all testified to the effect that they had not authorized *The New York Times*, Philip Randolph, the "Committee to Defend Martin Luther King," etc., nor any other person to place their names on the advertisement, and in fact did not see the contents of the advertisement until receipt of the letter from the plaintiff.

They all testified that after receiving the letter demanding a retraction of the advertisement they had not replied thereto, not had they contacted any person or group concerning the advertisement or its retraction.

AMOUNT OF DAMAGES

[45] Under assignment of error No. 81, *The Times* argues those grounds of its motion for a new trial asserting that the damages awarded the plaintiff are excessive, and the result of bias, passion, and prejudice.

In *Johnson Publishing Co. v. Davis, supra*, Justice Stakely in rather definitive discussion of a court's approach to the question of the amount of damages awarded in libel actions made the following observations:

> "* * * The punishment by way of damages is intended not alone to punish the wrongdoer, but as a deterrent to others similarly minded. *Liberty National Life Insurance Co. v. Weldon*, supra; *Advertiser Co. v. Jones*, supra [267 Ala. 171, 100 So.2d 696, 61 A.L.R.2d 1346]; *Webb v. Gray*, 181 Ala. 408, 62 So.194."

> "Where words are libelous per se and as heretofore stated we think the published words in the present case were libelous per se, the right to damages results as a consequence, because there is a tendency of such libel to injure the person libeled in his reputation, profession, trade or business, and proof of such pecuniary injury is not required, such injury being implied. *Advertiser Co. v. Jones*, supra [169 Ala. 196, 53 So.759]; *Webb v. Gray*, supra; *Brown v. Publishers: George Knapp & Co.*, 213 Mo. 655, 112 S.W. 474; *Maytag Co. v. Meadows Mfg. Co.*, 7 Cir., 45 F.2d 299."

> "Because damages are presumed from the circulation of a publication which is libelous per se, it is not necessary that there be any correlation between the actual and punitive damages. *Advertiser Co. v. Jones*, supra; *Webb v. Gray*, supra; *Whitcomb v. Hearst Corp.*, 329 Mass. 193, 107 N.E.2d 295."

> "The extent of the circulation of the libel is a proper matter of consideration by the jury in assessing plaintiff's damages. *Foerster v. Ridder*, Sup., 57 N.Y.S.2d 668; *Whitcomb v. Hearst Corp.*, supra."

> * * * * * *

> "In *Webb v. Gray*, supra [181 Ala. 408, 62 So.196], this court made it clear that a different rule for damages is applicable in libel than in malicious prosecution cases and

SUPREME COURT
OF ALABAMA,
AUGUST 1962

other ordinary tort cases. In this case the court stated in effect that in libel cases actual damages are presumed if the statement is libelous per se and accordingly no actual damages need be proved.

* * * * * *

"In *Advertiser Co. v. Jones*, supra, this Court considered in a libel case the claim that the damages were excessive and stated: 'While the damages are large in this case we cannot say they were excessive. There was evidence from which the jury might infer malice, and upon which they might award punitive damages. This being true, neither the law nor the evidence furnishes us any standard by which can ascertain certainly that they were excessive. The trial court heard all of this evidence, saw the witnesses, observed their expression and demeanor, and hence was in a better position to judge of the extent of punishment which the evidence warranted than we are, who must form our conclusions upon the mere narrative of the transcript. This court, in treating of excessive verdicts in cases in which punitive damages could be awarded. through Justice Haralson spoke and quoted as follows: 'There is no legal measure of damages in cases of this character.'"

* * * * * *

"The Supreme Court of Missouri considered the question in *Brown v. Publishers: George Knapp & Co.*, 213 Mo. 655, 112 S.W. 474, 485, and said: 'The action for libel is one to recover damages for injury to man's reputation and good name. It is not necessary, in order to recover general damages for words which are actionable per se, that the plaintiff should have suffered any actual or constructive pecuniary loss. In such action, the plaintiff is entitled to recover as general damages for the injury to his feelings which the libel of the defendant has caused and the mental anguish or suffering which he had endured as a consequence thereof. *So many considerations enter into the awarding of damages by a jury in a libel case that the courts approach the question of the excessiveness of a verdict in such case with great reluctance.* The question of damages for a tort especially in a case of libel or slander is peculiarly within the province of the jury, and unless the damages are so unconscionable as to impress the court with its injustice, and thereby to induce the court to believe the jury were actuated by prejudice, partiality, or corruption, it rarely interferes with the verdict.'". (Emphasis supplied.)

In the present case the evidence shows that the advertisement in question was first written by a professional organizer of drives, and rewrit-ten, or "revved up" to make it more "appealing." *The Times* in its own files had articles already published which would have demonstrated the falsity of the allegations in the advertisement. Upon demand by the Governor of Alabama, *The Times* published a retraction of the advertisement insofar as the Governor of Alabama was concerned. Upon receipt of the letter from the plaintiff demanding a retraction of the allegations in the advertisement, *The Times* had investigations made by a staff corespondent, and by its "string" correspondent. Both made a report demonstrating the falsity of the allegations. Even in the face of these reports, *The Times* adamantly refused to right the wrong it knew it had done the plaintiff. In the trial below none of the defendants questioned the falsity of thc allegations in the advertisement.

On the other hand, during his testimony it was the contention of the Secretary of *The Times* that the advertisement was "substantially correct." In the face of this cavalier ignoring of the falsity of the advertisement, the jury could not have but been impressed with the bad faith of *The Times*, and its maliciousness inferable therefrom.

While in the Johnson Publishing Co. case, supra, the damages were reduced by was of requiring a remittitur, such reduction was on the basis that there was somc clcment of truth in part of the alleged libelous statement. No such reason to mitigate the damages is present in this case.

It is common knowledge that as of today the dollar is worth only 50 cents or less of its former value.

The Times retracted the advertisement as to Governor Patterson, but ignored this plaintiff's demand for retraction. The matter contained in the advertisement was equally false as to both parties.

The Times could not justify its nonretraction as to this plaintiff by fallaciously asserting that the advertisement was substantially true, and further, that the advertisement as presented to *The Times* bore the names of endorsers whose reputation for truth it considered good.

The irresponsibility of these endorsers in attaching their names to this false and malicious advertisement cannot shield The Times from its irresponsibility in printing the advertisement and scattering it to the four winds.

[46] All in all we do not feel justified in mitigating the damages awarded by the jury, and

approved by the trial judge below, by its judgment on the motion for a new trial, with the favorable presumption which attends the correctness of the verdict of the jury where the trial judge refuses to grant a new trial. *Housing Authority of City of Decatur v. Decatur Land Co.*, 258 Ala. 607, 64 So.2d 594.

In our considerations we have examined the case of *New York Times Company v. Conner*, (5CCA) 291 F.2d 492 (1961), wherein the Circuit Court of Appeals for the Fifth Circuit, relying exclusively upon *Age Herald Publishing Co. v. Huddleston*, 207 Ala. 40, 92 So. 193, 37 A.L.R. 898, held that no cause of action for libel arose in Alabama where the alleged libel appeared in a newspaper primarily in New York.

This case overlooks, or ignores, the decisions of this court in *Johnson Publishing Co. v. Davis*, 271 Ala. 474, 124 So.2d 441, wherein this court rejected the argument that the whole process of writing, editing, printing, transportation and distribution of a magazine should be regarded as one libel, and the locus of such libel was the place of primary publication. This court further,

with crystal clarity, held that *Age Herald Publishing Co. v. Huddleston*, supra, concerned a venue statute, and that venue statutes do not apply to foreign corporations not qualified to do business in Alabama.

The statement of Alabama law in the *Conner* case, supra, is erroneous in light of our enunciation of what is the law of Alabama as set forth in the *Johnson Publishing Company* case, supra. This erroneous premise, as we interpret the *Conner* case, renders the opinion faulty, and of no persuasive authority in our present consideration.

> "The laws of the several states, except where the Constitution or treaties of the United States or Acts of Congress otherwise require or provide, shall be regarded as rules of decision in civil actions in the courts of the United States, in cases where they apply." Sec. 1652, Title 28, U.S.C.A., 62 Stat. 944.

It is our conclusion that the judgment below is due to be affirmed, and it is so ordered.

Affirmed.

Livingston, C. J., and Simpson and Merrill, JJ., concur.

SUPREME COURT
OF ALABAMA,
AUGUST 1962

U.S. SUPREME
COURT,
OCTOBER 1963

BRIEF FOR THE
PETITIONER

In the Supreme Court of the United States

October Term, 1963

No. 39

THE NEW YORK TIMES COMPANY,
PETITIONER,
V.
L. B. SULLIVAN, RESPONDENT

ON WRIT OF CERTIORARI TO THE SUPREME COURT OF ALABAMA

BRIEF FOR THE PETITIONER

LOUIS M. LOEB
T. ERIC EMBRY
MARVIN E. FRANKEL
RONALD S. DIANA
DORIS WECHSLER
LORD, DAY & LORD
BEDDOW, EMBRY & BEDDOW
OF COUNSEL

HERBERT BROWNELL
THOMAS F. DALY
25 BROADWAY
NEW YORK 4, NEW YORK

HERBERT WECHSLER
435 WEST 116TH ST.
NEW YORK 27, NEW YORK
ATTORNEYS FOR PETITIONER
THE NEW YORK TIMES COMPANY

Index

OPINIONS BELOW

The opinion of the Supreme Court of Alabama (R. 1139) is reported in 273 Ala. 656, 144 So. 2d 25. The opinion of the Circuit Court, Montgomery County, on the petitioner's motion to quash service of process (R. 49) is unreported. There was no other opinion by the Circuit Court.

JURISDICTION

The judgment of the Supreme Court of Alabama (R. 1180) was entered August 30, 1962. The petition for a writ of certiorari was filed November 21, 1962 and was granted January 7, 1963. 371 U.S. 946. The jurisdiction of this Court is invoked under 28 U.S.C. 1257 (3).

U.S. SUPREME
COURT,
OCTOBER 1963

BRIEF FOR THE
PETITIONER

QUESTIONS PRESENTED

1. Whether, consistently with the guarantee of freedom of the press in the First Amendment as embodied in the Fourteenth, a State may hold libelous *per se* and actionable by an elected City Commissioner published statements critical of the conduct of a department of the City Government under his general supervision, which are inaccurate in some particulars.

2. Whether there was sufficient evidence to justify, consistently with the constitutional guarantee of freedom of the press, the determination that published statements naming no individual but critical of the conduct of the "police" were defamatory as to the respondent, the elected City Commissioner with jurisdiction over the Police Department, and punishable as libelous *per se.*

3. Whether an award of $500,000 as "presumed" and punitive damages for libel constituted, in the circumstances of this case, an abridgment of the freedom of the press.

4. Whether the assumption of jurisdiction in a libel action against a foreign corporation publishing a newspaper in another State, based upon sporadic news gathering activities by correspondents, occasional solicitation of advertising and minuscule distribution of the newspaper within the forum state, transcended the territorial limitations of due process, imposed a forbidden burden on interstate commerce or abridged the freedom of the press.

Constitutional and statutory provisions involved The constitutional and statutory provisions involved are set forth in Appendix A, *infra*, pp. 91–95.

STATEMENT

On April 19, 1960, the respondent, one of three elected Commissioners of the City of Montgomery, Alabama, instituted this action in the Circuit Court of Montgomery County against *The New York Times,* a New York corporation, and four co-defendants resident in Alabama, Ralph D. Abernathy, Fred L. Shuttlesworth, S. S. Seay, Sr., and J. E. Lowery. The complaint (R. 1) demanded $500,000 as damages for libel allegedly contained in two paragraphs of an advertisement (R. 6) published in *The New York Times* on March 29, 1960. Service of process was attempted by delivery to

an alleged agent of *The Times* in Alabama and by substituted service (R. 11) pursuant to the "long-arm" statute of the State. A motion to quash, asserting constitutional objections to the jurisdiction of the Circuit Court (R. 39, 43–44, 47, 129) was denied on August 5, 1960 (R. 49). A demurrer to the complaint (R. 58, 67) was overruled on November 1, 1960 (R. 108) and the cause proceeded to a trial by jury, resulting on November 3 in a verdict against all defendants for the full $500,000 claimed (R. 862). A motion for new trial (R. 896, 969) was denied on March 17, 1961 (R. 970). The Supreme Court of Alabama affirmed the judgment on August 30, 1962 (R. 1180).[1] The Circuit Court and the Supreme Court both rejected the petitioner's contention that the liability imposed abridged the freedom of the press.

1. The nature of the publication   The advertisement, a copy of which was attached to the complaint (R. 1, 6), consisted of a full page statement (reproduced in Appendix B, *infra* p. 97) entitled "Heed Their Rising Voices," a phrase taken from a *New York Times* editorial of March 19, 1960, which was quoted at the top of the page as follows: "The growing movement of peaceful mass demonstrations by Negroes is something new in the South, something understandable … Let Congress heed their rising voices, for they will be heard."

The statement consisted of an appeal for contributions to the "Committee to Defend Martin Luther King and the Struggle for Freedom in the South" to support "three needs—the defense of Martin Luther King—the support of the embattled students—and the struggle for the right-to-vote." It was set forth over the names of sixty-four individuals, including many who are well known for achievement in religion, humanitarian work, public affairs,

---

[1] Libel actions based on the publication of the same statements in the same advertisement were also instituted by Governor Patterson of Alabama, Mayor James of Montgomery, City Commissioner Parks and former Commissioner Sellers. The James case is pending on motion for new trial after a verdict of $500,000. The Patterson, Parks and Sellers cases, in which the damages demanded total $2,000,000, were removed by petitioner to the District Court. That court sustained the removal (195 F. Supp. 919 [1961]) but the Court of Appeals, one judge dissenting, reversed and ordered a remand (308 F. 2d 474 [1962]). A petition to review that decision on certiorari is now pending in this Court. *New York Times Company* v. *Parks and Patterson,* No. 687, October Term, 1962, No. 52, this Term.

U.S. SUPREME
COURT,
OCTOBER 1963

BRIEF FOR THE
PETITIONER

trade unions and the arts. Under a line reading "We in the South who are struggling daily for dignity and freedom warmly endorse this appeal" appeared the names of twenty other persons, eighteen of whom are identified as clergymen in various southern cities. A New York address and telephone number were given for the Committee, the officers of which were also listed, including three individuals whose names did not otherwise appear.

The first paragraph of the statement alluded generally to the "non-violent demonstrations" of Southern Negro students "in positive affirmation of the right to live in human dignity as guaranteed by the U.S. Constitution and the Bill of Rights." It went on to charge that in "their efforts to uphold these guarantees, they are being met by an unprecedented wave of terror by those who would deny and negate that document which the whole world looks upon as setting the pattern for modern freedom.... ."

The second paragraph told of a student effort in Orangeburg, South Carolina, to obtain service at lunch counters in the business district and asserted that the students were forcibly ejected, tear-gassed, arrested en masse and otherwise mistreated.

The third paragraph spoke of Montgomery, Alabama and complained of the treatment of students who sang on the steps of the State Capitol, charging that their leaders were expelled from school, that truckloads of armed police ringed the Alabama State College Campus and that the College dining-hall was padlocked in an effort to starve the protesting students into submission.

The fourth paragraph referred to "Talla-hassee, Atlanta, Nashville, Savannah, Greensboro, Memphis, Richmond, Charlotte and a host of other cities in the South," praising the action of "young American teenagers, in face of the entire weight of official state apparatus and police power," as "protagonists of democracy."

The fifth paragraph speculated that "The Southern violators of the Constitution fear this new, non-violent brand of freedom fighter ... even as they fear the upswelling right-to-vote movement," that "they are determined to destroy the one man who more than any other, symbolizes the new spirit now sweeping the South—the Rev. Dr. Martin Luther King, Jr., world-famous leader of the Montgomery Bus Protest." It went on to portray the leadership role of Dr. King and

the Southern Christian Leadership Conference, which he founded, and to extol the inspiration of "his doctrine of non-violence."

The sixth paragraph asserted that the "Southern violators" have repeatedly "answered Dr. King's protests with intimidation and violence" and referred to the bombing of his home, assault upon his person, seven arrests and a then pending charge of perjury. It stated that "their real purpose is to remove him physically as the leader to whom the students and millions of others—look for guidance and support, and thereby to intimidate *all* leaders who may rise in the South", concluding that the defense of Dr. King "is an integral part of the total struggle for freedom in the South."

The remaining four paragraphs called upon "men and women of good will" to do more than "applaud the creative daring of the students and the quiet heroism of Dr. King" by adding their "moral support" and "the material help so urgently needed by those who are taking the risks, facing jail and even death in a glorious reaffirmation of our Constitution and its Bill of Rights."

2. The allegedly defamatory statements Of the ten paragraphs of text in the advertisement, the third and a portion of the sixth were the basis of respondent's claim of libel.

(a) The third paragraph was as follows:

"In Montgomery, Alabama, after students sang 'My Country, 'Tis of Thee' on the State Capitol steps, their leaders were expelled from school, and truckloads of police armed with shot-guns and tear-gas ringed the Alabama State College Campus. When the entire student body protested to state authorities by refusing to re-register, their dining hall was padlocked in an attempt to starve them into submission."

Though the only part of this statement that respondent thought implied a reference to him was the assertion about "truckloads of police" (R. 712), he undertook and was permitted to deal with the paragraph in general by adducing evidence depicting the entire episode involved. His evidence consisted mainly of a story by Claude Sitton, the southern correspondent of *The Times*, published on March 2, 1960 (R. 655, 656-7, Pl. Ex. 169, R. 1568), a report requested by *The Times* from Don McKee, its "stringer" in Montgomery, after institution of this suit was threatened (R. 590–593, Pl. Ex. 348, R. 1931–1935), and a later telephoned report from

Sitton to counsel for *The Times,* made on May 5, after suit was brought (R. 593–595, Pl. Ex. 348, R. 1935–1937).

This evidence showed that a succession of student demonstrations had occurred in Montgomery, beginning with an unsuccessful effort by some thirty Alabama State College students to obtain service at a lunch counter in the Montgomery County Court House. A thousand students had marched on March 1, 1960, from the College campus to the State Capitol, upon the steps of which they said the Lord's Prayer and sang the National Anthem before marching back to the campus. Nine student leaders of the lunch counter demonstration were expelled on March 2 by the State Board of Education, upon motion of Governor Patterson, and thirty-one others were placed on probation (R. 696–699, Pl. Ex. 364, R. 1972–1974), but the singing at the Capitol was not the basis of the disciplinary action or mentioned at the meeting of the Board (R. 701). Alabama State College students stayed away from classes on March 7 in a strike in sympathy with those expelled but virtually all of them returned to class after a day and most of them re-registered or had already done so. On March 8, there was another student demonstration at a church near the campus, followed by a march upon the campus, with students dancing around in conga lines and some becoming rowdy. The superintendent of grounds summoned the police and the students left the campus, but the police arrived as the demonstrators marched across the street and arrested thirty-two of them for disorderly conduct or failure to obey officers, charges on which they later pleaded guilty and were fined in varying amounts (R. 677–680, 681, 682).

A majority of the student body was probably involved at one time or another in the protest but not the "entire student body". The police did not at any time "ring" the campus, although they were deployed near the campus on three occasions in large numbers. The campus dining hall was never "padlocked" and the only students who may have been barred from eating were those relatively few who had neither signed a pre-registration application nor requested temporary meal tickets (R. 594, 591).

The paragraph was thus inaccurate in that it exaggerated the number of students involved in the protest and the extent of police activity and intervention. If, as the respondent argued (R.

743), it implied that the students were expelled for singing on the steps of the Capitol, this was erroneous; the expulsion was for the demand for service at a lunch counter in the Courthouse. There was, moreover, no foundation for the charge that the dining hall was padlocked in an effort to starve the students into submission, an allegation that especially aroused resentment in Montgomery (R. 605, 607, 949, 2001, 2002, 2007).

(b) The portion of the sixth paragraph of the statement relied on by respondent read as follows:

> "Again and again the Southern violators have answered Dr. King's peaceful protests with intimidation and violence. They have bombed his home, almost killing his wife and child. They have assaulted his person. They have arrested him seven times—for 'speeding,' 'loitering' and similar 'offenses.' And now they have charged him with 'perjury'—a *felony* under which they could imprison him for *ten* years."

As to this paragraph, which did not identify the time or place of the events recited, but which respondent read to allude to himself because it also "describes police action" (R. 724), his evidence showed that Dr. King's home had in fact been bombed twice when his wife and child were at home, though one of the bombs failed to explode—both of the occasions antedating the respondent's tenure as Commissioner (R. 594, 685, 688); that Dr. King had been arrested only four times, not seven, three of the arrests preceding the respondent's service as Commissioner (R. 592, 594–595, 703); that Dr. King had in fact been indicted for perjury on two counts, each carrying a possible sentence of five years imprisonment (R. 595), a charge on which he subsequently was acquitted (R. 680). It also showed that while Dr. King claimed to have been assaulted when he was arrested some four years earlier for loitering outside a courtroom (R. 594), one of the officers participating in arresting him and carrying him to a detention cell at headquarters denied that there was a physical assault (R. 692–693)—this incident also antedating the respondent's tenure as Commissioner (R. 694).

On the theory that the statement could be read to charge that the bombing of Dr. King's home was the work of the police (R. 707), respondent was permitted to call evidence that the police were not involved; that they in fact

U.S. SUPREME
COURT,
OCTOBER 1963

BRIEF FOR THE
PETITIONER

dismantled the bomb that did not explode; and that they did everything they could to apprehend the perpetrators of the bombings (R. 685–687)—also before respondent's tenure as Commissioner (R. 688). In the same vein, respondent testified himself that the police had not bombed the King home or assaulted Dr. King or condoned the bombing or assaulting; and that he had had nothing to do with procuring King's indictment (R. 707–709).

3. The impact of the statements on respondent's reputation As one of the three Commissioners of the City of Montgomery since October 5, 1959, specifically Commissioner of Public Affairs, respondent's duties were the supervision of the Police Department, Fire Department, Department of Cemetery and Department of Scales (R. 703). He was normally not responsible, however, for day-to-day police operations, including those during the Alabama State College episode referred to in the advertisement, these being under the immediate supervision of Montgomery's Chief of Police—though there was one occasion when the Chief was absent and respondent supervised directly (R. 720). It was stipulated that there were 175 full time policemen in the Montgomery Police Department, divided into three shifts and four divisions, and 24 "special traffic directors" for control of traffic at the schools (R. 787).

As stated in respondent's testimony, the basis for his role as aggrieved plaintiff was the "feeling" that the advertisement, which did not mention him or the Commission or Commissioners or any individual, "reflects not only on me but on the other Commissioners and the community" (R. 724). He felt particularly that statements referring to "police activities" or "police action" were associated with himself, impugning his "ability and integrity" and reflecting on him "as an individual" (R. 712, 713, 724). He also felt that the other statements in the passages complained of, such as that alluding to the bombing of King's home, referred to the Commissioners, to the Police Department and to him because they were contained in the same paragraphs as statements mentioning police activities (R. 717–718), though he conceded that as "far as the expulsion of students is concerned, that responsibility rests with the State Department of Education" (R. 716).

In addition to this testimony as to the respondent's feelings, six witnesses were permitted to express their opinions of the connotations of the statements and their effect on respondent's reputation.

Grover C. Hall, editor of the Montgomery Advertiser, who had previously written an editorial attacking the advertisement (R. 607, 613, 949), testified that he thought he would associate the third paragraph "with the City Government—the Commissioners" (R. 605) and "would naturally think a little more about the police commissioner" (R. 608). It was "the phrase about starvation" that led to the association; the "other didn't hit" him "with any particular force" (R. 607, 608). He thought "starvation is an instrument of reprisal and would certainly be indefensible … in any case" (R. 605).

Arnold D. Blackwell, a member of the Water Works Board appointed by the Commissioners (R. 621) and a businessman engaged in real estate and insurance (R. 613), testified that the third paragraph was associated in his mind with "the Police Commissioner" and the "people on the police force"; that if it were true that the dining hall was padlocked in an effort to starve the students into submission, he would "think that the people on our police force or the heads of our police force were acting without their jurisdiction and would not be competent for the position" (R. 617, 624). He also associated the statement about "truck-loads of police" with the police force and the Police Commissioner (R. 627). With respect to the "Southern violators" passage, he associated the statement about the arrests with "the police force" but not the "sentences above that" (R. 624) or the statement about the charge of perjury (R. 625).

Harry W. Kaminsky, sales manager of a clothing store (R. 634) and a close friend of the respondent (R. 644), also associated the third paragraph with "the Commissioners" (R. 635), though not the statement about the expulsion of the students (R. 639). Asked on direct examination about the sentences in the sixth paragraph, he said that he "would say that it refers to the same people in the paragraph that we look at before," i.e., to "The Commissioners," including the respondent (R. 636). On cross-examination, however, he could not say that he associated those statements with the respondent, except that he thought that the reference to arrests "implicates the Police Department … or the authorities that would do that—arrest folks for speeding and loitering and such as that" (R. 639-640). In general, he would "look at" the respondent when he saw "the Police Department" (R. 641).

H. M. Price, Sr., owner of a small food equipment business (R. 644), associated "the statements contained" in both paragraphs with "the head of the Police Department," the respondent (R. 646). Asked what it was that made him think of the respondent, he read the first sentence of the third paragraph and added: "Now, I would just automatically consider that the Police Commissioner in Montgomery would have to put his approval on those kind of things as an individual" (R. 647). If he believed the statements contained in the two paragraphs to be true, he would "decide that we probably had a young Gestapo in Montgomery" (R. 645–646).

William M. Parker, Jr., a friend of the respondent and of Mayor James (R. 651), in the service station business, associated "those statements in those paragraphs" with the City Commissioners (R. 650) and since the respondent "was the Police Commissioner," he "thought of him first" (R. 651). If he believed the statements to be true, he testified that he would think the respondent "would be trying to run this town with a strong arm—strong armed tactics, rather, going against the oath he took to run his office in a peaceful manner and an upright manner for all citizens of Montgomery" (R. 650).

Finally, Horace W. White, proprietor of the P. C. White Truck Line (R. 662), a former employer of respondent (R. 664), testified that both of the paragraphs meant to him "Mr. L. B. Sullivan" (R. 663). The statement in the advertisement that indicated to him that it referred to the respondent was that about "truck-loads of police," which made him think of the police and of respondent "as being the head of the Police Department" (R. 666). If he believed the statements, he doubted whether he "would want to be associated with anybody who would be a party to such things" (R. 664) and he would not re-employ respondent for P. C. White Truck Line if he thought that "he allowed the Police Department to do the things the paper say he did" (R. 667, 664, 669).

None of the six witnesses testified that he believed any of the statements that he took to refer to respondent and all but Hall specifically testified that they did not believe them (R. 623, 636, 647, 651, 667). None was led to think less kindly of respondent because of the advertisement (R. 625, 638, 647, 651, 666). Nor could respondent point to any injury that he had suffered or to any sign that he was held in less esteem (R. 721–724).

Four of the witnesses, moreover, Blackwell, Kaminsky, Price and Parker, saw the publication first when it was shown to them in the office of respondent's counsel to equip them as witnesses (R. 618, 637, 643, 647, 649). Their testimony should, therefore, have been disregarded under the trial court's instruction that the jury should "disregard … entirely" the testimony of any witness "based upon his reading of the advertisement complained of here, only after having been shown a copy of same by the plaintiff or his attorneys" (R. 833). White did not recall when he first saw the advertisement; he believed, though he was not sure, that "somebody cut it out of the paper and mailed it" to him or left it on his desk (R. 662, 665, 668). Only Hall, whose testimony was confined to the phrase about starving students into submission (R. 605, 607), received the publication in ordinary course at *The Montgomery Advertiser* (R. 606, 726–727).

4. The circumstances of the publication The advertisement was published by *The Times* upon an order from the Union Advertising Service, a reputable New York advertising agency, acting for the Committee to Defend Martin Luther King (R. 584–585, 737, Pl. Ex. 350, R. 1957). The order was dated March 28, 1960, but the proposed typescript of the ad had actually been delivered on March 23 by John Murray, a writer acting for the Committee, who had participated in its composition (R. 731, 805). Murray gave the copy to Gershon Aaronson, a member of the National Advertising Staff of *The Times* specializing in "editorial type" advertisements (R. 731, 738), who promptly passed it on to technical departments and sent a thermo-fax copy to the Advertising Acceptability Department, in charge of the screening of advertisements (R. 733, 734, 756). D. Vincent Redding, the manager of that department, read the copy on March 25 and approved it for publication (R. 758). He gave his approval because he knew nothing to cause him to believe that anything in the proposed text was false and because it bore the endorsement of "a number of people who are well known and whose reputation" he "had no reason to question" (R. 758, 759–760, 762–763). He did not make or think it necessary to make any further check as to the accuracy of the statements (R. 765, 771).

U.S. SUPREME COURT, OCTOBER 1963

BRIEF FOR THE PETITIONER

When Redding passed on the acceptability of the advertisement, the copy was accompanied by a letter from A. Philip Randolph, Chairman of the Committee, to Aaronson, dated March 23 (R. 587, 757, Def. Ex. 7, R. 1992) and reading:

> "This will certify that the names included on the enclosed list are all signed members of the Committee to Defend Martin Luther King and the Struggle for Freedom in the South.

> "Please be assured that they have all given us permission to use their names in furthering the work of our Committee."

The routine of *The Times* is to accept such a letter from a responsible person to establish that names have not been used without permission and Redding followed that practice in this case (R. 759). Each of the individual defendants testified, however, that he had not authorized the Committee to use his name (R. 787–804) and Murray testified that the original copy of the advertisement, to which the Randolph letter related, did not contain the statement "We in the South ... warmly endorse this appeal" or any of the names printed thereunder, including those of these defendants. That statement and those names were added, he explained, to a revision of the proof on the suggestion of Bayard Rustin, the Director of the Committee. Rustin told Murray that it was unnecessary to obtain the consent of the individuals involved since they were all members of the Southern Christian Leadership Conference, as indicated by its letterhead, and "since the SCLC supports the work of the Committee ... he [Rustin] ... felt that there would be no problem at all, and that you didn't even have to consult them" (R. 806–809). Redding did not recall this difference in the list of names (R. 767), though Aaronson remembered that there "were a few changes made ... prior to publication" (R. 739).

The New York Times has set forth in a booklet its "Advertising Acceptability Standards" (R. 598, Pl. Ex. 348, Exh. F, R. 1952) declaring, *inter alia*, that *The Times* does not accept advertisements that are fraudulent or deceptive, that are "ambiguous in wording and ... may mislead" or "[a]ttacks of a personal character." In replying to the plaintiff's interrogatories, Harding Bancroft, Secretary of *The Times*, deposed that "as the advertisement made no attacks of a personal character upon any individual and otherwise met the advertising acceptability standards

promulgated" by *The Times*, D. Vincent Redding had approved it (R. 585).

Though Redding and not Aaronson was thus responsible for the acceptance of the ad, Aaronson was cross-examined at great length about such matters as the clarity or ambiguity of its language (R. 741–753), the court allowing the interrogation on the stated ground that "this gentleman here is a very high official of *The Times*," which he, of course, was not (R. 744). In the course of this colloquy, Aaronson contradicted himself on the question whether the word "they" in the "Southern violators" passage refers to "the same people" throughout or to different people, saying first "It is rather difficult to tell" (R. 745) and later: "I think now that it probably refers to the same people" (R. 746). Redding was not interrogated on this point, which respondent, in his Brief in Opposition, deemed established by what Aaronson "conceded" (Brief in Opposition, p. 7).

The Times was paid "a little over" $4800 for the publication of the advertisement (R. 752). The total circulation of the issue of March 29, 1960, was approximately 650,000, of which approximately 394 copies were mailed to Alabama subscribers or shipped to newsdealers in the State, approximately 35 copies going to Montgomery County (R. 601–602, Pl. Ex. 348, R. 1942–1943).

5. The response to the demand for a retraction On April 8, 1960, respondent wrote to the petitioner and to the four individual defendants, the letters being erroneously dated March 8 (R. 588, 671, 776, Pl. Ex. 348, 355–358, R. 1949, 1962–1968). The letters, which were in identical terms, set out the passages in the advertisement complained of by respondent, asserted that the "foregoing matter, and the publication as a whole charge me with grave misconduct and of [*sic*] improper actions and omissions as an official of the City of Montgomery" and called on the addressee to "publish in as prominent and as public a manner as the foregoing false and defamatory material contained in the foregoing publication, a full and fair retraction of the entire false and defamatory matter so far as the same relates to me and to my conduct and acts as a public official of the City of Montgomery, Alabama."

Upon receiving this demand and the report from Don McKee, the *Times* stringer in Montgomery referred to above (p. 7), petitioner's counsel wrote to the respondent on April 15, as follows (R. 589, Pl. Ex. 363, R. 1971):

Dear Mr. Commissioner:

Your letter of April 8 sent by registered mail to The New York Times Company has been referred for attention to us as general counsel.

You will appreciate, we feel sure, that the statements to which you object were not made by The New York Times but were contained in an advertisement proffered to The Times by responsible persons.

We have been investigating the matter and are somewhat puzzled as to how you think the statements in any way reflect on you. So far, our investigation would seem to indicate that the statements are substantially correct with the sole exception that we find no justification for the statement that the dining hall in the State College was "padlocked in an attempt to starve them into submission."

We shall continue to look into the subject matter because our client, The New York Times, is always desirous of correcting any statements which appear in its paper and which turn out to be erroneous.

In the meanwhile you might, if you desire, let us know in what respect you claim that the statements in the advertisement reflect on you.

Very truly yours,

Lord, Day & Lord

The respondent filed suit on April 19, without answering this letter.

Subsequently, on May 9, 1960, Governor John Patterson of Alabama, sent a similar demand for a retraction to *The Times,* asserting that the publication charged him "with grave misconduct and of [*sic*] improper actions and omissions as Governor of Alabama and Ex-Officio Chairman of the State Board of Education of Alabama" and demanding publication of a retraction of the material so far as it related to him and to his conduct as Governor and Ex-Officio Chairman.

On May 16, the President and Publisher of *The Times* wrote Governor Patterson as follows (R. 773, Def. Ex. 9, R. 1998):

Dear Governor Patterson:

In response to your letter of May 9th, we are enclosing herewith a page of today's New York Times which contains the retraction and apology requested.

As stated in the retraction, to the extent that anyone could fairly conclude from the adver-

tisement that any charge was made against you, The New York Times apologizes.

Faithfully yours,

ORVIL DRYFOOS

The publication in *The Times* (Pl. Ex. 351, R. 1958), referred to in the letter, appeared under the headline "Times Retracts Statement in Ad" and the subhead "Acts on Protest of Alabama Governor Over Assertions in Segregation Matter." After preliminary paragraphs reporting the Governor's protest and quoting his letter in full, including the specific language of which he complained, the account set forth a "statement by The New York Times" as follows:

The advertisement containing the statements to which Governor Patterson objects was received by The Times in the regular course of business from and paid for by a recognized advertising agency in behalf of a group which included among its subscribers well-known citizens.

The publication of an advertisement does not constitute a factual news report by The Times nor does it reflect the judgment or the opinion of the editors of The Times. Since publication of the advertisement, The Times made an investigation and consistent with its policy of retracting and correcting any errors or misstatements which may appear in its columns, herewith retracts the two paragraphs complained of by the Governor.

The New York Times never intended to suggest by the publication of the advertisement that the Honorable John Patterson, either in his capacity as Governor or as ex-officio chairman of the Board of Education of the State of Alabama, or otherwise, was guilty of "grave misconduct or improper actions and omission." To the extent that anyone can fairly conclude from the statements in the advertisement that any such charge was made, The New York Times hereby apologizes to the Honorable John Patterson therefor.

The publication closed with a recapitulation of the names of the signers and endorsers of the advertisement and of the officers of the Committee to Defend Martin Luther King.

In response to a demand in respondent's pre-trial interrogatories to "explain why said retraction was made but no retraction was made on the demand of the plaintiff," Mr. Bancroft, Secretary of *The Times,* said that *The Times* published the retraction in response to the Governor's demand "although in its judgment no statement in said advertisement referred to

U.S. SUPREME COURT, OCTOBER 1963

BRIEF FOR THE PETITIONER

U.S. SUPREME
COURT,
OCTOBER 1963

BRIEF FOR THE
PETITIONER

John Patterson either personally or as Governor of the State of Alabama, nor referred to this plaintiff [Sullivan] or any of the plaintiffs in the companion suits. The defendant, however, felt that on account of the fact that John Patterson held the high office of Governor of the State of Alabama and that he apparently believed that he had been libeled by said advertisement in his capacity as Governor of the State of Alabama, the defendant should apologize" (R. 595–596, Pl. Ex. 348, R. 1942). In further explanation at the trial, Bancroft testified: "We did that because we didn't want anything that was published by The Times to be a reflection on the State of Alabama and the Governor was, as far as we could see, the embodiment of the State of Alabama and the proper representative of the State and, furthermore, we had by that time learned more of the actual facts which the ad purported to recite and, finally, the ad did refer to the action of the State authorities and the Board of Education presumably of which the Governor is ex-officio chairman … " (R. 776–777). On the other hand, he did not think that "any of the language in there referred to Mr. Sullivan" (R. 777).

This evidence, together with Mr. Bancroft's further testimony that apart from the statement in the advertisement that the dining hall was padlocked, he thought that "the tenor of the content, the material of those two paragraphs in the ad … are … substantially correct" (R. 781, 785), was deemed by the Supreme Court of Alabama to lend support to the verdict of the jury and the size of its award (R. 1178).

6. The rulings on the merits The Circuit Court held that the facts alleged and proved sufficed to establish liability of the defendants, if the jury was satisfied that the statements complained of by respondent were published of and concerning him. Overruling a demurrer to the complaint (R. 108) and declining to direct a verdict for petitioner (R. 728–729, 818), the court charged the jury (R. 819–826) that the statements relied on by the plaintiff were "libelous per se"; that "the law implies legal injury from the bare fact of the publication itself"; that "falsity and malice are presumed"; that "[g]eneral damages need not be alleged or proved but are presumed" (R. 824); and that "punitive damages may be awarded by the jury even though the amount of actual damages is neither found nor shown" (R. 825). While the court instructed, as requested, that "mere negligence or carelessness

is not evidence of actual malice or malice in fact, and does not justify an award of exemplary or punitive damages" (R. 836), it refused to instruct that the jury must be "convinced" of malice, in the sense of "actual intent" to harm or "gross negligence and recklessness" to make such an award (R. 844). It also declined to require that a verdict for respondent differentiate between compensatory and punitive damages (R. 846).

Petitioner challenged these rulings as an abridgment of the freedom of the press, in violation of the First and the Fourteenth Amendments, and also contended that the verdict was confiscatory in amount and an infringement of the constitutional protection (R. 73–74, 898, 929–930, 935, 936–937, 945–946, 948). A motion for new trial, assigning these grounds among others (R. 896–949), was denied by the Circuit Court (R. 969).

The Supreme Court of Alabama sustained these rulings on appeal (R. 1139, 1180). It held that where "the words published tend to injure a person libeled by them in his reputation, profession, trade or business, or charge him with an indictable offense, or tends to bring the individual into public contempt," they are "libelous per se"; that "the matter complained of is, under the above doctrine, libelous per se, if it was published of and concerning the plaintiff" (R. 1155); and that it was actionable without "proof of pecuniary injury …, such injury being implied" (R. 1160–1161). It found no error in the trial court's ruling that the complaint alleged and the evidence established libelous statements which the jury could find were "of and pertaining to" respondent (R. 1158, 1160), reasoning as follows (R. 1157):

> "We think it common knowledge that the average person knows that municipal agents, such as police and firemen, and others, are under the control and direction of the city governing body, and more particularly under the direction and control of a single commissioner. In measuring the performance or deficiencies of such groups, praise or criticism is usually attached to the official in complete control of the body."

The Court also approved the trial court's charge as "a fair, accurate and clear expression of the governing legal principles" (R. 1167) and sustained its determination that the damages awarded by the verdict were not excessive (R. 1179). On the latter point, the Court endorsed a statement in an earlier opinion that there "is no legal measure of damages in cases of this character" (R. 1177) and held to be decisive that "The Times in its own files had articles already published which would have demonstrated the falsity of the allegations in the advertisement"; that "The Times retracted the advertisement as to Governor Patterson, but ignored this plaintiff's demand for retraction" though the "matter contained in the advertisement was equally false as to both parties"; that in "the trial below none of the defendants questioned the falsity of the allegations in the advertisement" and, simultaneously, that "during his testimony it was the contention of the Secretary of The Times that the advertisement was 'substantially correct'" (R. 1178).

Petitioner's submissions under the First and the Fourteenth Amendments (assignments of error 81, 289–291, 294, 296, 298, 306–308, 310; R. 1055, 1091–1094, 1096–1097, 1098) were summarily rejected with the statements that the "First Amendment of the U.S. Constitution does not protect libelous publications" and the "Fourteenth Amendment is directed against State action and not private action" (R. 1160).

7. The jurisdiction of the Alabama courts
Respondent sought to effect service in this action (R. 11) by delivery of process to Don McKee, the *New York Times* stringer in Montgomery, claimed to be an agent under § 188, Alabama Code of 1940, title 7 (Appendix A, *infra,* pp. 91–92), and by delivery to the Secretary of State under § 199(1), the "long-arm" statute of the State (Appendix A, *infra,* pp. 92–95). Petitioner, appearing specially and only for this purpose, moved to quash the service on the ground, among others, that the subjection of *The Times* to Alabama jurisdiction in this action would transcend the territorial limitations of due process in violation of the Fourteenth Amendment, impose a burden on interstate commerce forbidden by the Commerce Clause and abridge the freedom of the press (R. 39, 43–44, 47; see also, *e.g.,* R. 129).

The evidence adduced upon the litigation of the motion (R. 130–566) established the following facts:

Petitioner is a New York corporation which has not qualified to do business in Alabama or designated anyone to accept service of process there (R. 134–135). It has no office, property or employees resident in Alabama (R. 146, 403–404, 438–439). Its staff correspondents do,

however, visit the State as the occasion may arise for purposes of newsgathering. From the beginning of 1956 through April, 1960, nine correspondents made such visits, spending, the courts below found, 153 days in Alabama, or an average of some thirty-six man-days per year. In the first five months of 1960, there were three such visits by Claude Sitton, the staff correspondent stationed in Atlanta (R. 311–314, 320, Pl. Ex. 91–93, R. 1356–1358) and one by Harrison Salisbury (R. 145, 239, Pl. Ex. 117, R. 1382). *The Times* also had an arrangement with newspapermen, employed by Alabama journals, to function as "stringers," paying them for stories they sent in that were requested or accepted at the rate of a cent a word and also using them occasionally to furnish information to the desk (*e.g.,* R. 175, 176) or to a correspondent (R. 136–137, 140, 153, 154). The effort was to have three such stringers in the State, including one in Montgomery (R. 149, 309) but only two received payments from *The Times* in 1960, Chadwick of *South Magazine,* who was paid $155 to July 26, and McKee of *The Montgomery Advertiser,* who was paid $90, covering both dispatches and assistance given Salisbury (R. 140, 143, 155, 159, 308–309, 441). McKee was also asked to investigate the facts relating to respondent's claim of libel, which he did (R. 202, 207). The total payments made by petitioner to stringers throughout the country during the first five months of 1960 was about $245,000 (R. 442). Stringers are not treated as employees for purposes of taxes or employee benefits (R. 439–440, 141–143).

The advertisement complained of in this action was prepared, submitted and accepted in New York, where the newspaper is published (R. 390–393, 438). The total daily circulation of *The Times* in March, 1960, was 650,000, of which the total sent to Alabama was 394–351 to mail subscribers and 43 to dealers. The Sunday circulation was 1,300,000, of which the Alabama shipments totaled 2,440 (Def. Ex. No. 4, R. 1981, R. 401–402). These papers were either mailed to subscribers who had paid for a subscription in advance (R. 427) or they were shipped prepaid by rail or air to Alabama newsdealers, whose orders were unsolicited (R. 404–408, 444) and with whom there was no contract (R. 409). *The Times* would credit dealers for papers which were unsold or arrived late, damaged or incomplete, the usual custom being for the dealer to get the irregularities certified by the railroad baggage man upon a card provided by *The*

U.S. SUPREME COURT, OCTOBER 1963

BRIEF FOR THE PETITIONER

U.S. SUPREME
COURT,
OCTOBER 1963

BRIEF FOR THE
PETITIONER

Times (R. 408–409, 410–412, Pl. Ex. 276–309, R. 1751–1827, R. 414, 420–426), though this formality had not been observed in Alabama (R. 432–436). Gross revenue from this Alabama circulation was approximately $20,000 in the first five months of 1960 of a total gross from circulation of about $8,500,000 (R. 445). *The Times* made absolutely no attempt to solicit or promote its sale or distribution in Alabama (R. 407–408, 428, 450, 485).

The Times accepted advertising from Alabama sources, principally advertising agencies which sent their copy to New York, where any contract for its publication was made (R. 344–349, 543); the agency would then be billed for cost, less the amount of its 15% commission (R. 353–354). The New York Times Sales, Inc., a wholly-owned subsidiary corporation, solicited advertisements in Alabama, though it had no office or resident employees in the State (R. 359–361, 539, 482). Two employees of Sales, Inc. and two employees of *The Times* spent a total of 26 days in Alabama for this purpose in 1959; and one of the Sales, Inc. men spent one day there before the end of May in 1960 (R. 336–338, Def. Ex. 1, R. 1978, 546, 548–551). Alabama advertising linage, both volunteered and solicited, amounted to 5471 in 1959 of a total of 60,000,000 published; it amounted to 13,254 through May of 1960 of a total of 20,000,000 lines (R. 342–344, 341, Def. Ex. 2, R. 1979). An Alabama supplement published in 1958 (R. 379, Pl. Ex. 273, R. 1689–1742) produced payments by Alabama advertisers of $26,801.64 (R. 380). For the first five months of 1960 gross revenue from advertising placed by Alabama agencies or advertisers was $17,000 to $18,000 of a total advertising revenue of $37,500,000 (R. 443). The gross from Alabama advertising and circulation during this period was $37,300 of a national total of $46,000,000 (R. 446).

On these facts, the courts below held that petitioner was subject to the jurisdiction of the Circuit Court in this action, sustaining both the service on McKee as a claimed agent and the substituted service on the Secretary of State and rejecting the constitutional objections urged (R. 49, 51–57, 1139, 1140–1151). Both courts deemed the newsgathering activities of correspondents and stringers, the solicitation and publication of advertising from Alabama sources and the distribution of the paper in the State to constitute sufficient Alabama "contacts"

to support the exercise of jurisdiction (R. 56–57, 1142–1147). They also held that though petitioner had appeared specially upon the motion for the sole purpose of presenting these objections, as permitted by the Alabama practice, the fact that the prayer for relief asked for dismissal for "lack of jurisdiction of the subject matter" of the action, as well as want of jurisdiction of the person of defendant, constituted a general appearance and submission to the jurisdiction of the Court (R. 49–51, 1151–1153).

SUMMARY OF ARGUMENT

I.

Under the doctrine of "libel per se" applied below, a public official is entitled to recover "presumed" and punitive damages for a publication found to be critical of the official conduct of a governmental agency under his general supervision if a jury thinks the publication "tends" to "injure" him "in his reputation" or to "bring" him "into public contempt" as an official. The publisher has no defense unless he can persuade the jury that the publication is entirely true in all its factual, material particulars. The doctrine not only dispenses with proof of injury by the complaining official, but presumes malice and falsity as well. Such a rule of liability works an abridgment of the freedom of the press.

The court below entirely misconceived the constitutional issues, in thinking them disposed of by the propositions that "the Constitution does not protect libelous publications" and that the "Fourteenth Amendment is directed against State action and not private action" (R. 1160). The requirements of the First Amendment are not satisfied by the "mere labels" of State law. *N.A.A.C.P.* v. *Button,* 371 U.S. 415, 429 (1963); see also *Beauharnais* v. *Illinois,* 343 U.S. 250, 263–264 (1952). The rule of law and the judgment challenged by petitioner are, of course, state action within the meaning of the Fourteenth Amendment.

If libel does not enjoy a talismanic insulation from the limitations of the First and Fourteenth Amendments, the principle of liability applied below infringes "these basic constitutional rights in their most pristine and classic form." *Edwards* v. *South Carolina,* 372 U.S. 229, 235 (1963). Whatever other ends are also served by freedom of the press, its safeguard "was fashioned to assure unfettered interchange of ideas for the bringing about of political and social changes desired by the people." *Roth* v. *United States,* 354 U.S. 476, 484 (1957). It is clear that the political expression thus protected by the fundamental law is not delimited by any test of truth, to be administered by juries, courts, or by executive officials. *N.A.A.C.P.* v. *Button, supra,* at 445; *Cantwell* v. *Connecticut,* 310 U.S. 296, 310 (1940). It also is implicit in this Court's decisions that speech or publication which is critical of governmental or official action may not be repressed upon the ground that it diminishes the reputation of those officers whose conduct it deplores or of the government of which they are a part.

The closest analogy in the decided cases is provided by those dealing with contempt, where it is settled that concern for the dignity and reputation of the bench does not support the punishment of criticism of the judge or his decision, whether the utterance is true or false. *Bridges* v. *California,* 314 U.S. 252, 270 (1941); *Pennekamp* v. *Florida,* 328 U.S. 331, 342 (1946); *Wood* v. *Georgia,* 370 U.S. 375 (1962). Comparable criticism of an elected, political official cannot consistently be punished as a libel on the ground that it diminishes his reputation. If political criticism could be punished on the ground that it endangers the esteem with which its object is regarded, none safely could be uttered that was anything but praise.

That neither falsity nor tendency to harm official reputation, nor both in combination, justifies repression of the criticism of official conduct was the central lesson of the great assault on the short-lived Sedition Act of 1798, which the verdict of history has long deemed inconsistent with the First Amendment. The rule of liability applied below is even more repressive in its function and effect than that prescribed by the Sedition Act: it lacks the safeguards of criminal sanctions; it does not require proof that the defendant's purpose was to bring the official into contempt or disrepute; it permits, as this case illustrates, a multiplication of suits based on a single statement; it allows legally limitless awards of punitive damages. Moreover, reviving by judicial decision the worst aspect of the Sedition Act, the doctrine of this case forbids criticism of the government as such on the theory that top officers, though they are not named in statements attacking the official conduct of their agencies, are presumed to be

hurt because such critiques are "attached to" them (R. 1157).

Assuming, without conceding, that the protection of official reputations is a valid interest of the State and that the Constitution allows room for the "accommodation" of that interest and the freedom of political expression, the rule applied below is still invalid. It reflects no compromise of the competing interests; that favored by the First Amendment has been totally rejected, the opposing interest totally preferred. If there is scope for the protection of official reputation against criticism of official conduct, measures of liability far less destructive of the freedom of expression are available and adequate to serve that end. It might be required, for example, that the official prove special damage, actual malice, or both. The Alabama rule embraces neither mitigation. Neither would allow a judgment for respondent on the evidence that he presents.

The foregoing arguments are fortified by the privilege the law of libel grants to an official if he denigrates a private individual. It would invert the scale of values vital to a free society if citizens discharging the "political duty" of "public discussion" (Brandeis, J., concurring in *Whitney* v. *California,* 274 U.S. 357, 375 [1927]) did not enjoy a fair equivalent of the immunity granted to officials as a necessary incident of the performance of official duties.

Finally, respondent's argument that the publication is a "commercial advertisment," beyond the safeguard of the First Amendment, is entirely frivolous. The statement was a recital of grievances and protest against claimed abuse dealing squarely with the major issue of our time.

II.

Whether or not the rule of liability is valid on its face, its application in this case abridges freedom of the press. For nothing in the evidence supports a finding of the type of injury or threat to the respondent's reputation that conceivably might justify repression of the publication or give ground for the enormous judgment rendered on the verdict.

Complaining broadly against suppression of Negro rights throughout the South, the publication did not name respondent or the Commission of which he is a member and plainly was not meant as an attack on him or any other individual. Its protests and its targets were impersonal: "the police," "the state authorities," "the Southern violators." The finding that these collective generalities embodied an allusion to respondent's personal identity rests solely on the reference to "the police" and on his jurisdiction over that department. But the police consisted of too large a group for such a personal allusion to be found. The term "police" does not, in fact, mean all policemen. No more so does it mean the Mayor or Commissioner in charge. This fatal weakness in the claim that the respondent was referred to by the publication was not cured by his own testimony or that of his six witnesses; they did no more than express the opinion that "police" meant the respondent, because he is Commissioner in charge. These "mere general asseverations" (*Norris* v. *Alabama*, 294 U.S. 587, 595 [1935]) were not evidence of what the publication said or what it reasonably could be held to mean.

Even if the statements that refer to "the police" could validly be taken to refer to the respondent, there was nothing in those statements that suffices to support the judgment. Where the publication said that "truckloads" of armed police "ringed the Alabama State College Campus," the fact was that only "large numbers" of police "were deployed near the campus" upon three occasions, without ringing it on any. And where the statement said "They have arrested him seven times," the fact was that Dr. King had been arrested only four times. That these exaggerations or inaccuracies cannot rationally be regarded as tending to injure the respondent's reputation is entirely clear. The advertisement was also wrong in saying that when "the entire student body protested to state authorities by refusing to re-register, their dining hall was padlocked in an attempt to starve them into submission." Only a few students refused to re-register and the dining hall was never padlocked. But none of these erroneous assertions had a thing to do with the police and even less with the respondent. It was equally absurd for respondent to claim injury because the publication correctly reported that some unidentified "they" had twice bombed the home of Dr. King, and to insist on proving his innocence of that crime as the trial court permitted him to do.

That the respondent sustained no injury in fact from the publication, the record makes entirely clear.

Even if there were in this record a basis for considering the publication an offense to the respondent's reputation, there was no rational relationship between the gravity of the offense and the size of the penalty imposed. A "police measure may be unconstitutional merely because the remedy, although effective as means of protection, is unduly harsh or oppressive." Brandeis, J., concurring in *Whitney* v. *California*, 274 U.S. 357, 377 (1927). The proposition must apply with special force when the "harsh" remedy has been explicitly designed as a deterrent of expression. Upon this ground alone, this monstrous judgment is repugnant to the Constitution.

III.

The assumption of jurisdiction in this action by the Circuit Court, based on service of process on McKee and substituted service on the Secretary of State, transcended the territorial limits of due process, imposed a forbidden burden on interstate commerce and abridged the freedom of the press.

There was no basis for the holding by the courts below that petitioner forfeited these constitutional objections by making an involuntary general appearance in the cause. The finding of a general appearance was based solely on the fact that when petitioner appeared specially and moved to quash the attempted service for want of jurisdiction of its person, as permitted by the Alabama practice, the prayer for relief concluded with a further request for dismissal for "lack of jurisdiction of the subject matter of said action." That prayer did not manifest an intention to "consent" or to make "a voluntary submission to the jurisdiction of the court," which the Alabama cases have required to convert a special into a general appearance. *Ex parte Cullinan*, 224 Ala. 263, 266 (1931). The papers made entirely clear that the sole ruling sought by the petitioner was that it was not amenable to Alabama jurisdiction, as a New York corporation having no sufficient contact with the State to permit the assertion of jurisdiction *in personam* in an action based upon a publication in New York.

Moreover, even if petitioner could validly be taken to have made an involuntary general appearance, that appearance would not bar the claim that in assuming jurisdiction of this action the state court imposed a forbidden burden on interstate commerce or that it abridged the freedom of the press. *Davis* v. *Farmers Co-operative Co.*, 262 U.S. 312 (1923); *Michigan Central R. R. Co.* v. *Mix*, 278 U.S. 492, 496 (1929); *Denver & R. G. W. R. Co.* v. *Terte*, 284 U.S. 284, 287 (1932).

The decisions of this Court do not support the holding that the sporadic newsgathering activities of correspondents and stringers of *The Times* in Alabama, the occasional solicitation and publication of advertising from Alabama sources and the minuscule shipment of the newspaper to subscribers and newsdealers in the State constitute sufficient Alabama contacts to satisfy the requirements of due process.

The petitioner's peripheral relationship to Alabama does not involve "continuous corporate operations" which are "so substantial and of such a nature as to justify suit against it on causes of action arising from dealings entirely distinct from those activities." *International Shoe Co.* v. *Washington*, 326 U.S. 310, 318 (1945); *Perkins* v. *Benguet Mining Co.*, 342 U.S. 437 (1952). Hence, if the jurisdiction is sustained, it must be on the ground that the cause of action alleged is so "connected with" petitioner's "activities within the state" as to "make it reasonable, in the context of our federal system of government, to require the corporation to defend the particular suit which is brought there." *International Shoe Co.* v. *Washington, supra*, at 319, 317. There is no such connection. Here, as in *Hanson* v. *Denckla*, 357 U.S. 235, 252 (1958), the "suit cannot be said to be one to enforce an obligation that arose from a privilege the defendant exercised in" the State. The liability alleged is not based on any activity of correspondents or stringers of *The Times* in covering the news in Alabama; and such activity does not rest on a privilege the State confers, given the rights safeguarded by the Constitution. Nor is this claim connected with the occasional solicitation of advertisements in Alabama. Finally, the negligible circulation of *The Times* in Alabama does not involve an act of the petitioner within the State. Copies were mailed in New York to Alabama subscribers or shipped in New York to newsdealers who were purchasers, not agents of *The Times*.

Even if the shipment of the paper may be deemed an act of the petitioner in Alabama, it does not sustain the jurisdiction here affirmed. The standard of *International Shoe* is not "simply mechanical or quantitative"; its application "must depend rather upon the quality and nature of the activity in relation to the fair and orderly administration of the laws which it was the purpose of the due process clause to insure" (326 U.S. at 319). Measured by this standard, a principle which would require, in effect, that almost every newspaper defend a libel suit in almost any jurisdiction of the country, however trivial its circulation there may be, would not further the "fair and orderly administration of the laws". To the extent that this submission prefers the interest of the publisher to that of the plaintiff, the preference is one supported by the First Amendment. It also is supported by the fact that the plaintiff's grievance rests but fancifully on the insubstantial distribution of the publication in the forum, as distinguished from its major circulation out of state.

The decision in *McGee* v. *International Life Ins. Co.*, 355 U.S. 220 (1957) does not govern the disposition here. The contract executed in *McGee* constituted a continuing legal relationship between the insurer and the insured within the State, a relationship which the States, with the concurrence of Congress, have long deemed to require special regulation. *Hanson* v. *Denckla, supra*, at 252; *Travelers Health Assn.* v. *Virginia*, 339 U.S. 643 (1950). *Scripto* v. *Carson*, 362 U.S. 207 (1960), relied on by respondent, is totally irrelevant to the problem of judicial jurisdiction.

The need for reciprocal restraints upon the power of the States to exert jurisdiction over men and institutions not within their borders is emphasized in our society by the full faith and credit clause of the Constitution. An Alabama judgment in this case would have no practical importance were it not enforceable as such in States where the petitioner's resources are located. Thus jurisdictional delineations must be based on grounds that command general assent throughout the Union. No standard worthy of such general assent sustains the jurisdiction here.

If negligible state circulation of a paper published in another state suffices to establish jurisdiction of a suit for libel threatening the type of judgment rendered here, such distribution interstate cannot continue. So, too, if the interstate movement of correspondents provides a factor tending to sustain such jurisdiction, as the court below declared, a strong barrier to such movement has been erected. In the silence of Congress, such movement and distribution are protected by the commerce clause against burdensome state action, unsupported by an over-

U.S. SUPREME COURT, OCTOBER 1963

BRIEF FOR THE PETITIONER

riding local interest. Such a burden has been imposed here.

Newsgathering and circulation are both aspects of the freedom of the press, safeguarded by the Constitution. Neither can continue unimpaired if they subject the publisher to foreign jurisdiction on the grounds and of the scope asserted here. Accordingly, the jurisdictional determination is also repugnant to the First Amendment.

ARGUMENT

The decision of the Supreme Court of Alabama, sustaining the judgment of the Circuit Court, denies rights that are basic to the constitutional conception of a free society and contravenes a postulate of our federalism.

We submit, first (Points I and II), that the decision gives a scope and application to the law of libel so restrictive of the right to protest and to criticize official conduct that it abridges the protected freedom of the press.

We argue, secondly (Point III), that in requiring petitioner to answer in this action in the courts of Alabama, the decision violates the territorial restrictions that the Constitution places on State process, casts a forbidden burden on interstate commerce and also abridges freedom of the press.

I. The decision rests upon a rule of liability for criticism of official conduct that abridges freedom of the press.

Under the law of libel as declared below, a public official is entitled to recover "presumed" and punitive damages for a publication found to be critical of the official conduct of a governmental agency under his general supervision if a jury thinks the publication "tends" to "injure" him "in his reputation" or to "bring" him "into public contempt" as an official. The place of the official in the governmental hierarchy is, moreover, evidence sufficient to establish that his reputation has been jeopardized by statements that reflect upon the agency of which he is in charge. The publisher has no defense unless, as respondent noted in his Brief in Opposition (p. 18, n. 10), he can persuade the jury that the publication is entirely true in all its factual, material particulars. *Ferdon* v. *Dickens*, 161 Ala. 181, 185, 200–201 (1909); *Kirkpatrick* v. *Journal Publishing Company*, 210 Ala. 10, 11 (1923); *Alabama Ride Company* v. *Vance*, 235 Ala. 263,

265 (1938); *Johnson Publishing Co.* v. *Davis*, 271 Ala. 474, 495 (1960). Unless he can discharge this burden as to stated facts, he has no privilege of comment. *Parsons* v. *Age-Herald Pub. Co.*, 181 Ala. 439, 450 (1913). Good motives or belief in truth, however reasonable, are relevant only in mitigation of punitive damages if the jury chooses to accord them weight. *Johnson Publishing Co.* v. *Davis, supra,* at 495. A claim of truth which is regarded as unfounded affords evidence of malice, fortifying the presumption that applies in any case (R. 1178).

We submit that such a rule of liability works an abridgment of the freedom of the press, as that freedom has been defined by the decisions of this Court.

First: The State Court's misconception of the constitutional issues The reasons assigned by the Court below give no support to its rejection of petitioner's constitutional objections.

The accepted proposition that "[t]he Fourteenth Amendment is directed against State action and not private action" (R. 1160) obviously has no application to the case. The petitioner has challenged a State rule of law applied by a State court to render judgment carrying the full coercive power of the State, claiming full faith and credit through the Union solely on that ground. The rule and judgment are, of course, State action in the classic sense of the subject of the Amendment's limitations. See *N.A.A.C.P.* v. *Alabama,* 357 U.S. 449, 463 (1958); *Barrows* v. *Jackson,* 346 U.S. 249, 254 (1953); *Shelley* v. *Kraemer,* 334 U.S. 1, 14 (1948).

There is no greater merit in the other reason stated in the Court's opinion, that "the Constitution does not protect libelous publications." Statements to that effect have, to be sure, been made in passing in opinions of this Court. See *Konigsberg* v. *State Bar of California,* 366 U.S. 36, 49 (1961); *Times Film Corporation* v. *City of Chicago,* 365 U.S. 43, 48 (1961); *Roth* v. *United States,* 354 U.S. 476, 486 (1957); *Beauharnais* v. *Illinois,* 343 U.S. 250, 266 (1952); *Pennekamp* v. *Florida,* 328 U.S. 331, 348–349 (1946); *Chaplinsky* v. *New Hampshire,* 315 U.S. 568, 572 (1942); *Near* v. *Minnesota,* 283 U.S. 697, 715 (1931). But here, no less than elsewhere, a "great principle of constitutional law is not susceptible of comprehensive statement in an adjective." *Carter* v. *Carter Coal Co.,* 298 U.S. 238, 327 (1936) (dissenting opinion of Cardozo, J.).

The statements cited meant no more than that the freedom of speech and of the press is not a universal absolute and leaves the States some room for the control of defamation. None of the cases sustained the repression as a libel of expression critical of governmental action or was concerned with the extent to which the law of libel may be used for the protection of official reputation. The dictum in *Pennekamp* that "when the statements amount to defamation, a judge has such remedy in damages for libel as do other public servants" left at large what may amount to defamation and what remedy a public servant has. *Beauharnais* alone dealt with the standards used in judging any kind of libel, sustaining with four dissenting votes a state conviction for a publication held to be both defamatory of a racial group and "liable to cause violence and disorder." Mr. Justice Frankfurter's opinion took pains to reserve this Court's "authority to nullify action which encroaches on freedom of utterance under the guise of punishing libel"—adding that "public men are, as it were, public property," that "discussion cannot be denied and the right, as well as the duty, of criticism must not be stifled." 343 U.S. at 263–264. Those reservations, rather than the judgment, are apposite here.

Throughout the years this Court has measured by the standards of the First Amendment every formula for the repression of expression challenged at its bar. In that process judgment has been guided by the meaning and the purpose of the Constitution, interpreted as a "continuing instrument of government" (*United States* v. *Classic,* 313 U.S. 299, 316 [1941]), not by the vagaries or "mere labels" of state law. *N.A.A.C.P.* v. *Button,* 371 U.S. 415, 429 (1963). See also Mr. Chief Justice Warren in *Trop* v. *Dulles,* 356 U.S. 86, 94 (1958). Hence libel, like sedition, insurrection, contempt, advocacy of unlawful acts, breach of the peace, disorderly conduct, obscenity or barratry, to name but prime examples, must be defined and judged in terms that satisfy the First Amendment. The law of libel has no more immunity than other law from the supremacy of its command.

Second: Seditious libel and the Constitution If libel does not enjoy a talismanic insulation from the limitations of the First and Fourteenth Amendments, the principle of liability applied below, resting as it does on a "common law concept of the most general and undefined nature" (*Cantwell* v. *Connecticut,* 310 U.S. 296, 308 [1940]), infringes "these basic constitutional rights in their most pristine and classic form." *Edwards* v. *South Carolina,* 372 U.S. 229, 235 (1963).

Whatever other ends are also served by freedom of the press, its safeguard, as this Court has said, "was fashioned to assure unfettered interchange of ideas for the bringing about of political and social changes desired by the people." *Roth* v. *United States,* 354 U.S. 476, 484 (1957). Its object comprehends the protection of that "right of freely examining public characters and measures, and of free communication among the people thereon," which, in the words of the Virginia Resolution, "has ever been justly deemed the only effectual guardian of every other right." 4 *Elliot's Debates* (1876), p. 554. The "opportunity for free political discussion" and "debate" secured by the First Amendment (*Stromberg* v. *California,* 283 U.S. 359, 369 [1931]; *DeJonge* v. *Oregon,* 299 U.S. 353, 365 [1937]; *Terminiello* v. *Chicago,* 337 U.S. 1, 4 [1949]), extends to "vigorous advocacy" no less than "abstract" disquisition. *N.A.A.C.P.* v. *Button,* 371 U.S. 415, 429 (1963). The "prized American privilege to speak one's mind, although not always with perfect good taste," applies at least to such speech "on all public institutions." *Bridges* v. *California,* 314 U.S. 252, 270 (1941). "To many this is, and always will be, folly; but we have staked upon it our all." L. Hand, J., in *United States* v. *Associated Press,* 52 F. Supp. 362, 372 (S.D.N.Y. 1943). That national commitment has been affirmed repeatedly by the decisions of this Court, which have recognized that the Amendment "must be taken as a command of the broadest scope that explicit language, read in the context of a liberty-loving society, will allow" (*Bridges* v. *California, supra,* at 263); and that its freedoms "need breathing space to survive." *N.A.A.C.P.* v. *Button, supra,* at 433.

It is clear that the political expression thus protected by the fundamental law is not delimited by any test of truth, to be administered by juries, courts, or by executive officials, not to speak of a test which puts the burden of establishing the truth upon the writer. Within this sphere of speech or publication, the constitutional protection does not turn upon "the truth, popularity, or social utility of the ideas and beliefs which are offered." *N.A.A.C.P.* v. *Button, supra,* at 445. See also *Speiser* v. *Randall,* 357 U.S. 513, 526 (1958). The Amendment "pre-

U.S. SUPREME COURT, OCTOBER 1963

BRIEF FOR THE PETITIONER

U.S. SUPREME
COURT,
OCTOBER 1963

BRIEF FOR THE
PETITIONER

supposes that right conclusions are more likely to be gathered out of a multitude of tongues, than through any kind of authoritative selection." *United States* v. *Associated Press, supra,* at 372. As Mr. Justice Roberts said in *Cantwell* v. *Connecticut,* 310 U.S. 296, 310 (1940):

> "In the realm of religious faith, and in that of political belief, sharp differences arise. In both fields the tenets of one man may seem the rankest error to his neighbor. To persuade others to his own point of view, the pleader, as we know, at times, resorts to exaggeration, to vilification of men who have been, or are, prominent in church or state, and even to false statement. But the people of this nation have ordained in the light of history, that, in spite of the probability of excesses and abuses, these liberties are, in the long view, essential to enlightened opinion and right conduct on the part of the citizens of a democracy."

These affirmations are the premises today of any exploration of the scope of First Amendment freedom undertaken by this Court. It is implicit in those premises that speech or publication which is critical of governmental or official action may not be repressed upon the ground that it diminishes the reputation of the officers whose conduct it deplores or of the government of which they are a part.

The closest analogy in the decided cases is provided by those dealing with contempt.[2] It is settled law that concern for the dignity and reputation of the bench does not support the punishment of criticism of the judge or his decision (*Bridges* v. *California, supra,* at 270), though the utterance contains "half-truths" and "misinformation" (*Pennekamp* v. *Florida, supra,* 328 U.S. at 342, 343, 345). Any such repression must be justified, if it is justified at all, by danger of obstruction of the course of justice; and such danger must be clear and present. See also *Craig* v. *Harney,* 331 U.S. 367, 373, 376, 389 (1947); *Wood* v. *Georgia,* 370 U.S. 375, 388, 389, 393 (1962). We do not see how comparable criticism of an elected, political official may consistently be punished as a libel on the ground that it diminishes his reputation.[3] The supposition that judges are "men of fortitude, able to thrive in a hardy climate" (*Craig* v. *Harney, supra,* at 376) must apply to commissioners as well.

These decisions are compelling not alone for their authority but also for their recognition of the basic principle involved. If political criticism could be punished on the ground that it endangers the esteem with which its object is regarded,

none safely could be uttered that was anything but praise.

The point was made in classic terms in Madison's Report on the Virginia Resolutions (4 *Elliot's Debates,* p. 575):

> "... it is manifestly impossible to punish the intent to bring those who administer the government into disrepute or contempt, without striking at the right of freely discussing public characters and measures; because those who engage in such discussions, must expect and intend to excite these unfavorable sentiments, so far as they may be thought to be deserved. To prohibit the intent to excite those unfavorable sentiments against those who administer the government, is equivalent to a prohibition of the actual excitement of them; and to prohibit the actual excitement of them is equivalent to a prohibition of discussions having that tendency and effect; which, again, is equivalent to a protection of those who administer the government, if they should at any time deserve the contempt or hatred of the people, against being exposed to it, by free animadversions on their characters and conduct... ."

If criticism of official conduct may not be repressed upon the ground that it is false or that it tends to harm official reputation, the inadequacy of these separate grounds is not surmounted by their combination. This was the basic lesson of the great assault on the short-lived Sedition Act of 1798, which first crystallized a national awareness of the central meaning of the First Amendment. See, *e.g.,* Levy, *Legacy of Suppression* (1960), p. 249 *et. seq.;* Smith, *Freedom's Fetters* (1956).

That Act declared it a crime "if any person shall write, print, utter or publish ... any false, scandalous and malicious writing or writings against the government of the United States, or either house of the Congress ..., or the President ..., with intent to defame the said government, or either house of the said Congress, or the said President, or to bring them or either of them,

---

[2] *Cf.* Kalven, *The Law of Defamation and the First Amendment,* in *Conference on the Arts, Publishing and the Law* (U. of Chi. Law School), p. 4: "It is exactly correct to regard seditious libel, which has been the most serious threat to English free speech, as defamation of government and government officials. It is at most a slight extension of terms to regard contempt of court by publication as a problem of defamation of the judicial process."

[3] Statements about officials dealing with purely private matters unrelated to their official conduct or competence might raise different questions, not presented here.

into contempt or disrepute; or to excite against them, or either or any of them, the hatred of the good people of the United States… ." It specifically provided that the defendant might "give in evidence in his defence, the truth of the matter contained in the publication charged as a libel", a mitigation of the common law not achieved in England until Lord Campbell's Act in 1843. It also reserved the right of the jury to "determine the law and the fact, under the direction of the court, as in other cases," accepting the reform effected by Fox's Libel Act of 1792. Act of July 14, 1798, Secs. 2, 3; 1 Stat. 596. These qualifications were not deemed sufficient to defend the measure against a constitutional attack that won widespread support throughout the nation.

In the House debate upon the bill, John Nicholas of Virginia warned that a law ostensibly directed against falsehood "must be a very powerful restriction of the press, with respect to the publication of important truths." Men "would be deterred from printing anything which should be in the least offensive to a power which might so greatly harass them. They would not only refrain from publishing anything of the least questionable nature, but they would be afraid of publishing the truth, as, though true, it might not always be in their power to establish the truth to the satisfaction of a court of justice." 8 *Annals of Congress* 2144. Albert Gallatin delineated the same peril, arguing that "the proper weapon to combat error was truth, and that to resort to coercion and punishments in order to suppress writings attacking … measures …, was to confess that these could not be defended by any other means." *Id.* at 2164. Madison's Report reiterates these points, observing that some "degree of abuse is inseparable from the proper use of every thing; and in no instance is this more true than in that of the press." 4 *Elliot's Debates,* p. 571. Summing up the position in words that have echoed through the years, he asked (*ibid.*):

> "Had Sedition Acts, forbidding every publication that might bring the constituted agents into contempt or disrepute, or that might excite the hatred of the people against the authors of unjust or pernicious measures, been uniformly enforced against the press, might not the United States have been languishing, at this day, under the infirmities of a sickly Confederation? Might they not, possibly, be miserable colonies, groaning under a foreign yoke?"

Though the Sedition Act was never passed on by this Court, the verdict of history surely sustains the view that it was inconsistent with the First Amendment. Fines levied in its prosecutions were repaid by Act of Congress on this ground. See, *e.g., Act of July 4, 1840, c. 45, 6 Stat. 802 (fine imposed on Congressman Matthew Lyon refunded to his heirs).[4] Its invalidity as "abridging the freedom of the press" was assumed by Calhoun, reporting to the Senate on February 4, 1836, as a matter "which no one now doubts." Report with Senate bill No. 122, 24th Cong., 1st Sess. p. 3. The same assumption has been made upon this Court. Holmes, J., dissenting in *Abrams* v. *United States,* 250 U.S. 616, 630 (1919); Jackson, J., dissenting in *Beauharnais* v. *Illinois,* 343 U.S. 250, 288–289 (1952). See also Cooley, *Constitutional Limitations* (8th ed. 1927), p. 900; Chafee, *Free Speech in the United States* (1941), pp. 27–29. These assumptions reflect a broad consensus that, we have no doubt, is part of present law.

Respondent points to Jefferson's distinction between the right of Congress "to control the freedom of the press," which Jefferson of course denied, and that remaining in the States, which he admitted. Brief in Opposition, p. 19; see *Dennis* v. *United States,* 341 U.S. 494, 522, n. 4 (1961) (concurring opinion). That distinction lost its point with the adoption of the Fourteenth Amendment and the incorporation of the First Amendment freedoms in the "liberty" protected against state action. See, *e.g., Bridges* v. *California,* 314 U.S. 252, 268 (1941); *Edwards* v. *South Carolina,* 372 U.S. 229, 235 (1963). The view that there may be a difference in the stringency of the commands embodied in the two Amendments (Jackson, J., in *Beauharnais* v. *Illinois, supra,* 343 U.S. at 288; Harlan, J., concurring in *Alberts* v. *California,* 354 U.S. 476, 501, 503 [1957]) has not prevailed in the decisions of this Court. Even if it had, we think it

U.S. SUPREME COURT, OCTOBER 1963

BRIEF FOR THE PETITIONER

---

[4] The Committee reporting the bill described its basis as follows (H.R. Rep. No. 86, 26th Cong., 1st Sess., p. 3 (1840)): "All that now remains to be done by the representatives of a people who condemned this act of their agents as unauthorized, and transcending their grant of power, to place beyond question, doubt, or cavil, that mandate of the constitution prohibiting Congress from abridging the liberty of the press, and to discharge an honest, just, moral, and honorable obligation, is to refund from the Treasury the fine thus illegally and wrongfully obtained from one of their citizens… ."

See also Acts of June 17, 1844, cc. 136 and 165, 6 Stat. 924 and 931.

U.S. SUPREME
COURT,
OCTOBER 1963

BRIEF FOR THE
PETITIONER

plain that there could be no reasonable difference in the strength of their protection of expression against "frontal attack or suppression" (Harlan, J., dissenting in *N.A.A.C.P.* v. *Button, supra,* 371 U.S. at 455) of the kind with which we are concerned.

The rule of liability applied below is even more repressive in its function and effect than that prescribed by the Sedition Act. There is no requirement of an indictment and the case need not be proved beyond a reasonable doubt. It need not be shown, as the Sedition Act required, that the defendant's purpose was to bring the official "into contempt or disrepute"; a statement adjudged libelous *per se* is *presumed* to be "false and malicious," as the trial court instructed here (R. 824). There is no limitation to one punishment for one offensive statement, as would be required in a criminal proceeding. Respondent is only one of four commissioners, including one former incumbent, not to speak of the former Governor, who claim damages for the same statement. The damages the jury may award them if it deems the statement to apply to their official conduct are both general and punitive—the former for a "presumed" injury to reputation (R. 1160) and the latter "not alone to punish the wrongdoer, but as a deterrent to others similarly minded" (R. 1176). Such damages, moreover, are fettered by "no legal measure" of amount (R. 1177). It does not depreciate the stigma of a criminal conviction to assert that such a "civil" sanction is a more repressive measure than the type of sentence the Sedition Act permitted for the crime that it purported to define. Here, as in *Bantam Books, Inc.* v. *Sullivan,* 372 U.S. 58, 70 (1963), the "form of regulation … creates hazards to protected freedoms markedly greater than those that attend reliance upon the criminal law."

It should be added that the principle of liability, as formulated by the Supreme Court of Alabama, goes even further than to punish statements critical of the official conduct of individual officials; it condemns the critique of government as such. This is accomplished by the declaration that it is sufficient to sustain the verdict that in "measuring the performance or deficiencies" of governmental bodies, "praise or criticism is usually attached to the official in complete control of the body" (R. 1157). On this thesis it becomes irrelevant that the official is not named or referred to in the publication. The

most impersonal denunciation of an agency of government may be treated, in the discretion of the jury, as a defamation of the hierarchy of officials having such "complete control." A charge, for example, of "police brutality," instead of calling for investigation and report by supervising officers, gives them a cause of action against the complainant, putting him to proof that will persuade the jury of the truth of his assertion. Such a concept transforms the law of defamation from a method of protecting private reputation to a device for insulating government against attack.

When municipalities have claimed that they were libeled, they have met the answer that "no court of last resort in this country has ever held, or even suggested, that prosecutions for libel on government have any place in the American system of jurisprudence." *City of Chicago* v. *Tribune Co.,* 307 Ill. 595, 601 (1923). See also *City of Albany* v. *Meyer,* 99 Cal. App. 651 (1929). That answer applies as well to converting "libel on government" into libel of the officials of whom it must be composed. The First Amendment, no less than the Fifteenth, "nullifies sophisticated as well as simple-minded modes" of infringing the rights it guarantees. *Lane* v. *Wilson,* 307 U.S. 268, 275 (1939); *Bates* v. *Little Rock,* 361 U.S. 516, 523 (1960); *Louisiana ex rel. Gremillion* v. *N.A.A.C.P.,* 366 U.S. 293, 297 (1961).

If this were not the case, the daily dialogue of politics would become utterly impossible. That dialogue includes, as Mr. Justice Jackson said, the effort "to discredit and embarrass the Government of the day by spreading exaggerations and untruths and by inciting prejudice or unreasoning discontent, not even hesitating to injure the Nation's prestige among the family of nations." *Communications Assn.* v. *Douds,* 339 U.S. 382, 423 (1950) (opinion concurring and dissenting in part). Sound would soon give place to silence if officials in "complete control" of governmental agencies, instead of answering their critics, could resort to friendly juries to amerce them for their words. Mr. Justice Brewer, in calling for the "freest criticism" of this Court, employed a metaphor that is apposite: "The moving waters are full of life and health; only in the still water is stagnation and death." *Government by Injunction,* 15 Nat. Corp. Rep. 848, 849 (1898). The First Amendment guarantees that motion shall obtain.

Third: The absence of accommodation of conflicting interests For the reasons thus far stated we contend that an expression which is critical of governmental conduct is within the "core of constitutional freedom" (*Kingsley Pictures Corp.* v. *Regents,* 360 U.S. 684, 689 [1959]) and may not be prohibited directly to protect the reputation of the government or its officials. A threat to such reputation is intrinsic to the function of such criticism. It is not, therefore, a "substantive evil" that a State has power to prevent by the suppression of the critical expression (*cf., e.g., Schenck* v. *United States,* 249 U.S. 47, 52 [1919]; *Dennis* v. *United States,* 341 U.S. 494, 506–507, 508–510 [1951]); nor does the protection of such reputation provide one of those "conflicting governmental interests" with which the protected freedom must "be reconciled" or to which it may validly be made to yield. *Konigsberg* v. *State Bar,* 366 U.S. 36, 50 n. 11 (1961); *Gibson* v. *Florida Legislative Comm.,* 372 U.S. 539, 546 (1963).

If this submission overstates the scope of constitutional protection, it surely does so only in denying that there may be room for the accommodation of the two "conflicting interests" represented by official reputation and the freedom of political expression. But even under a standard that permits such accommodation, the rule by which this case was judged is inconsistent with the Constitution.

This conclusion follows because Alabama's law of libel *per se,* as applied to the criticism of officials as officials, does not reconcile the conflicting interests; it subordinates the First Amendment freedom wholly to protecting the official. It reflects no compromise of the competing values which we assume, *arguendo,* a State may validly attempt to balance. The interest favored by the First Amendment has been totally rejected, the opposing interest totally preferred. But here, as elsewhere in the area which is of concern to the First Amendment, the breadth of an abridgment "must be viewed in the light of less drastic means for achieving the same basic purpose." *Shelton* v. *Tucker,* 364 U.S. 479, 488 (1960); *Speiser* v. *Randall,* 357 U.S. 513 (1958); *cf. Dean Milk Co.* v. *City of Madison,* 340 U.S. 349, 354 (1951). If there is room for the protection of official reputation against criticism of official conduct, measures of liability far less destructive of the freedom of expression are available and adequate to serve that end.

The Court of Appeals for the District of Columbia adopted such a standard as its version of the common law of libel in *Sweeney* v. *Patterson,* 128 F. 2d 457 (1942), dismissing a complaint based on a statement charging a Congressman with anti-Semitism in opposing an appointment. Judge Edgerton, joined by Judges Miller and Vinson, noted that "the cases are in conflict" but declared that "in our view it is not actionable to publish erroneous and injurious statements of fact and injurious comment or opinion regarding the political conduct and views of public officials, so long as no charge of crime, corruption, gross immorality or gross incompetence is made and no special damage results. Such a publication is not 'libelous per se.' "The position was placed upon the ground that "discussion will be discouraged, and the public interest in public knowledge of important facts will be poorly defended, if error subjects its author to a libel suit without even a showing of economic loss. Whatever is added to the field of libel is taken from the field of free debate." 128 F. 2d at 458. These are, we argue, grounds which are of constitutional dimension.

The same position was taken by Judge Clark, dissenting in *Sweeney* v. *Schenectady Union Pub. Co.,* 122 F. 2d 288 (2d Cir. 1941), affirmed by an equal division of this Court. 316 U.S. 642 (1942). Deprecating the "dangerous ... rationale of the decision that a comment leading an appreciable number of readers to hate or hold in contempt the public official commented on is libelous per se," he concluded that "the common-law requirement of proof of special damages gives" the commentator "the protection he needs, while at the same time it does prevent him from causing really serious injury and loss by false and unfair statements." 122 F. 2d at 291, 292.

Other courts have shown solicitude for the freedom to criticize the conduct of officials by requiring that the aggrieved official prove the critic's malice, abrogating the presumptions and strict liability that otherwise obtain.[5] This

---

[5] *Gough* v. *Tribune-Journal Company,* 75 Ida. 502, 510 (1954); *Salinger* v. *Cowles,* 195 Iowa 873, 890–891 (1923); *Coleman* v. *MacLennan,* 78 Kan. 711, 723 (1908) (frequently cited as a leading case); *Bradford* v. *Clark,* 90 Me. 298, 302 (1897); *Lawrence* v. *Fox,* 357 Mich. 134, 142 (1959); *Ponder* v. *Cobb,* 257 N.C. 281, 293 (1962); *Moore* v. *Davis,* 16 S.W. 2d 380, 384 (Tex. Civ. App. 1929). Applying the same rule to candidates for public office, see *Phoenix Newspapers* v. *Choisser,* 82 Ariz. 271, 277 (1957); *Friedell* v. *Blakeley Printing Co.,* 163 Minn. 226, 231 (1925); *Boucher* v. *Clark Pub. Co.,* 14 S.D. 72, 82 (1900). And *cf. Charles Parker Co.* v. *Silver City Crystal Co.,* 142 Conn. 605, 614 (1955) (same privilege against private

U.S. SUPREME COURT, OCTOBER 1963

BRIEF FOR THE PETITIONER

U.S. SUPREME
COURT,
OCTOBER 1963

BRIEF FOR THE
PETITIONER

approach draws a line between expression uttered with the purpose of harming the official by an accusation known to be unfounded, and expression which is merely wrong in fact, with denigrating implications. It thus makes an essential element of liability an intent similar to that which elsewhere has been deemed necessary to sustain a curb on utterance (see, *e.g., Dennis* v. *United States, supra,* at 516; *Smith* v. *California,* 361 U.S. 147 [1959]; *cf. Wieman* v. *Updegraff,* 344 U.S. 183 [1952]) and relieves the defendant of an evidential and persuasive burden of a kind that has been held to be excessive (*Speiser* v. *Randall,* 357 U.S. 513 [1958]), assimilating the criteria of libel law in both respects to those demanded by the Constitution in related fields.

Whether either of these mitigated rules of liability for criticism of official conduct, or both in combination, would conform to First Amendment standards, need not be determined in this case. The Alabama rule embraces neither mitigation. Neither would allow a judgment for respondent on the evidence on which he rests his claim.

Fourth: The relevancy of the official's privilege The arguments we have made are fortified by recollection of the privilege the law of libel grants to an official if he denigrates a private individual. In *Barr* v. *Matteo,* 360 U.S. 564, 575 (1959), this Court held the utterance of a federal official absolutely privileged if made "within the outer perimeter" of the official's duties. The States accord the same immunity to statements of their highest officers, though some differentiate their lowlier officials and qualify the privilege they enjoy, taking the position urged by the minority in the *Matteo* case. But all hold that all officials are protected unless actual malice can be proved.[6]

The ground of the official privilege is said to be that the threat of damage suits would otherwise "inhibit the fearless, vigorous, and effective administration of policies of government," that,

in the words of Judge Learned Hand (*Gregoire* v. *Biddle,* 177 F. 2d 579, 581 [2d Cir. 1949]), "'to submit all officials, the innocent as well as the guilty, to the burden of a trial and to the inevitable danger of its outcome, would dampen the ardor of all but the most resolute, or the most irresponsible, in the unflinching discharge of their duties.'" *Barr* v. *Matteo, supra,* at 571. Mr. Justice Black, concurring, also related the official privilege to the sustenance of "an informed public opinion," dependent on "the freedom people have to applaud or to criticize the way public employees do their jobs, from the least to the most important." 360 U.S. at 577.

It would invert the scale of values vital to a free society if citizens discharging the "political duty" of "public discussion" (Brandeis, J., concurring in *Whitney* v. *California,* 274 U.S. 357, 375 [1927]) did not enjoy a fair equivalent of the immunity granted to officials as a necessary incident of the performance of official duties. The threat of liability for actionable statement is assuredly no less of a deterrent to the private individual (*cf. Farmers Union* v. *WDAY,* 360 U.S. 525, 530 [1959]), who, unlike the official, must rely upon his own resources for defense. And, as Madison observed in words that are remembered, "the censorial power is in the people over the Government, and not in the Government over the people." 4 *Annals of Congress* 934. See also *Report on the Virginia Resolutions* (1799), 4 *Elliot's Debates* (1876), pp. 575–576. "For the same reason that members of the Legislature, judges of the courts, and other persons engaged in certain fields of the public service or in the administration of justice are absolutely immune from actions, civil or criminal, for libel for words published in the discharge of such public duties, the individual citizen must be given a like privilege when he is acting in his sovereign capacity." *City of Chicago* v. *Tribune Co.,* 307 Ill. 595, 610 (1923). The citizen acts in his "sover-

---

corporation allegedly libeled in political broadcast). Scholarly opinion, while describing as still a "minority view" in libel law this requirement that a plaintiff officer or candidate prove actual malice, has favored it with substantial unanimity. See, *e.g.,* 1 Harper and James, *The Law of Torts* (1956), pp. 449–450; Noel, *Defamation of Public Officers and Candidates,* 49 Col. L. Rev. 875, 891–895 (1949); *cf. Developments in the Law: Defamation,* 69 Harv. L. Rev. 875, 928 (1956).

[6] *E.g.,* according absolute privilege, *Catron* v. *Jasper,* 303 Ky. 598 (1946) (county sheriff); *Schlinkert* v. *Henderson,* 331 Mich. 284 (1951) (member of liquor commission); *Hughes* v.

Bizzell, 189 Okla. 472, 474 (1941) (president of state university); *Montgomery* v. *Philadelphia,* 392 Pa. 178 (1958) (deputy commissioner and city architect). Limiting officers below state cabinet rank to a qualified privilege, see, *e.g., Barry* v. *McCollom,* 81 Conn. 293 (1908) (superintendent of schools); *Mills* v. *Denny,* 245 Iowa 584 (1954) (mayor); *Howland* v. *Flood,* 160 Mass. 509 (1894) (town investigating committee); *Peterson* v. *Steenerson,* 113 Minn. 87 (1910) (postmaster). See generally, 1 Harper and James, *The Law of Torts* (1956), pp. 429–30; *Prosser on Torts* (2d ed., 1955), pp. 612–13; *Restatement, Torts,* § 591.

eign capacity" when he assumes to censure the officialdom.

Fifth: The protection of editorial advertisements Though the point was not taken by the court below, respondent argues that the fact that the statement was a paid advertisement deprives it of protection "as speech and press." Brief in Opposition, p. 19. The argument is wholly without merit.

The decisions invoked by respondent have no bearing on this case. *Breard* v. *Alexandria,* 341 U.S. 622 (1951), dealt with a regulation of the place, manner and circumstances of solicitation of subscriptions, not with the repression of a publication on the basis of its content, the ideas that are expressed. *Valentine* v. *Christensen,* 316 U.S. 52 (1942), involved a handbill soliciting the inspection of a submarine which its owner exhibited to visitors on payment of a stated fee. An ordinance requiring a permit for street distribution of commercial advertising was sustained as applied to him. It is merely cynical to urge that these determinations bar protection of the statement involved here.

The statement published by petitioner was not a "commercial" advertisement, as it is labeled by respondent. It was a recital of grievances and protest against claimed abuses dealing squarely with the major issue of our time. The fact that its authors sought to raise funds for defense of Dr. King and his embattled movement, far from forfeiting its constitutional protection, adds a reason why it falls within the freedom guaranteed. *Cf. N.A.A.C.P.* v. *Button, supra,* 371 U.S. at 429–431, 439–440. That petitioner received a payment for the publication is no less immaterial in this connection than is the fact that newspapers and books are sold. *Smith* v. *California,* 361 U.S. 147, 150 (1959); *cf. Bantam Books Inc.* v. *Sullivan,* 372 U.S. 58, 64, n. 6 (1963).

It is, of course, entirely true that the published statement did not represent or purport to represent assertions by petitioner, but rather by the sponsoring Committee and the individuals whose names appeared. But since the publisher is held no less responsible than are the sponsors, it must surely have the same protection they enjoy. *Cf. Barrows* v. *Jackson,* 346 U.S. 249 (1953). The willingness of newspapers to carry editorial advertisements is, moreover, an important method of promoting some equality of practical enjoyment of the benefits the First Amendment was intended to secure. *Cf. Lovell* v.

Griffin, 303 U.S. 444 (1938); *Schneider* v. *State,* 308 U.S. 147 (1939); *Talley* v. *California,* 362 U.S. 60 (1960). The practice encourages "the widest possible dissemination of information from diverse and antagonistic sources," which the First Amendment deems "essential to the welfare of the public." *Associated Press* v. *United States,* 326 U.S. 1, 20 (1945). It has no lesser claim than any other mode of publication to the freedom that the Constitution guarantees.

II. Even if the rule of liability were valid on its face, the judgment rests on an invalid application.

Assuming, *arguendo,* that the freedom of the press may constitutionally be subordinated to protection of official reputation, as it would be by the rule of liability declared below, the rule is nonetheless invalid as applied, upon the record in this case. Nothing in the evidence supports a finding of the type of injury or threat to the respondent's reputation that, on the assumption stated, justifies repression of the publication. And even if there were a basis for discerning such a threat, there was no ground for the enormous judgment rendered on the verdict.

First: The scope of review These submissions fall within the settled scope of review by this Court when it is urged that a federal right has been denied "in substance and effect" by a state court. *Norris* v. *Alabama,* 294 U.S. 587, 590 (1935). If the denial rests on findings of fact which are in law determinative of the existence of the federal right, those findings must be adequately sustained by the evidence. *Norris* v. *Alabama, supra; Fiske* v. *Kansas,* 274 U.S. 380 (1927); *Herndon* v. *Lowry,* 301 U.S. 242, 259–261 (1937). If the denial rests on a conclusion or evaluation governing the application of controlling federal criteria, this Court will make its own appraisal of the record to determine if the facts established warrant the conclusion or evaluation made. *Bridges* v. *California,* 314 U.S. 252, 263, 271 (1941); *Pennekamp* v. *Florida,* 328 U.S. 331, 335, 345–346 (1946); *Craig* v. *Harney,* 331 U.S. 367, 373–374 (1947); *Watts* v. *Indiana,* 338 U.S. 49, 50 (1949) (plurality opinion); *Kingsley Pictures Corp.* v. *Regents,* 360 U.S. 684, 708 (1959) (concurring opinion); *Wood* v. *Georgia,* 370 U.S. 375, 386 (1962); *Edwards* v. *South Carolina,* 372 U.S. 229 (1963).

The decision below that the publication libeled the respondent does not, therefore, foreclose the questions whether, on the facts estab-

U.S. SUPREME COURT, OCTOBER 1963

BRIEF FOR THE PETITIONER

lished by the record, it contained a statement "of and concerning" the complainant and, if so, whether such statement injured or jeopardized his reputation to an extent that, as a matter of the First Amendment, justified its punitive repression by the judgment rendered in the Circuit Court. *Bridges* v. *California, supra.* As in the contempt cases, this Court "must weigh the impact of the words against the protection given by the principles of the First Amendment... ." *Pennekamp* v. *Florida, supra,* at 349.

Second: The failure to establish injury or threat to respondent's reputation An appraisal of this record in these terms leaves no room for a determination that the publication sued on by respondent made a statement as to him, or that, if such a statement may be found by implication, it injured or jeopardized his reputation in a way that forfeits constitutional protection.

The publication did not name respondent or the Commission of which he is a member and it plainly was not meant as an attack on him or any other individual. Its protests and its targets were impersonal: "the police," the "state authorities," "the Southern violators." The finding that these collective generalities embodied an allusion to respondent's personal identity rests solely on the reference to "the police" and on his jurisdiction over that department. See pp. 7, 9, 10–14, 23–24, *supra.* But the police consisted of a force of 175 full-time officers, not to speak of a Chief responsible for the direction of their operations. See p. 10, *supra.* Courts have not hitherto permitted the mere designation of a group so large to be regarded as a reference to any member, least of all to one related to it only by an ultimate responsibility for its control or management.[7] While this result may well involve an element of judgment as to policy, regardful of "the social interest in free press discussion of matters of general concern" (*Service Parking Corp.* v. *Washington Times Co.,* 92 F. 2d at 505), it rests as well upon a common sense perception of the safety that numbers afford against a truly harm-

ful denigration. The term "police" does not in fact mean all policemen. No more so does it mean the Mayor or Commissioner in charge.

This fatal weakness in the allegation that respondent was referred to by the publication was not cured by his own testimony or that of his six witnesses, four of whom first saw the publication in the office of his counsel. See p. 14, *supra.* We have detailed that testimony in the Statement (*supra,* pp. 11–14) and shall not repeat it *in extenso* here. It was at best opinion as to the interpretation of the writing. No witness offered evidence of an extrinsic fact bearing upon the meaning of an enigmatic phrase or the identity of someone mentioned by description. *Cf., e.g., Hope* v. *Hearst Consolidated Publications, Inc.,* 294 F. 2d 681 (2d Cir. 1961). The weight of the testimony does not, therefore, transcend the ground of the opinions, which was no more than the bare *ipse dixit* that "police" meant the respondent, since he is Commissioner in charge.

Respondent's own conception of the meaning of the language went beyond this, to be sure. His view was that if one statement in a paragraph referred to the police, the other statements must be read to make the same allusion. Thus he considered that the declaration "They have bombed his home" meant that the bombing was the work of the police, because the paragraph contained the statement that "[t]hey have arrested him seven times"; and arrests are made by the police. See pp. 9, 11, *supra.*

We think it is enough to say that these "mere general asseverations" (*Norris* v. *Alabama,* 294 U.S. 587, 595 [1935]) were not evidence of what the publication said or what it reasonably could be held to mean. The problem, on this score, is not unlike that posed in *Fiske* v. *Kansas, supra,* where in determining the "situation presented" on the record, this Court read the crucial document itself to see if it possessed the attributes that had produced its condemnation (274 U.S. at 385). So read, this publication was a totally impersonal attack upon conditions, groups and institutions, not a personal assault of any kind.

Even if the statements that refer to "the police" could validly be taken to refer to the respondent, there was nothing in those statements that suffices to support the judgment. Assertions that were shown to have been accurate by the respondent's evidence cannot be relied on to establish injury to his official or his

---

[7] See, *e.g., Service Parking Corp.* v. *Washington Times Co.,* 92 F. 2d 502 (D.C. Cir. 1937); *Noral* v. *Hearst Publications, Inc.,* 40 Cal. App. 2d 348 (1940); *Fowler* v. *Curtis Publishing Co.,* 182 F. 2d 377 (D. C. Cir. 1950); *McBride* v. *Crowell-Collier Pub. Co.,* 196 F. 2d 187 (5th Cir. 1952); *Neiman-Marcus* v. *Lait,* 13 F.R.D. 311, 316 (S.D.N.Y. 1952); *cf. Julian* v. *American Business Consultants, Inc.,* 2 N.Y. 2d 1 (1956); *Weston* v. *Commercial Advertiser Assn.,* 184 N. Y. 479, 485 (1906). See also *Restatement of Torts,* § 564, Comment *c; Prosser on Torts* (2d ed. 1955), pp. 583–584.

private reputation; if the truth hurts that surely is a hurt the First Amendment calls on him to bear.[8] Hence, the whole claim of libel rests on two discrepancies between the material statements and the facts. Where the publication said that "truckloads" of armed police "ringed the Alabama State College Campus," the fact was that only "large numbers" of police "were deployed near the campus" upon three occasions, without ringing it on any. See p. 8, *supra.* And where the statement said "They have arrested him seven times," the fact was that Dr. King had been arrested only four times. Three of the arrests had occurred, moreover, before the respondent came to office some six months before the suit was filed. See pp. 9, 10, *supra.* That the exaggerations or inaccuracies in these statements cannot rationally be regarded as tending to injure the respondent's reputation is, we submit, entirely clear.

None of the other statements in the paragraphs relied on by respondent helps to make a colorable case. The advertisement was wrong in saying that when "the entire student body protested to state authorities by refusing to re-register, their dining hall was padlocked in an attempt to starve them into submission." This was, indeed, the gravamen of the resentment that the publication seems to have inspired in Montgomery. See p. 9, *supra.* A majority of students did engage in the protest against the expulsions, but only a few refused to re-register, the dining hall was never "padlocked" and, perforce, there was no "attempt to starve" the students "into submission." See p. 8, *supra.* But none of these admittedly erroneous assertions had a thing to do with the police and even less with the respondent. He testified himself that "as far as the expulsion of students is concerned, that responsibility rests with the State Depart-

ment of Education" (R. 716). If that was so, as it clearly was, it must have been no less the responsibility of the "State authorities," who are alone referred to in the offending sentence, to have padlocked the dining hall, as it alleged. There certainly is no suggestion, express or implied, that the imaginary padlock was attached by the police.

The statement that "the Southern violators have answered Dr. King's peaceful protests with intimidation and violence" was thought by the respondent to refer to himself only because "it is contained in a paragraph" which also referred to arrests (R. 717–718), a point on which his testimony is, to say the least, quite inexplicit, totally ignoring the fact that the paragraph did not even fix the time of the events recited or purport to place them in Montgomery. But whatever the respondent brought himself to think, or badgered Aaronson to say on cross-examination (see p. 17, *supra*), the statement cannot reasonably bear such a construction. The term "Southern violators of the Constitution" was a generic phrase employed in the advertisement to characterize all those whose alleged conduct gave rise to the grievances recited, whether private persons or officials. There was no suggestion that the individuals or groups were all the same, any more than that they were the same in Orangeburg as in Atlanta or Montgomery.

For the same reason, there was no basis for asserting that the statement that "they" bombed his home, assaulted him and charged him with perjury pointed to respondent as the antecedent of the pronoun, though the trial court pointedly permitted him to prove his innocence upon these points. See p. 10, *supra.* There was, to be sure, disputed evidence respecting a police assault but this related to an incident occurring long before respondent was elected a Commissioner (see pp. 9–10, *supra*). Beyond dispute, there were two bombings of King's home and he was charged with perjury. Indeed, to raise funds to defend him on that charge, which proved to be unfounded, was the main objective of the publication. See p. 6, *supra.*

It is, in sum, impossible in our view to see in this mélange of statements, notwithstanding the inaccuracies noted, any falsehood that related to respondent and portended injury to his official reputation. That he sustained no injury in fact was made entirely clear by his own evidence. The most that his witnesses could say was that

---

[8] This is recognized in part by Alabama law itself, despite the strictness of the rule respecting truth as a defense, since evidence of truth must be received in mitigation under the general issue. Ala. Code of 1940, title 7, § 909; see *Johnson Publishing Co.* v. *Davis,* 271 Ala. 474, 490 (1960). The problem has been met in England by enlarging the defense. See Defamation Act, 1952, 15 & 16 Geo. 6 & 1 Eliz. 2, ch. 66, § 5: "In an action for libel or slander in respect of words containing two or more distinct charges against the plaintiff, a defence of justification shall not fail by reason only that the truth of every charge is not proved if the words not proved to be true do not materially injure the plaintiff's reputation having regard to the truth of the remaining charges." See also *Report of the Committee on the Law of Defamation* (1948) cmd. 7536, p. 21.

they would have thought less kindly of him *if* they had believed the statements they considered critical of his official conduct. They did not in fact believe them and respondent did not fall at all in their esteem. In Alabama, no less than in Virginia, "the militant Negro civil rights movement has engendered the intense resentment and opposition of the politically dominant white community," as this Court said in *N.A.A.C.P.* v. *Button, supra,* 371 U.S. at 435. This publication was, upon its face, made on behalf of sympathizers with that movement. That such a statement could have jeopardized respondent's reputation anywhere he was known as an official must be regarded as a sheer illusion, not a finding that has any tangible support. In the real world, the words were utterly devoid of any "impact" that can weigh "against the principles of the First Amendment." *Pennekamp* v. *Florida, supra,* 328 U.S. at 349.

Respondent adduced as an aspect of his grievance that *The Times* made a retraction on demand of Governor Patterson but failed to do so in response to his demand. See pp. 18–22, *supra.* It is enough to say that if the statement was protected by the Constitution, as we contend it was, no obligation to retract could be imposed. Beyond this, however, there was an entirely reasonable basis for the distinction made. Petitioner selected Governor Patterson as "the proper representative" of Alabama to be formally assured that *The Times* did not intend the publication to reflect upon the State. It also took account of the fact that the Governor was chairman ex-officio of the State Board of Education; and that the "state authorities" had been referred to in the sentence claiming that the dining hall was padlocked. See pp. 21–22, *supra.* A distinction based upon those grounds was not invidious as to respondent. Far from exacerbating any supposed injury to him, as the court below believed (R. 1178), the retraction was a mollifying factor, weakening, if not erasing, the statement as to anyone who thought himself concerned.

Third: The magnitude of the verdict Even if we are wrong in urging that there is no basis on this record for a judgment for respondent, consistently with the protection of the First Amendment, the judgment of $500,000 is so shockingly excessive that it violates the Constitution.

That judgment was rendered, as we have shown, without any proof of injury or special damage. General damages simply were "presumed" and the jury was authorized to levy damages as punishment in its discretion. The trial court refused to charge that the jury should—or even could in its discretion—separately assess compensatory and punitive damages (R. 847, 864, Nos. 59 and 60). Since there was no rational foundation for presuming any damages at all[9], it is both legally correct and factually realistic to regard the entire verdict as a punitive award. *Cf. Stromberg* v. *California,* 283 U.S. 359, 367–368 (1931).

Viewing the publication as an offense to the respondent's reputation, as we do for purposes of argument, there was no rational relationship between the gravity of the offense and the size of the penalty imposed. *Cf. Crowell-Collier Pub. Co.* v. *Caldwell,* 170 F. 2d 941, 944, 945 (5th Cir. 1948). The court below declined, indeed, to weigh the elements of truth embodied in the publication in appraising the legitimacy of the verdict, contrary to its action in a recent case involving charges that a private individual was guilty of grave crimes. *Johnson Publishing Co.* v. *Davis,* 271 Ala. 474, 490 (1960). It chose instead to treat petitioner's assertion of belief in the substantial truth of the advertisement, so far as it might possibly have been related to respondent, as evidence of malice and support for the size of the award. See pp. 22, 24, *supra.*

The judgment is repugnant to the Constitution on these grounds. As Mr. Justice Brandeis said, concurring in *Whitney* v. *California,* 274 U.S. 357, 377 (1927), a "police measure may be unconstitutional merely because the remedy, although effective as means of protection, is unduly harsh or oppressive." The proposition must apply with special force when the "harsh" remedy has been explicitly designed as a deterrent of expression. It is, indeed, the underlying basis of the principle that "the power to regulate must be so exercised as not, in attaining a permissible end, unduly to infringe the protected freedom." *Cantwell* v. *Connecticut,* 310 U.S. 296, 304, 308 (1940). That

---

[9] It is relevant in this connection to recall that the entire circulation of *The Times* in Alabama was 394 copies, 35 in Montgomery County (R. 836). Even on the theory of the court below, the reference to "police" could hardly have been read to refer to respondent anywhere but in Montgomery, or at most in Alabama.

principle has been applied by this Court steadily in recent years as measures burdening the freedoms of expression have been tested by "close analysis and critical judgment in the light of the particular circumstances" involved. *Speiser* v. *Randall*, 357 U.S. 513, 520 (1958). See also, *e.g., Grosjean* v. *American Press Co.*, 297 U.S. 233 (1936); *N.A.A.C.P.* v. *Alabama*, 357 U.S. 449 (1958); *Smith* v. *California*, 361 U.S. 147, 150–151 (1959); *Bates* v. *Little Rock*, 361 U.S. 516 (1960); *Shelton* v. *Tucker*, 364 U.S. 479 (1960); *cf. Winters* v. *New York*, 333 U.S. 507, 517 (1948).

Even when the crucial freedoms of the First Amendment have not been at stake, this Court has made clear that a penalty or money judgment may deprive of property without due process where it is "so extravagant in amount as to outrun the bounds of reason and result in sheer oppression." *Life & Casualty Co.* v. *McCray*, 291 U.S. 566, 571 (1934). A statutory penalty recoverable by a shipper has not been permitted to "work an arbitrary, unequal and oppressive result for the carrier which shocks the sense of fairness the Fourteenth Amendment was intended to satisfy... ." *Chicago & N.W. Ry.* v. *Nye Schneider Fowler Co.*, 260 U.S. 35, 44–45 (1922). See also *Missouri Pacific Ry. Co.* v. *Tucker*, 230 U.S. 340, 350–351 (1913); *St. Louis, I. Mt. & So. Ry. Co.* v. *Williams*, 251 U.S. 63, 66–67 (1919). The idea of government under law is hardly older than the revulsion against "punishment out of all proportion to the offense... ." Douglas, J., concurring in *Robinson* v. *California*, 370 U.S. 660, 676 (1962). Such punishment was inflicted here, compounding the affront this judgment offers to the First Amendment.

It is no hyperbole to say that if a judgment of this size can be sustained upon such facts as these, its repressive influence will extend far beyond deterring such inaccuracies of assertion as have been established here. This is not a time—there never is a time—when it would serve the values enshrined in the Constitution to force the press to curtail its attention to the tensest issues that confront the country or to forego the dissemination of its publications in the areas where tension is extreme.

Respondent argued in his Brief in Opposition (pp. 25–26) that the Seventh Amendment bars this Court from considering the size of an award based on the verdict of a jury. The very authorities he cites make clear that any insulation of a verdict from review does not extend to situations where it involves or reflects error of law. See, *e.g., Fairmount Glass Works* v. *Cub Fork Coal Co.*, 287 U.S. 474, 483–485 (1933); *Chicago, B. & Q. Railroad* v. *Chicago*, 166 U.S. 226, 246 (1897). See also *Dimick* v. *Schiedt*, 293 U.S. 474, 486 (1935); *A. & G. Stevedores* v. *Ellerman Lines*, 369 U.S. 355, 364, 366 (1962). Abridgment of the freedom of the press is surely such an error; and in determining if an abridgment has occurred, it makes no difference what branch or agency of the State has imposed the repression. *N.A.A.C.P.* v. *Alabama*, 357 U.S. 449, 463 (1958); *Bantam Books, Inc.* v. *Sullivan*, 372 U.S. 58, 68 (1963). Indeed, the current of authority today regards the Seventh Amendment as inapplicable generally to appellate review of an excessive verdict, viewing the denial of relief below as an error of law. See, *e.g., Southern Pac. Co.* v. *Guthrie*, 186 F. 2d 926, 931 (9th Cir. 1951); *Dagnello* v. *Long Island Rail Road Company*, 289 F. 2d 797, 802 (2d Cir. 1961); *cf. Affolder* v. *New York, Chicago & St. L. R. Co.*, 339 U.S. 96, 101 (1950); 6 *Moore's, Federal Practice* (2d ed. 1953), pp. 3827–3841. That general problem is not presented here because this excess contravenes the First Amendment.

III. The assumption of jurisdiction in this action by the Courts of Alabama contravenes the Constitution.

In sustaining the jurisdiction of the Circuit Court, the courts below held that petitioner made an involuntary general appearance in this action, subjecting its person to the jurisdiction and forfeiting the constitutional objections urged. They also rejected those objections on the merits, holding that petitioner's contacts with Alabama were sufficient to support State jurisdiction in this cause, based either on the service of process on McKee as a purported agent or on the substituted service on the Secretary of State. The decision is untenable on any ground.

First: The finding of a general appearance The motion to quash stated explicitly that petitioner appeared "solely and specially for the purpose of filing this its motion to quash attempted service of process in this cause and for no other purpose and without waiving service of process upon it and without making a general appearance and expressly limiting its special appearance to the purpose of quashing the attempted service upon it in this case ..." (R. 39, 47). The grounds of the motion related to no other issue than that of petitioner's amenability to Alabama

U.S. SUPREME
COURT,
OCTOBER 1963

BRIEF FOR THE
PETITIONER

jurisdiction in this action as a New York corporation, neither qualified to do nor doing business in the State (R. 40–45, 47). The prayer for
relief (R. 45–46) was not, however, limited to
asking that the service or purported service of
process be quashed and that the action be dismissed "for lack of jurisdiction of the person" of
petitioner. It concluded with a further request
for dismissal for "lack of jurisdiction of the subject matter of said action" (R. 46). That prayer,
the courts held, converted the special appearance into a general appearance by operation of
the law of Alabama (R. 49–51, 1151–1153).

This ruling lacks that "fair or substantial
support" in prior state decisions that alone suffices to preclude this Court's review of federal
contentions held to be defeated by a rule of state
procedure. *N.A.A.C.P.* v. *Alabama,* 357 U.S. 449,
455–457 (1958). The governing principle of
Alabama practice was declared by the court
below in *Ex parte Cullinan,* 224 Ala. 263 (1931),
holding that a request for "further time to
answer or demur or file other motions," made by
a party appearing specially, did not constitute a
general appearance waiving constitutional
objections later made by motion to quash.
Noting that a non-resident's objection to the
jurisdiction "is not a technical one … but is an
assertion of a fundamental constitutional right,"
the court said the question involved was one "of
consent or a voluntary submission to the jurisdiction of the court," an issue of "intent as evidenced by conduct," as to which "the intent and
purpose of the context as a whole must control."
224 Ala. at 265, 266, 267. See also *Ex parte
Haisten,* 227 Ala. 183, 187 (1933); *cf. Sessoms
Grocery Co.* v. *International Sugar Feed Company,* 188 Ala. 232, 236 (1914); *Terminal Oil Mill
Co.* v. *Planters W. & G. Co.,* 197 Ala. 429, 431
(1916). For a waiver to be inferred or implied,
when the defendant appears specially to move to
set aside service of process, he must have taken
some "action in relation to the case, disconnected with the motion, and which recognized the
case as in court." *Lampley* v. *Beavers,* 25 Ala. 534,
535 (1854).

Petitioner's prayer for relief neither "recognized the case as in court" nor evidenced "consent or voluntary submission" to the
jurisdiction. On the contrary, the papers made
entirely clear that the sole ruling sought by the
petitioner was that it was not amenable to
Alabama's jurisdiction, as a New York corpora-

tion having no sufficient contact with the State
to permit the assertion of jurisdiction *in personam* in an action based upon a publication in
New York.

The doctrine of *Ex parte Cullinan* has not
been qualified by any other holding of the
court below before the instant case. It is, on the
other hand, confirmed by cases in which a defendant appearing specially has joined a motion to quash for inadequate service with a plea
in abatement challenging the venue of the
action—without the suggestion that the plea
amounted to a general appearance, though the
question that it raised was characterized by
the court below as one of "jurisdiction of the
subject matter." *St. Mary's Oil Engine Co.* v.
Jackson Ice and Fuel Co., 224 Ala. 152, 155, 157
(1931). See also *Seaboard Air Line Ry.* v.
Hubbard, 142 Ala. 546, 548 (1904); *Dozier
Lumber Co.* v. *Smith-Isburg Lumber Co.,* 145
Ala. 317 (1905); *cf. Johnson Publishing Co.* v.
Davis, 271 Ala. 474, 490 (1960); *Ex parte Textile
Workers Union of America,* 249 Ala. 136, 142
(1947). Indeed, the precise equivalent of the
prayer of the motion in this case was used in
Harrub v. *Hy-Trous Corporation,* 249 Ala. 414,
416 (1947), without arousing an objection to
adjudication of the issue as to jurisdiction of
the person, raised on the special appearance.
Beyond this, the late Judge Walter B. Jones, who
presided in this case at Circuit, reproduced
these very motion papers in the 1962 supplement to his treatise on Alabama practice, as a
form of "Motion to Quash Service of Process
by Foreign Corporation," without intimation
that the prayer addressed to lack of jurisdiction
of the subject matter waived the point respecting jurisdiction of the person. 3 Jones,
Alabama Practice and Forms (1947) § 11207.1a
(Supp. 1962).

There is, moreover, a persuasive reason why
a foreign corporation challenging its amenability to suit in Alabama by substituted service on
the Secretary of State should conceive of its
objection as relating in a sense to jurisdiction of
the subject matter of the action. The statute
(Ala. Code of 1940, title 7, § 199[1]) itself speaks
in terms of the sufficiency of service on the
Secretary "to give to any of the courts of this
state jurisdiction over the cause of action and
over such non-resident defendant" (Appendix
A, *infra,* p. 94). Hence a contention that the
statute is inapplicable or invalid as applied goes,

in this sense, to jurisdiction of the cause as well as jurisdiction of the person.[10] *Cf. St. Mary's Oil Engine Co.* v. *Jackson Ice & Fuel Co., supra,* at 155; *Boyd* v. *Warren Paint & Color Co.,* 254 Ala. 687, 691 (1950). The one conclusion is implicit in the other, not the product of a separate inquiry involving separate grounds.

Against all these indicia of Alabama law, ignored in the decisions of the courts below, the authorities relied on are quite simply totally irrelevant. None involved the alleged waiver of a constitutional objection. Except for *Blankenship* v. *Blankenship,* 263 Ala. 297, 303 (1955), where the court specifically declined to consider whether the appearance had been general or special, deeming the issue immaterial upon the question posed, none involved a special appearance. In *Thompson* v. *Wilson,* 224 Ala. 299 (1932), the defendant, a resident of Alabama, had not even purported to appear specially or attempted to question the court's jurisdiction of his person; his sole objection, taken by demurrer, was to the court's competence to deal with the subject matter of the action and to grant relief of the type asked. In *Vaughan* v. *Vaughan,* 267 Ala. 117, 120, 121 (1957), referred to by the Circuit Court, the movant failed to limit her appearance, leading the court to distinguish *Ex parte Haisten, supra,* on this ground. The additional decisions cited by respondent (Brief in Opposition, p. 36) are no less irrelevant. Neither *Kyser* v. *American Surety Co.,* 213 Ala. 614 (1925) nor *Aetna Insurance Co.* v. *Earnest,* 215 Ala. 557 (1927) involved a special appearance or dealt with a challenge to service of process on constitutional grounds.

The California and North Carolina cases cited and quoted below (*Olcese* v. *Justice's Court,* 156 Cal. 82 [1909]; *Roberts* v. *Superior Court,* 30

Cal. App. 714 [1916]; *Dailey Motor Co.* v. *Reaves,* 184 N.C. 260 [1922]) and the similar decisions referred to in the annotation cited (25 A.L.R. 2d 838–842), to the extent that they treated a challenge to the jurisdiction of the subject matter as a general appearance, all involved situations where the defendant's objection was deemed to ask for relief inconsistent with the absence of jurisdiction of the person or to raise a separate "question whether, considering the nature of the cause of action asserted and the relief prayed by plaintiff, the court had power to adjudicate concerning the subject matter of the class of cases to which plaintiff's claim belonged." *Davis* v. *O'Hara,* 266 U.S. 314, 318 (1924); *cf. Constantine* v. *Constantine,* 261 Ala. 40, 42 (1954). That no such question was presented here the motion papers make entirely clear.

The situation is, indeed, precisely analogous to that presented in the *Davis* case. There the defendant, Director General of Railroads, appeared specially for the purpose of objecting to the jurisdiction of the district court "over the person of the defendant and over the subject matter of this action," on the ground that in the circumstances the Director was immune to suit in the county where action was brought. The Nebraska courts treated the reference to subject matter as a general appearance, waiving the immunity asserted. *O'Hara* v. *Davis,* 109 Neb. 615 (1923). This Court reversed, holding that there "was nothing in the moving papers to suggest that the Nebraska court had no jurisdiction to try and determine actions, founded on negligence, to recover damages for personal injuries suffered by railway employees while engaged in the performance of their work" (266 U.S. at 318). So here, there was nothing in the papers to suggest that the petitioner questioned the competence of the Circuit Court to "exercise original jurisdiction ... of all actions for libel...." (Ala. Code, title 13, § 126). The point was only that petitioner, because it is a foreign corporation having only a peripheral relationship to Alabama, was immune to jurisdiction in the action brought.

For the foregoing reasons, we submit that the decision that petitioner made an involuntary general appearance does not constitute an adequate state ground, barring consideration of the question whether Alabama has transcended the due process limitations on the territorial extension of the process of her courts. *Cf. Wright* v.

---

[10] It should be noted also that prior to the enactment of Ala. Code, title 7, § 97 in 1907, Alabama denied her courts jurisdiction over actions against foreign corporations which did not arise within the State. See *McKnett* v. *St. Louis & San Francisco Ry.,* 292 U.S. 230, 231 (1934). The bar to foreign causes was raised, however, only to suits "in which jurisdiction of the defendant can be legally obtained in the same manner in which jurisdiction could have been obtained if the cause of action had arisen in this state." The claim that McKee was not an "agent" for purposes of service under Ala. Code, title 7, § 188 (Appendix A, *infra,* p. 92), if valid, thus implied a defect of subject matter jurisdiction of this cause of action, which petitioner submitted arose at the place of publication in New York. Compare the statement by the court below upon this point (R. 1179) with *New York Times Company* v. *Conner,* 291 F. 2d 492, 494 (5th Cir. 1961).

Georgia, 373 U.S. 284 (1963); *N.A.A.C.P.* v. *Alabama, supra; Staub* v. *City of Baxley,* 355 U.S. 313 (1958); *Davis* v. *Wechsler,* 263 U.S. 22 (1923); *Ward* v. *Love County,* 253 U.S. 17 (1920).[11]

Moreover, even if petitioner could validly be taken to have made an involuntary general appearance by the prayer for dismissal on the ground of lack of jurisdiction of the subject matter, that appearance would not bar the claim that in assuming jurisdiction of this action the state court has cast a burden upon interstate commerce forbidden by the Commerce Clause. That point is independent of the defendant's amenability to process, as this Court has explicitly decided in ruling that the issue remains open, if presented on "a seasonable motion," notwithstanding the presence of the corporation in the State or its appearance generally in the cause. *Davis* v. *Farmers Cooperative Co.,* 262 U.S. 312 (1923); *Michigan Central R.R. Co.* v. *Mix,* 278 U.S. 492, 496 (1929). See also *Denver & R.G.W.R. Co.* v. *Terte,* 284 U.S. 284, 287 (1932) (attachment); *Canadian Pacific Ry. Co.* v. *Sullivan,* 126 F. 2d 433, 437 (1st Cir.), *cert. denied,* 316 U.S. 696 (1942) (agent designated to accept service); *Zuber* v. *Pennsylvania R. Co.,* 82 F. Supp. 670, 674 (N. D. Ga. 1949); *Pantswowe Zaklady Graviozne* v. *Automobile Ins. Co.,* 36 F. 2d 504 (S.D.N.Y. 1928) (commerce objection relates to jurisdiction of subject matter); 42 Harv. L. Rev. 1062, 1067 (1929); 43 *id.* 1156, 1157 (1930). For the same reason, we submit, an implied general appearance would not bar the litigation of petitioner's contention, seasonably urged upon the motion, that by taking jurisdiction in this action, the courts below denied due process by abridging freedom of the press; that

------

[11] It should be noted that the Circuit Court also found a waiver of petitioner's special appearance in its application for mandamus to review an order directing the production of documents demanded by respondent to show the extent of petitioner's activities in Alabama. R. 50–51; see also R. 29–39, Pl. Ex. 311–313, R. 1835–1858. The Supreme Court's opinion is silent on this point, presumably in recognition of the proposition that an action must be "disconnected" with the motion to support an inference of waiver. *Lampley* v. *Beavers, supra; cf. Ford Motor Co.* v. *Hall Auto Co.,* 226 Ala. 385, 388 (1933). It would obviously thwart essential self-protective measures if an effort to obtain review of an allegedly abusive ancillary order were regarded as a waiver of the prime submission. *Cf. Ex parte Spence,* 271 Ala. 151 (1960); *Ex parte Textile Workers of America,* 249 Ala. 136 (1947); *Ex parte Union Planters National Bank and Trust Co.,* 249 Ala. 461 (1947). See *Fay* v. *Noia,* 372 U.S. 391, 432, n. 41 (1963).

also is an issue independent of the presence of petitioner in Alabama or its amenability to process of the court.

Second: The territorial limits of Due Process The courts below held that the sporadic newsgathering activities of correspondents and stringers of *The Times* in Alabama, the occasional solicitation and publication of advertising from Alabama sources and the minuscule shipment of the newspaper to subscribers and newsdealers in the State (*supra,* pp. 25–27) constitute sufficient Alabama contacts to permit the exercise of jurisdiction in this action, without transcending the territorial limits of due process.

This assertion of state power finds no sanction in this Court's decisions governing the reach of state authority, despite the relaxation in the limits of due process that we recognize to have occurred in recent years. Neither the "flexible standard" of *International Shoe Co.* v. *Washington,* 326 U.S. 310 (1945), as it was called in *Hanson* v. *Denckla,* 357 U.S. 235, 251 (1958), nor any of its later applications, sustains, in our submission, the extreme determination here.

It is plain, initially, that the petitioner's peripheral relationship to Alabama does not involve "continuous corporate operations" which are "so substantial and of such a nature as to justify suit against it on causes of action arising from dealings entirely distinct from those activities." *International Shoe Co.* v. *Washington, supra,* at 318. The case bears no resemblance to *Perkins* v. *Benguet Mining Co.,* 342 U.S. 437 (1952), where the central base of operations of the corporation, including its top management, was in the State where suit was brought. It hardly can be argued that *The New York Times* has such a base in Alabama, where, according to this record, it enjoys 6/100ths of one per cent of its daily circulation and 2/10ths of one per cent of its Sunday circulation and where the sources of 46/1000ths of one per cent of its advertising revenue are found (R. 402, 444–445). The occasional visits of correspondents to the State to report on events of great interest to the nation places *The Times* in Alabama no more than in Ankara or Athens or New Delhi, where, of course, similar visits occur.

Hence, if the jurisdiction here asserted is sustained, it must be on the ground that the alleged cause of action is so "connected with" petitioner's "activities within the state" as to "make it reasonable, in the context of our federal system of government, to require the corporation to defend the particular suit which is brought there." *International Shoe Co. v. Washington, supra,* at 319, 317. See also *Blount* v. *Peerless Chemicals (P.R.) Inc.,* 316 F. 2d 695, 700 (2d Cir. 1963); *L. D. Reeder Contractors of Ariz.* v. *Higgins Industries, Inc.,* 265 F. 2d 768, 774–775 (9th Cir. 1959); *Partin* v. *Michaels Art Bronze Co.,* 202 F. 2d 541, 545 (3d Cir. 1953) (concurring opinion).

There is, in our view, no such connection. Here, as in *Hanson v. Denckla, supra,* at 252, the "suit cannot be said to be one to enforce an obligation that arose from a privilege the defendant exercised in" the State. The liability alleged by the respondent certainly is not based on any activity of correspondents or stringers of *The Times* in covering the news in Alabama; and neither entering the State for such reporting, nor the composition nor the filing of reports rests on a privilege the State confers, given the rights safeguarded by the Constitution. Nor is this claim of liability connected with the occasional solicitation of advertisements in Alabama. The advertisement in suit was not solicited and did not reach *The Times* from anyone within the State. There remains, therefore, only the negligible circulation of *The Times* in Alabama on which to mount an argument that this suit relates to the exercise by the petitioner of "the privilege of conducting activities within" the State. *International Shoe Co. v. Washington, supra,* at 319.

We contend that this circulation did not involve the exercise of such a privilege. Copies of the paper were mailed to subscribers from New York or shipped from there to dealers who were purchasers, not agents of *The Times.* Such mailing and shipment in New York were not activity of the petitioner within the State of Alabama. See, *e.g., Putnam v. Triangle Publications, Inc.,* 245 N. C. 432, 443 (1957); *Schmidt* v. *Esquire, Inc.,* 210 F. 2d 908, 915, 916 (7th Cir. 1954), *cert. denied,* 348 U.S. 819 (1954); *Street & Smith Publications, Inc.* v. *Spikes,* 120 F. 2d 895, 897 (5th Cir.), *cert. denied,* 314 U.S. 653 (1941); *Cannon* v. *Time, Inc.,* 115 F. 2d 423, 425 (4th Cir. 1940); *Whitaker* v. *Macfadden Publications, Inc.,* 105 F. 2d 44, 45 (D. C. Cir. 1939); *Buckley* v. *New York Times Co.,* 215 F. Supp. 893 (E. D. La. 1963); *Gayle* v. *Magazine Management Co.,* 153 F. Supp. 861, 864 (M. D. Ala. 1957); *Brewster* v. *Boston Herald-Traveler Corp.,* 141 F. Supp. 760, 761, 763 (D. Me. 1956); *cf. Erlanger Mills* v. *Cohoes Fibre Mills, Inc.,* 239 F. 2d 502 (4th Cir. 1956); *L. D. Reeder Contractors of Ariz.* v. *Higgins Industries, Inc.,* 265 F. 2d 768 (9th Cir. 1959); *Trippe Manufacturing Co.* v. *Spencer Gifts, Inc.,* 270 F. 2d. 821, 823 (7th Cir. 1959). Whether Alabama may, upon these facts, declare the petitioner responsible for an Alabama "publication" by causing or contributing to the dissemination of those papers in the State is not, of course, the issue. That is a problem of the choice of law[12] which is entirely distinct from the question here presented: whether by its shipment in and from New York petitioner "avails itself of the privilege of conducting activities within the forum State, thus invoking the benefits and protections of its laws." *Hanson* v. *Denckla, supra,* at 253. A State may be empowered to apply its law to a transaction upon grounds quite insufficient to establish "personal jurisdiction over a non-resident defendant," as *Hanson (ibid.)* makes clear. If this were not the case, each of the individual non-resident signers of the advertisement might also be amenable to Alabama's long-arm process, not to speak of every author of a publication sold within the State. See *Calagaz* v. *Calhoon,* 309 F. 2d 248, 254 (5th Cir. 1962). That would, indeed, entail the "demise of all restrictions on the personal jurisdiction of state courts," an eventuality that this Court has declared the trend of its decisions does not herald. *Hanson* v. *Denckla, supra,* at 251. The avoidance of that outcome calls, at least, for a sharp line between a liability based on an act performed within the State and liability based on an act without, which merely is averred to have an impact felt within.[13] Surely the papers

---

[12] Courts have been no less perplexed than commentators by the conflicts problems incident to multi-state dissemination of an alleged libel; and some have sought to solve them by a "single publication" rule, fixing the time and place of the entire publication when and where the first and primary dissemination occurred. See, *e.g., Hartmann* v. *Time, Inc.,* 166 F. 2d 127 (3d Cir. 1947), *cert. denied,* 334 U.S. 838 (1948); *Insull* v. *New York World-Telegram Corp.,* 273 F. 2d 166, 171 (7th Cir. 1959), *cert. denied,* 362 U.S. 942 (1960); *cf. Mattox* v. *News Syndicate Co.,* 176 F. 2d 897, 900, 904–905 (2d Cir.), *cert. denied,* 338 U.S. 858 (1949). See also, *e.g.,* Prosser, *Interstate Publication,* 51 Mich. L. Rev. 959 (1953); Leflar, *The Single Publication Rule,* 25 Rocky Mt. L. Rev. 263 (1953); Note, 29 U. of Chi. L. Rev. 569 (1962).

[13] *Cf.* L. Hand, J., in *Kilpatrick* v. *Texas & P. Ry. Co.,* 166 F. 2d 788, 791–792 (2d Cir. 1948): "It is settled that, given the proper procedural support for doing so, a state may give judgment in personam against a non-resident, who has only passed through its territory, if the judgment be upon a liability incurred while he was within its borders. That, we con-

mailed to subscribers were delivered to them by petitioner when they were posted in New York. *Cf.* 1 *Williston on Contracts* (3d ed. 1957) § 81, p. 268. So, too, the delivery to carriers in New York for shipment to Alabama dealers, pursuant to their orders, can at most be said to have contributed to sales made by the dealers, but those sales were not the acts of the petitioner in Alabama. *Cf. United States* v. *Smith,* 173 Fed. 227, 232 (D. Ind. 1909). That is a matter to be judged in terms of a "practical conception" of the needs of our federalism, not "the 'witty diversities' ... of the law of sales." Holmes, J., in *Rearick* v. *Pennsylvania,* 203 U.S. 507, 512 (1906).

Assuming, however, that the shipment of *The Times* to Alabama may be deemed an act of the petitioner within that State, we still do not believe the jurisdiction here affirmed can be sustained. In *International Shoe* this Court made clear that the new standard there laid down was not "simply mechanical or quantitative" and that its application "must depend rather upon the quality and nature of the activity in relation to the fair and orderly administration of the laws which it was the purpose of the due process clause to insure" (326 U.S. at 319). See also *Hanson* v. *Denckla, supra,* at 253. The opinion left no doubt that, as Judge Learned Hand had previously pointed out (*Hutchinson* v. *Chase & Gilbert,* 45 F. 2d 139, 141 [2d Cir. 1930]), an "'estimate of the inconveniences' which would result to the corporation from a trial away from its 'home' or principal place of business is relevant in this connection" (326 U.S. at 317). Measured by this standard, a principle which would require, in effect, that almost every news-

paper defend a libel suit in almost any jurisdiction of the country, however trivial its circulation there may be, would not further the "fair and orderly administration of the laws." The special "inconvenience" of the foreign publisher in libel actions brought in a community with which its ties are tenuous need not be elaborated. It was perspicuously noted by the court below in a landmark decision more than forty years ago, confining venue to the county where the newspaper is "primarily published." *Age-Herald Publishing Co.* v. *Huddleston,* 207 Ala. 40, 45 (1921). This record surely makes the "inconvenience" clear.

We do not blink the fact that this submission focuses upon the hardship to the foreign publisher and that the plaintiff faces hardship too in litigating far from home. But if these conflicting interests call for balance in relation to the "orderly administration of the laws," there are substantial reasons why the interest of the publisher ought here to be preferred. In the first place, it is the forum which is seeking to extend its power beyond its own borders, carrying the burden of persuasion that the "territorial limitations on the power of the respective states" (*Hanson* v. *Denckla, supra,* at 251) are respected in the extension made. Secondly, the burden cast upon the publisher can only operate to thwart the object of the First Amendment by demanding the cessation of a circulation that entails at best no economic benefit—depriving the state residents who have an interest in the foreign publication of the opportunity to read. Thirdly, the plaintiff's grievance rests but fancifully on the insubstantial distribution of the publication in the forum, as distinguished from its major circulation out of state. If that grievance is to be assigned a locus, it is hardly where 394 copies were disseminated when the full 650,000 were regarded as relevant to the *ad damnum* (R. 2, 3, 601, 945) and a reason for sustaining the award (R. 1176, 1179). The difficulties presented by libel actions based on multi-state dissemination are notorious enough (see, *e.g., Zuck* v. *Interstate Publishing Corp.,* 317 F. 2d 727, 733 [2d Cir. 1963]), without permitting suit against a foreign publisher in every jurisdiction where a copy of the allegedly offending publication has been sold. Finally, but not the least important, this is not an action merely seeking redress for an injury allegedly inflicted on the plaintiff. Its dominant object is to punish the defendant, as the damages demanded made quite clear. Hence,

ceive, rests upon another principle. The presence of the obligor within the state subjects him to its law while he is there, and allows it to impose upon him any obligation which its law entails upon his conduct. Had it been possible at the moment when the putative liability arose to set up a piepowder court pro hac vice, the state would have had power to adjudicate the liability then and there; and his departure should not deprive it of the jurisdiction in personam so acquired. On the other hand, in order to subject a non-resident who passes through a state to a judgment in personam for liabilities arising elsewhere, it would be necessary to say that the state had power so to subject him as a condition of allowing him to enter at all, and that for this reason his voluntary entry charged him generally with submission to the courts. As a matter of its own law of conflicts of law, no court of one country would tolerate such an attempt to extend the power of another; and, as between citizens of states of the United States, constitutional doubts would arise which, to say the least, would be very grave... ."

the considerations that would be decisive against "long-arm" jurisdiction in a criminal proceeding ought to be persuasive here.

The courts below thought the foregoing arguments against the jurisdiction answered by the decision of this Court in *McGee* v. *International Life Ins. Co.,* 355 U.S. 220 (1957), where suit on an insurance contract was sustained in California against a non-resident insurer, based on the solicitation and the consummation of the contract in the State by mail. But that decision certainly does not control the disposition of this case. The contract executed in *McGee* constituted a continuing legal relationship between the insurer and the insured within the State, a relation which the States, with the concurrence of Congress (15 U.S.C. §§ 1011–1015, 59 Stat. 33), have long deemed to require special state regulation. *Hanson* v. *Denckla, supra,* at 252; *Travelers Health Assn.* v. *Virginia,* 339 U.S. 643 (1950). The liability asserted here derives from no such continuing relationship with someone in the State; and newspaper publication, including circulation (*Lovell* v. *Griffin,* 303 U.S. 444 [1938]; *Talley* v. *California,* 362 U.S. 60 [1960]), far from being exceptionally subject to state regulation, is zealously protected by the First Amendment.

Respondent also relies heavily on *Scripto* v. *Carson,* 362 U.S. 207 (1960) (Brief in Opposition, pp. 39, 41) but the reliance plainly is misplaced. That decision dealt with the minimum connection necessary to permit a State to impose on an out-of-state vendor the compensated duty to collect a use tax due from purchasers on property shipped to them in the State. It held the duty validly imposed where sales were solicited within the State, deeming *General Trading Co.* v. *State Tax Comm'n.,* 322 U.S. 335 (1944) controlling though the salesmen were "independent contractors" rather than employees of the vendor. No issue of judicial jurisdiction was involved. This "familiar and sanctioned device" (322 U.S. at 338) of making the distributor the tax collector for the State he exploits as a market plainly casts no burden comparable to the exercise of jurisdiction *in personam,* with the implications such a jurisdiction has. If the problems were analogous, the relevant decision here would be *Miller Bros. Co.* v. *Maryland,* 347 U.S. 340 (1954), where the imposition of the duty was invalidated because there was "no invasion or exploitation of the con-

sumer market" (*id.* at 347) by the out-of-state vendor. The *New York Times* does not solicit Alabama circulation (*supra,* p. 27); it merely satisfies the very small, local demand.

Viewed in these terms, a different question might be posed if it were shown that the petitioner engaged in activities of substance in the forum state, designed to build its circulation there. *Cf.* Mr. Justice Black, dissenting in part in *Polizzi* v. *Cowles Magazines, Inc.,* 345 U.S. 663, 667, 670 (1953); see also *WSAZ, Inc.* v. *Lyons,* 254 F. 2d 242 (6th Cir. 1958). That would involve a possible analogy to other situations where a foreign enterprise exploits the forum as a market and the cause of action is connected with such effort (*Hanson* v. *Denckla, supra,* at 251–252), though the punitive nature of the action and the special situation of the press must still be weighed. It also would confine the possibilities of litigation to places where the foreign publisher has had the opportunity to build some local standing with the public. No such activities, effort or opportunity existed here.

In a federated nation such as ours, the power of the States to exert jurisdiction over men and institutions not within their borders must be subject to reciprocal restraints on each in the interest of all. *Cf.* L. Hand, J., in *Kilpatrick* v. *Texas & P. Ry. Co.,* p. 81, footnote, *supra.* The need for such restraints is emphasized in our system by the full faith and credit clause of the Constitution. If Alabama stood alone it would be impotent in such a case as this to render any judgment that would be of practical importance to petitioner. What makes this judgment vitally important is the fact that if it is affirmed it is enforceable as such in States where the petitioner's resources are located. Thus jurisdictional delineations must be based on grounds that command general assent throughout the Union; otherwise full faith and credit will become a burden that the system cannot bear. No standard worthy of such general assent sustains the assumption of jurisdiction in this cause.

Third: The burden on commerce In forcing the petitioner to its defense of this case in Alabama, the state court has done more than exceed its territorial jurisdiction. It has also cast a burden on interstate commerce that the commerce clause forbids.

It takes no gift of prophecy to know that if negligible state circulation of a paper published in another state suffices to establish jurisdiction

U.S. SUPREME COURT, OCTOBER 1963

BRIEF FOR THE PETITIONER

of a suit for libel, threatening the type of judgment rendered here, such distribution interstate cannot continue. So, too, if the interstate movement of correspondents provides a factor tending to sustain such jurisdiction, as the court below declared, a strong barrier to such movement has been erected. Both the free flow of interstate communications and the mobility of individuals are national interests of supreme importance. In the silence of Congress, their protection against burdensome state action, unsupported by an overriding local interest, is the duty of the courts. *Fisher's Blend Station* v. *Tax Commission*, 297 U.S. 650, 654–655 (1936); *Edwards* v. *California*, 314 U.S. 160 (1941). In neither area may a State "gain a momentary respite from the pressure of events by the simple expedient of shutting its gates to the outside world." *Id.* at 173. An attempt to isolate a State from strangers or their publications is no less offensive to the commerce clause than the attempts at economic isolation which have been repeatedly condemned. See, *e.g.*, *Minnesota* v. *Barber*, 136 U.S. 313 (1890); *Baldwin* v. *G. A. F. Seelig, Inc.*, 294 U.S. 511, 527 (1935); *H. P. Hood & Sons* v. *DuMond*, 336 U.S. 525 (1949); *Dean Milk Co.* v. *City of Madison*, 340 U.S. 349 (1951).

This Court has not hitherto considered a case where the mere assumption of jurisdiction in a transitory action threatened an embargo of this kind. It has, however, held that the subjection of a carrier to suit, whether *in personam* or *in rem*, in a jurisdiction where it is engaged in insubstantial corporate activities may impose an excessive burden upon commerce, because of the special inconvenience and expense incident to the defense of litigation there. *Davis* v. *Farmers Co-operative Co.*, 262 U.S. 312 (1923); *Atchison, Topeka & Santa Fe Ry.* v. *Wells*, 265 U.S. 101 (1924); *Michigan Central R.R. Co.* v. *Mix*, 278 U.S. 492 (1929); *Denver & R. G. W. R. Co.* v. *Terte*, 284 U.S. 284, 287 (1932); *cf. International Milling Co.* v. *Columbia Transportation Co.*, 292 U.S. 511 (1934). See also *Sioux Remedy Co.* v. *Cope*, 235 U.S. 197 (1914); *Erlanger Mills* v. *Cohoes Fibre Mills, Inc.*, 239 F. 2d 502 (4th Cir. 1956); *Overstreet* v. *Canadian Pacific Airlines*, 152 F. Supp. 838 (S.D.N.Y. 1957). The burdens deemed excessive in those cases were as nothing compared to the burden imposed here, for which, as we have shown above (pp. 83–84), there is no overriding local interest.

Respondent argued in his Brief in Opposition (p. 42) that the cases holding that jurisdiction may be an excessive burden became moribund with the pronouncement in *International Shoe*. His contention finds no support in that opinion and ignores *Southern Pacific Co.* v. *Arizona*, 325 U.S. 761, 781 (1945), where a few months before the *Shoe* decision Chief Justice Stone alluded to the *Davis* and like cases, otherwise affirming the protective principle for which they stand. The need for that protective principle has, indeed, been increased by the progressive relaxation in due process standards. For the considerations leading to that relaxation have to do with the appropriate relationship between a State and foreign enterprise and individuals. They are entirely inapposite in the situation where an interest of the Nation is impaired.

Fourth: The freedom of the press We have argued that the jurisdictional determination violates the Constitution, judged by standards that apply to enterprise in general under the constitutional provisions limiting state power in the interest of our federalism as a whole. We need not rest, however, on those standards. Newsgathering and circulation are both aspects of the freedom of the press, safeguarded by the Constitution. Neither can continue unimpaired if they subject the publisher to foreign jurisdiction on the grounds and of the scope asserted here. The decision is, accordingly, repugnant to the First Amendment.

This Court has often held state action inconsistent with the First Amendment, as embodied in the Fourteenth, when it has "the collateral effect of inhibiting the freedom of expression, by making the individual the more reluctant to exercise it" (*Smith* v. *California*, 361 U.S. 147, 151 [1959])—though the action is otherwise consistent with the Constitution. Scienter is not generally deemed a constitutional prerequisite to criminal conviction, but a measure of liability for the possession of obscene publications was invalidated on this ground in *Smith* because of its potential impact on the freedom of booksellers. The allocation of burden of proof in establishing a right to tax-exemption fell in *Speiser* v. *Randall*, 357 U.S. 513 (1958) because it was considered in the circumstances to "result in a deterrence of speech which the Constitution makes free." *Id.* at 526. Compulsory disclosure requires a showing of a more compelling state interest when it tends to inhibit freedom of association than in other situations where disclosure may be forced (see, *e.g., Gibson* v. *Florida Legislative Comm.,* 372 U.S. 539 [1963]; *Talley* v. *California,* 362 U.S. 60 [1960]); and its extent may be more limited. *Shelton* v. *Tucker,* 364 U.S. 479 (1960). Regulation of the legal profession that would raise no question as applied to the solicitation of commercial practice must comply with stricter standards insofar as it inhibits association for the vindication of fundamental rights. *N.A.A.C.P.* v. *Button,* 371 U.S. 415 (1963).

The principle involved in these familiar illustrations plainly applies here. If a court may validly take jurisdiction of a libel action on the basis of sporadic newsgathering by correspondents and trivial circulation of the publication in the State, it can and will do so not only when the plaintiff has a valid cause of action but also when the claim is as unfounded and abusive as the claim presented here. The burden of defense in a community with which the publication has no meaningful connection and the risk of enormous punitive awards by hostile juries cannot be faced with equanimity by any publisher. The inevitable consequence must be the discontinuance of the activities contributing to the assumption of the jurisdiction. The interest of a State in affording its residents the most convenient forum for the institution of such actions cannot justify this adverse impact on the freedom that the First Amendment has explicitly secured. See also pp. 83–84, *supra.* The occasional solicitation of advertising in the State, being wholly unrelated to respondent's cause of action, does not augment the interest of the State in providing the forum challenged here.

CONCLUSION

For the foregoing reasons, the judgment of the Supreme Court of Alabama should be reversed, with direction to dismiss the action.

Respectfully submitted,

Louis M. Loeb

T. Eric Embry

Marvin E. Frankel

Ronald S. Diana

Doris Wechsler

Lord, Day & Lord

Beddow, Embry & Beddow

Of Counsel

Herbert Brownell

Thomas F. Daly

Herbert Wechsler

Attorneys for Petitioner

The New York Times Company

APPENDIX A

CONSTITUTIONAL AND STATUTORY PROVISIONS INVOLVED

Constitution of the United States

Article I, Section 8:

The Congress shall have power * * *

To regulate Commerce with foreign Nations, and among the several States * * *.

* * * * *

Amendment I

Congress shall make no law respecting an establishment of religion, or prohibiting the free exercise thereof; or abridging the freedom of speech, or of the press; or the right of the people peaceably to assemble, and to petition the Government for a redress of grievances.

* * * * *

Amendment XIV

Section 1. All persons born or naturalized in the United States, and subject to the jurisdiction thereof, are citizens of the United States and of the State wherein they reside. No State shall make or enforce any law which shall abridge the privileges or immunities of citizens of the United States; nor shall any State deprive any person of life, liberty, or property, without due process of law; nor deny to any person within its jurisdiction the equal protection of the laws.

Alabama Code of 1940 Title 7

188. How corporation served When an action at law is against a corporation the summons may be executed by the delivery of a copy of the summons and complaint to the president, or other head thereof, secretary, cashier, station agent or any other agent thereof. The return of the officer executing the summons that the person to whom delivered is the agent of the corporation shall be prima facie evidence of such fact and authorize judgment by default or otherwise without further proof of such agency and this fact need not be recited in the judgment entry. (1915, p. 607.)

* * * * *

199(1). Service on non-resident doing business or performing work or service in state Any non-resident person, firm, partnership, general or limited, or any corporation not qualified under the Constitution and laws of this state as to doing business herein, who shall do any business or perform any character of work or service in this state shall, by the doing of such business or the performing of such work, or services, be deemed to have appointed the secretary of state, or his successor or successors in office, to be the true and lawful attorney or agent of such non-resident, upon whom process may be served [in any action accrued or accruing from the doing of such business, or the performing of such work, or service, or as an incident thereto by any such non-resident, or his, its or their agent, servant or employee.][14] Service of such process shall be made by serving three copies of the process on the said secretary of state, and such service shall be sufficient service upon the said non-resident of the state of Alabama, provided that notice of such service and a copy of the process are forthwith sent by registered mail by the secretary of the state to the defendant at his last known address, which shall be stated in the affidavit of the plaintiff or complainant hereinafter mentioned, marked "Deliver to Addressee Only" and "Return Receipt Requested," and provided further that such return receipt shall be received by the secretary of state purporting to have been signed by said non-resident, or the secretary of state shall be advised by the postal authority that delivery of said registered mail was refused by said non-resident; and the date on which the secretary of state receives said return receipt, or advice by the postal authority that delivery of said registered mail was refused, shall be treated and considered as the date of service of process on said non-resident. The secretary of state shall make an affidavit as to the service of said process on him, and as to his mailing a copy of

the same and notice of such service to the non-resident, and as to the receipt of said return receipt, or advice of the refusal of said registered mail, and the respective dates thereof, and shall attach said affidavit, return receipt, or advice from the postal authority, to a copy of the process and shall return the same to the clerk or register who issued the same, and all of the same shall be filed in the cause by the clerk or register. The party to a cause filed or pending, or his agent or attorney, desiring to obtain service upon a non-resident under the provisions of this section shall make and file in the cause, an affidavit stating facts showing that this section is applicable, and stating the residence and last known post-office address of the non-resident, and the clerk or register of the court in which the action is filed shall attach a copy of the affidavit to the writ or process, and a copy of the affidavit to each copy of the writ or process, and forward the original writ or process and three copies thereof to the sheriff of Montgomery county for service on the secretary of state and it shall be the duty of the sheriff to serve the same on the secretary of state and to make due return of such service. The court in which the cause is pending may order such continuance of the cause as may be necessary to afford the defendant or defendants reasonable opportunity to make defense. Any person who was a resident of this state at the time of the doing of business, or performing work or service in this state, but who is a non-resident at the time of the pendency of a cause involving the doing of said business or performance of said work or service, and any corporation which was qualified to do business in this state at the time of doing business herein and which is not qualified at the time of the pendency of a cause involving the doing of such business, shall be deemed a non-resident within the meaning of this section, and service of process under such circumstances may be had as herein provided.

The secretary of state of the state of Alabama, or his successor in office, may give such non-resident defendant notice of such service upon the secretary of state of the state of Alabama in lieu of the notice of service hereinabove provided to be given, by registered mail, in the following manner: By causing or having a notice of such service and a copy of the process served upon such non-resident defendant, if found within the state of Alabama, by any offi-

---

[14] Following the decision in *New York Times Company* v. *Conner* 291 F. 2d 492 (5th Cir. 1962) the statute was amended by substituting the following language for the bracketed portion: [in any action accrued, accruing, or resulting from the doing of such business, or the performing of such work or service, or relating to or on an incident thereof, by any such non-resident, or his, its or their agent, servant or employee. And such service shall be valid whether or not the acts done in Alabama shall of and within themselves constitute a complete cause of action.] The amendment applied "only to causes of action arising after the date of the enactment" and therefore has no bearing on this case.

cer duly qualified to serve legal process within the state of Alabama, or if such non-resident defendant is found without the state of Alabama, by a sheriff, deputy sheriff, or United States marshal, or deputy United States marshal, or any duly constituted public officer qualified to serve like process in the state of the jurisdiction where such non-resident defendant is found; and the officer's return showing such service and when and where made, which shall be under oath, shall be filed in the office of the clerk or register of the court wherein such action is pending.

Service of summons when obtained upon any such non-resident as above provided for the service of process herein shall be deemed sufficient service of summons and process to give to any of the courts of this state jurisdiction over the cause of action and over such non-resident defendant, or defendants, and shall warrant and authorize personal judgment against such non-resident defendant, or defendants, in the event that the plaintiff prevails in the action.

The secretary of state shall refuse to receive and file or serve any process, pleading, or paper under this section unless three copies thereof are supplied to the secretary of state and a fee of three dollars is paid to the secretary of state; and no service shall be perfected hereunder unless there is on file in the office of the secretary of state a certificate or statement under oath by the plaintiff or his attorney that the provisions of this section are applicable to the case. (1949, p. 154, §§ 1, 2, appvd. June 23, 1949; 1951, p. 976, appvd. Aug. 28, 1951; 1953, p. 347, § 1, appvd. Aug. 5, 1953.)

**U.S. SUPREME COURT,
OCTOBER 1963**

**BRIEF FOR THE
PETITIONER**

COMMITTEE TO
DEFEND MLK AND
THE STRUGGLE
FOR FREEDOM IN
THE SOUTH

Heed Their Rising Voices

YOUR HELP IS URGENTLY NEEDED . . . NOW!!

—m—

"The growing movement of peaceful mass demonstrations by Negroes is something new in the South . . . . Let Congress heed their rising voices, for they will be heard." —New York Times editorial Saturday, March 19, 1960

As the whole world knows by now, thousands of Southern Negro students are engaged in widespread non-violent demonstrations in positive affirmation of the right to live in human dignity as guaranteed by the U.S. Constitution and the Bill of Rights. In their efforts to uphold these guarantees, they are being met by an unprecedented wave of terror by those who would deny and negate that document which the whole world looks upon as setting the pattern for modern freedom. . . .

In Orangeburg, South Carolina, when 400 students peacefully sought to buy doughnuts and coffee at lunch counters in the business district, they were forcibly ejected, tear-gassed, soaked to the skin in freezing weather with fire hoses, arrested en masse and herded into an open barbed-wire stockade to stand for hours in the bitter cold.

In Montgomery, Alabama, after students sang "My Country, 'Tis of Thee" on the State Capitol steps, their leaders were expelled from school, and truckloads of police armed with shotguns and tear-gas ringed the Alabama State College Campus. When the entire student body protested to state authorities by refusing to re-register, their dining hall was padlocked in an attempted to starve them into submission.

In Tallahassee, Atlanta, Nashville, Savannah, Greensboro, Memphis, Richmond, Charlotte, and a host of other cities in the South, young American teenagers, in face of the entire weight of official state apparatus and police power, have boldly stepped forth as protagonists of democracy. Their courage and amazing restraint have inspired millions and given a new dignity to the cause of freedom.

Small wonder that the Southern violators of the Constitution fear this new, non violent brand of freedom fighter . . . even as they fear the upswelling right-to-vote movement. Small wonder that they are determined to destroy the one man who, more than any other, symbolizes the new spirit now sweeping the South—the Rev. Dr. Martin Luther King, Jr., world-famous leader of the Montgomery Bus Protest. For it is his doctrine of non-violence which has inspired and guided the students in their widening wave of sit-ins; and it [is] this same Dr. King who founded and is president of the Southern Christian leadership Conference—the organization which is spearheading the surging right-to-vote movement. Under Dr. King's direction the Leadership Conference conducts Student Workshops and Seminars in the philosophy and technique of non-violent resistance.

Again and again the Southern violators have answered Dr. King's peaceful protests with intimidation and violence. They have bombed his home almost killing his wife and child. They have assaulted his person. They have arrested him seven times—for "speeding," "loitering" and similar "offenses." And now they have charged him with "perjury"—a felony under which they could imprison him for ten years. Obviously, their real purpose is to remove him physically as the leader to whom the students and millions of others—look for guidance and support, and thereby to intimidate all leaders who may rise in the South. Their strategy is to behead this affirmative movement, and thus to demoralize Negro Americans and weaken their will to struggle. The defense of Martin Luther King, spiritual leader of the student sit-in movement, clearly, therefore, is an integral part of the total struggle for freedom in the South.

Decent-minded Americans cannot help but applaud the creative daring of the students and the quiet heroism of Dr. King. But this is one of those moments in the stormy history of Freedom when men and women of good will must do more than applaud the rising-to-glory of others. The America whose good name hangs in the balance before a watchful world, the America whose heritage of Liberty these Southern Upholders of the Constitution are defending, is our America as well as theirs. . .

We must heed their rising voices—yes—but we must add our own.

We must extend ourselves above and beyond moral support and render the material help so urgently needed by those who are taking the risks,

facing jail, and even death in a glorious re-affir-
mation of our Constitution and its Bill of Rights.

We urge you to join hands with our fellow
Americans in the South by supporting, with
your dollars, this Combined Appeal for all three
needs—the defense of Martin Luther King—the
support of the embattled students—and the
struggle for the right to vote.

Stella Adler

Raymond Pace Alexander

Harry Can Arsdale

Harry Belafonte

Julie Belafonte

Dr. Algernon Black

Marc Blitztein

William Branch

Marlon Brando

Mrs. Ralph Bunche

Diahann Carroll

Dr. Alan Knight Chalmers

Richard Coe

Nat King Cole

Cheryl Crawford

Dorothy Dandridge

Ossie Davis

Sammy Davis, Jr.

Ruby Dee

Dr. Philip Elliott

Dr. Harry Emerson Fosdick

Anthony Franciosa

Lorraine Hansbury

Rev. Donald Harrington

Nat Hentoff

James Hicks

Mary Hinkson

Van Heflin

Langston Hughes

Morris Lushewitz

Mahalia Jackson

Mordecai Johnson

John Killens

Eartha Kitt

Rabbi Edward Klein

Hope Lange

John Lewis

Viveca Lindfors

Carl Murphy

Don Murray

John Murray

A.J. Muste

Frederick O'Neal

L. Joseph Overton

Clarence Pickett

Shad Polier

Sidney Poitier

A. Philip Randolph

John Raitt

Elmer Rice

Jackie Robinson

Mrs. Eleanor Roosevelt

Bayard Rustin

Robert Ryan

Maureen Stapleton

Frank Silvera

Hope Stevens

George Tabori

Rev. Gardner C. Taylor

Norman Thomas

Kenneth Tynan

Charles White

Shelley Winters

Max Youngstein

**WE IN THE SOUTH WHO ARE
STRUGGLING DAILY FOR DIGNITY
AND FREEDOM WARMLY ENDORSE
THIS APPEAL**

Rev. Ralph D. Abernathy (Montgomery, Ala.)

Rev. Fred L. Shuttlesworth (Birmingham, Ala.)

Rev. Kelley Miller Smith (Nashville, Tenn.)

Rev. W. A. Dennis (Chattanooga, Tenn.)

Rev. C. K. Steele (Tallahassee, Fla.)

Rev. Matthew D. McCollom (Orangeburg, S. C.)

Rev. William Holmes Borders (Atlanta, Ga.)

Rev. Douglas Moore (Durham, N. C.)

Rev. Wyatt Tee Walker (Petersburg, Va.)

Rev. Walter L. Hamilton (Norfolk, Va.)

I. S. Levy (Columbia, S. C.)

Rev. Martin Luther King, Sr. (Atlanta, Ga.)

Rev. Henry C. Bunton (Memphis, Tenn.)

Rev. S. S. Seay, Sr. (Montgomery, Ala.)

COMMITTEE TO
DEFEND MLK AND
THE STRUGGLE
FOR FREEDOM IN
THE SOUTH

COMMITTEE TO
DEFEND MLK AND
THE STRUGGLE
FOR FREEDOM IN
THE SOUTH

Rev. Samuel W. Williams (Atlanta, Ga.)

Rev. A. L Davis (New Orleans, La.)

Mrs. Katie E. Whickham (New Orleans, La.)

Rev. W. H. Hall (Hattiesburg, Miss.)

Rev. J. E. Lowery (Mobile, Ala.)

Rev. T. J. Jemison (Baton Rouge, La.)

**COMMITTEE TO DEFEND MARTIN
LUTHER KING AND THE STRUGGLE FOR
FREEDOM IN THE SOUTH**

**312 WEST 125TH STREET, NEW YORK
27, N.Y.UNIVERSITY 6–1700**

Chairmen: A. Philip Randolph, Dr. Gardner C. Taylor; *Chairmen of Cultural Division*: Harry Belafonte, Sidney Poitier; *Treasurer*: Nat King Cole; *Executive Director*: Bayard Rustin; *Chairmen of Church Division*: Father George B. Ford, Rev. Harry Emerson Fosdick, Rev. Thomas Kilgore, Jr., Rabbi Edward E. Klein; *Chairman of Labor Division*: Morris Iushewitz.

In the Supreme Court of the United States

October Term, 1963

No. 39

THE NEW YORK TIMES COMPANY,
PETITIONER,

V.

L. B. SULLIVAN, RESPONDENT

ON WRIT OF CERTIORARI TO THE SUPREME COURT OF ALABAMA

BRIEF FOR RESPONDENT

STEINER, CRUM & BAKER,
1109-25 FIRST NATIONAL BANK BUILDING,
MONTGOMERY 1, ALABAMA,
CALVIN WHITESELL,
MONTGOMERY, ALABAMA,
OF COUNSEL.
ROBERT E. STEINER III,
SAM RICE BAKER,
M. ROLAND NACHMAN JR.,
ATTORNEYS FOR RESPONDENT

Respondent adopts petitioner's statement of "Opinions Below" and "Jurisdiction."

QUESTIONS PRESENTED

1. Does a newspaper corporation have a constitutionally guaranteed absolute privilege to defame an elected city official in a paid newspaper advertisement so that the corporation is immune from a private common law libel judgment in a state court in circumstances where, because of the admitted falsity of the publication, the newspaper is unable to plead or prove state afforded defenses of truth, fair comment, privilege or retraction (to show good faith and eliminate punitive damages), and where the corporation has retracted the same false material for another admittedly "on a par" with the city official?

2. When the only claimed invasion of a corporation's constitutional rights is that a city official successfully sued it for damages in a private civil action for libel in a state court in circumstances described in Question 1, and when the corporation does not contend that the state trial proceedings have been unfair, has there been an abridgement of the corporation's constitutional rights under the First and Fourteenth Amendments?

3. Are libelous utterances in a paid newspaper advertisement within the area of constitutionally protected speech and press?

4. When an admittedly false newspaper advertisement published in circumstances described in Question 1 charges that city police massively engaged in rampant, vicious, terroristic and criminal actions in deprivation of rights of others, is a state court holding in a private common law libel action that such an utterance is libelous as a matter of state law—leaving to

U.S. SUPREME
COURT,
OCTOBER 1963

BRIEF FOR
RESPONDENT

the jury the questions of publication, identification with the police commissioner, and damages—an infringement of the newspaper's constitutional rights?

5. When a paid newspaper advertisement published in circumstances described in Question 1 contains admittedly false charges described in Question 4 about police action in a named city, may this Court consistently with its decisions and the Seventh Amendment review on certiorari a state jury finding, in a trial concededly fair, that the publication is "of and concerning" the city police commissioner whose name does not appear in the publication, and an award of general and punitive damages to him, when this state jury verdict embodied in a final state judgment has been approved by the state's highest appellate court?

6. May this Court consistently with its decisions and the Seventh Amendment re-examine facts tried by a state jury in a trial concededly fair, when those findings have been embodied in a final state judgment affirmed by the highest state appellate court, and when review is sought on assertions that the verdict is wrong and the general and punitive libel damages merely excessive?

7. When a foreign corporation makes a general appearance in a private state civil action against it, according to state law consistent with the majority view of all states, is there an adequate independent state ground as to jurisdiction over this foreign corporation?

8. Even if there had been no general appearance as described in Question 7, when a foreign newspaper corporation continuously and systematically gathers news by resident and transient correspondents, solicits advertising in person and by mail, and distributes its newspapers for sale in the forum state, and when some of these activities are incident to the cause of action in suit, has this foreign corporation sufficient contacts with the forum state so that suit against it is fair in accordance with decisions of this Court so explicit as to leave no room for real controversy?

STATUTES INVOLVED

Statutes referred to in this brief are contained in an appendix hereto.

STATEMENT

In the New York Times of March 29, 1960, there appeared a full-page advertisement, "warmly endorsed" by the four petitioners in

No. 40, entitled, "Heed Their Rising Voices."[1] Charging generally "an unprecedented wave of error," the advertisement said of Montgomery:

> "In Montgomery, Alabama, after students sang 'My Country, 'Tis of Thee' on the State Capitol steps, their leaders were expelled from school, and truckloads of police armed with shotguns and tear-gas ringed the Alabama State College Campus. When the entire student body protested to state authorities by refusing to re-register, their dining hall was padlocked in an attempt to starve them into submission.

> * * * * * * *

> "Again and again the Southern violators have answered Dr. King's peaceful protests with intimidation and violence. They have bombed his home almost killing his wife and child. They have assaulted his person. They have arrested him seven times—for 'speeding,' 'loitering' and similar 'offenses.' And now they have charged him with 'perjury'—a **felony** under which they could imprison him for **ten years.**"

Respondent, police commissioner of Montgomery, asked $500,000 as damages for this libel from the New York Times and the four "warm endorsers."

After a lengthy hearing the trial court held on August 5, 1960, that the New York Times was amenable to suit in Alabama. It had made a general appearance the court found. And, moreover, its business activities in Alabama, some of which had given rise to the cause of action, were sufficient contacts under due process standards to permit service on a Times string correspondent residing in Alabama, and on the Secretary of State under the Alabama Substituted Service Statute[2] (R. 49–57).

After its demurrers had been overruled (R. 108) the Times filed six separate pleas to the complaint (R. 99–105). Although truth regardless of motive is a complete defense to a libel suit in Alabama (see infra), the Times and its co-defendants filed no plea of truth. Although privilege and fair comment are defenses in Alabama in appropriate circumstances (see infra), the Times and its co-defendants did not plead these defenses. At the conclusion of the trial a jury returned a verdict against all defendants for

---

[1] App. B of Petitioner's brief, p. 97.
[2] Title 7, § 199 (1), Code of Alabama. The Times has conceded throughout adequate notice and opportunity to defend.

U.S. SUPREME
COURT,
OCTOBER 1963

BRIEF FOR
RESPONDENT

$500,000, and the trial court entered a judgment against all defendants in this amount.[3] Petitioner does not assert here any due process defects in these trial proceedings, and does not attack the motives and conduct of the jury.

The Times filed a motion for new trial, which was overruled (R. 970); the petitioners in No. 40 filed motions for new trial, but allowed them to lapse (R. 984, 998, 1013, 1028).

The Alabama Supreme Court affirmed the judgment as to all defendants (R. 1180).

The Times complains in this Court: (1) The holdings of the Alabama courts that the publication was libelous per se and the jury verdict that it was "of and concerning" respondent abridged its guaranties under the 1st and 14th Amendments, and (2) it was not amenable to suit in Alabama.

I. Merits

Since the Times has told this Court that the whole libel rests on two discrepancies—mere "exaggerations or inaccuracies"[4] in the course of an "impersonal"[5] discussion "plainly" not meant as an attack on any individual,[6] respondent will state **this** case.[7]

This lawsuit arose because of a wilful, deliberate and reckless attempt to portray in a full-page newspaper advertisement, for which the Times charged and was paid almost $5,000, rampant, vicious, terroristic and criminal police action in Montgomery, Alabama, to a nationwide public of 650,000. The goal was money-raising. Truth, accuracy and long-accepted standards of journalism were not criteria for the writing or publication of this advertisement. The defamatory matter (quoted R. 580–81) describes criminal police action because some college students innocently sang "My Country

'Tis of Thee" from the Alabama State Capitol steps. The innocent singers were expelled from school; police ringed their campus by truckloads armed with shotguns and tear gas;[8] and their dining hall was padlocked to starve the students into submission. All statements charge violation of the students' rights.

The Times is not candid when it tells this Court (Brief p. 7) that "the only part" of the foregoing statement "that Respondent thought implied a reference to him was the assertion about 'truckloads of police.'" Respondent made entirely clear that he considered the padlocking charge—and all other charges except expulsion—as applicable to him as well (R. 716). The Times is also absolutely inaccurate when it tells this Court that respondent's evidence "consisted mainly" (Brief p. 7) of a story by Sitton and a report by McKee. Respondent's evidence also included the Times' answers to interrogatories; respondent's own testimony, and that of his numerous witnesses; the testimony of all of the Times' trial witnesses; the statements and judicial admissions of its attorneys; and the testimony of John Murray who testified for the individual petitioners.

The advertisement in another paragraph charges that the perpetrators of the foregoing alleged barbarisms were the same persons who had intimidated Martin Luther King; bombed his home; assaulted his person; and arrested him. All statements charge criminal conduct. Although the Times' brief tells this Court that the pronoun "they" does not point to respondent, and that such a jury finding is "absurd" (Brief p. 33), the jury was able to make the connection from the Times' own witness, Gershon Aaronson. He conceded that the word "they" as it appeared repeatedly in the quotation in the ad "refers to the same persons" (R. 745).[9]

---

[3] Of course, this joint judgment is not collectible more than once. The facts giving rise to liability of petitioners in No. 40 will be related in a separate brief.

[4] Brief, p. 33.

[5] Brief, p. 32.

[6] Ibid.

[7] Respondent, accordingly, will not dignify beyond this comment the "statement" contained in the briefs of the friends of the Times. They are literally second editions of the advertisement and do not even purport to be confined to accurate summaries of the record.

    The American Civil Liberties Union Brief, for example, draws most of its statement from newspaper articles, offered by the Times on its motion for new trial, and excluded below. The correctness and propriety of the ruling are not

challenged. The brief simply cites the material as evidence anyway. Such practice presumably fosters the "fair trials" to which the organization is "devoted" (Brief, pp. 1 and 2). The other *amici* briefs are consumed with unrelated cases, entirely outside the record, and with inaccurate and incomplete characterizations of and quotations from a scant fraction of the testimony in this case.

[8] The Times apparently hopes to de-emphasize the ad's false allegations that the police were armed with shotguns and tear gas. It describes the ad as speaking of "truckloads of armed police …" (Brief, pp. 5 and 62. See also p. 8).

[9] The Times argues here, remarkable to say, that the jury should have disregarded Aaronson's testimony, because another witness, Redding, was *not* interrogated on the point (Brief, p. 17).

U.S. SUPREME
COURT,
OCTOBER 1963

BRIEF FOR
RESPONDENT

Accordingly, the same police and the same police commissioner committed or condoned these alleged acts. And a jury unanimously agreed with Aaronson.

In a vain attempt to transfer these devastating statements from the constitutionally unprotected area of socially useless libel, where they belong, to the arena of constitutionally protected speech, where they obviously have no place, the Times and its friends employ various soothing phrases to describe the advertisement. It is called "political expression" and "political criticism" (pp. 29 and 30) of "public men" (p. 41); "the daily dialogue of politics" (p. 50); "a critique of government as such"; "criticism of official conduct" and "of the government" (pp. 30 and passim); "the most impersonal denunciation of an agency of government" (p. 50); a "recital of grievances and protests against claimed abuse dealing squarely with the major issue of our time" (pp. 31 and 57); "an expression which is merely wrong in fact with denigrating implications" (p. 54); an "appeal for political and social change" (A.C.L.U. brief, p. 13); a "critique of attitude and method, a value judgment and opinion" (A.C.L.U. brief, p. 29).

But the ordinary, unsophisticated reader of this ad was bound to draw the plain meaning that such shocking conditions were the responsibility of those charged with the administration of the Montgomery Police Department—respondent and the other two city commissioners. Any other conclusion is impossible. The Times itself can suggest no other reference, except to the police generally, and police are under the direct control and supervision of respondent. Indeed, the Times brief (p. 44) characterizes the ad as "criticism of an elected political official ..." and

observes that this official should be hardy enough to take it without suing for libel.

A description of such conduct, at war with basic concepts of decency and lawful government, inevitably evokes contempt, indignation, and ridicule for the person charged with the administration of police activities in Montgomery. And obviously this was the precise intent of the authors of the advertisement. One of them, John Murray, so testified.[10]

Significantly, none of the Times' witnesses, and none of the petitioners in No. 40, all of whom testified, presented any evidence designed to show that the statements from the ad were true. Certainly, the individual petitioners in No. 40, two of whom lived in Montgomery, had no reason to withhold testimony harmful to respondent.

The reference to respondent as police commissioner is clear from the ad. In addition, the jury heard the testimony of a newspaper editor (R. 602, et seq.); a real estate and insurance man (R. 613, et seq.); the sales manager of a men's clothing store (R. 634, et seq.); a food equipment man (R. 644, et seq.); a service station operator (R. 649, et seq.); and the operator of a truck line for whom respondent had formerly worked (R. 662, et seq.). Each of these witnesses stated that he associated the statements with respondent, and that if he had believed the statements to be true, he would have considered such conduct reprehensible in the extreme.[11]

Unless the Times is asking this Court to assume the functions of a jury and to weigh the credibility of this relevant testimony, nothing could be more irrelevant than the time and place of the witnesses' first inspection of the ad. Even so, the Times has had to adjust the testimony to make its dubious point,[12] and it seems to forget that all of its witnesses were its own employees.

---

[10] "Q. (After reading the first paragraph quoted in the complaint) Was that the way that paragraph was when you first got it with the memorandum or did you give it that added touch for appeal?

"A. Well, it would be a little difficult at this time to recall the exact wording in the memorandum but the sense of what was in the memorandum was certainly the same as what is in here. We may have phrased it a little differently here and there.

"Q. I see. Your purpose was to rev it up a little bit to get money, I take it.

"A. Well, our purpose was to get money and to make the ad as—to project it in the most appealing form from the material we were getting.

"Q. Whether it was accurate or not really didn't make much difference, did it?

"A. Well, that did not enter the—it did not enter into consideration at all except we took it for granted that it was accurate—we took it for granted that it was accurate—they were accurate—and if they hadn't been—I mean we would have stopped to question it. I mean we would have stopped to question it—We had every reason to believe it" (R. 814–815).

[11] One stated, for example: "I don't think there is any question about what I would decide. I think I would decide that we probably had a young Gestapo in Montgomery" (R. 646).

[12] For example, Blackwell testified (R. 619): "He called me into his office and showed me this ad and at that time I indicated that I had seen the ad before but I don't remember just where and under what circumstances ..."

Undoubtedly the demonstrable falsity of the statements prevented pleas of truth or privilege or fair comment. Indeed, the Times published a retraction of the same paragraphs for Governor Patterson on May 16, 1960 (R. 596 and 1958–1961):

> "Since publication of the advertisement, The Times made an investigation and consistent with its policy of retracting and correcting any errors or misstatements which may appear in its columns, herewith retracts the two paragraphs complained of by the Governor."

The Times asked its Montgomery string correspondent, McKee, for an investigation. On April 14, 1960, five days before suit was filed, McKee advised that the statements in the first quoted paragraph of the ad were false; and that King had been arrested twice by the Montgomery police for loitering and speeding and twice by the Sheriff's office for violation of the State boycott law and on charge of income tax falsification—a charge on which he was subsequently acquitted. Nevertheless, the Times, instead of retracting, wrote respondent that with the exception of the padlocking statement the rest of the quoted material was "substantially correct" (R. 589).

Later the Times directed another investigation by its regional correspondent, Claude Sitton. While the Times now speaks in this Court of "discrepancies" and "inaccuracies" in two instances, Sitton reported on May 4, 1960, that the first quoted paragraph of the advertisement "appears to be virtually without any foundation" (R. 594). There was no suggestion of involvement of respondent or any other city commissioner, or public employee under their charge, in the matters in the second quoted paragraph.

The Times then retracted for Governor Patterson, but not for respondent. The Times attempted to explain its inconsistency:

> "The defendant ... felt that on account of the fact that John Patterson held the high office of Governor of the State of Alabama and that he apparently believed that he had been libeled by said advertisement in his capacity as Governor of the State of Alabama, the defendant should apologize" (R. 595–596).

When confronted with this answer to interrogatories, Harding Bancroft, then secretary of The New York Times, could give no reason for the different treatment of Governor Patterson and respondent. They were "on a par." But there was a retraction for Patterson and not for respondent (R. 779).[13]

Undisputed trial testimony showed that respondent and the other commissioners and the Montgomery police had nothing to do with the King bombings; that a city detective had helped dismantle a live bomb which had been thrown on King's front porch (R. 685); and that the department had exerted extraordinary efforts to apprehend the persons responsible (R. 686–687). The occurrence of this event before respondent took office simply compounds the libelous nature of this advertisement which seeks to portray such matters as current actions which "they" took. The ordinary reader, chronologically unsophisticated, would clearly associate the acts with the current city government.

Another police officer testified without contradiction that no one had assaulted King when he had been arrested for loitering outside the courtroom (R. 692–693).

Frank Stewart, State Superintendent of Education, testified without contradiction that students had not been expelled from school for singing on the capitol steps (R. 700).

The uncontroverted testimony of falsity was so overwhelming that counsel for the Times

---

Price testified: " ... I saw copies of the two paragraphs myself prior to that time" (R. 648).

Respondent's counsel himself asked Parker whether he had seen the ad "before in my office" (R. 649) but not whether this was the first occasion; and counsel for the Times did not cross-examine on the point, presumably because its counsel had also talked to Parker before the trial (R. 651).

13 The Times brief, in its lengthy attempt to explain its inconsistency (pp. 21–22), presents an incomplete and inaccurate summary of Bancroft's testimony. It omits the following (R. 779):

"Q. Is there anything contained in this sentence in the Interrogatories that I just read to you which differentiates in any manner the position of Governor Patterson in his suit with Commissioner Sullivan in the present suit?

"A. As I read the thing, the answer is no.

"Q. They are put on a par, aren't they, Governor Patterson and this Plaintiff?

"A. Yes.

"Q. But there was a retraction for Governor Patterson and there was no retraction for this Plaintiff. That is correct, isn't it?

"A. That is correct."

U.S. SUPREME
COURT,
OCTOBER 1963

BRIEF FOR
RESPONDENT

repeatedly brought out from witnesses that the statements quoted from the ad were not true. Moreover, he stated that truth was not in issue in the case because it had not been pleaded (A compendium of counsel's statements is in Appendix B of the brief in opposition, pp. 48–52). Counsel would not and could not have made such statements if the quoted portions of the ad had been true or if they had contained only a few "discrepancies" or "exaggerations."

Undeterred, however, in the teeth of these judicial admissions, Harding Bancroft maintained to the end an equivocal position about the correctness of the ad, with the exception of the padlocking statement.[14] The Times' brief, on the contrary, candidly recites (pp. 62–65) a chronicle of the ad's falsities in addition to the padlocking statement.

Because of this testimony, when the Times **six months before** had retracted the **same** statements on the basis of the **same** investigation as "errors and misstatements" (R. 595–596, 1958–1961), the court below characterized Bancroft's performance as "cavalier ignoring of the falsity of the advertisement" which surely impressed the jury "with the bad faith of the Times, and its maliciousness inferable therefrom" (R. 1178). The Times is absolutely incorrect when it argues that this statement of the Court was based upon the selected portion of

Bancroft's testimony excerpted on pages 21 and 22 of its brief.

Sullivan himself testified that the matters contained in the ad were false (R. 705–709); that the statements reflected "upon my ability and integrity, and certainly it has been established here that they are not true" (R. 713).

The bombing statement "referred to me and to the Police Department and the City Commissioners" (R. 718). Similarly, the other matters contained in the second quoted paragraph of the ad related to him "by virtue of being Police Commissioner and Commissioner of Public Affairs."

When asked on cross-examination whether he felt that the ad had a "direct personal reference" to him, his answer was, and it is the simple answer which any normal reader of the ad would give:

> "It is my feeling that it reflects not only on me but on the other Commissioners and the community. ... When it describes police action, certainly I feel it reflects on me as an individual" (R. 724).

Moreover:

> "I have endeavored to try to earn a good reputation and that's why I resent very much the statements contained in this ad which are completely false and untrue" (R. 722).

The circumstances under which this ad was cleared for publication show a striking departure from the Times' usual meticulous screening process. So that it will print only what is "fit to print," the Times has codified an elaborate set of "advertising acceptability standards" (R. 597–601), designed "to exclude misleading, inaccurate, and fraudulent advertisements and unfair competitive statements in advertising. The chief purpose of this policy of The Times is to protect the reader and to maintain the high standards of decency and dignity in its advertising columns which The Times has developed over the years."

To be as charitable as possible, it is remarkable that no person connected with The Times investigated charges that as part of "a wave of terror," public officials in Montgomery, because students sang "My Country 'Tis of Thee" from the Capitol steps, expelled the students from school; ringed their campus with truckloads of police armed with shotguns and tear gas; padlocked dining halls to starve them into submission; and thereby maintained continuity with

[14] When asked whether the Times took the position that the ad's statements, with this exception, were "substantially correct," Bancroft first said: "I think it is a pretty hard question to answer" (R. 781). Then, the Times ... "doesn't know anything more than what is set forth in these two responses which our stringer and correspondent there, which are annexed to the Answers to the Interrogatories and we don't have any additional knowledge to that" (R. 782). Next: "I really think I have to answer the question by saying I don't know" (R. 782). Then: "[I]t is awfully difficult to define what The Times thinks," but The Times' lawyers had seemed to indicate on April 15, 1960, that the statements were substantially correct (R. 784). He concluded (R. 785): "I find it terribly difficult to be able to say that The Times, as such, believes something is true or is not true. Now, all I can tell you is what the sources of The Times' knowledge are, and the sources are The Times' knowledge—the complete sources as far as I know, are the two annexes attached to the Answers to the Interrogatories. Now, if you asked me would I use the words 'substantially correct,' now, I think I probably would, yes. The tenor of the content, the material of those two paragraphs in the ad which have been frequently read here are not substantially incorrect. They are substantially correct. Now, what sort of words I can use to give you an answer that would satisfy you, I don't know."

earlier days in which they had bombed King's home, assaulted his person, and arrested him on baseless charges.

Over sixty names appeared on the ad; none of these persons was contacted. A regional correspondent in Atlanta, who the Times admits had written news reports about racial difficulties in Montgomery, was not questioned. The Times had a string correspondent in Montgomery. It directed him to give an immediate report on the demand for retraction. But he was not asked for prior information or investigation.

In its answer to interrogatories, the Times specified sixteen contemporaneous news stories of its own as "relating to certain of the events or occurrences referred to in the advertisement" (R. 586). Aaronson, Redding, and Bancroft—the three Times witnesses—had never bothered to look at any of this news material before publishing the ad.

Aaronson, an employee on the national advertising staff, who first received the ad, testified that he did not read it (R. 741), but simply "scanned it very hurriedly" (R. 742).

Because he knew nothing which would lead him to believe that these monstrous statements were false (R. 758), Vincent Redding, head of the Advertising Acceptability Department, did not check with any of the signers of the ad; or with the regional correspondent in Atlanta; or with the string correspondent in Montgomery; or with the sixteen newspaper stories on file in his office (R. 763–765):

> "Q. Mr. Redding, wouldn't it be a fair statement to say that you really didn't check this ad at all for accuracy?"
>
> "A. That's a fair statement, yes" (R. 765).

One wonders whether the performance of Messrs. Aaronson, Redding and Bancroft inspired the American Civil Liberties Union comment that the Times had suffered "liability without fault" (Brief, p. 26), and the Washington Post evaluation that " … the undisputed record facts disclose that the advertisement was published under circumstances which, by no stretch of the imagination could be characterized as anything other than complete good faith" (Brief, p. 6).

Testimony of John Murray, one of the authors of the ad, and erstwhile Hollywood "scenarist" and Broadway lyricist (R. 815), describing the manner in which the ad was composed, has been quoted previously (Footnote 10, *supra*).

Thus, this "appealing" congeries of monstrous and now undefended falsehoods was sent to The New York Times. Upon payment of almost five thousand dollars, it was published without any investigation as a full-page advertisement in The New York Times of March 29, 1960. Six hundred and fifty thousand copies of it circulated to the nation as part of "All the news that's fit to print." And its purveyors sat back to await the financial return on their investment in "free speech".

II. Jurisdiction

General appearance Petitioner, by moving to dismiss the action because the Alabama court was said to have no jurisdiction of the subject matter, made a general appearance in this case and thereby consented to the jurisdiction of the Alabama courts over its corporate person. This was the holding of both courts below. In addition, the trial court held that by bringing a mandamus action in the Supreme Court of Alabama unrelated to questions of personal jurisdiction, the Times had compounded its general appearance (R. 49–51). The holdings below, as will be demonstrated, accord with Alabama cases as well as those in a majority of the states.

The Times calls this general appearance "involuntary" (Brief, p. 75). But the Times in its brief in the Alabama Supreme Court (p. 54) said:

> "Accordingly, while the motion made it clear that the only grounds for the motion were the defects in the mode of service, the prayer asserted the consequences of these defects—a lack of jurisdiction not only over the person but also over the subject matter."

And the Times still makes the subject matter argument in this Court (Brief, p. 73):

> "Hence a contention that the statute is inapplicable or invalid as applied goes, in this sense, to jurisdiction of the cause as well as jurisdiction of the person."

Validity of service of process on The New York Times The courts below held that service on the string correspondent, McKee, and on the Secretary of State were valid. The trial court held that the Times had been sued on a cause of action "incident to" its business in Alabama (R. 55); and the "manifold contacts which The Times maintains with the State of Alabama" make it amenable to this process and suit in the Alabama courts, commenced by service on McKee and on the Secretary of State, "regardless

U.S. SUPREME
COURT,
OCTOBER 1963

BRIEF FOR
RESPONDENT

of its general appearance" (R. 51). The trial court found:

> " … an extensive and continuous course of Alabama business activity—news gathering; solicitation of advertising; circulation of newspapers and other products. These systematic business dealings in Alabama give The Times substantial contact with the State of Alabama, considerably in excess of the minimal contacts required by the Supreme Court decisions. … The Times does business in Alabama" (R. 56–57).

The Alabama Supreme Court affirmed on this point, after extensive findings regarding the business activities of the Times in Alabama (R. 1140–1147). It adopted, as had the trial court, the test of *Consolidated Cosmetics v. D-A Publishing Company*, 186 F. 2d 906, 908 (7th Cir. 1951):

> "The functions of a magazine publishing company, obviously, include gathering material to be printed, obtaining advertisers and subscribers, printing, selling and delivering the magazines for sale. Each of these, we think, constitutes an essential factor of the magazine publication business. Consequently if a non-resident corporation sees fit to perform any one of those essential functions in a given jurisdiction, it necessarily follows that it is conducting its activities in such a manner as to be subject to jurisdiction."

The court below concluded (R. 1149–1150):

> "The evidence shows that The Times sent its papers into Alabama, with its carrier as its agent, freight prepaid, with title passing on delivery to the consignee. See Tit. 57, Sec. 25, Code of Alabama 1940; 2 Williston on Sales, Sec. 279 (b), p. 90. Thence the issue went to newsstands for sale to the public in Alabama, in accordance with a long standing business practice.

> "The Times or its wholly owned advertising subsidiary, on several occasions, had agents in Alabama for substantial periods of time soliciting, and procuring in substantial amounts advertising to appear in The Times.

> "Furthermore, upon the receipt of the letter from the plaintiff demanding a retraction of the matter appearing in the advertisement, The Times had its string correspondent in Montgomery, Mr. McKee, investigate the truthfulness of the assertions in the advertisement. The fact that Mr. McKee was not devoting his full time to the service of The Times is 'without constitutional significance.' Scripto, Inc. v. Carson, Sheriff, et al., 362 U.S. 207."

Moreover, the court below found (R. 1151):

> "In the present case the evidence shows that the publishing of advertisements was a substantial part of the business of The Times, and its newspapers were regularly sent into Alabama. Advertising was solicited in Alabama. Its correspondent McKee was called upon by The Times to investigate the truthfulness or falsity of the matters contained in the advertisement after the letter from the plaintiff. The acts therefore disclose not only certain general conditions with reference to newspaper publishing, but also specific acts directly connected with, and directly incident to the business of The Times done in Alabama."

The exhaustive findings of fact contained in the opinions of both Alabama courts are fully substantiated in the record, and are not challenged in the Times Brief. In a qualitative sense, the test of *International Shoe Co. v. Washington*, 326 U.S. 310, 319–320, these decisions below were clearly correct. The Times from 1956 through April, 1960, conducted an extensive and continuous course of business activity in Alabama. The annual revenue was over twice as great as the $42,000 which this Court found sufficient to establish adequate Florida contacts in *Scripto v. Carson*, 362 U.S. 207.

SUMMARY OF ARGUMENT

I.

The commercial advertisement in suit sought to, and did, portray criminal and rampant police state activity—an "unprecedented wave of terror"—resulting from students singing "My Country 'Tis of Thee" from the state capitol steps. This falsely alleged "wave of terror" against innocent persons was said to include expulsion from school; ringing of a college campus with truckloads of police armed with shotguns and tear gas; padlocking of the dining hall to starve protesting students into submission; and the arrest of Martin Luther King for loitering and speeding by those who had also bombed his home, assaulted his person and indicted him for perjury. The ad did not name respondent, but massive, terroristic and criminal acts of the police carry the sure meaning to the average, reasonably intelligent reader that the police activity is that of the police commissioner.

A. Alabama libel laws provided petitioner with the absolute defense of truth and with the privilege of fair comment. Petitioner did not plead or attempt to prove truth or fair comment. Its attorneys suggested in open court that the defamatory matter was not true and would not be believed, and that truth was not in issue. The Times itself, in a contemporaneous retraction for another person whom it considered to be "on a par" with respondent, admitted that the material in the ad was erroneous and misleading.

Alabama law provides for untruthful and unprivileged defamers an opportunity to retract and thereby to eliminate all damages except special. Though the Times retracted for another "on a par," it refused to do so for respondent.

The Times makes no claim that it was denied a fair and impartial trial of this libel action, and raises no question of procedural due process.

In these circumstances, no provision of the Constitution of the United States confers an absolute immunity to defame public officials. On the contrary, this Court has repeatedly held that libelous utterances are not protected by the Constitution. *Beauharnais v. Illinois*, 343 U.S. 250; *Near v. Minnesota*, 283 U.S. 697, 715; *Konigsberg v. State Bar of California*, 366 U.S. 36, 49–50; *Roth v. U.S.*, 354 U.S. 476, 483; *Chaplinsky v. New Hampshire*, 315 U.S. 568, 571–572; *Barr v. Matteo*, 360 U.S. 564; *Farmers Union v. WDAY, Inc.*, 360 U.S. 525; and *Pennekamp v. Florida*, 328 U.S. 331, 348–349. Historical commentary on "freedom of the press" accords. See, Thomas Jefferson to Abigail Adams in 1804; Thomas Jefferson's Second Inaugural Address (1805); Chafee, Book Review, 62 Harvard L. Rev. 891, 897, 898 (1949). Moreover, commercial advertisements are not constitutionally protected as speech and press. *Valentine v. Chrestensen*, 316 U.S. 52, 54; and *Breard v. City of Alexandria*, 341 U.S. 622, 643. Because such libelous utterances are not constitutionally protected speech, "it is unnecessary, either for us or for the state courts, to consider the issues behind the phrase 'clear and present danger.' " *Beauharnais v. Illinois*, 343 U.S. 250, 266.

B. It is fantasy for petitioner to argue that the ad which falsely charged respondent, as police commissioner, with responsibility for the criminal and rampant "unprecedented wave of terror" is "the daily dialogue of politics" and mere "political criticism" and "political expression." If the Times prevails, any false statement about any public official comes within this protected category. The absolute immunity would cover false statements that the Secretary of State had given military secrets to the enemy; that the Secretary of the Treasury had embezzled public funds; that the Governor of a state poisoned his wife; that the head of the public health service polluted water with germs; that the mayor and city council are corrupt; that named judges confer favorable opinions on the highest bidder; and that a police commissioner conducted activities so barbaric as to constitute a wave of terror.

C. Since the Times did not invoke Alabama defenses of truth, fair comment or privilege, the question of the constitutional adequacy of these defenses is entirely academic. Nevertheless, Alabama libel law conforms to constitutional standards which this Court has repeatedly set and to the libel laws of most states. "Only in a minority of states is a public critic of Government even qualifiedly privileged where his facts are wrong." *Barr v. Matteo*, 360 U.S. 564, 585 (dissenting opinion of Chief Justice Warren). The constitution has never required that states afford newspapers the privilege of leveling false and defamatory "facts" at persons simply because they hold public office. The great weight of American authority has rejected such a plea by newspapers. *Burt v. Advertiser Company*, 154 Mass. 238, 28 N. E. 1, 4 (opinion by Judge, later Mr. Justice Holmes); *Post Publishing Company v. Hallam*, 59 F. 530, 540 (6th Cir. 1893) (opinion by Judge, later Mr. Chief Justice Taft); *Washington Times Company v. Bonner*, 86 F. 2d 836, 842 (D. C. Cir. 1936); *Pennekamp v. Florida*, 328 U.S. 331, 348–349: "For such injuries, when the statements amount to defamation, a judge has such remedy in damages for libel as do other public servants."

D. Alabama's definition of libel *per se* as a false publication which tends to injure the person defamed in his reputation, which brings him into public contempt as a public official, or which charges him with a crime, is a familiar one and accords with that of most states. This Court approved it in *Beauharnais v. Illinois*, 343 U.S. 250, 257, n. 5, citing *Grant v. Reader's Digest*, 151 F. 2d 733, 735 (2d Cir. 1945), opinion by Judge Learned Hand; *Hogan v. New York Times*, 313 F. 2d 354, 355 (2d Cir. 1963). The presumption of general damages from libel *per se* is the majority rule throughout the country. *Developments in the Law—Defamation*, 69 Harvard L. Rev. 875 at 934 and 937; 3 *Restatement of Torts*, § 621, pp. 313–316.

E. In Alabama, as elsewhere, punitive damages and general damages, where there has been no retraction, are permitted, and the jury is given broad discretion in fixing the amount of the award. *Reynolds v. Pegler*, 123 F. Supp. 36, 38,

U.S. SUPREME
COURT,
OCTOBER 1963

BRIEF FOR
RESPONDENT

U.S. SUPREME
COURT,
OCTOBER 1963

BRIEF FOR
RESPONDENT

affirmed 223 F. 2d 429 (2d Cir.), cert. den. 350 U.S. 846; *Faulk v. Aware, Inc.,* 231 N. Y. S. 2d 270; and *Beauharnais v. Illinois,* 343 U.S. 250, 266. In assessing punitive damages, the jury may properly consider the nature and degree of the offense, as well as the higher moral consideration that these damages may deter such illegal practices in the future. The award in this case is but a fraction of two recent libel awards in the *Faulk* case and by a Georgia Federal jury of more than three million dollars, with punitive damages alone of two and one-half million dollars and three million dollars respectively.

This Court has always considered itself barred by the Seventh Amendment of the Constitution from setting aside state and federal damage awards as inadequate or excessive. *Chicago, B. & Q. v. Chicago,* 166 U.S. 226, 242–243; *Fairmount Glass Works v. Cub Fork Coal Co.,* 287 U.S. 474; *Neese v. Southern Ry.,* 350 U.S. 77. Many other cases are cited in this brief.

There is no constitutional infirmity in Alabama procedure which preserves the jury's long-standing common law right to return a general verdict. *Statement of Mr. Justice Black and Mr. Justice Douglas,* 31 F. R. D. 617 at 618–619.

In setting punitive damages, the jury could properly contrast the judicial admissions of the Times' attorneys that the advertisement was false and the Times' retraction of the same matter for another person as misleading and erroneous, with the trial testimony of the secretary of the corporation that the advertisement was substantially correct with the exception of one incident described in the ad.

II.

It is patently frivolous for the Times to argue that no ordinary person of reasonable intelligence could read the advertisement in suit as referring to the Montgomery police commissioner. Certainly the jury is not required as a matter of law to hold that the ad is not of and concerning respondent. Its finding is entitled to all of the safeguards of the Seventh Amendment. *Gallick v. B. & O. R. Co.,* 372 U.S. 108; *Chicago B. & Q. R. Co. v. Chicago,* 166 U.S. 226 at 242–243; and *Fairmount Glass Works v. Cub Fork Coal Co.,* 287 U.S. 474. While the ad's reference is clear enough, the jury heard witnesses who associated respondent with its false allegations. *Hope v. Hearst Consolidated Publications,* 294 F. 2d 681

(2d Cir.), cert. denied 368 U.S. 956; *Chagnon v. Union Leader Corp.,* 103 N. H. 426, 174 A. 2d 825, 831–832, cert. denied 369 U.S. 830.

This Court in *Beauharnais v. Illinois,* 343 U.S. 250, and courts generally, have held that a plaintiff need not be named in a defamatory publication in order to have a cause of action for libel. *Cosgrove Studio, Inc. v. Pane,* 408 Pa. 314, 182 A. 2d 751, 753; *Hope v. Hearst Consolidated Publications,* supra; *Nieman-Marcus v. Lait,* 13 F. R. D. 311 (S. D. N. Y. 1952); *National Cancer Hospital v. Confidential, Inc..* 136 N. Y. S. 2d 921; *Weston v. Commercial Advertisers,* 184 N. Y. 479, 77 N. E. 660; *Bornmann v. Star Co.,* 174 N. Y. 212, 66 N. E. 723; *Chapa v. Abernethy* (Tex. Civ. App.), 175 S. W. 165; *Gross v. Cantor,* 270 N. Y. 93, 200 N. E. 592; *Fullerton v. Thompson,* 119 Minn. 136, 143 N. W. 260; *Children v. Shinn,* 168 Iowa 531, 150 N. W. 864; *Reilly v. Curtiss,* 53 N. J. 677, 84 A. 199; 3 *Restatement of Torts,* § 564 (c), p. 152; and *Developments in the Law— Defamation,* 69 Harvard L. Rev. 894 et seq.

III.

A. The courts below held that under Alabama practice the Times appeared generally in the action because it objected to jurisdiction of the subject matter as well as to jurisdiction of the person. This holding, which accords with the majority rule (25 A. L. R. 2d 835 and 31 A. L. R. 2d 258) is an adequate independent state ground as to jurisdiction over the Times which bars review of that question. *Herb v. Pitcairn,* 324 U.S. 117, 125–126; *Murdock v. Memphis,* 20 Wall. 590, 626; *Fox Film Corporation v. Muller,* 296 U.S. 207, 210; *Minnesota v. National Tea Company,* 309 U.S. 551, 556–557. A state court's interpretation of its own law is binding here. *Fox River Paper Company v. Railroad Commission,* 274 U.S. 651, 655; *Guaranty Trust Company v. Blodgett,* 287 U.S. 509, 513; *United Gas Pipeline Company v. Ideal Cement Company,* 369 U.S. 134.

B. Even if the Times had not made a general appearance in this case, effective service of process on a Times string correspondent residing in Alabama and on the Secretary of State of Alabama under a Substituted Service Statute, Title 7, § 199 (1), Alabama Code of 1940 as amended, is based on decisions of this Court so explicit as to leave no room for real controversy. Suit against the Times in Alabama accorded with traditional concepts of fairness and orderly administration of the laws. *International Shoe Company v. Washington,* 326 U.S. 310, 319;

McGee v. International Insurance Company, 355 U.S. 220; *Scripto v. Carson*, 362 U.S. 207; *Travelers Health Association v. Virginia*, 339 U.S. 643. The Times maintained three resident string correspondents in Alabama, and, since 1956, carried on an extensive, systematic and continuous course of business activity there, including news gathering, solicitation of advertising and circulation of newspapers and other products. It performed all of the functions of a newspaper outlined in *Consolidated Cosmetics v. D. A. Publishing Company*, 186 F. 2d 906, 908 (7th Cir. 1951). Its business activity produced more than twice the revenue which Scripto derived from Florida (see *Scripto v. Carson*, 362 U.S. 207), and its regular employees combined their efforts with those of independent dealers to produce this result.

It would be manifestly unfair to make respondent bring his libel suit in New York instead of in his home state where the charges were likely to harm him most. See Justice Black's dissenting opinion in *Polizzi v. Cowles Magazines*, 345 U.S. 663, 667.

When other business corporations may be sued in a foreign jurisdiction, so may newspaper corporations on similar facts. This Court has refused newspaper corporations special immunity from laws applicable to businesses in general. *Mabee v. White Plains Publishing Co.*, 327 U.S. 178, 184 (Fair Labor Standards Act); *Associated Press v. N. L. R. B.*, 301 U.S. 103 (National Labor Relations Act); and *Lorain Journal Company v. United States*, 342 U.S. 143 (Anti-trust laws).

ARGUMENT

I. The Constitution confers no absolute immunity to defame public officials

The New York Times, perhaps the nation's most influential newspaper, stooped to circulate a paid advertisement to 650,000 readers—an advertisement which libeled respondent with violent, inflammatory, and devastating language. The Times knew that the charges were uninvestigated and reckless in the extreme. It failed to retract for respondent with subsequent knowledge of the falsity of the material in the advertisement. Yet it retracted as misleading and erroneous the same defamatory matter for another "on a par."

Petitioner was unable to plead truth; or fair comment; or privilege. Alabama provides these classic defenses so that the press may be free

within the rubric of its libel laws.[15] Since petitioner did not invoke these Alabama defenses, its belated attack on their constitutional adequacy is hollow and entirely academic. Nevertheless, the Alabama law of libel conforms to constitutional standards which this Court has repeatedly set and to the libel laws of most states. "Only in a minority of states is a public critic of Government even qualifiedly privileged where his facts are wrong."[16] Moreover, "[t]he majority of American courts do not give a privilege to a communication of untrue facts, or to a comment based on them, even though due care was exercised in checking their accuracy."[17] *A fortiori* there is no such privilege where there was no check whatever. (See Aaronson, Redding and Bancroft testimony).

The Times' trial attorneys conceded that truth was not in issue; and made plain to the jury that the material was so patently false as to be unbelievable in the community. No defendant attempted to introduce testimony to substantiate the charges. The Times does not claim that it was denied a fair and impartial trial of the libel action. The petition raises no question of procedural due process.

> "This cause was tried in the courts of [the state] in accordance with regular court procedure applicable to such cases. The facts were submitted to a jury as provided by the constitution and laws of that State, and in harmony with the traditions of the people of this nation. Under these circumstances, no proper interpretation of the words 'due process of law' contained in the Fourteenth Amendment can justify the conclusion that appellant has been deprived of its property contrary to that 'due process.'"[18]

Libelous utterances have no constitutional protection The Times does not seek review of a

---

[15] Substantial truth in all material respects is a complete defense if specially pleaded. *Ferdon v. Dickens*, 161 Ala. 181, 49 So. 888; *Kirkpatrick v. Journal Publishing Company*, 210 Ala. 10, 97 So. 58; *Alabama Ride Company v. Vance*, 235 Ala. 263, 178 So. 438.

Privilege and fair comment, too, are defenses, if specially pleaded. *Ferdon v. Dickens*, supra; *W. T. Grant v. Smith*, 220 Ala. 377, 125 So. 393.

A retraction completely eliminates punitive damages. Title 7, Sections 913–917, Alabama Code (App. A. p. 67).

[16] Chief Justice Warren, dissenting in *Barr v. Matteo*, 360 U.S. 564, 585.

[17] *Developments in the Law—Defamation*, 69 Harvard L. Rev. 877, 927 (1956).

[18] *United Gas Public Service Company v. Texas*, 303 U.S. 123, 153, Black J. concurring.

U.S. SUPREME
COURT,
OCTOBER 1963

BRIEF FOR
RESPONDENT

federal question—substantial or otherwise. For libelous utterances have never been protected by the Federal Constitution. Throughout its entire history, this Court has never held that private damage suits for common law libel in state courts involved constitutional questions.[19] Respondent vigorously disputes the Times' assertion that this Court is wrong in its history (Brief, pp. 44–48), and that the constitutional pronouncements in those cases are mere "adjectives" and statements "made in passing" (Brief, p. 40). Respondent is confident that this Court meant what it said in *Roth v. U.S.*, 354 U.S. 476, 483, for example:

> "In light of this history it is apparent that the unconditional phrasing of the First Amendment was not intended to protect every utterance. This phrasing did not prevent this Court from concluding that libelous utterances are not within the area of constitutionally protected speech (citation)."

Again in *Konigsberg* this Court pronounced that it "has consistently recognized [that] … certain forms of speech [have] been considered outside the scope of constitutional protection." 366 U.S. 36, 50, citing *Beauharnais* and *Roth*.

Moreover, commercial advertisements are not constitutionally protected as speech and press, since there is no real restraint on speech and press where commercial activity is involved. *Valentine v. Chrestensen*, 316 U.S. 52, 54; *Breard v. City of Alexandria*, 341 U.S. 622, 643.[20] The Times has termed the citation of these cases "frivolous" and "cynical" (Brief, pp. 31 and 57). But its analysis of *Valentine v. Chrestensen* is incomplete—the other side of the handbill protested a city department's refusal of wharfage facilities. And the Times itself classified the ad as a commercial one, and submitted it to the Advertising Acceptability Department and to the standards of censorship which that department is supposed to impose. The Times charged the regular commercial advertising rate of almost five thousand dollars, scarcely as "an important method of promoting some equality of practical enjoyment of the benefits the First Amendment was intended to secure" (Brief, p. 58).

This Court last term in *Abernathy v. Patterson*, 368 U.S. 986, declined to review a decision of the Court of Appeals, 295 F. 2d 452, 456–457, which had held this very publication unprotected constitutionally as a libelous utterance. The Court of Appeals stated that the only

constitutional claim could be one relating to the conduct of the trial.

In 1804, Thomas Jefferson wrote to Abigail Adams, referring to his condemnation of the Sedition Act of 1798:

> "Nor does the opinion of the unconstitutionality and consequent nullity of that law remove all restraint from the overwhelming torrent of slander which is confounding all vice and virtue, all truth and falsehood in the U.S. The power to do that is fully possessed by the several state legislatures. It was reserved to them, and was denied to the general government, by the constitution according to our construction of it. While we deny that Congress have a right to control the freedom of the press, we have ever asserted the right of the states, and their exclusive right, to do so."[21]

Again in his second inaugural address on March 4, 1805, Jefferson said:

> "No inference is here intended that the laws provided by the States against false and defamatory publications should not be enforced; he who has time renders a service to public morals and public tranquility in reforming these abuses by the salutary coercions of the law; but the experiment is noted to prove that, since truth and reason have maintained their ground against false opinions in league with false facts, the press, confined to truth, needs no other legal restraint; the public judgment will correct false reasonings and opinions on a full hearing of all parties; and no other definite line can be drawn between the inestimable liberty of the press and its demoralizing licentiousness."[22]

A century and a quarter later, Justices Holmes and Brandeis joined Chief Justice Hughes, who spoke for the Court in *Near v. Minnesota*, 283 U.S. 697, 715:

> "But it is recognized that punishment for the abuse of the liberty accorded to the press is essential to the protection of the public, and that the common law rules that subject the

---

[19] *Beauharnais v. Illinois*, 343 U.S. 250; *Near v. Minnesota*, 283 U.S. 697, 715; *Konigsberg v. State Bar of California*, 366 U.S. 36, 49–50; *Roth v. U.S.*, 354 U.S. 476, 483; *Chaplinsky v. New Hampshire*, 315 U.S. 568, 571–572.

[20] Lower Federal court decisions accord. *Pollak v. Public Utilities Commission*, 191 F. 2d 450, 457 (D. C. Cir. 1951); *E. F. Drew & Co. v. Federal Trade Commission*, 235 F. 2d 735, 740 (2d Cir. 1956), cert. den. 352 U.S. 969.

[21] Quoted in *Dennis v. U.S.*, 341 U.S. 494, 522, n. 4, and in *Beauharnais v. Illinois*, 343 U.S. 250, 254, n. 4.

[22] I *Messages and Papers of the Presidents*, Joint Committee on Printing, 52nd Congress, pp. 366, 369 (1897).

libeler to responsibility for the public offense, as well as for the private injury, are not abolished by the protection extended in our constitutions."

Twenty years thereafter, this Court upheld an Illinois criminal group libel statute which had been applied to one who had distributed a pamphlet charging that Negroes as a class were rapists, robbers, carriers of knives and guns, and users of marijuana. *Beauharnais v. Illinois,* 343 U.S. 250, 266:

> "Libelous utterances, not being within the area of constitutionally protected speech, it is unnecessary, either for us or for the State courts, to consider the issues behind the phrase 'clear and present danger.' "

Since *Beauharnais,* as the table contained in Appendix A of respondent's brief in opposition shows, this Court has declined to review forty-four libel cases coming from the state and federal courts. It has reviewed three. Two of them[23] resulted in a holding that certain lower echelon federal executive personnel had an absolute privilege. The third[24] held that a radio and television station, which gave equal time to all political candidates because of the dictates of § 315 of the Federal Communications Act, was absolutely immune, by virtue of the same act, from state libel suits growing out of any such broadcasts.

The Times and its powerful corporate newspaper friends obviously realize that history and precedent support the holding below that this libelous advertisement is not constitutionally protected. They assert, therefore, at least for themselves and others who conduct the business of mass communication, an absolute privilege to defame all public officials—even in paid advertisements; even when the defamation renders the classic defenses of truth, fair comment and privilege unavailable; even when there is no retraction to show good faith. They urge this Court to write such a fancied immunity into the constitution—at least for themselves, for they are silent on whether this new constitutional protection is to extend to ordinary speakers and writers. The obvious consequence of such a holding would be the confiscation of the rights of those defamed to assert their traditional causes of action for defamation in state courts.

The Times attempts to cloak this defamatory advertisement with constitutional respectability. The ad is called "the daily dialogue of politics" and mere "political criticism" and "political expression." Surely desperation leads the Times

so to characterize a charge that respondent, as police commissioner, was responsible for the criminal and rampant "unprecedented wave of terror" which this ad sought to portray falsely.

If the Times prevails, then any statement about any public official becomes "the daily dialogue of politics," "political expression and criticism" and "a critique of attitude and method, a value judgment and opinion." The absolute immunity would cover false statements that the Secretary of State had given military secrets to the enemy; that the Secretary of the Treasury had embezzled public funds; that the Governor of a state poisoned his wife; that the head of the public health service polluted water with germs; that the mayor and city council are corrupt; that named judges confer favorable opinions on the highest bidder; and that a police commissioner conducted activities so barbaric as to constitute a wave of terror. If a state court indulges in "mere labels" without constitutional significance when it holds such utterances libelous, and if such defamatory statements about "public men" are to be protected as legitimate and socially useful speech, then the Times and its friends urge this Court to "convert the constitutional Bill of Rights into a suicide pact."[25]

Clearly, Congress and this Court did not find such a constitutional immunity, hence Section 315 and *Farmers Union v. WDAY,* 360 U.S. 525. The very reason for such Congressionally conferred immunity was the "widely recognized" existence of causes of action for libel by defamed candidates for public office "throughout the states" (360 U.S. 525 at 535). This Court found that Congress had given immunity because broadcasters would have too much difficulty determining whether a particular equal time broadcast was defamatory in terms of relevant state law. 360 U.S. 525 at 530. Surely this Court

---

[23] *Barr v. Matteo,* 360 U.S. 564; and *Howard v. Lyons,* 360 U.S. 593.

[24] *Farmers Union v. WDAY, Inc.,* 360 U.S. 525.

[25] Jackson, J. dissenting in *Terminiello v. Chicago,* 337 U.S. 1, 37.

The Times wrongly argues that Mr. Justice Frankfurter's caveat in *Beauharnais* was designed for such a purpose (Brief, p. 41). He examined the hypothetical dangers of permitting statutes which outlawed libels of political parties. Justice Frankfurter observed that such attempts would "raise quite different problems not now before us" (343 U.S. 250, 264), and it was in this context that he observed that the doctrine of fair comment would come into play "since political parties, like public men, are, as it were, public property." The case at bar, too, presents far different problems.

U.S. SUPREME COURT, OCTOBER 1963

BRIEF FOR RESPONDENT

U.S. SUPREME
COURT,
OCTOBER 1963

BRIEF FOR
RESPONDENT

did not decide *WDAY* on an assumption that the Constitution already provided such immunity absent a "clear and present danger."

Beauharnais, 343 U.S. 250 at 266, disposes of petitioner's "clear and present danger" cases (pp. 13–15) involving criminal prosecutions for breach of peace, criminal syndicalism and contempt of court.[26] Indeed, the background of one of them, *Pennekamp v. Florida,* 328 U.S. 331, 348–349, sharply distinguishes these cases from the one at bar. This Court told Pennekamp that even those hardy judges described by petitioner could bring private suits for defamation in state courts. "For such injuries, when the statements amount to defamation, a judge has such remedy in damages for libel as do other public servants."[27]

Pennekamp—editor of the Miami Herald—ignored this warning. Perhaps he assumed, as does the Times, that the official's remedy was "left at large," and that there was an absolute privilege to level not only fair but false and defamatory criticism at public officials. Pennekamp discovered that he was wrong, and that the remedy had been brought in tow, when his paper libeled a prosecuting attorney who recovered $100,000 in damages. *Miami Herald v. Brautigam* (Fla.), 127 So. 2d 718. Even though Pennekamp and his paper were able to plead fair comment and truth, and claimed the editorial expression as their own,[28] this Court declined to review despite the same First and Fourteenth Amendment arguments which the Times advances in its brief. 369 U.S. 821.

Two of this Court's greatest figures rejected a contention that newspapers should have an absolute privilege to defame public officials and a consequent absolute immunity from private libel suits. Mr. Justice, then Judge Holmes, in *Burt v. Advertiser Company,* 154 Mass. 238, 28 N. E. 1, 4, upholding a trial court charge to the jury

that newspaper statements of fact, as distinguished from opinion, if false, were not privileged, said:

> "But what the interest of private citizens in public matters requires is freedom of discussion rather than of statement. Moreover, the statements about such matters which come before the courts are generally public statements, where the harm done by a falsehood is much greater than in the other case."

> "If one private citizen wrote to another that a high official had taken a bribe, no one would think good faith a sufficient answer to an action. He stands no better, certainly, when he publishes his writing to the world through a newspaper, and the newspaper itself stands no better than the writer."

Mr. Chief Justice, then Judge Taft, upholding a similar trial court charge in *Post Publishing Company v. Hallam,* 59 F. 530, 540 (6th Cir., 1893), wrote:

> "[I]f the [absolute] privilege is to extend to cases like that at bar, then a man who offers himself as a candidate must submit uncomplainingly to the loss of his reputation, not with a single person or a small class of persons, but with every member of the public, whenever an untrue charge of disgraceful conduct is made against him, if only his accuser honestly believes the charge upon reasonable ground. We think that not only is such a sacrifice not required of everyone who consents to become a candidate for office, but that to sanction such a doctrine would do the public more harm than good."

Judge Taft rejected the argument, urged here by the Times and its newspaper friends, that the privilege of fair comment "extends to statement of fact as well as comment" when made by one "who has reasonable grounds for believing, and does believe, that [the public officer or candidate] has committed disgraceful acts affecting his fitness for the office he seeks" (59 F. 530 at 540).

---

[26] *Cantwell v. Connecticut,* 310 U.S. 296; *DeJonge v. Oregon,* 299 U.S. 353; *Bridges v. California,* 314 U.S. 252; *Pennekamp v. Florida,* 328 U.S. 331; *Craig v. Harney,* 331 U.S. 367; *Wood v. Georgia,* 370 U.S. 375; *Edwards v. South Carolina,* 372 U.S. 229; *Terminiello v. Chicago,* 337 U.S. 1; *Whitney v. California,* 274 U.S. 357; *Stromberg v. California,* 283 U.S. 359. While *Cantwell* is cited by the Times for the proposition that political expression is not limited by any test of truth, it omits the more relevant observation just following:

> "There are limits to the exercise of these liberties. The danger in these times from the coercive activities of those who in the delusion of racial or religious conceit would incite violence and breaches of the peace in order to deprive others of

their equal right to the exercise of their liberties, is emphasized by events familiar to all. These and other transgressions of those limits the states appropriately may punish" (at p. 310).

[27] Surely the Times does not assert seriously that this Court "left at large" what may amount to defamation and what remedy a public servant has (Brief, p. 41). He has the same remedy under the laws of his state that any other citizen has.

[28] In the Supreme Court of Alabama, the Times literally disavowed the advertisement as its utterance: "The ad was not written by anyone connected with The Times; it was not printed as a report of facts by The Times, nor as an editorial or other expression of the views of The Times" (Reply Brief, p. 12).

Judge Taft's admonitions still obtain, as Chief Justice Warren observed, in the majority of the states which hold that a public critic of government "is not even qualifiedly privileged where his facts are wrong." *Barr v. Matteo,* 360 U.S. 564, 585. Alabama is in accord with the great weight of state and federal authority.[29]

A noted commentator, Professor Zechariah Chafee, an old and close friend of free speech and press, also disagrees with the Times' law and history:

> "Especially significant is the contemporaneous evidence that the phrase 'freedom of the press' was viewed against a background of familiar legal limitations which men of 1791 did not regard as objectionable, such as damage suits for libel. Many state constitutions of this time included guaranties of freedom of speech and press which have been treated as having approximately the same scope as the federal provisions. Some of these, as in Massachusetts, were absolute in terms, while others, as in New York, expressly imposed responsibility for the abuse of the right. The precise nature of the state constitutional language did not matter; the early interpretation was much the same. Not only were private libel suits allowed, but also punishments for criminal libel and for contempt of court. For instance, there were several Massachusetts convictions around 1800 for libels attacking the conduct of the legislature and of public officials. This evidence negatives the author's idea of a firmly established purpose to make all political discussion immune."[30]

The Times can cite no authority holding that the Federal Constitution grants it an absolute privilege to defame a public official.

The advertisement was libelous per se The Times and its friends complain that the court below has held libelous *per se* a publication which is false, which tends to injure the person defamed in his reputation, which brings him into public contempt as an official, and which charges him with crime. Such a standard, they argue, is a common law concept of the most general and undefined nature. But this Court in *Beauharnais v. Illinois,* 343 U.S. 250, 257, n. 5, approved Judge Learned Hand's definition of libel in *Grant v. Reader's Digest,* 151 F. 2d 733, 735 (2d Cir. 1945), "in accordance with the usual rubric, as consisting of utterances which arose 'hatred, contempt, scorn, obloquy or shame,' and the like." Such a definition, this Court held, was a familiar—not a general and undefined—common law pronouncement.

The Times objects because the court decided the question of whether the publication was libelous *per se.* But the Times' contention opposes *Baker v. Warner,* 231 U.S. 588, 594. And see *Beauharnais,* 343 U.S. 250, 254:

> "Similarly, the action of the trial court in deciding as a matter of law the libelous character of the utterance, leaving to the jury only the question of publication, follows the settled rule in prosecutions for libel in Illinois and other States."

The Times complains because Alabama presumes general damages from a publication libelous *per se,* including the uncertain future damage of loss of job. This is the law generally.[31]

This publication charged a public official in devastating fashion with departing from all civilized standards of law and decency in the administration of his official duties. The correctness of the determination below that it is libelous *per se* is underscored by *Sweeney v. Schenectady Union Publishing Company,* 122 F. 2d 288, affirmed 316 U.S. 642. There a statement that a Congressman opposed a federal judicial appointment because of anti-Semitism was held libelous *per se* as a matter of law.

Very recently this same Court in *Hogan v. New York Times,* 313 F. 2d 354, 355 (2d Cir. 1963), observed that the Times did not even contest on appeal a district court holding that its news article describing a dice game raid of two policemen as a Keystone cop performance was "libelous per se as a matter of law."

Clearly the court below has correctly applied the Alabama common law of libel—law which accords in all relevant particulars with that of many other states.

---

[29] See *Washington Times Company v. Bonner,* 86 F. 2d 836, 842 (D. C. Cir. 1936).

[30] Chafee, Book Review, 62 Harvard L. Rev. 891, 897–898 (1949) (Footnotes omitted).

[31] Commentators precisely oppose the Times' view. See Note, *Exemplary Damages in the Law of Torts,* 70 Harvard L. Rev. 517, 531 (1957), where it was observed that a requirement of correlation between actual and punitive damages "fails to carry out the punitive function of exemplary damages, since it stresses the harm which actually results rather than the social undesirability of the defendant's behavior."

See, *Developments in the Law—Defamation,* 69 Harvard L. Rev. 875, at 934, et seq. And see ibid. at 937: "Because defamation is a tort likely to cause substantial harm of a type difficult to prove specifically, courts will allow a substantial recovery of general damages on a presumption of harm even though the plaintiff offers no proof of harm." See also 3 *Restatement of Torts,* § 621, pp. 313–316.

U.S. SUPREME
COURT,
OCTOBER 1963

BRIEF FOR
RESPONDENT

Damages awarded by the jury may not be disturbed The Times' objection that punitive damages in libel should not be imposed to deter the libeler and others like him from similar misconduct does not square with *Beauharnais*, 343 U.S. 250, 263. The Alabama test is precisely that of *Reynolds v. Pegler*, 123 F. Supp. 36, 38, affirmed 223 F. 2d 429 (2d Cir.), cert. den. 350 U.S. 846.[32] There the jury brought back one dollar compensatory damages and $175,000 in punitive damages.

In its argument that the size of this verdict impinges its constitutional rights, the Times has ignored a recent New York decision refusing to disturb a verdict of $3,500,000, of which the sum of $2,500,000 was punitive damages, against a publication and another for stating that plaintiff was linked to a Communist conspiracy. *Faulk v. Aware, Inc.*, 231 N. Y. S. 2d 270, 281:

> "In libel suits, of course, punitive damages have always been permitted in the discretion of the jury. The assessment of a penalty involves not only consideration of the nature and degree of the offense but the higher moral consideration that it may serve as a deterrent to anti-social practices where the public welfare is involved. The jury, representing the community, assesses such a penalty as, in its view, is adequate to stop the practices of defendants and others having similar designs."

The New York Times did not condemn the *Faulk* verdict—seven times as great as the one at bar—as heralding the demise of a free press. Instead, the Times applauded the verdict as "having a healthy effect."[33]

Quite recently a Federal jury returned a libel verdict of $3,060,000 in favor of a former college athletic director who was charged with rigging a football game. The specified punitive damages were $3,000,000, even higher than those in the *Faulk* case.[34]

Another commentator has observed that in England "the survival of honorific values and standards of communal decency keep defamation at a minimum and subject it, when it raises its head, to staggering jury verdicts." Riesman, *Democracy and Defamation*, 42 Columbia L. Rev. 727, 730.

It is appropriate here to remind this Court that it has always considered itself barred by the Seventh Amendment from setting aside state and federal jury damage awards as inadequate or excessive. *Chicago, B. & Q. v. Chicago*, 166 U.S.

226, 242–243 ($1 verdict in condemnation proceeding); *Fairmount Glass Works v. Cub Fork Coal Co.*, 287 U.S. 474 (and cases cited); *St. Louis, etc., Ry. Co. v. Craft*, 237 U.S. 648; *Maxwell v. Dow*, 176 U.S. 581, 598; *Southern Ry. v. Bennett*, 233 U.S. 80, 87; *Herencia v. Guzman*, 219 U.S. 44, 45; *Eastman Kodak v. Southern Photo Materials*, 273 U.S. 359; *L. & N. v. Holloway*, 246 U.S. 525; cf. *Neese v. Southern Ry.*, 350 U.S. 77. See also, *Justices v. U.S. ex rel. Murray*, 9 Wall. 274, said by this Court to be one of many cases showing "the uniform course of decision by this Court for over a hundred years in recognizing the legal autonomy of state and federal governments." *Knapp v. Schweitzer*, 357 U.S. 371, 378–379.

In an attempt to avoid this precedent, the Times first cites a series of cases which hold statutory penalties subject to judicial review as excessive—cases obviously having nothing to do with appellate review of jury verdicts.[35]

Next the Times urges that respondent's cases permit appellate review of excessive jury damage awards as errors of law (Brief, p. 69). But the cases themselves are otherwise. They cite, as examples of errors of law, awards which exceed the statutory limits; or are less than the undisputed amount; or are pursuant to erroneous instructions on measure of damages; or are in clear contravention of instructions of the court. *Fairmount Glass Works v. Cub Fork Coal Company*, 287 U.S. 474, 483–484. Another case, *Chicago, B. & Q. RR. v. Chicago*, 166 U.S. 226, 246, holds instead:

---

[32] "Punitive or exemplary damages are intended to act as a deterrent upon the libelor so that he will not repeat the offense, and to serve as a warning to others. They are intended as punishment for gross misbehavior *for the good of the public* and have been referred to as a 'sort of hybrid between a display of ethical indignation and the imposition of a criminal fine.' *Punitive damages are allowed on the ground of public policy and not because the plaintiff has suffered any monetary damages for which he is entitled to reimbursement; the award goes to him simply because it is assessed in his particular suit.* The damages may be considered expressive of the community attitude towards one who wilfully and wantonly causes hurt or injury to another" (Emphasis supplied; footnotes omitted).

[33] Editorial of June 30, 1962, p. 18.

[34] *New York Times*, August 21, 1963, p. 1.

[35] *Life & Casualty Co. v. McCray*, 291 U.S. 566; *Chicago and N. W. Ry. v. Nye Schneider Fowler Company*, 260 U.S. 35; *Mo. Pac. Ry. Co. v. Tucker*, 230 U.S. 340; *St. Louis, etc. Ry. v. Williams*, 251 U.S. 63. The other case cited for this purpose is a criminal case dealing with the Sixth Amendment. *Robinson v. California*, 370 U.S. 660 (Brief, p. 68).

"We are permitted only to inquire whether the trial court prescribed any rule of law for the guidance of the jury that was in absolute disregard of the company's right to just compensation."

Another case, *Dimick v. Schiedt,* 293 U.S. 474, did not hold that the question of excessive or inadequate verdicts was one of law, but on the contrary that it was "a question of fact." 293 U.S. 474 at 486. And *A. & G. Stevedores v. Ellerman Lines,* 369 U.S. 355, 360, cited by the Times, stated that the Seventh Amendment "fashions 'the federal policy favoring jury decisions of disputed fact questions.'"

The Times then argues that this Court may review the amount of damages because alleged abridgment of freedom of the press must take precedence over the Seventh Amendment (Brief, p. 69). It cites no authority for this amazing argument—one which scarcely accords with this Court's observation in *Jacob v. City of New York,* 315 U.S. 752 and 753:

"The right of jury trial in civil cases at common law is a basic and fundamental feature of our system of federal jurisprudence which is protected by the Seventh Amendment. A right so fundamental and sacred to the citizen, whether guaranteed by the Constitution or provided by statute, should be jealously guarded by the courts."

The Times quickly moves on to an argument almost as tenuous, namely, that modern authority "regards the Seventh Amendment as inapplicable generally to appellate review of an excessive verdict ..." (Brief, p. 69). The premise clashes with *Neese v. Southern Ry.,* 350 U.S. 77, as well as with such cases as *Fairmount, supra,* 287 U.S. 474, 481:

"The rule that this Court will not review the action of a federal trial court in granting or denying a motion for a new trial for error of fact has been settled by a long and unbroken line of decisions; and has been frequently applied where the ground of the motion was that the damages awarded by the jury were excessive or were inadequate." (Footnotes omitted.)

Finally, the Times complains that there was constitutional infirmity in the failure of the Alabama court to permit special interrogatories to the jury on damages, and thereby to deprive the jury of its right to return a general verdict.[36] Surely there is no constitutional defect in Alabama's adherence to the common law general verdict so recently eulogized by Justices Black and Douglas when they condemned an extension of the practice of submitting special interrogatories to federal juries:

"Such devices are used to impair or wholly take away the power of a jury to render a general verdict. One of the ancient, fundamental reasons for having general jury verdicts was to preserve the right of trial by jury as an indispensable part of a free government. Many of the most famous constitutional controversies in England revolved around litigants' insistence, particularly in seditious libel cases, that a jury had the right to render a general verdict without being compelled to return a number of subsidiary findings to support its general verdict. Some English jurors had to go to jail because they insisted upon their right to render general verdicts over the repeated commands of tyrannical judges not to do so."[37]

Accordingly, a review of the damages awarded by the jury in this case is beyond the powers of this Court. Moreover, the verdict, as the court below held, conforms to the general damages suffered by the respondent and to the wrong which the Times committed. The Times does not claim here that the jury was motivated by passion or prejudice or corruption or any improper motive. Two state courts have found that it was not.

The jury was no doubt struck by the amazing lack of concern and contrition exhibited by the Times' representatives at the trial, and it certainly contrasted their conduct. The Times' attorneys did not plead truth; did not attempt to introduce evidence of truth; suggested in cross-examination of respondent's witnesses that the matter was untrue and would not be believed; stated in open court that truth was not in issue; and could not plead fair comment or privilege. The Times retracted the same matter as erroneous and misleading for another person whom it considered to be "on a par" with respondent. But the secretary of the corporation, who had signed its answers to interrogatories, said that with the exception of the padlocking incident he believed the matters in the ad were not substantially incorrect.

U.S. SUPREME COURT, OCTOBER 1963

BRIEF FOR RESPONDENT

---

[36] *Johnson Pub. Co. v. Davis,* 271 Ala. 474, 496, 124 So. 2d 441; *All States Life Ins. Co. v. Jaudon,* 230 Ala. 593, 162 So. 668; *Little v. Sugg,* 243 Ala. 196, 8 So. 2d 866; *Spry v. Pruitt,* 256 Ala. 341, 54 So. 2d 701.

[37] Statement of Mr. Justice Black and Mr. Justice Douglas on the Rules of Civil Procedure and the Proposed Amendments, 31 F. R. D. 617, at 618–619.

Even more recently the conduct of the Times' business has warranted judicial condemnation. *Hogan v. New York Times,* 313 F. 2d 354, 355–356 (2d Cir. 1963):

> "We believe that sufficient evidence existed to sustain the jury verdict on either of the two possible grounds upon which its decision that defendant abused its qualified privilege might have been based: (1) improper purpose in publishing the article, or (2) reckless disregard for the truth or falsity of the story, amounting to bad faith."

The Times had its chance to retract and eliminate punitive damages, but chose not to do so for this respondent though it retracted for another person "on a par." A restriction of respondent to special damages would compound the evils described by Mr. Chafee in the following statement which he quoted with approval:

> " 'To require proof of special damages would mean virtual abolition of legal responsibility for inadvertent newspaper libel. Newspaper slips are usually the result of reprehensible conduct of members of the defendant's organization. To deny plaintiffs recovery for retracted libel unless they prove special damages, is to do away with newspapers' financial interest in accuracy. The tendency towards flamboyance and haste in modern journalism should be checked rather than countenanced. If newspapers could atone legally for their mistakes merely by publishing corrections, the number of mistakes might increase alarmingly… ' "[38]

II. There is no ground for reviewing a jury determination that the advertisement was "of and concerning" the Plaintiff

The Times' assertion that this Court should decide as a matter of constitutional law that the jury which tried this case was wrong in finding that the advertisement was "of and concerning" respondent is astounding. Respondent will not repeat here the thorough discussion of the testimony analyzing the false allegations of the ad and their reference to respondent as police commissioner of Montgomery. Apparently a reading of this testimony has now impressed even the Times. It has omitted from its brief on the merits the cases of *Thompson v. Louisville,* 362 U.S. 199, and *Garner v. Louisiana,* 368 U.S. 157, cited in its petition for certiorari for the proposition that there was no evidence to support the verdict.

Again the Times seeks to overturn imbedded constitutional principles. This case has been tried

in a state court according to admittedly proper court procedure, and a jury has decided the facts. This Court simply does not go behind these factual determinations and review a state court judgment, entered on a jury verdict and affirmed by the highest state appellate court. *Chicago, B. & Q. R. Co. v. Chicago,* 166 U.S. 226 at 242–243; *United Gas Public Service Co. v. Texas,* 303 U.S. 123, 152–153 (Black, J., concurring); *Fairmount Glass Works v. Cub Fork Coal Co.,* 287 U.S. 474; *Maxwell v. Dow,* 176 U.S. 581, 598.[39]

When this Court in *Gallick v. B. & O. R. Co.,* 372 U.S. 108, 9 L. Ed. 2d 618, 627, held that its duty was to reconcile state jury findings "by exegesis if necessary," it surely assigned no lesser place to the Seventh Amendment than that described by Justices Black and Douglas:

> "The call for the true application of the Seventh Amendment is not to words, but to the spirit of honest desire to see that constitutional right preserved. Either the judge or the jury must decide facts and to the extent that we take this responsibility, we lessen the jury function. Our duty to preserve this one of the Bill of Rights may be peculiarly difficult, for here it is our own power which we must restrain."[40]

Similar principles permeated the judicial philosophy of Judge Learned Hand:

> "And so only the most unusual circumstances could justify judicial veto of a legislative act … or a jury verdict. Hand's standard for intervention was essentially the same in both

---

[38] Quoted in Chafee, *Possible New Remedies for Errors in the Press.* 60 Harvard L. Rev., 1, 23.

[39] The Times seeks to circumvent these cases—and the 7th Amendment—by citing inapposite cases dealing with review here of state court conclusions as to a federal right where facts inadequately support the conclusion. *Norris v. Alabama,* 294 U.S. 587; *Wood v. Georgia,* 370 U.S. 375; *Craig v. Harney,* 331 U.S. 367; *Pennekamp v. Florida,* 328 U.S. 331; *Bridges v. California,* 314 U.S. 252; *Edwards v. South Carolina,* 372 U.S. 229—cases involving state court (not jury) determinations of questions of discrimination in the selection of a grand jury, and of the existence of a clear and present danger; *Watts v. Indiana,* 338 U.S. 49—a state court determination as to a coerced confession; *Herndon v. Lowry,* 301 U.S. 242—a case invalidating a conviction because the criminal statute prescribed "no reasonably ascertainable standard of guilt" (at 264); and *Fiske v. Kansas,* 274 U.S. 380— overturning a conviction under a criminal syndicalism act where the prosecution had introduced no evidence other than a preamble of the constitution of the Industrial Workers of the World which this Court found to be no evidence to support the conviction.

[40] *Galloway v. United States,* 319 U.S. 372, 407 (Black, Douglas and Murphy, JJ., dissenting).

cases. It came simply to this: if there was room for doubt, legislation—like a verdict—must stand, however, mistaken it might seem to judges. Ambivalence in the law was the province of jury and legislature—the two authentic voices of the people. Judicial intervention was permissible only when a court was prepared to hold that **no** reasonable mind could have found as the legislature or jury did find."[41]

Regarding falsity, the statements in the ad have been discussed exhaustively in this brief. The Times was unable to plead truth; and conceded falsity before the trial by its retraction to Governor Patterson and at the trial through the statements of its attorneys. It is surely paradoxical for the Times to assert in this Court that the record is so "devoid" of evidence of falsity as to invoke the certiorari jurisdiction of this Court. Nothing could be more idle than to debate with the Times and its friends the question of whether Alabama imposes the burden of proving truth on the wrong party, when the Times by its judicial admissions has conceded falsity.[42]

Moreover, this record reveals this ad's devastating effect on respondent's reputation among those who believed it. Courts have easily and effectively dealt with the Times' argument that the publication was not libelous or injurious because it was not believed in the community (Brief, p. 65).[43] Perhaps the Times would also argue that those in a crowded theater who did not see or smell smoke would not believe a person who yelled "fire."

It is patently frivolous for the Times to argue that no ordinary person of reasonable intelligence[44] could possibly read this advertisement as referring to the Montgomery police commis-

sioner. Nor is a jury bound by the Federal Constitution to take the Times' construction of these words after its attorneys have completed a sanitizing operation in an attempt to dull the cutting edges of these words.[45]

Beauharnais v. Illinois, 343 U.S. 250, teaches that a libel plaintiff need not be named in the defamatory publication. There the criminal prosecution was for defamation of the entire Negro race.[46]

It is difficult to believe that the Times is serious when it argues that this record is entirely devoid of evidence to support the jury finding that these defamatory words were of and concerning respondent.

The ad sought to, and did, portray criminal and rampant police state activity resulting from the singing of "My Country, 'Tis of Thee" from the State Capitol steps. It sought to portray, and did, a resultant "wave of terror" against innocent persons—expulsion from school; ringing of the campus of Alabama State College with truckloads of police armed with shotguns and tear gas; and padlocking of the dining hall to starve protesting students into submission. And the ad returned to Montgomery in the second quoted paragraph to charge that pursuant to the same "wave of terror," those who had arrested King for loitering and speeding also had bombed his home, assaulted his person, and indicted him for perjury.[47]

The effect of this publication was as deadly as intended—to instill in the minds of the readers the conclusion that these acts had been perpetrated by Montgomery city officials, specifically the police commissioner. The Times

---

[41] Mendelson, *Learned Hand: Patient Democrat,* 76 Harvard L. Rev. 322, 323–324 (1962).

[42] Completely inapposite, therefore, are the Times' citations of *Speiser v. Randall,* 357 U.S. 513 and *Bantam Books, Inc. v. Sullivan,* 372 U.S. 58, regarding inadequate state procedures where the speech or writing itself may be limited.

[43] See e.g. *Reynolds v. Pegler,* 123 F. Supp. 36, 37–38, affirmed 223 F. 2d 429 (2d Cir.), cert. denied 350 U.S. 846:

"'A person may be of such high character that the grossest libel would damage him none; but that would be no reason for withdrawing his case from the wholesome, if not necessary, rule in respect of punitive damages …'

To adopt the contrary view … would mean that a defamer gains a measure of immunity no matter how venomous or malicious his attack simply because of the excellent reputation of the defamed; it would mean that the defamer, motivated by actual malice, becomes the beneficiary of that unassailable reputation and so escapes punish-

ment. It would require punitive damages to be determined in inverse ratio to the reputation of the one defamed."

[44] This is the test everywhere. See *Albert Miller & Co. v. Corte,* 107 F. 2d 432, 435 (5th Cir. 1939), which holds that Alabama cases to this effect accord with libel law generally. See also *Peck v. Tribune Co.,* 214 U.S. 185 (where the wrong person was named); *Grant v. Reader's Digest,* 151 F. 2d 733 (2d Cir. 1945); *Spanel v. Pegler,* 160 F. 2d 619 (7th Cir. 1949); 3 *Restatement of Torts,* § 580, Comments (b) and (c), pp. 205–207.

[45] Authorities in Footnote 44.

[46] See also *Cosgrove Studio, Inc. v. Pane,* 408 Pa. 314, 182 A. 2d 751, 753: "The fact that the plaintiff is not specifically named in the advertisement is not controlling. A party defamed need not be specifically named, if pointed to by description or circumstances tending to identify him… ."

[47] Even Gershon Aaronson of the Times so read "they" as used in this paragraph of the advertisement (R. 745).

can suggest no one else except the police, whose massive acts in the public mind are surely the work of the commissioner. The connotation is irresistible—certainly not, as the Times argues, completely devoid of rationality.

Moreover, the jury heard witnesses who made the association. *Hope v. Hearst Consolidated Publications,* 294 F. 2d 681 (2d Cir.), cert. denied 368 U.S. 956; *Chagnon v. Union Leader Corp.,* 103 N. H. 426, 174 A. 2d 825, 831–832, cert. denied 369 U.S. 830.

Respondent sued as a member of a group comprising three city commissioners. Libel suits by members of private or public groups of this size are widely permitted. The decision below accords with the law generally.[48]

III. This case provides no occasion for excursions from this record and from accepted constitutional standards.

In a desperate effort to secure review in this Court, the Times and its friends go outside the record and refer this Court to other libel suits pending in Alabama. With the exception of two brought by the other Montgomery commissioners, all are erroneously and uncandidly labeled "companion cases."[49]

But the effort is as revealing as it is desperate. Clearly, petitioner feels that this case, standing on its own, does not present grounds for review.

These cases are not yet tried. There are different plaintiffs; different defendants; different publications; different communications media; different forums; different attorneys; different issues;[50] no final judgment in any; and a trial on the merits in only one of them. The Times urges

this Court to jettison libel laws that have existed since the founding of this Republic, and hold: (a) there is an absolute privilege to defame public officials, at least those living in Alabama; (b) private libel suits for defamation are available to all citizens of the United States in state courts according to state libel laws, but not to persons who happen to hold public office in Alabama; (c) plaintiffs in those cited cases shall be deprived of their rights to have their libel cases heard on their merits.

The Times seems to hint to this Court that because the publication contained statements regarding racial tensions, the law of libel should perforce "confront and be subordinated to" a constitutional privilege to defame.[51] Surely in a field so tense, truthful statements by huge and influential newspapers are imperative. For as this Court said in *Beauharnais,* 343 U.S. 250 at 262:

> "Only those lacking responsible humility will have a confident solution for problems as intractable as the frictions attributable to differences of race, color or religion."

The confrontation which the jury hoped to achieve was the confrontation of the Times with the truth.

The enormity of petitioner's wrong is clear. Hopefully the decision below will impel adherence by this immensely powerful newspaper to high standards of responsible journalism commensurate with its size.

> "A free press is vital to a democratic society because its freedom gives it power. Power in a democracy implies responsibility in its exercise. No institution in a democracy, either governmental or private, can have absolute

---

[48] *Hope v. Hearst Consolidated Publications,* 294 F. 2d 681 (2d Cir.), cert. denied 368 U.S. 956 (One of Palm Beach's richest men caught his blonde wife in a compromising spot with a former FBI agent); *Nieman-Marcus v. Lait,* 13 F. R. D. 311 (S. D. N. Y. 1952) (immoral acts attributed to department store's 9 models and 25 salesmen); *National Cancer Hospital v. Confidential, Inc.,* 136 N. Y. S. 2d 921 (libelous article about "hospital" gave cause of action to those who conducted hospital); *Weston v. Commercial Advertisers,* 184 N. Y. 479, 77 N. E. 660 (4 coroners); *Bornmann v. Star Co.,* 174 N. Y. 212, 66 N. E. 723 (charges about a hospital stall with 12 doctors in residence); *Chapa v. Abernethy* (Tex. Civ. App.), 175 S. W. 165 (charges about a posse); *Gross v. Cantor,* 270 N. Y. 93, 200 N. E. 592 (12 radio editors); *Fullerton v. Thompson,* 119 Minn. 136, 143 N. W. 260 (State Board of Medical Examiners, of which there were 9); *Children v. Shinn,* 168 Iowa 531, 150 N. W. 864 (Board of Supervisors); *Reilly v. Curtiss,* 53 N. J. 677, 84 A. 199 (an election board).

Commentators have agreed. See 3 *Restatement of Torts,* Sec. 564 (c), p. 152:

"[A] statement that all members of a school board or a city council are corrupt is sufficiently definite to constitute a defamatory publication of each member thereof." And see *Developments in the Law—Defamation,* 69 Harvard L. Rev. 894, et seq.

[49] Times' petition for certiorari, p. 19. Even the Times does not follow the reckless averment of its friends that this suit is part of an "attempt by officials in Alabama to invoke the libel laws against all those who had the temerity to criticize Alabama's conduct in the intense racial conflict" (Brief of Washington Post, p. 8).

[50] For example, the Times retracted for Patterson, but not for respondent. Obviously, the Times, while guilty of clear inconsistency, has nevertheless in Patterson's case sought to eliminate punitive damages by retraction, as permitted by Alabama statute.

[51] Times petition, p. 20 and *amici* briefs generally.

power. Nor can the limits of power which enforce responsibility be finally determined by the limited power itself. (Citation.) In plain English, freedom carries with it responsibility even for the press; freedom of the press is not a freedom from responsibility for its exercise. Most State constitutions expressly provide for liability for abuse of the press's freedom. That there was such legal liability was so taken for granted by the framers of the First Amendment that it was not spelled out. Responsibility for its abuse was imbedded in the law. The First Amendment safeguarded the right."[52]

These freedoms are amply protected when a newspaper in a state court can plead and prove truth; can plead and prove fair comment; and can plead and prove privilege. Even when it cannot, it can retract, show its good faith, and eliminate punitive damages. Alabama thus provides the very safeguards which, the Times and its friends argue, are essential to protect petitioner's constitutional rights.

When it can do none of these, and when it has indeed defamed in a commercial advertisement, no constitutional right, privilege or immunity expounded by this Court during its entire history shields a newspaper from damages in a common law libel suit.

The Times and its cohorts would have this Court abandon basic constitutional standards which have heretofore obtained and which Justice Harlan recently described:

"No member of this Court would disagree that the validity of state action claimed to infringe rights assured by the Fourteenth Amendment is to be judged by the same basic constitutional standards whether or not racial problems are involved."[53]

IV. The Times was properly before the Alabama courts.

1. Because both courts below held that the Times had made a general appearance,[54] an adequate independent state ground as to jurisdiction over the Times in this suit is a bar to review here. *Herb v. Pitcairn,* 324 U.S. 117, 125–126; *Murdock v. Memphis,* 20 Wall. 590, 626; *Fox Film Corporation v. Muller,* 296 U.S. 207, 210; *Minnesota v. National Tea Company,* 309 U.S. 551, 556–557.

The Times intended to assert, and did, that the trial court was without jurisdiction of the subject matter of this action. Indeed, the Times still argues in this Court that there was no juris-

diction of the subject matter (Brief, p. 63). This act, alone, is a general appearance in Alabama and in a majority of state courts. In addition, the Times compounded its general appearance by other activities in the Alabama courts unrelated to the claimed lack of personal jurisdiction.

Petitioner argues that the Alabama Supreme Court has incorrectly interpreted its own decisions, and that the decision below is in error. This is obviously the wrong forum for such an argument.[55]

But even if an examination of state law were appropriate, the court below followed its earlier cases. Alabama has held, as have other states, that there is a clear distinction between jurisdiction of the person and subject matter. *Constantine v. Constantine,* 261 Ala. 40, 42, 72 So. 2d 831. A party's appearance in a suit for any purpose other than to contest the court's jurisdiction over the person is a general appearance.[56]

The Alabama cases cited by the Times do not conflict with the decisions below. One case holds that a request for extension of time to file pleadings is not a general appearance;[57] another recognized that defendant might have converted a special appearance into a general appearance, but held that even so a circuit court had authority to set aside a default judgment within thirty days, and denied an extraordinary writ;[58] a third involved a limited attack on "the court jurisdiction over the person of defen-

---

[52] Frankfurter J., concurring in *Pennekamp v. Florida,* 328 U.S. 331, 355–356 (Footnotes omitted).

[53] *NAACP v. Button,* 371 U.S. 415, 9 L. Ed. 2d 405, 427 (dissenting opinion of Harlan, Clark and Stewart, J. J.).

[54] A state court's interpretation of its own case law is binding here. *Fox River Paper Company v. Railroad Commission,* 274 U.S. 651, 655; *Guaranty Trust Company v. Blodgett,* 287 U.S. 509, 513; *United Gas Pipeline Company v. Ideal Cement Company,* 369 U.S. 134.

Texas, for example, long provided that any appearance at all was a general appearance. *York v. Texas,* 137 U.S. 15, 20.

[55] See Footnote 54.

[56] *Kyser v. American Surety Company,* 213 Ala. 614, 616, 105 So. 689; *Blankenship v. Blankenship,* 263 Ala. 297, 303, 82 So. 2d 335; *Thompson v. Wilson,* 224 Ala. 299–300, 140 So. 439; *Aetna Insurance Company v. Earnest,* 215 Ala. 557, 112 So. 145. And see *Vaughan v. Vaughan,* 267 Ala. 117, 121, 100 So. 2d 1:

"[R]espondent … by not limiting her appearance and by including non-jurisdictional as well as jurisdictional grounds in her motion to vacate has made a general appearance and has thereby waived any defect or insufficiency of service."

[57] *Ex Parte Cullinan,* 224 Ala. 263, 139 So. 255.

[58] *Ex Parte Haisten,* 227 Ala. 183, 149 So. 213.

U.S. SUPREME COURT, OCTOBER 1963

BRIEF FOR RESPONDENT

dant;"[59] one did not even consider the question, since apparently neither the trial judge nor the parties had noticed it;[60] one discussed the proper way to plead misnomer;[61] and in the last two the defendants conceded jurisdiction of the person.[62]

Moreover, there is nothing novel about the Alabama holding of general appearance. This Court in such cases as *Western Loan & Savings Company v. Butte, etc. Mining Company*, 210 U.S. 368, 370 and *Davis v. Davis*, 305 U.S. 32, 42, as well as leading text writers,[63] and the majority of the jurisdictions of this country have recognized the binding effect of this rule.[64]

Petitioner argues that the general appearance ground is an untenable non-federal one. Its cases simply do not support its contention. No novel state procedure, of which a party could not fairly be deemed to have been apprised, thwarted all means of raising a federal question.[65] Nor is the Alabama rule—in accord with the majority one—an "arid ritual of meaningless form."[66] Clearly beside the point is a case where an admitted special appearance by a party, an officer appointed to run the railroads for the federal government, was not deemed by the state court to be a special appearance for his successor.[67]

Nor do petitioner's cases (pp. 76–77) support the contention that even if there had been jurisdiction by consent because of the general appearance, the commerce clause forbids its exercise. These cases simply hold that a carrier must be given an opportunity to make a seasonable objection to court jurisdiction, and cannot be deprived of doing so by state machinery making a special appearance a general one. Cf. *York v. Texas*, 137 U.S. 15, 20. Alabama does permit a special appearance, and does not prevent a "seasonable motion." But when a foreign corporation makes, instead, a general appearance, the commerce clause does not bar the exercise of court jurisdiction by consent.

Davis v. O'Hara, 266 U.S. 314, 318, discussed by the Times (Brief, pp. 74–75) involved Nebraska, not Alabama law, and held that under Nebraska practice a special appearance was not required to object to jurisdiction over the person.

2. Even if the Times had not made a general appearance in this case, effective service of process is based on decisions of this Court so explicit as to leave no room for real controversy. The Times, having already argued that this Court should cast aside its many decisions permitting libel suits against newspapers, now asks this Court to cast aside its cases permitting tort actions against foreign corporations in states where those corporations do business. In short, the Times seeks absolute immunity on the merits, and jurisdictional immunity from suit outside New York state.

The crucial test is simple. Did the Times have sufficient business contacts with Alabama so that suit against it there accorded with traditional concepts of fairness and orderly administration of the laws? *International Shoe Company v. Washington*, 326 U.S. 310, 319. The court below, and indeed the trial court, after painstaking analysis of the jurisdictional facts of record, held that there were sufficient contacts. The qualitative functions of a newspaper outlined in *Consolidated Cosmetics v. DA Publishing*

---

[59] *St. Mary's Oil Engine Company v. Jackson Ice & Fuel Company*, 224 Ala. 152, 155, 138 So. 834. See also *Sessoms Grocery Co. v. International Sugar Feed Co.*, 188 Ala. 232; *Terminal Oil Mill Co. v. Planters, etc. Co.*, 197 Ala. 429; and *Dozier Lumber Co. v. Smith-Isberg Lumber Co.*, 145 Ala. 317, also cited by the Times.

[60] *Harrub v. Hy-Trous Corp.*, 249 Ala. 414, 31 So. 2d 567.

[61] *Ex Parte Textile Workers*, 249 Ala. 136, 142, 30 So. 2d 247.

[62] *Seaboard Ry. v. Hubbard*, 142 Ala. 546, and *Johnson Publishing Co. v. Davis*, 271 Ala. 474, 124 So. 2d 441.

[63] *Restatement of Conflict*, § 82, Comment (b); and Kurland, *The Supreme Court, The Due Process Clause and The In Personam Jurisdiction of State Courts*, 25 U. of Chicago L. Rev. 569, 575:

"The mere appearance of a defendant in a lawsuit for a purpose other than to attack the jurisdiction of the court over him is considered a voluntary submission to the court's power."

[64] 25 A. L. R. 2d 835, 838 and 31 A. L. R. 2d 258, 265. New York itself prior to statutory amendment, held in *Jackson v. National Grain Mutual Liability Company*, 299 N. Y. 333, 87 N. E. 2d 283, 285:

"Under its special appearance, the defendant company could do nothing but challenge the jurisdiction of the Justice's court over its person ... (citation). Hence by its attempt to deny jurisdiction of the subject of the action, the company waived that special appearance and submitted its person to the jurisdiction of the court."

Civil Practice Act, § 273 (a), was necessary to enable a litigant to combine in New York an attack on jurisdiction of the person and of the subject matter without appearing generally in the action. *Ray v. Fairfax County Trust Company*, 186 N. Y. S. 2d 347.

[65] *NAACP v. Alabama*, 357 U.S. 449, and *Wright v. Georgia*, 373 U.S. 284.

[66] *Staub v. City of Baxley*, 355 U.S. 313, 320.

[67] *Davis v. Wechsler*, 263 U.S. 22.

Company, 186 F. 2d 906, 908 (7th Cir. 1951), were carried on in Alabama.

The Times plainly maintained an extensive and continuous pattern of business activity in Alabama at least since 1956. The resident string correspondents and staff correspondents, who repeatedly came into Alabama, were a unique and valuable complement to the news gathering facilities of the Associated Press and United Press and other wire services upon which smaller newspapers rely. Such widespread news gathering facilities unquestionably increase the scope and detail of the Times' news columns, and enhance, accordingly, its prestige, its circulation, and the prices which it can command in the advertising market. In turn, these far-flung news gathering tentacles subject the Times to potential suit in the states into which they reach. If financial reward comes to the Times from its on-the-spot news coverage in Alabama, it is fair that citizens of Alabama should be able to sue the Times here when it has wronged them.

Scoffing at the quantitative size of its business activities in Alabama, the Times apparently ignored the most recent pronouncement of this Court in *Scripto v. Carson,* 362 U.S. 207, cited by the courts below. *Scripto* derived less than half of the revenue from Florida which the Times has derived from Alabama—and regular employees of the Times have combined their efforts with those of independent dealers to produce this result.

The Times attempts to distinguish *Scripto* by the inaccurate observation that "no issue of judicial jurisdiction was involved" (Brief p. 85). But this Court's opinion in *Scripto* stated that the Florida courts had "held that appellant does have sufficient jurisdictional contacts in Florida [to be made a collector of use tax] … We agree with the result reached by Florida's courts" (362 U.S. 207, 208). While the Times would argue that due process standards for jurisdiction to sue are stricter than those for jurisdiction to make a tax collector out of a foreign corporation, objective commentators have not agreed. The due process clause "might well be deemed to impose more stringent limitations on collection requirements than on personal jurisdiction."[68]

One contract negotiated entirely by mail with a predecessor company gave California sufficient contact with a successor insurance company. A default judgment against it was upheld. *McGee v. International Insurance Company,* 355

U.S. 220.[69] Mail transactions alone enabled a Virginia Securities Commission to regulate an out-of-state insurance company. *Travelers Health Association v. Virginia,* 339 U.S. 643. And this Court, as noted in the decision below, commented upon more enlightened concepts resulting in expanded scope of state jurisdiction over foreign corporations. *McGee v. International Insurance Company,* 355 U.S. 220, 222–223. Moreover, state activity through the means of independent contractors, as distinguished from agents or employees, is without constitutional significance. *Scripto v. Carson,* 362 U.S. 207, 211. The Times does not cite *Scripto* on this point, but it is nevertheless the law.

A recent decision, interpreting Alabama's Substituted Service Statute, *Callagaz v. Calhoon,* 309 F. 2d 248, 256 (5th Cir. 1962) observed:

> "Since [*Travelers Health* and *McGee*] it is established that correspondence alone may establish sufficient contacts with a state to subject a non-resident to a suit in that state on a cause of action arising out of those contacts."

Justice Black's dissenting opinion in *Polizzi v. Cowles Magazines,* 345 U.S. 663, 667, considered a magazine publisher subject to Florida libel suit, under old or new concepts, when its only contact there was two circulation road men who checked retail outlets in a multi-state area which included Florida. Presumably no reporting or advertising solicitation was carried on. Mr. Justice Black's opinion, which has been widely quoted as expressive of the prevailing view, found it manifestly unfair to make the plaintiff "bring his libel suit in a federal district court in the corporation's home state of Iowa … [and not] in a federal court in the state where Polizzi lived and where the criminal charges were likely to do him the most harm" (345 U.S. 663 at 668).

Obviously the case at bar does not present an instance of "forum shopping" such as was

---

[68] *Developments in the Law—Federal Limitations on State Taxation of Interstate Business,* 75 Harvard L. Rev. 953, 998 (1962).

[69] Noteworthy is the fact that the foreign corporation held amenable to California process had never solicited or done any insurance business in California apart from the policy involved. The "continuing legal relationship" on the basis of which the Times attempts to distinguish *McGee* (Brief, p. 84) could not possibly consist of more than transmission of premiums by mail. Such "continuing legal relationship" scarcely compares with the vastly more extensive and continuing relationship which the Times maintained with Alabama according to evidence going back to 1956.

faced by Judge Hand in *Kilpatrick v. T. & P. Ry. Co.*, 166 F. 2d 788 (2d Cir. 1948). The court's remarks (quoted Brief, p. 81) were directed to a Texas plaintiff, injured in Texas, who had brought his suit in New York. Even so, the district court was reversed for dismissing the plaintiff's action.

McKee, an Alabama resident, conducted all of the usual activities of a stringer for the New York Times. In addition, he performed the delicate task, to which he "naturally" fell heir, of investigating respondent's demand for retraction. The Times was efficaciously brought into court by service on McKee. It is inconceivable, for example, that if while helping Harrison Salisbury obtain material for his Alabama stories, Don McKee had run an automobile into a plaintiff, the Times could have escaped liability by maintaining that McKee was an independent contractor.

Similarly substituted service under the Alabama statute[70] was valid. Alabama business activity of the Times preceded and followed the printing of this libelous material in New York. The ad itself was supposedly cleared on the basis of prior news gathering; it was later sent into Alabama by the Times, with a carrier as its agent, freight prepaid, with title passing on delivery to the consignee. Thence the issue went to newsstands for sale to the Alabama public, in accordance with the longstanding business practice of the Times.[71]

Scripto v. Carson, 362 U.S. 207, lays to rest the significance of any contention that sales to the public in Alabama were through the medium of independent contractors. It is not necessary for this Court to reach the question of whether isolated newsstand sales, disconnected from any other business activity in Alabama, would be a sufficient contact to sustain substituted service. This is not the case. For the Times has also solicited advertising and gathered news in a systematic and continuous fashion, and has thereby established a firm business connection with Alabama.[72]

Due process and the commerce clause do not immunize the Times from Alabama suit.

As *Polizzi* makes clear, newspapers are not to be in a special category. When other corporations may be sued in a foreign jurisdiction, so may they on similar facts. Newspaper corporations are no more entitled to the favored position which the Times and its friends would accord them than they are entitled to many other preferences for which they have unsuccessfully argued. In *Mabee v. White Plains Publishing Co.,* 327 U.S. 178, 184, this Court held: "As the press has business aspects, it has no special immunity from laws applicable to business in general." This case concerned the applicability of the Fair Labor Standards Act to newspapers. This Court has likewise held newspaper corporations subject to the National Labor Relations Act, *Associated Press v. N. L. R. B.,* 301 U.S. 103 and to the anti-trust laws, *Lorain Journal Company v. United States,* 342 U.S. 143.

Hanson v. Denckla, 357 U.S. 235, relied upon by the Times as contrary to the decisions below, is easily distinguishable. As this Court pointed out, there was no solicitation of business in Florida by the foreign corporation, either in person or by mail. In the case at bar the Times solicited business in both manners. The cause of action in *Hanson v. Denckla* did not arise out of an act done or transaction consummated in the forum. On the contrary, this cause of action arose out of the very distribution of the newspapers by the Times in Alabama. Surely the Times cannot contend that its introduction of these newspapers in Alabama was involuntary.[73] The

---

[70] Title 7, § 199 (1), Code of Alabama.

[71] If the cases cited by the Times (Brief, pp. 79–80) are supposed to conflict with the decision below, they conflict also with the decisions of this Court cited in this section of respondent's brief and by the court below. They conflict, too, with such cases as *Paulos v. Best Securities, Inc.* (Minn.), 109 N. W. 2d 576; *WSAZ v. Lyons,* 254 F. 2d 242 (6th Cir. 1958); *Gray v. American Radiator Corporation,* 22 Ill. 2d 432, 176 N. E. 2d 761; *Sanders Associates, Inc. v. Galion Iron Works,* 304 F. 2d 915 (1st Cir. 1962); *Beck v. Spindler* (Minn.), 99 N. W. 2d 670; and *Smyth v. Twin State Improvement Corporation,* 116 Vt. 569, 80 A. 2d 664. Moreover, the court in *Insull v. New York World-Telegram,* 273 F. 2d 166, 169 (7th Cir. 1959), indicated that its result would have been different if the newspa-

per "employ[ed] or ha[d] any reporters, advertising solicitors or other persons who are located in Illinois ..."

[72] A remarkably similar case is *WSAZ v. Lyons,* 254 F. 2d 242 (6th Cir. 1958), cited by the courts below. There the court upheld a Kentucky libel judgment against a foreign television station which had beamed the libelous television matter into Kentucky from outside the state. Service was had under a Kentucky statute covering causes of action "arising out of" or "connected" with the doing of business by foreign corporations in Kentucky. The court cited *McGee* and *International Shoe.* Moreover, it held irrelevant the fact that Kentucky produced only 1.03 per cent of the total annual advertising revenue.

[73] But compare Times Brief, p. 81.

foreign corporation in *Hanson v. Denckla* had received no benefit from the laws of the forum. The manifold business activities of the Times—news gathering, solicitation of advertising and distribution—have received the protection of Alabama laws.

Finally (Brief, pp. 86–88) the Times suggests that even though it might be amenable to suit in Alabama under due process standards, the commerce clause nevertheless bars the Alabama action. The most recent decision of this Court cited in support of this proposition was handed down in 1932. It seems scarcely necessary to observe that this Court, which has developed enlightened standards giving expanded scope to jurisdiction over foreign corporations in such cases as *International Shoe, McGee, Travelers Health* and *Scripto* will not grant review to turn the clock back to 1932, and invoke the rigid concepts of earlier days under the aegis of the commerce clause. And the Times must concede that this Court has not "hitherto" held that tort actions against foreign corporations—fairly subject to *in personam* jurisdiction—are unconstitutional as undue burdens on interstate commerce (Brief, p. 87).

Accordingly, even without a general appearance, the Times would have presented no unsettled federal question of jurisdiction for review by this Court on certiorari.

CONCLUSION

For the foregoing reasons it is respectfully submitted that the writ of certiorari should be dismissed as improvidently granted; in the alternative, respondent respectfully submits that this case should be affirmed.

Respectfully submitted,

ROBERT E. STEINER III,

SAM RICE BAKER,

M. ROLAND NACHMAN JR.,

Attorneys for Respondent.

STEINER, CRUM & BAKER,

CALVIN WHITESELL,

Of Counsel.

CERTIFICATE

I, M. Roland Nachman, Jr., of Counsel for Respondent, and a member of the bar of this Court, hereby certify that I have mailed copies of the foregoing Brief and of respondent's Brief in No. 40, *Abernathy v. Sullivan*, air mail, postage prepaid, to Messrs. Lord, Day & Lord, Counsel for petitioner, at their offices at 25 Broadway, New York, New York. I also certify that I have mailed a copy of the foregoing Brief, air mail, postage prepaid, to Edward S. Greenbaum, Esquire, 285 Madison Avenue, New York, New York, as attorney for American Civil Liberties Union and the New York Civil Liberties Union, as *amici curiae;* to Messrs. Kirkland, Ellis, Hodson, Chaffetz & Masters, attorneys for The Tribune Company, as *amicus curiae,* at their offices at 130 East Randolph Drive, Chicago 1, Illinois; and to William P. Rogers, Esquire, attorney for The Washington Post Company, as *amicus curiae,* at his office at 200 Park Avenue, New York 17, New York.

This … day of October, 1963.

… … … … … … … … … .. .

M. Roland Nachman Jr.,

Of Counsel for Respondent.

APPENDIX A

Title 7, Section 909 of the Code of Alabama:

"TRUTH OF THE WORDS, ETC., EVIDENCE UNDER THE GENERAL ISSUE.—In all actions of slander or libel, the truth of the words spoken or written, or the circumstances under which they were spoken or written, may be given in evidence under the general issue in mitigation of the damages."

Truth specially pleaded is an absolute bar to a civil libel action, *Webb v. Gray,* 181 Ala. 408, 62 So. 194; *Ripps v. Herrington,* 241 Ala. 209, 212, 1 So. 2d 899; *Johnson Publishing Co. v. Davis,* 271 Ala. 474, 124 So. 2d 441.

Title 7, Section 910 of the Code of Alabama:

"LIBEL OR SLANDER; DEFAMATORY MATTER.—In an action for libel or slander, it shall be sufficient to state, generally, that the defamatory matter was published or spoken of the plaintiff; and if the allegation be denied, the plaintiff must prove, on the trial, the facts showing that the defamatory matter was published or spoken of him."

Title 7, Section 913 of the Code of Alabama:

"RETRACTION MITIGATES DAMAGES.—The defendant in an action of slander or libel may prove under the general issue in mitigation of damages that the charge was made by mistake or through inadvertence, and that he has retracted the charge and offered amends before suit by publishing an apology in a newspaper when the charge had been thus promulgated, in a prominent position; or

U.S. SUPREME
COURT,
OCTOBER 1963

BRIEF FOR
RESPONDENT

verbally, in the presence of witnesses, when the accusation was verbal or written, and had offered to certify the same in writing."

Title 7, Section 914 of the Code of Alabama:

"AGGRIEVED PERSON MUST GIVE NOTICE TO PUBLISHERS OF ALLEGED LIBEL BEFORE VINDICTIVE DAMAGES CAN BE RECOVERED.—Vindictive or punitive damages shall not be recovered in any action for libel on account of any publication concerning the official conduct or actions of any public officer, or for the publication of any matter which is proper for public information, unless five days before the bringing of the suit the plaintiff shall have made written demand upon the defendant for a public retraction of the charge or matter published; and the defendant shall have failed or refused to publish within five days in as prominent and public a place or manner as the charge or matter published occupied, a full and fair retraction of such charge or matter."

Title 7, Section 915 of the Code of Alabama:

"WHEN ACTUAL DAMAGES ONLY RE-COVERABLE.— If it shall appear on the trial of an action for libel that an article com-

plained of was published in good faith, that its falsity was due to mistake and misapprehension, and that a full correction or retraction of any false statement therein was published in the next regular issue of said newspaper, or in case of daily newspapers, within five days after service of said notice aforesaid, in as conspicuous a place and type in said newspaper as was the article complained of, then the plaintiff in such case shall recover only actual damages."

Title 7, Section 916 of the Code of Alabama:

"RECANTATION AND TENDER; EFFECT OF.—If the Defendant, after or before suit brought, make the recantation and amends recited in the preceding sections, and also tender to the plaintiff a compensation in money, and bring the same into court, the plaintiff can recover no costs, if the jury believe and find the tender was sufficient."

Title 7, Section 917 of the Code of Alabama:

"EFFECT OF TENDER RECEIVED.—The receipt of the money tendered, if before suit brought, is a bar to the action; if after suit, releases the defendant from all damages and costs, except the costs which accrued before the tender and receipt of the money."

In the Supreme Court of the United States

October Term, 1963

No. 40

RALPH D. ABERNATHY,
FRED L. SHUTTLESWORTH,
S. S. SEAY, SR., AND
J. F. LOWERY, PETITIONERS,
V.
L. B. SULLIVAN, RESPONDENT

ON WRIT OF CERTIORARI TO THE SUPREME COURT OF ALABAMA

BRIEF FOR THE PETITIONERS

Harry H. Wachtel,
Samuel R. Pierce Jr.,
Joseph B. Russell,
David N. Brainin,
Stephen J. Jelin,
Clarence B. Jones,
David G. Lubell,
Charles B. Markham,
Wachtel & Michaelson,
Battle, Fowler, Stokes & Kheel,
Lubell, Lubell & Jones,
Of Counsel.
Of Counsel.
I. H. Wachtel,
Charles S. Conley,
Benjamin Spiegel,
Raymond S. Harris,
Attorneys for Petitioners.
1100 - 17th St., N.W.
Washington, D.C. 20036

Index

—⚍—

Petitioners Abernathy, Shuttlesworth, Seay, and Lowery submit this brief for reversal of the judgment of the Supreme Court of Alabama entered on August 30, 1962, which affirmed a $500,000 libel judgment for punitive damages entered on November 3, 1960 in the Circuit Court of Montgomery County, Alabama against petitioners and The New York Times Company, their co-defendant, in a suit for alleged libel, based on an advertisement (R. 6, 1925; reproduced in Appendix A *infra*, p. 63) printed in The New York Times on March 29, 1960, appealing for contributions to aid the civil rights movement in the South.

OPINIONS BELOW

The Trial Court (Circuit Court of Montgomery County) did not write an opinion. Its judgment is printed at R. 862. The Opinion of the Alabama Supreme Court (R. 1139) affirming said judgment is reported at 273 Ala. 656.

JURISDICTION

The judgment of the Supreme Court of Alabama was entered on August 30, 1962 (R. 1180). The petition for writ of certiorari was filed on November 21, 1962 and was granted on January 7, 1963, 371 U.S. 946 (R. 1194). The jurisdiction of this Court rests upon 28 U. S. C. § 1257(3).[1]

QUESTIONS PRESENTED[2]

1. May the State of Alabama, under the guise of civil libel prosecutions, suppress criticism of the political conduct of unnamed public officials, consistently with the guaranteed freedoms of speech, press, assembly and association of the First and Fourteenth Amendments?

2. Were petitioners' rights to due process of law, as guaranteed by the Fourteenth Amendment, violated by a $500,000 punitive judgment against them upon a record devoid of evidence of authorization, consent, publication or malice on their part or of pecuniary damage to respondent?

3. Does the rule of law adopted by the State of Alabama below, requiring total strangers to the challenged publication, to procure and study it and, under pain of $500,000 punitive damages, "retract" any claimed libel therein, impose an arbitrary and onerous burden which unconstitutionally infringes petitioners' rights under the First and Fourteenth Amendments?

4. Were the rights of Negro petitioners to equal protection, due process of law and fair and impartial trial under the Fourteenth Amendment violated by the trial of the suit brought against them by a white public official of Montgomery (i) in a segregated Courtroom, rife with racial bias and community hostility, (ii) before an all-white jury (from which Negro citizens were intentionally and systematically

excluded), and (iii) before a trial judge, not properly qualified, who has stated from the Bench that the Fourteenth Amendment is inapplicable in Alabama Courts, which are governed by "white man's justice"?[3]

CONSTITUTIONAL AND STATUTORY PROVISIONS INVOLVED

The Constitutional provisions involved are the First, Fourteenth and Fifteenth Amendments to the United States Constitution which are set forth in Appendix B, *infra,* pp. 65–66.

The Statutes involved are Title 7, Sections 913–16 of the Code of Alabama (i.e., the Alabama "Retraction" Statute) and Title 14, Sections 347 and 350 thereof (i.e., the Alabama "Criminal Libel" Statute) which read as follows:

Title 7, Section 913 of the Code of Alabama:

"RETRACTION MITIGATES DAMAGES.— The defendant in an action of slander or libel may prove under the general issue in mitigation of damages that the charge was made by mistake or through inadvertence, and that he has retracted the charge and offered amends before suit by publishing an apology in a newspaper when the charge had been thus promulgated, in a prominent position; or verbally, in the presence of witnesses, when the accusation was verbal or written, and had offered to certify the same in writing."

Title 7, Section 914 of the Code of Alabama:

"AGGRIEVED PERSON MUST GIVE NOTICE TO PUBLISHERS OF ALLEGED LIBEL BEFORE VINDICTIVE DAMAGES CAN BE RECOVERED.—Vindictive or punitive damages shall not be recovered in any action for libel on account of any publication

---

[1] By letter of the Clerk of this Court dated August 9, 1963, the time of petitioners to file this brief has been extended to September 9, 1963.
[2] Influenced by the landmark decisions of this Court in the "sit in" cases (n. 6, *infra*), *NAACP* v. *Button,* 371 U.S. 415 and *Johnson* v. *Virginia,* 373 U.S. 61 among others, and the historic events which have taken place since the filing of the petition for writ of certiorari herein on November 21, 1962, petitioners have in this brief consolidated the five questions there presented to this Court so as to focus their argument on the all-pervasive issue of the impingement on and serious threat to their First and Fourteenth Amendment rights.
[3] Judge Jones *On Courtroom Segregation,* 22 The Alabama Lawyer, No. 2, pp. 190–192 (1961), which reprints "Statement made from the Bench of the Circuit Court of Montgomery County, February 1, 1961, ..." during the trial of the related libel action by Mayor Earl James of Montgomery against The New York Times Company and the four Negro petitioners herein. On March 17, 1961, Judge Jones entered his order denying the new trial application herein (R. 970).

concerning the official conduct or actions of any public officer, or for the publication of any matter which is proper for public information, unless five days before the bringing of the suit the plaintiff shall have made written demand upon the defendant for a public retraction of the charge or matter published; and the defendant shall have failed or refused to publish within five days in as prominent and public a place or manner as the charge or matter published occupied, a full and fair retraction of such charge or matter."

Title 7, Section 915 of the Code of Alabama:

"WHEN ACTUAL DAMAGES ONLY RECOVERABLE.—If it shall appear on the trial of an action for libel that an article complained of was published in good faith, that its falsity was due to mistake and misapprehension, and that a full correction or retraction of any false statement therein was published in the next regular issue of said newspaper, or in case of daily newspapers, within five days after service of said notice aforesaid, in as conspicuous a place and type in said newspaper as was the article complained of, then the plaintiff in such case shall recover only actual damages."

Title 7, Section 916 of the Code of Alabama:

"RECANTATION AND TENDER; EFFECT OF.—If the defendant, after or before suit brought, make the recantation and amends recited in the preceding sections, and also tender to the plaintiff a compensation in money, and bring the same into court, the plaintiff can recover no costs, if the jury believe and find the tender was sufficient."

Title 14, Section 347 of the Code of Alabama:

"LIBEL.—Any person who publishes a libel of another which may tend to provoke a breach of the peace, shall be punished, on conviction, by fine and imprisonment in the county jail, or hard labor for the county; the fine not to exceed in any case five hundred dollars, and the imprisonment or hard labor not to exceed six months."

Title 14, Section 350 of the Code of Alabama:

"DEFAMATION.—Any person who writes, prints, or speaks of and concerning any woman, falsely imputing to her a want of chastity; and any person who speaks, writes, or prints of and concerning another any accusation falsely and maliciously importing the commission by such person of a felony, or any other indictable offense involving moral turpitude, shall, on conviction, be punished by fine not exceeding five hundred dollars, and imprisonment in the county jail, or sentenced to hard labor for the county, not

exceeding six months; one or both, at the discretion of the jury.

STATEMENT

Numerous recent decisions of this Court[4] have focused sharply on the intense nationwide efforts to secure the constitutional rights of Negroes, and on the numerous unconstitutional acts committed in various Southern states to frustrate these efforts. The four petitioners herein are Negro ministers (resident in Alabama at all relevant times) and religious and spiritual leaders of the movement to secure civil rights in Alabama and throughout the South.

1. The nature of the publication

To enlist public support and raise funds for the legal defense of Dr. Martin Luther King, Jr. (who shortly before had been indicted in Alabama for perjury)[5,] and in aid of the nonviolent demonstrations against racial segregation, a New York group called "The Committee to Defend Martin Luther King and the Struggle for Freedom in the South" ("Committee" hereinafter), with which petitioners had no connection, caused to be printed and published in The New York Times ("*The Times*" hereinafter) on March 29, 1960, an advertisement entitled: "Heed Their Rising Voices" (R. 6; Pl. Ex. 347 at R. 1925, reproduced in full in Appendix "A" p. 63, *infra*). The advertisement commented on the activities of *unnamed* governmental authorities, in cities in a number of Southern states, designed to stifle the then-current protest demonstrations[6] against segregation by students in various Southern institutions (including Alabama State College at Montgomery). In commenting on such activities, the advertise-

---

[4] *United States* v. *Alabama,* 373 U.S. 545; *United States* v. *Barnett,* 373 U.S. 920; *NAACP* v. *Alabama,* 357 U.S. 449; *Louisiana ex rel. Gremillion* v. *NAACP,* 366 U.S. 293; *Fair* v. *Meredith,* 305 F. 2d 341 (C. A. 5), cert. den., 371 U.S. 828; *Brown* v. *Board of Education,* 347 U.S. 483; *Holmes* v. *City of Atlanta,* 350 U.S. 879; *Cooper* v. *Aaron,* 358 U.S. 1; *Morgan* v. *Virginia,* 328 U.S. 373.

[5] Dr. King was later acquitted of this charge (R. 680).

[6] See Pollitt, *Dime Store Demonstrations: Events and Legal Problems of First 60 days,* Duke L. J. 315 (Summer, 1960), describing in detail (at 323–325) repressive acts and statements of Alabama public officials.

This Court has already reversed as unconstitutional a number of such repressive actions of officials of various Southern States including Alabama. *Shuttlesworth* v. *City of Birmingham,* 373 U.S. 262; *Gober* v. *City of Birmingham,* 373 U.S. 374; *Peterson* v. *City of Greenville,* 373 U.S. 244; *Garner* v. *Louisiana,* 368 U.S. 157; *Lombard* v. *Louisiana,* 373 U.S. 267.

ment used the broad, generic term "Southern violators of the Constitution".

The ad referred to the harassments to which Rev. King had been subjected, including arrests, imprisonment, the bombings of his home, and the then-pending perjury indictment, and concluded with an appeal for contributions to be sent to the Committee's office in New York in support of Dr. King's defense, the desegregation movement, and the voter registration drive in the South.

Under the text of the appeal appeared the names of some sixty eminent sponsors (including Mrs. Eleanor Roosevelt, Drs. Harry Emerson Fosdick, Mordecai Johnson, Alan Knight Chalmers and Algernon Black, and Messrs. Raymond Pace Alexander, Elmer Rice and Norman Thomas).

Below the list of sponsors appeared the caption "We in the south who are struggling daily for dignity and freedom warmly endorse this appeal", under which caption were printed the names of eighteen (18) ministers from various Southern states, including the four petitioners.

The appeal concludes with the following plea for funds:

> "We must extend ourselves above and beyond moral support and render the material help so urgently needed by those who are taking the risks, facing jail, and even death in a glorious re-affirmation of our Constitution and its Bill of Rights.

> "We urge you to join hands with our fellow Americans in the South by supporting, with your dollars, this Combined Appeal for all three needs—the defense of Martin Luther King—the support of the embattled students—and the struggle for the right-to-vote."

2. The evidence concerning publication

The undisputed record facts demonstrate that the names of petitioners were added to the advertisement without consultation with them and without their authorization or consent (R. 788–90; 792–4; 797–8; 801–2; 806–10; 824–5; 1175). Indeed, the record is clear that their first knowledge of *The Times* ad came when they received in the mail respondent Sullivan's identical letters which had been posted on or about April 8, 1960, and which were admittedly misdated "March 8, 1960" (Pl. Exs. 355–8, R. 1962–7). Moreover, these letters did not contain a copy of the ad, but merely quoted out of context the two paragraphs on which Sullivan based

his complaint, and demanded that each petitioner "publish in as prominent and public a manner" as *The Times* ad, "a full and fair retraction of the entire false and defamatory matter …" (R. 1962–8). Petitioners could not possibly comply with this demand; and, before they could consult counsel or even receive appropriate advice in regard thereto, suit was instituted by respondent on April 19, 1960 (R. 789; 793; 798; 801–3).

The undisputed record facts further show a complete lack of connection between petitioners and the publication of the advertisement. The typescript was submitted to *The Times* by one John Murray (R. 732), with a space order from The Union Advertising Service (R. 736). Names of sponsors (the Committee) were typed at the foot (R. 739). Accompanying (or submitted shortly following) the typescript was a letter, signed by A. Philip Randolph, (R. 739, 756–757) purporting to authorize the use of the names of the "signed members of the Committee" as sponsors (R. 1992). It is not disputed that petitioners' names did not appear on the manuscript as submitted (R. 806–7). Petitioners' names were subsequently placed on the advertisement by one Bayard Rustin, on his own motion, without any consultation with petitioners as shown by the undisputed evidence (R. 808–810) and the findings of the Court below (R. 1174–5). No representative of *The Times* ever asked petitioners whether they had consented to this use of their names (R. 754–5, 770, 790, 793, 797–8, 802).

None of the petitioners saw the *full text* of the advertisement prior to the commencement on April 19, 1960 of respondent Sullivan's suit (R. 789, 793, 798, 801); petitioners' first notice of *The Times* ad (and only of the language complained of) came from Sullivan's aforementioned misdated letters mailed on or about April 8, 1960 (R. 789, 793, 798, 802). Petitioners each wholly denied any knowledge of the ad prior to its publication, any consent to the use of their names and any responsibility for its publication (R. 788–90, 792–4, 795, 797–8, 801–2). Respondent in no way disputed these record facts which are confirmed in the opinion of the Court below (R. 1174–5).

3. The alleged libel

The Times ad in suit, without identifying or naming any particular individual or fixing any particular time period, refers to various incidents of claimed repression in numerous cities throughout the South, commencing with "Orangeburg, South Carolina" and continuing on to "Montgomery, Alabama" and "Tallahassee, Atlanta, Nashville, Savannah, Greensboro, Charlotte and a host of other cities in the South… ."

On October 5, 1959, respondent Sullivan became one of the City Commissioners of Montgomery, Alabama (R. 694). Nowhere in *The Times* ad in suit was respondent Sullivan or any other southern official referred to by name or office. Many of the repressive actions in Montgomery, referred to in the ad, occurred prior to Sullivan's term of office, as Sullivan himself admitted (R. 703–19).

The entire *gravamen* of Sullivan's complaint (which alleged no special damage but sought $500,000 as punitive damages) concerned the following two paragraphs of the advertisement (*i.e.*, the third and sixth), which were alleged to be defamatory:

> "In Montgomery, Alabama, after students sang 'My Country, 'Tis of Thee' on the State Capitol steps, their leaders were expelled from school, and truckloads of police armed with shotguns and tear-gas ringed the Alabama State College Campus. When the entire student body protested to state authorities by refusing to re-register, their dining hall was padlocked in an attempt to starve them into submission."

> *********

> "Again and again the Southern violators have answered Dr. King's peaceful protests with intimidation and violence. They have bombed his home almost killing his wife and child. They have assaulted his person. They have arrested him seven times—for 'speeding', 'loitering' and similar 'offenses'. And now they have charged him with 'perjury'—a *felony* under which they could imprison him for *ten years*." (R. 2–4).

Although Sullivan's complaint (R. 2–3) and his letters to petitioner demanding retraction (R. 1962–7) suggest that the above quoted paragraphs followed one another in consecutive order in *The Times* ad in suit, the record fact is that the first paragraph quoted is separated from the second by two lengthy paragraphs comprising almost a complete column of the ad—one relating to events in numerous cities in Southern states other than Alabama, and the other lauding Dr. King as the "world famous leader of the Montgomery Bus Protest" and the symbol of

"the new spirit now sweeping the South" (Pl. Ex. 347, R. 1923–6, reproduced in full in Appendix "A" hereto).

Moreover, Sullivan's entire claim of libel rests on the following minor discrepancy: whereas the ad said that "truckloads" of armed police "ringed the Alabama State College Campus," the fact was that "on three occasions they [police] were deployed near the Campus in large numbers" (R. 594).

Clearly no distinction of substance can validly be drawn between police "ringing" the campus and being "deployed near the campus in large numbers"—particularly in the context of comment and criticism of official conduct on this most vital public issue.

Further, the ad said that Dr. King was arrested "seven times". The testimony was that he was arrested three or four times in Montgomery, Alabama (three of which arrests admittedly occurred prior to the respondent's term of office) (R. 592, 594–5); but there is nothing in the text or context of the advertisement which either requires or permits the inference that the seven arrests occurred in Montgomery or anywhere else in Alabama. Other alleged inaccuracies in the ad were conceded by respondent Sullivan to refer to matters within the jurisdiction of the State Education Department or other agencies, and to matters occurring long prior to respondent's taking office (R. 684–5, 688, 694, 701, 716, 719, 725).

None of Sullivan's witnesses (four of whom first saw the ad when called to the office of plaintiff's counsel shortly before the trial to be prepared as witnesses) testified that they believed the ad, or that they thought any less of respondent by reason of its publication (R. 623, 625, 636, 638, 644, 647, 651, 667).

4. Biased trial and judgment

Alabama has enacted sweeping racial segregation laws,[7] which reflect the community hostilities and prejudices that were funneled

---

[7] See Southern School News, August 1960, Vol. 9, No. 2, p. 1, (no desegregation in Alabama schools);

Alabama Code Recompiled 1958, Title 44 § 10 (Segregation of paupers) *id.*, Title 45 §§ 52, 121–3 (Segregation of prisoners) *id.*, Title 48 § 186 (Segregation of railroad waiting rooms) *id.*, Title 48 §§ 196–7 (Segregation of railroad coaches) *id.*, Title 48 § 301 (31a) (Segregation of motor busses) *id.*, Title 51 § 244 (Accounts of poll taxes paid by each race must be kept separate) *id.*, Title 52 § 613(1)

U.S. SUPREME COURT, OCTOBER 1963

BRIEF FOR THE PETITIONERS

U.S. SUPREME
COURT,
OCTOBER 1963

BRIEF FOR THE
PETITIONERS

into the Courtroom. Continuous denunciations of the defendants and of the material in the advertisement appeared in Montgomery newspapers prior to the trial, and continued throughout the trial and while the defendants' motions for new trial and appeals were pending (R. 1999–2243; 871–89). The trial itself took place in a carnival-like atmosphere, with press photographers in the Courtroom taking pictures of all the jurors for the two local newspapers (R. 951, 955), and television cameras following the jury to the very door of the juryroom[8] (R. 889–90, 2242). Two Montgomery newspapers, one on its front page, carried the names of the jurors (R. 2079–80, 952).

This suit was tried in November 1960, in Montgomery County, before Judge Walter B. Jones, and an all-white jury. The Trial Judge himself was a member of the jury commission of Montgomery County, the group responsible for the selection of the jury panel (R. 936, 971), from which Negroes have been intentionally and systematically excluded.

Respondent Sullivan's counsel was permitted by the Trial Judge, without restraint, over objections of petitioners' counsel, to indulge in such inflammatory appeals to racial bias as the mispronunciation of the word "Negro" as "Nigra" and "Nigger" in the presence of the jury, (R. 579–80), and in an invidious reference in his summation to purported events in the Congo (R. 929–30, 939–41). The Opinion of the Alabama Supreme Court below, in condoning such conduct, accepts counsel's lame excuse that he pronounced "the word 'negro' " as he did because that was the way he had pronounced it "all my life"[9] (R. 1168–9).

Throughout the proceedings below, petitioners took all possible steps to preserve their constitutional rights. They demurred to the complaint (R. 15–24) and filed Amended Demurrers (R. 74–99); their demurrers, as amended, were all overruled (R. 108–9). They made numerous proper objections and excepted to the repeated admission of improper testimony of respondent's witnesses (R. 1102–09). They twice moved to exclude plaintiffs' evidence (R. 109–14, 728, 816), which motions were denied (R. 728, 816–17). They made motions for special findings (R. 114–18) and submitted written requests to charge (see R. 827); they made due and timely objections and exceptions to the denial of their motions and requests. Petitioners moved (see, *e.g.*, R. 109–14; 728, 816) for a dismissal at the end of plaintiff's case and for a directed verdict at the conclusion of the entire case, which motions were denied (R. 728, 816–18). Each petitioner duly and timely submitted a motion for new trial (R. 970–1028) on which Judge Jones refused to rule. This evasion of duty by the trial court was, in turn, seized upon by the Alabama Supreme Court as a pretext for denying review (R. 1169–70).

The treatment afforded petitioners' motions for new trial underlines the repeated denial to petitioners of proper opportunity to be heard below. On December 2, 1960 petitioners properly and timely made, filed and submitted motions for new trials. Petitioners duly appeared, in compliance with Title 13, Sec. 119 of the Alabama Code, on December 16, 1960, the day to which said motions (and the motions of their co-defendant, The New York Times) had been continued. On March 3, 1961, the day on which, the general understanding was, the motions of petitioners and The New York Times would be heard together, the Trial Court heard extensive argument on behalf of The New York Times in support of its motion for a new trial and then refused to hear petitioners' counsel, or permit him to argue, or allow him even to make a statement for the record (R. 895–6). Despite the fact that he had petitioners' papers properly before him, Judge Jones erroneously refused repeated demands by petitioners' counsel for rulings on their motions for new trials (R. 984, 998–9, 1013, 1027–8). On March 17, 1961, Judge Jones denied the Times' motion for a new trial (R. 970); arbitrarily, he never ruled on petitioners' motions (R. 895–6).

All of the foregoing rulings were properly objected to and challenged, and embodied in petitioners' Assignments of Error to the Ala-

---

(Segregation of delinquents) *id.,* Title 45 § 4 (Segregation of tubercular patients) *id.,* Title 45 § 248 (Segregation of patients in mental institutions) *cf. Green* v. *State,* 58 Ala. 190 (no intermarriage).

[8] The Judicial Conference of the United States strongly condemned such practices "as inconsistent with fair judicial proceedings ..." by resolution adopted at its meeting in March 1962 (See New York Law Journal, July 13, 1962, at p. 1).

[9] *Cf. Screws* v. *United States,* 325 U.S. 91, 135, where Mr. Justice Murphy stated in dissent: "As such, he [Robert Hall, a Negro citizen] was entitled to all the respect and fair treatment that befits the dignity of man, a dignity that is recognized and guaranteed by the Constitution." [Brackets added].

bama Supreme Court, duly filed therein and affixed to the certified transcript Record duly submitted and filed with this Court (R. 1100–1132).

In this setting and notwithstanding the complete absence of any evidence of or legal basis for liability of petitioners or any showing of actual damage suffered by respondent, the jury, upon the clearly erroneous instructions of the Trial Judge (R. 819–28), on November 3, 1960 rendered a one sentence verdict in "favor of the plaintiff" in the sum of $500,000 (R. 862), on which the Trial Judge entered judgment[10] (R. 863).

SUMMARY OF ARGUMENT

The State of Alabama and its public officials have developed refined and sophisticated schemes of repression, striking directly at the rights of free speech and press, the roots of our democracy. To silence people from criticizing and protesting their wrongful segregation activities, Alabama officials now seek to utilize civil libel prosecutions which require still less proof than was required under the infamous Sedition Act of 1798, 1 Stat. 596.

The libel prosecutions and enormous judgment herein are clearly induced by Alabama's massive "cradle to grave" statutory system of racial segregation, and clearly constitute another "ingenious" scheme by the State of Alabama and its public officials to suppress criticism of the political conduct of Southern public officials. As such, they clearly constitute prohibited state action and cannot be protected from review by mere labels such as "libel per se."

The preferred First and Fourteenth Amendments' freedoms of speech, press, assembly and association are the very cornerstone of the Bill of Rights. Moreover, the constitutional protection of criticism of the political conduct and actions of public officials extends even to exaggerations and inaccuracies.

Since " … public men are as it were, public property" (*Beauharnais* v. *Illinois,* 343 U.S. 250, 263), criticism and defamation of their official conduct is clearly within the protections guaranteed by the First and Fourteenth Amendments. The judgment and proceedings below clearly abridge these basic constitutional protections, especially in view of the vital public interest in the integration struggle, the role of petitioners as spiritual leaders of the non-violent resistance movement, and the unconscionable penalty imposed below.

In addition to their patent disregard of these preferred constitutional protections, the Alabama Courts rendered and affirmed the judgment below on a record devoid of evidence of publication by petitioners, evidence of their consent to or authorization of publication, or evidence of damage of any kind to respondent due to the publication of the alleged libel. This disregard is all the more flagrant where the libel alleged is based solely on one claimed minor discrepancy in an advertisement (which is substantially correct) that nowhere mentions respondent by name or refers to him by office or title. Further, they attempted to meet petitioners' defenses that they had not published the ad and that it was not libelous, by adopting definitions of libel, libel per se and ratification, so strained, vague and detached from established legal principles as to amount in and of themselves to unconstitutional infringements of petitioners' rights.

Moreover, imposition of such liability because of petitioners' silence abridges petitioners' First Amendment rights of free association and belief.

Coupled with all of these violations of basic rights is the fact that the trial proceedings patently denied petitioners due process and equal protection of laws. Clearly, when four Negro ministers are sued by a white City Commissioner for an ad seeking support for Dr. Martin Luther King, and the case is tried in a segregated court room in Montgomery, Alabama, during a Civil War Centennial, before an all-white jury and a trial judge elected at polls from which Negroes were excluded, and when that very Judge states that "white man's justice" governs in his court and permits respondent's counsel to say "Nigger" and "Nigra" to the jury, then the Fourteenth Amendment does indeed become the "pariah" that the Trial Judge below called it. (See n. 20, pp. 26–27, *infra*; n. 3, p. 3, *supra*).

U.S. SUPREME COURT, OCTOBER 1963

BRIEF FOR THE PETITIONERS

---

[10] *The Times*' Trial Counsel stated that the Sullivan verdict "could only have been the result of the passion and prejudice revived by that celebration [the Centennial Commemoration] and other events embraced within that Civil War celebration" and the failure of the Court to adjourn the trial even during the day "while ceremonies took place changing the name of the Court Square to "Confederate Square" (R. 2222); and again that plaintiff [Sullivan] "was allowed to present the case to the jury as a sectional conflict rather than as a cause of action for libel" (R. 944).

U.S. SUPREME
COURT,
OCTOBER 1963

BRIEF FOR THE
PETITIONERS

ARGUMENT

I. This court must nullify schemes which encroach on freedom of utterance under the guise of punishing libel The century-long struggle of the Negro people for complete emancipation and full citizenship has been met at each step by a distinct pattern of resistance, with only the weapons changing, from lynching, violence and intimidation, through restrictive covenants, Black Codes,[11] and Jim Crow laws, to avoidance, "interposition," "nullification," tokenism and open contempt. Into this pattern, the case at bar fits naturally as a further refinement.

In recent years, when tremendous advances have occurred, "when growing self-respect has inspired the Negro with a new determination to struggle and sacrifice until first-class citizenship becomes a reality" (King, *Stride Toward Freedom* 154 (1958)), when there has come "an awakening moral consciousness on the part of millions of white Americans concerning segregation" (*id.*, p. 154), a national crisis has developed. This crisis was created when the aspirations of the Negroes were met "with tenacious and determined resistance" by "the guardians of the status quo," which "resistance grows out of the desperate attempt of the White South to perpetuate a system of human values that came into being under a feudalistic plantation system which cannot survive" today (*id.*, pp. 155, 156, 158).[12]

Because the essence of this brief is that the civil libel prosecutions involved herein constitute another of the "evasive schemes for racial segregation whether attempted 'ingeniously' or 'ingenuously'" (*Cooper* v. *Aaron*, 358 U.S. 1, 18), we believe it pertinent and material to view this "scheme" historically, in the "mirror"[13] of the Supreme Court's approach and reaction to other, related "schemes" to preserve segregation.

Even if consideration be limited to the fields of education, voting and housing, such "evasive schemes" have been struck down because of this Court's conviction that "constitutional rights would be of little value if they could be thus indirectly denied" (*Smith* v. *Allwright*, 321 U.S. 649, 664).

Thus, the "separate but equal" concept of *Plessy* v. *Ferguson*, 163 U.S. 537 (1896) entrenched segregation in schools until 1954[14] when this Court, in *Brown* v. *Board of Education*, 347 U.S. 483, enunciated the fundamental constitutional principle that racial segregation in the field of public education stamped Negroes with a "badge of inferiority" and violated the equal protection of the laws guaranteed by the Fourteenth Amendment.

For almost a decade, to this very day, there has been "massive resistance" to this decision. (Mendelson, *Discrimination* 40 (1962); also see *id.*, pp. 33–68 *passim*). The State of Alabama has been a leader of the resistance. This Court in 1958 was compelled to observe that the constitutional rights of school children "can neither be nullified openly and directly by state legislators or state executives or judicial officers, nor nullified indirectly by them through evasive schemes

---

[11] Immediately following the Civil War, the former slave owners sought to replace the shackles of slavery "with peonage and to make the Negroes an inferior and subordinate economic caste … [T]he consequences of slavery were to be maintained and perpetuated." Konvitz, *A Century of Civil Rights* 15 (1961); see also Franklin, *From Slavery to Freedom* 299 (1956); Du Bois, *Black Reconstruction* 381–525 (1935).

[12] "The articulate and organized group, however, was the one favoring the maintenance of the caste system, and it used boycotts, effective appeals to the Southern legislatures, violence and *other means to resist the changes.* In general this group is larger and more effective in the Deep South … [Emphasis Added]

"All of the continuing leaders of the Southern resistance are persons with some traditional and legitimate authority. They apparently have a strong racist ideology, and strong personal desires to keep the Negro subordinate …" *Postscript Twenty Years Later* to Myrdal, *The American Dilemma* XXXVII (1962).

[13] "The Court is a good mirror, an excellent mirror, of which historians for some reason have little availed themselves, of

the struggle of dominant forces outside the Court." Mr. Justice Frankfurter, as quoted in the preface of Vose, *Caucasians Only* (1959).

[14] The 1960 Report of the U.S. Commission on Civil Rights (1863–1963 Freedom to the Free—Century of Emancipation) p. 5, refers to the period of 1875–1900 as "Reaction, Redemption and Jim Crow," when "the former masters would have mastered the techniques of maintaining separation of the races through the agencies of the law." It was the period when "the Supreme Court was becoming attuned to the changing temper of the times" (*Id.*, p. 62). See, *e.g.*, *Slaughterhouse Cases*, 83 U.S. 36 (1873); *United States* v. *Reese*, 92 U.S. 214 (1876); *Cruikshank* v. *United States*, 92 U.S. 542 (1876); *Civil Rights Cases*, 109 U.S. 3 (1883); and *Plessy* v. *Ferguson*, 163 U.S. 537 (1896). But note the sole dissent of the first Mr. Justice Harlan which foreshadowed the reversal in the *Brown* case 58 years later. " … [I]n view of the Constitution, in the eye of the law, there is in this country no superior, dominant, ruling class of citizens. There is no caste here. Our Constitution is color-blind, and neither knows nor tolerates classes among citizens. In respect of civil rights, all citizens are equal before the law" (*Id.*, p. 559).

for segregation whether attempted 'ingeniously or ingenuously'" (Cooper v. Aaron, 358 U.S. 1, 17) [Emphasis added]. In 1960, this Court in a unanimous memorandum made it clear that it would brook no further delay through the series of laws based upon the "concept" of "interposition" (Bush v. Orleans School Board, 364 U.S. 500). Dilatory requests for review have been refused. "Tokenism" as a device is under challenge.[15]

The resistance techniques have taken many forms, some subtle and others overt, including contempt of federal court orders by the Governors of Alabama and Mississippi which required the use of federal troops to enforce basic constitutional rights. Ironically, the resistance took the equitable concept of "all deliberate speed," (Brown v. Board of Education, 349 U.S. 294, 301), which this Court proffered as a shield, and converted it to a sword. It was employed not for "consideration" of a "prompt and reasonable start towards full compliance" (349 U.S. at 300), but for resistance and nullification. This Court in its last term recognized that the concept of "all deliberate speed" had been abused and subverted. Watson v. City of Memphis, 373 U.S. 526.[16]

This Court has been vigilant, as it pledged it would be in Cooper v. Aaron, supra, to invalidate direct and indirect schemes seeking to preserve racial segregation.[17] Such vigilance must now be directed against the "civil libel" scheme so "ingeniously" and "ingenuously" and to date successfully employed as a weapon against the Negro petitioners and The New York Times.

Similarly, in the realm of Negro voting rights and other appurtenances of full citizenship, this Court has exposed the use of "evasive schemes" designed to nullify and sterilize Negro civil rights.

After this Court struck down a Texas law which bluntly denied the Negro the right to vote in a Democratic Party primary (Nixon v. Herndon, 273 U.S. 536), circumvention and more subtle means were employed. When these too failed to pass this Court's scrutiny (Nixon v. Condon, 286 U.S. 73), Texas repealed all such laws and fell back successfully to the legal sanctuary of "private action", placing the device beyond the reach of the Fourteenth Amendment (Grovey v. Townsend, 295 U.S. 45).

But, several years later, in 1944, this Court in Smith v. Allwright, 321 U.S. 649, overcame the "private action" device by going behind the white primary. Mr. Justice Reed aptly described this Court's searching approach to nullification of constitutional rights by indirection (321 U.S. at 664):

> "The United States is a constitutional democracy. Its organic law grants to all citizens a right to participate in the choice of elected officials without restriction by any state because of race. This grant to the people of the opportunity for choice is not to be nullified by a state through casting its electoral process in a *form* which permits a private organization to practice racial discrimination in the election. *Constitutional rights would be of little value if they could be thus indirectly denied*" (Emphasis added).

Foreshadowing the aftermath of Brown v. Board of Education, supra, Smith v. Allwright "aroused a storm of denunciation in the south, participated in by members of Congress, governors and others who proclaimed that 'white supremacy' must be preserved. They threatened that the decision would be disregarded or circumvented." Fraenkel, *The Supreme Court and Civil Liberties* 31 (1963). Thus, each "evasive scheme" thereafter employed to achieve discrim-

U.S. SUPREME COURT, OCTOBER 1963

BRIEF FOR THE PETITIONERS

---

[15] "This Court ... condemns the Pupil Placement Act when, with a fanfare of trumpets, it is hailed as the instrument for carrying out a desegregation plan while all the time the entire public knows that in fact it is being used to maintain segregation by allowing a little token desegregation" (Bush v. Orleans Parish School Board, 308 F. 2d 491, 499 (CA 5)).

[16] Mr. Justice Goldberg stated "Brown never contemplated that the concept of 'deliberate speed' would countenance indefinite delay in elimination of racial barriers in schools, let alone other public facilities not involving the same physical problems or comparable conditions. [373 U.S. 526, 530]

" ... Hostility to the constitutional precepts underlying the original decision was expressly and firmly pretermitted as such an operative factor... ." [Id., p. 531]

"Most importantly, of course, it must be recognized that even the delay countenanced by Brown was a necessary, albeit

significant, adaptation of the usual principle that any deprivation of constitutional rights calls for prompt rectification. The rights here asserted are, like all such rights, *present* rights; they are not merely hopes to some *future* enjoyment of some formalistic constitutional promise. The basic guarantees of our Constitution are warrants for the here and now and unless there is an overwhelmingly compelling reason, they are to be promptly fulfilled." (Id., pp. 532–3).

[17] Thus, for example, peonage and involuntary servitude imposed through ingenious subterfuges, whether by contract or otherwise, have been stripped of their "casting" and branded violations of the Thirteenth Amendment. This Court went behind the basic agreement between private individuals—being alert and vigilant to subtle means of reimposing slavery. Bailey v. Alabama, 219 U.S. 219; Taylor v. Georgia, 315 U.S. 25; Pollack v. Williams, 322 U.S. 4.

U.S. SUPREME
COURT,
OCTOBER 1963

BRIEF FOR THE
PETITIONERS

ination in primary machinery was struck down. See *Terry* v. *Adams,* 345 U.S. 461; Fraenkel, *supra,* p. 31; Myrdal, *The American Dilemma* 479–86 (1944).[18]

In addition to the right to vote, full citizenship includes the right of jury service. Southern efforts to restrict and prevent jury service by Negroes reflect a similar pattern of resort to the full arsenal of "evasive schemes" after the passage of direct laws denying Negroes service on juries was barred by this Court. *Strauder* v. *West Virginia,* 100 U.S. 303. It was in this context that this Court first observed that it would not tolerate discrimination "whether accomplished ingeniously or ingenuously." *Smith* v. *Texas,* 311 U.S. 128, 132; see also *Norris* v. *Alabama,* 294 U.S. 587; *Cassell* v. *Texas,* 339 U.S. 282; *Avery* v. *Georgia,* 345 U.S. 559. Even the finding of a state court that no discrimination existed did not bar this Court from going behind the facade to unmask, after review of the facts, subtle techniques for achieving denial of impartial jury. *Ross* v. *Texas,* 341 U.S. 918; *Shepherd* v. *Florida,* 341 U.S. 50.

Grand jury selections which directly or indirectly discriminated were interdicted. *Smith* v. *Texas, supra; Eubanks* v. *Louisiana,* 356 U.S. 584.

This Court overcame the artifice of gerrymandering which is in essence an "evasive scheme" to disenfranchise Negroes. *Gomillion* v. *Lightfoot,* 364 U.S. 339; and in *Baker* v. *Carr,* 369 U.S. 186, it has begun to grapple with more subtle, deeply entrenched means of effective disenfranchisement. In the same spirit, this Court did not permit voting registrars who committed wrongful acts to be insulated from liability by the designation of "private persons." *United States* v. *Raines,* 362 U.S. 17.

Finally, in the realm of housing, the use of artificial forms and "legalisms" as techniques for perpetuating discrimination was struck down. Racially restrictive zoning ordinances were declared illegal. *Buchanan* v. *Warley,* 245 U.S. 60; *Harmon* v. *Tyler,* 273 U.S. 668. In this field, the label of "private action" on racially restrictive covenants remained an impregnable fortress for discrimination for many decades (cf. *Civil Rights Cases,* 109 U.S. 3; Vose, *Caucasians Only* (1959)). Through racially restrictive covenants, efforts of Negroes to move out of slums and ghettoes to find better homes and schools were effectively and "legally" thwarted.[19]

In *Shelley* v. *Kraemer,* 334 U.S. 1, 19, this Court breached the walls of the fortress protecting these obnoxious covenants and held that the "private action" of contracting parties, when enforced by state courts, resulted in state action, saying: "active intervention of the state courts supported by the full panoply of state power" resulted in state action in the full and complete sense of the phrase.

Again, as with *Smith* v. *Allwright* and *Brown* v. *Board of Education,* both *supra,* a landmark declaration of positive constitutional right and privilege was met by resistance. A search was on to nullify, interpose or circumvent. (Vose, *op. cit., supra,* 227–34). This Court, five years later, in 1953 had to stem a tide of damage suits which had victimized those who "breached" the racial covenants. *Barrows* v. *Jackson,* 346 U.S. 249. Mr. Justice Minton, in a decision which bears close scrutiny as applicable to the case at bar, concluded that the grant of damages by a state court constituted state action under the Fourteenth Amendment; that to allow damages against one who refuses to discriminate "would be to encourage the use of restrictive covenants. To that extent, the State would act to put its sanction behind the covenants … [T]he Constitution confers upon no individual the right to demand action by the State which results in the denial of equal protection of laws to other individuals" (346 U.S. at 254–60).

The foregoing discussion of "ingenious" efforts to find "evasive schemes" for segregation was intended to place the case at bar in true perspective. It brings to the fore Mr. Justice Frankfurter's statement, in *Beauharnais* v. *Illinois, supra,* that this Court "retains and exercises authority to nullify action which encroaches on freedom of utterance under the *guise* of punishing libel" (343 U.S. at 263–4) [Emphasis added]. We submit that the civil libel prosecutions involved in the case at bar represent just such a "guise"; that they fall squarely within the

---

[18] This text under the heading "Southern Techniques for Disfranchising of Negroes" refers not only to evasive legal schemes but to "violence, terror and intimidation" as the effective means used to disfranchise Negroes in the South (p. 485).

[19] A leading Negro newspaper, "The Chicago Defender," is quoted in Vose, *Caucasians Only:* "These covenants have been responsible for more human misery, more crime, more disease and violence than any other factor in our society. They have been used to build the biggest ghettoes in history. They have been used to pit race against race and to intensify racial and religious prejudice in every quarter" (p. 213).

pattern of devices and subterfuges which this Court has struck down in the realm of education, peonage, voting rights and housing, and must strike down here.

II. The proceedings below constitute prohibited state action and, together with the concepts of libel enunciated by the Alabama courts, unconstitutionally abridge freedoms of press, speech, assembly and association

A. Prohibited state action is clearly involved To insulate this case against critical review by this Court, the erroneous assertion was made in the courts below[20] that there is an absence of "state action" and that this is merely a "private action of libel." This contention has no validity.

In *Shelley* v. *Kraemer*, 334 U.S. 1, 14, the Court stated:

> "That the action of *state courts and of judicial officers in their official capacities is to be regarded as action of the State within the meaning of the Fourteenth Amendment, is a proposition which has long been established by decisions of this Court.*" [Emphasis added].

****

> "We have no doubt that there has been state action in these cases in the full and complete sense of the phrase." (*Id.,* p. 19).

See *Barrows* v. *Jackson,* 346 U.S. 249, 254 (state court suit between private parties, seeking damages for breach of a racially restrictive covenant, held barred by the Fourteenth Amendment); *American Federation of Labor* v. *Swing,* 312 U.S. 321 (state court's enforcement of a common law policy held state action within the Fourteenth Amendment); accord: *Bridges* v.

California, 314 U.S. 252; *Wood* v. *Georgia,* 370 U.S. 375.

Moreover, the action by respondent Sullivan and the actions and pronouncements of other public officials (including the Attorney General and Governor of the State of Alabama) *in and of themselves* clearly constitute "State action" within the concepts enunciated by this Court in *Lombard* v. *Louisiana,* 373 U.S. 267.

The record herein notes that the instant case was instituted by Sullivan several days after the public announcement by Attorney General Gallion of Alabama that, on instructions from Governor Patterson, he was examining the legal aspects of damage actions by the State against the New York Times and others based on the advertisement here involved (R. 1999, 2001). The related companion libel suits filed by Mayor James, Commissioner Parks, former Commissioner Sellers and Governor Patterson, as well as the instant case, were instituted soon thereafter. All of these suits were based on substantially identical claims of libel and were instituted against petitioners and The New York Times based on the same advertisement, in the same circuit court of Montgomery County. (See *Parks* v. *New York Times,* 195 F. Supp. 919 (M. D. Ala.), rev'd on other grounds, 308 F. 2d 474 (C. A. 5), cert. pending; *Abernathy* v. *Patterson,* 295 F. 2d 452 (C. A. 5), cert. den., 368 U.S. 986).

Governor Patterson's complaint prays for damages in the sum of $1,000,000, and the Parks and Sellers and James complaints each pray for $500,000 damages.

Four other libel suits were instituted by Birmingham officials, seeking a total of $1,300,000 in damages, based on articles on racial tensions by Harrison Salisbury in *The Times.* Alabama officials have also filed libel actions against the Columbia Broadcasting System, seeking $1,500,000 in damages based on a television news program devoted, in part, to the difficulties experienced by Negro citizens of Montgomery in registering to vote. *Morgan, Connor & Waggoner* v. *CBS, Inc.* (N. D. Ala., So. Div.) Civ. Nos. 10067–10069S; *Willis & Ponton* v. *CBS, Inc.* (M. D. Ala., No. Div.) Civ. Nos. 1790–1791N.

On May 22, 1960, shortly after the institution of the above-described actions against petitioners and *The Times,* the Montgomery Advertiser (a prominent local newspaper) stated editorially:

---

[20] Trial Judge Jones' disregard of the guarantees and requirements of the Fourteenth Amendment is understandable in view of his shockingly biased statement from the Bench during the trial of the related *James* case (n. 3 at p. 3, *supra*): "… [T]*he XIV Amendment has no standing whatever in this court, it is a pariah and an outcast,* if it be construed to … direct … this Court as to the manner in which … its internal operations [requiring racial segregation in seating persons in the courtroom] … shall be conducted …"

****

"We will now continue the trial of this case under the laws of the State of Alabama, and not under the XIV Amendment, and in the belief and knowledge that *the white man's justice* … will give the parties … equal justice under law." *Judge Jones on Courtroom Segregation,* 22 The Alabama Lawyer, 190 at pp. 191–2 (1961) [Emphasis and brackets added].

U.S. SUPREME COURT, OCTOBER 1963

BRIEF FOR THE PETITIONERS

U.S. SUPREME
COURT,
OCTOBER 1963

BRIEF FOR THE
PETITIONERS

"The Advertiser has no doubt that the recent checkmating of The Times in Alabama will impose a restraint upon other publications which have hitherto printed about the South what was supposed to be." (R. 2025).

It is difficult to believe that this flood of libel prosecutions instituted by public officials of the State of Alabama was simply a spontaneous, individual response to a critical newspaper advertisement. One is compelled to conclude that these actions by public officials are part of a concerted, calculated program to carry out a policy of punishing, intimidating and silencing all who criticize and seek to change Alabama's notorious political system of enforced segregation (See n. 7, p. 12, *supra*).

The Sullivan case, considered in conjunction with the activities of the other Alabama city and state officials, is clearly within the state action doctrine enunciated in the *Lombard* case, *supra*. "A State or a city may act as authoritatively through its executive as through its legislative body" (373 U.S. at 273). Clearly, Alabama has interceded, by its judiciary and its city and state officials, to put state sanctions behind its racial segregation practices.

Once the shelter of "private action" is removed from the "libel" judgment below, that judgment and its affirmance are exposed as another "scheme" to abridge the petitioners' basic constitutional rights of free political expression.

B. The First and Fourteenth Amendments protect criticism and discussion of the political conduct and actions of public officials Since this Court in the public interest accords to public officials immunity from libel (*Barr* v. *Matteo*, 360 U.S. 564), the same public interest must insure a corresponding protection to those who criticize public officials.[21]

Public officials, backed not only by the full power of their offices but also by the aura of power, must be held to strictest account. To expect such account to be received dispassionately and dealt with in polite phrases by press and public is to deny effective criticism and comment.

In *Roth* v. *United States,* 354 U.S. 476, 484, this Court ruled that the First and Fourteenth Amendments were "fashioned to assure unfettered interchange of ideas for the bringing about of political and social changes desired by the people."

In Justice Hughes' classic statement is found support for the key role of political discussion:

> "[I]mperative is the need to preserve inviolate the constitutional rights of free speech, free press and free assembly in order to maintain the opportunity for free political discussion to the end that government may be responsive to the will of the people and that changes, if desired, may be obtained by peaceful means. Therein lies the security of the Republic, the very foundation of consti-

---

[21] *Cf.* Chief Justice Warren's comment in his dissent: " ... The public interest in limiting libel suits against officers in order that the public might be adequately informed is paralleled by another interest of equal importance: that of preserving the opportunity to criticize the administration of our Government and the action of its officials without being subjected to unfair—and absolutely privileged—retorts. If it is important to permit government officials absolute freedom to say anything they wish in the name of public information, it is at least as important to preserve and foster public discussion concerning our Government and its operation" (at p. 584).

See also *Douglas, The Right of The People* 25 (1961), quoting "as the true spirit of the Bill of Rights":

"In times like those through which we have recently passed, the doctrine of fair comment should be extended as far as the authorities will permit. With unprecedented social and governmental conditions, our own institutions threatened, national legislators who participate in the formation of governmental policies should be held to the strictest official accountability. History has shown that this is promoted through free exercise of the right to criticize official acts. The people furnish the legislators with an extensive and expensive secretariat, give them the right to use the mails at public expense. Their colleagues are generous in granting leave to

print. With these opportunities for personal praise and propaganda, opposition newspapers and editorial writers should not be limited to weak, tepid, and supine criticism and discussion" (*Hall* v. *Binghamton Press Co.*, 263 App. Div. 403, 411, (3d Dept.)).

See also *Hall* v. *Binghamton, supra,* 263 App. Div. at pp. 412–13 (concurrence of Justice Bliss) for an eloquent dictum on this subject:

"Ours is a representative government, and one who assumes to represent our citizens in a legislative hall must expect that his acts will be commented upon and criticized.... Freedom of speech and press are guaranteed to us in our form of government, and it is the right of the free press to criticize severely and of a free citizenry to speak plainly to and of its representatives.... If the press or our citizens honestly believe that the acts of a legislative representative lend comfort to our nation's enemies there must be no question about the right to tell him just that in no uncertain terms. Queasy words will not do. How else can a democracy function? If the citizens believe such acts may be setting up a government of Quislings, they must have the right to say so. It is one of the verities of democracy that eternal vigilance is the price of liberty. The courts may not muzzle those who maintain such vigilance. Great issues require strong language."

tutional government" (*De Jonge* v. *Oregon*, 299 U.S. 353, 365).

Such criticism and discussion of the actions of public officials are constitutionally protected not only against prior restraint but also against subsequent punishment. *Wood* v. *Georgia, supra; Schneider* v. *State*, 308 U.S. 147; *Bridges* v. *California*, 314 U.S. 252; *Grosjean* v. *American Press Co.*, 297 U.S. 233, 243–245; *Near* v. *Minnesota*, 283 U.S. 697, 707; *Thornhill* v. *Alabama*, 310 U.S. 88; *Cantwell* v. *Connecticut*, 310 U.S. 296.

Perhaps more than any other issue in the history of the United States, the demand of Negro Americans to be granted full rights as citizens, from the slave revolts through the Abolition Movement and the Civil War to the present non-violent movement, has been a most graphic witness to these observations by Justice Jackson:

> "... a function of free speech under our system of government is to invite dispute. It may indeed best serve its high purposes when it induces a condition of unrest, creates dissatisfaction with conditions as they are, or even stirs people to anger. Speech is often provocative and challenging. It may strike at prejudices and preconceptions and have profound unsettling effects as it presses for acceptance of an idea." *Terminello* v. *Chicago*, 337 U.S. 1, 4.

This Court ruled in *Cantwell, supra*, that the Fourteenth Amendment invalidates state court judgments "based on a common law concept of the most general and undefined nature" (310 U.S. at 308) used by those on one side of "sharp differences" to penalize those on the other side. It concluded that:

> "... the people of this nation have ordained in the light of history, that, in spite of the probability of excesses and abuses, these liberties are, in the long view, essential to enlightened opinion and right conduct on the part of citizens of a democracy" (310 U.S. at 310).

This Court has repeatedly recognized that the preferred First and Fourteenth Amendment freedoms of speech, press, assembly and association are the very cornerstone of the Bill of Rights and our entire democratic heritage (*Wood* v. *Georgia, supra; Thomas* v. *Collins*, 323 U.S. 516; *Schneider* v. *State*, 308 U.S. 147, 161; *De Jonge* v. *Oregon, supra*, 364); and that the constitutional protection of such criticism of public officials extends even to "half truths," "misinformation," exaggerations and inaccuracies (*Pennekamp* v. *Florida*, 328 U.S. 331; *Bridges* v. *California*, 314

U.S. 252; *Cantwell* v. *Connecticut*, 310 U.S. 296, 310). "Freedom of petition, assembly, speech and press could be greatly abridged by a practice of meticulously scrutinizing every editorial, speech, sermon or other printed matter to extract two or three naughty words on which to hang charges of 'group libel'" (Mr. Justice Black, dissenting, in *Beauharnais* v. *Illinois*, 343 U.S. 250, 273).

Neither the State of Alabama nor any other state may foreclose the exercise of these basic constitutional rights by the appellation of "libel per se" or any other like label (*NAACP* v. *Button*, 371 U.S. 415, 429; *Wood* v. *Georgia*, 370 U.S. 375, 386; *Craig* v. *Harney*, 331 U.S. 367; *Norris* v. *Alabama*, 294 U.S. 587).

As this Court ruled in *NAACP* v. *Button, supra:*

> "A State cannot foreclose the exercise of constitutional rights by mere labels" (371 U.S. at 429).

The decision and judgment below clearly conflict with these prior decisions.

Indeed, as emphasized by the context in which they arose, the proceedings below are nothing more than a subterfuge to employ legal sanctions, and the fear of legal sanctions, to silence criticism of the official conduct of public officials, and to thus, revive, in new guise, the heinous, long-proscribed doctrines of "Seditious Libel." This tyrannical device and its civil counterpart, Scandalum Magnatum (described in Odgers, *Libel and Slander* 65 (6th Ed. 1929)), have long been considered barred by the preferred constitutional guarantees of freedom of speech, press, assembly and association embodied in the First and Fourteenth Amendments (see Holmes, J., in *Abrams* v. *United States*, 250 U.S. 616, 630; *De Jonge* v. *Oregon*, 299 U.S. 353, 365; *Sillars* v. *Collier*, 151 Mass. 50; Chafee, *Free Speech in the United States* 27–29 (1941); Schofield, *"Freedom of Press in the United States,"* ESSAYS ON CONSTITUTIONAL LAW AND EQUITY 540–541 (1921)). They must not now be permitted resurrection for any purpose, much less that repressive use attempted here.

This Court's recent decision in *Wood* v. *Georgia, supra*, restates and reaffirms the well-established doctrine that criticism of the official conduct of public officials is protected against state infringement by the First and Fourteenth Amendments. There, the Court found these Amendments protected Sheriff Wood's written accusations to a Grand Jury that the Superior

U.S. SUPREME COURT, OCTOBER 1963

BRIEF FOR THE PETITIONERS

U.S. SUPREME
COURT,
OCTOBER 1963

BRIEF FOR THE
PETITIONERS

Court Judges of Georgia were guilty of abusing their offices, misusing the state criminal law, attempted intimidation of Negro residents, fomenting racial hatred, "race baiting" and "physical demonstrations such as used by the Ku Klux Klan." In so holding, this Court said, per Mr. Chief Justice Warren:

> "Men are entitled to speak as they please on matters vital to them; errors in judgment or unsubstantiated opinions may be exposed, of course, but not through punishment for contempt for the expression. *Under our system of government, counterargument and education are the weapons available to expose these matters, not abridgement of the rights of free speech and assembly.*" (370 U.S. at 389) [Emphasis added].

A fortiori, The Times advertisement, which contained no official's name, no charge of crime or corruption in office, but rather which treated of vital and significant issues of the times, must fall well within that constitutionally protected ambit. Nor can any reasonable representation be made, to remove this case from that protected area, that *The Times* advertisement created any likelihood of immediate danger of conflict or violence. (*Whitney* v. *California,* 274 U.S. 357).

Further, the enormous sum of $500,000, awarded as punitive damages on a record so thoroughly devoid of crucial evidence, is wholly unconscionable. Such penalty by way of punitive damages (which, the jury was charged, constitutes "punishment" designed to deter defendants and others (R. 825–6)) represents a grave impairment of free expression and an unconstitutional restraint upon "the public need for information and education with respect to the significant issues of the times" (*Thornhill* v. *Alabama,* 310 U.S. at 102, quoted with approval in *Wood* v. *Georgia, supra*). The mere threat[22] of such "punishment" is far greater than the $400 fine and 20-day sentence for contempt which this Court has reversed as violative of the First and Fourteenth Amendments. (*Wood* v. *Georgia, supra.* See also *Barrows* v. *Jackson,* 346 U.S. 249; *Grosjean* v. *American Press Co.,* 297 U.S. 233).

The Alabama Supreme Court sustained the $500,000 verdict and judgment solely as proper "punitive damages" (R. 1175–9).[23] The technical and formal distinction that this huge penalty was imposed through civil rather than criminal libel prosecution is, in this situation, disingenuous at best, and lends no support to the judgment below.

For both this Court and the Circuit Court of Appeals have recognized that both civil and criminal libel prosecutions may encroach on the preferred rights guaranteed by the First and Fourteenth Amendments. See, *e.g., Beauharnais* v. *Illinois,* 343 U.S. 250, 263–4 (criminal); *Sweeney* v. *Patterson,* 128 F. 2d 457 (C. A., D. C.), cert. den., 317 U.S. 678 (civil).

In *Beauharnais* this Court stated:

> "'While this Court sits' it retains and exercises authority to nullify action which encroaches on freedom of utterance under the guise of punishing libel. Of course discussion cannot be denied and the right, as well as the duty, of criticism must not be stifled." (343 U.S. at 263, 264)

and significantly added in a footnote:

> "If a statute sought to outlaw libels of political parties, quite different problems not now before us would be raised. For one thing, the whole doctrine of fair comment as indispensable to the democratic political process would come into play [citing cases]. Political parties, like public men, are, as it were, public property." (*Id.,* p. 263, n. 18).

Criticism and discussion of the actions of public officials are a *sine qua non* of the democratic process.[24] It may fairly be said that the genius of our Bill of Rights lies precisely in its guarantee of the right to speak freely on public issues and to criticize public officials' conduct on the assumption that only an informed people is fit to govern itself. First Amendment freedoms

---

[22] In *Farmers Ed. & Coop. Union* v. *WDAY,* 360 U.S. 525, 530, this Court said: "Quite possibly, if a station were held responsible for the broadcast of libelous material, all remarks even faintly objectionable would be excluded out of an excess of caution." See also Riesman, *Democracy and Defamation: Fair Game and Fair Comment,* 42 Colum. L. Rev. 1282 (1943): There is a "need for protecting political and economic criticism against intimidation by the libel laws" (at p. 1309) " ... smaller journals, struggling along on subsidies or barely managing on their own, are, of course, highly vulnerable to a libel suit ..." (at p. 1310).

[23] Sullivan proved no special damages. Moreover, his testimony and that of his witnesses left little doubt that there was no injury to his reputation or standing in the community; more than likely, the contrary was true (R. 625, 638, 647, 651, 666, 721–4).

[24] "In dealing with governmental affairs, or the fitness of a political candidate for office, the law, however, has come to recognize a very broad privilege to comment freely and even criticize harshly. On matters of public concern, the expression of ideas may not be suppressed just because someone decides that the ideas are false. In that way we encourage the widest and broadest debate on public issues." Douglas, *A Living Bill of Rights* 26 (1961).

are "the most cherished policies of our civilization"[25] "vital to the maintenance of democratic institutions."[26]

This Court has recognized that the right to speak out for the civil rights of Negro citizens, and against those in public or private life who would deny them, is under bitter attack in Southern States, and has acted to protect that right in a long line of cases. *Gibson* v. *Florida Legislative Investigation Committee*, 372 U.S. 539; *NAACP* v. *Button*, 371 U.S. 415; *Shelton* v. *Tucker*, 364 U.S. 479; *Bates* v. *City of Little Rock*, 361 U.S. 516; *NAACP* v. *Alabama*, 357 U.S. 449.

In *Button*, this Court stated:

"We cannot close our eyes to the fact that the militant Negro civil rights movement has engendered the intense resentment and opposition of the politically dominant white community …" (371 U.S. at 435).

In *Bates*, this Court noted that:

"Freedoms such as these are protected not only against heavy-handed frontal attack, but also from being stifled by more subtle governmental interference." (361 U.S. at 523).

The award of punitive damages to a criticized official may well be more subversive of the freedom to criticize the government than is compelled disclosure of affiliation, which this Court has ruled inconsistent with the First Amendment in the cases cited above. See also *Gibson, supra; West Va. Board of Education* v. *Barnette*, 319 U.S. 624.

Indeed, "punishment by way of damages … not alone to punish the wrongdoer, but as a deterrent to others similarly minded,"[27] where such damages are subject to "no legal measure,"[28] exceeds even the criminal punishment of Seditious Libel. For here the "fine" is limited only by the complainant's *ad damnum* clause, and may be imposed without indictment or proof beyond a reasonable doubt. The Alabama courts require neither an intent to bring the official "into contempt or disrepute," as in the Sedition Act (Act of July 14, 1798, 1 Stat. 596), nor any proof of actual injury to reputation. The Trial Court below ruled the ad libelous *per se*, and instructed the jury (R. 823) that it was to be presumed to be "malicious." Further, the Court below ruled it was legally sufficient to constitute libel *per se* that the criticism, "if believed,"[29] would "tend to injure … [the official] in his reputation."[30]

Were the libel theory of the Alabama courts below allowed to stand, the danger to freedom of written expression would be tremendous. Its infection would spread quickly and disastrously, bringing suit next for slander for spoken words. A veritable blackout of criticism, a deadening conformity, would follow inexorably. It requires little imagination to picture the destructiveness of such weapons in the hands of those who, only yesterday, used dogs and fire hoses in Birmingham, Alabama against Negro petitioners leading non-violent protests against segregation practices.

C. Vagueness and indefiniteness of standards require reversal of the judgment below
Such vague rules of liability, as were employed in the Trial Court's judgment and upheld in the Alabama Supreme Court's affirmance, restrict the exercise of First Amendment rights more seriously than would have the penalties stricken down in *Wood, supra,* or *Cantwell, supra,* or the compulsory disclosure prohibited in *Gibson, supra.* For the uncertainty created thereby is even greater than that involved in the following cases in which this Court has found vagueness constitutionally offensive.

In *NAACP* v. *Button*, 371 U.S. 415, a Virginia statute was condemned on the ground that the conduct it prohibited was "so broad and uncertain" as to "lend itself to selective enforcement against unpopular causes." As the Court said in *Button, supra:*

"Broad prophylactic rules in the area of free expression are suspect [citing cases]. Precision of regulation must be the touchstone in an area so closely touching our most precious freedoms." (371 U.S. at 435).

Similarly, in *Bantam Books, Inc.* v. *Sullivan*, 372 U.S. 58, 71, the Court struck down a statute ostensibly designed to shield youthful readers from obscenity on the ground that the statutory mandate was "vague and uninformative," leaving the distributor of books "to speculate" as to whether his publication fell within the statute.

Perhaps the most telling of all statements on this point is contained in the dissent of Messrs. Justice Reed and Douglas in *Beauharnais:*

U.S. SUPREME COURT, OCTOBER 1963

BRIEF FOR THE PETITIONERS

---

[25] *Bridges* v. *California*, 314 U.S. 252, 260.

[26] *Schneider* v. *State*, 308 U.S. 147, 161.

[27] Ala. Sup. Ct. (R. 1176)

[28] *Ibid.* (R. 1177)

[29] *Ibid.* (R. 1162–3)

[30] *Ibid.* (R. 1155)

U.S. SUPREME
COURT,
OCTOBER 1963

BRIEF FOR THE
PETITIONERS

" ... Racial, religious, and political biases and prejudices lead to charge and countercharge, acrimony and bitterness. If words are to be punished criminally, the Constitution at least requires that only words or expressions or statements that can be reasonably well defined, or that have through long usage an accepted meaning, shall furnish a basis for conviction.

"These words—'virtue,' 'derision,' and 'obloquy'—have neither general nor special meanings well enough known to apprise those within their reach as to limitations on speech [citing case]. Philosophers and poets, thinkers of high and low degree from every age and race have sought to expound the meaning of virtue, but each teaches his own conception of the moral excellence that satisfies standards of good conduct. Are the tests of the Puritan or the Cavalier to be applied, those of the city or the farm, the Christian or non-Christian, the old or the young? Does the Bill of Rights permit Illinois to forbid any reflection on the virtue of racial or religious classes which a jury or a judge may think exposes them to derision or obloquy, words themselves of quite uncertain meaning as used in the statute? I think not. A general and equal enforcement of this law would restrain the mildest expressions of opinion in all those areas where 'virtue' may be thought to have a role. Since this judgment may rest upon these vague and undefined words, which permit within their scope the punishment of incidents secured by the guarantee of free speech, the conviction should be reversed." *Beauharnais* v. *Illinois,* 343 U.S. 250, 283–284.

Accordingly, on grounds of vagueness and uncertainty alone, the judgment below must be reversed.

D. Respondent's erroneous contentions as to the defense of truth Respondent, in opposing certiorari, contended that the availability of the defense of truth suffices to protect the First Amendment freedoms against encroachment by a common law libel action. This argument has been rejected by the courts and by history. *Sweeney* v. *Patterson,* 128 F. 2d 457, 458 (C. A., D. C.), cert. den., 317 U.S. 678, held:

"Cases which impose liability for *erroneous reports of the political conduct of officials* reflect the obsolete doctrine that the governed must not criticize their governors ... Information and discussion will be discouraged, and the public interest in public knowledge of important facts will be poorly defended if error subjects its author to a libel suit without even a showing of economic

loss. *Whatever is added to the field of libel is taken from the field of free debate."* [Emphasis added].

To the same argument, raised in defense of the Sedition Act of 1798, James Madison replied:

" ... [A] very few reflections will prove that [the Sedition Act's] baneful tendency is little diminished by the privilege of giving in evidence the truth of the matter contained in political writings."

* * * * *

"But in the next place, it must be obvious to the plainest minds; that opinions, and inferences, and conjectural observations, are not only in many cases inseparable from the facts, but may often be more the objects of the prosecution than the facts themselves; or may even be altogether abstracted from particular facts; and that opinions and inferences, and conjectural observations, cannot be subjects of that kind of proof which appertains to facts, before a court of law." (*Kentucky-Virginia Resolutions and Mr. Madison's Report of 1799,* Virginia Commission on Constitutional Government 71 (1960)).

Respondent's case confirms Madison's observations, resting as it does on one minor inaccuracy in *The Times* ad and the strained inferences there from of respondent and his witnesses.

Nor, as this Court has expressly stated in *NAACP* v. *Button, supra,* is the truth of ideas and beliefs a precondition for their constitutional protection:

" ... For the Constitution protects expression and association without regard to the race, creed or political or religious affiliation of the members of the group which invokes its shield, or to the truth, popularity or social utility of the ideas and beliefs which are offered." (371 U.S. at 444–5).

And the use by the Alabama Supreme Court (R. 1178) of the testimony of the Secretary of The Times, that the advertisement was "substantially correct" (R. 785), to sustain both an inference of malice and the $500,000 verdict, is best rebutted by Judge Clark in his cogent dissent in *Sweeney* v. *Schenectady Union Pub. Co.,* 122 F. 2d 288, 292 (C. A. 2), aff'd per curiam by an equally divided Court, 316 U.S. 642.

"I do not think it an adequate answer to such a threat against public comment, which seems to me necessary if democratic processes are to function, to say that it applies only to false statements. For this is comment and inference, ... and hence not a matter of explicit proof or disproof. The public official will always regard himself as not bigoted, and will so testify, sincerely enough. And then the burden of proving the truth of the defense will rest upon the commentator, who must sustain the burden of proving his inference true. If he fails in even a minority of the suits against him—as the sporting element in trials to juries susceptible to varying shades of local opinion would make probable—he is taught his lesson, and a serious brake upon free discussion established."

In sum, this Court must not permit a discredited technique of oppression, no matter how "subtle" or sophisticated or refined its new guise (*Bates* v. *Little Rock, supra,* at 523) to be restored as an effective device for men in office to

" ... injure and oppress the people under their administration, provoke them to cry out and complain; and then make that very complaint the foundation for new oppression and prosecutions."[31]

III. The judgment and proceedings below violate petitioners' First and Fourteenth Amendment rights in that the record is devoid of evidence of authorization or publication of the ad in suit, and they require of total strangers to the publication expression of disbelief and disavowal

A. Lack of evidence as denial of Due Process of Law The record below is devoid of probative evidence of authorization or publication by any of the petitioners of the alleged libel or of any malice on their part (see pp. 8–12, *supra*).

In examining this record, District Judge Johnson, in *Parks* v. *New York Times Co.,* 195 F. Supp. 919 (M. D. Ala.), rev'd on other grounds by a two to one decision, 308 F. 2d 474 (C. A. 5), petition for cert. pending, (No. 687, 1962 Term, renumbered No. 52, 1963 Term), found and ruled as follows (pp. 922–3):

"This Court reaches the conclusion that from the evidence presented upon the motion to remand in each of these cases there is no legal basis whatsoever for the claim asserted against the resident defendants Abernathy, Shuttlesworth, Seay, Sr., and Lowery [petitioners herein]. *From the facts available to this Court, no liability on the part of the four resident defendants existed under any recognized theory of law; this is true even with the application of the Alabama 'scintilla rule'.*"

* * * * *

"They were neither officers nor members of the Committee, and had not authorized the

committee, or Murray, or The New York Times, or anyone else to use their names in such a manner. *Neither resident defendant knew his name had been used until some time after the publication of the article in question. The theory that the article was authorized and that the individual resident defendants had authorized the use of their names through the Southern Christian Leadership Conference is without any evidentiary basis whatsoever. As a matter of fact, all the evidence is to the contrary and uncontradicted.*" [Emphasis and brackets supplied].[32]

The courts below relied on the unfounded premise that the petitioners were linked with the advertisement in question by the letter from A. Philip Randolph (R. 1948–9; 1992), which the Alabama Supreme Court seized upon and characterized as a certification that the petitioners had consented to the use of their names in the advertisement (R. 1170). On the contrary, however, it is undisputed that the letter referred to "signed members of the Committee" and that the petitioners' names were not attached thereto (R. 805–10, 818).

Therefore, as their names were used without their knowledge or consent (R. 754–5, 806–10), the assertion of the court below (R. 1170) that the Randolph letter certified petitioners' permission to use their names is clearly groundless and constitutes distorted fact finding.

In *Stein* v. *New York,* 346 U.S. 156, 181, this Court set forth the established rule:

"Of course, this Court cannot allow itself to be completely bound by state court determination of any issue essential to decision of a

---

[31] Andrew Hamilton, Argument to the Jury, *Zenger's Trial,* 17 How. St. Tr. 675, 721–2.

[32] The majority decision of the 5th Circuit Court of Appeals in *Parks* v. *New York Times, supra,* is clearly shown by the Opinion to rest on matters not contained in the Record in this case (see 308 F. 2d 478, at 479, 482), and the issue there considered was the question of "colorable liability" of petitioners to defeat removal to the federal courts of other libel suits.

In fact, the two majority judges in the *Parks* case had before them the complete Record in the *Sullivan* case at bar and took no issue with District Judge Johnson's findings and decision that, on that Record, there was not a scintilla of evidence or any "recognized theory of law" to support any claim against petitioners (195 F. Supp. 919, 922). This is further confirmed by the dissenting Opinion of Judge Ainsworth in the *Parks* case, which states in relevant part:

"The majority opinion apparently agrees with the principal findings of fact of the court below [*i.e.,* of District Judge Johnson as quoted above] ...", 308 F. 2d 474, 483 [brackets added].

claim of federal right, else federal law could be frustrated by distorted fact finding."

Accord: *Wood* v. *Georgia,* 370 U.S. 375; *Craig* v. *Harney,* 331 U.S. 367; *Pennekamp* v. *Florida,* 328 U.S. 331.

As indicated, the judgment against petitioners clearly lacks any rational connection with, and is in fact directly contrary to, the undisputed record facts. Accordingly, the result below conflicts with this Court's decisions in *Thompson* v. *Louisville,* 362 U.S. 199; *Postal Telegraph Cable Co.* v. *City of Newport, Ky.,* 247 U.S. 464; *Tot* v. *United States,* 319 U.S. 463.[33]

Since there is no rational evidentiary support in the record for the finding that petitioners authorized the use of their names as sponsors of the advertisements, the judgment below clearly violates the "due process" requirements of the Fourteenth Amendment and must be set aside for lack of evidence. *Garner* v. *Louisiana,* 368 U.S. 157; *Thompson* v. *Louisville,* 362 U.S. 199.

B. Prejudicial rulings below concerning "ratification;" silence as consent Absent any evidence that petitioners published or authorized publication of the advertisement at issue, and in the face of uncontroverted evidence that petitioners' names were used without authorization or consent, the trial court improperly charged the jury (R. 824–5):

> "… although you may believe … that they did not sign this advertisement and did not authorize it, yet it is the contention of the plaintiff … that the four individuals … after knowing of the publication of the advertisement and after knowing of its content, ratified the use of their names … and we here define ratification as the approval by a person of a prior act which did not bind him but which was professedly done on his account or in his behalf whereby the act, the use of his name, the publication, is given effect as if authorized by him in the very beginning. Ratification is really the same as a previous authorization and is a confirmation or approval of what has been done by another on his account."

---

[33] In *Williams* v. *Tooke,* 108 F. 2d 758, 759 (C. A. 5), cert. den., 311 U.S. 655, the established rule was cogently restated as follows:

"[I]f a case between private parties is arbitrarily and capriciously decided, in violation of settled principles of law and contrary to undisputed facts, though the court so deciding had jurisdiction over the suit, the judgment may be in violation of the 14th Amendment. *Postal Telegraph Cable Co.* v. *Newport, Ky.,* 247 U.S. 464, 38 S. Ct. 566, 62 L. ed. 1215."

Petitioners duly excepted, and the Trial Judge duly granted an exception, to this crucial and prejudicial portion of the oral charge (R. 829); but the Supreme Court of Alabama nevertheless refused to rule thereon, on the purported ground that the "attempted exception was descriptive of the subject matter only, and is too indefinite to invite our review" (R. 1168).

The quoted oral charge rests solely on the silence of petitioners for approximately eight days, between their receipt, on or about April 11, 1960 (R. 799), of respondent's demand for retraction, and April 19, 1960, the date of commencement of respondent's suit; for the record is wholly devoid of any other act or omission of petitioners subsequent to the publication of the advertisement. Thus, the charge invited the jury to impose liability on petitioners solely on the basis of their silence subsequent to publication of the advertisement. But such silence does not have sufficient rational connection with the publication of the advertisement to satisfy the Due Process Clause of the Fourteenth Amendment, nor can the erroneous refusal of the Alabama Supreme Court to rule on petitioners' exceptions and Assignments of Error preclude review by this Court.

Moreover, the trial judge, contrary to established principles, in effect directed the jury to find the New York Times' ad in suit "libelous per se" (R. 823); and the Supreme Court of Alabama, while finding this charge "confused" and "invasive" of the province of the jury (R. 1166–7), still refused to find prejudice to petitioners (R. 1167).

Such erroneous and prejudicial rulings by the courts below unconstitutionally infringed petitioners' basic rights in their gross misapplication of controlling decisions of this Court, and in the oppressive and unreasonable judgment they buttressed. No state court can, particularly on such evidence, exact a price of $500,000 for *eight* days' silence and remain consistent with the First and Fourteenth Amendments.

Nor do petitioners' failures to reply constitute a ratification. Governing authority is clear that a prerequisite of "ratification" (even in contract cases) is knowledge by the "ratifying" party of all the relevant facts involved. Petitioners did not have such knowledge here (R. 787–804). Neither respondent nor the Courts below cited any applicable authority to negate this accepted definition of ratification. (*Cf. A. B. Leach & Co.*

v. *Peirson*, 275 U.S. 120; and see *Angichiodo* v. *Cerami*, 127 F. 2d 849, 852 (C. A. 5)).

C. Compulsory disclosure of belief

Moreover, any such attempt to require petitioners to retract or deny publication fatally conflicts with the freedoms of thought and association guaranteed by the Constitution and the decisions of this Court. *Gibson* v. *Florida Legislative Investigation Committee; NAACP* v. *Button; Talley* v. *California; Bates* v. *City of Little Rock; NAACP* v. *Alabama; West Va. Board of Education* v. *Barnette; De Jonge* v. *Oregon,* all *supra.*

The applicability of the doctrine of these cases to a failure to retract or deny cannot be seriously disputed. It is patent that compelled expression of disbelief, such as would result from imposition of liability for failure to retract a publication neither made nor authorized, is at least as dangerous as compulsion to disclose belief (*Talley* v. *California, supra; NAACP* v. *Alabama, supra*) or express belief (*West Va. Board of Education* v. *Barnette, supra*). This Court has ruled such compulsions unconstitutional.

These cases guarantee petitioners freedom to believe in the aims of the advertisement as well as freedom to associate themselves with others to accomplish such aims. As this Court said in *Gibson* (*supra*, 544):

> "This Court has repeatedly held that rights of association are within the ambit of the constitutional protections afforded by the First and Fourteenth Amendments (citing cases). The respondent Committee does not contend otherwise, nor could it, for, as was said in *NAACP* v. *Alabama, supra,* 'it is beyond debate that freedom to engage in association for the advancement of beliefs and ideas is an inseparable aspect of the "liberty" assured by the Due Process Clause of the Fourteenth Amendment, which embraces freedom of speech.' 357 U.S. at 460. *And it is equally clear that the guarantee encompasses protection of privacy of association …*" [Emphasis added].

Respondent, abetted by the coercive power of the State of Alabama, cannot constitutionally compel petitioners to decide within an *eight* day period whether or not to associate themselves publicly with, or dissociate themselves from, an advertisement seeking to achieve goals which petitioners may constitutionally support, especially under penalty of imputing malice to them and of punitive damages. Certainly no such compulsion can be constitutionally imposed on petitioners to make such disavowal of an ad, the full text of which they had not seen. Any such application of the Alabama retraction statutes cited by respondent (Title 7, Sections 913–16 of the Code of Alabama, at pp. 4–5, *supra*), or any such "rule of evidence" as respondent seeks to apply, would deprive petitioners of their right to obtain a copy of the advertisement, study the content thereof, investigate the accuracy of the statements claimed to be false, analyze the effect of the advertisement, consult with legal counsel, and—in the light of such study, investigation, analysis and consultation—decide either to deny publication, support the advertisement, remain silent or adopt some other course of conduct consistent with their consciences and beliefs.

The Alabama statutes as herein applied compelled petitioners to choose between public dissociation from beliefs and ideas and the legal imputation that they are associated with such beliefs and ideas. The First and Fourteenth Amendments, as interpreted in the controlling decisions cited above, prohibit such compulsory disclosure of association or dissociation.

Moreover, the Alabama "retraction statute" requires in part that defendant shall "publish … in as prominent and public a place or manner as the charge or matter published occupied, a full and fair retraction of such charge or matter." (Title 7, Section 914 of the Code of Alabama, set forth in full at p. 4, *supra*).

Assuming *arguendo* that petitioners might have been willing to "retract," it was clearly impossible for them to meet the conditions imposed by the Alabama statute. To make such retraction would require petitioners to place and pay for an advertisement in *The Times.* The record (together with the subsequent attachments and levies on petitioners made by respondent Sullivan) indicates that the limited salaries of petitioners would probably have made the cost of such an advertisement prohibitive to them. Accordingly, the Alabama retraction statute, as applied in the case at bar, clearly appears to discriminate against the indigent and in favor of the wealthy. It is, thus, apparent that the Alabama retraction statutes, as so applied against petitioners, deny equal protection of law in violation of the Fourteenth Amendment. *Cf. Gideon* v. *Wainwright,* 372 U.S. 335.

This Court has repeatedly held that freedom of thought and belief is absolute (*Cf. Cantwell* v. *Connecticut, supra,* 303; *West Va. Board of Education* v. *Barnette, supra*). Whatever may be

U.S. SUPREME
COURT,
OCTOBER 1963

BRIEF FOR THE
PETITIONERS

the power of the State to restrict or compel actions, the right to remain silent as to a choice of such conflicting beliefs is absolutely protected. The statement at issue here is a constitutionally protected expression of opinion on important public issues. However, even if this case involved a statement not within the safeguards of the First and Fourteenth Amendments, failure during an *eight* day period to deny publication could not sustain liability for publication of a claimed libel, without unconstitutionally restricting freedom of belief and association. *Gibson, supra; NAACP* v. *Alabama, supra.*

IV. Petitioners' rights to Due Process and Equal Protection of Law and to a fair and impartial trial as guaranteed by the Fourteenth Amendment were flagrantly violated and abridged by the proceedings below

Petitioners submit that their trial below was a "race trial," in which they were from first to last placed in a patently inferior position because of the color of their skins.

Throughout the trial below, the jury had before it an eloquent assertion of the inequality of the Negro in the segregation of the one room, of all rooms, where men should find equality, before the law. This Court's landmark decision in *Brown* v. *Board of Education, supra,* gave Constitutional recognition to the principle that segregation is inherently unequal; that it denies Negroes the equal protection of the law, stamps them with a "badge of inferiority" and deprives them of the full benefits of first-class citizenship.

In *Johnson* v. *Virginia, supra,* this Court specifically held:

> "Such a conviction [for contempt for refusing to sit in a Negro section of the court room] cannot stand, for it is no longer open to question that a State may not constitutionally require segregation of public facilities [Citing cases]. State-compelled segregation in a court of justice is a manifest violation of the State's duty to deny no one the equal protection of its laws." 373 U.S. at 62 [Brackets added].

Where Sullivan, a white public official, sued Negro petitioners represented by Negro counsel before an all-white jury, in Montgomery, Alabama, on an advertisement seeking to aid the cause of integration, the impact of courtroom segregation could only denote the inferiority of Negroes and taint and infect all proceedings, thereby denying petitioners the fair and impartial trial to which they are constitutionally enti-

tled. And such courtroom segregation has been judicially noted to be a long-standing practice in the state courts of Alabama,[34] as well as throughout the South.[35]

In such a context and in light of Alabama's massive system of segregation,[36] the segregated courtroom, even if it be the immediate result of the acts of private persons in "voluntarily" segregating themselves, must be viewed as the direct result of state action and policy in contravention of the Equal Protection Clause. *Lombard* v. *Louisiana,* 373 U.S. 267. Here, as in *Lombard,* state policy and action has dictated, and is legally responsible for, the "private act" of segregation.

State courts and judges have an affirmative duty to secure the equal protection of laws (*Gibson* v. *Mississippi,* 162 U.S. 565, 586), which duty cannot be sidestepped, as below, by ignoring, or merely failing to discharge, the obligation. *Burton* v. *Wilmington Parking Authority,* 365 U.S. 715. Such duty can only be a more stringent obligation when the violation of equal protection occurs within the judge's own courtroom.

Compounding this unconstitutional segregation were the racial animosities of the community which the Trial Judge permitted, indeed encouraged, to enter and pervade the courtroom. See pp. 12–15, *supra.* The conclusion is inescapable that the trial denied petitioners equal protection and due process of law. *Irvin* v. *Dowd,* 366 U.S. 717; *Marshall* v. *United States,* 360 U.S. 310; *Shepherd* v. *Florida,* 341 U.S. 50, 54–5; *Craig* v. *Harney,* 331 U.S. 367.[37]

The conduct of the trial itself emphasized the race and racial inferiority of petitioners. In his summation to the jury, respondent's counsel, without so much as a rebuke from the Bench, made the following highly prejudicial and inflammatory remark:

> "In other words, all of these things that happened did not happen in Russia where the police run everything, they did not happen in the Congo where they still eat them, they happened in Montgomery, Alabama, a law-abiding community." (R. 929–30, 941).

---

[34] See *U.S. ex rel Seals* v. *Wiman,* 304 F. 2d 53 (C. A. 5), cert. den., 372 U.S. 915.

[35] See *Johnson* v. *Virginia, supra.*

[36] See n. 7, p. 12, *supra.*

[37] Nor does it matter whether the cause of such denial was state action or private action (see *Moore* v. *Dempsey,* 261 U.S. 86, 91) such as inflammatory local newspaper reports. See *Irvin* v. *Dowd, supra.*

Respondent's counsel was also permitted by the Trial Judge, without restraint and over the objections of petitioners' counsel, to mispronounce the word "Negro" as "Nigra" and "Nigger" in the presence of the jury (R. 579–80). The acceptance by the Court below of the lame excuse that this was "the way respondent's counsel had always pronounced it all his life" (R. 580) is directly in conflict with the decisions of this Court. Customs or habits of an entire community (and, *a fortiori*, of an individual) cannot support the denial of constitutional rights. *Cooper* v. *Aaron*, 358 U.S. 1; *Eubanks* v. *Louisiana*, 356 U.S. 584, 588.

More than fifty years ago in *Battle* v. *United States*, 209 U.S. 36, 39, Justice Holmes noted that racist epithets should never be permitted in a court of law, and that the trial judge should prevent such prejudicial and offensive conduct:

> "Finally, an exception was taken to an interruption of the judge, asking the defendant's counsel to make an argument that did not tend to degrade the administration of justice. The reference was to an appeal to race prejudice and to such language as this: 'You will believe a white man not on his oath before you will a negro who is sworn. You can swallow those niggers if you want to, but John Randolph Cooper will never swallow them.' The interruption was fully justified."

The very use of the term "Nigger" in referring to a defendant or a witness has been recognized by numerous state appellate courts to constitute prejudicial, reversible error. See, *e.g.*, *Taylor* v. *State*, 50 Tex. Crim. Rep. 560, *Harris* v. *State*, 96 Miss. 379; *Collins* v. *State*, 100 Miss. 435; *Roland* v. *State*, 137 Tenn. 663; *Hamilton* v. *State*, 12 Okla. Crim. Rep. 62.

Perhaps the most subtle and personally offensive example of racial derogation is the seeming difference in the Judge's forms of address to the various trial attorneys. Petitioners' trial counsel, all of whom are Negroes, were never addressed or referred to as "Mister" but always impersonally; indeed, in the transcript they are peculiarly referred to as "Lawyer" (*e.g.*, "Lawyer Gray," "Lawyer Crawford"); whereas all white attorneys in the case were consistently and properly addressed as "Mister" (see, *e.g.*, R. 787–90). Such suggested purposeful differentiation by the Judge himself not only would appear to classify Negro petitioners and their counsel as somehow different; it strongly intimates to all present, including the jurors, that in Alabama courts the Negro

practitioner at the bar may be a "lawyer" but is not quite a man to be dignified as "mister."

Furthermore, the systematic and intentional exclusion of Negroes from the jury panel itself again stamped the Negro petitioners inferior and unequal, and inevitably denied them a fair trial. From *Norris* v. *Alabama*, 294 U.S. 587, decided by this Court in 1935, through the recent *U.S. ex rel. Seals* v. *Wiman*, 304 F. 2d 53, cert. den., 372 U.S. 915, the federal judiciary has struck down, as violative of the Equal Protection Clause, the systematic exclusion of Negroes from the jury panels of Alabama.

Such exclusion is "an evil condemned by the Equal Protection Clause" (*Akins* v. *Texas*, 325 U.S. 398, 408), which violates the basic constitutional guarantee of a "fair trial in a fair tribunal" (*In re Murchison*, 349 U.S. 133, 136). For such exclusion deprived petitioners of a tribunal of impartial and indifferent jurors from the locality without discrimination (*Strauder* v. *West Virginia*, 100 U.S. 303; see *Irvin* v. *Dowd*, 366 U.S. 717), and firmly rooted in the minds of all those within the courtroom (most significantly, the twelve white jurors) that Negroes are unqualified to sit and render justice over their fellow citizens (*Strauder* v. *West Virginia*, *supra*; see *Cassell* v. *Texas*, 339 U.S. 282).

The denial of a fair trial is still further evidenced by the illegal election of the trial judge, even under the Alabama Constitution, which requires the lawful election of a judge as a prerequisite to his exercise of judicial power.[38] Yet, as the federal judiciary has recognized, the State of Alabama unconstitutionally deprives Negroes of their franchise. *Alabama* v. *United States*, 304 F. 2d 583, aff'd 371 U.S. 37.[39] And the United States Civil Rights Commission has documented in detail the county by county exclusion of qualified Negroes from the Alabama electorate.[40]

---

[38] Ala. Const. of 1901, Sec. 152.

[39] Thereinbelow the U.S. District Court stated (192 F. Supp. 677, 679 (M. D. Ala.)):

> "The evidence in this case is overwhelming to the effect that the State of Alabama, acting through its agents, including former members of the Board of Registrars of Macon County, has deliberately engaged in acts and practices designed to discriminate against qualified Negroes in their efforts to register to vote."

[40] 1961 Report of U.S. Civil Rights Commission (see p. 26 for paragraph summary of voting registration discrimination in Montgomery County). The detailed factual findings of this eminent government agency are entitled to consideration by

U.S. SUPREME COURT, OCTOBER 1963

BRIEF FOR THE PETITIONERS

Such long-standing exclusion of Negroes from voting in elections for State judges insured that the Trial Judge, in whom was vested "justice" in the form of the "atmosphere of the court room,"[41] would reflect, as in fact he did, the prejudice of the dominant, white community that elected him.

In this atmosphere of hostility, bigotry, intolerance, hatred and "intense resentment of the … white community …,"[42] can anyone expect or believe that an all-white jury could render a true and just verdict? It is inconceivable that these twelve men, with the attention of the whole community of their friends and neighbors focused on them, would be able to give their attention to the complex shadings of "truth," malice, fair comment and to the nuances of libel *per se,* injury to reputation and punitive damages despite the absence of proof of pecuniary damages. These twelve men were not, in fact or probably in their own minds, a jury of "peers" of petitioners, but rather an instrumentality for meting out punishment to critics of the political activities of their elected City Commissioner.

The provision of Section 2 of the Fourteenth Amendment, providing for reduction in representation in the event of denial of the right to vote in a federal election or in the election of "the Executive and Judicial officers of a State" is, in part, an implicit recognition that those so elected cannot sit as representatives of those discriminated against, and, therefore, cannot claim full representation. (*Cf. Baker* v. *Carr,* 369 U.S. 186).

In the case at bar, the Trial Judge was not only passively elected by a dominant, prejudiced, white electorate; he actively participated in the perpetuation of white supremacy within the State courts of Alabama. At the very time Trial Judge Jones was considering petitioners' motions for a new trial, he stated in a companion libel case to this one that the Fourteenth Amendment was "a pariah," and inapplicable in proceedings in Alabama State courts which are governed by "white man's justice."[43]

Given the cumulative pressure of all of these forms and techniques of emphasizing petitioners' racial inequality, it is clear that petitioners could not possibly receive a fair trial. The answer prescribes the remedy; for "the apprehended existence of prejudice was one inducement which led to the adoption of the Fourteenth Amendment," *U.S. ex rel. Goldsby* v. *Harpole,* 263 F. 2d 71, 81 (C. A. 5), cert. den., 361 U.S. 838; see also *Shelley* v. *Kraemer, supra.* **Jurisdiction to redress flagrant violations of fundamental constitutional rights "is not to be defeated under the name of local practice"**[44] Petitioners properly presented numerous objections to all these violations of fundamental rights, to the segregated courtroom, the racial bias and community hostility which pervaded the trial, the improper newspaper and television coverage of the trial,[45] the intentional and systematic exclusion of Negroes from the jury and from voting, the illegal election and improper qualification of the presiding Trial Judge and the *ad hominem* appeals of respondent's attorneys. Such abridgments of due process and equal protection were not and could not be waived and, under established authority, are properly before this Court for review.

These violations are inherent and implicit in the trial transcript, and too obvious for this Court not to notice. And, they are shockingly manifest outside the transcript as well. For, three decades after the decision in *Norris* v. *Alabama, supra,* one need only read *U.S. ex rel. Seals* v. *Wiman, supra,* to learn that Alabama still excludes Negroes from juries; *Alabama* v. *United States,* 304 F. 2d 583 (C. A. 5), aff'd 371 U.S. 37, to learn that Negroes are still excluded from voting in Alabama. In fact, state enforced racial segregation is the rule for all areas of public and civil activity,[46] a rule that will not, assuredly, be changed voluntarily by the officials of that state, if recent history is any accurate basis for prediction.[47]

---

this court. See *H. J. Heinz Co.* v. *NLRB,* 311 U.S. 514. The attempt to conceal the voting record of Montgomery County from federal government inspection is a fact also known to the federal courts. See *Alabama* v. *Rogers,* 187 F. Supp. 848 (M. D. Ala.), aff'd 285 F. 2d 430 (C. A. 5), cert. den. 366 U.S. 913.

[41] Judge Learned Hand in *Brown* v. *Walter,* 62 F. 2d 798, 799–800 (C. A. 2); See also *Herron* v. *Southern P. Co.,* 283 U.S. 91, 95.

[42] *NAACP* v. *Button, supra* at 435.

[43] See n. 3, p. 3, *supra* and n. 20, pp. 26–7, *supra.*

[44] *Davis* v. *Wechsler,* 263 U.S. 22, 24.

[45] See pp. 12–15, *supra* and n. 10 at p. 15, *supra.*

[46] See n. 7, p. 12, *supra.*

[47] Desegregation of the State University of Alabama was only achieved with the direct assistance of federal law enforcement authorities, and in the face of vigorous dissent by Alabama public officials. *Alabama* v. *United States,* 373 U.S. 545.

Public facilities in Alabama have been desegregated only after court litigation, and over strenuous opposition of state and local authorities. See: *Browder* v. *Gayle,* 142 F. Supp. 707 (M. D. Ala.), aff'd 352 U.S. 903, reh. den., 352 U.S. 950;

This Court has held repeatedly that violations of fundamental constitutional rights, which plainly appear on the record, are properly reviewable whether or not state "local forms" of practice have been complied with. *Fay* v. *Noia*, 372 U.S. 391; *Williams* v. *Georgia*, 349 U.S. 375; *Terminello* v. *Chicago*, 337 U.S. 1; *Patterson* v. *Alabama*, 294 U.S. 600; *Blackburn* v. *Alabama*, 361 U.S. 199; *U.S. ex rel. Goldsby* v. *Harpole*, 263 F. 2d 71 (C. A. 5), cert. den., 361 U.S. 838.

Moreover, where, as hereinabove shown, petitioners have raised objections as best they can, and have put the issues plainly before this Court, established authority requires review of these objections, even if they were not raised strictly in accordance with local forms of practice and procedural technicalities. *Rogers* v. *Alabama*, 192 U.S. 226. In *Rogers*, a Negro's objection to the selection of the Grand Jury, because Negroes had been excluded from the list of eligible persons, was stricken by the Alabama Court as not in statutorily prescribed form. This Court reviewed the objection and reversed the judgment below, even though it "assume[d] that this section was applicable to the motion," saying (p. 230):

"It is a necessary and well-settled rule that the exercise of jurisdiction by this court to protect constitutional rights cannot be declined when it is plain that the fair result of a decision is to deny the rights."

Accord: *Brown* v. *Mississippi*, 297 U.S. 278, 285; *Davis* v. *Wechsler, supra; American Ry.*

Express Co. v. *Levee*, 263 U.S. 19, 21; *Ward* v. *Love County*, 253 U.S. 17, 22.

As this Court held in *Davis* v. *Wechsler, supra*, at p. 24:

" ... the assertion of Federal rights, when plainly and reasonably made, is not to be defeated under the name of local practice."

CONCLUSION

Petitioners respectfully submit that the headlong clash between the proceedings and judgment below and the United States Constitution as interpreted by this Court requires reversal of the judgment and dismissal of respondent's suit herein, in order to preserve and protect those rights which are the Constitution's greatest gift.

Respectfully submitted,

I. H. WACHTEL,
CHARLES S. CONLEY,
BENJAMIN SPIEGEL,
RAYMOND S. HARRIS,
Attorneys for Petitioners.
1100 - 17th St., N.W.
Washington, D.C. 20036
HARRY H. WACHTEL,
SAMUEL R. PIERCE JR.,
JOSEPH B. RUSSELL,
DAVID N. BRAININ,
STEPHEN J. JELIN,
CLARENCE B. JONES,
DAVID G. LUBELL,
CHARLES B. MARKHAM,
WACHTEL & MICHAELSON,
BATTLE, FOWLER, STOKES & KHEEL,
LUBELL, LUBELL & JONES,
Of Counsel.

APPENDIX B

Constitutional and statutory provisions involved

The constitutional provisions herein involved are the First, Fourteenth and Fifteenth Amendments to the Constitution of the United States, which read as follows:

* * * * *

Baldwin v. *Morgan*, 251 F. 2d 780 (C. A. 5); *Baldwin* v. *Morgan*, 287 F. 2d 750 (C. A. 5); *Gilmore* v. *City of Montgomery*, 176 F. Supp. 776 (M. D. Ala.), modified and aff'd, 277 F. 2d 364 (C. A. 5); *Boman* v. *Birmingham Transit Co.*, 280 F. 2d 531 (C. A. 5); *Lewis* v. *The Greyhound Corp.*, 199 F. Supp. 210 (M. D. Ala.); *Sawyer* v. *City of Mobile, Alabama*, 208 F. Supp. 548 (S. D. Ala.); *Shuttlesworth* v. *Gaylord*, 202 F. Supp. 59 (N. D. Ala.), aff'd *sub. nom. Hanes* v. *Shuttlesworth*, 310 F. 2d 303 (C. A. 5); *Cobb* v. *Montgomery Library Board*, 207 F. Supp. 880 (M. D. ala.).

Alabama has failed to desegregate its public school system in compliance with the mandate of this Court in *Brown* v. *Board of Education, supra*, and has purposefully passed a series of statutes designed to evade compliance therewith. (See Alabama Code, Title 52 § 61 (13) authorizing the closing of integration-threatened schools by boards of education; *Id.*, Title 52 § 197(1)–(30) providing for secession of individual schools from local and state systems and for their organization into independent districts; *Id.*, Title 52 § 61(20) permitting allocation of education funds to private schools, etc.) See also *Statistical Summary, November 1961*, Southern Education Reporting Service, 5–6.

Amendment I

Congress shall make no law respecting an establishment of religion, or prohibiting the free exercise thereof; or abridging the freedom of speech, or of the press; or the right of the people peaceably to assemble, and to petition the Government for a redress of grievances.

* * * * *

Amendment XIV

Section 1. All persons born or naturalized in the United States, and subject to the jurisdiction thereof, are citizens of the United States and of the State wherein they reside. No State shall make or enforce any law which shall abridge the privileges or immunities of citizens of the United States; nor shall any State deprive any person of life, liberty, or property, without due process of law; nor deny to any person within its jurisdiction the equal protection of the laws.

Section 2. Representatives shall be apportioned among the several States according to their respective numbers, counting the whole number of persons in each State, excluding Indians not taxed. But when the right to vote at any election for the choice of electors for President and Vice President of the United States, Representatives in Congress, the Executive and Judicial officers of a State, or the members of the Legislature thereof, is denied to any of the male inhabitants of such State, being twenty-one years of age, and citizens of the United States, or in any way abridged, except for participation in rebellion, or other crime, the basis of representation therein shall be reduced in the proportion which the number of such male citizens shall bear to the whole number of male citizens twenty-one years of age in such State.

Section 3. No person shall be a Senator or Representative in Congress, or elector of President and Vice President, or hold any office, civil or military, under the United States, or under any State, who, having previously taken an oath, as a member of Congress, or as an officer of the United States, or as a member of any State legislature, or as an executive or judicial officer of any State, to support the Constitution of the United States, shall have engaged in insurrection or rebellion against the same, or given aid or comfort to the enemies thereof. But Congress may by a vote of two-thirds of each House, remove such disability.

Section 4. The validity of the public debt of the United States, authorized by law, including debts incurred for payment of pensions and bounties for services in suppressing insurrection or rebellion, shall not be questioned. But neither the United States nor any State shall assume or pay any debt or obligation incurred in aid of insurrection or rebellion against the United States, or any claims for the loss or emancipation of any slave; but all such debts, obligations and claims shall be held illegal and void.

Section 5. The Congress shall have power to enforce, by appropriate legislation, the provisions of this article.

Amendment XV

Section 1. The right of citizens of the United States to vote shall not be denied or abridged by the United States or by any State on account of race, color, or previous condition of servitude.

Section 2. The Congress shall have power to enforce this article by appropriate legislation.

In the Supreme Court of the United States

October Term, 1963

No. 40

RALPH D. ABERNATHY ET AL., PETITIONERS,
V.
L. B. SULLIVAN, RESPONDENT

ON WRIT OF CERTIORARI TO THE SUPREME COURT OF ALABAMA

BRIEF FOR RESPONDENT[1]

STEINER, CRUM & BAKER,
1109–25 First National Bank Building,
Montgomery 1, Alabama,
CALVIN WHITESELL,
Montgomery, Alabama
Of Counsel.
ROBERT E. STEINER III.,
SAM RICE BAKER,
M. ROLAND NACHMAN JR.,
Attorneys for Respondent

OPINIONS BELOW

The opinion of the Supreme Court of Alabama (R. 1139) is reported in 273 Ala. 656, 144 So. 2d 25.

JURISDICTION

Petitioners have sought to invoke this Court's jurisdiction under 28 U.S.C., § 1257 (3).

QUESTIONS PRESENTED

1. Will this Court review a state jury verdict in a private common law libel action, embodied in a final state judgment and affirmed by a state's highest appellate court, when alleged federal questions asserted in this Court were not timely raised below in accordance with state procedure, and when there is nothing in the record to support the allegations of the petition and brief?

2. Is there a constitutionally guaranteed absolute privilege to defame an elected city official, under guise of criticism, in a paid newspaper advertisement so that participants in the publication of this defamation are immune from private common law libel judgment in a state court in circumstances where, because of the admitted falsity of the publication, the participants are unable to plead truth, privilege or retraction (to show good faith and eliminate punitive damages)?

3. Are libelous utterances in a paid newspaper advertisement within the area of constitutionally protected speech and press?

4. When persons whose names appear on a defamatory newspaper advertisement as "warm endorsers" of the advertisement do not deny participation in its publication in response to a

[1] To conserve the time of this Court the brief filed by this respondent in No. 39, New York Times Company v. Sullivan, will be referred to throughout this brief when the same issues have been covered there.

demand for retraction which charges publication, and ratify by silence, and when there is other evidence of authority for use of their names on the advertisement, will this Court re-examine a state jury verdict of liability in a private common law libel action, embodied in a final judgment affirmed by the highest state appellate court on a record which a Federal Court of Appeals has found to contain state questions of "substance" which could "go either way." on a bare assertion that the same record is totally devoid of evidence of petitioners' participation in the publication of this defamatory advertisement?

5. When an admittedly false newspaper advertisement charges that city police massively engaged in rampant, vicious, terroristic and criminal actions in deprivation of the rights of others, is a state court holding in a private common law libel action that such an utterance is libelous as a matter of state law—leaving to the jury the questions of publication, identification with the police commissioner, and damages—an infringement of constitutional rights of a participant in the publication of the libel?

6. When a paid newspaper advertisement published in circumstances described in Questions 2 and 4 contains admittedly false charges described in Question 5 about police action in a named city, may this Court consistently with its decisions and the 7th Amendment review on certiorari a state jury finding that the publication is "of and concerning" the city police commissioner whose name does not appear in the publication, and an award of general and punitive damages to him, when this state jury verdict embodied in a final state judgment has been approved by the state's highest appellate court?

7. May this Court consistently with its decisions and the 7th Amendment re-examine facts tried by a state jury when those findings have been embodied in a final state judgment affirmed by the highest state appellate court, and when review is sought on assertions that the verdict is wrong and the general and punitive libel damages merely excessive?

STATUTES INVOLVED

Statutes referred to in this brief are contained in an appendix.

STATEMENT

Petitioners, whose names appeared in a paid advertisement in the New York Times of March 29, 1960 (described in No. 39) as "warm endorsers" of the material contained in the advertisement, were joined as co-defendants in a common law libel action against The New York Times. The nature of the ad as a defamation, and not a political expression; its extensive falsity, not one "minor discrepancy" (Brief pp. 11, 17 and 42);[2] its reference to respondent; the questions of libel *per se* and truth as a limitation on libelous utterances; the circumstances of the ad's composition, publication and distribution; and other relevant facts of record are fully discussed in respondent's brief in No. 39. As observed there, these petitioners, two residents of Montgomery, and all residents of Alabama, introduced no testimony whatever to attempt to substantiate in any manner the truth of the defamatory material in the advertisement. Nor did they plead specially truth, or privilege.

The jury returned a joint verdict against The New York Times and petitioners in accordance with Alabama procedure,[3] for Five Hundred Thousand Dollars, and the trial court entered a judgment thereon.

In the case which was tried below, as distinguished from the case which petitioners attempt to bring in this Court, the only alleged defect of due process which petitioners asserted at the trial was a contention that there was an entire absence of evidence connecting them with the publication of the advertisement.

Petitioners filed motions for new trial but allowed them to lapse (R. 984, 999, 1013, 1028). Petitioners' assertion that there was a "general understanding" (Brief, pp. 14–15) which should have prevented this lapse and which was violated by the trial court and presumably by respondent's attorneys is absolutely contrary to fact. The record is barren of even a hint of such an understanding. The record shows that petitioners' then attorneys (none of whom have

---

[2] Petitioners are entirely inaccurate in their observation that other "alleged inaccuracies in the ad were conceded by respondent Sullivan to refer to matters within the jurisdiction of the State Education Department or other agencies, and to matters occurring long prior to respondent's taking office" (Brief, p. 12).

[3] Such a joint verdict against joint tort-feasors is required by Alabama procedure, *Bell v. Riley Bus Lines*, 257 Ala. 120, 57 So. 2d 612. It is, of course, collectible only once.

appeared in this Court) made no attempt to continue the motion within each thirty day period as required by Alabama statutory and case law. The Times' attorneys obviously were unaware of such an "understanding" since they continued The Times' motion from January 14, 1961 to February 10, 1961 (R. 968) and from February 10, 1961 to March 3, 1961 (R. 968), when the motion was heard. Moreover, none of the assignments of error in the Supreme Court of Alabama relating to their motion for new trial (R. 1100–1132) even mentioned that there was any "understanding." Clearly there was not. And clearly the motion lapsed.[4]

The court below affirmed the judgment as to all defendants.

At the trial petitioners denied any connection with the publication of the advertisement. But contrary to what petitioners would have this Court believe, their denial was far from "undisputed", as this record and the following summary of it make clear. Certainly the jury was not required as a matter of law to believe petitioners' protestations of innocence.

Respondent showed at the trial that the names of the petitioners were on the advertisement. They did not reply to respondent's demand for retraction, and their silence in the face of the demand's inculpatory charges that each published the libel under circumstances normally calling for a reply, was evidence from which a jury could find that they had admitted the statements contained in the demand, namely, that they had published the material in the ad. Their failure to deny publication—not their failure to retract—is the basis of the admission.

Moreover, petitioners' silence, and their failure in any manner to disavow the advertisement, constituted a ratification.

In addition, a letter from A. Philip Randolph (R. 587) went to the jury without objection from petitioners as part of The Times' answer to an interrogatory asking for authorization from the signers of the advertisement.[5]

Though petitioners recite that "undisputed" evidence (Brief, pp. 8 and 46) established that their names were not on the Randolph letter, and called the contrary finding below "distorted," the sworn answers to the interrogatories were in evidence, and Times witness Redding, according to the Times' brief in this Court, "did not recall this difference in the list of names …" (Times Brief in No. 39, p. 16).

A witness for the Times, Aaronson, testified without objection from petitioners, that the Randolph letter was a "written communication confirming the fact that the persons whose names were given here had authorized it" (R. 739), and that such a letter was "our usual authorization" (R. 740). Murray, the author of the ad, a witness for petitioners, testified that the executive director of the committee which inserted the ad, one Bayard Rustin, had stated that the southern ministers, including petitioners, did not have to be contacted or consulted since they were all members of the Southern Christian Leadership Conference, and supported the work of the committee (R. 809).

While not in this record, the report of *Abernathy v. Patterson,* 295 F. 2d 452 (5th Cir.), cert. den. 368 U.S. 986, shows that the complaint of these petitioners in that case verified by oath of Petitioner Abernathy strongly underlines the correctness of the jury verdict.[6]

U.S. SUPREME
COURT,
OCTOBER 1963

BRIEF FOR
RESPONDENT

---

[4] Title 13, § 119, Code of Alabama, 1940 (App. A. p. 29); *Mount Vernon Woodbury Mills v. Judges,* 200 Ala. 168, 75 So. 916; *Ex parte Margart,* 207 Ala. 604, 93 So. 505; *Southern Ry. Co. v. Blackwell,* 211 Ala. 216, 100 So. 215.

[5] This letter stated:

"This will certify that the names included on the enclosed list are all signed members of the Committee to Defend Martin Luther King and The Struggle for Freedom in the South. Please be assured that they have all given me permission to use their names in furthering the work of our Committee."

[6] The painstaking analysis of the Court of Appeals revealed:
1. "(The complaint) alleges that on or about March 29, 1960, 'supporters of the plaintiffs and the movement for equality which they lead' inserted in The New York Times a paid advertisement …" (295 F. 2d at 453).

2. The advertisement "purports to be signed by twenty ministers including the four plaintiffs" (295 F. 2d at 454).

3. "The complaint then alleges: 'The defendants … conspired and planned … to deter and prohibit the plaintiffs and their supporters as set forth above, from utilizing their constitutional rights and in particular their right to access to a free press, by instituting fraudulent actions in libel against the plaintiffs …' " (295 F. 2d at 454).

4. "Irreparable damage is alleged, as follows: ' … (b) … the plaintiffs herein … will be deterred from using the media of a free press and all other rights guaranteed under the 1st Amendment …' " (295 F. 2d at 454).

5. "The relief prayed for is as follows: ' … (c) … Restraining each of the defendants … from engaging in the aforesaid conspiracy designed to deter and prohibit the plaintiffs from exercising rights guaranteed by the 1st and

U.S. SUPREME
COURT,
OCTOBER 1963

BRIEF FOR
RESPONDENT

The foregoing states the facts relating to this case.

The following matters, stated by petitioners to be in this case, are not.

A. Matters outside the record which petitioners did not raise in the trial court, but attempted to raise for the first time in the Supreme Court of Alabama

1. An alleged racially segregated court room. There is nothing in the record to support this. It was not raised in the trial court. Had it been, respondent would have strongly controverted the allegation as entirely untrue.[7]

2. An alleged "atmosphere of racial bias, passion and hostile community pressures" (Petition, p. 2). This was not raised in the trial court. There was no motion for change of venue, continuance, or for mistrial, though three lawyers represented the petitioners and five represented The New York Times at the trial (R. 567–568). Their silence in this regard speaks eloquently for the fair and impartial manner in which the trial judge conducted the trial. There is nothing in the record to support this allegation.

3. Alleged improper newspaper and television coverage at the trial. This was not raised in the trial court, nor were there motions for mistrial, change of venue, or continuance. There is nothing in the record to support the allegations. Had there been timely trial motions attacking the propriety of newspaper and television coverage of the trial, respondent would have strongly controverted them.

4. Alleged intentional and systematic exclusion of Negroes from the jury. This was not raised in the trial court and there is nothing in the record to support the allegation. Had the allegation been made, respondent would have strongly controverted it.[8]

5. Alleged unqualified trial judge—illegally elected and illegally a member of the county jury commission. This matter was not raised in the trial court. There was no motion seeking disqualification of the trial judge. There is nothing in the record to support the allegation. Had the charge been made in timely fashion, it would have been strongly controverted.

6. Alleged improper closing argument of one of the attorneys for respondent. There is nothing in the trial record about this. No objection to any argument of any attorney is in the record. There was no motion for mistrial. Had such objection or motion been made, respondent would have strongly controverted any suggestion of an improper argument. It is noteworthy that the Times makes no such allegation in this Court.

The record references contained in petitioners' brief on some of these points concern testimony offered by The Times in support of its motion for new trial, after petitioners' motion had lapsed. As the court below held, the trial court correctly excluded such evidence under the well-settled Alabama rule that only when newly discovered evidence is the basis for a motion for new trial is the trial court permitted to extend the hearing to matters not contained in the record of the trial.[9] Obviously the Times and these petitioners realize that the trial court ruling was correct. No petitioner challenges the ruling of the courts below here. Unlike the Times, however, these petitioners simply cite this rejected material as evidence anyway, and ask this Court to consider matters outside the record which were not raised in the trial below.

14th Amendments with respect to freedom of speech, press …' " (295 F. 2d at 455).

6. "As has been noted (on page 454), the plaintiffs' claim of irreparable injury and loss is based (1) upon the claim that 'the plaintiffs and the Negro citizens of the State of Alabama will be deterred from using the media of a free press …' " (295 F. 2d at 456).

7. "Libelous utterances or publications are not within the area of constitutionally protected speech and press. The plaintiffs' claim that they will be deterred from using the media of a free press must therefore be predicated upon their claims of denial of a fair and impartial trial of the libel actions and the absence of a plain, adequate and complete remedy at law" (295 F. 2d at 456–457).

7 Petitioners tell this Court that court room segregation "has been judicially noted to be a longstanding practice in the

state courts of Alabama …" (Brief, p. 53). They cite *U.S. ex rel. Seals v. Wiman,* 304 F. 2d 53 (5th Cir. 1962). But that case specifically held that the question of a segregated courthouse, there sought to be raised, "[was] not presented to the State courts on the appeal from the judgment of conviction, on the petition for leave to file coram nobis, or in any other manner. Those questions cannot therefore be considered here" (304 F. 2d at 56).

8 When this question was appropriately raised in a recent case, the method of selecting Montgomery County juries passed constitutional muster in this Court. *Reeves v. Alabama,* 355 U.S. 368, dismissing the writ of certiorari "as improvidently granted."

9 (R. 1165) citing *Thomason v. Silvey,* 123 Ala. 694, 26 So. 644; and *Alabama Gas Company v. Jones,* 244 Ala. 413, 13 So. 2d 873.

B. Matters outside the record which petitioners did not seek to raise in the trial court or in the Supreme Court of Alabama

1. Petitioners object to the court reporter's transcript designation of their attorneys as "Lawyer." This matter was not raised in either court below. The record was obviously transcribed by the court reporter after the trial was over. It was prepared at the instance of The New York Times; filed by The Times with the clerk of the trial court; and "joined in" by these petitioners (R. 1031). Under Alabama procedure, these petitioners had an opportunity to make any objection to the transcript which they desired, and to bring the matter to the attention of the trial court for ruling.[10] Moreover, the transcript, noting appearances, refers to these, and all other attorneys, as "Esq." (R. 567–568).

Obviously these designations by the court reporter are his own, and were made after the trial had closed. They do not purport to be, nor are they, quotations of the manner of address used by the attorneys in the case or by the trial judge. A search of the record reveals that only an attorney for the New York Times used this form of address in the proceedings before the trial court without a jury.[11]

2. Petitioners object to an alleged statement by the trial judge regarding "white man's justice," said to have been made by him three months after this trial concluded. The matter was not raised in either court below. There was no motion to disqualify the judge.

But this record **does** reveal that this judge stated to the jury in his oral charge (R. 819–20):

"Now, one other thing I would like to say although I think it is hardly necessary—one of the defendants in this case is a corporate defendant and some of the others belong to various races and in your deliberation in arriving at your verdict, all of these defendants whether they be corporate or individuals or whether they belong to this race or that doesn't have a thing on earth to do with this case but let the evidence and the law be the two pole stars that will guide you and try to do justice in fairness to all of these parties here. They have no place on earth to go to settle this dispute except to come before a Court of our country and lay the matter before a jury of twelve men in whose selection each party has had the right to participate and out of all the jurors we had here at this term of Court, some fifty jurors, the parties here have selected you because they have confidence in your honesty, your integrity, your judgment and your common sense. Please remember, gentlemen of the jury, that all of the parties that stand here stand before you on equal footing and are all equal at the Bar of Justice."

3. The allegation that there was a "general understanding" about petitioners' motion for new trial has already been covered. The point was not raised in either court below.

4. The allegation that an all-white jury deprived petitioners of their rights. This allegation was not made in either court below. Any such allegation of misconduct on the part of the jury would have been strongly controverted by respondent.

5. The pendency of other libel suits is a matter entirely outside this record; and not presented in either court below. The utter desperation involved in this attempt to bring in other libel suits is fully discussed in respondent's Brief in Opposition in No. 39. The argument will not be repeated here. The baseless and totally unfounded charge that this case is "part of a concerted, calculated program to carry out a policy of punishing, intimidating and silencing all who criticize and seek to change Alabama's notorious political system of enforced segregation" (Brief, p. 29) is simply a figment of the imagination of petitioners and their appellate lawyers. The charge is totally without foundation in the record or in fact. Significantly, none of the numerous attorneys representing the Times and these petitioners at the trial even questioned respondent about such a preposterous matter.

6. Alleged "deliberate, arbitrary, capricious, and discriminatory misapplications of law" (Petition, p. 12). It is impossible to determine what the reference is. It cannot have been raised in either court below.

It is not clear from petitioners' brief whether they claim that these matters outside the record (sub-heads "A" and "B") were raised by "steps" said to have been taken "to preserve their constitutional rights" (Brief, p. 14). Petitioners summarize these "steps" as demurrers to the complaint; objections to the admission of evidence; motions to exclude evidence as insufficient; motions for

U.S. SUPREME COURT, OCTOBER 1963

BRIEF FOR RESPONDENT

---

[10] Title 7, § 827 (1a), Alabama Code, Appendix A, p. 27.

[11] "Mr. Embry: … I will read Lawyer Gray's examinations" (R. 550).

"Mr. Embry: At this time, your Honor, Lawyer Gray said, 'That's all' " (R. 551).

U.S. SUPREME
COURT,
OCTOBER 1963

BRIEF FOR
RESPONDENT

special jury findings; written requests to charge the jury; and motions for directed verdict in their favor (Brief, p. 14). Obviously, such "steps" could not raise the foregoing points in "A" and "B" under any known rules of practice. It is perfectly plain that the questions were never presented at the trial. And later observations that the questions are "inherent and implicit in the trial transcript" (Brief, p. 59), and "shockingly manifest outside the transcript as well" (Brief, p. 60), reveal clearly that petitioners, too, know these matters were never raised, and are not part of the record before this Court.

C. Matters raised below but concluded to petitioners' apparent satisfaction at the time

This category relates to the pronunciation of the word "Negro." This entirely spurious objection vanished when, whatever the pronunciation had been, the pronouncing attorney was told to "read it just like it is" (R. 579). That was the end of the matter. No further objection was lodged by counsel for these petitioners, even though respondent's counsel spoke the word on at least a dozen additional occasions.[12] Moreover, there is nothing in the record to show precisely how the word was pronounced.

D. Matters foreclosed from the statement of facts by virtue of petitioners' improper procedure below

When petitioners allowed their motions for new trial to lapse, they were foreclosed from raising questions regarding alleged excessiveness of the verdict or alleged insufficiency of the evidence.[13]

SUMMARY OF ARGUMENT[14]

I.

When the only defect of procedural due process asserted at the trial was an alleged entire absence of evidence connecting petitioners with the publication of the ad, they cannot go outside the record and seek to present to this Court new

matters—none of which were raised in the trial court, and many of which were not asserted in the Supreme Court of Alabama. Included in this category are those arguments in this Court which allege a segregated trial courtroom; a hostile and prejudiced trial atmosphere; improper newspaper and television coverage of the trial; illegal composition of the jury; improper argument of one of the lawyers for respondent; improper court reporter's designation of petitioners' attorneys in the appellate transcript of the record prepared many months **after** the trial was over; improper statements allegedly made by the trial judge three months **after** the trial had ended; pendency of other libel suits by different plaintiffs, against different defendants, regarding different publications, in different communications media, brought in different forums, with different attorneys, and different issues; illegal election of the trial judge.

Had these allegations been made before or during the trial, they would have been strongly controverted. Since these assertions of alleged federal questions were not made in timely fashion, this Court will not go outside the record to consider them. *Stroble v. California*, 343 U.S. 181, 193–194 (charges of inflammatory newspaper accounts and community prejudice); *Michel v. Louisiana*, 350 U.S. 91 (systematic exclusion of Negroes from grand jury panels not raised in time); *Edelman v. California*, 344 U.S. 357, 358–359 (vagueness of vagrancy statute not raised at the trial); *Stembridge v. Georgia*, 343 U.S. 541, 547 (federal rights asserted for first time in state appellate court); *Bailey v. Anderson*, 326 U.S. 203, 206–207 (same holding); *Herndon v. Georgia*, 295 U.S. 441, 443 (trial court rulings not preserved in accordance with state practice); *Hanson v. Denckla*, 357 U.S. 235, 243–244.

Since petitioners allowed their motions for new trial to lapse, they may not question the size of the verdict against them or the sufficiency of the evidence. *State v. Ferguson*, 269 Ala. 44, 45, 110 So. 2d 280; *Shelley v. Clark*, 267 Ala. 621, 625, 103 So. 2d 743.

Moreover, it is noteworthy that the Times does not argue that the trial proceedings were defective or that they were other than fair and impartial.

II.

The only federal question of due procedure raised at the trial was whether there was **any** evi-

---

[12] R. 580; 581; 592; 593; 631; and 656.
[13] *State v. Ferguson*, 269 Ala. 44, 45, 110 So. 2d 280; *Shelley v. Clark*, 267 Ala. 621, 625, 103 So. 2d 743.
[14] Respondent refers this Court to his summary of argument in New York Times Company v. Sullivan, No. 39, where applicable. Respondent has there set out a summary of the constitutional questions relating to the substantive Alabama law of libel as applied in this case. Those arguments will not be repeated in this brief.

dence connecting petitioners with the publication of the ad. Positive evidence of authority for the use of their names on the ad, supplemented by evidence of their conduct and admissions, proved the case against petitioners for submission to a jury.

Their names were on the ad; and the Randolph letter, according to the Times' answers to interrogatories, showed authorization.

In addition, petitioners did not reply to Sullivan's demand for retraction which expressly charged them with publication. Their silence in the face of the inculpatory charges contained in this demand, under circumstances normally calling for a reply, was evidence from which a jury could find an admission of the statements contained in the letters demanding retraction. This failure to deny publication—not their failure to retract—is the basis of admission. A litigant will not be heard to say that his extrajudicial statements or conduct, inconsistent with his position taken at the trial, is so little worthy of credence that the trier of fact should not even consider them. *Parks v. New York Times Company,* 308 F. 2d 424 (5th Cir. 1962); *Perry v. Johnston,* 59 Ala. 648, 651; *Peck v. Ryan,* 110 Ala. 336, 17 So. 733; *Craft v. Koonce,* 237 Ala. 552, 187 So. 730; *Sloss-Sheffield Co. v. Sharp,* 156 Ala. 284, 47 So. 279; Annotation 70 A. L. R. 2d 1099; Wigmore on *Evidence,* § 1071; Morgan on Admissions, included in *Selected Writings on Evidence,* p. 829.

Closely allied to the doctrine of silence as admission is the equally well-established principle that one may ratify by silence and acquiescence the act of another, even though the persons involved are strangers. This Alabama rule applies whether or not there is a pre-existing agency relationship. *Parks v. New York Times Company,* 308 F. 2d 424 (5th Cir. 1962); *Birmingham News Co. v. Birmingham Printing Co.,* 209 Ala. 403, 407, 96 So. 336, 340–341; *Goldfield v. Brewbaker Motors* (Ala. App.), 36 Ala. App. 152, 54 So. 2d 797, cert. denied 256 Ala. 383, 54 So. 2d 800; *Woodmen of the World Ins. Co. v. Bolin,* 243 Ala. 426, 10 So. 2d 296; *Belcher Lumber Co. v. York,* 245 Ala. 286, 17 So. 2d 281; 1 *Restatement of Agency 2d,* Sec. 94, page 244; Comments (a) and (b); 3 *Restatement of Agency 2d* (App. pages 168 and 174).

III.

Libelous utterances are not within the area of constitutionally protected speech and press. *Roth v. United States,* 354 U.S. 476, 483; *Beauharnais v. Illinois,* 343 U.S. 250, 256; *Chaplinsky v. New Hampshire,* 315 U.S. 568, 571–572; *Konigsberg v. State Bar of California,* 366 U.S. 36, 49–50; *Near v. Minnesota,* 283 U.S. 697, 715.

ARGUMENT

I. This court will not go outside the record to consider federal questions which were not timely raised in accordance with state procedure

This brief should be stricken for failure to comply with Rule 40 (5) of the Rules of this Court.[15] In addition to the matters outside the record which were not raised in the trial court, and in some instances not even in the Supreme Court of Alabama, petitioners' brief contains lengthy expositions of cases and other materials relating to racial matters involving peonage, education, voting, housing and zoning, public transportation, parks, libraries, petit and grand jury service, municipal boundaries, and reapportionment. In the aggregate, such material and excursions from the record consume almost forty-five per cent of petitioners' brief.

Quite apart from the duty of attorneys to confine issues and discussions to matters appearing in the record, particularly when seeking review in this Court, it is noteworthy that not one of the attorneys appearing here for these petitioners was their counsel in the trial court and none was present there. These appellate attorneys are, therefore, peculiarly unqualified to comment on matters not in the record.

This Court will surely note that the brief of The New York Times in No. 39 does not support petitioners' characterization of the trial proceedings. Several of its attorneys were personally present at the trial; participated in it; and know how it was conducted. They make no complaints of trial unfairness.

This is the second time petitioners have brought their baseless charges here. Their petition in *Abernathy v. Patterson,* 368 U.S. 986, climaxed a

---

[15] "Briefs must be compact, logically arranged with proper headings, concise, and free from burdensome, irrelevant, immaterial, and scandalous matter. Briefs not complying with this paragraph may be disregarded and stricken by the Court."

parade of these same groundless attacks through the entire federal judiciary. The District Court called them "impertinent"; the Court of Appeals upheld that court's dismissal of the complaint, 295 F. 2d 452 and this Court denied certiorari.

It is too elemental for argument that this Court will not go outside the record to consider alleged federal questions which were not timely raised in accordance with state procedure. *Stroble v. California,* 343 U.S. 181, 193–194 (charges of inflammatory newspaper accounts and community prejudice); *Michel v. Louisiana,* 350 U.S. 91 (systematic exclusion of Negroes from grand jury panels not raised in time); *Edelman v. California,* 344 U.S. 357, 358–359 (vagueness of vagrancy statute not raised at the trial); *Stembridge v. Georgia,* 343 U.S. 541, 547 (federal rights asserted for first time in state appellate court); *Bailey v. Anderson,* 326 U.S. 203, 206–207 (same holding); *Herndon v. Georgia,* 295 U.S. 441, 443 (trial court rulings not preserved in accordance with state practice); *Hanson v. Denckla,* 357 U.S. 235, 243–244:

> "We need not determine whether Florida was bound to give full faith and credit to the decree of the Delaware Chancellor since the question was not seasonably presented to the Florida court. Radio Station WOW v. Johnson, 326 U.S. 120, 128."

Thus, aside from the question of whether petitioners have an asserted absolute privilege to defame public officials under the guise of criticism, and thereby to avoid Alabama libel laws—a matter fully discussed in respondent's brief in No. 39, incorporated herein by reference—the only question which petitioners can argue on this record is whether it is "devoid of probative evidence of authorization or publication by any of the petitioners of the alleged libel or of any malice on their part" (Brief, p. 44).

As this Court held in *Garner v. Louisiana,* 368 U.S. 157, 163–164:

> "As in Thompson v. Louisville (citation), our inquiry does not turn on a question of sufficiency of evidence to support a conviction, but on whether these convictions rest upon **any evidence** which would support a finding that the petitioners' acts caused a disturbance of the peace." (Emphasis supplied.)

II. There was ample evidence of petitioners' publication for submission to a jury

Positive evidence of authority for use of their names on the ad, supplemented by evidence of their conduct and admissions, proved the case against petitioners for submission to a jury.

Their names were on the ad; they did not reply to Sullivan's demand for a retraction which expressly charged them with publication, and their silence in the face of the inculpatory charges contained in the demand for retraction, under circumstances normally calling for a reply, was evidence from which a jury could find an admission of the statements contained in the letters demanding retraction. This admission came from their failure to deny publication—not their failure to retract.

Moreover, their silence and their failure in any manner to disavow the ad constituted a ratification.

The Randolph letter, according to The Times' answers to interrogatories, showed authorization. Testimony of Murray and of The Times' witness, Aaronson, has been cited. Clearly such evidence permitted a jury to decide where the truth lay. And, as pointed out, the sworn complaint in *Abernathy v. Patterson,* 295 F. 2d 452 (5th Cir.), cert. denied 368 U.S. 986, strongly corroborated the correctness of this verdict.

The Alabama trial court and Supreme Court held that there was a jury question on the issue of petitioners' liability as participants in the publication. The Court of Appeals in *Parks v. New York Times Company,* 308 F. 2d 474 (5th Cir. 1962), held that the position of this respondent in the state courts had substance, and that on the question of liability of these petitioners the judgment could "go either way" (308 F. 2d at 480–481). This is the classic situation for jury determination.

It is impossible to understand petitioners' assertion here that the Court of Appeals reversed the District Court "on other grounds" (Brief, p. 44). This erroneous assertion is simply in direct conflict with the holding of the Court. Moreover, in view of the Court's extensive and exhaustive discussion of silence in the face of the inculpatory charges in the demand for retraction as evidence from which a jury could "infer ratification or adoption" (308 F. 2d at 479), it is inconceivable that petitioners argue here (Brief, p. 45) that *Parks* "is clearly shown by the Opinion to rest on matters not contained in the Record in this case …" The very record on the merits in this case was introduced in the District Court in *Parks.*

The Alabama courts and the Federal Court of Appeals were clearly correct. Petitioners, in their lengthy brief, do not even attempt to challenge the legal authorities cited by respondent in his brief in opposition (pp. 15–18) except to say that they are inapplicable (Brief, pp. 48–49). But they are not, and give solid support to the jury finding of petitioners' liability.

A. Silence as admission

1. Petitioners' silence was an admission. This failure to deny publication—not their failure to retract—is the basis of the admission. Petitioners seem unable to distinguish between a retraction and a denial of publication. It is as simple as the rationale of admissions—that a litigant will not be heard to say that his extrajudicial statements or conduct inconsistent with his position taken at the trial, is so little worthy of credence that the trier of facts should not even consider them.[16]

The Legislature of Alabama, too, has given considerable importance to a demand for retraction in libel cases. Title 7, § 914, Code of Alabama (App. A of Brief in No. 39). The plaintiff in a libel suit such as this may not obtain punitive damages unless he seeks retraction from the defendant; and a defendant may eliminate his liability for punitive damages by retracting.

In much less compelling circumstances, *Gould v. Kramer*, 253 Mass. 433, 149 N. E. 142, 144, held that an admission of the truth of a letter charging defendant with authorship of another letter which had defamed the plaintiff could be considered from the silence of the defendant on receiving the written charge. This suit sought damages for false and malicious statements made by the defendant about the plaintiff in a letter to plaintiff's employer. Defendant contended that he had not signed or authorized the libelous matter contained in the letter.

While the principle of silence as an admission has been held not to obtain when the inculpatory statement was made in an unanswered letter, a well-recognized exception to this letter principle occurs where the unanswered letter contains a demand, or where it is part of a mutual correspondence.[17]

2. The absurd argument in petitioners' brief (pp. 49–52) that this rule of admissions—long a part of the law of evidence throughout this country—somehow violates a fancied federal right deserves no answer. It is undoubtedly based upon the inability of petitioners to distinguish between a denial of publication and a retraction. A denial does not involve a "dissociation" of belief in the underlying subject matter. If one has published a defamatory statement, he can and should be liable for civil damages in a common law libel action. If he had nothing to do with the defamatory publication, he certainly knows it, and is in a position to deny promptly. In short, these petitioners could have done exactly what they did at the trial—deny publication in an answer to the letter charging it.

Moreover, petitioners' argument that the retraction statute imposes too great a financial burden upon them is equally frivolous. If these petitioners had wanted a forum as wide as that of the advertisement, they could have written, most inexpensively, a letter to the New York Times for publication and there explained their alleged innocence.

These petitioners in response to the demand for retraction were not called upon to restate their views of the subject matter if in fact they had not participated in the publication. All the demand required in order to avoid this well established rule of evidence was a denial of publication. This is the rule of liability about which petitioners here complain. It involves no federal question whatever. It is as plain and simple a question of a state rule of evidence as can be imagined.

B. Petitioners ratified and acquiesced in the use of their names on the advertisement

Closely allied to the doctrine of silence as an admission is the equally well established principle that one may ratify by silence and acquiescence the act of another even though the persons involved are strangers. Alabama authorities and those elsewhere are thoroughly

---

[16] See *Perry v. Johnston,* 59 Ala. 648, 651; *Peck v. Ryan,* 110 Ala. 336, 17 So. 733; *Craft v. Koonce,* 237 Ala. 552, 187 So. 730; *Sloss-Sheffield Co. v. Sharp,* 156 Ala. 284, 47 So. 279; Annotation 70 A. L. R. 2d 1099; Wigmore on *Evidence,* § 1071; Morgan on *Admissions,* included in *Selected Writings on Evidence,* p. 829.

[17] See annotations in 8 A. L. R. 1163; 34 A. L. R. 560; 55 A. L. R. 460. Alabama, too, recognizes this exception to the letter rule. See *Denson v. Kirkpatrick Drilling Co.,* 225 Ala. 473, 479–480, 144 So. 86, and *Fidelity & Casualty Co. v. Beeland Co.,* 242 Ala. 591, 7 So. 2d 265. Among the cases cited for this exception to the letter rule in *Beeland* are *Leach & Co. v. Pierson,* 275 U.S. 120, which recognizes an exception to the unanswered letter rule where the letter contains a demand.

explored in *Parks v. New York Times Company,* 308 F. 2d 474, 480 (5th Cir. 1962).[18]

This Alabama rule applies whether or not there is a pre-existing agency relationship, and thereby accords with the law set out in Professor Warren A. Seavey's notes to Restatement of Agency 2d, cited in footnote eighteen.

Obviously, the foregoing matters involve plain questions of state law, and present no occasion for the exercise of certiorari jurisdiction. If there was **any** evidence against petitioners, there is no federal question. Two Alabama Courts and one Federal Court of Appeals have held there was.[19] Apposite is this Court's observation in *Stein v. New York,* 346 U.S. 156, 181:

> "Of course, this Court cannot allow itself to be completely bound by state court determination of any issue essential to decision of a claim of federal right, else federal law could be frustrated by distorted fact finding. But that does not mean that we give no weight to the decision below, or approach the record de novo or with the latitude of choice open to some state appellate courts, such as the New York Court of Appeals."

This case does not entitle petitioners to ask this Court to sit as a jury and substitute its collective judgment for that of the jury which tried this case.

III.

Respondent is reluctant to dignify by comment the statements in petitioners' brief which vilify respondent and his attorneys for bringing this libel suit. Surely, this Court will note the striking fact that nowhere in this lengthy and vituperative document is there the slightest suggestion that these petitioners, or indeed The New York Times, even attempted to introduce any testimony to substantiate the truth of the matters contained in the paid advertisement.

Respondent cares deeply about freedom of press and speech. And he is also concerned that these basic freedoms do not degenerate into a license to lie. As a commentator cited by petitioners has observed: "In the rise of the Nazis to power in Germany, defamation was a major weapon." Riesman, *Democracy and Defamation,* 42 Columbia L. Rev. 727, 728.

As venerable as John Peter Zenger is the imbedded constitutional principle that libelous utterances are not within the area of constitutionally protected speech and press.[20]

CONCLUSION

For the foregoing reasons it is respectfully submitted that the writ of certiorari should be dismissed as improvidently granted; in the alternative, respondent respectfully submits that this case should be affirmed.

Respectfully submitted,

ROBERT E. STEINER III,

SAM RICE BAKER,

M. ROLAND NACHMAN JR.,

Attorneys for Respondent.

STEINER, CRUM & BAKER,

CALVIN WHITESELL,

Of Counsel.

I, M. Roland Nachman, Jr., of Counsel for Respondent, and a member of the bar of this Court, hereby certify that I have mailed copies of the foregoing Brief and of Respondent's Brief in No. 39, The New York Times Company v. Sullivan, air mail, postage prepaid, to I. H. Wachtel, Esquire, Counsel for petitioners, at his office at 1100 17th Street N. W., Washington, D.C. I also certify that I have mailed a copy of the foregoing Brief, air mail, postage prepaid, to Edward S. Greenbaum, Esquire, 285 Madison Avenue, New York, New York, as attorney for American Civil Liberties Union and the New York Civil Liberties Union, as *amici curiae.*

This ... day of October, 1963.

M. Roland Nachman Jr.,

Of Counsel for Respondent.

---

[18] These and others are: *Birmingham News Co. v. Birmingham Printing Co.,* 209 Ala. 403, 407, 96 So. 336, 340–341; *Goldfield v. Brewbaker Motors* (Ala. App.), 36 Ala. App. 152, 54 So. 2d 797. cert. denied 256 Ala. 383, 54 So. 2d 800; *Woodmen of the World Ins. Co. v. Bolin,* 243 Ala. 426, 10 So. 2d 296; *Belcher Lumber Co. v. York,* 245 Ala. 286, 17 So. 2d 281; 1 Restatement of Agency 2d, Sec. 94, page 244, comments (a) and (b); 3 Restatement of Agency 2d (App. pages 168 and 174).

[19] It is, of course, elemental that signers of an advertisement—or those who later ratified the use of their names—would be liable for its publication since every individual participant in the publication of a defamatory statement, except a disseminator, is held strictly liable. *Peck v. Tribune Co.,* 214 U.S. 185; *Developments in the Law—Defamation,* 69 Harvard L. Rev. at 912.

[20] *Roth v. United States,* 354 U.S. 476, 483; *Beauharnais v. Illinois,* 343 U.S. 250, 256; *Chaplinsky v. New Hampshire,* 315 U.S. 568, 571–572; *Konigsberg v. State Bar of California,* 366 U.S. 36, 49–50; *Near v. Minnesota,* 283 U.S. 697, 715.

APPENDIX A

Title 7, Section 827 (1), of the Code of Alabama:

"BILLS OF EXCEPTION ABOLISHED IN CERTAIN COURTS; TRANSCRIPT OF EVIDENCE.—Bills of exception in the trial of cases at law in the circuit court and courts of like jurisdiction and all other courts of record having a full time court reporter and from which appeals lie directly to the court of appeals or the supreme court of Alabama, in the state of Alabama, are hereby abolished. If a party to a cause tried in such court desires to appeal from a judgment rendered, he shall, within five days after he perfects his appeal give notice to the court reporter, in writing, that he desires to appeal and request the evidence to be transcribed. The court reporter shall then promptly transcribe the evidence, including objections, oral motions, rulings of the court, and the oral charge of the court, certify the same and file it with the clerk within sixty days from the date on which the appeal was taken, or within sixty days from the date of the court's ruling on the motion for a new trial, whichever date is later. He shall also identify and copy all documents offered in evidence in the order in which offered. The evidence so transcribed and certified and filed shall be a part of the record, and assignments of error may be made as though the transcript constituted a bill of exceptions. If the reproduction of documents offered in evidence, such as maps or photographs, be difficult or impracticable, the court reporter shall so certify, and the clerk shall thereupon attach the original or a photostatic copy thereof to the transcript on appeal, and such original or photostatic copy thereof shall be a part of the transcript on appeal. If bulky or heavy objects be offered in evidence as exhibits which are not capable of being attached to the transcript, the court reporter shall certify that such exhibits are bulky or heavy objects which are not capable of being attached to the transcript; that he has identified them as part of the transcript on appeal. The court reporter shall include in his certificate a statement that he has notified both parties or their attorneys of record of the filing of the transcript of testimony. (1943, p. 423, § 1, effective Sept. 1, 1943; 1951, p. 1527, § 1, appvd. Sept. 12, 1951; 1956, 1st Ex. Sess., p. 43, § 1, appvd. Feb. 9, 1956.)"

Title 7, Section 827 (1a) of the Code of Alabama:

"EXTENSION OF TIME FOR FILING TRANSCRIPT; OBJECTIONS TO TRANSCRIPT; HEARING AND RULINGS THEREON.—The period of time within which the reporter must file the transcript may be extended by the trial court for cause. Within ten (10) days after the filing with the clerk of the certified transcript by the court reporter, either party may file with the clerk objections to the certified transcript, with his certificate that he has notified the opposing party, or attorney of record, that the same will be called to the attention of the trial court at a specified time and place. If no objections are filed within such ten (10) days the transcript shall be conclusively presumed to be correct. The hearing of objections and the ruling of the court thereon shall be concluded within a period of ninety (90) days from the date of the taking of the appeal, provided that this period may be extended by the trial court for cause. The trial court shall endorse its ruling on the transcript, sign the same, all within said ninety (90) days period, except as hereinbefore provided. Any ruling of the trial court upon such requested hearing, as well as any ruling on objections to a succinct statement, provided for in section 827 (c) of this title, shall be reviewable, with error duly assigned by the dissatisfied party upon the appeal of the cause, and the evidence upon such hearing shall be duly certified by the court reporter. (1951, p. 1528, § 2, appvd. Sept. 12, 1951.)"

Title 13, Section 119 of the Code of Alabama:

"EXECUTION ON JUDGMENT; NEW TRIAL MUST BE ASKED IN THIRTY DAYS.—After the lapse of ten days from the rendition of a judgment or decree, the plaintiff may have execution issued thereon, and after the lapse of thirty days from the date on which a judgment or decree was rendered, the court shall lose all power over it, as completely as if the end of the term had been on that day, unless a motion to set aside the judgment or decree, or grant a new trial has been filed and called to the attention of the court, and an order entered continuing it for hearing to a future day; provided that in any county in which the trial judge did not reside on the date of the trial such motion may be filed in the office of the clerk, or register, of the court of the county having jurisdiction of said cause, within thirty days from the date of the rendition of the judgment or decree, and the court shall lose all power over it sixty days after the date of the rendition of such judgment or decree as completely as if the end of the term had been on that day unless such motion is called to the attention of the court and an order entered continuing it for hearing to a future date. (1915, p. 707; 1939, p. 167.)"

U.S. SUPREME
COURT,
MARCH 1964

New York Times Company v. Sullivan

CITE AS 84 S.CT. 710 (1964)

—ᗰ—

THE NEW YORK TIMES COMPANY,
PETITIONER,
V.
L. B. SULLIVAN.

RALPH D. ABERNATHY ET AL.,
PETITIONERS,
V.
L. B. SULLIVAN.

NOS. 39, 40.

Argued Jan. 6 and 7, 1964.
Decided March 9, 1964.
376 U.S. 254

William P. Rogers and Samuel R. Pierce, Jr., New York City, for petitioner in No. 40.

Herbert Wechsler, New York City, for petitioners in No. 39.

M. Roland Nachman, Jr., Montgomery, Ala., for respondent.

Mr. Justice Brennan delivered the opinion of the Court.

We are required in this case to determine for the first time the extent to which the constitutional protections for speech and press limit a State's power to award damages in a libel action brought by a public official against critics of his official conduct.

Respondent L. B. Sullivan is one of the three elected Commissioners of the City of Montgomery, Alabama. He testified that he was "Commissioner of Public Affairs and the duties are supervision of the Police Department, Fire Department of Scales." He brought this civil libel action against the four individual petitioners, who are Negroes and Alabama clergymen, and against petitioner the New York Times Company, a New York corporation which publishes the *New York Times* a daily newspaper. A jury in the Circuit Court of Montgomery County awarded him damages of $500,000, the full amount claimed, against all the petitioners, and the Supreme Court of Alabama affirmed. 273 Ala. 656, 144 So.2d 25.

Respondent's complaint alleged that he had been libeled by statements in a full-page adver-tisement that was carried in the *New York Times* on March 29, 1960.[1] Entitled "Heed Their Rising Voices," the advertisement began by stating that "As the whole world knows by now, thousands of Southern Negro students are engaged in widespread non-violent demonstrations in positive affirmation of the right to live in human dignity as guaranteed by the U.S. Constitution and the Bill of Rights." It went on to charge that "in their efforts to uphold these guarantees, they are being met by an unprecedented wave of terror by those who would deny and negate that document which the whole world looks upon as setting the pattern for modern freedom. * * *" Succeeding paragraphs purported to illustrate the "wave of terror" by describing certain alleged events. The text concluded with an appeal for funds for three purposes: support of the student movement, "the struggle for the right-to-vote," and the legal defense of Dr. Martin Luther King, Jr., leader of the movement, against a perjury indictment then pending in Montgomery.

The text appeared over the names of 64 persons, many widely known of their activities in public affairs, religion, trade unions, and the performing arts. Below these names, and under a line reading "We in the south who are struggling daily for dignity and freedom warmly endorse this appeal," appeared the names of the four individual petitioners and of 16 other persons, all but two of whom were identified as clergymen in various Southern cities. The advertisement was signed at the bottom of the page by the "Committee to Defend Martin Luther King and the Struggle for Freedom in the South," and the officers of the Committee were listed.

Of the 10, paragraphs of text in the advertisement, the third and a portion of the sixth were the basis of respondent's claim of libel. They read as follows:

Third paragraph:

"In Montgomery, Alabama, after students sang 'My Country, 'Tis of Thee' on the State Capitol steps, their leaders were expelled from school, and truckloads of police armed with shotguns and tear-gas ringed the Alabama State College Campus. When the entire student body protested to state authorities by refusing to re-register, their dining hall was padlocked in an attempt to starve them into submission."

Sixth paragraph:

---

[1] A replica of the advertisement follows this document.

"Again and again the Southern violators have answered Dr. King's peaceful protests with intimidation and violence. They have bombed his home almost killing his wife and child. They have assaulted his person. They have arrested him seven times—for 'speeding,' 'loitering' and similar 'offenses.' And now they have changed him with 'perjury'—a *felony* under which they could imprison him for *ten years.* * * *"

Although neither of these statements mentions respondent by name, he contended that the word "police" in the third paragraph referred to him as the Montgomery Commissioner who supervised the Police Department, so that he was being accused of "ringing" the campus with police. He further claimed that the paragraph would be read as imputing to the police, and hence to him, the padlocking of the dining hall in order to starve the students into submission.[2] As to the sixth paragraph, he contended that since arrests are ordinarily made by the police, the statement "They have arrested [Dr. King] seven times" would be read as referring to him; he further contended that the "They" who did the arresting would be equated with the "They" who committed the other described acts and with the "Southern violators." Thus, he argued, the paragraph would be read as accusing the Montgomery police, and hence him, of answering Dr. King's protests with "intimidation and violence," bombing his home, assaulting his person, and charging him with perjury. Respondents testified that they read some or all of the statements as referring to him in his capacity as Commissioner.

It is uncontroverted that some of the statements contained in the two paragraphs were not accurate descriptions of events which occurred in Montgomery. Although Negro students staged a demonstration on the State Capital steps, they sang the National Anthem and not "My Country, 'Tis of Thee." Although nine students were expelled by the State Board of Education, this was not for leading the demonstration at the Capitol, but for demanding service at a lunch counter in the Montgomery County Courthouse on another day. Not the entire student body, but most of it, had protested the expulsion, not by refusing to register, but by boycotting classes on a single day; virtually all the students did register for the ensuing semester. The campus dining hall was not padlocked on any occasion, and the only students who may have been barred from eating there were the few

who had neither signed a preregistration application nor requested temporary meal tickets. Although the police were deployed near the campus, and they were not called to the campus in connection with the demonstration on the State Capitol steps, as the third paragraph implied. Dr. King had not been arrested seven times, but only four; and although he claimed to have been assaulted some years earlier in connection with his arrest for loitering outside a courtroom, one of the officers who made the arrest denied that there was such an assault.

On the premise that the charges in the sixth paragraph could be read as referring to him, respondent was allowed to prove that he had not participated in the events described. Although Dr. King's home had in fact been bombed twice when his wife and child were there, both of these occasions antedated respondent's tenure as Commissioner, and the police were not only not implicated in the bombings, but had made every effort to apprehend those who were. Three of Dr. King's four arrests took place before respondent became Commissioner. Although Dr. King had in fact been indicted (he was subsequently acquitted) on two counts of perjury, each of which carried a possible five-year sentence, respondent had nothing to do with procuring the indictment.

Respondent mad no effort to prove that he suffered actual pecuniary loss as a result of the alleged libel.[3] One of his witnesses, a former employer, testified that if he had believed the statements, he doubted whether he "would want to be associated with anybody who would be a party to such things that are stated in that ad," and that he would not re-employ respondent if he believed "that he allowed the Police Department to do the things that the paper say he did." But neither this witness nor any of the others testified that he had actually believed the statements in their supposed reference to respondent.

The cost of the advertisement was approximately $4800, and it was published by the *Times*

---

[2] Respondent did not consider the charge of expelling the students to be applicable to him, since "that responsibility rests with the State Department of Education."

[3] Approximately 394 copies of the edition of the *Times* containing the advertisement were circulated in Alabama. Of these, about 35 copies were distributed in Montgomery County. The total circulation of the Times for that day was approximately 650,000 copies.

U.S. SUPREME
COURT,
MARCH 1964

upon an order from a New York advertising agency acting for the signatory Committee. The agency submitted the advertisement with a letter from A. Philip Randolph, Chairman of the Committee, certifying that the persons whose names appeared on the advertisement had given their permission. Mr. Randolph was known to the *Times'* Advertising Acceptability Department as a responsible person, and in accepting the letter as sufficient proof of authorization it followed its established practice. There was testimony that the copy of the advertisement which accompanied the letter listed only the 64 names appearing under the text, and that the statement, "We in the south * * * warmly endorse this appeal," and the list of names thereunder, which included those of the individual petitioners, were subsequently added when the first proof of the advertisement was received. Each of the individual petitioners testified that he had not authorized the use of his name, and that he had been unaware of its use until receipt of respondent's demand for a retraction. The manager of the Advertising Acceptability Department testified that he had approved the advertisement for publication because he knew nothing to cause him to believe that anything in it was false, and because it bore the endorsement of "a number of people who are well known and whose reputation" he "had no reason to question." Neither he nor anyone else at the *Times* made an effort to confirm the accuracy of the advertisement, either by checking it against recent Times news stories relating to some of the described events or by any other means.

Alabama law denies a public officer recovery of punitive damages in a libel action brought on account of a publication concerning his official conduct unless he first makes a written demand for a public retraction and the defendant fails or refuses to comply. Alabama Code, Tit. 7, § 914. Respondent served such a demand upon each of the petitioners. None of the individual petitioners responded to the demand, primarily because each took the position that he had not authorized the use of his name on the advertisement and therefore had not published the statements that respondent alleged had libeled him. The Times did not publish a retraction in response to the demand but wrote respondent a letter stating, among other things, that "we * * * are somewhat puzzled as to how you think the statements in any way reflect on you," and "you might, if you desire, let us know in what respect

you claim that the statements in the advertisement reflect on you." Respondent filed this suit a few days later without answering the letter. The Times did, however, subsequently publish a retraction of the advertisement upon the demand of Governor John Patterson of Alabama, who asserted that the publication charged him with "grave misconduct and * * * improper actions and omissions as Governor of Alabama and Ex-Officio Chairman of the State Board of Education of Alabama." When asked to explain why there had been a retraction for the Governor but not for respondent, the Secretary of the Times testified: "We that because we didn't want anything that was published by the *The Times* to be a reflection on the State of Alabama and the Governor was, as far as we could see, the embodiment of the State of Alabama and the proper representative of the State and, furthermore, we had by that time learned more of the actual facts which the ad purported to recite and, finally, the ad did refer to the action of the State authorities and the Board of Education presumably of which the Governor is the ex-officio chairman * * *." On the other hand, he testified that he did not think that "any of the language in there referred to Mr. Sullivan."

The trial judge submitted the case to the jury under instructions that the statements in the advertisement were "libelous per se" and were not privileged, so that petitioners might be held liable if the jury found that they had published the advertisement and that the statements were made "of concerning" respondent. The jury was instructed that, because the statements were libelous *per se*, the law * * * implies legal injury from the bare fact of publication itself," "falsity and malice are presumed," general damages need not be alleged or proved but are presumed," and "punitive damages may be awarded by the jury even though the amount of actual damages is neither found nor shown." An award of punitive damages—as distinguished from "general" damages, which are compensatory in nature—apparently Alabama law, and the judge charged that "mere negligence or carelessness is not evidence of actual malice or malice in fact, and does not justify an award of exemplary or punitive damages." He refused to charge, however, that the jury must be "convinced" of malice, in the sense of "actual intent" to harm or "gross negligence and recklessness," to make such an award, and he also refused to require that a verdict for respondent differentiate between compensatory and punitive damages. The judge rejected petitioners' contention that his rulings abridged the freedoms of speech and of the press that are guaranteed by the First and Fourteenth Amendments.

In affirming the judgment, the Supreme Court of Alabama sustained the trial judge's rulings and instructions in all respects. 273 Ala. 656, 144 So.2d. 25. It held that "[w]here the words published tend to injure a person libeled by them in his reputation, profession, trade or business, or charge him with an indictable offense, or tends to bring the indictable offense, or tends to bring the individual into public contempt," they are "libelous per se"; that "the matter complained of is, under the above doctrine, libelous per se, if it was published of and concerning the plaintiff;" and that it was actionable without "proof of pecuniary injury * * *, such injury being implied." Id., at 673, 676, 144 So.2d, at 37, 41. It approved the trial court's ruling that the jury could find that statements to have been made "of and concerning" respondent, stating: "We think it common knowledge that the average person knows that municipal agents, such as police and firemen, and others, are under the control and direction of the city governing body, and more particularly under the direction and control of a single commissioner. In measuring the performance or deficiencies of such groups praise or criticism is usually attached to the official in complete control of the body." Id., at 674–675, 144 So.2d at 39. In sustaining the trial court's determination that the verdict was not excessive, the court said that malice could be inferred from the *Times* "irresponsibility" in printing the advertisement while "*The Times* in its own files had articles already published which would have demonstrated the falsity of the allegations in the advertisement"; from the *Times'* failure to retract for respondent while retracting for the Governor, whereas the falsity of some of the allegations was then known to the *Times* and "the matter contained in the advertisement was equally false as to both parties"; and from the testimony of the *Times'* Secretary that apart from the statement that the dining hall was padlocked, he thought the two paragraphs were "substantially correct." Id., at 686–687, 144 So.2d, at 50–51. The court reaffirmed a statement in an earlier opinion that "There is no legal measure of damages in case of this character." Id., at 686, 144 So.2d, at 50. It rejected petitioners' constitutional contentions with the brief statements that "The First Amendment of the U.S. Constitution does not protect libelous publications" and "The Fourteenth Amendment is directed against State action and not private action." Id., at 676, 144 So.2d, at 40.

[1, 2] Because of the importance of the constitutional issues involved, we granted the separate petitions for certiorari of the individual petitioners and of the *Times*. 371 U.S. 946, 83 S.Ct. 510, 9 L.Ed.2d 496. We reverse the judgment. We hold that the rule of law applied by the Alabama courts is constitutionally deficient for failure to provide the safeguards for freedom of speech and of the press that are required by the First and Fourteenth Amendments in a libel action brought by a public official against critics of his official conduct.[4] We further hold that under the proper safeguards the evidence presented in this case is constitutionally insufficient to support the judgment for respondent.

I.

[3] We may dispose at the outset of two grounds asserted to insulate the judgment of the Alabama courts from constitutional scrutiny. The first is the proposition relied on by the State Supreme Court—that "The Fourteenth Amendment is directed against State action and not private action." That proposition has no application to this case. Although this is a civil lawsuit between private parties, the Alabama courts have applied a state rule of law which petitioners claim to impose invalid restrictions on their constitutional freedoms of speech and press. It matters not that that law has been applied in a

---

[4] Since we sustain the contentions of all the petitioners under the First Amendment's guarantees of freedom of speech and of the press as applied to the States by the Fourteenth Amendment, we do not decide the questions presented by the other claims of violation of the Fourteenth Amendment. The individual petitioners contend that the judgment against them offends the Due Process Clause because there was no evidence to show that they had published or authorized the publication of the alleged libel, and that the Due Process and Equal Protection Clauses were violated by racial segregation and racial bias in the courtroom. The Times contends that the assumption of jurisdiction over its corporate person by the Alabama courts overreaches the territorial limits of the Due Process Clause. The latter claim is foreclosed from our review by the ruling of the Alabama courts that the *Times* entered a general appearance in the action and thus waived its jurisdictional objection; we cannot say that this ruling lacks "fair or substantial support" in prior Alabama decisions. See *Thompson v Wilson*, 224 Ala. 299, 140 So. 439 (1932); compare *N. A. A. C. P. v Alabama*, 357 U.S. 449, 454–458, 78 S.Ct. 1163, 2 L.Ed.2d 1488.

U.S. SUPREME COURT, MARCH 1964

U.S. SUPREME
COURT,
MARCH 1964

civil action and that it is common law only, though supplemented by statute. See, e. g., Alabama Code, Tit. 7, §§ 908–917. The test is not the form in which state power has been applied but, whatever the form, whether such power has in fact been exercised. See Ex parte Virginia, 100 U.S. 339, 346–47, 25 L.Ed. 676; *American Federation of Labor v. Swing*, 312 U.S. 321, 61 S.Ct. 568, 85 L.Ed. 855.

The second contention is that the constitutional guarantees of freedom of speech and of the press are inapplicable here, at least so far as the *Times* is concerned, because the allegedly libelous statements were published as part of a paid, "commercial" advertisement. The argument relies on *Valentine v. Chrestensen*, 316 U.S. 52, 62 S.Ct. 920, 86 L.Ed. 1262, where the Court held that a city ordinance forbidding street distribution of commercial and business advertising matter did not abridge the First Amendment freedoms, even as applied to a handbill having a commercial message on one side but a protest against certain official action on the other. The reliance is wholly misplaced. The Court in Chrestensen reaffirmed the constitutional protection for "the freedom of communicating information and disseminating opinion"; its holding was based upon the factual conclusions that the handbill was "purely commercial advertising" and that the protest against official action had been added only to evade the ordinance.

The publication here was not a "commercial" advertisement in the sense in which the word was used in Chrestensen. It communicated information, expressed opinion, recited grievances, protested claimed abuses, and sought financial support on behalf of a movement whose existence and objectives are matters of the highest public interest and concern. See *N. A. A. C. P. v. Button*, 371 U.S. 415, 435, 83 S.Ct. 328, 9 L.Ed.2d 405. That the Times was paid for publishing the advertisement is as immaterial in this connection as in the fact that newspapers and books are sold. *Smith v. California* 361 U.S. 147, 150, 80 S.Ct. 215, 4 L.Ed.2d 205; cf. *Bantam Books, Inc. v. Sullivan*, 372 U.S. 58, 64, n. 6, 83 S.Ct. 631, 9 L.Ed.2d 584. Any other conclusion would discourage newspapers from carrying "editorial advertisements" of this type, and so might shut off an important outlet for the promulgation of information and ideas by persons who do not themselves have access to publishing facilities—who wish to exercise their freedom of speech even though they are not members of the press. Cf. *Lovell v. City of Griffin*, 303 U.S. 444, 452, 58 S.Ct. 666, 82 L.Ed. 949; *Schneider v. State*, 308 U.S. 147, 164, 60 S.Ct. 146, 84 L.Ed. 155. The effect would be to shackle the First Amendment in its attempt to secure "the widest possible dissemination of information from diverse and antagonistic sources." *Associated Press v. United States*, 326 U.S. 1, 20, 65 S.Ct. 1416, 1424, 89 L.Ed. 2013. To avoid placing such a handicap upon the freedoms of expression, we hold that if the allegedly libelous statements would otherwise be constitutionally protected from the present judgment, they do not forfeit that protection because they were published in the form of a paid advertisement.[5]

Under Alabama law as applied in this case, a publication is "libelous per se" if the words "tend to injure a person * * in his reputation" or to "bring [him] into public contempt;" the trial court stated that the standard was met if the words are such as to "injure him in his public office, or want of official integrity, or want of fidelity to a public trust * *." The jury must find that the words were published "of and concerning" the plaintiff, but where the plaintiff is a public official his place in the governmental hierarchy is sufficient evidence to support a finding that his reputation has been affected by statements that reflect upon the agency of which he is in charge. Once "libel per se" has been established, the defendant has no defense as to stated facts unless he can persuade the jury that they were true in all their particulars. *Alabama Ride Co. v. Vance*, 235 Ala. 263, 178 So. 438 (1938); *Johnson Publishing Co. v. Davis*, 271 Ala. 474, 494–495, 124 So.2d 441, 457–458 (1960). His privilege of "fair comment" for expressions of opinion depends on the truth of the facts upon which the comment is based. *Parsons v. Age-Herald Publishing Co.*, 181 Ala. 439, 450, 61 So. 345, 350 (1913). Unless he can discharge the burden of proving truth, general damages are presumed, and may be awarded without proof of pecuniary injury. A showing of actual malice is apparently a prerequisite to recovery of punitive damages, and the defendant may in any event forestall a punitive award by a retraction meeting the statutory requirements. Good motives and belief in truth do not negate an

---

[5] See American Law Institute, Restatement of Torts, § 593, Comment b (1938).

U.S. SUPREME
COURT,
MARCH 1964

inference of malice, but are relevant only in mitigation of punitive damages if the jury chooses to accord them weight. *Johnson Publishing Co. v. Davis,* supra, 271 Ala., at 495, 124 So.2d, at 458.

The question before us in whether this rule of liability, as applied to an action brought by a public official against critics of his official conduct, abridges the freedom of speech and of the press that is guaranteed by the First and Fourteenth Amendments.

[5] Respondent relies heavily, as did the Alabama courts, on statements of this Court to the effect that the Constitution does not protect libelous publications.[6] Those statements do not foreclose our inquiry here. None of the cases sustained the use of libel laws to impose sanctions upon expression critical of the official conduct of public officials. The dictum in *Pennekamp v. Florida,* 328 U.S. 331, 348–349, 66 S.Ct. 1029, 1038, 90 L.Ed. 1295, that "when the statements amount to defamation, a judge has such remedy in damages for libel as do other public servants," implied no view as to what remedy might constitutionally be afforded to public officials. In *Beauharnais v. Illinois,* 343 U.S. 250, 72 S.Ct. 725, 96 L.Ed. 919, the Court sustained an Illinois criminal libel statute as applied to a publication held to be both defematory of a racial group and "liable to cause violence and disorder." But the Court was careful to note that it "retains and exercises authority to nullify action which encroaches on freedom of utterance under the guise of punishing libel"; for "public men, are, as it were, public property," and "discussion cannot be denied and the right, as well as the duty, of criticism must not be stifled." Id., at 263–264, 72 S.Ct. at 734, 96 L.Ed. 919 and n. 18. In the only previous case that did present the question of constitutional limitations upon the power to award damages for libel of a public official, the Court was equally divided and the question was not decided. *Schenectady Union Pub. Co. v. Sweeney,* 316 U.S. 642, 62 S.Ct. 1031, 86 L.Ed. 1727. In deciding the question now, we are compelled by neither precedent nor policy to give any more weight to the epithet "libel" than we have to other "mere labels" of state law. *N. A. A. C. P. v. Button* , 371 U.S. 415, 429, 83 S.Ct. 328, 9 L.Ed.2d 405. Like insurrection,[7] contempt,[8] advocacy of unlawful acts,[9] breach of the peace,[10] obscenity,[11] solicitation of legal business,[12] and the various other formulae for the repression of expression that

have been challenged in this Court, libel can claim no talismanic immunity from constitutional limitations. It must be measured by standards that satisfy the First Amendment.

[6–8] The general proposition that freedom of expression upon public questions is secured by the First Amendment has long been settled by our decisions. The constitutional safeguard, we have said, "was fashioned to assure unfettered interchange of ideas for the bringing about of political and social changes desired by the people." *Roth v. United States,* 354 U.S. 476, 484, 77 S.Ct. 1304, 1308, 1 L.Ed.2d 1498. "The maintenance of the opportunity for free political discussion to the end that government may be responsive to the will of the people and that changes may be obtained by lawful means, an opportunity essential to the security of the Republic, is a fundamental principle of our constitutional system." *Stromberg v. California,* 283 U.S. 359, 369, 51 S.Ct. 532, 536, 75 L.Ed. 1117. "[I]t is a prized American privilege to speak one's mind, although not always with perfect good taste, on all public institutions," *Bridges v. California,* 314 U.S. 252, 270, 62 S.Ct. 190, 197, 86 L.Ed. 192, and this opportunity is to be afforded for "vigorous advocacy" no less than "abstract discussion." *N. A. A. C. P. v. Button,* 371 U.S. 415, 429, 83 S.Ct. 328, 9 L.Ed.2d 405. The First Amendment, Said Judge Learned Hand, "presupposes that right conclusions are more likely to be gathered out of a multitude of tongues, than through any kind of authoritative selection. To many this is, and always will be, folly; but we have staked upon it our all." *United States v. Associated Press,* 52 F.Supp. 362, 372

---

[6] *Konigsberg v. State Bar of California,* 366 U.S. 36, 49, and n. 10, 81 S.Ct. 997, 6 L.Ed.2d 105; *Times Film Corp. v. City of Chicago,* 365 U.S. 43, 48, 81 S.Ct. 391, 5 L.Ed.2d 403; *Roth v. United States,* 354 U.S. 476, 486–487, 77 S.Ct. 1304, 1 L.Ed.2d 1498; *Beaubarnais v. Illinois,* 343 U.S. 250, 266, 72 S.Ct. 725, 96 L.Ed. 919; *Pennekamp v. Florida,* 328 U.S. 331, 348–349, 66 S.Ct. 1029, 90 L.Ed. 1295; *Chaplinsky v. New Hampshire,* 315 U.S. 568, 572, 62 S.Ct. 766, 80 L.Ed. 1031; *Near v. Minnesota,* 283 U.S. 697, 715, 51 S.Ct. 625, 75 L.Ed. 1357.

[7] *Herndon v. Lowry,* 301 U.S. 242, 57 S.Ct. 732, 81 L.Ed. 1066.

[8] *Bridges v. California,* 314 U.S. 252, 62 S.Ct. 190, 86 L.Ed. 192; *Pennekamp v. Florida,* 328 U.S. 331, 66 S.Ct. 1029, 90 L.Ed. 1295.

[9] *De Jonge v. Oregon,* 299 U.S. 353, 57 S.Ct. 255, 81 L.Ed. 278.

[10] *Edwards v. South Carolina,* 372 U.S. 229, 83 S.Ct. 680, 9 L.Ed.2d 697.

[11] *Roth v. United States,* 354 U.S. 476, 77 S.Ct. 1304, 1 L.Ed.2d 1498.

[12] *N. A. A. C. P. v. Button,* 371 U.S. 415, 83 S.Ct. 328, 9 L.Ed.2d 405.

U.S. SUPREME
COURT,
MARCH 1964

(D.C.S.D.N.Y.1943). Mr. Justice Brandeis, in his concurring opinion in *Whitney v. California*, 274 U.S. 357, 375–376, 47 S.Ct. 641, 648, 71 L.Ed. 1095, gave the principle its classic formulation:

> "Those who won our independence believed * * * that public discussion is a political duty; and that this should be a fundamental principle of the American government. They recognized the risks to which all human institutions are subject. But they knew that order cannot be secured merely through fear of punishment for its infraction; that it is hazardous for its infraction; that it is hazardous to discourage thought, hope and imagination; that fear breeds repression; that repression breeds hate; that hate menaces stable government; that the path of safety lies in the opportunity to discuss freely supposed grievances and proposed remedies; and that the fitting remedy for evil counsels is good ones. Believing in the power of reason as applied through public discussion, they eschewed silence coerced by law—the argument of force in its worst form. Recognizing the occasional tyrannies of governing majorities, they amended the Constitution so that free speech and assembly should be guaranteed."

[9] Thus we consider this case against the background of a profound national commitment to the principle that debate on public issues should be uninhibited, robust, and wide-open, and that it may well include vehement, caustic, and sometimes unpleasantly sharp attacks on government and public officials. See *Terminiello v. Chicago*, 337 U.S. 1, 4, 69 S.Ct. 894, 93 L.Fd. 1131; *De Jonge v. Oregon*, 299 U.S. 353, 365, 57 S.Ct. 255, 81 L.Ed. 278. The present advertisement, as an expression of grievance and protest on one of the major public issues of our time, would seem clearly to qualify for the constitutional protection. The question is whether it forfeits that protection by the falsity of some of its factual statements and by its alleged defamation of respondent.

[10] Authoritative interpretations of the First Amendment guarantees have consistently refused to recognize an exception for any test of truth—whether administered by judges, juries, or administrative officials—and especially one that puts the burden of proving truth on the speaker. Cf. *Speiser v. Randall*, 357 U.S. 513, 525–526, 78 S.Ct. 1332, 2 L.Ed.2d 1460. The constitutional protection does not turn upon "the truth, popularity, or social utility of the ideas and beliefs which are offered." *N. A. A. C. P. v. Button*, 371 U.S. 415, 445, 83 S.Ct. 328, 344,

9 L.Ed.2d 405. As Madison said, "Some degree of abuse is inseparable from the proper use of every thing; and in no instance is this more true than in that of the press." *4 Elliot's Debates on the Federal Constitution* (1876), p. 571. In *Cantwell v. Connecticut*, 310 U.S. 296, 310, 60 S.Ct. 900, 906, 84 L.Ed. 1213, the Court declared:

> "In the realm of religious faith, and in that of political belief, sharp differences arise. In both fields the tenets of one man may seem the rankest error to his neighbor. To persuade others to his own point of view, the pleader, as we know, at times, resorts to exaggeration, to vilification of men who have been, or are, prominent in church or state, and even to false statement. But the people of this nation have ordained in the light of history, that, in spite of the probability of excesses and abuses, these liberties are, in the long view, essential to enlightened opinion and right conduct on the part of the citizens of a democracy."

That erroneous statement is inevitable in free debate, and that it must be protected if the freedoms of expression are to have the "breathing space" that they need * * * to survive," *N. A. A. C. P. v. Button*, 371 U.S. 415, 433, 83 S.Ct. 328, 338, 9 L.Ed.2d 405, was also recognized by the Court of Appeals for the District of Columbia Circuit in *Sweeney v. Patterson*, 76 U.S.App.D.C. 23, 24, 128 F.2d 457, 458 (1942), cert. denied, 317 U.S. 678, 63 S.Ct. 160, 87 L.Ed. 544. Judge Edgerton spoke for a unanimous court which affirmed the dismissal of a Congressmen's libel suit based upon a newspaper article charging him with anti-Semitism in opposing a judicial appointment. He said:

> "Cases which impose liability for erroneous reports of the political conduct of officials reflect the obsolete doctrine that the governed must not criticize their governors. * * * The interest of the public here outweighs the interest of appellant or any other individual. The protection of the public requires not merely discussion, but information. Political conduct and views which some respectable people approve, and others condemn, are constantly imputed to Congressman. Errors of fact, particularly in regard to a man's mental states and processes, are inevitable. * * * Whatever is added to the field of libel is taken from the field of free debate."[13]

---

[13] See also Mill, *On Liberty* (Oxford: Blackwell, 1947), at 47:
"* * * [T]o argue sophistically, to suppress facts or arguments, to misstate the elements of the case, or misrepresent the opposite opinion * * * all this, even to the most aggravated degree, is so continually done in perfect good faith, by

[11, 12] Injury to official reputation error affords no more warrant for repressing speech that would otherwise be free than does factual error. Where judicial officers are involved, this Court has held that concern for the dignity and reputation of the courts does not justify the punishment as criminal contempt of criticism of the judge or his decision. *Bridges v. California*, 314 U.S. 252, 62 S.Ct. 190, 86 L.Ed. 192. This is true even though the utterance contains "half-truths" and "misinformation." *Pennekamp v. Florida*, 328 U.S. 331, 342, 343, n. 5, 345, 66 S.Ct. 1029, 90 L.Ed. 1295. Such repression can be justified, if at all, only by a clear and present danger of the obstruction of justice. See also *Craig v. Harney*, 331 U.S. 367, 67 S.Ct. 1249, 91 L.Ed. 1546; *Wood v. Georgia*, 370 U.S. 375, 82 S.Ct. 1364, 8 L.Ed.2d 569. If judges are to be treated as "men of fortitude, able to thrive in a hardy climate," *Craig v. Harney*, supra, 331 U.S., at 376, 67 S.Ct., at 1255, 91 L.Ed. 1546, surely the same must be true of other government officials, such as elected city commissioners.[14] Criticism of their official conduct does not lose its constitutional protection merely because it is effective criticism and hence diminishes their official reputations.

[13, 14] If neither factual error nor defamatory content suffices to remove the constitutional shield from criticism of official conduct, the combination of the two elements is no less inadequate. This is the lesson to be drawn from the great controversy over the Sedition Act of 1798, 1 Stat. 596, which first crystallized a national awareness of the central meaning of the First Amendment. See Levy, *Legacy of Suppression* (1960), at 258 et seq.; Smith, *Freedom's Fetters* (1956), at 426, 431 and *passim*. That statute made it a crime, punishable by a $5,000 fine and

persons who are not considered, and in many other respects may not deserve to be considered, ignorant or incompetent, that it is rarely possible, on adequate grounds, conscientiously to stamp the misrepresentation as morally culpable; and still less could law presume to interfere with this kind of controversial misconduct."

[14] The climate in which public officials operate, especially during a political campaign, has been described by one commentator in the following terms: "Charges of gross incompetence, disregard of the public interest, communist sympathies, and the like usually have filled the air; and hints of bribery, embezzlement, and other criminal conduct are not infrequent." Noel, *Defamation of Public Officers and Candidates*, 49 Col.L.Rev. 875 (1949).

For a similar description written 60 years earlier, see Chase, *Criticism of Public Officers and Candidates for Office*, 23 Am.L.Rev. 346 (1889).

five years in prison, "if any person shall write, print, utter or publish * * * any false, scandalous and malicious writing and writings against the government of the United States, or either house of the Congress * * *, or the President * * *, with intent to defame * * * or to bring them, or either of them, into contempt or disrepute; or to excite against them, or either or any of them, the hatred of the good people of the United States." The Act allowed the defendant the defense of truth, and provided that the jury were to be judges both of the law and the facts. Despite these qualifications, the Act, was vigorously condemned as unconstitutional in an attack joined in by Jefferson and Madison. In the famous Virginia Resolutions of 1798, the General Assembly of Virginia resolved that it

> "doth particularly protest against the palpable and alarming infractions of the Constitution, in the two late cases of the 'Alien and Sedition Acts,' passed at the last session of Congress * * *. [The Sedition Act] exercises * * * a power not delegated by the Constitution, but, on the contrary, expressly and positively forbidden by one of the amendments thereto—a power which, more than any other, ought to produce universal alarm, because it is levelled against the right of freely examining public characters and measures, and of free communication among the people thereon, which was ever been justly deemed the only effectual guardian of every other right." *4 Elliot's Debates*, supra, pp. 553–554.

Madison prepared the Report in support of the protest. His premise was that the Constitution created a form of government under which "The people, not the government, possess the absolute sovereignty." The structure of the government dispersed power in reflection of the people's distrust of concentrated power, and of power itself at all levels. This form of government was "altogether different" from the British form, under which the Crown was sovereign and the people were subjects. "Is it not natural and necessary, under such different circumstances," he asked, "that a different degree of freedom in the use of the press should be contemplated?" *Id.*, pp. 569–570. Earlier, in a debate in the House of Representatives, Madison had said: "If we advert to the nature of Republican Government, we shall find that the censorial power is in the people over the Government, and not in the Government over the people." *4 Annals of Congress*, p. 934 (1794). Of the exercise

U.S. SUPREME COURT, MARCH 1964

of that power by the press, his Report said: "In every state, probably, in the Union, the press has exerted a freedom in canvassing the merits and measures of public men, of every description, which has not been confined to the strict limits of the common law. On this footing the freedom of the press has stood; on this foundation it yet stands * * *." *4 Elliot's Debates*, supra, p. 570. The right of free public discussion of the stewardship of public officials was thus, in Madison's view, a fundamental principle of the American form of government.[15]

Although the Sedition Act was never tested in this Court,[16] the attack upon its validity has carried the day in the court of history. Fines levied in its prosecution were repaid by Act of Congress on the ground that it was unconstitutional. See, e. g., Act of July 4, 1840, c. 45, 6 Stat. 802, accompanied by H.R. Rep. No. 86, 26th Cong., 1st Sess. (1840). Calhoun, reporting to the Senate on February 4, 1836, assumed that its invalidity was a matter "which no one now doubts." Report with Senate bill No. 122, 24th Cong., 1st Sess., p. 3. Jefferson, as President, pardoned those who had been convicted and sentenced under the Act and remitted their fines, stating: "I discharged every person under punishment or prosecution under the sedition law, because I considered, and now consider, that law to be a nullity, as absolute and as palpable as if Congress had ordered us to fall down and worship a golden image." Letter to Mrs. Adams, July 22, 1804, *4 Jefferson's Works* (Washington ed.), pp. 555, 556. The invalidity of the Act has also been assumed by Justices of this Court. See Holmes, J., dissenting and joined by Brandeis, J., in *Abrams v. United States*, 250 U.S. 616, 630, 40 S. Ct. 17, 63 L.Ed. 1173; Jackson, J., dissenting in *Beauharnais v. Illinois*, 343 U.S. 250, 288–289, 72 S.Ct. 725, 96 L.Ed. 919; Douglas, *Constitutional Limitations* (8th ed., Carrington, 1927), pp. 899–900; Chafee, *Free Speech in the United States* (1942), pp. 27–28. These views reflect a broad consensus that the Act, because of the restraint it imposed upon criticism of government and public officials, was inconsistent with the First Amendment.

[15] There is no force in respondent's argument that the constitutional limitations implicit in the history of the Sedition Act apply only to Congress and not to the States. It is true that the First Amendment was originally addressed only to action by the Federal Government, and that

Jefferson, for one, while denying the power of Congress "to control the freedom of the press," recognized such a power in the States. See the 1804 Letter to Abigail Adams quoted in *Dennis v. United States*, 341 U.S. 494, 522, n. 4, 71 S.Ct. 857, 95 L.Ed. 1137 (concurring opinion). But this distinction was eliminated with the adoption of the Fourteenth Amendment and the application to the States of the First Amendment's restrictions. See e. g., *Gitlow v. New York*, 268 U.S. 652, 666, 45 S.Ct. 625, 69 L.Ed. 1138; *Schneider v. State*, 308 U.S. 147, 160, 60 S.Ct. 146, 84 L.Ed. 155; *Bridges v. California*, 314 U.S. 252, 268, 62 S.Ct. 190, 86 L.Ed. 192; *Edwards v. South Carolina*, 372 U.S. 229, 235, 83 S.Ct. 680, 9 L.Ed.2d 697.

[16, 17] What a State may not constitutionally bring about by means of a criminal statue is likewise beyond the reach of its civil law of libel.[17] The fear of damage awards under a rule such as that invoked by the Alabama courts here may be markedly more inhibiting than the fear of prosecution under a criminal statute. See *City of Chicago v. Tribune Co.*, 307 Ill. 595, 607, 139 N.E. 86, 90 (1923). Alabama, for example, has a criminal libel law which subjects to prosecution "any person who speaks, writes, or prints of and concerning another any accusation falsely and maliciously importing the commission by such person of a felony, or any other indictable offense involving moral turpitude," and which allows as punishment upon conviction a fine

---

[15] The Report on the Virginia Resolutions further stated:

"[I]t is manifestly impossible to punish the intent to bring those who administer the government into disrepute or contempt, without striking at the right of freely discussing public characters and measures; * * * which, again, is equivalent to a protection of those who administer the government, if they should at any time deserve the contempt or hatred of the people, against being exposed to it, by free animadversions on their characters and conduct. Nor can there be a doubt * * * that a government thus intrenched in penal statutes against the just and natural effects of a culpable administration, will easily evade the responsibility which is essential to a faithful discharge of its duty.

"Let it be recollected, lastly, that the right of electing the members of the government constitutes more particularly the essence of a free and responsible government. The value and efficacy of this right depends on the knowledge of the comparative merits and demerits of the candidates for public trust, and on the equal freedom, consequently, of examining and discussing these merits of the candidates respectively." *4 Elliot's Debates*, supra, p. 575.

[16] The Act expired by its terms in 1801.

[17] Cf. *Farmers Educational and Cooperative Union of America v. WDAY*, 360 U.S. 525, 535, 79 S.Ct. 1302, 3 L.Ed.2d 1407.

not exceeding $500 and a prison sentence of six months. Alabama Code, Tit. 14, § 350. Presumably a person charged with violation of this statute enjoys ordinary criminal-law safeguards such as the requirements of an indictment and of proof beyond a reasonable doubt. These safeguards are not available to the defendant in a civil action. The judgment awarded in this case—without the need for any proof of actual pecuniary loss—was one thousand times greater than the maximum fine provided by the Alabama criminal statute, and one hundred times greater than that provided by the sedition Act. And since there is no double-jeopardy limitation applicable to civil lawsuits, this is not the only judgment that may be awarded against petitioners for the same publication.[18] Whether or not a newspaper can survive a succession of such judgments, the pall of fear and timidity imposed upon those who would give voice to public criticism is an atmosphere in which the First Amendment freedoms cannot survive. Plainly the Alabama law of civil libel is "a form of regulation that creates hazards to protected freedoms markedly greater than those that attend reliance upon the criminal law." *Bantam Books, Inc. v. Sullivan,* 372 U.S. 58, 70, 83 S.Ct. 631, 639, 9 L.Ed.2d 584.

[18] The state rule of law is not saved by its allowance of the defense of truth. A defense for erroneous statements honestly made is no less essential here than was the requirement of proof of guilty knowledge which, in *Smith v. California,* 361 U.S. 147, 80 S.Ct. 215, 4 L.Ed.2d 205, we held indispensable to a valid conviction of a bookseller for possessing obscene writings for sale. We said:

> "For if the bookseller is criminally liable without knowledge of the contents, * * * he will tend to restrict the books he sells to those he has inspected; and thus the State will have imposed a restriction upon the distribution of constitutionally protected as well as obscene literature. * * * and the bookseller's burden would become the public's burden, for by restricting him the public's access to reading matter would be restricted. * * * [H]is timidity in the face of his absolute criminal liability, thus would tend to restrict the public's access to forms of the printed word which the State could not constitutionally press directly. The bookseller's self-censorship, compelled by the State, would be a censorship affecting the whole public, hardly less virulent for being privately administered. Through it, the distribution of all books,

both obscene and not obscene, would be impeded." (361 U.S. 147, 153–154, 80 S.Ct. 215, 218, 4 L.Ed.2d 205.)

A rule compelling the critic of official conduct to guarantee the truth of all his factual assertions—and to do so on pain of libel judgments virtually unlimited in amount—leads to comparable "self-censorship." Allowance of the defense of truth, with the burden of proving it on the defendant, does not mean that only false speech will be deterred.[19] Even courts accepting this defense as an adequate safeguard have recognized the difficulties of adducing legal proofs that the alleged libel was true in all its factual particulars. See, e.g., *Post Publishing Co. v. Hallam,* 59 F. 530, 540 (C.A.6th Cir. 1893); see also Noel, *Defamation of Public Officers and Candidates,* 49 Col.L. Rev. 875, 892 (1949). Under such a rule, would-be critics of official conduct may be deterred from voicing their criticism, even though it is believed to be true and even though it is in fact true, because of doubt whether it can be proved in court or fear of the expense of having to do so. They tend to make only statements which "steer far wider of the unlawful zone." *Speiser v. Randall,* supra, 357 U.S., at 526, 78 S.Ct. at 1342, 2 L.Ed.2d 1460. The rule thus dampens the vigor and limits the variety of public debate. It is inconsistent with the First and Fourteenth Amendments.

[19, 20] The constitutional guarantees require, we think, a federal rule that prohibits a public official from recovering damages for a defamatory falsehood relating to his official conduct unless he proves that the statement was made with "actual malice"—that is, with knowledge that it was false or with reckless disregard of whether it was false or not. An oft-cited statement of a like rule, which has been adopted by a number of state courts,[20] is found in the Kansas

---

[18] *The Times* states that four other libel suits based on the advertisement have been filed against it by others who have served as Montgomery City Commissioners and by the Governor of Alabama; that another $500,000 verdict has been awarded in the only one of these cases that has yet gone to trial; and that the damages sought in the other three total $2,000,000.

[19] Even a false statement may be deemed to make a valuable contribution to public debate, since it brings about "the clearer perception and livelier impression of truth, produced by its collision with error." Mill, *On Liberty* (Oxford: Blackwell, 1947), at 15; see also Milton, *Areopagitica, in Prose Works* (Yale, 1959), Vol. II, at 561.

[20] E. g., *Ponder v. Cobb,* 257 N.C. 281, 299, 126 S.E.2d 67, 80 (1962); *Lawrence v. Fox,* 357 Mich. 134, 146, 97 N.W.2d 719,

case of *Coleman v. MacLennan,* 78'Kan. 711, 98 P. 281 (1908). The State Attorney General, a candidate for re-election and a member of the commission charged with the management and control of the state school fund, sued a newspaper publisher for alleged libel in an article purporting to state facts relating to his official conduct in connection with a school-fund transactions. The defendant pleaded privilege and the trial judge, over the plaintiff's objection, instructed the jury that

> "where an article is published and circulated among voters for the sole purpose of giving what the defendant believes to be truthful information concerning a candidate for public office and for the purpose of enabling such voters to cast their ballot more intelligently, and the whole thing is done in good faith and without malice, the article is privileged, although the principal matters contained in the article may be untrue in fact and derogatory to the character of the plaintiff; and such a case the burden is on the plaintiff to show actual malice in the publication of the article."

In answer to a special question, the jury found that the plaintiff had not proved actual malice, and a general verdict was returned for the defendant. On appeal the Supreme Court of Kansas, in an opinion by Justice Burch, reasoned as follows (78 Kan., at 724, 98 P., at 286);

> "[I]t is of the utmost consequence that the people should discuss the character and qualifications of candidates for their suffrages. The importance to the state and to

society of such discussions is so vast, and the advantages derived are so great that they more than counterbalance the inconvenience of private persons whose conduct may be involved, and occasional injury to the reputations of individuals must yield to the public welfare, although at times such injury may be great. The public benefit from publicity is so great and the chance of injury to private character so small that such discussion must be privileged."

The court thus sustained the trial court's instruction as a correct statement of the law, saying:

> "In such a case the occasion gives rise to a privilege qualified to this extent. Any one claiming to be defamed by the communication must show actual malice, or go remediless. This privilege extends to a great variety of subjects and includes matters of public concern, public men, and candidates for office." 78 Kan., at 723, 98 P., at 285.

Such a privilege for criticism of official conduct[21] is appropriately analogous to the protection accorded a public official when *he* is sued for libel by a private citizen. In *Barr v. Matteo,* 360 U.S. 564, 575, 79 S.Ct. 1335, 1341, 3 L.Ed.2d 1434, this Court held the utterance of a federal official to be absolutely privileged if made "within the outer perimeter" of his duties. The States accord the same immunity to statements of their highest officers, although some differentiate their lesser officials and qualify the privilege they enjoy.[22] But all hold that all officials are protected unless actual malice can be proved. The rea-

---

725 (1959); *Stice v. Beacon Newspaper Corp.,* 185 Kan. 61, 65–67, 340 P.2d 396, 400–401, 76 A.L.R.2d 687 (1959); *Bailey v. Charleston Mail Assn.,* 126 W.Va. 292, 307, 27 S.E.2d 837, 844, 150 A.L.R. 348 (1943); *Salinger v. Cowles,* 195 Iowa 873, 889, 191 N.W. 167, 174 (1922); *Snively v. Record Publishing Co.,* 185 Cal. 565, 571–576, 198 P. 1 (1921); *McLean v. Merriman,* 42 S.D. 394, 175 N.W. 878 (1920). Applying the same rule to candidates for public office, see, e. g., *Phoenix Newspapers v. Choisser,* 82 Ariz. 271, 276–277, 312 P.2d 150, 154 (1957); *Friedell v. Blakely Printing Co.,*163 Minn. 226, 230, 203 N.W. 974, 975 (1925). And see *Chagnon v. Union-Leader Corp.,* 103 N.H. 426, 438, 174 A.2d 825, 833 (1961), cert. denied, 269 U.S. 830, 82 S.Ct. 846, 7 L.Ed.2d 795.

The consensus of scholarly opinion apparently favors the rule that is here adopted. E. g., 1 Harper and James, *Torts,*§ 5.26, at 449–450 (1956); Noel, *Defamation of Public Officers and Candidates,* 49 Col.L.Rev. 875, 891–895, 897, 903 (1949); Hallen, *Fair Comment,* 8 Tex.L.Rev. 41, 61 (1929); Smith, *Charging Against Candidates.*18 Mich.L.Rev. 1, 115 (1919); Chase, *Criticism of Public Officers and Candidates for Office,* 23 Am.L.Rev. 346, 367–371 (1889); Cooley, *Constitutional Limitations* (7th ed., Lane, 1903), at 604, 616–628. But see, e.g., American Law Institute, *Restatement of Torts,* § 598,

Comment a (1938) (reversing the position taken in Tentative Draft 13, § 1041(2) (1936); Veeder, *Freedom of Public Discussion,* 23 Harv.L.Rev. 413, 419 (1910).

[21] The privilege immunizing honest misstatements of facts is often referred to as a "conditional" privilege to distinguish it from the "absolute" privilege recognized in judicial, legislative, administrative and executive proceedings. See, e.g., Prosser, *Torts* (2d ed., 1955), § 95.

[22] See 1 Harper and James, *Torts,*§ 5.23, at 429–430 (1956). Prosser, *Torts,* (2d ed., 1955), at 612–613; American Law Institute, *Restatement of Torts* (1938), § 519.

We have no occasion here to determine how far down into the lower ranks of government employees the "public official" designation would extend for purposes of this rule, or otherwise to specify categories of persons who would or would not be included. Cf. *Barr v. Matteo,* 360 U.S. 564, 573–575, 79 S.Ct. 1335, 1340–1341, 3 L.Ed.2d 1434. Nor need we here determine the boundaries of the "official conduct" concept. It is enough for the present case that respondent's position as an elected city commissioner clearly made him a public official, and that the allegations in the advertisement concerned what was allegedly his official conduct as Commissioner in charge of the Police Department. As to

son for the official privilege is said to be that the threat of damage suits would otherwise "inhibit the fearless, vigorous, and effective administration of policies of government" and "dampen the ardor of all but the most resolute, or the most irresponsible, in the unflinching discharge of their duties."*Barr v. Matteo*, supra, 360 U.S., at 571, 79 S.Ct., at 1339, 3 L.Ed.2d 1434. Analogous considerations support the privilege for the citizen-critic of government. It as much his duty to criticize as it is the official's duty to administer. See *Whitney v. California*, 274 U.S. 357, 375, 47 S.Ct. 641, 648, 71 L.Ed. 1095 (concurring opinion of Mr. Justice Brandeis), quoted supra, pp. 720, 721. As Madison said, see supra, p. 723, "the censorial power is in the people over the Government, and not in the Government over the people." It would give public servants an unjustified preference over the public they serve, if critics of official conduct did not have a fair equivalent of the immunity granted to the officials themselves.

We conclude that such a privilege is required by the First and Fourteenth Amendments.

III.

[21–23] We hold today that Constitution delimits a State's power to award damages for libel in actions brought by public officials against critics of their officials against critics of their official conduct. Since this is such an action,[23] the rule requiring proof of actual malice is applicable. While Alabama law apparently requires proof of actual malice for an award of punitive damages,[24] where general damages are concerned malice is "presumed." Such a pre-

sumption is inconsistent with the federal rule. "The power to create presumptions is not a means of escape from constitutional restrictions,"*Bailey v. Alabama*, 219 U.S. 219, 239, 31 S.Ct. 145, 151, 55 L.Ed. 191; "[t]he showing of malice required for the forfeiture of the privilege is not presumed but is a matter for proof by the plaintiff * *," *Lawrence v. Fox*, 357 Mich. 134, 146, 97 N.W.2d 719, 725 (1959).[25] Since the trial judge did not instruct the jury to differentiate between general and punitive damages, it may be that the verdict was wholly an award of one or the other. But it is impossible to know, in view of the general verdict returned. Because of this uncertainty, the judgment must be reversed and the case remanded. *Stromberg v. California*, 283 U.S. 359, 367–368, 51 S.Ct. 532, 535, 75 L.Ed. 1117; *Williams v. North Carolina*, 317 U.S. 287, 291–292, 63 S.Ct. 207, 209–210, 87 L.Ed. 279; see *Yates v. United States*, 354 U.S. 298, 311–312, 77 S.Ct. 1064, 1073, 1 L.Ed. 2d 1356; *Cramer v. United States*, 325 U.S. 1, 36, n. 45, 65 S.Ct. 918, 935, 940, 89 L.Ed. 1441.

[24–26] Since respondent may seek a new trial, we deem that considerations of effective judicial administration require us to review the evidence in the present record to determine whether it could constitutionally support a judgment for respondent. This Court's duty is not limited to the elaboration of constitutional principles; we must also in proper cases review the evidence to make certain that those principles have been constitutionally applied. This is such a case, particularly since the question is one of alleged trespass across "the line between speech which may legitimately be regulated."

---

the statements alleging the assaulting of Dr. King and the bombing of his home, it is immaterial that they might not be considered to involve respondent's official conduct if he himself had been accused of perpetrating the assault and the bombing. Respondent does not claim that the statements charged him personally with these acts; his contention is that the advertisement connects him with them only in his official capacity as the Commissioner supervising the police, might be equated with the "They" who did the bombing and assaulting. Thus, if these allegations can be read as referring to respondent at all, they must be read as describing his performance of his official duties.

[24] *Johnson Publishing Co. v Davis*, 271 Ala. 474, 487, 124 So.2d 441, 450 (1960). Thus the trial judge here instructed the jury that "mere negligence or carelessness is not evidence of actual malice or malice in fact, and does not justify an award of exemplary or punitive damages in an action for libel."

The court refused, however, to give the following instruction which had been requested by the *Times:*

"I charge you * * * that punitive damages, as the name indicates, are designed to punish the defendant, the New York Times Company, a corporation, and the other defendants in this case, * * * and I further charge you that such punitive damages may be awarded only in the event that you, the jury, are convinced by a fair preponderance of the evidence that the defendant * * * was motivated by personal ill-will, that is actual intent to do the plaintiff harm, or that the defendant * * * was guilty of gross negligence and recklessness and not of just ordinary negligence or carelessness in publishing the matter complained of so as to indicate a wanton disregard of plaintiff's rights."

The trial court's error in failing to require any finding of actual malice for an award of general damages makes it unnecessary for us to consider the sufficiency under the federal standard of the instructions regarding actual malice that were given as to punitive damages.

[25] Accord, *Coleman v. MacLennan*, supra, 78 Kan., at 741, 98 P., at 292; *Gough v. Tribune-Journal Co.*, 75 Idaho 502, 510, 275 P.2d 663, 668 (1954).

U.S. SUPREME
COURT,
MARCH 1964

Speiser v. Randall, 357 U.S. 513, 525, 78 S.Ct. 1332, 1342, 2 L.Ed.2d 1460. In cases where that line must be drawn, the rule is that we "examine for ourselves the statements in issue and the circumstances under which they were made to see * * * whether they are of a character which the principles of the First Amendment, as adopted by the Due Process Clause of the Fourteenth Amendment, protect." *Pennekamp v. Florida,* 328 U.S. 331, 335, 66 S.Ct. 1029, 1031, 90 L.Ed. 1295; see also *One, Inc. v. Olesen,* 355 U.S. 371, 78 S.Ct. 364, 2 L.Ed.2d 352; *Sunshine Book Co. v. Summerfield,* 355 U.S. 372, 78 S.Ct. 365, 2 L.Ed.2d 352. We must "make an independent examination of the whole record," *Edwards v. South Carolina,* 372 U.S. 229, 235, 83 S.Ct. 680, 683, 9 L.Ed.2d 697, so as to assure ourselves that the judgment does not constitute a forbidden intrusion on the field of free expression.[26]

[27] Applying these standards, we consider that the proof presented to show actual malice lacks the convincing clarity which the constitutional standard demands, and hence that it would not constitutionally sustain the judgment for respondent under the proper rule of law. The case of the individual petitioners requires little discussion. Even assuming that they could constitutionally be found to have authorized the use of their names on the advertisement, there was no evidence whatever that they were aware of any erroneous statements or were in any way reckless in that regard. The judgment against them is thus without constitutional support.

As to the *Times,* we similarly conclude that the facts do not support a finding of actual malice. The statement by the *Times'* Secretary that, apart from the padlocking allegation, he

thought the advertisement was "substantially correct," affords no constitutional warrant for the Alabama Supreme Court's conclusion that it was a "cavalier ignoring of the falsity of the advertisement [from which], the jury could not have but been impressed with the bad faith of *The Times,* and its maliciousness inferable therefrom." The statement does not indicate malice at the time of the publication; even if the advertisement was not "substantially correct"— although respondent's own proofs tend to show that it was—that opinion was at least a reasonable one, and there was no evidence to impeach the witness' good faith in holding it. *The Times'* failure to retract upon respondent's demand, although it later retracted upon the demand of Governor Patterson, is likewise not adequate evidence of malice for constitutional purposes. Whether or not a failure to retract may ever constitute such evidence, there are two reasons why it does not here. *First,* the letter written by the *Times* reflected a reasonable doubt on its part as to whether the advertisement could reasonably be taken to refer to respondent at all. *Second,* it was not a final refusal, since it asked for an explanation on this point—a request that respondent chose to ignore. Nor does the retraction upon the demand of the Governor supply the necessary proof. It may be doubted that a failure to retract which is not itself evidence of malice can retroactively become such by virtue of a retraction subsequently made to another party. But in any event that did not happen here, since the explanation given by the *Times'* Secretary for the distinction drawn between respondent and the Governor was a reasonable one, the good faith of which was not impeached.

Finally, there is evidence that the *Times* published the advertisement without checking its accuracy against the news stories in the *Times'* own files. The mere presence of the stories in the files does not, of course, establish that the *Times* "knew" the advertisement was false, since the state of mind required for actual malice would have to be brought home to the persons in the *Times'* organization having responsibility for the publication of the advertisement. With respect to the failure of those persons to make the check, the record shows that they relied upon their knowledge of the good reputation of many of those whose names were listed as sponsors of the advertisement, and upon the letter from A. Philip Randolph, know to them as a responsible individual, certifying that the use of the names

---

[26] Seventh Amendment does not, as respondent contends, preclude such an examination by this Court. That Amendment, providing that "no fact tried by a jury, shall be otherwise reexamined in any Court of the United States, than according to the rules of the common law," is applicable to state cases coming here. *Chicago, B. & Q. R. Co. v. Chicago,* 166 U.S. 226, 242–243, 17 S.Ct. 581, 587, 41 L.Ed. 979; cf. *The Justices v. Murray,* 9 Wall. 274, 19 L.Ed. 658. But its ban on re-examination of facts does not preclude us from determining whether governing rules of federal law have been properly applied to the facts. "[T]his Court will review the finding of facts by a State court * * * where a conclusion of law as to a Federal right and a finding of fact are so intermingled as to make it necessary, in order to pass upon the Federal question, to analyze the facts." *Fiske v. Kansas,* 274 U.S. 380, 385–386, 47 S.Ct. 655, 656–657, 71 L.Ed. 1108. See also *Haynes v. Washington,* 373 U.S. 503, 515–516, 83 S.Ct. 1336, 1344, 10 L.Ed.2d 513.

was authorized. There was testimony that the persons handling the advertisement was nothing in it that would render it unacceptable under the *Times'* policy of rejecting advertisements containing "attacks of a personal character;"[27] their failure to reject it on this ground was not unreasonable. We think the evidence against the *Times* supports at most a finding of negligence in failing to discover the misstatements, and is constitutionally insufficient to show the recklessness that is required for a finding of actual malice. Cf.*Charles Parker Co. v. Silver City Crystal Co.,* 142 Conn. 605, 618, 116 A.2d 440, 446 (1955); *Phoenix Newspapers, Inc. v. Choisser,* 82 Ariz. 271, 277–278, 312 P.2d 150, 154–155 (1957).

[28] We also think the evidence was constitutionally defective in another respect: it was incapable of supporting the jury's finding that the allegedly libelous statements were made "of and concerning" respondent. Respondent relies on the words of the advertisement and the testimony of six witnesses to establish a connection between it and himself. Thus, in his brief to this Court, he states:

> "The reference to respondent as police commissioner is clear from the ad. In addition, the jury heard the testimony of a newspaper editor * * *; a real estate and insurance man * * *; the sales manager of a men's clothing store * * *; a food equipment man * * *; a service station operator * * *; and the operator of a truck line for whom respondent had formerly worked * * *. Each of these witnesses stated that he associated the statements with respondent * *." (Citations to record omitted).

There was no reference to respondent in the advertisement, either by name or official position. A number to respondent in the advertisement, either by name or official position. A number of the allegedly libelous statements— the charges that the dining hall was padlocked and that Dr. King's home was bombed, his person assaulted, and a perjury prosecution instituted against him—did not even concern the police; despite the ingenuity of the arguments which would attach this significance to the word "They," it is plain that these statements could not reasonably be read as accusing respondent of personal involvement in the acts in question. The statements upon which respondent principally relies as referring to him are the two allegations that did concern the police or police functions: that "truckloads of police * * * ringed the Alabama State College Campus" after the

demonstration on the State Capitol steps, and that Dr. King had been arrested * * * seven times." These statements were false only in that the police had been "deployed near" the campus but had not actually "ringed" it and had not gone there in connection with the State Capitol demonstration, and in that Dr. King had been arrested only four times. The ruling that these discrepancies between what was true and what was asserted were sufficient to injure respondent's reputation may itself raise constitutional problems, but we need not consider them here. Although the statements may be taken as referring to the police, they did not on their face make even an oblique reference to respondent as an individual. Support for the asserted reference must, therefore, be sought in the testimony of respondent's witnesses. But none of them suggested any basis for the belief that respondent himself was attacked in the advertisement beyond the bare fact that he was in overall charge of the Police Department and thus bore official responsibility for police conduct; to the extent that some of the witnesses thought respondent to have been charged with ordering or approving the conduct or otherwise being personally involved in it, they based this notion not on any statements in the advertisement, and not on any evidence that he had in fact been so involved, but solely on the unsupported assumption that, because of his official position, he must have been.[28] This reliance on the bare

---

[27] *The Times* has set forth in a booklet its "Advertising Acceptability Standards." Listed among the classes of advertising that the newspaper does not accept are advertisements that are "fraudulent or deceptive," that are "fraudulent or deceptive," that are "ambiguous in wording and * * * may mislead," and that contain "attacks of a personal character." In replying to respondent's interrogatories before the trial, the Secretary of the Times stated that "as the advertisement made no attacks of a personal character upon any individual and otherwise met the advertising acceptability standards promulgated," it had been approved for publication.

[28] Respondent's own testimony was that "as Commissioner of Public Affairs it is part of my duty to supervise the Police Department and I certainly feel like it [a statement] is associated with me when it describes police activities." He thought that "by virtue of being Police Commissioner and Commissioner of Public Affairs," he was charged with "any activity on the part of the Police Department." "When it describes police action, certainly I feel it reflects on me as an individual." He added that "It is my feeling that it reflects not only on me but on the other Commissioners and the community."

Grove C. Hall testified that to him the third paragraph of the advertisement called to mind "the City government—

U.S. SUPREME
COURT,
MARCH 1964

fact of respondent's official position[29] was made explicit by the Supreme Court of Alabama. That court, in holding that the trial court "did not err in overruling the demurrer [of the *Times*] in the aspect that the libelous matter was not and concerning the [plaintiff,]" based its ruling on the proposition that:

> "We think it common knowledge that the average person knows that municipal agents, such as police and firemen, and others, are under the control and direction of the city governing body, and more particularly under the direction and control of a single commissioner. In measuring the performance or deficiencies of such groups, praise or criticism is usually attached to the official in complete control of the body." 273 Ala., at 674–675, 144 So.2d, at 39.

[29] This proposition has disquieting implications for criticism of governmental conduct. For good reason, "no court of last resort in this country has ever held, or even suggested, that prosecutions for libel on government have any place in the American system of jurisprudence." *City of Chicago v. Tribune Co.*, 307 Ill. 595, 601, 139 N.E. 86, 88, 28 A.L.R. 1368 (1923). The present proposition would sidestep this obstacle by transmuting criticism of government, however impersonal it may seem on its face, into personal criticism, and hence potential libel, of the officials of whom the government is composed. There is no legal alchemy by which a State may

thus create the cause of action that would otherwise be denied for a publication which, as respondent himself said of the advertisement, "reflects not only on me but on the other Commissioners and the community." Raising as it does the possibility that a good-faith critic of government will be penalized for his criticism, the proposition relied on by the Alabama courts strikes at the very center of the constitutionally protected area of free expression.[30] We hold that such a proposition may not constitutionally be utilized to establish that an otherwise impersonal attack on governmental operations was a libel of an official responsible for those operations. Since it was relied on exclusively here, and there was no other evidence to connect the statement with respondent, the evidence was constitutionally insufficient to support a finding that the statements referred to respondent.

The judgment of the Supreme Court of Alabama is reversed and the case is remanded to that court for further proceedings not inconsistent with this opinion.

Reversed and remanded.

Mr. Justice Black, with whom Mr. Justice Douglas joins (concurring).

I concur in reversing this half-million-dollar judgment against the New York Times Company and the four individual defendants. In reversing the Court holds that "the Constitution delimits a

---

the Commissioners," and that "now that you ask it I would naturally think a little more about the police Commissioner because his responsibility is exclusively with the constabulary." It was "the phrase about starvation" that led to the association; "the other didn't hit me with any particular force."

Arnold D. Blackwell testified that the third paragraph was associated in his mind with "the Police Commissioner and the police force. The people on the police force." If he had believed the statement about the padlocking of the dining hall, he would have thought "that the people on our police force or the heads of our police force were acting without their jurisdiction and would not be competent for the position." I would assume that the Commissioner had ordered the police force to do that and therefore it would be his responsibility."

Harry W. Kaminsky associated the statement about "truckloads of police" with respondent "because he is the Police Commissioner." He thought that the reference to arrests in the sixth paragraph "implicates the Police Department, I think, or the authorities that would do that— arrest folks for speeding and loitering and such as that." Asked whether he would associate with respondent a newspaper report that the police had "beat somebody up or assaulted them on the streets of Montgomery," he replied; "I

still say he is the Police Commissioner and those men are working directly under him and therefore I would think that he would have something to do with it." In general, he said, "I look at Mr. Sullivan when I see the Police Department."

H. M. Price, Sr., testified that he associated the first sentence of the third paragraph with respondent because: "I would just automatically consider that the Police Commissioner in Montgomery would have to put his approval on those kind of things as an individual."

William M. Parker, Jr. testified that he associated the statements in the two paragraphs with "the Commissioners of the City of Montgomery," and since respondent "was the Police Commissioner," he "thought of him first." He told the examining counsel: "I think if you were the Police Commissioner I would have thought it was speaking of you."

Horace W. White, respondent's former employer, testified that the statement about "truck-loads of police" made him think of respondent "as being the head of the Police Department." Asked whether he read the statement as charging respondent himself with ringing the campus or having shotguns and tear-gas, he replied: "Well, I thought of his department being charged with it, yes, sir. He is the head of the Police Department as I understand it." He further said that the reason he would have been unwilling to re-employ respondent if he had believed the advertisement was "the

State's power to award damages for libel in actions brought by public officials against critics of their official conduct." Ante, p. 727. I base my vote to reverse on the belief that the First and Fourteenth Amendments not merely "delimit" a State's power to award damages to "public officials against critics of their official conduct" but completely prohibit a State from exercising such a power. The Court goes on to hold that a State can subject such critics to damages if "actual malice" can be proved against them. "Malice," even as defined by the Court, is an elusive, abstract concept, hard to prove and hard to disprove. The requirement that malice be proved provides at best an evanescent protection for the right critically to discuss public affairs and certainly does not measure up to the sturdy safeguard embodied in the First Amendment. Unlike the Court, therefore, I vote to reverse exclusively on the ground that the *Times* and the individual defendants had an absolute, unconditional constitutional right to publish in the *Times* advertisement their criticisms of the Montgomery agencies and officials. I do not base my vote to reverse on any failure to prove that these individual defendants signed the advertisement or that their criticism of the Police Department was aimed at the plaintiff Sullivan, who was then the Montgomery City Commissioner having supervision of the city's police; for present purposes I assume these things were proved. Nor is my reason for reversal the size of the half-million-dollar judgment, large as it is. If Alabama has constitutional power to use its civil libel law to impose damages on the press for criticizing the way public officials perform or fail to perform their duties, I know of no provision in the Federal Constitution which either

expressly or impliedly bars the State from fixing the amount of damages.

The half-million-dollar verdict does give dramatic proof, however, that state libel laws threaten the very existence of an American press virile enough to publish unpopular views on public affairs and bold enough to criticize the conduct of public officials. The factual background of this case emphasizes the imminence and enormity of that threat. One of the acute and highly emotional issues in this country arises out of efforts of many people, even including some public officials, to continue state-commanded segregation of races in the public schools and other public places, despite our several holdings that such a state practice is forbidden by the Fourteenth Amendment. Montgomery is one of the localities in which widespread hostility to desegregation has been manifested. This hostility has sometimes extended itself to persons who favor desegregation, particularly to so-called "outside agitators," a term which can be made to fit papers like the *Times*, which is published in New York. The scarcity of testimony to show that Commissioner Sullivan suffered any actual damages at all suggests that these feelings of hostility had at least as much to do with rendition of this half-million-dollar verdict as did an appraisal of damages. Viewed realistically, this record lends support to an inference that instead of being damaged Commissioner Sullivan's political, social, and financial prestige has likely been enhanced by the *Times*' publication. Moreover, a second half-million-dollar libel verdict against the Times based on the same advertisement has already been awarded to another Commissioner. There a jury again gave the full amount claimed. There is no reason to believe that there are not more such huge verdicts lurking just around the corner for the *Times* or any other newspaper or broadcaster which might dare to criticize public officials. In fact, briefs before us show that in Alabama there are now pending eleven libel suits by local and state officials against the *Times* seeking $5,600,000, and five such suits against the Columbia Broadcasting System seeking $1,700,000. Moreover, this technique for harassing and punishing a free press—now that it has been shown to be possible—is by no means limited to cases with racial overtones; it can be used in other fields where public feelings may make local as well as out-of-state newspapers easy prey for libel verdict seekers.

---

fact that he allowed the Police Department to do the things that the paper say he did."

[29] Compare *Ponder v. Cobb*, 257 N.C. 281, 126 S.E.2d 67 (1962).

[30] Insofar as the proposition means only that the statements about police conduct libeled respondent by implicitly criticizing his ability to run the Police Department, recovery is also precluded in this case by the doctrine of fair comment. See American Law Institute, Restatement of Torts (1938), § 607. Since the Fourteenth Amendment requires recognition of the conditional privilege for honest misstatements of fact, it follows that a defense of fair comment must be afforded for honest expression of opinion based upon privileged, as well as true, statements of fact. Both defenses are of course defeasible if the public official proves actual malice, as was not done here.

U.S. SUPREME
COURT,
MARCH 1964

In my opinion the Federal Constitution has dealt with this deadly danger to the press in the only way possible without leaving the free press open to destruction—by granting the press an absolute immunity for criticism of the way public officials do their public duty. Compare *Barr v. Matteo*, 360 U.S. 564, 79 S.Ct. 1335, 3 L.Ed.2d 1434. Stopgap measures like those the Court adopts are in my judgment not enough. This record certainly does not indicate that any different verdict would have been rendered here whatever the Court had charged the jury about "malice," "truth," "good motives," "justifiable ends," or any other legal formulas which in theory would protect the press. Nor does the record indicate that any of these legalistic words would have caused the courts below to set aside or to reduce the half-million-dollar verdict in any amount.

I agree with the Court that the Fourteenth Amendment made the First applicable to the States.[1] This means to me that since the adoption of the Fourteenth Amendment a State has no more power than the Federal Government to use a civil libel law or any other law to impose damages for merely discussing public affairs and criticizing public officials. The power of the United to do that is, in my judgment, precisely nil. Such was the general view held when the First Amendment was adopted and ever since.[2] Congress never has sought to challenge this viewpoint by passing any civil libel law. It did pass the Sedition Act in 1798,[3] which made it a crime—"seditious libel"—to criticize federal officials or the Federal Government. As the Court's opinion correctly points out however, ante, pp. 722–723, that Act came to an ignominious end and by common consent has generally been treated as having been a wholly unjustifiable and much to be regretted violation of the First Amendment. Since the First Amendment is now made applicable to the States by the Fourteenth, it no more permits the States to impose damages for libel than it does the Federal Government.

We would, I think, more faithfully interpret the First Amendment by holding that at the very least it leaves the people and the press free to criticize officials and discuss public affairs with impunity. This Nation of our elects many of its important officials; so do the States, the municipalities, the counties, and even many precincts. These officials are responsible to the people for the way they perform their duties. While our Court has held that some kinds of speech and writings, such as "obscenity," *Roth v. United States*, 354 U.S. 476, 77 S.Ct. 1304, 1 L.Ed.2d 1498, and "fighting words," *Chaplinsky v. New Hampshire*, 315 U.S. 568, 62 S.Ct. 766, 85 L.Ed. 1061, are not expression within the protection of the First Amendment,[4] freedom to discuss public affairs and public officials is unquestionably, as the Court today holds, the kind of speech the First Amendment was primarily designed to keep within the area of free discussion. To punish the exercise of this right to discuss public affairs or to penalize it through libel judgments is to abridge or shut off discussion of the very kind most needed. This Nation, I suspect, can live in peace without libel suits based on public discussions of public affairs and public officials. But I doubt that a country can live in freedom where its people can be made to suffer physically or financially for criticizing their government, its actions, or its officials. "For a representative democracy ceases to exist the moment that the public functionaries are by any means absolved from their responsibility to their constituents; and this happens whenever the constituent can be restrained in any manner from speaking, writing, or publishing his opinions upon any public measure, or upon the conduct of those who may advise or execute it."[5] An unconditional right to say what one pleases about public affairs is what I consider to be the minimum guarantee of the First Amendment.[6]

I regret that the Court has stopped short of this holding indispensable to preserve our free press from destruction.

---

[1] See cases collected in *Speiser v. Randall*, 357 U.S. 513, 530, 78 S.Ct. 1332, 1344, 2 L.Ed.2d 1460 (concurring opinion).

[2] See, e. g., 1 Tucker, *Blackstone's Commentaries* (1803), 297–299 (editor's appendix). St. George Tucker, a distinguished Virginia jurist, took part in the Annapolis Convention of 1786, sat on both state and federal courts, and was wisely known for his writings on judicial and constitutional subjects.

[3] Act of July 14, 1798, 1 Stat. 596.

[4] But see *Smith v. California*, 361 U.S. 147, 155, 80 S.Ct. 215, 219, 4 L.Ed.2d 205 (concurring opinion); *Roth v. United States*, 354 U.S. 476, 508, 77 S.Ct. 1304, 1321, 1 L.Ed.2d 1498 (dissenting opinion).

[5] 1 Tucker, *Blackstone's Commentaries*(1803), 297 (editor's appendix; cf. Brant, *Seditious Libel: Myth and Reality*, 39 N.Y.U.L.Rev. 1.

[6] Cf. Meiklejohn, *Free Speech and Its Relation to Self-Government* (1948).

Mr. Justice Goldberg, with whom Mr. Justice Douglas joins (concurring in the result).

The Court today announces a constitutional standard which prohibits "a public official from recovering damages for a defamatory falsehood relating to his official conduct unless he proves that the statement was made with 'actual malice'—that is, with knowledge that it was false or with reckless disregard of whether it was false or not." Ante, at p. 726. The Court thus rules that the Constitution gives citizens and newspapers a "conditional privilege" immunizing nonmalicious misstatements of fact regarding the official conduct of a government officer. The impressive array of history[1] and precedent marshaled by the Court, however, confirms my belief that the Constitution affords greater protection than that provided by the Court's standard to citizen and press in exercising the right of public criticism.

In my view, the First and Fourteenth Amendments to the Constitution afford to the citizen and to the press an absolute, unconditional privilege to criticize official conduct despite the harm which may flow from excesses and abuses. The prized American right "to speak one's mind," cf. *Bridges v. California,* 314 U.S. 252, 270, 62 S.Ct. 190, 197, 86 L.Ed. 192, about public officials and affairs needs "breathing space to survive," *N.A.A.C.P. v. Button,* 371, U.S. 415, 433, 82 S.Ct. 328, 338, 9 L.Ed.2d 405. The right should not depend upon a probing by the jury of the motivation[2] of the citizen or press. The theory of our Constitution is that every citizen may speak his mind and every newspaper express its view on matters of public concern and may not be barred

from speaking or publishing because those in control of government think that what is said or written is unwise, unfair, false, or malicious. In a democratic society, one who assumes to act for the citizens in an executive, legislative, or judicial capacity must expect that his official acts will be commented upon and criticized. Such criticism cannot, in my opinion, be muzzled or deterred by the courts at the instance of public officials under the label of libel.

It has been recognized that "prosecutions for libel on government have [no] place in the American system of jurisprudence." *City of Chicago v. Tribune Co.,* 307 Ill. 595, 601, 139 N.E. 86, 28 A.L.R. 1368. I fully agree. Government, however, is not an abstraction; it is made up of individuals—of governors responsible to the governed. In a democratic society where men are free by ballots to remove those in power, any statement critical of government. If the rule that libel on government has no place in our Constitution is to have real meaning, then libel on the official conduct of the governors likewise can have no place in our Constitution.

We must recognize that we are writing upon a clean slate.[3] As the Court notes, although there have been "statements of this Court to the effect that the Constitution does not protect libelous publications * * * [n]one of the cases sustained the use of libel laws to impose sanctions upon expression critical of the official conduct of public officials." Ante, at p. 719. We should be particularly careful, therefore, adequately to protect the liberties which are embodied in the First and Fourteenth Amendments. It may be

U.S. SUPREME
COURT,
MARCH 1964

---

[1] I fully agree with the Court that the attack upon the validity of the Sedition Act of 1798, 1 Stat. 596, "has carried the day in the court of history," ante, at p. 723, and that the Act would today be declared unconstitutional. It should be pointed out, however, that the Sedition Act proscribed writings which were "false, scandalous *and malicious.*" (Emphasis added.) For prosecutions under the Sedition Act charging malice, see e. g., Trial of Matthew Lyon (1798), in Wharton, *State Trials of the United States* (1849), p. 333; Trial of Thomas Cooper (1800), in *id,* at 684; Trial of James Thompson Callender (1800), in *id,* at 688.

[2] The requirement of proving actual malice or reckon disregard may, in the mind of the jury, add little to the requirement of proving falsity, a requirement which the Court recognizes not to be adequate safeguard. The thought suggested by Mr. Justice Jackson in *United States v. Ballard,* 322 U.S. 78, 92–93, 64 S.Ct. 882, 889, 88 L.Ed. 1148, is relevant here; "[A]s a matter of either practice or philosophy I do not see how we can separate an issue as to what is believed from considerations as to what is believable. The most convincing

proof that one believes his statements is to show that they have been true in his experience. Likewise, that one knowingly falsified is best proved by showing that what he said happened never did happen." See note 4, infra.

[3] It was not until *Gitlow v. New York,* 268 U.S. 652, 45 S.Ct. 625, 69 L.Ed. 1138, decided in 1925, that it was intimated that the freedom of speech guaranteed by the First Amendment was applicable to the States by reason of the Fourteenth Amendment. Other intimations followed. See *Whitney v. California,* 274 U.S. 357, 47 S.Ct. 641, 71 L.Ed. 1095; *Fiske v. Kansas,* 274 U.S. 380, 47 S.Ct. 655, 71 L.Ed. 1108. In 1931 Chief Justice Hughes speaking for the Court in *Stromberg v. California,* 283 U.S. 359, 368, 51 S.Ct. 532, 535, 75 L.Ed. 1117, declared; "It has been determined that the conception of liberty under the due process clause of the Fourteenth Amendment embraces the right of free speech." Thus we deal with a constitutional principle enunciated less than four decades ago, and consider for the first time the application of that principle to issues arising in libel cases brought by state officials.

U.S. SUPREME
COURT,
MARCH 1964

urged that deliberately and maliciously false statements have no conceivable value as free speech. That argument, however, is not responsive to the real issue presented by this case, which is whether that freedom of speech which all agree is constitutionally protected can be effectively safeguarded by a rule allowing the imposition of liability upon a jury's evaluation of the speaker's state of mind. If individual citizens may be held liable in damages for strong words, which a jury finds false and maliciously motivated, there can be little doubt that public debate and advocacy will be constrained. And if newspapers, publishing advertisements dealing with public issues, thereby risk liability, there can also be little doubt that the ability of minority groups to secure publication of their views on public affairs and to seek support for their causes will be greatly diminished. Cf. *Farmers Educational & Coop. Union v. WDAY, Inc.*, 360 U.S. 525, 530, 79 S.Ct. 1302, 1305, 3 L.Ed.2d 1407. The opinion of the Court conclusively demonstrates the chilling effect of the Alabama libel laws on First Amendment freedoms in the area of race relations. The American Colonists were not willing, nor should we be, to take the risk that "[m]en who injure and oppress the people under their administration [and] provoke them to cry out and complain" will also be empowered to "make that very complaint the foundation for new oppressions and prosecutions." The Trial of John Peter Zenger, 17 Howell's St. Tr. 675, 721–722 (1735) (argument of counsel to the jury). To impose liability for critical, albeit erroneous or even malicious, comments on official conduct would effectively resurrect "the obsolete doctrine that the governed must not criticize their governors." Cf. *Sweeney v. Patterson*, 76 U.S.App.D.C. 23, 24, 128 F.2d 457, 458.

Our national experience teaches that repressions breed hate and "that hate menaces stable government." *Whitney v. California*, 274 U.S. 357, 375, 47 S.Ct. 641, 648, 71 L.Ed. 095 (Brandeis, J., concurring). We should be ever mindful of the wise counsel of Chief Justice Hughes:

> "[I]mperative is the need to preserve inviolate the constitutional rights of free speech, free press and free assembly in order to maintain the opportunity for free political discussion, to the end that government may be responsive to the will of the people and that changes, if desired, may be obtained by peaceful means. Therein lies the security of

the Republic, the very foundation of constitutional government."*De Jonge v. Oregon*, 299 U.S. 353, 365, 57 S.Ct. 255, 260, 81 L.Ed. 278.

This is not to say that the Constitution protects defamatory statements directed against the private conduct of a public official or private citizen. Freedom of press and of speech insures that government will respond to the will of the people and that changes may be obtained by peaceful means. Purely private defamation has little to do with the political ends of a self-governing society. The imposition of liability for private defamation does not abridge the freedom of public speech or any other freedom protected by the First Amendment.[4] This, of course, cannot be said "where public officials are concerned or where public matters are involved. * * * * [O]ne main function of the First Amendment is to ensure ample opportunity for the people to determine and resolve public issues. Where public matters are involved, the doubts should be resolved in favor of freedom of expression rather than against it." *The Right of the People* (1958), p. 41.

In many jurisdictions, legislators, judges and executive officers are clothed with absolute immunity against liability for defamatory words uttered in the discharge of their public duties. See, e. g., *Barr v. Matteo*, 360 U.S. 564, 79 S.Ct. 1335, 3 L.Ed.2d 1434; *City of Chicago v. Tribune Co.*, 307 Ill., at 610, 139 N.E., at 91. Judge Learned Hand ably summarized the policies underlying the rule:

> "It does indeed go without saying that an official, who is in fact guilty of using his powers to vent his spleen upon others, or for any other personal motive not connected with the public good, should not escape liability for the injuries he may so cause; and, if it were possible in practice to confine such complaints to the guilty, it would be monstrous to deny recovery. The justification for doing so is that is impossible to know

---

[4] In most cases, as in the case at bar, there will be little difficulty in distinguishing defamatory speech relating to private conduct form that relating to official conduct. I recognize, of course, that there will be a gray area. The difficulties of applying a public-private standard are, however, certainly, of a different genre from those attending the differentiation between a malicious and nonmalicious state of mind. If the constitutional standard is to be shaped by a concept of malice, the speaker takes the risk not only that the jury will inaccurately determine his state of mind but also that the injury will fail properly to apply the constitutional standard set by the elusive concept of malice. See note 2, supra.

whether the claim is well founded until the case has been tried, and that to submit all officials, the innocent as well as the guilty, to the burden of a trial and to the inevitable danger of its outcome, would dampen the ardor of all but the most resolute, or the most irresponsible, in the unflinching discharge of their duties. Again and again the public interest calls for action which may later find himself hard to put to it to satisfy a jury of his good faith. There must indeed be means of punishing public officers who have been truant to their duties; but that is quite another matter from exposing such as have been honestly mistaken to suit by anyone who has suffered from their errors. As is so often the case, the answer must be found in a balance between the evils inevitable in either alternative. In this instance it has been thought in the end better to leave unredressed the wrongs done by dishonest officers than to subject those who try to do their duty to the constant dread of retaliation. * * *

"The decisions have, indeed always imposed as a limitation upon the immunity that the official's act must have been within the scope of his powers; and it can be argued that official powers, since they exist only for the public good, never cover occasions where the public good is not their aim, and hence that to exercise a power dishonestly is necessarily to overstep its bounds. A moment's reflection shows, however, that that cannot be the meaning of the limitation without defeating the whole doctrine. What is meant by saying that the officer must be acting within his power cannot be more than that the occasion must be such as would have justified the act, if he had been using his power for any of the purposes on whose account it was vested in him. * * *" *Gregoire v. Biddle,* 2 Cir., 177 F.2d 579, 581.

If the government official should be immune from libel actions so that his ardor to serve the public will not be dampened and "fearless, vigorous, and effective administration of policies of government" not be inhibited, *Barr v. Matteo,* supra, 360 U.S. at 571, 79 S.Ct. at 1339, 3 L.Ed.2d 1434, then the citizen and the press should likewise be immune from libel actions for their criticism of official conduct. Their ardor as citizens will thus not be dampened and they will be free "to applaud or to criticize the way public employees do their jobs, from the least to the most important."[5] If liability can attach to political criticism because it damages the reputation of a public official, then no critical citizen can safely utter anything but faint praise about the government or its officials. The vigorous criticism by press and citizen of the conduct of the government of the day by the officials of the day will soon yield to silence if officials in control of government agencies, instead of answering criticisms, can resort to friendly juries to forestall criticism of their official conduct.[6]

The conclusion that the Constitution affords the citizen and the press an absolute privilege for criticism of official conduct does not leave the public official without defenses against unsubstantiated opinions or deliberate misstatements. "Under our system of government, counterargument and education are the weapons available to expose these matters, not abridgment * * * of free speech * * *." *Wood v. Georgia,* 370 U.S. 375, 389, 82 S.Ct. 1364, 1372, 8 L.Ed.2d 569. The public official certainly has equal if not greater access than most private citizens to media of communication. In any event, despite the possibility that some excesses and abuses may go unremedied, we must recognize that "the people of this nation have ordained in the light of history, that, in spite of the probability of excesses and abuses, [certain] liberties are, in the long view, essential to enlightened opinion and right conduct on the part of the citizens of a democracy." *Cantwell v. Connecticut,* 310 U.S. 296, 310, 60 S.Ct. 900, 906, 84 L.Ed. 1213. As Mr. Justice Brandeis correctly observed, "sunlight is the most powerful of all disinfectants."[7]

For these reasons I strongly believe that the Constitution accords citizens and press an unconditional freedom to criticize official conduct. It necessarily follows that in a case such as this, where all agree that the allegedly defamatory statements related to official conduct, the judgments for libel cannot constitutionally be sustained.

U.S. SUPREME COURT, MARCH 1964

---

[5] Mr. Justice Black concurring in *Barr v. Matteo,* 360 U.S. 564, 577, 79 S.Ct. 1335, 1342, 3 L.Ed.2d 1434, observed that: "The effective functioning of a free government like ours depends largely on the force of an informed public opinion. This calls for the widest possible understanding of the quality of government service rendered by all elective or appointed public officials or employees. Such an informed understanding depends, of course, on the freedom people have to applaud or to criticize the way public employees do their jobs, from the least to the most important."

[6] See notes 2, 4, supra.

[7] See Freund, *The Supreme Court of the United States* (1949), p. 61.

ROE v. WADE

ROE V. WADE

ISSUE

Abortion

HOW TO USE MILESTONES IN THE LAW

This section allows readers to investigate the facts, the arguments, and the legal reasoning that produced the *Roe v. Wade* decision. It also sheds light on the roles and required skills of attorneys and judges in resolving disputes.

As you read this section, you may wish to consider the following issues:

- How did the appellant's description of the issues before the Court, or questions presented, differ from the appellee's descriptions?

- How did the courts and the two parties differ in describing the meaning of particular prior cases to the present case?

- How did the holdings (conclusions of law) of the district court differ from those of the Supreme Court?

- On what points in the Supreme Court's majority opinion do the concurring and dissenting justices agree and disagree?

- How would you decide this case?

THIS CASE IN HISTORY

Roe versus Wade may be the most well known and the most controversial decision of the modern Supreme Court. With this decision, the Court recognized a woman's right to obtain an abortion under certain circumstances. Virtually from the moment it was handed down, *Roe v. Wade* has divided lawyers, politicians, and the public into those who support the decision and those who would like it overturned, either by the Supreme Court itself or by act of the legislature. A judge's or politician's position on the subject of abortion has played a major role in countless appointments and elections. After the decision and for the rest of his life, the opinion brought its author, Justice Harry Blackmun, an unending stream of mail both praising and vilifying him for the decision.

Roe v. Wade

JANE ROE, PLAINTIFF,
V.
HENRY WADE, DEFENDANT,
V.
JAMES HUBERT HALLFORD, M.D.,
INTERVENOR.

JOHN DOE AND MARY DOE, PLAINTIFFS,
V.
HENRY WADE, DEFENDANT.

CIV. A. NOS. 3–3690–B, 3–3691–C.
UNITED STATES DISTRICT COURT,
N. D. TEXAS,
DALLAS DIVISION.
JUNE 17, 1970.

—⚍—

Action for judgment declaring Texas abortion laws unconstitutional and to enjoin their enforcement. The three-judge District Court held that laws prohibiting abortions except for purpose of saving life of a mother violated right secured by the Ninth Amendment to choose whether to have children and were unconstitutionally overwhelmed and vague, but Court would abstain from issuing injunction against enforcement of the laws.

Order accordingly.

Linda N. Coffee, Dallas, Tex., Sarah Weddington, Austin, Tex., for plaintiffs.

Fred Bruner, Daugherty, Bruner, Lastelick & Anderson, Ray L. Merrill, Jr., Dallas, Tex., for intervenor.

John B. Tolle, Asst. Dist. Atty., Dallas, Tex., Jay Floyd, Asst. Atty. Gen., Austin, Tex., for defendant.

Before Goldberg, Circuit Judge, and Hughes and Taylor, District Judges.

—⚍—

PER CURIAM:

Two similar cases are presently before the Court on motions for summary judgment pursuant to Rule 56 of the Federal Rules of Civil Procedure. The defendant in both cases is Henry Wade, District Attorney of Dallas County, Texas. In once action plaintiffs are John and Mary Doe, and in the other Jane Roe and James Hubert Hallford, M.D., intervenor.[1]

[1] From their respective positions of married couple, single woman, and practicing physician, plaintiffs attack Articles 1191, 1192, 1193, 1194, and 1196 of the Texas Penal Code,[2] hereinafter referred to as the Texas Abortion Laws. Plaintiffs allege that the Texas Abortion Laws deprive married couples and single women of the right to choose whether to have children, a right secured by the Ninth Amendment.

Defendant challenges the standing of each of the plaintiffs to bring this action. However, it appears to the Court that Plaintiff Roe and plaintiff-intervenor Hallford occupy positions *vis-a-vis* the Texas Abortion Laws sufficient to differentiate them from the general public. Compare Pierce v. Society of Sisters, 268 U.S. 510, 45 S.Ct. 1678, 14 L.Ed.2d 510 (1965),[3] with Frothingham v. Mellon, 262 U.S. 447, 43 S.Ct. 597, 67 L.Ed. 1078 (1923). Plaintiff Roe filed her portion of the suit as a pregnant woman wishing

---

[1] On March 3, 1970, plaintiff Jane Roe filed her original complaint in CA-3-3690–B umder the First Fourth, Fifth, Eighth Ninth, and Fourteenth Amendments to the United States Constitution. She alleged jurisdiction to be conferred upon the Court by Title 28, United States Code, Sections 1331, 1343, 2201, 2202, 2281, and 2284 and by Title 42, United States Code, Section 1983. On April 22, plaintiff Roe amended her complaint to sue "on behalf of herself and all others similarly situated."

On March 23, James Hubert Hallford, M.D., was given leave to intervene. Hallford's complaint recited the same constitutional and jurisdictional grounds as the complaint to plaintiff Roe. According to his petition for intervention, Hallford seeks to represent "himself and the class of people who are physicians, licensed to practice medicine under the laws of the State of Texas and who fear future prosecution."

On March 3, 1970, plaintiffs John and Mary Doe filed their original complaint in CA-3-3691–C. The complaint of plaintiffs Doe recited the same constitutional and jurisdic-

tion grounds as had the complaint of plaintiff Roe in CA-3-3690 and, like Roe, plaintiffs Doe subsequently amended their complaint so as to assert a class action.

Plaintiffs Roe and Doe have adopted pseudonyms for purposes of anonymity.

[2] *Article 1191 Abortion*

If any person shall designedly administer to a pregnant woman of knowingly procure to be administered with her consent any drug or medicine, or shall use towards her any violence or means whatever externally or internally applied, and thereby procure an abortion, he shall be confined in the penitentiary not less than two more than five years; if it be done without her consent, the punishment shall be doubled. By "abortion" is meant that life of the fetus or embryo shall be destroyed in the woman's womb or that a premature birth thereof be caused.

Article 1192 Furnishing the Means

Whoever furnishes the means for procuring an abortion knowing the purpose intended is guilty as an accomplice.

to exercise the asserted constitutional right to choose whether to bear the child she was carrying. Intervenor Hallford alleged in his portion of the suit that, in the course of daily exercise of his duty as a physician and in order to give his patients access to what he asserts to be their constitutional right to choose whether to have children, he must act so as to render criminal liability for himself under the Texas Abortion Laws a likelihood. Dr. Hallford further alleges that Article 1196 of the Texas Abortion Laws is so vague as to deprive him of warning of what produces criminal liability in that portion of his medical practice and consultations involving abortions.

[2] On the basis of plaintiffs' substantive contentions,[4] it appears that there then exists a "nexus between the status asserted by the litigant[s] and the claim[s] [they present]." Flast v. Cohen, 392 U.S. 83, 102, 88 S.Ct. 1942, 20 L.Ed.2d 947 (1968).

[3] Further, we are satisfied that there presently exists a degree of contentiousness between Roe and Hallford and the defendant to establish a "case of actual controversy" as required by Title 28, United States Code, Section 2201. Golden v. Zwickler, 394 U.S. 103, 89 S.Ct. 956, 22 L.Ed.2d 113 (1969).

Each plaintiff seeks a relief, *first*, a judgment declaring Texas Abortion Laws unconstitutional on their face and *second*, an injunction against their enforcement. The nature of the relief requested suggests the order in which the issues presented should be passed upon[5]. Accordingly, we see the issues presented as follows:

I. Are plaintiffs entitled to a declaratory judgment that the Texas Abortion Laws are unconstitutional on their face?

II. Are plaintiffs entitled to an injunction against the enforcement of these laws?

Article 1193 Attempt at Abortion

If the means used shall fail to produce an abortion, the offender is nevertheless guilty of an attempt to produce abortion, provided it be shown that such means were calculated to produce that result, and shall be fined not less than one hundred nor more than one thousand dollars.

Article 1194 Murder in Producing Abortion

If the death of the mother is occasioned by an abortion so produced or by an attempt to effect the same it is murder.

Article 1196 By Medical Advice

Nothing in this chapter applies to an abortion procured or attempted by medical advice for the purpose of saving the life of the mother.

I.

Defendants have suggested that this Court should abstain from rendering a decision on plaintiffs' request for a declaratory judgment. However, we are guided to an opposite conclusion by the authority of Zwickler v. Koota, 389 U.S. 241, 248–249, 88 S.Ct. 391, 19 L.Ed.2d 444 (1967):

"The judge-made doctrine of abstention * * * sanctions * * * escape only in narrowly limited 'special circumstances' * * * is the susceptibility of a state statute of a construction by the state courts that would avoid or modify the constitutional question."

The Court in Zwickler v. Koota subsequently quoted from United States v. Livingston, 179 F.Supp. 9, 12–13 (E.D.S.C.1959):

"Regard for the interest and sovereignty of the state and reluctance needlessly to adjudicate constitutional issues may require a federal District Court to abstain from adjudication if parties may avail themselves of an appropriate procedure to obtain state interpretation of state laws requiring construction. * * * The decision [Harrison v. N.A.A.C.P., 360 U.S. 167, 79 S.Ct. 1025, 3 L.Ed.2d 1152], however, is not a broad encyclical commanding automatic remission to the state courts of all federal constitutional question, it is the duty of a federal court to decide the federal question when presented to it. Any other course would impose expense and long delay upon the litigants without hope of its bearing fruit."[6]

[4] Inasmuch as there is no possibility that state question adjudication in the courts of Texas would eliminate the necessity for this Court to pass upon plaintiffs' Ninth Amendment claim or Dr. Hallford's attack on Article 1196 for vagueness, abstention as to their request for declaratory judgment is unwarranted. Compare City of Chicago v. Atchison, T. & S. F. R. Co., 357 U.S. 77, 84, 78 S.Ct. 1063, 2 L.Ed.2d 1174 (1958), with Reetz v. Bozanich, 397 U.S. 82, 90 S.Ct. 788, 25 L.Ed.2d 68 (1970).

[3] By the authority of *Griswold*, Dr. Hallford has standing to raise the rights of his patients, single women and married couples, as well as rights of his own.

[4] "[I]n ruling on standing, it is both appropriate and necessary to look to the substantive issues * * * to determine whether there is a logical nexus between the status asserted and the claim sought to be adjudicated." Flast v. Cohen, 392 U.S. 83, 102, 88 S.Ct. 1942, 20 L.Ed.2d 947 (1968).

[5] Zwickler v. Koota, 389 U.S. 241, 254, 88 S.Ct. 391, 19 L.Ed.2d 444 (1967); Cameron v. Johnson, 390 U.S. 611, 615, 88 S.Ct. 1335, 20 L.Ed.2d 182 (1968).

[6] 389 U.S.at 250–251, 88 S.Ct. at 396–397. (Citations omitted).

[5] On the merits, plaintiffs argue as their principal contention[7] that the Texas Abortion Laws must be declared unconstitutional because they deprive single women and married couple of their rights secured by the Ninth Amendment[8] to choose whether to have children. We agree.

The essence of the interest sought to be protected here is the right of choice over events which, by their character and consequences, bear in a fundamental manner on their privacy of individuals. The manner by which such interests are secured by the Ninth Amendment is illustrated by the concurring opinion of Mr. Justice Goldberg in Griswold v. Connecticut, 381 U.S. 479, 492, 85, S.Ct. 1678 14 L.Ed.2d 510 (1965):

> "[T]he Ninth Amendment shows a belief of the Constitution's authors that *fundamental*-rights exist that ate not expressly enumerated in the first eight amendments and intent that the list of rights included there not be deemed exhaustive." * * *

> "The Ninth Amendment simply shows the intent of the Constitution's authors that other *fundamental* personal rights should not be denied such protection or disparaged in any other way simply because they are not specifically listed in the first eight constitutional amendments." (Emphasis added.)[9]

Relative sanctuaries for such "fundamental" interests have been established for the family,[10] the marital couple[11] and individual.[12]

Freedom to choose in the matter of abortions has been accorded the status of a "fundamental" right in every case coming to the attention of this Court where the question has been raised. Babitz v. McCann, 312 F.Supp. 725 (E.D. Wis.1970); People v. Belous, 80 Cal. Reptr. 354, 458 P.2d 194 (Cal.1969); State v. Munson, (South Dakota Circuit Court, Pennington County, Aoril 6, 1970). *Accord*, United States v. Vuitch, 305 F.Supp. 1032 (D.D.C.1969). The California Supreme Court in *Belous* stated:

> "The fundamental right of the woman to choose whether to bear children follows from the Supreme Court's and this court's repeated acknowledgment of a 'right of privacy' or 'liberty' in matters related to marriage, family, and sex." 80 Cal.Rptr. at 359, 458 P.2d at 199.

The District Court in *Vuitch* wrote:

> "There has been * * * an increasing indication in the decisions of the Supreme Court of the United States that as a secular matter a woman's liberty and right of privacy extends to family, marriage and sex matters and may well include the right to remove an unwanted child at least in early stages of pregnancy." 305 F.Supp.at 1035.

Writing about Griswold v. Connecticut, *supra*, and the decisions leading up to it, former Associate Justice Tom C. Clark observed:

> "The result of these decisions is the evolution of the concept that there is a certain zone of individual privacy which is protected by the Constitution. Unless the State has a compelling subordinating interest that outweighs the individual rights of human beings, it may not interfere with a person's marriage, home, children and day-to-day living habits. This is one of the most fundamental concepts that the Founding Fathers had in mind when they drafted the Constitution."[13]

---

[7] Aside from their Ninth Amendment an dvagueness arguments, plaintiffs have presented an array of constitutional arguments. However, as plaintiffs conceded in oral argument, these additional arguments are peripheral to the main issues. Consequently, they will not be passed upon.

[8] "The enumeration in the Constitution, of certain rights shall not be contrued to deny or disparage others retained by the people."

[9] At 492, 85 S.Ct. at 1686 the opinion states: "In determining which rights are fundamental, judges are not left at large to decide cases in light of their personal and private notions. Rather, they must look to the 'traditions and [collective] conscience of our people' to detetmine whether a principle is 'so rooted [there] * * * as to be ranked as fundamental.' Snyder v. [Commonwealth of] Massachusetts, 291 U.S. 97, 105 [54 S.Ct. 330, 78 L.Ed. 674]. The inquiry is whether a right invilved 'is of such a character that it cannot be denied without violating those "fundamental principles of liberty and justice which lie at the base of all our civil and political institutions." * * *' Powell v. Alabama, 287 U.S. 45, 67 [53 S.Ct. 55, 77 L.Ed. 158]."

[10] Pierce v. Society of Sisters, 268 U.S. 510, 45 S.Ct. 571, 69 L.Ed. 1070 (1925); Meyer v. Nebraska, 262 U.S. 390, 43 S.Ct. 625, 67 LEd. 1042 (1923); and Prince v. Commonwealth of Massachusetts, 321 U.S. 158, 64 S.Ct. 438, 88 L.Ed. 645 (1944).

[11] Loving v. Commonwealth of Virginia, 388 U.S. 1, 87 S.Ct. 1817, 18 L.Ed.2d 1010 (1967); Griswold v. Connecticut, 381 U.S. 479, 85 S.Ct. 1678, 14 L.Ed.2d 510 (1965); and Buchanan v. Batchelor, 308 F.Supp. 729 (N.D.Tex.1970).

[12] Skinner v. Oklahoma, 316 U.S. 535, 62 S.Ct. 1110, 86 L.Ed. 1655 (1942); and Stanley v. Georgia, 394 U.S. 557, 89 S.Ct. 1243, 22 L.Ed.2d 542 (1969).

[13] Religion, Morality, and Abortion: A Constitutional Appraisal, 2 Loyola Univ. L.Rev. 1, 8 (1969). Mr. Justice Clark goes on to write, "* * * abortion falls within that sensitive area of privacy—the marital relation. One of the basic values of this privacy is birth control, as evidence by the *Griswold* decision. Griswold's act was to prevent formation of the fetus. This, the Court found, was constitutionally protected. If an individual may prevent contraception, why can he not nullify that conception when prevention has failed?" *Id.* at 9.

[6] Since the Texas Abortion Laws infringe upon plaintiffs' fundamental right to choose whether to have children, the burden is on the defendant to demonstrate to the satisfaction of the Court that such infringement is necessary to support a compelling state interest.[14] The defendant has failed to meet this burden.

To be sure, the defendant has presented the Court several compelling justifications for state presence in the area of abortions. These include the legitimate interests of the state in seeing to it that abortions are performed by competent persons and in adequate surroundings. Concern over abortion of the "quickened" fetus may well rank as another such interest. The difficulty with the Texas Abortion Law is that, even if they promote these interest,[15] they far outstrip these justifications in their impact by prohibiting all *all* abortions except those performed "for the purpose of saving the life of the mother."[16]

[7–9] It is axiomatic that the fact that a statutory scheme serves permissible or even compelling state interests will not save it from the consequences of unconstitutional overbreadth. *E. g.*, Thornhill v. Alabama, 310 U.S, 88, 60 S.Ct. 736, 84 L.Ed. 1093 (1940); Buchanan v. Batchelor, 308 F.Supp. 729 (n.D.Tex. 1970). While the Ninth Amendment right to choose to have an abortion is not unqualified or unfettered, a statute designed to regulate the circumstances of abortions must restrict its scope to compelling state interests. There is unconstitutional overbreadth in the Texas Abortion Laws because the Texas Legislature did not limit the scope of the statutes to such interests. On the contrary, the Texas statutes, in their monolithic interdiction, sweep far beyond any areas of compelling state interest.

[10] Not only are the Texas Abortion Laws unconstitutionally overbroad, they are also unconstitutionally vague. The Supreme Court has declared that "a statute which either forbids or requires the doing of an act in terms so vague that men of common intelligence must necessarily guess at its meaning and differ as to its application violates the first essential of due process of law." Connally v. General Construction Co., 269 U.S. 385, 391, 46 S.Ct. 126, 70 L.Ed. 322 (1926). "No one may be required at peril of life, liberty or property to speculate as to the meaning of penal statutes. All are entitled to be informed as to what the State commands or forbids." Lanzetta v. New Jersey, 306 U.S. 451, 453, 59 S.Ct. 618, 83 L.Ed. 888 (1939). *See also* Giaccio v. Pennsylvania, 382, U.S. 399, 402–403, 86 S.Ct. 518, 15 L.Ed.2d. 447 (1966). Under this standard the Texas statutes fail the vagueness test.

The Texas Abortion Laws fail to provide Dr. Hallford and physicians of his class with proper notice of what acts in their daily practice and consultation will subject them to criminal liability. Article 1196 provides:

> "Nothing in this chapter applies to an abortion procured or attempted by medical advice for the purpose of saving the life of the mother."

It is apparent that there are grave and manifold uncertainties in the application of Article 1196. How *likely* must death be? Must death be certain if the abortion is not performed? Is it enough that the woman could not undergo birth without an ascertainably higher possibility of death than would normally be the case? What if the woman threatened suicide if the abortion was not performed? How *imminent* must death be if the abortion is not performed? It is sufficient if having the child will shorten the life of the woman by number of years. These questions simply cannot be answered?

The grave uncertainties in the application of Article 1196 and the consequent uncertainty concerning criminal liability under the related abortion statutes are more than sufficient to render the Texas Abortion Laes unconstitutionally vague in violation of the Due Process Clause of the Fourteenth Amendment.

II.

We come finally to a consideration of the appropriateness of plaintiffs' request for injunc-

---

[14] "In a long series of cases this Court has held that where fundamental personal liberties are involved, they may not be abridged by the States simply on a showing that a regulatory statute has some rational relationships to the effectuation of a proper state purpose. 'Where there is a significant encroachment upon personal liberty, the State may prevail only upon showing a subordinating interest which is compelling,' Bates v. [City of] Little Rock, 361 U.S. 516, 524, [80 S.Ct. 412, 4 L.Ed.2d 480]." Griswold v. Conneticut, 381 U.S. 479, 497, 85 S.Ct. 1678, 14 L.Ed.2d 510 (1965) (concurring opinion of Mr. Justice Goldberg). *See also* Kramet v. Union Free School District, 395 U.S. 621, 89 S.Ct. 1886, 23 L.Ed.2d. 583 (1969).

[15] It is not clear whether the Texas laws presently serve the interests asserted by the defendant. For instance, the Court gathers from a reading of the challenged statutes that they presently would permit an abortion "for the purpose of saving the life of the mother" to be performed *anywhere* and quite possibly by *one other than a physician*.

[16] Article 1196.

tive relief. Plaintiffs have suggested in oral argument that, should the Court declare the Texas Abortion Laws unconstitutional, that the decision would of itself warrant the issuance of an injunction against state enforcement of the statutes. However, the Court is of the opinion that is must abstain from granting the injunction.

Clearly, the question whether to abstain concerning an injunction against the enforcement of state criminal laws is divorced from concerns of abstention in rendering a declaratory judgment. Quoting from Zwickler v. Koota,

> "[A] request for a declaratory judgment that a state statute is overbroad on its face must be considered independently of any request for injunctive relief against enforcement of that statue. We hold that a federal district court has the duty to decide the appropriateness and merits of the declaratory request irrespective of its conclusion as to the propriety of its issuance of the injunction." 389 U.S. at 254, 88 S.Ct. at 399

[11] The strong reluctance of federal courts to interfere with the process of state criminal procedure was reflected in Dombrowski v. Pfister, 380 U.S. 479, 484–485, 85 S.Ct. 1116, 1120–21, 14 L.Ed.2d 22(1965):

> "[T]he Court has recognized that federal interference with a State's good-faith administration of its criminal laws is peculiarly inconsistent with our federal framework. It is generally to be assumed that state courts and prosecutors will observe constitutional limitations as expounded by this Court, and that the mere possibility of erroneous initial application of constitutional standards will usually not amount to the irreparable injury necessary to justify a disruption of orderly state proceedings."

This federal policy of non-interference with state criminal prosecutions must be followed except in cases where "statutes are justifiably attacked on their face as abridging free expressions," or where statues are justifiably attacked "as applied for the purpose of discouraging protected activities." Dombrowski v. Pfister, 380 U.S. at 489–490, 85 S.Ct. at 1122.

[12] Neither of the above prerequisites can be found here. While plaintiffs' first substantive argument rests on notions of privacy which are to a degree common to the First and Ninth Amendments, we do not believe that plaintiffs can seriously argue that the Texas Abortion Laws are vulnerable "on their face as abridging free expression."[17] Further, deliberate application of the statues "for the purpose of discouraging protected activities" has not been alleged. We therefore conclude that we must abstain from issuing an injunction against enforcement of the Texas Abortion Laws.

CONCLUSION

In the absence of any contested issues of fact, we hold that the motions for summary judgment of the plaintiff Roe and plaintiff-intervenor Hallford should be granted as to their request for declaratory judgment. In granting declaratory relief, we find the Texas Abortion Laws unconstitutional for vagueness and overbreadth, though for the reasons herein stated we decline to issue an injunction. We need not here delineate the factors which could qualify the right of a mother to have an abortion. It is sufficient to state that legislation concerning abortion must address itself to more than a bare negation of that right.

JUDGMENT

This action came on for hearing on motions for summary judgment before a three-judge court composed of Irving L. Goldberg, Circuit Judge, Sarah T. Hughes and W. M. Taylor, Jr., District Judges. The defendant in both cases is Henry Wade, District Attorney of Dallas County, Texas. In one action plaintiffs are John and Mary Doe, husband and wife, and in the other Jane Roe and James Hubert Hallford, M.D., intervenor.

The case having been heard on the merits, the Court, upon consideration of affidavits, briefs and arguments of counsel, finds as follows:

Findings of Fact

(1) Plaintiff Jane Roe, plaintiff-intervenor James Hubert Hallford, M.D., and the members of their respective classes have standing to bring this lawsuit.

(2) Plaintiffs John and Mary doe failed to allege facts sufficient to create a present controversy and therefore do not have standing.

(3) Articles 1191, 1192, 1193, 1194, and 1196 of the Texas Penal Code, hereinafter referred to as

---

[17] "[T]he door is not open to all who would test the validity of state statues or conduct a federally supervised pre-trail of a state prosecution by the simple expedient of allerging that the prosecution somehow affects First Amendement rights." Porter v. Kimzey, 309 F.Supp. 993, 995 (N.D.Ga.1970).

the Texas Abortion Laws, are so written as to deprive single women and married persons of the opportunity to choose whether to have children.

(4) The Texas Abortion Laws are so vaguely worded as to produce grave and manifold uncertainties concerning the circumstances which would produce criminal liability.

Conclusions of Law

(1) This case is a proper one for a three-judge court.

(2) Abstention, concerning plaintiffs' request for a declaratory judgment, is unwarranted.

(3) The fundamental right of single women and married persons to choose whether to have children is protected by the Ninth Amendment, through the Fourteenth Amendment.

(4) The Texas Abortion Laws infringe upon this right.

(5) The defendant has not demonstrated that the infringement of plaintiffs' Ninth Amendment rights by the Texas Abortion Laws is necessary to support a compelling state interest.

(6) The Texas Abortion Laws are consequently void on their face because they are unconstitutionally overbroad.

(7) The Texas Abortion Laws are void on their face because they are vague in violation of the Due Process Clause of the Fourteenth Amendment.

(8) Abstention, concerning plaintiffs' request for an injunction against the enforcement of the Texas Abortion Laws, is warranted.

It is therefore ordered, adjudged and decreed that: (1) the complaint of John and Mary Doe be dismissed; (2) the Texas Abortion Laws are declared void on their face for unconstitutional overbreadth and for vagueness; (3) plaintiffs' application for injunction be dismissed.

In the Supreme Court of the United States

October Term, 1970

No. .....

JANE ROE, JOHN DOE, AND MARY DOE,
APPELLANTS,
JAMES HUBERT HALLFORD, M.D.,
APPELLANT-INTERVENOR,
V.
HENRY WADE, APPELLEE.
ON APPEAL FROM THE UNITED STATES
DISTRICT COURT FOR THE NORTHERN
DISTRICT OF TEXAS

BRIEF FOR APPELLANT

Roy Lucas
The James Madison Constitutional Law Institute
Four Patchin Place
New York, N.Y. 10011

Norman Dorsen
School of Law, New York University
Washington Square South
New York, N.Y. 10003

Linda N. Coffee
2130 First National Bank Building
Dallas, Texas 75202

Sarah Weddington
3710 Lawton
Austin, Texas 78731

Roy L. Merrill, Jr.
Daugherty, Bruner, Lastelick & Anderson
1130 Mercantile Bank Building
Dallas, Texas 75201

Attorneys for Appellants

TABLE OF CONTENTS

Introduction

BRIEF FOR APPELLANT

Appellants bring this direct appeal from a judgment entered June 17, 1970, by a statutory three-judge United States District Court for the Northern District of Texas. The judgment appealed from granted these Appellants (Plaintiffs below) a declaration that the Texas anti-abortion statues were unconstitutional on their face, by reason of overbreath affecting fundamental individual rights, and that provisions in the statue suffered from unconstitutional uncertainty. However, the judgment denied a permanent injunction which had been sought as necessary in aid of the District Court's jurisdiction to enjoin future enforcement of the statute declared invalid. Appellants submit this Statement to show that this is a direct appeal over which this Court has jurisdiction, and that the appeal presents important and substantial federal questions which merit plenary review.

CITATION TO OPINIONS BELOW

The June 17, 1970, opinion of the statutory three-judge United States District Court for the Northern District Texas is not yet reported. The text of the decision is set out in the Appendix, *infra*, at 7a.

U.S. SUPREME
COURT,
OCTOBER 1970

BRIEF FOR
APPELLANT

U.S. SUPREME
COURT,
OCTOBER 1970

BRIEF FOR
APPELLANT

JURISDICTION

(i) On March 3, 1970, Appellant Jane Roe filed her original complaint,[1] basing jurisdiction on 28 U.S. C. § 1343(3) (1964 ed.), and complementary remedial statutes, 28 U.S.C. § 1983 (1964 ed.). On the same day Appellants John and Mary Doe filed a complaint predicting federal jurisdiction on the same statutes. On March 23, 1970, the District Court granted leave for Appellant James H. Hallford, M.D., to intervene as a party-plaintiff, on the basis of a complaint alleging a class action and the same jurisdictional grounds set out above. Subsequently, on April 22, 1970, Appellant Jane Roe amended her complaint to sue "on behalf of herself and all others similarly situated" (App. at 8a n. 1). Appellants John and Mary Doe also amended their complaints to asserts a class action (*Id.*). All Appellants, from their respective position as married couples, pregnant single women, and practicing physicians asked that the Texas antiabortion statutes[2] be declared unconstitutional on their face, and for an injunction against future enforcement of the statutes. A statutory three-judge United States District Court was requested and convened pursuant to 28 U.S.C. §§ 2281, 2284 (1964 ed.).

(ii) The final judgment of the statutory three-judge District Court, granting Appellants' request for a declaratory judgment, but denying any injunctive relief, was entered on June 17, 1970 (App. at 4a). On Monday, August 17, 1970, all Appellants filed with the United States District Court for the Northern District of Texas notices of appeal to this Court (App. at 1a), pursuant to 28 U.S.C. § 2101(b) (1964 ed.), and SUP. CT. RULES 11, 34 (July 1, 1970 ed.), 398 U.S. 1015, 1021, 1045 (1970 ed.). A protective appeal to the United States Court of Appeals for the Fifth Circuit was noticed on July 23, 1970, by Appellant Hallford (App. at 23a), and on July 24, 1970, by Appellant Jane Roe (App. at 21a).

(iii) Jurisdiction of this Court to review by direct appeal the three-judge District Court's final judgment denying a permanent injunction is conferred by 28 U.S.C. § 1253 (1964 ed.).

(iv) Cases which sustain the jurisdiction of this Court are: *Evans* v. *Cornman*, 398 U.S. 419, 420 (1970); *Goldberg* v. *Kelly*, 397 U.S. 254, 261 (1970); *Carter* v. *Fury Comm'n of Greene County*, 396 U.S. 320, 328, (1970); *Moore* v. *Ogilivie*, 394 U.S. 814, 815–16 (1969); *Williams* v. *Rhodes*, 393 U.S. 23, 26–28 (1968); *Dinis* v. *Volpe*, 389 U.S. 570 (1968) (per curiam); *Hale* v. *Bimco Trading Co.*, 306 U.S. 375, 376–78 (1939).

STATUTES INVOLVED

2A TEXAS PENAL CODE art. 1196, at 436 (1961):

> Nothing in this chapter applies to an abortion procured or attempted by medical advice for the purpose of saving the life of the mother.

2A TEXAS PENAL CODE art. 1191, at 429 (1961):

> If any person shall designedly administer to a pregnant woman or knowingly procure to be administered with her consent any drug or medicine, or shall use towards her any violence or means whatever externally or internally applied, and thereby procure an abortion, he shall be confined in the penitentiary not less than two nor more than five years if it be done without her consent, the punishment shall be doubled. By 'abortion' is meant that the life of the fetus or embryo shall be destroyed in the woman's womb or that a premature birth thereof be caused.

2A TEXAS PENAL CODE art. 1192, at 433 (1961):

> Whoever furnishes the means for procuring an abortion knowing the purpose intended is an accomplice.

2A TEXAS PENAL CODE art. 1193, at 434 (1961):

> If the means used shall fail to produce an abortion, the offender is nevertheless guilty of an attempt to produce abortion, provided it be shown that such means were calculated to produce that result, and shall be fined not less than one hundred nor more than one thousand dollars.

2A TEXAS PENAL CODE art. 1194, at 435 (1961):

> If the death of the mother is occasioned by an abortion so produced or by an attempt to effect the same it is murder.

QUESTIONS PRESENTED

I. Whether the Three-Judge Court Should Have Enjoined Future Enforcement of the Texas Anti-Abortion Laws, Which the Court Had Declared Unconstitutional, Where an Injunction

---

[1] The complaint and all other documents referred to in this Jurisdictional Statement are part of the record on appeal.
[2] The statutes, set out verbatim, *infra*, at 4–5, are 2A TEXAS PENAL CODE arts. 1191–1194, 1196, at 429–36 (1961).

was Necessary in Aid of the Court's Jurisdiction, Proper to Effectuate the Declaratory Judgment, and Needed to Prevent Irreparable Injury to Important Federal Rights of the Class of Pregnant Women Who Are or Will be Seeking Abortions, and the Class of Physicians Who are Forced to Reject such Women as Patients Because of a Reasonable Fear of Prosecution.

II. Whether a Married Couple, and Others Similarly Situated, Have Standing to Challenge the Texas Anti-Abortion Laws, Where Said Laws Have a Present and Destructive Effect on their Marital Relations, They are Unable to Utilize Fully Effective Contraceptive Methods, Pregnancy Would Seriously Harm the Woman's Health, and Such a Couple Not Obtain Judicial Relief in Sufficient Time After Pregnancy to Prevent Irreparable Injury.

STATEMENT OF THE CASE

Appellants brought three actions on behalf of three variously situated classes of Plaintiffs.

John and Mary Doe, a childless married couple, sued on behalf of themselves and all others similarly situated. Mary Doe has a neural-chemical disorder which renders pregnancy a threat to her physical and mental health, although not to her survival. Her physician has so advised her, and has also advised against using oral contraceptives. The alternate means of contraception used by John and Mary Doe is subject to a significant risk of failure. In such event, Mary Doe would like to, but legally could not, obtain a therapeutic abortion in a suitable medical facility in Texas. The probability of contraceptive failure in the class represented by Mary Doe is unquestionably high, when the size of the class is considered. Also, the limitations of judicial relief for a pregnant woman seeking an abortion are well known.[3] For Mary Doe and others in her

positions, a pre-pregnancy ruling on the validity of the Texas anti-abortion laws was the only ruling that could grant her the relief she would be seeking. Any other decision would simply be too late to prevent irreparable injury. Accordingly, John and Mary Doe brought an action for declaratory and injunctive relief against the present effect of the Texas statutes on their marital relations, and the inevitable future effect the statutes would have, in the certain event that a member of the class would become pregnant and not qualify for a legal abortion in Texas.

Jane Roe, an unmarried pregnant woman, also brought an action of the same nature, on her own behalf and for all others similarly situated. Jane Roe had been unable to obtain a legal abortion in a medical facility in Texas, because her survival was not threatened by continued pregnancy, and no hospital would perform the abortion, in light of the Texas anti-abortion statutes.[4] Jane Roe was financially unable to journey to another jurisdiction with less restrictive laws on abortion, and according had no recourse other than continuing an unwanted pregnancy, or risking her life and health at the hands of a non-medical criminal abortionist.

James H. Hallford, M.D., intervened as a Plaintiff, representing himself and other licensed Texas physicians similarly situated. Dr. Hallford's interest was twofold. As a physician, he is requested by patients, on a regular and recurring basis, to arrange for medically induced abortions in hospitals or other appropriate clinical facilities. This he cannot do, for several reasons. The Texas anti-abortion statues are unclear in their potential application to the situations in which patients request abortions. Consequently, both physician and hospital must exercise special caution to avoid prosecution. Also, the potential sweep of the statutes is so drastic that the only

U.S. SUPREME
COURT,
OCTOBER 1970

BRIEF FOR
APPELLANT

---

[3] The period between pregnancy detection, which normally occurs after the fourth week, and the safest time for a therapeutic abortion, before the twelfth week, leaves little time for judicial deliberation. With the notable exception of the Seventh Circuit, courts have declined to render a decision on behalf of a pregnant woman in the limited time available. In the present case, the first complaint was filed March 3, 1970, and followed after fifteen full weeks by a decision in the merits, June 17, 1970. Compare *Doe* v. *Randall*, 314 F. Supp. 32 (D. Minn. 1970) (nearly five weeks between decision and complaint); *Doe* v. *Randall*, *Doe* v. *Lefowitz*, 69 Civ. 4423 (S.D.N.Y. Dec. 12, 1969) (per curiam) (preliminary injunction denied until all factual materials developed by deposition); and *California* v. *Belous*, 71 Cal. 2d—, 458 P.2d 194, 80

Cal. Rptr. 354 (1969) (argument March 3, 1969; decision September 5, 1969); with *Doe* v. *Scott*, No. 18382 (7th Cir.Mar. 30, 1970) (per curiam), *rev'g* 310 F. Supp. 688 (N.D. Ill. Mar. 27, 1970) (order entered in three days where pregnancy caused by rape).

[4] While Texas does not punish the woman who persuades a physician to abort her, the anti-abortion statutes impose a felony sanction of up to five years for physician. 2A TEXAS PENAL CODE art. 1191, at 429 (1961). Moreover, the physician risks cancellation of his license to practice. 12B TEXAS CIV. STAT. art. 4505, at 541 (1966); *id.* art. 4506, at 132 (Supp. 1969–70). Also, the hospital can lose its operating license for permitting an illegal abortion with its facilities. 12B TEXAS CIV. STAT. art. 4437f, § 9, at 216 (1966).

U.S. SUPREME
COURT,
OCTOBER 1970

BRIEF FOR
APPELLANT

clear case of legal abortion is one in which the patients is near to certain death. These cases are rare; hence the typical patient's case will be legally uncertain, or of certain illegality. To avoid the realistic possibility of severe penal and administrative sanctions, the physician must turn away typical patient. Since the conscientious physicians knows full well that such a patient may seek out an incompetent non-medical abortionist, thereby endangering her life or health, he will continually be forced by the statute to breach his professional duty of care to the patient.[5] To rectify this invasion of the physician-patient relationship, Dr. Hallford brought this action to enjoin future enforcement of the Texas anti-abortion statutes, against himself, or against any other physician similarly situated.

Dr. Hallford's second interest in bringing the action was to seek relief against two indictments outstanding against him on abortion charges[6] Under Texas law, a physicians charged with abortion is presumed guilty, if the State is able to establish the fact of the abortion. The physician, in such a case, must admit complicity in the act, waive his privilege against self-incrimination, and defend on the basis that the abortion was "procured or attempted by medical advice for the purpose of saving the life of the [woman]." 2A TEXAS PENAL CODE art. 1196, at 436 (1961). Decisions such as *Veevers* v. *State*, 354 S.W.2d 161 (Tex. Ct. Crim. App. 1962), hold that the Article 1196 exception is an affirmative defense, which the physician must raise and prove. In numerous respects, this settled state-law practical deprives a physician of essential constitutional rights. Moreover, state practice invades the privacy of physician and patient by exposing intimate and confidential associations

to the public glare of a criminal trial. In addition, the possibility of conviction carries with it the revocation of the physician's license before appeal. These elements of state practice render defense to criminal abortion charges a wholly inadequate means of vindicating the physician's constitutional rights. Accordingly, Dr. Halliford brought the present actions filed by Jane Roe, John Doe, and Mary Doe. The cases were consolidated, and argued together.

Essentially, the federal questions raised by each individual Plaintiff were raised by all. The complaints charged that the Texas anti-abortion statutes deprived physicians and patients of rights protected by the First, Fourth Fifth, Eighth, Ninth and Fourteenth Amendments, as construed by this Court in decisions such as *Griswold* v. *Connecticut*, 381 U.S. 479 (1965).[7] Defendants interposed objections to the standing of each Plaintiff, the propriety of adjudications versus abstention, the ripeness of the dispute for present decision, and the propriety of injunctive relief

A statutory three-judge court, convened in response to Plaintiffs' request for injunctive relief from the Texas anti-abortion statutes, granted a declaratory judgment that the statutes were unconstitutionally vague and overbroad.

After dealing with the jurisdictional questions of standing,[8] ripeness,[9] and abstention,[10] raised by the Defendants, the three-judge court stated:

> [T]he Texas Abortion Laws must be declared unconstitutional because they deprive single women and married couples of their right, secured by the Ninth Amendment, to choose whether to have children

Reliance was placed on decisions by this Court establishing "[r]elative sanctuaries for such 'fundamental' interests [as] the family,[11]

---

[5] If prior cases on abortion prosecutions in Texas are a reliable index, patients who are turned away by physicians have recourse only to an assortment of quacks. *See, e.g., Fletcher* v. *State*, 362 S.W.2d 845 (Tex. Ct. Crim. App. 1962) (non-physician using crude techniques in "cottage on the river"; hysterectomy necessary to prevent girl's death); *Catching* v. *State*, 364 S.W.2d 691 (Tex. Ct. Crim. App. 1962) (non-physician; police found "tool box containing several catheters, a knitting needle, and other items").

[6] *State* v. *Hallford*, Nos. C–69–2524–H & C–69–5307–IH (Tex. Crim. Ct., Dallas County).

[7] In the brief on the merits, Appellants will more fully elaborate this complex substantive constitutional point. For purposes of this Statement, however, it is sufficient to not that *Griswold* has been applied in the abortion context by numerous state and federal courts. *See* cases cited in notes 31–37, *infra*, and accompanying text.

[8] Jane Roe, the pregnant Plaintiff, and Dr. Hallford, had standing because they "occupy positions *vis-à-vis* the Texas Abortion Laws sufficient to differentiate them from the general public." App. at 9a Also, on authority of *Griswold*, Dr. Hallford had standing to raise the "rights of his patients, single women and married couples, as well as rights of his own." App. at 9a n. 3. John and Mary Doe, however, were held to lack standing. App. at 5a.

[9] The district court was "satisfied that there presently exists a degree of contentiousness between Roe and Hallford and the defendant to establish a 'case of actual controversy' . . " App. at 10a

[10] *Zwickler* v. *Koota*, 389 U.S. 241, 248–49 (1967), was sufficient authority to preclude abstention. App. at 11a.

[11] *See Pierce* v. *Society of Sisters*, 268 U.S. 510 (1925); *Meyer* v. *Nebraska*, 262 U.S. 390 (1923); *Prince* v. *Massachusetts*, 321 U.S. 158 (1944), all cited by the district court. App. at 13a.

the marital couple,[12] and the individual."[13] Further precedent was found in similar decisions by other federal and state courts,[14] as well as a major treatment of *Griswold* in the abortion setting by Retired Justice Tom C. Clark, see Clark, *Religion, Morality, and Abortion: A Constitutional Appraisal*, 2 LOYOLA UNIV. (L.A.) L. REV. 1 (1969).

Not only were the statues overbroad, and not justified by a narrowly drawn compelling State interest, but the language of the statutes was unconstitutionally vague. Although a physician might lawfully perform an abortion "for the purpose of saving the life of the [pregnant woman],"[15] the circumstances giving rise to such necessity were far from clear. The district court detailed a few of the more apparent ambiguities:

> How *likely* must death be? Must death be certain if the abortion is not performed? Is it enough that the woman could not undergo birth without an ascertainably higher possibility of death that would normally be the case? What if the woman threatened suicide if the abortion was not performed? How *imminent* must death be if the abortion is not performed? Is it sufficient if having the child will shorten the life of the woman by a number of years? These questions simply cannot be answered.

App. at 71a.

After finding the Texas anti-abortion statues unconstitutional on two grounds, the district court considered the propriety of injunctive relief. Acting on the assumption that *Dombroski* v. *Pfister*, 380 U.S. 479 (1965)

controlled, the court refused to enjoin any present or future enforcement of the statutes. Appellants have brought this appeal to review the denial of injunctive relief.

THE QUESTIONS ARE SUBSTANTIAL

The present appeal presents important and unresolved federal questions which have not been but should be determined by this Court. A district court's refusal to enjoin present and future enforcement of a statute declared facially unconstitutional raises important issues for the vindication by federal courts of rights guaranteed by the Constitution. Decisions by this Court have not in recent years clarified the propriety of federal injunctive relief against state criminal statutes outside the pristine speech area of the First Amendment. A decision by this Court is needed, particularly where, as here, the injunction was sought by some Appellants who were total strangers to any pending prosecutions, and by one Appellant for whom defense of state court prosecution would be a wholly inadequate means of vindicating his federally protected rights.

In addition, the substantive issues in the case, which will surely be raised for further review by Appellee, are novel issues of profound national import, affecting the lives of many thousands of American citizens each year. Further, the same issues are presented in four appeals already docketed,[16] a variety of conflicting decisions in the lower courts,[17] and a host of pending actions in federal and state lower courts.

---

[12] *See Griswold* v. *Connecticut*, 381 U.S. 479 (1965).

[13] See *Skinner* v. *Oklahoma*, 316 U.S. 535 (1942); *Stanley* v. *Georgia*, 394 U.S. 557 (1969).

[14] *See, e.g., McCann* v. *Babbitz*, 310 F. Supp. 293 (E.D.Wis.) (per curiam), *appeal docketed*, 38 U.S.L.W, 3524 (U.S. June 20, 1970) (No. 297, Oct. 1970 Term); *United States* v. *Vuitch*, 305 F. Supp. 1032 (D.D.C. 1969), *ques, of juris. postponed to merits*, 397 U.S. 1061, *further juris. questions propounded*, 399 U.S. 923 (1970); *California* v. *Belous*, 71 Cal. 2d—, 458 P.2d 194, 80 Cal. Rptr. 354 (1969), *cert denied* 397 U.S, 915 (1970).

[15] 2A TEXAS PENAL CODE art 1196, at 36 (1961).

[16] (1) *United States* v. *Vuitch*, No. 84, arises under a differently worded felony abortion statute, however, and poses numerous alternate grounds for affirmance other than the central questions presented here, of overbreadth and vagueness.

(2) *McCann* v. *Babbitz*, No. 297, was decided at the federal district court level on grounds virtually the same as those below in the present case. It appears in *McCann*, however, that the appeal was taken by the State solely from the granting of a declaratory judgment for Dr. Babbitz. No

appeal was taken from denial of an injunction, as 28 U.S.C. § 1253 (1964 ed.), would seem to require, and as this Court twice held last Term, *Mitchell* v. *Donovan*, 398 U.S. 427 (1970) (per curiam), *vacating* 300 F. Supp. 1145 (D. Minn. 1969), with directions enter a fresh judgment of dismissal, to enable appellants to appeal to the Eighth Circuit; *Rockeller* v. *Catholic Medical Center*, 397 U.S. 820 (1970) (per curiam).

(3) *Hodgson* v. *Randall*, No. 728, is an appeal from a three-judge federal court decision refusing to enjoin state court prosecution of a physician who sought federal relief before performing a hospital therapeutic abortion for German measles indications, and long before the state indictment.

(4) *Hodgson* v. *Minnesota*, No. 729, involves the same subject matter as No. 728, and is an appeal from the Supreme Court of Minnesota's denial of a writ of prohibition to a state trial court which had upheld the constitutionality of an abortion statute, where unconstitutionality was the defense to the charges.

[17] *See* cases cited in not 31–37, *infra*, and accompanying text.

U.S. SUPREME
COURT,
OCTOBER 1970

BRIEF FOR
APPELLANT

INTRODUCTION

In the remainder of this Jurisdictional Statement, Appellants will show that the questions presented are substantial, and merit plenary review by the full Court. Because of the novelty and complexity of the issues, and the limited function of a Jurisdictional Statement, this showing will not undertake to develop all arguments in depth.

I. The three-judge court should have enjoined future enforcement of the Texas anti-abortion laws, which the court had declared unconstitutional, because an injunction was necessary in aid of the court's jurisdiction, proper to effectuate the declaratory judgment, and needed to prevent irreparable injury to important federal rights of the class of pregnant women who are or will be seeking abortions, and the class of physicians who are forced to reject such women as patients out of a reasonable fear of prosecution

A. The subject matter of the merits involves important and substantial federal constitutional questions. On the merits, Appellants argued successfully that decisions by this Court, construing the First, Fourth, Ninth, and Fourteenth Amendments supported a claim that the Texas anti-abortion statutes swept too broadly and thereby invaded rights protected by the Constitution (Pay out 5a, 6a, 12a-16a).[19] Moreover, the statues in question were held to be so vague and indefinite as to violate the

Fourteenth Amendment due process guarantee of reasonably specific legislation (App. at 5a, 6a, 16a-18a). That guarantee is particularly significant where, as here, important personal rights are at stake, and an impermissibly vague statute operates to inhibit a wide range of constitutionally protected conduct.[20]

Ultimately, the substantive question presented is whether a State may enact a felony statute to punish a physician, a woman, and her husband, with five years in state prison, where the couple requests, and the physician performs, a therapeutic surgical procedure to abort a pregnancy which the couple did not want, but were unable to prevent.[21] Under *Griswold v. Connecticut*, 381 U.S. 479 (1965), it is clear that a husband and wife[22] are constitutionally privileged to control the size and spacing of their family by contraception. The failure of contraception, however, is commonplace.[23] Authoritative estimated are that between 750,000 and 1,000,000 births each year are unwanted.[24] These are in addition to the 200,000 to 1,000,000 unwanted pregnancies which are estimated to end in abortion induced outside of the clinical setting.[25] Taken together, some 950,000 to 2,000,000 unwanted births plus non-clinical abortions occur yearly. Accordingly, one must conclude that restrictive anti-abortion statutes, such as the Texas law in question here, drastically affect the conduct of literally millions of American citizens.

---

[18] *See* cases cited in not 38, *infra*.

[19] In particular, Appellants relied upon the reasoning of *Griswold* v. *Connecticut*, 381 U.S. 479 (1965), where this Court invalidated a state law prohibiting use of contraceptive devices, because the law swept too broadly and invaded "a relationship lying within the zone of privacy created by several fundamental constitutional guarantees." 381 U.S. at 485.

[20] The most reliable estimates hold that fewer than 10,000 hospital therapeutic abortions are performed yearly, in states where there has been no abortion law reform. *See* Tietze, *Therapeutic Abortions in the United States*, 101 Am.J. OBST. and GYNEC. 784, 787 (1968). These constitute a minute proportion of all unwanted pregnancies which face American couples each year. Those excluded from hospitals have two alternatives: continuation of unwanted pregnancy, or extra-hospital, probably illegal, induced abortion.

[21] The woman is not an accomplice under Texas law, but other participants, including her husband, are fully liable. *See Willingham* v. *State*, 33 Tex. Crim. 98, 25 S.W. 424 (1894) (woman neither principal nor accomplice).

[22] *Griswold* was silent on the more significant problem of access by unmarried persons to contraceptives. A result of non-access, and failure, is the birth of over 100,000 illegitimate children yearly to girls age nineteen or younger. *See*

U.S. Bureau of the Census: Statistical Abstract of the United States: 1969, Table 59, at 50 (90th ed. 1969).

Outside of the state judiciary in Massachusetts, authorities have uniformly held the *Griswold* rationale applicable to litigants who had not entered into the marriage contract. *Compare Baird* v. *Eisenstadt*, — F.2d—, No. 7578 (1st Cir. July 6, 1970) (invalidating Massachusetts statute which outlawed distribution of contraceptives to the unmarried), *Mindel* v. *United States Civil Service Comm'n*, 312 F. Supp. 485 (N.D. Calif. 1970) (reinstating postal clerk who had been dismissed for cohabitation without benefit of marriage), *and* the present case, *Roe* v. *Wade*, — F. Supp.—, Civ. No. 3–3690–B (N.D. Tex. June 17, 1970) (per curiam) (Texas anti-abortion statutes "deprive single women and married couples of their right, secured by the Ninth Amendment, to choose whether to have children.", *with Sturgis* v. *Attorney General*, 260 N.E.2d 687, 6900 (Mass.1970) (directly contrary to federal decision *Baird*).

[23] If a married couple is to have private control over numbers and spacing of children, induced abortion is absolutely necessary as a backstop to contraceptive failure. For compilation of contraceptive failure rates according to method used, see P. EHRLICH AND A. EHRLICH, POPULATION RESOURCES ENVIRONMENT 218–19 and TABLE 9–1 (1970); N. EAST-

U.S. SUPREME
COURT,
OCTOBER 1970

BRIEF FOR
APPELLANT

The national significance of the issues in this case can be also be inferred from increased activity within the medical profession, and in the legislatures. On June 25, 1970, the House of Delegates of the American Medical Association voted to permit licensed physicians to perform abortions in hospitals, with sole additional qualification that two other physicians can be consulted.[26] Physicians were cautioned, however, not to violate existing state statues, forty-seven of which are far more restrictive.[27] Three states in 1970—New York, Alaska, and Hawaii—removed, for the most part, any criminal penalties which might previously have been imposed upon physicians for performing abortions in appropriate medical facilities.[28] From 1967 to 1970, twelve states had adopted therapeutic abortion statutes similar to that of the Model Penal Code's 1962 Proposed Official Draft. More recently, on August 4, the Commissioner on Uniform State Laws issued a Second Tentative Draft of a Uniform Abortion Act. The Act sanctioned abortions by licensed physicians "within 24 weeks after the commencement of the pregnancy; or of after 24 weeks . . ." under the circumstances set out in the Model Penal Code proposal.

These developments bear witness to the importance of the issues presented here.

While policy-making and legislative bodies have debated the issue of abortion, courts, confined to the constitutional framework, have been asked to resolve the questions of individual and legislative power which are presented here. Although the questions framed in this case have not been decided[30] by this Court, numerous federal and state decisions attest to the substantiality of the federal questions. Moreover, the sometimes sharp divisions in the courts below illustrate further the need for a decision at this level. In showing that the Court has jurisdiction, and that the questions are substantial, Appellants will outline the divisions among lower courts.

In September, 1969 the Supreme Court of California became the first appellant court to recognize the constitutional stature of a "fundamental right of the woman to choose whether to bear children. . . ."[31] The *Belous* court found this right implicit in this Court's "repeated acknowledgment of a 'right of privacy' or 'liberty' in matters related to marriage, family, and sex."[32]

More recently, three different decisions by statutory three-judge federal courts have invalidated restrictions on access to medical abortion in Wisconsin and Georgia, as well as in the present case from Texas. The first, *McCann* v. *Babbitz*,[33] recognized in that jurisdiction a woman's

> "basic right reserved to her under the ninth amendment to decide whether she should carry or reject an embryo which has not yet quickened." 310 F. Supp. at 302

MAN AND L. HELLMAN, WILLIAMS OBSTETRICS 1068–75 (13th ed. 1966); Hardin, *History and Future of Birth Control*, 10 PERSPECTIVES IN BIOLOGY & MED. 1, 7–13 (1966); Tietze, *Clinical Effectiveness of Contraceptive Methods*, 78 AM. J. OBST. AND GYNEC. 650 (1959).

[24] The most recent scholarly examination of unwanted birth magnitudes will appear in a forthcoming issue of SCIENCE. A summary of these findings by Dr. Charles F. Westoff of Princeton University's Office of Population Research, analyzing in 1965 National Fertility Study, appeared in the N.Y.Times, Oct. 29, 1969, at 25, col. 3.

[25] Secret induced abortions are inherently incapable of quantification. Nonetheless, one can be certain that the number is very high. For estimates, see Fisher, *Criminal Abortion*, in ABORTION IN AMERICA 3–6 (H. Rosen ed. 1967); M. CALERONE (ed.), ABORTION IN THE UNITED STATES 180 (1958); P. GEBHARD *et al.*, PREGNANCY, BIRTH AND ABORTION 136–37 (1958); F. TAUSSIG, ABORTION: SPONTANEOUS AND INDUCED 25 (1936); Regine, *A Study of Pregnancy Wastage*, 13 MILBANK MEM. FUND QUART. No. 4, at 347–65 (1935).

[26] *See* N.Y. Times, June 26, 1970, at 1, col. 1. The statement has not yet been published in an official A.M.A. document. A recent issue of the J.A.M.A. noted that only 26 physicians had resigned from the body because of new policy. 213 J.A.M.A. 1242 (Aug. 24, 1970).

[27] For analysis of abortion laws in the United States prior to the most recent changes, See Lucas, *Laws of the United States*, in I ABORTION IN A CHANGING WORLD 127 (R. Hall ed. 1970); George, *Current Abortion Laws: Proposals and Movements for Reform*, 17 W. RES. L. REV. 371 (1966).

[28] *See, e.g.*, N.Y. PENAL LAW § 125.05(3), at 79 (McKinney Supp. 1970–71).

[29] *See* MODEL PENAL CODE § 230.3(2) (Proposed Official Draft, 1962). The states are Arkansas, New Mexico, North Carolina, Oregon, South Carolina, and Virginia.

On least eight occasions this Court has declined to review state court decisions which involved restrictive anti-abortion laws.

The eight denials are: *Mucie* v. *Missouri*, 398 U.S. 938 (June 1, 1970), *denying cert. to* 448 S.W.2d 879 (Mo. 1970) (manslaughter abortion conviction where patient died); *California* v. *Belous*, 397 U.S. 915 (Feb. 24, 1970), *denying cert. to* 71 Cal. 2d —, 458 P.2d 194, 80 Cal. Rptr. 354 (1969) (statute repealed after prosecution commenced); *Molinaro* v. *New Jersey*, 396 U.S. 365 (Jan. 19, 1979) (per curiam), *dismissing appeal from* 54 N.J. 246, 254 A.2d 792 (1969) (defendant jumped bail after appeal filed); *Knight* v.*Louisiana Bd. of Medical Examiners*, 395 U.S. 933 (June 2, 1969), *denying*

U.S. SUPREME
COURT,
OCTOBER 1970

BRIEF FOR
APPELLANT

McCann grew out of the prosecution of a physician, but the three-judge court had no difficulty holding that a physician has standing to assert the rights of pregnant patients.[34]

The second recent federal decision is the present case, *Roe* v. *Wade*,[35] declaring the Texas anti-abortion statutes unconstitutional on the similar ground that

> "they deprive single women and married couples of their right, secured by the Ninth Amendment, to choose whether to have children."

A third federal decision, *Doe* v. *Bolton*,[36] followed *Belous, McCann,* and *Roe,* holding:

> "[T]he concept of personal liberty embodies a right to privacy which apparently is also broad enough to include the decision to abort a pregnancy.

> "...[T]he reasons for an abortion may not be proscribed..."

Numerous lower courts have followed this lead, in both federal and state disputes.[37] In addition, three-judge courts have been requested and/or convened in a number of states to consider questions quite similar to those raised here.[38] The convening of a statutory court, of course, requires that the questions presented be "substantial."[39]

Scholarly commentary also recognizes that these issues are tremendous national importance, and "substantial" in the sense of warranting determination by this Court. Retired Justice Clark addressed himself to the applicability of *Griswold* in the abortion context more than a year ago.[40] According to Justice Clark's analysis,

> "*Griswold's* act[41] was to prevent formation of the fetus. This, the Court found, was constitutionally protected. If an individual may prevent conception, why can he not nullify that conception when prevention fails?"[42]

To examine Justice Clark's hypothetical question in full constitutional context, and to decide the propriety of injunctive relief in this case, the Court should note probable jurisdiction, and set the matter down for full briefing and argument.

B. Having determined the merits in appellants' favor, the three-judge court should have enjoined future enforcement of the invalid. Not only do the substantive issues in this case involve important federal questions, but the remedy following judgment also presents a novel point of which this Court has not clearly ruled.

Although no state proceedings were pending or imminently threatened against Appellants Jane Roe, John Doe, and Mary Doe, or members of their respective classes, the District Court declined to grant any injunctive relief whatever. This denial of necessary relief is contrary to decisions by this Court, and has the probable effect of inviting federal-state friction, rather than lessening such untoward interaction.

cert. to 252 La. 889, 214 So.2d 716 (1968) (per curiam) (federal questions not properly raised and preserved); *Morin* v. *Garra,* 395 U.S. 935 (June 2, 1969), *denying cert. to* 53 N.J. 82 (1968) (per curiam) (same); *Moretti* v. *New Jersey,* 393 U.S. 952 (Nov. 18, 1968), *denying cert. to* 52 N.J. 182, 244 A.2d 499 (1968) (conspiracy conviction; abortion to have been performed by barber); *Fulton* v. *Illinois,* 390 U.S. 953 (Mar. 4, 1968), *denying cert, to* 84 Ill. App.2d 280, 228 N.E.2d 203 (1967); *Carter* v. *Florida,* 376 U.S. 648 (Mar. 30, 1964), *dismissing appeal from* 150 So.2d 787 (Fla. 1963).
[31] *California* v. *Belous,* 71 Cal. 2d —, —. 458 P.2d 194, 199, 80 Cal. Rptr. 354, 359 (1969), *cert denied,* 397 U.S. 915 (1970). *Belous,* a state court appeal of a conspiracy conviction of a physician, involved a statute worded almost identically to that in the present case.
One year earlier, a California trial court had ruled that the Eighth and Fourteenth Amendments prohibited license revocation proceedings against physicians who had performed hospital approved abortions on patients exposed in early pregnancy to German measles. The opinion of the trial court, however, simply enumerated those Amendments among various conclusions of law, without supporting the conclusions with any attempt at reasoned analysis. Nonetheless, the result, and the factual similarities between that and the present case, are of interest. *See Shively* v. *Board of*

Medical Examiners, No. 590333 (Calif. Super, Ct., San Fran. County Sept. 24, 1968) (not reported), *on remand from* 65 Cal. 2d 475, 421 P.2d 65, 55 Cal. Rptr. 217 (1968) (granting physicians' motions for discovery, without reference to merits).
[32] 71 Cal. 2d at —, 458 P.2d at 199, 80 Cal. Rptr. at 359, *citing, e.g., Griswold* v. *Connecticut,* 381 U.S. 479 (1965); *Loving* v. *Virginia,* 388 U.S. 1, 12 (1967); *Skinner* v. *Oklahoma ex rel. Williamson,* 316 U.S. 535, 536 (1942).
[33] 310 F.Supp. 293 (E.D. Wis. 1970) (per curiam), *appeal docketed,* 38 U.S.L.W. 3524 (U.S. June 20, 1970) (No. 297, Oct. 1970 Term).
[34] The standing of a physician to assert a patient's rights along with his own follows from *Griswold* v. *Connecticut,* 381 U.S. 479, 481 (1965), and *Barrows* v. *Jackson,* 346 U.S. 249, 257 (1953). On this standing point, lower court decisions involving abortion laws all agree. *See also Planned Parenthood Ass'n of Phoenix* v. *Nelson,* Civ. No. 70–334 PHX (D. Ariz. Aug. 24, 1970) (per curiam); *Doe* v. *Bolton,* — F. Supp. —, Civ. No. 13676 (N.D. Ga. July 31, 1970) (per curiam); *United States ex rel. Williams* v. *Follette,* 313 F. Supp. 269, 273 (S.D.N.Y. May 12, 1970).
[35] — F. Supp. —, Civ. No. 3–3690–B (N.D. Tex. June 17, 1970) (per curiam).
[36] — F. Supp. —, Civ, No. 13676 (N.D. Ga July 31, 1970) (per curiam).

Moreover, the denial of injunctive relief to Dr. Hallford was equally improper, as he had requested an injunction against the commencement of any future prosecutions. As to charges then pending against Dr. Hallford, an injunction would have been proper in addition, for reasons which shall appear more fully hereinafter

Relying entirely on *Dombrowski* v. *Pfister*, 380 U.S. 479 (1965), the three-judge court recognized a "federal policy of non-interference with state criminal prosecutions [which] must be followed except in cases where 'statutes are justifiably attacked on their face as abridging free expression,' or where statutes are justifiably attacked 'as applied for the purpose of discouraging protected activities.'" 380 U.S. at 489–90. The quote from *Dombrowski*, however, was not pertinent, for Appellants' principal thrust was not against pending prosecutions, but against any *future* enforcement and effects of the challenged statutes. The pregnant Plaintiff, Jane Roe, for example, could never be prosecuted under Texas law regardless of the number of abortions she underwent, but the statute, unless enjoined, would have the effect of keeping her from obtaining an abortion.

For the most part, Appellants were strangers to any existing or contemplated prosecutions. Their chief controversy was over the drastic impact of the statutes on their lives, not any possibility of imminent enforcement. In *Dom-browski*, the appellants were actively threatened with prosecution, and an injunction would necessarily have abated that threat by operating directly on law officers who stood ready to go forward with existing indictments. Accordingly, "special circumstances" were necessary to justify the conclusion ultimately reached.

If, however, *Dombrowski* had been purely a challenge to quantifiable and recurring effects of a state criminal statute, without the pendency of criminal charges, the case would have been different. This is shown by the ease with which this Court has reversed lower courts that refused declaratory and injunctive relief against loyalty oath statutes backed by criminal sanctions. *See Keyishian* v. *Board of Regents*, 385 U.S. 589 (1967); *Baggett* v. *Bullitt*, 377 U.S.360, 365–66 (1964). Injunctive relief against the statute in *Dombrowski* would have presented no special problem, if the statute had been a loyalty oath backed by the very same criminal penalties, and no indictments had been waiting in the wings.

Dombrowski falls in the middle ground between (1) injunctive actions which are filed and completed prior to the commencement of any state criminal proceedings, and (2) actions which are filed after "proceedings in a State court,"[43] are underway. The *Dombrowski* case itself was filed but not completed before State proceedings began.[44] Hence, while *Dombrowski* acknowledged that "[28 U.S.C. § 2283 (1964

U.S. SUPREME
COURT,
OCTOBER 1970

BRIEF FOR
APPELLANT

---

[37] *See, eg., State* v. *Munson* (S.D. 7th Jud. Cir., Pennington County Apr. 6, 1970) (Clarence P. Coper, F.) (recognizing the woman's "' private decision whether to bear her unquickened child'"); *Statev. Ketchum* (Mich. Dist. Ct. Mar 30, 1970) (Reid, F.) ("the statute as written infringes on the right of privacy in the physician-patient's right to safe relationship, and may violate the patient's right to safe and adequate medical advice and treatment"); *Commonwealthv. Page*, Centre County Leg. J. at 285 (Pa. Ct. Comm. Pl., Centre County July 23, 1970) (Campbell, P.F.) ("the abortion statute interferes with the individual's private right to have or not to have children."); *People v. Gwynne*, No. 176601 (Calif. Mun. Ct., Orange County Aug. 13, 1970) (Schwab, F.); *People v. Gwynne*, No. 173309 (Calif. Mun. Ct., Orange County June 16, 1970) (Thomson, F.); *People v. Barksdale*, No. 33237C (Calif. Mun. Ct., Alameda County Mar. 24, 1970) (Foley, F.); *People v. Robb*, Nos. 149005 and 159061 (Calif, Mun. Ct., Orange County Jan. 9, 1970) (Mast, F.); *People v. Anast*, No. 69–3429 (Ill. Cir. Ct., Cook County, 1970) (Dolezal, F.) (holding the Illinois abortion statute "unconstitutional (1) for vagueness; and (2) for infringing upon a woman's right to control her body."); *cf. United States v. Vitch*, 305 F. Supp. 1032 (D.D.C. 1969), *ques. of juris. postponed to merits*, 397 U.S. 1061, *further juris. questions propounded*, 399 U.S. 923 (1970); *United States ex rel. Williams v. Follette*, 313 F. Supp.

269, 272–73 (S.D.N.Y. 1970) (questions substantial, but habeas petitioner-physician remitted to state courts).

[38] *See, e.g., Gwynne* v. *Hicks*, Civ. No. 70–1088–CC (C.D. Calif., filed May 18, 1970); *Arnold v. Sendak*, IP 70–C-217 (S.D. Ind., filed Mar. 29, 1970); *Corkey v. Edwards*, Civ No. 2665 (W.D.N.C., filed May 12, 1970); *YMCA of Princeton v. Kugler*; Civ. No. 264–70 (D.N.J., filed Mar. 5, 1970); *Hall v. Lefkowitz*, 305 F. Supp. 1030 (S.D.N.Y. 1969), *dismissed as moot* Op. No. 36936 (S.D.N.Y. July 1, 1970) (per curiam) (statute repealed); *Benson v. Johnson*, Civ. No. 70–226 (D. Ore., filed Aug. 4, 1970); *Doe v. Dunbar*, Civ. No. C-2402 (D. Colo., filed July 2, 1970); *Henrie v. Blankenship*, Civ. No. 70–C-211 (N.D. Okla., filed July 6, 1970); *Planned Parenthood Ass'n of Phoenix v. Nelson*, Civ. No. 70–334 PHX (D. Ariz. Aug. 24, 1970) (per curiam); *Ryan v. Specter*, Civ. No. 70–2527 (E.D. Pa., filed Sept. 14, 1970); *Doe v. Rampton*, Civ. No. 234–70 (D. Utah, filed Sept. 16, 1970).

[39] *Idlewild Bon Voyage Corp.* v. *Epstein*, 370 U.S. 713, 715 (1962) (per curiam).

[40] Tom C. Clark, *Religion, Morality, and Abortion: A Constitutional Appraisal*, 2 LOYOLA UNIV. (L.A.) L. Rev. 1–11 (1969).

[41] Although it is a minor point, Griswold was the Executive Director of Planned Parenthood in the *Griswold* case. It was the physician, the late Dr. Buxton of the Yale Medical School

ed.)], and its predecessors do not preclude injunctions against the institution of state court proceedings, but only bar stays of suits already instituted,"[45] this Court nonetheless required "special circumstances" to justify interference with a criminal proceeding begun shortly after the federal complaint was filed.

The present case lies chronologically in the earliest of the categories, (1), because, as to the bulk of relief sought against future enforcement of the anti-abortion statute, state proceedings have never been contemplated. Appellants were thus in the same position as petitioners contesting a loyalty oath that was backed by criminal sanctions. Their entitlement to an injunction against future enforcement should have followed as a matter of course. Put another way, Appellants were "strangers to [any pending] state court proceedings." *Hale* v. *Bimco Trading Co.*, 306 U.S. 375, 378 (1939) (Frankfurter, *F.*).[46] The fact of pending prosecutions against other physicians, or against Dr. Hallford based upon alleged past conduct, had no bearing on Appellant's request for prospective injunctive relief.

Accordingly, the three-judge court should have undertaken an inquiry as to the propriety of injunctive relief without reference to *Dombrowski* v. *Pfister*, and without any greater concern for hypothetical federal-state friction than exists in the ordinary case where state judicial machinery has not entered the controversy.

Indeed, denial of injunctive relief was an open invitation for Texas authorities to maintain existing enforcement policies. Should this have occurred against Dr. Hallford, or any other physician member of the class he represented, a federal injunction would have been sought from the district court as "necessary in aid of its jurisdiction, or to protect or effectuate its"[47] declaratory judgment invalidating the statute. A confrontation between federal and state judiciary might then have ensued. To avoid such a possibility, the three-judge court should have enjoined future enforcement of the statute on June 17, 1970, when it ruled the statute invalid. In other words, an injunction *ab initio* would have prevented federal-state conflict, and enhanced the very policy the three-judge court thought it was following be denying the injunction.

A further reason for having granted the injunction was to avoid irreparable injury to individuals in the class of Jane Roe, and to physicians deterred by the ongoing possibility that the State might continue to enforce the statute until the controversy was determined by *this* court. Without a coercive order on record, Texas law enforcement authorities are free to ignore the declaratory judgment rendered below, because the judgment is subject to possible reversal here. It requires no argument to show that a declaratory judgment by this Court ends the controversy,[48]

---

who had examined the patients and the prescribed contraceptive devices.

[42] Clark, *supra*, not 40, at 9.

[43] 28 U.S.C. § 2283 (1964 ed).

[44] While *Dombrowski* did not clarify the thorny definitional problems surrounding the concept of a "proceeding" in a state court, the Court did hold that at least an indictment must be returned. The federal complaint came before the indictments in *Dombrowski*, and was held to relate back where a district court erroneously dismissed the complaint. An almost identical situation in the abortion context is before this Court in *Hodges* v. *Randall*, No. 728, docketed Sept. 21, 1970, where law enforcement authorities secured the dismissal of a federal action for want of a case or controversy, and proceeded within two days to obtain an indictment against a physician who had been a federal plaintiff.

[45] 380 U.S. at 484 n. 2.

[46] *Hale* teaches that strangers to state proceedings may secure federal injunctive relief against a state statute, even though the effect of the federal decision may be to confuse cases pending at the same time before the highest court of the state. *Hale* affirmed a three-judge court decision enjoining enforcement of a Florida statute although "the injunction in effect stayed proceedings in the Supreme Court of Florida." 306 U.S. at 376.

[47] 28 U.S.C. § 2283 (1964 ed.).

[48] A decision by this Court on the propriety of injunctive relief, however, is necessary for guidance of lower courts in similar future controversies. Otherwise, the law of the district courts would be final law in all cases where the merits were correctly resolved, but an injunction improperly denied. In addition, as commentators have frequently observed, this Court has not resolved a sufficient variety of cases concerning the parameters of 28 U.S.C. § 2283 (1964 ed.), to provide answers to questions such as those presented here. The criteria for commencement of "proceedings in a State court," for example, are uncertain, as is the relevance of a State proceeding brought after a federal complaint. Also, the extent to which the anti-injunction statute affects declaratory judgments is in dispute, as well as the availability of injunctions against future prosecutions where one or more indictments is outstanding, or prosecutions threatened. Similarly, the availability of injunctive relief against prosecutions which threaten to inhibit wide areas of constitutionally protected conduct outside the First Amendment context is uncertain. For a more comprehensive review of the need for further guidelines from this Court in these areas, see Stickgold, *Variations on the Theme of Dombrowski v. Pfister: Federal Intervention in State Criminal Proceedings Affecting First Amendment Rights*, 1968 WIS. L. REV. 369; Brewer, *Dombrowski v. Pfister: Federal Injunction Against*

but such judgments at the district court level carry much less practical import.

Appellant Dr. Hallford sought not only an injunction against future enforcement of the Texas anti-abortion statutes, but also an injunction to bar the commencement of State proceedings against him based upon two outstanding indictments. This request for injunctive relief presents several substantial questions which merit review by this Court.

Assuming that the district court improperly denied an injunction directed generally against future enforcement of the anti-abortion laws, one question is whether that injunction, if entered, should cover the commencement of prosecution under the aforesaid indictments. Whether a bare indictment, returned from the secrecy of a grand jury, alone constitutes a "proceeding in a State court" is an open question.[49] If there is no "proceeding," as this Court found in *Dombrowski*, the degree of irreparable injury needed to justify an injunction must apparently be considered nonetheless. Here, unlike *Dombrowski*, law enforcement authorities have not to date gone forward with prosecutions; hence the degree of friction between state federal judicial systems is considerably lessened.

Also here, as in *Griswold* v. *Connecticut*,[50] and unlike *Dombrowski*, the permissible range of leeway for State regulation of marital and personal privacy is small. While government may regulate many facets of speech coupled with conduct, there is much doubt whether government can so intrude into the domain of privacy. Thus, to allow any prosecution at all of Dr. Hallford is to permit the State in invade the privacy of physician and patient in an area where the district court concluded that the State had little business at all.

State Prosecution in Civil Rights Cases—A New Trend in Federal-State Judicial Relations, 34 FORDHAM L. REV. 71 (1965); Note, *The Federal Anti-Injunctions Statute and Declaratory Judgments in Constitutional Litigations*, 83 HARV L. REV. 1870 (1970); Comment, *Federal Injunctions Against State Actions*, 35 GEO. WASH. L. REV. 744 (1967).

[49] Taken together, *Dombrowski*, 380 U.S. at 484 n. 2, and *Hill* v. *Martin*, 296 U.S. 393, 403 (1935), suggest that a "proceeding" begins at some time after indictment. Respectable authorities argue that the indictment or information is an administrative act, done *ex parte* and in secrecy; hence, no "proceeding" exists until trial or arraignment, when both parties are first before a "State court." See Brewer, *supra* note 48, at 92; Comment, 35 GEO. WASH. L. REV. at 766–67.

[50] 381 U.S. 479 (1965).

If one assumes that 28 U.S.C. § 2283 (1964 ed.), is *prima facie* a bar to an injunction on Dr. Hallord's behalf, the further question remains whether, notwithstanding § 2283, an injunction would be "necessary in aid of [the three-judge court's] jurisdiction," or "to protect or effectuate" the outstanding declaratory judgment. On this theory, since the court had jurisdiction to the grant an injunction on behalf of all parties, it would be incongruous to exclude Dr. Hallford. Indeed, the alleged patients who were aborted, according to the two indictments, might be able to enjoin the compulsion of process against them in order to protect their privacy.

In light of the above, the questions presented in this case, both on the merits, and with respect to relief, are substantial, novel, and hitherto unresolved by this Court. Accordingly, the Court should not probable jurisdiction, and set the case down for plenary review.

II. A married couple, and others similarly situated, have standing to challenge the Texas anti-abortion laws, because said laws have a present and destructive effect on their marital relations, they are unable to utilize fully effective contraceptive methods, pregnancy would seriously harm the woman's health, and such a couple could not obtain judicial relief in sufficient time after pregnancy to prevent irreparable injury.

A further aspect of the judgment below is presented on this appeal. In one part of the lower court's opinion is the holding that "Dr. Hallford has standing to raise the rights of his patients, single women and married couples, as well as rights of his own" (App. at 9a n.3). Yet, the judgment states that "[p]laintiffs John and Mary Doe failed to allege facts sufficient to create a present controversy and therefore do not have standing" (App. at 5a). Accordingly, both declaratory and injunctive relief were denied as to John and Mary Doe.

John and Mary Doe alleged a present impact of the Texas anti-abortion laws on their marital relations which, when considered in light of their assertion of the interests of a class, created a present controversy over a future right to relief in the event Mary Doe or another class member became pregnant.

This statement has already pointed out, *supra* at 6–7, that the judicial machinery is not equipped to grant relief to a party such as Mary Doe after she becomes pregnant. The only

U.S. SUPREME
COURT,
OCTOBER 1970

BRIEF FOR
APPELLANT

meaningful relief must be forthcoming prior to the twelfth week of pregnancy. While twelve weeks is a lengthy period of time, pregnancy is rarely detected before the fourth week, and often not until considerably later, depending upon the degree of medical sophistication of the patient.

Based upon an assumed size of the class represented by Mary Doe, and the known failure rate of the contraceptive she used, it would not be speculative to assume that one or more members of the class would be or become pregnant during the litigation. To assume to the contrary, as the district court did, was not only medically unsound, but served to elevate "ripeness" requirements to an unnecessarily high point, namely a point which deprived the entire class of relief sought simply because no class member stepped forward as pregnant. Indeed, Jane Roe, the pregnant plaintiff, won a judgment which proved meaningless to her, because it was too late.

Ample precedent, moreover, could have been found to conclude that a present controversy existed between the Does and Appellees. Not only should the lower court have considered "'the hardship of denying judicial relief,'"[51] but the dilemma faced by the class of Mary Does when they become pregnant is "'capable of repetition, yet evading review' . . ." *Moore* v. *Ogilvie*, 394 U.S. 814, 816 (1969). The situation, admittedly difficult if one ignores its uniqueness, is nonetheless one in which the "mere possibility of [recurrence] . . . serves to keep the case alive." *United States* v. *W.T. Grant Co.*, 345 U.S. 629, 633 (1953). To the extent that the lower court, almost without discussion, rejected the standing of John and Mary Doe for want of an Article III case or controversy, the court erred. To the Does the case was and is a very real one. The was never

---

[51] Friendly, F., in *Toilet Goods Ass'n* v. *Gardener*, 360 F.2d 677, 684 (2d Cir. 1966), *aff'd*, 387 U.S. 167, 170 (1967).

an absence of adversity. The relief requested had significant meaning for the Does throughout, and the denial of the relief could provide harmful precedent for similar situations. Accordingly, this Court should reverse the determination below, after noting jurisdiction to consider the claim by John and Mary Doe that they too were entitled to declaratory and injunctive relief.

CONCLUSION

For the reasons set out in this Jurisdictional Statement, the Court should note probable jurisdiction, and set the case down for plenary consideration with briefs on the merits and oral argument.

Respectfully submitted,

ROY LUCAS
The James Madison Constitutional Law Institute
Four Patchin Place
New York, N.Y. 10011

NORMAN DORSEN
School of Law
New York University
Washington Square
New York, N.Y. 10003

LINDA N. COFFEE
2130 First National Bank Building
Dallas, Texas 75202

SARAH WEDDINGTON
3710 Lawton
Austin, Texas 78731

ROY L. MERRILL, JR.
Daugherty, Bruner, Lastelick and Anderson
1130 Mercantile Bank Building
Dallas, Texas 75201
Attorneys for Appellants

In the Supreme Court of the United States

No. 78–18, 1971 Term

—⁂—

Jane Roe, John Doe, Mary Doe, and
James Hubert Hallford, M.D.
Appellants,
vs.
Henry Wade, District Attorney of Dallas County, Texas
Appellee.

**On Direct Appeal from the United States District Court
for the Northern District of Texas**

Brief for Appellee

STATEMENT OF THE CASE

Appellant Jane Roe instituted an action, suing on behalf of herself and all others similarly situated, contending she was an unmarried pregnant female who desired to terminate her pregnancy by "abortion"and that she was unable to secure a legal abortion in the State of Texas because of the prohibitions of the Texas Penal Code, Articles 1191, 1192, 1193, 1194, and 1196.[1] She further contends she cannot afford to travel to another jurisdiction to secure a legal abortion.[2]

Appellants John and Mary Doe instituted their action, suing on behalf of themselves and all others similarly situated, contending they were a childless married couple and that Appellant Mary Doe's *physician had advised her to avoid pregnancy because of a neural-chemical disorder.*[3] They further contend *their physician has further advised against the use of birth control pills* and, though they are now practicing an alternative method of contraception, *they understand* there is nevertheless a significant risk of contraceptive failure.[4] They contend that *should* Appellant Mary Doe become pregnant, she would want to terminate such pregnancy by abortion and would be unable to do so in the State of Texas because of the above prohibitory statutes.[5]

Appellant James Hubert Hallford, M.D., filed his Application for Leave for Intervene in Appellant Roe's action[6] and his Application was granted.[7] He contends he is in the active practice of medicine and contends of the Texas Abortion Laws are a principal deterrent to physicians and patients in their relationship in connection with therapeutic hospital and clinical abortions.[8] Appellant Hallford was under indictment in two (2) cases in Dallas County, Texas, charged with offense of abortion in violation of the Statutes in issue.[9]

In substance, Appellants contended in their Complaints filed in the lower court that (1) the Texas Abortion Laws are unconstitutionally vague and uncertain on their face, (2) they deprive a woman of the "fundamental right to choose whether and when to bear children," (3) they infringe upon a woman's right to personal privacy and privacy in the physician-patient relationship, (4) they deprive women and their physicians of rights protected by the First, Fourth, Fifth, Ninth, and Fourteenth Amendments to the Constitution of the United States.[10]

Appellants sought declaratory relief that the Texas Abortion Laws were unconstitutional in violation of the Constitution of the United States and injunctive relief against the future enforcement of such Statutes.[11] They prayed that a three-judge court be convened to hear and determine their causes of action.[12]

Appellee Henry Wade filed his Answer to Appellant Roe's Complaint[13] his Motion to Dismiss the Complaint of Appellants John and Mary Doe[14] and his Answer to Appellant Hallford's Complaint.[15] The State of Texas was granted leave to respond to the Appellants' Complaints and filed its Motion to Dismiss all Complaints and its alternative plea for Judgment on the Pleadings.[16] Both Motions to Dismiss challenged the standing of Appellants John and Mary Doe[17] and the State of Texas'

U.S. SUPREME
COURT, 1971

BRIEF FOR
APPELLEE

---

[1] A. 11 (The Statutes in issue are commonly referred to as the Texas Abortion Laws and are set out verbatim, *infra*, at pp. 5–6).

[2] A. 12.

[3] A. 16.

[4] A. 16–17.

[5] A. 17.

[6] A. 22–23.

[7] A. 36.

[8] A. 28.

[9] A. 30. (These cases are still pending.)

[10] A. 12–13, 19–20, 31, 34.

[11] A. 14, 20–21, 34.

[12] A. 13, 20–21 34.

[13] A. 37–39.

[14] A. 40–41.

[15] A. 42–46.

[16] A. 47–49.

[17] A. 40, 48.

Motion to Dismiss challenged the standing of Appellants Roe and Hallford.[18] In addition, the State of Texas' Motion to Dismiss asserted that Appellants (1) failed to state a claim upon which relief may be granted, (2) failed to raise a substantial Constitutional question, (3) failed to show irreparable injury and the absence of an adequate remedy at law, and (4) Appellant Hallford's Complaint was barred by 38 U.S.C. 2283.[19]

In the course of proceeding in the lower court, Appellants filed their Motions for Summary Judgment.[20] In support of Appellant Jane Doe's Motion for Summary Judgment, she filed her affidavit[21] and an affidavit of one Paul Carey Trickett, M.D.[22] Appellant Hallford Filed his affidavit in support of his Motion for Summary Judgment[23] and annexed copies of the indictments pending against him.[24]

The cases were consolidated and processed to a hearing before the Honorable Irving L. Goldberg, Circuit Judge, and the Honorable Sarah T. Hughes and W.M. Taylor, Jr., District Judges.[25] Neither the Appellants nor the Appellee offered any evidence at such hearing [26] and arguments were presented by all parties. The Court tendered its Judgment[27] and Opinion[28] on June 17, 1970.

Appellants filed Notice of Appeal to this Court pursuant to the provisions of 28 U.S.C. 1253.[29] Appellants Roe and Hallford and Appellee Wade filed Notice of Appeal to the United State Court of Appeals for the Fifth Circuit.[30] Appellants filed their Motion to Hold Appeal to Fifth Circuit of Appellee Wade in Abeyance Pending Decision by the Supreme Court of the United States[31], which Motion was granted.[32]

The lower court found that Appellants Roe and Hallford and the *member of their respective classes*[33] had standing to bring their lawsuits, but Appellants John and Mary Doe had failed to allege facts sufficient to create a present controversy and did not have standing.[34] That court held the Texas Abortion Laws unconstitutional in that they deprived single women and married persons of the right to choose whether to have children in violation of the Ninth Amendment to the Constitution of the United States and that such Laws were void on their face for unconstitutional overbreadth and vagueness.[35] The court denied Appellants' applications for injunctive relief.[36]

STATUES IN ISSUES

The Texas Abortion Laws and the statutes in issue are contained in the Texas Penal Code and consist of the following:

Article 1191. Abortion

If any person shall designedly administer to a pregnant woman or knowingly procure to be administered with her consent any drug or medicine, or shall use toward her any violence or means whatsoever externally or internally applied, and thereby procure an abortion, he shall be confined in the penitentiary for not less than two nor more than five years; if it be done without her consent, the punishment shall be doubled. By "abortion" is meant that the life of the fetus or embryo shall be destroyed in the woman's womb or that a premature birth shall be caused.

Art. 1192. Furnishing the Means

Whoever furnishes the means for procuring an abortion knowing the purpose intended is guilty as an accomplice.

Art. 1193. Attempt at Abortion

If the means used shall fail to produce and abortion, the offender is nevertheless guilty of an attempt to produce abortion, provided it be shown that such means was calculated to produce that result, and shall be fined not less that one hundred nor more than one thousand dollars.

Art. 1194 Murder in Producing Abortion

If the death of the mother is occasioned by an abortion so produced or by an attempt to effect the same it is murder.

---

[18] A. 48.
[19] A. 47–48.
[20] 50, 59–60.
[21] A. 56–60. (an alias affidavit)
[22] A. 51–55.
[23] A 61–72.
[24] A 73, 74.
[25] A. 75–110.
[26] A. 77.
[27] A. 124–126.
[28] A. 111–132.
[29] A. 127–129.
[30] A. 133, 134, 135.
[31] A. 136–138.
[32] A. 139–140. (The Court of Appeals has taken no further action in these cases).
[33] A. 124.
[34] A. 124
[35] A. 125–126.
[36] A. 126.

Art. 1196. By Medical Advice

Nothing in this chapter applies to an abortion procured or attempted by medical advice for the purpose of saving the life of the mother.[37]

QUESTIONS PRESENTED

In Appellee's opinion the questions presented may be precisely stated as follows:

I. Whether appellants Jane Roe, and John and Mary Doe, present a justiciable controversy in their challenge to the Texas abortion laws?

II. Whether the court should enjoin the enforcement of the Texas abortion laws as to appellant Hallford in the light of pending state criminal charges?

III. Did the district court err in refusing to enjoin future enforcement of the Texas abortion laws after declaring such laws unconstitutional?

IV. Whether this court can consider plenary review of an entire case when a lower court grants declaratory relief holding a state statue unconstitutional, but refuses to enjoin future enforcement of such statute, and the appeal to this court is from that portion of the judgment denying injunctive relief?

V. Whether articles 1191, 1192, 1193, 1194 and 1196 of Texas penal code are void on their face because of unconstitutional overbreadth and vagueness?

VI. Whether the constitution of the United States guarantees a woman the right to abort an unborn fetus?

VII. Whether the state of Texas has a legitimate interest in preventing abortion except under the limited exception of "an abortion procured or attempted by medical advice for the purpose of saving the life of the mother?"

SUMMARY OF ARGUMENT

Appellant Jane Roe has not presented a justiciable controversy admitting of specific relief for this Court in her challenge to the Texas Abortion Laws. She has not shown that she has sustained or is immediately in danger of sustaining some direct injury as a result of enforcement of the Texas Abortion Laws. Any cause of action that she may have had is not established by the record and has been mooted by the termination of her pregnancy.

Appellants John and Mary Doe's cause of action is based on speculation and conjecture and they also have shown they have sustained or are immediately in danger of sustaining some direct injury as a result of enforcement of the Texas Abortion Laws essential to standing and a justiciable controversy.

Appellant Hallford is under indictment in two cases for violation of the statutes he attacks in the controversy before the Court. The Court should abstain from exercising jurisdiction under the principles enunciated in *Younger* v. *Harris*, etc. Appellant Hallford is not entitled to assert a cause of action on behalf of his patients in the physician-patient relationship.

For a federal court to grant injunctive relief against the enforcement of a state statute, there must be a clear and persuasive showing of unconstitutionally and irreparable harm. The lower court can divorce injunctive and declaratory relief under its equity power and declare a statute unconstitutional, yet refuse to enjoin the enforcement of such statute.

Once a federal court has assumed jurisdiction of a cause, it may properly assume jurisdiction of the entire controversy and render a decision on all questions presented and involved in the case. If this Court determines that is has jurisdiction to consider the denial of injunctive relief to Appellants by the lower court, it may consider the constitutionality of the Texas Abortion Laws determined to be unconstitutional by the Court below.

The Texas Abortion Laws are not violative of the Constitution of the United States as being unconstitutionally vague and overbroad. *United States* v. *Vuitch* is decisive of the issues in the case as to vagueness and overbreadth.

Though the right of "marital privacy" and "personal privacy" are recognized, they have never been regarded as absolute. The "right to privacy" is a relative right that, in the matter of abortion, is not attached to an express right guaranteed under the Constitution of the United States. The right to life of the unborn child is superior to the right of privacy of the mother.

U.S. SUPREME COURT, 1971

BRIEF FOR APPELLEE

---

[37] The omitted article, Article 1195, concerns destruction of the vitality or life of a child in a state of being born and before actual, birth, which such child would otherwise have been born alive.

U.S. SUPREME
COURT, 1971

BRIEF FOR
APPELLEE

The state has a legitimate, if not compelling, interest in prohibiting abortion except under limited circumstances. In the light of recent findings and research in medicine, the fetus is a human being and the state has an interest in the arbitrary and unjustified destruction of this being.

ARGUMENT

I. Appellants Jane Roe, John and Mary Doe, have not presented a justiciable controversy in their challenge to the Texas abortion laws

A. Justiciability and standing   Article III of the Constitution of the United States limits the judicial power of Federal Courts to "cases" and "controversies." This has been construed by the courts to prohibit the giving of advisory opinions. *Flast v. Cohen,* 392 U.S. 83 (1968); *Bell v. Maryland,* 378 U.S. 226 (1964); *United States v, Fearful,* 365 U.S. 146 (1961). There must be a real and substantial controversy admitting of specific relief as distinguished from an opinion advising what the law would be upon a hypothetical state of facts. *Aetna Life Insurance Company v, Hayworth,* 300 U.S. 227 (1937); accord, *Public Service Commission of Utah v. Wycoff Company,* 344 U.S. 237 (1952); *Baker v. Carr,* 369 U.S. 186 (1962); *Golden v. Zwickler,* 394 U.S. 103 (1969). Correctively, a party challenging a statute as invalid must show that he has sustained or is immediately in danger of sustaining some direct injury as a result of the statue's enforcement before a three-judge court or any Federal court can entertain the action, *Frothingham v. Mellon*[38] 262 U.S. 447 (1923); *Ex parte Levitt,* 302 U.S. 633 (1937); *Fairchild v. Hughes* 258 U.S. 126 (1922); *Poe v. Ullman,* 367 U.S. 497 (1961). In a per curiam opinion this Court stated in *Ex Parte Levitt*:

> "It is an established principle that to entitle a private individual to invoke the judicial power to determine the validity of executive or legislative action he must show that he has sustained, or is immediately in danger of sustaining, a direct injury as the result of that action and *it is not sufficient that he has merely a general interest common to all members of the public.*" (Emphasis added). 302 U.S. at 634.

In *Flask v. Cohen,* supra, this Court gave careful consideration to the nexus between *standing* and *justiciability* and stated that "Standing is an aspect of justiciability and, as such, the problem of standing is surrounded by the same complexities and vagaries that inhere in justiciability." 392 U.S. at 98–99. Most proba-

bly, the best known decision of this Court on standing is *Frothingham v. Mellon,* supra, in which Mrs. Frothingham claimed that she was a taxpayer of the United States and sued to restrain payments from Treasury to the several states which chose to participate in a program created by the Maternity Act of 1921. She claimed that Federal government lacked power to appropriations would cause an unconstitutional increase in her future taxes. After considerations of the interest of an individual taxpayer, remoteness, and other issues, this Court finally stated that its power to declare statutes unconstitutional exists only where the statute is involved in a justiciable case, and that to present such a case the plaintiff "must be able to show, not only that the statute is invalid, but that he has sustained or is immediately in danger of sustaining some direct injury as the result of its enforcement, and not merely that suffers in some indefinite way in common with the people generally." 262 U.S. at 488. See, *Cramp v. Board of Public Instruction,* 368 U.S. 278 (1961); *Baker v. Carr,* supra; *National Association for the Advancement of Colored People v. Button,* 271 U.S. 415 (1963).

A Review and analysis of the decisions on standing indicated they are not easy to reconcile on the facts. It is frequently stated that to have standing a party must be able to demonstrate injury to a legally protected right or interest. *Tennessee Electric Power Co. v. Tennessee Valley Authority,* 306 U.S. 118 (1937); *Alabama Power Company v. Ickes,* 302 U.S. 464 (1938); *Perkins v. Lukens Steel Co.,* 310 U.S. 113(1940).

B. Standing of Appellants John and Mary Doe   Applying the standards of justiciability and standing stated above, an examination of the cause of action asserted by Appellants John and Mary Doe discloses they do not have standing. In their Complaint they contend they are a childless married couple and Mary Doe was not pregnant at the time.[39] Their cause of action is based upon their fear of contraceptive failure resulting in pregnancy to Mary Doe at a time *when they are not properly prepared to accept the responsibilities of parenthood* and upon the *advice of their physician to avoid pregnancy until her health condition improves.*[40] The record is

---

[38] This case is usually referred to as *Massachusetts v. Mellori*.
[39] A. 16.
[40] A. 17.

wholly lacking in proof of these contentions. The lower court properly and correctly denied standing to these Appellants upon finding they failed to allege facts sufficient to create a present controversy.[41]

Initially, it may be states that neither Appellants Doe nor Roe can be prosecuted under the Texas Abortion Laws for securing an abortion or for attempted abortion. *Gray v. State*, 178 S.W. 337 (Tex.Crim. 1915); *Shaw v, State*, 165 S.W. 930 (Tex.Crim. 1914). Appellants John and Mary Doe's cause of action is based upon speculation that these Appellants will not at that time be prepared for parenthood and, further, that Appellant Mary Doe's health condition at that time will be impaired by pregnancy. These speculative fears cannot support a caused of action. See, *Younger v. Harris*, 401 U.S. 37 (1971); *Golden v. Zwickler*, supra. For a court to decide the merits of Appellants John and Mary Doe's cause of action would result in giving an advisory opinion upon a hypothetical state of facts contrary to Federal Constitutional limitations and this Court's holding in *Flask v. Cohen*, supra, and cases cited, supra, at p. 9.

C. Standing of Appellant Jane Roe Appellant Jane Roe occupies a more unique position in regard to standing. She filed her Amended Complaint in the District Court on April 22, 1970,[42] and an "alias affidavit" on May 21, 1970.[43] *The only support in the record for her contentions and allegations giving rise to her cause of action is found in her Amended Complaint and her "alias affidavit."* The affidavit filed after the commencement of her action indicates she did not desire an abortion at the time of its filing.[44] This affidavit further shows that Appellant Roe had been pregnant for several months prior to its filing.[45] The hearing was held before the three-judge panel on July 22, 1970,[46] some four and one-half (4 and a half months after the filing of her Original Complaint[47] and on November 3, 1971, some twenty (20) months will have expired since the filing of said Original Complaint. There is no indication in the record the Appellant Jane Roe was pregnant at the time of the hearing on July 22, 1970, and it can be reasonably concluded that she is not now pregnant.[48]

The argument that Appellant Jane Roe has not presented a justiciable controversy to give her standing is not intended to be fictitious or spurious. If her statements in her affidavit did not moot her cause of action, resort may be had to *Golden v. Zwickler*, supra, wherein this Court stated:

> "The District Court erred in holding that Zwickler was entitled to declaratory relief if the elements essential to that relief existed '[w]hen this action was initiated.' The proper inquiry was whether a 'controversy' requisite to relief under the Declaratory Judgement Act existed at the time of the hearing on remand." 394 U.S. at 108.[49]

Golden v. Zwickler indicated that this Court should consider an issue as to standing *at the time* it reviews the case and not when the suit was filed. This is supported to some extent by *Bryan v. Austin*. 354 U.S. 933 (1957), wherein Plaintiffs sought to have a South Carolina statute declared unconstitutional and, pending appeal, the statute in question was repealed. In a per curiam opinion this Court stated that the repeal of the statute in issue after the decision of the District Court rendered the cause moot. *Atherton Mills v. Johnston*, 259 U.S. 13 (1922), involved a suit for injunctive relief to prevent the discharge of a minor employee because of the Child Labor Act of 1919, which was challenged as being invalid. While the case was on appeal, the minor employee involved became of age. This Court held that the case became moot by the lapse of time and the case could not be considered by the Court.

Mootness deprives a federal court of its judicial power since no case or controversy exists. *Mechling Barge Lines, Inc., v. United States*, 368 U.S. 3224 (1961); *Local No. 8–6 v. Missouri*, 361 U.S. 363 (1960); *Flast v. Cohen*, supra; *Parker v. Ellis*, 362 U.S. 574 (1960).

D. Class action aspects It is questionable whether the requirements of Rule 23, Fed. Rules Civ. Proc., have been complied with in connection with Appellants Roe and John and Mary Doe's attempt to bring their suits as class actions. These Appellants have alleged the pre-

---

[41] A. 124.

[42] A. 10.

[43] A. 56.

[44] "At the time I filed the lawsuit I wanted to terminate my pregnancy by means of an abortion. . ." (A. 57) and "I wanted to terminate my pregnancy because. . ." (A. 57).

[45] "Each month I am barely able to make ends meet" (A. 58).

[46] A. 77.

[47] Docket Entries in CA-3–3690–B (A-1).

[48] The Court may desire to take judicial notice of this fact.

[49] This case was reversed and remanded with direction to enter a new judgment dismissing the complaint.

requisites required in Rule 23 (a),[50] but have not designated whether their actions are (b) (1) or (b) (2) actions under Rule 23. Again, the record is wholly void of any showing of the propriety of class action relief and the only other mention of this aspect of the case is found in the lower court's judgment as follows:

> "(1) Plaintiff Jane Roe, plaintiff-intervenor James Hubert Hallford, M.D. and the members of their respective classes have standing to bring this lawsuit." (A. 124).[51]

The 1966 amendments to Rule 242 require the judgment in a (b) (1) or (b) (2) class action to include and describe those whom the court finds to be members of the class. In a Rule 23 (b) (3) class action the 1966 amendments require the judgment include and specify or describe those to whom notice was directed, as required by Rule 23 (c) (2), and who have not requested exclusion, and who are found by the court to be members of the class.

In *Hall v. Beals*, 396 U.S. 45 (1969), this Court had before it on direct appeal a case involving new residents of the State of Colorado, who had moved into the State four (4) or five (5) months prior to the November, 1968 presidential election. They were refused permission to vote because of a Colorado statute imposing a six (6) months residency requirement. They commenced a suit as a class action challenging the constitutionality of the statute. A three-judge court upheld the constitutionality of the statute. Thereafter, the election was held, and the State statute was amended to reduce the residency requirement for a presidential election to two (2) months. This Court, in a per curiam opinion, held that, aside from the fact that the election had been held, the case was rendered moot by the amendment to the statute that reduced the residency requirement to two (2) months, and under which the Appellants could vote, since the case had lost its character as a present, live controversy, notwithstanding that the Appellants had denominated their suit as a class action and had expressed opposition to residency requirements in general. In *Golden v. Zwickler*, supra, a distributor of anonymous handbills criticizing a congressman's voting record sought a declaratory judgment concerning the constitutionality of a New York statute which penalized the distributor of anonymous literature in connection with an election campaign. While the case was pending, the congressman left the House of Representatives and accepted a term as a justice on the Supreme Court of New York. The United States District Court held that the distributor was nevertheless entitled to a declaratory judgment because a genuine controversy had existed as the commencement of the action. This Court held there was no "controversy" of "sufficient immediacy and reality" to warrant a declaratory judgment and, in addition, stated as follows:

> "It is not enough to say, as did the District Court, that nevertheless Zwickler has a 'further and far broader right to a general adjudication of unconstitutionality. . . [in] [h]is *own interest as well as that of others* who would with like anonymity practice free speech in a political environment. . . .' The constitutional question, First Amendment or otherwise, must be presented in the context of a specific live grievance." (Emphasis added). 394 U.S. at 118.

See, *Burrows v. Jackson*, 346 U.S. 249 (1953).

The Federal Constitution limitation in Article III cannot be extended or limited by asserting a "class action" under Rule 23. Rule 82, Fed. Rules Civ. Proc., in referring to the preceding rules, including Rule 23, provides in part that "These rules shall not be construed to extend or limit the jurisdiction of the United States district courts or the venue of actions therein. . ."

II. This court should refuse declaratory and injunctive relief to Appellant James Hubert Hallford, M.D.

In Indictment No. 2023 A, Appellant James Hubert Hallford stands charged by the State of Texas with performing an abortion on Frances C. King,[52] and in Indictment No. 556 J with performing an abortion on Jane Wilhelm.[53] He sought and obtained leave to intervene in Appellant Roe's action[54] seeking a permanent injunction against the enforcement of the Texas Abortion Laws,[55] but reserving a right to make an application for an interlocutory injunction.[56] In reality, Appellant Hallford is seeking to avoid

---

[50] A. 12, 19.

[51] Appellant Hallford's Complaint makes no mention of class action relief. (A. 24–35).

[52] A. 73.

[53] A. 74.

[54] A. 22, 36.

[55] A. 34.

[56] A. 34 (it is submitted that Appellant Hallford reserved this right in the event the pending cases were set for trial).

criminal prosecution in the criminal cases pending against him.

Historically there has been great reluctance by the federal courts to interfere in the operations of a state court. *Stefanelli v. Minard*, 342 U.S. 117 (1951). General principles should be enough to show that an independent federal action is not an appropriate means to raise what should be a state court defense, but this does not stand alone. A statute almost as old as the Republic, the Anti-Injunction Act of 1793, has, with some variations in language over the years, provided that a court of the United States "may not grant an injunction to stay proceedings in a State court . . ." 28 U.S.C. 2283. This statute is no happenstance. It is a "limitation of the power of federal courts dating almost from the beginning of our history and expressing an important Congressional policy—to prevent friction between state and federal courts" *Oklahoma Packing Co. v. Oklahoma & Elec. Co.*, 309 U.S. 4 (1940).

Appellant Hallford's Complaint allegations do not justify the conclusion that any criminal charges have been brought against him in bad faith or under any conditions that would place his case within *Dombrowski's* "special circumstances." *Dombrowski v. Pfister*, 380 U.S. 479 (1965). There is no relationship worthy of note in the allegations contained in Paragraph 14 of this Complaint[57] to *Dombrowski's* "special circumstances." He appears to indicate that the State of Texas must negate the exception provided in Article 1196, supra,[58] and that he cannot offer medical testimony to bring him within the purview of the exception.

In *Atlantic Coast Line R. Co. v. Engineers*, 398 U.S. 281 (1970), the railroad obtained a state injunction against a union's picketing and the union sought and obtained in the Federal District Court an injunction against the enforcement of the state court injunction. The Court of Appeals for the Fifth Circuit affirmed the Federal District Court's judgment and, on certiorari, this Court reversed and remanded stating as follows:

> "First, a federal court does not have inherent power to ignore the limitations of Section 2283 and to enjoin state court proceedings interfere with a protected federal right or

invade an area preempted by federal law, even when the interference is unmistakably clear. This rule applies regardless of whether the federal court itself has jurisdiction over the controversy, or whether it is ousted from jurisdiction for the same reason that the state court is." (Omitting authority). 398 U.S. at 294.-295.

The above principle of federal abstention is further enunciated in *Spinally Motor Sales Co., Inc., v. Dodge*, 295 U.S. 89 (1935); *Cameron v. Johnson*, 390 U.S. 611 (1968); *Shaw v. Garrison*, 293 F.Supp. 937 (E.D.La. 1968); *City of Greenwood v. Peacock*, 384 U.S. 8080 (1966).

Most recently, this Court has announced certain guidelines on the subject of federal court interference with pending state criminal proceedings in what is sometimes referred to as the "February 23rd Decisions." *Younger v. Harris*, supra, *Samuels v. Mackell*, 401 U.S. 66 (1971); *Boyle v. Landry*, 401 U.S. 77 (1971); *Dyson v. Stein*, 401 U.S. 200 (1971); *Perez v, Ledesma*, 401 U.S. 82 (1971); *Bryne v. Karalexis*, 401 U.S. 216 (1971). These cases very strongly indicate the availability of federal injunctive relief against pending state criminal prosecutions has been severely curtailed even in the area of First Amendment rights of expression. Thus, federal interference, even to the extent of granting preliminary restraining orders and convening three judge courts is by far the exception rather than the rule.

The above cases further indicate that, independent of any obstacles posed by the federal anti-injunction statute, the primary prerequisite to federal court intervention in the present context, is a showing or irreparable injury. Even irreparable injury is insufficient unless it is "both great and immediate." In *Younger v. Harris*, supra, this Court stated as follows:

> "Certain types of injury, in particular, the cost, anxiety, and inconvenience of having to defend against a single criminal prosecution, could not by themselves be considered 'irreparable' in the special legal sense of that term. Instead, the threat to the Plaintiff's federally protected rights must be one that cannot be eliminated by his defense against a single criminal prosecution." 401 U.S. at 46.

Accord, *Byrne v. Karalexis*, supra.

Samuels v. Mackell, supra, considered declaratory relief prayed for in relation to the federal court's reluctance to interfere with pend-

U.S. SUPREME
COURT, 1971

BRIEF FOR
APPELLEE

---

[57] A. 30.

[58] See Article 1196, supra, at p. 6 containing the exception "procured or attempted by medical advice for the purpose of saving the life of the mother."

ing state criminal proceedings and this Court stated:

> "We therefore hold that, in cases where the state criminal prosecution was begun prior to the federal suit, same equitable principles relevant to the propriety of an injunction must be taken into consideration by federal district courts in determining whether to issue a declaratory judgment, and that *where an injunction would be impermissible under these principles, declaratory relief should be denied as well.* . . . Ordinarily, however, the practical effect of the two forms of relief will be virtually identical, and the basic policy against federal interference with pending state criminal prosecutions will be frustrated as much by a declaratory judgment as it would be by an injunction." (Emphasis added). 401 U.S. at 73.

Nor can Appellant rely upon his patients' rights, which a statute supposedly threatens. See *Glisten v. Ullman*, 318 U.S. 44 (1943); accord, *Golden v. Zwicker*, supra; *Burrows v. Jackson*, supra.

Applying the guidelines set forth in *Younger v. Harris*, supra, and the other "February 23rd Decisions," this Court can properly conclude Appellant Hallford has not suffered, nor under the present state of the record, will suffer both great and immediate irreparable injury of the nature required to authorize federal injunctive or declaratory relief. His case is precisely the type to which this Court was addressing itself in the recent pronouncements condemning, except in very limited circumstances, federal court equitable injunctive and declaratory interference with pending state criminal prosecutions.

III. The United States District Court did not err in refusing to enjoin future enforcement of the Texas abortion laws after declaring such laws unconstitutional.

This Court has been unwaivering in holding that a three-judge court cannot consider an action for injunctive relief under 28 U.S.C. 2281 on its merits without a preliminary showing of irreparable harm and no adequate legal remedy. In *Spielman Motor Sales Co. Inc., v. Dodge*, supra, a suit requesting a three-judge court to rejoin a New York district attorney from instituting criminal prosecutions against certain defendants under an alleged unconstitutional state statute, this court affirmed the lower court's dismissal of the action and stated:

> "The general rule is that equity will not interfere to prevent the enforcement of a criminal statute even though unconstitutional. . . To

justify such interference there must be exceptional circumstances and a clear showing that an injunction is necessary in order to afford adequate protection of constitutional rights." 295 U.S. at 95.

In *Mayo v. Lakeland Highlands Canning Co., Inc.*, 309 U.S. 310 (1940), a suit was brought before a three-judge court seeking to enjoin the Florida Agriculture Commission from enforcing an alleged unconstitutional state statute. This Court reversed the lower court's disposition on the merits and made the following observation:

> "The legislation requiring the convening of a court of three judges in cases such as this was intended to insure that the enforcement of a challenged statute should not be suspended by injunction except upon a clear and persuasive showing of unconstitutionality and irreparable injury." 309 U.S. at 318–319.

Accord, *Beal v. Missouri Pacific Railroad Corporation*, 312 U.S. 45 (1961); *Douglas v. City of Jeannette*, 319 U.S. 157 (1943); *Bryne v. Karalexis*, supra; *Dyson v, Stein*, supra; *Samuels v. Mackell*, supra; *Younger v. Harris*, supra.

The lower court cited *Dombrowski v. Pfister*, supra, and *Zwickler v. Koota*, 389 U.S. 241 (1967), as authority for the court to divorce injunctive and declaratory relief,[59] In *Powell v. McCormick*, 395 U.S. 486 (1969), this Court held that a court may grant declaratory relief even though it chooses not to issue an injunction or mandamus. 395 U.S. at 504. See, *United Public Workers v. Mitchell*, 330 U.S. 75 (1947).

IV. This court can consider plenary review of the entire case when a lower court grants declaratory relief holding a state statute unconstitutional, but refuses to enjoin future enforcement of such statute, and the appeal to this court is from that portion of the judgment denying injunctive relief.

Should this Court determine that it has jurisdiction to consider the propriety of injunctive relief in this case, it can properly assume jurisdiction of this entire controversy and render a decision on all questions involved in this case, including the constitutionally of the Texas Abortion Laws. Appellee joins Appellants in requesting this Court reach the issue of the Constitutionality of the Texas Abortion Laws. Appellee is in a somewhat awkward procedural position in that it lost on the merits in the lower

---

[59] A. 121, 122.

court as to declaratory relief and neither the grant nor the refusal of a declaratory judgment, without more, will support a direct appeal to this Court under 28 U.S.C. 1253. *Mitchell v. Donovan*, 398 U.S. 427 (1970); *Gunn v. University Committee*, 399 U.S. 383 (1971). Appellee has the avenue of appeal to the Fifth Circuit.[60] Should this Court in the present case hold that the lower court properly grant declaratory relief but improperly denied injunctive relief, it then might bed faced, at least indirectly, with the consideration and decision of the same constitutional issues that are being directly raised by the Appellee in the Court of Appeals for the Fifth Circuit.

Though not directly in point, *Public Service Commission of Utah v. Wycoff Co.*, supra, lends support to the premise that a federal court has the right, power, and authority to decide and determine the entire controversy and all the issues and questions involved in a case of which it has properly acquired jurisdiction. Accord, *Just v. Chambers*, 312 U.S. 383 (1941), *Florida Lime and Avocado Growers v. Jacobson*, 362 U.S. 73 (1960); cf, *Hartford Accident & Indemnity Company v. Southern Pacific Company*, 273 U.S. 207 (1927); *British Transport Commission v. United States*, 354 U.S. 129 (1957). In *Sterling v. Constantin*, 287 U.S. 378 (1932); this Court stated that:

> "As the validity of provisions of the state constitution and statutes, if they could be deemed to authorize the action of the Governor, was challenged, the application for injunction was properly heard by three judges. Straton v. St. Louis S. W. R. Co., 282 U.S. 10, 75 L. Ed. 135, 51 S.Ct. 8. The jurisdiction of the District Court so constituted, and of this Court upon appeal, extends to every question involved, whether of state or federal law, and enables the *court to rest its judgment on the decisions of such of the questions as in its opinion effectively dispose of the case." (Omitting authority). 287 U.S. at 393–394.

V. Articles 1191, 1192, 1193, 1194 and 1196 of the Texas Penal Code are not unconstitutional on their face because of overbreath and vagueness.

---

[60] Appellee has appealed to the United States Court of Appeals for the Fifth Circuit (A. 135) and this appeal is being held in abeyance pending a decision of this Court (A. 139–140).

The possible vagueness of state abortion statutes which allow for such a procedure only when the life, or in some cases, health, of the expectant mother is threatened has recently come under judicial scrutiny in a number of instances. One author, in commenting on the decision of the California Supreme Court in *People v. Belous*, 71 Cal. Rptr. 354, 458 P.2d 194 (1969), cert.denied, 397 U.S. 915 (1970), stated as follows:

> "In attempting to define the phrase 'necessary to preserve ... life ...' the California Supreme Court first examined the isolated words of the statute, and concluded that no clear meaning of 'necessary' and 'preserve' could be ascertained. It is not surprising that a seriatim examination of the words convinced the court that the phrase was vague. Necessity is a relative concept and must refer to a particular object to be meaningful. Nor can the word 'preserve' be understood out of context. In the abstract, such words are not just vague, they are meaningless. Taken in context, however, these words do have meaning. The object of the necessity in this statute is 'to preserve life.' The term is defined by its object—life." 118 U. Penn. L. Rev. 643, 644 (1970).

There is some inherent vagueness in many homicide laws, such as laws which define justifiable homicide as self-defense, or those which differentiate between first- and second-degree murder. The courts, like society, however, have learned to live with a certain element of inevitable vagueness in all laws and have learned to apply it reasonably. See, *Lanzetta v. New Jersey*, 306 U.S. 451 (1939); *Connally v. General Construction Company*, 269 U.S. 385 (1926). In order for a statute to be unconstitutionally vague, it must be so vague and lacking in standards so as to compel men of ordinary intelligence to guess as its meaning. *Adderley v. Florida*, 385 U.S. 39 (1967); *Cameron v. Johnson*, supra.

A number of three-judge panels have been convened recently to consider the constitutionality of abortion laws which allowed for the performance of such operations only when the life of the mother was threatened by continuance of the pregnancy. While one such court, in dealing with such a law in Wisconsin, did hold the statute to be unconstitutional on other grounds, it said that whatever vagueness existed in the law was not sufficient, of itself. for a declaration of unconstitutionality. *Babbitz v. McCann*, 310 F.Supp. 293 (E.D. Wis. 1970). The court observed:

"We have examined the challenged phraseology and are persuaded that it is not indefinite or vague. In our opinion, the word 'necessary' and the expression 'to save the life of the mother' are both reasonably comprehensible in their meaning." 310 F.Supp. at 297.

Accord, *Rosen v. Louisiana State Board of Medical Examiners*, 318 F.Supp. 1217 (E.D. La. 1970).

In *United States v. Petrillo*, 332 U.S. 1 (1947), this Court said:

"[That] there may be marginal cases in which it is difficult to determine the side of the line on which a particular fact situation falls is no sufficient reason to hold the language too ambiguous to define a criminal offense, *Robinson v, United States*, 324 U.S. 282, 285, 286, 89 L.Ed. 944, 946, 947, 65 S. Ct. 666. It would strain the requirement for certainty in criminal law standards too near the breaking point to say that it was impossible judicially to determine whether a person knew when he was willfully attempting to compel another to hire unneeded employees." (Omitting authority). 332 U.S. at 7–8.

See *Jordan v. DeGeorge*, 341 U.S. 223 (1951); *United States v. Ragen*, 314 U.S. 513 (1942); *United States v. Wurzback*, 280 U.S. 396 (1930).

This court below did not have the advantage of this Court's decision in *United States v. Vuitch*, 402 U.S. 62 (1971), at the time it handed down its decision in this case. In *Vuitch* this Court reversed the decision of a district court judge who had found that the District of Columbia abortion law was unconstitutionally vague. The exception clause in *Vuitch* stated in part "unless the same were done as necessary for the preservation of the mother's life or health."[61] Though this Court directed its attention to the word "health," its holding should be dispositive of the case at bar in that the exception clause is less certain of meaning that the exception found in the Texas Abortion Laws. This Court in *Vuitch* further disposed of the contention of the physician that once an abortion is performed he is "presumed guilty."

VI. The Constitution of the United States does not guarantee a woman the right to abort an unborn fetus.

A. The interest of marital privacy   One must recognize the interest of a husband and wife in preserving their conjugal relations from state interference, an interest which, in *Griswold v. Connecticut*, 381 U.S. 479 (1965), was found to be violated by Connecticut's statute forbidding the use of contraceptives. This law interfered with the most private aspect of the martial relation, sexual intercourse, making it criminal for a couple to engage in sexual intercourse when using contraceptives. In contrast, the usual statute restricting abortions does not affect the sexual relations of a couple except under some circumstances and only for a limited time. Prevention of abortion does not entail, therefore, state interference with the right of marital intercourse, nor does enforcement of the statute requiring invasions of the conjugal bedroom.

Assuming arguendo that there are other marital rights the state must respect, may it then be urged that the right of marital privacy includes the freedom of a married couple to raise and educate a child they do not want, or commit infanticide, incest, engage in pandering and the like. Family privacy, like personal privacy, is highly valued, but not absolute. The new media publicize the events that occur when a family is victimized by criminals though they seek seclusion. *Time v. Hill*, 385 U.S. 374 (1967). The family may not practice polygamy,[62] may not prohibit schooling for a child,[63] or prohibit the child's labor,[64] or expose the community or a child to communicable disease.[65] In *Gleitman v. Cosgrove*, 49 N.J. 22, 227 A.2d 689 (1967), the unborn child's right to live came into conflict with family privacy. The Gleitmans contended that their doctor failed to warn that Mrs. Gleitman was suffering from German measles and this failure deprived the family of the opportunity of terminating the pregnancy. They alleged the child was born with grave defects as a result of the doctor's omission. The court stated as follows:

"The right to life is inalienable in our society. . . .

We are not faced here with the necessity of balancing the mother's life against that of her child. The sanctity of the single human life is the decisive factor in this suit in tort. Eugenic considerations are not controlling. We are not talking here about the breeding of prize cattle. It may have been easier for the mother and less expensive for the father to have terminated the life of their child while he was an embryo, but these alleged detriments cannot stand against

---

[61] 22 D C Code 201.

[62] *Reynolds v. United States*, 98 U.S. 145 (1879).

[63] *Prince v. Massachusetts*, 321 U.S. 158 (1944).

[64] Id.

[65] Id.

the preciousness of a single human life to support a remedy in tort." 227 A.2d at 693.

B. Physician-patient relationship Proponents of abortion-on-demand assert that anti-abortion laws unlawfully intrude into the privacy of the physician-patient relationship. They assume necessarily that the doctor treating a pregnancy owes an obligation of good medical care to only one patient, the pregnant woman.

In *Jones v. Jones*, 208 Misc. 721, 144 N.Y.S.2d 820 spout. 1955), the court stated (concerning an unborn child) as follows:

> "...became a patient of the mother's obstetrician, as well as the mother herself. In so holding, I can think of the infant as a third-party beneficiary of the mother-doctor contract or perhaps a principal for whom the mother acted as agent." 144 N.Y.S.2d at 826.

As a patient of the obstetrician, the child may recover damages for a prenatal injury suffered as the result of the negligence of his doctor. *Sylvia v. Gobeille*, 101 R.I. 76, 220 A.2d 222 (1966); *Seattle-First National Bank v. Rankin*, Wash. 2d 288, 367 P.2d 835 (1962). It is elemental that a doctor cannot be freed from legal restraints in making socio-moral judgments. The state may regulate the medical profession to protect the health and welfare of all its citizens. See *Wasmuth v. Allen*, 14 N.Y.2d 391, 200 N.E.2d 756, 252 N.Y.S.2d 65 (1964), appeal dismissed, 379 U.S. 11 (1964); *Barksy v. Board of Regents*, 347 U.S. 442 (1954). Appellant's contentions of intrusion upon physicians-patient relationship are not self-sustaining and must be associated with and connected to a violation of some basic right.

C. The interests of the woman Personal privacy is an exalted right but, as in marital privacy, it has never been regarded as absolute. A person may be subjected to a "stop and frisk" though it constitutes an intrusion upon his person,[66] or a person may be required to submit to a vaccination,[67] and a blood sample may forcibly be extracted from the body of an individual arrested for suspicion of driving while intoxicated.[68] A woman has been required to submit to a blood transfusion necessary to preserve her life in order that her small child shall not be left without a mother.[69] The "right of privacy" is a highly cherished right—however one which is nowhere expressly mentioned in the Constitution of the United States or its amendments. Numerous examples in tort and criminal law indicate the right to privacy is a relative right.[70] A woman cannot in privacy, even though she harm no other person, legally utilize or even posses certain forbidden drugs, such as LSD or heroin. The right to privacy was considered a mere relative right by the framers of the Constitution. Had they not considered the right to privacy a mere relative right, they would have carefully defined additional protection for the small portion of the right to privacy protected by the guarantee against unreasonable search and seizure. In *Katz v. United States*, 389 U.S. 347 (1967), referring to searches and seizures, stated that the Fourth Amendment to the Constitution of the United States cannot be translated into a general constitutional "right of privacy." See, *Lewis v. United States*, 385 U.S. 206 (1966).

When the "right of privacy" is attached to an "express right" such as the "right of freedom of religion" a very strong constitutional basis exists for upholding the "right"—except when in conflict with the most basic and fundamental of all rights—the "right to life." In *Raleigh Fitkin-Paul Morgan Memorial Hospital v. Anderson*, 42 N.J. 421, 201 A.2d 537 (1964), cert. denied, 377 U.S. 985 (1964), the New Jersey Supreme Court was asked to decide just such an issue—a conflict between the mother's privacy and the life of the unborn child. The issue was whether the rights of a child *in utero* were violated by the pregnant woman's refusal on religious grounds to submit to a blood transfusion necessary preserve the lives of both the mother and the unborn child. The Court's finding favored the right to life of the unborn child over the pregnant woman's freedom of religion and stated:

> "The blood transfusions (including transfusions made necessary by the delivery) may be administered if necessary to save her life or the life of the child, as the physician in charge at the time may determine." 201 A.2d at 538.

D. The human-ness of the fetus The crux of the moral and legal debate over abortion is, in essence, the right of the woman to determine whether or not she should bear a particular child versus the right of the child to life. The proponents of liberalization of abortion laws speak of

---

[66] *Terry v. Ohio*, 392 U.S. 1 (1968).

[67] *Jacobson v, Massachusetts*, 197 U.S. 11 (1905).

[68] *Schmerber v. California*, 384 U.S. 757 (1966).

[69] *Application of President and Directors of Georgetown, Col.*, 331 F.2d 1000 (D.C. Cir, 1966), cert. denied, 377 U.S. 978 (1964).

[70] See Tort Law limitations on the Right of Privacy as outlined in *Prosser on Torts*, 3rd Edition, 1964, Chapter.

the fetus as "a blob of protoplasm" and feel it has not right to life until it has reached a certain stage of development.[71] On the other hand, the opponents of liberalization maintain the fetus is human from the time of conception, and so interruption of pregnancy cannot be justified from the time of fertilization. It most certainly seems logical that from the stage of differentiation, after which neither twinning nor recombination will occur, the fetus implanted in the uterine wall deserves respect as a human life. If we take the definition of life as being said to be present when an organism shows evidence of individual animate existence, then from the blastocyst stage the fetus qualifies for respect. It is alive because it has the ability to reproduce dying cells. It is human because it can be distinguished from other non-human species, and once implanted in the uterine wall it requires only nutrition and time to develop into one of us.

The recent recognition of autonomy of the unborn child has led to the development of new medical specialties concerning the unborn child from the earliest stages of the pregnancy.[72*] Modern obstetrics has discarded as unscientific the concept that the child in the womb is but tissue of the mother. Dr. Liley, the New Zealand pediatrician, who perfected the intra-uterine transfusion, has said:

> "Another medical fallacy that modern obstetrics discards is the idea that the pregnant woman can be treated as a patient alone. No problem in fetal health or disease can any longer be considered in isolation. At the very least two people are involved, the mother and her child." Liley, H.M.I.: *Modern Motherhood*, Random House, Rev. Ed. 1969.

Yet the attack on the Texas statute assumes this discredited scientific concept and argues that abortions should be considered no differently than any medical measure taken to protect maternal health, (see appellants brief pp. 94–98) thus completely ignoring the developing human being in the mother's womb.

The court has also abandoned that concept in *Kelly v. Gregory*, 282 App.Div. 542, 125 N.Y.S.2d 696 (1953), wherein the court stated:

> "We ought to be safe in this respect in saying that legal separability should begin where there is biological separability. We know something more of the actual process of conception and fetal development now than when some of the common law cases were decided; and what we know makes it possible

to demonstrate clearly that separability begins at conception.

> "The mother's biological contribution from conception on is nourishment and protection; but the fetus has become a separate organism and remains so throughout its life. That it may not live if its protection and nourishment are cut off earlier than the viable stage of its development is not to destroy its separability; it is rather to describe the conditions under which life will not continue." 125 N.Y.S.2d at 697.

It is our task in the next subsections to show how clearly and conclusively modern science—embryology, fetology, genetics, perinatology, all of biology—establishes the humanity of the unborn child. We submit that the data not only shows the constitutionality of the Texas legislature's effort to save the unborn from indiscriminate extermination, *but in fact suggests a duty to do so*. We submit also that no physician who understands this will argue that the law is vague, uncertain or overbroad for he will understand that the law calls upon him to exercise his art for the benefit of his *two patients*: mother *and* child.

From conception the child is a complex, dynamic, rapidly growing organism. By a natural and continuous process the single fertilized ovum will, over approximately nine months, develop into the trillions of cells of the newborn. The natural end of the sperm and ovum is death unless fertilization occurs. At fertilization a new and unique being is created which, although receiving one-half of its chromosomes from each parent, is really unlike either.[73]

About seven to nine days after conception, when there are already several hundred cells of the new individual formed, contact with the uterus is made and implantation begins. Blood cells begin at 17 days and a hear as early as 18 days. This embryonic heart which begins as a

---

[71] This is given variously as from 12 weeks to 28 weeks of intrauterine life, and some apparently feel it has no life at all until after full-term delivery.

[72] Gairdner, Douglas: *Fetal Medicine: When Is To Practice It*, J. Obster, and Gynec. Brit. Commonwealth, 75:1123–1124, Dec. 1968.

*The citations in this and the following are according to Medical Journal Practice.

[73] Ingelman-Sundberg, Axel, and Wirsen, Cloes: *A Child Is Born: The Drama of Life Before Birth*, photos by Lennart Nilsson, Dell Publishing Co., New York, 1965. Arey, Leslie B.:*Developmental Anatomy*, 6th Ed. Philadelphia W.B. Saunders Co. 1954 Chap. II IV. Patten, Bradley M.: *Human Embryology*, 3rd Ed. McGraw-Hill Book Co. New York, 1968 Chap. VII.

simple tube starts irregular pulsations at 24 days, which, in about one week, smooth into a rhythmic contraction and expansion.[74] It has been shown that the ECG on a 23 mm embryo (7.5 weeks) presents the existence of a functionally complete cardiac system and the possible existence of a myoneurol or humor regulatory mechanism. All the classic elements of the adult ECG were seen.[75] Occasional contractions of the heart in a 6 mm (2 week) embryo have been observed as well as tracing exhibiting the classical elements of the ECG tracing of an adult in a 15 mm embryo (5 weeks).[76]

Commencing at 18 days the developmental emphasis is on the nervous system even though other vital organs, such as the heart, are commencing development at the same time. Such early development is necessary since of the nervous system integrates the action of all other systems. By the end of the 20th day the foundation of the child's brain, spinal cord and entire nervous system will have been established. By the 6th week after conception this system will have developed so well that it is controlling movement of the baby's muscles, even though the woman may not be aware that she is pregnant. By the 33rd day the cerebral cortex, that part of the central nervous system that governs motor activity as well as intellect may be seen.

The baby's eyes begin to form at 19 days. By the end of the first month the foundation of the brain, spinal cord, nerves and sense organs is completely formed. By the 28 days the embryo has the building blocks for 40 pairs of muscles situated from the base of its skull to the lower end of its spinal column. By the end of the first month the child has completed the period of relatively greatest size increase and the greatest physical change of a lifetime. He or she is ten thousand times larger than the fertilized egg and will increase its weight six billion times by birth, having in only the first month gone from the one cell state to millions of cells.[78]

Shettles and Rugh describes this first month of development as follows:

> "This, then, is the greatest planning period, when out of apparently nothing comes evidence of a well integrated individual, who will form along certain well tried patterns, but who will, in the end, be distinguishable from every other human being virtue of ultra microscopic chromosomal difference." Rugh, Robert, and Shettles, Landrum B., with Richard N. Einhorn: *From Conception To Birth: The Drama of Life's Beginnings, supra* at p. 35.

By the beginning of the second month the unborn child, small as it is, looks distinctly human. Yet, by this time the child's mother is not even aware that she is pregnant.[79]

As Shettles and Rugh state:

> "And as for the question, 'when does the embryo become human?' The answer is that is *always* had human potential, and *no other*, from the instant the sperm and the egg came together because of its chromosomes." (Emphasis in original). Id at p. 40.

At the end of the first month the child is about 1/4 of an inch in length. At 30 days the primary brain is present and the eyes, ears, and nasal organs have started to form. Although the heart is still incomplete, it is beating regularly and pumping blood cells through a closed vascular system.[80] The child and mother do not exchange blood, the child having from a very early point in its development its own and complete vascular system.[81]

U.S. SUPREME
COURT, 1971

BRIEF FOR
APPELLEE

[74] Ingelman-Sunberg, Axel and Wirsen, Cloes: *A Child Is Born: The Drama of Life Before Birth, supra.*

[75] Arey, Leslie B.: *Developmental Anatomy*, supra. Patten, Bradley M.: *Human Embryology*, supra. Rugh, Robert, and Shettles, Landrum B., with Ronald N. Einhorn: *From Conception To Birth: The Drama of Life's Beginnings*, Harper and Row, New York 1971. Straus, Rueben, et al: *Direct Electrocardiographic Recording of A Twenty-Three Millimeter Human Embryo*, The American Journal of Cardiology, September 1961, pp. 443–447.

[76] Marcel, M.P., and Exchaquet, J.P.: *L'Electrocardiogramme Du Foetus Human Avec Un Ca De Double Rythne Auriculair Verifie*, Arch. Mal. Couer, Paris 31: 504, 1938.

[77] Arey, Leslie B.: *Developmental Anatomy*, supra. Rugh, Robert, and Shettles, Landrum B., with Richard N. Einhorn:*From Conception To Birth: The Drama of Life's Beginnings*, supra. Flannagan, G.L.: *The First Nine Months Of Life*, Simon and Schuster, 1962.

[78] Arey, Leslie B.: *Developmental Anatomy*, supra. Patten, Bradley M.: *Human Embryology*, supra. Rugh, Robert, and Shettles, Landrum B., with Richard N. Einhorn: *From Conception To Birth: The Drama of Life's Beginnings*, supra. Ingelman-Sundberg, Axel, and Wirsen, Cloes: *A Child Is Born: The Drama Of Life Before Birth*, supra. Flannagan, G.L.: *The First Nine Months Of Life*, supra.

[79] Ingelman-Sundberg, Axel, and Wirsen, Cloes: *A Child Is Born: The Drama Of Life Before Birth*, supra.

[80] Arey Leslie B.: *Developmental Anatomy*, supra.

[81] Arey Leslie B.: *Developmental Anatomy*, supra. Patten Bradley M.: *Human Embryology*, supra. Rugh, Robert, and Shettles, Landrum B., with Richard N. Einhorn: *From Conception To Birth: The Drama of Life's Beginnings*, supra. Marcel, M.P., and Exhaquet, J.P.: *L'Electrocardiogramme Du Foetus Human Avec Un Cas De Double Rythme Auriculaire Verife*, supra. Flannagan, G.L.: *The First Nine Months of Life*, supra.

Earliest reflexes begin as early as the 42nd day. The male penis begins to form. The child is almost 1/2 inch long and cartilage has begun to develop.[82]

Even at 5 1/2 weeks the fetal heartbeat is essentially similar to that of an adult in general configuration. The energy output is about 20% that of the adult, but the fetal heart is functionally complete and normal by 7 weeks. Shettles and Rugh describe the child at this point of its development as a 1–inch miniature doll with a large head, but gracefully formed arms and legs and an unmistakably human face.[83]

By the end of the seventh week we see a well proportioned small scale baby. In its seventh week, it bears the familiar external features and all the internal organs of the adult, even though it is less an inch long and weighs only 1/30th of an ounce. The body has become nicely rounded, padded with muscles and covered by a thin skin. The arms are only as long as printed exclamation marks, and have hands with fingers and thumbs. The slower growing legs have recognizable knees, ankles and toes.[84]

The new body not only exists, it also functions. The brain in configuration is already like the adult brain and sends out impulses that coordinate the function of the other organs. The brain waves have been noted at 43 days.[85] The heart beast sturdily. The stomach produces digestive juice. The liver manufactures blood cells and the kidney begins to function by extracting uric acid from the child's blood.[86] The muscles of the arms and body can already be set in motion.[87]

After the eighth week no further primordia will form; *everything* is already present that will

be found in the full term baby.[88] As one author describes this period:

> "As human face with eyelids half closed as they are in someone who is about to fall asleep. Hands that soon will begin to grip, feet, trying their first gentle kicks." Rugh, Roberts, and Shettles, Landrum B., with Richard N. Einhorn: *From Conception To Birth: The Drama of Life's Beginnings*, supra at p. 71.

From this point until adulthood, when full growth is achieved somewhere between 25 and 27 years, the changes in the body will be mainly in dimension and in gradual refinement of the working parts.

The development of the child, while very rapid, is also very specific. The genetic pattern set down in the first day of life instructs the development of a specific anatomy. The ears are formed by seven weeks and are specific, and may resemble a family pattern.[90] The lines in the hands start to be engraved by eight weeks and remain a distinctive feature of the individual.[91]

The primitive skeletal system has completely developed by the end of six weeks.[92] This marks the end of the child's embryonic (from Greek, to swell or teem within) period. From this point, the child will be called a fetus (Latin, young one or off spring).[93]

In the third month, the child becomes very active. By end of the month he can kick his legs, turn his feet, curl and fan his toes, make a fist, move his thumb, bend his wrist, turn his head, squint, frown, open his mouth, press his lips tightly together.[94] He can swallow and drinks the amniotic fluid that surrounds him. Thumb sucking is first noted at this age. The first respiratory motions move fluid in and out of his

[82] Arey, Leslie B.: *Developmental Anatomy*, supra. Patten, Bradley M.:*Human Embryology*, supra.

[83] Rugh, Robert, and Shettles, Landrum B., with Richard N. Einhorn: *From Conception To Birth: The Drama of Life's Beginnings*, supra at p. 54.

[84] Arey Leslie B.: *Developmental Anatomy*, supra. Patten Bradley M.: *Human Embryology*, supra. Rugh, Robert, and Shettles, Landrum B., with Richard N. Einhorn: *From Conception To Birth: The Drama of Life's Beginnings*, supra. Ingelman-Sundberg, Axel, and Wirsen, Cloes: *A Child Is Born: The Drama Of Life Before Birth*, supra.

[85] Still, J.W.:J. Washington Acad. Sci, 59:46, 1969.

[86] Flannagan, G.L.: *The First Nine Months Of Life*, supra. Gesell, Arnold: *The Embryology of Behavior*, Harper and Bros. Publishers, 1945, Chap. IV, V, VI, X.

[87] Hooker, Davenport: *The Prenatal Origin of Behavior*, Univ. of Kansas Press, 1952.

[88] Rugh, Robert, and Shettles, Landrum B., with Richard N. Einhorn: *From Conception To Birth: The Drama of Life's Beginnings*, supra at p.71.

[89] Arey, Leslie B.: *Developmental Anatomy*, supra. Potter, Edith: *Pathology Of The Fetus And Infant*, Year Book Publishers Inc., Chicago, 1961.

[90] Streeter, Geo. L.: *Developmental Of The Auricle In The Human Embryo*, Contributions to Embryology, Vol. XIII No. 61, 1921.

[91] Miller, James, R.: *Dermal Ridge Patterns: Tecnique For Their Study In Human Fetuses*, J. Pediatric, Vol. 73, No. 4, Oct. 1969, pp. 6114–616.

[92] Arey, Leslie B.: *Developmental Anatomy*, supra. Patten, Bradley M.: *Human Embryology*, supra.

[93] Patten, Bradley M.: *Human Embryology*, supra.

[94] Hooker, Davenport: *The Prenatal Origin of Behavior*; supra.

lungs with inhaling and exhaling respiratory movements.

The movement of the child has been recorded at this early stage by placing delicate shock recording devices on the mother's abdomen and direct observations have been made by the famous embryologist, Davenport Hooker, M.D. Over the last thirty years, Dr. Hooker has recorded the movement of the child on film, some as early as six weeks of age. His films show that prenatal behavior develops in an orderly progression.

The prerequisites for motion are muscles and nerves. In the sixth to seventh weeks, nerves and muscles work together for the first time.[97] If the area of the lips, the first to become sensitive to touch, is gently stroked, the child responds by bending the upper body to one side and making a quick backward motion with his arms. This is called a total pattern response because it involves most of the body, rather than a local part. Localized and more appropriate reactions such as swallowing follow in the third month. By the beginning of the ninth week, the baby moves spontaneously without being touched. Sometimes his whole body swings back and forth for a few moments. By eight and a half weeks the eyelids and the palms of the hands become sensitive to touch. If the eyelid is stroked, the child squints. On stroking the palm, the fingers close into a small fist.[98]

In the ninth and tenth weeks, the child's activity leaps ahead. Now if the forehead is touched, he may turn his head away and pucker up his brow and frown. He know his full use of his arms, and can bend the elbow and wrist

independently. In the same week, the entire body becomes sensitive to touch.[99]

The twelfth week brings a whole new range of responses. The baby can now move his thumb in opposition to his fingers. He now swallows regularly. He can pull up his upper lip, the initial step in the development of the sucking reflex.[100] By the end of the twelfth week, the quality of muscular response is altered. It is no longer marionette-like or mechanical—the movements are now graceful and fluid, as they are in the newborn. The child is active and the reflexes are becoming more vigorous. All this is before the mother feels any movement.[101]

Every child shows a distinct individuality in his behavior by the end of the third month. This is because the actual structure of the muscles varies from baby to baby. The alignment of the muscles of the face, for example, follow an inherited pattern. The facial expressions of the baby in his third month are already similar to the facial expressions of his parents.[102]

Further refinements are noted in the third month. The fingernails appear. The child's face becomes much prettier. His eyes, previously far apart, now move closer together. The eyelids close over the eyes. Sexual differentiation is apparent in both internal and external sex organs, and primitive eggs and sperm are formed. The vocal cords are completed. In the absence of air they cannot produce sound; the child cannot cry aloud until birth, although he is capable of crying long before.[103]

From the twelfth to the sixteenth week, the child grows very rapidly.[104] His weight increases six times, and he grows to eight to ten inches in height. For this incredible growth spurt the child

---

[95] Flannagan, G.L.: *The First Nine Months Of Life*, supra. Hooker, Davenport: *The Prenatal Origin of Behavior*; supra

[96] Hooker, Davenport: *The Prenatal Origin of Behavior*; supra. Hooker, Davenport: *Early Human Fetal Behavior With A Preliminary Note On Double Simultaneous Fetal Stimulation*, Proceedings of the Association for Research in Nervous and Mental Disease, Baltimore The Williams and Wilkins Co., 1954. Gesell, Arnold, M.D., Amatruda, C.S., M.D.: *Developmental Diagnosis*, P.S. Hoeber, 1958 pp. 8–9.

[97] Arey, Leslie M.: *Developmental Anatomy*, supra.

[98] Hooker, Davenport: *Early Human Fetal Behavior With A Preliminary Note On Double Simultaneous Fetal Stimulation*, supra. Hooker Davenport: *The Prenatal Origin of Behavior*; supra. Flannagan, G.L.: *The First Nine Months Of Life*, supra. Hooker, Davenport: *The Origin Overt Behavior*, Ann Arbor, Univ. of Michigan Press, 1944.

[99] Hooker, Davenport: *The Prenatal Origin of Behavior*, supra.

[100] Gairdner, Douglas: *Fetal Medicine: Who Is To Practice It*, supra.

[101] Gairdner, Douglas: *Fetal Medicine: Who Is To Practice It*, supra. Hooker, Davenport: *The Origin Overt Behavior*; supra

[102] Flannagan, G.L.: *The First Nine Months Of Life*, supra. Still J.W.: J. Washington Acad. Sci., supra. Gesell, Arnold: *The Embryology of Behavior*, supra.

[103] Arey, Leslie M.: *Developmental Anatomy*, supra. Flannagan, G.L.: *The First Nine Months Of Life*, supra. Patten, Bradley M.: *Human Embryology*, supra. Gairdner, Douglas: *Fetal Medicine: Who Is To Practice It*, supra.

[104] Hellman, L.M., et al.: *Growth And Development Of The Human Fetus Prior To The 20th Week of Gestation*, Am. J. Obstet. and Gynec. Vol. 103, No. 6, March 15, 1969, pp. 789–800.

needs oxygen and food. This he receives from his mother through the placental attachment—much like he receives food from her after he is born. His dependence does not end with expulsion into the external environment.[105] We now know that he placenta belongs to the baby, not the mother, as was long thought.[106]

In the fifth month, the baby gains two inches in height and ten ounces in weight. By the end of the month he will be about one foot tall and will weigh one pound. Fine baby hair begins to grow on his eyebrows and on his head and a fringe of eyelashes appear. Most of the skeleton hardens. The baby's muscles become larger his mother finally perceives his many activities.[107] The child's mother come to recognize the movement and can feel the baby's head, arms and legs. She may even perceive a rhythmic jolting movement—fifteen to thirty per minute. This is due to the child his coughing.[108] The doctor can now hear the heartbeat with is stethoscope.[109]

The baby sleeps and wakes just as it will after birth.[110] When he sleeps he invariably settles into his favorite position called his "lie." Each baby has a characteristic lie[111] When he awakens he moves about freely in the buoyant fluid turning from side to side, and frequently head over heel. Sometimes his head will be up and sometimes it will be down. He may sometimes be aroused from sleep by external vibrations. He may wake up from a loud tap on the tub when his mother is taking a bath. A loud concert or the vibrations of a washing machine may also stir him into activity.[112] The child hears and recognizes his mother's voice before birth.[113] Movements of the mother, whether locomotive, cardiac or respiratory, are communicated to the child.[114]

In the sixth month, the baby will grow about two more inches, to become fourteen inches tall. He will also begin to accumulate a little fat under his skin and will increase his weight to a pound and three-quarters. This month the permanent teeth buds come in high in the gums behind the milk teeth. Now his closed eyelids will open and close, and his eyes look up, down and sideways. Dr. Liley of New Zealand feels that the child may perceive light through the abdominal wall.[115] Dr. Still has noted that electroencephalographic waves have been obtained in forty-three to forty-five day old fetuses, and so conscious experience is possible after this date.[116]

In the sixth month, the child develops a strong muscular grip with his hands. He also starts to breathe regularly and can maintain respiratory response for twenty-four hours if born prematurely. He may even have a slim change of surviving in an incubator. The youngest children known to survive were between twenty to twenty-five weeks old.[117] The concept of *viability* is not a static one. Dr. Andre Hellegers of Georgetown University states that 10% of children born between twenty weeks and twenty-four weeks gestation will survive.[118] Modern medical intensive therapy has salvaged many children that would have been considered non-viable only a few years ago. The concept of an artificial placenta may be a reality in the near future and will push the date of viability back even further, and perhaps to the earliest stages of gestation.[119] After twenty-four to twenty-eight weeks the child's chances of survival are much greater.

This review has covered the first six months of life. By this time the individuality of this human being should be clear to all unbiased

[105] Arey, Leslie M.: *Developmental Anatomy*, supra. Patten, Bradley M.: *Human Embryology*, supra.

[106] Gairdner, Douglas: *Fetal Medicine: Who Is To Practice It*, supra.

[107] Arey, Leslie M.: *Developmental Anatomy*, supra.

[108] Flannagan, G.L.: *The First Nine Months Of Life*, supra. Gairdner, Douglas: *Fetal Medicine: Who Is To Practice It*, supra.

[109] Arey, Leslie M.: *Developmental Anatomy*, supra. Flannagan, G.L.: *The First Nine Months Of Life*, supra.

[110] Petre-Quadens, O., et al.: *Sleep In Pregnancy: Evidence Of Fetal Sleep Characteristics*, J. Neurologic Science, 4:600–605, May, June, 1967.

[111] Gairdner, Douglas: *Fetal Medicine: Who Is To Practice It*, supra.

[112] Flannagan, G.L.: *The First Nine Months Of Life*, supra.

[113] Wood, Carl: *Weightlessness: Its Implications For The Human Fetus*, J. Obstetrics and Gynecology of the British

Commonwealth, 1970 Vol. 77, pp. 333–336. Liley, Albert W.: *Auckland MD To Measure Light And Sound Inside Uterus*, Medical Tribune Report, May 26, 1969.

[114] Wood, Carl: *Weightlessness: Its Implications For The Human Fetus*, supra.

[115] Liley, Albert W.: *Auckland MD To Measure Light And Sound Inside Uterus*, supra.

[116] Still, J.W,: Washington Acad. Sci., supra.

[117] Flannagan, G.L.: *The First Nine Months Of Life*, supra.

[118] Monroe, *Canadian Medical Association's Journal*, 1939. Hellegers, Andre. M.D.: *National Symposium On Abortion*, May 15, 1970, Prudential Plaza, Chicago, Illinois.

[119] Zapol, Warren, and Kolobow, Theodore: *Medical World News*, May 30, 1969. Alexander, D.P.; Britton, H.G.; Nixon, D.A.; *Maintenance Of Sheep Fetuses By An Extra Cororeal Circuit For Periods Up To 24 Hours*, Am. J. Obstet. and Gynec, Vol. 102, No. 7, Dec. 1968, pp. 969–975.

[120] *Fetology: The Smallest Patients, The Sciences*, published by

observers. When one views the present state of medical science, we find that the artificial distinction between born and unborn has vanished. The whole thrust of medicine is in support of the motion that the child in its mother is a distinct individual in need of the most diligent study and care, and that he is also a patient whom science and medicine treat just as they do any other person.

This review of the current medical status of the unborn serves us several purposes. Firstly, it shows conclusively the humanity of the fetus by showing that human life is a continuum which commences in the womb. There is no magic in birth. The child is as much a child in those several days before birth as he is those several days after birth. The maturation process, commenced in the womb, continues through the post-natal period, infancy, adolescence, maturity and old age. Dr. Arnold Gesell points out in his work that no king ever had any other beginning than have had all of us in our mother's womb.[121] Quickening is only a relative concept which depends upon the sensitivity of the mother, the position of the placenta, and the size of the child.*

VII. The state of Texas has a legitimate interest in prohibiting abortion except by medical advice for the purpose of "saving the life of the mother."

There seems little argument necessary if one can conclude the unborn child is a human being with birth but a convenient landmark in a continuing process—a bridge between two stages of life. The basic postulates from which the Appellees' arguments proceed are : (1) the pregnant woman has a right of control over her own body as a matter of privacy guaranteed to her by the Constitution of the United States; and (2) this right cannot be interfered with by the state since the state cannot demonstrate any compelling interest to justify its intrusion. The contrary position is the state's interest in preventing the arbitrary and unjustified destruction of an unborn child—a living human being in the very earliest stages of its development. Whatever personal right of privacy a pregnant woman may have with respect to the disposition and use of her body must be balanced against the personal right of the unborn child to life.

Whatever the metaphysical view of it is, or may have been, it is beyond argument the legal concepts as to the nature and rights of the unborn

child have drastically changed, based on expanded medical knowledge, over the last 2,500 years.

In addition to the provisions of 22 D C Code 201,[122] the Congress of the United States has clearly indicated a firm general policy of the Federal government against abortion: 18 U.S.C. 1461 provides in part as follows:

> "Every obscene, lewd, lascivious, indecent, filthy or vile article, matter, thing, device or substance; and—
>
> Every article, instrument, substance, drug medicine, or thing which is advertised or described in a manner calculated to lead another to use or apply it for preventing conception or producing *abortion*, or for any indecent or immoral purpose; and
>
> Every description calculated to induce or incite a person to so use or apply any such article, instrument, substance, drug, medicine, or thing—
>
> Is declared to be nonmailable matter and shall not be conveyed in the mails or delivered from any post office or by any letter carrier.
>
> . . . ." (Emphasis added).

It most seriously argued that the "life" protected by the Due Process of Law Clause of the Fifth Amendment includes the life of the unborn child. Further, it would be a denial of equal protection of law not to accord protection of the life of a person who had not yet been born but still in the womb of its mother. If it is a denial of equal protection for a statute to distinguish between a thief and an embezzler under a

---

the New York Academy of Sciences, Vol.8 No. 10, Oct. 1968, pp. 11–15. Gairdner, Douglas: *Fetal Medicine: Who Is To Practice It*, supra.

[121] Gesell, Arnold: *The Embryology Of Behavior*, supra. *If the court is interested in the actual medical history on nineteenth century legislative opposition to abortion, it may consult the American Medical Association, 1846–1951 *Digest of Official Actions* (edited F.J.L. Blasingame 1959), p. 66, where a list of the repeated American Medical Association attacks on abortion are compiled. It will be seen that the great medical battle of the nineteenth century was to persuade legislatures to eliminate the requirement of quickening and to condemn abortion from conception, see Isaac M. Quimbly *Introduction to Medical Jurisprudence*, Journal of American Medical Association, August 6, 1887, Vol. 9, p. 164 and H.C. Markham *Foeticide and Its Prevention*, ibid. Dec. 8, 1888, Vol. 11, p. 805. It will be seen that the Association unanimously condemned abortion as the destruction of "human life", American Medical Association, *Minutes of the Annual Meeting* 1859, The American Medical Gazette 1859, Vol. 10, p. 409.

[122] The District of Columbia abortion statute in issue in *United States v. Vuitch*

statute providing for the sterilization of the one and not the other,[123] then it is surely a denial of equal protection for either the state or federal government to distinguish between a person who has been born and one living in the womb of its mother.

In *Katz v. United States*, supra, this Court, after concluding that the Fourth Amendment cannot be translated into a general constitutional "right to privacy" and after making reference to other forms of governmental intrusion,[124] stated that ". . . the protection of a person's *general* right to privacy—his right to be let alone by other people—is, like the protection of his property and his very life, left largely to the law of the individual States." 389 U.S. at 352. Compare *Kovacs v. Cooper*, 336 U.S. 77 (1949).

If it be true the compelling state interest in prohibiting or regulating abortion did not exist at one time in the stage of history, under the result of the findings and research of modern medicine, a different legal conclusion can now be reached. The fact that a statute or law may originally have been enacted to serve one purpose does not serve to condemn it when the same statute, with the passage of time, serves a different but equally valid public purpose. See *McGowan v. Maryland*, 366 U.S. 420 (1961).

CONCLUSION

For the reasons above stated Appellee submits that the appeal from the judgment of the lower court denying injunctive relief to the appellants should be affirmed; that this Court consider plenary review of this entire case and reverse the judgment of the court below declaring Articles 1191, 1192, 1193, 1194, and 1196 of the Texas Penal Code unconstitutional and enters its order accordingly.

Respectfully submitted,

CRAWFORD C. MARTIN
Attorney General of Texas

HENRY WADE
Criminal District Attorney
Dallas County Government Center
Dallas County, Texas

JOHN B. TOLLE
Assistant District Attorney
Dallas County Government Center
Dallas, Texas 75202

NOLA WHITE
First Assistant Attorney General

ALFRED WALKER
Executive Assistant

ROBERT C. FLOWERS
Assistant Attorney General

JAY FLOYD
Assistant Attorney General
P.O. Box 12548, Capitol Station
Austin, Texas, 78711
Attorney for Appellee

---

[123] *Skinner v. Oklahoma*, 316 U.S. 535 (1942).
[124] Note 5 at page 510.

In the Supreme Court of the United States

NO. 70–18, 1972 TERM

—∾∾—

Jane Roe, John Doe, Mary Doe, and
James Hubert Hallford, M.D.
Appellants

v.

Henry Wade, District Attorney of Dallas County, Texas
Appellee

On Appeal from the United States District Court for
the Northern District of Texas

Supplemental Brief for Appellants

STATEMENT

The instant case was argued before this Court on December 13, 1971. It is a direct appeal from the decision of a three-judge federal panel declaring the Texas abortion law to be unconstitutional but refusing to grant injunctive relief and denying standing to Appellants Doe.

On June 27, 1972, the case was restored to the calendar for reargument. 40 U.S.L.W. 3617. Reargument is scheduled for October 11, 1972.

Several pertinent decisions have been rendered since the submission of Appellants' original brief. This supplemental brief is submitted to inform the Court of those decisions.

Request for injunctive relief

As to their request for injunctive relief, Appellants would once again point out that the injunction requested was one against *future* prosecutions only. Appellant Hallford had *not* requested injunctive relief to prevent continuation of the state criminal charge pending against him.

The continuing situation in Texas

Despite the District Court holding in June, 1970, that the Texas abortion law is unconstitutional, in November, 1971, the Texas Court of Criminal Appeals ('Texas' highest criminal court), in *Thompson v, State*, No. 44,071 (Tex. Ct. Crim. App., Nov. 2, 1971), *petition for cert. filed*, 40 U.S.L.W. 3532 (U.S. March 20, 1972) (No. 71–1200), rendered a decision which directly contradicted that of the District Court. Without interpreting the abortion statue, the Texas court held that the Texas law was not vague. It specifically did not reach the issue of privacy but held the State has a compelling interest in protecting the fetus through legislation.

Since the District Court refused to grant injunctive relief and since there is now a direct dichotomy between state federal decisions, Texas physicians continue to refuse to perform abortions for fear of prosecution. During the last nine months of 1971, 1,658 Texas women travelled to New York to obtain abortions. Texas women continue to be unable to obtain abortion procedures in Texas and thereby continue to suffer irreparable injury.

Actions regarding abortion

At its 1972 Midyear Meeting, the American Bar Association House of Delegates approved the Uniform Abortion Act as drafted by the National Conference of Commissioners on Uniform State Laws. 58 A.B.A.J. 380 (1972). The Uniform Abortion Act allows termination of pregnancy up to twenty weeks of pregnancy and thereafter for reasons such as rape, incest, fetal deformity, and the mental or physical health of the woman.

The Rockefeller Commission on Population and the American Future has recommended that the matter of abortion should be left to the conscience of the individual concerned. *Abele v. Markle*, 342 F. Supp. 800, 802 (D. Conn. 1972).

ARGUMENT

I. Recent cases support appellants' contentions regarding standing

In the oral argument before the three-judge panel, the attorney for Henry Wade, the sole defendant herein, admitted that Appellant Dr. Hallford has standing and that Appellant Roe has standing as an individual and as the representative of the class. (A. 104). The defendent-appellee did not accede standing to John and Mary Doe.

Several recent cases support Appellants' arguments regarding standing.

This Court, in *Eisenstadt v. Baird*, 405 U.S. 438 (1972) held that Appellee Baird had standing to assert the rights of unmarried persons denied access to contraceptives even though he was not a physician or pharmacist and was not an unmarried person denied access to contraceptives.

U.S. SUPREME
COURT, 1972

SUPPLEMENTAL
BRIEF FOR
APPELLANTS

Just as Baird was allowed to raise the rights of persons who were affected by the statute but who were affected but who were not subject to prosecution thereunder, here Appellant Hallford should be allowed to raise, in addition to his own constitutional claims, the claims of women who are vitally affected by the Texas abortion law but now subject to prosecution thereunder.

Young Women's Christian Association v. Kugler, 342 F.Supp. 1048 (D.N.J. 1972), declared the New Jersey abortion laws unconstitutional. Such laws prohibited persons from causing miscarriage "without lawful justification."

Saying that "the alleged deprivations of unconstitutional rights depend upon the contingency of pregnancy," 342 F.Supp. at 1056, the Court dismissed all the women plaintiffs since none alleged pregnancy. There is no indication that any had alleged status as persons wishing to give advice or assistance to women seeking abortions.

The Court recognized that all the physician plaintiffs, two of whom had lost their licenses to practice medicine and one of whom was incarcerated at the time of the action, had standing to raise the constitutional questions both on behalf of and pertaining to themselves and their women patients.

The plaintiff physicians alleged that they had been forced to turn away patients seeking advice and information about the possibility of obtaining abortions, as have Dr. Hallford and the classes he represents in the instant case. Dr. Hallford and his fellow physicians are also subject to prosecution under the law if they should perform an abortion that a jury finds was not for the purpose of saving the life of the woman.

Dr. Hallford should be recognized to have standing to litigate the constitutional claims of his class of physicians and those of women patients.

In *Abele v. Markle*, 342 F.Supp. 800 (D. Conn. 1972), the Connecticut anti-abortion statutes were declared to be unconstitutional. Much like the Texas law, the statutes prohibited all abortions except those necessary to preserve the life of the mother or fetus. Prior to the District Court's consideration of the merits the Circuit Court held that pregnant women and medical personnel desiring to give advice and aid regarding abortions had standing to challenge to statute. *Abele v. Markle*, 452 F.2d 1121 (2 Cir. 1971).

In this Texas case, Appellant Jane Roe was pregnant when the action was filed. Appellants John and Mary Doe in their complaint outlined their desire to actively participate in organizations giving advice and counselling regarding abortions, along with information to specifically assist in securing abortion. (A. 18). Although the Connecticut abortion laws more specifically applied to giving aid, advice, and encouragement to bring about abortion, Texas law is such that Appellants Doe have been effectively stopped from giving such aid, advice, and encouragement for fear of being subjected to prosecution under either 1 Texas Penal Code art. 70 (1952) as accomplices to the crime of abortion, or 3 Texas Penal Code art 1628 (1953) for conspiring to commit the crime of abortion. (A. 19). Like the Connecticut medical personnel desiring to give advice and aid regarding abortions, Appellants Doe should be recognized to have standing to challenge the Texas law.

In *Poe v. Menghini*, 339 F.Supp. 986 (D. Kan. 1972), the three-judge panel recognized that two women who were pregnant when the action was commenced and a doctor had standing to challenge certain restrictions applicable to the performance of abortions. In the instant case, Appellant Jane Roe, who was pregnant when the action was commenced, and Appellant Dr. Hallford would correspondingly have standing to challenge the Texas abortion laws.

Beecham v. Leahy, 287 A.2d 836 (Vt. 1972), declared unconstitutional the Vermont abortion law, which, like Texas law, made abortion a criminal offense unless the same is necessary to preserve the life of the woman. The Vermont statute stated that the woman was not liable to the penalties prescribed by the section.

The plaintiffs in *Beecham* were an unmarried pregnant woman who wanted an abortion and a physician who, except for the law, was willing to terminate the pregnancy but who had not done so and who (unlike Appellant Dr. Hallford) was not the subject of pending state criminal action. The Court held that unmarried pregnant woman had standing but that the physician did not. There is no indication in the opinion as to whether or not the physician sought to adjudicate the rights of his patients, which other cases have allowed.

Regarding the woman the Court said:

By reducing her rights to ephemeral status without confronting them, the ability of the plaintiff to produce a case or controversy in the ordinary sense is likewise frustrated. She cannot sue the doctor for an action by him that cannot be compelled. She is not herself subject to legal action, by statutory exemption. Yet a very real wrong, in the eyes of the law, exists . . . Therefore, . . . we declare that she is entitled to proceed in her action founded on her petition. . . .287 A.2d at 840.

Appellant Jane Roe was similarly found by the lower court to have standing. She, too, was pregnant, had sought but been unable to find a physician to terminate the pregnancy, was not subject to state prosecution, and yet had suffered a very real wrong.

II. The right to seek and receive medical care for the protection of health and well-being is a fundamental personal liberty

As shown in the original brief of Appellants, the Texas abortion law effectively denies Appellants Jane Roe and Mary Doe access to health care.

Although under Texas case law it is not a crime for a pregnant woman to terminate her own pregnancy or to persuade someone else to perform an abortion on her, the Texas law effectively denies her assistance of trained medical personnel in doing what she is otherwise legally allowed to do.

The Supreme Court in Vermont, in *Beecham v. Leahy, supra,* observed that:

> On the one hand the legislation, by specific reference, leaves untouched in the woman herself those rights respecting her own choice to bear children now coming to be recognized in many jurisdictions... *Yet, tragically, unless her life itself is at stake, the law leaves her only to the recourse of attempts at self-induced abortion, uncounselled and unassisted by a doctor, in a situation where medical attention is imperative.* 287 A.2d at 839 (emphasis added).

The woman is guilty of no crime in Texas, although by case law rather than by statute. Tragically, Texas women effectively prevented from securing the services of a doctor when medical expertise and experience are imperative to avoid such pitfalls as the piercing of the uterine wall and infection. By preventing the availability of medical assistance, the state effectively endangers the health and well-being of citizens in direct contravention of their best interests and fundamental rights.

III. The Texas abortion law violates fundamental rights of privacy

As the opinion of this Court in *Eisenstadt v. Baird, supra,* states:

> If the right of privacy means anything, it is the right of the *individual,* married or single, to be free from unwanted governmental intrusion into matters so fundamentally affecting a person as the decision whether to bear or begat a child. 405 U.S. 438.

In *Vuitch v. Hardy,* Civil No. 71–1129–Y (D. Md. June 22, 1972), the Court stated: "However, this Court is convinced that a woman does have a constitutionally protected, 'fundamental personal right' to seek an abortion," citing *Griswold* and the above language from Eisenstadt.

Y.W.C.A. v. Kugler, supra, resulted in the New Jersey abortion law being declared unconstitutional in part as a violation of rights of privacy.

> The scope of interests found to be constitutionally protected by the Supreme Court demonstrates that it views both the sanctity of the individual's person and his relationships within a family as so vital to our free society that they should be ranked as fundamental, or implicit in the concept of ordered liberty. 342 F.Supp at 1071.

> Accordingly, we are persuaded that the freedom to determine whether to bear a child and to terminate a pregnancy in its early stages is so significantly related to the fundamental individual and family rights already found to exist in the Constitution that it follows directly in their channel and requires recognition. Whether a constitutional right of privacy this area is conceptualized as a family right, as in *Griswold,* as a personal and individual right, or as deriving from both sources is of no significance and applies equally to all women regardless of marital status, for the restriction on abortion by the New Jersey statutes immediately involves and interferes with the protected areas of both family and individual freedom. Hence we hold that a woman has a constitutional right of privacy recognizable under the Ninth and Fourteenth Amendments to determine for herself whether to bear a child or to terminate a pregnancy in its early stages, free from unreasonable interference by the State. 342 F.Supp at 1072.

The fundamental impact of the question of abortion on women was emphasized by the *Abele* Connecticut panel:

> The decision to carry and bear a child has extraordinary ramifications for a woman. Pregnancy entails profound physical changes.

Childbirth presents some danger to life and health. Bearing and raising a child demands difficult psychological and social adjustments. The working or student mother must curtail or end her employment or educational opportunities. The mother with an unwanted child may find that it overtaxes her and her family's financial or emotional resources. *Thus, determining whether or not to bear a child is of fundamental importance to a woman.* 342 F.Supp. at 801 (emphasis added).

As the lower Court found in the instant case, the Texas abortion law must be declared unconstitutional because it deprives women of their right, secured by the Ninth and Fourteenth Amendments, to choose whether or not to carry a pregnancy to term.

I. The Texas statute does not advance any state interest of compelling importance in a manner which is narrowly drawn.

The legislative purposes that the Texas abortion law was meant to serve are not altogether clear. No legislative history specifically applicable to Texas is available.

Appellee during the oral argument before the lower court said the State has only one interest, that of protecting the unborn (A. 104–05). Appellee's brief and Dec. 13th argument before this Court advance no other State interest.

It is important to note that Appellee give no authority whatsoever that even tends to establish that the purpose of the Texas legislature in adopting the abortion law was in fact what Appellee suggests.

On the other hand, Appellants' original brief establish that the purpose of the Texas legislature in adopting the abortion law was in fact what Appellee suggests.

On the other hand, Appellants' original brief establishes that the legislative purpose in other states was to protect the pregnant woman from the dangers of antiseptic surgery.

Further *Watson v, State*, 9 Tex. App. 237 (Tex. Crim. App. 1880), states that the *woman* is the *victim* of the crime of abortion.

People v. Nixon, Dkt. No. 9579 (Ct. App. 2 Div., Aug. 23, 1972), involved a challenge to the constitutionality of the Michigan abortion statute making a criminal actions terminate a pregnancy unless the same was necessary to preserve the life of the woman. The Court concluded that the "so-called 'abortion' statute was not intended to protect the 'rights' of the unquick-ened fetus" but rather that the obvious purpose was to protect the pregnant woman.

The Court pointed out that the woman was not subject to prosecution for self-induced abortion and concluded:

> . . .it must be assumed that the harm the statute was attempting to punish ran only to the woman and not to the fetus. If the statute were intended to protect the continued existence of the fetus, then there would be no reason for exempting the woman from prosecution. Opinion at 4, n.9.

Similarly, since self-abortion is not a crime in Texas, it is not logical to assume that the purpose of the legislature in passing the so-called "abortion" law was to protect the fetus. It is logical that the legislative purpose was to protect the woman and her health.

Appellants' original brief establishes that the Texas abortion law no longer serves to protect the health of the pregnant woman; in fact it is a hindrance to health.

Even if Appellee could establish that the legislative purpose of the Texas abortion law was to protect the life of the unborn, the state certainly cannot meet its burden of proving that the statute now has a compelling interest in such regulation not that the law is sufficiently narrow.

The fetus, as such, is not and never has been protected in Texas, with the possible exception of the abortion statutes. In Texas, the so-called protections for the "unborn child" are dependent on the live birth of the child. Thus under Texas law, once born a child may have rights retroactive to the time prior to birth but such rights are meant to benefit those who have survived birth.

Under the criminal laws of Texas, the fetus is given little protection. Self-abortion is not a crime, and the pregnant woman who seeks or receives the help of others in terminating her pregnancy is guilty of no crime. Even the severity of the penalty for another having performed an abortion depends upon whether or not the woman consented to the procedure.

To destroy the life of a fetus has never been considered as homicide in Texas. In order to obtain a murder conviction, the state must ". . . prove that the child was born alive; (and) that it had an existence independent of the mother . . ." *Harris v, State*, 28 Tex. App. 308, 309, 12 S.W. 1102, 1103 (1889). In *Wallace v. State*, 7 Tex. App. 570, 10 S.W. 255 (1880), the mother strangled her child with string. The court overturned her murder conviction, saying that the state failed to prove either that the child was born live or that the actual childbirth process had been completed before the child was killed.

Texas courts are not alone in following the common law rule that a child must be born alive to be the subject of the crime of murder. *State v. Dickinson*, 28 Ohio St. 2d 65, 275 N.E.2d 599 (1971); *Keeler v. Superior Court*, 2 Cal. 3d 619, 470 P.2d 662, 87 Cal. Rptr. 481 (1970); *Clark v. State*, 117 Ala. 1, 23 So. 671 (1898); *Abrams v, Foshee*, Clark 274 (Iowa 1856). In those cases where a person has actually been convicted of a crime for causing the death of a fetus, it has not been under the regular homicide statute but under some special statutory provision, such as a feticide statute. Most feticide statutes have as one of their essential elements a *malicious intent to kill the mother. Passley v. State*, 194 Ga. 327, 21 S.E.2d 230 (1942); *State v. Harness*, 280 S.W.2d 11 (Mo. 1955). An intent to cause a miscarriage without an intent to kill the woman would not be sufficient to sustain a conviction of feticide. The penalties under such statutes are also generally lighter than those prescribed by the homicide laws.

Viewed from another angle, there are ironical contradictions between some Texas criminal laws, and the abortion law. As stated in *Abele v. Markle, supra*, "(t)he statutes force a woman to carry to natural term a pregnancy that is the result of rape or incest. Yet these acts are prohibited by the state at least in part to avoid the offspring of such unions." 342 F.Supp at 804.

Similarly, Texas makes rape and incest criminal offenses, 2A Texas Penal Code, art 1183 at 372 (1961), and 1 Texas Penal Code, art. 495, at 553 (1952), and prohibits the marriage of persons closely related, Texas Family Code section 2.21, at 17 (1971). Persons who have any infectious condition of syphilis or other veneral disease cannot obtain a marriage license. Texas Family Code, section 1.21, at 9, and 1.31 at 11 (1972).

The fetus gets no more protection under Texas tort laws than it does under Texas criminal law. The Texas courts did not recognize a right to recover for injuries received prior to birth until 1967 (113 years after the Texas abortion law was enacted) in *Leal v. C.C. Pitts Sand and Gravel, Inc.*, 429 S.W.2d 820 (Tex. 1967). *Leal* involved a wrongful death action brought by the parents of a child who died two days after birth as the result of pre-natal injuries received in an automobile collision. In allowing the wrongful death action, the Texas Supreme Court held that the child, *had it lived*, could have maintained an action for damages for the pre-natal injuries.

In *Delgado v. Yandell*, 468 S.W.2d 475 (Tex. Civ. App. 1971), the Texas Supreme Court approved the holding of the Court of Civil Appeals that a cause of action does exist for pre-natal injuries sustained at any pre-natal stage *provided the child is born alive and survives*. The damages in such a case are not paid to the fetus; they are compensation to a *living* child for having to spend all or a part of his life under a disability caused prior to birth by another's wrongful act.

Thus the claimed "rights" of the fetus in the tort area are actually rights which may only be exercised by a live child after birth or are the right of bereaved potential parents to be compensated for their loss.

Though much has been written concerning the property rights of the fetus, these rights are really legal fictions which have developed to protect the rights of living children. In order to receive the benefit of its supposed rights, the fetus must be born alive. There has never been a case in Texas where a fetus which stillborn or destroyed through miscarriage or abortion has been treated as a person for the purpose of determining property rights. When certain kinds of inheritances are involved, even unconceived children can be considered to have some property "rights" in that they may receive a legacy on their subsequent birth. *Byrn v. New York City Health & Hospitals Corp.*, No. 210 72 (Ct. App. 1972). However, this has not prevented the United States Supreme Court from finding a constitutional right on the part of a woman to practice contraception. *Griswold v. Connecticut*, 38 U.S. 479 (1965).

There are other areas where Texas does not treat a fetus as a person. For example, under the rules of the Texas Welfare Department, a needy pregnant woman cannot get welfare payments for her unborn child. The state compels the birth of the child, yet does not provide the assistance often needed to produce a healthy child.

Texas does not regard the fetus as a person and had made no attempt to put the fetus on an equal footing with a living child.

Several courts have recently dealt directly with the question of whether the fetus is a person within the meaning of the United States Constitution. Arguably this Court's opinion in *Vuitch* implicitly rejected the claim that the fetus is a person under the Fifth and Fourteenth Amendments.

McGarvey v. Magee-Womens Hospital, Civil Action No. 71–196 (W.D.Pa. Mar. 17, 1972), held that the embryo or fetus is not a person or citizen within the meaning of the Fourteenth Amendment or the Civil Rights Act.

In *Byrn v. New York City Health & Hospitals Corp., supra*, the issue whether children in embryo are and must be recognized as legal persons or entities entitled under the State and Federal Constitutions to a right to life. The Court's conclusion was the Constitution does not confer or require legal personality for the unborn.

The Appellee has failed to produce any authority for the proposition that the fetus is considered a person under the Constitution. There is evidence in the Constitution that "person" applies only to a live born person. The clause requiring a decennial census says "the whole number must be counted. U.S. Const. Art. I, § 2, Cl. 3. From the first census in 1790 to the present, census takers have counted only those born. Means, *The Phoenix of Abortional Freedom*, 17 N.Y.L. Forum 335, 402–03 (1971).

Although on its face, the Texas abortion law applies any time after conception, the Brief for Appellee submitted to this Court at page 30 states:

> It most certainly seems logical that from the stage of differentiation . . . the fetus implanted in the uterine wall deserves respect as a human life.

Here Appellee seems to suggest that the law should apply instead only after implantation. Yet on page 32 Appellee devotes a paragraph to describing the "child" during the seven to nine days *before* implantation. During oral argument Appellee suggested that the Texas hospitals intervene to terminate pregnancy when a rape victim is brought in (Tr. 47–48), although there is no exception for rape in the Texas statute.

Appellee's ambivalence is but on indication that the statute does not evidence a compelling interest which could not be protected by less restrictive means.

V. The Texas abortion law is unconstitutionally vague

In *Thompson v. State, supra*, the Texas Court of Criminal Appeals upheld the conviction of a physician who allegedly had performed an abortion. The court held, relying on *United States v. Vuitch*, 402 U.S. 62 (1971), that the Texas abortion law was not vague.

The Court in *Thompson* erred. Whether or not a statute is vague is to be determined from the standpoint of the person who is considering performing an act. The Supreme Court in *Vuitch* emphasized that a doctor's day-to-day task was one of consideration for the *health* of his patients; the District of Columbia statute allowed physicians to act to preserve the life or *health* of patients. Texas, however, allows physicians to act only when necessary to protect *life*; that is not the sort of criteria physicians are accustomed to dealing with. From the physician's standpoint, as the District Court in this case pointed out, there are many uncertainties inherent in the language of the statute. Vuitch is not authority for upholding the Texas abortion law.

Further, in *Vuitch* the Court upheld the D.C. statute as interpreted by the lower courts to include both mental and physical health. In Texas there has been no interpretation of the Texas statute. *Thompson* does not even discuss application of the statute.

Recent decisions have declared laws in New Jersey and Florida to be unconstitutionally vague. In *Y.W.C.A. v. Kugler, supra*, a federal panel declared vague to the New Jersey statute against performing an abortion "unless the same shall have been necessary to preserve the life of the mother" was declared unconstitutionally vague by the Florida Supreme Court in *State v. Barquet*, 262 So.2d 432 (1972).

The Florida court said that "if the statutes contained a clause reading 'necessary to the preservation of the mother's life *or health*' instead of the clause necessary 'to preserve *the* life,' the statutes could be held constitutional. . ." 262 So.2d at 433.

Chaney v. Indiana, No. 1171 S 321 (Ind. July 24, 1972), however, rejects the vagueness arguments as to a non-medical person.

VI. The Texas abortion law places an unconstitutional burden of proof in the physician

Appellant's original brief details the unconstitutionality of placing upon the physician charged with allegedly performing an abortion the burden of showing that the procedure was necessary for the purpose of saving the life of the woman. Although the burden of proof issue was not before, them, the Texas Court of Criminal Appeals in a footnote in *Thompson, supra*, recognized that the *Vuitch* case does call into question the validity of Texas' statutory scheme as to who has the burden of proof on the exemption.

CONCLUSION

For the reasons stated in Appellants' original brief and this supplemental brief, this Court should reverse the lower court's judgment denying standing to Appellants Doe and denying injunctive relief; declare that the Texas Abortion Statutes, Art 1191, 1192, 1193, 1194 and 1196, Texas Penal Code, violate the United States Constitution; and remand with instructions that a permanent injunction against enforcement of said statutes be entered.

Respectfully submitted,

ROY LUCAS
Law Institutional Madison Constitutional Law Institute
230 Twin Peaks Blvd.
San Francisco, California 94114

SARAH WEDDINGTON
JAMES R. WEDDINGTON
709 West 14th
Austin, Texas 78701

LINDA N. COFFEE
2130 First Nat'l Bank Bldg.
Dallas, Texas 75202

FRED BRUNER
ROY L. MERRILL, JR.
Daughtery, Bruner, Lastelick and Anderson
1130 Mercantile Bank Bldg.
Dallas, Texas 75201
Attorneys for Appellants

U.S. SUPREME
COURT, 1972

SUPPLEMENTAL
BRIEF FOR
APPELLANTS

U.S. SUPREME
COURT,
JANUARY 1973

Roe v. Wade

CITE AS 93 S.CT. 705 (1973)

—⚓—

410 U.S. 113, 35 L.Ed.2d 147

Jane Roe, et al., Appellants,
v.
Henry Wade.
No. 70–18.

Argued Dec. 13, 1971.
Reargued Oct. 11, 1972.
Decided Jan. 22, 1973.

Rehearing Denied Feb. 26, 1973.
See 410 U.S. 959, 93 S.Ct. 1409.

Action was brought for a declaratory and injunctive relief respecting Texas criminal abortion laws which were claimed to be unconstitutional. A three-judge United States District Court for the Northern District of Texas, 314 F.Supp. 1217, entered judgment declaring laws unconstitutional and an appeal was taken. The Supreme Court, Mr. Justice Blackmun, held that the Texas criminal abortion statutes prohibiting abortions at any stage of pregnancy except to save the life of the mother are unconstitutional; that prior to approximately the end of the first trimester the abortion decision and its effectuation must be left to the medical judgement of the pregnant woman's attending physician, subsequent to approximately the end of the first trimester the state may regulate abortion procedure in ways reasonably related to maternal health, and at the stage subsequent to viability the state may regulate and even proscribe abortion except where necessary in appropriate medical judgment for preservation of life or health of mother.

Affirmed in part and reversed in part.

Mr. Chief Justice Burger, Mr. Justice Douglas and Mr. Justice Stewart filed concurring opinions.

Mr. Justice White filed a dissenting opinion in which Mr. Justice Rehnquist joined.

Mr. Justice Rehnquist filed a dissenting opinion.

Supreme Court was not foreclosed from review of both the injunctive and declaratory aspects of case attacking constitutionally of Texas criminal abortion statutes where case was properly before Supreme Court on direct appeal from decision of three-judge district court specifically denying injunctive relief and the arguments as to both aspects were necessarily identical. 28 U.S.C.A. 1253.

With respect to single, pregnant female who alleged that she was unable to obtain a legal abortion in Texas, when viewed as of the time of filing of case and for several months thereafter, she had standing to challenge constitutionality of Texas criminal abortion laws, even though record did not disclose that she was pregnant at time of district court hearing or when the opinion and judgment were filed, and she presented a justiciable controversy; the termination of her pregnancy did not render case moot. Vernon's Ann.Tex.P.C. arts. 1191–1194, 1196.

Usual rule in federal cases is that an actual controversy must exist at stages of appellate or certiorari review and not simply at date action is initiated.

Where pregnancy of plaintiff was a significant fact in litigation and the normal human gestation period was so short that pregnancy would come to term before usual appellate process was complete, and pregnancy often came more than once to the same woman, fact of that pregnancy provided a classic justification for conclusion of nonmootness because of termination.

Texas physician, against whom there were pending indictments charging him with violations of Texas abortion laws who made no allegation of any substantial and immediate threat to any federally protected right that could not be asserted in his defense against state prosecutions and who had not alleged any harassment or bad faith prosecution, did not have standing to intervene in suit seeking declaratory and injunctive relief with respect to Texas abortion statutes which were claimed to be unconstitutional. Vernon's Ann.Tex.P.C. arts. 1191–1194, 1196.

Absent harassment and bad faith, defendant in pending state criminal case cannot affirmatively challenge in federal court the statutes under which state is prosecuting him.

Application for leave to intervene making certain assertions relating to a class of people was insufficient to establish party's desire to intervene on behalf of class, where the complaint failed to set forth the essentials of class suit.

Childless married couple alleging that they had no desire to have children at the particular time because of medical advice that the wife should avoid pregnancy and for other highly personal reasons and asserting an inability to obtain a legal abortion in Texas were not, because of the highly speculative character of their position, appropriate plaintiffs in federal district court suit challenging validity of Texas criminal abortion statutes. Vernon's Ann.Tex.P.C. arts. 1191–1194, 1196.

Right to personal privacy or a guarantee of certain areas or zones of privacy does exist under Constitution, and only personal rights that can be deemed fundamental or implicit in the concept of odered liberty are included in this guarantee of personal privacy; the right has some extension to activities relating to marriage. U.S.C.A.Const. Amends. 1, 4, 5, 9, 14, 13, § 1.

Constitutional right to privacy is broad enough to encompass woman's decision whether or not to terminate her pregnancy, but the woman's right to terminate pregnancy is not absolute since state may properly assert important interests in safeguarding health, in maintaining medical standards and in protecting potential life, and at some point in pregnancy these respective interests become sufficiently compelling to sustain regulation of factors that govern the abortion decision. U.S.C.A.Const. Amends. 9, 14.

Where certain fundamental rights are involved, regulation limiting these rights may be justified only by a compelling state interest and the legislative enactments must be narrowly drawn to express only legitimate state interests at stake.

Word "person" as used in the Fourteenth Amendment does not include the unborn. U.S.C.A.Const. Amend. 14.

Prior to approximately the end of the first trimester of pregnancy the attending physician in consultation with his patient is free to determine, without regulation by state, that in his medical judgment the patient's pregnancy should be terminated, and if that decision is reached such judgment may be effectuated by an abortion without interference by the state.

From and after approximately the end of the first trimester of pregnancy a state may regulate abortion procedure to extent that the regulation reasonably relates to preservation and protection of maternal health.

If state is interested in protecting fetal life after viability it may go so far as to proscribe abortion during that period except when necessary to preserve the life or the health of the mother.

State criminal abortion laws like Texas statutes making it a crime to procure or attempt an abortion except an abortion on medical advice for purpose of saving life of the mother regardless of stage of pregnancy violate due process clause of Fourteenth Amendment protecting right to privacy against state action. U.S.C.A.Const. Amend, 14; Vernon's Ann.Tex.P.C. arts. 1191–1194, 1196.

State in regulating abortion procedures may define "physician" as a physician currently licensed by State and may proscribe any abortion by a person who is not a physician as so defined.

Conclusion that Texas criminal abortion statue proscribing all abortions except to save life of mother is unconstitutional meant that the abortion statutes as a unit must fall, and the exception could not be struck down separately for then the state would be left with statue proscribing all abortion procedures no matter how medically urgent the case. Vernon's Ann.Tex.P.C. arts. 1191–1194, 1196.

SYLLABUS*

A pregnant single woman (Roe) brought a class action challenging the constitutionality of the Texas criminal abortion laws, which proscribe procuring or attempting an abortion except on medical advice for the purpose of saving the mother's life. A licensed physician (Hallford), who had two state abortion prosecutions pending against him, was permitted to intervene. A childless married couple (the Does), the wife not being pregnant, separately attacked the laws, basing alleged injury on the future possibilities of contraceptive failure, pregnancy, unpreparedness for parenthood, and impairment of the wife's health. A three-judge District Court, which consolidated the actions,

---

* The syllabus constitutes no part of the opinion of the Court but has been prepared by the Reporter of Decisions for the convenience of the reader. See United States v. Detroit Timber & Lumber Co., 200 U.S. 321, 337, 26 S.Ct. 282, 287, 50 L.Ed. 409.

held that Roe and Hallford, and members of their classes, had standing to sue and presented justiciable controversies. Ruling that declaratory, thought not injunctive, relief was warranted, the court declared the abortion statutes void as vague and overbroadly infringing those plaintiffs' Ninth and Fourteenth Amendment rights. The court ruled the Does' complaint not justiciable. Appellants directly appealed to this Court on the injunctive rulings, and appellee cross-appealed from the District Court's grant of declaratory relief to Roe and Hallford. *Held*:

1. While 28 U.S.C. § 1253 authorizes no direct appeal to this Court from the grant or denial of declaratory relief alone, review is not foreclosed when the case is properly before the Court on appeal from specific denial of injunctive relief and the arrangements as to both injunctive and declaratory relief are necessarily identical. pp. 711–712.

2. Roe has standing to sue; the Does and Hallford do not. pp. 712–715.

(a) Contrary to appellees's contention, the natural termination of Roe's pregnancy did not moot her suit. Litigation involving pregnancy, which is "capable of repetition, yet evading review," is an exception to the usual federal rule that an actual controversy must exist at review stages and not simply when the action is initiated. pp. 712–713.

(b) The District Court correctly refused injunctive, but erred in granting declaratory, relief to Hallford, who alleged no federally protected right not assertable as a defense against the good-faith state prosecutions pending against him. Samuels v. Mackell, 401 U.S. 66, 91 S.Ct. 764, 27 L.Ed.2d 688. pp. 713–714.

(c) The Does' complaint, based as it is on contingencies, any one or more of which may not occur, is too speculative to present an actual case or controversy.

3. State criminal abortion laws, like those involved here, that except from criminality only a life-saving procedure on the mother's behalf without regard to the stage of her pregnancy and other interests involved violate the Due Process Clause of the Fourteenth Amendment, which protects against state action the right to privacy, including a woman's qualified right to terminate her pregnancy. Though the State cannot override that right, it has legitimate interests in protecting both the pregnant woman's health and the potentiality of human life, each of which interests grows and reaches a "compelling" point at various stages of the woman's approach to term. pp. 726–732.

(a) For the stage prior to approximately the end of the first trimester, the abortion decision and its effectuation must be left to the medical judgment of the pregnant woman's attending physician. pp. 731–732.

(b) For the stage subsequent to approximately the end of the first trimester, the State, in promoting its interest in the health of the mother, may, if it chooses, regulate the abortion procedure in ways that are reasonably related to maternal health. pp. 731–732.

(c) For the stage subsequent to viability the State, in promoting its interest in the potentiality of human life, may, if it chooses, regulate, and even proscribe, abortion except where necessary, in appropriate medical judgment, for the preservation of the life or health of the mother. pp. 732–733.

4. The State may define the term "physician" to mean only a physician currently licensed by the State, and may proscribe any abortion by a person who is not a physician as so defined. pp. 732–733.

5. It is unnecessary to decide the injunctive relief issue since the Texas authorities will doubtless fully recognize the Court's ruling that the Texas criminal abortion statutes are unconstitutional. p. 733.

314 F.Supp. 1217, affirmed in part and reversed in part.

Sarah R. Weddington, Austin, Tex., for appellants.

Robert C. Flowers, Asst. Atty. Gen. of Texas, Austin, Tex., for appellee on reemergence.

Jay Floyd, Asst. Atty. Gen., Austin, Tex., for appellee on original argument.

Mr. Justice BLACKMUN delivered the opinion of the Court.

This Texas federal appeal and its Georgia companion, Doe v. Bolton, 410 U.S. 179, 93 S.Ct. 739, 35 L.Ed.2d 201, present constitutional challenges to state criminal abortion legislation. The Texas statutes under attack here are typical of those that have been in effect in many States for approximately a century. The Georgia statutes, in contrast, have a modern cast and are a legislative product that, to an extent at least, obviously reflects the influences of recent attitudinal change, of advancing medical knowledge and techniques, and of new thinking about an old issue.

We forthwith acknowledge our awareness of the sensitive and emotional nature of the abortion controversy, of the vigorous opposing views, even among physicians, and of the deep and seemingly absolute convictions that the subject inspires. One's philosophy, one's experiences, one's exposure to the raw edges of human existence, one's religious training, one's attitudes toward life and family and their values, and the moral standards one establishes and seeks to observe, are all likely to influence and to color one's thinking and conclusions about abortion.

In addition, population growth, pollution, poverty, and racial overtones tend to complicate and not to simplify the problem.

Our task, of course, is to resolve the issue by constitutional measurement, free of emotion and of predilection. We seek earnestly to do this, and because we do, we have inquired into, and in this opinion place some emphasis upon, medical and medical-legal history and what that history reveals about man's attitudes toward the abortion procedure over the centuries. We bear in mind, too, Mr. Justice Holmes' admonition in his now-vindicated dissent in Lochner v. New York, 198 U.S. 45, 76, 25 S.Ct. 539, 547, 49 L.Ed. 937 (1905):

"[The Constitution] is made for people of fundamentally differing views, and the accident of our finding certain opinions natural and familiar, or novel, and even shocking, ought not to conclude our judgment upon the question whether statutes embodying them conflict with the Constitution of the United States."

I

The Texas statutes that concern us here art Arts. 1191–1194 and 1196 of the State's Penal Code,[1] Vernon's Ann.P.C. these make it a crime to "procure an abortion," as therein defined, or to attempt one, except with respect to "an abortion procured or attempted my medical advice for the purpose of saving the life of the mother." Similar statutes are in existence in a majority of the States.[2]

Texas first enacted a criminal abortion statue in 1854. Texas Laws 1854, c. 49, § 1, set forth in 3 H. Gammel, Laws of Texas 1502 (1898). This was soon modified into language that has remained substantially unchanged to the present time. See Texas Penal Code of 1857, c. 7, Arts. 531–536; G. Paschal, Laws of Texas, Arts. 2192–2197 (1866); Texas Rev.Stat., c. 8, Arts. 536–541 (1879); Texas Rev.Crim.Stat., Arts. 1071–1076 (1911). The final article in each of these compilations provided the same exception, as does the present Article 1196, for an abortion by "medical advice for the purpose of saving the life of the mother."[3]

II

Jane Roe[4] a single woman who was residing in Dallas County, Texas, instituted this federal

---

[1] "Article 1191. Abortion.

"If any person shall designedly administer to a pregnant woman or knowingly procure to be administered with her consent any drug or medicine, or shall use towards her any violence or means whatever externally or internally applied, and thereby procure an abortion, he shall be confined in the penitentiary not less than two nor more than five years; if it be done without her consent; the punishment shall be doubled. By 'abortion' is meant that the life of the fetus or embryo shall be destroyed in the woman's womb or that a premature birth thereof be caused.

"Art. 1192. Furnishing the means."

"Whoever furnishes the means for procuring an abortion knowing the purpose is intended is guilty as an accomplice."

"Art. 1193. Attempt at abortion."

"If the means used shall fail to produce an abortion, the offender is nevertheless guilty of an attempt to produce abortion, provided it be shown that such means were calculated to produce that result, and shall be fined not less than one hundred nor more than one thousand dollars."

"Art. 1194. Murder in producing abortion."

"If the death of the mother is occasioned by an abortion so produced or by an attempt to effect the same it is murder."

"Art. 1196. By medical advice."

"Nothing in this chapter applies to an abortion procured or attempted by medical advice for the purpose of saving the life of the mother."

The foregoing Articles, together with Art. 1195, compose Chapter 9 of title 15 of the Penal Code. Article 1195, not attacked here reads:

"Art. 1195. Destroying unborn child."

"Whoever shall during parturition of the mother destroy the vitality or life in a child in a state of being born and before actual birth, which child would otherwise have been born alive, shall be confined in the penitentiary for life or for not less than five years."

[2] Ariz.Rev.Stat.Ann. § 13–211 (1956); Conn.Pub.Act No. 1 (May 1972 special session) (in 4 Conn.Leg.Serv. 677 (1972)), and Conn.Gen.Stat.Rev. §§ 53–29, 53–30 (1968) (or unborn child); Idaho Code § 18–601 (1948); Ill.Rev. Stat., c. 38, § 23–1 (1971); Ind.Code § 35–158–1 (1971); Ky.Rev.Stat. § 436.020 (1962); La.Rev.Stat. § 37:1285(6) (1964) (loss of medical license) (but see § 14–87 (Supp.1972) containing no exception for the life of the mother under the criminal statute); Me.Rev.Stat.Ann., Tit. 17, § 51 (1964); Mass.Gen. Laws Ann., c. 272, § 19 (1970) (using the term "unlawfully"

U.S. SUPREME
COURT,
JANUARY 1973

action in March 1970 against the District Attorney of the county. She sought a declaratory judgment that the Texas criminal abortion statutes were unconstitutional on their face, and an injunction restraining the defendant from enforcing the statutes.

Roe alleged that she was unmarried and pregnant; that she wished to terminate her pregnancy by an abortion "performed by a competent, licensed physician, under safe, clinical conditions"; that she was unable to get a "legal" abortion in Texas because her life did not appear to be threatened by the continuation of her pregnancy; and that she could not afford to travel to another jurisdiction in order to secure a legal abortion under safe conditions. She claimed that the Texas statutes were unconstitutionally vague and that they abridged her right of personal privacy, protected by the First, Fourth, Fifth, Ninth, and Fourteenth Amendments. By an amendment to her complaint Roe purported to sue "on behalf of herself and all other women similarly situated."

James Hubert Hallford, a licensed physician, sought and was granted leave to intervene in Roe's action. In his complaint he alleged that he had been arrested previously for violations of the Texas abortion statutes and that two such prosecutions were pending against him. He described conditions of patients who came to him seeking abortions, and he claimed that for many cases he, as a physician, was unable to determine whether they fell within or outside the exception recognized by Article 1196. He alleged that, as a consequence, the statutes were vague and uncertain, in violation of the Fourteenth Amendment, and that they violated his own and his patients' rights to privacy in the doctor-patient relationship and his own right to practice medicine, rights he claimed were guaranteed by the First, Fourth, Fifth, Ninth, and Fourteenth Amendments.

John and Mary Doe,[5] a married couple, filed a companion complaint to that of Roe. They also named the District Attorney as defendant, claimed like constitutional deprivations, and sought declaratory and injunctive relief. The Does alleged that they were a childless couple; that Mrs. Doe was suffering from a "neural-chemical" disorder; that her physician had "advised her to avoid pregnancy until such time as her condition has materially improved" (although a pregnancy at the present time would not present "a serious risk" to her life); that, pursuant to medical advice, she had discontinued use of birth control pills; and that if she should become pregnant, she would want to terminate the pregnancy by an abortion performed by a competent, licensed physician under safe, clinical conditions. By an amendment to sue "on behalf of themselves and all couples similarly situated."

---

construed to exclude an abortion to save the mother's life, Kudish v. Bd. of Registration, 356 Mass. 98, 248 N.E.2d 264 (1969); Mich.Comp.Laws § 750.14 (1948); Minn.Stat. § 617.18 (1971); Mo.Rev.Stat. § 559.100 (1969); Mont.Rev. Codes Ann. § 94–401 (1969); Neb.Rev.Stat. § 28–405 (1964); Nev.Rev. Stat. § 200.220 (1967); N.H.Rev.Stat. Ann. § 585:13 (1955); N.J.Stat.Ann. § 2A:87–1 (1969) ("without lawful justification"); N.D.Cent.Code §§ 12–25–01, 12–25–02 (1960); Ohio Rev.Code Ann. § 2901.16 (1953); Okla.Stat.Ann., Tit. 21, § 861 (1972–1973 Supp.); Pa.Stat. Ann., Tit 18, §§ 4718, 4719 (1963) ("unlawful"); R.I.Gen.Laws Ann. § 11–3–1 (1969); S.D.Comp.Laws Ann. § 22–17–1 (1967); Tenn.Code Ann. §§ 39–301, 39–302 (1956); Utah Code Ann. §§ 76–2–1, 76–2–2 1953); Vt.Stat.Ann., Tit. 13, § 101 (1958); W.Va.Code. Ann. § 61–2–8 (1966); Wis.Stat. § 940.04 (1969); Wyo.Stat.Ann. §§ 6–77, 6–78 (1957).

[3] Long ago, a suggestion was made that the Texas statutes were unconstitutionally vague because of definitional deficiencies. The Texas Court of Criminal Appeals disposed of that suggestion peremptorily, saying only,

"It is also insisted in the motion in arrest of judgment that the statue in unconstitutional and void, in that it does not sufficiently define or describe the offense of abortion. We do not concur with counsel in respect to this question." Jackson v. State, 55 Tex.Cr.R. 79, 89, 115 S.W. 262, 268 (1908).

The same court recently has held again that the State's abortion statutes are not unconstitutionally vague or overboard. Thompson v. State, 493 S.W.2d 913 (1971), appeal docketed, No. 7101200. The court held that "the State of Texas has a compelling interest to protect fetal life"; the Art. 1191 "is designed to protect fetal life"; that the Texas homicide statutes, particularly Art. 1205 of the Penal Code, are intended to protect a person "in existence by actual birth" and thereby implicitly recognize other human life that is not "in existence by actual birth"; that the definition of human life is for the legislature and not the courts; that Art. 1196 "is more definite than the District of Columbia statute upheld in [United States v.] Vuitch" (402 U.S. 62, 91 S.Ct. 1294, 28 L.Ed.2d 601); and that the Texas statute "is not vague and indefinite or overboard." A physician's abortion conviction was affirmed.

In 493 S.W.2d, at 920 n. 2, the court observed that any issue as to the court observed that any issue as to the burden of proof under the exemption of Art. 1196 "is not before us." But see Veevers v. State, 172 Tex.Cr.R. 162, 168–169, 354 S.W.2d 161, 166–167 (1962). Cf. United States v. Vuitch, 402 U.S. 62, 69–71, 91 S.Ct. 1294, 1298–1299, 28 L.Ed.2d 601 (1971).

[4] The name is a pseudonym.

[5] These names are pseudonyms.

The two actions were consolidated and heard together by a duly convened three-judge district court. The suits thus presented the situations of the pregnant single woman, the childless couple, with the wife not pregnant, and the licensed practicing physician, all joining in the attack on the Texas criminal abortion statutes. Upon the filing of affidavits, motions were made for dismissal and for summary judgment. The court held that Roe and members of her class, and Dr. Hallford, had standing to sue and presented justiciable controversies, but that the Does had failed to allege facts sufficient to state a present controversy and did not have standing. It concluded that, with respect to the requests for a declaratory judgment, abstention was not warranted. On the merits, the District Court held that the "fundamental right of single women and married persons to choose whether to have children is protected by the Ninth Amendment, through the Fourteenth Amendment," and that the Texas criminal abortion statutes were void on their face because they were both unconstitutionally vague and constituted an overbroad infringement of the plaintiff's Ninth Amendment rights. The court then held that abstention was warranted with respect to the requests for an injunction. It therefore dismissed the Does' complaint, declared the abortion statutes void, and dismissed the application for injunctive relief. 314 F.Supp. 1217, 1225 (N.D. Tex.1970).

The plaintiffs Roe and Doe and the intervenor Hallford, pursuant to 28 U.S.C. § 1253, have appealed to this Court from the part of the District Court's judgment denying the injunction. The defendant District Attorney has purported to cross-appeal, pursuant to the same statue, from the court's grant of declaratory relief to Roe and Hallford. Both sides also have taken protective appeals for the Fifth Circuit. That court ordered the appeals held in abeyance pending decision here. We postponed decision on jurisdiction to the hearing on the merits. 402 U.S. 941, 91 S.Ct. 1610, 29 L.Ed.2d 108 (1971).

III

It might have been preferable if the defendant, pursuant to our Rule 20, had presented to us a petition for certiorari before judgment in the Court of Appeals with respect to the granting of the plaintiffs' prayer for declaratory relief. Our decisions in Mitchell v. Donovan, 398 U.S. 427, 90 S.Ct. 1763, 26 L.Ed.2d (1970), and Gunn v. University Committee, 399 U.S. 383, 90 S.Ct. 2013, 26 L.Ed.2d 684 (1970), are to the effect that § 1253 does not authorize an appeal to this Court from the grant or denial of declaratory relief alone. We conclude, nevertheless, that those decisions do not foreclose our review of both the injunctive and the declaratory aspects of a case of this kind when it is properly here, as this one is, on appeal under § 1253 from specific denial of injunctive relief, and the arguments as to both aspects are necessarily identical. See Carter v. Jury Comm'n 396 U.S. 320, 90 S.Ct. 518, 24 L.Ed.2d 549 (1970); Florida Lime and Avocado Growers, Inc. v. Jacobsen, 362 U.S. 73; 80–81, 80 S.Ct. 568, 573–574, 4 L.Ed.2d 568 (1960). It would be destructive of time and energy for all concerned were we to rule otherwise. Cf. Doe v. Bolton, 410 U.S. 179, 93 S.Ct. 739, 35 L.Ed.2d 201.

IV

We are next confronted with issues of justiciability, standing, and abstention. Have Roe and the Does established that "personal stake in the outcome of the controversy," Baker v. Carr, 369 U.S. 186, 204, 82 S.Ct. 691, 703, 7 L.Ed.2d 663 (1962), that insures that "the dispute sought to be adjudicated will be presented in an adversary context and in a form historically viewed as capable of judicial resolution," Flast v. Cohen, 392 U.S. 83, 101, 88 S.Ct. 1942, 1953, 20 L.Ed.2d 947 (1968), and Sierra Club v. Morton, 405 U.S. 727, 732, 92 S.Ct. 1361, 1364, 31 L.Ed.2d 636 (1972)? And what effect did the pendency of criminal abortion charges against Dr. Hallford in state court have upon the propriety of the federal court's granting relief to him as a plaintiff-intervenor?

[2] A. *Jane Roe.* Despite the use of the pseudonym, no suggestion is made that Roe is a fictitious person. For purposes of her case, we accept as true, and as established, her existence; her pregnant state, as of the inception of her suit in March 1970 and as late as May 21 of that year when she filed an alias affidavit with the District Court; and her inability to obtain a legal abortion in Texas.

Viewing Roe's case as of the time of its filing and thereafter until as late as May, there can be little dispute that it then presented a case or controversy and that, wholly apart from the class aspects, she, as a pregnant single woman thwarted by the Texas criminal abortion laws, had standing to challenge those statutes. Abele v. Markle, 452 F.2d 1121, 1125 (CA2 1971); Crossen v. Breckenridge, 446 F.2d 833, 838–839 (CA6 1971); Poe v. Menghini, 339 F. Supp. 986, 990–991 (D.C.Kan. 1972). See Truax v. Raich, 239 U.S. 33, 36 S.Ct. 7, 60 L.Ed. 131 (1915). Indeed, we do not read the appellee's brief as really asserting anything to the contrary. The "logical nexus between the status asserted and the claim sought to be adjudicated," Flast v. Cohen, 392 U.S., at 102, 88 S.Ct., at 1953, and the necessary degree of contentiousness, Golden v. Zwickler, 394 U.S. 103, 89 S.Ct. 956, 22 L.Ed.2d 113 (1969), are both present.

The appellee notes, however, that the record does not disclose that Roe was pregnant at the time of the District Court hearing on May 22, 1970,[6] or on the following June 17 when the court's opinion and judgment were filed. And he suggests that Roe's case must now be moot because she and all other members of her class are no longer subject to any 1970 pregnancy.

[3] The usual rule in federal cases is that an actual controversy must exist at stages of appellate or certiorari review, and not simply at the date the action is initiated. United States v. Munsing-wear, Inc., 340 U.S. 36, 71 S.Ct. 104, 95 L.Ed. 36 (1950); Golden v. Zwickler, *supra*; SEC v. Medical Committee for Human Rights, 404 U.S. 403, 92 S.Ct. 577, L.Ed.2d 560 (1972).

[4] But when, as here, pregnancy is a significant fact in the litigation, the normal 266–day human gestation period is so short that the pregnancy will come to term before the usual appellate process is complete. If that termination makes a case moot, pregnancy litigation seldom will survive much beyond the trial stage, and appellate review will be effectively denied. Our law should not be that rigid. Pregnancy often comes more than once to the same woman, and in the general population, if man is to survive, it will always be with us. Pregnancy provides a classic justification for a conclusion of nonmootness. It truly could be "capable of repetition, yet evading review." Southern Pacific Terminal Co. v. ICC, 219 U.S. 498, 515, 31 S.Ct. 279, 283, 55 L.Ed. 310 (1911). See Moore v. Ogilvie, 394 U.S. 814, 816, 89 S.Ct. 1493, 1494,

23 L.Ed.2d 1 (1969); Carroll v. President and Commissioners of Princess Anne, 393 U.S. 175, 178–179, 89 S.Ct. 347, 350, 351, 21 L.Ed.2d 325 (1968); United States v. W. T. Grant Co., 345 U.S. 629, 632–633, 73 S.Ct. 894, 897–898, 97 L.Ed. 1303 (1953).

We, therefore, agree with the District Court that Jane Roe had standing to undertake this litigation, that she presented a justiciable controversy, and that the termination of her 1970 pregnancy has not rendered her case moot.

[5] B. *Dr. Hallford.* The doctor's position is different. He entered Roe's litigation as a plaintiff-intervenor, alleging in his complaint that he:

> "[I]n the past has been arrested for violating the Texas Abortion Laws and at the present time stands charged by indictment with violating said laws in the Criminal District Court of Dallas County, Texas to-wit: (1) The State of Texas vs. James H. Hallford, No. C—69–5307–IH, and (2) The State of Texas vs. James H. Hallford, No. C—69–2524–H. In both cases the defendant is charged with abortion ..."

In his application for leave to intervene, the doctor made like representations as to the abortion charges pending in the state court. These representations were also repeated in the affidavit he executed and filed in support of his motion for summary judgment.

[6] Dr. Hallford is, therefore in the position of seeking, in a federal court, declaratory and injunctive relief with respect to the same statutes under which he stands charged in criminal prosecutions simultaneously pending in state cout. Although he stated that he has been arrested in the past for violating the State's abortion laws, he makes no allegation of any substantial and immediate threat to any federally protected right that cannot be asserted in his defense against the state prosecutions. Neither is there any allegation of harassment or bad-faith prosecution. In order to escape the rule articulated in the cases cited in the next paragraph of this opinion that, absent harassment and bad faith, a defendant in a pending state criminal case cannot affirmatively challenge in federal court the statutes under which the State is prosecuting him, Dr. Hallford seeks to distinguish his status as a "potential future defendant" and to assert only the latter for standing purposes here.

We see no merit in that distinction. Our decision in Samuels v. Mackell, 401 U.S. 66, 91

---

[6] The appellee twice states in his brief that the hearing before the District Court was held on July 22, 1970. Brief for Appellee 13. The docket entries, App. 2, and the transcript, App. 76, reveal this to be an error. The July date appears to be the time of the reporter's transcription. See App. 77.

S.Ct. 764, 27 L.Ed.2d 688 (1971), compels the conclusion that the District Court erred when it granted declaratory relief to Dr. Hallford instead of refraining from so doing. The court, of course, was correct in refusing to grant injunctive relief to the doctor. The reasons supportive of that action, however, are those expressed in Samuels v. Mackell, *supra*, and in Younger v. Harris, 401 U.S. 37, 81 S.Ct. 746, 27 L.Ed.2d 669 (1971); Boyle v. Landry, 401 U.S. 77, 91 S.Ct. 758, 27 L.Ed.2d 696 (1971); Perez v. Ledesma, 401 U.S. 82, 91 S.Ct. 674, 27 L.Ed.2d 701 (1971); and Byrne v. Karalexis, 401 U.S. 216, 91 S.Ct. 777, 27 L.Ed.2d 792 (1971). See also Dombrowski v. Pfister, 380 U.S. 479, 85 S.Ct. 1116; 14 L.Ed.2d 22 (1965). We note, in passing that *Younger* and its companion cases were decided after the three-judge District Court decision in this case.

[7] Dr. Hallford's complaint in intervention, therefore, is to be dismissed.[7] He is remitted to his defenses in the state criminal proceedings against him. We reverse the judgment of the District Court insofar as it granted Dr. Hallford relief and failed to dismiss his complaint in intervetnion.

[8] C. *The Does*. In view of our ruling as to Roe's standing in her case, the issue of the Doe's standing in their case has little significance. The claims they assert are essentially the same as those of Roe, and they attack the same statutes. Nevertheless, we briefly note the Doe's posture.

Their pleadings present them as a childless married couple, the woman not being pregnant, who have no desire to have children at this time because of their having received medical advice that Mrs. Doe should avoid pregnancy, and for "other highly personal reasons." But they "fear . . . they may face the prospect of becoming parents." And if pregnancy ensues, they "would want to

terminate" it by an abortion. They assert an inability to obtain an abortion legally in Texas and, consequently, the prospect of obtaining an illegal abortion there or of going outside Texas to some place where the procedure could be obtained legally and competently.

We thus have as plaintiffs a married couple who have, as their asserted immediate and present injury, only an alleged "detrimental effect upon [their] marital happiness" because they are forced to "the choice of refraining from normal sexual relations or of endangering Mary Doe's health through a possible pregnancy." Their claim is that sometime in the future Mrs. Doe might become pregnant because of possible failure of contraceptive measures, and at that time in the future she might want an abortion that might then be illegal under the Texas statutes.

This very phrasing of the Doe's position reveals its speculative character. Their alleged injury rests on possible future contraceptive failure, possible future pregnancy, possible future unpreparedness for parenthood, and possible future impairment of health. Any one or more of these several possibilities may not take place and all may not combine. In the Doe's estimation, these possibilities might have some real or imagined impact upon their marital happiness. But we are not prepared to say that the bare allegation of so indirect an injury is sufficient to present an actual case or controversy. Younger v. Harris, 401 U.S., at 41–42, 91 S.Ct., at 749; Golden Zwickler, 394 U.S., at 109–110, 89 S.Ct., at 960; Abele v. Markle, 452 F.2d, at 1124–1125; Crossen v. Breckenridge, 446 F.2d, at 839. The Doe's claim falls far short of those resolved otherwise in the cases that the Does' urge upon us, namely, Investment Co. Institute v. Camp, 401 U.S. 617, 91 S.Ct. 1091, 28 L.Ed.2d 367 (1971); Association of Data Processing Service Organizations, Inc. v. Camp, 397 U.S. 150, 90 S.Ct. 827, 25 L.Ed.2d 184 (1970); and Epperson v. Arkansas, 393 U.S. 87, 89 S.Ct. 266, 21 L.Ed.2d 228 (1968). See also Truax v. Raich, 239 U.S. 33, 36 S.Ct. 7, 60 L.Ed. 131 (1915).

The Does therefore are not appropriate plaintiffs in this litigation. Their complaint was properly dismissed by the District Court, and we affirm that dismissal.

V

The principal trust of appellant's attack on the Texas statutes is that they improperly invade a right, said to be possessed by the pregnant

U.S. SUPREME
COURT,
JANUARY 1973

---

[7] We need not consider what different result, if any, would follow if Dr. Hallford's intervention were on behalf of a class. His complaint in intervention does not purport to assert a class suit and makes no reference to any class apart from an allegation that he "and others similarly situated" must necessarily guess at the meaning of Art. 1196. His application for leave to intervene goes somewhat further, for it asserts that plaintiff Roe does not adequately protect the interest of the doctor "and the class of people who are physicians . . . [and] the class of people who are . . . patients . . ." The leave application, however, is not the complaint. Despite the District Court's statement to the contrary, 314 F.Supp., at 1225, we fail to perceive the essentials of a class suit in the Hallford complaint.

U.S. SUPREME
COURT,
JANUARY 1973

woman, to choose to terminate her pregnancy. Appellant would discover this right in the concept of personal "liberty" embodied in the Fourteenth Amendment's Due Process Clause; or in personal, marital, familial, and sexual privacy said to be protected by the Bill of Rights or its penumbras, see Griswold v. Connecticut, 381 U.S. 479, 85 S.Ct. 1678, 14 L.Ed.2d 510 (1965); Eisenstadt v. Baird, 405 U.S. 438 (1972); *id*, at 460, 92 S.Ct. 1029, at 1042, 31 L.Ed.2d 349 (White, J., concurring in result); or among those rights reserved to the people be the Ninth Amendment, Griswold v. Connecticut, 381 U.S., at 486, 85 S.Ct., at 1682 (Goldberg, J., concurring). Before addressing this claim, we feel it desirable briefly to survey, in several aspects, the history may afford us, and then to examine the state purposes and interests behind the criminal abortion laws.

VI

It perhaps is not generally appreciated that the restrictive criminal abortion laws in effect in a majority of States today are of relatively recent vintage. Those laws, generally proscribing abortion or its attempt at any time during pregnancy except when necessary to preserve the pregnant woman's life, are not of ancient or even of common-law origin. Instead, they derive from statutory changes effected, for the most part, in the latter half of the 19th century.

1. *Ancient attitudes.* These are not capable of precise determination. We are told that at the time of the Persian Empire abortifacients were known and that criminal abortions were severely punished.[8] We are also told, however, that abortion was practiced in Greek times as well as in the Roman Era,[9] and that "it was resorted to without scruple."[10] The Ephesian, Soranos, often described as the greatest of the ancient gynecologists, appears to have been generally opposed to Rome's prevailing free-abortion practices. He found it necessary to think first of the life of the mother, and he resorted to abortion when, upon this standard, he felt the procedure advisable.[11] Greek and Roman law afforded little protection to the unborn. If abortion was prosecuted in some places, it seems to have been based on a concept of a violation of the father's right to his offspring. Ancient religion did not bar abortion.[12]

2. *The Hippocratic Oath.* What then of the famous Oath that has stood so long as the ethical guide of the medical profession and that bears the name of the great Greek (460(?)-377(?)

B.C.), who has been described as the Father of Medicine, the "wisest and the greatest practitioner of his art," and the "most important and most complete medical personality of antiquity," who dominated the medical schools of his time, and who typified the sum of the medical knowledge of the past?[13] The Oath varies somewhat according to the particular translation, but in any translation the content is clear: "I will give no deadly medicine to anyone if asked, nor suggest any such counsel; and in like manner I will not give to a woman a pessary to produce abortion,"[14] or "I will neither give a deadly drug to anybody if asked for it, nor will I make a suggestion to this effect. Similarly, I will not give to a woman an abortive remedy."[15]

Although the Oath is not mentioned in any of the principal briefs in this case or in Doe v. Bolton, 410 U.S. 179, 93 S.Ct. 739, 35 L.Ed.2d 201, it represents the apex of the development of strict ethical concepts in medicine, and its influence endures to this day. Why did not the authority of Hippocrates dissuade abortion practice in his time and that of Rome? The late Dr. Edelstein provides us with a theory:[16] The Oath was not uncontested even in Hippocrates' day; only the Pythagorean school of philosophers frowned upon the related act of suicide. Most Greek thinkers, on the other hand, commended abortion, at least prior to viability. See Plato, Republic, V, 461; Aristotle, Politics, VII, 1335b 25. For the Pythagoreans, however, it was a matter of dogma. For them the embryo was animate form the moment of conception, and abortion meant destruction of a living being.

---

[8] A. Castiglioni, A History of Medicine 84 (2d ed. 1947), E. Krumbhaar, translator and editor (hereinafter Castiglioni).
[9] J. Ricci, The Genealogy of Gynaecology 52, 84, 113, 149 (2d ed. 1950) (herein after Ricci); L. Lader, Abortion 75–77 (1966) (hereinafter Lader); K. Niswander, Medical Abortion Practices in the United States, in Abortion Practices in the United States, in Abortion and the Law 37, 38–40 (D. Smith ed. 1967); G. Williams, The Sanctity of Life and the Criminal Law 148 (1957) (herein after Williams); J. Noonan, An Almost Absolute Value in History, in the Morality of Abortion 1, 3–7 (J. Noonan ed. 1970) (hereinafter Noonan); Quay, Justifiable Abortion-Medical and Legal Foundations, (pt. 2), 49 Geo.L.J. 395, 406–422 (1961) (hereinafter Quay).
[10] L. Edelstein, The Hippocratic Oath 10 (1943) (hereinafter Edelstein). But see Castiglioni 227.
[11] Edelstein 12; Ricci 113–114, 118–119; Noonan 5.
[12] Edelstein 13–14.
[13] Castiglioni 148.
[14] *Id.*, at 154.
[15] Edelstein 3.
[16] *Id.*, at 12, 15–18.

The abortion clause of the Oath, therefore, "echoes Pythagorean doctrines," and "[i]n no other stratum of Greek opinion were such views held or proposed in the same spirit of uncompromising austerity."[17]

Dr. Edelstein then concludes that the Oath Originated in a group representing only a small segment of Greek opinion and that it certainly was not accepted by all ancient physicians. He points out that medical writings down to Galen (A.D. 130–200) "give evidence of the violation of almost every one of its injunctions."[18] But with the end of antiquity a decided change took place. Resistance against suicide and against abortion became common. The Oath came to be popular. The emerging teachings of Christianity were in agreement with the Pythagorean ethic. The Oath "became the nucleus of all medical ethics" and "was applauded as the embodiment of truth." Thus, suggests Dr. Edelstein, it is "a Pythagorean manifesto and not the expression of an absolute standard of medical conduct."[19]

This, it seems to us, is a satisfactory and acceptable explanation of the Hippocratic Oath's apparent rigidity. It enables us to understand, in historical context, a long-accepted and revered statement of medical ethics.

3. *The common law.* It is undisputed that at common law, abortion performed *before* "quickening"—the first recognizable movement of the fetus *in utero*, appearing usually from the 16th to the 18th week of pregnancy[20]—was not an indictable offense.[21] The absence of a common-law crime for pre-quickening abortion appears to have developed from a confluence of earlier philosophical, theological, and civil and canon law concepts of when life begins. These disciplines variously approached the question in terms of the point at which the embryo or fetus became "formed" or recognizably human, or in terms of when a "person" came into being, that is infused with a "soul" or "animated." A loose concensus evolved in early English law that these events occurred at some point between conception and live birth.[22] This was "mediate animation." Although Christian theology and the canon law came to fix the point of animation at 40 days for a male and 80 days for a female, a view that persisted until the 19th century, there was otherwise little agreement about the precise time of formation or animation. There was agreement, however, that prior to this point the fetus was to be regarded as part of the mother, and its destruction, therefore, was not homicide. Due to continued uncertainty about the precise time when animation occurred, to the lack of any empirical basis for the 40–80–day view, and perhaps to Aquinas' definition of movement as one of the two first principles of life, Bracton focused upon quickening as the critical point. The significance of quickening was echoed by

---

[17] *Id.*, at 18; Lader 76.

[18] Edelstein 63.

[19] *Id.*, at 64.

[20] Dorland's Illustrated Medical Dictionary 1261 (24th ed. 1965).

[21] E. Coke, Institutes III *50; 1 W. Hawkins, Pleas of the Crown, c. 31, § 16 (4th ed. 1762); 1 W. Blackstone, Commentaries *129–130; M. Hale, Pleas of the Crown 433 (1st Amer. ed. 1847). For discussion of the role of the quickening concept in English common law, see Lader 78; Noonan 223–226; Means, The Law of New York Concerning Abortion and the Status of the Foetus, 1964–1968: A Case of Cessation of Constitutionality (pt. 1), 14 N.Y.L.F. 411, 418–428 (1968) (hereinafter Means I); Stern, Abortion: Reform and the Law, 59 J.Crim.L.C. & P.S. 84 (1968) (hereinafter Stern): Quay 430–432; Williams 152.

[22] Early philosophers believed that the embryo or fetus did not become formed and begin to live until at least 40 days after conception for a male and 80 to 90 days for a female. See, for example, Aristotle, Hist.Anim. 7.3.583b; Gen.Anim. 2.3.736, 2.5.741; Hippocrates, Lib. de Nat.Puer., No. 10. Aristotle's thinking derived from his three-stage theory of life: vegetable, animal, rational. The vegetable stage was reached at conception, the animal at "animation," and the rational soon after live birth. This theory together with the 40/80 day view, came to be accepted by early Christian thinkers.

The theological debate was reflected in the writings of St. Augustine, who made a distinction between *embryo inanimatus*, not yet endowed with a soul, and *embryo animatus*. He may have drawn upon Exodus 21:22. At one point, however, he expressed the view that human powers cannot determine the point, during fetal development at which the critical change occurs. See Augustine, De Origine Animae 4.4 (Pub.Law 44.527). See also W. Reany, The Creation of the Human Soul, c. 2 and 83–86 (1932); Huser, The Crime of Abortion in Canon Law 15 (Catholic Univ. of America, Canon Law Studies No. 162, Washington, D.C., 1942).

Galen, in three treaties related to embryology, accepted the thinking of Aristotle and his followers. Quay 426–427. Later, Augustine on abortion was incorporated by Gratian into the Decretum, published about 1140. Decretum Magistri Gratiani 2.32.2.7 to 2.32.2.10, in 1 Corpus Juris Canonici 1122, 1123 (A. Friedberg, 2d ed. 1879). This Decretal and the Decretals that followed were recognized as the definitive body of canon law until the new Code of 1917.

For discussion of the canon-law treatment, see Means I, pp. 411–412; Noonan 20–26; Quay 426–430; see also J. Noonan, Contraception: A History of Its Treatment by the Catholic Theologians and Canonists 18–29 (1965).

U.S. SUPREME
COURT,
JANUARY 1973

later common-law scholars and found its way into the received common law in this country.

Whether abortion of a *quick* fetus was a felony at common law, or even a lesser crime, is still disputed. Bracton, writing early in the 13th century, thought it homicide.[23] But the later and predominant view, following the great common-law scholars, has been that it was, at most, a lesser offence. In a frequently cited passage, Coke took the position that abortion of a woman "quick with childe" is "a great misprision, and no murder"[24] Blackstone followed, saying that while abortion after quickening had once been considered manslaughter (though not murder), "modern law" took a less severe view.[25] A recent review of the common-law precedents argues, however, that those precedents contradict Coke and that even post-quickening abortion was never established as a common-law crime.[26] This is of some importance because while most American courts ruled, in holding or dictum, that abortion of an unquickened fetus was not criminal under their received common law,[27] others followed Coke instating that abortion of a quick fetus was a "misprision," a term they translated to mean "misdemeanor."[28] That their reliance on Coke on this aspect of the law was uncritical and, apparently in all the reported cases, dictum (due probably to the paucity of common-law prosecutions for post-quickening abortion), makes it now appear doubtful that abortion was ever

firmly established as a common-law crime even with respect to the destruction of a quick fetus.

4. *The English statutory law.* England's first criminal abortion statute, Lord Ellenborough's Act, 43 Geo. 3, c. 58, came in 1803. It made abortion of a quick fetus, § 1, a capital crime, but in §2 it provided lesser penalties for the felony of abortion before quickening, and thus preserved the "quickening" distinction. This contrast was continued in the general revision of 1828, 9 Geo. 4, c. 31, § 13. It disappeared, however, together with the death penalty, in 1837, 7 Will. 4 & 1 Vict., c. 85, § 6, and did not reappear in the Offenses Against the Person Act of 1861, 24 & 25 Vict., c. 100, § 59, that formed the core of English anti-abortion law until the liberalizing reforms of 1967. In 1929, the Infant Life (Preservation) Act, 19 & 20 Geo. 5, c. 34, came into being. Its emphasis was upon the destruction of "the life of a child capable of being born alive." It made a willful act performed with the necessary intent a felony. It contained a proviso that one was not to be found guilty of the offense "unless it is proved that the act which caused the death of the child was not done in good faith for the purpose only of preserving the life of the mother."

A seemingly notable development in the English law was the case of Rex v. Bourne, [1939] 1 K.B. 687. This case apparently answered in the affirmative the question whether an abortion necessary to preserve the life of the pregnant

---

Bracton took the position that abortion by blow or poison was homicide "if the foetus be already formed and animated and particularly if it be animated." 2 H. Bracton, De Legibus et Consuetudinibus Angliae 279 (T. Twiss ed. 1879), or, as a later translation puts it, "if the foetus is already formed or quickened, especially if it is quickened," 2 H. Bracton, On the Laws and Customs of England 341 (S. Thorne ed. 1968). See Quay 431: see also 2 Fleta 60–61 (Book 1, c. 23) (Selden Society ed. 1955).

[24] E. Coke, Institutes III * 50.

[25] 1 W. Blackstone, Commentaries *129–130.

[26] Means, The Phoenix of Abortional Freedom: Is a Penumbral or Ninth Amendment Right About to Arise from the Nineteenth-Century Legislative Ashes of a Fourteenth-Century Common-Law Liberty?, 17 N.Y.L.F. 335 (1971) (hereinafter Means II). The author examines the two principal precedents cited marginally by Coke, both contrary to his dictum, and traces the treatment of these and other cases by earlier commentators. He concludes that Coke, who himself participated as an advocate in an abortion case in 1601, may have intentionally misstated the law. The author even suggests a reason: Coke's strong feelings against abortion, coupled with his determination to assert common-law (secular) jurisdiction to assess penalties for an offense that tradition-

ally had been an exclusively ecclesiastical or cannon-law crime. See also Lader 78–79, who notes that some scholars doubt that the common law ever was applied to abortion; that the English ecclesiastical courts seem to have lost interest in the problem after 1527; and that the preamble to the English legislation of 1803, 43 Geo. 3, c. 58, § 1, referred to in the text, *infra*, at 718, states that "no adequate means have been hitherto provided for the prevention and punishment of such offenses."

[27] Commonwealth v. Bangs, 9 Mass. 387, 388 (1812); Commonwealth v. Parker, 50 Mass. (9 Metc.) 263, 265–266 (1845); State v. Cooper, 22 N.J.L. 52, 58 (1849); Abrams v. Foshee, 3 Iowa 274, 278–280 (1856); Smith v. Gaffard, 31 Ala. 45, 51 (1857); Mitchell v. Commonwealth, 78 Ky. 204, 210 (1879); Eggart v. State, 40 Fla. 527, 532, 25 So. 144, 145 (1898); State v. Alcorn, 7 Idaho 599, 606, 64 P.1014, 1016 (1901); Edwards v. State, 79 Neb. 251, 252, 112 N.W. 611, 612 (1907); Gray v. State, 77 Tex.Cr.R. 221, 224, 178 S.W. 337, 338 (1915); Miller v. Bennett, 190 Va. 162, 169, 56 S.E.2d 217, 221 (1949). Contra Mills v. Commonwealth, 13 Pa. 631, 633 (1850); State v. Slagle, 83 N.C. 630, 632 (1880).

[28] See Smith v. State, 33 Me. 48, 55 (1851); Evans v. People, 49 N.Y. 86, 88 (1872); Lamb v. State, 67 Md. 524, 533, 10 A. 208 (1887).

woman was expected from the criminal penalties of the 1861 Act. In his instructions to the jury, Judge Macnaghten referred to the 1929 Act, and observed that the Act related to "the case where a child is killed by a willful act at the time when it is being delivered in the ordinary course of nature," *Id.*, at 691. He concluded that the 1861 Act's use of the word "unlawfully," imported the same meaning expressed by the specific proviso in the 1929 Act, even though there was no mention of preserving the mother's life in the 1861 Act. He then constructed the phrase "preserving the life of the mother" broadly, that is, "in a reasonable sense," to include a serious and permanent threat to the mother's *health*, and instructed the jury to acquit Dr. Bourne if it found he had acted in a good-faith belief that the abortion was necessary for this purpose. *Id.*, at 693–694. The jury did acquit.

Recently, Parliament enacted a new abortion law. This is the Abortion Act of 1967, 15 & 16 Eliz. 2, c. 87. The Act permits a licensed physician to perform an abortion where two other licensed physicians agree (a) "that the continuance of the pregnancy would involve risk to the life of the pregnant woman, or of injury to the physical or mental health of the pregnant woman or any existing children of her family, greater than if the pregnancy were terminated," or (b) "that there is a substantial risk that if the child were born it would suffer from such physical or mental abnormalities as to be seriously handicapped." The Act also provides that, in making this determination, "account may be taken of the pregnant woman's actual or reasonably foreseeable environment." It also permits a physician, without the concurrence of others, to terminate a pregnancy where he is of the good-faith opinion that the abortion "is immediately necessary to save the life or to prevent grave permanent injury to the physical or mental health of the pregnant woman."

5. *The American law.* In this country, the law in effect in all but a few States until mid-19th century was the pre-existing English common law. Connecticut, the first State to enact abortion legislation, adopted in 1821 that part of Lord Ellenborough's Act that related to a woman "quick with child."[29] The death penalty was not imposed. Abortion before quickening was made a crime in the State only in 1860.[30] In 1828, New York enacted legislation[31] that, in two respects, was to serve as a model for early anti-abortion

statutes. First, while barring destruction of an unquickened fetus as well as a quick fetus, it made the former only a misdemeanor, but the latter second-degree manslaughter. Second, it incorporated a concept of therapeutic abortion by providing that an abortion was excused if it "shall have been necessary to preserve the life of such mother, or shall have been advised by two physicians to be necessary for such purpose." By 1840, when Texas had received the common law,[32] only eight American States had statutes dealing with abortion.[33] It was not until after the War Between the States the legislation began generally to replace the common law. Most of these initial statutes dealt severely with abortion after quickening. Most punished attempts equally with completed abortions. While many statutes included the exception for an abortion thought by one or more physicians to be necessary to save the mother's life, that provision soon disappeared and the typical law required that the procedure actually be necessary for that purpose.

Gradually, in the middle and late 19th century the quickening distinction disappeared from the statutory law of most States and the degree of the offense and the penalties were increased. By the end of the 1950's a large majority of the jurisdictions banned abortion, however and whenever performed, unless done to save or preserve the life of the mother.[34] The exceptions, Alabama and the District of Columbia, permitted abortion to preserve the mother's health.[35] Three States permitted abortions that were not "unlawfully" performed or that were not "without lawful justification," leaving inter-

---

[29] Conn.Stat., Tit. 20 § 14 (1821).

[30] Conn.Pub.Acts, c. 71, § 1 (1860).

[31] N.Y.Rev.Stat., pt. 4, c. 1, Tit. 2, Art. 1, § 9, p. 691, and Tit. 6, § 21, p. 694 (1829).

[32] Act of Jan. 20, 1840, § 1, set forth in 2 H. Gammel, Laws of Texas 177–178 (1898); see Grigsby v. Reib, 105 Tex. 597, 600, 153 S.W. 1124, 1125 (1913).

[33] The early statutes are discussed in Quay 435–438. See also Lader 85–88; Stern 85–86; and Means II 375–376.

[34] Criminal abortion statutes in effect in the States as of 1961, together with historical statutory development and important judicial interpretations of the state statutes, are cited and quoted in Quay 447–520. See Comment, A Survey of the Present Statutory and Case Law on Abortion: The Contradictions and the Problems, 1972 U.Ill.L.F. 177, 179, classifying the abortion statutes and listing 25 States as permitting abortion only if necessary to save or preserve the mother's life.

[35] Ala.Code Tit. 14, § 9 (1958); D.C. Code Ann. § 22–201 (1967).

pretation of those standards to the courts.[36] In the past several years, however, a trend toward liberalization of abortion statutes has resulted in adoption, by about one-third of the States, of less stringent laws, most of them patterned after the ALI Model Penal Code, § 230.3,[37] set forth as Appendix B to the opinion in Doe v. Bolton, 410 U.S. 205, 93 S.Ct. 754.

It is thus apparent that at common law, at the time of the adoption of our Constitution, and throughout the major portion of the 19th century, abortion was viewed with less disfavor than under most American statutes currently in effect. Phrasing it another way, a woman enjoyed a substantially broader right to terminate a pregnancy than she does in most States today. At least with respect to the early stage of pregnancy, and very possibly without such a limitation, the opportunity to make this choice was present in this country well into the 19th century. Even later, the law continued for some time to treat less punitively an abortion procured in early pregnancy.

6. *The position of the American Medical Association.* The anti-abortion mood prevalent in this country in the late 19th century was shared by the medical profession. Indeed, the attitude of the profession may have played a significant role in the enactment of stringent criminal abortion legislation during that period.

An AMA Committee on Criminal Abortion was appointed in May 1857. It presented its report, 12 Trans. of the Am.Med.Assn. 73–78 (1859), to the Twelfth Annual Meeting. That report observed that the Committee had been appointed to investigate criminal abortion "with a view to its general suppression." It deplored abortion and its frequency and it listed three causes of "this general demoralization.":

"The first of these causes is a wide-spread popular ignorance of the true character of the crime—a belief, even among mothers themselves, that the foetus is not alive till after the period of quickening.

"The second of the agents alluded to is the fact that the profession themselves are frequently supposed careless of foetal life . . .

"The third reason of the frightful extent of this crime is found in the grave defects of our laws, both common and statute, as regards the independent and actual existence of the child before birth, as a living being These errors, which are sufficient in most instances to prevent conviction, are based, and only based, upon mistaken and exploded medical dogmas. With strange inconsistency, the law fully acknowledges the foetus in utero and its inherent rights, for civil purposes; while personally and as criminally affected, it fails to recognize it, and to its life as yet denies all protection." *Id.*, at 75–76.

The Committee then offered, and the Association adopted, resolutions protesting "against such unwarrantable destruction of human life," calling upon state legislatures to revise their abortion laws, and requesting the cooperation of state medical societies "in pressing the subject." *Id.*, at 28, 78.

In 1871 a long and vivid report was submitted by the Committee on Criminal Abortion. It ended with the observation, "We had to deal with human life. In a matter of less importance we could entertain no compromise. An honest judge on the bench would call things by their proper names. We could do no less," 22 Trans. of the Am.Med.Assn. 258 (1871). It proffered resolutions, adopted by the Association, *id.*, at 38–39, recommending, among other things, that it "be unlawful and unprofessional for any physician to induce abortion or premature labor, without the concurrent opinion of at least

---

[36] Mass.Gen.Laws Ann. c. 272, § 19 (1970); N.J.Stat.Ann. § 2A:87–1 (1969); PA.Stat.Ann. Tit. 18, §§ 4718, 4719 (1963).
[37] Fourteen States have adopted some form of the ALI statute. See Ark.Stat.Ann. §§ 41–303 to 41–310 (Supp.1971); Calif. Health & Safety Code §§ 25950–25955.5 (Supp.1972); Colo. Rev.Stat.Ann. §§ 40–2–50 to 40–2–53 (Cum.Supp.1967); Del. Code Ann. Tit. 24 §§ 1790–1793 (Supp. 1972); Florida Law of Apr. 13, 1972, c. 72–196, 1972 Fla.Sess.Law Serv., pp. 380–382; Ga.Code §§ 26–1201 to 26–1203 (1972); Kan.Stat.Ann. § 21–3407 (Supp.1971); Md.Ann.Code, Art. 43, §§ 137–139 (1971); Miss.Code Ann. § 2223 (Supp.1972); N.M.Stat.Ann. §§ 40A–5–1 to 40A–5–3 (1972); N.C.Gen. Stat. § 14–45.1 (Supp.1971); Ore.Rev. Stat. §§ 435.405 to 435.495 (1971); S.C.Code Ann. §§ 16–82 to 16–89 (1962 and Supp.1971);

Va.Code Ann. §§ 18.1–62 to 18.1–62.3 (Supp.1972). Mr. Justice Clark described some of these States as having "fed the way." Religion, Morality, and Abortion: A Constitutional Appraisal, 2 Loyola U. (L.A.) L.Rev. 1, 11 (1969).

By the end of 1970, four other States had repealed criminal penalties for abortions performed in early pregnancy by a licensed physician, subject to stated procedural and health requirements. Alaska Stat. § 11.15.060 (1970); Haw.Rev.Stat. § 453–16 (Supp.1971); N.Y.Penal Code § 125.05, subd. 3 (Supp.1972–1973); Wash.Rev.Code §§ 9.02.060 to 9.02.080 (Supp.1972). The precise status of criminal abortion laws in some States is made unclear by recent decisions in state and federal courts striking down existing state laws, in whole or in part.

one respectable consulting physician, and then always with a view to the safety of the child—if that be possible," and calling "the attention of the clergy of all denominations to the perverted views of morality entertained by a large class of females—aye, and men also, on this important question."

Except for periodic condemnation of the criminal abortionist, no further formal AMA action took place until 1967. In that year, the Committee on Human Reproduction urged the adoption of a stated policy of opposition to induced abortion, except when there is "documented medical evidence" of a threat to the health or life of the mother, or that the child "may be born with incapacitating physical deformity or mental deficiency," or that a pregnancy "resulting from legally established statutory or forcible rape or incest may constitute a threat to the mental or physical health of the "patient," two other physicians "chosen because of their recognized professional competency have examined the patient and have concurred in writing," and the procedure "is performed in a hospital accredited by the Joint Commission on Accreditation of Hospitals." The providing of medical information by physicians to state legislatures in their consideration of legislation regarding therapeutic abortion was "to be considered consistent with the principles of ethics of the American Medical Association." This rec-

ommendation was adopted by the House of Delegates. Proceedings of the AMA House of Delegates 40–51 (June 1967).

In 1970, after the introduction of a variety of proposed resolutions, and of a report from its Board of Trustees, a reference committee noted "polarization of the medical profession on this controversial issue"; division among those who had testified; a difference of opinion among AMA councils and committees; "the remarkable shift in testimony" in six months, felt to be influenced "by the rapid changes in state laws and by the judicial decisions which tend to make abortion more freely available," and a feeling "that this trend will continue." On June 25, 1970, the House of Delegates adopted preambles and most of the resolutions proposed by the reference committee. The preambles emphasized "the best interests of the patient," "sound clinical judgment," and "informed patient consent," in contrast to "mere acquiescence to the patient's demand." The resolutions asserted that abortion is a medical procedure that should be performed by a licensed physician in an accredited hospital only after consultation with two other physicians and in conformity with state law, and that no party to the procedure should be required to violate personally held moral principles.[38] Proceedings of the AMA House of Delegates 220 (June 1970). The AMA Judicial Council rendered a complementary opinion.[39]

---

[38] "Whereas, Abortion, like any other medical procedure, should not be performed when contrary to the best interests of the patient since good medical practice requires due consideration for the patient's welfare and not mere acquiescence to the patient's demand; and

"Whereas, The standards of sound clinical judgment, which, together with informed patient consent should be determinative according to the merits of each individual case; therefore be it.

"RESOLVED, That abortion is a medical procedure and should be performed only by a duly licensed physician and surgeon in an accredited hospital acting only after consultation with two other physicians chosen because of their professional competency and in conformance with standards of good medical practice and the Medical Practice Act of his State; and be it further

"RESOLVED, that no physicians or other professional personnel shall be compelled to perform any act which violates his good medical judgment. Neither physician, hospital, nor hospital personnel shall be required to perform any act violative of personally-held moral principles. In these circumstances good medical practice requires only that the physician or other professional personnel withdraw from the case so long as the withdrawal is consistent with good med-

ical practice." Proceedings of the AMA House of Delegates 220 (June 1970).

[39] "The principles of Medical Ethics of the AMA do not prohibit a physician form performing an abortion that is performed in accordance with good medical practice and under circumstances that do not violate the laws of the community in which he practices.

"In the matter of abortions, as of any other medical procedure, the Judicial Council becomes involved whenever there is alleged violation of the Principles of Medical Ethics as established by the House of Delegates."

"UNIFORM ABORTION ACT

"Section 1. [Abortion Defined: When Authorized.]

"(a) 'Abortion' means the termination of human pregnancy with an intention other than to produce a live birth or to remove a dead fetus.

"(b) An abortion may be performed in this state only if it is performed:

"(1) by a physician licensed to practice medicine [or osteopathy] in this state or by a physician practicing medicine [or osteopathy] in the employ of the government of the United States or of this state, [and the abortion is performed [in the physician's office or in a medical clinic, or] in a hospital approved by the [Department of Health] or operated

U.S. SUPREME
COURT,
JANUARY 1973

7. *The position of the American Public Health Association.* In October 1970, the Executive Board of the APHA adopted Standards for Abortion Services. These were five in number:

a. Rapid and simple abortion referral must be readily available through state and local public health departments, medical societies, or other non-profit organizations.

b. An important function of counseling should be to simplify and expedite the provision of abortion services; it should not delay the obtaining of these services.

c. Psychiatric consultation should not be mandatory. As in the case of other specialized medical services, psychiatric consultation should be sought for definite indications and not on a routine basis.

d. A wide range of individuals from appropriately trained, sympathetic volunteers to highly skilled physicians may qualify as abortion counselors.

e. Contraception and/or sterilization should be discussed with each abortion patient." Recommended Standards for Abortion Services, 61 Am.J.Pub.Health 396 (1971).

Among factors pertinent to life and health risks associated with abortion were three that "are recognized as important":

a. the skill of the physician,

b. the environment in which the abortion is performed, and above all

c. the duration of pregnancy, as determined by uterine size and confirmed by menstrual history." *Id.*, at 397.

It was said that "a well-equipped hospital" offers more protection "to cope with unforeseen difficulties than an office or clinic without such resources. . . . The factor of gestational age is of overriding importance." Thus, it was recommended that abortions in the second trimester and early abortions in the second trimester and early abortions in the presence of existing medical complications be performed in hospitals as inpatient procedures. For pregnancies in the first trimester, abortion in the hospital with or without overnight stay "is probably the safest practice." An abortion in an extramural facility, however, is an acceptable alternative "provided arrangements exist in advance to admit patients promptly if unforeseen complications develop." Standards for an abortion facility were listed. It was said that at present abortions should be performed by physicians or osteopaths who are licensed to practice and who have "adequate training." *Id.*, at 398.

8. *The position of the American Bar Association.* At its meeting in February 1972 the ABA House of Delegates approved, with 17 opposing votes, the Uniform Abortion Act that had been drafted and approved the proceeding August by the Conference of Commissioners on Uniform State Laws. 58 A.B.A. J. 380 (1972). We set forth the Act in full in the margin.[40] The Conference has appended an enlightening Prefatory Note.[41]

VII

Three reasons have been advanced to explain historically the enactment of criminal abortion laws in the 19th century and to justify their continued existence.

It has been argued occasionally that these laws were the product of a Victorian social con-

---

by the United States, this state, or any department, agency, or political subdivision of either;] or by a female upon herself upon the advice of the physician; and

"(2) within [20] weeks after the commencement of the pregnancy [or after [20] weeks only if the physician has reasonable cause to believe (i) there is a substantial risk that continuance of the pregnancy would endanger the life of the mother or would gravely impair the physical or mental health of the mother, (ii) that the child would be born with grave physical or mental defect, or (iii) that the pregnancy resulted form rape or incest, or illicit intercourse with a girl under the age of 16 years].

"Section 2. [*Penalty.*] Any person who performs or procures an abortion other than authorized by this Act is guilty of a [felony] and, upon conviction thereof, may be sentenced to pay a fine not exceeding [$1,000] or to imprisonment [in the state penitentiary] not exceeding [5 years], or both.

"Section 3. [*Uniformity of Interpretation.*] This Act shall be construed to effectuate its general purpose to make uniform the law with respect to the subject of this Act among those states which enact it.

"Section 4. [*Short Title*]. This Act may be cited as the Uniform Abortion Act.

"Section 5. [*Severability.*] If any provision of this Act or the application thereof to any person or circumstance is held invalid, the invalidity does not affect other provisions or applications of this Act which can be given effect without the invalid provision or application, and to this end the provisions of this Act are severable.

"Section 6. [*Repeal*]. The following acts and parts of acts are repealed:

"(1)

"(2)

"(3)

"Section 7. [*Time of Taking Effect*]. This Act shall take effect _____."

[41] "This Act is based largely upon the New York abortion act following a review of the more recent laws on abortion in several states and upon recognition of a more liberal trend in laws on this subject. Recognition was given also to several

U.S. SUPREME
COURT,
JANUARY 1973

cern to discourage illicit sexual conduct. Texas, however, does not advance this justification in the present case, and it appears that no court or commentator has taken the argument seriously.[42] The appellants and *amici* contend, moreover, that this is not a proper state purpose at all and suggest that, if it were, the Texas statutes are overboard in protecting it since the law fails to distinguish between married and unwed mothers.

A second reason is concerned with abortion as a medical procedure. When most criminal abortion laws were first enacted, the procedure was a hazardous one for the woman.[43] This was particularly true prior to the development of antisepsis. Antiseptic techniques, of course, were based on discoveries by Lister, Pasteur, and others first announced in 1867, but were not generally accepted and employed until about the turn of the century. Abortion mortality was high. Even after 1900, and perhaps until as late as the development of antibiotics in the 1940's, standard modern techniques such as dilation and curettage were not nearly so safe as they are today. Thus, it has been argued that a State's real concern in enacting a criminal abortion law was to protect the pregnant woman, that is, to restrain her from submitting to a procedure that placed her life in serious jeopardy.

Modern medical techniques have altered this situation. Appellants and various *amici* refer to medical data indicating that abortion in early pregnancy, that is, prior to the end of the first trimester, although not without its risk, is now relatively safe. Mortality rates for women undergoing early abortions, where the procedure is legal, appear to be as low as or lower than the rates for normal childbirth.[44] Consequently, any interest of the State in protecting the woman from an inherently hazardous procedure, except when it would be equally dangerous for her to forgo it, has largely disappeared. Of course, important state interests in the areas of health and medical standards do remain. The State has a legitimate interest in seeing to it that abortion, like any other medical procedure, is performed under circumstances that insure maximum safety for the patient. This interest obviously extends at least to the performing physician and his staff, to the facilities involved, to the availability of after-care, and to adequate provision for any complication or emergency that might arise. The prevalence of high mortality rates at illegal "abortion mills" strengthens, rather than weakens, the State's interest in regulating the conditions under which abortions are performed. Moreover, the risk to the woman increases as her pregnancy continues. Thus, the State retains a definite interest in protecting woman's own health and safety when an abortion is proposed at a late stage of pregnancy.

The third reason is the State's interest—some phrase it in terms of duty—in protecting prenatal life. Some of the argument for this justification rests on the theory that a new human life is present from the moment of conception.[45] The State's interest and general obligation to

---

decisions in state and federal courts which show a further trend toward liberalization of abortion laws, especially during the first trimester of pregnancy.

"Recognizing that a number of problems appeared in New York, a shorter time period for 'unlimited' abortions was advisable. The time period was bracketed to permit the various states to insert a figure more in keeping with the different conditions that might exist among the states. Likewise, the language limiting the place or places in which abortions may be performed was also bracketed to account for different conditions among the states. In addition, limitations on abortions after the initial "unlimited' period were placed in brackets so that individual states may adopt all or any of these reasons, or place further restrictions upon abortions after the initial period.

"This Act does not contain any provision relating to medical review committees or prohibitions against sanctions imposed upon medical personnel refusing to participate in abortions because of religious or other similar reasons, or the like. Such provisions, while related, do not directly pertain to when, where, or by whom abortions may be performed; however, the Act is not drafted to exclude such a provision by a state wishing to enact the same."

[42] See for example, YWCA v. Kugler, 342 F.Supp. 1048, 1074 (D.C.N.J.1972); Abele v. Markle, 342 F.Supp. 800, 805–806 (D.C.Conn.1972) (Newman, J., concurring in result), appeal docketed, No. 72–56; Walsingham v. State, 250 So.2d 857, 863 (Ervin J., concurring) (Fla. 1971); State v. Gedicke, 43 N.J.L. 86, 90 (1881); Means II 381–382.

[43] See C. Haagensen & W. Lloyd, A Hundred Years of Medicine 19 (1943).

[44] Potts, Postconceptive Control of Fertility, 8 Int'l J. of G. & O. 957, 967 (1970) (England and Wales); Abortion Mortality, 20 Morbidity and Mortality 208, 209 (June 12, 1971) (U.S. Dept. of HEW, Public Health Service) (New York City); Tietze, United States: Therapeutic Abortions, 1963–1968, 59 Studies in Family Planning 5, 7 (1970); Tietze, Mortality with Contraception and Induced Abortion, 45 Studies in Family Planning 6 (1969) (Japan, Czechoslovakia, Hungary); Tietze & Lehfeldt, Legal Abortion in Eastern Europe, 175 J.A. M.A. 1149, 1152 (April 1961). Other sources are discussed in Lader 17–23.

[45] See Brief of Amicus National Right to Life Committee; R. Drinan, The Inviolability of the Right to Be Born, in Abortion and the Law 107 (D. Smith ed. 1967); Louisell,

protect life then extends, it is argued, to prenatal life. Only when the life of the pregnant mother herself is at stake, balanced against the life she carries within her, should the interest of the embryo or fetus not prevail. Logically, of course, a legitimate state interest in this area need not stand or fall on acceptance of the belief that life begins at conception or at some other point prior to live birth. In assessing the State's interest, recognition may be given to the less rigid claim that as long as at least *potential* life is involved, the State may assert interests beyond the protection of the pregnant woman alone.

Parties challenging state abortion laws have sharply disputed in some courts the contention that a purpose of these laws, when enacted, was to protect prenatal life.[46] Pointing to the absence of legislative history to support the contention, they claim that most state laws were designed solely to protect the woman. Because medical advances have lessened this concern, at least with respect to abortion in early pregnancy, they argue that with respect to such abortions the laws can no longer be justified by any state interest. There is some scholarly support for this view of original purpose.[47] The few state courts called upon to interpret their laws in the late 19th and early 20th centuries did focus on the State's interest in protecting the woman's health rather than in preserving the embryo and fetus.[48] Proponents of this view point out that in many States, including Texas,[49] by statute or judicial interpretation, the pregnant woman herself could not be prosecuted for self-abortion or for cooperating in an abortion performed upon her by another.[50] They

claim that adoption of the "quickening" distinction through received common law and state statutes tacitly recognizes the greater health hazards inherent in late abortion and impliedly repudiates the theory that life begins at conception.

It is with these interests, and the weight to be attached to them, that this case is concerned.

VIII

[9] The Constitution does not explicitly mention any right to privacy. In a line of decisions, however, going back perhaps as far as Union Pacific R. Co. v. Botsford, 141 U.S. 250, 251, 11 S.Ct. 1000, 1001, 35 L.Ed. 734 (1891), the Court has recognized that a right of personal privacy, or a guarantee of certain areas or zones of privacy, does exist under the Constitution. In varying contexts, the Court or individual Justices have, indeed, found at least the roots of that right in the First Amendment, Stanley v. Georgia, 394 U.S. 557, 564, 89 S.Ct. 1243, 1247, 22 L.Ed.2d 542 (1969); in the Fourth and Fifth Amendments, Terry v. Ohio, 392 U.S. 1, 8–9, 88 S.Ct. 1868, 1872–1873, 20 L.Ed.2d 889 (1968), Katz v. United States, 389 U.S. 347, 350, 88 S.Ct. 507, 510, 19 L.Ed.2d 576 (1967); Boyd v. United States, 116 U.S. 616, 6 S.Ct. 524, 29 L.Ed. 746 (1886), see Olmstead v. United States, 277 U.S. 438, 478, 48 S.Ct. 564, 572, 72 L.Ed. 944 (1928) (Brandeis, J., dissenting); in the penumbras of the Bill of Rights, Griswold v. Connecticut, 381 U.S., at 484–485, 85 S.Ct., at 1681–1682; in the Ninth Amendment, *id.*, at 486 85 S.Ct. at 1682 (Goldberg, J., concurring); or in the concept of liberty guaranteed by the first section of the Fourteenth Amendment, see Meyer v. Nebraska, 262 U.S. 390, 399, 43 S.Ct. 625, 626, 67 L.Ed. 1042 (1923). These decisions make it clear that only personal rights that can be deemed "fundamental" or "implicit in the concept of ordered liberty," Palko v. Connecticut, 302 U.S. 319, 325, 58 S.Ct. 149, 152, 82 L.Ed. 288 (1937), are included in this guarantee of personal privacy. They also make it clear that the right has some extension to activities relating to marriage, Loving v. Virginia, 388 U.S. 1, 12, 87 S.Ct. 1817, 1823, 18 L.Ed.2d 1010 (1967); procreation, Skinner v. Oklahoma, 316 U.S. 535, 541–542, 62 S.Ct. 1110, 1113–1114, 86 L.Ed. 1665 (1942); contraception, Eisenstadt v. Baird, 405 U.S., at 453–454, 92 S.Ct., at 1038–1039; *id.*, at 460, 463–465, 92 S.Ct. at 1042, 1043–1044 (White, J. concurring in result); family relationships, Prince v. Massachusetts, 321 U.S. 158, 166, 64

Abortion, The Practice of Medicine and the Due Process of Law, 16 U.C.L.A.L.Rev. 233 (1969); Noonan 1.

[46] See, *e.g.*, Abele v. Markle, 342 F.Supp. 800 (D.C.Conn. 1972), appeal docketed, No. 72–56.

[47] See discussions in Means I and Means II.

[48] See, *e.g.*, State v. Murphy, 27 N.J.L. 112, 114 (1858).

[49] Watson v. State, 9 Tex.App. 237, 244–245 (1880); Moore v. State, 37 Tex. Cr.R. 552, 561, 40 S.W. 287, 290 (1897); Shaw v. State, 73 Tex.Cr.R. 337, 339, 165 S.W. 930, 931 (1914); Fondren v. State, 74 Tex.Cr.R. 552, 557, 169 S.W. 411, 414 (1914); Gray v. State, 77 Tex.Cr.R. 221, 229, 178 S.W. 337, 341 (1915). There is no immunity in Texas for the father who is not married to the mother. Hammett v. State, 84 Tex.Cr.R. 635, 209 S.W. 661 (1919); Thompson v. State, Tex.Cr.App., 493 S.W.2d 913 (1971), appeal pending.

[50] See Smith v. State, 33 Me., at 55; In re Vince, 2 N.J. 443, 450, 67 A.2d 141, 144 (1949). A short discussion of the modern law on this issue is contained in the Comment to the ALI's Model Penal Code § 207.11, at 158 and nn. 35–37 (Tent.Draft No. 9, 1959).

[51] Tr. of Oral Rearg. 20–21.

S.Ct. 438, 442, 88 L.Ed. 645 (1944); and child rearing and education, Pierce v. Society of Sisters, 268 U.S. 510, 535, 45 S.Ct. 571, 573, 69 L.Ed. 1070 (1925), Meyer v. Nebraska, *supra*.

[10] This right of privacy, whether it be founded in the Fourteenth Amendment's concept of personal liberty and restrictions upon state action, as we feel it is, or, as the District Court determined, in the Ninth Amendment's reservation of rights to the people, is board enough to encompass a woman's decision whether or not to terminate her pregnancy. The detriment that the State would impose upon the pregnant woman by denying this choice altogether is apparent. Specific and direct harm medically diagnosable even in early pregnancy may be involved. Maternity, or additional offspring, may force upon the woman a distressful life and future. Psychological harm may be imminent. Mental and physical health may be taxed by child care. There is also the distress, for all concerned, associated with the unwanted child, and there is the problem of bringing a child into a family already unable, psychologically and otherwise, to care for it. In other cases, as in this one, the additional difficulties and continuing stigma of unwed motherhood may be involved. All these factors the woman and her responsible physician necessarily will consider in consultation.

On the basis of elements such as these appellant and some *amici* argue that the woman's right is absolute and that she is entitled to terminate her pregnancy at whatever time, in whatever way, and for whatever reason she alone chooses. With this we do not agree. Appellant's arguments that Texas either has no valid interest at all in regulating the abortion decision, or no interest strong enough to support any limitation upon the woman's sole determination, are unpersuasive. The Court's decisions recognizing a right of privacy also acknowledge that some state regulation in areas protected by that right is appropriate. As noted above, a State may properly assert important interests in safeguarding health, in maintaining medical standards, and in protecting potential life. At some point in pregnancy, these respective interests become sufficiently compelling to sustain regulation of the factors that govern the abortion decision. The privacy right involved, therefore, cannot be said to be absolute. In fact, it is not clear to us that the claim asserted by some *amici* that one has an

unlimited right to do with one's body as one pleases bears a close relationship to the right of privacy previously articulated in the Court's decisions. The Court has refused to recognize an unlimited right of this kind in the past. Jacobson v. Massachusetts, 197 U.S. 11, 25 S.Ct. 358, 49 L.Ed. 643 (1905) (vaccination); Buck v. Bell, 274 U.S. 200, 47 S.Ct. 584, 71 L.Ed. 1000 (1927) (sterilization).

We, therefore, conclude that the right of personal privacy includes the abortion decision, but that this right is not unqualified and must be considered against important state interests in regulation.

We note that those federal and state courts that have recently considered abortion law challenges have reached the same conclusion. A majority, in addition to the District Court in the present case, have held state laws unconstitutional, at least in part, because of vagueness or because of overbreadth and abridgment of rights. Abele v. Markle, 342 F.Supp. 800 (D.C.Conn.1972), appeal docketed, No. 72–56; Abele v. Markle, 351 F.Supp. 224 (D.C.Conn. 1972), appeal docketed, No. 72–730; Doe v. Bolton, 319 F.Supp. 1048 (N.D.Ga.1970), appeal decided today, 410 U.S. 179, 93 S.Ct. 739, 35 L.Ed.2d 201; Doe v. Scott, 321 F.Supp. 1385 (N.D.Ill.1971), appeal docketed, No. 70–105; Poe v. Menghini, 339 F.Supp. 986 (D.C.Kan. 1972); YWCA v. Kugler, 342 F.Supp. 1048 (D.C.N.J. 1972); Babbitz v. McCann, 310 F.Supp. 293 (E.D.Wis.1970), appeal dismissed, 400 U.S. 1, 91 S.Ct. 12, 27 L.Ed.2d 1 (1970); People v. Belous, 71 Cal.2d 954, 80 Cal.Rptr. 354, 458 P.2d 194 (1969), cert. denied, 397 U.S. 915, 90 S.Ct. 920, 25 L.Ed.2d 96 (1970); State v. Barquet, 262 So.2d 431 (Fla.1972).

Others have sustained state statutes. Crossen v. Attorney General, 344 F. Supp. 587 (E.D.Ky. 1972), appeal docketed, No. 72–256; Rosen v. Louisiana State Board of Medical Examiners, 318 F.Supp. 1217 (E.D.La.1970), appeal docketed, 70–42; Corkey v. Edwards, 322 F.Supp. 1248 (W.D.N.C.1971), appeal docketed, No. 71–92; Steinberg v. Brown, 321 F.Supp. 741 (N.D.Ohio 1970); Doe v. Rampton, 366 F.Supp. 189 (Utah 1971), appeal docketed, No. 71–5666; Cheaney v. State, Ind., 285 N.E.2d 265 (1972); Spears v. State, 257 So. 2d 876 (Miss.1972); State v. Munson, S.D., 201 N.W.2d 123 (1972), appeal docketed, No. 72–631.

Although the results are divided, most of these courts have agreed that the right of privacy, however based, is broad enough to cover the abortion decision; that the right, nonetheless, is not absolute and is subject to some limitations; and that at some point the state interests as to protection of health, medical standards, and prenatal life, become dominant. We agree with this approach.

[11] Where certain "fundamental rights" are involved, the Court has held that regulation limiting these rights may be justified only by a "compelling state interest," Kramer v. Union Free School District, 395 U.S. 621, 627, 89 S.Ct. 1886, 1890, 23 L.Ed.2d 583 (1969); Shapiro v. Thompson, 394 U.S., 618, 634, 89 S.Ct. 1322, 1331, 22 L.Ed.2d 600 (1969); Sherbert v. Verner, 374 U.S. 398, 406, 83 S.Ct. 1790, 1795, 10 L.Ed.2d 965 (1963), and that legislative enactments must be narrowly drawn to express only legitimate state interests at stake. Griswold v. Connecticut, 381 U.S., at 485, 85 S.Ct., at 1682; Aptheker v. Secretary of State, 378 U.S. 500, 508, 84 S.Ct. 1659, 1664, 12 L.Ed.2d 992 (1964); Cantwell v. Connecticut, 310 U.S. 296, 307–308, 60 S.Ct. 900, 904–905, 84 L.Ed. 1213 (1940); see Eisenstadt v. Baird, 405 U.S., at 460, 463–464, 92 S.Ct., at 1042, 1043–1044 (White, J., concurring in result).

In the recent abortion cases, cited above, courts have recognized these principles. Those striking down state laws have generally scrutinized the State's interests in protecting health and potential life, and have concluded that neither interest justified broad limitations on the reasons for which a physician and his pregnant patient decide that she should have an abortion in the early stages of pregnancy. Courts sustaining state laws have held that the State's determinations to protect health or prenatal life are dominant and constitutionally justifiable.

IX

The District Court held that the appellee failed to meet his burden of demonstrating that the Texas statute's infringement upon Roe's rights was necessary to support a compelling state interest, and that, although the appellee presented "several compelling justifications for state presence in the area of abortions," the statutes outstripped these justifications and swept "far beyond any areas of compelling state interest." 314 F.Supp., at 1222–1223. Appellant and appellee both contest that holding. Appellant, as has been indicated, claims an absolute right that bars

any state imposition of criminal penalties in the area. Appellee argues that the State's determination to recognize and protect prenatal life form and after conception constitutes a compelling state interest. As noted above, we do not agree fully with either formulation.

A. The appellee and certain *amici* argue that the fetus is a "person" within the language and meaning of the Fourteenth Amendment. In support of this, they outline at length and in detail the well-known facts of fetal development. If this suggestion of personhood is established, the appellant's case, of course, collapses, for the fetus' right to life would then be guaranteed specifically by the Amendment. The appellant conceded as much on reargument.[51] On the other hand, the appellee conceded on reargument,[52] that no case could be cited that holds that a fetus is a person within the meaning of the Fourteenth Amendment.

The Constitution does not define "person" in so many words. Section 1 of the Fourteenth Amendment contains three references to "person." The first in defining "citizens," speaks of "persons" born or naturalized in the United States." The word also appears both in the Due Process Clause in the Equal Protection Clause. "Person" is used in other places in the Constitution: in the listing of qualifications for Representatives and Senators, Art. I § 2, cl. 2, and § 3, cl. 3; in the Apportionment Clause, Art. I, § 2, cl. 3;[53] in the migration and Importation provision, Art. I, § 9, cl. 1; in the Emolument Clause, Art. I, § 9, cl. 8; in the Electors provisions, Art. II, § 1, cl. 2, and the provision outlining qualifications for the office of President, Art. II, § 1, cl.5; in the Extradition provisions, Art. IV, § 2, cl. 2, and the superseded Fugitive Slave Clause 3; and in the Fifth, Twelfth, and Twenty-second Amendments, as well as in §§ 2 and 3 of the Fourteenth Amendment. But in nearly all these instances, the use of the word is such that it has application only postnatally. None indicates, with any assurance, that it has any possible prenatal application.[54]

---

[52] Tr. of Oral Rearg. 24.

[53] We are not aware that in the taking of any census under this clause, a fetus has ever been counted.

[54] When Texas urges that a fetus is entitled to Fourteenth Amendment protection as a person, it faces a dilemma. Neither in Texas nor in any other State are all abortions prohibited. Despite broad proscription, an exception always

[12] All this, together with our observation, *supra*, that throughout the major portion of the 19th century prevailing legal abortion practices were far freer than they are today, persuades us that the word "person," as used in the Fourteenth Amendment, does not include the unborn.[55] This is in accord with the results reached in those few cases where the issue has been squarely presented. McGarvey v. Magee-Womens Hospital, 340 F.Supp. 751 (W.D.Pa.1972); Byrn v. New York City Health & Hospitals Corp., 31 N.Y.2d 194, 335 N.Y.S.2d 390, 286 N.E.2d 887 (1972), appeal docketed, No. 72–730. Cf. Cheaney v. State, Ind., 285 N.E.2d at 270; Montana v. Rogers, 278 F.2d 68, 72 (CA7 1960), aff'd sub nom. Montana v. Kennedy, 366 U.S. 308, 81 S.Ct. 1336, 6 L.Ed.2d 313 (1961); Keeler v. Superior Court, 2 Cal. 3d 619, 87 Cal.Rptr. 481, 470 P.2d 617 (1970); State v. Dickinson, 28 Ohio St. 2d 65, 275 N.E.2d 599 (1971); Indeed, our decision in United States v. Vuitch, 402 U.S. 62, 91 S.Ct. 1294, 28 L.Ed.2d 601 (1971), inferentially is to the same effect, for we there would not have indulged in statutory interpretation favorable to abortion in specified circumstances if the necessary consequence was the termination of life entitled to Fourteenth Amendment protection.

This conclusion, however, does not of itself fully answer the contentions raised by Texas, and we pass on to other considerations.

B. The pregnant woman cannot be isolated in her privacy. She carries an embryo and, later, a fetus, if one accepts the medical definitions of the developing young in the human uterus. See Dorland's Illustrated Medical Dictionary 478–479, 547 (24th ed. 1965). The situation therefore is inherently different from marital intimacy, or bedroom possession of obscene material, or marriage, or procreation, or education, with which *Eisenstadt* and *Griswold, Stanley, Loving, Skinner* and *Meyer* were respectively concerned. As we have intimated above, it is reasonable and appropriate for a State to decide that at some point in time another interest, that of health of the mother or that of potential human life, becomes significantly involved. The woman's privacy she possesses must be measured accordingly.

Texas urges that, apart form the Fourteenth Amendment, life begins at conception and is present throughout pregnancy, and that, therefore, the State has a compelling interest in protecting that life from and after conception. We need not resolve the difficult question of when life begins. When those trained in the respective disciplines of medicine, philosophy, and theology are unable to arrive at any consensus, the judiciary, at this point in the development of man's knowledge, is not in a position to speculate as to the answer.

It should be sufficient to note briefly the wide divergence of thinking on this most sensitive and difficult question. There was always been strong support for the view that life does not begin until live birth. This was the belief of the Stoics.[56] It appears to be the predominant, though not the unanimous, attitude of the Jewish faith.[57] It may be taken to represent also the position of a large segment of the Protestant community, insofar as that can be ascertained; organized groups that have taken a formal position on the abortion as a matter for the conscience of the individual and her family.[58] As we have noted, the common law found greater significance in quickening. Physicians and their scientific colleagues have regarded that event with less interest and have tended to focus either upon conception, upon live birth, or upon the interim point at which the fetus becomes

---

exists. The exception contained in Art. 1196, for an abortion procured or attempted by medical advice for the purpose of saving the life of the mother, is typical. But if the fetus is a person who is not to be deprived of life without due process of law, and if the mother's condition is the sole determinant, does not the Texas exception appear to be out of line with the Amendment's command

There are other inconsistencies between Fourteenth Amendment status and the typical abortion statue. It has already been pointed out, n. 49, *supra*, that in Texas the woman is not a principal or an accomplice with respect to an abortion upon her. If the fetus is a person, why is the woman not a principal or an accomplice? Further, the penalty for criminal abortion specified by Art. 1257 of the Texas Penal Code. If the fetus is a person, may the penalties be different?

[55] Cf. the Wisconsin abortion statute, defining "unborn child" to mean "a human being from the time of conception until it is born alive," Wis.Stat. § 940.04(6) (1969), and the new Connecticut statue, Pub. Act No. 1 (May 1972 Special Session), declaring it to be the public policy of the State and the legislative intent "to protect and preserve human life from the moment of conception."

[56] Edelstein 16.

[57] Lader 97–99; D. Feldman, Birth Control in Jewish Law 251–294 (1968). For a stricter view, see I. Jakobovits, Jewish Views on Abortion, in Abortion and the Law 124 (D. Smith ed. 1967).

[58] Amicus Brief for the American Ethical Union et al. For the position of the National Council of Churches and of other denominations, see Lader 99–101.

"viable," that is, potentially able to live outside the mother's womb, albeit with artificial aid.[59] Viability is usually placed at about seven months (28 weeks) but many occur earlier, even at 24 weeks.[60] The Aristotelian theory of "mediate animation," that held sway throughout the Middle Ages and the Renaissance in Europe, continued to be official Roman Catholic dogma until the 19th Century, despite opposition to this "ensoulment" theory from those in the Church who would recognize the existence of life from the moment of conception.[61] The latter is now, of course, the official belief of the Catholic Church. As one brief *amicus* discloses, this is a view strongly held by many non-Catholics as well, and by many physicians. Substantial problems for precise definition of this view are posed, however, by new embryological data that purport to indicate that conception is a "process" over time, rather than an event, and by new medical techniques such as menstrual extraction, the "morning-after" pill, implantation of embryos, artificial insemination, and even artificial wombs.[62]

In areas other than criminal abortion, the law has been reluctant to endorse any theory that life, as we recognize it, begins before live birth or to accord legal rights to the unborn except in narrowly defined situations and except when the rights are contingent upon live birth. For example, the traditional rule of tort law denied recovery for prenatal injuries even though the child was born alive.[63] That rule has been changed in almost every jurisdiction. In most States, recovery is said to be permitted only if the fetus was viable, or at least quick, when the injuries were sustained, though few courts have squarely so held.[64] In a recent development, generally opposed by the commentators, some

States permit the parents of a stillborn child to maintain an action for wrongful death because of prenatal injuries.[65] Such an action, however, would appear to be one to vindicate the parents' interest and is thus consistent with the view that the fetus, at most, represents only the potentiality of life. Similarly, unborn children have been recognized as acquiring rights or interests by way of inheritance or other devolution of property, and have been represented by guardians *ad litem*.[66] Perfection of the interests involved, again, has generally been contingent upon live birth. In short, the unborn have never been recognized in the law as persons in the whole sense.

X

In view, of all this, we do not agree that, by adopting one theory of life, Texas may override the rights of the pregnant woman that are at stake. We repeat, however, that the State does have an important and legitimate interest in preserving and protecting the health of the pregnant woman, whether she be a resident of the State or a nonresident who seeks medical consultation and treatment there, and that it has still *another*-important and legitimate interest in protecting the potentiality of human life. These interests are separate and distinct. Each grows in substantiality as the woman approaches term and, at a point during pregnancy, each becomes "compelling."

[13, 14] With respect to the State's important and legitimate interest in the health of the mother, the "compelling" point, in the light of present medical knowledge, is at approximately the end of the first trimester. This is so because of the now-established medical fact, referred to above at 725, that until the end of the first trimester mortality in abortion may be less than mortality in normal childbirth. It follows that,

---

[59] L. Hellman & J. Pritchard, Williams Obstetrics 493 (14th ed. 1971); Dorland's Illustrated Medical Dictionary 1689 (24th ed. 1965).

[60] Hellman & Pritchard, *supra*, n. 59, at 493.

[61] For discussions of the development of the Roman Catholic position, see D. Callahan, Abortion: Law, Choice, and Morality 409–447 (1970); Noonan 1.

[62] See Brodie, The New Biology and the Prenatal Child, 9 J.Family L. 391, 397 (1970); Gorney, The New Biology and the Future of Man, 15 U.C.L.A.L. Rev. 273 (1968); Note, Criminal Law—Abortion—The "Morning-After Pill" and Other Pre-Implantation Birth-Control Methods and the Law, 46 Ore.L.Rev. 211 (1967); G. Taylor, The Biological Time Bomb 32 (1968); A. Rosenfeld, The Second Genesis 138–139 (1969); Smith, Through a Test Tube Darkly; Artificial Insemination and the Law, 67 Mich.L. Rev. 127

(1968); Note, Artificial Insemination and the Law, 1968 U.Ill.L.F. 203.

[63] W. Prosser, The Law of Torts 335–338 (4th ed. 1971); 2 F. Harper & F. James, The Law of Torts 1028–1031 (1956); Note, 63 Harv.L.Rev. 173 (1949).

[64] See cases cited in Prosser, *supra*, n. 63, at 336–338; Annotation, Action for Death of Unborn Child, 15 A.L.R.3d 992 (1967).

[65] Prosser, *supra*, n. 63, at 338; Note, The Law and the Unborn Child: The Legal and Logical Inconsistencies, 46 Notre Dame Law. 349, 354–360 (1971).

[66] Louisell, Abortion, The Practice of Medicine and the Due Process of Law, 16 U.C.L.A.L.Rev. 233, 235–238 (1969); Note, 56 Iowa L.Rev. 994, 999–1000 (1971); Note, The Law and the Unborn Child, 46 Notre Dame Law, 349, 351–354 (1971).

from and after this point, a State may regulate the abortion procedure to the extent that the regulation reasonably relates to the preservation and protection of maternal health. Examples of permissible state regulation in this area are requirements as to the qualifications of the person who is to perform the abortion; as to the licensure of that person; as to the facility in which the procedure is to be performed, that is, whether it must be a hospital or may be a clinic or some other place of less-than-hospital status; as to the licensing of the facility; and the like.

This means, on the other hand, that, for the period of pregnancy prior to this "compelling" point, the attending physician, in consultation with his patient, is free to determine, without regulation by the State, that, in his medical judgment, the patient's pregnancy should be terminated. If that decision is reached, the judgment may be effectuated by an abortion free of interference by the State.

[15] With respect to the State's important and legitimate interest in potential life, the "compelling" point is at viability. This is so because the fetus then presumably has the capability of meaningful life outside the mother's womb. State regulation protective of fetal life after viability thus has both logical and biological justifications. If the State is interested in protecting fetal life after viability, it may go so far as to proscribe abortion during that period, except when it is necessary to preserve the life or health of the mother.

[16] Measured against these standards, Art. 1196 of the Texas Penal Code, in restricting legal abortions to those "procured or attempted by medical advice for the purpose of saving the life of the mother," sweeps too broadly. The statute makes no distinction between abortions early in pregnancy and those performed later, and it limits to a single reason, "saving" the mother's life, the legal justification for the procedure. The statue, therefore, cannot survive the constitutional attack made upon it here.

This conclusion makes it unnecessary for us to consider the additional challenge to the Texas statute asserted on grounds of vagueness. See United States v. Vuitch, 402 U.S., at 67–72, 91 S.Ct., at 1296–1299.

XI

To summarize and to repeat:

1. A state criminal abortion statute of the current Texas type, that excepts from criminali-

ty only a *life-saving* procedure on behalf of the mother, without regard to pregnancy stage and without recognition of the other interests involved, is violative of the Due Process Clause of the Fourteenth Amendment.

(a) For the stage prior to approximately the end of the first trimester, the abortion decision and its effectuation must be left to the medical judgment of the pregnant woman's attending physician.

(b) For the stage subsequent to approximately the end of the first trimester, the State, in promoting its interest in the health of the mother, may, if it chooses, regulate the abortion procedure in ways that are reasonably related to maternal health.

(c) For the stage subsequent to viability, the State in promoting its interest in the potentiality of human life may, if it chooses, regulate, and even proscribe, abortion except where it is necessary, in appropriate medical judgment, for the preservation of the life or health of the mother.

[17] 2. The State may define the term "physician," as it has been employed in the proceeding paragraphs of this Part XI of this opinion, to mean only a physician currently licensed by the State, and may proscribe any abortion by a person who is not a physician as so defined.

In Doe v. Bolton, 410 U.S. 179, 93 S.Ct. 739, 35 L.Ed.2d 201, procedural requirements contained in one of the modern abortion statutes are considered. That opinion and this one, of course, are to be read together.[67]

This holding, we feel, is consistent with the relative weights of the respective interests involved, with the lessons and examples of medical and legal history, with the lenity of the common law, and with the demands of the profound problems of the present day. The decision leaves

---

[67] Neither in this opinion nor in Doe v. Bolton, 410 U.S. 179, 93 S.Ct. 739, 35 L.Ed.2d 201, do we discuss the father's rights, if any exist in the constitutional context, in the abortion decision. No paternal right has been asserted in either of the cases, and the Texas and the Georgia statutes on their face take no cognizance of the father. We are aware that some statutes recognize the father under certain circumstances. North Carolina, for example, N.C.Gen.Stat. § 14–45.1 (Supp.1971), requires written permission for the abortion from the husband when the woman is a married minor, that is, when she is less than 18 years of age, 41 N.C.A.G. 489 (1971); if the woman is an unmarried minor, written permission from the parents is required. We need not now decide whether provisions of this kind are constitutional.

the State free to place increasing restrictions on abortion as the period of pregnancy lengthens, so long as those restrictions are tailored to the recognized state interests. The decision vindicates the right of the physician to administer medical treatment according to his professional judgment up to the points where important state interests provide compelling justifications for intervention. Up to those points, the abortion decision in all its aspects is inherently, and primarily, a medical decision, and basic responsibility for it must rest with the physician. If an individual practitioner abuses the privilege of exercising proper medical judgment, the usual remedies, judicial and intra-professional, are available.

XII

[18] Our conclusion that Art. 1196 is unconstitutional means, of course, that the Texas abortion statutes, as a unit, must fall. The exception of Art. 1196 cannot be struck down separately, for then the State would be left with a statute proscribing all abortion procedures no matter how medically urgent the case.

Although the District Court granted appellant Roe declaratory relief, it stopped short of issuing an injunction against enforcement of the Texas statutes. The Court has recognized that different considerations enter into a federal court's decision as to declaratory relief, on the other. Zwickler v. Koota, 389 U.S. 241, 252–255, 88 S.Ct. 391, 397–399, 19 L.Ed.2d 22 (1965). We are not dealing with a statute that, on its face, appears to abridge free expression, an area of particular concern under *Dombrowski* and refined in Younger v. Harris, 401 U.S., at 50, 91 S.Ct., at 753.

We find it unnecessary to decide whether the District Court erred in withholding injunctive relief, for we assume the Texas prosecutorial authorities will give full credence to this decision that the present criminal abortion statutes of that State are unconstitutional.

The Judgment of the District Court as to intervenor Hallford is reversed, and Dr. Hallford's complaint in intervention is dismissed. In all other respects, the judgment of the District Court is affirmed. Costs are allowed to the appellee.

It is so ordered.

Affirmed in part and reversed in part.

Mr. Justice STEWART, concurring.

In 1963, this Court in Ferguson v. Skrupa, 372 U.S. 726, 83 S.Ct. 1028, 10 L.Ed.2d 93, purported to sound the death knell for the doctrine of substantive due process, a doctrine under which many state laws had in the past been held to violate the Fourteenth Amendment. As Mr. Justice Black's opinion for the Court in *Skrupa* put it: "We have returned to the original constitutional proposition that courts do not substitute their social and economic beliefs for the judgment of legislative bodies, who are elected to pass laws." *Id.,* at 730, 83 S.Ct., at 1031.[1]

Barely two years later, Griswold v. Connecticut, 381 U.S. 479, 85 S.Ct. 1678, 14 L.Ed.2d 510, the Court held a Connecticut birth control law unconstitutional. In view of what had been so recently said in *Skrupa,* the Court's opinion in *Griswold* understandably did its best to avoid reliance on the Due Process Clause of the Fourteenth Amendment as the ground for decision. Yet the Connecticut law did not violate any provision of the Bill of Rights, nor any other specific provision of the Constitution.[2] So it was clear to me then, and it is equally clear to me now, that the Griswold decision can be rationally understood only as a holding that the Connecticut statute substantively invaded the "liberty" that is protected by the Due Process Clause of the Fourteenth Amendment.[3] As so understood, *Griswold* stands as one in a long line of pre-*Skrupa* cases decided under the doctrine of substantive due process, and I now accept it as such.

---

[1] Only Mr. Justice Harlan failed to join the Court's opinion, 372 U.S., at 733, 83 S.Ct., at 1032.

[2] There is no constitutional right of privacy, as such. "[The Fourth] Amendment protects individual privacy against certain kinds of governmental intrusion, but its protections go further, and often have nothing to do with privacy at all. Other provisions of the Constitution protect personal privacy from other forms of governmental invasion. But the protection of a person's *general* right to privacy—his right to be let alone by other people—is like the protection of his property and of his very life, left largely to the law of the individual States." Katz v. United States, 389 U.S. 347, 350–351, 88 S.Ct. 507, 510–511, 19 L.Ed.2d 576 (footnotes omitted).

[3] This was also clear to Mr. Justice Black, 381 U.S., at 507, (dissenting opinion); to Mr. Justice Harlan, 381 U.S., at 499, 85 S.Ct., at 1689 (opinion concurring in the judgment); and to Mr. Justice White, 381 U.S., at 502, 85 S.Ct., at 1691 (opinion concurring in the judgment). See also Mr. Justice Harlan's thorough and thoughtful opinion dissenting from dismissal of the appeal in Poe v. Ullman, 367 U.S. 497, 522, 81 S.Ct. 1752, 1765, 6 L.Ed.2d 989.

"In a Constitution for a free people, there can be no doubt that the meaning of 'liberty' must be broad indeed." Board of Regents v. Roth, 408 U.S. 564, 572, 92 S.Ct. 2701, 2707, 33 L.Ed.2d 548. The Constitution nowhere mentions a specific right of personal choice in matters of marriage and family life, but the "liberty" protected by the Due Process Clause of the Fourteenth Amendment covers more than those freedoms explicitly named in the Bill of Rights. See Schware v. Board of Bar Examiners, 353 U.S. 232, 238–239, 77 S.Ct. 752, 755–756, 1 L.Ed.2d 796; Pierce v. Society of Sisters, 268 U.S. 510, 534–535, 45 S.Ct. 571, 573–574, 69 L.Ed.1070; Meyer v. Nebraska, 262 U.S. 390, 399–400, 43 S.Ct. 625, 626–627, 67 L.Ed. 1042. Cf. Shapiro v. Thompson, 394 U.S. 618, 629–630, 89 S.Ct. 1322, 1328–1329, 22 L.Ed.2d 600; United States v. Guest, 383 U.S. 745, 757–758, 86 S.Ct. 1170, 1177–1178, 16 L.Ed.2d 239; Carrington v. Rash, 380 U.S. 89, 96, 85 S.Ct. 775, 780, 13 L.Ed.2d 675; Aptheker v. Secretary of State, 378 U.S. 500, 505, 84 S.Ct. 1659, 1663, 12 L.Ed.2d 992; Kent v. Dulles, 357, U.S. 116, 127, 78 S.Ct. 1113, 1118, 2 L.Ed.2d 1204; Bolling v. Sharpe, 347 U.S. 497, 499–500, 74 S.Ct. 693, 694–695, 98 L.Ed. 884; Truax v. Raich, 239 U.S. 33, 41, 36 S.Ct. 7, 10, 60 L.Ed. 131.

As Mr. Justice Harlan once wrote: "[T]he full scope of the liberty guaranteed by the Due Process Clause cannot be found in or limited by the precise terms of the specific guarantees elsewhere provided in the Constitution. This 'liberty' is not a series of isolated points pricked out in terms of the taking of property; the freedom of speech, press, and religion; the right to keep and bear arms; the freedom from unreasonable searches and seizures; and so on. It is a rational continuum which, broadly speaking, includes a freedom from all substantial arbitrary impositions and purposeless restraints . . . and which also recognizes, what a reasonable and sensitive judgment must, that certain interests require particularly careful scrutiny of the state needs asserted to justify their abridgment." Poe v. Ullman, 367 U.S. 497, 543, 81 S.Ct. 1752, 1776, 6 L.Ed.2d 989 (opinion dissenting from dismissal of appeal) (citations omitted). In the words of Mr. Justice Frankfurter, "Great concepts like . . . 'liberty' . . . were purposely left to gather meaning from expertise. For they relate to the whole domain of social and economic fact, and the statesmen who founded this Nation knew too well that only a stagnant society remains unchanged." National

Mutual Ins. Co. v. Tidewater Transfer Co., 337 U.S. 582, 646, 69 S.Ct. 1173, 1195, 93 L.Ed. 1556 (dissenting opinion).

Several decisions of this Court make clear that freedom of personal choice in matters of marriage and family life is one of the liberties protected by the Due Process Clause of the Fourteenth Amendment. Loving v. Virginia, 388 U.S. 1, 12, 87 S.Ct. 1817, 1823, 18 L.Ed.2d 1010; Griswold v. Connecticut *supra*: Pierce v. Society of Sisters, *supra*; Meyer v. Nebraska, *supra* . See also Prince v. Massachusetts, 321 U.S. 158, 166, 64 S.Ct. 438, 442, 88 L.Ed. 645; Skinner v. Oklahoma, 316 U.S. 535, 541, 62 S.Ct. 1110, 1113, 86 L.Ed. 1655. As recently as last Term, in Eisenstadt v. Baird, 405 U.S. 438, 453, 92 S.Ct. 1029, 1038, 31 L.Ed.2d 349, we recognized "the right of the *individual*, married or single, to be free from unwarranted governmental intrusion into matters so fundamentally affecting a person as the decision whether to bear or beget a child." That right necessarily includes the right of a woman to decide whether or not to terminate her pregnancy. "Certainly the interests of a woman in giving of her physical and emotional self during pregnancy and the interests that will be affected throughout her life by the birth and raising of a child are of a far greater degree of significance and personal intimacy than the right to send a child to private school protected in Pierce v. Society of Sisters, 268 U.S. 510, 45 S.Ct. 571, 69 L.Ed. 1070 (1925), or the right to teach a foreign language protected in Meyer v. Nebraska, 262 U.S. 390, 43 S.Ct. 625, 67 L.Ed. 1042 (1923)." Abele v. Markle, 351 F.Supp. 224, 227 (D.C. Conn.1972).

Clearly, therefore, the Court today is correct in holding that the right asserted by Jane Roe is embraced within the personal liberty protected by the Due Process Clause of the Fourteenth Amendment.

It is evident that the Texas abortion statute infringes that right directly. Indeed, it is difficult to imagine a more complete abridgment of a constitutional freedom than that worked by the inflexible criminal statute now in force in Texas. The question then becomes whether the state interests advanced to justify this abridgment can survive the "particularly careful scrutiny" that the Fourteenth Amendment here requires.

The asserted state interests are protection of the health and safety of the pregnant woman, and protection of the potential future human

U.S. SUPREME
COURT,
JANUARY 1973

life within her. These are legitimate objectives, amply sufficient to permit a State to regulate abortions as it does other surgical procedures, and perhaps sufficient to permit a State to regulate abortions more stringently or even to prohibit them in the late stages of pregnancy. But such legislation is not before us, and I think the Court today has thoroughly demonstrated that these state interests cannot constitutionally support the broad abridgment of personal liberty worked by the existing Texas law. Accordingly, I join the Court's opinion holding that that law is invalid under the Due Process Clause of the Fourteenth Amendment.

Mr. Justice REHNQUIST, dissenting.

The Court's opinion brings to the decision of this troubling question both extensive historical fact and a wealth of legal scholarship. While the opinion thus commands my respect, I find myself nonetheless in fundamental disagreement with those parts of it that invalidate the Texas statute in question, and therefore dissent.

I

The Court's opinion decides that a State may impose virtually no restriction on the performance of abortions during the first trimester of pregnancy. Our previous decisions indicate that a necessary predicate for such an opinion is a plaintiff who was in her first trimester of pregnancy at some time during the pendency of her lawsuit. While a party may vindicate his own constitutional rights, he may not seek vindication for the rights of others. Moose Lodge No. 107 v. Irvis, 407 U.S. 163, 92 S.Ct. 1965, 32 L.Ed.2d 627 (1972); Sierra Club v. Morton, 405 U.S. 727, 92 S.Ct. 1361, 31 L.Ed.2d 636 (1972). The Court's statement of facts in this case makes clear, however, that the record in no way indicates the presence of such a plaintiff. We know only that plaintiff Roe at the time of filing her complaint was a pregnant woman; for aught that appears in this record, she may have been in her *last* trimester of pregnancy as of the date the complaint was filed.

Nothing in the Court's opinion indicates that Texas might not constitutionally apply its proscription of abortion as written to a woman in that stage of pregnancy. Nonetheless, the Court uses her complaint against the Texas statute as a fulcrum for deciding that States may impose virtually no restrictions on medical abortions performed during the *first* trimester

of pregnancy. In deciding such a hypothetical lawsuit, the Court departs from the longstanding admonition that it should never "formulate a rule of constitutional law broader than is required by the precise facts to which it is to be applied." Liverpool, New York & Philadelphia S.S. Co. v. Commissioners of Emigration, 113 U.S. 33, 39, 5 S.Ct. 352, 355, 28 L.Ed. 899 (1885). See also Ashwander v. TVA, 297 U.S. 288, 345, 56 S.Ct. 466, 482, 80 L.Ed. 688 (1936) (Brandeis, J., concurring).

II

Even if there were a plaintiff in this case capable of litigating the issue which the Court decides, I would reach a conclusion opposite to that reached by the Court. I have difficulty in concluding, as the Court does, that the right of "privacy" is involved in this case. Texas, by the statute here challenged, bars the performance of a medical abortion by a licensed physician on a plaintiff such as Roe. A transaction resulting in an operation such as this in not "private" in the ordinary usage of that word. Nor is the "privacy" that the Court finds here even a distant relative of the freedom from searches and seizures protected by the Fourth Amendment to the Constitution, which the Court has referred to as embodying a right to privacy. Katz v. United States, 389 U.S. 347, 88 S.Ct. 507, 19 L.Ed.2d 576 (1967).

If the Court means by the term "privacy" no more than that the claim of a person to be free from unwanted state regulation of consensual transactions may be a form of "liberty" protected by the Fourteenth Amendment, there is no doubt that similar claims have been upheld in our earlier decisions on the basis of that liberty. I agree with the statement of Mr. Justice STEWART in his concurring opinion that the "liberty," against deprivation of which without due process the Fourteenth Amendment protects, embraces more than the rights found in the Bill of Rights. But that liberty is not guaranteed absolutely against deprivation, only against deprivation, without due process of law. The test traditionally applied in the area of social and economic legislation is whether or not a law such as that challenged has a rational relation to a valid state objective. Williamson v. Lee Optical Co., 348 U.S. 483, 491, 75 S.Ct. 461, 466, 99 L.Ed. 563 (1955). The Due Process Clause of the Fourteenth Amendment undoubtedly does place a limit, albeit a broad one, on legislative power to enact laws such as this. If the Texas statute were to prohibit an abortion even where the mother's life is in jeopardy, I have little doubt that such a statute would lack a rational relation to a valid state objective under the test stated in *Williamson, supra.* But the Court's sweeping invalidation of any restrictions on abortion during the first trimester is impossible to justify under the standard, and the conscious weighing of competing factors that the Court's opinion apparently substitutes for the established test is far more appropriate to a legislative judgment than to a judicial one.

The Court eschews the history of the Fourteenth Amendment in its reliance on the "compelling state interest" test. See Weber v. Aetna Casualty & Surety Co., 406 U.S. 164, 179, 92 S.Ct. 1400, 1408, 31 L.Ed.2d 768 (1972) (dissenting opinion). But the Court adds a new wrinkle to this test by transposing it from the legal considerations associated with the Equal Protection Clause of the Fourteenth Amendment to this case arising under the Due Process Clause of the Fourteenth Amendment. Unless I misapprehend the consequences of this transplanting of the "compelling state interest test," the Court's opinion will accomplish the seemingly impossible feat of leaving this area of the law more confused than it found it.

While the Court's opinion quotes from the dissent of Mr. Justice Holmes in Lochner v. New York, 198 U.S. 45, 74, 25 S.Ct. 539, 551, 49 L.Ed. 937 (1905), the result it reaches is more closely attuned to the majority opinion of Mr. Justice Peckham in that case. As in *Lochner* and similar cases applying substantive due process standards to economic and social welfare legislation, the adoption of the compelling state interest standard will inevitably require this Court to examine the legislative policies and pass on the wisdom of these policies in the very process of deciding whether a particular state interest put forward may or may not be "compelling." The decision here to break pregnancy into three distinct terms and to outline the permissible restrictions the State may impose in each one, for example, partakes more of judicial legislation than it does of a determination of the intent of the drafters of the Fourteenth Amendment.

The fact that a majority of the States reflecting, after all the majority sentiment in those States, have had restrictions on abortions for at least a century is a strong indication, it seems to me, that the asserted right to an abortion is not

"so rooted in the traditions and conscience of our people as to be ranked as fundamental," Snyder v. Massachusetts, 291 U.S. 97, 105, 54 S.Ct. 330, 332, 78 L.Ed. 675 (1934). Even today, when society's views on abortion are changing, the very existence of the debate is evidence that the "right" to an abortion is not so universally accepted as the appellant would have us believe.

To reach its result, the Court necessarily has had to find within the Scope of the Fourteenth Amendment a right that was apparently completely unknown to the drafters of the Amendment. As early as 1821, the first state law dealing directly with abortion was enacted by the Connecticut Legislature. Conn.Stat., Tit. 22, §§ 14, 16. By the time of the adoption of the Fourteenth Amendment in 1868, there were at least 36 laws enacted by state or territorial legislatures limiting abortion.[1] While many States have amended or updated their laws, 21 of the laws on the books in 1868 remain in effect today.[2] Indeed, the Texas statute struck down today was, as the majority notes, first enacted in 1857 and "has remained substantially unchanged to the present time." *Ante,* at 710.

There apparently was no question concerning the validity of this provision or of any of the other state statutes when the Fourteenth Amendment was adopted. The only conclusion possible from this history is that the drafters did not intend to have the Fourteenth Amendment

---

[1] Jurisdictions having enacted abortion laws prior to the adoption of the Fourteenth Amendment in 1868:

    1. Alabama—Ala.Acts, c.6, § 2 (1840).

    2. Arizona—Howell Code, c. 10 § 45 (1865).

    3. Arkansas—Ark.Rev.Stat. c. 44, div. III, Art. II, § 6 (1838).

    4. California—Cal.Sess.Laws, c. 99 § 45, p. 233 (1849–1850).

    5. Colorado (Terr.)—Colo.Gen.Laws of Terr. of Colo., 1st Sess., § 42, pp. 296–297 (1861).

    6. Connecticut—Conn.Stat. Tit. 20, §§ 14, 16 (1821). By 1868, this statute had been replaced by another abortion law. Conn.Pub.Acts, c. 71, §§ 1, 2, p. 65 (1860).

    7. Florida—Fla.Acts 1st Sess., c. 1637, subc. 3, §§ 10, 11, subc. 8, §§ 9, 10, 11 (1868), as amended, now Fla.Stat.Ann. §§ 782.09, 782.10, 797.01, 797.02, 782.16 (1965).

    8. Georgia—Ga.Penn.Code, 4th Div., § 20 (1833).

    9. Kingdom of Hawaii—Hawaii Pen. Code, c. 12, §§ 1, 2, 3 (1850).

    10. Idaho (Terr.)—Idaho (Terr.) Laws, Crimes and Punishments §§ 33, 34, 42, pp. 441, 443 (1863).

    11. Illinois—Ill.Rev. Criminal Code §§ 40, 41, 46, pp. 130, 131 (1827). By 1868, this statute had been replaced by a subsequent enactment. Ill.Pub.Laws §§ 1, 2, 3, p. 89 (1867).

U.S. SUPREME
COURT,
JANUARY 1973

withdraw form the States the power to legislate with respect to this matter.

III

Even if one were to agree that the case that the Court decides were here, and that the enunciation of the substantive constitutional law in the Court's opinion were proper, the actual disposition of the case by the Court is still difficult to justify. The Texas statute is struck down *in toto*, even though the Court apparently concedes that at later periods of pregnancy Texas might

impose these selfsame statutory limitations on abortion. My understanding of past practice is that a statute found to be invalid as applied to a particular plaintiff, but not unconstitutional as a whole, is not simply "struck down" but is, instead, declared unconstitutional as applied to the fact situation before the Court. Yick Wo v. Hopkins, 118 U.S. 356, 6 S.Ct. 1064, 30 L.Ed. 220 (1886); Street v. New York, 394 U.S. 576, 89 S.Ct. 1354, 22 L.Ed.2d 572 (1969).

For all of the foregoing, reasons, I respectfully dissent.

---

12. Indiana—Ind.Rev.Stat. §§ 1, 3, p. 224 (1838). By 1868 this statute had been superseded by a subsequent enactment. Ind.Laws, c. LXXXI, § 2 (1859).

13. Iowa (Terr.)—Iowa (Terr.) Stat., 1st Legis., 1st Sess., § 18, p. 145 (1838). By 1868, this statute had been superseded by a subsequent enactment. Iowa (Terr.) Rev.Stat., c. 49, §§ 10, 13 (1843).

14. Kansas (Terr.)—Kan. (Terr.) Stat., c. 48, §§ 9, 10, 39 (1855). By 1868, this statute had been superseded by a subsequent enactment. Kan. (Terr.) Laws, c. 28, §§ 9, 10, 37 (1859).

15. Louisana—La.Rev.Stat., Crimes and Offenses § 24, p. 138 (1856).

16. Maine—Me.Rev.Stat., c. 160, §§ 11, 12, 13, 14 (1840).

17. Maryland—Md. Laws, c. 179, § 2, p. 315 (1868).

18. Massachusetts—Mass.Acts & Resolves, c. 27 (1845).

19. Michigan—Mich.Rev.Stat., c. 153, §§ 32, 33, 34, p. 662 (1846).

20. Minnesota (Terr.)—Minn. (Terr.) Rev.Stat., c. 100 §§ 10, 11, p. 493 (1851).

21. Mississippi—Miss.Code, c. 64 §§ 8, 9, p. 958 (1848).

22. Missouri—Mo.Rev.Stat., Art. II, §§ 9, 10, 36, pp. 168, 172 (1835).

23. Montana (Terr.)—Mont. (Terr.) Laws, Criminal Practice Acts § 41, p. 184 (1864).

24. Nevada (Terr.)—Nev. (Terr.) Laws, c. 28 § 42, p. 63 (1861).

25. New Hampshire—N.H.Laws, c. 743, § 1, p. 708 (1848).

26. New Jersey—N.J.Laws, p. 266 (1849).

27. New York—N.Y.Rev.Stat., pt. 4, c. 1, Tit. 2, §§ 8, 9, pp. 12–13 (1828). By 1868, this statute had been superseded. N.Y.Laws, c. 260, §§ 1, 2, 3, 4, 5, 6, pp. 285–286 (1845); N.Y.Laws, c. 22 § 1, p. 19 (1846).

28. Ohio—Ohio Gen.Stat §§ 111(1), 112(2), p. 252 (1841).

29. Oregon—Ore.Gen.Laws, Crim.Code, c. 43, § 509, p. 528 (1845–1964).

30. Pennsylvania—Pa.Laws No. 374 87, 88, 89 (1860).

31. Texas—Tex.Gen.Stat.Dig., c. VII, Arts. 531–536, p. 524 (Oldham & White 1859).

32. Vermont—Vt.Acts No. 33, § 1 (1846). By 1968, this statute had been amended. Vt.Acts No. 57, §§ 1, 3 (1867).

33. Virginia—Va.Acts, Tit. II, c. 3, § 9, p. 96 (1848).

34. Washington (Terr.)—Wash. (Terr.) Stats., C. II, §§ 37, 38, p. 81 (1854).

35. West Virginia—Va.Acts, Tit. II, c. 3, § 9, p. 96 (1848).

36. Wisconsin—Wis.Rev.Stat., c. 133, §§ 10, 11 (1849). By 1868, this statute had been superseded. Wis.Rev.Stat., c. 164, §§ 10, 11; c. 169, §§ 58, 59 (1858).

[2] Abortion laws in effect in 1868 and still applicable as of August 1970:

1. Arizona (1865).
2. Connecticut (1860).
3. Florida (1868).
4. Idaho (1863).
5. Indiana (1838).
6. Iowa (1843).
7. Maine (1840).
8. Massachusetts (1845).
9. Michigan (1846).
10. Minnesota (1851).
11. Missouri (1835).
12. Montana (1864).
13. Nevada (1861).
14. New Hampshire (1848).
15. New Jersey (1849).
16. Ohio (1841).
17. Pennsylvania (1860).
18. Texas (1859).
19. Vermont (1867).
20. West Virginia (1848).
21. Wisconsin (1858).

ISBN 0-7876-6378-6

90000

For Reference

Not to be taken from this room